Neoliberalism Inequality And Authoritarianism

Jon Kofas

Published by The Little French eBooks, 2024.

NEOLIBERALISM INEQUALITY AND AUTHORITARIANISM

First edition. September 3, 2024.

ISBN: 979-8230997740

Written by Jon Kofas.

Also by Jon Kofas

Phantom of Apocalypse: A Dystopian novel
Links on a Chain
Neoliberalism Inequality And Authoritarianism

NEOLIBERALISM

INEQUALITY

AND AUTHORITARIANISM

Jon V. Kofas

NEOLIBERALISM, INEQUALITY, AND AUTHORITARIANISM

Jon V. Kofas

Published by The Little French eBooks

Cover Art by The Little French eBooks

NEOLIBERALISM

INEQUALITY

AND AUTHORITARIANISM

Jon V. Kofas

Table of Contents

PREFACE

Before the Great Recession of 2007-2008, neoliberalism was a term that academics, journalists, and analysts working for think tanks or international organizations used to articulate how the new phase of capitalism impacted society. Experiencing the transformation's impact daily, the public accepted neoliberalism as the new norm. Unaware of the global transition from Keynesian social welfare to the neoliberal corporate welfare state, people fell into the mold of more rapid redistributive economics from the bottom up.

After the Great Recession of 2008, the intensified crisis of the neoliberal political economy, and the rise of illiberal democracy (regime under an electoral system curtailing popular consent and civil liberties legislatively and through the courts) intensified. Given the rapid pace of social and political changes, academics, journalists, analysts, and businesspeople examined more closely the neoliberal model's impact not just on the economy, but society as a whole.

In search of a link between the rise of authoritarianism and the institutionalization of neoliberalism, social scientists debated the inexorable relationship between the two. This was especially after Donald Trump's presidential victory in 2016, emboldening a global wave of rightwing populism as a movement and regime, but also as it impacted the media which unapologetic advocated or stealthily promoted the GOP candidate. Rhetorically opposed globalization to consolidate the disgruntled popular base, Trump and other populist politicians in the US and around the world pursued privatization of public enterprises, tax cuts for the wealthiest, an accommodative monetary policy as another form of subsidy benefiting institutional borrowers, and business deregulation resulting in higher profits amid deteriorating labor and environmental conditions.

In the name of market efficiency and economic competition during China's global economic ascendancy, policies associated with authoritarianism became mainstream within the G-7 and in developing nations. The origin of the slippery slope toward US authoritarianism took place during the early Cold War when Senator Joseph McCarthy in the early 1950s used Communism as the pretext to impose sociopolitical conformity at home and support covert operations and overt military intervention globally.

Under neoliberalism, and especially after the terrorist strikes in the US on 9/11/2001, the US-led global war on terrorism and military intervention in Iraq and Afghanistan distracted people from stagnant living standards and downward social mobility during a period of rapid and massive income transfer from the lower classes to the wealthiest. Regardless of empirical evidence compiled by international organizations, the media, political, business, and community leaders promoting neoliberal transformation insisted that the US was the world's beacon of freedom and democracy.

Beyond the disconnect between the projected hollow image and verifiable evidence, there is the link between neoliberalism and autocratization, namely, the erosion of democratic institutions and policies within an electoral system on the path of authoritarianism owing to the neoliberal phase of capitalism responsible for the global trend of rapid capital concentration and rising inequality. The historical antecedents for the erosion of democratic institutions and renewed efforts toward monopoly capitalism after the twin shocks of the Great Depression and WWII culminated in the neoliberal experiment in Chile in the 1970s, and then in the UK toward the end of the decade and the US in the beginning of the 1980s.

The US emerged as the world's most powerful economic power in the 1940s when Europe and Japan were at their nadir. Global transformation policy was the catalyst to cement Pax Americana's preeminence during the

East-West confrontation. Relying on the Bretton Woods System established in 1944 to manage the capitalist world economy under America's aegis, all presidents from Truman to Biden used its unprecedented economic and military power to integrate as many countries as possible under its orbit of influence. The goal was also to prevent countries from allying with the USSR and/or China after Mao's victory in the Civil War in 1949, and even non-aligned countries after the Bandung Conference in 1955.

The ideological justification for US global integration of the non-Communist world started at the end of WWII when Japan Europe, and their colonies in Asia and Africa had collapsed and needed reconstruction aid. Exploiting public fear of the emerging Communist bloc, especially after 1949 when Mao's Red Army prevailed over Chiang Kai-shek's nationalists, and the USSR successfully tested the atomic bomb, the US government and the entire establishment from Wall Street to mainstream media discouraged workers from supporting leftist organizations, trade unions, or political parties anywhere in the world. The class war that neoliberalism institutionalized had its origins in the early Cold War during the zenith of Pax Americana, inexorably linked to geopolitics from its origin.

Combined with a wave of decolonization in Asia and Africa, the world order remained in a bipolar superpower division from the Truman-Stalin era until the collapse of the Soviet bloc in 1991 amid the ascendancy of global neoliberal transformation. Undercutting the convergence of liberalism and democracy that the New Deal forged in the 1930s, neoliberalism became institutionalized after the capitalist class and mainstream political parties used the pretext of the crises of capital accumulation in the 1970s, amid the concurrent energy crisis and stagflation to launch a class war and dismantle the Keynesian state.

The US retreat from Vietnam, the oil embargo of 1973, the Iranian and Nicaraguan revolutions, and USSR troops in Afghanistan, all in 1979, exacerbated capitalism's systemic contradictions in the US-Western European core, thereby setting the stage for neoliberalism first in the UK under Prime Minister Margaret Thatcher and then in the US under President Ronald Reagan. Partly because China shifted economic development strategies after the Mao-Nixon visit of 1972, but also because northwest Europe and Japan had become much stronger relative to the US in the 1950s, the East-West Cold War world order was already multipolar at the economic level by the 1970s.

As evidenced not only by northwest Europe and Japan's economic ascendancy, but also OPEC's global leverage, and the non-aligned bloc's "South-South" cooperation intended to modify the historical dependency relationships with the former colonial powers, the world capitalist system's multipolar nature weakened the US economically despite its continued military preeminence. Along with northwest Europe, the US chronic balance of payments deficits and defense spending from the beginning of the Korean War to the end of the Vietnam War, combined with the nuclear arms race contributed to lower capital returns as Europe and Japan were increasing global market share. Despite an average of 3.7% GDP growth from 1950 to 1973 in the US, the period from 1973 to 1992 witnessed a 2.2% GDP growth rate and 0.9% business productivity.[1]

The US-based multi-dimensional crisis had a global impact. The combination of the Bretton Woods System and military Keynesianism (diverting the surplus from social welfare to raise defense spending amid the nuclear arms race) hastened capitalism's contradictions and slowed civilian economic growth amid chronic rising balance of payments deficits and weakened the dollar as the world's preeminent reserve currency.

Refusing to further devalue its currency, in May 1971, Germany left the Bretton Woods System. In August 1971, President Richard Nixon delinked the dollar as a reserve currency from the gold standard. To control inflation,

Nixon ordered three-month wage-price controls, while imposing a 10% import surcharge as insurance not to disadvantage US-made products amid the fluctuating exchange rates. Replacing the fixed exchange rate system with a floating responsible for sinking the greenback by one-third in the 1970s was part of the pretext to abandon Keynesianism.[2]

With the relative decline of US global economic power amid the Vietnam War in the 1970s, there was a grassroots movement for popular sovereignty in the Southern Hemisphere, especially in South Africa where apartheid was another tool of race-based working-class exploitation. South African apartheid had some similarities with the US. Other parts of Muslim northern Africa and sub-Saharan Africa were inspired by Gamal Abdel Nasser, Indonesia's Sukarno, India's Nehru, and other non-aligned leaders defying the bipolar Cold War world order that the US and USSR were using to manage the world balance of power.

Popular sovereignty and social inclusion, democracy with all its limitations during the Cold War, and classical liberalism placing all emphasis on the individual above social class, never existed except at the theoretical level. Even in the Scandinavian countries, which consistently rank among the most committed to democracy, the hierarchical social structure reflects the essence of the political economy that neoliberalism inherited from the Bretton Woods System. The Bretton Woods conference (July 1944), which created the International Monetary Fund (IMF) and the World Bank, established the antecedents for neoliberalism by scaling back on Keynesian policies of social welfare, accelerated privatization of public entities, and government bolstering businesses by sub-contracting and outsourcing services otherwise carried out in the public sector. Through monetary stabilization and development loans, the multilateral financial institutions' role was paramount in influencing the fiscal, trade, investment, and labor policy of its member countries, especially of the Global South. Indirectly coordinating and managing the world economy with the full support of private financial markets, the US government and its junior partners dominated the IMF and World Bank both instrumental in transformation policy.

Essential elements in IMF-World Bank loan conditionality included decentralization of state power and minimal business regulation. Antecedents to neoliberalism included the free flow of goods and capital between national borders with minimal tariff barriers and a reduction in business taxes with a simultaneous rise in consumption taxes. Impacting the Keynesian welfare state, the twin international financial institutions promoted reducing the labor force in public agencies, opposed policies favoring trade unions and safeguards for both workers and the environment, and advocated a skeletal social safety net including social security, education, and health care. Permitting the market to determine services otherwise included in a social welfare state, especially health care, was the epitome of market hegemony over the state.[3]

Diluting Keynesian social welfare policies was a gradual process after the US-based Bretton Woods System established the institutional mechanisms to manage international monetary stability and economic development on behalf of the private sector which benefited from such policies intended to redistribute income from labor to capital and from the Global South periphery to the core countries. IMF and World Bank policies of the first three postwar decades helped pave the way for neoliberal transformation. The financial institutions applied policies selectively in developing nations, but not in the advanced capitalist countries, and not in those countries which the US deemed of geopolitical significance.

Western Europe, Japan, South Korea, and Taiwan, all countries that the US chose to reconstruct and reindustrialize for geopolitical and trade considerations, were not subject to IMF-World Bank monetarism-free trade policies. Allowing developmentalism based on import-substituting industrialization, Washington injected capital into these nations instead of de-capitalizing which would have forced them into chronic balance of payments deficits and external financial dependency conditions, as was the case with Latin America and Africa. Furthermore, IMF-World Bank conditionality never interfered with parasitic military Keynesian policies in any country undergoing austerity.

Although the IMF and World Bank linked market-based policies to stabilization and development loans, the institutionalization of full-fledged global neoliberal transformation started with UK Prime Minister Margaret Thatcher in 1979, and US President Ronald Reagan in 1981. This was after a neoliberal experiment in Chile in the second half of the 1970s. By the late 1980s when the Soviet bloc collapsed, neoliberals celebrated the triumph of capitalism and seized the opportunity to integrate the former Communist countries under neoliberal transformation's global reach. Against the background of the new doctrine of deregulation and privatization, governments around the world shifted resources from social welfare to corporate subsidies under a state conducting fiscal and monetary policy to accommodate market hegemony over mainstream institutions.[4]

After UK and US conservative governments institutionalized neoliberalism in the 1980s, liberal and center-left political parties globally pursued transformation in the 1990s amid the euphoria of the Communist bloc's collapse. Following Reagan's lead, neoliberal governments promised "trickle-down" economic prosperity, a theory prompting John Kenneth Galbraith to observe that: *"if one feeds the horse enough oats, some will pass through to the road for the sparrows."*[5] History proved that neoliberals delivered a chronic rise in inequality under the existing stratified social structure and uneven development in the world economy. Promises of protecting the environment, democracy, and human rights were as hollow as trickle-down economics which was originally part of Will Rogers's satire about capitalism during the Great Depression.[6]

As much in the US and UK, as in Brazil, India, Hungary, Turkey, Russia, former Soviet republics, and indeed most countries in the world, aspects of authoritarianism behind the thin veil of representative democracy are rooted in structural dynamics of the neo-classical political economy's contradictions and empirical conditions in deteriorating social relations. Other than historical antecedents of the global rightwing populist tide in core countries, neoliberalism has had an impact on all aspects of society. From social structure to popular culture, commodifying one's identity as a consumer-citizen seeking fulfillment in narcissistic and increasingly virtual reality endeavors, neoliberalism's global reach has had a far-reaching impact even in traditional societies.

Contrary to liberal and center-left claims that "progressive neoliberalism" is the antidote to rightwing populism, the dynamics of the neoliberal political economy transcend conservative, centrist, or center-left politics, all of which operate under the larger umbrella of the same social contract. All mainstream political parties have been responsible collectively for the consolidation of the model whose tentacles reach every aspect of society.

Regardless of political obfuscation by liberals blaming conservatives and vice versa, the systemic cause of the rise in inequality and authoritarianism is intertwined with policies of capital concentration and reliance on aspects of governance designed to serve the political economy amid class war intended to transfer income from the lower classes to the wealthy. The amazing aspect is that a segment of the lower classes supported such policies, aspiring to join the wealthy. Giuseppe Ricotta calls it "punitive populism", part of neoliberal control strategies both in rhetoric and practice at all levels of government.[7]

One could dismiss such control strategies as symptomatic of high tech's application to the state's bureaucratic mechanisms. However, at the core rests an ideology molding society to have it serve the political economy benefiting the world's richest 1% who own half of the wealth on the planet.[8] In *"Neoliberalism – the ideology at the root of all our problems,"* George Monbiot correctly points out that neoliberalism's pervasiveness as an ideology *"arose as a conscious attempt to reshape human life and shift the locus of power."*[9]

No matter what criteria one considers, for the working class and a segment of the middle class, life in the UK has changed for the worse after Thatcher's term in office. Apologists present the ideology as neutral and natural, reflecting human nature, as though Heaven dropped the neoliberal social contract to Earth for humanity's salvation. Promising a hierarchical society in which competitive capabilities determine the individual's socioeconomic status, the neoliberal utopia is riddled with contradictions, including the promise of freedom and prosperity vs. the reality of the degree of freedom and prosperity that socioeconomic status determines, as was the case before neoliberalism.

Built into the development model which has contributed to an increasingly politically polarized and socioeconomically unequal society, liberal democracy's erosion has been the inevitable consequence of the political economy's contradictions manifesting themselves in the promise of prosperity vs. the reality of class war and inequality. Contrary to the nebulous rhetoric of the 'free market' doing its magic, neoliberalism relies heavily on the state to mold social relations. In every endeavor, from fiscal to monetary policy and from education to religious policy, the goal has been to maintain capital concentration, minimize popular opposition to rising inequality, and foster institutional conformity.

In reaction to the liberal pluralistic-diversity political camp operating within the neoliberal political economy, the evolving social contract has normalized rising inequality on a world scale, social marginalization, and class war in the name of market efficiency. Representing big capital, the media and establishment analysts incessantly debate whether the pluralist-diversity model best serves society amid a shrinking social welfare safety net, or a rightwing populist regime promising salvation. Each political camp reinforces the other and both serve the same social contract.

Socioeconomic polarization precedes political polarization. This was evident in President Donald Trump's America, Prime Minister Narendra Modi's India, and Jair Bolsonaro's Brazil, among other authoritarian governments from Hungary to Turkey and from Kazakhstan to Myanmar where Western neoliberal transformation led to a military coup in February 2021.[10] Espousing a pluralist–diversity-pro-environment model, while aiming at the same neoliberal socioeconomic goals as rightwing populists, French President Emmanuel Macron's *La Republique En Marche* and Canada's Justin Trudeau's Liberal Party, as two examples in the same political camp, serve the same neoliberal goals as their rightwing counterparts around the world.

Whether under the pluralist or the authoritarian model, neoliberalism represents what Barrington Moore described during the Vietnam War era as a capitalist reactionary route in response to the struggle for capital appropriation and accumulation. To protect the capitalist class after the market crash of 1929, several countries fell under totalitarianism or a variety of authoritarian regimes. Fearing that the Bolshevik Revolution had inspired a global social revolution, the capitalist class, bourgeois politicians, the church, and many mainstream institutions supported totalitarianism promising salvation from trade unions and socialism. National and international conditions are not identical in the early 21st century as in the interwar, but there are some similar macroeconomic and sociopolitical trends.[11]

Barrington Moore's observation that capitalism's reactionary route is singularly focused on appropriation and accumulation entails that the political economy's goal transcends any concern to preserve liberal democracy as much in the interwar totalitarian era as under neoliberal transformation. Integrated geographically and demographically more thoroughly than at any time in its 500-year history, the capitalist world economy under the neoliberal phase has led society toward authoritarianism under the thin veil of liberal democracy.

Contrary to liberal analysis that the bourgeois democracy crisis stems from a combination of fringe groups and voter apathy, the problem extends into the socioeconomic elites' interference and manipulation of elections, as well as institutional forms of subtly coerced social conformity. Combined with marginalized extreme groups propagating against democracy and demanding authoritarianism, neoliberalism has manifested clear signs that it is incongruent with democracy and compatible with authoritarianism which it breeds. Although it has existed under the liberal-pluralist state, while doing so neoliberalism's contradictions generate the antecedents to authoritarianism.

Liberal democratic society's multi-dimensional crisis goes to the heart of neoliberalism's myriad of contradictions hastening geographic and social polarization. This has led to the rebellion of many in the capitalist class against the liberal bourgeois institutional order intertwined with Keynesian policies. An inevitable development, authoritarianism as a vehicle to carry out class war means expanding the unfettered markets against the reality of downward social mobility and chronic erosion of the social safety net.

Launching a counterrevolution against the institutional order, a segment of the capitalist class has become what Dutch cultural theorist Johan Huizinga (*Homo Ludens: A Study of the Play-Element of Culture* (2016) described during the Great Depression as the sadistic elite striving to preserve its privileges by lashing out at the working class, especially trade unionists. Beyond the manifestation of narcissistic and psychopathic traits that the model foments not just among the capitalist class but across all of society finding expression in social relations, neoliberalism reinforces sociopathic behavior. Several psychologists and social scientists have concluded that in the predatory market value system, neoliberalism finds expression across all institutions impacting the individual's psyche.[12]

Molding the mass consciousness that the root cause of systemic calamities befalling society rests with migrants, racial, ethnic, and religious minorities, women, and recalcitrant trade unionists, the neoliberal counterrevolution from above is multidimensional considering liberals and even progressive neoliberals have been a part of it. Because of identity politics in both the liberal-pluralist and rightwing populist camps, and because policies of both camps are designed to undermine working-class solidarity, the hegemonic social class, the political class, the media, and mainstream national and international organizations working toward the same goal of appropriation and accumulation are the reasons that the neoliberal order remains in force globally.

America's gradual retreat from the core of the capitalist world system amid China's rapid economic ascendancy also hastened authoritarian neoliberalism and its embrace of ultra-nationalist tendencies. As will be seen in the next chapters, China experienced phenomenal economic growth, upward social mobility, and elimination of extreme poverty from Jiang Zemin (1993-2003) to Xi Jinping (2013-present). China's rapid economic ascendancy posed a challenge not only to US hegemony but its junior partners scrambling to keep their companies competitive by seeking greater market share. Rooted in global integration for the sake of national economic development, China's long-term development has not entailed shared sacrifice amid industrialization's benefits that the state celebrates as a collective achievement.

As much as they demand that China must adopt the neo-classical transformation model, liberal and progressive Western elements support the pluralist neoliberal political parties which promise to deliver the same goals under a policy mix that includes Keynesianism. Except for a few countries, especially Scandinavian, the goal has been to maintain a skeletal social safety net and inclusive social structure to mitigate class conflict and market disequilibrium.

Further confusing those concerned about whether neoliberalism falls in the domain of a progressive, liberal, or authoritarian political umbrella, culture wars have been intertwined with identity politics and green economy issues that neoliberal governments and international organizations, including the World Bank, have co-opted. Added to mixed reactions about the US-led campaign to slow China's ascendancy, major corporate leaders like Morris Chang, Taiwan Semiconductor founder, argued in 2023 that de-globalization is a reality under a post-neoliberal fragmented world economy.[13]

These debates invariably shift the focus from neoliberal policies responsible for chronic downward social mobility to the slowing of capital appropriation and accumulation on a world scale. They further contribute to the debate of the "lesser evil" choice between liberal and rightwing populist regimes, although both aim at the same socioeconomic goals. Rejecting elitist culture and embracing popular culture often finding expression in "identity politics", Friedrich Hayek, the most important apostle of neoliberal ideology, did not reject cultural pluralism as part of the political economy in the same manner that he rejected the Enlightenment's rationalism and liberal democracy. On the contrary, he viewed culture as a useful tool for popular mobilization behind the neoliberal model.

It is common to find capitalists and corporations readily accepting Hayek's popular culture theory based on evolutionist assumptions. Just as readily, they embrace the neoliberal order beneath the multilayered cloak of a trendy culture - clothing, music, lifestyle choices, etc. – intertwined with identity politics, camouflaging the political economy's ultimate goal of market hegemony, class war, and rising inequality. While Hayek dismissed the constructivist theory (cultural context determines empirical reality/knowledge) of culture in favor of the Darwinian evolutionist theory, the capitalist system in its neoliberal phase is the quintessence of constructivism. [14]

Along with socioeconomic fiscal conservatives, nationalists, militarists, and technocrats, cultural conservatives also reject democracy's collectivist assumptions. Historically, they have identified more with libertarian James M. Buchanan promoting authoritarian neoliberalism than with Walter Lippmann who brought the first group of neoliberal thinkers together in Paris in 1938. Although there are libertarian neoliberals who do not identify with Buchanan advocating supremacy of property over people, the libertarian policy does aim at cultural discrimination against workers and minorities.

Because of the populist rhetorical rejection of globalization and diversity-based cultural identity, many confuse libertarianism with radicalism. Some of the confusion in the progressive camp has aspects of the counterculture of the 1960s; a thin coating over what the reactionary core beneath. The pluralist political and business neoliberal elite has been as effective in carrying out politically and socioeconomically polarizing policies as authoritarian neoliberals who use culture wars as a catalyst to mobilize the popular base.[15]

Liberal pluralists and rightwing populists have deliberately used culture wars to undercut class solidarity and mobilize support for the pro-market model molding the entire institutional structure. In the US, the political and business class has historically used politics of race, nationalism, ethnicity, and religion, especially Evangelicals as catalysts to mobilize the right made up mostly of whites. In India, Hindu vs. Muslim, especially as expressed in Hindutva has been the catalyst for rightwing populism under Prime Minister Narendra Modi's regime. In mobilizing the masses behind authoritarian neoliberalism, religion, and culture have played a catalytic role. Effectively subordinating class consciousness to culture wars and using it as a mechanism of class war, conservative and liberal political parties alike have delivered a mass popular base behind the neoliberal social contract.

Without the mass media and social media's role in mass indoctrination, education, and religious institutions, political distraction and indoctrination would be very difficult. Redefining citizenship based on market-based criteria, neoliberalism has reduced all human endeavors, including social relations and individuals, healthy and gravely ill, into "cash-value" commodities. Recognizing society only in its monolithic market dimension, neoliberalism accepts Max Weber's disdain for bureaucracy, although serving the corporate welfare state bureaucracy is important in neoliberal transformation.[16]

By subordinating, if not obviating, community rights, human rights, and civil rights to the marketplace, neoliberalism has de-politicized and alienated the automaton-like citizens at the bottom of the socioeconomic ladder who recognize that the social contract excludes them from the privileged mainstream; a class war objective at the core of neoliberalism. The irony of undermining human rights and community rights is that the movements defending dissidents and community rights took off concurrently with the neoliberal transformation. This was only a trojan horse concealing the transition from the Keynesian state to the neoliberal corporate welfare state.

Another social conformity mechanism has been integrating neoliberal doctrines into constitutions by invoking "constitutional originalism" as a means of weakening the central government and Keynesian remnants while decentralizing state power. Especially in the US where social relations under states' rights with layers of racist undertones, the concept has a divisive past. It is infused with neoliberal doctrines, constitutional originalism reinforced and legitimized the populist right culminating in Trump's election and the Republican Party embracing aspects of authoritarianism, including regimenting press and academic freedom, voter suppression targeting minorities, election interference, high concentration of power in the executive, and manipulation of the judicial branch and entire criminal justice system.[17]

The success of neoliberalism has been that its apologists in all venues from media to education have convinced a large segment of the masses to accept its definition of self and a mythology analogous to Calvinist salvation for the market-oriented predestined souls. At the same time, neoliberal advocates have effectively neutralized both Keynesians and progressives advocating some form of social safety net. This is in part because the fall of the Soviet bloc coincided with the rise of neoliberalism under the US-centered world order emerging during the presidency of George H. W. Bush. At the same time, China's ascendancy as the main driver of capitalist development, seemingly validated the Western neoliberal argument about accepting social contract as the norm globally, despite Beijing's political economy resting on a hybrid model.[18]

With a special focus on the US, this study offers an overview of some aspects of neoliberal transformation's global reach from the 1980s to the early 2020s. Contrary to apologists' claims about neoliberalism as the panacea, the Great Recession of 2008 and its lingering aftermath, the COVID-19 pandemic which required a collective response with the state assuming a central role to save capitalism from self-destruction, and the Western sanctions against Russia after the latter invaded Ukraine provides ample proof of the myths and glaring contradictions that have been detrimental to society's welfare throughout the world.

Refusing to reevaluate the neoliberal model in the face of such global tragedies, the state, international financial institutions, including the IMF, World Bank, and World Trade Organization (WTO), and stock markets, especially Wall Street, preach profit against addressing rising inequality and authoritarianism. The widespread misery of the majority living in fear under monetary and fiscal austerity after 2008, the economic and health consequences of the COVID-19 pandemic, and global stagflation amid the Russian war in Ukraine in the 2020s were opportunities to amass even greater profits under a model thriving on chaos and disorder.[19]

The media, corporate and political lobbyists, business consultants, think tanks and business-linked academics have been dogmatic about perpetuating the very system that failed amid early 21st-century crises and led societies deeper into authoritarianism's embrace. Contrary to optimistic scenarios that the global economic crisis of 2008 and the pandemic, supply-chain bottlenecks, war in Ukraine, and Western sanctions would lead to systemic changes mitigating socioeconomic marginalization under the neoliberal model, none of these predictions came true. Even during the pandemic that shattered the myth about the state's role as essential for collective public health and an end to vaccine apartheid at the expense of the Global South, neoliberals dogmatically insisted on adherence to a socially-destructive model born out of a sociopathic hysteria against the concept of the "social" which Hayek dismissed as a *"weasel word par excellence."*[20]

The ultimate contradiction of neoliberalism is market hegemony over the state and outsourcing public agency functions to buttress the private sector unable to survive on its own without massive public income transfer from labor and the middle class. Furthermore, neoliberalism theoretically entails a decentralized state structure and a weak social welfare component with a strong corporate welfare dimension. When factoring into the mix of geopolitics amid the US-China competition, the state's role becomes even more significant. This has been the case in the US-China inimical relationship which the US has used as the pretext to withhold technology transfers, especially semiconductors. Competition to secure rare earth elements neodymium and praseodymium used for medical devices, motors, and turbines has been a part of the US-China rivalry as well.[21]

In the struggle for global hegemony, the US has responded differently from China. The Chinese government consults the corporate sector in pursuing pro-business economic policy by central planning and social development goals. In the US, corporate lawyers and lobbyists draft regulations that government agencies and elected officials endorse. Globally, neoliberals demand even lower tariffs, the end of price controls, privatization of public assets, accommodative monetary policy, corporate welfare incentives, and state intervention to bail out larger businesses, especially banks. At the same time, where geopolitics transcends the global market to serve national capitalism, tariffs become policy benefiting corporations of the country imposing them. Not only is there no Keynesian regulatory state except for geopolitical considerations, but as Craig Berry argues analyzing neoliberalism in the UK, the "substitutive state" has taken over statecraft.[22]

If neoliberalism stopped with the "substitutive state", one could argue that its apologists are merely building upon and expanding Adam Smith's (*An Inquiry into the Causes of The Wealth of Nations*, 1776) laissez-faire ideology by creating a hybrid model to efface all traces of the Keynesian state. Intending to save the bourgeois social order and avert social revolution, Keynes (*The General Theory of Employment, Interest, and Money*, 1936) offered a holistic vision of society beyond employment theory, inflation, aggregate demand, and output, all of them ultimately aiming to save capitalism from inherent contradictions and the bourgeois social order and civilization.

Hardly a theory of everything like Stephen Hawking's unifying astrophysics cosmological model explaining nature's interwoven interactions, neoliberalism's global reach into markets, government, and institutions including religion, and culture is far from what 18th and 19th-century liberals envisioned. It is farther afield from any ambitious goals rooted in rationalist Enlightenment principles upon which modern Western Civilization was built.

The "theory of everything" construct goes to the heart of the debate on whether neoliberalism is merely a finance ideology or an all-inclusive model subsuming every institution more rigidly than any previous phase of capitalism. Other symptoms of the neoliberal transformation's global reach include a shift in labor-capital relations under the economy's financialization and rentier capitalism. The quintessence of capitalism's parasitic nature under its neoliberal phase, financialization places all emphasis on the financial market's preponderate role in the economy, while rentier capitalism entails concentrated ownership of key assets reducing the majority to servile status.[23]

Contrary to claims that neoliberals favor a weakened state structure as a means of strengthening capital, they only advocate a weak social welfare and regulatory state in the name of market efficiency; a concept narrowly defined to exclude regulatory mechanisms applied to business. Corporate welfare, corporate bailouts, and commodifying domestic and foreign policy to buttress the corporate sector are integral parts of the neoliberal state which is more bureaucratically parasitic than the Keynesian social welfare state. This is partly because the former outsources services previously carried out by the state bureaucracy at a much higher cost to the consumer without public scrutiny and accountability of a public entity.

Yet, the US and the West argue that China's state bureaucracy is burdensome to the private sector merely because Beijing has been pursuing a hybrid development model integrating much of the world economy under its aegis. Competing with the Washington Consensus neoliberal model, the Chinese mixed economic model (Beijing Consensus, followed by the Belt and Road Initiative, BRI) has resulted in competition with the US-led Western coalition. Confined with IMF austerity, deregulation-privatization, and anti-labor policies that the US urged Latin American governments to adopt, after 1989 the Washington Consensus became globalized at the same time that China was integrating rapidly into the world economy.[24]

The resounding success of the Beijing development model has been evident in its rapid rise to global hegemony. Going beyond the Shanghai Cooperation Organization (SCO), representing the largest regional block with close to half of the world's population and more than 30% of global GDP[1], the model has come at the expense of workers domestically and globally, while aiming at upward social mobility and poverty elimination at home. US-China competition aside, inherent dynamics slowing capital accumulation in the Western core, neoliberalism has been on the path of authoritarianism as a means of realizing even greater concentrated capital and global market share at the expense of workers. Ironically, to deflect attention from Western neoliberalism, Western politicians and analysts castigate China as an authoritarian anomaly in an otherwise 'democratic' neoliberal world.

1. https://en.wikipedia.org/wiki/GDP

Resorting to sanctions, tariffs, technology transfer restrictions, and investment regulatory obstacles, precluding third countries from signing contracts with Chinese firms, to mention just a few tactics, US-G-7 and NATO members leverage to gain global market advantage works short term. This is merely by weakening the target seeking continued integration while undermining the global neoliberal transformation model, thus, self-defeating. Besides the dollar's prevalence as a reserve currency in the IMF Special Drawing Rights basket over other currencies, choosing to buy government bonds as a means of strengthening one reserve currency over the other, combined with sanctions and a myriad of national security restrictions on trade, and punishing third parties that violate such restrictions are all examples of how the neoliberal state sabotages the transformation model's global reach by opting for trade fragmentation as a short-term strategy.

To reach domestic social consensus and serve national capitalism's appetite for market share by using geopolitical considerations as a pretext, neoliberalism deviates from its own free market principles which are hardly meaningful both at the microeconomic and macroeconomic level. The very contradictions involving greater reliance on state intervention entail losing the ability to deliver on capital appropriation and accumulation on a world scale, amid eroding consumer-citizen freedom and mobility which neoliberalism claims is at the core of sociopolitical consensus. After the dot.com bubble of 2000 and the Great Recession of 2008, deepening systemic contradictions caused market disequilibrium amid the shifting core of the world economy. Greater inequality under the rise of autocratization coincided with US-NATO interventionism in 2010 and into the 2020s.

In the post-WWII era, Pax Americana's management of the world economy with the help of the multilateral institutions, while simultaneously the US has been leveraging its military superpower status ran its course of maturity and set course toward decline. The pattern of Pax Americana's twilight was not so different from Pax Britannica's during the Age of Imperialism (1870-1914) when Germany, the US, and Japan emerged as newly industrialized powers challenging the British Empire with London as the world's financial center. Under neoliberalism coinciding with the war on terror replacing the Cold War, Pax Americana provided greater impetus for the rise of authoritarianism on a world scale, including parts of Asia where there was a rise in domestic struggles and conflicts.[25]

Although the capital has always gone where it realizes the highest, safest, and most promising return on investment, everything from war, sanctions, tariffs, and geopolitical considerations impedes its flow on whose logic neoliberalism operates. This is not to suggest that non-market factors related to foreign and defense policy are divorced from capital accumulation on a world scale as a goal. Under exigent geopolitical conditions, the nation-state supersedes the market to serve it, both short-term and especially longer-term. Hence, inherent contradictions inevitably arise, as the US-China competition has demonstrated in the early 21st century.

A US-China power struggle amid rising geopolitical tensions in a multipolar world capitalist system poses challenges for the Global South states decision is whether to serve the militarized declining Pax Americana-led trading blocs or to opt for trade and investment terms under Chinese tutelage promising better terms of a dependency relationship. No matter which regional trading bloc countries choose, conditions rooted in global trade fragmentation dilute the neoliberal transformation's global reach.

Neoliberalism, the highest stage of capitalism of the late 20th-early-21st century, encompasses all of the structural aspects of late-19th-early-20th century imperialism. Liberal reformist (John Hobson) and Marxist intellectuals Rosa Luxemburg, Rudolf Hilferding, V.I. Lenin, and Karl Kautsky described the Age of Imperialism as detrimental to the working class and society. History proved them correct, given that imperialism inevitably led to wars of imperialism culminating in WWI and to the Bolshevik Revolution. Amid its underlying crisis and dangerous course of global division for markets and raw materials, combined with heightened militarism, neoliberalism's contradictions amid a US-led massive arms buildup amounting to 40% of the world's total defense spending is as dangerous as the British-German arms race during the Boer War in South Africa (1899-1902).

Behind the thin ideological veil of free efficient market and non-state intervention, neoliberalism relies heavily on state power which has surrendered policy and many essential functions of public agencies to corporations and the billionaire investor class. Corporations aggressively seeking markets at any cost, including the risk of mutually destructive wars for the entire world economy, as was the case of Russia's invasion of Ukraine in 2022, are ominous signs of a self-destructive model taking society down with it.

Promoting global integration for resource concentration, neoliberalism is caught up in the myth of its own making about boundless growth which is nothing more than resource allocation from the bottom up on a world scale. Along with geopolitics fragmenting the world economy, and incessant class war manifesting itself in everything from declining workers' living standards to attack on social justice, neoliberalism contains the seeds of the model's demise as it serves an ever-smaller percent of the population, repressing the majority, undercutting the Enlightenment ideal of improving human welfare through liberal-democratic institutions in the age of mass politics.

Introduction: An Overview of Neoliberalism's Historical Antecedents

Rooted in the 19th century Age of Imperialism that produced monopolies, trusts, and cartels, neoliberal ideology is counterrevolution against liberal democracy and the working class in reaction not just to fear of socialism, but of Keynesianism. The ideology on which an eclectic blend of policies is based began taking shape in Europe during the Great Depression amid the global popularity of Keynesian policies and the fear of the Bolshevik Revolution spreading beyond the USSR. By the early Cold War amid the East-West world order, neoliberalism found the perfect political environment to propagate its ideology.[26]

If one accepts the wave theory that Nikolai Kondratieff (*Long Wave Cycle*, 1926) developed to explain capitalism's long cycles of 40-60 years, neoliberalism was the outgrowth of new technology from the late 1970s to the present. Even if Kondratieff's technologically/scientific wave theory is taken at face value, there are questions about cycles so rigidly tied to a time frame, complicated by the short-term and intermediate contracting cycles determining the long cycle's course, duration, and above all the role of capital accumulation in the process.

In *The Curve of Capitalist Development* (1923), Leon Trotsky writes: "*Entire epochs of capitalist development exist when several cycles are characterized by sharply delineated booms and weak, short-lived crises. As a result, we have a sharply rising movement of the basic curve of capitalist development. There are epochs of stagnation when this curve while passing through partial cyclical oscillations, remains on approximately the same level for decades. And finally, during certain historical periods the basic curve, while passing as always through cyclical oscillations, dips downward as a whole, signaling the decline of productive forces.*"

Although neoliberalism on the surface appears to fit into the Kondratieff cycle theory because it roughly coincides with the new technology era following the long wave of Keynesianism, and it is rather typical of past cycles building on existing layers of capitalist development. An even more atomistic, anti-social, and anti-labor ideology than classical liberalism found in the works of Adam Smith, David Ricardo (*On the Principles of Political Economy and Taxation*, 1817) and John Stuart Mill (*On Liberty*, 1859), neoliberalism was initially a reaction to the Bolshevik Revolution's global influence, the rise of the welfare state in the 1930s and Keynesian macroeconomics that most capitalists and politicians wanted diluted, if not eliminated.

In August 1938, French and American scholars participated in a colloquium - *Comité international d'étude pour le renouveau du libéralisme* (CIERL) which American journalist/political analyst Walter Lipmann headlined in Paris. Ideological nuances emerged between the faction that Lippmann and Austrian scholar Friedrich Hayek headed against that of militant anti-Keynesian Étienne Mantoux and the "Manchester School" economists, especially Ludwig von Misses who favored "pure market" economics without any state involvement.

Making the state-backed market the core of the social contract, everything in society from personal freedoms and rights to privileges rested on the market, without a social safety net or the state assuming any stimulative role in the economy through public enterprises to address unemployment amid contracting cycles. The welfare-state bureaucracy was the enemy to be replaced with a business-welfare state structure aiming to shift public resources to support private capital. This was based on the theme of private appropriation of public income and greater redistribution from labor to capital.[27]

Arising from the chaos of transitioning out of the war economy to the unregulated civilian economy in the 1920s during postwar reconstruction, American interwar isolationism combined with lingering chaotic market-based conditions in Europe and the colonies, global dislocation was a prescription for economic disaster. The 1920s was the decade of market preeminence with trading blocs, uncoordinated, if not clashing central bank monetary policies, and reckless bank lending linked to unregulated stock market speculation.

Against the background of minimal government market interference and lack of international monetary coordination, world trade fragmentation, banking speculation and rising tariffs, a deep cyclical economic depression was inevitable, built into the system. The political question was whether to save capitalism under an authoritarian regime and sacrifice liberal democracy, try to save both, or possibly face social revolution as did Russia in 1917, if nothing else succeeded within the system intended to preserve the capitalist system.

As a result of the stock market and banking speculation, combined with the debt crisis in the Caribbean and Latin America, the New York stock market crashed in 1929, unveiling jungle capitalism beneath the illusion of postwar economic expansion. Governments and politicians around the world, especially in the US, found the solution in Keynesian economics to sustain the capitalist system and preserve social harmony by building and strengthening the social welfare state with the support of trade unions. It was against this backdrop that neoliberalism as an ideology emerged to reaffirm the validity of a political economy in ruins. At the Paris conference that Lippmann hosted, one of the proposals was to convert the social welfare Keynesian state into a corporate welfare state. The far-fetched idea in 1938, the corporate welfare state proposal became institutionalized four decades after Lippmann's Paris conference.[28]

After WWII, the Truman administration focused on integrating as many countries as possible under America's aegis to manage the capitalist world economy through various programs, including the Bretton Woods System. The Truman Doctrine, the Marshall Plan, and the General Agreement on Tariffs and Trade (GATT), all with geopolitical and geoeconomic goals, intended to generate capitalist growth. However, they were also a means to prevent workers from gravitating toward trade unionism and leftist movements, guiding them instead toward the pro-business mainstream.

Breaking from FDR's policies, Truman was responsible for promulgating the Cold War and laying the groundwork to shift from social welfare Keynesianism to military Keynesianism, prioritizing the defense sector as Pax Americana's global geopolitical and geoeconomic leverage. Using the Cold War as justification, President Dwight Eisenhower continued to strengthen the military-industrial complex which absorbed the surplus capital and mitigated contracting economic cycles. By the late 1950s, the balance of payments surplus of the late 1940s turned into a chronic deficit. The IMF privately informed the Eisenhower administration that the chronic current account deficits placed the dollar's integrity as a reserve currency at risk and posed long-term problems to the US and global economy.[29]

Continuing to roll back Keynesianism at home, the US expected the rest of the world to go along with the transformation policy by IMF and World Bank guidelines on economic development, trade, fiscal, monetary, foreign investment, and labor policy. The two international lending institutions based their policies on a free-market model which necessarily entailed eroding the Keynesian welfare state, reducing tariffs, opening the economy to foreign capital, weakening and/or privatizing public enterprises, and weakening trade unions.

A prelude to neoliberalism, the strategy intended to strengthen capital, especially multinational enterprises at the expense of workers in core nations and periphery alike. Against the background of the nascent Soviet-American confrontation, Austrian scholars Hayek, Ludwig von Mises, and Karl Popper, along with American economists George Stigler and Milton Friedman reignited the neoliberal flame by forming the Mont Pelerin Society, which coincided with the Truman Doctrine and IMF launching global operations in 1947.[30]

Three years before the Mont Pelerin meeting held in Switzerland, Hayek published *The Road to Serfdom,* castigating as "authoritarian" not just Soviet Union and socialism in any form, but Keynesianism for its extensive income redistribution policy component, and the social welfare system as part of market equilibrium strategy. Ignoring the fiscal structure's historic role as an instrument of hierarchical income distribution at the core of the market economy, Hayek criticized Western progressives for advancing the thesis of Nazism as a manifestation of the "dying capitalist system". Somewhat typical of early Cold War thinking, his critique implied that the enemy was not the Nazi state, but socialism and Keynesianism that defeated the Axis Powers.

Among scholars arguing that neoliberalism was not consistent with Adam Smith's laissez-faire economics, French philosopher/historian Michel Foucault noted that neoliberalism advocated market construction through active political intervention. From Harry Truman to Jimmy Carter, the US, Western Europe, and most of the capitalist world pursued a policy mix that retained a weakened social welfare component as a means of sustaining the market and sociopolitical equilibrium during the Soviet-American confrontation.

Once Margaret Thatcher took office in 1979 and Ronald Reagan in 1981, fundamental differences between classical liberalism and neoliberal ideology intended to transform the world looked very different from what Foucault had speculated. In *Critiquer Foucault: Les années 1980 et la tentation néoliberale,* Daniel Zamora points out that Foucault betrayed the left by mis-analyzing neoliberalism. This was during the post-Vietnam Western economic and foreign policy malaise marked by defaulting all structural problems to Keynesianism, without uttering a word about military Keynesianism.

After Thatcher took over, she adopted Freidman's monetarist dogma and Hayek's harsh anti-society (anti-Keynesian) beliefs. Long before Thatcherism, IMF policies contained neoliberal elements imposed on developing nations trying to secure monetary stabilization loans in return for adopting austerity measures as a prelude to borrowing from private financial institutions. The IMF's long-standing practice entailed income transfer from the working class to domestic and foreign businesses, and from the periphery to the metropolis.

Disillusioned with Keynesian capitalism, Foucault ignored such important historical facts, perhaps because IMF-World Bank policy and its impact on the Global South was outside of his research focus. Although he delivered the lectures (*The Birth of Biopolitics,* 1979) before Thatcher and Reagan implemented neoliberal policies, his initial analysis of neoliberalism was in part a reaction to the French and global economic crisis of the 1970s. Like many analysts, Foucault was in search of an alternative model to the stagnation of Keynesian statism that yielded low growth under high inflation without offering much growth prospects after the Arab-Israeli War of 1973 and the OPEC reaction precipitating the oil crisis.

Foucault did not place the proper weight on several salient factors, including the arms race and containment militarism that the US and its junior partners had embraced as a cause of stagflation. This oversight further obfuscated the larger picture of the world capitalist system's postwar evolution, including the empirically baseless assumption that the development model after Keynesianism would somehow benefit society more. Nor did he take into account that the IMF and World Bank had already established the foundation for neoliberalism on a world scale since the late 1940s and the transition was about to start in the UK and US. At the very least, he could have considered that neoliberals were using Chile as an experiment when Foucault was writing.[31]

For its part, the US had another pretext to pursue "military Keynesianism" to manage its imperial interests; most notably, to maintain growing non-Western markets, and access to energy and minerals for industrial expansion. As reflected in the chronic balance of payments deficits and the dollar's artificially high value and subject of international speculative profiteering, the price paid for military Keynesianism was to drain precious resources from the civilian economy. No country other than the US enjoyed the privilege of borrowing on its own currency, in essence writing a blank check when the account showed deficient funds. Given the dollar's global use for trade and investment, the value was artificially high amid chronic current account deficits at the expense of its partners, causing trade imbalances due to the artificial value that the dollar determined.[32]

Two years after Nixon de-linked the dollar from gold in August 1971, a Western-wide economic dislocation followed the energy crisis of 1973. In retaliation for the US supplying Israel weapons during the Yom Kippur War (October 1973), the OPEC oil embargo triggered the energy crisis which turned into a global economic crisis. Against the background of the post-Vietnam stagflation economy, the capitalist class was eager to further weaken the Keynesian social welfare state that on the surface appeared to be the cause of limiting capitalist appropriation. In the absence of catalytic geopolitical developments, neoliberalism would not have taken place based solely on Keynesianism's failure to deliver optimal returns to capital and economic growth, as Foucault argued in his lectures.[33]

The convergence of geopolitics and economics played a salient role in the weakening of the US at the core of the world capitalist system. Neoliberalism's embryonic evolution took place against such a global context at the end of the Vietnam War amid internal dynamics determining each country's struggle with economic growth that appeared to be part of a long cycle that had run its course. From the late 19th century to the present, the geopolitical-geoeconomic nexus and shifting core in the world system have played a contributing role in the social structure cycles of capitalist appropriation and accumulation.

Most studies on neoliberalism have a trans-Atlantic (northwest Europe-US-Canada) focus, placing secondary significance on the periphery's role; a thesis which several scholars developed, among them Samir Amin (*Accumulation and Development*, 1974). While the state's role assumes great significance in the political economy, the unequal relationship based on the patron-client (core-periphery) integration model is considered only on the margins, if at all. Policy transition from the Keynesian era to neoliberalism required not just the international financial institutions setting the ideological groundwork, but forging of a political consciousness at the national level in developed and developing nations.[34]

Contrary to the neoliberal model's claims under Thatcher and Reagan, no economy in history has ever existed in the absence of the state's interference in terms of fiscal, monetary, trade, investment, labor, and tariff policy. From Lipmann's Paris Colloquium to the IMF and World Bank analysts preaching the gospel of free enterprise as a means of making neoliberalism widely acceptable in developing countries, neoliberal apostles have been deceiving governments and the world, if not themselves. Neoliberalism engenders and preserves market hegemony over every sector for the sake of securing appropriation and accumulation at labor's expense. From the 1980s to the present, the neoliberal political economy's goal has been to mold all institutions, public and private, while transforming society by re-writing the social contract.[35]

Ever since Hayek's conference in Mont Pelerin, neoliberals have failed to address the contradiction of transitioning from the social welfare state to corporate welfare, while insisting that they are advocates of free enterprise. Promising that market hegemony would result in society's 'modernization' whose benefits would filter down to all classes, commonly baptized "trickle-down economics" under Reagan, the result has been a wider socioeconomic gap, marginalization, and democracy's steady decline along with living standards, while rightwing populism was gaining momentum.[36]

Replete with modernization theory assumptions, a theory that emerged after WWII when the US took advantage of its preeminent global superpower status to impose a transformation model on much of the non-Communist world, neoliberal ideology was creeping into the mainstream in the 1970s. In an influential work entitled *The Stages of Economic Growth: A Non-Communist Manifesto*, (1960), Cold War liberal Walt Rostow articulated the modernization development model that neoliberal ideology ultimately absorbed.

At the center of the US-Communist rivalry rested the struggle for global markets, raw materials, especially strategic minerals, and geopolitical advantage to secure economic benefits. Transcending macroeconomic perimeters, Rostow's modernization theory was based on imperialist assumptions about the Western patron-client model which reflected US global hegemony determining the world order through both economic and military means. This necessarily entailed supporting military Keynesianism as a means of undermining and ultimately defeating the Communist bloc. Although the enemy was hardly a monolith, considering the Sino-Soviet split after 1956, which coincided with the Hungarian Revolution against the USSR, it was in the US interest to present Communism as monolithic to justify the Western geopolitical and geoeconomic bloc.[37]

The challenge for the post-WWII bourgeois political class operating on consensus-building assumptions was to mobilize a popular base that would afford legitimacy to the social contract with a Cold War dimension intertwined with the political economy. The issue for mainstream political parties was never whether there was systemic injustice with the social contract. Rather, it was the degree to which the masses would be co-opted through various methods to support the status quo at home and the capitalist world order against the Communist bloc. In so far as Keynesian social welfare remained a viable policy, it was to stimulate consumer demand that political parties needed as a tool to prevent working-class radicalization.

Considering that America's social contract reflected the Soviet-American confrontation justifying military Keynesianism, it was inevitable that all non-Communist countries would follow the Western superpower's lead. Foucault's assumptions about the quasi-statist model's bankruptcy by the 1970s notwithstanding, the Cold War, especially the Vietnam War which much of the world opposed, was both a contributing factor to the decadence and fanatic dogmatism of that era, while serving as an impetus for the neoliberal model's global ascendancy.

"A generation ago," Josh Friedman and Michael Lind pointed out, *"the country's [USA] social contract was premised on higher wages and reliable benefits, provided chiefly by employers. In recent decades, we've moved to a system where low wages are supposed to be made bearable by low consumer prices and a hodgepodge of government assistance programs. But as dissatisfaction with this arrangement has grown, it is time to look back at how we got here and imagine what the next stage of the social contract might be."*[38]

Disagreeing only on how best to achieve capital accumulation, while retaining sociopolitical conformity, Keynesianism and neoliberalism operated under the same social order. Friedman and Lind's argument illustrates how some analysts easily misinterpret nuances within the social contract, attributing them to the covenant's macroeconomic goals. Similar to the view expressed in the article above, the *New America Foundation's* publications identify specific aspects of Arthur Schlesinger's Cold War militarist policies enmeshed with social welfare Keynesianism.

This mix represents the evolving social contract and the new reality of the US at the core of global capitalism. Rooted in the 19th-century Manifest Destiny philosophical doctrine, American political elites and academics in their quest to justify foreign intervention and the patron-client relationship with the Global South assumed that the US had earned the right to determine the world balance of power under the Cold War-Bretton Woods transformation model.[39]

Identifying the Cold War-Bretton Woods social contract with a specific set of policies under various administrations reflecting the nuances of political class strategies to mobilize popular support and forge political consensus, some analysts contend that the European Union-wide social contract advanced neoliberalism following in Thatcher's footsteps. In the name of the transformation's global reach, European Union members subordinated their national sovereignty to the regional bloc as the best means to remain globally competitive collectively. This was the best route for European companies to reduce their tax/tariff costs, increase market share, and use the bloc as leverage internationally.

Apologists of Pax Americana maintain that from the Marshall Plan in 1948 to Charles de Gaulle withdrawing France from NATO's military structure in 1966, Europe owed its ascendancy to the US as its senior economic and strategic partner. A gesture of symbolic significance about Europe's relative rising strength, de Gaulle's gesture coincided with the waning of the dollar's value and the US's weakened economic role. Mutual ideological, political, geopolitical, and economic interests kept relations cordial between the US and its European partners. Through the regional economic union, Europe pursued globalization as aggressively as the US, Japan, Australia, and Canada.[40]

Neoliberal transformation's global reach was more challenging for the US and its G-7 partners to impose on developing nations. This is because the patron-client relationship between the core and periphery entailed uneven terms of trade at the expense of the Global South's "dependency" on the industrialized West. Rooted in 19th-century imperialism, the patron-client relationship became more pronounced under the neoliberal status quo, demanding a weakened state structure catering only to businesses under diluted national sovereignty.

Not only had the patron-client model failed to deliver on the promise of post-WWII socioeconomic development and social justice, but it perpetuated external dependence on the Global South, cyclical debt crises, and chronic underdevelopment by focusing on financing finished products by exporting raw materials. In part, the cyclical debt crises that IMF austerity and policies caused in part meant greater dependence and borrowing with downward pressure on wages and lower living standards.[41]

A unique exception to global neoliberal transformation, China, which embraced aspects of neoliberalism at home, linked its economy to the world capitalist system and benefited more from neoliberal globalization than the rest of the world. Following the shift from a command economy under Chairman Mao to developmentalist capitalist reforms under Deng Xiaoping (1982-1987), and an increasingly mixed economy under Jiang Zemin (1989-2002), rapid industrial development in the nascent stage of global ascendancy coincided with neoliberal transformation.

China's average annual per capita income was $195 in 1980, about the same as India's at the time that neoliberalism was reinventing the UK. Indicative of a remarkable achievement in rapid economic development and upward mobility, in comparison with downward mobility in the West, by 2021, China outpaced the world in GDP at $27.2 trillion against the US at $23 trillion, measured in purchasing power parity (PPP).[42]

Partnering with private companies, and engaged in compulsory technology transfer, Chinese state-owned enterprises helped the country's rapid domestic economic development and global integration, while also pursuing social development and massive domestic and international infrastructure programs. Consolidating its indispensable position in the neoliberal world economy under a mixed model with statist policies that the Communist Party was coordinating in a partially planned economy, China's goal has been to out-compete the G-7 group and to closely integrate as much of the world as possible, above all Asia and Eurasia. From an economy comparable to the average in the Global South, China leaped forward to the semi-periphery by the Great Recession of 2008.

Thereafter, it began competing with the US head-to-head, matching it in GDP-PPP terms by 2016, and consistently surpassing it. China's astronomic economic rise prompted a renewed US-led Cold War containment policy while continuing to engage China economically. Indicative of far-reaching interdependence, from which neither party could disengage, both Washington and Beijing have tried to influence other governments and international organizations, including the WTO, World Bank, and IMF, all of which modified Beijing's behavior in geoeconomics from which China benefited.[43]

Long before the trans-Atlantic core countries institutionalized neoliberalism and before China's global integration, IMF-imposed austerity linked to monetary stabilization loans was the leverage to compel developing nations to weaken the social safety net while transferring income from the working class to capital. IMF fiscal adjustment around the world helped China absorb surplus capital at a time when several governments turned to Beijing for trade and investment deals owing to cheap labor and a growing domestic market. IMF austerity linking monetary stabilization loans as a prerequisite for development loans from the World Bank and private markets credit rating was similar to imperialist financial control that prevailed in the 19th century. One key difference is that China indirectly benefited without suffering the austerity stigma attached to the IMF whose policies Beijing has supported.[44]

Narrowly focused on market efficiency, rarely do IMF austerity apologists mention fiscal adjustment and neoliberalism's far-reaching social costs or the erosion of democracy. Representing big capital focused on the promise of allowing the market to do its magic to advance capital at any social and political cost, Milton Friedman and other neoliberals were deliberately oblivious to downward pressure on working-class living standards. A testament to neoliberalism's smooth transition within the social structure, the general public took it for granted that the political economy operated in the background like passing clouds before the rain.

George Monbiot of *The Guardian* raised a few basic questions about the degree to which the general public has remained mystified when it comes to the social contract under which society operates. "*Neoliberalism: do you know what it is? Its anonymity is both a symptom and cause of its power. It has played a major role in a remarkable variety of crises: the financial meltdown of 2007-2008, the offshoring of wealth and power, of which the Panama Papers offer us merely a glimpse, the slow collapse of public health and education, resurgent child poverty, the epidemic of loneliness, the collapse of ecosystems, the rise of Donald Trump. But we respond to these crises as if they emerge in isolation, apparently unaware that they have all been either catalyzed or exacerbated by the same coherent philosophy; a philosophy that has – or had – a name. What greater power can there be than to operate namelessly?*"[45]

Whether under the liberal-pluralist Western umbrella where remnants of Keynesian social welfare remain, or under a regime claiming the "electoral democracy" label, but imposing authoritarian policies, the political and social elites' strategy disagreements are about dogmatic rightwing culturally-determined ideology of social exclusion vs. inclusive populism of identity politics. The disagreements serve to distract and further confuse the public, while the political leadership of opposing camps represents the neoliberal social contract.[46]

Throughout the Western World, conservative and liberal political parties and the media have been celebrating neoliberalism's triumph which Communism's fall validated, especially for Pax Americana. By the end of the 1990s amid the dot.com bubble, it became obvious that history was not "ending", not any time soon, as Francis Fukuyama (*The End of History*) was speculating in 1992. In retrospect, history was merely starting a new chapter of concentrated capital and intensified class war. Besides weakened progressive parties, middle-class and working-class living standards experienced chronic decline amid the rise of the populist right and an effective co-optation strategy of both liberals and conservatives.[47]

Globalization enthusiasts never mention Chile where the IMF and the neoliberal Chicago Boys caused misery on a wide scale during the US-backed dictatorship of Augusto Pinochet (1973-1990). A dictatorship that neoliberal apostles Friedrich Hayek, Milton Friedman, and James Buchanan supported, Pinochet's regime proved neoliberalism's transformation from the Frieberg School (Ordo-liberalism School) of Walter Eucken, Franz Böhm, and Hans Großmann-Doerth intending to reinvigorate classical liberalism in the 1930s to the identification of neoliberalism with a brutal dictatorship. The neoliberal model in a Third World country could hardly have any resemblance to what would take place in the trans-Atlantic core. Nevertheless, authoritarian Chile was neoliberalism's laboratory that the Western political, media, and business establishment hailed as a success.[48]

Refusing to acknowledge that class war has been responsible for a wider socioeconomic chasm and rightwing populism, neoliberal apologists dismiss any criticism and resistance to neoliberal authoritarianism. Although illiberal democracy found a home in the traditional conservative camp in core and periphery alike by adapting to local conditions, liberals and rightwing populists have supported neoliberal goals, but not the same political strategies leading to autocratization. Despite divergence on cultural issues finding expression through identity politics, the common goals converging has contributed to apathy and cynicism that has benefited the far right and alienated the left.[49]

Under Thatcher and Reagan, the UK and US governments privatized public enterprises and outsourced services. Neoliberals insisted that the government-owned too much of the economy, over-regulated it, and choked economic growth by protecting labor with a costly social safety net. As part of market efficiency, neoliberals promoted deregulation and elimination or at least reduction of anti-corruption laws for business violations in everything from work safety to environmental issues, and from banking allowing for multi-layered scandals in stock market abuses. By lowering taxes on the wealthy, transferring massive capital from welfare programs to corporate subsidies, and pursuing a low-interest-rate policy, the state helped to strengthen capital at labor's expense, all along legalizing previously illegal financial crimes.[50]

Aggravating the debt-to-GDP ratio, especially when adding massive defense spending to the mix, rising public debt entailed weaker currency and further downward pressure on wages failing to keep pace with inflation. Public debt became another state subsidy for the private sector at the expense of workers and the middle class. The media and mainstream analysts used the issue to justify further trimming everything from cutting social security to raising health care costs, arguing that social welfare is a parasitic impediment to economic growth.[51]

In a brief article entitled, *"How the Welfare State Became the Neoliberal Order"*, Pablo Preluca notes that consequences of the transition transcend the narrow boundaries of development models and are at the heart of social and institutional relations. *"Neoliberalism could be seen as a reaction: not against developmental plans, but against the balance of power—that is, the power of workers about the power of capital—that underpinned the welfare state."*[52]

As much in the US as in Europe, workers have been the target of deeper cuts in compensation and benefits. At the same time that most countries have raised the retirement age, the state targeted pension reform, collective bargaining, and the right to strike. Slashing social programs and unemployment benefits which neoliberals view as "work disincentives" started during the 1980s, continuing throughout the world until the mass UK and French labor protests in 2023. Regardless of the political regime, the trans-Atlantic transformation model began to redefine the social contract for the entire world, undertaking a massive transfer of income. Through market ethics individualized while rejecting the Keynesian social context, neoliberalism redefined the social contract solely around capital's interests, thus reshaping the social order on a world scale.[53]

Since the early 1950s, IMF currency stabilization loans and World Bank development loans represent neoliberalism's historical continuity and were instrumental in the erosion of the social safety net and social justice. Working with large banks and multilateral institutions like the IMF and World Bank which use loans as leverage to impose neoliberal policies on debtor nations desperate to become credit-worthy, raise capital in the private markets, and attract foreign investment, developing nations acquiesce to the neoliberal social contract. The results include financial dependence, unequal terms of trade, and an endless debt-borrowing cycle. The working class suffers downward living standard pressures and governments become more authoritarian to counter popular resistance to neoliberal austerity.[54]

Using the pretext of reducing public debt by reducing public sector spending invariably has meant dismissing workers and curtailing regulation on foreign capital investment. Preconditions to qualify not only IMF currency stabilization loans, but World Bank project loans, among other government-guaranteed and/or consortium loans, entailed the unavoidable bait of neoliberal policies. Contrary to promises of reducing debt, IMF austerity aggravated public debt and kept developing nations economically weak and externally dependent on low living standards.[55]

The oil embargo of 1973 resulted in quadrupled price per barrel which coincided with the US withdrawing from Vietnam, the revolutions in Iran and Nicaragua in 1979, and the USSR sending troops to support the pro-Moscow Afghan regime (People's Democratic Party of Afghanistan) a devastating impact not only on the American establishment but on how the rest of the world viewed the US. The socioeconomic and political elites in the US were concerned about the weakened economy amid the post-Vietnam malaise and about losing the investment world's trust.

Instead of addressing the structural problems by reexamining exorbitant defense spending, capital concentration, and economic and social development strategies toward growth, neoliberal advocates proposed slashing social welfare and taxes paid by corporations and the richest individuals as a means of strengthening capital. Meanwhile, the US raised defense spending from $113 billion in 1978 to $300 billion during Reagan's last year in office. Thatcher also pursued militarist policies, partly as a means to enforce unpopular neoliberal policies, including the privatization of public firms, undercutting middle class and workers' living standards, but also to support the defense sector.[56]

Coinciding with post-Vietnam pessimism about Pax Americana's future, neoliberalism's nascent stage provided a new impetus for defense spending. In "War profiteering: the neoliberal militarism" Jordi Calvo Rufanges points out that, contrary to commonly-held views, defense spending is not strictly limited to the military budget, as many assume. Such spending involves many sectors from scientific research and development to consultants and banks.

"Hence, when it comes to military spending, military R&D, companies and military industries, and arms purchases, we have to pay attention not only to the defense budgets of the states but also to budgets of other ministries such as industry. Together they finance the whole military business cycle. The other elements that form a part of the cycle are the arms trade, which also includes financial institutions that hold the entire cycle, as well as shareholders of military enterprises that finance the industry operations and the arms trade."[57]

Beginning with the Thatcher-Reagan era, every sector from government agencies to universities, and from hospitals to corporate-linked charitable organizations emulated the business management model. Especially in the US, hospitals treat patients, including mental patients, as customers. As part of social welfare cuts, the Reagan administration released mental patients from public institutions thereby creating a homelessness problem along with the failed PR war on drugs campaign. Promoting neoliberal policies globally as part of "good governance", a euphemism for self-regulating markets and limited state welfare programs, the US identified neoliberal transformation with democracy and castigated any system deviating from market orthodoxy.[58]

Celebrating the twilight of the welfare state in the 1980s, to maximize profits the entire institutional structure was deliberately injurious to the working class and the environment. As the Soviet bloc crumbled in the late 1980s, neoliberals felt optimistic about the transformation model's global reach. In the 1990s, several Eastern European and trans-Caucasus countries went from the Soviet bureaucratic socialist system to neoliberal authoritarianism with a highly hierarchical social structure.[59]

Blurring the lines between legitimate and illegal business, and seeking to profit from privatized public assets, state-linked oligarch capitalist practices undermined any possibility of an inclusive democracy focused on social development. Western banks, real estate, and other corporations laundering Eastern European money were part of the same neoliberal mold identified with democracy. Oligarchs became the new privileged class, contributing to systemic corruption throughout the world, especially in G-7 countries where they invested in various sectors from taxis to high tech, from the stock market to real estate to launder money.[60]

Unconcerned about the social consequences of rising socioeconomic inequality and autocratization becoming the norm, neoliberals remained committed to unfettered market hegemony at any social and political cost. In pursuit of consolidating transformation on a world scale, the neoliberal politicians and media preached subordinating to the market popular sovereignty and consent from which the state's legitimacy emanates. Precipitating downward social mobility that extended into the middle class, neoliberalism's emancipatory promise was to strengthen capital.

Even when stock market and banking deregulation led to recurring banking crises and global economic contractions from the mid-1980s to the Great Recession of 2008, and on to the US regional banking crisis of 2023, neoliberals blamed the remnants of the welfare system, and the government for fiscal and monetary policy, along with restrictive banking regulations. Predictably, the neoliberal solution was to provide even greater safeguards and incentives to capital in the form of corporate subsidies, greater tax cuts, deregulation, and outsourcing of public services to the private sector. Similar neoliberal reactions and proposed solutions were evident from the pandemic of 2020 to the global stagflation of 2022-2023.[61]

Molding the social environment and hegemonic culture reflecting the hierarchical class structure and market-driven social marginalization, the neoliberal social contract became more entrenched from the Great Recession to the stagflation of 2022-2023, resulting from the US-led coalition trying to save neoliberalism by violating its globalization imperative and resorting to fragmented weaponized bloc trading. Symptomatic of central bank policy and capitalist appropriation, inflation's monetary and price-formation dimension resulted in strengthening the strongest sectors within the capitalist world economy, thus leading toward increased capital concentration.[62]

As reflected in sharp defense budget increases by the G-7, especially the US, Germany, France, and Japan, reinforced military Keynesianism took precedence over social development. Emboldened that there was no competing ideology from any government challenging capitalism after the fall of the Soviet bloc, Western neoliberals aggressively pursued globalization under the deregulation-corporate welfare and anti-labor policies. All along, they insisted that supporting capital entailed economic growth and job creation.[63]

Within the neoliberal world economy, China which pursued a hybrid model and resisted US-led pressure to adopt unfettered neoliberalism, benefited more than the rest of the world from globalization. Its policy mix to achieve economic growth took into account upward social mobility, including wiping out extreme poverty, never a goal of any neoliberal government. Coinciding with China's economic ascendancy, neoliberalism's global reach appeared to favor the US-based unipolar world order. By the Great Recession of 2008, it was evident that the Trans-Atlantic core was undergoing a deep structural crisis. Because China was the catalyst in mitigating the global recession's impact to serve its own economic stabilization and employment goals, there was no doubt about a shift in the world capitalist system's core from the G-7 to China, with India desperately fighting not to be left behind the global competition.[64]

Considering that China's mixed economic model accounted for its astronomic rise in the 21st century at a time of G-7 decline, Beijing took advantage of globalization, making optimal use of its human capital and vast internal market to leverage trade and foreign investment policy. Fearing that China was challenging the unipolar US-based world order, the US-G-7 goal was to impose the Washington Consensus on Beijing's one-party state to strengthen capital and weaken the state, thereby preserving the waning unipolar world order.

Without much economic leverage to force the trans-Atlantic neoliberal model on China, the US fallback position was to drive Beijing toward higher defense spending and deprive it of markets where the US had influence. If undercutting the civilian economy to speed up its eventual demise worked against the Soviet Union, the US assumption was that it would also work against China's reluctance to adopt the Washington Consensus.[65]

Besides China limiting defense spending to well under 2% of GDP and focusing on combining import-substituting industrialization and export-oriented growth along with massive spending on domestic and Asian infrastructural development, other countries experimented with developmental policies on a much smaller scale while protecting the social safety net. Most of the EU members retained aspects of the social welfare state, while some of the former Soviet republics, including Russia, the trans-Caucasus, Eurasian, and several Eastern European countries pursued authoritarian neoliberalism, often following the advice of Western consultants, most of them linked to governments, IMF, or World Bank.

Neoliberal policies were tailored to clientelist politics and crony capitalism in the Middle East, Africa, and Asia where pluralism and multi-party traditions were not very strong historically owing to colonial or semi-colonial rule. As analyzed in the next chapters, the executive branch used the office to reward small cliques, including top military and police officials, as well as relatives and loyal political associates within the bureaucracy and private sector. This left some Western multinationals and governments vehemently objecting to difficulties competing within such a clientelist system, demanding greater access to market share.[66]

Whether under a neoliberal authoritarian state like Hungary under Viktor Orban, a clientelist-patronage state in the Middle East like Egypt under Abdel Fatah al-Sisi, or any pluralist regime in Western Europe, 'market omnipotence theory' has been the catalyst under the umbrella of the neoliberal social contract in the first two decades of the 21st century.

As Harvey Cox put it in "The Market as God", there are parallels between the neoliberal dogma and St. Augustine's City of God (426 A.D.), written as a Christian apologia during the Fall of the Roman Empire, promising an eternity of bliss to the faithful. Despite its catastrophic results for workers and the environment, neoliberal divination's appeal in collective faith for market efficiency is a transcendent experience and rests partly on dogmatism linked to the infallible political economy promising deliverance from community obligations and emancipation of the individual. [67]

Despite the neoliberal serial crises as they unfolded from the savings and loan crisis of the late 1980s, the "dot-com bubble" of the late 1990s, the Great Recession of 2008, the tragedy of the COVID-19 pandemic erupting late in 2019, and the Russian invasion of Ukraine followed by global stagflation due to US-led sanctions, the neoliberal social order further consolidated gains as authoritarianism experienced a global surge.[68]

It would have been unthinkable in the Thatcher-Reagan decade for two presidential contenders in France's election (April 2022) to represent the center-right pluralist neoliberal camp of incumbent Emanuel Macron facing challenger Marine Le Pen of the neo-Fascist National Rally. Even more inconceivable, in September 2022, Italy elected Giorgia Meloni, the first postwar pro-Fascist Prime Minister, in a coalition that Fratelli d'Italia led to victory. In the same year, Hungary's rightwing prime minister Viktor Orban easily won reelection, and Sweden Democrats, a neo-Nazi party, became the second most popular in a country known for its strong democratic commitment. These elections signaled that neoliberalism's continued impact in core and periphery alike, while the progressive movements have not scored comparable victories.[69]

Against the political backdrop of pluralism vs authoritarianism political competition taking place under the neoliberal umbrella, sociopolitical, economic, and cultural polarization has benefited the far right whose rise is symptomatic of the transformation's global reach in all facets of society. Contrary to what some political analysts were predicting about the pandemic resulting in a return to democratic politics and a compassionate society where greater social justice would ensue from the Great Recession to the pandemic, the entrenched economic elites and political class became more determined to strengthen finance capital while crushing any opposition regardless of whether it came from leftist critics advocating systemic change or Keynesian reformists. Disillusionment among the waning middle class and even a segment of workers led to the rise of far-right political parties and regimes.[70]

Especially after the Great Recession, the rise of populist rightwing regimes alarmed liberal and progressive politicians about what socioeconomic polarization would entail for the political consensus under the neoliberal model. While the capitalist class remained united in its goal for capitalist appropriation and class war, it has been divided about how best to achieve it and preserve social conformity.

A number of European neo-fascist parties insist that they operate within a democracy, including "Sweden Democrats", Slovenian Democratic Party, Hungary's Fidesz[1]-Christian Democratic People's Party[2], the Freedom Party of Austria, Czech Freedom and Direct Democracy, the Progress Party of Norway, Netherlands Forum for Democracy, to mention some of the more important ones. The liberal pluralist camp has been willing to preserve some of the most essential elements of the Keynesian welfare state, including social security, health care, and education, with some entitlement programs such as unemployment benefits and veterans' programs, but nothing resembling pre-Thatcher-Reagan era conditions.[71]

As a means of safeguarding and expanding their interests under an authoritarian regime, neoliberals have also been using traditional conservative and rightwing ideology and political strategy to mobilize popular support. The US Democratic Party, British Labour Party, Canada and Australia's Liberal parties, and France's La République En Marche have been moving closer to the rightwing populist positions on economic, social, and cultural issues ranging from lower tolerance on immigration to regimenting labor unions. The pluralist camp's neoliberal policies drove disgruntled voters to the populist-exclusionary far right promising punitive measures against migrant workers, trade unionists, environmentalists, Muslims, and alternative lifestyle advocates.[72]

Part of the convergence between the pluralist and rightwing political parties can be explained by campaign financing sources linked to corporate interests. Ranging from religious to anti-abortion, and varieties of nationalist/nativist elements to anti-migrant xenophobes, rightwing groups emerged during the embryonic stage of neoliberalism largely because of Western geopolitical and economic destabilization in the Middle East and Africa, at a time of chronic downward social mobility.

Although neoliberalism has resulted in rising inequality and loss of public confidence in the social contract, the mass media has so obfuscated these core issues that despite general agreement on credibility based on the social contract's lack of fairness and equity, many working-class voters fail to see the common denominator of class solidarity amid class war. Instead, they blame groups within the working class, including trade unionists, and support either the inclusionary pluralist or the exclusionary authoritarian neoliberal political parties aiming at the same neoliberal economic goals. [73]

More likely to survive under an authoritarian regime than a pluralist one, the neoliberal order will eventually collapse under the weight of its contradictions and declining legitimacy among an ever-larger segment of the population opposing it amid inter-elite conflicts. COVID-19 demonstrated that without massive public funding in every sector from vaccine subsidies to the hospitality sector, the "free market" left to its own devices is incapable of surviving. It is not simply a matter of one crisis but of successive ones each more severe and widespread. If the state's role is to pour public funding to buttress the private sector, it necessarily follows that the state's function is to safeguard and augment private capital, while maintaining a minimal social safety net to maintain social conformity.[74]

Adding to the model's inherent contradictions, the geopolitical dimensions of the US-China global competition and Western sanctions promoting block trading and higher global defense spending are signaling the twilight of neoliberal transformation as the model is withering from an inability to resolve its contradictions. The Great Recession, followed by popular resistance from 'Occupy Wall Street' to the Arab Spring, from global anti-IMF austerity protests to trade

1. *https://en.wikipedia.org/wiki/Fidesz*

2. *https://en.wikipedia.org/wiki/Christian_Democratic_People%27s_Party_(Hungary)*

union strikes and rallies, and from chronic downward social mobility to geopolitical international rivalry have strengthened economic nationalism to the degree some question the waning model's ability to survive under the new dimension of increasing fragmentation.

In his essay on economic nationalism in the age of neoliberalism, Yorgos Rizopoulos, argues that if one scratches the thin surface of nationalist rhetoric, there is not much substance to the apprehension of returning to the protectionist interwar era policies. "Currently, the United States conducts policies guided by geopolitical considerations which can have significant consequences on the modalities of globalization. However, in general, the material base for classic protectionism is undermined and the probability of thorough nationalist policies is low..."[75]

Although conditions are very different today than in the interwar era, there are some disturbing parallels specifically with trading blocs, overvalued weaponized reserve currencies, and rising nationalism among neoliberalism's contradictions sounding the alarm for its inevitable demise. Even before Russia invaded Ukraine in February 2022, the US and China were engaged in a fierce global competition for core hegemony in the capitalist system. Unable to compete with China's Belt and Road Initiative (BRI) and the race for tech superiority, the US resorted to sanctions, tariffs, and a proxy war against Russia which is China's most important geostrategic ally.

To rally support around the inherently weak dollar and waning Western-centered global trade block relying on the preeminence of semiconductors, artificial intelligence, biotechnology, financial services, electric vehicles, and to a lesser extent liquified natural gas, the US compelled its trading partners to become more dependent on the US while selectively blocking Chinese foreign investments, reshoring operations from China to the home base or other countries.

Similar to the early Cold War, the geopolitical and geoeconomic landscape of the 2020s is intended to strengthen Pax Americana. In the name of trans-Atlantic strategic, economic, and political solidarity, the US has been buying time. Great Britain did the same with the Sterling Area in the 1930s, refusing to accept the structural shift in the world capitalist system. The inherently weak but overvalued weaponized dollar has a few similarities with Britain's Commonwealth interwar experience of using the colonies and the Commonwealth countries to save the beleaguered British Empire.

Given that the Great Depression and WWII dealt the final blows to the aging empire at a time when the US was already the world economy's core, all efforts of British revival were futile. Bloc trading, global economic fragmentation, and economic nationalism at least in some symbolic forms for most countries, backfire and undermine capitalism on a world scale today as they did in the interwar. Even under such challenging conditions, the neoliberal transformation's global reach continues to thrive but hardly looks promising.[76]

Historically, great powers have collapsed under the weight of domestic and foreign policies riddled with contradictions which the political and social elites defend because they are invested in the status quo. As they become more desperate and aggressive in the pursuit to maintain fading glory, the elites become increasingly sadistic, taking out their frustrations institutionally on the masses, exactly as Johan Huizinga observed in Homo Ludens, (1938).

As sociopathic sadism finds expression in public policy and social and international relations, the lives of the people become increasingly difficult. In the twilight of their power, imperial networks become desperate, aggressive, and reckless. Divisions among the elites about the manner to preserve the status quo filter down to the rest of the population. Knowing that they are especially dependent on countries under their aegis to maintain waning power at home, great powers in decline become increasingly aggressive, refusing to address the root causes of decline. Opting for military solutions in their inability to compete economically undermines public confidence in the social contract and results in declining credibility.

As the declining power, the US has been using military means and varieties of economic measures exposing contradictions in the transformation model amid the struggle to retain global hegemony. Inexorably operating within the same capitalist world system, development models also reflect the power struggle not only of political parties in their quest to manage the political economy but also inter-elite competition either to maintain or modify the status quo.

In the second half of the 2010s, the BREXIT movement, British conservatives, and far-right elements demanding withdrawal from the EU seemed to illustrate a lack of support for neoliberalism among the political and socioeconomic elites. This was farthest from reality. The BREXIT proponents overriding concern was that neoliberalism under EU market restrictions hindered the model at the national level and prevented optimal economic benefits, while national income was unevenly distributed causing socioeconomic imbalances.

The same mode of thinking prevailed among some capitalists in other countries within Europe and beyond. Before BREXIT and the rise of rightwing populism in the US, Brazil, India, and Eastern Europe, among other countries, neoliberal nationalism precipitated democracy's decline in every single case. This reflected the model's exhaustion with alternatives for capitalist appropriation and accumulation, while also trying to mobilize citizens behind the social contract. An elite-led counterrevolutionary movement, neoliberalism will not survive longer than Keynesianism. The evidence is very clear as it creates perpetual crises while reproducing itself.

Slowly drowning in the chaotic contradictions of inter-class alliances and policies contributing to rising inequality and authoritarianism, combined with increasingly aggressive reliance on geopolitics to resolve such contradictions through market expansion under coercive conditions points to the model's twilight. The problem is that locally and globally, the elites' sociopathic sadism makes the path to neoliberal decline more difficult for the working class and challenging for the shrinking middle class.[77]

CHAPTER I:

The Social Contract, Neoliberal Ideology and Development Models

Social Contract Theory

At the G-20 meeting in March 2020, World Bank President David Malpass promoted neoliberal policies as an economic remedy for the impact of COVID-19. *"Countries will need to implement structural [neoliberal] reforms to help shorten the time to recovery and create confidence that the recovery can be strong. For those countries that have excessive regulations, [social welfare] subsidies, licensing regimes, trade protection or litigiousness as obstacles, we will work with them to foster markets, choice, and faster growth prospects during the recovery."*[78]

The World Bank president's neoliberal promotional speech revealed apprehension that the pandemic could expose the social contract's continued detrimental impact on the middle class and working class. This was especially so in poorer nations accusing the rich Western countries of practicing vaccine apartheid. Although policy nuances in different countries reflect the institutions, social relations, and hegemonic culture, the neoliberal social contract is the common driving force throughout the world. Departing from the historical social contract's theoretical perimeters, neoliberalism has redefined capitalism's narrow boundaries.

Eighteenth-century social contract theory was a manifestation of classical liberal ideology intended to empower the middle class. Along with limited government, liberty through mainstream public inclusion/participation and the potential of upward social mobility were at the core of classical liberal theory. The result of neoliberal policy is forging social relations based on social inequality and political division for the sake of market hegemony at the expense of a docile working class. Because the judicial and legislative branches of government and the entire mainstream institutional structure take into account capital's essential role, some scholars have argued that capitalism's neoliberal phase could be described as neo-feudalism – social relations with the state-protected privileged propertied class determining the fate of the working population.[79]

A reflection of the political economy and social structure, modern social contract theory has its origins in the transition from subsistence agriculture under the feudal-manorial social order to commercial agriculture and the emergence of long-distance trade under capitalism in what originally Fernand Braudel, and later Immanuel Wallerstein described as the long 16th century (1452-1630) of social discontinuity. Departing from the feudal-manorial order lasting from the fall of the Roman Empire in the fifth century to the end of the Black Death in the fifteenth century, Hugo Grotius (1583-1645) argued that northwest Europe's political order was rooted in a social contract. This was a means of advancing the natural rights of individuals bound together under one government for society's welfare.[80]

Reflected in the nascent phase of early 17th-century capitalist Holland, the view that sovereignty rests with the governed assumed coherent philosophical dimensions in the work of John Locke, father of Western Liberalism and precursor of the Enlightenment. Refining social contract theory, Locke argued that sovereignty rests with the people whose consent affords government legitimacy. While consent theory predates capitalism, theory from practice differs. In theory, there is the impression of an all-encompassing doctrine of the collective citizenry.

Given Locke's criteria for property ownership linked to political rights under the social contract, inequality is built into the bourgeois social contract. It is far harsher in daily life than it appears in theory.[81]

Analyzing the relationship between the individual and the state, some scholars maintain that the social contract is about the degree to which the government advances a set of social and economic policies intended to benefit the governed. Although this is the social contract's theoretical assumption, the problem arises when the governed lose confidence in the state's legitimacy; an important point that Locke analyzed during the Glorious Revolution of 1688-1690 in *Two Treatises of Government*. Deconstructing the subject of popular sovereignty, the classical liberal definition links property qualifications to individual liberties and accordingly to social and political privileges. Besides hierarchical criteria, the assumption of a capitalist social order stems from citizens' consent for the sake of social harmony, safety, and security, and presumably from economic growth, instead of chaos under a sovereign above public accountability.[82]

Building on Locke's liberal philosophy and opposed to the tyranny of France's Absolute Monarchy, Jean-Jacques Rousseau wrote in *The Social Contract* (1762) that: *"Man is born free, but everywhere in chains."* The statement reflects the views of many Enlightenment thinkers who believed that society's modernization was not possible in the absence of a social contract taking into account "natural rights", presumably of all people on whose consent the sovereign's legitimacy rests. Rousseau's approach to government by consent by the totality evolved into merit-based criteria by placing the common interest (General Will) above the individual but without clarification of what constituted the abstract "General Will".

Departing from Locke's liberalism based on property ownership and individualism at the core of his political thought, in the *Discourse on Inequality,* (1754) Rousseau rejected wealth as the sole criterion of value in society. He maintained that appropriation rests at the root of institutionalized inequality and oppression of individuals against community interest. Like Locke, Rousseau recognized the state's role as an *"association which will defend the person and goods of each member with the collective force of all."* The basis of social contract theory accounts for the sovereign power's legitimacy and justice, thus resulting in public acceptance of the status quo regardless of social inequality.[83]

As the division of labor underwent systemic changes owing to successive industrial and social revolutions, social contract theory evolved in the last two centuries. From the first Industrial Revolution in 18th century England to the European-wide social revolutions of 1848 and down to the counterrevolutionary neoliberal transformation, working-class co-optation into bourgeois political parties as a popular base in the age of mass politics has identified social contract's goal with capital. In theory, acknowledging the "rights of the people", a political concept projecting the appearance of egalitarianism, capitalism always operated under varieties of regimes from absolute monarchy to social democracy. This further beclouds the argument about capitalism's presumed harmony under a Lockean liberal regime to the exclusion of others.[84]

The late 19th-century second industrial revolution precipitated the creation of large enterprises and the rise of the trade union movement amid greater division and specialization of labor. Big business created the need for a bureaucratic regulatory state with agencies intended to stabilize and grow capitalism amid predatory oligopolistic practices undermining market conditions and social relations, especially amid international competition for markets. Nineteenth-century northwest European, US and Japanese industrialization resulted in the expansion of the middle class acting as a buffer between capital and the working class subservient to the social contract theoretically predicated on upward social mobility.

Combined with inherent contradictions in capitalism regarding economic growth, which implies shared prosperity, capitalism's cyclical contractions on a world scale (the 1840s, 1870s, and 1890s), diluted the social contract's promise of upward social mobility more in the colonized Global South than in the Western metropolis. Given the political economy's structure, industrial, scientific, and technological progress benefited primarily the upper echelons in the social order with the greatest consumption power enjoying the derivative benefits of favorable public policy. The second industrial revolution's impact on the international division of labor resulted in upward social mobility in the advanced capitalist countries at the expense of the Global South.[85] Factoring in race, ethnicity, gender, urban/rural divide, and religion, working-class marginalization remained a permanent dimension of social relations in exclusionary politics. Along with imperialist policies determining the world division of labor, surplus value is the underlying factor in the mode of production.[86]

The impact of WWI, American isolationism, the British Sterling Area-Commonwealth bloc, and lack of central banks' coordination, combined with hyper speculation by banks and stock markets contributed to interwar economic dislocation amid a rush by the Great Powers to make up for losses suffered during the decade of war and reconstruction. The rise of the Axis Powers (Italy, Germany, and Japan), and authoritarian regimes throughout the world in the interwar era reflected capitalism's crisis contributing to the public's loss of confidence in Enlightenment Age liberal principles.[87]

To the degree that the Keynesian model restored some stability in social relations to preserve capitalism under the Enlightenment's philosophical foundation, many leaders from Roosevelt's New Deal to French President Leon Blum's working class-middle class coalition under *Front Populaire* (1936-1940), and Chile's President Pedro Aguirre Cerda's *El Frente Popular* (1938-1941), accepted the Keynesian social contract as the new norm.

In a weaker form, the Keynesian welfare state prevailed in what Eric Hobsbawm called the postwar 'golden age of capitalism" (*The Age of Extremes: The Short Twentieth Century, 1914–1991),* until the post-Vietnam global energy crisis precipitating a capitalist-manufactured accumulation crisis. In the 1970s, the nature of the accumulation crisis centered around "deficient surplus value" owing to stimulative aggregate demand arising from the stimulative Vietnam War economy. Considering that inflation-adjusted wage rates remained stagnant from the mid-1960s to the mid-1970s, labor costs were not a factor in the capital accumulation crisis.[88]

With the advent of Anglo-American neoliberalism in the 1980s, government, media, and mainstream institutions indoctrinated the public throughout the world to reject the Keynesian social contract as obsolete and an obstacle to economic growth. To a considerable degree, military Keynesianism undermined the welfare state more in the US than in Northwest Europe. Neo-classical advocates insisted that left to its own devices, the market adjusts eventually, even during high unemployment and market disequilibrium.[89]

By the 1970s, at the national and international levels, a loss of confidence in the social contract was manifested in the breakdown of the postwar bourgeois consensus. Despite the oil crisis of 1973, neo-corporatist Japan emerged as a global export power by 1977. While some countries, especially France, were concerned about the US using its global dollar dominance to maintain economic hegemony at the expense of the rest of the world, Japan challenged competitors seeking market share. By the end of the 1970s, the welfare state lapsed into crisis only in so far as capitalists viewed it as a burden against their stagnant profit margins.[90]

For apologists of the market economy, the remedy was slashing social welfare and keeping a lid on wages, along with a fiscal policy favoring the higher income groups, which came down to income transfer from labor to capital. Eager to accommodate capital, conservatives moved to the extreme right embracing neoliberalism and populism to justify radical slashing of the social safety net and reducing the tax burden on the rich. This was first tested in the UK and the US, driving some centrists to embrace conservatism because they feared the reactionary far right. The center-left became part of the liberal center. Consequently, socioeconomic and political polarization accompanied the shift from Keynesianism to neoliberalism.[91]

While the transition was gradually becoming apparent to the general public by the early 21st century, there was also no doubt about the rise of right-wing populism in several countries. The seeds of authoritarian neoliberalism were sown during the 1980s but continued during the pluralist Clinton-Blair era when a neoliberal Gilded Age manifested itself in the hegemonic culture permeating society during the high-tech decade of the 1990s.

From North America to historically progressive Scandinavian countries with a very strong social welfare safety net in comparison with the rest of the world, the shift from Keynesianism to neoliberalism was unmistakable. Amid stagnant wages, rising social marginalization, and erosion of popular sovereignty, the neoliberal opium of the people was the culture of atomism and yuppie techno-homogeneity replacing the diverse counterculture of the 1960s.[92]

Instead of a collective body to which the state must respond, the neoliberal social contract substituted citizens with the libertarian concept of individual producer/consumer. Commodifying and monetizing the citizenship concept, social contract theory was essential in forging consumer-citizen consent for the social contract. Substituting the classical liberal concept of the state's accountability to the people for submission to the market, neoliberalism disparaged the concepts of "public welfare" and popular sovereignty. No matter the populist rhetoric distracting the public from the ideology's goal, neoliberalism's practical aim was to downsize democracy as a consequence of downsizing Keynesian welfare.[93]

As Regina Queiroz argues, *"It also points to the importance of the political category of "the sovereign people", which is all the greater where illiberal and undemocratic political alternatives jockey to fill the vacuum left by a system that, at its ideological core, cannot acknowledge the common good."* [94] Dismissing the assumption of "public value governance" at the core of the classical liberal and Keynesian social contract, neoliberals regard it as antithetical to the hegemonic market.[95]

Rejecting the theoretical premise of the "common good" as a political goal, or at least a moral ideal, the neoliberal social contract only recognizes the individual consumer-citizen, not society. Yet, class war is at the center of its strategy, manifesting itself in various domains from labor policy to fiscal policy. Since the dawn of civilization, the individual was never divorced from the community's social fabric, no matter the dogmatic attempts by Western apologists of capitalism to justify the atomistic value system.

Just as religion was intertwined with the identity of the faithful in Western Christendom of the Middle Ages, and the theocentric value system, modern secular ideology under capitalism fulfills a similar goal. Some scholars have criticized neoliberalism as a secular religion, *"sacralization of the market"*, as Luca Mavelli calls it. Mainstream politicians, business people, educators, journalists, and even clergy around the world have embraced aspects of the neoliberal ideology and adjusted their operations accordingly. While government bureaucracies validate it, the media and all mainstream institutions reinforce it, hegemonic culture promotes and projects it as the norm. [96]

Neoliberal Ideology

In an interview in 1987, UK Prime Minister Margaret Thatcher reflected on the views of Friedrich Hayek whose ideology profoundly influenced her. *"They are casting their problems at society. And, you know, there's no such thing as society. There are individual men and women and there are families. And no government can do anything except through people, and people must look after themselves first. It is our duty to look after ourselves and then, also, to look after our neighbors."[97]*

In her official capacity, Thatcher articulated the absence of social collective and conscience, recognizing only individual interests that transcend society. In *Politics,* Aristotle argues that society precedes the individual. Human beings are social creatures, forming social organizations to continually build society and share common goals for the good of all, at least theoretically as an ethical imperative. If no society precedes the individual, then Thatcher was not elected prime minister to lead a country with common institutions and goals for a society that transcends the individual as Jean-Jacques Rousseau argued in *The Social Contract* (1762), reflected the philosophical spirit of the Enlightenment.

Implicit in Thatcher's *"there is no society"* comment is Hayek's dismissal of the "social" as a "weasel" concept, reflecting an elitist anti-Keynesian and anti-working-class ideology. This goes beyond the social contract concept of popular consent from which political legitimacy emanates, as Locke articulated in *Two Treatises of Government* (1688). Neoliberal ideology is not only at odds with Locke's philosophy, but opposed to John Stuart Mill's *Considerations of Representative Government* (1861) which argues that government's goal is the common good and greatest happiness for all citizens.[98]

Neoliberalism deviated not just from late 19th-century utilitarianism and reformist liberalism during the second industrial revolution (1870-1914) amid changes in social relations, it was a reactionary ideology so militantly against Keynesianism that its inspiration was monopoly capitalism and repackaging of Social Darwinism. Neoliberal transformation necessarily entails not only commercial Darwinism, but at its core the ideology is based on inequality and the perpetual transfer of income from the laboring classes to capital. Serving and subsidizing the self-regulated commercial Darwinist markets, neoliberalism redefined the concept of governance by usurping public policy to serve capital.[99]

Beyond the ideological perimeters of classical liberalism, Thatcher's neoliberal ideology defies common sense of interwoven community interests and ignores that society molds human beings as social animals. Institutional conditions regiment individual behavior not only through legal enforcement mechanisms but through the hegemonic culture that indoctrinates the individual into conformity. From natural disasters and pandemics to socioeconomic crises, the individual's fate is intertwined with society.

Even Emile Durkheim, who did not view society as the totality of its citizens, recognized the validity of the collective conscience behind which rests social currents, rules, and norms; all indicative that society regulates the individual as part of political and institutional socialization. Sacrificing society for the sake of strengthening capitalism, neoliberal ideologues reject Hegel's view of the social contract that the state preserves society by safeguarding general or universal interests transcending the individual, an Enlightenment-era concept influencing 19th-century political thought.

For neoliberals, the Hegelian view that people gain rights after a historical social struggle is an anathema. Hayek makes a distinction between 'true individualism' identified with John Locke, Adam Smith, David Hume, and Edmund Burke versus 'false individualism' of 18th-century French among other continental writers emphasizing reason that led to 19th-century socialism. The Enlightenment's emphasis on the application of reason and scientific approach to solve society's problems was intellectually dishonest; at least, according to Hayek who had no moral qualms supporting Chile's military dictator Pinochet.[100]

As the new temples of neoliberal dogma that no one must question, stock exchanges and investment financial institutions are society's catalysts to the narrowly defined concept of progress. Vilifying the working class and pauperism reflecting individual failure and obstruction to economic progress, the precursor to neoliberal class war can be found in the early industrial policy of England's "Poor Laws" (1834 Poor Law Amendment Act). Manifestations of industrial capitalism's 'progress', the British Parliament enacted such laws to punish poor adults and children alike by confining them to workhouses of forced labor under unhealthy and dangerous conditions in exchange for housing and food.[101]

Industrial Revolution apologists contended that poverty was a reflection of individual character flaws, not structural conditions resulting in subsistence wages. A contemporary version of 19th-century industrial capitalism's anti-poor and anti-working-class statement, Republican Senator Chuck Grassley defended tax cuts to the wealthy while berating workers for lack of sound financial decisions and moral lapses. *"I think not having the* estate tax[1] *recognizes the people that are investing — as opposed to those that are just spending every darn penny they have, whether it's on booze or women or movies."[102]*

Rightwing class-war rhetoric had a large audience to which the GOP Iowa senator was appealing. Unlike the liberal experiment, Keynesian social welfare ideology never faulted the poor for structural poverty which capitalism causes.[103] Grounded in laissez-faire and social Darwinist principles that affirm social progress as defined by material self-interest based on the metaphysics of racial and biological superiority, neoliberalism challenged the liberal institutional consensus.

Along with Ludwig von Mises and Karl Popper, Friedrich Hayek became Europe's ideological apostles reconfiguring classical liberalism into a neoliberal ideology that subverted democracy from the French Revolution to the Great Depression. Considering that even amid the Great Depression there was fierce political and business opposition to Keynesianism, neoliberalism emerged at a key juncture in the postwar era when there was neither economic depression nor war to justify continuing with Keynesian social welfare policies. Other than Western-inculcated fear of Communism as a means to engender sociopolitical conformity, the dawn of capitalism's golden age offered the right environment for neoliberal philosophers like Popper to replace Keynesianism.[104]

Best known for *"The Open Society and its Enemies"* (1945), Popper decried interwar Fascism, Nazism and Communism. Adamantly against the Keynesian consensus as he was against Marxism, Popper's views reflected the Red Scare and Cold War political climate. Supporting Western capitalist hegemony as a means of preventing the spread of Soviet Communism's anti-capitalist propaganda, Popper, among the few pioneer neoliberal

1. https://www.huffingtonpost.com/topic/estate%20tax

intellectuals of his generation, rejected Keynesianism and Socialism, refusing to acknowledge that the logical result of neoliberal policies intended to strengthen capital would unavoidably erode liberal democracy and degrade social justice.

Where Hayek found social justice meaningless, Popper only rejected the means that socialists employed to achieve it as a transcendent ethical goal. Part of the 20th-century philosophical school that decried political and scientific dogmatism, Popper had no problem promoting neoliberal dogmatism and justifying it based on "negative utilitarianism", namely, minimizing suffering as a public policy goal, rather than state mechanisms maximizing happiness through material security.

Criticizing Plato and Marx's utopianism, Popper maintained that the goal of their philosophy was social engineering. Although from different perspectives and centuries apart, Plato and Marx placed social justice's ethical, political, and social dimensions at the center of their political philosophy. By contrast, neoliberal thinkers cannot reconcile class-war ideology with any dimension of social justice for it is an obstacle to capitalist appropriation.[105]

Aiming for more than citizens' mechanical compliance, neoliberal ideology projects the illusion that individual life matters, but not individuals as part of working-class solidarity. To actualize neoliberal myths of a utopian world that emulates the marketplace in every aspect of one's existence, the ideology aims to retain the privileges of the billionaire's neoliberal subjectivity rather than address the unemployed worker's plight.

"The transition from organized capitalism to neoliberal hegemony over the recent period has brought about a corresponding transformation in subjectivity." Jim McGuigan maintains. *"Leading celebrities, most notably high-tech entrepreneurs, for instance, operate in the popular imagination as models of achievement for the aspiring young. They are seldom emulated in real life, however, even unrealistically so. Still, their famed lifestyles and heavily publicized opinions provide guidelines to appropriate conduct in a ruthlessly competitive and unequal world."*[106]

Promising the opportunity for upward social mobility, neoliberals try to convince voters around the world that the corporate welfare state is the only hope for a better life, while the Keynesian social welfare state is parasitic and market-inefficient obstructing capital growth. Many in the middle class and a segment of the working class, especially in former Communist bloc countries where people entertain an idealized vision of bourgeois society, accept the neoliberal transformation model as the norm. Just as readily, they accept the myth that the individual, not the political economy embedded in the social contract is responsible for structural problems determining social relations.

Empirical evidence aside, the myth of individual self-blame rather than systemic causes from structural exploitation prevails, even more so in the former Soviet bloc than in the West. In 2019, Eastern Europeans earned 65 percent of the EU's average national income. From 1980 to 2017, Europe's poverty rose from 20 to 22 percent, while the income of the richest one percent grew twice as fast as the bottom half of the population. Despite downward living standards pressure, the majority of voters support EU integration operating under neoliberalism and its expansion on a patron-client division basis, regardless of rising illiberal democracy.[107]

Ideologically, neoliberalism differs from liberal democracy as it evolved in late 19th century Western Europe, the US, Canada, and Australia. During the era of William Gladstone, a four-term prime minister between 1868 and 1894, the ideology of liberal democracy became closely identified with his reformist policies. This was especially after the Reform Act of 1884–85 granted the vote to agricultural workers, and the Redistribution Act[2] of 1885 called for representation based on 50,000 voters per member in the legislative constituency[3].[108]

Reflecting the need to professionalize government bureaucracies and mitigate the effects of monopoly capitalism in society, Gladstone's reformist brand of liberalism spread to the European continent and the US. The evolving liberal ideology during the Second Industrial Revolution ushered in progressivism which redefined the state's role as an arbiter intended to harmonize inter-class and intra-class interests. In the era of monopoly capitalism, trusts, and cartels precipitating socioeconomic disequilibrium at a time of a rapidly growing lower middle class and a mass consumer economy, reformist politicians were concerned that capitalism was a victim of its predatory practices.[109]

Unlike liberalism's ideological redefinition assigning regimented market perimeters to ensure balanced inter-sector growth during the progressive era, contemporary neoliberal ideology decries the state as an obstacle to market efficiency leading to growth. Inspired by English conservative opponent of the French Revolution Edmund Burke, and diehard anti-Keynesians Hayek, Popper, Friedman, and especially Walter Eucken also promoted ordoliberalism, a juridic-political institutional mechanism for finance-dominated accumulation and a model for heavy reliance on the monetary order to achieve optimal economic outcomes. All of them were aware that monetary policy was another mechanism to subsidize capital and strengthen finance-dominated accumulation tantamount to class war. The process entailed higher unemployment and depressed aggregate demand mostly in consumer spending, while strengthening the cash-rich strongest business at the expense of the credit-dependent weaker ones, thus resulting in oligopoly capitalism.[110]

Largely responsible for the mutation of 19th-century liberalism under the neoliberal umbrella operating within different political modalities aiming at the same goals, ordoliberalism invariably entails social disorder and chaos governance, leading toward monopoly capitalism. Another ideological dimension favoring concentration, the financialization of the economy entails that the financial sector, especially the stock market, has a preeminent role in determining economic policy and measuring the nation's wealth largely according to securities speculation which the state subsidizes in various forms from monetary to fiscal policy, not to mention bailouts.[111]

Turning back the clock on the regulatory aspects Progressive Era's centralization, expansion, and professionalization of the bureaucratic state to accommodate big business and the expanding consumer base amid changing demographics in industrialized nations, neoliberals advocate a bureaucratic framework popular among capitalists and political supporters from the dawn of the English Industrial Revolution to America's Gilded Age (1870-1900) when there were no state mechanisms to regulate monopolies in transportation, mining, food and drugs, child labor, especially work-related health and safety.

Unlike progressive liberals advocating a professional merit-based state structure with robust regulatory agencies to harmonize the market economy and minimize monopolies' role in oil, mining, transportation, tobacco, among industries precipitating market disequilibrium and inequality, neoliberals dogmatically advocate a fundamentalist dogma that would restore unfettered market hegemony. Despite efforts to make liberal democracy more inclusive and tolerant of previously excluded groups, the Progressive Era's goal was not social justice, but rationalizing the economy.

2. https://www.britannica.com/topic/Redistribution-Act

3. https://www.merriam-webster.com/dictionary/constituency

Advocates recognized that market rationalization with the state as a catalyst for stability would strengthen evolving consumer capitalism. Nor was the Progressive Era free of racism, sexism, and ethnocentrism in the Age of Imperialism when US states permitted schools to teach Herbert Spencer's Social Darwinism, racist pseudo-science. Emulating Gilded Age wealth concentration and government promoting big capital, neoliberalism tossed out rationalizing the economy and broadening the social consensus, subordinating the consumer-citizen to its market hegemony ideology.[112]

The theme of markets over states at the core of neoliberal ideology evolved in the UK and the US in the 1980s. The driving force behind the market hegemony thesis was economist John Williamson. Affiliated with the corporate-funded Peterson Institute for International Economics think tank, he articulated the "Washington Consensus" in 1989. By the time that the Washington Consensus was the ideological foundation for the transformation model, neoliberal ideology was already a policy in the UK and the US. Suffering through the US Savings and Loan crisis in the 'lost decade' of rising debt, a form of subsidy for the capitalist class oblivious to cycles of debt that IMF-style austerity was precipitating mostly in the Global South, several Latin America countries embraced the Washington Consensus which perpetuated greater dependence, underdevelopment, inequality, and authoritarianism.[113]

Encouraging governments around the world to adopt the Washington Consensus, the IMF, World Bank, Western governments, and multinational corporations were using financial, trade, investment, and geopolitical leverage to impose the transformation model's international conformity across all mainstream institutions. Embedded in the Washington Consensus ideology, financialization was one of its dimensions that led to the Great Recession. Coinciding with the demise of the Soviet bloc, China's thorough integration into the world economy included joining the WTO in 2001, two decades after the IMF and World Bank had recognized it. Market apologists insisted that there was no alternative to the neoliberal dogma under the aegis of the US-based "unipolar" world order.[114]

Although the Washington Consensus quickly swept much of the world, by June 2016 the IMF admitted that the development model had been oversold on false premises. In September 2022, the IMF criticized conservative Prime Minister Liz Truss for proposing tax cuts mostly to the rich, thereby raising the public debt, and risking rising inequality at a time when the Bank of England was raising interest rates to control inflation, a factor in contributing to inequality.

Whether in a developed nation with a reserve currency like the UK, Lebanon, or Sri Lanka, neoliberalism delivers capitalist appropriation at the cost of rising social inequality. Although neoliberalism sunk Sri Lanka into chaos in 2022-2023, the IMF imposed more austerity along with a series of neoliberal measures in March 2023. Despite UN and World Bank programs presumably designed to reduce global poverty and inequality, neoliberal policies created greater poverty.[115]

Similar to the elites of the Gilded Age, neoliberals are oblivious to rising inequality and to authoritarian politicians who campaign the wealthy finance. Harboring disdain for the working class, they reject even in principle social responsibility on the part of the market accountable only to shareholders. Equating capitalist appropriation and concentration with progress achievable through market efficiency, neoliberals demand that capital must remain above public accountability. An instrument promoting income redistribution from the bottom up and capital concentration, government policies reflect the model's goals, regardless of consequences on rising social and geographic inequality and what this entails for social harmony and democracy.[116]

While neoliberal ideologues castigate the welfare state and decry using government resources for social welfare, they believe that capitalists are entitled to appropriate public capital in various forms from low tax rates to corporate welfare. This is because they operate on the assumption that capital, not labor, is production's catalyst. Neoliberal ideology perpetuates the myth of non-government interference, while corporations demand subsidies, and low tax rates, which in many cases amounts to zero tax liability because of loopholes. In addition, corporations demand legal and judicial protections not accorded to labor unions or labor subcontracting. Naturally, the underlying assumption of corporate welfare entitlement is that the national interest rests exclusively with capital whereas labor is capital's designated enemy in the quest to maximize profits.[117]

Even after the Great Recession exposed neoliberalism as a model thriving on chaos, which business analysts praise as 'disruptive capitalism', apologists of the system insisted that the cause of the recession was over-regulation, not enough privatization, public sector outsourcing contracts for businesses, corporate welfare, or low taxes. More ironic, they blamed central banks and regulatory agencies whose policies are designed to advance capital. Rather than pointing to the contradictions in the political economy for the cyclical crisis, and influential banks and corporations providing public policy advice, neoliberal apologists beat the same old drum of the non-existent Keynesian state.[118]

Whether under a liberal-pluralistic political model or the rightwing populist, neoliberal hegemony entails employing every government and international organization mechanism in the advancement of international capital. As Riad Azar points out, *"The common denominator is the empowering of elites over the masses with the assistance of international forces through military action or financial coercion—a globalized dialectic of ruling classes."* [119]

The war against Keynesianism was accompanied by sharply higher campaign donations that drove conservatives, liberals alike, and various center-left political parties to embrace neoliberal ideology as the guiding light for public policy to remold society. To mobilize the middle class and workers behind the neoliberal model, traditional conservative parties revert to an eclectic ideological mix of nationalism, militarism, and economic and cultural conservatism. Hiding behind the cultural and economic conservatism fig leaf, conservative parties flirt with racism, xenophobia, sexism, anti-intellectualism, and anti-humanism. This has been a part of the populist ideological mix intended to obfuscate neoliberalism's class war impact on labor and marginalized groups.[120]

Such an eclectic ideological mix was typical of interwar Fascism and varieties of authoritarian movements and regimes. Fully endorsing the neoliberal ideology as the catalyst to economic growth, pluralist liberals differentiated themselves from the populist right by emphasizing social inclusion and support for modest social development. Rejecting cultural conservatism, but not economic or class war goals concealed behind identity politics, liberals historically celebrate individualism which includes cultural/lifestyle diversity and equal rights within the context of the merit-based philosophy and market economy. Although neoliberalism's short history has shown that it can easily coexist both with rightwing populism and multicultural liberal regimes, the latter has proved more effective in de-radicalizing and coopting the progressives.[121]

While Austrian and American neoliberals redefined classical liberalism against the background of Keynesianism, Lippmann's political theory was based on the rule of law as the framework for the "free market"; itself as an elite-manufactured concept, as he acknowledged public consent (*Public Opinion* (1922). This marked the categorical rejection of collectivism not only of Bolshevism but any ideology based on populist ultra-nationalism. [122]

Influenced by the shock of the Bolshevik Revolution, the rise of totalitarianism in Italy and Germany, and Keynesian economics to address the Great Depression's multifaceted systemic problems, Lippmann's interwar ideological redefinition of classical liberalism presaged the 21st-century debate about neoliberalism's compatibility with liberal democracy. In this respect, right-wing populists have been closer to Hayek's ideological vein.

Neoliberal disdain even for terms like "democratism", a concept used to describe Lenin's view of Socialist power resting on grassroots workers' soviets, revealed that liberalism was itself problematic. Advocating that the state must impose "negative freedoms" and avoid "positive" ones, Hayek's ideological support for illiberal democracy extended to the US-backed Chilean dictator Pinochet (1973-1990), after a CIA coup replaced duly-elected Salvador Allende.[123]

"[Hayek] couched his defense of Pinochet in a broader context of supporting democracy only insofar as it contributes to the formation and maintenance of a liberal market order: "In Modern times there have of course been many instances of authoritarian governments under which personal liberty was safer than under democracies". He offers Salazar's "early government" in Portugal as an example and suggests that there are many democracies in Eastern Europe, Africa, and South America and Asia that fail to protect personal liberty."[124]

Claiming that he preferred a "liberal", by which he meant neoliberal, dictator like Pinochet to a *"democratic government lacking in liberalism"*, Hayek, Friedman, James Buchanan, and Theodore Schultz of the Chicago School made no apologies about opposing pluralism and the Keynesian state as obstacles to free market fundamentalism. Justifying support for dictatorship by making a distinction between liberty, a term-limited to market freedom, and democracy associated with a social safety net, they subordinated democracy to capitalist appropriation, laying the political groundwork for authoritarianism in the name of market freedom.[125]

From the fall of the Communist bloc in 1991, to US-led sanctions on Russia in 2022, neoliberal authoritarianism found expression in many former Communist countries, including Hungary, Poland, Georgia, Moldova, Belarus, Azerbaijan, Kazakhstan, Armenia, and Kyrgyzstan. The same ideological debate was also at the core of the centrist vs. rightwing neoliberals whether in Trump's America, Jair Bolsonaro's Brazil, Emmanuel Macron's France, or Narendra Modi's India. The irony is that the West moved rapidly toward economic integration of former Communist countries, under the guise of 'democratizing' when in fact neoliberalism was on the agenda, not democracy.[126]

The most glaring contradiction of the neoliberal ideology is the ostensible celebration of free market fundamentalism as the panacea against the reality of a corporate welfare system and rigorous state interventionism to support capitalist appropriation. Resulting in massive income transfer from the bottom layers of society to the wealthiest few, this contradiction compels neoliberals in politics and media to engage in mass distraction and focus on identity politics, the cult of personality, militarism, and police-state methods, nativism and racism, culture wars, 'clash of civilization' and 'end of history' theories which reinforced the trans-Atlantic neoliberal transformation.[127]

Considering the four decades of wage stagnation and massive downsizing of public sector jobs (1980-2020) in the US, EU, India, and Latin America, ideological distraction served its purpose. In 2021-2022, employers, the media, and pundits tried to distract the public about downward social mobility by arguing there were jobs but people were rejecting them, leaving the impression that people are lazy and prefer to collect unemployment or welfare. By the end of 2022-early 2023, layoffs, especially in high tech, combined with wages failing to keep pace with inflation, proved the hollow propaganda regarding "labor shortages". OECD reported that inflation-adjusted wages rose 6% from 1990 6% from 1990 to 2022, whereas net wealth for the richest 1% rose from 23.5% in 1990 to 31.9% in 2022.[128]

Defending neoliberal ideology against the reality of rising inequality, academics, journalists, and politicians advanced different theories on the need to continue consolidating the model into the institutional mainstream. Swept away by the enthusiasm of the Soviet bloc's fall and China's thorough integration into the world capitalist economy, Daniel Bell, in *The End of Ideology* (2000), argued that the world returned to old religious and ethnic conflicts around which ideologies have been molded.

Bell maintains that China's integration into the global capitalist system encouraged Western neoliberals. *"It's the end of ideology in China. Not the end of all ideology, but the end of Marxist ideology. China has many social problems, but the government and its people will deal with them in pragmatic ways, without being overly constrained by ideological boundaries. I still think there's a need for a moral foundation for political rule in China - some sort of guiding ideal for the future - but it won't come from Karl Marx."*[129]

Besides Bell proclaiming the end of Marxist ideology, one of the most widely circulated ideological celebrations of the neoliberal era in the 1990s came from Francis Fukuyama's *The End of History*. History has proved that the end of history theory was a premature celebration of Pax Americana's triumph in Fukuyama's highly imaginative work. Another theoretical weapon in the ideological arsenal of Western neoliberals and neoconservative militarists, in 2019, Fukuyama, whose earlier work has some traces of Hayek's ideological influence, acknowledged that rightwing populism was a threat to liberal democracy.[130]

Favoring an ethics-guided foreign policy, in a post-Trump study, Fukuyama rejected cynical realism in resurgent Cold War policy. Merely because the Soviet bloc's fall coincided with neoliberalism's ascendancy and the unipolar world order, Fukuyama along with other Western analysts in the 1990s imagined Paradise on earth under a unipolar world order. Short-sighted scholarship in the 1990s and early 2000s sang the praises of neoliberal transformation intertwined with Communism's downfall.

Regardless of far-reaching structural problems, including the savings and loan crisis (1986-1995), the speculative derivatives market rooted in the economy's parasitic financialization, insider trading, dot.com bubble, and the infamous ERNON scandal, and above all the Great Recession, costing the taxpayers billions, the fault was never with the neoliberal political economy. No matter what, the problem always rests with the few bad apples and bad governments failing to prevent the crises of capitalism. Fukuyama's faint attempts to walk back some of the more egregious aspects of the 'end of history' theory in *Liberalism and Its Discontents* (2022) did not address social contract. Offering only the caveat of the dangers of the far right, he included the left in the same category, as though there is moral equivalence or the latter had any role in neoliberal policy.[131]

Among others swept away by the end of the Soviet bloc, which became synonymous with the 'end of history', Fukuyama provided the ideological fig leaf for global transformation under the "new world order" in which US unipolar hegemony presumably meant that neoliberalism's global reach was a fait accompli for eternity. At least for the 1990s, the Western bourgeoisie breathed a sigh of relief under an integrated world in which the Washington Consensus would somehow magically solve humanity's problems; and all simply because the bipolar Cold War order no longer existed to challenge Western capitalism.

While Bell, Fukuyama, and other academics, journalists, and politicians celebrated the triumph of Western hegemony, they overlooked the chronic rising inequality and capitalist contradictions of their own time, conditions leading to the Great Recession of 2008, and the rising global tide of illiberal democracy. In their eagerness to denounce Hegelian historicism, they manipulated the concept from a philosophical to a political one, deliberately ignoring the reality of inequality and authoritarian conditions of the liberal Western world.[132]

An integrative world system on a quest for perpetually higher accumulation, capitalism makes it necessary to absorb all countries under the same model that the Western metropolis is pursuing. Enthusiastic about integrating China under global capitalism, Milton Friedman and other globalization proponents, including the IMF, World Bank, and private investors, made repeated efforts through economic, political, and geopolitical means to inculcate the merits of the neoliberal model in China as well as other former Communist countries. These were the same individuals who had no reservations about supporting neoliberal authoritarianism in Chile. [133]

Deeply integrated into the world economy, the Chinese Communist Party rejected the Washington Consensus. Such a model would result in the withering of the strong centralized state's role as a driving force for economic planning domestically and globally, and it would keep social development to a minimum. Before finally embracing the new ideology, Japan and South Korea, and to a lesser degree Taiwan had also resisted neoliberal transformation.

Unlike their neighbors closely linked to the US, China maintained a mixed economy that took into account a heavy dose of statist policies to ensure the government's role in managing the economy. Determining social relations, powerful state-owned enterprises, and the government's major role in privately owned firms distinguished China from its neighbors. Taking full advantage of neoliberalism in the rest of the world, China's globalization under an export-oriented growth strategy combined with import substitution, heavy state involvement in the economy, and social development raised the GDP and living standards very rapidly.[134]

"Departing from the Maoist emphasis on local self-sufficiency," economist Isabella Webber notes, *"the reformers have reintegrated China's vast resources into the global division of labor and have thereby integrated China into neoliberal globalization. However, this integration is based on the premise of being controllable and controlled by the Chinese state and the CCP. The Chinese reform paradigm that emerged in the first decade of reform is marketization under the primacy of the state and not of private property. The market and private property are meant to serve the state's developmentalist agenda. This form of marketization has reintegrated China into neoliberal globalization without, however, pursuing a wholesale adaptation of neoliberal economic policies."*[135]

Just as Mao used nationalism to mobilize the masses in support of the revolution in the 1940s, Deng Xiaoping's *"reform and opening up"* policy at the end of 1978 relied on nationalism to achieve social consensus for capitalist integration. All leaders thereafter employed a similar social consensus strategy. A strong element in ideological indoctrination, Western liberal and rightwing populist neoliberals also used nationalism to mobilize the masses in favor of transformation amid the dilution of the Keynesian state. Although there have been different political approaches about how best to achieve social consensus to promote neoliberal policies within a country and trade/currency blocs like the eurozone, the transformation model's goals remained the same.[136]

Embracing both globalization and nationalism, capitalism's neoliberal phase entails a borderless world for tariff-free trade and capital flows within the international institutional structure of the WTO, World Customs Organization, OECD, UN Conference on Trade and Development, (UNCTAD), IMF, and World Bank. Despite operating within the Westphalian system's nation-state confines, capital has always been predicated on the same basic principles of accumulation on a world scale. However, the periphery has always been subject to uneven terms of trade at the mercy of the metropolis.[137]

Dependent on patron-client integration, or interdependent inter-core relations, national economic development and the integrity of harmonious sociopolitical relations transcends international capital expansion under the neoliberal model. At the same time, neoliberalism needs the nation-state as a vehicle for pro-business fiscal and monetary policy at the national level and to redistribute income nationally. The nation-state further regiments the disparate social interests in a hierarchical society operating under the premise of liberal democratic principles, while serving as a vehicle to negotiate commercial agreements for an expanding market share in a competitive international field.[138]

Whether in the form of sanctions, tariffs, capital investment restrictions, etc., geopolitical rivalries, especially among great powers competition for markets and balance of power, necessarily entail that economic nationalism and alliance trading blocs dilute and distort the neoliberal model. An ideology incorporating globalization under more favorable conditions for capital since the Age of Imperialism, neoliberalism is responsible for political and cultural nationalism as essential leverage on which politicians rely to forge social consensus. A salient factor in promoting nationalism, geopolitics has made it easier for the nation-state as a catalyst in the transition from Keynesianism to neoliberalism.[139]

Besides the reorganized nation-state, neoliberal ideology has co-opted *Ideological State Apparatuses* (ISA), including religious, health, educational, and cultural institutions, among others in all sectors of society, as well as NGOs. Arguing that ISAs perpetuate the capitalist social order, Louis Pierre Althusser, captured the essence of such mechanisms that help to indoctrinate and mobilize the masses in support of the status quo. Along with ideology as a driving force to keep citizens faithful to the social contract, institutional repression in varying forms is a parallel mechanism that the state uses to impose conformity.

While peoples' material concerns play a role in dictating political orientation, it would be misguided to dismiss ideology and culture. Along with various cultural influences, including religion deeply ingrained into society shaping peoples' worldviews while keeping them docile, regardless of class, race, ethnicity, gender, or lifestyle differences, the media and social media's role is of paramount importance. Although Althusser articulated the theory in 1970 *"Idéologie et appareils idéologiques d'État (Notes pour une recherche)"*, a decade before the neoliberal institutionalization in the Thatcher-Reagan era, it is more relevant in the neoliberal era, given the ideology's geographical and socio-cultural reach.[140]

Combined with the state's repressive mechanisms – police networks, security, and armed forces – ISA enforces conformity wherein social repression and exploitation operate within the boundaries that the state defines as 'legal', thereby affording them normative status within the social hierarchy. While global neoliberal transformation has taken place relying on indoctrination, repressive mechanisms manifested in economic and social policy have been at the core of IMF-directed or government-imposed austerity measures resulting in massive income transfer from the working class to capital.[141]
Ideology plays a key role in engendering mass conformity to policies resulting in income concentration, structural exploitation, and marginalization. At the core of the neoliberal value system rests the premise that modernization transcends social development and social justice. Even if the sacrifice means higher inequality, the neoliberal assumption is that society's welfare measured against corporate finance as the driver for progress is worth it. Although during the neoliberal transformation, corporate scandals reached unprecedented levels, the state promoted the neoliberal model in every sector at the expense of labor and the middle class. Economic chaos, greater inequality, and political polarization were inevitable.[142]

Almost three decades after neoliberal capitalism took precedence over the state, the Great Recession further exposed the systemic crisis owing to a combination of factors from financialization to banking deregulation in the 1980s, all related to the market infallibility dogma that the state implemented and businesses practiced. From 1980 to 1994, 1617 banks collapsed costing the public $160 billion. Comparing the very few bank failures under the Keynesian regulatory state versus the floodgates of failures under the neoliberal regime raises suspicions about the latter. International financial organizations and governments were as keenly aware of the root causes of the crisis as bank executives. Instead of foregoing the opportunity for greater profit knowing the government would bail them out, they dug in their heels and remained on the course of high-risk adventures placing investments in sectors even more speculative than previously, including cryptocurrency.[143]

In "*The Great Transformation*" (1944), Karl Polanyi argued that if the market is the sole mechanism determining the fate of human beings, society will be demolished. The inexorable symbiosis between the economy and social relations, formal transactions embedded in informal social transactions is characterized by the marked absence of social control over production and distribution with the only goal to realize greater profits. Neoliberal transformation is predicated on embeddedness for its success in securing popular consensus amid class war.[144]

As Polanyi described about the Great Depression, unchecked market forces resulted in society's demolition. Ironically, remnants of the Keynesian state helped to mitigate the depth of the Great Recession to which deregulation had contributed, especially in banking and hedge funds investing in derivatives. Instead of absorbing the surplus capital through the fiscal system from big capital to stimulate growth and market equilibrium, the state offered more neoliberal policies responsible for the deep economic contraction in the first place. Long before the neoliberal era, the IMF and World Bank had been imposing austerity, deregulation, privatization, weakened social safety net, and currency devaluation in the Global South, thus, devaluing assets, including labor costs, for the benefit of large domestic and foreign investors. IMF and World Bank whose policies converged with the neoliberal model before institutionalization, resulted in greater inequality, foreign economic dependence under chronic balance of payments deficits, cyclical debt crises, and authoritarianism.[145]

The consequences of neoliberal policies are not limited to downward social mobility and marginalization. Chronically weakening economies in the metropolis amid capital concentration, much weaker in the periphery, and sinking deeper in debt in the quest to bail out banks and insurance companies engaging in speculative activities of dubious legality have been the result of the neoliberal model. Where the IMF imposed austerity, neoliberalism precipitated authoritarian policies under elected regimes in developing nations that further eroded the social safety net. From November 2007 to May 2014, this was also the case with core countries in severe economic dislocation, measured in terms of job loss and recovery.[146]

Discrediting Keynesian ideology and undermining its policies in favor of neoliberalism in developing nations since the 1970s, the IMF and World Bank undercut the state's ability to initiate economic and social development initiatives and weakened trade unions as the vanguard for such policies to promote privatization.[147] As part of global transformation under cyclical austerity, regardless of whether the IMF formalized socioeconomic inequality with austerity measures or not, the neoliberal dogma's legacy was autocratization. As a consequence of capital's hegemony over the state, class war, socioeconomic inequality, and rightwing populism became as prevalent globally, amid a weakened social welfare state.[148]

After the CIA-sponsored coup in September 1973, the weak state structure was more evident in Chile. The 'Chicago Boys' imposed the neoliberal model with a resounding success by the criteria of its advocates, Friedman, Hayek, and Buchanan, among others. Once Pinochet privatized the social security system, banks, and other state enterprises, reduced tariffs, surrendered central bank functions to private banks, cut taxes on the wealthy, and weakened the labor unions, the dictatorship resorted to violence to silence dissenting voices.[149]

The result of massive income transfer from the working class and public enterprises to private domestic and foreign firms was that as a percent of nominal GDP external debt ratio rose from a low of 23.9% when the CIA helped to overthrow Salvador Allende to an astonishing 115.6% in 1985; all in the name of market efficiency. Despite such disastrous results, by the 1990s, neoliberalism became the prevailing doctrine among Latin American political and economic elites under US sponsorship. At the cost of rising cyclical debt, inequality, and poverty, neoliberal ideology prevailed because the local elites hoped to advance their interests closely integrated with those of international capital.[150]

Long before the neoliberal model advocates landed on Chile's shores, spreading the 'pure market' gospel across the Latin American republics, northwest Europe and the US largely determined the region's terms of trade as they did terms of trade in Africa where speculative commodities brokers in London, New York, and Chicago, not the producers, decided on raw material prices. Foreign-based companies dominating the export-oriented Latin American economies based on the primary sector, with a weak and primarily foreign-owned manufacturing sector, keep the region chronically dependent with low living standards in comparison to the G-7 countries.[151]

Considering Latin America's history of external dependence, the IMF, World Bank, and the 'Chicago Boys' institutionalized wholesale privatization of public enterprises while making sure that the republics remained trapped in debt cycles as policy leverage impacting all of society. Given the historical context, neoliberalism was not a radical departure from the IMF-World Bank post-WWII policy. "*Neoliberalism supplied the general justification for the transfer of public assets and state-owned enterprises, paid for with public savings, even in areas considered "taboo" and untouchable until a few years ago, such as electricity, aviation, oil, or telecommunications.*"[152]

In the name of upholding the virtues of neoliberalism as the ideology that replaced Keynesianism, the model's apologists contended that global transformation would lift the entire integrated economy from the trans-Atlantic core to the Global South. Lofty claims of development and higher living standards notwithstanding, the Washington Consensus delivered a wider income gap on a world scale amid long-standing downward pressure on wages under authoritarian policies. Although the world economy was growing from the fall of the Soviet Bloc to the Lehman Brothers collapse unleashing the Great Recession, all along amid the crisis, the richest one percent in the world benefited at the expense of the bottom two-thirds.[153]

From the Washington Consensus to China's Belt and Road Initiative

Under the umbrella of the five-century-old capitalist economy, there have been different models of development reflecting its evolving phases. From the transition of subsistence agriculture to cash crops for export and long-distance trade to the neoliberal phase of financialization where the financial sector and development models emerge out of capitalism's crises. Although neoliberals invoke Adam Smith's free enterprise economic theory, analysis of his work representing market fundamentalism is a distortion of what he wrote in *An Inquiry into the Nature and Causes of the Wealth of Nations.*[154]

From classical economists Adam Smith, David Ricardo, and John Stuart Mill, to neoliberal apostles Hayek, von Misses, and Friedman, the promise of development models is predicated on a system that best serves capital by extracting the most surplus value from labor. Promising to maintain a social order presumably by minimizing sociopolitical chaotic conditions that compromise mass conformity, neoliberal policies precipitate market disorder, inefficiency, and chaos. Besides ideology determining what constitutes the best development model, methodology criteria that reflect measuring the wealth of a nation are important. For example, in 2019, US per capita GDP was at $65,000. However, 50% of workers earned less than $35,000, and 28% of the population earned under $25,000, a figure below the poverty line for a family of four.[155]

Economic growth, trade, capital investment expansion, and unemployment statistics reflect capital expansion, not social development excluded from the neoliberal experiment. Like sins measured against pious deeds to secure eternal life in Paradise, the political and socioeconomic elites use averaged GDP statistics to identify the wealth of the nation as a deliberate obfuscation to deceive and distract the working class about material conditions. Regardless of their actual financial situation, the wealth effect symbolism, which includes assets from housing to stocks and retirement funds for the more affluent, influences the psychology of most people.

Using trickle-down economics, Keynesian economist John Kenneth Galbraith compared it to giving a horse enough oats in the bag hanging from its neck, so that seeds dropping on the ground feed the passing sparrows. Neoliberal supply-side economics manipulates labor and goods supply by reducing taxes and providing multiple benefits to corporations as the vehicle delivers "trickle-down" benefits. More than four decades of neoliberal propaganda about the model's success trickling down does not erase the empirical reality that in the 1970s, half of Americans were earning more than their parents, while in 2019, this figure dropped to a mere 8 percent.[156]

The neoliberal model encountered resistance among countries that saw merit in preserving aspects of Keynesian developmentalism. In the age of neoliberal transformation, neo-mercantilism and varieties of developmental policies have found support in a few countries. At the forefront of neo-mercantilism, China pursued a balance of payments surplus, stock-piled gold, and foreign reserves, vigorously engaged in protecting national entities against competition, and pursued an export-oriented growth strategy by providing subsidies to companies and keeping a fairly docile labor force through unions linked to the state through the All-China Federation of Trade Unions (ACFTU).[157]

Few countries combined developmentalism with aspects of the neoliberal model while maintaining a strong commitment to steady social development parallel to economic growth. At the CCP plenary session of 2016, China announced the 13th Five-Year Plan (2016-2020) that it was the world's largest industrial economy, trader of goods, and holder of foreign exchange reserves. Acknowledging the end of high growth rates, the regime announced transitions in the industrial structure and labor policy with an emphasis on greater income distribution amid slower economic growth emanating from exports. That was based on the expectation of a reduced trade surplus with the US which had turned negative on offshoring and over-reliance on China as a trading partner. Other nations, including Brazil, India, Russia, South Africa, and Singapore, pursued a policy mix that included aspects of neo-mercantilism to achieve an economic miracle similar to China's, without emphasizing the social development component.[158]

Neoliberal transformation in the interest of large businesses was not very different than 19th-century economic imperialism, minus the costs and complications of colonial rule. In China's case, the Communist Party's underlying assumption was that embracing Western-style neoliberalism at home would mean submitting to a model responsible for the erosion of US global economic hegemony. After all, China derived the benefits of globalization, without embracing the Washington Consensus, while managing to eliminate extreme poverty by the end of the 2010s as the government had promised and raising living standards even in the Western and south-Western provinces.[159]

From the US perspective, the US-led China competition over trade, industrial, tech, investment, and monetary policies was about Beijing subverting neoliberal orthodoxy by pursuing a policy mix with a heavy dose of statism and realizing a trade surplus with the G7, especially the US. China continued the historic five-year plans for economic and social development while benefiting from neoliberal global markets and opening windows of opportunity to foreign investors. By comparison, Singapore's developmentalism with a dose of statism was also a deviation from neoliberal orthodoxy, as other developmentalist models in some Asian and Latin American countries. However, Singapore and countries pursuing mixed policies never carried the same global significance as China, nor did they pose any challenge to US hegemony.[160]

As a result of globalization under the neoliberal model, especially after 2008, most of the world suffered rising poverty and inequality, while China was the exception. Framing this issue into a global perspective in terms of social mobility, an OECD study concluded that mass anxiety stemmed from the public impression that the middle class did not benefit from the political economy. Lagging salaries were not catching up with the rising cost of living especially in housing, health, and education.

"In 2009 the middle class included 1.8 billion people, with Europe (664 million), Asia (525 million) North America (338 million) accounting for the highest number of people belonging to this group. ... The size of the "global middle class" will increase from 1.8 billion in 2009 to 3.2 billion by 2020 and 4.9 billion by 2030. The bulk of this growth will come from Asia: by 2030 Asia will represent 66% of the global middle-class population and 59% of middle-class consumption, compared to 28% and 23%, respectively in 2009..."[161]

The OECD study confirmed contradictions between neoliberalism's promise to expand the middle class against the reality of downward social mobility. Relegating the concept of development to capital expansion and "selective democracy" implying an oligarchic system serving the privileged capitalist class, a segment of the middle class and workers have accepted selective democracy because they are bombarded with consumerist indoctrination embedded in the hegemonic culture. Hence, the neoliberal model has redefined the norms and obviated popular democracy in the name of fealty to the market under a hierarchical social structure.[162]

Neoliberalism's greatest accomplishment is that it has co-opted the middle class and workers under various mainstream political parties aiming at the same development model goal. As Ali Kadri points out. *"Selective democracy, the rule of the few personifying capital is not democracy. ... The central working-class casts a vote for the imperialist class, which violently underprice and overconsume man and nature. Needless to say, cheaper underpriced commodities from the developing world buttress the purchasing power of central wage earners. And as material circumstances influence consciousness, the central working-class adopts an ideological prism that mirrors the short-termism of corporate profit making."*[163]

A paradox in development models, horizontal economic growth (expanding/scaling products and services within the existing market) without social development benefiting the majority in society has been capitalism's historical reality and one that developed countries promote at the expense of the periphery. The patron-client integration model has resulted in the periphery's dependence on raw materials exports to finance imported finished products and service foreign loans. Latin America, Africa, and much of Asia have suffered worse inequality under the uneven terms of trade with core countries. Similarly, neoliberalism has exacerbated the patron-client-integration model which resulted in perpetual underdevelopment and dependence of the Global South on the core countries. [164]

Because neoliberal capitalism has precipitated higher levels of structural inequality and autocratization in many countries, including the US and UK that prided themselves as pillars of liberal democracy, scholarly and journalistic interest in development models' impact on society assumed greater importance after the Great Recession. This is especially in light of China's rapid economic growth based on the Beijing Consensus and then the Belt and Road Initiative as an alternative to the trans-Atlantic neoliberal experiment. Four years before the 2008 crisis, Joshua Cooper Ramo used the term Beijing Consensus to explain the differences between China's development strategy and the Washington Consensus.[165]

Stressing innovation, steady economic growth, expansion based on global integration, and self-determination as part of a mixed economy, the Beijing Consensus includes the state as a key player in economic and social development. This is not to suggest that cheap labor and a vast domestic market attractive to foreign investors have not played catalytic roles in China's rapid industrial development. Although multinational corporations took advantage of cheap and forced labor under a regimented Chinese labor force, India also has a vast domestic market and cheap labor without a social development program. Unlike China, India failed to achieve rapid development to the degree that it could challenge US global hegemony as did China. Although in the 1980s, India and China were at comparable development levels, with India leading in some areas, the key was the divergent development models in the two countries with India following a path closer to the Western neoliberal model.[166]

Resisting neoliberalism's emphasis on market hegemony over the state, even after joining the World Trade Organization in December 2001, the Chinese Communist Party (CCP) feared diluting the state's power, while strengthening the private sector, especially with foreign companies in every sector from high tech to due diligence services involving services in the complex relationship of the private sector and government bureaucracies.

Considering that the state's economic interventionism lessened the shock to its economy and the world in 2008, the Great Recession validated some of the premises of the Beijing Consensus.[167]

In 2013, the Belt and Road Initiative (BRI) replaced the Beijing Consensus. With at least 150 countries involved, many of which signed trade and investment contracts with Chinese public and private companies, and 32 international organizations, BRI represents the essence of globalization. Despite Western criticism of economic nationalism, in 2002, the China-ASEAN Free Trade Area (CAFTA) signed the first three free trade agreements to promote rapid mutual development with a trade volume of $54 billion until 2013. When the agreement expired, Beijing introduced the BRI initially involving 60 countries with an estimated $8 trillion global investment. While Chinese companies are the main beneficiaries, foreign companies play a role, muting criticism that BRI has come at the expense of international capitalism.[168]

Accommodating foreign capital and adhering to WTO, IMF, and World Bank guidelines, by the sheer volume of its role as the world's second-largest economy in nominal value, and first in PPP terms, China left no doubt that BRI along with its role in the BRICS and the Shanghai Cooperation Organization would afford it global dominance. Because Beijing has influenced the multilateral organizations to adjust their policies to accommodate its development model, Western authoritarian neoliberals oppose the Bretton Woods system that paved the way for neoliberalism which they associate with the old liberal world order inadvertently strengthening the Chinese economy listed as 'developing', which permits it to enjoy favorable international trade treatment reserved for Third World African and Latin American countries.[169]

Besides leveraging its dominant global trade role, China also relies on multilateral institutions where it has preeminent influence, including the Asian Infrastructure Investment Bank (AIIB), the BRICS' New Development Bank (NDB), Regional Comprehensive Economic Partnership (RCEP), Forum for Asia, the Conference on Interaction and Confidence Building Measures in Asia. While US foreign policy has been confrontational toward China, relying on military intimidation in the South China Sea, geopolitical and geoeconomic containment combined with continued trade engagement has meant increased measures to limit US semiconductor chips exports for artificial intelligence applications and supercomputers, as well as discouraging investment in Chinese semiconductor companies.[170]

Well aware that China will eventually replace the US as the global hegemonic power in the 21st century, the US has moved to consolidate power within trade agreements resorting to Cold War-style containment strategies resulting in economic fragmentation. The price for combined containment and engagement policy has been to undercut globalization, hurting the US and its economic partners as much as China.

To compensate for losses owing to various highly costly and counterproductive Western containment mechanisms, China has been expanding the domestic market and forging new trade partnerships with the Global South. Western analysts recognize that US-G7 containment aimed at China has limited impact because international capital circumvents such barriers. Because of neoliberal globalization, US-allied interdependence with China is so deep that any option other than cooperation would be disastrous for the major players and the rest of the world.[171]

Ostensibly concerned that the Beijing model entails capitalism under state rule violates "democratic principles" and human rights in the Xinjiang Uygur Autonomous Region, the US-led campaign historically castigated the

Communist Party for subordinating individual freedoms to economic development. Western criticism would carry a great deal more weight, except that in 2018, there were 52 Fortune 500 companies, and a year later, 69 European companies operating in the province. In short, Western companies are exploiting cheap labor in a province that the West accuses of human rights violations. While China ranks very low in human rights, Western allies Egypt, Saudi Arabia, and Israel are not much better. Although the US has used human rights as foreign policy leverage, China has continued to make economic inroads in the Middle East for market share where historically the US was dominant.[172]

"For Beijing," John Liu observes, *"its success legitimizes its model as an alternative to the liberal values of the West, an idea the U.S. and its allies have resisted. It's a debate that plays out on a variety of fronts, from combating the Covid-19 pandemic to reining in Big Tech."[173]* Because of the pandemic and geopolitical developments after Russia invaded Ukraine in February 2022, several of China's BRI individual projects changed amid aggressive attempts to dilute neoliberal globalization and forge trade blocs.

Combined with the military focus on trans-Atlantic geopolitical and economic solidarity, and complimented by an Indo-Pacific Framework Agreement (May 2022) as regional leverage against China's expanding influence, economic nationalism, and regional bloc solidarity have been attempts to slow down China's race for global economic hegemony. However, even the US closest allies question the wisdom of forcing countries into binary zero-sum games where either the US or China emerge as winners. Vague on specifics, and nothing comparable to economic development on the scale of BRICS, US-forged geopolitical trade blocs based on the fear of China taking over the world undermine neoliberal globalization. Nevertheless, the capital remained free-flowing within neoliberal policies at the national and within and between bloc-trade groups.[174]

Among many US-Western criticisms of China is that the political economy is the product of authoritarianism, while the trans-Atlantic neoliberal model promotes democracy. The history of both core and periphery where the neoliberal model has been implemented from the 1980s to the present has shown that it promotes inequality, social marginalization, and autocratization. This is not to argue that the Beijing Consensus and the BRI have operated outside the confines of capitalist appropriation. In this regard, Karl Kautsky's revisionist theory about the unpreparedness of the working class to take over the state as a vehicle of capitalism is valid as applied to China as well as to parliamentary systems where authoritarian liberalism is the actual governance model behind the façade of the electoral system.[175]

From the Thatcher-Reagan era to the present, neoliberalism's message was anti-democratic, replete with rightwing populist messages, advocating the withering of the welfare state and forging a strong state in the service of capital.[176] *"The 'authoritarian' state,"* Hermann Heller argues, *"claims to amount to a truly non-partisan and just state—by contrast with the democratic party state... No state that is determined to secure 'the free labor power of those people active in the economy' will be allowed to retreat from it; rather, it will have to act in an authoritarian way."[177]*

Regardless of the Washington Consensus vs Beijing Consensus-BIR, development models do not have the same impact on class relations and governance in the core as in the periphery. In Latin America, which has been under external economic dependence within the confines of the patron-client integration model, neoliberalism has had a greater detrimental impact on the working class and society as a whole than in the US which derives the benefits of uneven terms of trade with the periphery, resulting in uneven development for the latter.[178]

Projecting the impression that the benefits of the neoliberal model are somehow fairly distributed among the population, despite the "trickle down" form, whether in the US, EU, or Latin America, neoliberal apologists promote the myth that the system works fairly for all based on a universal set of rules, abilities, ambitions, and above all economic status and access to capital. Yet, from Hayek to Friedman, neoliberal apostles make no apologies that social classes do not derive nor do they deserve equal benefits within the social contract. Nor do they acknowledge that neoliberalism leads to greater inequality and authoritarianism.[179]

Developmentalism in the Semi-periphery: Asian Tigers and BRICS

Geopolitical asymmetry reflects geoeconomic power and the political economy which determines the course of the former. With the support of the national and comprador bourgeoisie from Spain under King Philip II (1556-1598) to 21st century India, semi-periphery states have historically balanced their position between core and periphery to secure market advantages within the periphery and in the metropolis. This has been a means of climbing closer to the core of the world capitalist economy benefiting the national and comprador bourgeoisie who play an important role in the patron-client integration model.[180]

During the era of neoliberalism, the Asian Tigers (South Korea, Taiwan, Hong Kong, and Singapore) and BRICS (Brazil, Russia, India, China, and South Africa) took advantage of their semi-periphery status to strengthen national capitalism. Resorting to some of the worst practices of international capitalism affecting the working class, these countries experienced upward social mobility but at labor's expense.

Although China emerged as the undisputed beneficiary, the others experienced some level of upward social mobility at a time when the trans-Atlantic core was on a steady downward mobility trend. Besides exacerbating foreign debt and external dependence on the Global South, the neoliberal model's market hegemony weakened the Western core. This was also the case in Japan, Taiwan, and South Korea, all of which adopted neo-corporatist strategies where the state played a key role in outlining a blueprint of the economy, but abandoned them for neoliberalism.[181]

As the Soviet bloc was collapsing rapidly in the late 1980s-early 1990s, Japan, South Korea, and Taiwan, along with Singapore and Hong Kong emerged as significant regional economic players. Except for Japan, in the first three decades of the Cold War, South Korea, Taiwan, Hong Kong, and Singapore integrated rapidly into the world economy, developing the secondary and tertiary sectors of production and focusing on exports. Under a strong centralized developmental state, combining authoritarianism and an inclusive institutional structure, by the 1990s, they became the envy of the Third World for a brief period, before China overshadowed them.[182]

The 'Asian Tiger' model entailed government investment in certain industries intended to meet internal demand and expanded exports to realize a balance of payments surplus. Considering that the government subsidized select companies and allowed others to operate with chronic deficits, Asian Tiger neo-mercantilist policies focused on long-term domestic self-sufficiency instead of short-term profits. In many respects, this was a model similar to Japan's. To influence financial institutions, while choosing specific companies to support, the state steered resources and production through public ownership.[183]

Hardly surprisingly, Western neoliberals opposed Asian Tiger neo-mercantilism where government involvement in trade, finance, and investment promoted certain sectors. Intended to promote national capitalism, while still allowing foreign capital investment, the Asian Tigers aimed at strengthening national capitalism by maintaining a strong state structure and keeping a weakened social safety net to maintain popular consensus. Where labor share rose modestly in Hong Kong from 1990 to 2017, it declined in South Korea, Taiwan, and Singapore.[184]

Initially based on import-substitution strategies prevalent in many countries amid the Great Depression, in the late 1940s-early 1950s, developmentalism resulted in state support of the steel industry, shipbuilding, and manufacturing, combining capital-intensive and labor-intensive export-oriented growth sectors. In varying degrees, this model found its way to Russia, India, and Spain in the 1990s, and Brazil and Argentina after the dotcom bubble of 1999-2000. Along with South Korea, Taiwan, Singapore, and Hong Kong, the BRICS combined aspects of neo-mercantilism and neoliberalism in the 1990s when much the rest of the world was embracing it owing to IMF, World Bank, Western corporate and government pressures to pursue privatization under fiscal austerity and monetarism.[185]

Besides relatively rapid GDP growth in the 1990s, the Asian Tigers experienced the fastest middle-class expansion in the continent. With national economic growth and development promising to translate into individual prosperity, the quasi-statist governments used nationalism as a catalyst to mobilize popular support for export-oriented and importing-substituting developmentalism. An obstacle to the US-led transformation model, a Western campaign undermined the Asian Tigers so that their model would not spread to other parts of the world. *"Western speculators then took down the vulnerable countries one by one in the "Asian crisis" of 1997-98. China alone was left as an economic threat to the Western neoliberal model, and it is this existential threat that is the target of the trade and currency wars today."*[186]

Amid its struggle to affirm a quasi-statist developmental model deviating from neoliberalism, China learned an important lesson observing the US-led Western reaction to the Asian Tigers during the 1990s. Navigating through the rough waters of the neoliberal world economy, the Asian Tigers used their semi-periphery status to circumvent some burdensome terms of dependence on the trans-Atlantic core by relying on multilateral foreign economic policies and the comprador bourgeois class as its link to foreign investment. Complying with neoliberal globalization, especially the extent to which foreign capital would play a role in economic development, they hoped to benefit the domestic economy. By introducing limits on foreign firms, while subsidizing domestic ones, they were able to strengthen the national bourgeoisie and accommodate the comprador class whose interests were tied to the metropolis. These measures were sufficient to satisfy international financial institutions.[187]

Operating within the capitalist world system, the Asian Tigers model further illustrates that the ideological divide between Western capitalism against Eastern Communism was in essence about global hegemony of markets, raw materials, and geopolitics under the aegis of the US and its G7 partners and their allies. To circumvent foreign capital domination and inordinate foreign dependence comparable to Latin America under the US patron-client model, the Asian Tigers leveraged their semi-periphery status. However, they did not have the strength to escape dependence on the metropolis, ultimately benefiting China more than their national economies.

Besides IMF-recommended currency devaluations amid speculation along with hyper speculation amid hyper speculation, the levels of corruption and crony capitalism contributed to the Asian financial crisis of 1997-1998. Given the integrated world economy, the crisis quickly spread outside the continent. Widespread corruption among US and European corporations and lack of oversight and accountability exposed the neoliberal model imbued with flaws that had ripple effects globally. The nail in the Asian Tiger's coffin was IMF austerity, especially for Thailand, Indonesia, and South Korea.

By 2000 when the dot.com bubble burst, the era of the Asian Tigers was already in twilight. Accompanied by "rescue packages" in 1997, IMF austerity carried the usual neoliberal conditionality terms to qualify for stabilization loans. Interestingly, it was not the neoliberal core US and EU, but semi-periphery neo-mercantilist China that emerged as the clear winner regionally and globally because its economy was far too strong to cave under international pressure. Although the dot-com bubble cut China's GDP growth from 14.2% in 1992 to 7.7% in 1999, that was still phenomenal compared with the rest of the world.[188]

Considering China's continued economic expansion sweeping along most Asian economies, US-led efforts to undermine the Asian Tigers model backfired in areas difficult to anticipate in so far as China benefited from austerity imposed on the Asian Tigers. At the same time, the US and EU's quest to integrate former Soviet bloc countries under the Washington Consensus model failed to yield the desired geopolitical and economic benefits for the West, much less engender liberal democracy as advertised.

Besides large corporate interests, especially the defense industry, autocratization followed the path of the neoliberal model in the periphery, most notably in the former Soviet republics. Although Europe and the US tried to integrate many of the former Soviet republics, regardless of any commitment to democracy and human rights, China played a far greater role economically. This was not only because of geography and a government plan to integrate Eurasia, but China's terms of trade and investment deals in comparison to those of the West, China or the West neoliberalism and autocratization went hand in hand.[189]

In "The Political Economy of Neoliberalism and illiberal democracy" Gary Jacobs, argues: *"Despite the rhetoric of the Washington Consensus, the fall of the Berlin Wall, the collapse of communism and dissolution of Soviet authoritarianism did not mark a final vindication and victory for Western democratic neoliberalism... Globalization, financialization, global mergers and acquisitions, shadow banking, international tax havens, the policy bias favoring energy-intensive automation, maximizing shareholder value, state capture, oligarchy, and plutocracy have fueled soaring levels of economic inequality and insecurity."*[190]

Despite the dot.com bubble and abundance of evidence that the neoliberal commitment to capital accumulation transcends human rights and democracy, the myth of the neoliberal model's triumph equated with electoral system politics persists among Western politicians, the media, IMF, World Bank, and the business sector. Supply-side economists, IMF-World Bank monetarists, and free market purists celebrated the benefits of taming the "Asian Tigers", while at the same time integrating the former Communist bloc and China under the aegis of the capitalist system. All along, US policymakers assumed that there would be problems in other countries embracing neoliberal transformation as the new norm.

Despite the developmental state in Asian Tiger countries, neoliberalism's global reach still had a significant impact. Income transfer from social welfare programs to corporate welfare, tax rate reductions, and loopholes for the wealthy remained at the core of neoliberal policy. As David Harvey points out in *"Neoliberalism as Creative Destruction"*, not only does the model impact fiscal, monetary, and economic policy, but in the quest to transform society, it remolds all institutions to facilitate the social contract, establishing its norms while molding peoples' identity. Neoliberalism's global reach undermined the quest of the Asian Tigers to solidify their role in the semi-periphery of the world economy.[191]

Presumably operating under an open, free, and democratic society where the market operates with minimal government intervention, neoliberalism established the foundation for blurring the lines between liberal democracy and authoritarian liberalism. This was the case in Hong Kong with its unique relationship to the mainland, South Korea, Singapore, and Taiwan observing the formalities of parliamentary government while pursuing policies identified with authoritarianism.[192]

By deregulating and legalizing financial activities otherwise predatory, crying out for regulation, the state became an unapologetic advocate of jungle capitalism, often ignoring both ethical and legal considerations. Elected governments in advanced and underdeveloped countries alike proved that legalized corrupt corporate and financial activities are not confined to small authoritarian countries. Such practices are inherent in neoliberal globalization where the main actors are the political elites, elected or not, promoting deregulation, privatization, and fiscal and corporate subsidies.[193]

Using Peru as a case study, Peter Leys points to capitalism's inherent contradictions immersed in corruption with the neoliberal state at the heart of it. *"Peru's neoliberal dream has turned into a nightmare, one in which society ceases to exist and politicians are no longer seen to represent anybody, simply acting on behalf of their financial interests — and those of their allies — at the expense of the common good. Hope for the future does not lie in the present interim government, but in the growth of political engagement from Peru's younger generation and the politics of the street, outside the sphere of conventional parties."[194]*

Well known for their history of authoritarian capitalism and endemic corruption, several Latin American countries, among them Mexico, Brazil, and Argentina, accepted the neoliberal model only to suffer a severe economic crisis in the late 1990s and 2000s for the latter two. In 1994, Mexico underwent severe currency devaluation during the 'Tequila Crisis', impacting much of Latin America. Borrowing $50 billion in IMF bailout, Mexico's cyclical debt crisis took place 11 years after the 1983 IMF structural adjustment presumably to stop the bleeding which only opened deeper wounds. The country was worse off after the adjustment, with currency devaluation in 1994 taking place just one year after Mexico signed the North American Free Trade Agreement (NAFTA), thereby making its assets cheaper for the US and Canada.[195]

Mexico's example was typical for all of Latin America. After the US-supported Argentinian military coup of March 1976, the country experimented with the IMF-proposed neoliberal model that Chile's Pinochet had implemented. The experiment resulted in deindustrialization, foreign debt explosion, and a sharp drop in living standards. By 1998, Argentina lapsed into an economic depression lasting until 2002. Because of the deposit freeze, adopting a flexible exchange rate, and partly because of public debt default, a massive drop in consumer demand especially in real estate, but in most sectors sent the country into a deep crisis. At the peak of the deep economic contraction, more than half of the people lived below the poverty line. The middle class and workers paid the price for neoliberal legal and illegal activities carrying the IMF's dogmatic stamp of legitimacy behind which was Wall Street, international and local finance capital.[196]

During the 1990s, under presidents Fernando Alfonso Collor de Mello and Fernando Henrique Cardoso[1], Brazil followed a path similar to Argentina's. With an inflation rate of just under 3000%, neoliberal populist President Collor's approval dropped from 71% in 1989 to 9% in 1992[2] at which point the Senate removed him from office on corruption charges initially brought up by his brother.[197] From Brazil to Argentina and Peru under Alberto Fujimori (1990-2000), rightwing populism forged sociopolitical consensus behind the transformation

1. https://en.wikipedia.org/wiki/Fernando_Henrique_Cardoso

2. http://datafolha.folha.uol.com.br/opiniaopublica/1992/06/1222335-avaliacao-governo-collor---1992.shtml

model that allowed foreign capital to dominate mining and public utilities resulting from the privatization of state enterprises. Disillusioned segments of the working class and the middle class accepting the growth and prosperity myth blindly backed Fujimori's neoliberal authoritarianism in Peru as many Brazilians fell for the myths of prosperity that Collor and Cardoso were promoting. After twelve years of a constitutional government, Fujimori engaged in self-coup (Fujimorazo) in 1992. Using the pretext of the growing 'threat' by leftwing *Sendero Luminoso* (Shining Path), he suspended the constitution and institutionalized neoliberalism at an even greater pace.[198]

The Peruvian and Latin American elites inculcated fear into the public that any inclusionary center-left populist regime would scare businesses and invite higher unemployment and inflation. However, once in power, rightwing populist presidents like Fujimori could not possibly deliver the economic miracle promised in return for broad acceptance of the neo-classical model. As a substitute for the unfulfilled economic miracle, fear-mongering about the menacing left nationally and outside the country was the only populist tool to forge sociopolitical consensus.[199]

Taking into account the historical impact of developmental Argentinian economist Raul Prebisch (*The Economic Development of Latin America, 1950*) and Brazilian Celso Furtado (*Development and Underdevelopment*, 1964), Latin American policy-makers in the neoliberal era considered the interests of the national capitalist class and full employment goals along with an industrial policy designed to protect domestic firms through trade and investment, without hindering the open economy. The World Bank saw some merit in the neo-developmentalist model combining market mechanisms and state intervention intended to modernize and expand the economy. However, it was always within the framework of the neoliberal transformation. Brazil and Argentina's hybrid model that took into account aspects of developmentalism stabilized the weakened economy amid an expansionary cycle that ended during the Great Recession of 2007-2008.[200]

Under President Nestor Kirchner (2003-2007), Argentina forged a neo-developmental model that several countries had implemented in the 1980s but abandoned under pressure from the US, IMF, and multinational corporations. Coming from a labor union background, Brazil's most popular president, Luiz Inacio Lula da Silva (2003-2010), pursued a hybrid agenda with traits of inclusionary populism evident in other regimes from Hugo Chavez's Venezuela (2002-2013) to Evo Morales' Bolivia (2006-2019). Like Kirchner, Lula accommodated domestic and foreign capital through monetary, fiscal, and investment policy perpetuating the wage-productivity gap. His cabinet appointments, and especially Henrique Meireles as Central Bank president, signaled that populist campaign promises would not result in market disruptions.[201]

Considering that Brazil and Argentina had come out of the disaster of privatization, deregulation, and anti-labor policies to bolster national and foreign capital, Argentina's *"Kirchnerismo"* and Brazil's *"Lulismo"* had a great deal of traction among the masses hoping for relief from austerity. Although the inclusionary populist regimes readily accepted finance capitalism's preeminence within the context of the Keynesian social mix, they managed the contradictions fairly well because of global growth, largely owing to China's rapid expansion. The combination of China's gradual rise in the world economy and Venezuela's inclusionary populist tide under President Chavez (Chavismo) influenced other republics that economic development along Keynesian lines would strengthen national capitalism and lessen social exclusion.[202]

Many governments, including Lula's Brazil, Rafael Correa's Ecuador (2007-2017), and Turkey's Recep Tayyip Erdogan (2014-) blamed neoliberalism as the root cause behind the trans-Atlantic-based Great Recession. Partly because of the desire to have a more robust role of the state in the economy, after 2008, several countries reaffirmed their commitment to aspects of developmentalism, using nationalism as the catalyst for popular mobilization. However, they kept core neoliberal policies, including foreign capital investment incentives and a fiscal policy to attract such investment. Despite each country's unique political differences, to some extent, this was based on the playbook of the Asian Tigers.

Around the world, there were differences with the neo-developmentalist model. In comparison to the patronage state under Erdoğan's neo-Ottoman Sultanism, as one example of neoliberal authoritarianism, pro-labor inclusive populist Brazilian president Lula catering to foreign and domestic capital offered some hope for the masses because of the social development component in government, often more symbolic than real. Both models were swimming upstream in contradictions, but the common denominator between authoritarian neoliberalism and hybrid neo-developmentalism within the context of the neoliberal experiment was how they contributed to democracy intentionally and coincidentally or detracted from it.[203]

Neoliberal authoritarian Jair Bolsonaro (2019-2022) who succeeded Lula's successor Dilma Rousseff came to office at an opportune time partly because the far right had discredited and seriously distorted Lulismo, which Rousseff undermined in the quest to satisfy capital. Caught in the contradictions of inclusionary populist policies clashing with neoliberalism, Rousseff was unable to deal with unrest in various cities as early as August 2012. These culminated in the uprising of June 2013 against mass transit fare increases. Abandoning Lula's commitment to social development, she undercut Lulismo from within by adopting anti-inflation policies more in line with neoliberalism. Popular skepticism about Rousseff made it easier for her successor to proceed with authoritarian neoliberalism that many among the masses misinterpreted as anti-institutionalism, presumably yielding results and a sense of legitimacy that appeared to be lacking in Rousseff's policy mix.[204]

Similar trends prevailed in other republics, including post-Correa Ecuador. President Lenin Moreno's (2019-2021) neoliberal policies took center stage as they did in Bolsonaro's Brazil. In both Brazil and Ecuador, the underlying political strength of neoliberals was more entrenched among the elites which convinced enough voters to turn their back on inclusive developmental populists in favor of authoritarian capitalism promising to deliver more for the masses. Despite the public sector rescuing the neoliberal experiment after 2008, the combination of corruption and anti-institutional sentiment became part of rightwing populist rhetoric.[205]

China's Response to the Neoliberal Crisis

The global financial and trade structure makes it very difficult for countries to operate outside the institutional perimeters of the neoliberal model's global matrix of national and international public and private institutions. Especially for China benefiting from global integration combined with the ambitious domestic economic growth and social development agenda, circumventing some of Western neoliberalism's policy trappings requires constant revision of its hybrid model. To stimulate demand while keeping a balanced budget, Beijing decentralized the fiscal system and funded infrastructural development including education and health care, areas where the neoliberal West was slashing. Like other governments throughout the world, China privatized the majority of state-owned companies which became publicly listed and regulated. As leverage, the state retained a substantial role in economic planning and partial ownership.[206]

Hardly a model pro-labor regime, the Chinese government nevertheless promoted optimizing the necessary skilled labor force, while undertaking an enormous expansion of education compared with the rest of the world, with the possible exception of the Scandinavian countries and much of northwest Europe. Claims that the Beijing Consensus was tantamount to autarky was a convenient slogan, but no more accurate than the suggestion that it was another version of the trans-Atlantic neoliberal model which rested on geopolitics as economic leverage.

Under the neoliberal model, which modified the military-industrial complex to reflect even greater reliance on the corporate sector for private security and less regulatory oversight, US and Western defense spending rose sharply. Governments justified such spending increase by invoking the "war on terror" which each country defined as it wished to target domestic and foreign enemies, followed by the new Cold War against Russia and China, and NATO's global expansion prompting greater defense spending by those countries impacted. Whereas the US under the neoliberal model spent 3.7% on defense and demanded that NATO members spend a minimum of 3%, China spent 1.7%. Focusing on capital goods spending in the civilian sector, and infrastructure, and providing massive stimulus for the post-2008 crisis, Beijing did not deviate from economic expansion through global integration.[207]

Taking advantage of the Western neoliberal experiment's crisis, BRI appealed to Eurasian, Middle Eastern, African, and Latin American countries and even to countries well-integrated with the G7 whose corporations have substantial investments in China's global expansion. Unlike the US and EU, China refrained from geopolitical linkage, weaponized currency, and sanctions as leverage with trading partners. As the world's largest bilateral lender, Beijing provided loans for infrastructure linked to the primary sector of production, but also social infrastructure for the benefit of the working class and rural population.[208]

Linking everything to trade and investment, specifically to raw materials, market share, and key infrastructure access, Beijing often used loans as incentives for wider economic integration. Western governments and critics charged that China was using loans to reduce trading partners' financial and trade dependence. Since the 18th century (Treaty of Kuchuk-Kainarji, 1774) Western countries have been doing exactly what they accuse Beijing of doing in the 21st century. After 1947 the IMF, World Bank, the General Agreement on Tariffs and Trade (GATT), and various organizations, such as the UN Economic and Social Council presented their work as more apolitical and technocratic when in reality there was a political and economic agenda, just as is the case with China's global integration policy.[209]

Never challenging IMF-US-EU austerity programs imposed throughout the world, China worked within the guidelines that it helped modify so that they reflected its economic goals. In so far as its ultimate goal has been to integrate as much of the world economy as possible under its aegis, the Beijing Consensus-BRI played a major role in the rapidly growing private sector driving innovation and development. This was carried out without weakening the fiscal structure or transferring assets from social development to capital goods and infrastructure.

A class structure with labor at the bottom of the hierarchy, especially in rural areas and in the more sparsely populated less developed Western regions of Yunnan, Gansu, Tibet, Xinjiang, and Guizhou has meant uneven social and geographic development typical of capitalism. At the same time, Chinese companies do not have a good labor-management reputation inside the country or anywhere in the world. Anti-trade unionism has been the policy for it interferes with economic goals. The government only permits the All-China Federation of Trade Unions which is in essence an appendage of the state. Trade union officials at the local level have made efforts to represent labor and not the state's development agenda, but government policy favors capital relegating labor to a secondary role.[210]

Because of its rapid and successful rise to globalism, China influenced Vietnam, Cambodia, and Pakistan, among others in the continent to pursue hybrid development models. That other countries tried to emulate aspects of the Chinese development model was not welcome news in the US or any of the G7. In the first two decades of the 21st century, China increased its influence in all regional trading blocs and international financial organizations like the World Bank, especially after the IMF adopted the yuan as a reserve currency in October 2016.

Considering China's chronic trade surplus, especially with the US, the West accused China of currency manipulation, never reflecting on its such practices. While all countries and currency traders speculate thereby manipulating currency values, Beijing interfered less than Western governments because it served its integration and foreign investment goals to adopt a less intrusive posture. Contrary to populist rhetoric in the West, China's role strengthened and stabilized neoliberalism's global reach, especially after the trans-Atlantic-centered Great Recession caused chaos and misery across the world.[211]

Having surpassed the US in GDP measured in PPP terms in 2013, it was evident that China would eventually replace the US as the world's economic superpower. This is not only because it had all the preconditions, but it focused narrowly all of its policies around this goal, not allowing the US to divert it. US administrations from Obama to Biden contended that the rising Asian power constituted a "national security threat" to allied interests and the world order, namely because Beijing, not Washington would have preeminent influence in the world's economic balance of power.

Accusing Beijing of violating the human rights of Muslim Uyghurs in Xinjiang province, militarizing the South China Sea, and insisting that Taiwan is part of the one-China policy alarmed the US which historically considers itself both an Atlantic and Pacific power. Given America's own historical human rights record, and "cherry-picking" human rights diplomacy to suit geopolitical objectives, Beijing questioned the rival's motives that appeared as justifications for the US tariffs, sanctions, and containment policy which China viewed as a pretext to prevent its rapid economic ascendancy.[212]

Intellectual property rights 'theft' has been a hotly contentious subject, especially in high tech. It was never a secret that in some cases joint ventures with Chinese partners, tech sharing/transfer was a condition for investing. This has been a practice since the Industrial Revolution, and the US is one of the countries practicing it. The US rallied several Western allies against the Huawei corporation and other companies, including Sinno Electronics of Shenzhen Changsha Tianyi Space Science and Technology Research Institute.

Using the Russian war in Ukraine as a pretext in 2022, the US blacklisted more tech companies, including Connec Electronics, King Pai Technology, and Winning Electronics, all on national security grounds. In a US-led campaign for weaponized technology as an integral part of fragmented world trade undercutting neoliberal globalization, preventing third countries from signing contracts with Chinese tech firms, tech-sharing practices became the new leverage against the Chinese development model.[213]

Because China integrated African, Latin American, and Asian-Eurasian markets, multinational corporations had a vested interest in remaining in China. This includes US and EU-based tech multinationals receiving corporate subsidies and investing in China's tech sector. Regardless of Western governments' demands that Beijing comply with the trans-Atlantic neoliberal model, the corporate sector was pursuing its own agenda.

Given the mutual interests of the intra-core rivals and their allies, whether geopolitically linked to the US or China, the rivalry placed corporations, especially in Japan, South Korea, Indonesia, and the US among many others, in the position to chase profits across national borders while their governments' policy was to bolster their competitiveness through weaponized technology policies. Even with corporations circumventing their own governments' sanctions and blacklists, partly through investment in Chinese companies, inter-core rivalry undercuts the neoliberal model as it necessarily entails the consolidation of bloc trading, thereby undermining the WTO and multilateral organizations' rules. At the same time, sanctions and strong-arm investment policy tactics place doubts about where to invest in companies concerned about decoupling and reshoring.[214]

Digital technology, especially semiconductors, and artificial intelligence, but also the case of rare earth minerals required for high tech, have been at the heart of the US-China power struggle, despite US and Western-based companies investing heavily in China's technology sector. Just as important, China has 44 million metric tons of the world's seventeen rare earth minerals, while the US has just 1.5 million. The US has a clear technology edge, but it depends on China's rare earth elements (78% of total imports) needed for everything from rechargeable batteries to semiconductors and aerospace to clean energy.[215]

With the ability either to flood the market to discourage competition, or withhold supply for higher prices and/or act on other geopolitical considerations, the asymmetrical trade relationship affords China immense global leverage. US geopolitical considerations find expression in deliberate agitation in Taiwan and the South China Sea, as well as blacklisting Chinese companies military-linked to social media using national security, data privacy, and misinformation as a fig leaf.

In the name of freedom of the seas, a 21st-century version of the late 19th century US 'Open Door Policy' toward China has resulted in fragmented world trade under neoliberalism. Rattling Beijing when it comes to its geopolitical claims as a means of securing some peripheral advantage is just one dimension of the US destabilization strategy in Asia. Whether in the form of naval exercises, establishing new military bases in the Pacific, encouraging de-risking, decoupling, and re-shoring US destabilization policies have taken many forms. While resulting in Beijing taking selective action against certain US-based firms in China, transnational corporations seeking higher profit have remained committed to investment strategies circumventing US divesting-reshoring policy.[216]

No matter how one interprets various dimensions of the East-West confrontation on either side, China's transition from the semi-periphery to ascendancy into the core of the capitalist world system poses a serious challenge to trans-Atlantic global hegemony but breathes some strength into global capitalism in crisis. As of 2021, Beijing was holding more than one trillion dollars of the public US debt, second only to Japan, falling below one trillion by mid-2022. Direct and portfolio investments amounting to just under $400 billion, and the immense value of its domestic and third-party markets for US multinationals afford China far-reaching leverage.

China's dollar exchange reserves translate into deeper interdependence and leverage over the US that Beijing uses for optimal economic benefit. Amid the dollar's sharp rise in late September 2022, President Xi Jinping ordered banks to sell dollars as a means of supporting the renminbi or yuan; a measure designed more to restore some balance in hard currency impacting global trade than to transition away from the dollar. While neoliberalism apologists castigate China's "industrial socialism", a nebulous polemical term to differentiate it from Western neoliberalism, the Chinese economy is an integral part of the capitalist world economy with the corporate world benefiting from cheap labor, cheap raw materials, and a growing domestic market. The government's shift to lessen dependence on foreign trade by stimulating internal demand and capitalist development mixed with social development favors both domestic and foreign firms.[217]

The irony of the US-led neoliberal model is that it has weakened the welfare state structure and culture, partly in the hope of competing with the rest of the world. Because the US and the West could not possibly disengage from China's lucrative markets, low-cost labor, and cheap raw materials, agitating China into diverting resources from the civilian economy to defense has been a failed path. Sustaining a chronic balance of payments deficit to China's benefit, the US has no one to blame but its own policies of consumerism, financialization of the economy, debt-by-growth strategies, and corporations eager to make a quick profit which is why they are in business.

Along with the regulatory regime, and fiscal and monetary policy, the tans-Atlantic neoliberal state has permitted the corporate sector to alter the legal system and to enjoy input on spending levels in government agencies, from defense to environment. Western neoliberal transformation has molded public perception about the corporate world's monopoly on wisdom from which public policy emanates, including science and medicine, as the COVID-19 pandemic proved. Although the decades-long record has indubitably demonstrated that: *"neoliberalism applied to a corporate economy lowers investment, slows growth, heightens irresponsibility, intensifies worker coercion, and sharply raises economic inequality,"* neoliberal politicians, media, and business advocates insist on a more dogmatic course.[218]

Legitimizing market hegemony over the state and public institutions has entailed a retreat of the public sector amid big capital's global takeover. These conditions induced "social anomie", a Durkheim-based theory that explains how industrial development results in social dislocation and reduces trust in the state. Although there has been a drop in social trust even in China despite rapid industrial development resulting in widespread optimism, the Communist Party has employed state mechanisms to guide the economy and public opinion. Asking for the public's conformity in return for future rewards emanating from the capitalist marketplace, the state has relied as much on nationalism for capitalist development as Mao who cultivated nationalist sentiment linking the country's institutions from the semi-colonial past, especially during the self-sufficiency agricultural/industrial drive of the Great Leap Forward (1958-1961) era.[219]

Within the historical confines of central planning, the Chinese mixed model has consistently offered a combination of a growing internal market combined with social development and global integration under terms based largely on the neoliberal model. Promising more favorable conditions than what the Global North offers the Global South, China has also filled gaps where the US and its junior partners have stayed away for various reasons, above all low return on investment amid high risk. Common development under mutual support and cooperation has not translated into a partnership of equals at all. Chinese firms have not always met their obligations toward local producers or supported trade unionism overseas. The uneven China-Global South relationship and lack of pro-labor policies are not much different from what the West offers. Advocating for Chinese companies and projects linked to the BRI, the All-China Federation of Trade Unions (ACFTU) promotes capitalism at home and abroad, but has no impact on foreign trade unions.[220]

Western-based multinationals operating in China benefited from the host government's integration model and the state-controlled ACFTU regimenting workers toward conformity. Once President Bill Clinton withdrew human rights as a precondition for China's annual renewal in the most favored nation category in 1994 and approved permanent normal trade in 1998, the path opened for the WTO (December 2001) and China's global trade legitimacy.

Corporations had the green light to invest in China, integrating it more rapidly in the global economy. Regarding capital accumulation, from 1980 to 2020, China's GDP growth far outpaced that of the US and the rest of the world. Owing to internal and external market growth, China moved rapidly from the semi-periphery to the core of the world economy, which meant increased influence in global trade. Therein rest the essential causes of the US-led confrontation with Beijing that undermines both sides, although it does not necessarily slow down world trade despite damaging specific companies that governments target.[221]

Projecting the image of its development model with generous social benefits, the working class either in China or its trading partners has not seen the benefits of economic growth that businesses have enjoyed. In comparison with the G7, Beijing's labor policy ranks just below Japan and the US, both of the latter in the OECD's bottom tier. One of the contingencies of the EU-China Comprehensive Agreement on Investment (December 2020) was not only greater EU investment access in China's markets but that Beijing ratify two international conventions on "forced labor" and improve workers' conditions. That capitalist governments were making such a demand of the Chinese Communist Party is indicative of the degree to which Beijing is committed to the welfare of the proletariat vs. capitalist development. A job discrimination practice that the law permits in both the public and private sector, those over 35 years old have a more difficult time securing employment in a society that will eventually have to adjust its discriminatory practices with the demographics of an aging society.[222]

Whereas Western neoliberal politicians and policy analysts have argued that China's BRI is nothing more than an imperialist scheme intended to subjugate countries under its hegemony, the question is the degree to which Chinese imperialism actually serves Western imperialism, and more specifically corporations and investors in Chinese firms. Considering the 40,000 foreign companies in China, including 8,619 US firms, with about a quarter of a trillion dollars at the beginning of 2022, excluding foreign investments indirectly through Hong Kong. Chinese development has benefited from foreign capital which carries with it technological and scientific diffusion. If this were not the case, annual foreign direct investment (FDI) would not have risen from $1.4 billion in 1984 to $173 billion in 2021.[223]

Along with national private and state firms, international capital has benefited from Chinese labor conditions, and Free Trade Agreements (FTAs). As Minq Li put it, while China has *"an exploitative relationship with South Asia, Africa, and other raw material exporters, on the whole, China continues to transfer a greater amount of surplus value to the core countries in the capitalist world system than it receives from the periphery."*[224]

Fearing that China would replace the US as the world's preeminent economy in nominal GDP in the late 2020s to early 2030s, Washington has used tariffs and sanctions intended to force Beijing into full compliance with neoliberal transformation. The goal was to realize market hegemony and weaken the powerful Chinese state. US GDP was 15.74% of the world share in 2022, after adjusting for PPP, while China's share was 18.8%. The trends for the two rivals are projected to reflect declining US GDP and the reverse for China. Even fragmented trade policies and US-led Western punitive tariffs failed to slow down China's development and expansion and augment US-EU expansion.

Coercive and voluntary bloc trading and exclusionary pacts, which undermine the neoliberal model, have had a serious impact on China's global integration through BRI projects with multinational investments. In the first two decades of the 21st century, because the divergent development models favored Chinese growth and expansion, China's exports rose sharply, as did both direct and portfolio investment, in key sectors, including semi-conductors and artificial intelligence.[225]

During the Trump presidency, the glaring contradictions between economic nationalism and the purist neoliberal model were not lost on governments around the world. This included America's closest allies in the EU which expanded economic ties with China as the most indispensable economy on the planet. Under Trump's "America First" policy, tariffs targeted US enemies and allies alike. Under the guise of multilateralism, Biden continued and intensified economic nationalism by redefining the Washington Consensus to take geopolitics into account.

More committed to interventionism and neoconservative militarist solutions, Biden launched very broad anti-Russian and anti-Chinese sanctions. Lobbying third countries to reject collaboration agreements with Chinese firms on national security grounds, the Biden administration invoked national security more than Trump. Such efforts notwithstanding, China made inroads in Latin America, Africa, and especially Asia and Eurasia during the COVID-19 pandemic and the US-Western-led anti-Russia sanctions period.

To slow China's technological advantage, the Biden administration introduced "friend-shoring", a 19th-century spheres of influence concept applied during the Cold War when each side used the other as a pretext to impose hegemony over junior partners. In April 2022, US Treasury Secretary Janet Yellen proposed friend-shoring to "trusted countries", thereby lowering supply-chain risks to the US and junior partners. A concept that the US Agency for International Development introduced during the COVID-19 pandemic, the idea was to minimize supply chain problems, though the concept does not guarantee higher GDP, but actually may lead to losses.

A WTO study published during the Ukraine-Russia war estimated that friendshoring would shave off $4 trillion from world GDP or 5%, impacting hardest the Global South and the working class. Willing to permit such sacrifices on a world scale, the US has been focusing on slowing down China's progress in semiconductors and biotechnology. Aggressively promoting decoupling policy, the Biden administration discovered that this is not what businesses want, especially after spending years and a lot of money to enter the Chinese market.[226]

Without the cooperation of European, Japanese, South Korean, and Taiwanese semiconductor companies, not just governments, the US high-tech spheres of influence scheme falls apart, not to mention that it contradicts neoliberal transformation. To undermine China's semiconductor sector's upgrading ability in developing a 7-nm chip, the US needs what one tech analyst baptized 'Asia's chipmaking godfathers', among them Japan's Yukio Sakamoto who became disillusioned with Micron Technology corporation in 2019 and joined China's Tsinghua firm. In June 2022, he signed a deal with China's SwaySure company, dealing another blow to Biden's semiconductors global campaign to undercut Chinese firms.

Like most capitalists, the Japanese chipmaking godfather has been chasing the best investments, regardless of Pax Americana semiconductor zones of influence strategies, or even government subsidies with too many strings attached. While China accounts for a mere 15%, the US has a decisive semiconductor production advantage. Because the US knows that once factoring into the equation foreign-based firms and prospects for development, only zones of influence under a fragmented world trade system can slow down China. Zones of influence cannot deliver results, however, if corporations and investors do not cooperate, or if they do so with half-hearted measures.[227]

Not until Russia's war in Ukraine did the US plan to slow down China reveal its crude combination of late 19th-century imperialism and early Cold War recklessness in the multi-layered world of neoliberalism. The problem with such strategies is that billions of innocent people paid the price, including triple-digit inflation for several countries, especially in the Global South with Lebanon, Zimbabwe, and Sri Lanka taking major hits. The inter-core competition carries monumental risks of a global recession with much higher inequality, volatile reserve currencies, lower social mobility, and increased prospects for neoliberal authoritarianism. As a result of contradictions in Western strategies for hegemony, the neoliberal model itself has come under fire not just from critics, but neoliberals of different political camps.[228]

CHAPTER II:

Neoliberalism's Path to Authoritarianism

Illiberal Democracy in Neoliberal Society

Behind the thin veneer of neoliberalism, which many of its apologists either assume or pretend is consistent with liberal democracy, rests social destabilization, inequality, and authoritarianism. After Donald Trump won the election in 2016, some political analysts were drawing comparisons with the Eighteenth Brumaire of Louis Bonaparte coup in 1851. While the closest that Trump came to a coup was on 6 January 2021, his rise to office was a reflection of conditions similar to those of mid-19th century France.

"Both countries [19th century France and 21st century US] prepared the groundwork for the rise of authoritarian politics through the increasing desperation of poor and working people and a decimated left that subordinated itself to capitalist parties. In these outbreaks of common discontent, members of vulnerable groups found themselves lured in by the siren song of right-wing strongmen... Bonaparte had sympathy from proletarians and the petty bourgeoisie, who hailed him as the "scourge of Cavaignac"—the general who violently suppressed working class revolts and was a candidate of the Party of Order. Likewise, the disaffected white elements of the rural poor, workers and middle-class voters saw in Trump the scourge of Clinton's neoliberal agenda."[229]

Forging consensus among the nobility and bourgeoisie, Louis-Napoleon's internal coup to end constitutionalism with populist middle-class mobilization set a dangerous precedent for authoritarianism in the name of a non-existent popular mandate. After the storming of Congress on 6 January 2021, with the blessing of the White House, Trump's Bonapartism comparison became more evident for many people trying to make sense of what happened to the nation priding itself on division and separation of powers.[230]

Among many others in the traditionally conservative, populist-nationalist, technocratic, or some combination category, Hungary's Prime Minister Viktor Mihály Orban's (2010-present) authoritarian neoliberal regime falls in the same category as Trump's. Given the numerous contradictions in the neoliberal ideology, not the least of which are nationalism, militarism, and social exclusion, authoritarian liberalism becomes an inevitable mechanism to reconcile such contradictions while maintaining capital accumulation that exacerbates the very contradictions that the state endeavors to resolve.[231]

Combined with structural inequality at home, 19th-century imperialism undercut 18th-century philosophical tenets of popular sovereignty and social justice. From the First Opium War (1838) to the Boer War in South Africa (1899-1902), and to the Second Moroccan Crisis[1] (Agadir Crisis, 1911), among several other wars of imperialism, Western powers caused massive destruction and chaos in Asia and Africa, all of which eventually led to WWI and the twilight of northwest Europe as the core of the capitalist world economy. The advanced capitalist countries' struggle for markets and mastery of the Global South led to the demise of European hegemony and the dawning of the American century.

John Hobson (*Imperialism: A Study*, 1902) and Rosa Luxemburg (*The Accumulation of Capital: A Contribution to an Economic Explanation of Imperialism,* 1913) captured in their analysis capitalism's inherent social inequality

1. https://www.historycrunch.com/second-moroccan-crisis.html

within the belligerent countries and the forcible geographic expansion beyond its sovereign borders that led to imperialist wars. Neo-feudal labor relations under neoliberalism's class war have driven the declining inter-Atlantic core toward imperialist conditions with similar dynamics as the late 19th-early 20th century.[232]

John Bellamy Foster's *"Late Imperialism"* succinctly captures the neoliberal era's authoritarian path in the quest for market greater global share. *"There is no question that world capitalism has changed in the century since the First World War when Lenin developed his critique of the imperialist stage. Yet, this has to be seen in the context of a historical dialectic that embraces continuity as well as change. Imperialism is a historical as much as a theoretical category. ...today we are clearly in an era of late imperialism associated with generalized monopoly-finance capital; the globalization of production; new forms of surplus extraction from the periphery to the center; and epochal economic, military, and environmental challenges. The crises facing the system and human society as a whole are now so severe that they are creating new fissures in the state in both the advanced capitalist and emerging economies, with rapid growth of protofascist and neofascist tendencies, on the one hand, and a revival of socialism, on the other."*[233]

Just like scholars in the 21st century have been analyzing and searching for answers on the consolidation of imperialism and decline of democracy, after WWI, political economist Joseph Schumpeter tried to make sense of why Western civilization and the rationalist-liberal order crumbled under the weight of a series of smaller wars leading to global war and economic depression. Analyzing the relationship of the capitalist class with the state, Schumpeter, unlike Lenin and Luxemburg who viewed imperialism as the root cause of wars, maintained that imperialism was a 'will to power', an atavism not symptomatic of capitalism as Hobson, Luxemburg, and Lenin argued.

"The bourgeoisie did not simply supplant the sovereign, nor did it make him its leader, as did the nobility. It merely wrested a portion of its power from him and for the rest submitted to him. It did not take over from the sovereign the state as an abstract form of organization. The state remained a special social power, confronting the bourgeoisie. In some countries, it has continued to play that role to the present day. It is in the state that the bourgeoisie with its interests seeks refuge and protection against external and even domestic enemies. The bourgeoisie seeks to win over the state for itself, and in return serves the state and state interests that are different from its own."[234]

Whereas John Stuart Mill (*Principles of Political Economy,* 1871), advocated legal private property reform to promote a more egalitarian political economy, Schumpeter rejected the flirtation with the welfare state and economic distribution laws as an act of policymakers serving specific interests. Mill hoped for a futuristic society where social justice was taken into account. Schumpeter believed and probably hoped that innovation would save capitalism, dreading that under the liberal regime, the political economy would ultimately fail. It is precisely this fear and hope that neoliberals also entertain and which led some to embrace authoritarianism as a means of saving capitalism from its own "success" of concentrated capital accumulation.[235]

With the advent of interwar totalitarianism and militarism, Europeans experienced the unraveling of the Enlightenment Era's rationalist order that WWI had seriously wounded. Big capital's quest for higher profits accompanied by fear and disdain of workers as obstacles to capital expansion played a key role in interwar developments from the speculative 1920s to the depression of the 1930s. The same interwar motivating factors of big capital were present late 20th -early 21st century neoliberal era during which socioeconomic polarization accounted for the rapid spread of authoritarian capitalist policies to which IMF austerity contributed.[236]

Characterized by socioeconomic elitism, gender, racial, and ethnic inequality, limits on freedom of expression, human rights, and civil rights, the crisis of interwar liberal democracy was symptomatic of the crisis in capitalism and the struggle to save it. Just as the pursuit of concentrated capital accumulation under irreconcilable contradictions during the interwar era eroded liberal democracy and led to varieties of authoritarian regimes, similar contradictions exist under the neoliberal social contract.[237]

Tested in Chile during the Pinochet dictatorship, neoliberalism became the laboratory for the global transformation model. Vising Chile, Milton Friedman, James M. Buchanan, and Friedrich Hayek observed, advised, and tested neoliberal constitutionalism under the repressive Pinochet dictatorship. All of them presented it as best suited for the market economy. Friedman proclaimed neoliberal Chile a 'miracle'.

Latin American scholar Andre Gunder Frank published an open letter to Freidman (*Economic Genocide in Chile: Open Letter to Milton Friedman and Arnold Harberger,* 1976) about the well-documented atrocities in Chile. A few years before the UK and US institutionalized the model, testing full-blown neoliberalism under a military dictatorship raised questions about how this model could coexist under liberal democracy without incorporating aspects of authoritarianism to achieve sociopolitical conformity and capital accumulation goals.[238]

In *"The Political Economy of Neoliberalism and Illiberal Democracy"*, Garry Jacobs argues that although classical liberal economics operates in a pluralistic and presumably non-militaristic society, democracy is under siege as a result of the neoliberal transformation. "*The tolerance, openness, and inclusiveness on which modern democracy is founded are being rejected by candidates and voters in favor of sectarian, parochial fears and interests... Party politics has been polarized into a winner-take-all fight to the finish by vested interests and impassioned extremist minorities trying to impose their agendas on a complacent majority. Corporate power and money power are transforming representative governments into plutocratic pseudo-democracies. Fundamentalists are seizing the instruments of secular democracy to impose intolerant linguistic, racial, and religious homogeneity in place of the principles of liberty and harmonious heterogeneity that are democracy's foundation and pinnacle of achievement.*"[239]

To engender domestic sociopolitical conformity and achieve concentrated capital accumulation under more thorough global economic integration, neoliberals present the model as the vanguard of democracy. The question is not so much that the pluralist political camp under the neoliberal political umbrella pursues a strategy of populist inclusion to mobilize a popular base, while the rightwing promotes exclusionary policies. The degree to which each dilutes liberal-democratic institutions and normalizes authoritarianism under liberalism is really at issue. Both pluralists and rightwing populists share the common goal of the individual's institutional submission and molding of the consumer-citizen's subjective reality around the neoliberal ideology. Regardless of political mobilization strategies, this necessarily leads to authoritarianism because the system breeds resistance owing to rising inequality and exclusionary populism.[240]

Relying on traditional political, economic, religious, and cultural conservatism, exclusionary populism is the culmination of many factors. Some scholars have argued that the populist right is the offspring of neoliberalism, while others maintain that liberals are globalization promoters, and both serve the same social contract.[241] Baptizing populism "Populocracy", Catherine Fieschi stresses that its goal is to undermine collective endeavors required for various social and environmental issues. Under neoliberalism, 'Populocracy' has been symptomatic of and a reaction to globalization and culture wars that distract from the class struggle boiling just beneath the political/cultural surface.[242]

Rhetorically denouncing economic integration under market hegemony, populist rightwing politicians assert the importance of national capitalism and opposition to globalization. Operating within the perimeters of neoliberal policies, they promote capital accumulation as do globalization liberal pluralists. The differences between the two camps rest in co-optation strategies, with the populists resorting to socio-cultural and nationalist extremism, racism, ethnocentrism, Islamophobia, and religious bigotry as political strategies to mobilize the mass base.[243]

From Eastern Europe, South Asia, and Africa, to the Western Hemisphere, rightwing populist trends reflect a global triumph by a segment of neoliberal business people and the bourgeois political class with the corporate media incessantly propagating social cooptation and conformity. Unquestionably, there is a direct correlation between the internationalization of the Western neoliberal transformation model, especially in the post-Soviet world order, and the rise of populism reacting to the gap between what capitalism promises and the reality of chronic downward pressures on living standards amid an expanding world economy and wealth concentration. Considering that in 2021, the richest 1% own half of the world's net wealth, and the bottom 90% own just 15% of total wealth, neoliberalism's record speaks for itself.[244]

Not only the US, but Europe has been flirting with 'illiberal democracy' with politicians operating inside the electoral process as did Trump. During national elections in Bosnia in 1996, US diplomat Richard Holbrooke wondered about the former Yugoslav republics' rightwing path. *"Suppose the election was declared free and fair and those elected are "racists, fascists, separatists, who are publicly opposed to [peace and reintegration]. That is the dilemma."*[245]

Exactly twenty years after Holbrooke's remarks about *"racists, fascists, separatists"* in the Balkans, the US elected Trump, along with likeminded GOP local, state, and national politicians, rightwing judges, and school board members in favor of banning books that offend the sensibilities of racists. Manifesting itself in culture wars as a strategy to distract from the undercurrent of class war, the institutionalized rightwing populist wave deliberately undermined workers' solidarity and mobilized a mass voting base rooted in exclusionary populist ideology. A structural issue that transcends personalities, beginning with Reagan, autocratization was symptomatic of the link to neoliberal transformation. Considering that modern liberal democracy entails 'majoritarianism' with all the caveats regarding policy, authoritarianism is embedded in democracy, whether under Trump or any other elected head of state in the world.[246]

After the election of 2016, some mainstream political observers analyzing right-wing policies concluded that neoliberalism was leading toward a Fascist-like regime. Whether in the US, India, Brazil, Turkey, or Hungary, there is no leap of faith in how illiberal democracy's popularity flourished under the neoliberal social contract. In 2016, Manuela Cadelli, President of the Magistrates Union of Belgium, concluded that neoliberalism is a form of fascism. This is also the position of scholars, journalists, and progressive politicians arguing that the Trump administration pursued neoliberal policies with a populist ideological and cultural platform to keep a popular base loyal to the Republican Party that the mass base historically identified with the elite. Given America's changing demographics favoring the Democrats, the GOP moved to rightwing populism to remain competitive. This meant that the popular base moved to the cultural right of mainstream business conservatism which retained control of the party machinery.

"Fascism may be defined as the subordination of every part of the State to a totalitarian and nihilistic ideology." Manuela Cadelli wrote. *"I argue that neoliberalism is a species of fascism because the economy has brought under subjection not only the government of democratic countries but also every aspect of our thought. The state is now at the*

disposal of the economy and roof finance, which treat it as a subordinate and lord over it to an extent that puts the common good in jeopardy."[247]

Unleashing elements characteristic of the interwar Fascist era, neoliberalism drives society toward centralized autocracy. Mobilizing the middle class and elements of the working class, neoliberal authoritarian regimes start by neutralizing any widespread popular opposition. Interwar Italian Communist Party leaders Antonio Gramsci and Palmiro Togliatti concluded that Fascism was the outgrowth of advanced capitalism's crisis and a reactionary movement to exploit the disgruntled working class, along with the urban and rural petit bourgeoisie by forming their mass movement comprised of the same elements.

Largely because the institutional structure has conditioned them into conformity for survival, most people accept the status quo and identify with it, thus defending rather than criticizing it. Without grasping the neoliberal model's eclectic complexities, mass followers support the status quo under which it operates through political parties packaging transformation under different modalities. No matter how tyrannical, they accept political hegemony, in part because mainstream institutions present the status quo as the norm as part of the ideological-cultural dominant structure inculcated in mass consciousness.[248]

Just as it was difficult to survive under Italian Fascism and German Nazism for those opposing the regime and its institutions, it is no different under the neoliberal social contract. Exiled during the Mussolini regime, Palmiro Togliatti cautioned about vilifying workers who joined the ruling party merely out of the necessity to survive. Revolutionary syndicalism had been the first home of Fascist cadres who mobilized workers who placed their families' survival above ideology and party affiliation. Systemic exploitation ingrained into society passes as the norm to which neoliberal institutions assign legitimacy and expect social relations to proceed accordingly. Whether under liberal-pluralist or rightwing populism, subtle and overt neoliberal institutional repression targets workers, minority groups, migrants, and working-class women, demonizing and distracting the general public from the model's structural character and promoting inequality.[249]

As though social justice is a fad associated with a specific era of extreme socioeconomic conditions like the Great Depression, or the 1960s counterculture movement, mainstream media, neoliberal politicians, and the corporate community denounce those clamoring for human rights, progressive reform, and systemic change, wishing the return of the Keynesian state. Considering that the media reinforces and validates the legitimacy of the social contract, the political class and social elites enjoy the freedom to shape and normalize the state's neoliberal goals under a surveillance quasi-police state in the digital era.

In the age when people default surveillance capitalism to the same technology used to detect foreign enemies and domestic criminals, shaping consumer-citizens' subjective reality goes without notice in the mass consciousness for profit. Out of this consumer culture emerged "reality TV" which reinforces neoliberalism's commodified society.[250] As Nick Couldry put it, *"Reality TV ... is, in effect, a "secret theatre" of the neoliberal workplace, allowing the acting out in the form of ritualized play many of the skills required in the "flexible" work economy: "passion", emotional commitment, individual adaptability, the combination of team conformity and personal ambition.*[251]

Neoliberal culture has conditioned people to focus narrowly on their role as consumer citizens, not on the class-based institutional structure that determines social relations. Chatting on the cell phone, laptop, or iPad, the "reality TV" mindset reinforcing neoliberal values is among the market tools promoting consumer illusions about free will while inculcating the hegemonic culture molding free will. Partly because of the communications revolution in the digital age, neoliberal politicians, business people, corporate media, and various apologists with access to the public airwaves mold the consumer-citizen beyond loyalty to the social contract, not just into mechanical market observance but total institutional submission by reshaping the person's values and identity. Molding every aspect of society and the individual, neoliberal cultural appropriation is more thoroughly intrusive than Medieval religious and feudal/manorial institutions that shaped the worldview of peasants and serfs without the benefit of the means of communication available in the 21st century.[252]

As Anis Shivani points out, neoliberalism has succeeded in redefining subjectivity more than any past ideologies. *"Classical liberalism was successful too, for two and a half centuries, in people's self-definition, although communism and fascism succeeded less well in realizing the "new man." It cannot be emphasized enough that neoliberalism is not classical liberalism, or a return to a purer version of it, as is commonly misunderstood; it is a new thing, because the market, for one thing, is not at all free and untethered and dynamic in the sense that classical liberalism idealized it." [253]*

Amid the mostly symbolic UN "Millennium Campaign" (2000-present) to reduce global poverty within the neoliberal market, rising social inequality, political instability, and loss of public confidence in mainstream bourgeois parties created a new age of mass anxiety as much in the G7 as in the Global South. This was especially the case after the Great Recession, the COVID-19 pandemic outbreak, the Russian invasion of Ukraine, and the global stagflation/recession that ensued.[254]

To distract the public from neoliberalism at the root of downward social mobility, rightwing populists defaulted economic and social problems to minorities, migrants, workers, and marginalized groups, all defaulted to the 'angry voter' category. The result was a rise in human rights violations in the age of mass anxiety. Governments, political parties, mainstream media, social media, and popular entertainment reinforce sociocultural stereotypes and the concept of the hero and anti-hero Medieval archetypes with elements of glorified violence presented as cathartic for the individual.[255]

Representing the UN Human Rights agency, Prince Zeid bin Ra'ad al-Hussein reported that 2016 was a disastrous year for human rights. Largely because of the US-led global war on terror as a substitute for the Cold War reignited against both Russia and China, Samuel Huntington's *Clash of Civilizations* (1993) post-Cold War ideological construct became ingrained in the political consciousness of the institutional mainstream and cultural milieu, offering a sense of superiority to the declining West. *"In some parts of Europe, and the United States, anti-foreigner rhetoric full of unbridled vitriol and hatred, is proliferating to a frightening degree and is increasingly unchallenged. The rhetoric of fascism is no longer confined to a secret underworld of fascists, meeting in ill-lit clubs or on the 'deep net'. It is becoming part of normal daily discourse."[256]*

Because neoliberalism drove all mainstream political parties to the right, the progressive parties espousing a Keynesian state were not as radical during the neoliberal era as the Vietnam War's protest generation that aspired to social justice. Mainstream institutions have promoted the idea that society must reject anything outside the hegemonic market, as all institutions reflect. This goes beyond Karl Popper's neoconservative construct. Where sociopolitical conformity follows because survival outside the system is neither desirable nor viable is a method flirting with neo-totalitarianism. The contradiction of neoliberalism rests in the system's goal of integrating everyone into the mold, thereby leaving no room outside the social contract structurally based on social exclusion. [257]

The financial, political, and media support that certain corporations and wealthy individuals provide to conservative organizations explains why a segment of the middle class and even the working class constitute the expanding popular base of populist groups. Because democratic consensus breaks down as disparate elements among the private sector and public sector elite diverge, counterrevolution from within the extreme right becomes inevitable.[258]

"*Rather than subversion of the normative order causing suffering, rebellion or revolution that might establish a new nomos of shared life as a way of establishing a new governing logic, the dissociated elements of disintegrating democratic formations identify with the very power responsible for their subjection—capital, the state and, the strong leader. Thus, the possibility of fascism is not negated in neoliberal formations but is an ever-present possibility arising within it. Because the value of the social order as such is never in itself sufficient to maintain its constitution, it must have recourse to an external value, which is the order of the sacred embodied by the sovereign.*[259]

Published one year after the storming of the US Capitol, a public opinion poll indicated that 64% of those surveyed believed democracy was in crisis, and 70% believed that the US was 'failing'. The same percentage of Americans who stated that the country was 'failing', also believed that the economic system unfairly favors the wealthy. Public opinion surveys in several countries, including the US, indicate that most people do not favor the existing social contract rooted in neoliberal globalization that impacts everything from living standards and labor policy to the judicial system and foreign affairs.[260]

Many among the lower middle class and a segment of culturally-conservative workers have historically supported rightwing populism especially when there is a rise in inequality. Besides nationalism identified with the powerful elites as guardians of the national interest, segments of the middle class and the working class accept the neoliberal myth that salvation rests with the same social contract responsible for existing problems. As has been the case historically, religion and commercial "popular culture" played a key role in pulling the masses to the right. While widespread disillusionment with neoliberal globalization seems to be at the core of the rise of rightwing populism, the common denominator is downward social mobility and confusion about what or who is at fault. [261]

As Garry Jacobs argues, "*Even mature democracies show signs of degenerating into their illiberal namesakes. The historical record confirms that peaceful, prosperous, free, and harmonious societies can best be nurtured by the widest possible distribution of all forms of power—political, economic, educational, scientific, technological, and social—to the greatest extent to the greatest number. The aspiration for individual freedom can only be realized and preserved when it is married with the right to social equality. The mutual interdependence of the individual and the collective is the key to their reconciliation and humanity's future.*"[262]

With the mass communications panoply at their disposal, policymakers and promoters have indoctrinated the public that generally aligns with the neoliberal agenda, despite skepticism regarding specific policies and the media.[263] Considering the low level of public trust in the mainstream media, which most people regardless of political/ideological position view as propaganda rather than informational, cynicism about national and international institutions prevails.

Fomenting skepticism about the legitimacy of institutions plays into the rightwing ideology of disparate elements, especially those on the right, unwittingly or knowingly supporting the neoliberal social contract. In the eyes of the public, the fierce power struggle among mainstream political parties to manage the state on behalf of capital has undermined the credibility of the bourgeois political class whose policies run counter to the public interest and undercut voter preferences. For example, businesses relocating from one country to the other chasing maximum profits undermines the 'democratic' or populist political class commitment to strengthen the economy and secure jobs in the home base; a point that authoritarian neoliberals were making but pluralists quickly followed as well in supporting reshoring, especially from China.[264]

Operating under the illusion that political salvation comes from anti-institutionalist political messiahs, presumably those presenting themselves above politics, a version of 21st century Bonapartism, a segment of the disgruntled middle class and working class turn to rightwing populist politicians, without realizing that they too safeguard the neoliberal social contract as much as the liberals. This has been as evident in France where the neoliberal pluralist model focused on class war strengthened neo-Fascist Marine Le Pen's *Rassemblement National*, as in Trump's America where the Democratic Party's pluralist neoliberal policies became the rallying cry of populists.[265]

As *The Economist* points out, by 2016, widespread disillusionment with globalization policies drove people to the right in search of an enemy to blame for calamities that befell society. "*Beset by stagnant wage growth, less than half of respondents in America, Britain, and France believe that globalization is a "force for good" in the world. Westerners also say the world is getting worse. Even Americans, generally an optimistic lot, are feeling blue: just 11% believe the world has improved in the past year. The turn towards nationalism is especially pronounced in France, the cradle of liberty. Some 52% of the French now believe that their economy should not have to rely on imports, and just 13% reckon that immigration has a positive effect on their country. France is divided as to whether or not multiculturalism is something to be embraced. Such findings will be music to the ears of Marine Le Pen, the leader of the National Front, France's nationalist, Eurosceptic party. Current (and admittedly early) polling has her tied for first place in the 2017 French presidential race.*"[266]

Partly through lobbying efforts but primarily through the media, consulting firms, law offices representing charity organizations, and political action committees, the capitalist class provides a variety of support for right-wing politicians to mobilize the population behind simpleminded authoritarian solutions to society's complex multi-layered structural problems. Intertwined with neoliberal authoritarianism to obscure the fact that populists serve neoliberal transformation as faithfully as their liberal opponents, deep-rooted ideological and cultural traits float to the top.

Varieties of populism include 'Lepenism', Le Pen's *Rassemblement National*, Modism, Modi's Indian *Bharatiya Janata Party* (Indian Peoples' Party), and Trumpism in the US, all sharing conservative cultural traits and the cult of personality following as part of the popular base. The ultimate goal of all rightwing populists has been to camouflage deregulation, privatization, and corporate welfare, using the fiscal and monetary structure for capital accumulation and anti-labor policies under the guise of "protecting" workers from the tyranny of unionization. [267]

Having molded the popular base into accepting the party's ideological boundaries to include populists at the core, traditional conservatives in the US, UK, France, and all around the world followed a political course and tactics similar to those of interwar conservatives who eventually backed Fascism. Just as liberals refused to believe in the imminent rise of fascism as a movement amid the parliamentary system's collapse and capitalism's crisis of the 1920s, similarly, 21st-century liberals have not accepted populism's global trend as a symptom of neoliberalism's crisis.

In an article entitled *"Populism is not Fascism: But it could be a Harbinger"*, Sheri Berman points out that liberal bourgeois democracy around the world is losing ground to rightwing populism. This was as true in 2016 when Trump won the presidency, as in 2022 when Marine Le Pen was Macron's major presidential opponent or Giorgia Meloni of the neo-Fascist *Fratelli d'Italia* became Prime Minister. US and EU public opinion polls point to pessimism about democracy's future, as political polarization is taking root. Considering the rise of the far right across Europe and the US, public pessimism about democracy is justified.[268]

Drawing on parallels between fascism and populism, Ishay Landa (*The Apprentice's Sorcerer. Liberal Tradition and Fascism*, 2010) and Federico Finchelstein (*From Fascism to Populism*, 2019) point to liberal political economy containing the seeds of fascism, indoctrination, and mythology that replaces empirical reality. In the absence of analyzing structural socioeconomic, political, and cultural causes for the rise of authoritarianism during the neoliberal phase, it stands to reason that it is a marginal outgrowth of mainstream conservatism amid liberalism's decline.[269]

Just as Fascists and Nazis consolidated power with the considerable backing of industrialists and bankers during the interwar era, so did 21st-century populist politicians that wealthy individuals financed promise to protect and expand national capitalism by undercutting Keynesianism. Inherent neoliberal contradictions represent a desperate struggle to curb Keynesian social structure accumulation and expand capitalist appropriation. Indicative of the deepening neoliberal crisis, the state declares war on any institution diluting market hegemony, regardless of how injurious to bourgeois democracy.[270]

Richard D. Wolff contends that social conditions and conflicts within the nation-state determine the level of cooperation between the dominant class and state apparatus. *"In certain extreme conditions, a centralized State merged with a capitalist class of large, concentrated employers into a system called fascism. The 20th century saw several major examples of fascism's rise and fall. Now again, fascism looms as a possible resort of capitalism in trouble. Usually, the transition from decentralized to centralized States reflected social conditions in which dominant classes needed to strengthen State power to reproduce the system they dominated. They feared that otherwise, social conditions would provoke a collapse of their system and/or movements to a different economic system. In either case, their social dominance was at stake. Because that situation now looms on our historical agenda, so too does fascism."*[271]

Regardless of the rise in authoritarianism and the global rise in inequality, especially after the Great Recession of 2007-2008 and the pandemic of 2020-2022, neoliberal cheerleaders remained stuck in the unipolar World Order that the US forged in the 1990s. As long as capitalist appropriation continued, glittering on the surface but casting a dark shadow over the middle class and workers, neoliberal Gilded Age apologists stayed the course. The problem arose once statistics indicated that from 1978 to 2012, China's per capita GDP rose 40-fold, while US real GDP rose two-and-a-half times. During the same period, the entire Western neoliberal Gilded Age witnessed downward pressure on wages and social mobility.[272]

Relying on cheerleading Western-centered studies such as Samuel Huntington's "*The Clash of Civilizations and the Remaking of the World Order*" and Francis Fukuyama's "*End of History and the Last Man*", Western neoliberals celebrated the triumph of trans-Atlantic capitalism, projecting the impression of teleological salvation under Pax Americana's wings. *"In neoliberalism, the 'free market' is not merely a tool for exchange, but a purposeful force – guided by an 'invisible hand' – that strives toward a positive economic goal in ways that are beyond human understanding."*[273] Almost mystical analysis of a predatory system as though it has a will of its own reflects how mesmerized its followers have been, no matter the empirical evidence of rising inequality and authoritarianism.

The quest to articulate a unifying theory that explained the end of the Cold War and the emergence of the multi-polar order led some scholars right back to Cold War assumptions about the importance of maintaining Western global hegemony under Western aegis in every area from determining the balance of power to managing the transformation's global reach amid the integration of former Soviet republics into the Western orbit. The generically selective manufactured "war on terror" became the raison d'être to replace the East-West confrontation, thus perpetuating Pax Americana's post-Cold War institutional structure which the neoliberal model absorbed. A pretext to continue the policy of military Keynesianism of high defense budgets, military adventures, and weaponized trade and currency, the War on Terror followed by the new Cold War represented a remarkable continuity of the post-WWII World Order.[274]

Analyzing how neoliberalism integrated military Keynesianism into the "privatization model", James Cypher notes that like all other public sectors, the defense also fell in the same matrix. *"Neoliberals believe, a priori, that all public sector activities are inefficient and that (thanks to the regulating role of the free market) private sector activities are a model of efficiency. Hence, get the military out of every sort of activity to the fullest degree possible. This model is now in place in Iraq, where private contractors (operating an unofficial army with over a hundred thousand employees) have enjoyed unrestrained opportunities to amass quick profits. As a result, a new addition to the military-industrial complex—a vast constellation of contractors employing a shadow military with a vested interest in higher levels of military spending, particularly in the high-profit intervention/reconstruction business—has been created over the last fifteen years."*[275]

After the 9/11 jihadist attacks on US targets, the counter-terrorism regime with Homeland Security coordinating domestic and some foreign security operations took another turn toward illiberal democracy. What followed was a two-decade military occupation of Afghanistan and Iraq. Especially in Iraq's case, neoliberal transformation rested not on "free markets" but on a quasi-colonial military occupation. Looking for a pretext to continue expanding in the post-Cold War and increase defense spending, the military-industrial complex, already an integral part of the neoliberal-digital matrix, relied on the global market hegemony model amid the war on terror. [276]

Largely a pretext to perpetuate Pax Americana, but partly a mass distraction from structural problems in Western societies, the military-industrial complex became more prominent. High-tech applications in modernizing weapons entailed that tech companies were as eager to secure defense contracts as traditional weapons manufacturers. Deeply ingrained into the public consciousness, the 'war on terror' reinvigorated Pax Americana under the neoliberal political economy. Despite the path toward illiberal democracy justified in the name of the war on terror after the 9/11 attacks, old industries and high-tech, especially digital electronics and telecommunications, supported the merging of neoliberal policies with Cold War-style military Keynesian policies.[277]

The US defense, security, and intelligence agencies signed lucrative contracts either directly with corporations or through the Defense Advanced Research Projects Administration. Silent about such contracts with companies benefiting from corporate subsidies, politicians, the media, think tank analysts, and academics reverted to Cold War assumptions, linking military hegemony to US global economic role. This is where China entered the field 'threatening' the West because its economy was rapidly expanding. In this regard, the thesis of a country born of empire - land, trade, and war - and emulating the colonizing mother country, as William Appleman Williams articulates in *"Empire as a Way of Life"*, remained relevant from the early 19th to the early 21st century. The problem with the way of life rested in the reality that American power was at its zenith in 1945 from which point there was only a gradual decline that neoliberalism hastened.[278]

Because globalization under neoliberal policies evolved rapidly after the Reagan administration, the only question in the post-Cold War era was to forge domestic and international political consensus around the war on terror and to project aggressive interventionist policies as 'defensive' of the civilized Western World. As the US and NATO defense/intelligence budgets rose sharply after 9/11, there were more corporate subsidies and lucrative contracts to the defense industry because of the Homeland Security agency which in turn influenced the FBI and local police in so far as they behaved like the armed forces preparing to confront a foreign enemy. The convergence of military Keynesianism and neoliberalism hastened the erosion of the social welfare state along with liberal democracy under a militarized surveillance state. US police operating like combatants on the battlefield was in many respects militarism reflected in a more gun-violent society increasingly moving toward authoritarianism.[279]

‘Third Wave Democracy’ or Illiberal Democracy?

The waning of Keynesianism and the nascent phase of neoliberal globalization captured the attention of scholars throughout the world. Even before Roland Robertson’s *Globalization: Social Theory and Global Culture (1992),* which helped to coin the term, there were studies like *Global Reach: The Power of Multinational Corporations*, (1974) by Richard J. Barnett and Ronald E. Muller and *Global Rift: The Third World Comes of Age*, (1981) by L.S. Stavrianos dealing with globalization historically to illustrate the social impact of capitalism transcending national borders and the uneven North-South relationship.

It was against this background that Michel Foucault’s lectures (*The Birth of Biopolitics,* 1978-1979) reflected ambiguities about neoliberalism in the immediate post-Vietnam era when Keynesianism appeared to have reached its twilight. Since the 1980s, globalization apologists have been confident that neoliberalism and military Keynesianism would deliver a more ‘democratic’ and prosperous American-centered world. Official pronouncements by the US and its Western European allies to integrate the world under the Washington Consensus and geopolitical orbit were more a reflection of Communism’s fall than any substantive improvement either in social conditions, democracy, or global peace. After all, US global military engagement from Afghanistan to Syria in the first two decades of the 21st century proved that transformation precluded both economic development and that democratization under greater geopolitical stability was empty rhetoric.

A few scholars, most notably Noam Chomsky (*Profit over People: Neoliberalism and the Global Order,* 1999), maintain that the post-Cold War transition to the war on terror coinciding with the global neoliberal transformation represented a greater threat to democracy than did the old Cold War. By contrast, Samuel Huntington’s *The Third Wave: Democratization in the Late Twentieth Century*, (1991) was optimistic on every front about Pax Americana’s triumph and global democratization waves. By the end of the 2010s, the world was headed closer to where Chomsky feared than where Huntington had hoped. “Third Wave” democracy was part of first-wave neoliberalism during the Thatcher-Reagan counterrevolution, while the neoliberal class war was leading countries toward authoritarianism.[280]

Huntington credited US policy from Truman to Reagan for the success of integrating the world economically, politically, and geopolitically. Characterized by sweeping generalizations about ‘democracy’ equated with capitalism, his analysis of the transition from authoritarianism to 'democracy' reflects US-Western ideological assumptions divorced from empirical political and social realities in “Third Wave” countries - Portugal, Spain and Greece during the mid-1970s, Latin America, Philippines, South Korea, and Taiwan during the 1980s, and Eastern Europe after the Soviet bloc’s collapse.

The grand transition from authoritarianism to “Third Wave” democracy followed in the path of the First Wave of liberal democracy in Canada, Australia, and Italy after unification in 1860 and Germany after the unification through the War of 1870. Along with northwest European countries, the US and Argentina were in the “First Wave” from the late 19th century to the interwar era. “First Wave” democracy coincided with the “Age of Imperialism” and Social Darwinism amid the prevalence of racism and marginalization of minorities, women, and the working class.[281]

Considering the level of social marginalization, especially in the US under Jim Crow laws, cultural ethnocentrism permeated the mainstream along with anti-labor policies and institutional, legal, and cultural resistance to social justice. Like many Western liberal thinkers, Huntington equated democracy with the multi-party electoral system under capitalism where a limited number of citizens enjoy political rights to elect representatives from establishment party-selected candidates. All "First Wave" democratic countries had a philosophical commitment to "equality of opportunity" for upward social mobility as capitalism's promise, excluding women, ethnic, and racial groups. Despite the pre-selected pro-establishment candidates offered to citizens for their endorsement, the process afforded legitimacy to the democratic government of public consensus.[282]

The "Second Wave" took place from the end of WWII until the mid-1970s. This was the period when the US integrated a large number of countries under its military and economic orbit using the Communist bloc to justify Pax Americana's Western hegemony. To the degree that several countries adopted the market economy under an electoral system, they met Huntington's 'democracy' criteria. In the spring of 1974, the "Third Wave" began with Portugal's "Carnation Revolution". Later that summer, the "Third Wave" spread to Greece when the military junta collapsed after a disastrous military adventure in Cyprus that included staging a coup to install a junta while provoking a Turkish response in July-August 1974. In November 1975, Spain's dictator for life Francisco Franco died, followed by a representative government, competing with the southern European circle of bourgeois democracy.[283]

Several Latin American republics, most significantly Argentina in 1983 and Brazil in 1985, Taiwan in 1985, and the Philippines in 1986, transitioned from authoritarianism to representative government. In the 1990s, the former Soviet republics transitioned out of Communism into capitalism, thus, earning their democracy stipes. Equating democracy with global integration into the capitalist system and the Western electoral model, Huntington contended that the world was headed toward the path of pluralism. This was on the eve of neoliberal transformation. Four decades after the end of dictatorship in Southern Europe, history proved that far from democratic waves the seeds of illiberal democracy were planted during the "third wave" in Southern and Eastern Europe, in the East Asian semi-periphery, and even in the trans-Atlantic core.[284]

Reflecting US superpower status, the "modernization theory", which emerged during the early Cold War to justify Pax Americana's global reach, became a part of the "Third Wave" thesis. Celebrating both the end of Communism and neoliberalism's ascendancy, its goal was US global reach even before the neoliberal era precluded democratization and development. Huntington was as aware of this as Chomsky. Unlike the 'waves democracy' theoretician who accepted the premise of economically, politically, and militarily subservient relationship of the periphery to the advanced capitalist countries, Chomsky decried neo-imperialist premises. [285]

Ignoring socioeconomic and institutional inequality, especially for people of color and women, trans-Atlantic-centered "Third Wave" and "modernization theory" was predicated on economic growth taking place within the confines of Western-led trade structure based on uneven terms of trade and financial dependence. Even when judged by its criteria of social mobility, Horatio Alger's 19th-century rags to riches theme, structural inequality is built into the political economy. During the various waves of democracy operating under the modernization theory, working-class conditions have deteriorated. Furthermore, downward social mobility even in the US has been a harsh reality from the late 1970s to the present. Despite the myth of "liberal ascendancy" which market economy apologists equate with democracy, statistics of social marginalization tell a different story.[286]

In *Capitalism, Socialism and Democracy* (1942) Joseph Schumpeter advanced the argument of an *"elite model of participatory democracy"* in which the average person who lacks the intelligence of politics does not participate, while an elite minority does. If the will of the people is the product, not the motive power of the political process, then in practice democracy operates within an elitism model. This is as valid under neoliberalism as under Keynesianism when Schumpeter was writing.

Through the institutional structure and hegemonic culture, the elites manipulate and manufacture public opinion and consent, cultivating the illusion of popular consensus. From the post-WWII Keynesian liberal-democratic synthesis to the neoliberal model, there has been a remarkable continuity of social relations. As an ideological cooptation vehicle to suppress dissent, the Cold War was as efficacious under the neoliberal model priding itself on closing all avenues to dissent by transforming every institution from public education to popular culture.[287]

Manufactured and delivered through various institutions, the dialectic of consent and resistance became even more important under neoliberalism's all-inclusive transformation reach. The political and social elites were eager to convince the working class that transitioning from social welfare to corporate welfare would result in opportunities through trickle-down "voodoo economics" of simultaneous demand and supply side economics, which George H.W. Bush criticized before he joined the voodoo Reaganomics team.

Not to mention mainstream politicians and business people, Cold War scholars accepted modernization theory assumptions to explain the transition from traditional preindustrial societies to the modern industrial world. Just as readily, they accepted "Third Wave" democracy at the critical juncture of the Soviet bloc's collapse. Anything outside the neoliberal model was an obstacle to development and 'consumer democracy', no matter how to sound in achieving market equilibrium and social stability.[288]

Helping to promote neoliberal consumer democracy, the modernization theory was the best means to articulate US transformation goals at the core of IMF and World Bank loan policies contingent upon the recipient nation implementing neoliberal policies. To integrate as many countries under its aegis as possible, presumably for their good, a menacing enemy served as the catalyst reluctantly in many cases uniting countries behind Pax Americana. Condemning the Communist bloc, many Western scholars, journalists, and politicians took it for granted that democratization and modernization emanate from the capitalist core to the Global South under uneven global geographic and social development conditions. Therefore, democracy becomes intertwined with the social order of international finance capitalism.

Similar to the paternalistic Western assumptions on which the modernization theory was based, Walt Rostow's (*The Stages of Economic Growth: A Non-Communist Manifesto*, 1960) economic growth theory implies that development is narrowly defined to buttress capitalism in the core. Diffusion emanates from the industrialized countries to the less developed. This is presumably to achieve universal 'modernization' relying on Western techno-scientific skills. Operating under the patron-client model, however, the result has been that the patron core countries undermine the development of the periphery by keeping it financially and commercially dependent.[289]

A single development path based on exigent geopolitical considerations intertwined with geoeconomics, Rostow justified his implicit endorsement of imperialism in the name of anti-communism. Included in the economic growth stages, and Huntington's Third Wave thesis is the transition from the unindustrialized traditional primary-sector-driven Global South society to industrial capitalism under Western-style liberal democracy. Influential throughout the second half of the 20th century, Rostow's thesis was part of the mainstream in governments, international financial institutions, media, and academia, eventually, incorporated into the neoliberal paradigm.[290]

Without exception, countries falling into the "Third Wave" and Modernization theory framework, became even more thoroughly dependent economically, more socioeconomically polarized, and authoritarian. This is as true of Latin America under US hegemony as of Africa, Asia, the Middle East, and southern and eastern Europe serving as the periphery under northwest European and US preponderate influence.[291]

Even if one accepts the assumptions of modernization and Third Wave theories without analyzing the empirical evidence of each country's history, it is important to keep in mind Schumpeter's contention (*"Democratic Method"* and *Capitalism, Socialism, and Democracy*) that democracy, is an institutional arrangement for arriving at political decisions through consensus by the socioeconomic and political elites in which individuals acquire the power to determine who captures the popular vote. This top-down process is not very different than corporations competing for market share where the consumer chooses between products and services operating under similar rules and conditions based on what the market offers based on its terms. Along with the preeminent neoconservative Irving Kristol, his close associate Daniel Bell, Daniel P. Moynihan, and Huntington who authored the "Trilateral Study" relied on Schumpeter's top-down interpretation of democracy.[292]

Huntington's argument that from the "First Wave" of minimal democracy in the 19th century to the second wave (1945-1974) characterized by US economic hegemony during the Cold War takes into account autocratization elements present in every domain from the criminal justice system to health care and education. This is especially true as the institutional structure impacts minorities and the poor institutionally and culturally. At best, democracy in the context of "waves of democracy" and modernization theory provides a picture of the elites determining the social contract, presumably based on a version of what is good for capital is good for society. As another layer on the social contract, neoliberalism has resulted in more unequal social conditions under a crumbling liberal-democratic order.

Other than arrogance of superpower status making transformation policy possible for the rest of the world, "waves of democracy" is a Western construct rooted in capitalism, and bourgeois values and interests, rather than empirical analysis of the global diffusion of popular sovereignty and the material improvement of workers and middle class. The author of democratic waves and *Clash of Civilizations and the Remaking of World Order* (1996) theories struck just the right political bipartisan note during the 1990s when neoliberalism was on its global ascendancy trajectory, and no one challenged the US-based unipolar world order. Western Cold War ideological baggage with a heavy dose of cultural determinism in both theories prevented structural analysis of capitalism's global reach molding social relations in core and periphery alike.[293]

Southern Europe and Third-Wave Democracy

Third Wave democracy began with Portugal's "Carnation Revolution" (25 April 1975), marking the end of the corporative *Estado Novo*, a regime that started in 1933 when Hitler and FDR came to power. After seven years of a US-backed military junta, Greece returned to parliamentary rule in August 1974, just three months after the Carnation Revolution. Spain followed the same path as its southern European counterparts, in November 1975, after almost four decades of Franco's dictatorship. Besides corrupt anachronistic dictatorships stuck in interwar era rightwing fanaticism, the divergence between Southern Europe's geopolitical dependence on the US and economic dependence on Northwest Europe was part of the reason for transitioning to electoral politics.

The transition to a parliamentary system was related to the closer integration into northwest European economies, and the latter's ability to compete with the US as the patron military state behind the southern European dictatorships supported closer economic integration. Moving toward the European pluralist model where basic freedoms and human rights constituted the foundation of the new social contract, the Iberian countries and Greece appeared to embrace bourgeois democracy as part of economic modernization. This entailed cultural pluralism influenced by postwar "Americanization" as an integral part of a consumer society preparing for US-supported economic integration with northwest Europe during the immediate post-Vietnam and post-Watergate scandal had weakened the US.[294]

Although the working class and progressive students were the Carnation Revolution's popular base, by the end of November 1974, Portugal's traditional conservatives were firmly in control of the institutional structure. This left the country under the control of the capitalist class advocating economic integration with Europe and military dependence on US-NATO. Operating within the new cultural pluralist matrix, the same socioeconomic elite under the dictatorship transitioned to the parliamentary system with northwest Europe as the dominant economic force.[295]

After seven years of military rule (April 1967-August 1974), Greece joined Portugal's journey into Third Wave democracy, with considerable political influences from France's Charles De Gaulle era of the 1960s. With the failed military adventure in Cyprus (August 1974), which resulted in the island nation's division between the more affluent Greek-speaking south and the economically weak Turkish-speaking north, the US-backed military junta had outlived its political usefulness. Along with a few thousand Greek families owning most of the country's wealth, European and US corporations enjoyed preeminent policy influence. In this respect, Greece's path to democracy was along the same lines as Portugal's, with the former suffering one of the highest levels of public and private sector corruption in Europe but still managing to leverage what little it had with Europe and the US that historically value the country geopolitically.[296]

In November 1975, after the death of the dictator Francisco Franco (1939-1974), Spain joined Portugal and Greece in the transition to an electoral system with Spain in a category of its own owing to its much larger economy of $115 billion against $28.5 billion for Greece and just $19 billion for Portugal. Southern Europe's failed experiment with US-backed dictatorships had come to an end. This was largely because northwest Europe's political economy had matured to the degree that the economic integration of its southern neighbors previously under the US-patron-client integration model also entailed that they would have to be in alignment politically while remaining under the US-NATO strategic umbrella.[297]

As in the case of Portugal, the working class and college students in Greece and Spain were at the forefront of the anti-authoritarian mass movements, hoping for systemic change that never materialized. The Third Wave democracy construct has some commonalities across the region. However, each country's history, social relations, and role in the capitalist world economy differed, with Portugal and Greece having more in common economically with each other, than they did with Spain which was closer to Italy's position in the continent. Far from a Scandinavian-style liberal pluralistic society, especially the Swedish model of market equilibrium with social development, southern Europe did not experience a social revolution resulting in Nordic-style popular sovereignty. In all cases, the socioeconomic elites experienced no change in their role. The political transition did not entail a social transition, and new political elites catered to the interests of the national bourgeoisie by more thorough integration with northwest European capital.[298]

Given the increasingly integrated European economy under liberal-democratic regimes, southern Europe's dictatorships had outlived their usefulness to the national elites regionally and internationally. The established political parties in southern Europe coordinated policy more closely with northwest Europe and introduced institutional mechanisms to satisfy criteria for full economic and political integration into the European Economic Community (EEC) which evolved into the European Economic and Monetary Union after the Maastricht Treaty of February 1992, followed by the Treaty of the European Union in November 1993.[299]

Just as there was a rise in foreign capital investment in low-wage Portugal, the same was true of Greece which observed IMF and EEC guidelines about reducing external imbalances while permitting free flow of capital, lower taxes, and capital repatriation under more favorable terms. Because of the large domestic market, Spain benefited more from foreign capital investment, especially from Germany and the UK, than its southern European neighbors. From infrastructure to the primary and secondary sectors, substantial spending for public works and real estate construction along with stimulating consumer demand resulted in upward social mobility across southern Europe under socialist parties during the 1980s and early 1990s. Southern Europe's externally-dependent development was taking place at a time when the US and UK were institutionalizing neoliberalism. All along, the IMF and World Bank were recommending that these countries transition out of Keynesianism.

To qualify for entry into the eurozone under Maastricht Treaty conditions, living standards need to be raised all across the European periphery. Partly because northwest Europe was concerned about waves of southern European migration which amounted to a brain drain that enriched northwest European countries at the expense of the southern countries' taxpayers' spending to educate the individual migrating to the more affluent northwest, the interdependent integration model of lifting the weaker members closer to Europe's richer countries where per capita GDP levels was the basis of integration. This was in contrast with the patron-client model that the US pursued under NAFTA. Other integration agreements between the US and Latin America entailed that the richer northern neighbor was decapitalizing the republics south of the Rio Grande, imposing neoliberal policies that further exacerbated inequality.[300]

From the end of Southern European dictatorships in the mid-1970s to the global recession of 2008, deficit spending combined with an influx of northwest European public and private capital, and massive investment in real estate and construction resulted in higher living standards and middle-class expansion. However, this was partly because of northwest European public and private capital investment seeking higher returns. Externally dependent development in Portugal, Greece, and Spain hinged on heavy public domestic and foreign borrowing. Besides real estate, foreign capital investment in retail, mining, banking, and manufacturing industries fueled stock market speculation and expanded the consumer base.

With common market funding various projects from roads and bridges to tourism and agriculture, EEC/EU investment aimed to raise consumer demand and stimulate intra-European trade. Especially after joining the eurozone, Southern Europe's modest development helped in an expanding middle class but resulted in a large balance of payments deficits, and public debt. This was with the full approval of Western creditors and the European Central Bank, as long as there was policy compliance within the neoliberal integration model, and as long as the IMF approved of monetary and fiscal policy patterns.[301]

Considering the northwest European financial control of Southern Europe, massive capital outflows from the EU periphery to France and Germany were inevitable after the Great Recession and the IMF-EU-imposed austerity in the early 2010s. Neoliberal austerity resulted in the conversion of the EU interdependent model into the patron-client model resulting in the EU core-periphery chasm and hastening downward social mobility across the entire continent. As though there were no systemic differences between the northwest core and southern and eastern EU periphery economies, the European Monetary Union (EMU) had imposed uniform rules on all members, thereby forcing them into a north-south dependency relationship once the austerity wave swept across Europe.[302]

Combined with massive borrowing by economically weaker members, EU "demand-led growth" strategies reduced the southern and eastern European intermediate and periphery economies to client status providing interest capital for northwest European creditors. Because the neoliberal northwest core demanded that southern European public debt absorb private bank debt, the manipulated financial insolvency of the public sector became the leverage to impose deeper and wider neoliberal policies that drained capital from the periphery. Seeking to buttress their accounts that the "sub-prime" pre-2008 crisis and the loosely regulated lending craze had weakened, northwest European banks benefited from austerity imposed on Southern Europe where capital began flowing to the northwest, once the state domestic assets were selling at huge discounts.[303]

Even before the IMF-EU imposed austerity measures on the EU periphery, including on the low corporate tax the Irish Republic (2010-2011) aspiring to consolidate its intermediary economy similar to Spain in many respects, the stronger northwest EU members imposed the patron-client model of integration as leverage to serve their interests and to remain competitive with China and North America. Depleting assets from the EU periphery to buttress the core was a reflection of the northwest EU financial sector's need for reserves owing to massive losses from pre-2008 risky loans.

The patron-client model was a means to transfer capital inflows from southern Europe by slashing social welfare programs, cutting wages and social security benefits, and transferring private bank debt into public debt, all to pay creditors and provide subsidies to businesses. Austerity became the pretext to raise the retirement age, weaken collective bargaining, raid pension funds, and force the sale of lucrative public assets to private investors for pennies on the euro. In some cases, the state gifted the public asset in return for the private company, taking on the seller's debt which was the underwriter as a tax deduction on top of special agreements foregoing tax liability for several years.[304]

Under the patron-client model, austerity resulted in southern Europe's rapid decline in living standards and downward social mobility. A weaker welfare state and trade unions begrudgingly went along with institutions marking the transition from the diluted Keynesian state to the neoliberal corporate welfare state. This took place at the urging of the European Central Bank, IMF, western governments, US-based credit-rating agencies, and multinational corporations. Because neoliberal transformation rested on the internationally coordinated effort which was a political decision, the options before all countries, especially in the case of Europe's semi-periphery and periphery, were severely limited, considering that China also expected IMF-austerity compliance.[305]

Only because the solution came from the neoliberal policy regime, the post-2008 Great Recession sunk Spain, Greece, Portugal, and Italy deeper into debt. Third-wave democracy entailed high unemployment and a rise in inequality and poverty. Unable to find employment in their fields of study, college graduates in southern and eastern Europe sought work in northwest Europe, thereby contributing to the periphery's brain drain, in addition to the cost of educating students.

As much in southern Europe as in the rest of the continent, there was a rise in Euroscepticism and rightwing populism. Just as significant, the patron-client model, which the northwest EU imposed on the southern and eastern European semi-periphery and periphery resulted in political polarization. Austerity conditions that the EU imposed on Southern Europe were very similar to those imposed on Egypt, Morocco, Tunisia, Jordan, and Lebanon, all Mediterranean Partner Countries operating under various free trade agreements from the mid-1990s through the Great Recession.[306]

While in the North-African-Middle East countries, the effects of EU-IMF austerity were the Arab Spring uprising, in Europe there was a rise in rightwing political parties, quickly establishing a mass base sufficient to win parliamentary seats nationally and in the European Parliament. In 2012, two years after the EU and IMF imposed austerity in Greece, the neo-Nazi Golden Dawn (*Laïkós Sýndesmos–Chrysí Avgí*) became the country's third-largest party. Rooted in extreme nationalism and an anti-immigrant agenda, using violence, including extortion and targeted assassinations, Golden Dawn enjoyed financial backing from various sources including wealthy individuals.[307]

Founded in 2014 on an anti-immigrant, anti-Islam, anti-feminist, anti-gay, pro-life agenda, Spain's Vox was similar to *Democracia Nacional*, founded in 1995 and modeled after France's neo-Fascist National Rally[1]. With several rightwing groups inspired by the Salazar dictatorship (*Estado Novo*), it was no surprise that populist parties emerged in Portugal, Greece, and Spain, and all across Europe in reaction to the neoliberal austerity and globalization.[308]

Once the IMF-EU austerity programs imposed full-fledged neoliberalism across southern Europe, the gains of the 1980s-1990s for middle-class expansion and higher living standards for workers came to an end. Focused on the loss of national sovereignty against globalization and opposition to international organizations, the far right opposed the EU's monetary and fiscal austerity as symptoms of globalization. Advocating national capitalism, the extreme right blamed society's problems on the EU bloc made up of liberal globalization advocates. High on the list of villains, are African, Asian, Middle Eastern, and Eastern European migrant laborers driving down wages. Although the electorate became polarized, the majority in southern Europe continued to elect politicians

1. https://en.wikipedia.org/wiki/National_Rally

who executed neoliberal policies and supported EU integration. To capture the populist mass base, traditional conservative parties moved to the cultural right and became ultra-nationalist and militarist.[309]

The post-Great Recession austerity era resulted in the consolidation of a two-tiered EU economy. Northwest Europe constituted the minority core where finance capital was amassing income from the low-wage majority in the periphery which played into the hands of the populist rightwing. Adamantly against globalization, the right argued that Portugal, Greece, and Spain surrendered more of their national economy and public finances to national and global finance capital under the liberal order favoring migrants and decadent pluralism as causes for the economic decline. This was especially true of Greece and Portugal, "Third Wave" democracies reduced to virtual semi-colonies under IMF-EU (Franco-German) austerity (2010-2011), serving as a pretext for neoliberal transformation. The political cost was a sharp rise in political polarization, obviating the "Third Wave" theory which never rested on popular sovereignty and was nothing but a Western-centered construct lacking an empirical foundation in the non-Western world.[310]

From the dot.com stock market bubble in 1999-2000 to the global recession erupting in 2008, European banks, like their counterparts in the US and countries under neoliberalism's global reach pursued a lending policy designed to maximize interest and fee income because they knew that the state would cover their losses arising from non-performing loans. This took place amid the frenzy of the global economy's financialization, combined with high-risk lending reminiscent of the "dance of the millions" loans to Latin America in the 1920s. From construction and mortgage loans to business and consumer credit, banks were promoting loans without much focus on creditworthiness. Largely because banks anticipated taxpayer bailout, which is what took place, the practice was universal.

Combined with business loans to businesses across the board, housing loans in southern Europe, especially in Greece and Spain, brought about the banking crisis of non-performing loans that the state then converted into public debt. Although refinancing appeared to be in the public sector, private banks were at the root of the problem. However, governments, think tanks, mass media, and mainstream publications, in general, blamed the public sector, implying that the decadent Keynesian welfare state was at fault for sustaining a welfare-regulatory state asphyxiating business.[311]

The neoliberal solution was for the taxpayers to bail out banks through the government absorbing their debt because the banks and stockholders demanded a corporate welfare solution; hardly a "market efficiency" solution as neoliberals advertised. This is how the banking crisis turned into a sovereign debt crisis which entailed that southern European governments could not access private market lending unless undergoing IMF austerity first. Not only the IMF, but the U.S., and northwest European countries demanded that the state must bail out private financial institutions and pass on the cost to taxpayers. Therefore, the neoliberal-induced banking crisis was another pretext to pursue even more neoliberal policies of privatization of public assets, lower taxes on corporations and the very wealthy, greater market deregulation, and cuts in the social safety net and working-class wages and benefits.

After transferring private banking debt into public debt, on the advice of the international financial institutions and Western governments, debt was so unsustainable that the IMF, European Central Bank, and Germany demanded fiscal austerity to maintain the integrity of the common currency. Along with international financial institutions, the core states were acting on behalf of big banks as lenders to the banks in southern Europe, all enjoying the support of international financial rating firms Moody's, Fitch, and S&P. Therefore, the bailout was insurance to make sure that the taxpayers in southern Europe bail out private banks in northwest Europe.[312]

Besides using austerity to transfer income from the middle class and workers to banks, and capital from the periphery to the core, international financial institutions demanded that debtor nations reinforce neoliberal solutions guaranteed to sink them deeper into debt and continue to transfer income from the working class and middle class to further strengthen capital. Such a prescription allowed to institutional speculators to buy forcibly auctioned public assets at deeply discounted prices, not to mention immense profits by bondholders, considering that 60% of euro-denominated bonds constituted a large portion of the global bond market.

To justify austerity, the Greek government of Socialist Prime Minister George Papandreou (2009-2011), and all southern and eastern European governments, argued that loss of confidence in the domestic banking system would entail economic chaos, high unemployment and place risk all of the EU. Never suggesting that in return for the taxpayer bailout, the government must assume part ownership of the banks, European leaders justified using public money in a massive income transfer from the middle class and workers to investors. Southern European governments were well aware that austerity would mean a massive rise in public debt and chronic "dependent development", resulting in mass outward movement of young educated people seeking a better life beyond austerity. Historically, such scenarios were associated with the Global South suffering a shrinking middle class, especially from the mid-1970s to the mid-1990s, and again after the Great Recession.[313]

Mainstream politicians, media pundits, and business analysts on corporate payrolls insisted that the taxpayer had no choice but to gift the banks the bailout funds through the central bank which would then rely on the EU and IMF to meet liquidity requirements for the economy. Because IMF monetarist policy was not an option given the common currency, fiscal discipline resulted in lower wages and trimming of the social safety net; above all trimming wages and raiding workers' pension funds. Not only was there silence by the mainstream media when it came to the suggestion of capitalists sharing in the austerity sacrifice but there was also an expectation to strengthen the strongest elements in the private sector with the considerable and ongoing transfer of income from labor to the rich. Considering the high level of tax evasion and avoidance by the richest individuals and businesses, the austerity burden fell inordinately on the middle class and workers whose benefits the government slashed, attacked collective bargaining, and reduced the public labor force, thus aggravating inequality.[314]

"Portugal, for example, has reduced the number of private-sector workers covered by collective bargaining agreements from 1.9 million in 2008 to just 300,000 in 2012. Spain, meanwhile, has loosened restrictions on collective layoffs, and softened limits on extending temporary work, now allowing workers to work on fixed-term contracts for as many as four years. Ireland has frozen its minimum wage, and Greece — perhaps the ground zero of the anti-labor austerity movement — has shaved its minimum wage by a fourth."[315]

Weakened under the neoliberal political economy, trade unions suffered major setbacks because of austerity as the pretext to impose neoliberal policies. With French and German government support, the IMF, EU, and ECB demanded wage and benefit cuts throughout Europe. Targeting collective bargaining, raising the social security age, and reducing social benefits to dependents, the message to society was that labor must pay for the risks that banks were taking with public and depositors' money. Along with austerity-created unemployment, market conditions made it nearly impossible to maintain worker solidarity. Austerity became the perfect pretext for the war on the social safety net.[316]

Inspired by the US and UK neoliberal anti-labor policy model evolving since the 1980s, a weaker social welfare state meant deep cuts in social spending, while privatizing public enterprises from phones and utilities to lucrative state lottery operations, raising subsidies for businesses. Although several IMF-EU-imposed austerity measures were not compatible with European and international human rights laws, as a UN report confirmed, big capital prevailed on governments to proceed with neoliberal reforms that violated the law. Some courts across Europe overturned such laws in favor of the government, but neoliberal transformation prevailed in the age of Third Wave Democracy.[317]

Austerity and fast-track neoliberalism entailed that the EU further weakened the commitment to safeguard working-class living standards, social programs, and geographic inequality between the northwest core and the periphery in the continent's southern and eastern parts. At the same time, the patron-client model, which created a deeper divide between core and periphery, strengthened rightwing populist movements that blamed East European and non-white immigrants for taking jobs from citizens and driving down wages while burdening the welfare system amid an economic crisis. Such thinking reflects what the rightwing politicians, media, and pundits spew out to deflect attention from the corporate welfare state which shifts income from the bottom of the social ladder to the top.

Fearing the populist right, voters in Greece and Spain rallied around the center left that employed nebulous anti-IMF, and anti-neoliberal rhetoric, while refusing to pinpoint exactly what policies they would adopt to roll back austerity and neoliberalism. Once in power, the center-left followed neoliberal policies, arguing all along that it was protecting workers' rights. Greek general elections in January 2015 and Spain in December 2015 initially sent mild shock waves in the stock markets. This was especially true with bank stocks that benefited from consolidation and government bailouts as the state absorbed their debt, restored solvency, and adhered faithfully to austerity measures. Once it became clear that the inclusive-populist center-left parties complied with the neoliberal agenda, markets quickly bounced back.[318]

European politicians and investors knew that it was highly unlikely that the anti-austerity SYRIZA and Spain's PODEMOS governments, both coming to office with less than half of the popular vote, would not take their respective countries out of the EU. Remaining in the EU was an endorsement of neoliberalism and austerity. Nor would they oppose privatization and weakening the consumption power of the middle class and workers. Continuing the vacuous rhetoric about the evils of big capital, the Greek and Spanish progressive agenda of the inclusive populist center-left quickly transformed into a neoliberal pro-IMF monetarism-fiscal restructuring agenda, although with a commitment to preserve some elements of the weakened social safety net. The populist center-left mobilized voter support on an agenda that appealed to progressive liberals and leftists, running on rhetorical fumes instead of policy intended to improve living standards.[319]

Merely a rhetorical commitment of SYRIZA and PODEMOS to a leftist ideology completely divorced from policy, the respective governments fell back on the "lesser evil" theory, arguing that those on the neoliberal right were much worse for society. Not surprisingly, the media across the world labeled the center-left "radical left", "ultra-left" and anti-capitalist. Declaring solidarity with Venezuelan President Hugo Chavez, Bolivia's Evo Morales, and Ecuador's Rafael Correa, the EU's inclusionary populist regimes welcomed the comparisons to mobilize the progressive popular base.

Rejecting neoliberalism and US hegemony with which the development model was identified, southern European inclusionary populists justified complying with IMF-EU austerity because withdrawing from the common currency would have been much worse. Portugal, Greece, and Spain's options were to stay in the EU and embrace neoliberalism, or leave and endure the wrath of the entire Western World's punitive financial, trade, and investment measures at a time when Chinese companies were benefitting from EU austerity as much as northwest European capitalists.[320]

Desperate to mobilize popular support from the left and center-left, both Greece's SYRIZA party and Spain's PODEMOS party employed Socialist rhetoric as bait for the disgruntled working class and lower middle class against neoliberal policies. Once in power, these parties presented austerity and EU integration as unavoidable linkages against fear of the unknown. The rising tide of euro-skepticism as the domain of the far right afforded some ideological weight to the center left's arguments about their policies. Undermining social justice, the center-left's volatile face on EU integration and neoliberalism proved that the inclusionary populists were committed to the status quo. Especially symbolically, taking office mattered more than delivering pro-labor policies that the national and international business and political establishment opposed.[321]

Setting aside socialist and euro-skeptic rhetoric intended to win disgruntled mainstream voters, southern European regimes focused on trying to finesse contradictions of promising to change the neoliberal model from within, while pursuing 'neoliberalism light' which meant cracking down on corruption and holding the line on the social safety net a bit more than the conservatives. Although closer to Ecuador's Rafael Correa Delgado than to Germany's Angela Merkel model, SYRIZA, and PODEMOS were not so different in policy orientation and strategy than their Western liberal counterparts who openly embraced EU integration, globalization, and supported high defense expenditures during austerity.[322]

Cooperating fully with IMF-EU austerity, Portugal, Greece, and Spain accepted the patron-client integration economic and geopolitical model while keeping up the leftist rhetoric. Of the three countries, only Greece, economically the weakest in Southern Europe burdened with a GDP-debt ratio jumping from 109% in 2008 to 183% in 2017, agreed to US demands to spend 3% of the GDP minimum-required for defense as a NATO member. While Portugal spent close to 1.5% and Spain 1.2% of GDP on defense, Germany which insisted on rigid southern and eastern European austerity and whose banks benefited as a result, spent about the same as Portugal. Once it was evident that the only goal was to survive as a ruling political party instead of addressing systemic social and economic problems by injecting Keynesianism into the EU economy and altering the integration model, SYRIZA and PODEMOS lost credibility with the voter base.[323]

PODEMOS Prime Minister, Pablo Iglesias, continued to support his Greek counterpart Prime Minister Alexis Tsipras, and the predominantly *gauche caviar* Greek cabinet, with some ministers invested in Blackrock among other multinationals. Embracing austerity and neoliberal policies of privatization and deregulation on the pretext of using national assets to manage the national debt crisis for the benefit of the middle class and workers, SYRIZA and PODEMOS relied on a petty-bourgeois platform that quickly fell within the neoliberal mainstream. They accepted it as the norm along with the patron-client model that northwest Europe had imposed, effectively dividing the EU into northwest core against the southern and eastern European periphery, with Spain and Italy vying for influence in the semi-periphery.[324]

European center-left populist parties emerged out of a political need to fill a gap that neoliberalism and austerity had created by appealing mostly to middle-class voters fearing Communists and Eurosceptics alike. Once the

Greek and Spanish center-left parties went along with austerity and neoliberalism, voters realized the preponderating power of the EU bloc outside of which life would be worse, at least short-term.

From Greece and Spain to Portugal's Socialist Party and Italy's Five Star Movement with its reformist appeal, inclusionary populists projected the image of circumventing globalization by questioning the benefits of the EU bloc as an instrument of big capital. However, they did not form coalitions to pass legislation that would raise corporate taxes, protect wages, and reduce corporate subsidies and privatization. In both symbolic and a real sense, the inclusionary parties were not hostile to trade unions and workers, despite pursuing class war policies that perpetuated social marginalization and exclusion, while de-radicalizing middle-class and working-class voters.[325]

Under IMF-EU-imposed austerity which precipitated a decade-long economic recession, Greece and Spain suffered the highest official unemployment and structural semi-unemployment or under-employment rates in the EU. Besides sharply higher debt-to-GDP ratio under neoliberal austerity which meant higher taxes for the middle class and workers, all of Southern Europe along with Eastern Europe, suffered a very slow recovery, with sharply larger income gap, inequality, and rising poverty rates.[326]

With a strong manufacturing sector of $155 billion and $1.3 trillion GDP, Spain was in no way comparable to Greece whose manufacturing was 8% of GDP, or Portugal's 12% of GDP. However, Spain's dependent development and semi-periphery status in the world economy suffered a serious blow along with all of southern and eastern Europe, especially the GDP-to-debt ratio. It was not much better for Italy whose GDP-to-debt ratio touched 147.3% in 2022, in comparison to Spain at 115.6%, Portugal at 120.1%, Greece at 178.2%, while the EU area's GDP-to-debt ratio stood at 93%. Despite the leverage that both Italy and Spain enjoyed in the EU in comparison to Greece and Portugal, they also struggled as reflected in sociopolitical polarization and sharply rising popularity for the far right.[327]

Exploiting the rise of eastern European and Middle Eastern migrants in Europe, especially in Greece and Italy amid socioeconomic contraction, rightwing populism was neoliberalism's political underbelly. Combining the migrant and refugee issue with downward social mobility coinciding with Euroscepticism responsible for the neoliberal patron-client model of integration, the far right adopted leftist rhetoric to oppose neoliberal globalization. Although unique in its social relations despite some common sharing elements with the other EU members, the UK Brexit movement represents the epitome of rightwing anti-integration and anti-globalization. These elements found a home in the Republican party in 2016, the year that Trump became the head of the new far-right GOP that assumed his brand of populism.[328]

Despite the growing popularity of anti-globalization during austerity, the state in the eurozone became a vehicle to strengthen large businesses at the national level, especially within the EU core. Once people caught on to the myth of a strong euro benefiting everyone, when in fact benefited capital not labor, many on the right and the left turned against neoliberal monetarism. The common currency symbolized regional bureaucratic control of the nation-state. Meanwhile, billionaires and investment firms sought the opportunity amid sharp drops in public asset values to buy at immense discounts. In some cases, the state simply gifted such assets, in return for companies developing the property and/or business, and providing jobs to generate payroll and consumption taxes.[329]

Across Europe, income redistribution from the bottom to the top became the key issue for Eurosceptics on the right and the left. Segments of the media blamed mostly Germany but also the northwest EU that supported neoliberal policies and austerity. Exerting financial control as a mechanism to determine fiscal, monetary, trade, and labor policy from EU headquarters in Brussels angered nationalists and anti-globalists who opposed policies that impacted living standards and European cultural identity myths that Asian and African migrants were diluting by their presence.

Throughout Europe, neoliberalism became the stealthy systemic cause of rising xenophobia, especially targeting Muslims and non-whites, as though marginalized groups were responsible for IMF austerity and neoliberalism determining the international division of labor. While focusing on right-wing racists, misogynists, anti-environmentalists, alternative lifestyle advocates, and trade unionists, the mainstream media rarely criticized the transformation model for rising inequality and authoritarianism which was the price that workers paid for neoliberalism's survival.[330]

A pretext for adhering to neoliberalism, austerity was the thin veil behind which governments were hiding while selling public assets to domestic and foreign interests at huge discounts and declaring class warfare. Justifying giving away valuable public assets to billionaires and corporations, governments insisted that it was all for the worthy cause of creditworthiness that allowed companies and the wealthy to borrow at low rates to invest. Neither the media nor the government mentioned that individuals and corporations benefiting from public asset sales were tax evaders, insider stock market traders, and money launderers, who used lobbyists to influence public policy. The International Consortium of Investigative Journalists revealed in the Pandora Papers that in Spain alone there were 700 offshore companies evading taxes, many of which the government was rewarding with tax cuts and corporate subsidies.[331]

In addition to widespread tax evasion through offshore entities, shadow banking, of which an estimated 60% of the funds were linked to financial institutions represented another source of regulatory evasion. Unregulated non-bank financial companies utilized various means, including hedge funds, credit default swaps, and derivatives in which category J.P. Morgan leads the world and which rose sharply in the ten years before the Great Recession. Because the crisis of neoliberalism further weakened the social welfare state, the government was unable to use the leverage of publicly-owned assets amid a weakened fiscal structure to reduce unemployment and stimulate the economy. Massive capital transfers from Spain, Greece, and Portugal resulted in fiscal policies that drained income from the bottom of the socioeconomic ladder to strengthen capital.[332]

Although the populist center-left succumbed to neoliberal co-optation, exclusionary far-right populists became increasingly popular all across Europe, from the southern Balkans to the Baltic Sea states. As socioeconomic conditions deteriorated especially in southern and eastern Europe, more people lost confidence in the socially inclusive consensus around bourgeois parliamentarism. Hollow promises of protecting the waning social safety net became cliches that the far right used to ridicule progressives. The betrayal of the center-left resulted in greater political polarization that helped traditional conservatives who had moved closer to the far right. Throughout the 2010s, authoritarianism continued gaining momentum behind the thin veil of electoral politics. This was not just in countries that Samuel Huntington described as "Third Wave" democracies in the early 1990s, but across Europe, the trans-Caucasus region, and Eurasia.

As consumer demand dropped amid austerity, especially in the real estate and construction sector important for the southern European economy, income transfer from workers and the middle class and from the periphery to the core was a prescription for unsustainable GDP growth. In addition, GDP-to-debt ratios amid financialization undercut the productive economy and translated into chronic high unemployment and under-employment. This was more in Spain and Greece, less in Portugal and Italy. Depressed wages in the entire southern and eastern European periphery impacted the northwest core where labor was rapidly losing ground to capital amid an intensified class war targeting trade unions.[333]

Far from "Third Wave" democracy, de-politicization under autocratization distracted the public from the economic crimes against society by the financial elites and the political class advancing their privileged interests. Instead, the focus was on the power struggle between mainstream political parties disagreeing about how to best manage the neoliberal economy at the national level and within the EU, disagreeing on cultural and social issues including migrants who were mostly victims of US and NATO military intervention.[334]

Resorting to fear-mongering about non-Western, mostly non-white, non-Christian waves of migrants fleeing their countries, especially after Western-instigated military conflicts in the Middle East and Africa in the name of counter-terrorism, European conservative parties incorporated aspects of neo-fascism as a means of attracting support from middle class and working-class voters looking for an enemy to blame. Considering there were thirty Eurosceptic parties representing eighteen countries in the European Parliament, Euroscepticism moved from the far-right fringes to the conservative mainstream across various facets of society. Eurosceptics were concerned not only about the lack of national sovereignty and ethnic/cultural identity and 'purity', but about Brussels-imposed globalization on the member states for the benefit of multinational corporations.[335]

In the second half of the 2010s, especially after the BREXIT vote in June 2016, a segment of the Europhobic anti-globalization middle class and working class gravitated to the far right. Rejecting EU-IMF-imposed neoliberalism, they supported national capitalism and exclusionary politics. There was speculation that one or more of the periphery countries would follow the BREXIT route, perhaps one of the larger members like Italy with the EU's second-highest debt-to-GDP ratio. Despite the neoliberal integration model's impact on growing inequality, fear of the unknown outside the EU kept continental European members within the zone. In part, this was because the liberal integrationists in each country whose fortunes were tied to the EU launched an RP campaign against the far-right anti-integrationists.[336]

After the UK's conservative party agreed with the Eurosceptic far right to exit from the Franco-German-dominated EU, in varying degrees, and in several countries, liberal democracy was facing serious challenges. Besides sending a powerful message about the bloc's preponderate power over its members, the rightwing trend swept the conservative and even centrist parties farther to the right. Not just a rise in inequality after the Great Recession of 2008 and the onslaught of formal or informal austerity in the UK and all across the EU, but frustration with the lack of EU benefits trickling down socially and geographically drove a segment of Europeans to embrace rightwing populist propaganda about globalization's open borders undermining national economy and living standards. As it turned out, after BREXIT, the conservative politicians remained committed to neoliberal policies. Considering that real wages were below pre-2008 levels through 2022, BREXIT advocates were as committed to class war as liberal pluralists.[337]

European values, including democracy and equality, were vacuous slogans for neoliberal globalization enriching 628 billionaires collectively owning $3 trillion of European GDP amounting to $17 trillion, almost 18% of the total wealth in a continent with a population of 743 million. Meanwhile, of the 447 million in the EU, 94 million lived in poverty or social exclusion in 2020. For the far right, income disparity was not an issue, but multiculturalism and homogenized culture wiping out national identity were part of a campaign to mobilize popular support. Combined with the strong national sovereignty argument, behind the very effective culture wars which a segment of the EU elites propagated, the neoliberal model perpetuated class war. Intertwined with NATO, EU politicians and the media depoliticized the general population, especially co-opting or rendering the progressives silent.[338]

"Instead of strongly pushing back against this conservative approach," Max Bergmann observes, *"Europe's progressive parties have often embraced conservative framing—about debt or the European Union—only promising a softer touch or to do things better. A new dichotomy formed where being pro-European Union meant adhering to the EU austerity agenda. This gave political leaders in these countries very little economic room to maneuver or stimulate growth."[339]*

Although the neoliberal mainstream co-opted the progressive movement, some trade unions remained a voice of resistance from within the Eurosceptic camp. As the neoliberal regime attacked labor rights while working-class living standards stagnated amid rising corporate profits, popular discontent found expression either on the left or the far right. A form of rebellion against neoliberal globalization, the far right had opportunistically but effectively incorporated aspects of the leftist Eurosceptic rhetoric against international capital and EU bureaucrats representing globalization. Hastening a global rightwing populist movement, neoliberalism's contradictions were a manifestation of class war redirected and remolded by rightwing elites behind authoritarian movements in an attempt to save a crumbling destructive system with a liberal facade.[340]

Finding expression in various forms in a socioeconomically and geographically polarized Europe, the neoliberal phase of capitalism intensified class warfare. "Third Wave" democracy under neoliberalism resulted in the co-optation of the inclusionary southern European populist parties into the mainstream while invigorating rightwing populism. This was especially true of Hungary and Poland, but also core countries, including Italy under Giorgia Meloni's *Fratelli d'Italia* and France where Marine Le Pen's neo-Fascist *National Rally* is the reason that conservative and liberal parties moved to the right on the refugee and Muslim migrant issues. Just as Thatcher's conservatives who institutionalized neoliberalism moved to the far-right embracing BREXIT, in the second decade of the 21st century, continental Europe, including those of Southern Europe's far-right parties were the beneficiaries of neoliberalism's class warfare; hardly the flouring of new waves democracy sweeping Europe. [341]

The Arab Spring and Counter-Revolution

Besides southern Europe, the Middle East was another area where Western liberal democracy took root, at least, according to Samuel Huntington and those who hailed the triumph of the capitalist West spreading freedom and democracy across the world. While it is true that the far right in the West, especially in the US, relied on Huntington's 'Clash of Civilizations' cultural determinist theory immersed in Orientalist stereotypes, Huntington articulated an all-encompassing theory based on traditionalism against the post-Iranian revolution climate.

In the context of culture clashes inside the US, which were rooted in socioeconomic and political causes, Huntington's view of the Muslim East vs. Christian West thesis flowed from the American historical experience of the vilified minorities and marginalized populations. While he had collaborated with neoconservatives linked to America's white elite, he was reflecting and presaging rather than promoting rightwing populist culture wars, regardless of how some used his work.[342]

In an article entitled *"The Arab Spring: A Fourth Wave of Democratization"*, Ahmed Ibrahim Abushouk applied Huntington's theory to the Middle East and North Africa. Examining the possibility that the Arab Spring (December 2010-December 2012) could have been a fourth-wave democracy or a reversal to authoritarianism, Abushouk was optimistic about how history will judge the Arab Spring in the context of other revolutions.

Less optimistic scholars argue that the cause of the uprisings, which ostensibly the West welcomed publicly, but undermined through various covert channels, did not rest in democratization before 2010, but in the implementation of the neoliberal model. Hence, grassroots protests across northern Africa and the Middle East (Afro-Arab uprisings) can be understood against the background of local social relations and the neoliberal transformation's impact on the urban middle class and workers. In collaboration with international financial institutions, including the IMF, the authoritarian clientelist state serves as an instrument of maintaining a corrupt institutional structure that in combination with neoliberal policies exacerbated inequality.[343]

Even before the Great Recession of 2008, across the Middle East and North Africa, there was a gradual erosion of the social safety net manifested in lower wages, rising income inequality, weakening public enterprises, made worse by endemic corruption under paternalistic clientelist authoritarian regimes claiming to be democratic. Hardly the cause or even the most efficacious instrument in the Arab Spring, social media that many young people used in the digital age of instant global information networks helped to expand grassroots popular democracy movements. Although Egypt's Muslim Brotherhood did not play a key role in initiating the uprising, it gained subsequent political advantages, despite its reluctance to use social media. While important, technology's role was uneven in communicating sociopolitical issues across the Middle East-North African region and its demographic impact was limited.[344]

Amid widespread post-2008 hopelessness, the goal of young protesters, workers, and middle-class activists was popular sovereignty and social justice, along with official corruption under a government lacking transparency. Although neoliberal authoritarianism was a significant root cause of the Afro-Arab Spring, the result was more of the same, with greater civil strife and even greater external dependence. Besides the lack of centralized planning and execution, domestic reactionary, Saudi Arabian, and Israeli governments were concerned about uprisings in their land, and Western overt and covert interference undermined the movements. Eager to use the grassroots movements to present neoliberal transformation as democracy in action, Western governments and the media applauded the Afro-Arab Spring for opposing authoritarian states.

A Brooking Institution essay reflects the initial mindset of the West decidedly against the revolution, opting instead for economic reform which meant neoliberalism. *"How, then, does change occur? The United States and European policy communities coalesced around the notion of 'gradualism.' Nearly everyone said they supported the objective of Arab democracy but few seemed to think that anything creative or bold should be done to bring it about. It made more sense to focus on economic reform first and political change later. Perhaps it was just a matter of being realistic, of accepting that politics—and, by extension, foreign policy—was the art of the possible. The revolution was impossible."*[345]

Not surprisingly, there was silence on the status quo in Saudi Arabia, Bahrain, Kuwait, Oman, Qatar, and the United Arab Emirates, all as reactionary as any Arab Spring country. Once it became clear that the rebels' goal was popular democracy, free of local and international capitalist control, regional and Western governments turned against the uprising. As Seumas Milne aptly contended in an article published in *"The Guardian"* " Whatever the setbacks, the West never relinquishes its goal of controlling the Middle East for historic geopolitical and geoeconomic reasons.[346]

"Whilst democracy promotion has been seen as a pragmatic national interest, which was most prominently expressed after 11 September 2001," argues Oz Hassan, *"both transatlantic partners have a "conflict of interests" problem. In addition to promoting democracy, the US and EU, to greater and lesser extents, also seek to secure the free flow of energy into the global market, the movement of military and commercial traffic through the Suez Canal, to secure business contracts throughout the region, cooperation on immigration, military, counter-terrorism, and counter-proliferation policies, the security of regional allies such as Israel, and to contain hostile regimes such as Iran."* [347]

In December 2010, a street vendor's protest against local officials in Tunis provided the spark for the Afro-Arab Spring. Very quickly, street protests spread from the Tunisian capital to the rest of the country. Tunisian President Zine El Abidine Ben Ali, a corrupt Western-backed dictator for two decades, escaped to Saudi Arabia which was eager to maintain the status quo domestically by preventing change regionally. A working class-driven rebellion against authoritarian rule and Western economic exploitation under globalization, the Arab Spring included various groups that joined to bring about systemic change.[348]

"Defining it today in terms of "Arab springtime," Joseph N. Agbo and Jonathan O. Chimakonam commented, *"means that the Tunisian revolution would be a "Jasmine" revolution as the press calls it. "Jasmine" revolution, like when one spoke at the "Orange" revolution in the Ukraine, where one saw the manipulation of the masses by different factions of the Nomenklatura swapping power... What we see in North Africa is a response by the people, to internal stimuli—hunger, joblessness, hikes in prices goods-producing emotional states of hopelessness, helplessness,anger, and despondency that had to be externally expressed via these operations. Some analysts are even of the opinion, and we agree, that Ben Ali and Mubarak had to be eased out of office with the support of the United States so that the ruling class in both countries."*[349]

Some scholars reject the suggestion that the Tunisian uprising and the Afro-Arab Spring were a proletarian revolution like the Bolshevik or Cuban. A few deny that it was even against endemic corruption embedded in clientelism, anti-imperialist, anti-authoritarian, or a reaction against neoliberal transformation that had eroded the Keynesian state. Throughout the 1990s and in the first decade of the 21st century, Middle East-North African governments, especially Egypt, Tunisia, Jordan, Algeria, and Morocco, went along with IMF-World Bank austerity. Besides privatization of public enterprises and business deregulation, there were cuts in social welfare programs, all resulting in income transfer from labor to capital.[350]

In 1995, the EU promoted the Euro-Mediterranean Partnership (EMP), or 'Union for the Mediterranean' (UfM) as a free trade mechanism to stimulate greater integration between Europe and the Afro-Arab Mediterranean countries. Promising to raise living standards close to those of the EU, neither the EMP nor the IMF-World Bank programs delivered on social progress promises. Measured in verified statistics obviating neoliberal rhetoric, the result was a rise in inequality, lower wages for workers and the middle class, and limited social mobility for young college graduates amid income redistribution from the bottom to the small wealthy minority. The squeezed middle-class youth taking part in the mass protests against authoritarianism was reacting to neoliberal transformation hastening downward social mobility with no prospects for improved conditions. [351]

The more the Arab Spring was flowering the more Western bourgeois governments, especially the US with a long-standing strategy to retain regional control, supported Israeli policies against Palestinians and destabilization toward states it deemed enemies hedging their bets in favor of the mass movements. Hoping for emerging regimes friendlier to the West under neoliberal transformation, the US and Western Europe could not predict the outcome of the grassroots Arab Spring revolts, just as they could not predict the Iranian revolution in 1979.

After Tunisia's uprising, popular protests against other regional authoritarian governments in Egypt, Libya, and Yemen posed a threat to Western geopolitical and economic interests. During the chaos in Sunni-dominated countries experiencing social uprisings, Saudi Arabia had an ongoing rivalry for a regional balance of power with Iran which would benefit from turmoil in Arab countries. Mass disillusionment with Arab elites linked to Western economic and political interests drove thousands of people to the streets amid colonial-style US military occupation in Iraq and Afghanistan and uninterrupted Israeli settlement expansion in Palestinian territories. In addition, the regional economy had adopted the neoliberal model long before the uprising, which the crisis of 2008 proved detrimental in generating greater poverty and inequality.[352]

The Western premise that the Arab Spring was an opportunity for modernization had the aroma of neoliberal apologists salivating at the more thorough exploitation of Middle East-North African countries privatizing public entities and greater Western integration. Neoliberal assumptions identifying economic development with 'civilizing' the world through diffusion have similarities with Huntington's "waves of democracy" theory. Without the cooperation of the local political, military, and social elites, neoliberal transformation could not work in the Middle East-North African region any more than in Eastern Europe, Latin America, or the trans-Caucasus region.[353]

Rarely taking into account the bitter legacy of European colonialization and post-WWII US hegemony of the Middle East and Africa, and Islam which has been an ideology of colonial resistance, Western modernization theory scholars rarely focus on the social structure in the periphery molded by the capitalist system to serve core countries. Instead, they assume that compatibility between Christianity and democracy is rooted in Max Weber's thesis of intertwined bureaucracy and liberal democracy based on the Protestant ethic. Despite the empirical evidence in India, where Hinduism, Buddhism, and Islam are the main religions and where colonialism in which Christianity played a role left a far-reaching legacy of racism and jingoism, modernization theory disregards any possible linkage between Islam and liberal democracy.[354]

Even the most populous Muslim nation, Indonesia, after the end of General Haji Mohammad Suharto's dictatorship in 1998, embraced globalization and the neoliberal model. Suspending "Orientalism" racist assumptions, Western critics praised Islamic Indonesia's compatibility with Western democracy identified with capitalism. Along similar lines, the West has historically embraced Turkey, a NATO member and candidate for EU membership. This is despite its heritage and traditions with strong Muslim links between President Recep Tayyip Erdogan's authoritarian regime and foreign capital, especially from the G-7 countries and China.[355]

While the Arab Spring was unfolding, Western journalists and analysts were reporting that Muslim countries were undergoing democratization, a concept which presumably they identified with cultural and institutional Westernization. Difficult to determine whether the Afro-Arab Spring fell within Huntington's third or fourth wave, Ahmed Abushouk points out that it was a sort of 'wave democratization'.[356] The Arab Spring did not approximate the bourgeois top-down transition of Portugal, Spain, and Greece in the mid-1970s, aiming at regional economic integration to strengthen the European Community. In the post-2008 recession and especially after the IMF-EU austerity in several European countries in the early 2010s, Arab Spring countries lapsed into neoliberal nightmares that prompted grassroots mass protests.

Pursuing democratization, Arab protesters hoped to end clientelism, deregulation, privatization of state-owned firms, and international finance capital's preponderate influence. Particularly in the Middle East and North Africa, but also in non-Middle East Muslim countries, including Indonesia, Malaysia, and Pakistan, privatizing state-owned companies was a common neoliberal practice globally. A small clique of politicians, the military, police, and businessmen with substantial public policy influence used their positions to profit from state-linked businesses and contracts.[357]

Similar to the Iranian revolution of 1979 in which both secular and religious grassroots groups united against US-supported autocratic Mohammad Reza Shah Pahlavi, the Afro-Arab Spring uprisings were predominantly working class with young educated middle-class people eager for systemic change. Praising the Arab Spring as an extension of Iran's revolution, Supreme Leader Ayatollah Ali Khamenei labeled it a 'natural enlargement' of his country's uprising and an "Islamic awakening."

Iranian public statements notwithstanding, the Arab Spring movements were heterogeneous in ideological orientation, in which disparate groups demanded rights, including women at the heart of the movement. United more in what they opposed than in what they proposed, the Afro-Spring uprisings were similar in some respects to the European revolutions of 1848. It is not unusual in an uprising lacking in cohesive organization, centralized leadership, and planning to have the participants come together in what they oppose rather than what they propose to replace the existing regime.[358]

Grassroots opposition to authoritarianism reflected largely the urban-secular middle class vs. rural farmers and workers clinging to Islam as society's unifying force which in some respects made it easier for the armed forces, the police, and local business elites linked to the state and foreign capital to prevail over the disparate rebel groups. The question for modernization theory and 'democracy waves' is whether liberal and leftist ideologies, which inspired the uprisings, could deliver social justice because of the mass movement's heterogeneous composition taking place in Muslim countries.[359]

A foreign-assisted counterrevolution in every Afro-Arab Spring country sabotaged the uprisings. The result was greater socioeconomic inequality and political instability under authoritarian regimes. Not just in Egypt, but in countries subject to US-European direct or indirect military intervention, including Libya, Yemen, and Syria, the goal was to have pro-Western authoritarian rule under the neoliberal mold. Yet, it was all in the name of freedom and democracy. Countries with unfinished revolutions, including Egypt and Tunisia, lapsed into pre-Arab Spring political conditions, crushing hope for social change.

Lebanon, which did not have an uprising like Tunisia and Egypt, suffered a fate worse than all the rest, especially amid the pandemic and the inflationary impact of Russia's invasion of Ukraine. From the 1990s to the COVID-19 pandemic and Western sanctions against Russia, Lebanon's predatory neoliberal policies were the most extreme case of the transformation's global reach.

Led by the Saudi-linked billionaire Hariri family (patriarch, Rafic Bahaa El Deen Al Hariri), Lebanon suffered one of the world's worst economic disasters with triple-digit inflation. No matter the efforts of domestic, regional, and Western detractors it was all the fault of religious conflicts, attributed especially to Iranian-backed Hezbollah, the Lebanese Shia political party, the core issue was neoliberalism that benefited the plutocratic families. Under the neoliberal experiment, which resulted in capital concentrated among a few politically connected businessmen, the working class and middle class were devastated, as poverty skyrocketed from 11% in 2000 to 78% in 2022.[360]

Neoliberalism's resounding failure in Lebanon was similar to what took place in other Muslim countries after the Arab Spring. Whether subject to Western military operations as was the case in Libya. The US and Western European allies toppled Libyan leader Muammar Qaddafi, sinking the country into a chronic civil war; Saudi-US-UK military and financial aid as in Yemen resulted in the same scenario as Libya. Sabotage in Egypt and Tunisia to install pro-West regimes succeeded, while Western-Saudi-Turkish regime change operations in Syria failed. The common denominator was Western involvement with local political, military, and business elites to make sure that counterrevolution prevailed.

Domestic political factions vying for power, wealthy individuals at the local and regional level, and the reactionary pro-US Gulf States also contributed to the failed Afro-Arab uprisings. Considering the assumptions of "Third Wave" democracy regarding popular sovereignty, the Afro-Arab Spring uprisings were successful only in revealing the level of widespread popular discontent with local elites and Western geopolitical hegemony behind neoliberal transformation impacting the lives of millions.

Interpreting the Arab Spring as a reawakening and the Global South's challenge to the West, Egyptian-French economist Samir Amin argued that the US dreaded grassroots democracy and self-government for it entailed a blow to US imperial designs of neoliberal transformation's global reach. Amid the apparent overreach in Iraq and Afghanistan, militarism did not save the American imperial network from systemic decline in a multipolar world challenging Pax Americana. The success of the Afro-Arab Spring amid the US military occupation of Iraq and Afghanistan would have delivered a massive blow to America's role on a far wider scale than the Iranian revolution. The Arab Spring success would have meant a blow to Western-supported Israel, fearing the revolts could embolden Palestinians to rise against the apartheid state.[361]

Through various means, including NGOs posing as friendly democratic entities, the US in collaboration with Western European allies, Saudi Arabia, and Israel undermined the popular movements, while publicly the impression was one of either support or non-interference. Even more sinister, the US and UK used the Arab Spring to support regime change in Syria, unleashing civil war (2011-2019), using it to counter-balance Iranian influence regionally and determine control of oil in the northeast. Castigating Syrian president Bashar al-Assad's clientelist authoritarian regime, the US and Europe stayed silent when it came to authoritarianism in Saudi Arabia and the Gulf States which were backing jihadists trying to overthrow the Assad regime to deny Iran strengthening its regional balance of power influence.[362]

To prevail geopolitically and impose neoliberal transformation, the larger US Middle East destabilization strategy was to determine what type of regime would best suit Western geopolitical and economic interests in Afro-Arab countries. Securing Saudi Arabia and Israel's geopolitical support and denying the advantage to Russia and Iran backing the Assad regime, US considerations included Syria's energy sector, Iran's influence, and denying Russia the link to Syria.

Largely because regime change goals entailed working side-by-side with jihadists, Pax Americana's over-reach replete with contradictions between publicly-stated policy and on-the-ground practices backfired. Russia and Iran had the upper hand in Syria, once Turkey presented itself as a regional intermediary after switching sides from backing the Saudi-Western anti-Assad camp. Left behind was massive destruction and more than 13 million either refugees or internally displaced, allowing Russia and Iran to claim victory in defeating the Islamic State of Iraq and the Levant jihadists in a Middle East country where Western-backed destabilization failed. Remarkably, the US-European (UK and France) regime change Syrian operation was taking place against the failed US neoliberal militarist experiments in occupied Iraq and Afghanistan which had been the source of more jihadist activity.[363]

Regardless of how Western powers along with regional players viewed social movements in Islamic countries and how they manipulated them directly or through corporate and government-funded NGOs, political Islam remained a strong ideological force in society which played both a positive and negative role. This was not only true of Tunisia, but especially Egypt where the Muslim Brotherhood historically played a major role in the political landscape.[364]

An inclusionary populist promising stability, President Mohamed Morsi (June 2012 to July 2013.) succeeded pro-Western Mubarak. Former chairman of the Muslim Brotherhood's Freedom and Justice Party, Morsi enjoyed Muslim Brotherhood backing which was a blessing for power consolidation, a curse because the IMF and the Western political and business establishment adamantly opposed him. Initially taking a wait-and-see attitude toward the government, the West was waiting for the military to regroup before staging a coup. Egypt's military elite, most local businessmen, Israel, and the US viewed Morsi's regime as another Iran on Israel's doorstep. Western geopolitical and neoliberal advocates, reactionary regional governments, and the domestic elites, including the military and businesses, supported an authoritarian regime as the best way to safeguard their interests.[365]

In the absence of a dominant political ideology and broad grassroots movement under strong leadership to unify the people demanding popular sovereignty, Egyptian rebels rallied against the common enemy of systemic corruption under authoritarianism, but without a clear vision about how the Morsi government would govern. In cooperation with Saudi Arabia and the West, counterrevolutionary elements, including the military and business elites, opposed any regime change unless their economic and geopolitical interests were advanced.[366]

Morsi attempted to balance Western demands for neoliberal policies with an Islamic-based social justice domestic agenda. Western governments and the IMF were skeptical. Once evident that Morsi and the Muslim Brotherhood were leaning less toward neoliberalism and more toward social reform, the IMF refused monetary stabilization loans. That was a signal to investors to stay away from Egypt. At that juncture, the local elites rallied behind the reactionary Gulf states and a Western-backed military coup. On 3 July 2013, Egyptian army chief General Abdel Fattah al-Sisi led a military coup against Morsi's duly-elected government. General al-Sisi took office with the promise to carry out the Arab Spring reforms.[367]

Many identify Morsi's downfall with the Raaba Massacre (14 August 2013) marking the start of the Arab Spring's counterrevolutionary phase in Egypt. General al-Sisi's Health Ministry reported 235 dead protesters, 43 policemen, three journalists, and more than 2000 dead. Although the Raaba Massacre was far worse than Beijing's Tiananmen Square (1989), there was no outcry by US and European governments, or the Western media. Because the West and its Middle East allies adamantly opposed any semblance of democracy in Egypt which did not accommodate foreign and domestic capital along with US, Saudi, and Israeli geopolitical interests, the West dismissed the Raaba Massacre as an internal affair between government and alleged Islamist militants. [368]

Western reaction to Egypt's Raaba Massacre was one of support for law and order against Egyptian Muslim Brotherhood jihadists. Rewarding General al-Sisi for carrying out a successful coup that crushed all hope for anti-neoliberal and pro-democratic reform, the pluralist neoliberal Obama administration immediately granted $575 million in military aid to the dictatorship, allowing such action to speak for itself regarding US foreign policy.[369]

After the military coup, the authoritarian regime unleashed unrelenting repression against the Muslim Brotherhood and the working class, especially young middle-class Egyptians who demanded popular sovereignty. Despite ruling by decree, al-Sisi insisted that his government was democratic. In return for Western political and military support, he went along with neoliberalism and a pro-US-Israeli-Saudi foreign policy. Although Human Rights Watch and independent organizations condemned the regime as repressive, Egyptian capitalists and foreign corporate interests gained a great deal from their association with al-Sisi who forged close ties with the US-Saudi-Israel nexus against Iran allied with Russia and China. Linking his dictatorship's fortunes to US-NATO policy and neoliberal transformation, his reward was Western military aid, including German weapons transfers. For his part, the Egyptian leader reaffirmed geopolitical dependence on the West and continued support for national and foreign capital.[370]

Similar to the pro-West authoritarian regime of Hosni Mubarak (1981-2011), which walked a fine line between appeasing tycoons and generals, al-Sisi followed the existing cronyism path. Pursuing economic, diplomatic, and strategic cooperation with Israel and the Gulf States, and a commitment to neoliberal transformation within Egypt's political and economic tradition of clientelism, in 1992, Mubarak signed an agreement with the World Bank to adopt neoliberal policies, including privatizing several public enterprises. General al-Sisi followed Mubarak's policies but had difficulty navigating World Bank privatization demands with resistance from the top brass in the military.

Egypt's top generals owned 35 factories and other companies that they refused to privatize as the World Bank recommended. This sort of cronyism was widespread throughout the Middle East where inequality remained among the highest in the world, and where neoliberalism made the problem worse. In essence, the transformation was about how the domestic elites would divide the pie with international capital. Indicative of neoliberalism in the Middle East, in 2018 the richest 10% in fifteen countries owned 64% of income in comparison with 37% in Western Europe and 47% in the US.[371]

From 2014 to 2018 under General al-Sisi's tenure, poverty rose by almost 10%, while clientelism continued to thrive. *"Beyond the increased poverty and social deprivation of the average citizen,'* writes Maged Mandoor, *"the regime is bound to become more repressive and autocratic as it continues to impose these harsh policies. This in turn will fuel the rise of violent resistance to the state. Even if resistance does not crystallize into a coherent political movement, the level of social violence is bound to rise, leading to long-term destabilizing effects. Furthermore, the expansion of military-owned businesses leads to increased pressure on the civilian private sector as it struggles to compete with the military behemoth. This will have long-term structural impacts on the economy and the political system that will be difficult to reverse, ultimately outliving Sisi and his regime."*[372]

Survival for al-Sisi meant declaring war on workers and the poor; a policy within the perimeters of neoliberalism adapted to local conditions. Where it concerned the generals' business monopolies, the government modified Western neoliberal policies. In this respect, the business-military nexus in Egypt was similar to Turkey under the self-styled autocratic president Erdogan who fell back on the distant glory of the Sultans during the Ottoman Empire, distracting the working class from rising inequality with dreams of past glory when the state was closely associated with Islam.

Other Arab leaders tried to emulate Erdogan's neoliberal authoritarian model which seemed to be working better than the rest in the region. This was partly because the Turkish leader invited foreign capital investment with the lure of cheap labor and a large domestic market acting as a regional intermediary. Cleverly using Islamic populism, he presented Turkey as the alternative to China in the Middle East. Constantly agitating with neighboring countries from the trans-Caucasus to the Middle East and Aegean, especially with the perennial Kurdish minority question and incursions in Syria, Erdogan tried to balance all sides simultaneously.[373]

Unlike Erdogan, other Muslim leaders were blunt about reaching consensus while resorting to coercion. The ruling by decree since 2014, Tunisian President Kais Saied had staged a Bonapartist-style coup in the name of the "people". Against the corrupt dictatorship catering to domestic and foreign capital and complying with Western geopolitical goals and the IMF neoliberal program, protests took place throughout the second half of the 2010s against Kais Saied's authoritarian neoliberalism. On every occasion of dissent, Kais Saied responded with more authoritarian measures, securing tighter control of the police and the judiciary, while keeping the armed forces loyal.[374]

In Egypt's case, the armed forces enjoyed full control of the state which was not the case in Tunisia or Turkey. Top military officers played a major role in civilian businesses solely because of their positions in government made possible in large measure by market liberalization. A development comparable to that in Turkey, the fundamental differences between the three authoritarian populist regimes include Erdogan's neoliberalism with aspects of developmentalism to support the national bourgeoisie in his political power base. At the same time, he used Turkey's NATO membership as leverage but also forged close ties with Russia and China as a member of the Belt and Road Initiative project. With far fewer investments and operations from multinational corporations, and lacking Turkey's special relationship with the EU and US, al-Sisi and Kais Saied were more overtly authoritarian neoliberal, without the strong commitment to developmental and social development of Brazil's Lula.[375]

Theoretically inconsistent with the neoliberal model, military-owned companies existed before the Afro-Arab Spring but grew much faster during General al-Sisi's regime. Cooperating with the IMF and World Bank on neoliberal transformation, the Egyptian autocratic ruler accommodated foreign capital and introduced deep cuts in state welfare subsidies and other welfare measures impacting the middle and lower classes. Tunisia's Kais Saied followed a similar pattern as his Egyptian counterpart amid rising inequality and deeper debt that forced the country into the embrace of the IMF's demands for stricter adherence to fiscal discipline, privatization, deregulation, and corporate subsidies. Although Kais Saied and al-Sisi were authoritarian and crushed grassroots hope for popular democracy, Western politicians and media pundits rarely criticized them in the manner that they did Iran which operated outside the Western neoliberal and geopolitical network.[376]

Except for Yemen's unfinished revolution which turned into a protracted civil war, the Afro-Arab Spring failed in all countries. In collaboration with the armed forces and tycoons with a big stake in the regional economies, Israel, Saudi Arabia, and Western political and business interests, not the least of which were the oil and natural gas sectors, restored authoritarian neoliberalism. This took place with the IMF's considerable influence after the new regimes co-opted various groups through populist rhetoric appealing to religion and nationalism. Contrary to theoretical constructs that the Afro-Arab Spring approximated Huntington's waves of democracy, the democratic/social justice goals of the rebels never saw the light of day.[377]

Selectively applied as the explanation for supporting the post-Afro-Arab Spring elites that emerged from counterrevolution, Western neoliberal apologists demagogued the 'jihadist' theme intertwined with the US war on terror; a generic term allowing each government to define it as they wished. Western officials and analysts argued that ideally there must be an alternative to jihad as political opposition to corrupt regimes – authoritarian or elected - closely integrated economically and geopolitically with the West.

After the dust settled on the Afro-Arab Spring, crony capitalism was as prevalent as Western hegemonic influence, including from IMF neoliberal bureaucrats influencing policy. A euphemism for the secularized rebel youth movement, 'post-Islamism' in the era of the Afro-Arab Spring manifested itself in the rise of urbanization and the young generation embracing the latest communications technology as a means of grassroots organizing and consciousness-raising. However, they fell victim to digital era authoritarian neoliberalism coexisting under the traditional clientelism political tradition.[378]

Accepting some of the theoretical assumptions of the Modernization theory, French-Moroccan author Rachid Benzine was one of many in Europe representing the Afro-Arab Spring generation trying to make sense of the events in North Africa and the Middle East in the early 2010s. Following a long-standing tradition of Middle East scholars Bernard Lewis, Fazlur Rahman, and Edward Said, Rachid Benzine, as a critic of conventional scholarship, argued that the failure of the Afro-Arab Spring and more widely of the Islamic world was that it had not undergone cultural/intellectual revolution like Europe during the Renaissance, Scientific Revolution, and the Enlightenment. Partly because of nuanced interpretations of the Koran by conventional scholarship, and in response to specific historical events, Benzine linked intellectual/cultural evolution to social development as pertinent to Arab Spring's failure, adopting Antonio Gramsci's (*Prison Notebooks*) theory of cultural hegemony and cultural revolution.[379]

Not only does Modernization Theory fall short in explaining what took place during the Arab Spring, but it is far from the reality of what societies experience under authoritarian regimes linked to local economic, military, and political elites with ties to Saudi Arabia and Western governments determined to prevent any social change unless it accommodates their economic and geopolitical interests. Few scholars dispute that the Great Recession added fuel to the crisis of neoliberalism in the Middle East. However, there is disagreement regarding the underlying political, social, and cultural/religious causes and the degree to which ensuing authoritarian regimes worsened conditions for workers and the middle class.

Historically, some scholars have argued that transcending class, Islam has been the most important catalyst to popular resistance against authoritarian rule at home and in anti-imperialist struggles. The paradox is that Islam has been both a distraction issue from social justice and a reactionary sociopolitical force that has worked in favor of neoliberal transformation. Understandably, a heterogeneous popular movement against authoritarian regimes and a hierarchical social order would involve Islamist organizations at the grassroots level, as was the case with the post-Great Recession revolts.

The neoliberal West, Israel, and Saudi Arabia feared that the Afro-Arab Spring could have evolved along the lines of the Iranian Revolution of 1979. As a heterogeneous popular movement, the Iranian Revolution had the considerable participation of the Tudeh Party (Communist), even as other leftist groups held back support from what they perceived as a reactionary Islamic-dominated revolution planning to form a theocratic regime. Just as Iranian anti-imperialism manifested itself in nationalism intertwined with Islam, so was the case in the Afro-Arab Spring.[380]

Traditional developing countries like those experiencing uprisings in the 2010s never underwent a European-style Renaissance, Scientific Revolution, Enlightenment, and Industrial Revolution. Because the European colonial system determined the division of labor in Africa and the Middle East, the colonial government imposed monocultural economic structures (export-oriented economies inordinately dependent on one or a few exports). Trade was based on an uneven relationship between colonial masters and subjects molding the Islamic Middle East and northern Africa.[381]

Unlike Western Christendom, Muslim societies did not have a clash of science and religion. Many of the same themes found in the Enlightenment were part of Islamic societies much earlier. Nevertheless, it is the combination of the scientific/intellectual revolution with the industrial revolution resulting in a new division of labor and the national bourgeoisie in a weaker position in Islamic societies that emboldened the comprador bourgeoisie to support neoliberalism. In addition, Western colonialism's bitter divisive legacy, molding Muslim countries long after their official externally-influenced self-rule under export-dependent monocultural economies has contributed to the elites identifying their future with the West. Part of the external dependence legacy included inordinate defense sector spending, weakening the civilian economy, exacerbating income inequality, and breeding authoritarianism.[382]

Impossible to circumvent integration into the global market economy, which entails geopolitical and economic dependence under the neoliberal model, the rebels were caught in a myriad of contradictions that doomed the movement from the outset. Confronting such contradictions by trying to preserve cultural identity, while at the same time eliminating exploitation by the political and military elite in collaboration with a few powerful capitalists linked to Western interests, Afro-Arab rebels sought national sovereignty in the form of popular democracy and freedom from Western dependence that perpetuates the local elites.

Among other Islamic countries, Egypt's 'Fourth Wave' democracy and economic development was a construct by Western-based modernization theory apologists expressing optimism about neoliberalism's global reach. Crushing the hopes for social justice and democracy within the cultural milieu, counterrevolution prevailed much easier than it appeared against the background of grassroots protests. The comprador bourgeoisie, the military, police, and especially Western governments along with Saudi Arabia's long reach easily undermined factionalized movements that lacked solidarity and centralized organization and leadership in each country where the rebels took to the streets.[383]

Middle-class rebels were hoping for a system that would afford them greater opportunities while the working class wanted a much more interventionist social welfare state amid high unemployment, inequality, and chronically low living standards. Resulting in the absence of either national or regional solutions, the failure of the revolts reaffirmed the resiliency of ties between foreign capital with the national bourgeoisie and the security forces.[384] In the absence of some 21st-century version of Nasser's pan-Arabism ideological dream for Afro-Arab solidarity with a multilateral foreign economic policy as leverage against political/military fiefdoms using the state as an instrument for wealth concentration against the global neoliberal transformation, Egypt, Tunisia, and the entire Afro-Arab region would remain thoroughly integrated under the neoliberal global system until global economic fragmentation and geopolitics undermine neoliberal transformation. Such fragmentation took shape in the spring of 2023 after China brokered a rapprochement between Iran and Saudi Arabia, ending Syria's regional isolation and convincing Egypt to follow Saudi Arabia's lead in closer integration with China.[385]

Under the neoliberal model and observance of treaties by the Afro-Arab countries, economic integration has meant uninterrupted trade, aid, and greater geopolitical dependence on the West. However, China, which opposed social revolution as much as the local elites and the West, benefited from the uprisings even in Saudi Arabia which was free of a rebel movement. As a result of commercial contracts with private and government entities, trade with the entire region rose sharply. China played an increasingly influential role across the Middle East and Africa, while the West pursued geopolitical hegemony as leverage.[386]

Although the Afro-Arab Spring's goals of popular sovereignty and social justice were not realized, Westernization through commercialism - consumer products and services, pop cultural influences, telecommunications, social media, and technology - along with slashing the welfare state, were neoliberal substitutes. The perverse result of the uprisings was not less neoliberalism and authoritarianism, but its consolidation and expansion. By the end of the Arab Spring decade, youth unemployment and the region's socioeconomic polarization were higher than in 2010-2011 when middle-class youth and workers poured into the streets of Tunis and Cairo demanding social justice.[387]

The Afro-Arab Spring was a working-class-middle-class popular uprising against autocratic regimes whose legitimacy emanated from the military, police, a small group of very wealthy individuals, multinational corporations, and Western government military aid. The US and local elites' concept of sovereignty was identified with the early Cold War patron-client integration model modified to meet 21st-century neoliberal goals. Along the way, political Islam, the mixing of religion and politics, alienated a segment of the population partly because many did not want to replicate the Iranian theocracy model. A major dynamic in Arab cultural hegemony intended to preserve the local status quo while undergoing neoliberal transformation, political Islam was the catalyst for the mobilization of the masses. The lack of broad grassroots movements and the absence of ideological cohesiveness and organization prevented a victory over the combined domestic and foreign counterrevolutionary elements working within the transformation model.

CHAPTER III

Neoliberalism and Autocratization in the Global Metropolis

Financialization, Hedge Funds, and Neoliberalism

Emerging from the institutionalization of neoliberalism in the 1980s, "financialization" has been a catalyst in the crisis of capitalism and liberal democracy. Identified primarily with core countries that shifted from the secondary sector of production to finance capitalism as the economy's backbone, financialization has several layers interwoven in the political economy's mainstream impacting social relations, living standards, and the political landscape. Not only was financialization at the heart of the Great Recession, but it persisted despite band-aid regulatory measures. Insufficient to prevent bank failures, token regulations had virtually no impact on the fragile financial markets and economy as revealed by the shaky foundations of US and EU banks in March 2023.[388]

Modified by Keynesianism in the 1930s to mid-1940s, finance capitalism's preponderate influence determined economic policy and social relations since the late 19th century. Gradually in the 1980s, financialization entailed measuring the wealth of the nation not by the traditional GDP indicators (value of the primary, secondary, and tertiary sectors, creditworthiness, monetary stability, and growth prospects), but by the value of securities reflecting short-term global speculation and investor sentiment.[389]

Ultimately determined by the speculative immediacy of profit, financialization is not based on real economic indicators but on speculation which sidelines real economic indicators. Because financialization results in income transfer from the productive sectors of the economy to parasitic finance, the result is a higher level of inequality, rising debt, and more frequent and deeper recessionary cycles. Central banks carry out monetary policy to buttress the financialization on which the entire economy rests, thereby institutionalizing speculative risk and endorsing its parasitic nature. An equally significant impact, the state absorbs, at least in part, corporate debt and passes on the cost to the taxpayer. Hence, private debt conversion into public debt has been financialization's stealthy corporate welfare subsidy and another mechanism to transfer income from the bottom layers of society to the wealthiest investors.[390]

Profit decline owing in part to military Keynesianism in postwar America in exchange for greater market equilibrium, combined with the US sustaining chronic balance of payments deficits to support several countries for geopolitical consideration, contributed to the rise of financialization which was a fast and reckless way to put quick and high profits into the pockets of market investors.

Because financialization is global, it compromises national sovereignty by subordinating national economies to speculative international capital with the help of institutions like the IMF and the World Bank. Diluting and in some cases eliminating regulatory mechanisms intended to lessen capitalism's cyclical crises' impact, financialization has exacerbated such cycles. From the Thatcher-Reagan decade to the present, financialization has been one of the structural causes of downward social mobility and social exclusion. This is owing to income transfer from the bottom social strata to the top with the state's considerable role as a catalyst to capitalist appropriation primarily through fiscal, monetary, labor, and corporate welfare policies.[391]

Led by US monetary and fiscal policy designed to promote financial markets' centrality, the world has been adjusting to the new reality of state-subsidized hyper-market speculation taking precedence over productivity amid a weak regulatory regime and weak trade unions. Four years before the Great Recession, an IMF article faulted politically motivated regulation in the periphery for contributing to the cyclical crises of capitalism. The same article accepted financialization as the norm.

"In nearly every major financial crisis of the past decade—from East Asia to Russia, Turkey, and Latin America—political interference in financial sector regulation helped make a bad situation worse. Political pressures not only weakened financial regulation generally, but they also hindered regulators and the supervisors who enforce the regulations from taking action against banks that ran into trouble. In so doing, they crippled the financial sector in the run-up to the crisis, delayed recognition of the severity of the crisis, slowed needed intervention, and raised the cost of the crisis to taxpayers."[392]

On a world scale, there is a correlation between the share of wages in national income and sharply rising dividends, interest, and investor/corporate management compensation. Even when taking on unsustainable debt in conjunction with lower productivity and lack of sustainability, and even when breaking up a corporation and dismissing workers to add shareholder asset value, quarterly profits as opposed to book value on the balance sheet take precedence.[393] Financialization has resulted in skyrocketing top management salaries, outsourcing, offshoring, and replacing full-time labor with temporary and part-time workers. In 1965, worker-to-CEO pay disparity was 21 to 1, rising to 61 to 1 in 1989, rising to 399 to 1 in 2021.

"[Of the] 300 U.S. corporations that provided the lowest median pay in 2020, including large corporations such as Amazon and Starbucks —found that the CEO-to-worker pay gap at those companies grew wider last year compared with the year prior. The average gap between CEO and median worker pay among those 300 low-paying companies rose last year to 670-to-1, up from 604-to-1 in 2020, the report said. Forty-nine firms had ratios above 1,000-to-1 last year, the study showed."[394]

Aiming at unfettered capitalist appropriation, financialization's short-term speculative motives and market performance projection carry more weight than other considerations rooted in real economic data, market equilibrium, or efficiency that apologists proclaim as neoliberalism's goals. Symptomatic deregulation and the evolution of capitalism toward speculation, with the comfort of knowing the government will bail out the speculators, has resulted in a parasitic world of high finance and economy. Often bending laws and regulations or operating illegally, monetizing everything that can be profitable has contributed to recurring capitalist crises. This was the case from the S&L crisis of 1986-1995 to the Great Recession and regional banking crisis of 2023 in the US.[395]

Banks, insurance companies, and investment firms like Goldman Sachs deal in everything from the derivatives market to converting a country's sovereign debt into a surplus, thus deceiving both government regulators, the bond market, and IMF economists trying to assess monetary stability. As the *New York Times* reported, the involvement of Goldman Sachs in the collapse of Silicon Valley Bank in March 2023 revealed the extremely reckless and parasitic nature of financialization.

"As an adviser to Silicon Valley Bank, Goldman Sachs tried to pull off a last-minute capital raise[1] *last week [of 5 March 2023] to save the bank from collapse. But the Wall Street giant also had another role in the bank's final days,*

for which it is expected to collect a huge fee: It bought a cache of the bank's debt in a deal that ultimately led to concerns about the bank's viability. In exchange for buying $21.4 billion of debt from Silicon Valley Bank — which the failed lender booked at a loss of $1.8 billion — Goldman could make around $100 million, said people familiar with the matter, who requested anonymity because the information was confidential. That total remained in flux. Here's why: When buying bonds the way Goldman did, a bank usually acquires the debt at a discount to what it thinks it can sell it for. That discount is effectively a form of compensation for the risk the bank takes by putting the debt on its balance sheet. The bank then tries to sell the debt for as much as it can, and the difference between what it paid and what it brings in will determine the value of its reward."[396]

By creating the illusion of economic development based on speculative stock market performance, including colossal failures like SVB, financialization speeds up capital concentration and enriches speculators at the expense of society. Housing, education, pension systems, health care, and personal consumption are all negatively impacted by financialization that concentrates capital through speculation rather than producing anything from capital goods to consumer products and services.[397]

Although speculators and oligarchs predate the financialization of capitalism, their consolidation and ability to influence the course of neoliberal transformation's global reach impacting society's every domain has been notable because of financialization. A small percentage of financialization profits flow into key sectors to mold them and society into the neoliberal model. According to a US Federal Trade Commission study, policymakers have been weakening anti-trust measures since the 1970s, permitting the stock market's inordinate influence in public policy, especially monetary and fiscal policy. Along with corporate concentration, the modern global oligarchy has increased its power over society on a world scale. It is not just post-Soviet countries adopting the neoliberal authoritarian system that has experienced a rise in oligarchs. Pluralist Western countries where the term oligarch is rarely used have their share of plutocrats presenting themselves as savvy businesspeople commanding society's respect.[398]

Without mentioning income disparity, neoliberal apologists insist on perpetuating the myth that capitalists contribute more in taxes than the average worker. After all, capitalist philanthropists establish charity organizations, although those serve as tax-avoidance-evasion instruments.[399] Above all, capitalists "sacrifice" for the sake of "job creation" to keep a vibrant economy for the good of society which they identify with capital, not labor.

There is no mention of the neoliberal oligarchy defining the terms of the social contract and transforming the world economy to maintain the status quo of the tiny privileged minority overwhelmingly determining humanity's fate from the vanilla bean child-farm worker in Madagascar to the underpaid school teacher in Omaha, or the healthcare worker in Singapore; all subject to capitalist appropriation. Considering that corporations own securities in companies globally, capital concentration is far larger than it appears. In 2022, the bottom half of the US and European population owned a mere 2% of the wealth, while the richest 10% owned 65% of total wealth, and 76% in the world. Much of the oligarchy's concentrated wealth is invested in transnational corporations that determine public policy.[400]

---

1. https://www.nytimes.com/2023/03/14/business/dealbook/bank-stocks-rescue.html

"Transnational corporations control the states and their political subjects," Zarco Paic points out, *"with sovereignty rendered an illusion by the obsolescence of the modern project. Since the post-imperial order in the 21st century requires the expansion of total power rather than the fragmentation of freedom, it is necessary to explore the hybrid relationship between economics and politics."*[401]

Market speculation drives prices higher, especially essentials impacting the mass consumer, inevitability contributing to built-in booms and busts during which a small group of people can secure a legal and illegal means to profit. After the Great Recession, the *European Network and Debt and Development* (EURODAD) published an article critical of financialization and its impact on world hunger. *"Everybody talks about commodities – with the Agriculture Euro Fund you can benefit from the increase in value of the seven most important agricultural commodities." With this advertisement, the Deutsche Bank t tried in the spring of 2008 to attract clients for one of its investment funds. At the same time, there were hunger revolts in Haiti, Cameroon, and other developing countries, because many poor could no longer pay the exploding food prices. In fact, between the end of 2006 and March 2008, the prices for the seven most important commodities went up by 71 percent on average, for rice and grain the increase was 126 percent. The poor are most hit by the hike in prices. Whereas households in industrialized countries spend 10 -20 percent on food, in low-income countries they spend 60 - 80 percent. As a result, the World Bank forecasts an increase in the number of people falling below the absolute poverty line by more than 100 million. Furthermore, the price explosion has negative macroeconomic effects: deterioration of the balance of payment, fueling inflation and new debt."*[402]

Contributing to the neoliberal income transfer that has negatively impacted middle class and workers' living standards, and a cause of rising inequality, higher indirect and real estate taxes, and cuts in social programs, CEO compensation grew 1,460% from1978 to 2021, while real wages had about the same purchasing power in 1978 as in 2021. Using lobbyists and contributions to political campaigns, institutional and corporate investors have influenced public policy undermining the real economy while reproducing the neoliberal culture.[403]

Contrary to politicians, business analysts, and media spin that financialization is all about creating jobs, helping to "democratize" investment, and diffusing income to the middle class and workers, the record supports no such claims. A larger debtor class and social marginalization inevitably resulted from the process which would not exist were it not for the state permitting its existence and promoting it through central bank monetary policy and purchase of government bonds. It is hardly surprising that people from various ideological and political backgrounds believe that the political economy is rigged on behalf of the privileged plutocrats to maintain their status with the state's support.[404]

Throughout the world, liberal pluralist and authoritarian neoliberals use culture wars and identity politics as distractions from structural issues, including financialization. The neoliberal transformation's institutionalization has resulted in central banks' active alignment with capital to make financialization possible. Using monetary governance to buttress the process, the result has been capital concentration. From Eastern Europe to North America and from Japan to Indonesia, this widespread practice contributed to the subprime high-risk mortgage crisis and the Great Recession.[405]

Deemphasizing the significance of global power distribution based on the Westphalian nation-state model and regional economic/monetary blocs such as the EU, the neoliberals insist that the obsolete nation-state must submit to the international market hegemony for optimal private sector efficiency. At the same time, they demand central bank intervention – in essence another public subsidy – which entails national sovereignty subordination to international financialization of the economy.

The European Central Bank's quantitative easing which included government bond purchases among other securities from the Great Recession outbreak until the war in Ukraine, clearly projected the image of easy credit designed to stimulate growth. While quantitative easing helped stock market values without offering anything but illusions of wealth for the real economy, only investors benefited at the expense of the rest of society stuck with rising public debt.[406]

In an article entitled *"The Politics of Public Debt: Neoliberalism, capitalist development, and the Restructuring of the State"*, Wolfgang Streeck concludes that neoliberalism's systemic rewards provide a disincentive for capitalists to abandon financialization in favor of productivity. *"Why should the new oligarchs be interested in their countries' future productive capacities and present democratic stability if they can be rich without it, processing back and forth the synthetic money produced for them at no cost by a central bank for which the sky is the limit, at each stage diverting from it hefty fees and unprecedented salaries, bonuses, and profits as long as it is forthcoming — and then leave their country to its remaining devices and withdraw to some privately owned island?*[407]

To distract from the economy's financialization precipitating inequality and marginalization, liberals and rightwing populists have relied on identity politics while the media amplifies culture wars as a substitute for class struggle. An important difference between pluralists and rightwing populists in their approach to the state's role has been that the former advocate a strong legislative branch and a weaker executive. Regardless of pluralism identity politics and hollow populist nationalist slogans, both political camps support policies strengthening financialization, thus facilitating the convergence of capitalist class interests across national borders.[408]

Rhetoric about a weak state resulting from neoliberal policies aside, the state has been the catalyst for class hegemony and class warfare. Once Margaret Thatcher and Ronald Reagan weakened the Keynesian state and strengthened the corporate welfare state while openly declaring war on the working class, they simultaneously used the central bank's power to align more closely with financialization goals. Reckless speculation and risk with everything including lending allowed by Reagan's deregulation of the industry permitted fraud in S&Ls aware that the government would bail them out. Financialization's impact in the first S&L crisis in 1986 resulted in debtor class expansion, reaching its highest point after the subprime-mortgage-induced Great Recession in 2008 but the impact lingered into the 2010s. To facilitate the over-accumulation of capital in the name of free competition and market efficiency, governments followed the same Reagan-Thatcher disastrous prescription because the government guaranteed the deposits.[409]

Regardless of whether the ruling parties have co-opted trade unions, neoliberal policies have been targeting labor, fighting against trade unionism, collective bargaining, and raising the retirement age. Either former executives of the financial world from firms like Goldman Sachs instrumental globally in financialization schemes, or closely linked to financial firms, government officials in charge of economic policy have a mission to serve finance capital's interests. Because of financialization, there has been stagnation in the real economy except the defense sector in core countries. Behind the deceptive mask of public policy for the unspecified "common good", monopolist international finance capitalism is well protected by pluralist and rightwing populist politicians desperately vying for power.[410]

From 1980 to 2008, financialization created rapid income inequality amid massive capital concentration leading to the Great Recession and its lingering effects on society. According to the OECD: *From the late 1980s, the increase in income inequality became more widespread. The latest trends in the 2000s showed a widening gap between rich and poor not only in some of the already high-inequality countries like Israel and the United States, but also – for the first time – in traditionally low-inequality countries, such as Germany, Denmark, and Sweden (and other Nordic countries), where inequality grew more than anywhere else in the 2000s."*[411]

Valuing risk-adjusted earnings as part of capitalization has defined financialization which propelled investment banking to have a preponderate influence in monetary and fiscal policy. In turn, this resulted in restructuring society through income redistribution favoring the richest one percent. The Great Recession proved incontrovertibly that the neoliberal myth of market social efficiency was nothing more than a hoax when it pertained to 'social efficiency' and in essence another monopoly capitalism scheme.

Concurrent with growing income inequality, financialization created a large chronic debtor class that kept increasing as the capitalist crisis deepened. Indicative of peoples' desire to maintain living standards at certain levels, despite the inability to afford them, US personal debt reached $12.58 trillion in 2016, or 80% of GDP. Despite the economic recovery and relatively low unemployment in the second half of the 2010s-early 2020s, this trend was expected to continue higher, reflecting grossly uneven income distribution as government and corporate policy.

Combined with a fiscal structure burdening the middle class and working class, wage stagnation and higher costs of health, housing, and education drove more people into the debtor class, especially after the central banks began raising prices in 2022 to control inflation. Above all, stagflation/recessionary conditions of 2022-2023, bubbling for more than a decade because of near-zero prime rates and worsened by US-led sanctions against Russia, dealt a bigger blow to the chronic debtor class as higher interest rates depleted savings among the heavily indebted class. [412]

The rise of the chronic debtor class creates ambiguities about middle-class status and conceals downward mobility. According to Eugene Ludwig, a former Clinton administration official, the costs of household needs rose 64% in the first two decades of the 21st century, well above the inflation rate. *"We found that while people in 2001 maybe did have just a little bit of discretionary spending, by 2019 as a comparison, many households did not, particularly the ones with more children,"*[413]

Although some European countries, including Germany and Italy, have low household debt relative to GDP, many advanced and developing nations, including South Korea and Australia have experienced a sharp rise in personal debt. Contributing factors include stagnant wages, privatization and deregulation of public enterprises that resulted in higher consumer costs, and lower taxes on the wealthy with the burden falling on the mass consumer. Hence the creation of a permanent debtor class whose fortunes rest on maintaining steady employment and/or additional part-time employment to meet obligations and keep one step ahead of bankruptcy.[414]

In the late 20th-early 21st century, IMF austerity carrying loan conditionality imposed on developing and semi-developed nations added to a rising debtor class throughout the Global South and in parts of the Western metropolis. A study commissioned by the Bank for International Settlements concluded that in the first two decades of the 21st century, across Europe and other OECD countries, household debt relative to GDP rose very rapidly. For every one percent debt-to-GDP ratio, there is a corresponding drop in growth. This is especially dangerous once the debt-to-GDP ratio reaches 80%, burdening inordinately the middle class and workers on whose shoulders fall the burden of taxation relative to income. Just as in the US where financialization has been at the heart of the economy, in Europe the rise in household debt has taken place amid a rise in legal protection of creditors and withering protection for debtors.[415]

Maurizio Lazzarato's *The Making of the Indebted Man: An Essay on the Neoliberal Condition* (2012) argues that neoliberalism created a debtor-creditor relationship which has supplanted the worker-capitalist dichotomy; an argument that other scholars focusing on the financialization of the economy have made as well. Debt-capitalism, which Lazzarato makes a central theme of his work (*Governing by Debt*, 2015) has been a commoditized product of the financialization economy which contributes to crisis cycles for which the US and G7 try to find geopolitical solutions that in turn further aggravate the debt crises.

In the Keynesian phase of capitalism, public and private debt was a stimulant for growth amid the deep contracting economic cycle of the 1930s when it was necessary to stimulate consumer demand and stabilize employment. After 1980, financialization was a factor in the rise of a permanent chronic debtor class without stimulating economic growth or stabilizing employment. Evident after the Great Recession, financialization attracted the attention of some politicians and political observers who realized the convergence of the widening debtor class with a corresponding rich-poor income gap amid an expanding corporate welfare state.[416]

Thanks to easy credit and investor speculation, including cryptocurrency among other online mechanisms, neoliberals maintain that securities trading and investing have been democratized. The ultimate scam of financialization's speculative nature to hide taxable assets from authorities, cryptocurrency has been a means of money laundering and evading official channels. Indicative of the depth of corruption, but also the remarkable tolerance by the state and media complicity, the collapse of FTX, one of the world's largest trading firms using customer money to cover trade losses, and the arrest of its founder, Sam Bankman-Fried, in December 2022.[417] Bahamas-based FTX demonstrated the various levels of corruption as three of its top executives pleaded guilty to criminal charges that included money laundering, commodities, wire, and securities fraud, in addition to campaign law violations in a multi-billion-dollar scheme.[418]

"Many investors have been left penniless by FTX's collapse, with founder Sam Bankman-Fried estimating that $8 billion of funds[2] would be required to refund every depositor in full...Speculation is not something confined to pointless things like Bitcoin, or that only takes place on the stock market. It permeates the entire economy under capitalism, including life's necessities like housing and food, fueling rising rents and inflation... None of this speculation provides anything useful to society or enriches anyone but the super-rich. It is simply a means for myopic, self-interested capitalists to make a quick buck at everyone else's expense."[419]

Disagreeing about the central banks' role in speculative bubbles, apologists and critics alike agree that cryptocurrency reflects the entire stock market's speculative motif under financialization. The ultimate deregulated market mechanism to circumvent legal reporting channels, the crypto irony is that it emerged from the banking crisis of 2007-2008. Besides the numerous criminal activities involved in cryptocurrency, it deprives

2. *https://www.theguardian.com/technology/2022/nov/18/how-did-crypto-firm-ftx-collapse*

the economy of valuable assets that could otherwise be used for investment in the economy; something that J.P. Morgan's CEO, the master of derivatives, labeled *'hyped-up fraud'*.[420]

"In the weeks since Sam Bankman-Fried's cryptocurrency empire was revealed to be a house of lies, mainstream news organizations and commentators have often failed to give their readers a straightforward assessment of exactly what happened... It is now clear that what happened at the FTX crypto exchange and the hedge fund Alameda Research involved a variety of conscious and intentional fraud intended to steal money from both users and investors. That's why a recent New York Times interview was widely derided[3] for seeming to frame FTX's collapse as the result of mismanagement rather than malfeasance[4]. A ***Wall Street Journal*** *article bemoaned the loss of charitable donations[5] from FTX, arguably propping up Bankman-Fried's strategic philanthropic pose. Vox co-founder Matthew Yglesias, the court chronicler of the neoliberal status quo, seemed to whitewash his entanglements by crediting Bankman-Fried's money with helping Democrats[6] in the 2020 elections – sidestepping the likelihood that the money was effectively embezzled."[421]*

Neoliberalism determines monetary policy, terms of money supply, bond purchase, adjusting reserves, collateralized debt obligations, and quantitative easing, theoretically all mechanisms to stabilize the economy. In essence, neoliberal tentacles have supplanted central banks with rogue market forces that test legal limits and challenge reserve currencies. Representing the utopian dream of anarcho-libertarians influencing monetary policy, cryptocurrency investors are an important dimension of neoliberal ideology close to the heart of financialization. Techno-utopians envisioning the digital citizen in a neoliberal society favor a 'gypsy economy' operating on digital currency outside the purview of the state's regulatory reach where it is possible to transfer and hide money from the government while speculating to maximize profits.[422]

Like Hayek, Milton Friedman favored market forces determining monetary policy rather than having the government in that role coordinating the central banks' administrative structure to balance disparate market interests. Central banks have always catered to capital and responded to markets but take a broader perspective that includes equilibrium to soften the contracting cycle's impact. Hayek's proposal (*The Denationalization of Money*, 1976) called for the law of the 'free market' (monetary speculation) to determine the policy that would negatively impact working-class living standards by lifting regulatory mechanisms. In Hayek's model, government regulation and coordination of monetary policy would not constrain capital. In short, banking deregulation and monetary speculation would theoretically result in greater economic growth, no matter the consequences of inter-sector imbalances or legal and illegal activity owing to the absence of regulatory measures. In short, allows the formal economy to operate essentially like the informal or underground.[423]

Although the deregulated banking sector, including shadow banking, contributed to the crisis of 2008, the decentralized financial system that included cryptocurrency after the Great Recession transported financial trading into a new level of legalized corrupt and criminal activity, some of which operated enough within the law

---

3. https://beincrypto.com/new-york-times-breathless-love-letter-sbf-lambasted-crypto-community/

4. https://www.nytimes.com/2022/11/14/technology/ftx-sam-bankman-fried-crypto-bankruptcy.html

5. https://www.wsj.com/articles/sam-bankman-frieds-plans-to-save-the-world-went-down-in-flames-11669257574?reflink=e2twmkts

6. https://www.slowboring.com/p/some-thoughts-on-the-ftx-implosion

that stock exchanges did not feel embarrassed. From 2010 when crypto started trading until 2022 when FTX collapsed, the rise in criminal activity associated with crypto, especially money laundering operations involving organized crime to banks, rose sharply. In December 2017, the UK and EU warned that cryptocurrencies go beyond the boundaries of financialization into criminal enterprises, including money laundering, tax evasion, and varieties of scams involving billions of dollars.[424]

J.P. Morgan called it crypto-fraud, and they do know considering the fines they have paid in relationship with the company's promotion of mortgage-backed securities. Without the full support of the state, hyped crypto-fraud, would not be possible. In February 2023, the Biden administration announced a multibillion bailout of crypto-banks, raising eyebrows even among Wall Street's staunchest apologists. Silvergate Bank, Signature Bank, Ally Financial, and Provident Bancorp secured advances from the Federal Home Loan Banks (FHLB) whose goal is to invest in housing, jobs-growth businesses, and anything stimulating economic growth in all fifty states.[425]

Crypto-banks Silvergate Bank, Ally Financial, Signature Bank, and Provident Bancorp tapped into FHLB funds, which are FDIC-insured and liabilities passed on to the public in case of insolvency. By October 2022, FDIC knew that 24 financial institutions, among them most of the large banks, were active in crypto-currency and another 56 were on the fence. Not publicly traded, none of the crypto-banks mentioned above had filed SEC reports, making it difficult to determine the risk of their operations.[426]

Larry Thomspon[7], vice-chair of Signature Bank which received loans from the FHLB of New York, served as board chairman of Ledger X acquired by FTX US derivatives and was elected in FHBL of New York at the time that FTX declared bankruptcy in November 2022. In 2021, Thompson's bank was instrumental in helping several crypto banks through FHLB. *"It's unclear whether or not Thomspon recused himself from the advances given to Signature in 2022 — which* ***increased significantly*** *compared to the previous year. Indeed, with about $50 million in New York's FHLB stock, Signature[8]'s advances increased from $2.63 billion to $11.28 billion from 2021 to 2022. Meanwhile, Silvergate[9] shares increased in the FHLB of San Francisco, from $19 million in 2021 to almost $25 million the next year. According to American Banker, no advances were given in 2021 — but $4.3 billion in advances were offered[10] the following year."[427]*

Experiencing the same problems of corruption and financial strains involved in crypto as an instrument of criminal activity that the state protects, in the later part of 2010 Japan adopted a more cautious approach to crypto than Europe or the US. Indicative of investors' influence, Australia and a few other countries went for a much slower pace. Cryptocurrency reflects both the neoliberal ideology and capital accumulation goals gaining popularity among large and small speculators throughout the world. Circumventing the IMF basket of reserve currencies, cryptocurrency evades national and international legal accountability mechanisms for the transfer of money and tax liability, fulfilling a speculator's or a tax evader's dream.[428]

---

7. https://www.youtube.com/watch?v=baYpx8cjEZk

8. *https://investor.signatureny.com/pme/press-releases/news-details/2023/Signature-Bank-Reports-2022-Fourth-Quarter-and-Year-End-Results/*

9. *https://s23.q4cdn.com/615058218/files/doc_financials/2022/q3/fe57d23e-df43-4118-bffa-43ec28b9cad6.pdf*

10. *https://www.americanbanker.com/news/silvergate-bank-loaded-up-on-4-3-billion-in-fhlb-advances*

A tiny fraction of the global monetary system, cryptocurrency became important even for governments like Venezuela under President Nicolas Maduro (2013-) trying to pump liquidity into the oil-dependent economy suffering from hyperinflation, economic stagnation, and US sanctions throughout the 2010s. To circumvent US sanctions, in February 2018, Maduro launched the petro crypto-token. Although the government-backed Petro with oil, diamond, and gold revenues, the effort did not inspire confidence among consumers or investors.

In neighboring Colombia crypto accounted for an estimated 2% of GDP, largely because of drug-related use, but also an exchange currency system along the Colombia-Venezuelan border where illegal activity thrived. By the end of 2010, cryptocurrency became a trend in Brazil, Mexico, Argentina, Panama, and El Salvador with a 1370% rise for the Latin American republics between 2019 and 2021. Dropping 66% from November 2021 to June 2022, Latin Americans holding crypto suffered massive losses.[429]

Crypto and corruption are at the core of this dimension in the financialization economy. In August 2022, the Securities and Exchange Commission charged eleven people involved in a $300 million crypto-pyramid scheme. While this may seem impressive, the entire sector is not far off a pyramid scheme that the government indirectly subsidizes without regulating it in the same manner as banks. Although the US Justice Department has prosecuted organized crypto-criminals involving $2 billion in fraud, the aim has been to catch those circumventing US sanctions in different countries. If cryptocurrency can operate outside the purview of regulatory and central bank mechanisms, then trusting the private speculator and drug lord is as valid as the contention that the central bank's role and monetary centralization are superfluous.[430]

Central banking is a mechanism that 17th-century capitalists (Sweden's Riksens Ständers Bank, 1668, Bank of England, 1694) and their political representatives created for the market's harmonious operations. Not surprisingly, neoliberal apologists insist that the US and Western governments fighting foreign actors using crypto for illegal purposes must not undermine "innovation" by regulating cryptocurrency. Government regulators and those involved with crypto realize that 'innovation' is a pretext for evading the formal financial system's constraints and centralized regulation.[431]

Indicative of the neoliberal ideology's far-reaching impact on economic life, cryptocurrency reflects the extreme parasitic aspect of finance capitalism's quest for accumulation without any accountability. In an ironic twist, the very neoliberal forces that promote cryptocurrencies are on the defensive, partly because Mexican and Colombian drug cartels use it to launder money. Among countries on the US-Western sanctions list, various players, including oligarchs from the former Soviet republics and anti-Western governments use cryptocurrencies to circumvent Western legal restrictions.[432]

This is only one of neoliberalism's many contradictions that undermines the system that it theoretically serves. Another contradiction is lingering skepticism by mainstream financial institutions eager to maintain a monopoly of government-issued currency and leverage over the central banks, not to mention price volatility resulting from speculation. As the world's most important institutional promoter of neoliberalism, the IMF has cautioned not to dismiss cryptocurrencies because they could have a future, or actually 'be the future'. In this respect, China's central bank took the lead to issue a regulated digital yuan where wild speculation is taken out of the product. Although e-commerce company *Alibaba* and social network *Tencent* corporations support the digital yuan, there is a question as to its utility for the general public, given that there is no incentive as a mobile payment mode.[433]

Once the stagflation crisis took hold globally owing primarily to capitalism's cyclical nature, the combination of interest rate hikes and US-EU-led sanctions on Russia amid pandemic-related supply chain problems in 2022, cryptocurrencies crashed, thereby exacerbating global debt. Accounting for unfulfilled liabilities and derivatives in 2022, global debt was estimated at $3 quadrillion. The issue is not so much that cryptocurrency constituted a substantial portion of that debt, but that it is part of rising debt. *"Fool's Gold comes in many guises, whether it is in fake paper money, Ponzi investment schemes, fake and manipulated gold derivatives, Bitcoin, or just fake gold discoveries in Uganda..."*[434]

Among other factors, there is a correlation between the rise of cryptocurrency and the dollar's decline under financialization. Because the dollar represents about 60% of the world's central banks' foreign reserves, while the euro is only 20% and the Chinese renminbi 3%, the war with Ukraine showed that "de-dollarized" global trade can take place very rapidly, especially as the US growth prospects are not as promising as those of East Asia.

The Great Neoliberal Recession

After the IMF's *'Global Financial Stability Report'* of September 2006, every major international financial institution, government, and stock market trader knew that a recession was imminent. They took no precautions to mitigate its impact. Financialization operates on the "here and now profit mandate". Two years before the crisis, behind the IMF's concern were hedge funds and credit derivatives that brought down Lehman Brothers (August 2007-October 2008) holding $400 billion in credit default swaps which involved more than $600 billion in assets.

In May 2007, New York Federal Reserve governor Timothy Geithner knew the details of this catastrophe. Yet, he stated that credit derivatives were safe, praising every single neoliberal measure, and claiming that the world economy was delivering low inflation and high growth. Although the crisis proved Geithner wrong, his credentials with the IMF and his wholehearted support for using taxpayer money to help J. P. Morgan bought Bear Stearns (March 2008) endeared him to Obama who appointed him Treasury Secretary from 2009 to 2013. [435]

Geithner's German counterpart, Wolfgang Schäuble, a notorious dogmatic neoliberal among the architects of EU-IMF-imposed austerity in southern Europe, managed the transition from the interdependent pre-2008 EU model to the patron-client US model. Intended to support big capital at the expense of the working class and middle class, the patron-client model created a two-tiered EU, decapitalizing the south and east for the sake of strengthening northwest European financial institutions.

Shocking not only neoliberal critics, some of whom compared him to a Nazi Reich minister, Schäuble used the international financial system to subjugate the working class in open class warfare. Many raised eyebrows among pluralist neoliberals when he stated that *"saving lives should not be a paramount concern"* of the state. More circumspect than Schäuble who used language that some associated with the Nazi era, Geithner was as eager to promote the corporate welfare system through massive government subsidies amid the crisis.[436]

As late as 16 September 2008, J.P. Morgan, which had just received taxpayer money to buy Bear Stearns, offered Lehman $138 billion in "Federal Reserve-backed advances". This was a clear illustration of how the government was rewarding financial institutions with taxpayer money, even on the eve of the Great Recession, despite those institutions having played a role in the financial crisis.

As early as the autumn of 2006, financialization was out of control impacting Lehman. This was with the full knowledge of government agencies, big banks, and international financial institutions. Companies involved in credit swaps included American International Group (AIG), Pacific Investment, and Citadel Hedge Fund. Continuing to do business as usual, they fully expected a government bailout. Focused only on stock market indexes, the media kept singing the praises of "market efficiency"; a situation similar to the 1920s before the crash of 1929.[437]

Wild market speculation manifested itself partly in the form of hedge funds - unregulated mutual funds in all areas from energy to currencies, stocks, precious metals, and mortgages. Under the assumption that the government would come to their aid, emboldened corporations operated in a very loosely regulatory environment. Engaged in duplicitous accounting, they took immense risks with hedge funds operating beyond regulatory mechanisms. A small group of institutional investors exercised immense influence over the decision-making process in loosely regulated hedge funds where fraud is more likely to precipitate dislocation. Far from a victimless crime, millions lost their jobs and many more suffered wage cuts.[438]

In a *New York Times* article, entitled *"The Neoliberal Looting of America"*, published in July 2007, Mehrsa Baradaran argued that private equity managers caused the loss of 1.3 million jobs in the US because of liquidation and bankruptcies. *"As "leveraged buyout" firms took advantage of the new market for high-yield debt (better known as junk bonds) to buy and break up American conglomerates, capturing unprecedented wealth in fewer hands. The private equity industry embodies the neoliberal movement's values while exposing its inherent logic. Private equity firms use money provided by institutional investors like pension funds and university endowments to take over and restructure companies or industries. Private equity touches practically every sector[1], from housing[2] to health care to retail[3]. In pursuit of maximum returns, such firms have squeezed businesses for every last drop of profit, cutting jobs, pensions, and salaries where possible. The debt-laden buyouts privatize gains when they work, and socialize losses when they don't, driving previously healthy firms to bankruptcy and leaving many others permanently hobbled... In the last decade, private equity management has led to approximately 1.3 million job losses[4] due to retail bankruptcies and liquidation."*[439],

Considering the massive scope of the US-based global capitalist crisis, the media eventually covered Goldman Sachs, among other financial institutions responsible for selling high-risk products to clients, going beyond speculation into the domain of questionable legality. In April 2010, the Securities and Exchange Commission (SEC) accused the company of structuring and marketing synthetic *'collateralized debt obligation'.* Without ever disclosing to investors the particulars of the products while shorting them, the company linked them to subprime residential mortgage-backed securities.[440]

No matter the scandals' scope, Goldman Sachs retained its preeminent influence under the Bush and Obama administrations. Knowing that these high-risk products would decline in value, Wall Street institutions were shorting them to unsuspecting clients, deliberately withholding full disclosure. To make deficits appear as surpluses, Goldman Sachs was also responsible for striking deals with several countries around the world, including southern Europe. Falsifying public accounts in the same manner as accounting firms in the 1990s and early 2000s was a way to help corporations make debt appear as assets. The result was to deceive investors, while the taxpayer covered the losses.

Well aware of the investment banks' operations, EU and US regulators looked the other way. Eventually, the EU warned Goldman Sachs to stop the practice within member nations. Inaccurate current accounts threw off the EU's accounting of everything from the relationship of the European Central Bank with member states'

---

1. *https://www.bloomberg.com/news/features/2019-10-03/how-private-equity-works-and-took-over-everything*

2. *https://www.theatlantic.com/technology/archive/2019/02/single-family-landlords-wall-street/582394/*

3. *https://www.forbes.com/sites/andriacheng/2019/07/26/the-high-cost-of-private-equity-firms-retail-buyout-13-mln-jobs-study-finds/#a5c02393e59c943d6a75a9241140faca35299ac967834*

4. *https://www.washingtonpost.com/business/2019/07/24/private-equitys-role-retail-has-decimated-million-jobs-study-says/*

central banks, currency reserves, liquidity, and the size of subsidies that members were due to receive. The reason that Goldman Sachs operated with impunity was because of the immense support it enjoyed not only on stock exchanges globally but because everyone knew that the US and EU governments would only impose symbolic fines and allow it to operate.[441]

"They weren't murderers or anything," Matt Taibbi of *Rolling Stone* writes, *"they had merely stolen more money than most people can rationally conceive of, from their own customers, in a few blinks of an eye. But then they went one step further. They came to Washington, took an oath before Congress, and lied about it...This isn't just a matter of a few seedy guys stealing a few bucks. This is America: Corporate stealing is practically the national pastime, and Goldman Sachs is far from the only company to get away with doing it."[442]*

No Wall Street company defended the neoliberal dogma as vigorously as Goldman Sachs. Involved in scandals of the financialization economy, a Goldman Sachs director was involved in insider trading of hedge funds during the height of the financial crisis in 2008. Nevertheless, the incoming Obama administration relied on former Goldman Sachs executives for economic policy advice, knowing they had broken the law. Academics from prestigious universities were apologists for the investment firm. From Stanford University to Boston College, the firm had endowed faculty positions, historically donating millions to higher education and buying influence and public goodwill.[443]

Because the influence of hedge funds was far-reaching in the market, the assumption was that the federal government would rescue them. *Credit isn't extended to help people get ahead,"* Jodi Dean points out. *"It's the means for producing securitizable debt, which means financialization (one of the key features of neoliberalism) needs poor people, poor people cut off from public services and left to fend for themselves."[444]*

Aware of the dangers, the Federal Reserve still permitted such operations to spread. The bank knew about stock market volatility that drove many companies like AIG to engage in hedge fund speculation, exacerbating the vicious cycle. Considering the collapse of energy-trader ENRON, this was highly irregular. Not surprisingly, the government, investors, and the media quickly placed the crooked neoliberal ENRON experiment behind them, as new illegal activities continued involving banks, employees and their pensions, investors, and customers. Given that the public would absorb all the risk, jungle capitalism and corruption were not as risky for the company, as it appeared to the public.[445]

Not only through central bank intervention, as will be seen below, but governments throughout the world bailed out financial institutions and insurance companies transferring private debt on the backs of taxpayers. This was all at the expense of further slashing social welfare programs, and a sharp rise in public debt that undercut living standards and precipitate downward social mobility. As Senator Bernie Sanders noted about American-style neoliberal bailouts: "*Not one major Wall Street[5] executive went to jail for destroying our economy in 2008 as a result of their greed, recklessness, and illegal behavior. No. They didn't go to jail. They got a trillion-dollar bailout."[446]*

The central banks of the rest of the world were no more forthcoming than the US Federal Reserve. Although several European banks, among them Lloyds TSB, Deutsche Bank, and Bank of Cyprus, were involved in money laundering and insider trading, neither the European Central Bank nor individual central banks did much to

5. *https://www.rollingstone.com/t/wall-street/*

expose them. Because financial institutions globally were buying US-based issued real estate mortgages, it was inevitable that the financial crisis would have a global impact.[447]

Mario Draghi who in 2011 became European Central Bank president had worked for Goldman Sachs as VP and managing director when the company was involved in deceptively converting debt to make it appear as surplus on the books of EU governments. Involved in both Greece and Italy fudging the books to deceive EU regulators about the two countries' qualifications for euro-zone membership, Draghi left behind a trail of massive losses in derivatives. After two decades of distorting official figures, the real debtor status of Greece and Italy was far worse than it appeared officially. Enjoying a stellar reputation in business and government circles around the world, Draghi became Italy's prime Minister in 2019. Committed to all aspects of neoliberalism, three years before taking office, he declared that it was not his job or that of the ECB to regulate cryptocurrencies; a statement typical of the top EU bank regulator signaling to speculators that they were 'free to choose', to borrow the phrase from Friedman's book title in praise of neoliberalism.[448]

Goldman Sachs was also involved in Malaysia's sovereign fund 1MBD which the corrupt billionaire financier Jho Low helped to establish in 2009. Presumably for economic development, 1MBD raised $6.5 billion in bonds, diverting $4.5 billion into offshore and shell companies, some linked to Low. In a deal with US prosecutors in October 2019, Low gave up $900 million in seized assets, in exchange for leniency in the criminal case. In October 2020, the UK imposed a fine of Goldman Sachs $126 million, and the company agreed to pay $3 billion as part of a settlement for its role in the 1MBD corruption scandal.[449]

The institutionalization of corruption was neither an accident nor an enigma to regulators and law enforcement. After US-led sanctions on Russia, it became public that the US government knew a great deal of detail about the assets of Russian oligarch billionaires, thereby putting to rest the myth about the lack of information to go after financial crimes. *"A leaked FBI intelligence bulletin warned that a gap in U.S. rules aimed at fighting dirty money likely allows so-called "threat actors" to place funds with private investment firms. The FBI gave as an example of an unnamed New York-based private equity company that took in more than $100 million from a Russian business with alleged ties to organized crime. Now, this lack of insight into the $11 trillion U.S. private investment industry threatens to complicate the White House's push to punish the financial elite close to President Vladimir Putin over Russia's invasion of Ukraine. Anti-corruption groups and Treasury officials have pushed for private investments to act more like banks in rooting out money laundering. These private investments are increasingly important players in financial markets. Each year for the past decade, more money has been raised in private markets than in public markets, such as on stock exchanges, according to the Securities and Exchange Commission. Private markets now hold about half as many assets as all U.S. commercial banks, which stand at about $22.5 trillion in deposits."*[450]

Computer trading has made it possible for hundreds of billions of dollars to exchange hands daily globally. For a tiny investment, speculators were buying insurance, shorting certain stocks and government bonds, thus precipitating their decline. Risky mortgages and how they were traded led to the housing bubble. Lehman's role in subprime mortgages notwithstanding, the firm reflected a widespread international practice about how banking had evolved into a corrupt scheme under neoliberalism. Debt-packed bonds sold to investors came with the backing of the government. In 2006, the IMF warned that the world economy was headed for trouble, but the speculative trend intensified.[451]

For a small amount of investment, hedge funds were betting that AIG would decline and investors would walk away with billions in profits. Operating in 130 countries, AIG received half of its one trillion dollars in assets from the non-US market. While the US government decided that Lehman was not too big to fail, it did not arrive at the same conclusion about AIG. Hedge funds were also betting that countries with weak fiscal structures like southern and Eastern European governments unable to meet their bonded debt obligations would undergo austerity and be forced to further privatize public assets.[452]

Partly because big corporate donors and billionaires provided the funding for political campaigns, the US and other governments were reluctant to regulate hedge funds. The calamity of the AIG crisis was not a matter of "a few bad apples". Indicative of the neoliberal dogma, AIG, Goldman, and corporate apologists insisted that the government must permit the market to self-regulate because markets know best. Even more shocking for the general public paying to bail out market efficiency, neoliberal apologists expected government bailout of companies like AIG at the cost of higher public debt. The same corporate welfare neoliberals demanded cuts in social welfare programs while walking away with massive ill-gotten profits coming at taxpayers' expense.[453]

In January 2010, the Obama administration proposed tougher regulations for financial institutions investing in hedge funds. French President Nicolas Sarkozy concurred. Both Sarkozy and Obama knew that Greece's budget deficit was above 15% of GDP in 2009. The French government was facing imminent default on the 10-year bond and inability to service the debt with a potential EU-wide crisis brewing and difficult to contain.

Naturally, the neoliberal solution was not to cut corporate welfare and raise taxes on the richest 10%, but to slash social security, and social programs, and acquire higher debt. Some EU leaders agreed with Obama and Sarkozy, others hesitated to speculate how many countries were in the same situation as Greece. Short-term stock market reaction reflected the inordinate influence of hedge funds amid a brewing European-wide public debt crisis which the government bailout of private banks had created at the urging of the IMF and European Central Bank.[454]

In April 2010, the Securities and Exchange Commission and US Congress investigated Goldman Sachs for 'improperly' if not illegally manipulating the housing market. EU regulators were aware that Goldman worked with corrupt European politicians and influential investors. In addition, the EU had its banks overextended with risk loans, including in real estate. The neoliberal in the EU was not very different than in the US.[455]

In July 2010, the Dodd-Frank Act (*Emergency Economic Stabilization Act*) placed some regulatory measures back in the system to stop the sector's bleeding and restore investor confidence. However, it did not curb financialization or the long-standing neoliberal practice of corporate welfare and bailouts. Led by Goldman Sachs, which had given as much in campaign contributions to Obama as ENRON to the Bush campaign, Wall Street adamantly resisted regulation, demanding bailouts with minimal accountability for receiving public money.[456]

Partly because of the link between campaign financing and bank lobbyists dictating policy to elected officials, banking and hedge funds scandals made the Great Recession worse, leaving billions of people poorer. Not just in the US and Europe, but throughout the world, banking consolidation resulted in massive capital concentration. Ironically, "over banking" was a pretext often used to justify government and central bank support for consolidation which in essence made the financial oligopoly even more concentrated.

Because of the Great Recession, the largest five US investment banks became more influential in the international banking market. Exerting immense pressure on the entire financial sector, monetary, fiscal, and trade and labor policy, US banking giants' gains were at the expense of European banks which retreated, opening the way for US financial firms to dominate EU investment projects. Because of US banking international market share, combined with the weakening of most economies relative to the US, more than $23 trillion poured into the US between 2008 and 2016. This is in sharp contrast to $14 trillion for the 20 years before the Great Recession.[457]

Although the Great Recession exposed the neoliberal model as unproductive, socially parasitic, and politically antidemocratic, many critics were predicting its demise. Under different political approaches, governments reaffirmed their commitment to neoliberalism. *"Many governments, industries, and households are under debt bondage, with the result that societies are being drained of valuable resources to support and sustain the financialization of the economy. ...Everyone could strike it rich simply by borrowing or making highly speculative investments, but this in itself becomes a serious problem when financial scams and economic policy-making join hands to dictate the rules of the game and the structure and operation of any given economic environment. ...Yet the implications of this crisis continue to elude us, largely because many people are in the grip of neoliberal orthodoxy and refuse to acknowledge the need for large-scale economic, social, and political change."*[458]

Even after receiving roughly one-third of GDP in subsidies and loans, Wall Street firms demanded strict adherence to the neoliberal model. This meant minimal investment restrictions and corporate accountability. Adamantly against Dodd-Frank and the Wall Street Reform and Consumer Protection Act of July 2010, stock market professionals and investors did not want any mechanisms inhibiting the sort of speculation that led to the Great Recession. Although Dodd-Frank only reinstated state support regulations that Democrats and Republicans had dismantled, the same advocates demanding government bailouts insisted that even minimal regulation was a burden on capital.[459]

Market apologists contended that the "bank bail-in" system implemented in many countries around the world where banks used funds from depositors, bondholders, and unsecured creditors, combined with stress test capital reserves were sufficient to restructure internally and stay solvent for the duration. In essence, these mechanisms permitted banks to convert debt into equity thereby passing capital requirements; a ploy that had contributed to the crisis of 2008. Emphasizing the "growth imperative", a euphemism for guaranteed profit over other goals such as market equilibrium, social stability, ethical business practices, sustainable development, and environmental justice, neoliberal apologists maintained that any form of government regulation asphyxiates innovation and economic growth linked to a healthy economy and creating new jobs.[460]

Accompanied by the promise of future earnings, the artificially glittering quarterly reports were enough to keep institutional and retail investors coming back. Because speculative capital did not necessarily reflect productive capacity to support the investment built on a paper pyramid, it was only a matter of time before companies' actual values caught up with the hyper-inflated paper values. At the heart of the crisis was the economy's financialization which facilitated Ponzi schemes like that of Bernard L. Madoff Securities, the largest in history. The combination of media "pumping" highly speculative securities, insider trading, and capital accumulation via debt expansion, minimal regulatory oversight was the establishment's expected norm. Ponzi schemes were more widespread than Madoff, precipitating a massive global banking crisis that would then turn into austerity with governments requiring taxpayers to bail out financialization failures.[461]

With government approval often accompanied by corporate subsidies, European and US financial institutions, investment, and insurance firms underwent consolidation reflecting further concentration of wealth. In September 2008, British PM, Gordon Brown, approved Lloyds TSB's purchase of banking and insurance giant HBOS also the largest mortgage lender. The question was whether the prime minister's office knew that on 13 February 2009, Lloyds would request a bailout after it had purchased $17 billion 'bad debt' from HBOS, thus intentionally placing its corporate debt burden on the taxpayer's shoulders. There were similar cases in the US where the Bush administration urged banking consolidation to save financial institutions from state control while the government was taking all the risk. Similar scenarios played out in many countries around the world.[462]

In February 2019, the Australian government concluded that the financial sector was corrupt at every level. Involving everything from retail banking to the broader market, banking benefited from regulators who turned a blind eye to or were part of systemic corruption. In most countries, the lines between legal and illegal activities have become blurred. The political and corporate elites knew that the government would not take action against individuals and at best impose symbolic fines on the firm. Despite the Great Recession's manifesting a crisis in capitalism, in 2018, Trump loosened regulatory mechanisms about liquidity. This measure opened the floodgates for the 2022-2023 crisis in regional banks investing in cryptocurrency, risky startups, and real estate, among other speculative ventures. US banks suffered $620 billion in losses on securities out of $2.2 trillion total, or roughly one-third of capital. Technically insolvent, most banks were staying operational knowing the government was behind them.[463]

Although various EU government officials and bank experts insist that there is no possibility of contagion as there was in 2008 because EU regulation is stricter than in the US, the collapse of Credit Suisse coinciding with the US regional banking crisis was alarming. Another part of the world that was on shaky grounds was Japan, according to Robert Kiyosaki who cautioned the central bank's possible collapse. *"The biggest bank that's going to go down is Bank of Japan. Because the Bank of Japan carried the interest rates at, what, zero or whatever they did, [and] financed the derivatives markets. And the derivatives market, as Warren Buffett said about derivatives, they're weapons of mass financial destruction and the derivatives market in the world today, financed by the Bank of Japan, is a quadrillion [dollars]." "The Bank of Japan has been financing derivatives. Derivatives are a quadrillion [dollars]. That's 1000 trillion. So, we haven't seen the crash coming yet."[464]*

No matter the level of corruption and legalized criminal acts against investors, bank depositors, and society, banks, and the corporate sector have been capitalism's sacred temples beyond reproach. Nor is the issue apportioning blame to big capital which finances political campaigns and the merging of the political class with the financial elite. The political class, which overlaps with the socioeconomic class frames public policy around finance capitalism's perimeters, and sets legal consequences and punishment for illegal activities of white-collar crime reaching a nadir under neoliberalism. Not a few 'bad apples' from individual banks to regulatory agencies, or elected officials, but the neoliberal social contract is at the heart of the problem.[465]

Neoliberal 'Solution' to the Great Recession

Precipitated by hedge fund-traded derivatives in the mortgage market, and a popular backlash against neoliberal globalization and bloc trading, the nexus of the stock market and government stretched from the trans-Atlantic to the trans-Pacific. Although the Great Recession exposed neoliberalism's myths, contradictions, and illegal activities inherent in the political economy, both the business and political elites refused to alter the status quo and the model's core principles.[466]

Not on the radar screen of mainstream politicians, business people, media, and scholars celebrating neoliberalism's triumph after the fall of Communism, the Great Recession was telegraphing crisis signals as early as the dotcom bubble boiling over in the late 1990s. Falling into the class warfare trap, the political and business elites accepted as dogma optimizing capital accumulation identified with the national interest. Opposing regulatory and social safety guards, singularly focus on maximizing profit and celebrating the goal no matter the side effects on society.[467]

Because the economic crisis caused social and political instability, in 2008, a segment of the social elite and Democrat neoliberals viewed Obama's election as necessary to save the political economy by de-radicalizing disgruntled workers and the middle class while pursuing neoliberalism. Promising to end military occupation in Afghanistan, and respect human rights abroad and civil rights at home, Obama appeased anti-war liberals and world public opinion that had turned decidedly against the US because of the military occupation of Afghanistan and Iraq. Rather convincingly for a large segment of the population at home and globally, Obama employed peace and social justice rhetoric, leaving the impression that he would be less committed to military Keynesianism and corporate welfare, and more to peace and social welfare than his predecessor.[468]

As America's first black president, Obama represented symbolic hope for all marginalized masses at home and all opposed to racism and militarism. His cabinet appointments and policies proved that he was as committed to Wall Street and the military-industrial complex as Bill Clinton and George Bush. No different than any pluralist European neoliberals, especially Tony Blair who employed liberal and even leftist rhetoric to mobilize popular support, Obama fell in line with mainstream neoliberalism and militarism serving Wall Street faithfully while keeping the social justice rhetoric to placate the masses.[469]

Distorting diversity as a public principle to fit into the neoliberal mold by eliminating class from race and ethnicity, Obama advocated transcending racism within the confines of the entrepreneurial system. Pursuing such a course, he implicitly opposed class solidarity and precluded the majority of the marginalized population from escaping marginalization. The image projected was to offer the minority bourgeois community hope as a substitute for social justice for all. By appointing Timothy Geithner Treasury Secretary, and Lewis A. Sachs as special advisor, Obama signaled that neoliberal orthodoxy would remain as it had been since Reagan. A key individual in Tricadia Inc., Lewis A. Sachs supervised the company's operations in synthetic collateralized debt obligations sold to investors while the company bet against the products they sold.[470]

In an article analyzing the Obama administration's policies, Lionel D. Lyle stresses that the evidence of public policy points to the reality of a president who projected an inclusivist populist image but practiced neoliberalism exactly as all presidents from Reagan to George W. Bush. Loyal to Wall Street, Obama appointed Larry Summers, the quintessential Wall Street neoliberal, as chief White House Advisor. Nevertheless, he never let up on the hollow rhetoric about minorities, the poor, the rights of women, and the working people. Projecting emotional empathy, at least showing symbolic support and good intentions, actually worked for him more so than previous presidents.[471]

In the presidential race of 2008, Goldman Sachs, J. P. Morgan, Microsoft, and Citigroup were among the top contributors to Obama. Indicative of market hegemony over the state, in the case of Citizens United v. the Federal Elections Commission of January 2010, the US Supreme Court ruled that limiting corporate campaign contributions constitutes an infringement on free speech, thus overturning the Bipartisan Campaign Reform Act of 2002.

"The 10 most generous donors and their spouses ***injected $1.2 billion into federal elections*** *over the last decade. That tiny group of major donors accounted for 7 percent of total election-related giving in 2018, up from less than 1 percent a decade prior. The balance of political power shifted from political parties to outside groups that could spend unlimited sums to bolster their preferred candidates. Election-related spending from non-party independent groups* ***ballooned to $4.5 billion*** *over the decade. It totaled just $750 million over the two decades prior."*[472]

In a post–Citizens United political climate, corporate money had constitutional cover to assume even greater influence in public policy and suppress popular opposition to corruption stemming from large enterprises and wealthy individuals circumventing the law. At the time, the revelations of ties between rightwing Supreme Court justices and billionaires were not known, as they only became public in 2023. Even after the economic crimes associated with the crisis of 2007-2008, the Supreme Court's ruling signaled that the judicial branch would side with capital against society. Ignoring the legislative branch's faint attempts to rationalize capitalism, the Supreme Court placed the stamp of approval on neoliberalism as the new legal norm, dealing a terminal blow to social welfare ideology.[473]

By embracing the neo-classical dogma's ubiquitous application in society, the US Supreme Court was simultaneously endorsing the far-right wing dogma of *Citizens United.* Sending a clear message to Wall Street and elected officials that market hegemony, not liberal democracy, was at the heart of the social contract, the Supreme Court rejected the imperative of liberal democracy and social justice as constitutional law's foundation.

Among other decisions in the first two decades of the 21st century, the ruling of 2010 reflected the constitutional endorsement of deregulation, privatization of public assets, and corporate welfare with all the scandals that led to the Great Recession. The Supreme Court's decision to put the stamp of legitimacy on autocratization coincided with the GOP's move to the far right. This combination signaled to investors that capital transcends all other constitutional protections.[474]

Predisposed to govern as a pluralist neoliberal, employing Keynesian-New Deal and civil rights rhetoric, Obama undermined democracy as much as any Cold War Republican openly hostile to the Keynesian social welfare state while embracing parasitic military Keynesianism. Because inequality rose sharply under Obama whose policies never matched the rhetoric, he left a mixed legacy of relief that finally America elected a black president, but also unfulfilled hope and cynicism amid broken promises for upward social mobility and democracy. Allowing Larry Summers and Timothy Geithner to implement neoliberal policies on Wall Street's behalf, Obama missed the opportunity of the weakened private sector to trim the corporate welfare state and to end class warfare amid neoliberalism's global crisis.[475]

By reinforcing military Keynesianism, accompanied by direct and/or covert foreign intervention operations in the Middle East, Africa, Ukraine, and the trans-Caucasus region, while staying within the neoliberal mold of government subsidies to corporations and subcontracting public services, Obama was as mainstream as Bush in domestic and foreign affairs alike. Along with rising defense costs, corporate subsidies, tax evasion and avoidance by the wealthiest citizens and corporations accounted for the rising public debt. Obama went along with the Republicans and Wall Street who used debt as the pretext to continue slashing the welfare state and keep wages stagnant.[476]

Besides permitting corporations to use the state as a vehicle to buttress big capital through tax cuts, and corporate subsidies, Obama pursued an accommodating monetary policy, outsourcing federal public services to the private sector, and using geopolitical leverage to accomplish geoeconomic goals. Not that European governments did anything different, despite maintaining a more rigorous regulatory and social welfare system. In some cases, European governments took a stake in the bailed-out companies. Nevertheless, they did not pursue the Chinese model of the state's role in central economic planning. As the US economy improved owing to government support with the Federal Reserve rates keeping close to zero, banks and corporations pressured Obama and Congress to loosen government regulation on business, reverting to the same policies that led to the Great Recession.[477]

In *"From Neoliberalism to New Finance Capital,"* Stephen Maher and Scoot Aquanno point out that far from addressing the core issue at the root of the Great Recession, the US under Bush and Obama encouraged riskier assets, despite modestly regulating the banking industry and setting mechanisms to prevent another subprime-rate crisis. Working closely with large Wall Street firms like J. P. Morgan, Blackrock, and Vanguard, among others, the Obama administration permitted easier fusion of financial and industrial capital, essentially allowing the financialization of the economy to continue. As a result, the influential inter-sector corporate governance gained new strength under capitalism, while the state became more susceptible to Wall Street's demands for capital concentration. These measures, among Trump-era regional bank deregulation and Biden's refusal to reverse the course, resulted in the regional banking crisis of late 2022-early 2023.[478]

With the judicial branch of government solidly on the side of Wall Street, neoliberalism was far from dead, in contrast to some analysts' predictions after 2008. Far from learning from Madoff's Ponzi scheme, from 2008 to 2018, there were 811 such schemes involving $58 billion. *"To put that number in comparison, the $58 billion involved in those Ponzi schemes is just shy of Costa Rica's 2018 gross domestic product. These figures only account for Ponzi schemes in the United States - a country with one of the most aggressive and proactive regulatory frameworks - and thus the worldwide total is unfortunately most likely a multiple of this number."*[479]

Early in autumn 2008, many European politicians, business people, and pundits dismissed the Great Recession as an aberration confined to America's shores. This was partly a PR strategy to avoid public panic because European banks were heavily invested in US mortgage-backed securities, including toxic subprime products sold in the secondary market. In addition, banks had invested in housing, especially in the UK, Ireland, and across southern Europe, especially Spain.

As responsible for the transatlantic housing bubble as US financial institutions, European banks assumed that the entire Eurozone carried uniform risk, heavier for the southern and eastern European periphery than the northwest metropolis. Shifting from interdependence to the patron-client integration model, Germany, and France reduced the EU periphery's role to a relationship similar to US-Latin America. Countries with higher GDP and substantial northwest EU investment, like Spain and Ireland, enjoyed more influence than Greece, Portugal, and Bulgaria.[480]

When the Bush administration and the Federal Reserve Bank proposed a coordinated international bank bailout plan in early September 2008, European governments dismissed the idea. Within days, capitalist contagion spread from New York to the rest of the world, hitting some countries worse than others. Rumors of panic about the banks compelled the UK and Germany initially, with all others quickly following, to bail out the banks by offering guarantees. It was all in the name of saving the economy and jobs, rather than bailing out large firms.[481]

By the end of September 2008, it became apparent after the first signs of the US stock market meltdown that the epicenter of the Great Recession was the transatlantic neoliberal core. Fearing Asian contagion, China was scrambling to stop the bleeding, especially in the rapidly growing manufacturing, raw materials, and transportation sectors linked to the world economy. While Japan was facing a similar problem as the US and EU, China, as the rising economic power, enjoyed a large current account surplus which it used to maintain employment stability through heavy government stimulus.

To cushion the sluggish export sector, in December 2008, Beijing launched export-import trade in renminbi RMB in several provinces, including ASEAN[1] countries, Hong Kong, and Macau. For a brief period, Hong Kong banks appeared unsteady, made worse by currency speculation in Asian markets, including in Thailand. This quickly spread to Russia and Latin America. As Chinese factory production slowed, Beijing was weighing its options about the transatlantic turmoil, realizing the ripple effect on its economy and currency instability. By February 2009, China's exports fell 25.7%, accompanied by a comparable decline in imports, resulting in rising unemployment. [482]

As one of the most rapidly industrialized nations in history, China was facing a steep decline unless the government expanded domestic consumption and used the enormous trade surplus reserves to strengthen the world's core economies and the dollar as the preeminent reserve currency. After promulgating a domestic stimulus plan of $586 billion in November 2008, President Hu Jintao announced at the Asia-Pacific Economic Cooperation (APEC) summit that China was stimulating internal demand to raise imports with the explicit goal of stabilizing the transatlantic economies. This was necessary for economic, social, and political considerations both at home and to prevent even greater international trade collapse.[483]

To strengthen the dollar and stabilize US-China trade relations, China purchased more US Treasury bonds. Fearing China's inordinate economic influence in the US economy, some American politicians adamantly opposed selling Treasury bonds to the Chinese government, but there were no other buyers. Beyond a long-standing interest in US-China trade, Beijing was as aware as the US immediately after WWII, that its economy would fall into recession unless it helped its European trading partners.

---

1. https://en.wikipedia.org/wiki/Association_of_Southeast_Asian_Nations

A trading partner with 120 countries and more than 38,000 foreign companies, China's role became more significant because the Great Recession was taking its toll on the transatlantic countries and dragging down the world economy. Despite heavy state intervention to save the collapsing private sector, the APEC summit focused on neoliberal goals of free trade, privatization, and the state as a vehicle to strengthen business, not on labor suffering the brunt of the recession's effects.[484]

Operating under a mixed economic policy intended to maintain a strong state structure and regulated private sector, China had no choice but to minimize the damage to its economy by stabilizing the world economy. The US had played a similar role after WWII, but it was using geopolitics owing to the Cold War to line up client states behind it. Even before the crisis of 2008, Chinese money kept afloat Fannie Mae and Freddie Mac, the government-backed mortgage companies that bought mortgages from lenders and often packaged them into mortgage-back securities. After the crash of 2008, the China Investment Corporation (CIC) and the sovereign wealth fund with $2 trillion in holdings, invested in several foreign financial firms and foreign government bonds to stabilize currencies. As the US government approved a $15 billion bailout gift to automakers, the CIC was prepared to contain the damage of the transatlantic crisis's global impact regardless of Western neoliberal orthodoxy amid the exigencies of the crisis.[485]

The transatlantic core countries relied on China to stabilize their economies by keeping trade steady. This reality notwithstanding, Western politicians and neoliberal apologists contended that China's exchange surplus utilized to stabilize transatlantic countries existed because the terms of trade favored China at the expense of the world, especially given China's World Trade Organization (WTO) designation as a 'developing' instead of a developed economy. Unequal exchange on a world scale was not China vs. core nations and their satellites, as it was multinational corporations prevailing in exploiting the working class from core to periphery, with China continuing to play the intermediary role in global capitalism.[486]

After China joined the WTO in December 2001, it abided by existing terms of trade which historically favored the Trans-Atlantic core at the expense of the Global South. The US consistently criticized China's mercantilist policies that clash with neoliberalism, whereas Beijing insisted that it always complied with WTO and international trade agreements. Considering that multinational firms operating in China re-exported products and services globally, Chinese development came as a result of building its own capital goods and secondary sector partly by relying on foreign technology transfer as part of the investment agreement. China's unequal and exploitative economic relations with Africa, Latin America, the Middle East, Eastern Europe, and most of Asia, benefited transnational corporations along with Chinese firms in which the state had a stake.[487]

Unlike the neoliberal model resting heavily on parasitic financialization which was at the core of the crisis in 2008, the Chinese development model was multi-faceted, mostly relying on massive infrastructure and capital goods development, with the manufacturing/value-added sector and simultaneous expansion of the consumer base providing the trade surplus cash. To shield itself from trans-Atlantic-based market volatility, in 2009, China struck swap agreements with major trading partners, including Hong Kong, South Korea, Brazil and Argentina, the UK, Australia, and several former Soviet republics.

Gradually, the country moved toward high tech and high finance as the domestic consumer base was expanding with a major role of the state-owned enterprises. Always under the watchful eye of the state as a partner engaged in long-term economic planning and social engineering, Beijing pursued a mixed development model, using a liberal monetary policy and aggressive fiscal policy. China suffered less than the Western core during the recession and was able to lift trade partners like Australia and Brazil, and the entire world economy from Great Depression-style collapse. This was because it was the fastest way to recover its development path.[488]

A wake-up call for neoliberalism, the Great Recession did not modify the teleological propaganda linked to hollow "End of History" and "waves of democracy" theories. The fall of the Berlin Wall and the Communist bloc resulted in weaker democracy and greater socioeconomic inequality, while China was rapidly proving that the Beijing Consensus better suited the needs of the capitalist world economy than the Washington Consensus. As Gary Jacobs explains, with the advent of neoliberalism, the rise of illiberal democracy was inevitable.

"Globalization, financialization, global mergers and acquisitions, shadow banking, international tax havens, the policy bias favoring energy-intensive automation, maximizing shareholder value, state capture, oligarchy, and plutocracy have fueled soaring levels of economic inequality and insecurity. More importantly, they have shaken the roots of the social consensus that is the foundation of modern liberal democracies: polarizing and destabilizing society and throwing political processes into chaos... A return to unbridled capitalism is threatening the culture of liberal values and the functioning of democratic institutions. Even mature democracies show signs of degenerating into their illiberal namesakes."[489]

Neoliberal Autocratization against the Open Society

On the 10th anniversary of the Lehman Brothers collapse several journalists and academics reflected on the legacy of the economic crisis, rising income inequality, and illiberal democracy globally. Most analysts focused narrowly on specific financial firms like Lehman, AIG, and Goldman Sachs's involvement in the subprime crisis, and the banking sector. Others examined solely the subprime domain or nuances of banking and stock market regulation. So as not to offend the establishment, few took into the political economy in its entirety. Rarely was there any analysis about how the liberal and conservative regimes were following neoliberal policies responsible for the rise of illiberal democracy and how the media and think tanks helped to promote the transformation model responsible for the crisis?[490]

Very few journalists and academics acknowledged that there was a crisis of liberal democracy linked to the neoliberal economy. Most analysts debated whether the problem was with the liberal or authoritarian model of neoliberalism, or just the regulatory mechanisms not catching the banking sector's quasi-legal or illegal activities. In the otherwise 'pious' corporate world, the theory of a few "bad apples" always serves to distract from the decadent status quo, while failing to explain the multidimensional causes and consequences of the crisis operating in an otherwise 'market efficient' model. Some maintained that the problem was mainly with non-Western authoritarian countries failing to observe Western political and neoliberal institutions. Included in this non-Western category are China and Russia integrated into the capitalist system, upsetting the apple cart because neither operates under the Western liberal model.[491]

Interestingly, both French President Macron and US President Obama warned citizens that bourgeois democracy was lapsing toward illiberalism. However, neither took responsibility for their neoliberal policies exacerbating the very crisis about which they were warning. On 10 December 2017, Barak Obama admonished Americans not to follow a Nazi path. The speech was a clear reference to President Trump and the Republican Party leading America in a far-right direction with rhetoric and policies that encouraged a 'culture war' (*kulturkampf*) struggle by varieties of right-wingers from evangelicals to neo-Nazis against traditional conservatives and liberals. A reality that a few political observers acknowledged before Trump, socioeconomic polarization at the root of political polarization was another sign of America's slope toward Third Worldism that neoliberalism hastened.

"The combination of economic disruption, cultural disruption — nothing feels solid to people — that's a recipe for people wanting to find security somewhere. And sadly, there's something in all of us that looks for simple answers when we're agitated and insecure. The narrative that America at its best has stood for, the narrative of pluralism and tolerance and democracy and rule of law, human rights and freedom of the press and freedom of religion, that narrative, I think, is the more powerful narrative. The majority of people around the world aspire to that narrative, which is the reason people still want to come here." [492]

Obama pointed to differences between the Democratic Party's brand of pluralist neoliberalism and Trump's rightwing populism. He never acknowledged what he knew to be true, namely, that both models sought the same economic goals. Differing in rhetoric and modalities, both pluralist and populist neoliberals contributed to inequality and authoritarianism. Nor did Obama ever mention that policies that he and Bill Clinton pursued drove a segment of the population into the embrace of authoritarian neoliberalism, offering the illusion of the

American Dream. Merely because of defaulting all calamities befalling society on minorities, illegal immigrants, labor unions, environmentalists, feminists, and other groups lined up behind the Democratic Party, the right painted itself into the *kulturkampf* corner where it felt comfortable historically.

Arguing that the GOP alone was solely responsible for driving the country toward authoritarianism, Obama was perpetuating a myth disproved by contemporary American political and social history. Even worse, Obama knew that he was distorting reality, considering that he hired cabinet secretaries to pursue neoliberal policies leading America deeper into inequality and autocratization. Furthermore, he was propagating the myth that there is no choice outside of the neoliberal model. As far as Obama was concerned, Democrats were the lesser of two evils, and the market was the only vehicle to transcend racism. The question for voters was the degree to which the lesser of two evils choice precipitated inequality and authoritarianism in neoliberal America.[493]

"His [Obama's] deficit-reduction commission has created "a model for austerity," and he codified preventive detention in law, [Glen] Ford (Black Agenda Report) complained. "He's expanded the theaters of war in drone wars, and he's made an unremitting assault on international law. ...What will go down as his biggest contribution to history is a kind of merging of the banks and the state, with $16 trillion being infused into these banks, into Wall Street ... and the line between Wall Street and the federal government virtually disappearing."[494]

Distancing themselves from far-right fringe groups increasingly popular in the US, Europe, and other parts of the world, mainstream political leaders who embraced the pluralist neoliberal model condemned right-wing populism's pursuit of culture war. However, there was no self-criticism about using cultural determinism as part of the class war that liberals have also pursued. In April 2018, President Macron noted that there was a civil war between the forces of democracy and authoritarianism. Five years later, in April 2023, Macron's social security and labor policy prompted mass long-term labor protests and placed the country in a state of unrest not experienced since the civil unrest of May 1968. Even worse, the police killing of an Algerian teenager prompted massive riots in late Early July 2023, manifesting a very deep divide in society.[495]

In April 2018, in a speech before the European Parliament, Macron called on the EU to resist rightwing populism. Never mentioning the structural causes of illiberal democracy's rise, he focused on liberalism as the antidote. *"There is a fascination with the illiberal and it's growing all the time. I reject this idea that is spreading in Europe that democracy would be condemned to powerlessness. In the face of authoritarianism that everywhere surrounds us, the response is not authoritarian democracy but the authority of democracy."[496]*

One year before Macron delivered the speech on illiberal democracy, some of his prominent supporters accused him of pandering to the far right by *"rolling back the freedoms of information, opinion, belief, education, association, demonstration, and protest...To allow this attack on our freedoms and rights is to install what the neo-fascist extreme right dreams of an authoritarian state where the rule of law becomes a police state..."[497]*

Macron's France is not the only country where both liberal and conservative political parties have moved to the right to undermine liberal democracy in a socio-politically polarized society subject to the transformation's global reach. After all, Macron's labor policy in general, and raising the retirement age specifically in 2023, reflects the core of the neoliberal class war. Nor can this be dismissed because workers live longer, thus, they must work longer.[498]

Although both Obama and Macron acknowledged that the tilt toward authoritarianism was a global reality, neither reflected on their respective fiscal and labor policies that led to authoritarianism. Pluralist rhetoric keeps the facade of democracy, but policies strip off the mask. In the second half of the 20th century, Western democracy did not experience revitalization under neoliberalism, but a rapid pace toward authoritarianism. This is because of liberalism's unapologetic support for neoliberalism with large enterprises determining policy.[499]

In *"The Collapse of Neoliberalism"* Ganesh Staraman maintains that from 1997 to 2012, two-thirds of all industries became more concentrated. The COVID-19 pandemic resulted in even greater concentration, leaving critics to wonder how neoliberalism was molding society. *"Leading political scientists have declared that the U.S. is no longer best characterized as a democracy or a republic but as an oligarchy—a government of the rich, by the rich, and for the rich. The neoliberal embrace of individualism and opposition to "the collective society," as Margaret Thatcher put it, also had perverse consequences for social and political life. Humans are social animals. But neoliberalism rejects both the medieval approach of having fixed social classes based on wealth and power and the modern approach of having a single, shared civic identity based on participation in a democratic community."*[500]

Accusing Trump of emboldening varieties of neo-Fascists around the globe, European liberals ignored their policies that contributed to creating the economic and social antecedents for the rise of authoritarianism. Like Obama and his fellow Democrats, European pluralists drew sharp distinctions between their version and the rightwing populist neoliberalism version rooted in xenophobia, racism, Islamophobia, and sexism, all camouflaging capitalism's class war. Neoliberal pluralists have often accused right-wing populists of undercutting global integration principles by stressing economic nationalism and social exclusion with a particular focus on migrants and minorities. Prime Minister Tony Blair and Bill Clinton pursued the institutionalization of neoliberalism while they continued to replace social welfare with corporate welfare and tax cuts for the rich that contributed to the Great Recession and illiberal democracy.[501]

Institutionalizing neoliberalism under rightwing GOP populism and Trump's "personality cult" as a rallying point, the US sent the signal to nations around the world that authoritarianism could co-exist under the democracy label. Desperate for solutions to the crisis of neoliberalism, a segment of the US population increasingly turned to authoritarianism under the illusion that it would deliver social and cultural salvation by excluding certain segments from migrant laborers to social and cultural minorities. Everything from banning books to banning and criminalizing abortion, and issues linked to neoliberal health restructuring and redistributive social policies in the US became part of the populist agenda concealing neoliberalism's destructive contradictions.[502]

"But why are reproductive rights under attack from all sides, considering that the number of abortions is constantly decreasing and is connected to social inequality? In Hungary, where the social security system does not cover any contraception, several studies by the Central Statistical Office have shown that abortion is the only affordable method of birth control for poor women, minors, and women who already have several children." Yet the Hungarian government's new family policies have secured strong electoral support, as seen in the April 3 general election. In this way, illiberal governments have taken hold of redistributive social policies, which were previously the preserve of the left."[503]

Rejecting the claim of any similarities between neoliberalism and authoritarianism, mainstream politicians, media, and analysts have applauded the weakening of the Keynesian social welfare state. Deceptive and distracting populist rhetoric aside about the state as the enemy and the market as the superhero coming to the rescue of capitalists, the neoliberal state viciously attacked even fundamental universal human rights such as women's most fundamental rights regarding reproductive rights, as well as minority rights. In the US, ethnocentrism and racism worked at both blatant and subtle levels, as the 'critical race theory' debate proved popular with the white suburbanites otherwise claiming to be pluralists.

In "*Neoliberal Fascism: Free Markets and the Restructuring of Indian Capitalism,*" Shankar Gopalakrishnan observed that Hindu nationalism has been the catalyst for rightwing neoliberalism to mobilize popular support. "*Hindutva* [a term coined by Vinayak Damodar Savarkar in 1923 to assert exclusive Hindu dominance] "*is seen as an effort by neoliberalism, or perhaps more broadly by capitalism, to divert attention from class conflict, to divide and weaken working class struggles and to deflect class-driven anxieties on to minority communities. This approach is problematic in two senses. First, it does not explain why Hindutva organizations can develop a mass base, except to the extent that they are seen to be appealing to "historical identity" or "emotive" issues. The state exists* **only** *as the expression and guarantor of a collectivity founded around a transcendent principle: The ideal state is the guarantor of the Hindu Rashtra, a "nation" that exists as an organic and harmonious unity between "Hindus."*"[504]

To achieve its goal of mobilizing popular support, conservative and rightwing political parties coopted institutionalized religion not just in India but globally. Pursuing neoliberal populist policies under a pro-Wall Street and pro-militarist political umbrella, Christian Evangelical populists served as the popular base of the conservative establishment, strengthening the corporate-welfare state structure, ironically, while decrying 'big government'. Using the state to buttress big business, Reagan and Thatcher demanded that other countries follow a similar path of switching from social welfare to corporate welfare. Using the IMF and World Bank as vehicles to promote transformation worked very well with Global South countries.[505]

As an appendage of big business, the neoliberal state was closer to Giovanni Gentile's *La Dottrina del Fascismo* than to John Locke or John Stuart Mill's liberal philosophy. By shifting risk to the public sector, neoliberalism encourages corporate irresponsibility, corruption, and even illegal activity. In more than four decades, the system has demonstrated that its 'moral order' does not lessen but reinforces fraud, inequality, and illiberalism, all practices on which the neoliberal social contract is based.[506]

Even before Reagan and Thatcher institutionalized neoliberalism while promoting the corporate-welfare-militarist-police-state, the IMF and World Bank had been advising non-Western governments to pursue the deregulation, privatization, pro-big-business, and anti-labor path. Defense and domestic security were the only sectors that the IMF and World Bank rarely mentioned in monetary stabilization or development loan negotiations. Anything related to social welfare was on the chopping block. In less developed countries, the public sector was already weak and weakened further when the US and EU expected the implementation of neoliberal policies. Neoliberal transformation's global reach aggravated socioeconomic polarization and led to illiberal democracy more in the Global South than in the G7.[507]

Gaspar Miklos Tamas, a Romanian political philosopher of the George Lukacs-inspired Budapest School, contends that the global division of labor in the neoliberal era not only resulted in wealth transfer from the bottom up, it diminished national sovereignty and citizenship, especially in less developed nations. Given the perception of erosion of national sovereignty, illiberal democracy advocates promoted nationalism and xenophobia to compensate for the perception of "national weakness" linked to sovereignty.

"The new dual sate is alive and well: Normative State for the core populations of the capitalist center, and another State of arbitrary decrees for the non-citizens who are the rest. Unlike in classical fascism, this second State is only dimly visible from the first. The radical critique protesting that liberty within the Normative State is an illusion, although understandable, is erroneous. The denial of citizenship based not on exploitation, oppression, and straightforward discrimination, but on mere exclusion and distance, is difficult to grasp because the mental habits of liberation struggle for a more just redistribution of goods and powers are not applicable. The problem is not that the Normative State is becoming more authoritarian: rather, that it belongs only to a few."[508]

In the normative state where the elites institutionally exclude the minority in the name of the majority, the media projects the illusion of sociopolitical inclusion within the autocratization structure. Neoliberal transformation categorically rejects the Enlightenment tradition of natural rights (universal, fundamental, and inalienable) which is the essence of the bourgeois social contract. With police-state and militarist characteristics, the normative state, whether in the US, Western or Eastern Europe, Latin America, Africa, or Eurasia, is swept along by historical political trends enmeshed with neoliberal policies. Referencing such a trend, in January 2018, German Chancellor Angela Merkel's Christian Democratic Union (CDU) faced the prospect of rejuvenated neo-Nazi *Alternative fur Deutschland* (AfD), as did France with Marine Le Pen, Italy under Prime Minister Giorgia Meloni, among others, including the US under the Trumpist-transformed GOP.[509]

Rooted in the history and culture of national unification from the Franco-German war in 1870-71, German far-right politics, including the rise of the AfD, was symptomatic of neoliberal transformation whose very existence influenced mainstream political parties across Europe. Euroscepticism and the influx of migrants coming from countries where the West intervened militarily and/or undermined economically, contributed to the rise of the neo-Nazis from the fringes into the mainstream, targeting liberal democracy identified with globalization and neoliberalism.[510]

In the 2010s, no political group represented Europe's far-right ideological and political trend more dogmatically than the *Patriotische Europäer gegen die Islamisierung des Abendlandes* PEGIDA, (Patriotic Europeans Against the Islamification of the West). Along with AfD, PEGIDA found a home among disgruntled nationalists looking to blame migrants and non-white, non-Christian Europeans for all calamities that befell the working class and lower middle class as a result of the neoliberal transformation within the context of the embattled EU bloc. Especially after the global crisis of 2008, anti-migrant, anti-Islamist trends spread from Western to Eastern and Southern Europe.[511]

The rise of the populist right of the Western World and the Global South alike is a reaction to globalization diluting national sovereignty on the surface, but in fact, responsible for living standards erosion for the middle class and workers. Along with a disdain for liberal democracy and the illusion that authoritarianism will yield the right formula that transcends class, cultural and anti-establishment populism have been common features in neoliberal regimes of many countries.

Although the world economy operates under the neoliberal model, sovereignty at the core entails entitlement dreams of national hegemony over areas economically, politically, and/or militarily. The concept of national sovereignty for rightwing populists in the Global South has unique characteristics rooted in the post-colonial hegemonic culture and the country's traditions and mythology of national identity linked to comprador and national bourgeoisie. Turkey under Recep Tayyip Erdoğan, (2014-), the Philippines under Rodrigo Duterte (2016-2022), and Jair Bolsonaro (2019-22), among others, representing the local elites under a clientelist state accommodating foreign capital within the Western geopolitical zone of influence, demagogued the national sovereignty issue while pursuing neoliberal policies in the name of the 'people'.[512]

Scrambling to attract foreign investment, populist and liberal governments adjusted their policies to deregulation and privatization, corporate subsidies, low taxes, and weakened trade unions, all part of the class war thematic focus. From one country to the other, the modalities of how they carried out these policies differed, but not the result. The neoliberal institutional structure and culture have been the driving force behind the rise of illiberal democracy adapting to each country's traditions and social relations. Blaming minority low-paid workers, exclusionary nationalist-populists also argued that rapid income inequality would not take place if no globalization results in companies chasing low-cost labor.[513]

Along with declining workers' living standards, the national sovereignty vs. globalization issue has allowed national capitalists and especially multinational corporations to distract the public against the background of a market-dominated state structure. The populist far-right opportunistically took advantage of the nationalist trend amid falling wages, promising the illusion of quick and easy solutions under an authoritarian regime of social exclusion. Along with weakened national sovereignty in the age of globalization, national citizenship found expression in populist rightwing groups to compensate for withering socioeconomic and political rights.[514]

Although it would be an obvious mistake to lump together a neoliberal state with the Third Reich or Mussolini's Fascist regime, there are some similarities in political, socioeconomic, and cultural trends. Distinguishing the composition and goals of the parliamentary regime vs. the Fascist one-party state, Italian Fascism's theoretician Giovanni Gentile characterized the latter as '*totalitario*'; a term which applies more closely to Germany's Third Reich, the latter with the added dimension of anti-Semitism as a core ideological component. Arguing that ideology in the Fascist totalitarian state had a ubiquitous role in every aspect of life and power over people, Gentile and Mussolini viewed the state as the catalyst to a powerful nation that subordinated all institutions and the lives of citizens to its mold and value system.

Molding socioeconomic conditions that propelled to power interwar Fascists and Nazis, capitalism's cyclical crises repeated in the early 21st century. Under neoliberalism, the cultural groundwork and economic policies created the sociopolitical climate for the rise of the German AfD and PEDIGA and France's National Rally, Austrian Freedom Party, Italy's Northern League, Hungarian Civic Alliance Fidesz – Magyar Polgári Szövetség, among others that assumed mainstream role in the mainstream. The US Republican Party evolved from a businessman's traditional state-rights, church-and-flag party into a populist party incorporating the country's far-right fringe groups. Not as crude and extreme in its overt war against minorities and workers as the Third Reich, twenty-first-century rightwing populist parties have elements of both paramilitary groups and *polizeistaat*. Labor mobility aside, neoliberal capital accumulation and class-war-based social policies approximate the harshness of the interwar totalitarian regimes.[515]

To distract the public from the cyclical crises of capitalism and its inherent conflict with democracy, neoliberalism feeds on an assault on liberal democracy as a means for the market to prevail over the state. The popular expectation that capitalism must deliver on the promise of prosperity and security necessarily clashes with appropriation built into the system which manages to conceal appropriation by projecting competitive market valuation as the salient dynamic. Needless to point out, the competitive theory of value sidelines the state's role, above all ignoring capitalism as a social system and its five-century history of appropriation.[516]

The goal is to pretend that liberal democracy is the root of the systemic crisis rather than neoliberalism which liberal democracy has served as faithfully as the rightwing since the 1980s. Conformity to the neoliberal status quo and self-censorship during the digital age of mass communications has unfolded under far greater surveillance than in the interwar and with just as great difficulty to survive outside the system. Paradoxically, the far-right uses the liberal surveillance state to argue in favor of some opaque libertarian dystopia of individual autonomy under an authoritarian regime. The pervasive drive toward neoliberal conformity and digital self-control of the selfie culture has been an integral part of the market. Socially unattached, neoliberal market-determined culture has facilitated the evolution of the illiberal democratic state.[517]

Just as banks, industrialists, and large landowners collaborated closely with dictators in the 1930s to secure the existing social order, which the crisis of capitalism destabilized, neoliberal elites pursued the same goal under different strategies. While it operates in most countries within the parliamentary framework, neoliberalism functions better under authoritarianism which promotes its goals without compromise.

Partly because the elites fear grassroots dissent finding expression in organized labor or resistance groups, a segment of the capitalist class wants to preserve the social contract's democratic façade under identity politics as a substitute for universal civil rights, human rights, and social justice. This is especially significant for the political class as a strategy of popular mobilization. In either case, economic authoritarianism as the essence of neoliberalism, or *post-fascism* as Miklos Tamas calls it, has inescapably led to political authoritarianism.[518]

Comparisons of neoliberalism and interwar Fascism are often far-fetched when the goal of comparative analysis is polemics for the sake of making a political point. A loosely defined label, 'fascism' has degenerated to the degree that rightwing populists use it against progressives to indicate pluralistic dogmatism from the left. As a means of resolving the crisis of capitalism through autocratization methods, interwar fascism and neoliberalism aim at totalitarian institutional and cultural transformation on a world scale. Fascism is not market-driven but a state-driven ideology with a strong police-state and militarist component under a political party relying on a fringe political base at its core.[519]

The celebration of the irrational proclivity in human nature, especially under neoliberalism, contributed to the rise of authoritarianism with governments tilting toward fascist strategies and policies. One of the monumental contributions to the link between the rise of the irrational and authoritarianism, Georg Lukacs (*The Destruction of Reason*, 1923) presaged the age of mass irrationality of the interwar era that made possible the rise of Fascism and Nazism.

Operating under the democratic ideological and constitutional label, American society *"achieved a dictatorship of monopoly capitalism at least as firm as that which Hitler set up with tyrannic procedures. This smoothly functioning democracy, so-called, was created by the Presidential prerogative, the Supreme Court's authority in constitutional questions, the finance monopoly over the Press, radio, etc., and electioneering costs, which successfully prevented democratic parties from springing up beside the two parties of monopoly capitalism, and lastly the use of terroristic devices (the lynching system). And this democracy could, in substance, realize everything sought by Hitler without needing to break with democracy formally. In addition, there was the incomparably broader and more solid economic basis of monopoly capitalism."*[520]

Although the Cold War-militarist era of Pax Americana laid out the prolegomena of neoliberal irrationalism about political power, Vietnam left society in a deep-seated cynical state of malaise. Harboring disdain for the enemy in the Global South and Communist East, the post-Vietnam generation grew during the odd era of heightened militarism amid Pax Americana's twilight, especially evident by the late 2010s. The combination of Pax Americana's twilight and neoliberalism's emergence left many more cynical and readily accepting of the irrational which is what the counterrevolutionary political and business elites exploited.

Despite the absence of a dictatorship bringing together a segment of the masses and nationalist elite behind a political party with a militarist and 'law-and-order' ideological orientation, the corporate state hiding behind electoral democracy's façade is an instrument of what Sheldon Wolin describes as *"inverted totalitarianism"*, managed democracy with policies not so different substantively than those of classical interwar totalitarianism. Considering the increased role of security-intelligence-surveillance agencies in a presumably open society within the limitations of the consumer-citizen framework, contemporary neoliberalism under both the pluralist liberal and populist rightwing regimes shares some common elements with classical Fascism.[521]

A few weeks after the 9/11 tragedy, Congress passed the *USA Patriot Act*, without amendments. In the name of hunting down jihadists across the world, government and tech companies collaborated to expand domestic spying operations declared illegal up to that point. In February 2022, Senate testimony revealed that the CIA and National Security Agency (NSA) were spying on citizens unrelated to terrorism. This took place with the collaboration of high-tech companies that vehemently denied their role as conduits. Once the evidence surfaced to prove that it is not only Russian and Chinese companies collaborating with the state, US corporations resorted to hollow excuses about business complying with government and respecting privacy.[522]

Not surprisingly, the US surveillance focus was on minorities, especially Black Lives Matter, environmentalists, and other progressive groups. While predictive policing, or "Total Information Awareness," targets minorities and progressives, rightwing militia groups and neo-Nazis, which the FBI considers domestic terrorists, have not had surveillance priority for government agencies. As expected, corporate America benefits from securing billions in contracts linked to the surveillance state.[523]

To the tune of billions annually, the National Security Agency (NSA), CIA, and Department of Homeland Security (DHS) subcontract products and services to private companies. Once the media began exposing the surveillance state as a constitutional violation, disparate elements from neoliberal populists to Cold War liberals and militarist neoconservatives reinvented old national security rhetoric to fit contemporary global conditions with China at the center. Implicit that constitutional protections apply selectively, national security arguments never explained in detail to delineate multi-billion contracts and over-charges permit the state to carry on above public accountability mechanisms to determine the constitutionality of its acts when it comes to NSA and CIA intercepting phones and internet of its citizens.[524]

More subtle than the interwar totalitarian model and reflecting nuances of the evolving capitalist economy, the US internationalized aspects of inverted totalitarianism. This was apparent from the neoliberal and neoconservative convergence under Reagan to Biden who relied on neoliberals for domestic policy advice and neoconservatives for foreign affairs. Defense Secretary Caspar Weinberger's references to limited nuclear war, as long as the theater of war was on European soil, camouflaged the massive transfer of social welfare funding for defense buildup at a time that such spending would force Moscow to spend more and weaken the civilian economy. Within the neoliberal model, all presidents after Reagan pursued military Keynesianism and police-state methods under various domestic and national pretexts.[525]

After the US established DHS, police departments in cities throughout the US became militarized in every respect from illegal surveillance to suppressing dissent in the name of counterterrorism. The signal to the Global South was that a quasi-police American state was democratic facing ill-defined terrorism threats similar to the legal and tactical measures that apartheid South Africa and Israel employed against popular resistance.[526]

Almost a century after Italian Fascism and German Nazism, the transition of capitalism's global structure within a shifting core from the G7 to China entailed intense global competition for market share and geoeconomic advantage. The intense competition for markets drove companies to seek greater accumulation, pushing living standards down to compete with low-wage-emerging Asian economies. With the help of IMF-style austerity policies, capitalist appropriation was deeper historically in less developed countries than in the core. Under neoliberalism, however, the same process infected the advanced countries, resulting in socioeconomic polarization and authoritarianism, just beneath the thin layer of liberal democracy's legal and political structure. [527]

Because of digital technology, society's neoliberal transformation was more organized, rapid, and ubiquitous in comparison with interwar European Fascism. This is not only because of the state structure's collaborative relationship with capital. Digital technology and mass communications networks have enabled surveillance and imposed subtle forms of indoctrination tailored to each country's culture and traditions. Everything from manipulating global currency markets to monetizing the personal data of millions of people, neoliberalism's global reach, and its ability to reproduce itself despite capitalism's crisis and popular resistance has manifested itself in various sociopolitical venues.[528]

Although the West castigates its enemies when it comes to surveillance and digital authoritarianism, the high-tech corporate sector's cooperation with the state is not as dramatically different as media analysts try to convince the public amid the new East-West confrontation. In June 2013, the media revealed that the NSA had direct access to internet giants Google, Facebook[1], Apple, and others, using them to spy on people's emails, video chats, audio, documents, connection logs, etc.

The irony behind all of this was that the internet companies and the media were propagating the myth that the internet was "democratizing" the world, that companies respected peoples' privacy, while China and Russia were guilty of digital authoritarianism. The PR campaign was taking place as society was sliding toward an illiberal path with the help of giant tech companies tracking users and some "monetizing" personal data. Meanwhile, people generally ignored the details of privacy policies, projecting the impression that users had no problem with company terms.[529]

Western liberal democracy's inability to deliver optimistic messages about the future was directly linked to neoliberal sociopolitical shifts on a world scale. The COVID-19 pandemic exposed the crisis further amid declining living standards, expensive health care, higher household debt, and dismantled social safety net. Many around the world were cynical about the social contract and the state's role to protect citizens not from foreign and domestic subversives, but from the state in the service of the privileged class. Frustrated and angry, rightwing groups and varieties of charlatans on mainstream and social media turned their frustration not on the socioeconomic elite that the represented, but on migrants, ethnic, racial, and religious minorities, women, environmentalists, and liberal and progressive groups.[530]

1. https://www.theguardian.com/technology/facebook

Chronic downward social mobility and the absence of hope for improvement left the working class and the middle class desperate for political solutions. As cyclical contracting cycles entailed greater income inequality, social polarization undermined liberal democracy which was historically predicated on a fairly healthy working class and a strong middle class. Crammed into micro-apartments, essentially a storage closet that is unfit for human habitation in cities like Tokyo, London, or New York, college graduates experience the disappointment of inequitable income distribution and realize that upward mobility is elusive, regardless of college degrees. Decrying liberal democracy and embracing authoritarianism as the panacea, right-wing populist politicians promise punitive measures against the marginalized that they define as obstacles to economic progress and the root cause of falling wages.[531]

After the stock market crashed in the autumn of 2008, the *Wall Street Journal* dreaded a retreat from neoliberal policies, when in fact only modest corrective measures became policy. Ironically, liberals and progressives reached the same conclusion, looking to Obama as the new Franklin D. Roosevelt to save society from both an economic disaster and unpopular and expensive US military adventures that only enriched a few companies and left trillions in debt payments for the taxpayer. Although America's first black president turned out to be the new Clinton instead of another FDR, the global economic crisis of 2008 drove the GOP closer to populism with the advent of the Tea Party which the billionaire Koch brothers-funded along with energy and tobacco companies. Having converted public institutions at all levels into instruments of the capitalist class, neoliberalism marginalized Keynesian progressives as commentators about what policymakers needed to do, keeping the open society theory honest.[532]

The Great Recession prompted billionaires, with the Koch brothers leading the pack, to an intense right-wing media campaign against liberal democracy. Richard Fink, an academic administrator and Charles Koch's political adviser, was instrumental in converting the GOP into a Libertarian-populist movement. Convinced that disinformation is the key to a successful political party's popular mobilization strategy, the Fink-Koch strategy was to tap into universities in every state for intellectual support on policy, combined with a tightly controlled journalism network and grassroots alliances. Castigating liberal politicians and identity politics activists as the enemy of marketplace freedom ranked among the favorite distractions from the recession's structural causes. For the continuation of the neoliberal transformation, propagating in favor of social exclusion and social division, civic and religious rightwing political groups mobilized popular support to afford legitimacy to their cause.[533]

Presenting social justice, civil rights, equity, and popular democracy as obstacles to market progress, neoliberals in the US and its Western European partners insisted that the rest of the world must emulate the liberal-neoliberal brand based on inequality and authoritarianism. According to an OECD study on social justice, all members of the international organization experienced marked deterioration. Of 41 countries for poverty prevention, the US ranked 40th. Despite the lowest rankings of any advanced country in the world, preaching freedom and democracy under Pax Americana's neoliberal model never stopped.

"Freedom from poverty features as the first dimension in our index because it is such an essential component for agency and positive life outcomes. Since 2009, the US has continued to score scandalously poorly on poverty prevention (score: 2.44), ranking last in our current edition. "In recent years, there has been persistent poverty along with exceptionally large income gains for the top 1% and especially the top 0.1% of the income scale." The current overall population share at risk of poverty, 17.8% (rank: 40), has barely shifted over the past ten years. This lack of improvement is paralleled in two population groups. A similar share of children and youth (under 18) risk poverty today as 10 years ago: 21.2%

(rank: 37), "with 1.3 million children homeless." The share of seniors at risk of poverty has increased from 20.6% to 23.1% (rank: 36). With a rank of 37th and the worst score of the last 10 years (4.37), the US also fails miserably at counting the interests of both older and younger generations in public policies."[534]

Contrary to a great deal of speculation, de-legitimizing liberal democracy has not been the symptom of the cult of personality from the Thatcher-Reagan decade to Trump and Boris Johnson. Nor is the entire matter as simple as blaming media empires of right-wing billionaires like Rupert Murdock and Silvio Berlusconi. Corporate liberal media has always employed an equally effective indoctrination methodology to promote the same neoliberal goals, deradicalizing progressives by co-opting them as supporters of the social contract. As analyzed in another chapter, rightwing and liberal media empires have played a catalytic role in the class war and rising inequality on a world scale.[535]

Because the issue is structural, it is deeper than the far-right political class producing intellectually limited and emotionally unstable mendacious business-politics hustlers like Trump and Bolsonaro to distract from the continued downward living standards slope. Beyond the damage to the economy, there is a wider impact on society, as Israel's case demonstrates. Using the Palestinian Question to promote neoliberalism and illiberal democracy, Israel's Benjamin Netanyahu (King Bibi) repeatedly proved his commitment to authoritarianism. After his fifth election in November 2022, he tried to reform the judicial system which would entail openly proving his disdain for democracy and resolve to cover up the ongoing criminal trial for alleged fraud, bribery, and breach of trust.[536]

Philippines President Rodrigo Duterte (2018-2022), an authoritarian neoliberal, used crime as an issue to rally support, while Turkey's Erdogan and India's Modi used religion, to mention just three elected heads of state at the forefront of illiberal democracy under neoliberalism. Infamous for cultivating a personality cult, these leaders fall in the same broader category of neoliberal authoritarianism resorting to culture wars by promoting class warfare, and projecting an anti-establishment populist image when they are nothing more than counterrevolutionaries. [537]

Because neoliberalism dogmatically adheres to the principle and practice of market hegemony over the state as a precondition to progress synonymous with capital accumulation, there has been a merging of the political class with the capitalist class. From finance to law and lobbying, big capital representatives have been instrumental in drafting legislation impacting their industries and enjoying a preponderating voice in public policy. Inordinate corporate presence in public policy has resulted in eight men on earth owning as much wealth as the bottom half of the entire population, the neoliberal state has precipitated illiberalism because the state marginalizes voices opposing the neoliberal model.[538]

Not only does big capital have the dominant voice because it finances campaigns, but it also has a rôle in who presides over government agencies. This was key to everything from regulatory functions to awarding contracts to corporations and consulting firms. According to a UN report, neoliberal outsourcing of public services to private companies on a world scale has been detrimental in everything from water quality and price to education. *"The world has been fundamentally reordered by widespread neoliberal economics that has privatized basic public goods — social protections, education, pensions, and criminal justice among them — with often disastrous impacts on the human rights of the extremely poor, experts told the Third Committee (Social, Humanitarian, and Cultural) today." [539]*

Whether the Department (Ministry) of Labor, Commerce, Environmental Protection Agency, Labor, or Education, the goal has been to undermine the agency by removing obstacles to transferring public funds to businesses, outsourcing, privatizing agency functions, and hiring parasitic consultants to justify neoliberal policies. In the UK, the US, and India, outsourcing and privatization of public interest has been an integral part of the neoliberal model which has reshaped the corporate state to reflect market values and goals.

Transforming government agencies' entire institutional structure to fit the neoliberal mold has meant a shift in the definition of what constitutes legitimate public interest. Neoliberal hostility toward the public sector in its totality, especially those against pluralist liberal democracy, is directly linked to the populist emphasis on the irrational, anti-institutional, anti-labor, and anti-public welfare as the guiding force for public policy. Crossing the line by using the legal system to sue private schools for "indoctrinating" students with anti-racist curricula, parents and law firms in the US have been sending a signal that dancing on the fence of fascism is more acceptable than inclusive populism. Going a step further, the Mississippi House of Representatives essentially reintroduced Jim Crow enforcing racial segregation in Jackson, Mississippi where 83% of the population is black.[540]

A distraction from class warfare and income redistribution from the bottom up, exclusionary populism keeps the majority docile. Just as the government has been outsourcing public services to the private sector to buttress capital accumulation, the same process extends to citizens. Luca Mavelli's characterization of the *"neoliberal economization [which] turns states and individuals into entrepreneurial actors that attempt to maximize their value, not just in economic and financial but also in moral and emotional terms,"* captures the essence of the structure of the new state containing the seeds of illiberal democracy. An entrepreneurial agent on behalf of capital with historical roots, the neoliberal state does not operate on conventional notions of citizenship based on a liberal democratic social contract.[541]

Undermining the class-collaboration ethos in the socio-politically inclusive Keynesian social welfare state, as a means of extricating capitalism from systemic crisis, neoliberalism dilutes the mechanisms to assuage labor and the middle class, leaving only rightwing populist and liberal identity politics to distract and mobilize the masses behind the transformation model. Keynesianism was built on the model of military Keynesianism, reorienting labor to strengthen capitalism in crisis. Neoliberalism 'piggy-backs' on the Keynesian paradigm reversing its social welfare component to serve capital by taking into account the state's role as an instrument of capital accumulation based on the assumption of classical formulation theory of low wages as a means of reducing unemployment.[542]

Delegitimizing, indeed vilifying, the welfare state and displacing the social contract predicated on the theoretical principle of society's collective welfare has meant that the citizens can no longer rely on the state for social solutions. In everything from the economy to public health and public utilities, and from the environment to education, the neoliberal model calls for private sector reliance. In every domain, including running prisons and subcontracting defense and intelligence functions, the state takes a back seat to the private sector. more so than at any time since the late 19th century. Beyond a vehicle for society's technocratic-expertise solutions justified in the name of "market efficiency" and techno-rationality of hierarchical and exclusionary neoliberal capitalism, the model on larger policy issues impacts class relations to international relations where the state yields to capitalist appropriation interests.[543]

The media and mainstream institutions promote corporations and billionaires as society's saviors. This is regardless of their record of corruption and practices destructive to society, as was the case during the S & L crisis from the late 1980s to the early 2020s; from the dot.com bubble of the late 1990s, through the Great Recession, the pandemic, and the stagflation crisis of 2022-2023. Even while enduring climate change with immediate and long-term consequences for all species, the corporate media, the business elite, and corporate-sponsored pundits blame public policy, as though such policy is divorced from the interests of capital.

"From the vantage point of the ruling elites, it is even desirable that the population gets worked up about the greed of bankers, lashes out at the lying and hypocrisy of politicians, the intellectual corruption of journalists, or the cruelty or sadism of torture experts – that is, characteristics of persons who are products of deep-seated conditions and qualifications – and lose sight of the structural and institutional causes and consequently the real centers of power! Therefore, our urgent task is gaining insights into these structural conditions."[544]

Historically, rising inequality and political polarization paved the way for populist politicians to mobilize marginalized groups, merging the far right with the conservative mainstream. Under neoliberalism, globalization strengthened populists' skepticism of international organizations, trade/monetary blocks, and multilateralism especially as it pertained to climate change policies and goals, and conformity to the liberal institutional order. Swept away by polemical rhetoric demonizing marginalized, liberal, and progressive social groups, the popular base of the authoritarian right accepts vague promises that authoritarianism would deliver utopia by repressing minority communities. Claiming to deliver society from liberal pluralist multicultural decadence, the result of apocalyptic populism has permitted mainstream conservative elites publicly or privately to support the right as a means of perpetuating neoliberal transformation's global reach.[545]

Closely tied to identity politics and distracting from class war, there has been a proliferation of NGOs and civil society organizations during the neoliberal phase of capitalism. Although many NGOs project a progressive façade, often targets of rightwing populism, it is a myth that they do not serve the same neoliberal agenda as the right. Backed either by corporations or government promoting market-based individualism, liberal NGOs have contributed to the diffusion of the neoliberal transformation's global reach. It is hardly a coincidence that NGO proliferation took place during the institutionalization of neoliberal globalization, especially popular in the trans-Atlantic core.[546]

In the age of the internet and social media, neoliberal cultural hegemony promotes ahistorical and atomistic worldviews, venerating the billionaire oligarchy as society's heroes. At the same time, the culture of authoritarian neoliberalism worsens conditions for working people, the homeless, migrants, refugees, and marginalized groups. As it evolved from the 1980s to the present, the neoliberal culture created the 'hero-businessman'. Going a step beyond Joseph Schumpeter's concept of the 19th-century entrepreneur, (*Theorie der wirtschaftlichen Entwicklung. Eine Untersuchung über Unternehmergewinn, Kapital, Kredit, Zins und den Konjunkturzyklus,* 1911), the 21st neoliberal culture celebrates the businessman who takes advantage of the corporate welfare laws, tax avoidance and evasion, privatization of public utilities, deregulation impacting the environment and worker safety, and deregulated merger-and-acquisitions with the state subsidizing the merger, invariably linked to corporate political contributions. One of the most stealthy corporate welfare aspects has been the state appearing to be subsidizing the consumer in everything from energy-efficient cars to air conditioners and energy windows when in fact this is but a corporate subsidiary.[547]

The political and popular culture of the Great Depression and WWII vilified greedy businessmen and praised honest hard-working people, always within the political and economic institutional structure. Those elevated to heroic status in the neoliberal era would be social villains in novels and motion pictures during the Great Depression. The neoliberal social contract altered not just society's value system, but its political, legal, and legislative system to permit what were once society's criminals elevated into the hero-businessman cult around which charity organizations and media empires were built as protective castles shielding society's villains.

From Eastern Europe to the US, and from Latin America to the Indian subcontinent, the homogenized cult of the hero-businessman-oligarch is deeply inculcated in the mass consciousness. Rhetorically, governments claimed to support social programs and human development. The combination of the hegemonic culture's conditioning of the middle class and workers into an obsequious predisposition to accept neoliberal institutions and social hierarchy as "natural" has been very effective. Although illiberal politics assumes the historical traits of traditionalism, sociocultural conservatism, and nationalism in different countries – India, the US, Brazil, Turkey, Hungary, and France - the common denominator of social exclusion is essentially the same no matter how the ruling party presents the issue.[548]

Ideologically, liberal pluralists substitute class politics with identity politics, thereby affording legitimacy and normalizing the latter as a core theme in public discourse. To avoid social exclusion, many voters embrace a narrowly defined role of living in the "lesser-of-two-evils" universe. Class-based neoliberal inclusion of gender, race, ethnicity, religion, and lifestyle, all transcending class, succumbs to targeted expectations while surrendering hope for social justice in the neoliberal 'risk society'.[549]

Identity politics affords liberal pluralist governments the protective cloak to pursue class warfare in the form of privatization, deregulation, corporate welfare, bank/corporate bailouts, government agencies outsourcing work to corporations, and lower taxes for the wealthy along with monetary policy that has led toward monopoly capitalism. All along, the pluralist government insists that it represents the middle and working class through the framework of identity issues. This has been an effective means of co-opting social groups that would otherwise oppose neoliberalism in a class-based political context.

Despite the establishment's "feel good" inclusionary, or "hate-based" exclusionary identity politics, from the 1980s to the present, people gradually realized that their material lives did not improve. From 1978 to 2022, college tuition has risen 1,120%, medical care 601%, and housing 380%, while the average CEO pay reached 937% as minimum wage fell 5.5%. Cynicism, alienation, and de-politization replaced enthusiasm for social justice among some of the more progressive identity politics groups. Inadvertently, the rise in de-politization has benefited those favoring authoritarianism.[550]

Neoliberal culture has indoctrinated a segment of the public to accept the backsliding of liberal democracy, resulting in social exclusion and the permanent war on the working class. In all institutional and cultural facets, from politics and media to education and social organizations, neoliberal hegemony makes democracy's backsliding difficult to stop because it is normalized. This is the ideal recipe for diverting middle-class and working-class mass anxiety and anger directed away from inherent structural problems that neoliberalism creates, deflecting them onto the marginalized population and workers. Once the state implements a legal framework of regimentation of the socially marginalized groups, and once it is already institutionalized and at the core of cultural hegemony, there is the question of where it draws the line. How far it carries out policies of democratic backsliding to complete the circle toward a form of 21st-century totalitarianism under the thin veil of liberal democracy appears less of an enigma as the neoliberal model reveals its societal impact.[551]

CHAPTER IV:

Structural Exploitation under Neoliberalism

A Theoretical Introduction

A relationship of social dominance by elites over the rest of society subordinated for economic and political control through institutional and cultural determinants constitutes structural exploitation. Rationalizations for institutional exploitation include everything from patriotic loyalty to national security eliminating foreign and domestic impediments to economic progress, and pursuing ideal economic and social policies based on nature's competitive forces that exist in the animal kingdom and reflect human nature.[552]

From ancient Babylon when King Hammurabi codified the first laws in 1780 B.C. to Solon "the lawgiver" in 6th century BC Athens, and from the Napoleonic Code (1804) to the neoliberal era, the state can be the catalyst to social harmony and social fairness and justice built into traditions and social relations. In reality, however, the social contract, upon which the constitutional systems are based, legalizes the privileged class and gender-based hierarchical structure thereby normalizing it.

Expecting the faithful to believe that the hierarchical social structure was the will of God, the Medieval clergy and nobility kept serfs and peasants docile and fatalistic. In the ideal social contract, the theoretical assumption is one of a social structure based on fairness and justice for all aiming at common goals for society's welfare and progress. Philosophical principles, good intentions, and image projection notwithstanding, historical evidence clearly illustrates that equality and social justice are inexorably linked to social stratification symptomatic of the social contract.[553]

The Fourth Industrial Revolution's biotechnology, nanotechnology, quantum computing, and artificial intelligence theoretically serve all mankind rather than exploit more thoroughly and marginalize a large segment of humanity divided by class, race, and gender, among other exclusionist traits. The persistence of structural inequality under globalization challenges those with a social conscience and ethics rooted in humanist values to question what constitutes social progress and public interest. Furthermore, there is the question of whether the Fourth Industrial Revolution is simply another layer on top of the previous three operating under similar structural dynamics of social inequality, marginalization, and varieties of autocratization regimes from autocracy to liberal democracy.[554]

Based on social relations of production between commodity producers and labor exploitation through surplus value, structural exploitation is evident in every sector from farming to child labor, and from precarious work to women's sweatshops paying subsistence wages and exposing workers to unsafe conditions. Through the International Labor Organization and World Health Organization, the UN has issued several reports about the most egregious cases of labor exploitation, including child labor and human trafficking in the age of neoliberalism.[555]

Like all development models, neoliberalism constructs and perpetually reproduces its social reality. Considering that capitalist innovation's real goal is to devalue what currently exists, neoliberalism represents the endless struggle for higher profits which contributes to chronic structural exploitation. Creative destruction, *"industrial mutation that incessantly revolutionizes the economic structure from within, incessantly destroying the old one, incessantly creating a new one,"* is an inescapable trap as much under neoliberalism as in previous phases of capitalism, as Joseph Schumpeter observed in *Capitalism, Socialism and Democracy* (1942).[556]

Resting on classical liberal ideology with Christian-Libertarian tenets advocating that free will is the ultimate determining factor in human behavior, mainstream institutional and dominant cultural indoctrination are catalysts for neoliberalism to secure popular conformity. Neoliberal ideology's inherent contradiction is the emphasis on free choice, while the larger goal is to mold subjective reality within the institutional structure, which facilitates conformity and obviates free will. Irreconcilable aspects represent the contradictory goals of the desire to project a facade of popular sovereignty; at least one based on the consumer-citizen democracy, while pursuing capitalist appropriation under methods that necessitate public and private institutional hegemony.[557]

Ranging from the inability to forge greater social compromise and sustain economic stability, while enhancing upward social mobility, inherent contradictions expose the divergence between the promise of the neoliberal social contract's panacea for society and the reality of disempowering the working class and weakening the middle class. As distortions and contradictions within the system create large-scale social marginalization, cooperation and political mobilization of the masses under a progressive anti-neoliberal movement have not been as successful as right-wing political organizing.[558]

Owing to the state's role in regulating social conflict through coercion and a legal structure representing capital while pursuing class war, neoliberalism's inherent contradictions inescapably result in sociopolitical polarization. This has strengthened the far right more than the left. As a means of elevating the market and defaulting all problems in society to the state and its agencies which act merely as the market's instrument, establishment politicians, businesses, media, think tanks, and academic analysts encourage skepticism about the institutional structure's legitimacy. Mobilizing popular support in a process that projects the lure of free will, when in fact choice exists only within the neoliberal mold, helps to explain the political parties' difficulty in promoting the illusion of popular sovereignty where there is none, while simultaneously distracting from structural exploitation far more tangible in peoples' lives than popular sovereignty interpretations.[559]

Convinced that electoral system competition is the essence of democracy, a fluid concept with a very different set of dynamics in each country where the elites largely determine the selection of candidates through various means, above all money, the masses line behind competing elites representing the same social contract. This is especially evident in post-Communist Eastern Europe where the emerging capitalist class, ruling parties, and institutions identified 'democracy' with Western neoliberal capitalism and Western European institutions and consumerism. As long as a plurality passively acquiesces to the legitimacy of the social contract, even if in practice it is as socially unjust, as Viktor Orban's Hungary, for example, the status quo remains secure until systemic contradictions in the political economy and social relations make it unsustainable.[560]

From the post-2008 street protests in Bolivia, Argentina, and Ecuador, to Occupy Wall Street to the post-2010 mass anti-austerity demonstrations in Athens, Greece, and the indignados movement in Madrid, Spain, there has been a global reaction to the tyranny of neoliberal exploitation. The pandemic of 2020-2022, followed by the US-led sanctions imposed on Russia unleashed even more grassroots reaction. This included efforts to unionize America's Amazon and Starbucks workers to labor strikes in the UK, Spain, and France from autumn 2022 to winter-spring 2023. Against the preponderance of corporate news and analysis presented solely from the neoliberal prism, faint voices against structural exploitation rise above the relentless hollow rhetoric contradicting empirical reality in working peoples' material lives.[561]

Regardless of global labor protests, neoliberal transformation combined with the mass media's incessant efforts to shape the individual's worldview and subjective reality has succeeded in inculcating a new norm. The degree that dogmatism of the 'single-thought' process dominates not just neoliberal economics, but the very fabric of people's sense of humanity is a testament to market orthodoxy's success in transforming society against the reality of rising structural exploitation and growing inequality.[562]

In 38 OECD member countries, the richest 10% earned 9.5 times more than the poorest 10% in 2010 in comparison with the 7:1 rich-poor ratio in 1980 when neoliberalism was in its nascent stage. By 2021, the world's richest 10% had 52% of aggregate income, whereas the bottom 50% earned a mere 8%. As a result of the pandemic, followed by the US-led sanctions against Russia as punishment for invading Ukraine, the income gap widened globally as did poverty, considering that the world's richest 10% own 76% of the wealth.[563]

Taking the long view, inequality rose from 1820 to 1910 within countries and between rich and poor countries. From 1910 to 1980, wealth inequality declined, rising sharply from 1980 to 2020 which coincides with the neoliberal era. Borrowing from classical economists, neoliberals insist that workers are entrepreneurs selling their labor. Therefore, the 'neutral and efficient' marketplace determines workers' fate just as it does the billionaires' fate with the exception that the latter enjoy all the advantages of fiscal, monetary, investment, and labor policy.[564]

Implicit in the neoliberal argument about the market determining labor's value is the rejection of inequality as a symptom of the political economy and a function of a "natural" system in social relations. Furthermore, there is the implicit refusal to acknowledge private capital's hold on the state determining labor-management relations, along with fiscal and monetary policy as catalysts to uneven income distribution. Reflecting the capitalist world system's north-south division, the global south low-wage conditions excused based on surplus labor were far worse, partly because of a generally unhealthy and unsafe workplace environment in comparison with the core also under pressure amid the ubiquitous class war and weakened trade unions.[565]

Without intending to criticize the neoliberal regime and its impact on labor, Jonathan Malesic's essay captures some of the salient issues associated with the political economy's social impact. "*Secular, 21st-century residents of wealthy countries don't worry much about whether we're God's elect. But we're still trapped in the Calvinist cage... Like divine election, this type of status is an abstract condition that we cannot assign to ourselves, but one we hope others will recognize. When our status anxiety wells up, we reach back into our culture's religious heritage for a balm: hard, disciplined work. For example, Tristen Lee, a millennial-generation British public relations worker, tells*[1] *a too-familiar story of how long hours, lack of sleep, no real time off, and excessive rent keep her in the grind. "I throw my absolute heart and soul into" work, she writes. "I am so obsessed with reaching some notable level of success and hitting my financial targets, that I've forgotten how to enjoy life." Lee says she feels as if she has "something to prove – but to whom?" To herself, [Max] Weber [Die protestantische Ethik und der Geist des Kapitalismus] would say.*"[566]

---

1. *https://www.independent.co.uk/voices/millennials-burnout-gen-z-work-life-balance-holiday-income-snap-a9055471.html*

Proponents of the gig economy, short-term unprotected employment without benefits, have been promising techno-paradise from which the whole world can benefit. Far from the techno-paradise, conditions for workers in some respects resemble a return to the early 19th-century industrial capitalist pre-trade union era. The proliferation of the gig economy contract workers and "Uberization of labor" (freelance, without fixed salaries, benefits, or trade union and contract protection) has contributed to rising uneven income distribution. One of the most exploitative forms of labor, "Uberization" affords the feel-good delusion of ownership by the worker who assumes all the risk. Under this mode of labor-management relations, appropriation of productive forces is as significant as the economy's financialization that evolved as the norm exacerbating structural exploitation on a world scale.[567]

Commonly especially in the service sector rather than manufacturing, people often work two jobs, for contract workers overtime goes without compensation or benefits. For many involved in desk work, taking work home to keep up with the demands of the job is not uncommon. People have bought into the neoliberal myth of perpetual work enmeshed with the ideology of perpetual economic growth perversely intertwined with the narrowly defined neoliberal concept of progress and success. Characterized by unfettered capital concentration, the neoliberal concept of progress ultimately places the public debt burden on the public, thereby impacting the fiscal structure and social program cuts while strengthening the corporate welfare state.[568]

Coinciding with the digital revolution, neoliberal ideology has indoctrinated those generations that grew up under its institutional structure and value system. Dismissing the concept of 'public value governance' for it hinders economic growth, neoliberalism's goals proceed along the path of authoritarianism. This ideology and value system permeated forcefully the former Communist countries that lacked the experience of capitalism as it evolved from 1945 to 1990. Needless to say, the vision of a capitalist consumer paradise against the reality of low living standards for the majority under a weak social safety net was disillusioning.[569]

Thrust into the neoliberal way of life, the daily struggle for survival forces people to accept the status quo until it becomes part of their identity. Especially young people from the former Soviet republics to Western Europe and East Asia have accepted the assumption that the successful path to material progress is to emulate the stock-market and bitcoin speculators in a casino-style capitalist economy. The neoliberal imperative of "grow at any cost" necessarily entails that the capitalist class becomes more innovative in structural exploitation, lapsing toward greater institutionalized and private sector corruption at the expense of working people and the middle class.[570]

Concentrated Capital and Vertical-Growth Capitalism

The incentive for conformity to neoliberal transformation is predicated on the belief that the social benefits would be fairly distributed depending on the individual's assets, innovative spirit, and initiative. If not in the present, then at some point in the future, embracing neoliberalism will pay off. To prove that the system works, politicians, business people, the media, and establishment analysts point to stock market gains and to the wealth effect on the mass consumer who feels optimistic and borrows thereby raising consumption.

Grossly uneven income distribution and stagnant wages leading to the Great Recession did not have a major impact on consumption because of expanding credit amid falling savings rates. As reflected in the cumulative value of securities and real estate construction projects, the illusion of wealth keeps borrowing and consumption at high levels, but with record-high personal/household debt. Although this was the case after the stock market crashes of 1980, 1987, 1999-2000, 2008, and 2020, with each crash inequality rises and prospects for mobility decline, while finance capital becomes more concentrated.[571]

"Nevertheless, it is significant that the cash funds of corporations in the current phase of monopoly-finance capital far exceed profitable investment outlets. At the beginning of 2020, nonfinancial corporations were sitting on over 4 trillion dollars in cash; before the end of 2020, this had risen to over $5 trillion. According to the Federal Reserve Flow of Funds data, shown in Chart 2, total cash held by U.S. nonfinancial corporations as a share of gross domestic product (GDP)—much of it parked abroad in tax havens—has almost tripled between the early 1990s and the present."[572]

A small percentage of people on the planet (544 million out of 7 billion in 2009) owned securities, mostly Americans. Of those owning securities, a mere 10% owned 77% of global wealth. Except in times of market crashes when the socioeconomic impact is widespread, there is no correlation between upward stock market performance and living standards for the average person. Nevertheless, the corporate media, politicians, and analysts have inculcated into the mass consciousness that the correlation of good stock market performance is as meaningful for working people as the wages they earn. In the financialization economy, the "national interest" is equated with the speculative stock market. This projects the illusion that all is well with the world, as long as plutocracy is thriving, without necessarily investing in productive enterprises to realize horizontal growth.[573]

Measured by asset value minus debt, the S&P 500 index stood at 117 in 1982, rising to 2675 in December 2017. However, from 1982 to 2017, middle-class and workers' incomes declined. Despite a rise in productivity and immense profits reflected in the income gap between the bottom 90% vs. the top 10% for the same period, the striking divergence between the wealth accumulation of the top 1% and the decline of the bottom 90% demonstrates that the rise in the stock market confirms systemic exploitation. While neoliberal apologists dismiss wage exploitation, uneven income distribution is difficult to obfuscate simply by diverting focus on stock market or GDP growth figures.[574]

Indicative of accelerated structural exploitation under neoliberalism in comparison with the era of Keynesianism, a study compiled by the non-profit think tank *'Economic Policy Institute* stresses the historic divergence between productivity and real wages. While the top 0.01% of America realized 386% income growth between 1980 and 2014, the bottom 90% suffered a 3% real income drop. In 1980, the income share of the bottom 90% of

Americans stood at 65%, while the top 1% income share was 10%. By 2014, the bottom 90% held just half of the total income, while the top 1% owned 21%. The empirical evidence of a 40-year income trend cannot possibly be manipulated by rationalizations or defaulting blame on the slothful worker for failing to receive "proper training" to keep up with the changing technology, or any other early 19th-century explanation that distracts from structural causes in income distribution.[575]

The dramatic income divergence between labor and capital on a world scale took place under the full implementation of neoliberal transformation. Industrializing rapidly, China experienced upward social mobility and eliminated extreme poverty by the end of the 2010s, as the World Bank defines extreme poverty as under $2 a day. For the core countries, neoliberalism entailed de-industrialization amid massive offshoring to non-Western countries, especially Asia.[576]

Using the argument of "wage competition" in developing countries versus developed, Western-based corporations kept wages stagnant. Meanwhile, corporate profits soared along with tax evasion and tax havens sheltering between $21 and $32 trillion in a global economy of $85 trillion GDP in 2020. It is significant to note that this was during the period of high productivity globally amid the transition from social welfare to corporate welfare. Combined with a fiscal and monetary policy, privatization, deregulation, corporate welfare, offshoring, and outsourcing policies, higher worker productivity resulted in income transfer from labor to capital on a world scale.[577]

From 1973 to 2014, 80% of the US labor force suffered wage stagnation. During that same period, net productivity rose at an annual rate of 1.33%, a low rate in comparison to China benefiting US offshoring companies. *"Since 2000, the gap between productivity and pay has risen even faster. The net productivity growth of 21.6 percent from 2000 to 2014 translated into just a 1.8 percent rise in inflation-adjusted compensation for the median worker (just 8 percent of net productivity growth). Since 2000, more than 80 percent of the divergence between a typical (median) worker's pay growth and overall net productivity growth has been driven by rising inequality (specifically, greater inequality of compensation and a falling share of income going to workers relative to capital owners). Over the entire 1973–2014 period, rising inequality explains over two-thirds of the productivity–pay divergence."*[578]

The average corporate tax rate in the world was cut in half from 40% in 1980 to 22% in 2020. Because of loopholes in the tax codes and rampant tax evasion and avoidance, the effective rate was much lower than the official rate. This represents a massive transfer of wealth to the highest income brackets draining income share from the working class and middle class. During that same period, there was a systematic global diffusion of US tax policy lowering taxes on the rich and corporations, while labor and middle-class taxation trended higher. There has also been a similar global diffusion of corporate subsidies. The US government provided $19 billion to pharmaceutical companies for COVID-19 treatment and vaccine development, while European corporate subsidies for the COVID-19 vaccine cost taxpayers $12 billion. These funds were above and beyond subsidies for pipeline research and development of new drugs.[579]

Neoliberal transformation's impact on fiscal policy throughout the world goes beyond the core-periphery patron-client relationship and into the heart of molding the international division of labor, precipitating socioeconomic inequality and authoritarianism. Coinciding with the age of neoliberalism, the information economy has successfully distracted the vast majority. The goal was to convince the public that there is an element of egalitarianism in this mode although it generated more inequality. Predatory and more monopolistic than traditional industries, the digital economy has benefited from a lack of regulation, low taxes, and corporate welfare benefits ranging from subsidies to lucrative research and development grants, while the global "digital proletariat" has paid the price for digital monopoly capitalism.[580]

Under neoliberalism, capital concentration has resulted in more thorough exploitation of workers to the degree that social relations resemble America's Gilded Age (1870-1900) of monopoly capitalism. Before government-regulated companies, the Gilded Age was an era of inter-sector struggle for a larger share of the market - railroads against agriculture, forestry and mining, energy against manufacturing, etc. Under an expanded federal bureaucracy essential in rationalizing operations in everything from domestic commerce and foreign trade to preventing one sector from undercutting the rest of the economy and upsetting market equilibrium, the government intervened to protect capitalism from its inherent contradictions.[581]

As detrimental to labor in the early 21st as in the late 19th century, hegemonic culture has many manifestations of disdain for the working class from which it demands more appropriation in surplus value far greater than at any time in contemporary history. Relegating social responsibility associated with Keynesian economics to the realm of parasitic social welfare, neoliberalism presents corporate-supported sustainable development as a means of securing government subsidies for renewable energy, to respecting differences in lifestyle, culture, and religion within the social contract.[582]

Under the heading *"A 21st Century Social Contract"*, at the annual conference in 2017 where representatives from the 'Fortune 500', academia, think tanks, NGOs, and government, business consultancy group BSR provided the following vision: *"The nature of work is changing very rapidly. Old models of lifelong employment via business and a predictable safety net provided by the government are no longer assured in a new demographic, economic, and political environment. We see these trends most clearly in the rise of the "gig economy," in which contingent workers (freelancers, independent contractors, consultants, or other outsourced and non-permanent workers) are hired on a temporary or part-time basis. These workers make up more than 90 percent of new job creation in European countries, and by 2020, it is estimated that more than 40 percent of the U.S. workforce will be in contingent jobs."*[583]

Representing corporate executives, investors, and sponsors of sustainable development solutions within the neoliberal model, BSR applauded the aspirations and expectations of business people expecting even greater capital concentration amid an increasingly uberization of the workforce in the gig economy. According to a US government study published in 2019, the "independent contractor" labor force was 10 to 14 percent, depending on the survey source.[584]

Some studies estimate that "independent" or freelance workers constitute between 20 and 30 percent of the labor force. As this percentage rose parallel to income inequality, it has been a source of continued political polarization. Only a small percentage of the labor force constitutes the well-paid 'labor aristocracy' group which tends toward conformity to the social contract but fears losing out to robots and migrant laborers. Despite fear and anxiety about a bleak techno-science future as another mechanism to keep wages close to subsistence, if not below that level, and using child labor that further drives wages down, peoples' survival instinct compels them to adjust their lives around the neoliberal social contract.[585]

Mainstream institutions perpetuate the myth that the digital revolution - *'knowledge-based economy'* - of endless innovation, with a "creative destruction" dimension (innovation in production and marketing while making obsolete existing products as a means of accumulation) is the catalyst not only to economic growth but to civilization's preservation and society's welfare. Mesmerized by post-WWII scientific and technological advancements, in 1965, Alvin Weinberg, director of the Oakridge National Laboratory coined the term "technological fix"; a most appropriate term that neoliberal digital monopoly apologists present as the panacea and distraction from the realities of structural exploitation.[586]

The myth of technological innovation as the panacea for society's social and political ills is as old as the first industrial revolution in 18th century England. History has proved such myths hollow. Contrary to rhetoric about shared prosperity, from 1980 to 2020, the indisputable rising uneven income distribution statistics prove just the opposite. In 1980, world GDP was at $11 trillion, rising to $85 trillion in 2020. During that same period, average US household incomes rose by a mere 1% annually.[587]

Although Western European income distribution trends from 1980 to 2020 have not been as uneven as in the US, the richest 10% went from just under 30% of income share in 1980 to 36% in 2020, while the bottom 50% of income share dropped to 19% from 23% during the same period. From 1978 to 2022, college tuition rose 1,120%, medical care 601%, housing 380%; Meanwhile, average CEO pay rose 937%, minimum wage fell 5.5% and average work rose 10%. Despite massive innovation in digital, biotech, and energy sectors, socioeconomic polarization and environmental degradation persist at much higher rates today than in 1970 when Richard Nixon established the Environmental Protection Agency and Clean Air Act. Whether in the US, the European Union, or developing nations, the neoliberal promise of *'prospering together'* combined with the digital techno-fix as a cure for all has been a farce.[588]

With each passing recessionary cycle (1980-82, 1987, 1990-91, 2000-01, 2007-09, 2020-23), working-class living standards retreated, especially for pensioners. From 2000 to 2022, the buying power of Social Security dropped 36%. To keep up with living expenses, those who retired before 2000 would need an additional $500 a month. Meanwhile, the richest 1% in the US realized a five-fold increase in comparison with middle-class incomes.

The situation has been much worse for sub-Saharan Africa, Latin America, and much of Asia, including India, despite its rapid economic progress in poverty reduction. Although the techno-science panacea has proved a distraction from the reality of capital concentration, media, and establishment analysts have continued to promote the illusive "modernity as development" thesis confined primarily to a small segment of society while the rest take pride in living vicariously through that dream.[589]

Neoliberal myths about upward mobility across all segments of society notwithstanding, economic expansion and contraction result in greater capital concentration. Considering that the world economy under neoliberalism strengthened capital at labor's expense, massive income transfer from the working class and middle class to the richest 10 percent was inevitable.[590] During the 1948-1974 period when modified Keynesian policies were in effect, along with military Keynesianism, wages rose commensurately with productivity. Net productivity rose 61.8% from 1979 to 2020. Hourly pay grew 17.5%, adjusted for inflation, indicative of massive capitalist appropriation. During the neoliberal era of rise in inequality, CEO pay rose sharply as did household wealth for the richest 1%. After the Great Recession recovery, the household wealth of the poorest 50% rose just 2% while that of the richest 1% almost tripled.[591]

Using the data from 37 million businesses and investors globally, the Swiss Federal Institute of Technology isolated 43,060 multinationals and stockholders linking them directly or through investor networks with these companies. "*The model revealed a core of 1318 companies with interlocking ownerships. Each of the 1318 had ties to two or more other companies, and on average they were connected to 20. What's more, although they represented 20 percent of global operating revenues, the 1318 appeared to collectively own through their shares the majority of the world's large blue chip and manufacturing firms, the "real" economy, representing a further 60 percent of global revenues. When the team further untangled the web of ownership, it found much of it tracked back to a super-entity of 147 even more tightly knit companies (all of their ownership was held by other members of the super-entity) that controlled 40 percent of the total wealth in the network. "In effect, less than 1 percent of the companies were able to control 40 percent of the entire network."*[592]

Because of the combination of fiscal, monetary, and corporate welfare subsidies, but also labor policy and the transfer of billions from workers' pensions into the corporate coffers in the post-2008 Great Recession, capital concentration reached new levels in the 2010s as inequality was rising rapidly along with authoritarian neoliberal political parties and regimes. There is a direct correlation between capital concentration and retirement security erosion throughout the world from the 1980s to the 2020s. Because of social program cuts, along with private sector benefits reductions, and governments raiding workers' pensions during IMF austerity, wealth concentration and inequality became more pronounced after 2008.[593]

Because the predatory atomistic value system is an integral part of neoliberalism, advocates of the pure market ideology demand that the state must conduct policy on behalf of the capitalist class. This argument clearly illustrates that the model is predicated on class war and the state demanding the sacrifice of the many for the enrichment of the few. In *Liberalism in the Shadow of Totalitarianism* (2007) David Ciepley argues that the system's contradictions led to the authoritarian political model as its only option moving forward.

"Neoliberalism was born in reaction against totalitarian statism and matured at the University of Chicago into a program of state-reduction that was directed not just against the totalitarian state and the socialist state but also (and especially) against the New Deal regulatory and welfare state. ... But the contradiction between its individualist ideals and our corporate reality means that the effort to institutionalize it, oblivious to this contradiction, has induced deep dysfunction in our corporate system, producing weakened growth, intense inequality, and coercion. ... And when the ideological support of a system collapses—as appears to be happening with neoliberalism—then either the system will collapse, or new levels of coercion and manipulation will be deployed to maintain it. This appears to be the juncture at which we have arrived."[594]

Endemic Neoliberal Corruption in the Former Soviet Bloc

Hiding behind the great hoax of the 'market efficiency' thesis, economic crimes on a world scale have been an integral part of legalized structural exploitation. This is partly because of deregulation that has had governments turning a blind eye to everything from global illegal sales of cigarettes and gasoline to off-betting sports operations and money laundering involving some of the world's most prestigious banks, some of which used derivatives as the mechanism of choice.

In 2021, the Geneva-based Global Initiative network's empirical study on criminal activity concluded that globalization favored the illicit economy more than the legal economy. Paying lip service to tough law-and-order policy, neoliberals legalized large-scale business-related criminal activity ranging from the hedge funds scandals and money laundering in the US and Europe, to toxic waste in Mexico, Cote D'Ivoire and Italy, while permitting poisoned drinking water supply in Flint, Michigan, and Jackson, Mississippi in predominantly minority communities. These are crimes on a massive scale. While reporting such social crimes, the media also celebrates the winners who profit from them.[595]

Testing the limits of the criminal justice system, corporate criminals know that even if caught, the company pays a symbolic fine and keeps the profits. Although written before the Thatcher-Reagan nascent neoliberal era, the structuralist theory of the juridic-political superstructure of the state, Nicos Poulantzas (*L' État, le pouvoir, le socialism*, 1978) provides a useful theoretical framework for the reproduction of capitalist relations and remolding of the political class as enforcer. Borrowing from the neoliberal model's 'market efficiency' principle, the state bureaucracy emulates such efficiency to serve businesses while stigmatizing the working class, especially trade unionists, as the enemy of economic growth.[596]

Because of the neoliberal redefinition and remolding of the state, the class-based criminal justice system became even more punitive toward the working class and progressive groups. It demonstrated remarkable leniency toward white-collar crime involving hundreds of billions of dollars while becoming more brutal toward the marginalized population. Created under the neoliberal model, private prisons were flooded with working-class and minority inmates. Between 2000 and 2019, the US private prison population rose by 32%, in comparison with just a 3% increase in the entire prison population. There is a direct correlation between the decline of working-class and middle-class living standards and the rise in the punitive value system and policies reflecting neoliberalism's class war.[597]

Against the background of mass incarceration mostly of blue-collar and minority populations, neoliberal business ethics have whitewashed everything from financial and corporate fraud to offshore betting on "fixed" professional sports. Corporate investment, speculation on securities or commodities in certain cases involved laundered money from real estate drugs, illegal cigarettes, and weapons. While a small-time inner-city cannabis dealer rots in prison, cannabis trading on the stock market with heavy investments from Russian oligarchs like Roman Abramovich who helped establish the legalized industry is a celebrated market accomplishment. The symbiotic relationship between the political and business elites has redefined the concept of social justice to suit the corrupt interests of the capitalist class enjoying the state's protection for "elite deviance" commonly part of white-collar crime. Projecting the impression of the new norm, state bureaucracies are merely facilitators and enforcers of the neoliberal criminal justice model which courts of law also follow along the same ideological lines.[598]

Apologists of the social contract demand lengthy prison sentences for small-time neighborhood narcotics dealers. However, the same 'law-and-order' advocates have no qualms about the opioid drug companies costing the health care system billions of taxpayer dollars. Nor do they object to Wall Street-listed cannabis companies, but criminalize the small-time dealer. Even worse, the 'law-and-order' advocates never call for bank executives who launder billions from international narcotics trafficking to receive prison terms as they do for someone holding up the bank for a few hundred dollars. Besides Wachovia Bank (Wells Fargo acquired it during the crisis of 2008) involved in drug money laundering, the International Consortium of Investigative Journalists claimed that five major global banks funneled trillions of dollars in criminal funds from 2000 to 2017. In 2022, a year before its bankruptcy, Credit Suisse was laundering Bulgarian mafia drug money, a practice that the bank attributed to a single employee acting alone.[599]

Among mega banks in the US and EU, rate fixing (London Interbank Offered Rate (LIBOR) and the Euro Interbank Offered Rate (EURIBOR) by *Barclays* defrauded customers of billions as did Wells Fargo's fake accounts. Legally appropriating billions of dollars in the form of bailouts, the banks were benefiting from income transferred from the middle class and workers whose taxes governments used as corporate subsidies after banks defrauded customers and broke the law. Upon first impression, it seems enigmatic that there is acquiescence for large-scale white-collar crime with the institutional cover of the state's legitimacy.[600]

Perversely, mainstream media has conditioned the public to shrug off structural corruption and exploitation on a mass scale as an integral part of the social contract. Without any regard for the double standard and detrimental impact on the working class and middle class, the rationale has been that society is best served by market hegemony which often includes criminal activity legalized to accommodate neoliberalism. In the absence of the state as the catalyst for the creation of the neoliberal order, legalized white-collar criminal activity would not have been at the same high level.[601]

De-criminalization of white-collar crime predates neoliberalism, as does the celebration of the elites amid class war. Because of the wholesale transfer of power from the public sector to corporations, neoliberal structural exploitation assumed a higher level than it had since the late 19th century. Transferring sweeping policy powers from the public to the corporate sector, structural exploitation's tentacles have impacted every sector from labor and the environment to health, education, and foreign policy.[602]

Neoliberal apologists have been presenting the model as the purest and most efficient form of capitalism. The promise is a system free of corruption associated with statism, free of clientelism patronage politics, and free of bribery and the black-market economy associated with the political nexus of illegal business. Contrary to neoliberalism's moral order mythology, countries from Indonesia to South Africa, Brazil to India, and the US to Turkey have a history of far greater official and private-sector corruption under neoliberalism than what neoliberals condemn in the Keynesian state.[603]

Quick to hold the state accountable for any structural flaw in the political economy causing imbalances and social discontent, neoliberals defended the private sector as vigorously as the Catholic Church defended the dogma of Papal infallibility at the First Vatican Council in 1869. Financial institutions involved in money laundering and fraud, companies selling oil, tobacco, and guns, and illegal payments to public officials to secure contracts, especially in the lucrative defense sector, are minor infractions and the fault of the state failing in its official capacity.[604]

Because of market hegemony, many countries have passed legislation to legalize what were once corrupt practices associated with the world of high finance. Because of the blurring lines between legal and illegal activities, private sector corruption went mainstream enjoying the protection of the courts. Corporations from large automakers' emissions violation scandals, mega banks involved in derivatives by purchasing interest rate futures to hedge their position, stock market manipulation through insider trading, companies concealing money in tax havens, and billionaires fixing professional sports games by engaging in offshore betting are all part of the ocean of neoliberal corruption.

Difficult to determine where illegal activities end and legal ones begin, the mechanisms of accountability have often been in the hands of violators. Beyond shifting paradigms from the Keynesian to the neoliberal state, considering both aimed at the primacy of capital through different means, the criminal justice system evolved to support unfettered capitalist appropriation by continuing to vilify the worker and marginalized social groups, as had been the case historically before the New Deal and similar Keynesian programs around the world.[605]

Under a deregulated regime, illicit finance and trade circumvent government detection because of lenient and deferential policy toward capital, but also because governments do not spend resources on enforcement. Long before the neoliberal era, the criminal justice system always reflected the political economy. Neoliberalism did not invent the merging of official and private sector corruption under capitalism. However, its proclamations about law and order and the purity of the unfettered market ring hollow considering it has facilitated organized criminal activity and provided the stamp of legitimacy not only through legislative cover but through the judicial system from the lowest to the highest courts. As much in the core as in the periphery, such activities are especially noticeable in the former Communist bloc countries which used neoliberalism as cover for gangster-style capitalism.[606]

Ranking in the top ten most corrupt countries in the world, Russia managed to collapse neoliberal aspects with the Kremlin-linked oligarchic economy. Nowhere is neoliberalism as synonymous with gangster capitalism as in the former Communist bloc which transformed under the guidance of Western, especially US, advisors as soon as each country disengaged from the Soviet system.

In an empirical study of mass privatization and deregulation in former Communist countries, Patrick Hamm, David Stuckler, and Lawrence King maintain that once mass privatization depleted state revenue, public-private sector corruption increased along with poverty and inequality. "These findings contrast with the neoliberal prediction that rapid privatization would both promote firm restructuring and combat weak corporate governance, ultimately leading to stronger growth. They are, however, consistent with the leading post-mortem explanations (by both economists and sociologists) that weak institutions and poor governance were major causes of the post-communist economic recession."*[607]*

The former Soviet republics transitioned from decaying and stagnant centralized command economies to a chaotic private sector in a highly hierarchical socially polarized structure. As the only means of enabling their operations, post-Soviet government-linked oligarchs had appropriated massive capital from state enterprises. Going from a collectivist system of social safety net under a preponderate bureaucratized state to one that associated private property and consumerism with freedom and democracy projected the impression of Western liberalism limited to institutional and cultural superficialities. For most former Communist bloc republics, autocracy, or degrees thereof, coexisted with authoritarian neoliberalism.[608]

Consistent with neoliberalism in the former Communist bloc countries, capital accumulation entailed a form of an enclosure movement which meant massive privatization of all forms of state property. This accounted for the creation of kleptocrats, a small middle class in most countries, and a large but weak working class. Amid extreme social polarization, gangster capitalism operated in the name of neoliberal market reform. *'Professor Jeffrey Sachs and his capitalist provocateurs at the Harvard Institute for International Development (HIID)... advised Yegor Gaidar, Yeltsin's first economic czar, to dismantle quickly most of the controls and subsidies that had structured life for Soviet citizens for most of the century. Sachs predicted a more or less smooth transition to a normal western-style capitalism, once the initial shock of price decontrol was over."*[609]

With the assistance of Western academics and consultants, kleptocracy emerged from the ashes of the USSR, infecting other countries where oligarchs invested or laundered money. Crony capitalism took root in the oligarchic Kremlin leadership, especially in the 1990s under Boris Yeltsin, and in other former Soviet republics claiming to be democratic merely because they went through the motions of electoral representation.

Well-paid US and European advisors promoted the Washington Consensus in post-Communist countries, especially in the Russian Federation. Without commenting on neoliberalism, a US Department of Justice report on Russian organized crime reached the same conclusions as independent scholars. Russian links extended from the Kremlin and the oligarch-dominated formal economy to international businesses and political circles from Israel and Cyprus, to Western Europe and the US where money laundering operations were part of investing in varying forms.[610]

Unlike the rest of the world transitioning from varieties of Keynesian models to neoliberalism, the former Soviet republics went from a centrally-planned bureaucratic network straight into a private sector jungle with the five hundred most powerful Kremlin-connected oligarchs owning more wealth expropriated from the public than 99.8% of the population. The unapologetic private appropriation of public assets fell within the neoliberal model. Far from forging a society based on popular sovereignty, the overriding concern of Western advisors was how to integrate the economies to benefit Western-based multinational corporations.[611]

A dimension of the post-Communist transition included new private entities operating more or less like organized criminal enterprises. From sex trafficking to narcotics, and from energy to grain exports, endemic corruption and crime became intertwined with neoliberalism as the norm. Celebrating the end of the Soviet era and the dawning of capitalism, Western media was not questioning the political economy's gross inequality upon which the new political economy was based. Nor did the media dwell on the catastrophic social consequences of post-Communist society, forcing some to leave the country and others to engage in all sorts of illegal activities.[612]

Russia and the post-Communist republics preserved some of the old Communist bureaucratic state machinery apparatus on which the neoliberal state was built. Although the new system varied from fairly Westernized neoliberal Lithuania to paternalistic Eurasianist Kazakhstan, clientelist/crony capitalist elements operated between legality and criminality. Globalization and deregulation made the rapid spread of corruption easier with its merging of legitimate operations.[613]

Rather than focusing on endemic corruption and social dislocation under post-Soviet neoliberalism, Western politicians, media, and business analysts contended that it had not gone far enough to mirror the trans-Atlantic model as articulated in the Washington Consensus, and IMF-World Bank policies. Once the G.HW. Bush proclaimed the unipolar 'New World Order', post-Communist countries surrendered sovereignty to the neoliberal world system tailored under multi-level governance to suit local political conditions and social relations. It was precisely because the new elites betrayed popular democracy that post-Communist countries moved toward rightwing populism.[614]

A combination of dogmatic belief and naivete drove many analysts in East and West alike to emulate Western-style development and high living standards by creating a consume-oriented middle class. Especially given the formalization of post-Communist neoliberal marketization, while paying lip service to pluralist cultural-lifestyle issues, none of the post-Communist countries rose to the level of the trans-Atlantic core in living standards or democratic institutions modeled during the Keynesian era. Because the former Communist countries experienced unprecedented levels of inequality, the rise in the underground economy, and corruption, combined with the exodus of highly educated people to the West, a segment of the population turned to authoritarianism for salvation, while a few remained nostalgic for the Communist era.[615]

The combination of the Great Recession, Russia's economic crisis of 2014-2016 resulting from sharp rubble devaluation following the collapse in energy prices, and the simultaneous success of the Chinese global integration model sweeping across the former Soviet republics had a sobering effect on the post-Communist political elites' confidence in Western neoliberalism's impact on a state structure under market hegemony. Emulating the example of Russian President Vladimir Putin (2000-2008, 2012-present), several former republics from Belarus to Kazakhstan pursued populist authoritarianism under the neoliberal model, making it easier for the oligarchs to impose conformity amid rising social inequality.[616]

Not only in off-shore operations, but in everything from banking, real estate, professional sports, and other investments corruption outside the former Soviet bloc orbit entailed quick and easy profits for Western participants, even if much of it was illegal. In the absence of the neoliberal era of globalization and the growing shadow economy within Russia and throughout the region and much of the world, Russian gangster capitalist operations would have been more difficult. In their study of the globalization of Russian corruption, Paul Massaro and Amelie Rausing maintain that Western legal and financial loopholes permitted Russians to export corruption.

"The Russian brand of corruption thrives off of globalization and depends on access to the global financial system. Under this model, weak property rights and a lack of rule of law support a corrupt system at home, where markets are distorted and courts are politicized. State funds are looted and assets are acquired through corporate raiding and asset stripping. Cronies then siphon off national funds to safe havens outside of former Soviet countries. The failure to return ill-gotten assets, especially when they have been invested in the U.S. economy, diminishes the United States' democratic legitimacy and America's claim to be a champion of freedom."[617]

Considering that oligarchs in post-Communist countries invested legally and illegally in Western real estate, securities, banks, and various other enterprises from sports clubs and off-betting sports and high tech, the diffusion of corruption contributed to capital accumulation in the global economy where the boundaries between formal and informal economy are blurred. This is in part because the state either eliminated or diluted those lines to accommodate capital while hiding behind the thin veil of neoliberal orthodoxy and market efficiency rhetoric; a rationale that plays into populist politics of both the rightwing and liberal pluralists.

Neoliberalism and Corruption in Iraq and Indonesia

Although the pattern of neoliberal corruption has followed a similar path across the world, the nuances in the post-Communist countries are as important as those in Muslim countries. A part of local traditions, religious sectarianism, and political Islam, neoliberalism played an important role as much in Lebanon and Iraq as in Malaysia and Indonesia; the latter aspiring to compete with India and East Asian countries, especially China. The key to the transformation model's success has been commodifying cultural differences and subordinating local culture and traditions to the neoliberal superstructure.[618]

In May 1998, after President Suharto fell from power in Indonesia, and in March 2003 when the US invaded and occupied Iraq, endemic corruption in both Muslim countries provided unique perspectives of how neoliberalism's global reach impacted working-class living standards of Muslim society. Some question whether neoliberalism is compatible with Islamic doctrines, especially social service which includes helping those in need and in general lessening the suffering of others. Neoliberal apologists maintain that the eclectic aspects of the ideology transcend religion, ethnicity, geography, and culture. After all, history has proved that the political economy can exist under various local conditions and cultures. In so far as neoliberalism hastens capitalist crises, at a time when religion is suffering an institutional crisis amid a struggle with classical liberalism in a secularized world economy, the marriage of religion and neoliberalism seems mutually beneficial.[619]

Neoliberalism has molded Christianity, Judaism, Hinduism, and Islam under its image of the consumer-citizen culture, emphasizing personal choice and the self rather than community values and society's welfare. Delivering the 'Word of God', with a healthy dose of neoliberal 'faith-based development', Evangelical-sponsored NGOs have been active in developing countries. Within the marriage of neoliberalism and Christianity, there are historical influences from the theology of John Calvin and John Wesley to messianic capitalism evident in the speeches and writings of autocratization advocates. Prevalent in Christianity throughout the Western Hemisphere and Europe, this eclectic mixture is also present in Muslim countries across the Middle East, North Africa, and Asia. Besides political and religious groups, corporate and religious-funded NGOs have played a key role in this endeavor.[620]

Whereas neoliberal dogma places all focus on the amoral individual emulating an animal-like hierarchy with personal profit as the preeminent consideration above community welfare, Islamic civilization's principles have historically included social harmony, cooperation, and empathy for the less fortunate and those suffering. Because neoliberalism's only imperative is profit maximization and state intervention to strengthen capital at the community's expense, this objective obviates Islam's moral imperative with society's collective welfare as a core principle. Based on the social/legal code of Shariah law, anything injurious to society is morally repugnant, a principle that neoliberal ideology does not take into account.[621]

"Pious neoliberalism", or the elite-arranged marriage of institutional Islam and Hayek's pure market ideology manifesting itself through political parties, has been a vehicle through which neoliberal transformation succeeded in penetrating traditional Asian and African countries where religion transcends secularism. Despite the legacy of imperialism's transforming both religion and the concept of the secular in Muslim countries, neoliberalism has carried the stamp of international legitimacy because governments, the markets, and international organizations like IMF, WTO, and World Bank promoted through their institutional mechanisms. Amid market and social relations changes, industrial and technological developments modified the way that religious people as consumer-citizens express faith. Not just religious rituals, but teachings conform to the neoliberal value system of commodifying everything, including religion, which was never far from this modality, considering that religion and capitalism have historically influenced the culture in which they have co-existed for five centuries.[622]

With the considerable assistance of the World Bank, IMF, and private companies, the US military occupation authority forced Iraq to accept neoliberal measures as though it were a 19th-century colony. By contrast, in Indonesia's case, embracing neoliberalism was a political decision driven by the desire of the national and comprador bourgeoisie to compete with China, Japan, South Korea, and Taiwan through closer integration with both East and West. After three decades of President Suharto's dictatorship based on a patronage system, Indonesian capitalists aspired to industrial development intended to achieve rapid GDP growth comparable to East Asia.

Although Western countries were promoting neoliberal transformation both in Iraq and Indonesia, China ultimately benefited more than the West by reaching major trade and investment deals. For different reasons, both Indonesia and Iraq engaged in a balancing act between the US and China. Given China's very close ties with US arch-enemy Iran, it is ironic that the US neoliberal model and corruption in Iraq benefited China economically and Iran geopolitically. For its part, Indonesia recognized the benefits of acting as a bridge between China and the US, using its semi-periphery position as leverage in the world economy.[623]

Leaving aside the Bush administration's blatant distortion of the facts to justify US military intervention and regime change in Iraq, the costs were enormous to the US, its allies, bordering nations hosting refugees, and above all, to the people of Iraq enduring a brutal occupation whose only goal was geopolitical and geoeconomic exploitation in the hope of capturing Pax Americana's faded glory. The war-torn Middle East country became a neoliberal experiment and a strategic buffer zone to contain Iran and impose tighter control on the region, leaving US allies Israel and Saudi Arabia the region's major players.

While institutionalizing domestic intelligence/surveillance networks while using terrorism as a pretext, the US exported and tested the neoliberal security ideology in the Middle East. This was comparable to the counter-revolutionary ideology and institutional structure of the early Cold War under Truman. Besides think tanks such as the American Enterprise Institute, neoliberals advising the Bush administration insisted that there was a power struggle between globalization vs. jihad tribalism.[624]

Benjamin R. Barber who concocted the concept of 'jihad tribalism', and whose views became mainstream with Western liberals and Conservatives alike, argues that local struggles against neoliberalism as inevitable owing to disparate dynamics from nationalism and ethnic tribes to religious sectarianism. When analysts use the term "tribalism" as a critique of those resisting neoliberal globalization, it has connotations of resistance to 19th-century Western imperialism and underlying Social Darwinist assumptions concealed behind the term tribalism to justify the neoliberal version of Rudyard Kipling's "The White Man's Burden".

An example of the US-led neoliberal transformation model, nation-building in Iraq served a geopolitical goal as well, with the apparent Jihad vs. McWorld antagonism at the surface level. Considering the history of colonialism in Iraq and the entire Middle East whose fate the secret Sykes-Picot Agreement (1916) determined as a means of dividing the entire region into Western spheres of influence amid the Ottoman Empire's partition, in many respects US military occupation represented imperialism's historical continuity of destabilizing to control the Middle East.[625]

Putting aside the devastation of military invasion and occupation, the transformation model did not result in a sound economy, democratization, and social well-being, as neoliberals working for corporate-funded think tanks and the Bush administration had promised. However, not only did Iraq rank number one in the world for corruption by 2021, but it also suffered one of the world's worst post-WWII economic devastations because of the combination of destabilizing US nation-building schemes of conquest that perpetuated internal instability, and military occupation resulting in massive migration amid a sharp rise in poverty. Neoliberal corruption at gunpoint was in many respects worse than the clientelist political economy under US-deposed Saddam Hussein (1979-2003).[626]

Self-assigned responsibility to integrate Iraq into the world economy, mostly to benefit US-based companies and boost the Pentagon's morale, entailed that the US Coalition Provisional Authority (CPA) provided the legal framework to transform Iraqi institutions so that they serve international capital and US geopolitical interests, with the goal of counter-balancing Iran while looting Iraq. As part of the occupied country's constitution of 2005, the US imposed 112 laws on Iraq. At the same time, the IMF, World Bank, and WTO played a major role in coercing the occupied country into accepting austerity policies intended to benefit foreign corporations and large domestic capital, regardless of hardships to the vast majority.[627]

Known for its pro-neoliberal position, *The Economist* noted that *A shock program of economic reforms signals a radical departure for Iraq. The changes ... could see its battered economy transformed abruptly into a virtual free-trade zone. If carried through, the measures will represent the kind of wish list that foreign investors and donor agencies dream of for developing markets. Investors in any field, except for the all-important oil production and refining, would be allowed 100% ownership of Iraqi assets, full repatriation of profits, and equal legal standing with local firms. Foreign banks would be welcome to set up shop immediately or buy into Iraqi ventures.*[628]

Gatekeepers of the occupied country's economy, security, and legal system, US government contractors arranged for Iraqi oil to be sold to US corporations not at market prices, but on terms that the occupation authority decided. This meant "high-value, cost-plus" reconstruction contracts for which Iraq would pay with oil revenues. Similar to schemes that Europe and the US imposed on colonies semi-colonies and spheres of influence during the Age of Imperialism (1870-1914), "high-value, cost-plus" reconstruction contracts were intended to benefit US companies.[629]

Without taking into account the costs that the US military inflicted on Iraq, the US-CPA authority decided on the terms and price of Iraqi oil sold to US companies and reconstruction contracts awarded to US companies paid through Iraqi oil revenues. Even within the narrow boundaries of the neoliberal dogma's logic, the obvious contradiction of the transformation's global reach was its catalytic role in determining the lives of almost 30 million people without a voice to carve their destiny. The US insisted that it was exporting freedom and democracy to Iraq, while the entire world watched US troops delivering 'salvation' at gunpoint.[630]

Self-righteous moral superiority rhetoric aside, hollow "freedom and democracy" cliché proclamations could not conceal the US occupation authority ignoring the Geneva Conventions and international law. Subordinating Iraq's sovereignty to US corporations and the Defense Department was a violation of international law before the world to witness. Under the approval of the WTO and IMF, the US-CPA apostles of neoliberal dogma systematically appropriated Iraq's national wealth.

US-appointed auditors provided a stamp of legitimacy for US corporations to pillage Iraq's natural resources. Behind thinly-veiled neoliberal ideology rested state-supported corporate war crimes. Operating under the assumption that the imperialist power has the right to pillage, President Trump spoke openly about pillaging the oil resources of the Middle East as part of military intervention, crudely expressing a de facto condition that he wanted to be formalized as part of policy.[631]

Predictably, a percentage of Iraqi oil revenue found its way into bank accounts of US private contractors, some of whom did very little in return for Iraqi compensation. Money spent for bribery, embezzlement, and falsifying accounts, combined with legitimate expenses amounted to $12 billion. In a country where per capita GDP in 2010 was around $3000, and the poverty level around 25% with three million refugees, endemic neoliberal corruption was one more systemic burden that the US-CPA imposed on Iraq. This was not an ideal case of 'pious neoliberalism'. Instead, a case closer to neocolonial exploitation, which included war crimes, in the name of a Pax Americana nation-building in theory, while in essence destroying a nation.[632]

Under the nebulous Westphalian-sounding nation-building construct designed to make sure that money flowed through corrupt channels to contractors with whom the military occupying force collaborated, there was only neoliberal profiteering and externally imposed violence that replaced Saddam Hussein's military dictatorship with a puppet regime. Through various domestic coalitions and brutal force, Saddam's dictatorship maintained a modicum of social harmony between more than two dozen ethnic and religious groups by co-opting the elites from disparate groups. Under US military occupation, the US-imposed regime in Bagdad lacked any legitimacy, given that its base of support was very thin and facing the gunpoint of American marines. Because Iraq was the model to which the US and the West aspired amid the Afro-Arab Spring uprisings of the early 2010s, it is hardly surprising that some in the Iraqi political leadership positions, and throughout the Middle East and Africa, looked to China as a substitute for Western-imposed neoliberal orthodoxy.

Polarizing Iraqi society, the US invasion precipitated deeper endemic corruption under sectarian neoliberalism which ran parallel to Lebanon's transformation in the first two decades of the 21st century. Deregulated Iraqi markets, including labor, rent, debt, and international finance capitalism linked to the clientelist state catering to the sectarian comprador bourgeoisie. Not surprisingly, foreign and domestic mainstream analysts defaulted mass protests from 2019 to 2021 not to the decadence and divisiveness of neoliberal sectarianism and military occupation, but to rising public debt leading to a currency crisis. Even worse, "jihadist tribalist" politics, which Western mainstream analysts adopted to justify neocolonialism, was a term representing the mindset of Orientalism; a Western form of racism to absolve economic and war crimes in US-occupied Iraq.[633]

As much in Iraq as in Lebanon, Western neoliberals blamed everyone from fringe groups to Islamist politicians and regional players, but never the invaders shielding economic exploitation. In Lebanon's case, the fault always rested with the eternal enemy Iran owing to Lebanon's Shia political party Hezbollah, and its hostile relations with Israel. This is not to suggest that Iran did not entertain ambitions to determine the regional balance of power by meddling in Iraq, Syria, Yemen, Afghanistan, Azerbaijan, and Palestinian territories. Iran's role was defensive against the US-Israel-Saudi Arabian nexus and their regional allies that had imposed various containment measures in the Persian Gulf and Eastern Mediterranean.[634]

In October 2019, there were mass protests in Baghdad and Beirut against the corrupt ruling class of the respective countries. For the next two years, social unrest continued periodically, inviting the world's attention to a decadent ruling class operating under neoliberalism subsumed in the crony/clientelist structure linked to Saudi Arabia with US-Israel-Western European support. Protests did not bring any change in the neoliberal model or crony capitalism. Indicative of the entrenched traditional social and political elites competing for control, Lebanon's sectarianism kept society divided. Combined with existing crony capitalism, the neoliberal transformation had ruinous effects on workers and the middle class, precipitating a humanitarian crisis.[635]

The convergence of Islam and neoliberalism was common in Iraq, Lebanon, Turkey, Egypt, and Indonesia, transforming the economies of all under the same mold. Characterized by the promise of development and ending crony capitalism, after Suharto's fall in 1998, Indonesia's neoliberal presidents delivered greater capital concentration, more externally-dependent economic development, and continued endemic corruption accommodating foreign and national capitalists under the clientelist state.[636]

After three decades of authoritarian capitalism under Suharto, a new era of neoliberalism dawned, coinciding with the eve of the dot.com bubble. Promising an end to the web of corruption associated with the Suharto regime, transformation substituted authoritarian capitalist development with a new network of neoliberal corrupt practices, some in the name of land reform, others to secure 'free market democracy', and still others to compete with the East Asia countries. Following the advice of the World Bank, IMF, and Western firms, Indonesia's 'democratization', a euphemism for neoliberalism, promised ethical government open to foreign investment and free flow of capital under minimal regulation. Free-market economy and rapid urbanization were not much different than they had been under Suharto's patronage system; all of it coming at the expense of small farmers and the urban working class paying the price for neoliberal policies.[637]

Interwoven with foreign economic policy, Indonesia's neoliberal political economy is aimed at rapid growth with open borders for trade and capital investment. The capital incentives included weakened protection for workers under a new set of pro-business laws and diluted environmental and land rights protection. In the race to outdo Western neoliberal competitors and compete with East Asia by embracing the gig economy, post-Suharto governments sacrificed the working class and small farmers who had some protections from the late 1960s to the late 1990s. Phasing out Keynesian policies in favor of neoliberalism entailed forging a new consensus among the elites while promising workers and small farmers improved conditions in the future for sacrifices in the present. [638]

Marketed as a program to alleviate poverty and lift living standards, while strengthening local governance and empowering rural communities, from 1998 to 2006, the World Bank introduced the Kecamatan Development Program (KDP) in two phases. As the neoliberal transformation Trojan Horse, KDP was hardly unique. The World Bank had used a version of it in several Asian countries, including Afghanistan, as part of the larger neoliberal community development project to spread the gospel of Western neoliberal bliss to Asia with predictable disastrous results.[639]

Ten years of neoliberalism after Suharto, Indonesia, the world's 10th largest economy in PPP terms, joined the G-20. Considering the competitiveness level of several Asian countries struggling for a position in the semi-periphery, this was a major accomplishment for Indonesia. While it reduced extreme poverty from 25% where Suharto left it, to 10% before the global recession of 2008, paradoxically, inequality increased. Income growth was concentrated in the richest 20%, while the bottom 80% of 205 million people did not benefit from neoliberal vertical growth without social development. Based on living standards criteria, Indonesia did not compare favorably to many Asian nations, including the Asian Tigers (Hong Kong, Singapore, South Korea, and Taiwan) with which it was competing in industrialization, trade, and finance. The government focused on strengthening the secondary sector which accounted for half of GDP by 2012. Accompanied by almost doubling of urbanization from the end of the Suharto dictatorship to 2021, rising urban poverty amid decreased rural poverty was a mixed blessing in the first two decades of the 21st century.[640]

Under neoliberal transformation, the old guard continued to exert control and influence over public policy. Socioeconomic status and connections to the regime were exactly the way business was carried out under Suharto. In 2008, Suharto's old guard formed the Gerindra party embracing neoliberalism and representing Indonesia as a candidate in the BRICS group. As was the case in other Muslim countries, the Indonesian government and private companies stressed Islamic piety as a conformity tool within the Western neoliberal model, further politicizing Islam.[641]

The fundamental difference between Indonesia and other Muslim countries was its struggle to rise to the semi-periphery in the world capitalist system, relying on neoliberalism to accomplish the goal of industrial development, especially in the high-tech sector. In reality, the country was experiencing "dependent development" similar to what was taking place in Turkey and Brazil, with low-cost labor and a vast internal market as common denominators. The World Bank's praise of Indonesia as another "Asian miracle" owing to transitioning from the primary sector, especially agriculture, to industrial development continued in the early stage of neoliberal development. By 2000, computer exports amounted to twice the value of palm oil, historically the top export followed by coal briquettes, gold, and petroleum and gas.[642]

The Kecamatan Development Program was a tangible example of Indonesia's struggle to climb higher within the semi-periphery and compete with giant industrial exporters like South Korea and Taiwan focused on high tech and trying to keep up with Japan and China. Carrying the promise of rural uplifting, the project did not erase the general view that popular sovereignty was nonexistent when it pertained to economic development and government policies. On the contrary, it confirmed the general sense that the Jakarta political elite and large domestic and foreign businesses benefited from economic growth. Similar development patterns were also present in Erdogan's Turkey during his government's efforts to lift the country into the semi-periphery in the 2010s.[643]

Under the thin veil of "green economy" and sustainable development, neoliberal policies impacted Indonesia as much as other developing nations projecting an image that did not match economic and social realities. Behind the conservation rhetoric, rested World Bank projects designed within the neoliberal framework of green business opportunism. These included clearing lands along the Lamandau River Wildlife Reserve in Central Kalimantan to make space for the commercial exploitation of palm oil, in the name of environmentalism; a façade behind which rested commercial land privatization.[644]

Neoliberal promises from the World Bank, local politicians, and foreign investors aside, Indonesia did not become the new South Korea, as some had promised and many had hoped. Not only was South Korea's per capita GDP 3.2 times higher (2017) than Indonesia's, but South Korea moved swiftly toward the digital economy while Indonesia was de-industrializing. Because of market share loss in manufacturing, sinking to 20% in 2020 in comparison to 32% in 2002, Indonesia reverted to raw materials exports, especially nickel mostly to China.

Like other countries trying to strengthen the secondary sector of production where wages are higher than the primary sector, by 2017, Indonesia's dreams of rapid industrialization faded, switching its focus to the rapidly growing financial services and agriculture. Indicative of waning industrialization/high-tech dreams, palm oil became the largest export. By 2021, the service sector was 42% of GDP. In an intensely competitive world market, high-tech exports were once again a small segment of the export trade.[645]

Besides the World Bank and IMF promoting neoliberal policies, the WTO Agreement on Agriculture undermined the Indonesian coffee trade after the Great Recession. Insisting on open-market access, reduction of government subsidies for coffee producers, in the name of improving quality and competition, and removal of export subsidies resulted in weakening the small producers. Considering that the country ranked the fourth largest producer in the world, 90% of coffee farmers were listed as small and cooperatives, suffering a major blow to their livelihood.[646]

WTO coffee trade policies coincided with Indonesia's deindustrialization, while the service sector along with agriculture was becoming the economy's core in the 2010s. The result was uneven income distribution. Solid GDP growth notwithstanding, Anne Booth concluded that: *There is now little support for the argument that Indonesian growth in recent decades has been particularly egalitarian, at least by Asian standards.*"[647]

Added to rising uneven income distribution, in 2017, Indonesia ranked 90th out of 180 countries in endemic corruption. For a country promoting itself as the world's third-largest democracy, corruption, and inequality were worse under neoliberalism than when Suharto was in power. *Transparency International* concluded that all three branches of government had a corruption problem, with some of the same structural problems that existed under Suharto's dictatorship remaining society's permanent fixture.[648]

In the course of the neoliberal transformation, the old religious-cultural divide intensified and Indonesia's political arena reflected it. As a manifestation of inequality and uneven social development, polarization was an inescapable reality. Even the World Bank acknowledged that the richest 20% benefited from neoliberalism, while 80% of the 225 million Indonesians did not experience upward social mobility, even though average wages were higher than in Vietnam and Bangladesh. Suffering an economic slowdown amid the COVID-19 period, Indonesia experienced a modest spike arising from the demand that the war in Ukraine created. Because the level of foreign capital investment is lower than lower-labor-cost Asian competitors, international financial organizations and multinationals have used it as a pretext for more neoliberal measures using the state to return more capital to them.[649]

Neoliberalism's Subversion of the Liberal Social Order

Under neoliberal transformation, endemic corruption was as prevalent in Iraq and Indonesia as in the trans-Atlantic core. This includes the US whose ranking is the same as Chile's in Transparency International's global corruption perceptions index.[650] From Reagan's election in 1980 to Trump's victory in 2016, the gradual merging of authoritarian tendencies in the Republican Party represented a transition of far rightwing ideological tendencies becoming mainstream amid neoliberalism's institutionalization. Shortly after Trump took office, the liberal media called out the dangers of neoliberalism's path toward dismantling the liberal order to replace it with authoritarianism.[651]

In *The Principles of a Liberal Social Order* (1966), Friedrich Hayek made a strong case for pure-market liberalism. A decade later, his theory translated into policy in Chile under Pinochet's military dictatorship. Pinochet's Chile experienced an erosion of social rights with anomic impact on society at the expense of the working class. Advocating restrictions within liberal democracy, if not its elimination, Hayek's version of liberalism was in contrast to late 19th-century social liberalism arising in Germany, among other European countries in which working-class interests and social harmony were taken into account as the mass consumerist society was taking shape.[652]

More than four decades after the neoliberal transformation from Chile to the UK, US, India, and Brazil, Hayek's vision of a neoliberal society without democracy had evolved closer to reality. Susan George, president of the Transnational Institute, maintained that neoliberalism is rooted in Social Darwinism and undermines the liberal social contract not as it fits into an ideological mold but as it has evolved in Western civilization. Because powerful organizations, including the IMF, World Bank, and WTO have been the precursors to the neoliberal phase of capitalism and among its significant promoters, the liberal social contract infused with Keynesian elements lost mainstream credibility.

"Thanks to the debt crisis and the mechanism of conditionality, it [IMF] has moved from balance of payments support to being quasi-universal dictator of so-called "sound" economic policies, meaning of course neo-liberal ones. The World Trade Organisation was finally put in place in January 1995 after long and laborious negotiations, often rammed through parliaments that had little idea what they were ratifying. Thankfully, the most recent effort to make binding and universal neo-liberal rules, the Multilateral Agreement on Investment, has failed, at least temporarily. It would have given all rights to corporations, all obligations to governments, and no rights at all to citizens. The common denominator of these institutions is their lack of transparency and democratic accountability... It [neoliberalism] claims that the economy should dictate its rules to society, not the other way around. Democracy is an encumbrance, neo-liberalism is designed for winners, not for voters who, necessarily encompass the categories of both winners and losers."[653]

There is a chasm between the promise of political, and business leaders, and international organizations which profess that institutions are designed to benefit everyone against the reality of people's declining living standards. Once people realize that elected government abrogates the "representative covenant" by ignoring the social welfare of the majority, citizens view democracy as a sham. This scenario leads to apathy, cynicism, sociopolitical polarization, and the rise of right-wing populism.[654]

Consumerist freedom and democracy are predicated on the social hierarchy of income inequality and socioeconomic marginalization. People recognize that purchasing power parity means that the political economy determines their lives. For example, people are forced to live in tents in San Francisco where the average rent was $44,000 annually in 2023. In a city that spends as much money a year for about 7,500 homeless people as the cost of 10 houses after gentrification which drove prices so high that a working family could not afford housing, neoliberalism thrives among the political and business class that wants the homeless to disappear because they ruin the city's reputation.

Anti-working-class policies which the G7 and international organizations such as the IMF promote are integral parts of the neoliberal transformation's deleterious global reach filtering down to families living in tents from San Francisco to Rio de Janeiro's Favela hills. Against rising inequality and authoritarianism, monopoly capital and the state remain unyielding in pursuing neoliberalism, regardless of the chaos and destruction to society.[655]

Hiding behind neoclassical theory, institutions like Wells Fargo inflated their stock value by selling new accounts and charging extra fees and engaged in 'cross-selling' (millions of accounts opened under pretenses without customer consent and customer identity misuse). For such corrupt practices, the government rewarded the bank with taxpayer money. Even though the company dismissed more than 8,000 workers between 2011 and 2016 for failing to meet sales quotas, the Obama administration bailed out the bank to the tune of $36 billion on top of an estimated $25 billion in tax incentives to buy Wachovia Bank involved in laundering billions in Mexican drug money. In October 2012, the U.S. Attorney in the Southern District of New York sued the bank for hundreds of millions of dollars in fraud damages for illegally certifying more than 100,000 mortgages as eligible for federal mortgage insurance.[656]

The picture is not so different for Deutsche Bank, among many others across the world with a history of circumventing the law already heavily tilted in favor of finance capital. Especially for the European and US middle class, but also for Latin American and African nations statistics show that the neoliberal social contract emboldened and rewarded businesses' predatory practices while punishing labor and further regimenting freedom analogous to social status. This is in contrast to Hayek's theory defining freedom as the absence of coercion which is what takes place institutionally in the neoliberal class war climate.[657]

In the neoliberal world where institutional economic crime is protected and rewarded, and where the eight wealthiest individuals on the planet own as much wealth as the bottom 50% or 3.6 billion people, systemic exploitation and oppression are the norm. Any deviation is punished legally and in the marketplace. After reaching 805.5 million in 2005, world hunger began dropping to reach a low of 570.7 in 2013, but began to climb steadily thereafter, reaching 828 million in 2021, or roughly 10% of the world's population. This is mostly concentrated in sub-Saharan Africa, Latin America, and southern-southwestern Asia. Guardians of the neoliberal status quo, including the media, politicians, business, and community leaders castigate anyone questioning the social contract in which institutionalized exploitation and political oppression subtly or overtly as the norm.[658]

As the neoliberal political economy has resulted in a steady rising income gap and downward social mobility since the 1980s, with China as the world's notable exception, it is hardly surprising that a segment of the masses has accepted rightwing populists demonizing everyone from globalist liberals to migrants and environmentalists to women-rights advocates. Walking a fine line between bourgeois electoral politics and Fascism has been the norm not just in Eastern Europe and non-Western nations, but in northwest Europe and the US.[659]

Regardless of the relentless media campaign to ignore coverage of the neoliberal class war, while distracting the working class and middle class from rising inequality and authoritarianism undermining liberal-democratic societies, a segment of the population is aware at some level that they have common class interests. This is despite differences in everything from race, ethnicity, culture, religion, and personal lifestyle. Those looking for a scapegoat, emotional fulfillment expressing anger against the other as a form of psychotherapy, or deliberate distraction from structural issues drift toward the authoritarian camp.[660]

Despite violations of workers' rights, more broadly human rights, and structural exploitation, as the UN and international organizations have confirmed, liberal and authoritarian governments alike vigorously defend their policies for benefiting "society". The world has a serious problem when Sweden, which consistently ranks in the top five most democratic, worker-friendly, and one of the most socially just countries in the world, has experienced a rise in structural exploitation with a politically viable far-right party promoting anti-Muslim and anti-migrant propaganda, waiting in the wings to govern with the traditional conservatives. Whether a liberal democracy such as Sweden or more authoritarian Erdogan's Turkey and Orbán's Hungary, empirical data from various sources points to a rise in structural exploitation, thereby exposing the neoliberal model's inherent direction toward rightwing populism.[661]

According to the Pew Research Center, the world average of public satisfaction with government stood at 46% in 2017, the exact percentage in the US which ranks about the same as South Africa, much lower than neighboring Canada at 70% or Sweden at 79%. "*Publics around the globe are generally unhappy with the functioning of their nations' political systems. Across the 36 countries asked the question, a global median of 46% say they are very or somewhat satisfied with the way their democracy is working, compared with 52% who are not too or not at all satisfied. Levels of satisfaction vary considerably by region and within regions. Overall, people in the Asia-Pacific region are the most happy with their democracies. At least half in five of the six Asian nations where this question was asked expressed satisfaction. Only in South Korea is a majority unhappy (69%).*[662]

Combined with the immediacy of their perceived survival and aspirations, not necessarily their actual material interests, people make political decisions based on multiple considerations, including ideological, cultural, and political indoctrination, but aspirations of their preferred instead of actual identity. Assumptions of the rational and moral imperative, let alone the pursuit of social justice and collective welfare, are not necessarily the primary factors that people consider when deciding whether to camp under the liberal or rightwing populist tent or simply drift away from the bourgeois tents making hollow promises about social justice under the electoral system. From the fall of the Communist bloc to the present, the number of countries holding direct national elections has risen. However, the global average voter turnout fell significantly from 1990 to 2015, especially in core countries at the heart of the neoliberal model.[663]

Since the dawn of civilization, the hegemonic culture has indoctrinated the public to remain obsequious to authority from the nuclear family level and up. This is even against the reality of structural exploitation which becomes the norm and rarely challenged either from within the institutional structure or outside its perimeters. It is a tribute to cultural hegemony's triumph that so many accept neoliberalism's paradoxical premises, as though it were a mystical journey into the pursuit of Buddhism's nirvana. Operating within the institutional borders of social coercion and the need to survive, the masses succumb to consent-support of the institutional structure, knowing it is socially unjust. In part, this is because mainstream institutions prevent them from seeing alternatives to survival. Hence, structural exploitation under neoliberalism has worsened working-class and middle-class material conditions.[664]

Considering that the institutional power structure molds human behavior to minimize obstacles and maximize conformity to the state and social order, neoliberalism in the digital age has been more successful than any model under capitalism in indoctrinating, de-radicalizing, and co-opting the majority to support the transformation's global reach. As neoliberalism has successfully placed all of the burden on the individual, minimizing the community's role outside of identity politics, formal and informal structures operate within the new dogma. Hence, structural exploitation is internalized and becomes the fault of the victim, not objective social relations under the neoliberal political economy.[665]

During the ascendancy of neoliberalism in the 1980s, there was a simultaneous rise of the "self-help" ideology marketed, commercialized, and hailed as the postmodern miracle of the yuppie conspicuous consumption era. The rise of consumption-commodity fetishism coincided with the corresponding decrease in self-esteem. This became a commercial lifestyle and pop-art form in the nascent neoliberal era of the Thatcher-Reagan decade when self-identity underwent redefinition.[666]

In the $10-15 billion "self-help" industry of neoliberal commodified subjectivity, the combination of self-positivity and exploitation rooted in self-management theoretical constructs means that society is composed of "self-help" individuals bypassing not only social solidarity but accepting the premise of self-blame for structural conditions impacting their lives. Because neoliberalism places individual competition and self-help above all else, while claiming to celebrate the individual, it undermines her/him through disengagement and marginalization promoting alienation and social disconnection.[667]

"The University of Pennsylvania's Positive Psychology Center *offers resilience services*[1] *that claim to boost "cognitive and emotional fitness, strength of character, and strong relationships." In "Lean In: Women, Work, and the Will to Lead" (2013), Facebook COO Sheryl Sandberg advises women to take a leading role in corporate America, and urges men to support them. Resilience-informed urban projects uphold White suburban neighborhoods as the standard of resilience and use this standard to police and displace racialized communities (Bonds 2018). These resilience strategies encourage neoliberalism's victims to assimilate into the free-market economy, and they blame dissenters for failing or refusing to adapt."[668]*

In June 2022, Sandberg resigned after an internal investigation revealed that she had used corporate money to plan her wedding. Just another tech billionaire executive offering advice to average women on how to 'build character' and create a 'better society' while pursuing a private ethical path. Meanwhile, while Facebook executives insisted that the company followed the highest ethical standards, the platform was permitting posts by those responsible for genocide in Myanmar and allowing posts promoting ethnic violence in Sri Lanka. More than any other social media network, Facebook was responsible for a variety of rightwing propaganda and infamous "fake news" stories, according to a Princeton University-led study tracking postings from 2016 to 2020. [669]

---

1. *https://ppc.sas.upenn.edu/resilience-programs/resilience-skill-set*

In some countries, assimilation into the neoliberal mold took place under multiculturalism, while in others, neoliberalism took hold in the context of a more homogenous cultural and social exclusion within the confines of an authoritarian regime. Relying on traditional institutions from which to draw their popular base, populist political parties blame structural exploitation on the very victims of the system along with foreign enemies. As has been the case historically, a percentage of the disillusioned middle class and working class have embraced populist demagogues who presented authoritarianism as the panacea, attributing downward social mobility to individual failure.[670]

In neoliberal mythology, the capitalist is something like Thomas Hobbes' mythical godlike creature Leviathan, relying on market power to mold the recalcitrant public. Stroking the inflated business ego and projecting hope for riches above mere mortals, this cultural mythology is devoid of a social conscience, while reinforcing exploitative delusions about the individual's role against society's welfare. While many question the morality of structural exploitation, others subconsciously adopt a perverse interpretation of Friedrich Nietzsche's life-affirming creative will to power, along with the late 19th-century elitism that Hayek embraced to justify market hegemony and class war.[671]

Not just in the US and Europe, but across the world, neoliberal culture produced autocratization by subordinating liberal democracy to capital. Authoritarian neoliberal governments unapologetically espouse suppression of human rights and fundamental freedoms, while they enjoy the support of international organizations and multinational corporations as long as they proceed with the transformation goals. Far from camouflaging structural exploitation or trying to excuse it, liberal and rightwing parties alike demand that society celebrate the success of the comic-strip-style "superhero billionaire", as though it is a virtue to go through life benefiting from pro-capital policies at society's expense with public and private institutional support.[672]

Using GDP growth figures, it is common for politicians, media, and mainstream economics analysts to deceive the general public that there is an implied correlation between GDP growth and social development. "*In 2012 the United States spent an estimated 19.4% of GDP on such social expenditures, according to the Organization for Economic Cooperation and Development, the Paris-based industrial country think tank. Denmark spent 30.5%, Sweden 28.2% and Germany 26.3%. All of these nations have a lower central government debt-to-GDP ratio than that of the United States. Why the United States invests relatively less in its social safety net than many other countries and why those expenditures are even at risk in the current debate over debt reduction reflect Americans' conflicted, partisan, and often contradictory views on fairness, inequality, the role and responsibility of government and individuals in society and the efficacy of government action. Rooted in value differences, not just policy differences, the debate over the U.S. social contract is likely to go on long after the fiscal cliff issue has been resolved.*"[673]

Propagating the dogma of the fictionalized pure market society, neoliberalism apologists distort the empirical evidence of rising capital concentration and social inequality on a world scale Because society as a whole has been transformed, everything from the health care system and commercial popular culture promoting the neoliberal value system, imagining a world outside the neoliberal model is not realistic for the average person trying to survive. This is no different than people in Medieval Europe who could not conceive of a world different from the feudal/manorial order where the nobility and upper clergy determined society's fate. Considering mass cultural conditioning that marginalizes dissidents, it is no enigma that the social contract based on systemic inequality appears to be as "natural" as the earth and the sun.[674]

Under global neoliberal transformation since the 1980s, there has been a corresponding rise in authoritarianism which has undermined the myth of Western liberal democracy and hollow promises of a better society under market efficiency. The path to authoritarianism has been operating within a culturally pluralistic world and brings to the surface neoliberalism's authoritarian essence; that is, the very enemy that Karl Popper theoretically opposed in *The Open Society and Its Enemies*. As a means to disprove rather than offer final absolute answers, Popper's hollow "falsification" theory of science establishes the mythological foundation for Hayek's neoliberal ideology deceptively claiming political neutrality when it is quintessentially authoritarian targeting labor as the enemy of capital.[675]

Social Exclusion and Popular Resistance

In a study of social exclusion in Europe, sociologists Michelle Lamont and Jonathan Mijs argue that neoliberalism reinforces institutional animosity toward the poor and ethno-religious minorities, especially Muslims. Neoliberal transformation has had the same impact on social exclusion and subordination in Mexico and Chile as in the US, Europe, and Japan. Inherent to capitalism, social exclusion is a manifestation of the evolving political economy from the first industrial revolution in England to capitalism's neoliberal phase. Partly because the ideology was born against the background of Keynesianism and the social welfare state, class war became neoliberalism's main focus.[676]

American billionaire investor Warren Buffett has candidly acknowledged that class war from above aggressively aims to dismantle the social welfare state and transfer income from the bottom to the top. This is regardless of the detrimental social and political consequences.[677] Since the dawn of civilization when the elites controlling the state relegated the lower social strata of the population to the fringes, social exclusion has always existed. From ancient Babylon until the abolition of American slavery (1865) and the end of Russian serfdom (1861), social exclusion invariably involved a large segment of the population behind which was private gain camouflaged by ideology to justify it.

Long before the trade union movement secured a living wage, and some benefits and safety measures for the working class, the dynamics of industrial capitalism perpetuated social exclusion and subjugation. Since the 1980s, neoliberal policies have been a throwback to pre-trade union-era conditions. Creating a chronic debtor working class that operates under the assumption of integration into the mainstream, the neoliberal model entails social marginalization of the debtor working class. The neoliberal political economy is the catalyst to the creation of this condition that has aggressively dismantled the social welfare state offering a modicum of labor protection. Growing considerably in the late 1930s and early 1940s, the trade union movement began to decline and was co-opted by mainstream political parties during the Cold War. More than at any time since the 1920s, during the Thatcher-Reagan decade, trade unionism suffered setbacks owing to anti-labor and class warfare policies.[678]

Among the very obvious and striking cases of social exclusion coinciding with neoliberalism's ascendancy, post-apartheid South Africa provides a glimpse of how the native population continued to be exploited economically and that the end of racial apartheid did not end social injustice. Whites who enjoyed economic and institutional control agreed to end institutional discriminatory policies that excluded the majority non-white population. However, the white minority capitalist class continued to derive the economic benefits and enjoy institutional hegemony in post-apartheid society after 1994 when Nelson Mandela was president.

Along with the rest of the continent, post-Mandela neoliberal South Africa has marginalized the working class and lumpenproletariat made up primarily of people of color. Because apartheid ended at the time of the global neoliberal transformation, class relations pushed race into the background to ensure capitalism's continued success which accounted for South Africa becoming one of the BRICS members in 2011. Not surprisingly, the government presents BRICS membership as a great accomplishment, sufficient to make up for the neoliberal policies' impact on the working class.[679]

Just as it impacted the social structure in post-apartheid South Africa and the Global South under pressure from Western governments, the IMF, and multinational corporations, neoliberalism gave rise to a new precarious working class (lacking work-related security) in Europe and the US. Popular with scholars analyzing neoliberalism, the concept of precariousness has its origin with Fredrich Engels (*The Condition of the Working Class in England*, 1845) analyzing the industrial 'reserve' labor force one step above the lumpenproletariat. Reflecting globalization's molding of the division of labor, neoliberal-generated precarity has been the result of class war and market conditions.

Overqualified and struggling to secure steady employment in their field of academic training, especially amid recessionary cycles that last longer and/or run deeper, the newly educated working class has become part of the surplus labor force globally. Despite the historical tradition of a strong welfare state, trade unionism relatively free of government and business persecution, employment safety net, and social policies, Western Europe followed in the footsteps of the UK and US in labor relations. Using cyclical economic contractions as the pretext to roll back remnants of the Keynesian state, neoliberal class-war policies undermined the current working class and the next generation.[680]

"The neoliberal model and the effects of deregulated and global finance not only question the "European social model," write Elísio Estanque and Hermes Augusto Costa, *"but push sectors of the labor force – with the youngest and well-qualified being prominent – into unemployment or precarious jobs. ...the sociological and potential socio-political significance of these actions particularly as a result of the interconnections that such movements express, both in the sphere of the workplace and industrial system or whether with broader social structures, with special emphasis on the middle classes and the threats of 'proletarianization' that presently hang over them. ... labor relations of our time are crossed by precariousness and by a new and growing "precariat" which also gave rise to new social movements and new forms of activism and protest."[681]*

A growing chronic debtor class created the proletarianization of the college-educated middle class which contributed to downward wage pressure. Symptomatic of globalization, the debt economy amid stagnant wages and rising living standards exacerbated proletarianization and social exclusion, especially after the Great Recession. Downward social mobility's impact on the middle class naturally weakened liberal democracy because historically liberal democracy's base has been the middle class. Hayek-Freidman neoliberals evoking John Locke and Adam Smith had no use for democracy based on Voltaire and Jean-Jacques Rousseau's political philosophy. Their arguments have been more consistent with the reality of the political landscape as it has unfolded particularly under authoritarian neoliberal regimes.[682]

At all levels of government, public policy faithfully mimics the neoliberal model resulting in the proletarianization of the middle class amid class war. The neoliberal road to material salvation has resulted in an increasingly larger percentage of young adults living with relatives, postponing marriage, and having children, especially in the Western World. A staggering 20% of young Americans living with relatives is the largest number since the Great Depression. The situation is not very different in Europe, and worse in developing nations with a small middle class and a more family-dependent culture owing to economic conditions and traditional culture. [683]

Burdened with college loan debt, about half of the unemployed youth are unable to find work. Of those working, they do so outside the field of their academic training. According to the OECD, youth unemployment in the US is not confined to high school dropouts but includes college graduates. From southern Europe to North Africa, the neoliberal economy of massive capital concentration has created a new class of lumpenproletariat that has no assets and only carries debt. After 1980, personal bankruptcies rose sharply across the Western World. From 2009 to 2018, 10% of U.S. households filed for bankruptcy at least once, while the debt discharged during the period amounted to $2.03 trillion. The debt trend, including shadow debt, and debt from the non-payment of goods and services not reported to credit bureaus, reflects downward social mobility and has a far-reaching impact on the chronically indebted made worse with each recessionary cycle.[684]

Rising income inequality has been a reality in all OECD countries in the neoliberal era. Since the late 1970s, the working class suffered stagnation, while the middle class experienced much slower income growth relative to the two decades after WWII. After the economic crisis of 2008, conditions worsened and proletarianization rose across most countries. From health care to social security benefits and higher indirect taxes burdening workers and the middle class, the metrics in every domain reflected the rich-poor gap. According to the Rand Corporation, from the mid-1970s to the mid-2010s, America's richest 1% experienced an unprecedented rise in total wealth increase, while the bottom 90% of the income earners suffered a drop in income.[685]

From Mexico to India and the Arab World, proletarianization followed similar patterns in the US and Western Europe. Contract labor and "zero-hours" workers squeezed the petit bourgeois class whose working conditions resemble those of manual laborers. Except for China, the rural sector was subject to proletarianization much worse than the urban. This was partly because of the neoliberal 'enclosure movement' under the pretext of the green economy.

In India, Bangladesh, Sri Lanka, Eastern Europe, the Middle East, Africa, and Latin America, capital-intensive consolidation of agriculture entailed massive migration of rural population into urban centers. Such migration patterns contributed to small farmers' downward income pressure and social marginalization of the rural population. In 2011, 450 million of the 1.2 billion in India migrated within the country. Of those migrating, 78 million migrated into urban areas where they joined the precarious labor force. Contributing to rising pauperization throughout southern Asia and the Arab World amid the region's massive defense spending and minimal social spending, seventy million migrated into urban areas, exacerbating marginalization and proletarianization.[686]

During the second decade of the 21st century, neoliberalism in India created immense social dislocation and marginalization. The crisis started in the late-1980s-early1990s amid privatization and globalization when the government reduced farm subsidies and opened the market to foreign competition, as was IMF, World Bank, and WTO policy. As operational costs rose sharply, only large-scale commercial operations could compete. More than two-thirds of cotton, wheat, rice, and chickpea producers were unable to recover production costs.[687]

Making matters worse, Prime Minister Narendra Modi's regime introduced legislation allowing large corporations to assume even greater ownership of the primary sector of production. The result was displacing and/or reducing millions into laborers for large-scale commercial farm operations. By neoliberal doctrine, Modi weakened the regulatory regime through the *Essential Commodities (Amendment) Act* of 2020), among other measures strengthening large-scale agriculture.

Throughout the Indian subcontinent, with Sri Lanka and Bangladesh as the most egregious cases, legislation strengthening large commercial agriculture was prevalent at the World Bank and WTO's urging. In the name of market efficiency, but mainly because of state subsidies for large operations and, the rising cost of agricultural machinery, energy, seeds, pesticides, and fertilizers, only the large operations could be competitive. Moreover, the G7 convinced many Global South governments to plant commercial products for export. Both Sri Lanka and Bangladesh suffering a food deficit made up the difference with more expensive imports, suffering balance of payments deficits and creating conditions for fiscal austerity leading to further neoliberal measures.[688]

After the Great Recession, small Indian farmers and rural laborers engaged in mass demonstrations against policies involving cutting or eliminating subsidies resulting in consolidation of commercial agriculture and laws that would result in plunging farm prices. Organized by a group representing more than 200 Indian farm organizations, on 30 November 2018, tens of thousands marched amid the deepening of the agrarian crisis. The Modi government did not back down from its commitment to large enterprises. Undeterred by mass protests and people losing their livelihood, the government permitted massive agricultural investment by India's top two billionaires (*Mukesh Ambani and Gautam Adani),* both with a history of close ties to the rightwing regime.[689]

Appealing to Hindu nationalism, Modi tried to distract farmers and workers, many of whom had voted for him based on cultural/religious appeal. Intended to substitute small farm subsidies with corporate welfare oligopolistic firms as part of crony capitalism, neoliberal transformation in India enjoyed the World Bank's support which hypocritically was producing reports about the rise in rural poverty and food insecurity, while backing policies causing the calamities it described. A global phenomenon, neoliberalism in agriculture marked the end of India's 1960s Green Revolution aimed at food security while supporting small farmers and agricultural workers. Despite rhetoric about rising export crops benefiting the economy, the transition from traditional farming that displaced millions to horticulture and the production of fisheries, dairy, and poultry created massive dislocation and rising rural poverty.[690]

Largely because of shifts in the sector catering to the more affluent foodstuff demand in urban areas, Modi's agricultural policies resulted in a doubling of rural and urban household debt as a percent of GDP. In part, this reflected the stalling of modest upward mobility from 2000 to 2008. Although from 1990 to 2018, 170 million rose from poverty to the "vulnerable" category, inequality increased as did capital concentration in the hands of a few billionaires and millionaires. This is in contrast to China which eliminated extreme poverty and managed to create a middle class surging from 3% to 18% in the first decades of the 21st century. During the same period, India's middle class increased by only two percentage points, while the population rose from 1.05 billion in 2000 to 1.45 billion in 2022.[691]

Household Debt and Global Imbalances under Neoliberalism

From 1980 to 2020, $50 trillion more income wound up in the pockets of the richest Americans, while household debt rose. This was not the result of market efficiency, but government policies designed to strengthen monopoly capitalism. The massive transfer of wealth from the bottom up through various means from fiscal, monetary, and corporate welfare policy resulted in rising middle-class and working-class debt, combined with government debt burdening the popular classes. Intended to strengthen corporate America and the billionaire class at the expense of working people, class warfare worked exactly as the apostles of neoliberal ideology envisioned; exactly as it did in Pinochet's Chile in the 1970s where neoliberals first tested the experiment in various ministries from trade to labor.[692]

An astronomical rise in concentrated income, the richest 1% owned $41.52 trillion (2020), or 16 times more than the bottom half of the population. Government spending has been devoted to strengthening big capital in the name of competition and an unfettered market by delivering massive tax cuts from labor to the rich and corporations, along with an accommodative monetary policy and endless tax loopholes. On top of permitting tax avoidance and evasion by not pursuing the money trail to tax havens from Switzerland to the Cayman Islands, these measures created a gap between statutory and effective tax rates.[693]

Twice under Reagan and George W. Bush, and once under Obama and Trump, tax cuts resulted in unprecedented wealth transfer to the richest Americans. During the same period, public debt, inequality, and higher cost of living entailed lower living standards for the bottom two-thirds of the population. Considering that the average corporate rate was half in 2020 in comparison to 1980, a similar trend with variations was evident throughout the world. Contrary to vacuous claims about tax cuts for the rich and corporations resulting in GDP growth benefiting workers, forty years of data does not support such claims.[694]

Although the US ranks 7th among the world's most tax-friendly countries, fiscal and monetary policy was along the same lines as in many other countries. International competition to attract foreign investment under the neoliberal model sent governments scrambling to offer incentives, especially to high-tech corporate giants.[695] One result of the neoliberal fiscal structure was weaker GDP growth in many Western countries compared with China pursuing a mixed model with social development parallel to economic growth. Like the former Soviet republics, primitive capital accumulation was based on the state legally-sanctioned dissolution of public property expropriation giving rise to kleptocratic oligarchs, but maintaining a social safety net.

China evolved toward a blend of Russian-style oligarchic/gangster capitalism under a highly centrally-planned economy with a modicum of local community roles and social development policies. Interestingly, corruption in China is estimated at comparable levels to India which was more in line with the trans-Atlantic neoliberal model thus compromising its competitiveness with China. Whereas corruption in India precluded growth levels comparable to China and an economy geared to cater to the domestic and foreign markets without necessarily considering domestic food security and social safety net, the corruption factor did not hinder China's growth. Despite aspects of Russian-style gangster capitalism, Beijing was not pursuing market orthodoxy.[696]

Based on the empirical data gathered by international organizations, China's corruption is much higher than in the US. Under neoliberal transformation impacting the criminal justice system, the US, along with other Western countries legalized practices that are illegal in China. Hence, corruption legally defined is much higher in China. Although the organization conducting the empirical corruption study plays a role, the legal status of specific public and private sector practices explains the corruption index classification of the US vs. China.

After President Xi Jinping took power in 2012, there was a sweeping crackdown on more than 1.5 million government officials along with many in the private sector. This is indicative of the state's commitment to rationalize capitalism and project the image of the state's preeminence. Preventing corporations from having inordinate political influence through questionable legal practices sent the message to businesses that the state remained hegemonic. Unique to China, a preponderate state role would be unthinkable in the US. Wall Street would lose its hegemonic influence in government and elected officials would lose their privileges.

In the first half of 2022, 67 members of the US Congress were discovered to have violated the Stock Act of 2012 intended to prevent insider trading. The penalty is $200 which the Ethics Committee can waive. Even in blatant cases of elected officials and/or family members violating the Stock Act of 2012 insider trading. Before the outbreak of the COVID-19 pandemic, elected officials with advanced knowledge of what was about to take place, traded stocks on insider information. The consequences of their illegal activities were symbolic. With the occasional expulsion in egregious cases to keep the public believing in the system, financial crime goes largely unpunished.[697]

With all the problems of US public and private sector corruption before and after 2008, massive public debt as a result of bailing out large corporations further weakened the artificially strong dollar's prospects as the world's dominant reserve currency. During China's rapid economic ascendancy and prospects for growth in the first half of the 21st century, this trend continued parallel to the US public debt-to-GDP ratio increase, and low economic growth prospects. These conditions left a gap that China and the BRICS would eventually fill, surpassing G7 cumulative GDP both nominal and in PPP terms.

Combined with a sharp rise in household debt, neoliberalism exacerbated global imbalances on a world scale. Between 1980 and 2020, global debt nearly doubled, rising from $150 trillion to almost $300 trillion. While civilian-sector debt would presumably generate horizontal economic and social development, debt for defense and devoted to stimulating stock market financialization was parasitic undermining the real economy. *"Debt increases are particularly striking in advanced economies, where public debt rose from around 70 percent of GDP, in 2007, to 124 percent of GDP, in 2020. Private debt, on the other hand, rose at a more moderate pace from 164 to 178 percent of GDP, in the same period."*[698]

For most of the developed countries, especially the G7, public debt did not reflect productive investment yielding economic development with high-paying jobs to benefit society. In the US, 42% of public sector investment went to the defense sector; health care absorbed less than 20%, and infrastructure 4%. By contrast, China spends 8.7% of its budget on infrastructural development and one-fourth on defense development in comparison with the US.

In 2021, the US spent as much on defense as the next ten countries combined, with benefits limited to defense corporations and related sectors from high tech to law firms, advertising, and public relations. This only serves capital accumulation to the detriment of social development. Considering that the consumer-based economies of the developed nations engage most of the labor force in the service sector, ranging from part-time hospitality workers to high-paying high-tech workers, the social safety net ideally serves as a buffer from social marginalization.[699]

The US and other developed and semi-developed countries pursuing military Keynesian policies drive up debt which accounts for chronic balance of payment deficits and undercuts both the civilian economy and living standards. Parallel to the rise in public debt, individual and household debt among the middle and working classes has given rise to a large parasitic debt industry that relies on the government to make it profitable, thus, perpetuating the parasitic vicious circle.

In a study entitled *"Confining Social Insecurity: Neoliberalism and the Rise of the 21st Century Debtors' Prison,"* Genevieve LeBaron points out that the current situation conjures images of Charles Dickens novels. *"debt-buying firms have increasingly relied upon the state's legal system as a means of compelling individuals behind on their credit card payments, auto loans, and other bills to meet their obligations. In the past year alone, judges have signed off on more than 5,000 arrest warrants, incarcerating Americans for debts as small as $250. Far from being an anomalous phenomenon, as we argue in this article, the recent resurgence of the debtors' prison in the United States is one manifestation of a broader trend toward the coercive governance of the social insecurity generated by neoliberal social and economic policies."*[700]

A common practice from the American colonial era until 1833, debt imprisonment was a policy left up to each state to decide within the context of an anti-debtor national legal system. In the 18th and 19th centuries Great Britain, France, Germany, and the Netherlands, among other countries, adopted such punitive practices aimed mostly at the working class. The post-WII era of consumer protection and human rights opposed debtor prisons. Under different conditions, the neoliberal era restored the 19th-century punishment for the working poor, including children.

Between 2015 and 2022, child labor has risen 37% in the US, and law violations rose 400%, from 1012 to 3876. In Alabama, primarily children of migrants as young as 12 were working in an auto parts plant., and dozens in a meatpacking plant in Wisconsin. From Reagan to Biden, state legislatures have been rolling back restrictions on child labor impacting mostly black and Latino children. A study by the CATO Institute (2014) revealed that the billionaire DeVos family and the Koch brothers have spearheaded efforts to weaken child-labor laws impacting all children, especially blacks. The world's largest asset management firm, BLACKROCK, among other corporate giants has been employing children in factories in which they have investments.[701]

This is a very significant subject about which there is only peripheral coverage in the media, just as there is about the convergence of the financialization-based economy which ultimately led to skyrocketing public and household debt weakening both the middle class and the working class. Not surprisingly, the neoliberal state rewards corporate debt, while punishing workers, especially minorities, and family debt.[702]

As liberal democracy's backbone, the majority struggling to make monthly payments reveals how neoliberalism seriously undermines workers and the middle class in the US, as well as in 18 of the 26 EU member countries. Despite UN-sponsored *'Millennium Development Goals,'* and World Bank and IMF poverty-reduction loan programs to reduce inequality, the economic devastation of the COVID-19 pandemic took its toll on the middle class in Latin America, Africa, and most of Asia where capital concentration rose along with inequality.[703]

Under neoliberalism, financialization resulted in a divergence between financial markets and the real economy, surprisingly impacting the core which drained capital from the Global South and workers and the middle class to the richest owning most of the capital. Financialization led to rentier capitalism, thoroughly integrating the middle class and much of the working class into the credit economy, especially since the 1980s. The neoliberal model molded the larger debtor class to the degree that everything from housing and health to education and durable goods are part of the credit score system; a form of debt peonage that prevailed in the second half of the 19th century US and Mexico.

By creating a perpetual debtor class in the name of the neoliberal myth of perpetual growth, the thin veil of a thriving middle class exists to keep up appearances behind which rests a debtor class, downward social mobility, and rising child labor. Debt permits the weakened middle class to pursue the façade of a lifestyle suitable to the social status that society expects. As Atif Mian, Ludwig Straub, and Amir Sufi point out (*The Saving Glut of the Rich and the Rise in Household Debt*), there is a correlation between the richest one percent owning most of the income, and "dissavings" of the lower 90% of the population. According to a US Federal Reserve Board survey in 2020, 47% of Americans had a mere $400 to spare for emergencies. By 2021, 25% of the population had zero savings, and another 26% had enough for less than three months to cover expenses. Only 35% had sufficient funds to cover unexpected emergencies.[704]

In fast-paced growth in India, consumer debt rose 400% from 2014 to 2023. Considering that India suffers high inflation and unemployment along with low-paying jobs in a low-growth economic environment, especially in the secondary sector of production, rising personal/household debt is not a good indicator. *"Loans are being taken because families cannot meet their needs through their earnings. The data show that loans for heavy expenditure items—like buying homes or funding expensive education—are not exhibiting as much growth as loans for smaller, possibly retail, spending."*[705]

In the Social Darwinian laissez-faire struggle for survival, debt insecurity works to the benefit of the capitalist class which optimizes profits from a surplus labor force and makes money on household debt. In a society of weak trade unions, adult and child workers unprotected by the state, and wages close to subsistence levels, most people live with the neoliberal dream of tomorrow's anticipated riches, pushing aside today's reality. Officially, the EU and the US have 9.4% and 8.3% respectively of their labor force classified as working poor. However, in 2021, the poverty rate rose to 11.6% in the US, and 21.7% in the EU, mostly attributed to the pandemic.

In 2018, one-fourth of the US labor force was earning less than two-thirds of the median earnings. Official unemployment was 3.9%, reflecting the myth between low unemployment and presumed working-class prosperity. In a society with a weak social safety net in every sector from health to education, and rising income concentration among the top one percent, the middle class and working poor in chronic debt continue to enrich the top one percent. When breaking down the demographics of the debtor working poor, this necessarily conjures up the legacy of Social Darwinism at the core of the neoliberal model's class-war reality. [706]

Normalizing chronic debt as a way of life, neoliberalism is a guide on how to achieve false upward mobility in the present by postponing payment. As a speculative commodity that projects the facade of wealth, rising debt can be indicative of sluggish growth, but also of excessive spending as well as a fiscal policy not reflecting the state absorbing the surplus capital from the capitalist class.

Rising public debt illustrates capitalist resistance to taxation amid rising inequality and political apathy. The media, political, business, and educational institutions inculcate into the public consciousness that credit is extended to individuals, businesses, various public organizations, and nations to advance their economic goals and/or facilitate programs or projects. By making both private and public debt an integral part of the means of production, the neoliberal system has reshaped social relationships and subverted social equilibrium in democracy.[707]

Because the line of demarcation is blurred between consumption credit intended for commodity fetishism, and productive investment credit, a segment of the general public is either apathetic or entertains a favorable perspective on debt, not realizing the pitfalls involved for borrowers depending on income status. Under neoliberalism, credit has been a means to generate "securitized debt" intended to enrich the lending investors who assume no risk because the government bails out the banks. Another dimension of the public shouldering the burden of subsidizing capitalists, Fannie Mae introduced this product under Reagan in 1983.[708]

As Jodi Dean explains, collateralized debt rewards parasitic investment which deprives the real economy of investment capital to benefit billionaire speculators and investment firms. *"When a market is made for a specific designer instrument, like derivatives such as collateralized debt obligations and credit default swaps, the surplus risk shifts from being a byproduct to being* the product*; it occupies the place previously held by the asset. The riskiest tranches of a collateralized debt obligation (CDO) are the ones with the highest potential reward. When investors, particularly hedge funds and others looking for something too short, want them, banks look for more bad loans to buy, whether these loans are for houses, education, or municipal improvements. Low net worth individuals, people unlikely to be able to repay their loans, are necessary for high-risk loans."*[709]

Part of a policy that resulted in social asymmetrical power aiming to speed up capital accumulation, maintain market hegemony while generating greater social exclusion, and perpetuate class warfare, neoliberalism has exacerbated the chronically indebted middle class and working class. Servicing public loans has been among the causes of downward pressure on living standards in advanced and developing capitalist countries alike. While working-class debtors are criminalized, the state bails out capitalist debtors and rewards them with tax write-offs. This is another aspect of the corporate welfare state in support of "market efficiency".[710]

In 2021, aggregate debt of both private and public sectors on a world scale was just under $300 trillion in a global economy of $91 trillion, or 350% of the debt-to-GDP ratio. Driven by consumerism where neoliberalism has taken hold more than in the periphery, and where the illusion of upward mobility is widespread merely because of the average citizen's identification with the rich nation as a whole, the rapid rise of household debt has been widespread. In 2021, in the EU, for example, household debt stood at 62% of GDP and 78% in the US.

Because of downward mobility, 45% of those polled believed that the American Dream was attainable. As a result of wages measured against inflation declining in both Europe and the US, household debt has been rising resulting in a growing socioeconomic chasm and political polarization. European pessimism about the economy is not only confined to young and minorities seeking work that matches the cost of living, it is also regional with northwest Europeans having a great deal more faith that the system works, whereas this is not the case for the periphery in the south and east.[711]

While household debt is often but not always a reflection of a consumerist society, the digital economy is creating a surplus labor force that results in work instability and asymmetrical social relations. The Florida-based think tank and its lobbying arm, the Opportunity Solutions Project, have found remarkable success among Republicans in relaxing regulations that prevent children from working long hours in dangerous conditions. And they are gaining traction at a time when the Biden administration was scrambling to enforce existing labor protections for child labor rising under his presidency.[712]

Under the neoliberal political economy, child labor has been a topic that scholars have analyzed, but mostly in the Global South countries, especially in sub-Sahara Africa, Bangladesh, and Vietnam. This is not an issue that most people associate with the world's greatest democracy, as its leaders and media advertise. Yet, the US is moving in the same direction as the Global South, using the blatant lie of labor shortages when in fact the labor participation rate is at 62%.

It is indeed ironic that in several US states, the government has passed legislation permitting children as young as 14 to carry out hazardous work, including serving alcohol in bars. The same US government complaining about China's labor policies is permitting child labor law dilution benefiting US businesses whether domestically or their operations in China using child labor. As if this were not enough, the US media, politicians, and pundits preach 'democracy' to the rest of the world, never reflecting on its own anti-labor, anti-child, anti-women, anti-minority policies at the core of American society.[713]

Besides child labor under neoliberalism, unauthorized work has been another dimension in the labor domain. A study that Ryan Edwards and Francesc Ortega published in 2016, concluded that: *"unauthorized [US] workers are removed from each industry at a time reveals that these workers are responsible for about 3% of private-sector GDP, which amounts to approximately $5 trillion over 10 years. At first, the removal of unauthorized workers would reduce*

aggregate production by about 1.7%, but the loss would be magnified as employers downsize

the stock of capital to match the reduced workforce. These aggregate estimates hide

large differences across industries, largely reflecting the shares of unauthorized workers in

industry employment. Once capital has been adjusted, value-added in Agriculture, Construction and Leisure and hospitality would fall by 8-9%. However, the largest losses in dollars would take place in Manufacturing, Wholesale and retail trade, Finance and Leisure and

hospitality. Likewise, we also find large differences across states that largely reflect the

employment shares of unauthorized workers in each state, along with the state's industry

specialization."[714]

Based on a 2014 ILO study, 'forced labor' generated $150 billion in corporate profits annually. Along with the core's exploitation of the Global South, and US-NATO geopolitical instability which exacerbates labor conditions, 'free markets' account for imbalances in the unfree labor force. This includes low-paid Asian migrant workers in the Gulf States where thousands die each year, sex trafficking, and child labor. Ever since the British Abolition of the Slave Trade Act in 1807, advocates of industrial capitalism and liberal democracy maintained that slave labor is inconsistent with free labor markets and with the liberal social contract rooted in individual freedom. This inconsistency does not hold for 'unauthorized' labor. Furthermore, by creating a chronic debtor class, neoliberalism has transformed socioeconomic relations while promoting servile and child labor under illiberal democracy.[715]

Technology automation has been the pretext for capital concentration and downward living standards for the middle class and workers while creating more debtors trying to keep one step ahead of obligations. Especially given the safeguards and protections accorded to creditors in the past four decades, the financial system backed by a legal framework favors institutional creditors. Permitting financial institutions to set debt traps for consumers, the state has many blatant ways that it uses to criminalize debt and poverty. While the government has safety net guarantees for banks and the corporate sector which it subsidizes in various ways, working-class debt is a trap tantamount to an economic prison. Considering that creditworthiness is essential for everything from renting a home to securing a job, debt catches up with creditworthiness, even in the event of eventually paying off all debt.[716]

In Germany, the EU's strongest economy, it was not former Chancellor Angela Merkel who initiated the debt trap, but a center-left coalition before she came to office in 2005. The collapse of the East German Communist regime coincided with the Anglo-American campaign to have all governments adopt neoliberalism. Similar to Japan, Germany's corporatist model was not yielding the profits that corporations expected, so the government used reunification as the pretext to adopt neoliberalism, although there were already some policies in the works before 1989. A bourgeois counterrevolution, German neoliberalism entailed the weakening of the social safety net and the redefining of social relations. This was especially burdening the East German working class suffering high unemployment and insecurity in the few years after reunification.[717]

In an article entitled *"Torturing the Poor, German-Style"*, Thomas Klikauer stresses that the weakening of the social welfare state took place under the Social Democratic Party (SPD)-Green Party coalition (1998-2005) pursuing neoliberal policies. Although historically the SPD struck a compromise that would permit labor's social inclusion into the institutional mainstream, by the 1990s, the SPD was Europe's most important socialist party and fully embraced neoliberalism and Keynesian militarism, just as the British Labour Party and all European socialist parties.

Klilauer writes: *"Germany's chancellor [Gerhard] Schröder (SPD) –known as the "Comrade of the Bosses"– no longer sought to integrate labor into capitalism, at least not the Lumpenproletariat or precariate[1]. These sections of society are now deliberately driven into mass poverty, joining the growing number of working poor on a scale not seen in Germany perhaps since the 1930s."[718]*

Like many workers around the world who needed more than one job to meet debt payments and living expenses, three million Germans, up from 150,000 in 2003, lived in Europe's richest nation as part of a rising debtor underclass. Even before the austerity tide of the 2010s, Germany's working poor and lumpenproletariat had been increasing in numbers. Social exclusion and the expansion of the debtor class manifested themselves in the national elections of 2017 when for the first time since the interwar era a political party carrying the legacy of Nazism, the *Alternative fur Deutschland* (AfD), founded by an elite ultra-conservative group captured 13% of the vote to become the third-largest party.[719]

---

1. *https://www.youtube.com/watch?v=nnYhZCUYOxs*

Rejecting the link between market fundamentalism that both the SPD and German conservatives pursued since the late 1980s-early 1990s, neoliberal apologists insist that the AfD reflects a Western-wide anti-Muslim trend unrelated to social exclusion and neoliberal policies that have led to a rise in Germany's new working poor and lumpenproletariat.[720] Placing the AfD platform between neoliberalism and social populism, Ralf Havertz's essay captures the spirit of rightwing populist parties in all countries.

"The party now has adopted a strategy of ambivalence, representing neoliberal and social populist positions at the same time; and it can be expected that they will play with this ambiguity in the future. The party now has adopted a strategy of ambivalence, representing neoliberal and social populist positions at the same time; and it can be expected that they will play with this ambiguity in the future."[721]

Whether in Germany, the US, or elsewhere, there is no empirical foundation to the argument that rightwing populism is devoid of historical roots; that it is unconnected either to domestic or foreign policy, relying merely on demagogues' rhetoric for its existence. As much in Germany in the US, and across the world, the neoliberal model precipitated inequality and rightwing populism as it hastened social exclusion and the new chronic debtor class. The inevitable political clashes between neoliberal pluralism, which presents itself as democratic, on the one hand, and rightwing populism, on the other, do not aim at eliminating structural exploitation built into the social contract. Rather, the objective is how best to manage it and how to mobilize popular support to minimize grassroots popular opposition.[722]

CHAPTER V:

'De-democratization' under Neoliberalism

A Theoretical Framework

"De-democratization" is the withering of the liberal-democratic institutional structure, evolving under a hybrid regime that projects the image of democracy narrowly identified with the market economy. Whether one calls it "autocratization", as Anna Luhrmann and Stefan Lindberg, or reversion from democratic to undemocratic government, as Charles Tilly sees it, the result is the erosion of liberal democracy which is what has taken place under neoliberal transformation.[723]

Throughout the 20th century, de-democratization was taking place when multi-party systems and elected governments gave way to military or civilian dictatorships that the armed forces, police, and traditional elites supported. As neoliberalism undermines popular democracy, which implies undercutting public consent and inclusiveness in public policy decision-making, class warfare, rising inequality, and downward social mobility have been symptoms of the political economy.

Because of the implied identification of capitalism and liberal democracy, there is reluctance to recognize the correlation between neoliberalism and de-democratization. Even when evident in advanced Western countries, including the US, clinging to the mythology of Western liberal tradition and Jeffersonian democracy makes people feel safe about their ideological universe. Refusing to accept neoliberal democracy's crisis in managing social relations, or to acknowledge the hastening of authoritarianism, apologists of the transformation model do not see the rise in social exclusion and reduction in civil liberties as a salient issue. In *Undoing the Demos: Neoliberalism's Stealth Revolution* (2015), Wendy Brown points out the illusion of democracy is catalytic in liberalism, until neoliberalism strips it off layer by layer.

Western scholars, journalists, and politicians point to countries like Turkey under Recep Tayyip Erdogan, Myanmar under military commander-in-chief Min Aung Hlaing, and Kazakhstan's president Kassym-Jomart Tokayev as typical examples of authoritarianism. Once discounting cultural differences, Erdogan, Aung Hlaing, and Tokayev operate within the same neoliberal global economy, sharing common traits found in the liberal-democratic West. A closer historical analysis shows that beneath the surface there are common elements of de-democratization between the West where the mechanisms of institutional control are both more subtle and ubiquitous and corruption legalized to reflect the neoliberal value system, and the non-Western periphery where crony capitalism is intertwined with traditionalism, patronage, and paternalistic politics.[724]

Aside from religion, nationalism, militarism, and social exclusion as common traits that rightwing elites use wherever de-democratization has taken root, the larger question is about the advanced capitalist countries fostering authoritarianism under the guise of Western liberal norms. This is not only under the neoliberal model, but under capitalism predating the current ideology, especially with the US invoking the doctrine of exceptionalism. Contributing to Trump's 'America First' populist slogan, historically, exceptionalism entails that the US is on a unique mission with a divine mandate, as originally found in the Declaration of Independence (*...with a firm reliance on the Protection of Divine Providence).* Setting itself above and apart from the rest of the world, the American elites were never bound to follow the same rules that they dictated to other countries in conducting foreign or domestic policy and considering that exceptionalism along with Manifest Destiny and states' rights cultural and political tradition, authoritarianism is enmeshed in neoliberalism as part of politically-imposed historical faith in individualism and market forces, rather than collective welfare.[725]

Besides the US, other countries have historical roots in traditions where authoritarianism easily prevails within the electoral system. South Korea and Taiwan, which Westerners consider democratic primarily because of geopolitical and economic ties to the West, have aspects of cultural and institutional semi-authoritarianism within a system of neo-corporatism similar to postwar Japan. In response to the need for political consensus that permits further policy shifts at the expense of workers and the middle class, hybrid models have been as strong in the periphery as in the core, especially during the Trump administration, which exploited historical social exclusionary politics of racism, ethnocentrism, and anti-pluralism, targeting Muslims and non-whites.[726]

With a fairly robust social safety net and a commitment to social justice, even in Scandinavian countries, the right-wing neoliberal populist phenomenon has managed to foster sociopolitical divisions, in large measure because of rising inequality and marginalization. According to the 2021 report of Sweden's *Institute for Democracy and Electoral Assistance*, in the second half of the 2010s, *"many democratic governments suffer from backsliding by adopting their tactics of restricting free speech and weakening the rule of law, exacerbated by what threatens to become a "new normal" of Covid-19 restrictions. For the fifth consecutive year, the number of countries moving in an authoritarian direction exceeds the number of countries moving in a democratic direction. The number moving in the direction of authoritarianism is three times the number moving towards democracy."*[727]

Opposing the liberal-democratic ideology of Voltaire-Rousseau and the Enlightenment's emphasis on reason and science as catalysts to understand and solve society's problems, Hayek among other neoliberals viewed Enlightenment values promoting representative government as an obstacle to market efficiency. Ironically, Hayek's skepticism of religions' truth value did not extend to the market which he believed must be subject to manipulation for the sake of strengthening capital. It stands to reason that market manipulation necessarily entails social relations manipulation through the political process. Hence, an implied back-channel authoritarian tilt.[728]

From 1945 to 1990 many governments used the Cold War and the "East-West" bipolar world order as a pretext to suppress trade union rights and civil rights in the name of national security, thus silencing dissent. Decrying human rights violations by the Communist monolithic state, the US and its Western allies argued that national security transcends human rights and civil rights at home and especially abroad.

National security provided the pretext to violate human rights by supporting right-wing dictatorships. Mostly through covert operations, from 1947 and 1989, the US engaged in regime change operations 72 times, and carried out 251 military interventions, in some fashion, from 1991 to 2022. Claiming to support 'freedom and democracy', regime change operations and interventions were invariably to install pro-US regimes, regardless of their authoritarian and hostile position toward democracy.[729]

Intertwined with American "exceptionalism", the US selectively used human rights policy to promote the market economy on a world scale through policies that have often resulted in de-democratization in both core and periphery. As part of the neoliberal model's global reach, transformation intensified under the manufactured generic war on terror and the new containment Cold War policy aimed mostly at China and Russia. Iran, Cuba, Venezuela, and North Korea remained the lesser targets, with even lesser ones, including Somalia, Nicaragua,

Syria, and Sudan. Ironically, the "end of history" neoliberal era ushered in de-democratization on a global scale reinvigorating military Keynesianism.[730]

In the 2020 *"Democracy Report"*, the University of Gothenberg's V-Dem Institute, which is the world's largest collector of data on democracy, confirmed democracy's erosion in 26 countries. *"One-third of the world's population now lives in countries that are undergoing autocratization – the decline of democratic regime traits. Even in seven European countries – Bulgaria, Croatia, Czech Republic, Hungary, Poland, Romania, and Serbia – liberals have succeeded in weakening liberal democratic institutions substantially. Moreover, illiberal and authoritarian-leaning parties are on the rise in almost all European countries, threatening democratic institutions and norms."*[731]

Among many critics of neoliberalism, Wendy Brown has been among the most articulate scholars, arguing that neoliberal ideology prevails as much in the public sector as in every other, fomenting 'de-democratization'. Rather than citizens whose human rights the social contract guarantees as part of collective welfare, human beings are reduced to automaton extensions of a hierarchical economic system, more commodified today than they were in the nascent phase of industrial capitalism. This kind of ubiquitous transformation of the individual's identity under 'de-democratization' was evident in interwar totalitarian countries.[732]

"Neoliberalism is, both in principle and in practice," Jamie Peck and Nik Theodore point out, *"compatible with, and sometimes even productive of, authoritarian, despotic, paramilitaristic, and/or corrupt state forms and agents within civil society." By reducing neoliberalism "to a bundle of economic policies with inadvertent political and social consequences," analysts are liable to underestimate its role as a pervasive "political rationality that both organizes these policies and reaches beyond the market". Mobilizing and yet at the same time reaching beyond the market has long been an ideological hallmark of neoliberalism, the recurring manifestations of which are never identical but resound in ways that are nevertheless unmistakable."*[733]

Subtly interwoven into the institutional structure, in some respects even more so than in interwar totalitarian regimes because of modern technology and closer national and transnational integration of institutions in the digital era, neoliberalism has been suppressing civil rights and human rights in the name of market efficiency. To attract private investment, local and central government agencies assist with civil rights suppression, using the pretext of safer neighborhoods and cities, which implies targeting marginalized populations from the poor to the homeless as part of privatization development programs. Operating under the umbrella of all bourgeois political parties, regardless of rhetorical claims either opposing globalization or favoring social welfare, neoliberalism thrives because of the masks that political parties provide.[734]

The neoliberal surveillance state retains vestiges of pluralism and the façade of liberal democracy identified with electoral choice, consumerism, and cultural diversity. Just as the Fascist and Nazi parties convinced many Europeans to accept the totalitarian state because the options were Bolshevism or liberal democracy which could lead to Bolshevism, authoritarian neoliberals argue that de-democratization policies are intended to preserve traditional society and prevent the decadence of the liberal-pluralist culture.[735]

Whereas interwar totalitarian regimes did not permit protest and resistance, freedom of expression, and freedom of assembly, neoliberalism permits dissent within the narrow boundaries of institutional perimeters which have become increasingly regimented since the Thatcher-Reagan era. Celebrating the open society as the salvation from the tyranny of Keynesian social welfare democracy, pluralist neoliberals have been confronting a rightwing populist challenge, thereby exposing the contradictions of the transformation model preaching freedom while carrying on class-war policies resulting in de-democratization.

Along with due process and inclusive electoral politics, rejection of freedom of speech and assembly entails that de-democratization under the neoliberal socioeconomic structure exposes the philosophical contradictions of Karl Popper's neo-conservatism. Supporting deregulation, privatization, and market-based institutional criteria, neoconservatism and neoliberalism diverge on due process Machiavellianism, and the oligarchy that capitalism creates.

By the end of the 2010s, some neoconservatives were reluctant to support autocratization as it pertained to social exclusion. However, they were not at all reluctant to subordinate democracy and social justice to transcendent geoeconomic and geopolitical goals. As a pretext to reject institutional legitimacy, opportunistic populist manipulation of the COVID-19 pandemic was as close as many right-wingers came to expose their counterrevolutionary predilections. Considering that all bourgeois political parties have been moving to the right and setting the stage for de-democratization since the early Cold War with the official stamp of approval of the IMF peddling austerity which leads to economic and political polarization, the hybrid political model under the thin layer of democracy was difficult to conceal. This was especially after Trump's election legitimized authoritarianism as the new conservatism for the mainstream political arena.[736]

As Claudio Hallo has argued, de-democratization has been taking place under the many faces of liberal democracy because systemic change to achieve greater social justice is unthinkable for its goals are incongruent with capitalism. *"If the core of neoliberalism is a natural fact, as suggested by the ideology already embedded deep within our collective psyche, who can change it? Can you live without breathing, or stop the succession of days and nights? This is why Western democracy chooses among the many masks behind which is essentially the same liberal party. Change is not forbidden, change is impossible. Some consider this feature to be an insidious form of invisible totalitarianism."*[737]

Rooted in ultra-relativism and rejection of value systems, especially the criminal justice system influenced by social values, postmodernism opposition to reason, truth, empiricism and faith in progress, combined with consumer culture have inculcated into peoples' minds that they have never been so free.[738] Public opinion polls indicate that most people have never felt so helpless about determining their fate in a society; ironic given that neoliberalism promotes the primacy of the self-governing individual, not the community of which she/he is an integral part. This false premise is the basis for social science and goes to the heart of the mental construct about which Hayek was enthusiastic because it was based on Schumpeter's methodological individualism (*Das Wesen und der Hauptinhalt der theoretischenand Nationalökonomie*, 1909). The problem is in the contradictions, leaving those embracing such beliefs baffled when the theoretical test fails upon encountering daily life.

Quantitatively measured, consumerist freedom is based on materialist criteria at the individual level rather than any social criteria within the context of society's institutions. This comes at a cost not just to society as a whole, but to one's sense of social responsibility subordinated in the quest for atomistic pursuit. The neoliberal hegemonic culture's value system incessantly contributes to de-politization, de-democratization, and marginalization as the norm. Conspicuous consumption, including those going deeper into debt just to maintain consumer habits as social status, manifests a means to transcend or defy social status; at least, as reflected in real assets to experience a sense of vicarious social mobility that bourgeois society expects. Capitalism's universal characteristic, which neoliberal culture reinforces, social status, and identity linked to wealth have been part of the evolution of material culture in the last five hundred years.[739]

As though freedom operates objectively with the individual's ability to actualize one's free will transcending socioeconomic and political context, the media, government, educational, and cultural institutions, including churches absorbed by the neoliberal ideology, incessantly reinforce individual freedom as a core value, emphasizing cultural determinism, often under the veil of environmental determinism. Within the context of the neoliberal institutional structure, which obviates collective welfare, freedom is predicated on class, above all else, and free will is but an illusion, as Louis Althusser has argued. In a neoliberal society, where the atomistic values transcend the welfare of society, private profit has supplanted public interest. In such a social context, de-democratization has been the logical outcome.[740]

In *"The Unholy Alliance of Neoliberalism and Postmodernism"*, Hans van Zon argues that these Western World dominant ideologies have molded society since the 1980s. *"Neoliberalism by the commercialization of even the most sacred domains and postmodernism by its super-relativism and refusal to recognize any hierarchy in value or belief systems,"* has undermined society's course. Perversely, the counterrevolutionary ideology born out of panic that socialism was taking over the world has emulated the right-wing totalitarian model just as interwar fascism thrived under somewhat similar structural conditions.[741]

Through the creation of neoliberal policies and the remolding of institutions and culture that influence the collective consciousness, the convergence of neoliberalism and postmodernism have contributed to de-democratization more than either neoliberals or self-baptized postmodernists would care to admit. Because of market hegemony, pluralists and rightwing populists present the social contract as transcending politics. Presenting the ideologies as 'objective' forces, as they are laws of nature, the convergence of neoliberalism and postmodern skepticism has contributed to de-democratization. Consumer fetishism and the commoditized value of everything, most especially commoditized humans, at the core of the value system, inevitably devalue anthropocentric values and democracy.[742]

Cold War, Class War, and De-democratization

Enjoying unrivaled military and economic global power during the Cold War, the US imposed a transformation policy on the non-Communist world as a means of sustaining imperial hegemony in the name of Western anti-Communist solidarity contained the seeds of de-democratization institutionally and culturally. In 1947 when Harry Truman institutionalized the Soviet American confrontation, neoliberal thinkers gathered at Mont Pelerin to articulate strategies that would influence Western policy intended to efface the Keynesian model once and for all. Financed by some of Europe's wealthiest families, the Mont Pelerin Society grew in importance after its first meeting which coincided with the Truman Doctrine (March 1947) launching the Cold War, the anti-labor Taft-Hartley Act (June 1947, and the Marshall Plan (April 1948) intended to reintegrate Europe and its colonies and spheres of influence under the aegis of the US. As the new hegemon of Western Judeo-Christian civilization with a growing imperial network, American political, and socioeconomic elites saw merit in ideas found in Hayek's *The Road to Serfdom* (1944) calling for the state to intervene on capitalists' behalf to mitigate the contracting economic cycle.[743]

Given the imperial assumptions behind the US-led global transformation policy, the Cold War marked the beginning of de-democratization in the name of defending democracy. A counterrevolutionary ideology, neoliberalism would eventually impose mass political and geoeconomic conformity on a global level. Presenting the Communist global threat in Armageddon terms, the US pursued global transformation geopolitically and economically to strengthen Pax Americana, while the IMF, World Bank, and GATT were the instruments of integration and catalysts in neoliberalism's historical antecedents. Against such background, the Mont Pelerin Society was a continuation of 19th-century Euro-American imperial ambitions adapted to the realities of the mid-20th century global power structure. At the core of the capitalist world system and the zenith of its power in the mid-1940s, the US integrated most non-communist countries into the trans-Atlantic imperial orbit.[744]

Working with 460 organizations in 96 countries, Mont Pelerin's neoliberals influenced both centrist and rightwing political parties. The question of the degree to which the Mont Pelerin Society has historically contributed to de-democratization can be summed up by Corey Robin's contention that in an attempt to preserve hierarchy against the tide of popular democracy, conservatism undercuts the liberal order and pluralistic society at its core. Contrary to commonly held views, Corey Robin included, de-democratization did not emanate exclusively from the conservative camp that embraced neoliberal ideology. Rather, the liberal camp, whose political economy goals and foreign policy aims have been essentially the same as those of conservatives, has historically played a pivotal role.[745]

Pubic influence began with the Mont Pelerin Society's ideological support in various universities, including Stanford University's Hoover Institution, the University of Chicago, and Cambridge University. By advocating market fundamentalism, neoliberal academics supported the surrender of popular sovereignty to the financial hierarchy. This necessarily entailed the surrender of civil rights and human rights to a political economy devoid of any social justice criteria. In the amoral Machiavellian world of social contract-sanctioned "criminal virtue" that the political establishment and socioeconomic elite impose on society, it was inevitable that liberal democratic institutions would wither away for the sake of global economic integration intended to guarantee optimal capital return on investment.

Indicative of the perversion of values rooted in capitalist greed transcending any commitment to democracy and social justice, hegemonic culture celebrates those responsible for global social inequality and authoritarianism as society's heroes. It is as though time has stood still since Charles Dickens, Victor Hugo, and Upton Sinclair when robber baron monopolists harbored contempt for democracy and workers, viewing them as obstacles to capitalist accumulation. In class war reflected in public policy and corporate practice, 21st-century neoliberalism restored 19th-century capitalist disdain for humanity and popular democracy.[746]

Under neoliberalism's institutionalization since the 1970s in Chile, history is replete with examples of the gradual legitimization of activities that were undemocratic, if not illegal in the Keynesian era. To the degree that the lines between the legitimate economy and organized criminal activity are blurred, they reflect the flexible lines between legally-financed billionaire-backed elected officials, oligarchs, and drug lords laundering money in the world's largest banks real estate, and the stock market. In March 2022, Credit Suisse, one of the world's most trusted financial institutions for billionaires, oligarchs, and varieties of individuals concealing money from the authorities, had its legal department send letters to investors to *"destroy and permanently erase"* any confidential information linking the bank to Russian oligarchs' loans for their *"jets, yachts, real estate and/or financial assets."*

The odd aspect about these letters is that just a month earlier there were criminal charges about its involvement in a Bulgarian cocaine-money-laundering operation. In spring 2023, the bank sunk into the abyss, facing a run by depositors as it confronted bankruptcy, only to be saved by the government in a brokered deal allowing UBS to buy it, after securing 100 billion francs in government liquidity assistance.[747]

Hardly the first time, considering its nine major scandals from 1986 to 2022, Credit Suisse was not new to embarrassing stories about its remarkable ability to circumvent the law and pay billions in fines. Beyond the bank's internal data disclosed to the public about how the rich keep billions out of government oversight, widespread public skepticism of a rigged economy is based on cynicism on the part of voters who lose faith in institutions or turn to the far right for solutions. Mainstream institutions are swept up in the same corrosive wave to the degree that liberal-democratic society is reduced to a hybrid autocracy with democratic elements. Invariably, this phenomenon is associated with former Soviet republics but is commonly found globally.[748]

In *"Democratic Authoritarianism: Origins and Effects,"* Dawn Brancati focuses on non-Western societies before Trump, and the Panama Papers and Paradise Papers expose the depth of tax evasion and avoidance through tax havens by the socioeconomic and political elites who preach public virtue to the public while they engage in criminal activities. De-democratization takes place from within because the social contract's guardians undermine it, although they have it set up to serve their class interests. Overwhelming evidence for de-democratization points to the use of the hybrid model in which the authoritarian regime makes use of liberal bourgeois democratic institutions to enhance credibility and project legitimacy. From law enforcement to media education, the state's enhanced ability to govern through subtle means of engendering social conformity has had wide institutional support essential to preserve the neoliberal order.[749]

The Great Recession, COVID-19, and US-G7 sanctions in response to the Russian war in Ukraine hastened the global rightwing tilt along with rising inequality. Examining the topic from a Euro-centric perspective, many scholars associate authoritarianism and economic corruption with developing nations and the former Soviet republics. An integral part of hybrid politics, institutionalized kleptocratic capitalism is usually identified with the periphery where clientelism and patronage historically prevailed over a rules-based market economy largely as an extension of the core's economic and geopolitical hegemony. Kleptocratic capitalism's corrosive impact on the political institutions and social structure of the Global South has been symptomatic of the integrated capitalist world economy and imperialism's legacy in post-colonial regimes.[750]

Historically, it has been difficult to prove the magnitude of the behind-the-scenes political and business arrangements of clientelism and patronage whose tentacles reach globally. Despite the lack of transparency, and regardless of liberal-democratic or hybrid quasi-authoritarian regime, the catalyst to kleptocracy rests within the structure of the global political economy. Published in 2016, the Panama Papers covering more than 11 million offshore financial records of the richest people in the world provide definitive proof that kleptocracy is a substantial part, if not at the heart of the system. Although there is a well-documented pattern of government contracts to business in all domains, especially defense, kleptocracy has been at the core of the status quo, and not such a deviation from neoliberalism.[751]

In November 2017, the Paradise Papers added more evidence from 13.4 million documents about tax havens in Panama, Cyprus, Bermuda, Malta, and Luxemburg, among others, including Nevada and Wyoming. Besides ending the myth of kleptocracy as an exclusive Third World phenomenon, the leaked documents brought to light the nexus of world leaders, from former Prime Minister Silvio Berlusconi, President Donald Trump, Mexican billionaire Carlos Slim, Russian oligarch Roman Abramovich, and others with reputed ties to organized criminal networks and mainstream financial institutions and governments. Because the same social and political elites are engaged in illegal activities, pretending to support liberal democracy, middle-class and working-class voters understandably become cynical about the decadence of democracy.[752]

American liberals blame billionaires like the Koch brothers and the Mercer family for funding right-wing causes that contribute to society's de-democratization. However, liberal politicians have also been receiving campaign contributions from billionaires whose names are on the Panama Papers and Paradise lists. Despite the institutionalized kleptocracy as an integral part of the global political economy, the media presents the topic as an aberration, something about corrupt politicians and wealthy individuals, instead of the political economy and laws accommodating kleptocrats.[753]

Aside from political campaign contributions, historically the converging interests of the capitalist class and political class, and how such interests contribute to de-democratization are rarely topics for analysis in mainstream media. Perpetuating the myth that voters, not corporate interests, determine public policy, the media both manufactures consent, as Walter Lippmann argued a century ago (*Public Opinion*, 1922), and perpetuates it to sustain the social order.[754]

Under the neoliberal transformation's global reach, institutional and cultural de-democratization has resulted not only in replacing the corporate welfare state with market hegemony but in molding mass consciousness which de-democratization along with the kleptocratic political economy is a necessary precondition for the primacy of the "free-market individual".[755] Beyond the domain of politics and the market, de-democratization, kleptocracy, rightwing populism, and the personality cult endanger the very fabric of bourgeois society by determining the culture and value system that normalize such conditions. As a segment of society gravitates toward acceptance of rightwing solutions, others lapse into apathy, cynicism, and alienation.

Neoliberal myths guarantee that the masses accept the "winner-take-all" economics which leads to de-democratization with winner-take-all politics. Although progressive grassroots groups have been active in several countries, the hegemonic culture continues to determine neoliberalism's global reach behind a facade of pluralist inclusionary politics. Out of fear that the alternative is continued de-depoliticization, de-democratization, and eventual full-blown authoritarianism, the nonconformist progressives in the minority have moved to embrace the liberal-democratic status quo. Hardly anything resembling democracy, neoliberalism, which many progressives supported by throwing their vote behind liberal pluralists, led to de-democratization that liberals attribute solely to rightwing populism to deflect attention away from structural problems.[756]

The Popular Base of Authoritarianism

Among factors that shape political behavior, social class and cultural conditioning are catalysts in political identity tied to self-identity subject to various salient factors ranging from religion to ethnic affiliation and social/lifestyle associations. In the age of mass politics, political parties, the media, and mainstream institutions have convinced a segment of voters that sovereignty rests with the people rather than built into the social contract. Against the reality of downward social mobility affecting the middle class and workers, political mobilization of voters becomes especially important for mainstream political parties.[757]

Partly because of the highly integrated world economy and means of mass communication, popular discontent manifests itself in populist ideologies of social exclusion around the world. Liberals have been struggling to mobilize a popular base that includes progressives hoping to strengthen the social safety net and prevent authoritarianism. As democracy's failures under neoliberalism became more evident from the Trans-Atlantic core to the Global South, social groups became more disengaged from the mainstream political parties responsible for the crisis. Enjoying corporate and billionaire funding, the far right has exploited the neoliberal crisis to mobilize popular support.[758]

During the neoliberal "post-truth" era, amid de-democratization symptomatic of capitalism's structural crisis, mainstream and social media played a catalytic role in mass indoctrination. Relying on reactionary postmodernism and relativism to forge and disseminate the neoliberal consensus, rightwing populists have taken advantage of the neoliberal class war and policies imposing social conformity to steer the masses toward liberal-democratic anti-institutionalism. Above all, the inherent contradictions manifested egregious flaws in public policy affecting the lives of billions. Because of lingering economic contraction after 2008, the pandemic of 2020-2022, and the stagflation of 2022-2023, rising socioeconomic polarization further contributed to democracy's decline. This was so much so that the supposed chasm between Biden and Trump, or Macron and Le Pen was hardly noticeable in peoples' judging by peoples' material and political lives.[759]

The convergence of the Great Recession, the Eurozone banking/sovereign debt crisis of the 2010s, and rising global inequality prompted the quest for political solutions tilted heavily toward de-democratization within the neoliberal mainstream. Building on a popular base of extremist exclusionists, the right became more hostile toward the liberal-democratic consensus of tolerance, reserving animosity for globalization proponents, progressives, and marginalized groups.[760]

Neoliberalism's ascendancy precipitating the twilight of liberal democracy has followed a pattern in the decline of merit-based Enlightenment ideals. During the digital revolution, young people took for granted that the social contract operated on a merit-based system simply because the technology was presumably the great equalizer, just as Wall Street and media analysts presented it. Empirical evidence, however, shows that the digital revolution increased income and wealth inequalities, inordinately favoring capital at labor's expense.[761]

Depending on the country's historical experiences and cultural traditions, loss of confidence in the Western liberal value system manifested itself in various ways. Although neoliberalism had absorbed the mainstream institutions, some among the political and socioeconomic elites were eager to de-democratize society at the constitutional and cultural levels without taking into account civil rights and social justice. Others lapsed into a state of de-politization apathy, closer to neoliberalism's moral and political nihilistic core. Especially since 2008, public opinion polls in Western and non-Western countries indicated a low level of youth optimism about the institutional structure, especially public policy as a vehicle to help lift them socioeconomically under a more democratic society.[762]

Except for China where the level of public optimism and confidence was high because of steady long-term economic growth prospects, most of the world experienced an erosion of confidence in the status quo as the post-2008 economic effects impacted living standards. This trend favored the nationalist/populists lashing out against globalization and liberal democracy. Since Thatcher and Reagan's counterrevolution, neoliberal politicians have been promising upward mobility to millennials and Generation Z growing up in times of downward mobility and de-democratization as the norm.[763]

Especially for the G7 operating under the umbrella of a pluralist-liberal government where the promise of upward mobility has been elusive, political polarization intensified during the second decade of the 21st century. Partly because of the absence of tangible benefits in the material lives of the majority, combined with rising pessimism for better days ahead, a segment of the middle and working-class population turned to exclusionary populism as a form of popular resistance, without appreciating that populism was a distraction for neoliberalism's detrimental impact on their interests and reinforced class war.[764]

Demanding perpetual income redistribution from the bottom up through various fiscal, monetary, and other policies, the capitalist class fully supported downward pressure on middle-class and working-class income to recover recession-related capital losses. Consequently, the focus of liberal and conservative politicians was whether to further legitimize the authoritarian model as a means of managing the neoliberal political economy or to keep vestiges of pluralism linked to a social safety net that projects the image of a democratic society. Ultimately, the issue was about how the bourgeois state managed the growing inequality amid downward social mobility while maintaining a popular voting base.[765]

Contrary to liberal and rightwing media accounts, a segment of the working class and middle class gravitate toward authoritarianism with guidance from rightwing elites. Operating under the same neoliberal umbrella, the political class is almost indistinguishable in policy making. This leaves cultural and lifestyle issues, and liberal vs conservative rhetoric for voters to separate the two camps. A similar pattern of political polarization leading to de-democratization took place during the transition from liberal democracy to Fascism in Italy in the early 1920s and Germany in the early 1930s.

Once the Italian and German middle class began to fear that downward socioeconomic mobility meant descending toward the working class, the political reaction was to castigate the capitalist elites, while dreading the prospect of a socialist regime that would result in their proletarianization. As much during the interwar era as under neoliberalism, de-democratization has meant that the authoritarian regime adopts repressive measures at the expense of marginalized social groups, the working class, and dissidents advocating more equitable income distribution. Such measures project the impression that the status quo remains safe amid the unsafe conditions that capitalism creates.[766]

Beyond working within the parliamentary system and representing the same political economy, there are some social relations parallels between the interwar Fascist era and the twenty-first-century neoliberal era. In the quest to mobilize popular support amid disillusionment with the political class, anti-globalization in the form of nationalism became the rallying cry of authoritarian politicians. US-NATO-led geopolitical friction exacerbated the nationalist trends globally. The trends were apparent even before 2008, but especially after BREXIT and Trump's election, intensifying after Russia invaded Ukraine. These trends sent political signals that rightwing populism dominated the conservative mainstream.[767]

Regardless of political identity, middle-class and working-class inability to maintain living standards drove a percentage of voters in several countries to accept the mythology of rightwing rhetoric. By further punishing economically and marginalizing politically the weakest segments of society, somehow this would elevate the rest. Through the successful use of corporate media and social media, authoritarianism apologists deflected the public's attention by offering culture wars and tangible enemies as a substitute for a constructive policy that would reverse the downward social mobility inherent in neoliberal capitalism. Not just billionaire conservatives, but liberals were also feeding the culture wars as a distraction from the bankruptcy of the neoliberal model's class war and its pernicious social impact.[768]

Hardly a new propaganda tool, culture wars distraction goes to the heart of neoliberalism's failure to deliver a more robust middle class and higher living standards for all classes. Under conditions of sustained downward social mobility, immersed in cultural determinism that mainstream institutions, media, and academics were promoting, it was not surprising that a segment of the US lower middle class and workers turned to the far right by 2016.[769]

In *"Drivers of Authoritarian Populism in the United States,"* Dalibor Ruhak, Liz Kennedy, and Vikram Singh concluded that economic uncertainty in the middle-income population left it feeling squeezed by high-tech and globalization. *"This is consistent with the voting patterns observed in the 2016 U.S. presidential election, as Donald Trump received a large share of votes from the middle segments of the income ladders and from areas where jobs were under threat from automation."*[770]

In an article entitled *"The deceptive coherence of Marine Le Pen's electoral base"* Bilal Berady argues that the French middle class constituting the far-right voting base rallied behind the populist candidate for reasons similar to the American white middle class supporting Trump. Following the lead of conservative and rightwing politicians, a segment of the pessimistic middle class blamed "liberal elites" for pursuing globalization, while faulting progressives for demanding social justice, unionization, equal pay for equal work, and workplace safety.[771]

Besides failing to assess accurately capitalism's contradictions in undermining market equilibrium, political polarization, and lack of social justice, middle-class anxiety about downward mobility squeezed by big capital remained important elements that populist politicians and media propagandists exploited to strengthen the voting base. While blaming the liberal elites, a select few billionaire advocates of globalization and rightwing populists defaulted domestic structural problems to China which had not embraced the same trans-Atlantic neoliberal rules. Playing up nationalism around which the middle class and workers rally was a long-standing strategy that usually worked, except in cases like the severe economic dislocation of 2008 which caused greater polarization contributing to de-democratization.[772]

Besides the middle class, there is also a segment of the working class gravitating to right-wing populist parties. Ever since England's first industrial revolution, the higher-skilled working class (labor aristocracy) has historically aspired to join the petite bourgeoisie, at least for their progeny. The 19th-century labor aristocracy theory, which Friedrich Engels and Karl Kautsky popularized by analyzing the pro-establishment predisposition of skilled workers, helps to explain 21st-century trends among well-paid workers gravitating toward authoritarianism. According to one source, one-third of Trump voters in 2016 were in the salary category under $50000 annually. Despite Trump's blatant attack on labor unions, many of his supporters included union members, indicative that the more highly-paid workers gravitated toward the far-right candidate. Alienation within the liberal democratic social contract is the most important factor for a segment of the working class turning to the far right.[773]

Because workers make up a part of the rightwing populist base with percentages differing depending on the country, the media, rightwing parties, and mainstream analysts project the image that the working class is the bulk of the political base. Lower-paid workers generally support centrist or progressive policies. The lumpenproletariat has remained disillusioned and apathetic, thus susceptible to propaganda about the virtues of autocratization projecting dreams of grandeur with which the masses identify. More characteristic of the higher-paid working class than the middle class, anti-immigration, and anti-minority attitudes have been catalysts for mobilizing mass support by appealing to cultural/ethnic identity.[774]

The higher the level of downward social mobility, the more intense the biased attitudes on the part of some higher-paid workers who feel as threatened by the marginalized low-wage migrants, women, and minorities as they do by AI technology replacing them. Not just right-wing media and politicians, but especially mainstream liberals contribute to right-wing indoctrination by focusing on culture wars rather than global capitalism undercutting the working class in all countries, regardless of race, gender, religion, ethnicity, and lifestyle.[775]

Opposing the liberal pluralist institutional structure which they see as elitist and an obstacle to upward mobility, a segment of the petit bourgeoisie and working class blame the liberal world order for the decline of economic vitality and their status. Static notions of power asymmetry in a democratic society are obstacles to social justice, contributing to de-democratization. Reactionaries support hierarchical authoritarianism based on asymmetric power relationships that would serve narrow cultural and class interests while preserving cherished traditional conservative values. In the race for capital accumulation, especially amid a shifting of the core from the US-EU to China, political polarization and de-democratization are a byproduct of market hegemony generating socioeconomic polarization globally.[776]

After the Great Recession, the rise of right-wing populism was evident in several countries. Behind a very thin layer of 'democracy', rests a coercive system of a highly corrupt government forcibly displacing small farmers and suppressing labor rights to accommodate everything from foreign-owned casinos and resorts to auto manufacturing. Despite benefiting from global capitalist integration and being influenced by the culture of a 'free-trade' economy, Kazakhstan and Kyrgyzstan, Cambodia followed a course toward violent authoritarianism instead of Western pluralism. Although each country's neoliberal authoritarian regime reflected characteristics of its historical cultural and political traditions of socially hierarchal exclusion, they experienced capitalist appropriation in the primary sector of production, banking, and public utilities by local elites often in ventures with foreign investors. The result was a chronic widening income gap and downward social mobility as much in Central Asia as in Cambodia under regimes with more similarities to traditional paternalistic society and very few to Western liberalism.[777]

Just as the neoliberal transformation integrated the global economy more closely than ever, impacting all institutions and homogenizing the value system, it also globalized common traits of autocratization manifested differently in each country. For example, Brazil's military dictatorship (1964-1985) molded a segment of the population to the degree that Jair Bolsonaro was elected president in 2018 and worked with the traditional elites making neoliberal transformation possible. However, it was the government of Fernando Henrique Cardoso, both as finance minister under President Itamar Franco in 1993 and as president from 1995 to 2003, that abandoned developmentalism in favor of neoliberalism.[778]

Although he veered to the far-right camp, Bolsonaro continued Cardoso's neoliberal projects, taking them further to the degree that he alienated neoliberal pluralists because of massive deforestation estimated at 17% of the rainforest. An agribusiness ally, Bolsonaro permitted the exploitation of the Amazon's resources, combined with blunt attacks on the indigenous population to domestic and foreign companies either directly or as investors. Similar to Bolsonaro, Horacio Cartes, Paraguay's richest individual with a long history of legal and illegal activities from tobacco to currency and narcotics, relied on the country's deep authoritarian roots for his presidency (2013-2018). Not only in Latin America but globally, the authoritarian wave sweeping both Cartes and Bolsonaro into power, crushed popular dissent and commodified every aspect of policy. As much in Paraguay as in Brazil, the patronage system that predated neoliberal authoritarianism facilitated the process.[779]

Because neither country had cultural roots in liberal pluralism comparable to northwest Europe, Paraguay under Cartes, and Brazil under Bolsonaro provided more fertile ground for authoritarianism than the US and northwest Europe carrying the legacy of global militarist imperial expansion. Helped by the Republican Party at the local and state level, Trump consolidated power as a legitimate populist president pushing the limits on exclusionary populism within a traditional conservative party that had undergone neoliberal transformation since Reagan. Unlike the Latin American republics with a legacy of external dependence, the US historical experience with exclusionary populism was rooted in the politics of racism, ethnocentrism, aspects of libertarianism, and bipartisan foreign policy supporting Pax Americana.[780]

Refusing to incorporate a structuralist methodology in analyzing the rise of authoritarianism during the neoliberal era, some scholars maintain that Cartes and Bolsonaro were aberrations in their respective country's political culture, instead of the logical outgrowth. Although Cartes' neoliberal policies and governance strategies were not so different from Bolsonaro's or Trump's, in July 2022, the US blacklisted Cartes for corruption. Hardly political mutants, the neoliberal Latin American presidents emerged from their countries' institutional mainstream and reflected it in both the party base and key policies, as did Trump in the US.[781]

Like Cartes and Bolsonaro, Trump came into politics from the world of endemically corrupt business practices that he inherited from his father exploiting a system of government subsidies and tax avoidance schemes. The neoliberal environment made many such activities easier and more widespread. Once in office, Trump, like Cartes and Bolsonaro, continued the transformation model by stretching existing neoliberal norms beyond legal boundaries. Pursuing parallel activities of questionable legality for clientelist-style autocratization that commodified all aspects of public policy, these authoritarian neoliberal presidents faithfully served capital while advancing their family interests and those within their circle of big capital.[782]

Common structural traits in Paraguay, Brazil, and the US accounted for well-financed party machinery and a popular base misled by promises of eliminating obstacles to economic growth by attacking social welfare, the environment, workers, feminism, and pluralism. Silencing dissent, punishing advocates of civil and human rights, and promoting populism by relying on everything from religion and social conservatism to hate-filled rhetoric served the larger goal of neoliberal transformation. The individual heads of state were not nearly as significant as the neoliberal policies camouflaged beneath the "voters' choice" mythology that the political class and media promoted.[783]

Downward Social Mobility and the Rise of Authoritarianism in the US

Published on 15 June 2022, one of the most revealing public opinion polls shows that 55% of Democrats and 53% of Republicans stated that the US will *"cease to be a democracy"*, while only 25% considered it unlikely. The same survey indicates that the American people were not convinced the House Committee hearings of the 6 January 2021 mob attack on the capitol were intended to strengthen democracy. Instead, they viewed congressional hearings with skepticism because both parties were responsible for the institutional structure. Interestingly, public policy impacting the material needs of those polled are at the top of the dissatisfaction list. [784]

Indicative of public sentiment about the social contract, a Pew Research poll (December 2020) found that two-thirds in the US and France, 50 percent in the UK, and 40 percent in Germany believe that the government needs a complete overhaul or major reform. Except for Germany, in the other three core countries, no more than a quarter of the population felt satisfied with the political system. In 2022 and 2023 during the war in Ukraine, the situation deteriorated across Europe because of inflation and intensified anti-labor policies, especially in the UK with underpaid junior doctors and France raising the retirement age. The UK conservative government replaced workers on strike with scabs while promoting anti-strike legislation in Parliament. Amid incessant class war in the US, there was comparable trade union activity throughout 2022.[785]

From 2017 to 2022, public opinion polls indicate that between one-third and two-thirds of Americans believed that the political system needs minor to sweeping reforms. France is the only other country to show similar results during the same period. The common denominator between the US and France was Trump's GOP and Marine Le Pen's neo-Fascist National Rally party. While it is difficult to know what each person understands by the term 'democracy', respondents did not believe that the social contract represented people like them.

In another poll of 2019, the US ranked 10th from the bottom, right above Nigeria, as a functioning democracy, in the flawed category. Based on a 2022 opinion poll on democracy, Nigeria, with endemic corruption and an informal economy above fifty percent of the total, ranked higher than the US. For liberal pluralists, at least, this should have been an alarm bell that the social contract no longer inspires confidence in citizens. "*The 12 countries most dissatisfied with their democracy included four – Mexico, Greece, Brazil, and Spain – where eight in ten or more were dissatisfied with the state of democracy, and another five where six in ten or more expressed dissatisfaction: Tunisia, Italy, South Africa, Argentina, and Nigeria. The United States was close behind, with 58% expressing unhappiness with the way democracy is functioning.*"[786]

More so than the in rest of the world, in the US, the link between downward social mobility and the rise of neoliberal authoritarianism has been the subject of scholarly and political debate. As the US lapsed toward the hybrid authoritarian model while clinging to the 'the world's greatest democracy' label, the debate intensified especially as the historic bipartisanship began collapsing. Because the US has been at the core of the capitalist world economy since the mid-1940s, and it has the largest economy in nominal value only, a large stock of nuclear weapons, and a military presence in 159 countries, authoritarianism combined with hegemonic military and economic power alarms the entire world.

A public opinion poll conducted between February and April 2021 in 53 countries revealed that 44% of the 50,000 respondents feared that the US threatens democracy in their respective countries. By contrast, fear of Chinese influence was at 38% and Russian at 28%. Governments have been as skeptical of the US as the general public. According to a Cambridge University study of 137 countries, including 75 countries after Russia attacked Ukraine in February 2022, the world is divided between those in the West that were more supportive of the US and NATO, against much of the Global South representing 85% of the world's population and 40% of global GDP that supported China, Russia, or both. Largely because the US weaponized the dollar and its global financial and trade network, all in the name of national security, the mask came off Pax Americana, especially under Trump who indiscriminately launched ephemeral trade wars against foes and allies. The stated purpose was to "protect" – essentially subsidizing - everything from aluminum and steel to autos and high tech.[787]

Putting aside self-serving pronouncements by politicians, military, media, business analysts, and an assortment of those insisting that the US is the 'world's greatest democracy', the abolition of slavery evolved into an apartheid society (Jim Crow) until the Civil Rights Act of 1964, and race-based institutional structure as permanent fixtures of the hegemonic culture under the capitalist political economy. Reformers have historically aspired to fulfill the articles of the Constitution and the Bill of Rights for the sake of maintaining a sense of political integrity. Empirical data of class relations as well as other metrics, including the criminal justice system, reflect the hierarchical social/racial/ethnic structure.

In a recent book, *"Donald Trump and the Prospect for American Democracy,"* Arthur Paulson poignantly argues that America was never as democratic as its politicians, the media, or analysts contend. Under Trump's presidency of an imperial executive and weakened legislative branch, economic inequality and rightwing propaganda becoming mainstream made America even less democratic. Compared with Western Europe, Scandinavian countries, Canada, and New Zealand, the US does not project a favorable image as a democratic society, by any metrics of any international organization.[788]

Complicating the complex downward path toward autocratization, the US at the core of the world economy has been using its preeminent global military power, sanctions, the dollar, and trade as leverage. Many Americans accept the universal assumption that the US has the potential for economic prosperity translating into the realization of the American Dream for all, even under neoliberalism. In a Pew Research study in 2017, only 36% claimed to have achieved the American dream, depending on their definition, and 46% expected that they were on their way.

Measured against the actual data of downward social mobility from 1980 to 2020, the Pew study illustrates incredible public optimism based mostly on promise rather than current realities. It is hardly a secret that wealth concentration skyrocketed from Reagan to Trump, while wages remained stagnant and income share declined. The middle class declined from 47% to 36%, while the lower middle class went from 31% to 16%. These downward mobility statistics show the disconnect between reality and the aspiration of the American Dream. Social relations were not much better in neighboring Canada where the richest 20% owned 68% of the wealth and the bottom 40% accounted for just 2.7% in 2023.[789]

While the Canadian Dream is more within reach despite the erosion of the Keynesian state, the same does not hold for the US. Even Joseph Stiglitz, with a history as both a supporter and critic of neoliberal capitalism in different stages of his career, agreed that: *"America has become the advanced country not only with the highest level of inequality but one of those with the least equality of opportunity."*[790] Long before President Herbert Hoover made rugged individualism popular, the myth of the universally achievable American Dream dates back to the Declaration of Independence. Part of the myth is that upward mobility is possible like spiritual salvation as the ticket to Heaven. In the quest to become a rich nation offering the promise of upward mobility to all, upward mobility assumed significance during 19th-century industrialization.[791]

Divided on how to manage the economy, and diverging on cultural issues and the degree to which the social safety net must be maintained, Democrats and Republicans represent the same American Dream social construct, while catering to the privileged class. Differing on strategies to mobilize the masses falls within the perimeters of the neoliberal matrix, both political parties have sown the seeds of America's slippery slope to autocratization. As much as they are aware of the myth correlating the Calvinist work ethic with material success, a substantial segment, especially among young people who gravitated to Senator Bernie Sanders' campaign in 2016 and 2020, demonstrated that democracy intertwined with the American Dream is more of a myth than reality.[792]

Refusing to delve into the cultural, social, and political roots of authoritarianism, journalists and analysts from academia to the business community focus on the cult of personality, promoting 'unstable politician' theories intended to distract from structural causes and solutions that have led to autocratization over decades. Even in the aftermath of the Great Recession, there was not much analysis of the convergence of the sharp economic downturn, massive capital concentration, downward social mobility, and the rise of authoritarianism intertwined with neoliberalism. When Senator Sanders addressed some of these issues from a Keynesian perspective, mainstream media, analysts, and establishment Democrats dismissed him as a "socialist", a stigma which by implication afforded legitimacy to rightwing pro-business Trump and GOP politicians promoting authoritarian neoliberalism.[793]

Instead of focusing on the structural causes of the multidimensional crisis, the mainstream media and politicians focused on China's ascendancy as a convenient Cold War-style distraction for rising inequality, loss of high-paying manufacturing jobs, and downward mobility. Reviving the Cold War and strengthening military Keynesianism distracted from the structural crisis while affording the illusion that militarism was a way of life. Compelling friends and foes alike to adopt neoliberalism that would benefit US-based companies, at least short-term as though structural problems can be treated like corporate quarterly reports, thereby remaining on the path of the transformation model.[794]

Instead of addressing aggregate demand by supporting wage stability through consumer spending stimulus in the aftermath of the Great Recession, the US and other governments focused on reducing consumer demand. The result was to transfer capital from the weakest to the strongest banks and corporations, thereby feeding monopoly capital in a blatant appropriation process. Not just in the US, but in many OECD countries, workers' pension funds invested in stocks and bonds fell victim to the Great Recession. Pension "securitization" meant that workers' savings fed off the rising indebtedness of the workers and the middle class. In addition, raiding public pensions was ubiquitous throughout the world. Another form of corporate welfare, funds from pensions to bail out private financial institutions appeared like the government was trying to save the economy.[795]

Channeling the middle class and workers' anger about rising inequality toward the marginalized population, the Republican Party, like many of its conservative counterparts in other countries, fully embraced cultural populism. This took place beneath a thin veneer of narrowly defined anti-establishment populism and anti-elitism at the local and national levels. Historically a far-right strategy, the GOP went as far as to embrace aspects of classical interwar Fascism.

In February 2016, after quoting Benito Mussolini, Trump defended the quote of the Italian Fascist dictator. Lapsing into a hybrid political party with authoritarian aspects, the Republican party inculcated skepticism into the public's political consciousness regarding the legitimacy of the liberal institutional structure intertwined with globalization. According to a Pew Research study, the decline of trust in government filtered down to individual mistrust within one's class; this took place as a simultaneous rise in populism across the land prevailed.[796]

From the Reagan presidency to the Tea Party movement (2009-2014) and into Trump's presidential term, there were wealthy individuals involved in well-financed campaigns that forged the popular base for the reconfigured conservative party in a wide tent that included everyone from anti-abortionists and evangelicals to pro-gun, anti-environmentalist activists among other far-right fringe groups. Largely because of rising inequality, especially after 2008, the GOP's evolving cultural metamorphosis continued to integrate fringe white-supremacist-neo-Fascist elements with local and national networks hiding behind the flag and the cross. They were always there, but the old GOP kept them at arms-length, until Reagan, before full integration took place under Trump.[797]

Besides the sharp rise in official unemployment from 4.3% in 2007 to 9.6% in 2010, and the labor participation rate from 66% to 64% during the same period, American workers suffered a massive loss of income. Meanwhile, the richest 5% realized a 20% share of income gains from 2008 to 2020, relegating the American Dream to the realm of mythology. In the first months of the Great Recession, an average of 700,000 were losing their jobs each month, along with a 17% drop in average income. During the presidential election of 2012, Obama noted that economic recovery was in full swing. However, he candidly admitted that the richest 1% benefited, while the bottom 70% suffered continued income losses.[798]

Citing a University of California study, Obama conceded that from 2008 to 2013, 95% of the income benefits from his administration's policies went to the richest 1%. Less reluctant to accept responsibility for capital concentration policies that his administration implemented, he dwelled on the highly symbolic but vacuous identity politics rhetoric. It was the only means to maintain the party's popular base. In his second presidential term, he continued neoliberal policies and militarism with dead-end involvement in Syria for the sake of regime change. Higher-income inequality and greater cynicism settled in because he broke campaign promises about income inequality and strengthening social development. Obama continued pro-corporate, anti-labor, and pro-militarism policies leading to inequality, just as Bush and Clinton before him. The remarkable achievement was his ability, like that of Clinton, to project an image of a progressive Democrat representing the working class rather than Wall Street.[799]

Amid the unrelenting rising unequal economic climate, conservatives and right-wingers in the US and around the world called for a new order based on nationalism, anti-environmentalism, isolationism, militarism, traditionalism, messianic autocratic populism, and anti-institutionalism that the mainstream and social media helped to promote. As the world's only remaining superpower after the USSR collapsed, the US played a role in signaling a sharp political turn to the right. Deeply woven into the American political culture from early 19th century Manifest Destiny to neoliberal authoritarianism, these traits further enhanced rising geopolitical conflicts and trans-Atlantic rivalries with Russia and China, mostly as distractions and catalysts to mobilize voters but also to strengthen the defense sector as leverage amid intense global market share competition.[800]

Contemporary rightwing conspiracy theories about the liberal political and social elites trying to create a world government and threatening America's protestant cultural foundation and value system date back to the John Birch Society in the 1950s. Reaching an audience skeptical of the elites and any liberal identity politics group, old reactionary propaganda repackaged under neoliberalism weakened the centrist bourgeois pluralist consensus. This was largely because inequality kept rising. As conservatives moved farther to the right, centrists filled the gap of traditional conservativism. Amid downward social mobility, autocratization in the political arena spilled over to all institutions in society, co-opting the progressives under the center-right umbrella.[801]

In an empirical study using Western liberal criteria, Vanessa A. Boesse concluded that: *"The level of democracy enjoyed by the average global citizen in 2021 was down to 1989 levels. In 2021, autocracies were on the rise, harboring 70% of the world population, or 5.4 billion people. There was also a record number of countries autocratizing in 2021: 33 countries, home to 36% of the global population. In recent years, the EU seems to be facing its wave of autocratization, with 20% of its members autocratizing over the last decade. In addition to the continued downturn in global democracy, this article documents several signs that autocratization is changing in nature. Polarization increased substantially and significantly in 40 countries between 2011 and 2021, and our analysis indicates that polarization increasingly damages democracy especially recently and under anti-pluralist governments."*[802]

Partly because of disillusionment with the economic recovery benefiting the rich, exclusionary populism's popularity spread as rapidly in the US, as in the rest of the world. The symbolism of Trump's presidency inadvertently contributed to global skepticism about liberal elites whose economic interests transcend national boundaries under the neoliberal world order. Combining narrowly defined anti-establishment conspiracy theories with inflammatory cultural and socioeconomic populist rhetoric, illiberal democracy usually associated with the Third World has been a permanent fixture in mainstream American politics. Not only in the Republican Party's metamorphosis from Reagan to Trump, but in the judicial branch, law enforcement, armed forces, churches, schools, media, and social media rightwing populism's imprint is evident.[803]

Fully intending to transform the political landscape toward the far right, major corporations and two dozen billionaires have financially supported the Republican Party. Based on 2012 tax records, the billionaire Mercer-backed National Institute was funding the rightwing shell company Gravitas Maximus LLC, which in turn funded far-right Breitbart News, white supremacist groups, pollsters, and multi-layered local political campaigns. At the core of the Republican Party, plutocrats Robert Mercer and the Koch brothers funded Donor's Trust which in turn funneled money to ultra-rightwing Project Veritas.[804]

From Reagan to Trump, plutocratic populism veered toward an authoritarian path by mobilizing the shrinking popular base that appealed mostly to suburban voters, along with religious and cultural conservatives. To widen the white popular voting base and win elections amid a sharp rise in socioeconomic inequality, most traditional conservatives moved into the domain of culture wars at the core of their ideological warfare against labor and marginalized populations.

Billionaire-funded right-wing media became the promoter of faith-based groups, anti-abortion organizations, the KKK, neo-Nazis, Alt-right, neo-Confederates, and fringe groups that found a home within the GOP mainstream. Legislating voter exclusion at the state level, opposing criticism of institutionalized racism, while publicly supporting white supremacy through such means as banning progressive books, the Republican Party invoked traditionalism, religious fundamentalism, ethnocentrism, ultra-nationalism, and militarism. As long as the GOP helped to achieve sociopolitical consensus promoting conservative values by obfuscating and distracting from the underlying class war, wealthy individuals and businesses kept a low profile. Individuals with money proudly funded culture wars, with some contributing both to Republicans and Democrats to make sure of policy influence with both.[805]

Considering the steady downward social mobility of the middle class and workers, despite the post-Great Recession recovery in the early 2010s, the rightwing populist electoral challenge was to capture a popular base disgruntled with the Obama administration presenting an image of a progressive Democrat with eloquent delivery of Clintonesque inclusionary rhetoric to retain the popular base while governing as a pro-Wall Street-military neoliberal president.[806]

Defending the institutional structure safeguarding some social safety net measures such as the Affordable Care Act of 2010, which strengthened private insurance companies and did nothing to lower prescription drug costs, or address affordable universal health care, Obama's Clintonesque neoliberal Democratic Party rhetorically used the rising socioeconomic inequality issue only as a voting mobilization strategy. Even the Affordable Care Act had insurance companies' stamp of approval because it yielded to their interests. Democrats also defended the pluralism that Republicans were attacking as culturally corrosive. To protect the privileged billionaire and multi-millionaire class while suppressing the aspirations of the working class and the dwindling debt-ridden middle class, which dropped from 61% in 1971 to 50% in 2021, both political parties remained committed to corporate welfare capitalism and Keynesian militarism under different strategies.[807]

Except for minor issues, bipartisan consensus has been in force in everything from defense to fiscal and monetary policy. The two parties diverged on cultural and lifestyle issues or how much to continue slashing the social safety net and regulatory measures impacting the environment, women's reproductive rights, gun control, and school lunch waivers for millions of children, to mention some issues. Mostly at the rhetorical cliché level only as ideal goals, some neoliberal Democrats have supported the progressive FDR's New Deal and LBJ's Great Society.[808]

On the path to delegitimizing social justice by substituting core policies with the superficialities of identity politics symbolism, Democrats employ progressive rhetoric to co-opt voters and avoid addressing structural socioeconomic issues under the neoliberal counterrevolution that they support. Hence, they deliberately undermine middle-class and working-class social mobility and alienate the small progressive wing. Claiming to represent a pluralist society, the Democrats' goal was always to enforce the neoliberal model which they knew would continue to exacerbate inequality, thereby undermining liberal democracy. By contrast, the unapologetic GOP embraced populism as ideology and strategy, and autocratization as a goal to mobilize disgruntled voters. [809]

The Republican Party's hybrid politics forced the Democratic Party to fight for the conservation of the status quo ante and defend institutionalism; a position historically held by the GOP. Deliberately circumventing class politics, Democrats placed all emphasis on the superficialities and symbolism of identity politics with a strong emphasis on the culture war, which the media and the entire institutional structure promoted as well, feeding the populist movement with a class war distraction. Using its brand of exclusionary identity politics, the far right pointed to the 'decadence' of liberal identity political groups as a means to mobilize popular support and further divide society culturally while continuing to undermine class solidarity.[810]

As income distribution became increasingly uneven, despite rising GDP, the realization that the American Dream was elusive for the vast majoritywas inescapable. Populist support from the middle class and a segment of the working class, including many Evangelicals, had become part of the Republican Party mainstream since Reagan's election in 1980. The GOP strategy succeeded in part because Democrats were more divided between those committed to Wall Street employing hollow rhetorical promises about improving living standards, while progressives supported a more robust Keynesian social welfare state and weaker military-industrial complex.[811]

Reflecting the views of many progressive scholars, Noam Chomsky argued that while both parties moved to the right during the neoliberal era, the Republican call for "radical insurgency" necessarily entailed questioning not only institutionalism but liberal democracy's ideology and institutional structure. This phenomenon has been present in the UK, and across Europe. It was also something that Hayek supported in the 1970s and 1980s. Preferring military dictator Augusto Pinochet to duly-elected Salvador Allende, in his second visit to Chile in 1981, Hayek indicated to a local newspaper that there were problems with "unlimited democracy", a term open to interpretation. He added that the Western press had mischaracterized the military dictatorship's economic policies which were based on his ideology.[812]

Because the Republican Party had nothing to offer to the mass voters in the domain of social justice, there was no choice but to mobilize cultural conservatives from evangelicals to the fringe far-right elements. Backed by ultra-conservative pro-corporate, pro-gun, anti-environmentalist, anti-abortion justices, GOP disdain for grassroots democracy manifested itself in redistricting measures obviating majority rule and minimizing black voter influence, banning literature critical of institutional racism, among other exclusionary measures that unified the far right and serving as a recruitment tool.[813]

Because the Democratic Party has been supporting class-warfare policies, its strategy to preserve the heterogeneous popular base also relied on inculcating fear into voters about the GOP. Within the conservative camp, divisions reflect the views of some corporations concerned about losing a segment of the diverse middle-class consumer base. Some business campaign contributors to Republicans try to be circumspect about their support for authoritarian measures and fringe groups. In a world economy where race, ethnicity, gender, religion, and lifestyle are identified with the exclusionary populist camp, amid class war, there is corporate fear not to alienate the diverse consumer base.[814]

In the 2019-2020 campaign season, corporations spent $2.9 billion in lobbying and political donations. Most campaign contributions went to Biden. Donors agreed with his domestic and foreign policy intended to strengthen and stabilize capital without resorting to indiscriminate economic nationalism. Some in the business community had reservations about Trump's nationalism and unilateralism in foreign affairs undermining globalization and traditional allies. Nevertheless, the massive tax cuts of 2017 essentially placed close to $2 trillion of taxpayer money into the pockets of the richest 1%, making it difficult for billionaires and corporations not to donate to the GOP, despite Trump's flirtation with economic nationalism.[815]

Even at the rhetorical level, economic nationalism was not what many neoliberal businesspeople wanted to hear. The tipping point was Trump's 25% tariff on Canadian and Mexican steel and 10% tariff on aluminum. At the same time, he threatened a tariff war and went as far as to embrace Brexit in defiance of the EU's integrity. This was right after withdrawing from the Paris Agreement (2015) on climate, sending liberals into a frenzy, considering the multi-billion-dollar investments in the green economy. Amid antagonistic sanctions/tariff policy toward China, the indiscriminate tariff policy failed to achieve the intended result of greater investment at home by US companies and lowering the current account deficit.[816]

Rhetoric aside, Biden shared Trump's view that China constituted the real challenge to US economic hegemony, though they disagreed on confronting Russia. The question was whether to pursue unilateralism or multilateralism with block trade and defense networks to preserve Pax Americana. Both presidents also agreed on attracting investment, reshoring policy, strengthening US-based multinational corporations against competition, and maintaining a robust military-industrial complex.

Because both political parties maintained an unyielding commitment to the neoliberal model, they were very safe bets for Wall Street. To the degree that the Democratic establishment was willing to sustain vestiges of the welfare state without compromising neoliberal goals became an issue with Senator Sanders' supporters. While mainstream Democrats support cultural pluralism, as do progressives, they also support neoliberal economic policies that lead to higher inequality and inadvertently authoritarianism.[817]

Indebted for their elected seats to corporate donors, mainstream neoliberal Democrats are as accommodating to corporations and individual billionaires as the GOP. Neoliberalism's resounding political success has been the ability to bring under its umbrella the mainstream parties in support of the corporate counterrevolution intended to preserve the status quo.[818] Throughout the neoliberal era, in very subtle intentional, and inadvertent ways, the Democratic Party had contributed to the rise of hybrid authoritarian policies at labor's expense, concealed behind the pluralism mask. By supporting legislation to weaken labor, especially trade unions, while strengthening Wall Street legislatively, the Democrats and their liberal counterparts around the world promoted class warfare and corporate counter-revolution against democracy.

"This corporate counter-revolution is easiest to see in Democrats' enthusiastic support for Republicans' legislative response to the coronavirus crisis. Democrats' entire 2018 electoral campaign told America that the opposition party needed to win back Congress to block Trump's regressive agenda. And yet, when the Republicans proposed a bill to let Trump's appointees dole out government cash to their corporate allies with no strings attached[1], this same opposition party mustered not a single recorded vote[2] against the package. Not one. Thanks to that, Trump appointees and the Federal Reserve can now hand out $4tn[3] to politically connected corporations as they lay waste to our economy and steamroll progressive reforms. Private firms and fossil fuel companies[4] get new tax breaks as they buy elections and try to lock in permanent climate change."[819]

Financial support for Republicans and rightwing groups with access to the media from billionaires like Richard Uihlein, the Koch brothers, Isaac Perlmutter, the Mercer family, and Steve Wynn, among others, implies substantive policy differences between Republicans and Democrats. Because neoliberalism has absorbed the mainstream political parties, it is the main reason for the rise of de-politicization and de-democratization.

1. *https://www.forbes.com/sites/shivaramrajgopal/2020/03/31/the-500-billion-in-corporate-assistance-will-end-up-as-a-corrupt-cash-grab-if-we-dont-ask-the-right-questions/#a5c02393e59c943d6a75a9241140faca32969dfb55d4a*

2. *https://www.nytimes.com/2020/03/27/us/politics/coronavirus-house-voting.html*

3. *https://www.nytimes.com/2020/03/26/business/economy/fed-coronavirus-stimulus.html*

4. *https://www.bloomberg.com/news/articles/2020-05-15/-stealth-bailout-shovels-millions-of-dollars-to-oil-companies*

Furthermore, the absence of substantive policy differences in mainstream political parties explains, at least in part, the historical move of the entire political arena gravitating to the right amid continuing downward social mobility, especially for women and minorities. A reflection of a hybrid autocratization model, GOP strategies and policies betray any claim to democracy just because the illiberal model operates within an electoral system without necessarily taking into account the impact of policies designed to benefit capital.[820]

Mobilizing popular support for rightwing politics by questioning the institutional structure has its origin in the 1964 Republican presidential candidate of Senator Barry Goldwater who left a populist legacy. Although it would take another decade and a half, Goldwater moved the party to the cultural right and farther apart from the Rockefeller family's elite East-coast influence. Using cultural populism as a means to mobilize popular support and institutionalize neoliberalism and neoconservative militarist policies rooted in the 1950s "*Committee on the Present Danger*" (CPD) became part of the mainstream under Reagan.

Behind the ideology whose goal was to maintain a strong military-industrial complex, the CPD regrouped and was influential under Reagan. Under neoconservative leadership, the third CPD reconstituted in 2004 during the George W. Bush administration involved in Iraq and Afghanistan. In 2019, Trump's far-right advisor Steve Banon reconstituted a group calling itself CPD-China, using China's global economic ascendancy as the pretext for heighted military Keynesianism and neoliberal transformation with the US at the core of the world economy. [821]

Whereas there was upward social mobility when the bipartisan CPD was formulating policy in the 1950s under both Truman and Eisenhower, downward social mobility and rising inequality from Reagan to Biden led to hybrid authoritarianism. Structural problems revealed American society's traits associated with developing nations' governance structures and social relations. This includes institutional decadence, a rigged economy based on financialization schemes, legally murky activities of corporate America, and a debilitated social safety net amid rising social marginalization. Institutional, socioeconomic, and political corrosion under both political parties precipitated widespread cynicism leading a segment of the middle class and workers to embrace authoritarianism. This was partly as a form of extreme protest, but also a reflection of rightwing indoctrination inculcated in the mass consciousness.

Because of everything from a rise in white-collar and corporate crimes with widespread victim impact, to Trump encouraging a mass uprising to overturn the election results of 2020, de-democratization was as inevitable in the US as in France and the UK. Resorting to a combination of constitutional means by appealing to a corrupt Supreme Court, as the case of Citizens United in 2010 proved, to illegal acts by fringe far-right groups, the US descent toward Third Worldism was best illustrated when the rightwing mob of 6 January 2021 tried to stage a coup on behalf of the incumbent president. Converted into a paramilitary appendage of the presidency, the event appeared like an attempted coup from within the government, as law enforcement, security, and other off-duty public sector officials were involved. The lukewarm response by the FBI, Homeland Security, Pentagon, and the National Guard spoke louder than the counterrevolutionary rioters who temporarily seized Congress.[822]

Hardly an anomaly either within the GOP or the broader mainstream political culture, Trumpism became associated with a form of authoritarianism rooted in the cultural and political history of social exclusion. From the early Cold War to Trump's presidency, America's long path to de-democratization signaled a deeper and wider problem in a society whose elites struggle to project what is left of liberal democracy.[823]

To mobilize the masses and distract them from the incessant neoliberal class war. advocates of authoritarianism effectively rely on nationalism, religion, and traditionalism. Using the private sector's considerable leverage combined with public institutional co-optation, along with selective repression in a campaign of disinformation, the elite-driven authoritarian trend relies on populist myths and the cult of personality that the media, social media, liberals, and conservatives alike promote. This is an underlying symptom of institutional decay and a manifestation of misanthropic political and social elites willing to undermine liberal democracy to preserve the capitalist hierarchy.[824]

Similar to the Italian Fascist Party and the German Nazi Party, both products of their respective countries' hegemonic culture and institutions unable to reconcile capitalist society's postwar contradictions amid national socioeconomic and political crises, Trump was very much a product of a historical capitalist crisis that neoliberalism precipitated. The slogan *"Make America Great Again"* was not so different from populist slogans that dictators have used to project ultra-nationalist strength as part of a mass psychology and a substitute for policy intended to benefit workers and the middle class.

During the interwar era, Italian and German socioeconomic elites feared that their countries were weakening other advanced countries, which necessarily entailed the weakening of the elites. The social and political elites deluded themselves and the masses into believing that totalitarianism was the road to mythological 'greatness' that militarism and a police state could deliver. Similarly, the US neoliberal elite and those in the middle class and working class embraced Trumpism as they feared decline amid China's global ascendancy and the multipolar world power structure.[825]

From academic researchers of American political economy to the average voter, there has been a reluctant realization that the world's number one economy in nominal value has been experiencing chronic far-reaching structural problems. US military superpower status, the global financial and trade network, and dollar dominance camouflaged many underlying systemic problems. Ranking 36th in the social justice index out of 41 advanced countries in the world in 2019, and number one in poverty among advanced countries with an inequality gap comparable to South Africa illustrates America's deep-rooted structural problems.[826]

Ranking 27th in the world in healthcare and education, the US remains at the bottom when it comes to child poverty among 41 advanced nations. Unsafe living conditions, including unsafe drinking water in cities with large minority populations, exposed the ugly realities in Flynt, Michigan (2014-2016) and Jackson, Mississippi (2022) where the majority is made up of working poor minorities. Ranking 124th in the world in human rights, right below South Africa and slightly above Mauritius, neoliberal America is hardly the beacon of democracy that its political and business elites promote.[827]

Despite ranking very low among developed countries in every domain from affordable health, education, and housing, liberals and conservatives alike have historically refused to address systemic conditions on their own merits because they know exactly where the evidence leads and the policy shifts needed to change rising inequality. Preferring instead to perpetuate the myth about the 'world's greatest democracy' helps to assuage the masses and maintain conformity through vacuous populist rhetoric. As the institutional pull toward conformity clashes with the reality of rising inequality, the political solution has been to lead voters toward greater conformity to preserve the oppressive neoliberal status quo. After Trump's election, the question arose about how far to the right on the counterrevolutionary path to non-conformity with liberal democracy, and what dangers lay ahead about fascism becoming mainstream.

In March 2018, Tyler Cowen wrote in *POLITICO* that fascism could not possibly take root in the US. Even after four years of Trump in the White House, most analysts kept recycling the view that fascism was incongruent with US institutions, the division, and separation of powers, a value system based on individualism, and strong tendencies toward libertarianism, but without tolerance of lifestyles, or civil liberties.

No matter the evidence of civil rights and human rights violations, de-democratization ranging from voter suppression to refusal to prosecute right-wing terrorists, and FBI surveillance of citizens, are subtle forms of conformity that compels people toward self-censorship. Although most analysts refuse to acknowledge that the US had lapsed toward a hybrid authoritarian regime under the neoliberal political economy, it is difficult to explain the banning of books, abortion, the abortion pill, and including critical race theory in the curriculum. The erosion of civil liberties including freedom of the press, considering that the US ranks 48th out of 180 countries in freedom of the press, are not good signs of a liberal democracy.[828]

One argument against the possibility of Fascism in the US, an assumption made because of American Exceptionalism, revolves around the theme of the US government's large and unwieldy size. Another argument is that the US fought against the Axis Powers. Besides, Fascism is a very distinct interwar European ideology, movement, and regime with no roots in the US, at least not nearly as deep as in Europe. Cowen's assertion that fascists could not possibly control the vast US bureaucracy is based on the assumption that the bureaucracy can only operate under a pluralistic model and that civilian, military, and police bureaucrats are too heterogeneous to yield to Fascist proclivities. Government bureaucracies, especially those in the criminal justice and defense sectors, are bastions of the status quo. As Henry Giroux has observed, the alliance of government bureaucracy and corporate America has contributed to the consolidation of authoritarianism evident as early as George W. Bush's reelection in 2004.[829]

History has shown that, beyond the military and police, the bureaucracy in an authoritarian state is a part of the power base, including the armed forces and the police. Ignoring warnings from German Communists about the threat from the emerging Nazi party, mainstream German political parties and analysts in the 1920s argued that Germany would never tolerate an authoritarian regime, for it was simply not the sort of country to host such a regime. Prussian-German political culture steeped in militarism was precisely the sort of nation that met the preconditions for Nazi totalitarianism. Combined with populist nationalism and religious dogmatism, technocracy has been a vehicle of authoritarian neoliberalism as much in the US as in other parts of the world. [830]

Characterized by the domination of the small group of capitalists who subordinate the rest of society to their interests, institutional conformity has been a means to normalize social relations and inculcate the new norm into the mass psychology of the populist movement. This necessarily entails sociopolitical exclusion justified in the name of social harmony, law, and order. In essence, a hybrid authoritarian state, which rhetorically claims that social issues need technocratic solutions, presents itself as democratic and becomes the norm so people behave accordingly.[831]

Delinking structural socioeconomic problems from hybrid authoritarianism precludes analysis that would lead to a comprehensive understanding of how the US checks and balances system produced Trump who boastfully used authoritarian rhetoric, tactics, and policies to remold the entire party from the local to the national level. Based on the election results of 2020, about half of the voters accepted authoritarianism as a political solution, while the other half awaited its passing like a painful kidney stone. By 2022, more than half of the population doubted democracy's survival.

According to a Morning Consult poll, *"26% of the U.S. population qualified as highly right-wing authoritarian, Morning Consult research found, twice the share of the No. 2 countries, Canada and Australia."*[832] Even more alarming, an Axios-Momentive poll of January 2022 found that: "*Only a slim majority (55%) accepts Joe Biden as having legitimately won the 2020 election, down slightly from 58% a year ago.*"[833]

Politicians, corporate media, business, and academic analysts either gloss over or vehemently reject the reality that the neoliberal social contract has brought American society closer to authoritarianism under liberal democracy's thin veil. At the core of the institutional mainstream in every sector from business and politics to the criminal justice system rests autocratization which may not be important to many who view democracy as a consumer-citizen society unrelated to social justice. However, it is frightening for the consumer-citizen to contemplate a liberal bourgeois democracy lapsing toward autocratization that citizens will experience in their interactions with official bureaucracy. Hence, there is a tendency to over-compensate with Pax Americana's dreams of glory and identity politics, equating them with democracy.[834]

For many among the political and business elite and ordinary voters, the pro-Trump mass riot that resulted in storming the capitol on 6 January 2021 was a wake-up call that autocratization had finally arrived at Congress' doorstep. The White House, the FBI, and the Pentagon watched and waited for a few hours as the Trump-inspired rightwing mob ransacked the halls of Congress. Revealing its counterrevolutionary dimension, Trumpist Bonapartism, to borrow the term which Karl Marx applied to Louis Napoleon Bonaparte (*The Eighteenth Brumaire*), exposed the GOP's illiberal character, a fractured security apparatus because the FBI was not fully on board. The disturbing element about the attempted Trumpist-Bonapartist counterrevolution was that it enjoyed support among some GOP elected officials, elements of the bureaucracy, and a segment of the American elites who knew the cost of stripping off the democracy veil on that day.[835]

In an article in the *Intelligencer*, Rick Perlstein argues that the right-wing insurrection of 6 January 2021 has historical roots in conservative politics. "*In 2003, right-wingers won a demagogic campaign to recall California governor Gray Davis less than a year after his reelection. The campaign was driven by frantic claims on talk radio that Davis wanted to grant undocumented immigrants driver's licenses... The paramilitary wing of the party mobbed the Capitol seeking traitors to lynch. Meanwhile, the parliamentary wing, represented by the majority of the Republican members of the House and Senate who voted not to certify Biden's electoral votes, raised a clenched fist. Together, these two wings compose the right-wing model of governance — and at this model's heart lies the citizen as the bearer of violent threat.*"[836]

To be sure, the US was not at the point of Nazi-style burnings of 'un-German' books in May 1933, coinciding with the *Sturmabteilung* (SA) occupying trade union offices before Hitler ordered them dissolved to appease the elites. Although there is no centralized paramilitary organization like the Third Reich's SA, twenty-six states have banned books along with "Critical Race Theory" (CRT), while another eighteen states considered moving in that direction. Only eight of the fifty states have either never considered banning CRT. In addition, there is the loss of academic freedom, progressive faculty have lost their jobs, and self-censorship manifests the fear of losing one's job.[837]

The Eighteenth Brumaire did not repeat in the US on 6 January 2021. Common elements point to counterrevolution struggling to rattle a very conservative system evolving toward authoritarianism behind the thin layer of liberal democracy. The dogmatic response of most GOP officials and supporters revealed that authoritarianism is at the core of the mainstream, right below the thin layer. Preferring to build the cult of personality, as though there were no systemic problems at the core of the social contract, the Democratic Party focused narrowly on discrediting the GOP.

The US still permits freedom of speech that does not violate mainstream protocol. However, not just social media, but the entire institutional structure invariably leans more heavily toward rightwing than leftwing freedom of expression. GOP-controlled states banned terms like "global warming", "sustainability" and "climate change", adopting measures to curb lifestyle freedom of expression as well as depriving women of choice over their reproductive rights. In and of themselves, culture wars are indeed contrary to the republic's pluralist ideological foundations, but populist politicians them to distract from class warfare.[838]

Dominated by voices representing the status quo, the mass media and social media dwell on identity politics controversies, while drowning out progressive class-based dissent. Effective as a cooptation strategy, the media and institutional mainstream's cultural determinist assumptions along with identity politics are catalysts in middle-class and working-class 'false consciousness' which obfuscates the real nature of social relations based on structural exploitation.[839]

The US is not at the juncture where workers take loyalty oaths or are subjected to anything like the House on Un-American Activities which started under Franklin Roosevelt to investigate pro-Nazis and pro-Communists in the 1930s. During the 'Red Scare' era of the 1950s, the government under the leadership of Senator Joseph McCarthy was chasing Hollywood writers, actors, directors, journalists, and academics to send a strong warning regarding political dissent, even in the domain of the fine arts, literature, and mass entertainment. During the 'Red Scare' era, people knew as they do today that political conformity accompanied by self-censorship are precondition to secure and maintain employment across the public and private sectors. In this respect, superimposed false consciousness in the age of neoliberal identity politics only reinforces sociopolitical conformity.

Most definitely not a police state modeled after the Third Reich born from German culture and eclectic European rightwing ideologies, nevertheless the US has elements of an authoritarian-militarist state. In February 2015, the world discovered the nature of America's militarized police force when investigative reporting published a story about the Chicago police department's highly secretive Homan Square facility where treatment included detaining arrestees, some as young as 15, without due process, shackling them, denying access to legal counsel, torture, and deaths. They operated no differently than the US-operated Guantanamo Bay or the CIA "black sites" in Morocco.

On 17 April 2023, Oklahoma Governor Kevin Stitt asked for McCurtain County Sheriff Kevin Clardy, county Commissioner Mark Jennings, sheriff's investigator Alicia Manning, and Jail Administrator Larry Hendrix to resign after a local newspaper revealed that they were caught on tape discussing assassinating reporters and lamenting that lynching of blacks was illegal. Granted that practices described above are more characteristic of Latin American dictatorships, but they too used the interwar Fascist/Nazi model for their regimes.[840]

To the degree that the pluralistic society is interwoven with the market economy, molded by its culture and value system, the US may never reach the Third Reich's rigid institutionalization of *Polizeistaat*. Such a regime would expose myriads of contradictions in a consumerist culture permeating all social, geographic, and cultural sectors in a global consumer economy. To be sure, neoliberal pluralistic society has deviated from the Enlightenment's principles, including liberty, tolerance, and social development and progress.

Grassroots Resistance to Neoliberalism

Regardless of the deplorable conditions of displaced farmers in India, America's Amazon, Starbucks, or Apple workers trying to unionize, Lebanese workers protesting free economic zones designed to further exploit unprotected labor, or French workers pouring onto the streets against Macron's labor policy, exploitation in the name of market efficiency and resistance to neoliberal globalization is global has been intensifying globally. The results of the French National Assembly and the Colombian presidential election in June 2022, and Brazil in October 2022 were a form of resistance within the electoral system in the core and periphery where a large segment of the population is disgruntled owing to the impact of neoliberal policies in every domain from social to fiscal policy.[841]

Resistance has taken different forms beyond the ballot box. Workers at Amazon corporation in the US, small farmers all across the Indian subcontinent, students in Afro-Arab capitals, women's groups across Hungary and Slovakia, anti-IMF and anti-globalization activists in Hamburg, Germany, and environmentalists in New Zealand have been part of the global resistance movement to neoliberalism. Driven by deregulation, tax cuts for business, and privatization, IMF austerity met with resistance against neoliberalism in the "global south" and developed nations from the 1990s to the present.[842]

In Chile, the first country to experience mass protests against the neoliberal model, workers and middle-class progressives organized against the plundering of their country by domestic and foreign businesses under the CIA-installed General Augusto Pinochet (1973-1990). Austerity, privatization of public enterprises, public sector social benefit cuts, and higher indirect taxes resulted in higher costs for the mass consumer accompanied by anti-labor policies and the crushing of dissidents. Beyond what it entailed for working-class and middle-class living standards, austerity and privatization of public services took place under a rightwing regime that brutally crushed any form of criticism whether from politicians, journalists, or academics.[843]

In the 1990s, anti-neoliberal, anti-globalization popular resistance spread throughout Latin America. The *Ejército Zapatista de Liberación Nacional, EZLN* (Zapatista movement) uprising of 1994 in Chiapas, Mexico symbolized the challenge of the periphery to the New World Order's neoliberal transformation. Symbolically, the EZLN emerged on the day that the North American Free Trade Agreement (NAFTA) went into effect. Inspiring dissident movements around the globe, the anti-NAFTA and anti-globalization Zapatista movement called for workers' and middle-class solidarity in Latin America.[844]

Networking with other progressive movements to bring attention to globalization's impact on workers and environmental degradation, the Zapatistas, working through the *"Peoples' Global Action"* forum, came to the attention of social activists in advanced capitalist countries. Unlike the Zapatistas, anti-globalization activists in Western countries were less concerned about urban and rural worker exploitation and more about corporate hegemony in politics and environmental degradation which many opposed not as an issue intertwined with structural exploitation, but as part of identity politics. Nevertheless, global opposition to neoliberalism linked social justice and workers in the global south with environmental and bourgeois identity politics that preoccupied many northern hemisphere activists.[845]

The emergence of the *World Social Forum* (WSF) in Porto Alegre, Brazil, and its international popularity helped to bring into focus the convergence between neoliberalism, militarism, environmental degradation, and the exploitation of labor.[846] Despite its waning influence after a decade of activism, the WSF left an important legacy on grassroots resistance to the neoliberal world order. After the Great Recession of 2008, rightwing groups around the world incorporated some WSF issues into their populist nationalist-xenophobic agenda, including anti-globalization identified with the liberal order, opposition to international financial institutions like the IMF, World Bank, the World Trade Organization, and liberal billionaires like George Soros allegedly conspiring to create a world government.

"Millions of people across the globe are engaged at the grassroots level," Roberto Savio observed, *"hundreds of times more than related to the WSF. The great challenge is to connect with those working to change the present dire trends, making clear that we are not part of the same elite structures and, indeed, share the same enemy. The historic preconditions undergird the possibility of such a project, our visions of another world give it a direction, and the growing restlessness of countless ordinary people is a hopeful harbinger."*[847]

Besides WSF and the Zapatistas, there were other grassroots anti-neoliberal organizations, even before the economic crisis of 2008. Without much impact on policy, some anti-neoliberal groups found expression and mobilized followers through social media, which was a major means to spread the message globally. Active at the local level, these groups raised public awareness about policies that undermined workers and minorities. A few attempted to alter public policy through cooperation with state entities, and/or NGOs, but without much impact. The most important anti-neoliberal grassroots organizations were Brazil's Landless Workers' Movement *(Movimento dos Trabalhadores Rurais Sem Terra, MST),* South Africa's *Abahlali baseMjondolo, Western Cape Anti-Eviction Campaign, Landless Peoples' Movement,* Haiti's *Fanmi Lavalas,* and India's *Narmada Bachao Andolan.*[848]

In the Global South and the G7, some organizations were independent of government and business influence. Throughout the world, but especially in the Global South, small farmers were often victims of corporate farming that international institutions like the World Bank supported. Because governments were selling public land to commercial farming operations, some small farmers lost their livelihoods. To rally public support, grassroots groups employed social justice rhetoric and appealed to people concerned about large-scale environmentally hostile commercial agriculture.

Without the ability to change policy, these groups were fighting against commercial agriculture pillaging the environment and exploiting workers in the name of neoliberal progress, many hiding behind the sustainable development label. The anti-globalization movement and by implication anti-neoliberalism included elements from the entire political spectrum from left to ultra-right. From India to Bangladesh, from South Africa to Brazil, and from the US to the UK and France, much of the working class anti-neoliberal movement was directly or indirectly co-opted, often de-politicized by corporate-funded or government-funded local and international NGOs that used progressive rhetoric but their agenda was neoliberal.[849]

Promoting measures invariably in the domain of lifestyle, combined with some social welfare and civil rights issues such as women's rights, renter's rights, and sustainable development, the organizations operated within the neoliberal structure and did not aim at universal social inclusion. It was hardly a coincidence that globally the rise of NGOs coincided with the rise of neoliberalism in the 1990s, most trying to reform the status quo a la carte through identity politics.

Most NGOs operated under the guise of aiding the poor and the ill, protecting human rights, and the environment, and advocating for animals. Some did exactly what they advertised. Others were nothing more than well-funded fronts by wealthy individuals, corporate foundations, and governments promoting market-related issues. In some respects, 21st-century NGOs became the equivalent of 19th-century Western missionaries using their position as ideological preparatory work for a Western-based economy in the non-Western world.[850]

Advocating for marginalized groups, some NGOs and grassroots movements maintained that it is better to win on a single issue such as abortion, higher minimum wage, etc. at the cost of co-optation into the neoliberal system than to have nothing at all looking in from the outside. The assumption is that social exclusion can be mitigated, one issue at a time within the neoliberal institutional structure.[851]

Partly because governmental and non-governmental organizations have successfully co-opted grassroots movements often incorporating them into the mainstream political base, mass resistance to neoliberalism has not succeeded in modifying the status quo, despite social media, computers, and cell phones that permit instant communication globally. This was certainly the case with the Arab Spring uprisings that opposed privatization, deregulation, and social policies impacting everything from health care to housing rentals.[852]

Especially in developing nations where GDP growth translates into even greater wealth concentration and misery for urban and rural workers, the neoliberal transformation has been responsible for the deterioration of everything from health and education to housing for working people across the world. Despite such a monumental negative impact on a world scale, progressive-led resistance to counter neoliberalism has been relatively weak in comparison with the vociferous rightwing populists. In part, this is because a much larger percentage of workers are engaged in the informal economy in developing countries than in the core, with Africa leading the world in informal employment.

According to a study in *"Dying for Growth: Global Inequality and the Health of the Poor"*: *"100 countries have undergone grave economic decline over the past three decades. Per capita income in these 100 countries is now lower than it was 10, 15, 20, or in some cases even 30 years ago. In Africa, the average household consumes 20 percent less today than it did 25 years ago. Worldwide, more than 1 billion people saw their real incomes fall during the period 1980-1993."*[853]

After the US invasions of Afghanistan (October 2001) and Iraq (March 2002), the anti-neoliberalism movement became intertwined with the anti-war movement. On 15 February 2003, more than 11 million protested globally against US invasions identified with Western contempt for national sovereignty in the name of the vague and hypocritical concept of 'freedom' in select Muslim countries. All along, there was silence about Saudi Arabian authoritarianism and the plight of Palestinians living under apartheid conditions as numerous international organizations have determined along with the UN Special Rapporteur on the Right to Adequate Housing. Despite becoming part of the anti-war movement, resistance to corporate globalization remained limited against the background of rapid and ubiquitous neoliberal transformation.[854]

Globalization included not just the developed nations' efforts to impose market hegemony, but a trans-Atlantic military world order as an integral part of corporate globalization. During the war in Afghanistan, the US occupation of Iraq, and the US-NATO destabilization of Middle Eastern and African countries, the Great

Recession brought to the surface the links between militarism and globalization. Social resistance around the world adopted different approaches depending on the country's unique political and social issues.[855]

Even before the crisis of 2008, neoliberal global resistance found expression in opposition to the annual World Economic Forum (Davos) meetings of corporate and political elites as well as in protests against the G20; symbolic amounting to nothing and hardly receiving any press coverage. As the financial crisis of 2008 exposed the symbiotic nexus between big capital and the state whose role was a pillar of financial markets at the expense of society, the "occupy" movements spread to 950 cities in 82 countries. From anti-austerity demonstrations in Greece and Bulgaria in 2013-14, to South Africa's service delivery demonstrations in 2019, and India's civil service protests in the early 2020s, anti-neoliberal grassroots social movements found expression in different countries depending on hard-hit sectors and social impact.[856]

The global anti-neoliberal movement covered many groups, from the Occupy Wall Street movement against the social contract serving the richest 1%, to the streets of London protesting wage stagnation and downward social mobility; from the streets of Madrid's *'Indignados'* protesting IMF-EU-imposed austerity and privatization to Cairo's Tahrir Square. Global grassroots resistance went beyond opposition to the IMF austerity and governments bailing out commercial banks. The corrosiveness of liberal democracy concealing decadence of the social order has been a universal theme in global resistance to class war as the centerpiece of the neoliberal social contract.[857]

Depending on the nation's history and traditions, the nature of local institutions, and the degree to which people were impacted by neoliberal policies in a deregulated economy and weakened social safety net, anti-neoliberalism social movements assumed different forms. Even in Brazil, Russia, India, and South Africa experiencing relatively rapid growth from the early 1990s until the great recession of 2008, there was popular opposition to neoliberalism eroding living standards for workers, peasants, and the middle class.[858]

International grassroots organizations opposed policies that further integrated their countries into the world economy and marginalized the working class, especially in South Africa, Brazil, and India which showed promise of economic development confined to the capitalist class, with meager benefits for labor and parallel social development. To assuage and co-opt the masses, BRICS governments followed a policy mix combining neoliberalism and Keynesian developmentalist policies, with some social welfare policies.[859]

Combined with geopolitical opposition to US-NATO military interventionism, BRICS's policies were an attempt to keep the national bourgeoisie loyal to the regime as bloc trading increased in volume and profits. Naturally, corporations from non-BRICS countries also benefit from policies intended to generate growth, even if within the bloc. Projecting a commitment to national sovereignty while promising long-term economic development in return for labor's short-term sacrifice, the BRICS made a commitment to broader masses for social development. The US, EU, IMF, and World Bank pressured the BRICS to pursue neoliberal transformation for the sake of global integration presumably in society's best interest.[860]

Domestic and foreign businesses also pressured Brazil, India, and South Africa to embrace neoliberal policies and to confront grassroots opposition, rather than make concessions to labor and environmental groups. Considering that BRICS development policies accommodated domestic and foreign capital, grassroots opposition manifested itself in various resistance organizations, especially in Brazil, India, and South Africa where the state structure was not nearly as powerful as in Russia and China. Furthermore, unlike China which could point to tangible evidence of forthcoming economic development filtering down, Brazil and South Africa were not in a position to make such claims, with India making a bit more progress in poverty reduction than most Global South countries.[861]

By accentuating identity politics, the mainstream political parties and the media undermined many grassroots organizations. Environmental groups fell victim to corporate or government co-optation through NGOs. Brazil's *Landless Workers Movement* (MST) skillfully remained independent of both pro-labor President Luiz Inacio Lula da Silva and Dilma Rousseff (*Partido dos Trabalhadores*). Maintaining some programs to protect workers, the indigenous population, and the Amazon from commercial exploitation, Brazil's inclusionary populist government promoted the growth of domestic and foreign capital investment. A working-class hero for many, Lula was in power during the Great Recession which he blamed on the US and advanced capitalist countries. Anti-neoliberal rhetoric aside, Lula pursued policies accommodating big capital, while giving hope to anti-neoliberal groups by acknowledging that Western capitalism was in crisis.[862]

Although Brazil's MST supported some policies of both Lula and his successor Rousseff, their accommodations to foreign and domestic capital were indicative of the preponderating influence of IMF-World Bank-backed corporate interests. Rousseff used her and Lula's scandals involving Petrobras state oil company executives' bribes from construction firms awarded above-fair-value contracts as a key reason for the election of rightwing president Jair Bolsonaro. Under the advice of University of Chicago-trained Paulo Guedes involved with the dictatorship of Chilean President Pinochet, Bolsonaro's Brazil sank into a chaotic neoliberal inferno.[863]

Lula had come to power after the rise in inequality and economic polarization resulting from austerity and neoliberal policies of the 1990s. Although poverty was declining rapidly in the first half of the 1990s, IMF demands for a speedy transition to neoliberalism resulted in an upward trend of inequality. Lula's inclusionary populist policies of social protection addressed poverty, which dropped sharply along with income inequality from 2003 to 2014. Amid business pressure to abandon Keynesian measures of social safety nets, Lula's balancing act between capital and labor kept steady because of his persona as the common man's hero status that permitted him to prevail.[864]

Imposing high taxes on consumer goods, especially cars (65%) and prescription drugs (35%) amid a real-estate bubble four years after the US-European real estate bubble, Brazil had a high interest-rate environment and 7% inflation rate, resembling Argentina's *convertibility* of the 1990s. Like Brazil, Bolivarian republics including Venezuela, Ecuador, and Bolivia experienced convergence between the inclusionary populist parties, the working class, and grassroots anti-neoliberal groups as a counterweight to capital to maintain some Keynesian policies that big businesses and the IMF adamantly opposed. This was also prevalent across Southern Europe after the Great Recession of 2008, but it did not last.[865]

Corruption charges leading to a prison term (April-July 2018) tarnished Lula's reputation. However, it also helped him solidify popular support for the presidential run in 2022. In a worse predicament, his successor faced impeachment once the Chamber of Deputies accepted (2 December 2015) the petition and removal from office in May 2016. After going along with neoliberal austerity, including major job-creation infrastructure projects, Rousseff who had personalized the presidency and moved to the right of Lula, alienated the progressive camp. At the same time, small Brazilian businesses that had initially supported her presidency blamed her for slow economic growth. The combination of her poor balancing act between neoliberal austerity and impeachment paved the way for the neoliberal populist Bolsonaro to further divide society and present the inclusionary populists as corrupt hypocrites.[866]

"Bolsonaro took advantage of the austerity policies implemented between 2015 and 2018 by the government of Dilma Rousseff, Lula's successor. Bolsonaro also played on voters' feelings of insecurity by promoting a strongman image and strengthening social and cultural divisions and anti-migration sentiment. His variety of populism has resulted in the reversal of decades of economic development and climate adaptation[1] and one of the world's largest death rates related to COVID-19[2]."[867]

Rightwing political and media rhetoric aside about Lula and Rousseff, the MST persisted with the struggle against neoliberal policies that contributed to rising GDP heavily concentrated among the national and comprador bourgeoisie and foreign corporations. Other Latin American grassroots movements had mixed results; not much better than those in Brazil. Ecuador under President Rafael Correa of the *Alianza PAIS* tried to co-opt the left by yielding to big capital on some policy issues, as did Lula and Rousseff while pursuing a mixed neoliberal-developmentalist model as much as his Brazilian counterparts.

In inclusionary populist governments of Lula's Brazil, Venezuela's Hugo Chavez's (2002-2013) *El Movimiento V (Quinta) República*, Ecuador's Rafael Correa's Alianza PAIS (2007-2013), and Bolivia's Evo Morales' (2006-2019) *Movimiento al Socialismo,* the balancing act was indicative of the difficult policy choices under domestic and foreign pressures to follow neoliberal orthodoxy. Within varying degrees depending on the country, popular opposition to neoliberalism persisted across Latin America.

This included Mexico thoroughly integrated into the US-Canada NAFTA regional bloc, an outgrowth of neoliberal policies to pursue lower taxes, cheap labor, and minimal trade and environmental regulations. Not so unique to Latin America, the neoliberal transformation's global reach exacerbated the subterranean economy, especially in Mexico where NAFTA allowed importers and exporters to manipulate trade rules. As a result, capital flight skyrocketed from both legal and illegal activities.[868]

Partly because IMF-sponsored austerity has historically been reserved primarily for the Global South, but also because of the much larger middle class in the capitalist core in comparison with the periphery, anti-neoliberal activity in the advanced countries did not manifest itself in the same fashion as in developing nations. Historically, underdeveloped countries had a much stronger tradition of anti-imperialist, anti-elite movements with greater antagonism toward domestic and foreign capital than the disparate middle-class progressive movements in the metropolis, especially in the US lacking a strong left-wing and trade union tradition.

In their anti-neoliberal campaigns, South Africa's *Abahlali baseMjondolo* and Latin American trade unions stressed a working-class philosophy of needs rather than individual rights which is associated with bourgeois identity politics. Anti-corporate globalization in Nigeria, South Africa, Brazil, Mexico, and Argentina focused not just on the transformation of society under the inherently socially inequitable neoliberal political economy,

1. *https://www.cambridge.org/core/journals/environmental-conservation/article/brazils-new-president-and-ruralists-threaten-amazonias-environment-traditional-peoples-and-the-global-climate/F5C1E42BF9F6E6BDDB957B87601FC4F7*

2. *https://www.thelancet.com/journals/langlo/article/PIIS2214-109X(20)30285-0/fulltext*

but on the periphery's dependency on the core (the North-South divide under the patron-client model) determining everything from the terms of trade to the periphery's geopolitical fate.[869]

Popular resistance to neoliberalism in the EU and US has been a part of the anti-globalization movement which has historically included various groups from environmentalists to anti-IMF-World Bank, anti-Wall Street, and anti-military-industrial complex groups. Although there are some locally based groups like East Harlem-based *Justice in El Barrio* representing immigrants and low-income workers, there is no national anti-neoliberal grassroots movement and certainly no political party around to organize, other than the Democratic Party's Keynesian wing that Senator Sanders represents. There has often been convergence between anti-neoliberalism-anti-globalization issues which the same groups represent in the US among other countries. This is largely because neoliberal transformation coincided with the New World Order of a reinvigorated Pax Americana launching the global war on terror as a substitute for the old Cold War.[870]

Unlike the Republicans who proudly took credit for Reagan's de-institutionalization of Keynesianism, the Democrats rarely advertise their support for neoliberal policies. Under the thin veil of jobs growth initiatives and President Clinton's 'welfare reform', a euphemism for slashing entitlement programs, the Democratic Party in a circumspect manner promoted neoliberalism, while keeping up Keynesian rhetoric that appealed to labor. In the 1990s, Clinton did more to expand neoliberal policies while containing anti-corporate globalization grassroots resistance than Reagan and Bush combined. Rather than restoring some of Lyndon B. Johnson's "Great Society" programs that the Republicans had slashed in the 1980s-early 1990s, Clinton called for deeper cuts in the social safety net to keep the budgetary deficit under control amid the transfer of public funding for corporate welfare. [871]

He justified social program cuts based on expanding private sector opportunities. Freeing people from social welfare, limiting government bureaucracy as part of the privatization drive, and offering people chronically dependent on the government a chance to assume individual initiative to become integrated into the free market as workers instead of social welfare recipients was Clinton's selling point. Considering that the 1990s was a decade of slow wage growth relative to massive capital concentration, transfer from social welfare to corporate welfare, and a meteoric rise of the high-tech market, Clinton's neoliberal apologists tried to convince the voting base that against the background of the digital technological revolution the neoliberal model was the vehicle to reach the American Dream.[872]

Clinton's slogans, "reinventing government" and "mandate for change" were euphemisms for full-scale neoliberal transformation. In the name of "national prosperity", the Democrats asked the middle class and working class to accept the neoliberal social contract as the panacea. Promising growth and prosperity, Democrats continued globalization, pro-business policies, trimming public resources from health, education, and vital social programs while strengthening corporate welfare. Propagating the mythology of the neoliberal digital revolution regarding prosperity for all, Clinton completed the Reagan neoliberal revolution. All along, he managed to project an image of safeguarding Keynesian policies. Hence, the term *"Clintonism"* which captured the essence of his presidency, delivered the neoliberal social contract while claiming to support the Keynesian state.[873]

Crushing the hopes of progressives who demanded a modern version of a New Deal-style political, social, and economic policies, *"Clintonism"* persisted during the two-term Obama administration. Because Obama remained faithful to pro-business fiscal and monetary policy, corporate welfare, and military Keynesianism, by 2016, the progressive wing was thoroughly disillusioned with the Clinton-Obama-dominated party machine. Fearing the far-right GOP, some progressives stayed under the Democratic Party's umbrella.

Supporting government subsidies for fossil fuel companies, the Democratic Party opposed Senator Bernie Sanders' progressive agenda on taxes, universal healthcare, college-free tuition, a rise in the federal minimum wage, and climate-related investments linked to social welfare. Because voting independently or not voting at all would guarantee Republican electoral victories, the classic "lesser evil" option kept the Democrats competitive against the background of a rising rightwing tide. Combined with corporate support, the absence of substantive political alternatives, kept the neoliberal agenda moving forward.[874]

Skepticism with the neoliberal platform of establishment Democrats was not only on the part of the progressives, but with leftover elements of 'Occupy Wall Street', and a dozen other anti-neoliberal/anti-war groups that rallied behind Senator Sanders. A consistent representative of the Democratic Party's "New Deal" faction carrying the legacy from Henry Wallace in the 1940s to George McGovern in the 1970s, Sanders challenged the neoliberal establishment and the GOP during the presidential races of 2016 and 2020. An inclusionary social welfare populist, the New Deal Democrat senator was aware that the neoliberal establishment's deep roots extended from the political arena to all levels of the government bureaucracy, and from Wall Street and the media to all mainstream institutions.[875]

An advocate of the pluralist-diversity political model, the Senator from Vermont worked within the same neoliberal party whose policies and super-PAC-rooted strategies that he criticized. Although it needed the progressives to win, the Democratic Party and the liberal media dismissed Sanders' followers as idealists, anarchists, socialists, and extremists whose naïve dogmatism drove voters to the far right.

Challenging '*Clintonism*' and GOP rightwing populism, Sanders' inclusionary populist strategy was a means of mobilizing and co-opting middle-class and working-class voters with the hope of diluting the neoliberal core in case of a Democratic victory. Because of fear that a Clinton-style neoliberal government was better than an authoritarian neoliberal Republican administration, the strategy had more appeal in 2020 than in 2016. Sociopolitical polarization and frequent clashes which Trump and the GOP and the media had manufactured and promoted, resulted in an expansion not contraction of the populist base.[876]

Fearing a progressive backlash against neoliberalism, both the Democratic and Republican parties continued to perpetuate culture wars and identity politics. The result was to distract from corporate welfare, while the government subcontracted many functions of government agencies to corporations, and continued to slash the social safety net. To avoid class issues that Sanders was raising as a core strategy in inclusionary populism against Wall Street Democrats and GOP exclusionary populists, the media and the entire institutional mainstream kept the focus narrowly on personalities and identity politics.

Because there is nothing in the US similar to the anti-neoliberal leftwing grassroots groups in Brazil, Mexico, South Africa, or the Indian subcontinent, the absence of American grassroots movements operating autonomously and resisting co-optation by political parties has been a testament to the institutional power of the political class and wealthy donors financing political campaigns. To silence dissent, the same billionaire donors pour money into academic institutions, think tanks, and media promoting neoliberal conformity within the two-party system.[877]

The co-optation of American progressives into the neoliberal mainstream was in some respects similar to what took place in Europe after Thatcher's election. All European centrist and center-left governments fully embraced neoliberalism while retaining the liberal or socialist rhetoric. All across southern Europe, self-proclaimed leftist parties that came to power on an anti-neoliberal, anti-austerity platform did a volte-face once in power. They embraced austerity, deregulation, privatization, and corporate welfare. Rebaptizing the Democratic Party into the neoliberal model, 'Clintonism' betrayed the party's historic commitment to social justice. This was also true of 'Blairism' in the UK and other center-left parties all across continental Europe where liberal-pluralist political parties claimed to represent workers and the middle class.

Considering that Clinton and Blair de-radicalized the progressive wings of their respective parties and co-opted them into the neoliberal mold, it is historically inaccurate to argue that Thatcher and Reagan did more to de-democratize society than their liberal successors. From conservative to liberal and center-left, political parties embracing neoliberalism were able to co-opt the majority of the middle class and workers, thereby contributing to popular disillusionment and alienation while furthering neoliberalism's class warfare.

Undercutting popular solidarity against neoliberal transformation, the ruling parties weakened the grassroots movements as much in the US and EU, as across the rest of the world. This was indicative of the relative weakness of the left against the immense power of capitalism's hold on society through the ownership of mainstream, media, social media, and all institutions that viewed the neoliberal social contract as the new reality. It was also a testament to the relative strength of the far right that hijacked some issues such as anti-globalization from the left, but with emphasis on limiting migration from the Global South to the North.[878]

Rightwing anti-globalization rhetoric placed the progressives in a dilemma about abstaining from voting. The dilemma was whether to cast a ballot for a progressive candidate without the prospect of winning, or whether to vote for the neoliberal centrist because the rightwing candidate was more divisive, chaotic, and destructive for workers. In the US, the inevitable transformation of the Republican Party from a traditional conservative (Rockefeller Republicans, 1950-1970s), to a populist far rightwing party of dogmatism is indicative of the neoliberal model's far-reaching influence in transforming the entire political class, pulling all political parties to the right.[879]

Among many analysts, the lingering question has been whether the neoliberal model developed so many contradictions that it was itself the root cause of the crisis. Another issue is whether right-wing populists and centrists were scrambling to keep neoliberalism alive by competing to mobilize the popular base. Behind the vacuous populist rhetoric about democracy and prospects for socioeconomic mobility is the goal of even greater capital accumulation. Given neoliberalism's multifarious contradictions, especially political resistance to authoritarian neoliberalism, there is no cause to be optimistic either about the transformation model's imminent decay or the demise of the right wing. French National Assembly election results, the presidential election results of Colombia, both on 19 June 2022, and Brazil's election in October 2022 that resulted in Bolsonaro's defeat proved that the lesser of two evils dilemma is not exactly an endorsement for authoritarian neoliberalism, but the model remains strong even amid an increasingly fragmented world economy.[880]

"Marine Le Pen's National Front in France, the Danish People's Party, the Freedom Party in Austria, Viktor Orban's Fidesz Party in Hungary — abandoning parts of the old neoliberal programs advocating liberalization and less taxation that they had supported and now proclaiming they were for the welfare state and more protection of the economy from international engagements, but exclusively for the benefit of the people with "right skin color," the

"right culture," the "right ethnic stock," the "right religion. Essentially, it's the old "national socialist" class-inclusivist but racially and culturally exclusivist formula, whose consummate practitioner at present is Donald Trump. But, unfortunately, it works in our troubled times, as shown by the unexpected string of electoral successes of the far right that have pirated large sectors of social democracy's working-class base."[881]

Lapsing into despair after hoping for meaningful improvement in their material lives, it is understandable at the political, sociological, and psychological levels to appreciate why so many have become depoliticized. Especially in the lower middle class where anger is aimed at minorities and marginalized social groups, many place all hope on rightwing political parties naively believing in Messianic messages. When 70% of Americans in a public opinion poll indicated that the entire economy, not just Wall Street, is rigged to benefit billionaires and millionaires, the level of cynicism should not be surprising any more than political polarization.[882]

Considering the hegemonic culture's far-reaching societal impact, it is hardly a surprise that many people do not blame the institutional structure upon which the political economy is based, even if they have disdain for wealthy individuals benefiting from that system. Behind the illusion about marginalized populations causing society's problems, and beneath multiple layers of bourgeois issues ranging from property rights, consumer and privacy rights rests not a rigged economy, but a social contract whose goal of capital accumulation amid class warfare drives the masses toward conformity to the socially unjust institutional structure for no other reason than mere survival.[883]

CHAPTER VI:

The Neoliberal Model of Education

Commodified Education

Unleashing the creative potential for humanity's edification, education has the potential as an instrument of socialization and social progress. Historically, education has been an instrument of indoctrination, social engineering, and manipulation for socioeconomic exploitation by secular and religious social elites. This was the case from the religious schools of the Middle Ages to the post-industrial-revolution public schools based on the concept of educational mass production and to Harvard University's AI robot replacing classroom faculty in 2023. While technology has influenced modern education, the neoliberal model subsumed this domain with the introduction of government-subsidized private schools for profit. As will analyzed below, this has entailed defunding public schools, shifting resources indirectly to private schools, the student being reduced to a commodity, and the system operating within a business-style structure that mirrors the private sector's values and goals.[884]

Given that socialization is the catalyst for transmitting trans-cultural ideas through education, civilization is the process of socialization's philosophical underpinning. The question is the degree to which education is the product of cultural diffusion for the edification of the individual and society under a hierarchical social order. If education's goal is not cultural diffusion but the preservation of traditional culture and molding the individual into institutional conformity for the benefit of preserving the privileged elites, the status quo necessarily defines civilization's perimeters to benefit the elites.[885]

Not limited to higher education, neoliberal commodification has impacted the entire system in the US and other countries, partly because of neoliberalism's promotion by international organizations, especially the IMF and World Bank. Despite some countries struggling to exempt health and education from predatory state-subsidized privatization in the age of neoliberalism, maintaining traditional public institutions untouched by the neoliberal model has been very difficult. Because European and American academics and policymakers immersed in neoliberal ideology succeed by molding people into the new social contract, it should come as no surprise that the neoliberal transformation of the education system is inevitable.

Higher learning especially reflected the ideological, political, and cultural mainstream in the earliest European universities during the late Middle Ages (University of Bologna, 1088; University of Paris, c.1150; University of Oxford (1167) - even earlier for Arab universities (University of al-Qarawiyyin, 859; Al-Azhar University, 970). Dating back to the fourth century BC when Confucius created an academy that became the basis for various higher learning schools, Chinese higher education also served the institutional hierarchy, as it did in the West, presumably for the sake of order and harmony.[886]

Rooted in the social order, throughout the history of China and Europe, universities served the practical function of producing an educated population that enhances society's function and contributes to civilization. This is a much broader concept invariably linked to socialization and society's welfare, rather than neoliberalism's narrow market-rooted perimeters. Education's definition is different in the 21st century than it was in the 19th; and worlds apart from the Renaissance when Europeans first developed universities having learned a great deal from

Western Christendom's religious schools and Islam's advanced institutions. Founded in Fez Morocco by Fatima al-Firhi in 859 A.D., the first university (al-Qarawiyyin mosque-religious school) influenced education in the Iberian Peninsula and Western Christendom.[887]

Like all institutions throughout history, education reflects the hegemonic culture's values rooted in the social structure. Based on the Enlightenment era concept of universal, dogma-free, and critical thinking, education's ultimate goal is self-improvement and social development as catalysts to progress in every domain from medical science to the fine arts and literature. Although commodification predates neoliberalism and reflects industrial capitalism's demands for an educated labor force, the concept of applying purist market principles and reducing the entire system to a commodity subject to market forces reflects the transformation that began during the 1980s.

Beyond commodification, modern education has been an integral part of the arsenal of the elites' molding institutions around neoliberal ideology. Contrary to the Enlightenment methodology and goals of critical thinking permitting the individual to transcend the confines of social relations dialectically, neoliberal education regiments the individual's role in the manner that she/he fits in society as a consumer/citizen in the social hierarchy.[888]

As part of social policy transformation during the Thatcher-Reagan era, all schools, especially universities, started emulating the corporate structure, methodology, and goals. Neoliberal education entailed reducing full-time faculty and relying on adjuncts, bureaucratizing the institution, and shifting focus from improving the quality of teaching, to expanding physical facilities while treating the student as a customer whose tuition and student loans kept rising at the college level. At the same time, the chasm widened between rich and poor public schools at the primary and secondary levels.

In December 1985, the *Gramm–Rudman–Hollings Balanced Budget and Emergency Deficit Control Act* became the instrument to undertake social transformation based on the neoliberal model. Within varying degrees, depending on the country, education transformed from a public good to a commercial commodity no different than any other in the marketplace. Even for those who could afford college education's basic costs, it became increasingly difficult because of declining working-class incomes, and at the same time, college graduates failed to secure a job in their chosen field of academic training.[889]

The 21st-century neoliberal era is not like the mid-19th century when the Boston School Committee refused to admit Sarah Roberts, a five-year-old African-American girl based on race. More than race, socioeconomic conditions dictate that the quality of education is subject to the laws of the market, affording access to the wealthy and limiting opportunities to the working class. In some respects, the neoliberal era has traveled back in time to the world of Charles Dickens and Ida B. Wells. Especially in the US with a history of institutional racism deeply rooted in the culture, there is a de facto economic segregation of the education system. This is also in other countries with a similar history of ethnic segregation from South Africa to Israel, and to a lesser degree in advanced countries like Germany and France.[890]

Stressing education's market value, not its edification in the life of the student and society, neoliberals justify commodification as the key to individual progress. Critics castigate commodification's disastrous impact on social development, contributing to the culture of atomism. Under neoliberal transformation, education's 18th-century philosophical goals of intellectual and cultural self-enrichment for the edification of society have been replaced with the profit motive taking precedence over everything. Given the goal of neoliberal transformation, it makes sense that education from the elementary to post-graduate level has been a neoliberal target.[891]

Centered on personal creativity of making the individual socially, culturally, and politically aware, education has historically meant contributing intellectually and culturally to humanity and society for therein rests the key to social progress. While the Enlightenment's legacy is still present with individual teachers, institutionally those principles have taken a back seat to the market-centered theme of human capital efficiency. *"Human capital represents a subtle masking of social conflict,"* Marnie Holborow argues, *"and expresses metaphorically the commodification of human abilities and an alienating notion of human potential, both of which sit ill with the goals of education."*[892]

Combined with the skills-driven education panacea which promises, but fails to deliver the volume of high-value jobs, neoliberalism obfuscates underlying social conflict amid class war by blaming the student who is "free to choose", to borrow Milton Friedman's book title, rather than neoliberalism which determines the individual's choices. An advocate of the "School Choice Theory" and the voucher system long before neoliberal governments implemented it, Freidman believed that parents, not government, must make education decisions. This assumption is deliberately oblivious to the voucher system benefiting the wealthier students at the expense of the working class whose taxes subsidize the voucher system. Tested in Chile under Pinochet's dictatorship, Friedman's school choice theory of decentralized education based on the voucher plan resulted in advancing the affluent few, leaving the rest behind.[893]

Education's theoretical goal remains to cultivate intellectual, artistic, and cultural traits for the student's edification and society's benefit, not at its expense, although this is the result in many cases because of the nature of neoliberal social relations. The neoliberal educator is an instrument for value-added products, molding students for the marketplace as consumers, workers, and/or managers and capitalists. Operating on the assumption of managerial efficiency, as though schools are no different than corporations, treating faculty, staff, and students as human capital, the neoliberal strategy is comparable to programming automatons for profit. In a commodified society, this strategy applies to everything from social work, health, and medicine, to services impacting children in nurseries to older adults in nursing homes.[894]

The neoliberal objective is not only to create market-conscious students prepared to take her/his place in the marketplace hierarchy but also individuals immersed in the ideology of libertarian individualism which means self-identity placed against public welfare. The individual student fits into a hierarchical social order where the "winner-take-all" mindset permeates the mass consciousness. It is worth noting that the education system's neoliberal transformation has resulted in the corresponding involvement of corporations injecting their agenda to mold the entire system. Regardless of any benefit to society incidental only in so far as the profit dimension is involved, the corporate model promotes its own marketing, research, and economic interests in education.

With the pernicious goal to efface diversity, and pluralism, and to replace historical accuracy along with creativity as cultural enrichment with social engineering, influential far-rightwing individuals and various entities from churches to corporations have used the education system as a weapon in the neoliberal transformation model. Education has been a popular rallying cry of conservative and far-right in culture wars as a political mobilization strategy, especially in the US and the UK since the 1980s. As social construction and political interest convergence, race and cultural diversity in education have been successfully politicized both by liberals and conservatives. Both camps have used education to promote their version of neoliberalism along with their ideological and political preferences.[895]

Under exclusionary populist neoliberal regimes, the education system in several countries, including Hungary, Turkey, India and Brazil among other republics has been leaning toward nationalism and religious dogmatism in the service of neoliberal authoritarianism. Critical thinking based on anthropocentric values, academic freedom, pluralism, creativity, and scientific inquiry are subordinated to neoliberal values. The cliché neoliberal assumption that public schools have failed because of teachers' unions has been universally used to proceed with transformation. Whether in favor of the commodification model or not, there is a consensus that neoliberal transformation is a reality. Its impact reaches from right-wing political parties financed by organized religion, corporations, and billionaires who have transformed the education system as a weapon in the neoliberal crusade. [896]

After taking office, Prime Minister Narendra Modi used education as a political weapon of the Bharatiya Janata Party (BJP) within the neoliberal mold. Vikram Singh of India's *News Click* writes that: *"there is a silent conspiracy to completely dismantle the public education system in India. In the past four years, the policy paralysis of the government has gone hand in hand with the attempts to dismantle all decision-making bodies. The Rashtriya Uchhtar Shiksha Abhiyan (RUSA) was a UPA flagship program that has been carried forward by the BJP government. It replaces the pre-existing multiple funding mechanisms with one centralized mechanism."*[897]

Whether under Modi's BJP, or Erdogan's Justice and Development Party, authoritarian neoliberalism has been a vehicle of injecting religious and private education to satisfy market forces and neoliberal ideologues. Identifying with religion and the neoliberal transformation, education reform in both Turkey and India was a top priority which started before the two neoliberal authoritarian leaders took power. Within the first one hundred days of taking office, Modi announced a neoliberal transformation that included education reform. In traditional societies like India and Turkey, neoliberal transformation carried a heavy dose of religion – Hinduism for India, and Islam for Turkey - at the expense of deemphasizing human rights, diversity, and cultural tolerance. Using religion and cultural politics in education has been a tool not only to indoctrinate the masses but to mobilize them behind authoritarian neoliberalism and distract from class war and systemic inequality.[898]

Industrial capitalism's 19th-century apologists assumed that whatever was good for business was good for society. This was regardless of consequences to workers, small farmers, the environment, market equilibrium, or humanity's future. Like factories turning out manufactured products for profit, schools under the neoliberal model adopted the monolithic business management model based on early 19th-century industrial capitalist dogma. Naturally, the business model works very differently for the wealthy with access to the best schools from kindergarten to graduate school than it does for the working class at the bottom of the public funding priority list. Confined to the worst public schools in inner-city neighborhoods and rural areas, the poor find it difficult to use education as a social mobility instrument.[899]

As though choice was equally available to all regardless of socioeconomic status, race, gender, and ethnicity, neoliberal privatization of public education, especially under the voucher system and tuition tax credits, has come at the expense of public schools. Underfunding public education has undermined the quality of schools in working-class neighborhoods, while enriching private schools where, in many cases, working conditions and faculty compensation are as bad if not much worse than their counterparts in public schools. A reflection of neoliberalism's global reach, the corporatization of education cannibalized by the high-tech sector is not confined to private schools in the US but reaches across the entire spectrum of the education system in many countries.[900]

Especially in Latin America, Eastern Europe, and the Middle East, politicians and businesses have targeted education as a key institution and a catalyst to ideological and socioeconomic conformity to neoliberal policy enmeshed with conservative religious and secular ideology. The global neoliberal transformation has entailed an even more stratified system than public schools under the Keynesian state. The largest share of education resources, including allocation for modern physical facilities, computer technology, and the most qualified faculty wind up in the richest neighborhoods. Elected officials justify this based on higher taxes paid by wealthier residents, thus inadvertently acknowledging education policy's socioeconomic basis. Hence, neoliberal education has been a catalyst to inequality, instead of a vehicle for social mobility.[901]

Among other countries, Chile, the US, and the UK adopted the neoliberal model of education which the working class has been subsidizing so the wealthy can exercise 'free choice'. Because the poorest neighborhoods receive the least resources in elementary and secondary school, they have the lowest possibilities for a college education and upward social mobility. Pointing to the worst education outcomes in poor neighborhood public schools, neoliberals reject the argument of linking under-funded schools to poor student performance. Privatization, which has been the source of economic segregation and transferring income from the working class to the more affluent, has been justified in the name of exercising free choice.[902]

Education in Latin America, Africa, and the Middle East has been a part of the entrenched political structure and dependency ideology linking local elites to international capital and geopolitical alliances. Like other scholars, Moroccan social scientist Hicham Alaoui points out that the neoliberal model has resulted in policy reforms at the expense of teachers and students from the lower classes without access to the best schools. International financial institutions, including the IMF, World Bank, and international aid agencies promote the stratification process in the Arab World by imposing a linkage of such aid to neoliberal transformation. Like all domestic policy, education is intertwined with the regime's political patronage schemes which is no different than how other ministries operate. Just as important, the nature of the curriculum is tailored to the authoritarian regime under neoliberalism.[903]

The neoliberal model's impact on education has been subverted and adapted to local political and social conditions that further leave behind the working class. *"Arab educational systems are embedded in larger political structures,"* Hicham Alaoui argues. *"We call these structures "limited access orders," more commonly known as authoritarianism. Limited access orders operate by controlling the distribution of knowledge, which is the most precious resource, across vast segments of society. They see humanistic education, which delivers the skills needed for critical thinking and self-emancipation, as existential threats. An active, engaged, and empowered citizenry will question authority and demand answers to the pressing problems of their economy and state."*[904]

The downgrading of humanistic education and critical thinking has been characteristic of the neoliberal education curriculum. Even at that, the system has reverted to serving those who can buy access to quality private and public schools, while underfunded public schools intended for the working class become downgraded as a result of the policy. Those with the financial means avail themselves of private tutoring services, adding another layer into the rich-poor education chasm. The estimate for these services is at $123.8 billion in 2020, expected to rise above $200 billion by 2026. In South Korea, France, Turkey, and the US, to mention only a few countries, private tutoring is ubiquitous, experiencing a meteoric rise under neoliberal transformation. Those who can afford it, pay to achieve high scores in college entrance exams.[905]

In a comparative study of private tutoring in South Korea and the US, Jaekyung Lee points out that there is a difference in how the tutoring industry operates in different countries. Limited opportunities for the best schools lead those who can afford tutoring to academic remediation, a service that serves those who need it the least. Hence, private tutoring further undermines equal opportunities as it limits academic excellence to those with financial means. While the prevailing view in South Korea is that private tutoring threatens public education, despite the government's efforts to offer public tutoring, in the US hegemonic culture there is a tendency to view anything private in a positive light and anything public as inherently inferior and flawed. Even though it serves a limited number of students whose affluent parents can afford private tutoring, neoliberal apologists praise private education as the panacea for society.[906]

Budget cuts in public schools hit especially hard the working poor and minority communities. In part, the strategy has an ideological and political dimension. Trying to prove that the public school model is obsolete and a remnant of the Keynesian social welfare state, neoliberals adhere to Milton Friedman's view of education. In the Chilean experiment where Freidman played a role in policy, neoliberals contended that salvation rests with the charter school model reflecting the pure market dogma favoring a small percentage of the population.

Manipulation of public education policy through budgetary control results in the rise of delinquent behavior in underfunded schools. In turn, this reinforces the view of some elected officials that working-class and minority community students are potential psychiatric patients or even future candidates for prison incarceration. Despite the need for more funding in the weakest schools, as part of neoliberal social engineering, governments reduced funding, while pouring resources into the strongest ones.[907]

Class-based, education has also been tainted by racism and sexism. In *Capitalism and Freedom* (1962), Milton Friedman argued in favor of minimal publicly-subsidized education. If, in theory, one views education solely from the human capital perspective, then the individual, not society, must be responsible for the cost. If true to the theory, then fiscal policy cannot be designed to provide tax credits or any other form of subsidy, as neoliberals demand. Friedman and neoliberal supporters knew that taxpayer money must be redirected from public to private schools via the voucher system to benefit the wealthy at the expense of the working class and minorities. This practice precluded upward social mobility which they claim as a goal of their ideology. Behind the school choice model based on the voucher system in the US, there is a long-standing historical racist tradition promoting white supremacy. Without ever using racialized language, neoliberals hide behind the thin veil of class-warfare ideology which advocates the voucher system and other forms of public subsidies along with tax deductions for private education.[908]

The Rising Cost of Higher Education

Minimizing its social role within the limits of market perimeters, neoliberal transformation redefined education. It has redirected the focus to indoctrinate against publicly-funded schools from primary to university. Where large college endowments from corporations and billionaires are involved, the neoliberal model's impact has been even greater in higher education than in the primary and secondary school levels. To slash public funding for higher education, just as in primary and secondary, neoliberal managerial strategies took precedence over pedagogy. Especially in higher education, it is difficult to distinguish the non-profit institution from any private company charging the "consumer-student" a hefty price for services and investing endowment money in hedge funds, thus operating like a private company.[909]

The corresponding rise in higher education from the 1980s to the present has occurred against the background of stagnant wages, making college education a difficult proposition for working-class families hoping to have a better material life than the previous generation. *"Parents are finding their life savings dwindling under the strain. Young men and women are going further into debt than ever before, hoping that future earnings will make repayment relatively painless. All are wondering if the education students are receiving is worth the investment. And through it all, more and more taxpayers' dollars are being routed through state and Federal programs to fund grants and guaranteed loans."* [910]

Besides private tutoring with its multibillion-dollar industry growing rapidly, *"distance learning"* or online education is another outgrowth of the neoliberal model which has added a for-profit dimension to traditional public schools. In some cases, full or partial online degree schools are nothing more than factories selling degrees for low quality or no education throughout the world. Some such operations exist solely because there is government funding for student loans and direct student fees. In India, half of its graduates are not qualified for employment because of the fraudulent education system.[911]

To the degree that there are numerous services alerting students what to avoid, college scams and quasi-scams have become more widespread. One of the most famous scams involved Trump University supposedly offering instruction on becoming a real estate investor tycoon like Trump who inherited $413 million from his father but launched a university to teach people how to become self-made billionaires like him. In 2013, New York Attorney General Eric Schneiderman sued Trump for defrauding thousands of people out of millions at Trump University. In 2016, Schneiderman settled the case for $25 million in damages. In August 2019, the Harvard Law School blog reported that for-profit colleges had defrauded 96% of students. Partly because of the low quality of education, but also because of the loan default rate, the US Department of Education was concerned about the Federal Student Aid program keeping some institutions afloat that they would otherwise not exist.[912]

The incredible contradiction of neoliberalism is that politicians, businesses, and media, among other enthusiasts in the establishment matrix, constantly argue that education and skills are the keys to good jobs. At the same time, the same apologists support privatization of the education system which limits access and often compromises quality, depending on the for-profit institution. Because many businesses and government agencies either refuse to hire graduates of expensive fake schools with expensive fake degrees, or hire them temporarily and then dismiss them, both the college grad and taxpayers are shortchanged.

Globally where people receive degrees in every field, including medical science based on skeletal learning of the basics. Resulting of neoliberal dogma, public education's downgrading has diminished the quality of the educated population which then hurts society and the economy; one of neoliberalism's many contradictions. Spending $117 billion for education in 2020, compared with $1 trillion in the US, India's budget for public education hovers just under 3% in comparison with the government target of 6%. The problem has been a society-wide neoliberal deception that businesses and government have perpetuated to the detriment of students and society, considering that other than the scam institutions, no one benefits.[913]

Using Australia as a case study, Kristin Natalie and Robert Clarke point out that the market and the state under the neoliberal model are shaping the education system subordinated to the market economy's logic. *"The practices and technologies of online education can align with neo-liberal logic. A discourse of democratizing education can hide the ambiguities of online education, which can simultaneously increase socially disadvantaged groups' access to higher education, respond to the student consumers expectation of more online modes of learning enable universities to penetrate underdeveloped or inaccessible local and international markets and maximize efficiencies in teaching through the affordances of replication and scaling without associated staffing and infrastructure costs comment on flexible education generally applies to online education in particular: it is a "pedagogy and a marketing strategy as well as a form of work organization."*[914]

Neoliberal logic assumes the one-dimensional role of education in the service of capital accumulation while indoctrinating students to conform and enhance social contract goals. From the dynamics of industrial capitalism in the 18th and 19th centuries to the financialization of capitalism by the end of the 20th century, education has been subject to the laws of overproduction. Applied not just to commodities, but to the surplus labor force, the crisis of overproduction of the college-educated population in the metropolis coincided with the institutionalization of neoliberalism in the last two decades of the 20th century.[915]

Among other institutions, the World Bank has played an important role in promoting the neoliberal model of education. From Nepal to Brazil, and all around the world, the World Bank has been promoting autonomy in education as part of a broader transformation policy. Unlike UNESCO which accepts education's social value, the World Bank's goal has nothing to do with an improved institution for the edification of the student and society. Instead, the goal is to cut spending and shift the cost burden from the taxpayer to the student and private sources. This policy diminishes college opportunities for the working class dependent on public education as the most important institution for intellectual enrichment, greater appreciation of society as active critical thinkers, and upward social mobility.[916]

In the first two decades of the 21st century, Nepal and Brazil followed the World Bank's neoliberal recommendations not just about tuition, but on how to manage public universities using the corporate model. Under the pretext of "reducing education poverty" programs, the World Bank linked development loans to neoliberal reform. The university was obligated to link curriculum and programs to the private sector's goals and collaborate with businesses to meet their needs rather than pursue academic goals independent of the business agenda.[917]

As success and achievement are defined by "human capital theory" criteria, the goal of neoliberal education has been to mold the student from elementary through graduate school. Blaming educators and publicly-funded systems for the crisis of overproduction and 'underperformance', the neoliberal solution has been the "free marketplace", namely, government-subsidized private schools. Although historically education has been a catalyst for upward mobility, under neoliberalism, a segment of college graduates suffers downward mobility. Often graduating with debt and accepting jobs outside the field of academic training with lower wages if not seasonal or part-time work, the college graduate lives with the neoliberal winner-take-all law of the jungle world. The fate of the college graduate lapsing toward the chronic debtor class is part of a much larger framework that contributes to downward social mobility.[918]

Emulating the corporate model, the university administration has been operating under the ideology that focuses on the commodification, commercialization, and marketization of everything. Gradually after 1980, the commodification of everything became a reality. Priority in neoliberal higher education is usually based on scholarly outcomes, with those the institution values most as they are specifically linked to a business, government, or an institutional mainstream theme. Whether scholarly research pertains to a pharmaceutical or food company, studies analyzing the benefits or harm of chemical ingredients in a product, or analyzing the multifaceted aspects of drug-gang-related violence in the inner city, neoliberal themes narrowly focus on advancing predetermined goals to satisfy the study's sponsor. Rarely do such studies allow for open-ended conclusions. Methodologically, this is no different than consulting firms that corporations hire to reinforce predetermined strategies, goals, and objectives.

Either corporate or government agency-funded research has an obvious impact on the results of the project, thereby impeding academic freedom and compromising the integrity of scholarly research and curriculum. In more tangible terms, researchers know that funding is linked to conclusions that at the very least would not offend the sponsor whether it is a business, corporate-funded foundation, or government. At the core of the issue is not only academia's privatization, but its manipulation to fit the corporate and/or government objectives.[919]

Redefining the purpose and role of colleges and universities, neoliberalism has converted students into consumers, faculty into entrepreneurial workers, and administrators into corporate managers with an eye on the budget, not on the quality of education. The integrity of the curriculum intended for optimal benefits to the student remains important, but only relative to overriding goals. Academic freedom and critical thinking revolve around the perimeters of job performance as neoliberal goals define them. Instead of academic freedom with the theoretical goal of contributing to humanity's edification and environmental protection, the focus is to pursue these goals as long as they fall within the neoliberal matrix.

School and teacher accountability is quantitatively measured and narrowly based on the concept of "market competitiveness". Beyond the narrowly-defined "output metrics", faculty fall into a mold and are generally reluctant to cross the boundaries of intellectual exploration and creativity. As in any institution, academic conformity has rewards, while academic freedom is safe only within certain perimeters to which most faculty adhere instinctively like corporate employees.[920]

The neoliberal transformation has reduced the complexities of education to quantifiable data related to a business culture, methods, and goals. Both research publication rankings and student test scores as criteria for quality and success are mechanisms to redefine education under individualized outcomes metrics geared for a narrowly defined purpose. This means quantifying the learning process, confined not only to the advanced capitalist countries but the periphery emulating the core's institutional structure and values.[921]

With the passage of the Bayh-Dole Act (1980), higher education became an even greater appendage of the corporate world. Although taxpayer money in part funds research, neoliberal proponents present it as market-competitive. In reality, it is part of the larger corporate welfare model. Four years after the bipartisan Bayh-Dole Act, the National Cooperative Research Act (1984) extended antitrust status to joint university-business ventures.

Under this act, taxpayer money for privately held research was no longer subject to anti-trust violations. University research became a mirror of the deregulation/privatization corporate welfare model. In practice, it meant depriving faculty not just of autonomy and academic freedom, but surrendering to the corporate sector to advance their careers. The hierarchy of institutions receiving the most money in endowments and the establishment of academia carrying on the corporate agenda in their works speaks volumes about neoliberal hegemony.[922]

More than race, gender, religion, or ethnicity, socioeconomic status has been an obstacle to college access for qualified students. Besides the US with the highest college costs in 35 OECD member countries, costs have also been rising across Asia. Fueling inequality, private tutoring and private schools in Japan, Taiwan, and South Korea are similar to Western private schools as part of the global education marketization trend.[923]

From Chile, Belgium, Switzerland, and the former Soviet republics, to the Middle East, marketization has made education a luxury for working people. Dubai is among the most expensive countries, while Turkey, Israel, Qatar, Saudi Arabia, and the United Arab Emirates are along a similar path. From the more than eighty US-affiliated colleges and universities overseas, many institutions around the world have accepted the commodified neoliberal model, often at the urging of the World Bank and other international organizations such as the OECD and IMF.[924]

Anna Hoffman and Almantas Salamavicius point out that former Communist countries in central and eastern Europe embraced marketization and commodification even more aggressively than Western countries. "*The commodification of knowledge makes the economic role of universities and research institutions focal, strongly affecting the central European and Slovenian academic landscape. The tendencies of the current neo-liberalization of higher education are visible in decreasing governmental funding and the competitiveness it fuels, the increase of short-term contracts for academic staff, and scientific production governed by funding structures. However, I think that we should be careful about generalizing these processes since they take different forms in different environments. The neo-liberalization of academia is an ideologically and structurally multifaceted process that influences the daily work and lives of students and academic and administrative staff in different ways.*[925]

For most countries, education has never been a high priority like the defense sector, the stock market, commerce, or law enforcement. Because local, state, and central government spending for education has been historically low in developing nations, the wealthy in those countries send their children to domestic private schools, and then to Western universities. Historically, this phenomenon accounted for the "brain drain" from the periphery to the metropolis, perpetuating socioeconomic inequality in the country losing the educated/skilled labor force while enriching the advanced capitalist countries. Especially in countries undergoing austerity, neoliberal internationalization of higher education has exacerbated the brain drain at the Global South's expense.[926]

Neoliberal disdain for public education, as an integral part of the social welfare state, has made it an easy political and ideological target. By stigmatizing social welfare and inner-city public schools, both rightwing populists and liberal pluralists played a role in convincing the public to defund the weakest public schools. American historian of education Michael Katz argues that in the US, more than in other countries, there is a widespread neoliberal notion that social welfare and public schools are a stigma in comparison to private institutions that carry status, even if a number of them are worse than public schools.

"Welfare is the most despised public institution in America. Public education is the most iconic. To associate them with each other will strike most Americans as bizarre, even offensive. The link would be less surprising to nineteenth-century reformers for whom crime, poverty, and ignorance formed an unholy trinity against which they struggled. Nor would it raise British eyebrows. Ignorance was one of the "five giants" to be slain by the new welfare state proposed in the famous Beveridge Report. National health insurance, the cornerstone of the British welfare state, and the 1944 Education Act, which introduced the first national system of secondary education to Britain, were passed by Parliament only two years apart. Yet, in the United States, only a few students of welfare and education have even suggested that the two might stand together."[927]

The irony of stigmatizing the victims of social welfare is that capitalism creates inequality necessitating such programs. Unable to defend the political economy, capitalism's apologists blame the victims for systemic problems in the social contract. This is especially true in the US with its long history of racial/ethnic /gender/ working class institutional discrimination, especially in the domain of education which reflects cultural hegemony and is culturally determined.[928]

The corporate model of education, especially higher education, has had a detrimental impact on the tenured/ adjunct faculty ratio. Furthermore, highly paid administrators govern the university like corporate executives, the college bureaucracy continues to expand, and the focus is on physical facilities and equipment. Between 1993 and 2009, university administration in the US grew 10 times more than the full-time faculty. To fund the top-heavy bureaucratic structure, there was a sharp rise in adjunct faculty. This phenomenon was as pronounced in the US and UK as in other countries following the same corporate bureaucratization-managerial model largely responsible for rising tuition.[929]

With layers of vice-chancellors and assistant vice-chancellors, deans and assistant deans, directors, and assistant directors, among other titles, along with an army of clerical staff, the top-heavy system resembles the sort of bureaucracy that neoliberals criticize in the public sector. Predictably, this model resulted in diminished access for working-class students and skyrocketing student debt because the cost has risen sharply to support a parasitic bureaucracy and new facilities. Paying lip service to "market efficiency" mythology, neoliberals support the model lacking in substantive contributions to education but adhering to the ideology. Unlike many countries around the world where college education costs are very low, and in some cases free, the US and several Western countries experienced high costs once the downgrading public education began. Almost indistinguishable from a business, university management transformation was made possible because of a heavier reliance on the endowment, thus driving tuition and other fees higher.[930]

From 1978 to 2012, the increase in tuition and fees in US higher education was 1,120%. For the same period, inflation was less than ten times lower than college tuition, and much less if we excluded health care. Canada A reflection of the corporatization of colleges and universities, rising tuition was far above the level of inflation making higher education a luxury as much in the US as in several other countries pursuing the neoliberal model. [931]

Even with a single-digit in tuition increase in 2023, expenses for a US public university education are estimated at an average of $25,000 annually, $44,000 out of state, and $54,000 for private school. Advanced degrees are much higher. Medical degrees average between $250,000 and $350,000 for the complete program, excluding personal expenses. Although not as dramatic, there has been a corresponding rise in all OECD member nations, especially in the UK, Canada, Netherlands, Australia, New Zealand, Japan, and the Scandinavian countries. In continental Europe, the average cost of all English-taught bachelor's programs is $7,390 per year.[932]

"Students at [US] public four-year institutions paid an average of $3,190 in tuition for the 1987-1988 school year, with prices adjusted to reflect 2017 dollars. Thirty years later that average has risen to $9,970 for the 2017-2018 school year. That's a 213 percent increase. The difference is stark at private schools as well. In 1988, the average tuition for a private nonprofit four-year institution was $15,160, in 2017 dollars. For the 2017-2018 school year, it's $34,740, a 129 percent increase."[933]

For a family with two children in the US, college cost is the difference between owning a home and sending the children to college. Because of higher college tuition combined with stagnant incomes for the working class with modest gains for the middle class since the 1980s, the average household experienced a drop in income adjusted for inflation, while accumulating higher debt. Historically, the assumption is that college education is a worthy investment for upward mobility, not to mention the quest for knowledge about the world and self-discovery as basic to cultivating the mind and benefiting society.[934]

After the Great Recession, states slashed spending on higher education, raised corporate subsidies, and provided more tax breaks for upper-income groups, thereby creating greater inequality. Education's corporatization marginalized an even greater percentage of society's lower strata. According to a study by the Center on Budget and Policy Priorities: *"Overall state funding for public two- and four-year colleges in the school year ending in 2018 was more than $6.6 billion below what it was in 2008 just before the Great Recession fully took hold, after adjusting for inflation. In the most difficult years after the recession, colleges responded to significant funding cuts by increasing tuition, reducing faculty, limiting course offerings, and in some cases closing campuses. Funding has rebounded somewhat, but costs remain high and services in some places have not returned."*[935]

Despite contributing only 2% of the entire higher education budget, the US federal government has enormous leverage. At $170 billion of the estimated $520 billion in annual spending on higher education, the federal student loan program has a major impact on who receives a college degree and which schools are competitive. Student loan default rates range from 11.8% in 2012 to a low of 7.3% in 2018, affecting millions of families and hundreds of billions.[936]

Concurrently with the massive rise in household debt, between 2010 and 2020, the US student debt trend ran parallel with downward social mobility. This was largely owing to the absence of well-paying jobs across all of the economy, despite the revolution in the high-tech sector. For the majority of the politicians, the options are not to change existing conditions, but to allow companies and business people to determine higher education's future through their generous contributions. At Grinnell College where he served as a trustee, billionaire investor Warren Buffett raised its endowment from $8 million to $1 billion and eventually $2 billion. Nevertheless, the school kept tuition high. An excellent undergraduate liberal arts college, Grinnell's classroom instruction hardly derived much benefit from the endowment that went straight into physical facilities, equipment, and top-heavy administration/bureaucracy.[937]

Sociologist Betz Mintz maintains that American academia went through a multi-decade spending spree on buildings, invariably dedicated to wealthy donors as monuments in their memory for the community to admire. The construction of new buildings came at a huge cost to the quality of education. *"Between 2002 and 2012, interest payments almost doubled, growing from $6 billion to $11 billion[1] for four-year (nonprofit) schools. The University of Colorado, for example, owed approximately $1.5 billion in 2019, with 3.6.%[2] of its annual operating budget going towards debt servicing. Expanded student services are also common recruitment vehicles, and although they do not typically require large capital outlays, they fuel the growth of administrators. Defined narrowly, about 8.4%[3] of spending in private (nonprofit) four-year institutions and 4.9%[4] for comparable publics is on student services. This contributes to the decline in instructional spending as a percentage of total expenses in both the public and private (non-profit) sectors which, in 2017-2018, accounted for 27% and 31%[5] of four-year schools' budgets, respectively. Add to this nearly half a billion dollars[6] spent on advertising each year, and the role of competition and marketization in tuition escalation becomes clearer."*[938]

In an economy with $23 trillion GDP in 2021, college student debt increased by 100% in the 2010s to $1.7 trillion by September 2021. Efforts to undermine public education through various methods have created a debt crisis for young people even before they embark on a career. The persistent question remains whether the quality of education has improved under marketplace 'efficiency' which punishes the working class and minorities because of cuts in public school budgets especially in working-class and minority school districts. At the same time, low-paid teachers have been further reduced to proletariat status. Punishing the teacher as the scapegoat for systemic problems, the neoliberal model has added quantitative evaluation accountability mechanisms designed based on the business model, without taking into account institutional obstacles.[939]

As part of a neo-Keynesian platform, Senator Bernie Sanders repeatedly proposed free tuition along with free health care for all. He reasons that students are punished for going to college and graduating with massive debt

1. *http://debtandsociety.ucmerced.edu/publication/borrowing_against_the_future/*

2. *https://www.cu.edu/doc/fy-20-debt-ratio-reportfinalmay19pdf*

3. *https://nces.ed.gov/programs/digest/d19/tables/dt19_334.30.asp*

4. *https://nces.ed.gov/programs/digest/d19/tables/dt19_334.10.asp*

5. *https://nces.ed.gov/programs/coe/indicator_cuc.asp*

6. *https://www.brookings.edu/research/commercials-for-college-advertising-in-higher-education/#_853ae90f0351324bd73ea615e6487517__4c761f170e016836ff84498202b99827__853ae90f0351324bd73ea615e6487517_text_43ec3e5dee6e706af7766fffea512721_In_0bcef9c45bd8a48eda1b26eb0c61c869_20the_0bcef9c45bd8a48eda1b26eb0c61c869_20United_0bcef9c45bd8a48eda1b26eb0c61c869_20States_0bcef9c45bd8a48eda1b26eb0c61c869_2C_0bcef9c45bd8a48eda1b26eb0c61c869_20the_c0cb5f0fcf239ab3d9c1fcd31fff1efc_colleges_0bcef9c45bd8a48eda1b26eb0c61c869_20and_0bcef9c45bd8a48eda1b26eb0c61c869_20universities_0bcef9c45bd8a48eda1b26eb0c61c869_20is_0bcef9c45bd8a48eda1b26eb0c61c869_20unrelenting._6cff047854f19ac2aa52aac51bf3af4a_text_43ec3e5dee6e706af7766fffea512721_In_0bcef9c45bd8a48eda1b26eb0c61c869_202017_0bcef9c45bd8a48eda1b26eb0c61c869_2C_0bcef9c45bd8a48eda1b26eb0c61c869_20the_0bcef9c45bd8a48eda1b26eb0c61c869_20most_0bcef9c45bd8a48eda1b26eb0c61c869_20recent_c0cb5f0fcf239ab3d9c1fcd31fff1efc__0bcef9c45bd8a48eda1b26eb0c61c869_2C_0bcef9c45bd8a48eda1b26eb0c61c869_20outdoor_0bcef9c45bd8a48eda1b26eb0c61c869_2C_0bcef9c45bd8a48eda1b26eb0c61c869_20and_0bcef9c45bd8a48eda1b26eb0c61c869_20online_0bcef9c45bd8a48eda1b26eb0c61c869_20ads*

to start their lives in a hardly favorable job market. The Senator is correct that in terms of securing a job, a college degree in the 2020s is roughly equivalent to a High School degree in the 1950s-1960s when upward mobility was taking place.[940]

Adamantly against free education as part of the social welfare state, the business, political, and media establishment argues that raising taxes on the rich to pay tuition for the poor is 'socialism'. This is an old hypocritical argument because the same "socialism" critics support hundreds of billions in corporate bailouts and have no objection to taxpayer-subsidized private schools for the rich. An integral part of social justice, education goes to the core of the Enlightenment-based claim of maintaining the bourgeois merit-based system by developing the most creative minds to benefit humanity. If higher education is society's mirror and the source of progress, the neoliberal model has transformed it to reflect the values of the privileged capitalist class. Having redefined higher education's market-oriented goal and value system, neoliberalism has marginalized, if not demonized, non-market values and objectives aimed at collective rather than individual progress.[941]

Part of a transition from Keynesianism to neoliberal corporate welfare through various subsidies and tax reductions, education became an integral part of the transformation at the urging of businesses and international organizations, including the World Bank, IMF, and OECD. The UN has adopted a more critical perspective of neoliberal education's impact, especially in the Global South. In the US, state legislatures reduced budgetary allocations to colleges and universities, forcing them to seek funding from the private sector and to spend less on faculty salaries, while expanding physical facilities, in part to justify the expanding managerial structure.[942]

From faculty hiring to the bloated bureaucracy, everything reflects the ideological orientation and priorities linking the institution to local, national, and transnational businesses. To expand the endowments estimated at $648 billion in 2018, business donors' cooperation was essential. Although a very small percentage of the endowment went to the operating budget, the goal was to augment it as a symbol of the institution's prestige and a variable in the rankings, as though the endowment size was commensurate to the quality of education. Ironically, the transformation model based on market efficiency entails a bloated university bureaucracy around the endowment, to support the university presidents' main role as the promoter of the business model in education and business-dominated boards revolving around the size of the endowment, thereby justifying the costly administrative structure.[943]

In both public and private universities, one of the consequences of university endowments has been waste, fraud, abuse, and corruption by the administrators authorized to deal with endowments. With 170 US universities celebrating endowments totaling $807.332 billion in 2022, manipulation and in some cases corruption is widespread. The government and the private sector are well aware that there is systemic university corruption because the institution's focus is not on its mission to deliver the best education possible, but on accumulating more for the endowment, even if it means harming the institution, and widening the gap between salaries of administrators and faculty analogous to CEO-worker disparities.[944]

Powerless to do anything about corrupt university administration narrowly focused on the endowment to the school's detriment, faculty have reacted through the faculty senate or as in the case of Rutgers going on strike. "*Faculty at Rutgers University are on strike for the first time because the school refuses to pay instructors living wages. Meanwhile, the university keeps plowing more of its endowment into poorly performing hedge fund investments.*

Instead, Rutgers has pumped more than $246 million, or 12.6 percent, of its $1.9 billion[7] endowment investments into high-risk, high-fee hedge funds in just the past two years. The amount that the university has invested in hedge funds has more than doubled since 2020, from $213 million[8] to $459 million[9]."[945]

Behaving like corporate CEOs and treating academics as workers to be disciplined into the university's neoliberal mold, many college presidents and top administrators serve on boards of local and national businesses. Top university administrators distance themselves from the teacher-scholar that they treat with disdain. Behaving like politically-minded business people who have discovered that the key to academic excellence is enhancing the endowment, the neoliberal college administrator is at best indifferent to the teacher-scholar role, except in so far as it meets predetermined assessment guidelines. Like a bank executive or a politician vacuously talking about "education reform", university administrators advocate that higher education must be inexorably linked to the business community.

"*According to a 2008 survey by The Chronicle of Higher Education,*" *New York Times* reporter Graham Bowley writes, "*presidents from 19 of the top 40 research universities with the largest operating budgets sat on at least one company board. The trend is more widespread among public universities, but the private ones are catching up: the American Council on Education says that from 2001 to 2006, the proportion of presidents from all doctorate-granting institutions sitting on corporate boards rose to 52.1 percent from 47.8 percent at public institutions, and to 50.9 percent from 40.6 percent at private ones.*"[946]

There are many cases of blatant billionaire takeover cases of colleges and universities, among them the historically independent liberal arts-oriented Shimer College. In late 2007-2008, rightwing billionaire Barre Seid provided $825,000 to the school through an anonymous foundation. When Thomas Lyndsay, a Bush-era deputy chair of the National Endowment for the Humanities, became president he appointed a rightwing board of Trustees with financial ties to Seid. Faculty and students noticed that the school was evolving into an instrument of a billionaire with an agenda gradually eclipsing the long-standing history of academic freedom.

Not surprisingly, Shimer College began offering classes promoting neoliberal themes, including one called "*The Morality of Capitalism,* a course developed by faculty with ties to Herbert Walberg, chairman of the "free-market" think tank the Heartland Institute. In August 2022, the media reported that the Koch-brothers-affiliated Leonard Leo and Barre Seid tax-dodging network raised $1.65 billion for right-wing political campaigns.[947]

As in the rest of society, marketization, corporatization, and privatization permeated higher education because billionaires like Seid and the Koch brothers had substantial institutional influence, but also because the corporate-financed political class was promoting the same goals. Corporations and wealthy donors making campaign contributions to liberal and rightwing populists viewed education, especially higher education, as another form of corporate subsidy, part of the larger transformation model. Therefore, the commodification of higher education is as much a product of transformation's global reach, as the healthcare industry whose principal focus is maximizing profit.[948]

---

7. *https://emma.msrb.org/P21671638-P21285740-P21715822.pdf*

8. *https://emma.msrb.org/P11469441-P11139075-P11552080.pdf*

9. *https://emma.msrb.org/P21671638-P21285740-P21715822.pdf*

To deliver hope to the public where it is lacking institutionally as a reflection of the hierarchical political economy, neoliberals took advantage of the rags-to-riches myth within the meritocracy confines. Like many critics who have historically pointed out the obvious myths of meritocracy and the reality of social hierarchy, Clifton Mark arrives at the same conclusion. *"Meritocracy is the most self-congratulatory of distribution principles. Its ideological alchemy transmutes property into praise, and material inequality into personal superiority. It licenses the rich and powerful to view themselves as productive geniuses. While this effect is most spectacular among the elite, nearly any accomplishment can be viewed through meritocratic eyes. Graduating from high school, artistic success or simply having money can all be seen as evidence of talent and effort. By the same token, worldly failures become signs of personal defects, providing a reason why those at the bottom of the social hierarchy deserve to remain there."*[949]

Part of a perpetual neoliberal public relations campaign, meritocracy has provided the ideological shield for the privatization rationale and has served as a mechanism for social exclusion. The US college admissions scandals (2019-2020) involving bribery among other schemes including favoring faculty candidates and student applicants linked to endowment donations exposed the hypocrisy of meritocracy in America's top universities. Although these scandals revealed that neoliberalism has opened various avenues for the wealthy to circumvent the formal bureaucratic process, the institutions remain committed to the ideology responsible for corruption.[950]

Historically, wealthy individuals either made large donations to university endowments, scholarships, programs, etc., or engaged in more corrupt measures by having privileged applicants secure college entrance without meeting the criteria because of intermediaries involved, usually justified as 'unique circumstance' individuals. The more blatant college admissions scandals of the 2010s simply stripped the thin veil behind which social status prevailed as the sole criterion.[951]

Against the background of government cuts in public education, higher education's managerialism, corruption, and bribery involving private college admissions offices and prep consulting firms are all symptomatic of a decadent process. In a highly competitive job market for college graduates, endemic corruption at more subtle levels than bribery is a manifestation of the larger problem to which the business model of education gave birth.

Rather than contributing to the quality and breadth of education, the neoliberal commodification of college admissions has added another layer of 'market efficiency' mythology which is a thick layer of decadence. Although meritocracy remains a core value and the mode of operation, there are levels of decadence within the system that reflect neoliberal democracy and its institutions. Clinging to the noble goal of higher learning, universities are somewhat more skillful at handling their neoliberal image than other sectors.[952]

The Information Age, Bureaucratization, and Proletarianization of Higher Education

In a World Bank study on global education, of the one billion primary-school-aged children, 260 million had not received an education by 2019. Breaking down these global statistics, 80% of ten-year-old children in poor countries had no education, while 53% in middle-to-low income met the same fate. In rich and poor countries alike, economic factors determine education levels. As Richard March points out in a study on neoliberalism and education, social justice is never a consideration as it clashes with the model's goals.

"But even for the estimated billion children that do go to class every day, a lack of trained teachers, inadequate learning materials, makeshift classes, and poor sanitation facilities means schooling does not necessarily equal learning. This isn't just an issue for developing countries; in developed countries too, "high income is no guarantee of high educational quality[1]" and poverty and social exclusion[2] mean many students fall behind. In some wealthy European countries, such as the Netherlands for instance, there's a greater gap in the reading ability of 15-year-olds between schools than between children[3]. Why? Rich and poor families send their children to different schools. And globally, governments often underfund schools in remote or low-income areas[4], resulting in "well-resourced educational institutions catering to elite urban strata and poorly resourced institutions serving those in poorer or rural areas[5]".[953]

Camouflaging social marginalization in education, neoliberal apologists have been promoting high-tech as one of the drivers behind the neoliberal model that would theoretically serve as the great equalizer. Digital tech companies use technology as the panacea to transform the nature of education while the media and politicians peddle the same line of technological determinism to deliberately mitigate social class. A catalyst in advancing the neoliberal model to condition students into the new normal, technological determinism is the bait for companies to secure billions of dollars in contracts from schools throughout the world.[954]

A Nation at Risk (1983), by William Bennett, President Reagan's Education Secretary, coincided with the nascent phase of neoliberalism and the myth that computer science is the panacea behind transformation.[955] In the name of "market efficiency" since the 1980s, college administration has relied on technology in all endeavors, largely because of the corporate connection and business favorable disposition toward technology versus teachers. Using technology for fundraising, the technofix further helped to integrate the university with the market by identifying institutional progress with technology instead of quality teaching and research.

Estimated at $107 billion in 2021, the education tech market is expected to grow at 16.5% annually in the 2020s in everything from hardware and software to virtual distance-learning services and ebooks. Under neoliberal

---

1. *https://www.weforum.org/agenda/2018/10/inequality-of-education-in-the-uk-among-highest-of-rich-nations*

2. *https://theconversation.com/how-cradle-to-career-schools-provide-all-round-support-and-tackle-inequality-150795*

3. *https://www.unicef-irc.org/publications/pdf/an-unfair-start-inequality-children-education_37049-RC15-EN-WEB.pdf*

4. *https://www.unicef.org/media/63896/file/Addressing-the-learning-crisis-advocacy-brief-2020.pdf*

5. *https://jl4d.org/index.php/ejl4d/article/view/312*

transformation, high tech changed the culture in education globally. Technophiles have marketed digital technology not only as the presumed great equalizer but as the key to universal education. In practice, the system operates within neoliberal structural perimeters of inequality and marginalization. In the US, half of the bottom 51% of income group earning under $30,000 annually have no smartphone, and 40% of rural blacks and 23% of whites have no access to broadband. For this substantial segment of society, the technofix is possible only if they achieve a certain income level to integrate into the middle class.[956]

Accepting the assumption that competitiveness entails using the very latest technology as the panacea for structural problems, school administrators, politicians, and businessmen pay lip service to excellence in teaching. However, they place greater value on technology as the magic education formula. Without denying its utility, the machine on which humans rely affords the illusion that it is a substitute for intellectual and artistic creativity, and social functions rooted in the promotion of collective community interests. Deflecting from the social contract rooted in institutional inequality, neoliberal techno-enthusiasts contend that "disruptive" (neoliberal euphemism for chaotic market hegemony over society) technology is the panacea for education systems, as for all else ailing society from voter fraud to environmental pollution.[957]

Neoliberal apologists maintain that it is not social inequality but a knowledge and skills deficit holding back students in the global marketplace. There is an assumption that the business sector must determine what is best for society, and students must conform to and serve the neoliberal order. This is also the position of politicians, the media, and mainstream analysts. Statistical studies indicate that neoliberal education remains class-determined, rooted in social hierarchy with benefits mirroring it accordingly.[958]

After the COVID-19 outbreak forced more education systems online, the democratization theory myth was evident for the world to see, as Sarah Emerson of OneZero online tech magazine points out. *"Online learning is a multi-billion-dollar[6] that optimistically envisions[7] a future wherein education is propelled to greater heights by technology. Now, with an estimated 54 million students[8] currently out of school, these online learning tools are being put to the test — and it's clear that they are not the equalizing force that some entrepreneurs have imagined they could be."*[959]

Rather than lessen the problem, expensive technology has worsened the inequality gap. Published early in 2019, a UK National Education Opportunity Network's study found that half of England's universities have fewer than 5% poor white students. In the US, *"tracking (or "ability grouping") systems deny low-income students and students of color access to college-prep courses even when those classes are indeed offered in their schools. The GAO report analyzes what it calls "high-poverty schools" — those where at least three-quarters of the students live in poverty. This is itself the core problem. Any serious effort to close opportunity gaps must begin by addressing this concentrated poverty, as well as the associated racial segregation."*[960]

6. *https://www.forbes.com/sites/tjmccue/2018/07/31/e-learning-climbing-to-325-billion-by-2025-uf-canvas-absorb-schoology-moodle/#a5c02393e59c943d6a75a9241140faca3532e80b83b39*

7. *https://www.nytimes.com/2020/02/20/education/learning/education-technology.html*

8. *https://www.nbcnews.com/politics/meet-the-press/school-closures-skyrocket-nearly-54-million-students-sent-home-n1165946*

For high school-degreed students not attending college, the poverty rate was 13.2% in 2020, while for those attending some college 8.4.%. Technofix rhetoric aside, education inequality has been widening not just in the West, but in Japan and South Korea where private tutoring is a considerable cost for working families. The situation is not much better in Germany, Europe's wealthiest country which the OECD has classified as poor when it comes to education opportunities compared with other developed nations. Under the neoliberal model, the statistical correlation between social class and college education has remained.

Especially in the US, rising student debt has been the added dimension to education even below the college level. Contradicting the claim that either digital technology or distance learning has accounted for upward social mobility, in the course of 54 years, 1964-2018, in the US the average hourly wage difference between high-school and college graduates was a mere 11.7%. These statistics support Senator Sanders' theme that a college degree today is equivalent to a High School degree half a century ago. According to researchers, income inequality and a sharp decline in trade unions and collective bargaining explain the trend that technology has done nothing to rectify.[961]

Here to stay, digital technology and distance learning have helped many people in remote areas or without the means to attend a physical classroom setting. However, how courses are implemented under the neoliberal model has been to optimize profits for tech companies and further reduce education into a factory system. Corporations like Google, Microsoft, Dell, and Cisco Systems, among others, have been promoting digital education because it provides the cheapest, fastest, and most efficient labor force possible for the marketplace. Naturally, they focus narrowly on the field of training while diluting the broader classical liberal arts curriculum associated with a traditional liberal arts education.

An idea with only very few companies participating in the 1980s, by the early 21st century several thousand companies were part of custom learning in the US, Canada, and other countries. The convergence of custom learning or individualized narrowly-focused education and business influenced public policy with budgets reflecting the policy-targeted individual student outcomes, using business-model criteria and technology access to create market-ready students.[962]

Besides control over the curriculum and reinforcement of the corporate culture in schools, both online and physical facilities offering custom learning worked great for corporations. This is partly because the taxpayers subsidized the programs so businesses can have a pool of tailored-trained laborers at the taxpayers' expense. Theoretically, education enhances the student's pedagogical and life experiences, while permitting intellectual integrity whose goal is a well-rounded knowledge in the humanities, arts, and sciences. With the hybrid model of distance (online) learning and on-campus instruction, technology, skills, and natural sciences have been more prevalent along with business-related courses, deemphasizing humanities, social sciences, and the arts. Combined with loan programs, the highly competitive landscape of web-assisted programs and enormous costs related to technology have had an impact on underfunded public institutions.[963]

Using digital technology as the catalyst to transform the system on a world scale, Ben Williamson has made worthy scholarly contributions to the field. *"Powerful networks, consisting of big tech companies such as Google, Microsoft, and Facebook, international organizations including the OECD and UNESCO, as well as a global education industry of edu-businesses, consultancies, investors and technology providers, are coming together to define how education systems should respond to the crisis. But their objectives do not just focus on the short term. These pandemic power networks are developing new long-term policy agendas for how education systems globally should be organized long after the emergency ends."*[964]

In the first two decades of the 21st century, there was sharp growth in private institutions in many countries, including China, Brazil, Israel, and Poland, all operating under the neoliberal model, placing pressure on public schools to compete at that level. This development has been taking place as governments have been cutting spending for public colleges and universities, thereby forcing institutions to seek private resources.

Parallel to this development across the world, including in the US, there is a rise in specialized (technical-vocational) private schools. Operating under individual corporate contracts, schools tailor to a narrowly defined curriculum intended for the workforce. This trend has inadvertently undermined traditional liberal arts schools. As though they are programmed automatons ready to execute operations, students graduate ready for specific businesses, with minimal focus on the traditional arts, humanities, and social sciences that make them critical thinkers.[965]

With the advent of the neoliberal techno-education model, faculty have experienced the reality of what Mark Olssen, education policy expert, describes as the neo-liberalization of academic life that faculty find difficult to escape. However, techno-neoliberal model apologists maintain this is best for society because it enhances business growth which is tantamount to the progress of civilization.

"What is also likely to constrain higher education is the conservative implications neoliberalism has for student curriculum choice, which means that lots of areas of the curriculum and lots of academics from Classics, Philosophy, not to mention all the new so-called progressive paradigms of Gender Studies, Media Studies, and Culture Studies, are all going by the board. The Natural Sciences such as pure Math, and some forms of Physics and Chemistry are also having difficulties in recruiting students because students are now very careful in choosing their courses, to be relevant to their intended careers. Students, for the most part, are going to choose in agreement with their parents, and the broader families, and their parents are not going to want them to do subjects like Classics or even Philosophy; they want them to get the meal ticket."[966]

Besides weakening the traditional liberal arts education, the neoliberal model further restricts college access based on income. Even without various corruption schemes that came to light in the 2010s, shifting resources in advertising as part of "marketization" for recruiting, universities focusing on buildings and layers of "student services" were diverting funds from teaching to the Ponzi-style administrative bureaucracy.[967]

In an article entitled *"Bureaucrats and Buildings: the case for why college is so expensive"*, Carolyn Simon notes that aggregate instruction costs for US higher education in 1980-1981 amounted to $20.7 billion. Academic support totaled $13 billion, or 24% of the budget for administrative expenses vs. 41% for teaching. By 2014-2015, instructional costs ran up to $148 billion, while administrative stood at $122.3 billion. It was against such a background that the US college admissions corruption scandals emerged. Although endowment donors influenced the process even before the transformation from a faculty-driven to an administrative-driven university, institutional commodification contained the seeds of legalized manipulation, politicization, and corruption.[968]

Indicative of the proletarianization of higher education, salary discrepancy is one of the most scandalous aspects of the neoliberal model. In 2019-2020, the average salary for university presidents was $300,000. Full-time faculty averaged $85,000, while adjunct faculty salary was $7,789 per course. In 2018, at the University of California-San Diego, adjunct faculty earned $9000 per course, while the university president made $7 million, plus a lucrative expense account. Reflecting the "uberization" of employment in higher education, the sharp rise in part-time faculty has weakened faculty morale and governance by permitting business-style administrations to impose the transformation model which in turn further weakens faculty and expands a parasitic administration relying on a bureaucracy to do most of the administrative work.[969]

Under the neoliberal model, 75.5% of college faculty, or 1.3 million of the 1.8 million total are non-tenure track, and half of the non-tenure track are part-time without any benefits, earning salaries below manual laborers. No different than corporate CEOs making millions a year but adamantly opposed to raising the federal minimum wage, university administrators support the erosion of tenure and greater reliance on institutionally unprotected "contingent faculty" lacking the academic freedom of tenured faculty. In short, the university administration is immersed in the same class war mindset as corporate executives and mega investors in the stock market.[970]

Because adjunct faculty are not under any research obligations as tenure-track faculty, the quality of scholarship and teaching is not under the same criteria as full-time faculty. Administrators' overriding commitment has been the business model, not the quality of teaching and scholarship, except as it relates to a business or government agenda. More suited for the corporate sector, highly-paid administrators are often hired with an anti-academic if not anti-intellectual predisposition, thus deliberately sabotaging the institution's scholarly mission for the sake of conformity into the neoliberal mold.

Class warfare mindset permeates administrators' views who often encounter faculty in a similar antagonistic manner as corporate managers deal with workers. The result of neoliberal faculty disempowerment has been low morale and a perpetual struggle to maintain high academic standards against business-style consumerist metrics such as student retention and securing business and government links, as well as bringing research grants to the institution.[971]

A reflection of an overeducated, underpaid surplus labor force, the number of Ph. D.s in all advanced capitalist countries has been rising at the same time that the job market has been shrinking. This is partly because of the overproduction of individuals with advanced degrees, but also replacing full-time with contingent faculty, program cuts, and increasing the number of students in class. Employment statistics blatantly contradict the argument that the problem is not the political economy but the lack of an educated-skills labor force.[972]

Not just the trillion-dollar companies like Google, Apple, Microsoft, Amazon, and Oracle, but even multi-billion-dollar pharmaceutical company Eli Lilly, Detroit's automakers, the Koch brothers, the Mercer and Walton families, Sheldon Adelson, among other billionaires have enjoyed a ubiquitous role in molding universities. No matter the cost to the integrity of independent scholarship, academic freedom, and rising inequality of access, institutions compete for corporate money to strengthen their endowment.[973]

Besides using the university to spread the neoliberal gospel, billionaires also make donations and have the ability to influence everything from admissions policy to curriculum and ideological orientation. No matter how university public relations offices try to project an image of academic independence and money-free meritocracy as the ideal, the reality inside the institution tells a different story. *"Steven A. Cohen, the hedge fund billionaire, gave $5 million to USC in 2014, through his foundation. The university hailed the gift[9] at the time as the largest ever* *received by its School of Cinematic Arts for student aid. What the press release didn't note was that the gift followed the highly competitive school's decision to admit Cohen's twin daughters."*[974]

In April 2023, hedge fund manager Kenneth C. Griffin donated $300 million to Harvard which renamed the Graduate School of Arts and Sciences after the billionaire Republican contributor who had been an Obama supporter but switched to rightwing Florida governor Ron DeSantis. Besides generous donations in some cases linked to programs, in others to buildings, the larger issue has been an undue influence on curriculum and academic freedom. Not only humanities and social sciences faculty, but math, chemistry, biology, geology, and physics find it more difficult to secure research grants not linked to corporate or government agenda.[975]

As the government has been cutting funding to the National Science Foundation, National Endowment for the Humanities, and National Endowment for the Arts, all of which President Trump tried to eliminate, scholars found it difficult to pursue projects with no strings attached. The political decision to cut government funding to these foundations has been an integral part of the neoliberal strategy to reinforce higher education's reliance on the corporate sector and impose transformation. After its members resigned in protest over Trump's pro-white nationalist rally in Charlottesville, Virginia, Trump dissolved the advisory Committee on the Arts and the Humanities.[976]

In an article entitled *"Higher Education or Education for Hire? Corporatization and the Threat to Democratic Thinking"*, Joel Wetheimer writes: *"The effects of corporatization on the integrity of university research – especially in the sciences – has been well-documented elsewhere. Readers of* Academic Matters *are likely familiar with the many cases of scientific compromise resulting from private commercial sponsorship of research by pharmaceutical and tobacco companies. Indeed, faculty throughout North America are already deluged with requests or demands to produce research that is "patentable" or "commercially viable."*[977]

A land grant school, the University of Illinois-Champaign-Urbana campus is one of many public institutions heavily indebted to the private sector. Like other universities, the University of Illinois was not above securing corporate funding, even if it meant redefining academic integrity. For a school spending $700 million annually in research projects, the University of Illinois accepts substantial grants from agrichemical companies such as Monsanto and caters to the wishes of corporate donors regarding projects and internal decisions theoretically impacting the university's autonomy. Everything from hiring faculty specializing in genetically modified seeds and agrichemicals that would have a direct impact on multinational businesses to the nature and purpose of research is subject to the sponsor's influence.

This is just another low-cost corporate scheme of outsourcing research and development while passing partial cost on to the taxpayer. On the surface, it appears that there is nothing wrong with this process because private money lifts the burden from the taxpayer. However, a publicly tax-supported institution's work was never intended to serve the private corporation. In an ideal situation under the neoliberal model, the taxpayer is indirectly subsidizing corporations that drive the scientific research agenda of universities.[978]

In numerous articles, Wenonah Hauter, executive director of the *Food & Water Watch* NGO, points out that lobbyists control the agenda of public policy on food and agriculture, using the university to extend credibility to corporate practices. Arguing that scientific research requires impartial and unbiased research, Hauter notes that:

---

9. https://cinema.usc.edu/news/article.cfm?id=14503

"...like nearly every aspect of our modern food system, land-grant school funding has been overrun by narrow private interests... Private-sector funding not only corrupts the public research mission of land-grant universities but also distorts the science that is supposed to help farmers improve their practices and livelihoods. Industry-funded academic research routinely produces favorable results for industry sponsors. And since policymakers and regulators frequently cite these university studies to back up their decision-making, industry-funded academic research increasingly influences the rules that govern their business operations."[979]

Putting aside federal and state cuts for higher education, which have driven universities into dependence on wealthy donors and businesses, highly paid university administrators who serve on corporate boards incentivize faculty to forge closer ties with the private sector. Conducting business-sponsored research that enhances the corporate sector, the university administration compromises the integrity of research in almost every field from hard sciences to sports. Because 42% of the Board trustees at public universities come from large corporations, they make decisions about university governance by corporate values, and ideology. Their methods are far removed from the traditional academic freedom culture and the institution serving society rather than business. [980]

One of the main concerns that college administrators have had with Senator Bernie Sanders' proposal for free college tuition has been the inevitable reduction in the top-heavy bureaucracy which will not be needed to process student loans, scholarships, and fundraising for student aid. Amid the ascendancy of the neoliberal transformation from 1985 to 2005, the number of administrators rose by 85% and their attendant staff by 240%. [981]

Refusing to promote the relationship between education and democracy, and replacing the concept of active socially-conscious citizenship with the docile consumer-citizen, advocates of neoliberalism reject the connection between education and social and political change. Teaching is downgraded through quantification-based assessment oblivious to students' academic interests, aiming only to satisfy neoliberal consultants' criteria. Furthermore, vocational training linked to the digital economy has been upgraded amid full-fledged attacks on the concept of classical liberal education. Outside the perimeters of the capitalist "disruptor" aiming to innovate not just in digital technology and parasitic financialization schemes, but to facilitate transformation in all institutions amid a class war climate, the neoliberal model has no room for critical, reflective thinking challenging the institutional structure.[982]

Popular among voters under 30 years of age, especially college students, Senator Sanders connected with America's youth not just because of free college tuition and debt forgiveness proposals, but his adamant opposition to Wall Street controlling the institutional structure that determines people's lives. Although Sanders mobilized popular support for the mainstream Democratic Party in the 2010s, his popular base was more radical reflecting opposition to the social contract.

A Harvard University study in 2016 showed that 51% of individuals between 18 and 29 opposed capitalism and 33% stated support for socialism, as they understand the term, which is closer to Keynesian economics. As in many parts of the world, a segment of America's youth has been moving farther to the left of the neoliberal establishment, with another segment moving to the far right. Despite resistance to the transformation model, the neoliberal establishment has deep institutional roots. Meanwhile, the media incessantly propagates that there is no alternative to the social contract outside of the range between the pluralist liberal and the populist right.[983]

The Media and the Corporate Model of Education

Worth trillions of dollars in market capitalization, media, and social media companies contribute to mass conformity of the neoliberal social contract, including mass indoctrination to mold the education system as an integral part of the institutional structure. The convergence of the digital revolution in the 1990s and the global reach of neoliberal transformation helped to mold the "consumer citizen", of which neoliberal education has been an integral part. Market hegemony over the state also entailed minimizing social opposition to business domination in every domain, including education given its role in helping to shape public opinion.[984]

Like all institutions, the media and social media always project the illusion of personal choice. They are the driving forces behind engendering conformity within the institutional structure which precludes choice. Reporting on education, the media does not emphasize the individual's education for society's benefit but directly or indirectly focuses on market-oriented, class-based goals aiming to disparage public education while praising the private model. Necessary to afford legitimacy to the neoliberal social contract, dissent exists on the margins as a reminder that the neoliberal status quo is the norm.[985]

Denigrating public education as "inferior" to private schools and dismissing unionized educators as "elitist liberal" political tools with an agenda, the mass media consistently defends neoliberal schemes to transform education into a business and deviate from the classical model rooted in the Enlightenment's ideals. Either deliberately oblivious to the inequality that neoliberalism exacerbates, or blaming educators and privatization opponents, especially teachers' unions, for the system's problems, journalists and pro-business analysts present education's neoliberal transformation as a social enterprise under an economic imperative for the benefit of economic development.[986]

Not just the media, but the entire institutional structure has indoctrinated the public into accepting education's corporatization as a part of the "market efficiency" theory, a euphemism for slashing the budget of public schools and pouring taxpayer money into private education. In the absence of competing norms and values, neoliberalism has inculcated its agenda into the core of the education system, as it has in the cultural mainstream. Even those skeptical about the neoliberal model of education make school choice and college choice decisions based on the new norm because of the institutionally predetermined choices before them.[987]

Besides relying on corporate-funded consultants and think tanks for their expertise in neoliberal education's benefits, the media has systematically sided with Wall Street and its anti-union political agenda. This has been a means to delegitimize the public school system by presenting it as a dinosaur of the obsolete welfare state undercutting the globalized economy. Using nebulous slogans 'freedom of choice, market efficiency, and reform', the media has consistently echoed the dogma of market preeminence, without mentioning who benefits and who pays the price.[988]

As much in the US as in other countries, the open or subtle attack on public education carries an underlying class warfare dogma, in most countries with unmentioned racist/ethnocentric implications. It is mostly the wealthier children attending private schools that neoliberals want taxpayers to subsidize. Working-class students, especially from the minority working-class community, attend underfunded public schools. Just as important, the corporate neoliberal media has conditioned a segment of the middle class to associate public education with inferior-quality institutions promoting a liberal agenda. Because stigmatizing public schools is associated with minorities and working-class students, the general public easily falls into the neoliberal trap of demonizing public institutions, without delving into the systemic causes of the poor quality of public education.[989]

Exerting enormous influence in shaping education, the conservative Heritage Foundation and similar organizations represent corporate interests on which institutions rely for funding. By de-legitimizing public institutions associated with the Keynesian welfare state, the Heritage Foundation and others present privatization as the norm and anything public as an aberration. At the same time, there is a right-wing political agenda linked to neoliberal education. For example, Spain's *Fundación para el Análisis y los Estudios Sociales* (FAES), a business-funded neoliberal organization, is linked to the conservative *Partido Popular* working through the political class which has had a major role in shaping the dialogue that the media presents to the public about education.[990]

An extension of the corporate sector under its hegemony, the media which both reflects and reinforces transformation has played an important role in framing the debate of education's role. This is partly because international organizations, NGOs, and transnational corporations have been promoting it and using their influence to reorient government policy. As Rebecca A. Goldstein and her co-authors point out: *"Neoliberalism, its supporters, and the media have quite literally shaped how we think about, talk about, and engage in daily life at the local, economic, and civic levels. Further, its discourses have helped to constitute a new normal—employing neoliberalism at all levels of government to fix the never-ending crises of American society—even though those same neoliberal principles have helped to bring about those same crises."*[991]

Regardless of a specific media outlet's conservative or liberal ideological orientation, the promotion of the neoliberal education agenda has been a common goal. Liberal and rightwing media alike have been promoting the neoliberal consensus finding expression in policy intended to subordinate education to market hegemony. For example, the *Washington Post*, the *New York Times, and the Boston Globe,* adamantly opposed Senator Sanders' higher education proposals because it would entail institutionalizing a neo-Keynesian state while invalidating the entire neoliberal project.

Opposing Sanders' proposal to make public education a national priority, the liberal and rightwing media opposed college free tuition, universal student loan-debt forgiveness, permitting true academic freedom by de-linking curriculum and research from the private sector, lowering the vast college bureaucracy along with limits on sky-high administrative salaries, and lowering the growing number of adjunct faculty by hiring tenured-track staff.[992]

Presenting itself as America's premier liberal newspaper, the *New York Times* came out decidedly against Sanders' free tuition proposal, arguing that: *"free tuition means fewer resources to teach students. Unintended consequences could include reductions in need-based financial aid, which would harm the low- and middle-income students' free tuition is meant to help."*[993] The newspaper was not as adamant about corporate tax cuts, running articles both for and against.[994]

Although Sanders' plan would cover about 70% of college students at an estimated $75 billion annually, an amount split between the federal government and the states, the liberal media sided with Republicans, as did establishment Democrats who opposed a new tax on Wall Street speculation to fund public education. Conservative or liberal, the media never has a problem with high defense costs, corporate welfare, or tax cuts for the richest 1%.

Nevertheless, it decried free tuition and strengthened the social safety net. Where the liberal media generally attacked the 2017 tax cuts of nearly $2 trillion to the wealthy, the target of criticism was not Wall Street, but Trump personally. In a hollow effort to distract from corporate lobbyists advocating tax cuts benefiting corporate-owned media, the masters of manufactured consent vilified Trump at the personal level, while remaining fairly muted about big capital benefiting from the fiscal policy.[995]

Along with several prominent academics, some on the media's payroll, others on corporate-funded think tanks and consulting firms, all adamantly defended the neoliberal model of education as the irreversible new norm. The pretext was that free tuition would entail stifling innovation and creativity, undermining private colleges and universities in favor of public ones. The cliché argument revolved around "too much government" in higher education impeding entrepreneurship and depriving faculty and students of "freedom of choice". The most absurd argument is that free tuition would necessarily mean quality would suffer. Of the twenty-two countries providing free college tuition, including France and Germany, there is no evidence that the quality of education is suffering, considering that the aforementioned ranks among the world's top five.[996]

The occasional op-ed pieces in support of re-examining education as a public good, instead of a commodity subordinated to the market, is an exception to mainstream analysis. Important to validate the media's contention that it remains committed to pluralism, faint voices within the perimeters of dissent rarely go to the heart of the problem which is education's role in the political economy.[997]

Like the majority of Republicans and Democrats, the liberal and conservative media agrees with corporate America that "the economy cannot afford" to adopt the model of free public education, just as it cannot afford universal public health care available in nine African countries, but not the US. To provide universal public health care and/or free education would signal abandoning neoliberal transformation, marking the first step toward the Keynesian social welfare state. Instead, politicians and the media support government-subsidized private education, including for-profit online universities.

While true that not all private institutions are in the same category, with some of immense prestige as world-class operations, while others exist only thanks to taxpayer funding, providing low-quality education online. Highly influential in the media, the Brookings Institution, concluded that for-profit colleges have been a resounding failure. Nevertheless, Brookings did not call for their elimination for that would mean admitting the neoliberal model's failure.

"For-profit colleges have a long history of engaging in manipulative[1] behavior to preserve the flow of Title IV funds to their schools while providing their students a poor education. After the quadrupling of undergraduate enrollment[2] in for-profit colleges from 2000 to 2010, Obama-era regulations led to the closure of some high-profile schools[3] and a slight decline[4] in enrollment overall... Almost 60% of Black students[5] who took on student debt to attend a for-profit

1. *https://tcf.org/content/report/profit-college-story-scandal-regulate-forget-repeat/*

2. *https://nces.ed.gov/programs/coe/indicator_cha.asp*

3. *https://www.pbs.org/wgbh/frontline/article/another-for-profit-college-chain-closes-its-doors/*

school in 2004 defaulted on their loans by 2016, compared to only 36% of their white peers... The for-profit college sector has failed to prove its worth time and time again. Issues around racial inequity and the cost of higher education are at the forefront of America's current political debate." [998]

It is hardly surprising that the corporate-owned media reflects the position of think tanks and consultants on many issues including education, considering that these exist thanks to the corporate model. From mission statement to research agenda and curriculum, corporate America does not want to lose the influence it enjoys over universities. Just as millionaires and billionaires have a hold on the political arena through campaign finance, lobbying, and media ownership, billionaire donors with powerful pro-business, and often rightwing strings attached cultivate university links to strengthen their public influence.[999]

In Kentucky, Papa John's Pizza founder John Schnatter teamed up with the Koch Brothers Foundation to fund business school programs at the University of Louisville and the University of Kentucky. Both donations came with the caveat that the donors can stop funding if they do not feel that their mission – the teaching of free market economics and business practices – is being carried out to their satisfaction. To some, such stipulations imply that students will be taught by professors sympathetic to the political and economic views of the donors." [1000]

Despite the perception that there are multiple voices representing disparate class interests in the media, the trail of funding for many organizations leads right back to the largest corporations and billionaires supporting class warfare. Independent media presents dissident voices challenging mainstream interpretations, usually within the social contract's perimeters. Independent media's impact on society is minimal largely because it reaches a small audience in comparison with the ubiquitous corporate mainstream media and social media which project the illusion of the social norm that the public must trust. To convince parents, students, and society as a whole that there is no alternative to the dogma, media promotion of global market hegemony has been part of the indoctrination effort.[1001]

The largely economically determined education structure, especially higher education in the US, suggests that tax subsidies benefit the very few at the top to the detriment of the working class. At the bottom of the pyramid, the system shows it is socially unjust and dysfunctional. It is at the base of the pyramid where there is a mixture of poorly funded public schools and for-profit online colleges with graduation rates below the 20th percentile. At the bottom of the pyramid, the debt level is very high and the college degree does not mean very much in the competitive job market. Instead of pointing to systemic problems at the root of such results, the mainstream media focuses on the isolated "success stories", implying that it is the individual's fault for failing to excel in an otherwise dysfunctional hierarchical structure.[1002]

On occasion, mainstream media draws attention to the link between education and socioeconomic status. However, the focus is more on race, gender, and ethnicity, along with the importance of education in contributing to the individual's cash-value self-realization and growth potential with derivate benefits for society. When it comes to addressing the business model as the culprit for rising social inequality with education as part of the problem, there is rarely any criticism. The liberal media has criticized neoliberalism only in so far as it has delivered the education system closer to the embrace of the populist right in both advanced capitalist countries

---

4. https://nces.ed.gov/programs/coe/indicator_cha.asp

5. https://www.brookings.edu/wp-content/uploads/2018/01/scott-clayton-report.pdf

and the periphery. In essence, eliminating diversity and dissent in the liberal order, rightwing anti-institutional populism has impacted education, especially in most Republican-controlled states in the US but also the UK, Hungary, and India. One common thread among neoliberal populists is anti-intellectualism finding expression in education policy.[1003]

In the absence of systemic change in the political economy and hegemonic culture, the business model of education will remain. Considering the entrenched elites' tentacles stretch from business to government and across all institutions, neoliberal education persists, regardless of student debt and corruption scandals involving university administration resembling a Ponzi scheme. Techno-enthusiasts contend that AI robotics will make traditional classroom education and human teaching obsolete. Harvard is already putting that theory to the test and others will soon follow. With the rise of the global tide of rightwing populism, the current model's convergence with AI has been the antidote to the Enlightenment era's philosophical and moral principles, including universal human rights and social justice.[1004]

A populist book with impressionistic cliches pointing to flaws in higher education, Jason Brennan's *Cracks in the Ivory Tower: The Moral Mess of Higher Education* reflects not only the right but neoliberal critique that has been used to impose the business model. Ironically, the book describes education system flaws as symptomatic of the neoliberal status quo. In *Against Democracy* (2016), Jason Brennan dismisses democracy as *"unnecessary"* that must be replaced with "epistocracy"; a system where only "politically-informed" citizens would enjoy the privilege of voting.

A contemporary version of the ancient Athenian concept of "timocracy" emerging during the era of Solon the Lawgiver (circa 630-560 B.C.), epistocracy is a more palatable means to preserve the privileged capitalist class under the socio-politically polarizing neoliberal system. It is noteworthy that the mainstream media has used Brennan's thesis not only because he works for a university, but because the media eagerly promotes populist themes while hiding behind hollow academic constructs intended to justify the neoliberal hierarchy.[1005]

Given the need for a highly educated population in the digital era, colleges and universities have become more significant, yet, less useful as the graduating class is chasing gainful employment to match the degree. The significance of higher education has been partly in promoting the anti-institutional neoliberal populist agenda intended to build on capital accumulation. Not to diminish the immensely creative and beneficial work of individual faculty in teaching and research, or technology's considerable benefits for society. However, the more cynical superficial neoliberal thinking is that the California Community college system with full-time faculty is too costly to taxpayers. After all, students have computers and cell phones and use search engines as more cost-efficient and useful than a classic liberal arts college education. Besides, the employer trains employees and tailor-makes a student-worker to fit the corporate mold.

Neoliberals have been insisting that technology is a substitute for critical, creative, socially-conscious students who question the status quo instead of conforming. Better than a teacher with spontaneous creative thoughts interacting with students, neoliberal apologists claim that AI will provide efficiency at a lower cost. The neo-Luddite leftist reaction to techno-education and digital classroom aside, neoliberals focus on a profit-oriented system and aggressive class war that the media camouflages through liberal and rightwing identity politics. Beyond the ethical implications of 'blended learning' resting principally on digitization that corporations have been advancing, education's neo-liberalization is riddled with contradictions. This includes the promise of freedom and pluralism, both of which are principles that the model sacrifices because they clash with the profit motive.[1006]

Contrary to apologists claiming that digital exclusion is limited to those who choose owing to personal preferences, it is for the most part class-based and very difficult for people whose priority is just to survive inside the neoliberal matrix. *"Thinking and learning skills have become a feature of neoliberal selfhood, and are implicated in rendering individuals ready-made for a 21st century market. Thus, it is important to not only critique and transform the context in which HOT [higher order thinking,* self-regulated, critical thinkers, creative, and good problem solvers - all of which fall under the rubric of higher order thinking*] is learned and applied but also take explicit notice of the kinds of person that is inscribed. Both the communal self and historical non-self can serve as constructions of personhood that support a democratic vision of schooling."*[1007]

Against the background of downward social mobility, media representing the neoliberal political and social elites, even academics who know what the system entails are generally uncritical about the very narrow utilitarian definition of education. The result has been marginalization for those either priced out of the education market or forced into low-quality underfunded schools. Reduced to extensions of technology for the private sector to use and dispose of like commodities, regimentation of the students' creative potential and critical thinking along with a value system rooted in atomism without much regard for society's welfare is by far worse than underfunded schools.[1008]

CHAPTER VII:

Neoliberalism, Transhumanism, and Artificial Intelligence

AI Paradise or Digital Authoritarianism?

Artificial intelligence (AI) holds the promise of transforming science, technology, and everything from complex medical surgery and human genome sequencing and diagnostics, to emergency rescue operations, and just about every endeavor imaginable. While the excitement for AI's creative applications is justified, a cursory examination of the history of technology suggests that its benefits for the majority of the earth's population may fall far short of what techno-enthusiasts promise. In 18th century England, industry and technology enthusiasts such as industrialist Josiah Wedgewood made lofty promises of progress for humanity. Very quickly, Wedgewood's predictions turned into disappointment for the working class and millions of displaced peasants and small farmers. Even worse, Africans subject to the trans-Atlantic slave trade whose role was essential in cheap raw materials that made industrial capitalism possible derived no benefits.[1009]

AI's potential benefits in life's every domain notwithstanding, some have raised questions about killer robots, drone warfare, and robots in crowd control under authoritarian regimes. An integral part of the defense industry, digital tech companies have been competing for lucrative government contracts. In a socioeconomically and geographically polarized world, divided geopolitically in a struggle for geoeconomic advantages, AI will play a much larger transforming role than any technological innovation's benefits filtering down to mass uses. As the military and police also rely on AI technology, there is a debate about the digital paradise's promise of turning into an authoritarian nightmare. This is not just for countries currently under autocratic governments, but especially those claiming the label of democracy and struggling to postpone the inevitability of the political economy within a pluralist social structure leading to authoritarianism.[1010]

After mathematician Norbert Wiener (*Cybernetics or Control and Communication in the Animal and the Machine*, 1950) invented cybernetics in the 1940s, the scientific imagination understandably ran wild about the infinite possibilities for science, profit, and power. Profoundly influenced by the nascent Cold War political climate, Wiener, like other scientists of the early Cold War, was interested in cybernetics' application in everything from its impact on the military and technology in general to the application of cybernetics to understanding the brain. Governments, the military, law enforcement, intelligence networks, education, and businesses deem AI essential for progress, but the question is the term's definition. Since Wiener's publication, analytical studies have explored its implications on various dimensions of society, especially on social relations and nations, revealing a far less benevolent scenario than AI enthusiasts present.

Because of a skeletal neoliberal regulatory regime, AI applicability has the potential of surpassing the legal boundaries with large businesses using it for market manipulation to maximize profit. The world already has a glimpse of the future now. Legitimate questions include how the largest businesses would define AI policy and use it to undermine the smaller/weaker ones, as well as exploit workers and suppress dissent. Governments have used and will continue to use AI to amass greater power at the expense not just of other governments and corporations, but of their citizens, regardless of whether they are a one-party state like China, a two-party system like the US, or a multi-party system like France.[1011]

Government and business research analysts point to AI's potential to contribute 10-20 percent to additional world GDP growth. Estimated to add $6.4 trillion to the global economy by 2025, the global AI market's impact could reach $15.7 trillion by 2030. Considering that governments heavily subsidize AI research and development technology, it can be used to eradicate epidemics, famine, and natural disasters, and rescue people in difficult circumstances, among countless other tasks without pricing out all but wealthy clients. AI could free human beings from mundane tasks and elevate them creatively, culturally, and intellectually. Above all, AI could help end world hunger and extreme poverty, assuming this becomes a policy goal by governments.

Although AI has the potential to enhance social justice, the history of technology under capitalism indicates that AI will likely condemn society to social control and repression under a regime where the wealthy would benefit from the technology and use it to exploit and regiment the rest of the world's population. Under the existing neoliberal social contract, AI can result in upward social mobility for very few while sinking the vast majority into poverty and servitude, creating greater inequality, and facilitating authoritarianism in the name of progress.[1012]

Contrary to lofty promises about freedom and democracy, making life better for all, and the absence of an alternative to technological progress, the reality of algorithmic systems per se is not the issue. Rather, it is the social contract and social relations environment in which AI operates. This is one reason that the *World Economic Forum*, which has historically hosted large banks, corporations, and governments, raised ethical issues ranging from inequality, racism, and unpredictable nefarious uses of AI that can threaten humanity. After all, corporations and governments are the ones programming AI to realize the desired results.[1013]

Governments and corporations project an image of AI responsibility and accountability, but they did the same thing with the internet and social media. Behind beguiling PR rests digital authoritarianism in the name of public safety and national security. In April 2022, the US initiated an *"open, free, global, interoperable, reliable and secure"* internet of 60 countries. The ultimate goal was not digital transparency, but targeting China and Russia, while promoting a US-led bloc behind which were Western tech giants with a long record of disdain for democracy. One of the world's worst abusers of digital democracy, according to independent human rights organizations, Israel is actually on the US list of democracies. According to Amnesty International, the Israeli government has been using facial recognition AI systems to impose harsh restrictions on Palestinians as part of an ever-growing surveillance network intended to maintain apartheid and remove Palestinians from their homes by force.[1][1014]

Unlike the US with the means to use digital authoritarianism against its chosen domestic and foreign enemies, while exempting itself and close allies from the category, Malaysia provides a clear preview of what can take place. In 2018, the Royal Malaysia Police Cooperative signed a contract with China's Yitu Technology company to purchase facial recognition equipment using artificial intelligence. Determined to become a data-controlled society, the Malaysian government claimed that it used AI equipment to deter terrorism, enforce immigration restrictions, combat crime, and promote a healthy economy and education system.[1015]

Along Malaysia's path, China, South Korea, and Taiwan moved toward digital authoritarianism under different modalities and rationalizations. Distancing itself from China's technology governance model, Taiwan claims

1. https://www.amnesty.org/en/documents/mde15/5141/2022/en/

that it embraces digital democracy, not authoritarianism. Although less restrictive in internet freedom than China, Taiwan and South Korea operate under a neoliberal developmentalist regime that exacerbates both inequality and authoritarianism. The nexus between authoritarianism in police and military domains has the full cooperation of corporate partners like China's Baidu, which is Google's counterpart and the world's second-largest search engine.[1016]

The COVID-19 pandemic brought to the surface digital authoritarianism in China, Taiwan, and South Korea, and the course toward planned social control. This sort of surveillance is not so different than the subtle forms of autocratization in Western countries targeting dissident groups. Under different modalities, 176 countries are using AI surveillance. This is expected to rise 40 percent, mostly because police agencies will rely on digital technology in the 2020s. The COVID-19 pandemic placed the policy to the test in several countries and became the pretext to use it widely.[1017]

Besides digital authoritarianism as a function of collaboration between the state and the private sector, there is also the issue of companies using AI to determine not just social relations, but human destiny, as robots will monitor, warn, and regiment human behavior and decisions. While tech companies justify everything in the name of making life better for the consumer under the highest ethical standards, the history of technology is not as rosy. Beyond raising productivity like the cotton gin and steam engine during the first industrial revolution, digital technology has ubiquitous applications in every sector from mining and agriculture to manufacturing and transportation. From England's first industrial revolution in the 18th century to the present, automation's detrimental impact on workers is a sacrifice that technology apologists believe is well worth it.

In a classic study about the Industrial Revolution's impact on class relations, E.P. Thompson's *The Making of the English Working Class* (1963) raises some issues about technology, labor, and capital relevant in the neoliberal era. Like Thompson, scholars before and after him recognized the limitations of technical determinism. After all, technical innovation, although in the category of capital goods investment, is an integral part of the labor process linked to capital accumulation. Furthermore, technology, especially digital/AI, invariably leads to techno-authoritarianism as an integral part of neoliberalism. This is not just in Russia and China, as many Western analysts, along with the media and Western politicians contend, but globally. During the accelerated class war since the 1980s, there have been clear warning signs that digital authoritarianism under the neoliberal model could make everything much worse for both the working class and the middle class.[1018]

Under digital neoliberalism, society is experiencing the most far-reaching transformation since the 1940s when cybernetics was born as part of systems theory. Based in part on Ervin Laszlo[2]'s *Introduction to Systems Philosophy: Toward a New Paradigm of Contemporary Thought,* (1972), it helps to compartmentalize the automaton sector and deconstruct its role. Under the neoliberal political economy necessarily generating greater inequality, AI will precipitate greater social marginalization, as an MIT-Boston University study in 2020 found. *"...for every robot added per 1,000 workers in the U.S., wages decline by 0.42% and the employment-to-population ratio goes down by 0.2 percentage points — to date, this means the loss of about 400,000 jobs. The impact is more sizable within the areas where robots are deployed: adding one more robot in a commuting zone (geographic areas used for economic analysis) reduces employment by six workers in that area."[1019]*

2. https://en.wikipedia.org/wiki/Ervin_L%C3%A1szl%C3%B3

Like all technology, AI benefited from corporate welfare and contributed to concentrated capital and liberal democracy's erosion. Even those supporting AI research and development public funding are concerned that in the context of the neoliberal de-regulation model, AI under monopolistic corporate control working with the state is a potential prescription for digital authoritarianism. This is more evident when governments use 'national security' to justify surveillance on targeted citizens deemed a security risk. Even before the outbreak of COVID-19, Taiwan and Israel identifying with digital democracy behaved similarly to China when it came to surveillance.[1020]

Beyond the real prospect of a redistribution of the workforce, especially for unskilled labor, and the creation of a surplus labor force, and setting aside the philosophical issue of autonomy and identity, there is the larger question of mass commercial manipulation using AI algorithms, as well as the prospect for realignment of defense sectors relying on digital technology. Dan Smith, director of the Stockholm International Peace Research Institute, SIPRI, has expressed concern about AI's impact on strategic stability and impact on military doctrine.

"The world is undergoing a 'fourth industrial' revolution, characterized by rapid and converging advances in multiple technologies including artificial intelligence (AI), robotics, quantum technology, nanotechnology, biotechnology, and digital fabrication. How these technologies will be utilized remains a question that has not yet been fully answered. It is beyond dispute, however, that nuclear-armed states will seek to leverage these technologies for their national security."[1021]

High-tech companies have been lobbying even more vigorously for defense contracts than traditional military contractors whose firms have incorporated high-tech into defense systems. Modern defense entails increasing reliance on AI algorithms, which in turn translates into modernization of the military-industrial complex, not just in the US leading the world in defense spending, but all countries that can afford weapons modernization. On 8 March 2023, the US Intelligence and National Security Alliance held a meeting with OpenAI company executives to adopt the AI chatbot ChatGPT developed for US global security and intelligence operations. Using ChatGPT's predictive capabilities to interpret the world, the US is seeking to militarize an AI operation designed for civilian use.[1022]

As defense sectors around the world incorporate more sophisticated government-subsidized AI technology, the trend will continue feeding the arms competition. This was the case during the Reagan era coinciding with exorbitant military spending that dragged the rest of the world along during the dawning of neoliberal transformation. Because of the long-standing relationship between the defense and intelligence sector and technology that has civilian applications, such as the IBM computer during the Truman presidency, AI with countless possibilities for defense and intelligence is easy to justify receiving government subsidies.[1023]

Considering the oligopolistic nature of high tech, even some AI advocates question the wisdom of placing humanity's fate in multi-billion-dollar enterprises with vast political influence where it is difficult to discern private sector boundaries and government. Corporate priority is to secure government contracts and subsidies for everything from domestic and foreign surveillance to police-private security applications in predictive crime, and private prisons to precision-bombing drones.

Given that an estimated 6% of those in digital consulting are former politicians, along with defense and intelligence officials returning to defense and intelligence-related tech companies, especially in the lucrative digital industry, the revolving door of corporation government and/or back is an illustration of how the system works. No matter the rhetoric about policy decisions made on the "merits" which includes public safety, profit drives AI policy in all sectors.[1024]

Besides police security and military applications, all pointing to a future of enhanced digital authoritarianism, the AI-dependent biosynthetic revolution aims at immortality. Corporations will create androids closely resembling humans and biosynthetically engineered humans resembling automatons with organic and/or engineered parts in both. Along with a redefinition of self, depending on social class, AI will have a ubiquitous role in every aspect of society from food production/distribution to waste management, and from complex precision surgery to elderly care.[1025]

Businesses using AI contend that their only goal is to deliver quality of life for people in every field. However, the socioeconomic structure determines the harm/benefit ratio. AI corporations' lack of transparency in algorithmic processing leaves doubts about accountability, especially given the history of the invisible hand of corporate-programmed algorithms.[1026] According to the European Digital Rights group, governments have used AI to discriminate against marginalized populations.

"To this day in the EU, we have seen several similar, worrying practices, including the use of pseudo-scientific 'lie detection' technology piloted on migrants in the course of their visa application process. This is just one example where governments, institutions, and companies are extracting data from people in extremely precarious situations...Many of the most harmful AI applications rely on large datasets of biometric data as a basis for identification, decision-making, and predictions. What is new in Europe, however, is that such undemocratic projects could be legitimized by a policy agenda "promoting the uptake of AI" in all areas of public life."[1027]

Despite the ethical and economic concerns that psychologists, progressive politicians, theologians, and scientists have raised, AI is humanity's only future for those espousing Max More's philosophy of "transhumanism". A movement whose goal is to enhance the human condition physically, aesthetically, and intellectually through the application of scientific and technological means, transhumanism has potential applicability in various sectors with immense returns on investment. At the heart of the semiconductor competition, over which the US-China rivalry has been taking place from the Obama to the Biden administration, AI is essential for transhumanism and the potential of humankind's evolution.[1028]

Pervasive in the EU leading the world in AI spending as a bloc, the US is number one as an individual country with 46% global market share in 2021. Not just the West, but Japan, China, Taiwan, Russia, and South Korea are all in the race for the latest innovations to capture global market share. Taking place in the context of the neoliberal political economy, beyond its commercial potential, AI will further contribute to militarization and police-state methods on a world scale under the existing balance of power between the trans-Atlantic alliance against the China-led commercial-geopolitical Asia-Eurasian bloc.[1029]

Although profit and political power are the driving forces behind digital authoritarianism, it has assumed different forms in China, Russia, and India than in the US and northwest Europe. Operating under a one-party state, China is unique because it has been dealing with both authoritarian and liberal democratic countries through AI partnerships in the *'Belt and Road Initiative'* (BRI). *"In 2019, a Lowy Institute report[3] indicated that*

---

3. https://www.lowyinstitute.org/the-interpreter/belt-and-road-means-big-data-facial-recognition-too

126 countries and twenty-nine international organizations had signed more than 3,000 high-technology cooperation agreements under the BRI framework. What is less understood, however, is why established democracies like Austria, Ireland, and the Netherlands have joined more authoritarian countries in partnering with China, and whether the United States or EU could provide similar high-technology partnerships with developing nations."[1030]

Contrary to Western-centered perspectives, including the article above published by the *Carnegie Endowment for International Peace* about how technology has resulted in the cooperation of democracies with authoritarian countries, the issue is less about authoritarianism vs. democracy when it comes to AI's role in society and more about the degree of digital authoritarianism on a world scale, regardless of regime.

This is because of the transcendent political economy, geopolitical dimensions of economic policy, and democratic governments adopting policies no different than those of authoritarian states that they castigate. Considering that the US-China rivalry has molded the consciousness of journalism, academia, and businesses, Western and pro-Western academic institutions and the media tend to focus on digital authoritarianism in China and its close ally Russia. This focus deflects attention from the US, Japan, South Korea, Israel, India, Brazil, and other Western and Eastern European countries where aspects of digital authoritarianism are a matter of record. [1031]

Even before the Great Recession, several countries including the US were moving rapidly toward rightwing populism largely because corporate authoritarianism had spread from the board room to the broader institutional structure. "*Outside the heavily regulated political arena,*" Peter Bloom and Carl Rhodes point out, *"Americans have little opportunity to legitimately practice democracy or democratic decision-making. Instead for the majority of citizens, it is their boss and the demands of capital rather than voting or public deliberation that determine their everyday choices and long-term fate."*[1032]

Enticed by the prospect of higher profits and political power, corporations and governments embraced *"AI solutionism"*, as Oxford University AI researcher Vyacheslav Polonski has baptized humanity's algorithmic panacea. In 2023, global corporate investment was 13 times higher than in 2013. In 2015 total corporate global investment in AI stood at just under $13 billion, jumping to $276.1 billion in 2021, and projected to double by the mid-2020s. If public investment is taken into account, the US government alone spent $6 billion in 2021, mostly for defense-related projects. AI private sector and government investment was well over $100 billion in 2020.[1033]

Historically, most of that investment has been US-based, but after 2015, China, Taiwan, South Korea, Japan, EU, also accelerated budgetary allocations. In July 2022, the US House of Representatives passed a $280 billion bill in support of chip production, mostly to counter Chinese growth in the sector. Just a few weeks before US chip legislation to contain China's semiconductor sector, *The Japan Times* they were reported that in 2021 chip manufacturing equipment from foreign suppliers rose 58%. Despite trade obstacles intended to bolster US-based companies against Chinese competition, China has been the world's largest customer of chip-making gear during the Trump and Biden presidencies. A fundamental question has been the degree to which AI will contribute or further retard social development.[1034]

Social Consequences of AI under Neoliberalism

Arguably the most promising technology with a tiny fraction of the global GDP in 2010, AI has the potential to contribute as much as $15 trillion by 2030. Like all technology, AI is concentrated mostly in core countries which will retain the lion's share used to forge unequal terms of trade, carve out the largest market share, and other geopolitical advantages. On the surface, the nation-state rivalry over security-related semiconductor dominance seems preeminent. In essence, it is primarily about the multinational corporations' struggle for global market share. Even the more enthusiastic AI proponents realize that AI will increase capital and power concentration while diminishing popular sovereignty and social justice.[1035]

Operating within the existing hierarchical social structure, AI has incorporated social eugenics, universalizing human intelligence based on algorithms designed with preconceived notions of the corporation. This is not to suggest that AI will not benefit medical science for a hefty profit. It will chase profits as much in mass consumer products as in defense. *"Advocates of sociogenomics [social factors and processes affect genome activity] envision a prospect that not everyone will find entirely benevolent: health "report cards," based on your genome and handed out at birth, that predict your risk of various diseases and propensity for different behaviors. In the new social sciences, sociologists will examine the genetic component of educational attainment and wealth, while economists will envision genetic "risk scores" for spending, saving, and investment behavior."[1036]*

Another means of promoting eugenics is transhumanism science has started a race to transform science fiction dreams into a profitable reality. An extension of AI, neuromorphic computing mimicking the brain and nervous system has attracted substantial investment in semiconductor devices necessary to operate AI algorithms in a variety of sectors. Beyond motion pictures and video games, transhumanism has attracted investors seeking to capture market share in everything from self-driving cars to crop harvesting.[1037]

Either in the liberal pluralist or populist rightwing camp, neoliberal politicians have been supporting government subsidies for digital technology. Partly because the industry provided campaign contributions for Democrats, the Biden administration provided more subsidies than Trump. Very profitable companies, including IBM and Intel, lobbied for subsidies in AI, semiconductors, and quantum computing. The same high-tech companies securing taxpayer money for their operations adamantly oppose labor unions and social welfare. Like pharmaceutical companies, they consistently overcharge state and federal government agencies in project contracts, while engaging in off-shore tax evasion.[1038]

Whether US, European, or Chinese, high-tech companies realized billions in profits, on top of government subsidies and defense and non-defense agency contracts. Universities, government-funded research institutions, and privately-funded AI labs have been working to realize the futuristic dream of riches and glory, without worrying about the potential risks. A continuation of the fourth industrial revolution which combines cyber-physical systems[1] and the digital world, AI further normalizes the commodification of human beings using the pretext of technological progress upon which civilization's future rests.[1039]

1. https://en.wikipedia.org/wiki/Cyber-physical_system

AI enthusiasts, including Peter Norvig and Stuart J. Russell (*Artificial Intelligence: A Modern Approach*, 2021), emphasize only the benefits of AI. Like most AI enthusiasts, rarely do they take into account the neoliberal context in which the industry operates and what it entails for inequality and authoritarianism. Critics caution about real risks and unforeseen consequences already evident with the cybergeneration of infophiles addicted to cell phones, computers, tablets, video games, and any human-enhancing or human-free physical or intellectual endeavor.

Optimistic that AI will add, not eliminate jobs, the business-government think tank McKinsey Global Institute estimates that: *"the global average level of adoption and absorption implied by our simulation, AI has the potential to deliver additional global economic activity of around $13 trillion by 2030, or about 16 percent higher cumulative GDP compared with today. This amounts to 1.2 percent additional GDP growth per year. If delivered, this impact would compare well with that of other general-purpose technologies through history."*[1040]

Accepting cyberspace as parallel to or better than real-life experiences, the industry has conditioned the cyber-bourgeois generation to accept algorithms as the norm despite alienation from empirical reality. Separating the immediacy of physical reality from cyberspace, people become conditioned to live vicariously through the illusion of greater personal control from a distance via a digital device. It is precisely this predilection to transcend physical limitations through technology that has become the addictive norm and which high-tech companies have exploited in a minimally regulated environment. Beyond digital games and virtual reality entertainment, AI is laying the foundation for the continued global transformation under an economy dependent on the interconnectedness of AI systems in life's every domain.[1041]

Born during the digital neoliberal era, cybergeneration, especially in the metropolis, has normalized high-tech-related alienation. Weakening the collective conscious, digital technology under the individualistic neoliberal value system is *"the opiate of the masses and a source of disintegration, deviance, strain, and divisiveness,"* Karam Adibifar argues in *"Technology and Alienation in Modern-Day Societies"*. [1042]

The cyber-community has replaced the empirical experience where people escape through numerous cyberspace masks as entertainment. In comparison with the social conditioning of the pre-neoliberal era, cybergeneration's socialization has been intertwined with virtualization. Interacting in the real community, and developing a social conscience and empathy are part of the dogma of individualism molded by virtualization. The community's role in cyber-subjectivity is further diminished thereby converging with the neoliberal ideological agenda.[1043]

"A normative crisis characterizes the systems that work the techno-economic structures of the world. Carrying the DNA of cyber-libertarian and tech-utopian ambitions of Silicon Valley entrepreneurs, these structures point to the crying need for norms-building for a new data epoch, acknowledging the strengths and limitations of the human rights framework. Whether AI will be an autonomous weapon of social injustice or a powerful agent of autonomous societies depends on the stories we choose to weave and the parameters we decide to make worthy. Data as a master signifier is firmly located in social subjectivities carefully crafted and tirelessly nurtured by neo-liberal capitalism. In dismantling the AI that fuels 21st-century capitalism, democracy must find new master signifiers that inspire new subjectivities." [1044]

Children growing up with robots, holograms, and bioengineered humans will have a sense of reality far different than it was for their grandparents. In every respect, from individual to group identity, and from self-identity to sociopolitical consciousness, the baby-boomer generation growing up during the Keynesian welfare state did not see the world through the same 'selfie-culture' lenses of algorithms and alienation as the generation born in the early 21st century. Digital technology has molded the neoliberal generation of millennials and Generation Z differently than the TV-molded baby boomers in every respect, except for the capitalist social contract as the common denominator.[1045]

Henry Armand Giroux, one of the more astute analysts of the neoliberal model, stresses that selfie culture is symptomatic of consumerism, narcissism, and commodification. Superficial appearances notwithstanding, selfie culture is both a struggle to affirm one's identity amid commercial exploitation of self where the private sector defines the public domain and the preponderance of the surveillance society where nothing is private.

"The rise of selfies under the surveillance state is only one register of neoliberal-inspired flight from privacy. The critique of the flight from privacy fails to address how the growth of the surveillance state and its appropriation of all spheres of private life is connected to the rise of the punishing state, the militarization of American society, secret prisons, state-sanctioned torture, a growing culture of violence, the criminalization of social problems, the depoliticization of public memory, and one of the largest prison systems in the world, all of which "are only the most concrete, condensed manifestations of a diffuse security regime in which we are all interned and enlisted."[14][2] The authoritarian nature of the corporate-state surveillance apparatus and security system with its "urge to surveil, eavesdrop on, spy on, monitor, record, and save every communication of any sort on the planet" can only be fully understood when its ubiquitous tentacles are connected to wider cultures of control and punishment...and the increasing labeling of dissent as an act of terrorism in the U.S."[1046]

Not only is the sense of identity and community largely impacted by AI for all social classes, but technology has impacted everything from education to consumer patterns. Wealthier families have access to AI technology, and numerous digital devices in their homes to educate their children, while the rest of humanity lives a world apart. Like a loveable pet, the robot would become an integral part of the wealthy family's socialization. For the less affluent, AI technology will be out of reach except in the public domain under state agencies' control. Workers will be lesser beings than robots whose intelligence and functions are another privilege that the wealthy enjoy and value more than humans.[1047]

"According to a new academic research study, automation technology has been the primary driver in U.S. income inequality[3] over the past 40 years. The report, published by the National Bureau of Economic Research, claims that 50% to 70% of changes in U.S. wages, since 1980, can be attributed to wage declines among blue-collar workers who were replaced or degraded by automation. Artificial intelligence, robotics, and new sophisticated technologies have caused a wide chasm in wealth and income inequality. It looks like this issue will accelerate. For now, college-educated, white-collar professionals have largely been spared the fate of degreeless workers. People with a postgraduate degree saw their salaries rise, while "low-education workers declined significantly." According to the study, "The real earnings of men without a high-school degree are now 15% lower than they were in 1980."[1048]

To the degree that people take for granted the new norm, the link between digital technology and autonomous systems has already altered the labor market. AI has changed human engagement in professional, social, and

2. *https://www.counterpunch.org/#_edn14*

3. *https://www.nber.org/papers/w28920*

personal relationships. Digital agents, which corporations use to communicate with employees and customers, have conditioned users that surrendering control of their lives to corporate autonomous systems in the name of 'Fordist efficiency' (product standardization in assembly-line mass production amid alienating work) best serves their interests.

Because digital technology is under corporate control and the supervision of the state whose policies, rules, and regulations are also under corporate control, the leap of faith to market conformity is inevitable. Even as the new status quo ushers in authoritarianism just beneath the thin layer of consumerist democracy, neoliberal conformity will remain the goal. While those who can afford it prefer the obvious convenience of everything that digital life offers, there is still the issue not just of loss of control and alienation, but digital physical and psychological dependence behind which there is corporate manipulation impacting every aspect of life. [1049]

AI and the Job Market under Neoliberalism

When it comes to the AI debate between the techno-optimist and techno-pessimist camps, at the heart of the issue for the latter there is downward pressure on middle-class and working-class living standards. There is also the corresponding rise in independent contract workers (uberization) of the labor force, which AI will likely worsen. Precarity, which includes poorly paid, unprotected, and often vulnerable undocumented workers, has been one of the more pervasive forms of labor under neoliberalism invariably associated with socially insecure and marginalized migrant and minority populations, especially women. The rapidly changing flexible and insecure labor force that neoliberalism created has entailed placing accountability on the vulnerable worker. [1050]

"The structural precarisation of labor is a global process, which has taken place heterogeneously according to national contexts, sectors, qualifications, and labor market stratifications. Besides, young people, low-skilled older workers, and women, it has mainly affected migrants, who have suffered from labour precarity combined with the weakness of their legal and social status. At the same time, immigration is also involuntarily an agent of spreading and widening precarisation—often a testing ground where new forms of precarity are trialed before being extended to other groups of workers."[1051]

In so far as both AI and temporary and contract labor have been operating under the neoliberal regime, the result has been to maximize profit through 'labor efficiency' which entails the lowest possible labor cost and highest productivity level. Besides downward wage pressure owing to digital technology's contribution to efficiency by eliminating workers, the common denominator has been the redefinition of labor-management relations. This is where the convergence of AI and the unregulated independent contractor-worker model plays a significant role in the international division of labor's re-molding beyond the automaton's role in the displacement of low-skilled labor.

"Such working arrangements are growing in popularity – both with businesses seeking short-term help and with workers, who prefer a more flexible and independent working schedule. However, they are also causing controversy, since employers pay no social premiums and wage taxes and workers receive no minimum wage, sick leave, or protection from dismissal. Since independent contractors often do similar jobs as regular employees under similar conditions and policies, many courts in Europe tend to interpret such arrangements as employment relationships. Therefore, companies employing freelancers are at risk of reassessment by the social security authorities, or of claims from the worker before the labor court to requalify their relationship as permanent employment."[1052]

Conducting public policy impacting the digital economy in everything from transportation, media, and advertising, elected officials place priority on corporate interests which finance political campaigns. Because of the trend described above, France, and the Netherlands, among other countries, have been reexamining how to protect short-term self-employed workers. Investors and politicians have argued in favor of "corporate demand for efficiency" to justify government subsidies for AI research and development while overlooking multiple consequences on labor. An endorsement that the private sector knows best when it comes to labor-management relations, the corporate subsidy illustrates that government policy helps to shift costs from social programs to AI's R&D capital goods spending.[1053]

Neoliberal policies have encouraged continued expansion of contractor employees and part-time labor, and even reconsidering reducing the minimum age for work. In *Robots and Immigrants: Who Is Stealing Jobs?*, Kostas Maronitis[1] and Denny Pencheva[2] maintain that labor precarity under neoliberalism entails minimal labor security in comparison with what prevailed under the Keynesian state. Owing to the combination of contractor labor and AI, the entire workforce feels less secure, fearful, and docile, subject to a hierarchy with an even smaller well-paid 'labor aristocracy' segment. Already providing the systemic surplus pool to keep profits high, the unskilled, migrant, and minority workers will be in a more precarious position because of AI.[1054]

"With real innovation at hand, it can be difficult to distinguish nonsense from progress, but there are some telling signs. Companies declaring they're using AI to replace human workers, for instance, are almost always just papering over more serious internal problems. Their statements typically indicate they're thinking small, are looking to reduce their workforce anyway, or both. Take IBM, for example. Just this week its CEO Arvind Krishna said his company would pause hiring for back-office roles that AI might replace, suggesting[3] AI could take over as many as 7,800 positions. Technology this powerful should be able to make workers more productive, not unnecessary. And IBM itself sells that very idea to those who buy its Watson A.I. service. In its marketing materials[4], it says Watson helps "free up employees to focus on higher value work." The incongruity is revealing."[1055]

Following in the footsteps of Luddites smashing machines as the symbolic enemy of workers in England during the 1810s, some AI critics have distracted the public from structural issues by focusing solely on the machine. Public policy, not AI technology is the essential issue in labor relations. After all, the evidence is incontrovertible that workers have been enduring downward wage pressure before and after the gig economy under neoliberalism. [1056]

Naturally, human employment will not come to an end because of some AI apocalypse. Poorly paid, temporary, and contractor-worker jobs will likely multiply because government and businesses will use AI as a weapon in the neoliberal class war. Although AI is concentrated in the core where the consumer base is largest and most lucrative, the international division of labor will be further impacted, as it has been since the 1980s under deregulation and a withering social safety net.[1057]

One of the countries with a fairly well-developed digital sector, Japan provides a good insight into how the convergence of AI and neoliberalism has impacted the social structure. Along with Switzerland, South Korea, Norway, and Germany, Japan ranks among the top five countries in the world for job security, according to the OECD. Altering Japan's social contract under global neoliberal transformation was at the center of rising social inequality and insecurity. Digital technology was the thinly veiled pretext for capitalist appropriation.[1058]

---

1. https://www.amazon.com/s/ref=dp_byline_sr_book_1?ie=UTF8&field-author=Kostas+Maronitis&text=Kostas+Maronitis&sort=relevancerank&search-alias=books
2. https://www.amazon.com/s/ref=dp_byline_sr_book_2?ie=UTF8&field-author=Denny+Pencheva&text=Denny+Pencheva&sort=relevancerank&search-alias=books
3. *https://www.bloomberg.com/news/articles/2023-05-01/ibm-to-pause-hiring-for-back-office-jobs-that-ai-could-kill?utm_source=substack&utm_medium=email*
4. *https://www.ibm.com/watson?utm_source=substack&utm_medium=email*

By privatizing the National Railways, on 1 April 1987, Prime Minister Yasuhiro Nakasone delivered a major blow to the blend of Keynesianism and corporatism. A major privatization measure signalizing the neoliberal era's institutionalization, the move was a bottom-up political mechanism designed to break the railroad union. Nakasone patterned class warfare policy after Reagan who dismissed the Professional Air Traffic Controllers Organization on the first year he was in office. Four years later, Thatcher crushed the National Union of Mineworkers. An extension of the neoliberal model, Japan's fiscal policies favored capital to the detriment of the mass consumer exactly as in the UK and US.[1059]

To reward Nakasone for institutionalizing neoliberalism, the Reagan administration lifted 17% of trade sanctions on companies exporting to the US. The semiconductor sector benefited especially from US trade sanctions relief. Indicative of neoliberal corporate welfare practices, Japan's Semiconductor Industry Association lobbied the Reagan administration to fund tech representation in Tokyo.[1060]

Further endearing himself to Reagan neoliberals, Nakasone weakened the labor movement which in turn led to the twilight of Japan's Socialist Party and the inevitable rise of socioeconomic inequality amid the digital era's concurrent ascendancy. Continuing with deregulation, privatization, and corporate subsidies in the age of high tech and globalization, Nakasone often deflected attention from rising inequality by pointing to the digital revolution's promise of prosperity. Like Western countries, Japan experienced a decline in labor stability and a rise in part-time work, especially permanent part-time contract workers performing the equivalent of full-time work without the analogous compensation to keep their jobs.[1061]

Implementing AI in all sectors under the neoliberal model had a similar impact on labor relations as the implementation of robotics in automotive and electronics when Nakasone's policies determined Japan's management-labor relations. Predictably, neoliberal apologists argued that digital technology, not public policy was remolding terms of labor, resulting in more permanent part-timers responsible for production output comparable to full-time workers. As the catalyst to justify the labor force divided into a small percentage of well-paid permanent (indefinite duration contract) and poorly-paid "flexible" workers, neoliberalism further weakened the working class by breaking its solidarity and creating a subservient citizenry competing for 'right-to-work' stability.[1062]

Contrary to many analysts who maintain that AI has been the root cause of systemic social disruption, digital technology, much like the Spinning Jenny or the Cotton Gin during England's first industrial revolution, has been the pretext for more thorough capitalist appropriation. Subject to corporate and government decisions, realignment in the datafication and algorithmic management of workers is rationalized based on the technology. Naturally, the machine per se and its potential for a constructive or destructive role in society is simply another tool that capital uses for accumulation while further regimenting labor.[1063]

At the beginning of the 2020s, it is estimated that 34% of the US labor force, or 53 million 'freelance' workers were part of the precarity pool. By the end of the decade, this category could double. In part, this is because businesses and governments use AI to justify the evolving division of labor on a downward slope. It is possible that two-thirds of the workforce will not have benefits, labor protection, or job security; all policy-based issues taking place within the 'miracle' gig economy that entailed more thorough structural exploitation of labor.[1064]

According to a Gallup poll, only 40% of workers consider themselves to have "good jobs" which term includes security, adequate compensation, and benefits such as health care with drug coverage. Along with enthusiasm surrounding AI robotics which investors and corporations use as distractions for those negatively impacted, endless uses from games to medical applications and nuances of the technology have become a substitute for effective public policy improving peoples' material lives.[1065]

A constant debate and one that Philippe Aghion, Céline Antonin, and Simon Bunel raise in their case study on France, the question is whether AI robots are so different than automation in the 1970s. Their findings show that while theoretically possible for AI to increase employment, robotization overall increased unemployment from 1994 to 2014. "*We also find that non-educated workers are more negatively affected by automation than educated workers. This suggests that inappropriate labor market and education policies could reduce the positive impact of AI and automation on employment.*"[1066]

Robotics automation in the auto and electronics industries entailed the loss of well-paying manufacturing jobs in the 1970s-1980s. When the auto industry introduced robotics in the 1970s (MIT's "Silver Arm"), auto workers reacted like Luddites in early 19th-century English manufacturing towns of Yorkshire, Lancashire, Derbyshire, and Leicestershire. To drive down wages and benefits, and circumvent labor standards, robotics automation became the neoliberal pretext to weaken the strongest unions. According to the National Bureau of Economic Research, all US industries experiencing automation in the 1980s and 1990s resulted in wage loss of 50-70%. To justify the huge wage decline, businesses, politicians, and media insisted that workers needed retraining to acquire new job skills.[1067]

The transfer of factories to low-wage countries, especially from the US and Canada to Mexico's *maquiladora* manufacturing[5] operations focused on duty-free assembly plants with components for export was just a small part of manufacturing relocating to low-wage countries. Similarly, AI goes to the heart of how existing and new industries widen the rich-poor gap and core-periphery GDP chasm. Especially in less developed countries, resource allocation entails that the lower classes experience further marginalization in the world economy. At the same time, companies use low-wage countries as leverage to keep wages low in the metropolis.[1068]

In the absence of a meaningful social safety net and regulations to protect the working class, neither skilled nor unskilled workers are safe from rising inequality and neoliberal authoritarianism using robotics as a pretext to justify class war. Besides Amazon's poor safety record of delivery trucks in comparison with other companies, surveillance, and biometric monitoring accounts for primitive working conditions made possible by digital technology. "*Far from the sophisticated, sentient machines portrayed in media and pop culture, so-called AI systems are fueled by millions[6] of underpaid workers around the world, performing repetitive tasks under precarious labor conditions. And unlike the "AI researchers" paid six-figure salaries in Silicon Valley corporations, these exploited workers are often recruited out of impoverished populations and paid as little as $1.46/hour[7] after tax.*"[1069]

---

5. https://www.britannica.com/technology/manufacturing

6. https://www.gigeconomydata.org/basics/how-many-gig-workers-are-there

7. https://time.com/6147458/facebook-africa-content-moderation-employee-treatment/

Considering the demand for higher productivity at a lower wage cost, AI has accelerated under favorable government tax, corporate subsidy, and loose regulatory policies. The other side of the demographic concern is that the growing aging population in the G-7 countries concurrently taking place with overall growth expected to slow to the low single digits in the balance of the 2020s and perhaps 2030s. The business argument is that robotics will fill labor shortage needs, a view that corporations propagate to keep wages low. Contrary to AI apologists' claims, human-replacement robotics are not designed to serve humanity, but to ensure a surplus labor force and low wages which theoretically yield high profits, assuming an expanding middle-class consumer base.[1070]

"Lower fertility and increasing longevity have implications on the age population structure and, therefore, on the balance between savings and investment. Jointly with meager productivity growth, this implies a low natural rate of interest that conditions the effectiveness of monetary and fiscal policies, especially in a world of high debt. New technological changes (robots, artificial intelligence, automation) may increase productivity growth but are at the risk of having disruptive effects on employment and wages. The survey highlights the main mechanism by which demographic and technological changes, considered both individually and in conjunction, affect per capita growth and other macroeconomic variable."[1071]

Based on the experience of robotics manufacturing applications in the 1970s, labor throughout the world will feel the impact of AI human-replacement technologies in wage compensation, benefits, and work conditions.Digital technology and AI afford leverage for businesses to discourage unionization, just as was the case with robotics in the auto industry in the 1980s. Under the neoliberal regime, contradictions are already evident between the promise of social protection and upward mobility versus the reality of a continued decline in living standards. Rising inequality will continue to feed sociopolitical extremism and embolden authoritarianism which neoliberals view as the best guarantee against popular demand for inclusionary socially just policies.[1072]

In 2016, an Obama White House AI report proclaimed that the new technology would result in higher productivity. The same report expected AI to leave millions without work and precipitate greater inequality. Just as Silicon Valley created a small wealthy class without integrating the surplus labor force into living-wage conditions amid the widening rich-poor gap, and creating immense housing and living standards problems in the greater region around San Francisco, AI will exacerbate the existing trend. Rejecting pessimistic scenarios about AI, apologists insist that it has accelerated demand for machine learning and robotics engineers, and data scientists, among other professions.[1073]

Based on one estimate, in the 2020s, AI's job-stimulation trend is expected to create as many as 100 million jobs. This projection assumes geopolitical stability, the absence of US-led neo-mercantilist policies, workers "upskill" ready to meet industry requirements, and jobs that AI will create to replace those lost. AI optimism aside, according to an opinion poll, 72% of workers, especially in the area of insurance, personal services, transportation, and energy expect to lose their position within a decade because of AI. Only 26% expect job growth because of AI. Instead of examining how the political economy determines social structure, workers' apprehension has been misplaced by focusing on digital technology enmeshed in a neo-Luddite mindset. Determining AI's impact on the working class, personal identity, popular culture, and value system, neoliberalism has been and remains the most important catalyst.[1074]

Arguing that population will catch up to food production between 2030 and 2050, Malthusian theory apologists (Thomas Malthus, *An Essay on the Principle of Population*, 1798), maintain that AI can help with rapid food production. The prospect that AI application in agriculture is the only solution to feed the world is no different than similar contentions during England's 18th-century agricultural revolution that resulted in ownership concentration. Except for periodic famines in East Africa amid climate change, among war-ravaged areas like Yemen, Afghanistan, and Syria in the 2010s-early 2020s, history has shown that there is a world food surplus, except in unique circumstances including unusual drought, war, tariffs, wars, sanctions, and corporate profiteering.[1075]

The issue is not food sufficiency, but the profit motive precluding distribution to feed the world's population, periodic natural causes, and geopolitics. Therefore, the issue is not food production innovation using high tech, but the political economy and policies impacting food, and climate change. If the world population reaches 9.8 billion by 2050, 38% higher than in 2010, and climbs to 11.2 billion by the end of the century with the majority living in Africa and Asia where high levels of structural unemployment and high levels of inequality prevail, AI could be a lifesaver in many domains including climate guidance policies. By the same token, it could create even greater problems for the benefit of corporate profits.[1076]

Considering that population concentration will remain in Asia and Africa, it is easy to see how corporations and governments could use AI as a pretext to exert political, economic, military, economic, and cultural hegemony over other countries. Western xenophobic populist politicians and nativist groups could use AI as a pretext to keep Middle Easterners, Africans, Asians, and Latin Americans out of white-majority countries. With robots to the rescue of the Caucasian minority on the planet, heightened xenophobia will be another dimension of those looking for a pretext to rally right-wing populists behind authoritarian regimes. Even governments claiming to be liberal democratic in support of pluralism will be using AI to impose greater sociopolitical conformity.[1077]

Extending to an estimated 700 different fields, according to an Oxford University study, AI will result in many benefits in every field from dangerous rescue operations to health care. Just as the internet made it possible for a physician in Cleveland to provide live instructions to a colleague carrying out surgery in Rio de Janeiro, similarly, AI will result in life-saving miracles. The core issue is the social distribution of 'tech miracles', and how corporations and governments use AI to promote social justice or as policy leverage to punish a class of people or an entire nation. While there is no consensus on whether AI will negatively impact the middle or low-skilled labor force, there is agreement that corporations will shift resources from wages to capital goods.[1078]

In the era of fast-food restaurants, self-check-out supermarkets, and fast delivery, AI has already replaced workers with AI technology. Just as capitalists in early 19th-century England were using machines as leverage in labor policy, so did 21st-century corporations use AI for the same purpose. At the same time, there is no dispute that AI unlocked the immense potential for economic growth and development with derivative benefits for the general population. Especially in the Global South, women will pay the price for technological innovation amid the neoliberal class war.[1079]

In some respects, labor relations in the digital age are similar to the era of coerced labor in 18th-century Africa and the Western Hemisphere which provided cheap labor for England's industrialization. Not surprisingly, governments and the national bourgeoisie in the Southern Hemisphere are optimistic that AI will elevate their status closer to the core. Promising an expanding middle class, AI apologists see the rainbow across the Global South horizon.[1080]

Desperate to achieve economic development and upward social mobility, the middle class and workers alike, especially in the periphery are both afraid and mesmerized by the AI-techno fix as a substitute for public policy to address structural inequality. This is more so today than in the mid-20th century when Herbert Marcuse wrote *"One-Dimensional Man: Studies in the Ideology of Advanced Industrial Society."* *"Technological rationality reveals its political character as it becomes the great vehicle of better domination, creating a truly totalitarian universe in which society and nature, mind and body are kept in a state of permanent mobilization for the defense of this universe." [1081]*

In addition to a technofix as a substitute for public policy, historically the terms of trade based on the patron-client relationship between the advanced capitalist countries and the Global South determine workers' living standards. This is especially true when considering the weaponization of technology, trade, currency, and investment as policy tools in the neoliberal class war. As the *Newsweek* article below notes, AI as an extension of globalization continues to operate under the same principles of neoliberalism by accelerating the rich-poor gap on a world scale.

"AI has created a new set of blue-collar workers called data labelers who earn, on average, as low as $2 per hour, much lower than the U.S. federal minimum wage of $7.25 per hour. These are figures for the U.S., so it's anyone's guess how low workers get paid in India, the Philippines, and other countries in the global south where these data labelers reside...These low-skilled workers get peanuts compared to the millions earned by companies like Samasource, Scale AI, and Mighty AI. Data labeling startups are mushrooming [8] globally, but it remains to be seen if they will decrease the disparity in AI's money concentration. Much of the data labeling task is crowdsourced through platforms like Amazon[9] Mechanical Turk, where the earnings are sometimes disbursed as Amazon gift cards[10]."[1082]

An IMF study on AI and its impact on the socioeconomic and geographic gap is as pessimistic as studies by critics of AI implementation under the neoliberal model. As financing for AI rises to increase productivity and lower labor costs across all sectors, especially in advanced countries, corporations shift financing from the Global South, undermining labor-intensive traditional sectors and GDP growth prospects. *"Assuming robots replace unskilled labor but complement skilled workers, a permanent decline in the terms of trade in the developing region may emerge after the robot revolution. This is because robots will disproportionately displace unskilled workers, reducing their relative wages and lowering the price of the good that uses unskilled labor more intensively. The drop in relative price of its main output, in turn, acts as a further negative shock, reducing the incentive to invest and potentially leading to a fall not just in relative but in absolute GDP."[1083]*

Within the advanced capitalist countries and in their relations with the less developed nations, technology has always been a tool of social exploitation and imperial expansion. Under neoliberalism, AI will continue to exacerbate inequality and uneven development on a world scale. Saudi Arabia's NEOM-Line project provides an excellent example of how technology can coexist with and enhance tyranny. Planned an entire sustainable-AI-run city, NEOM-Line projects the image of techno-modernity behind which rests an authoritarian Medieval kingdom that ranks among the world's worst human rights violators.

---

8. *https://fortune.com/2020/02/04/artificial-intelligence-data-labeling-labelbox/*

9. *https://www.newsweek.com/topic/amazon*

10. *https://blog.mturk.com/amazon-mechanical-turk-workers-in-23-countries-outside-of-the-us-can-now-transfer-their-earnings-98ec29ef7f7f*

Completely ignoring Saudi Arabian authoritarianism and human rights record, techno-enthusiasts focus only on how AI will make the NEOM-Line possible, as though millions of human beings are not as important as the AI-run city. In May 2023, UN representatives sharply objected to the Saudi Arabian government's plan to execute three members of the Howeitat tribe who resisted evictions to make room for the NEOM project. Hardly an example of how a high-tech city as a model of modernity is also a democratic model, it is a monument to an authoritarian regime.[1084]

To justify corporate subsidies, international competition is at the top of the list followed by the promise of creating a techno-scientific paradise on earth that corporations, governments, the media, and techno-enthusiasts have been promoting. Trump's executive order *"Maintaining American Leadership in Artificial Intelligence"* called for *"sustained investment in AI R&D in collaboration with industry, academia, international partners and allies, and other non-Federal entities."* With the signing of one trillion-dollar infrastructure bill in November 2021, the Biden administration vastly expanded corporate welfare subsidies that Obama and Trump had also promoted. [1085]

Multinational corporations have been lobbying for more subsidies, while adamantly opposing publicly-funded universal insurance healthcare, free college tuition, college debt forgiveness, or any social safety net program. Among the many that have warned about the greater gap between rich and poor owing to robotics and AI, an Oxford University study estimates that automation will absorb approximately half of American jobs at a pace more rapid than the primary sector's commercialization during the first industrialization while uprooting the rural population.[1086]

In *"Robot Nation: Surviving the Greatest Socio-economic Upheaval of All Time,"* (2011), Stan Neilson[11] raises the question of the percentage of the population that will survive when corporations replace humans with robots. An even better question is whether companies will use AI to keep wages down and trade unions away. As government, businesses, and media identify AI with the future and national security without tangible derivative benefits for the majority of the population, AI resistance frontlines of populists and progressives fighting against the machine and the system supporting it will further aggravate sociopolitical polarization.[1087]

With built-in biases against marginalized groups, minorities, and the poor, robotic law enforcement will concentrate on actual and predictive crime because technology permits more rapid market-determined efficient marginalization. As has been the case under neoliberalism, billionaire-financed rightwing groups will co-opt anti-AI groups as authoritarianism's popular base against the wave of progressive grassroots neoliberal resistance. [1088]

Not the revolt of the robots, but of workers and marginalized groups could assume different forms in various countries to end neoliberalism's digital paradise. Fiction and non-fiction writers imagine robot rebellions against humans as a fantasy of technophiles concerned more about the machine as if it were human. This is itself a distraction from systemic exploitation. As class war intensifies, the possibility of a working-class and middle-class

---

11. https://www.amazon.com/s/

ref=dp_byline_sr_book_1?ie=UTF8&field-author=Stan+Neilson&text=Stan+Neilson&sort=relevancerank&search-alias=books

rebellion against high-tech companies and their political and institutional defenders is a plausible scenario, more likely as part of a broader social movement.[1089]

Transhumanism and Neoliberal Identity

Resting on the works of transhumanist neoliberal intellectuals, government representatives, businesses, and media maintain that with the advent of AI robotics, the evolution of digital culture and identity is already the new norm and the future. Transhumanism enthusiasts who favor technologies that would augment the human experience contend that people have always evolved under conditions that technology influences. Thanks to science and technology, humans continue to evolve toward a higher plane of existence both physically and mentally. Max More's definition of transhumanism stresses benefits as well as inherent risks, touching on justifications that AI investors, government, and industry have been advancing.

"The intellectual and cultural movement that affirms the possibility and desirability of fundamentally improving the human condition through applied reason, especially by developing and making widely available technologies to eliminate aging and to greatly enhance human intellectual, physical, and psychological capacities. The study of the ramifications, promises, and potential dangers of technologies that will enable us to overcome fundamental human limitations, and the related study of the ethical matters involved in developing and using such technologies.[1090]

Cyberculture communities, some incorporating environmentalists among other groups, have raised philosophical questions about identity, relationships, and values under the withering real culture vs. virtual reality as an alternative to real-life socialization. Considering that the neoliberal model diminishes rather than enhances socialization and popular participation, cultural determinism in the digitized universe is another layer within cultural hegemony shaping personal identity. Digital technology has been molding cultural lifestyles to create more compliant citizens, consumers, and workers.[1091]

Minimizing possible risks that AI poses to society, infophiles maintain that internet skeptics had similar concerns as those questioning AI. Some who argue that AI-forged cyberculture is egalitarian also contend that there is a counterculture movement within cyberculture validating its democratic nature and endless possibilities for cyber-identity transcending all else. In 2023, a public opinion poll found that just 9% of respondents believed that AI will benefit rather than harm society, while 41% believe it will do more harm and 46% equal harm to good ratio.[1092]

During the nascent era of the internet, there was no shortage of democratization theories, just as was the case in the embryonic phase of social media. Considering the global autocratization trend, internet, and social media democratization theories proved premature and hollow. After the coup of February 2021, Myanmar Military Junta was using digital technology to repress those demanding social justice, thus earning UN condemnation as a "digital dictatorship". US-based big tech corporations share citizens' information with governments, proving that the digital era has provided a public arena for all, contributing to rightwing populism, not democracy.[1093]

Peddling vacuous rhetoric about freedom and democracy, high-tech companies were not what they appeared. Although billionaires Peter Theil of Palantir Technologies and Elon Musk of TESLA did not conceal their right-wing ideological leanings. Others projected an image of pluralism. *As much as Silicon Valley likes to promote an image of innovative iconoclasm."* writes Julia Carrie Wong, *"companies have a herd mentality when it comes to political[1] or social issues[2]...TJ Rodgers, the founder of Cypress Semiconductor, and Scott McNealy, co-founder of Sun Microsystems, represent an earlier generation of conservative Silicon Valley... Other tech leaders, such as Oracle's Larry Ellison, Intel's Craig Barrett, Dell's Michael Dell, and AOL's Tim Armstrong, have been major donors to the GOP, while HP's Carly Fiorina and eBay's Meg Whitman have both run (unsuccessfully) for elected office as Republicans. The Thiel Foundation and Thiel Fellowship, led by Jack Abraham, and Palantir – a data analysis company whose clients include the US intelligence community and defense department – are other meeting grounds for the ideologically like-minded."*[1094]

Peter Thiel's patriotism reward was that his data company secured multibillion-dollar government contracts from intelligence agencies and the FBI, allowing the company to venture into the lucrative healthcare field. Coinciding with the rise of neoliberal authoritarianism, AI has been closely linked to intelligence and defense, but it has also facilitated criminal activity. The larger question is one of public accountability for both government and businesses using AI for commercial, social, and political manipulation, including illegal activities of cybercriminals, and crimes by the socioeconomic and political elites usually evading legal consequences.[1095]

From white-collar crime to disparate groups operating in everything from narcotics to human trafficking, and from neo-Nazi activities to nihilistic cults promoting suicide, all become more challenging with AI technology as the process makes it easier to evade legal avenues. Especially those using avatars, cybercriminals will have a much easier time exploiting others, only to have the digital industry sell more security programs to customers and government agencies eager to protect everything from bank accounts to personal documents. Cybercrime dwarfs what corporations and governments have been doing and will be doing with the help of AI at the expense of citizens in the name of security. The digital industry points to cybercriminal activity as a selling point for its products.[1096]

Among the many studies of potential abuses of AI, the British government commissioned a study (2012) directed by John Beddington on how the web has redefined human identity. Beddington concluded that web users deemed traditional identity based on community as less relevant. The study reinforces the conclusions of other empirical works that digital technology has reinforced neoliberal values of individualism.

Companies and political parties use the web to mobilize the population identifying with a particular sport or cultural event. Just as easily, modern means of communication have meant that thousands could be called into political action. This was the case with the Arab Spring uprisings, Occupy Wall Street, and European-wide protests. Whereas the internet permits users to share their identities more easily and freely, affording a sense of freedom lacking in interpersonal relations, digital interaction also accounts for alienation.[1097]

Given the prevalence of multi-trillion-dollar social media, web, and AI industries vested in commodifying human beings, there have been debates about what digital technology means to the average person's sense of identity, community, and citizenship. Like surreal characters in a Franz Kafka novel, or zombies in a cult horror film, technophiles are the physical extensions that afford legitimacy to digital reality, but inadvertently to digital alienation.[1098]

---

1. *https://www.theguardian.com/technology/2016/mar/03/silicon-valley-apple-fbi-encryption-airbnb-ebay-reddit-twitter*

2. *https://www.theguardian.com/sustainable-business/big-businesses-nike-cummins-backing-gay-marriage*

Manifestations of digital dependency, enthusiasts craving virtual reality more than empirical reality are seemingly satisfied with virtual relationships taking precedence over physical contact. If we accept the premise that to a large degree, the environment shapes human nature, then much of humanity is on the way to a digital world where transhumanism eventually could be the norm to which at least the middle class aspires. Within the digital norm, there is a question about how far human rights will retreat for workers and marginalized populations.[1099]

Even before the advent of the internet and AI, there were various institutional and cultural means, including religious dogma, nationalist ideology, race, ethnicity, gender, and personal aesthetics; all subject to manipulation for commerce and/or political ends. Eager to have robots behaving like the 'ideal human', scientists are trying to create a machine that closely emulates human intelligence, while the infophileand corporations aspire to a quasi-robotic existence for workers. Just as IT engineers program the robot to mimic human behavior, corporations, and neoliberal institutions program humans to mimic robots. For the employee-consumer, conformity is the business goal. This is similar to what religious institutions expect of the faithful and what the government expects from a compliant citizenry.[1100]

Just as corporate engineers program robots, social engineers and political propagandists use digital technology in the mass media and social media to program the masses into conformity. Concerned about digital technology's impact on the masses, Yuval Noah Harari[3], maintains that AI will create a class of "useless humans". Within the reach of commercial advertisers and political parties eager to mold public perceptions, AI is very useful in molding Harari's "useless humans". Except as a public or private institutional entity, for the vast majority AI is and will likely remain an out-of-reach tool.[1101]

In June 2023, the press revealed that a wealthy donor provided funding to install surveillance in synagogues, schools, and campus communities throughout the US, with the help of former FBI, CIA[4], Shin Bet, and Mossad agents. For the general population, the most notable access to AI has been online shopping, telecommunications services, the video-game industry, and various modes of transportation. Besides creating an Orwellian bubble society in the hands of a government only too eager to impose control, AI used in youth-oriented video game culture promotes a value system of aggressive individualism, fear, dread, and disdain for society, while celebrating the mythological high-tech superhero emulating a Medieval Beowulf prototype. Growing up in the age of neoliberalism, the video-game generation along with government and corporate surveillance provides a glimpse into how AI will shape society into sociopolitical and cultural conformity.[1102]

Ubiquitous in contemporary culture, digital games relying on AI for home use on TV, computers, iPads, cell phones, and gambling devices or the arcade have historically provided an outlet through interactive fantasies based on classical mythology and popular superhorse cartoons from around the world. Without questioning the often violent, at times misanthropic, and misogynist video games, the individual player feels a sense of power against external obstacles, resorting to aggressive resolution rather than reason guided by compassion when facing challenges. Nintendo ushered in the popularity of digital games in the nascent phase of neoliberalism. Reflecting themes and alienation of the individual from society and virtual reality connections taking precedence,

3. https://www.theguardian.com/profile/yuval-noah-harari

4. https://knewz.com/tag/cia/

video-game culture also mimics the battles against society's institutional forces that prevent the digital hero from prevailing in the quest for realization of the fantasy in the quest to defy conventions.[1103]

A dominant neoliberal theme, market hegemony over the state and society is a virtue and a goal for the "superhero player" of the digital game intertwined with one's identity. Some scholarly researchers have raised questions about an empathy deficit associated with video games. Vicariously enjoying watching pain and destruction on virtual human beings for the sake of "winner-take-all" games does not necessarily suggest mental imbalance. Nor is it a reflection of a constructive and positive outlook of self or society.

Amid the madness of demonizing those who stand in the way of redemptive violence inculcated into the minds of youth playing video games, there is a morality deficit. This is not only for the sake of profit on the part of the digital game corporations and distributors seeking to touch the player's nerve, but an issue of ideological orientation as well. The net result is the delivery of a value system consistent with neoliberalism and a populist rightwing ideology of libertarian freedom, devoid of a social conscience. The goal of domination through a process of violent antagonism with the amorphous virtual enemy as entertainment gives one pause about how the digital-neoliberal era has been influencing values.[1104]

Through AI-powered interactive video games or voice-activated devices, the generations growing up in the world of AI have been conditioned into virtual reality not just as entertainment, but as an integral part of the new norm in their lives. Naturally, they realize that the real community, which they cannot switch off like cell phones, is not as easily subject to commands. More receptive to karate lessons, guns, online gambling, and cryptocurrency, video game players have been conditioned by the neoliberal digital culture as much as non-video gamers to suppress empathy as an obstacle to the illusion of power. The same principles employed in digital games for decades apply to Blockchain technology, allowing speculators to trade at fast speeds and lower costs in a winner-take-all mindset. Making the entire experience like a videogame marks the triumph of "crypto-evangelists" as an integral part of the neoliberal political economy that has been part of the speculators' projected mystique.[1105]

Arguing that video games are not merely innocuous entertainment, Justin Schumaker points out that they have built-in ideological, political, social, and financial dimensions. *"As computer game culture exists in this period of limitless exploitation or swindling, the players' willingness to consume virtual goods is tied to the experience of fun$; these virtual goods are earned through the players' labor-play, masking the logic of exploitation to which they belong. While some companies have seen pushback against loot crates and excessive*

the proliferation of virtual goods40, they do not appear to be leaving the commercial market for

computer games, or significantly altering their business practices. They seem to assume the

player's desire to consume is infinite and inelastic. However, no acquisitive impulse, even one

mediated through virtual goods, can be truly inexhaustible. The conflict between the interests of players and game operators must eventually appear. Players will rebel and owners will retaliate."[1106]

Through a dystopian narrative rooted in the individual's quest to gain control over the other and prevail over the community, the global neoliberal transformation has left no stone unturned to mold the consumer from the school child playing a video game to the day trader speculating on the market. Conditioned by neoliberalism and infophilia, the identity of the post-1980s generations centers around the dominant digital culture to permit virtual self-expression while fostering sociopolitical conformity. Something analogous to a religious experience in the post-secular world mainly in the Global North, neoliberalism has absorbed religion's role that digital technology has molded. Freed from the confines of institutionalized religion, itself part of the neoliberal dogma, institutions serve the political economy behind the digital veil.[1107]

Beyond the AI engineering room, the AI global matrix includes everyone from the investment banker to the marketing and advertising salesman; from the politician voting to subsidize the industry to the aviation maintenance crew. Everything from its impact on education to mainstream and social media, and from medical surgery to facial recognition, AI's impact on social relations and culture has driven many researchers to emphasize public policy and business standards that must take into account the cultural norms in establishing AI ethics. Rarely mentioning anything related to social justice, most Western researchers and corporations focus on "privacy" and the environment.[1108]

Determining automation's governing patterns and for whose benefit, technology governance and AI-enhanced management systems have been within the domain of the corporation which the state protects and subsidizes. As corporations define it, privacy is a bourgeois preoccupation that ignores the larger issue of how AI hastens socioeconomic and geographic structural inequality. The approach to sociocultural AI has attracted scholarly interest in the nexus with neoliberal transformation, especially impacting the Global South where AI companies rely on cheap labor. Although many organizations including the International Labour Office (ILO), OECD, and World Bank have examined AI's role from various perspectives, not just from investors' interests, there is a reluctance to criticize the political economy under which AI operates, and a refusal to address socioeconomic and geographic exploitation.[1109]

Beyond the narrow field of consumer products and services, living in a world of algorithms for personal use has its costs mostly for the working class. The OECD estimates that 87% of all human activity can be automated. Adding 40,000 industrial robots annually to the existing 310,000, the US is on course to eliminate 73 million jobs by 2030, or 46% of the labor force as it stands in 2023. Globally, by 2021 there were 3.5 million industrial robots, representing a staggering 17% increase from the previous year.[1110]

As far as transhumanism apologists are concerned, AI robotics means that humans will be living a life of leisure. *"Many transhumanists[5] argue that advanced technologies will soon provide humanity with a means to evolve beyond its current physical and mental limitations. For transhumanist thinkers, the development of advanced computational technologies foreshadows a new era in which humans and machines evolve together[6]. Beyond the era of automation, perhaps we should begin to consider the possibilities of a future transhumanist economy[7] in which human evolution is the key to economic growth."*[1111]

AI-transhumanism has the potential to forge the creation of Thomas Hobbes' *Leviathan* (1651), a sea serpent symbolic of the authoritarian nature of the political economy of techno-repression of citizens, at least the vast majority not part of the privileged class. Using AI, the neoliberal elites have redefined the status quo with

5. *https://whatistranshumanism.org/*

6. *https://www.wired.co.uk/article/darpa-arati-prabhakar-humans-machines*

7. *https://www.youtube.com/watch?v=bTMS9y8OVuY*

remarkable ease, despite downward social mobility. Far from rebelling against a social contract in which the capitalist class is hegemonic, a large segment of the middle class and workers accept the new norm, thereby acquiescing to society's autocratization.[1112]

In April 2021, EU-AIDA (Artificial Intelligence in a Digital Age) produced a report warning about AI's multifarious impact on society. *"Against this background, the rapid uptake of AI by both public and private actors coupled with the ever-increasing availability of data raises a host of questions for the future evolution of democracies within and beyond the EU. From sentiment analysis to deep fakes, AI technologies can be used to both further and disrupt democratic participation and accountability, while also potentially amplifying trends of polarization and growing authoritarianism."*[1113]

Neoliberalism's monolithic definition of what it means to be human centers around the concept of "human capital". Beyond social class, AI uses human nature's myriad of contradictions for commercial purposes. Everything from the rational and irrational tendencies in consumption and electoral politics to instinctive spontaneous reactions, carefully planned education and career decisions, and emotional ventures to self-improvement ventures, all have become narrowly boxed into neoliberal subjectivity.[1114]

With robots as the ideal workers, market efficiency in the absence of social development is inevitable and a reality under authoritarian and liberal-democratic regimes. In a dystopian neoliberal society of profits under autocratization or authoritarianism, one where the automaton is the model for humans to emulate, capitalism with the help of AI technology is recreating a society where citizens are mere observers narrowly focused on consumer rights, instead of human rights, civil rights, environmental rights, and social justice.

"The most common transhumanist thesis is that human beings may eventually be able to transform themselves into different beings with abilities so greatly expanded from the current condition as to merit the label of posthuman beings. Transhumanism is a way of thinking about the future that is based on the premise that the human species in its current form does not represent the end of our development but rather a comparatively early phase. Transhumanism is a loosely defined movement that has developed gradually over the past two decades... The alliance between global neoliberalism and transhumanism is one of the most important challenges of our time."[1115]

Francesc Torralba Roselló, the above article's author, calls for a global techno-ethics regime to defend the principles of human dignity and equality against AI under corporate and government control with the potential to create greater inequality justified in the name of progress. Ethical issues aside, social and criminal justice institutional mechanisms, and above all the media, have conditioned people to accept anything the market offers as beneficial for society. As a contemporary substitute for religion and the new catalyst to keep people in conformity, the digital era under neoliberal transformation is the new secular religion capturing aspects of heavenly transformation on earth with the assistance of the machine against human limitations and a sense of individual alienation from the totality.[1116]

AI Alienation and Neoliberal Marginalization

Along with his collaborators in *Les Temps Modernes,* Simone de Beauvoir and Maurice Merleau-Ponty (*Phenomenology of Perception,* 1945), Jean-Paul Sartre addressed existential alienation in *Being and Nothingness* (1943), a topic most fitting in the era of AI and neoliberalism that the cyber-bourgeoisie immersed in alienation have embraced. Although Sartre, de Beauvoir and Merleau-Ponty's analysis of alienation inherent in the political economy reflects Western Europe in the turbulent first half of the 20th century, the core ideas are just as applicable in the cyber-world of the early 21st century. The digital era exacerbates the layers of mass delusions and social exclusions.[1117]

Whereas the French peasant in the 13th century was presumably content in the delusion of connectedness to the divine chain of being through clerical intercession and hoped for eternal Paradise, 21st-century humans are wired to the digital market-oriented logic and the culture of neoliberal hegemony. If cyber-delusions could be even more realistic and fulfilling than the religious ones of our ancestors 1000 years ago, there is nothing to stop structural exploitation. In the name of neoliberal cyber-culture, people embrace hope and delusions more readily, not only to cope with daily life, but because in a materialistic civilization, the potential rewards are more tangible than the promise of the afterlife in the Dark Ages.[1118]

Associated with the robotic work-related life and anxiety combined with neoliberalism's commodification of humans and objects alike, self-estrangement has become far worse in the 21st-century era of AI than it was in the 1840s when Karl Marx analyzed similar themes in *"Economic and Philosophical Manuscripts";* a work on which Sartre, Merleau-Ponty and de Beauvoir relied to analyze alienation in a modern capitalist society. The combination of rising inequality on a world scale and autocratization in countries clinging to the label of 'democracy' resemble patterns of interwar socioeconomic, political, and cultural patterns, some of which Fritz Lang captures in the dystopian film *Metropolis.*[1119]

Not only is the worker an extension of the machine but her/his source of purpose and fulfillment is intertwined with work, commodified without her/his awareness. Because the social contract is universal, the individual takes it for granted that it is normal and often seeks commodification to be within the mainstream. As much during the first industrial revolution as during the digital revolution, the worker is aware at some level that of her/his role in the lower echelons of society where the elites control all institutions and enjoy privileges that they accord themselves and institutionally exclude the working class. In the era of the social and geographic digital divide, algorithms increasingly determine the nature of the autocratization society's destiny.[1120]

"Algorithms decide which news we get to see and which politicians get to target us with hyper-specific election advertising. If we get to vote, we get to vote for the change a small number of billionaires in California would like to see in the world. It's not that the machines are coming for our jobs. The capitalists are coming for our jobs and machines are the tools they use to make it happen. But they also come for our societies, our workplaces, and our ways of living and we must resist those who use technology like AI against us at every turn."[1121]

Beyond threatening human identity and promoting self-estrangement, AI and biogenetic engineering reduce not just workers but also the elites into market-ready citizen-automatons. The difference is that workers are the exploited and the elites are the exploiters under the delusion that AI entails subjugation limited to the masses. After all, the elites have the means to benefit from the latest that science and technology have to offer and to manipulate human identity by influencing the institutional mainstream and social environment. In a position to exert power algorithmically, in a world transcending the mechanisms of institutional accountability to which ordinary people are subjected at the receiving end of digital technology, the social imbalance further strengthens the elites closing ranks to consolidate power.[1122]

With the advent of cyber-technology, the entire "gaming industry" - cloud, console, mobile, PC, VR/AR, and e-sports - has skyrocketed to mirror the capitalist system's financialization. Along with the rise in gaming, substance abuse involving illegal narcotics, opioids, and other prescription drugs has seen a sharp increase among the digitally-addicted Z generation. This is especially true within the affluent social strata striving to feel human in the age of alienating virtual reality. Research has confirmed the interconnectedness of substance abuse and behavioral digital addictions. Furthermore, there is a correlation between the necroculture of which transhumanism's cybereconomy's culture is an integral part and widespread substance abuse on a world scale. [1123]

Especially since the Reagan decade of yuppie culture in the 1980s, the cyber-generation became increasingly immersed in materialism, hedonism, and atomism. For a segment of that population, despair, and alienation were certain considerations linked to illegal narcotics and prescribed antidepressants among other psychiatric drugs, especially for young people. Between 1999 and 2016, half of the US states experienced a 30% rise in suicides, almost double the overall rate of the UK, and higher than most of Europe. While there are many reasons for suicide, the culture of materialism as a substitute for self-discovery, creativity, and contributions to social justice, substance abuse, and the unrealized American Dream leads to hopelessness, emptiness, and alienation. By further isolating the individual from the community, other than what exists digitally, the neoliberal cyber world has molded the individual like the automaton.[1124]

Governments, businesses, and proponents of AI argue that the goal of the new technology has never been to use it as an agent of alienation but to build robots that serve humanity. Performing everything from menial jobs to rescue operations and improving the quality of life for all has always been the selling point. Good intentions and public relations aside, loosely regulated AI falls within the same category as the rest of the business sector, especially high-tech. As it evolved under various regimes of the neoliberal umbrella, liberal democracy has been in crisis and deepening on a world scale.[1125]

In every sector from national intelligence services to local police, government agencies track foreign enemies and domestic dissidents, political activists, journalists, human rights, and environmental groups, among other suspects challenging the status quo, even within the perimeters of the law. AI spyware technology is part of digital civilization. After the rightwing riots of 6 January 2021, the FBI used the opportunity to grant a $14 million contract to a private firm to monitor not only the various rightwing elements posing a threat to public institutions but to Black Lives Matter which the FBI had already concluded was largely a peaceful organization. The same private sector organization existing because of government security contracts also went after peaceful abortion rights protesters.[1126]

Besides government agencies, schools surveil everyone from faculty to students. Family members spy on each other, making spyware technology as routine as the microwave oven. Israeli digital tech company NSO Group and its Pegasus malware division is an excellent case of how corporations use technology as a pretext to go above the law with the consent of the state. As the technology is capable to harvest a cell phone's data and switch on a phone's camera and microphone, its capabilities bypass any law, no matter the obligatory "we respect your privacy" statements. Like Israel, other countries using NSO-Pegasus have been spying on dissidents, journalists, and politicians, and conducting industrial espionage.[1127]

Besides human rights organizations taking notice of how governments use AI, some have raised alarm bells about Silicon Valley's attempts throughout the 2010s to sell AI spyware technology to educational institutions along with online technology. Naturally, this is all in the name of an "enhanced education" experience. *"Mark Zuckerberg's [FACEBOOK CEO] $100 million effort*[1] *to remake the school system in Newark, N.J., led to allegations of corruption along with limited evidence of improvement. AltSchool, an education company backed by Zuckerberg and top venture capital firms and founded by former Google executives, started closing*[2] *its 3D-printer-equipped classrooms in 2017 and got out of the business of operating schools entirely in 2019."*[1128]

The neoliberal thesis of the commoditization of everything raises the question of humans as workers and consumers living in the neoliberal amoral universe. Focusing narrowly on the self like a robot that corporations would like for workers to emulate, the worker/consumer citizen becomes an extension of the robot, without any sense of social responsibility, other than conformity to the social contract. Among AI enthusiast researchers, there are those adopting a neo-corporatist approach to a collaborative relationship between the AI robot and the human, as though there is an equivalency between machine and human in labor relations and human rights. "*Through such collaborative intelligence,*" H. James Wilson and Paul R. Daugherty point out, *"humans and AI actively enhance each other's complementary strengths: the leadership, teamwork, creativity, and social skills of the former, and the speed, scalability, and quantitative capabilities of the latter."*[1129]

Besides science-fiction fantasies for books and motion pictures, AI-human collaboration is based on the corporation's logic seeking labor-savings mechanisms and profit maximization. If digital technology makes all tasks from online ordering to digital dating, sex, and marriage readily accessible for the right price, devaluing and exploiting human beings in the AI era is a continuation of labor-management relations, representing continuity from the first industrial revolution era.[1130]

There is nothing inevitable about the polarizing impact of AI per se, any more than there was anything inherently polarizing about the steam engine in the 18th century or electricity in the 19th century. Technology operates within the framework of the political economy, not as an enclave in a parallel universe, or in a research lab. Structurally, the relationship between technology and capital was not much different in 19th-century Western Europe amid rapid technological advances when profits doubled in Great Britain because of stagnant wages during the Second Industrial Revolution.[1131]

Promising to raise living standards along with education levels, the policies of capital concentration in the AI era have already left people without access to affordable health care, housing, and education, no matter the progress of technology. These are not issues for "machine ethics" amid the fourth industrial revolution, as some have

1. *https://www.bloomberg.com/news/articles/2012-06-28/facebook-and-newark-schools-about-the-100-million*

2. *https://www.bloomberg.com/news/articles/2017-11-01/silicon-valley-tried-to-reinvent-schools-now-it-s-rebooting*

argued as a means to distract from AI's impact on the working class. Going to the heart of the neoliberal social contract, this is a matter of human rights, social justice, and popular democracy.[1132]

Whether airport security, self-driving vehicles, or human-substitute companions, liability for malfunctioning robots will be both a legislative policy issue and a legal one that the courts sort out. Given that the judicial system on a world scale reflects the neoliberal model, manufacturers and distributors have the advantage. Civil liberties are somewhere between minimal to non-existent when cell phones, computers, smart TVs, and even headsets permit governments and corporations to monitor people, and collect and commercialize personal data. AI technology has enhanced the existing surveillance society in which government and corporations have citizens under watch for profit and power. All along, they pledge to respect privacy.[1133]

Besides surveillance and robotic systems for the private sector, the state uses surveillance technology to contain dissent, mobilize popular support for its policies, and build consensus invariably to promote programs and safeguard the social contract. Desperately trying to hide behind the very thin veil of protecting the consumer/citizen and private property, government and corporations laid the foundations of a mass surveillance culture using the post-9/11 war on terror as a pretext.[1134]

Combined with the culture of mysticism surrounding the digital universe, the convergence of national security and surveillance capitalism under the neoliberal consensus of market hegemony has resulted in high demand for digital tech products and services. Some advocates of surveillance capitalism have been trying to convince the public that paternalistic neoliberalism is the necessary byproduct of digital technology as an integral part of society's mode of operation for both domestic safety and national security.[1135]

Contrary to those focused on AI technology per se as the villain, rather than on the political economy and social relations, two public opinion polls (2007 and 2016) indicate that the majority of Americans do not fear automatons, at least, not as motion pictures and science fiction books depict them in some demonic sense. The majority is not even concerned about how some journalists and analysts depict AI's dreaded possibility of taking over in some sort of dystopian universe. Respondents are more worried about people intentionally causing harm and/or exploiting others by relying on AI as tools, rather than the algorithms and programmed robots taking over the world to impose some Hellish rule.

Because living standards have been declining in the age of the internet whose proponents had been promising techno-paradise on earth, many question whether AI would improve material conditions for the majority. In a public opinion poll conducted in 2016, 53% of respondents replied that it was important to proceed with AI research and development, while 15% agreed with scientists warning that AI is potentially dangerous to dynamic social equilibrium. Another 20% did not see the need for AI, presumably because human beings are sufficient to carry out the same tasks as robots.[1136]

Some scientists estimate that by the end of this century, AI robots will have superhuman physical strength and intellectual capabilities beyond comprehension. There is speculation that automatons will make a segment of the population more intelligent. There is also concern that automatons will diminish intellectual, creative, and physical capabilities because the machine will think and work, rendering users useless. Advocates of AI argue that as biotechnology improves, it is likely that humans will evolve along with the automatons, or rather along analogous programming functions emulating them. There is also the prospect of modification for humans who can afford a form of AI-based eugenics.[1137]

Already in the pre-AI phase of a robotic society where the hegemonic culture is conditioning robotic citizens into conformity, profits drive corporations to pursue research and development while governments have been planning for "robot-soldiers" and "robocops". All domains in society, including religion will adapt to the new norm of AI technology, just as they did with the internet. Promising to provide miracles in human health for the sake of a 'wellness society', biosynthetic engineering fits into the mold.

Ironically, according to the CDC, both mental health and life expectancy in the US decreased precipitously in the first two decades of the 21st century amid the high-tech application of medical science and the 'wellness society PR drive. This was the period coinciding with downward pressure on living standards and high health care cost justified because high tech and prescription medication drove up prices. The inadequacy of health care amid the COVID-19 pandemic was another indicator that public policy is at the heart of the problem. The chasm between the vacuous rhetoric about AI creating a 'better society', and CDC statistics illustrates the contradictions and hollowness of the neoliberal social contract.[1138]

Historically, AI has raised public policy concerns about the many dimensions of the entire social structure that the new science and technology impacts in a socially uneven manner. Amid the inevitable severe economic contraction in the next contracting cycle, the possibility of mass uprisings will not be one that robots undertake. On orders from the government, robots and human security officers will suppress workers and marginalized minority populations resisting neoliberal oppression.

'It is important to remember that AIs are statistics-based programs that are 95% accurate at most—meaning that there is a 5% chance of errors occurring. He posed the question: 'Are we willing to accept such a high degree of probability when human lives are on the line?' ... Another danger of the mass implementation of AI is widespread unemployment, particularly among those with fewer qualifications and those engaged in routine work. This could lead to a sharp increase in antisocial behavior and crime. There is also a threat to those working in creative professions; for example, in India, AI has been used to develop designs for clothes and shoes that are more appealing to consumers and have a greater range of variety."[1139]

As a tool to afford the dream of transhumanism, AI sets the wealthy apart from the rest of humanity, allowing them to live as integral parts of the privileged AI techno-universe, bypassing the misery and drudgery of ordinary people's lives. Techno-flawlessness as a way of life emulating the automatons, some of whom would have either replaced or supplemented human partners, may sound like science fiction. This is big businesses attracting massive public subsidies and private investment while playing a key role in geopolitics.

Besides Stephen Hawking, writer and commentator James Barrat, mathematician Vernon Vinge, and Swedish philosopher Nick Bostrom, among others have raised concerns about humanity's future because AI has the potential to become autonomous and mark humanity's demise. Hardly an issue of imminent apocalypse, this is not about defining human beings so narrowly that they only fit into the mold of pre-civilization hunter-gatherers, or pre-industrial era serfs serving the Lord of the manor, subordinating mind and spirit to church and superstition. Neoliberalism at the core of the political economy and the state's role in society is far more frightening than the apocalyptic predictions of scientists and philosophers; it is about underlying causes for rising inequality and authoritarianism.[1140]

In a global economy shaping culture where the means of communication are instantly bringing people together, AI will have profound ramifications working as much in favor as against the elites by disparate counterrevolutionary groups using AI to bring about authoritarianism as the solution to all problems befalling humanity. Revolutionary movements, resistance, and protests will also change because of AI. No matter what the corporate world and bourgeois politicians promise about the miracle of the digital economy and AI as society's techno-fix, the dialectic will continue where the neoliberal model leads it, rather than carving its path. With undisputed ethical and material ambiguity, AI cuts both ways, as social engineering leads to unintentional consequences while struggling to regiment workers and marginalized groups.[1141]

"Data accumulation in the current political-economic order mimics capital accumulation: It is not for anything other than just accumulation. Data culture is an obsessive pursuit of data that acquires the mythical force of a revolution servicing capital. The race to corner mammoth volumes of diverse data sets hinges on the promise of new unforeseen connections that can materialize into avenues for profit. It is produced socially but owned privately. Wealth creation in data culture is predicated on a seamless sociality that knows no boundaries – countless individuals and collectives provide data, but it is still owned privately. It thrives on differentiation. Data provides capitalism with the material engine – in the form of AI – to perfect the art of sorting, segmenting, eliminating, targeting, optimizing, and finally, simplifying capitalism's relentless endeavor to optimize difference for the reproduction of social hierarchies."[1142]

Although creativity manifested in various domains has resulted in the edification of mankind throughout history, it also extends to the domain of weapons of mass destruction that no one with a social conscience can defend, regardless of perfidious rhetoric about freedom, democracy, and national security. This is something that nuclear physicist Robert Oppenheimer discovered after realizing the atomic bomb's potential to end life on earth, as did Albert Einstein, who also committed to international peace and nuclear disarmament. As an integral part of nuclear weapons, and with the rapidly changing technology's application to nuclear warheads, AI is about mesmerizing delusional necro-fascination even though it entails the possibility of ending life on the planet.[1143]

No matter what ethicists, politicians, theologians, and scientists argue, realistically, the only voice that matters in the AI industry is that of the business sector with its considerable army of well-paid lobbyists, analysts, consultants, PR staff, lawyers, and politicians safeguarding their interests which are identical with those of the business they represent. Among others, American billionaire Mark Cuban predicts that the world's first trillionaires will be those with the ability to master all marketing aspects of artificial intelligence and derivative industries. Such an appetizing dream of economic power has many venture capitalists investing in artificial intelligence research and development, comfortably knowing that taxpayer money is heavily subsidizing the industry.[1144]

The recognition that the industry of the future is operating under neoliberalism means that AI will continue to exacerbate social, economic, environmental, and political problems throughout the world. Even if AI never existed, there is no evidence that society was headed for a neoliberal Paradise on earth, as some apologists of the transformation model contend.[1145]

Human beings gravitate toward AI for a million reasons, not the least of which is related to media and to the entire institutional establishment inculcating the idea that by using AI humans may be able to approximate godlike qualities, at least in certain tasks. There is also a fascination to experience, even vicariously, what it is like to remain forever young and powerful through a super-intelligent machine; to be potentially as close to "aesthetically perfect" as possible; to live through the machine, manipulate, and defy the laws of nature. To the capitalist class, AI will allow enjoying the privilege of master automaton in the universe. Therein are some underlying political concerns for those delusional narcissists to the degree that they may feel as invincible as they believe the AI machine to be.

"Just as we are seeing a step function increase in the spread of AI, something else is happening: the rise of ultra-nationalism, rightwing authoritarianism, and fascism. All of these movements have shared characteristics, including the desire to centralize power, track populations, demonize outsiders, and claim authority and neutrality without being accountable. Machine intelligence can be a powerful part of the power playbook" Dirk Helbing and an auguste team, including Bruno Frey (Helbing, et. al. 2017) speculated about the fate of democracy in the era of Big Data and AI, in the pages of Scientific American, and were not what one might call optimistic. Plus, Oxford researcher, Vyacheslav Polonsky, told global elites at Davos, "how artificial intelligence silently took over democracy", as if they did not already know."[1146]

The universal presence of AI necessarily means that "freedom" and self-determination for the masses are delusional coping mechanisms, added to so many others. Workers and the middle class collectively determine their destiny is nothing but a myth within and outside the digital universe. Kai-Fu Lee, president of *Sinovation Venture's Artificial Intelligence Institute*, maintains that AI will make obsolete billions of jobs in every sector and create chaos in the global economy while resulting in astronomical wealth concentration. In a winner-take-all economy, AI operating under the neoliberal model has the potential to precipitate social and political disorder amid widespread unemployment and income inequality, thereby hastening authoritarianism and a new Dark Age of inequality under the brightness of the AI universe.[1147]

CHAPTER VIII:

Neoliberal Indoctrination, the Media and Social-Media

A *Historical Overview of Journalism*

Rejecting 19th-century philosophical concepts of the individual and society found not just in the works of socialist thinkers, but even in Emile Durkheim's *"Représentations individuelles et représentations collectives"* (1898), neoliberal dogma does not acknowledge collective consciousness as a social function necessary for consensus, social morality, or a legitimate foundation for authority.[1148] Not the sole catalysts in molding public opinion, mainstream, and social media have played the most important role in normalizing the neoliberal dogma and culture which precipitates rightwing populism. Mainly focused on reinforcing social property relations, identity, and aspirations of the individual against the state's responsibility to society with collective needs, normalizing neoliberal culture has been the major task of journalism behind the mask of "serving the public". [1149]

Even before the advent of neoliberalism, television and radio, film and video, digital media and computer games, public relations and marketing, journalism, and the business of publishing operated under the broad category of mainstream media. The overriding common denominator is in inculcating the idea into the consumer-citizen that the individual is invested in the vague notion of national prosperity, regardless of the rising rich-poor gap. As long as the individual adheres to neoliberal orthodoxy, even in developing nations where opportunities are severely limited for the vast majority, the "rags to riches dream" can theoretically become a reality.[1150]

Within the context in which the press operates, serves, and reflects the institutional structure, journalism has always played a role in molding public opinion. Regardless of self-serving hypocritical liberal doctrines about free press, objectivity, and 'public service', journalism has always operated within narrow class-based ideological confines, promoting a worldview and a value system of the privileged ruling class at the core.[1151]

Historically, journalism rarely covered the world outside the elites. When it did, it was always from the perspective of the hegemonic culture. Coinciding with the rise of the nation-state – Henry VIII's War of the Roses (1485) to The Peace of Westphalia 1648 - the advent of the printing press accounted for the first newspapers representing capitalism's mercantilist phase. European merchants printed stories about business conditions, while governments issued news bulletins. In 1605, Johann Carolus published *Relation aller Fürnemmen und gedenckwürdigen Historien*, followed by Caspara van Hulten's Amsterdam-based newspaper *Courante uyt Italien, Duytslandt, &c.* in 1618.

Although news, letters, and gazettes existed in the 17th and 18th centuries sporadically in northwest Europe, circulation was very low. Largely because of the small number of literate individuals estimated at 11% in 1500, and 60% in 1750, and also of lack of access and the publications' narrow focus and limited circulation. Embryonic class-based journalism centered around issues of the emerging bankers' and merchants' role in society. It was also a platform for political and religious ideas, public policy, and the lives of famous individuals. From the genesis of the press to the present, information was always an instrument impacting public opinion and policy on behalf of the class that the publication represented.[1152]

Western journalism's ideological foundations solidified in the Age of Reason when the bourgeoisie challenged the feudal/manorial social order and absolute monarchy representing the privileged upper clergy and nobility. The bourgeois challenge culminated in the French Revolution of 1789 and the European revolutions that followed throughout the 19th century. It is hardly an enigma that journalism mirrored Lockean liberal ideology, the nascent mercantile capitalist social order, institutions, and culture rapidly changing owing to England's industrialization. Transforming mercantile capitalism on the continent, and determining social relations while influencing international relations between northwest Europe and the colonial periphery influenced Europe's self-image as journalism reflected it.[1153]

As capitalism propelled the bourgeoisie to the forefront of society, the American War of Independence and the French Revolution of the late 18th century provided the pluralist ideological foundations for modern journalism. Always in the name of free speech which Voltaire and Thomas Jefferson advocated as liberal democracy's foundation, the old regime of the aristocratic privileged order and monarchy was the target of vehement criticism. After the European revolutions of 1848, the second industrial revolution across continental Western Europe swept along the industrialization of the US and Japan. European liberal ideology and social relations accounted for the liberal-bourgeois model of journalism in the Western World and European colonies and spheres of influence.[1154]

Whether journalistic coverage pertained to Britain's role in India and South Africa, France's role in Algeria and Indochina in the 19th and 20th centuries, or US colonial rule in the Philippines (1898-1946), Western journalistic principles did not apply to non-white, non-Western marginalized population, any more than they did to the Western working class, minorities, and women. The predominantly white male capitalist class viewed inequality and marginalization as the "norm" which is what contemporary journalism reflects.[1155]

Historically, part of journalism's role has been to promote the virtues of Western liberal democracy as the ideal system best suited under capitalism's 'natural' social order of wealthy males invariably from northwest Europe. Intertwined with the widely-held belief that man can apply the laws of nature to society and create a more rational institutional structure to serve humanity, the theme of the Enlightenment was universally narrowly applied in practice. In theory, the concept was universally inclusive. In practice, it excluded workers, minorities, women, migrants, and non-whites in developed nations and the Global South, although under much worse conditions the latter compared with the former. Many Western journalism scholars project the position of the socioeconomic and political elites that there is an inexorable link between mainstream news consumption and high-minded citizenship. An empirically unsubstantiated link, this obfuscates social relations dynamics.[1156]

Unique as a business claiming to deliver non-partisan coverage, journalism carried the special burden of molding public opinion, often resorting to disinformation, especially on issues of diplomacy, war, dissident movements, and social uprisings. Projecting the image that they represent the public as a watchdog of government, church, and private institutions, the press as an integral part of the business and political class molds public opinion to conform to the social contract. Part of the reason for journalism's commercialization was the Industrial Revolution and the rise in advertising stemming from the expansion of the consumer-based economy. As readership increased with universal education and the expansion of the middle class, political parties became newspaper patrons propagating their platform to the popular base.[1157]

The late 19th – early 20th-century drive for liberal democracy expanded to include universal voting under the parliamentary system. Combined with the rise of trade unionism and workers demanding political representation, the expanding middle class on which businesses relied to stimulate the consumer economy, led to the press covering marginalized elements. Part of the Progressive Era, reformist journalism covered everything from public and private sector corruption to unrepresented working people, women, and minorities. As big capital, especially trusts and cartels, made big government bureaucracy necessary, the voices of the disenfranchised and marginalized people found some representation in journalists questioning political and business corruption, and systemic institutional discrimination as a manifestation of a dysfunctional social contract.[1158]

Reflecting late 19th-century pluralism in its nascent stage, Progressive Era journalists demanded a more inclusive and participatory political process. Amid contradictions of Western imperial expansion, the Second Industrial Revolution and the rise of mass politics ushered in the age of mass communication. This was more the case with the expanding consumer middle class in the age of business concentration when marginalized social groups received some attention but not much when it pertained to public policy systemically marginalizing labor.

Therein was the challenge of apologists for monopoly capitalism in the form of international trusts and cartels whose interests the press reflects and promotes. Representing reformist journalism, a few faint voices criticized monopoly capitalism's social impact, reverting to 18th-century liberal democracy principles.[1159] As part of a mission to mold public opinion about the integrity of a liberal-democratic society, the "Muckraker" reformers of the Progressive Era had the burden to weave ideological, political, cultural, and socioeconomic developments in journalism that reflected emerging bourgeois pluralism in mass politics.[1160]

The "free press" slogan invoking the doctrine of journalistic objectivity and projecting the image of journalism serving the 'public interest', itself subject to definition depending on who is using the term, cannot be substantiated by the historical record. Rooted in liberal philosophy implying analysis above class and politics, these lofty claims have been and remain idle efforts to win universal public trust and legitimacy. Upton Sinclair's, *The Brass Check: A Study of American Journalism* (1919) pointed to a class-based institution promoting the elite and castigating workers captures the universal essence of the real code of journalist ethics. Three years later, Walter Lippmann (*Public Opinion*) did not go along with Sinclair's pro-labor perspective but agreed that journalism necessarily entails interpretation of the news with the intent of molding public opinion.

Rarely questioning its own ideological and political assumptions and the cultural milieu within which it operates, journalism is far from abiding by a code of ethics regarding reporting from a perspective above the institutional establishment's boundaries. Operating as a business and abiding by the rules of the regime and social contract, criticism of the institutional structure takes place within those perimeters, despite the news media anointing itself defender of the public interest.

Regardless of whether the public accepts bourgeois journalism's self-serving objectivity claims, the press perpetually indoctrinates, especially on issues of social class and foreign affairs. With heavy doses of nationalism and religion as integral parts of the hegemonic culture, often from a populist perspective, the media molds and manipulates public opinion no differently than a politician, priest, or salesman, thereby subtly contributing to institutional conformity. Not surprisingly, individuals, governments, or groups of different ideological and political orientations accuse each other of indoctrination and propaganda while for themselves attributing the 'free press' and 'objectivity' labels.[1161]

Father of modern American journalism and one of neoliberalism's original ideological forces, the influential journalist and political theorist Walter Lippmann had no illusions that the press manufactured consent. Nevertheless, he defended the social order and economic system that the state faithfully served. In the 1930s, the press even refrained from criticizing Western companies doing business with the Axis Powers and right-wing dictators like Spain's Francisco Franco, and Latin American dictators like Brazil's Getulio Vargas. Diverting focus from capitalism as the root cause of social problems, and the rise of fascism and authoritarianism, during the war, mainstream American press closed ranks with arch-enemy USSR.[1162]

By the time President Truman formally launched the Cold War with the Truman Doctrine in March 1947, the US had already established an international monetary and international trade order designed to promote US commercial interests. American 'patriotic journalism', which had operated on wartime conditions, simply continued under the Cold War shifting focus from the Axis Powers to the USSR. Engendering mass international conformity to the regime of anti-communism and the capitalist system and its values became the dogma of the new Western "free press". Synonymous with anti-Communism, the term "free press" embodied the Cold War definition of democracy and citizenship and justified the Pax Americana world order against the Communist bloc.[1163]

Despite hollow claims about freedom of expression, civil rights, human rights, women's rights, minority rights, workers' rights, or any issue about social justice, the core of mainstream media's coverage and theme was always conformity to the status quo which invariably conflicted with social justice goals. Given the persecution of dissidents during the McCarthy era (1950-1954), as a pretext to impose conformity on domestic and foreign policy, journalists became an instrument of the state, in addition to falling in line with the private sector's goal of consumerism. Although the Cold War ended in 1990, self-censorship conformist journalism remained. The only form of protest journalism and news analysis emanated from within the institutional structure with its ideological, political, and cultural baggage.[1164]

Drawing parallels between the institutionalization of McCarthyism and Trumpism, historian Beverly Cage writes: *"A Republican-controlled Senate voted to censure[1] Joseph McCarthy, one of their own, after four years of lies and vitriol. In that nobler age, the story goes, McCarthy's colleagues recognized the threat he posed to democratic institutions and political fair play and voted to bring an end not only to McCarthy's reign of terror but to the broader phenomenon of McCarthyism — just as many Democrats (and more than a few Republicans) hope that Trumpism will disappear, or at least diminish, once Trump himself leaves office. But the afterlife of McCarthyism is not nearly as clear-cut x— or as comforting for Trump opponents — as the legend might suggest... Far from bringing an end to McCarthyism, the 1954 Senate vote mainly pushed it out of Washington, and a new generation of right-wing activists took up his cause."*[1165]

From Truman to Regan, the global anti-Communist crusade, like the counter-terrorism crusade from Bush to Obama, followed by the new Cold War from Obama to Biden were at least in part convenient excuses to

---

1. https://www.senate.gov/artandhistory/history/common/censure_cases/133Joseph_McCarthy.htm

engender conformity in a society that subordinated liberal democratic principles and practices, including First Amendment rights, while reinforcing the social contract. Silencing dissent of any kind that questioned anything from the corporate world to the defense establishment has always been the norm. The difficult task for bourgeois journalism has been to present the veneer of public interest, individual freedoms, and democratic principles while forging support for the institutional structure.

Not just in foreign affairs, but in every domain, from sports and cultural events, and from the strategic balance of power to the race for global market share, the ideological East-West confrontation remained the model for neoliberal-era journalism. News through print, film, radio, TV, and digital was packaged to the degree that the same story covered by opposing camps would often not have common ground even on how the events unfolded. Reflecting and promoting the social contract, media in all countries is an appendage of private business interests and the state serving those interests.[1166]

Unlike former Communist regimes, or authoritarian governments where the average person's access to news and analysis was the state-controlled media, the Western model permitted dissenting voices of progressives and trade unionists. However, this was only as long as they embraced the social contract goals and operated within the institutional structure. Always circumspect of any capitalist criticism, Western media framed social, political, economic, and cultural issues in terms of a political economy beneficial to all of society, rather than the elite. The neoliberal media and social media empires of the 21st century inherited and built on this legacy, using pluralism as the distinguishing trait and equating it with 'objectivity'.[1167]

As Alexander Safford explains, contrary to what the media in Western countries wanted the public to believe, the journalistic monolith was not confined to the Communist bloc. *"The Red Scare" campaigns of the Western media were presented on every applicable media source. The use of print with easily de-codable and emotive images helped to redefine national identity as a virtuous and patriotic America, against a dangerous and destructive socialist east. The media distributed extreme propagandist slogans such as "Better Dead than Red!" This type of politicized propaganda served to cause hysteria over communism and nuclear war (Bernhard, 1999). It worked to subdue any domestic sympathy for the enemy or resistance to the conflict that usually occurs during war. It was a calculated action to maintain public antagonism towards the enemy and rejection of their political and economic policies. The media extended the propaganda to every aspect of Western life, from radio, film, television, and print to even schools."*[1168]

To distract from structural problems in the political economy and society, including inequality, racism, and marginalization of the poor and minorities, the mass media helped to perpetuate the myth of a Western paradise of freedom, democracy, and prosperity which never matches the reality of institutionalized endemic poverty, income inequality, and social marginalization. Under neoliberalism, this trend intensified. After 1990, all countries became thoroughly integrated into the capitalist system with nationalism remaining as the salient catalyst to mobilize public support for the status quo.[1169]

Neoliberal Media Ownership: The Myth of Free Market Democratization

Ideologically, culturally, and institutionally the Cold War media culture lingered into the neoliberal era thereby contributing to class warfare. Guardian of a non-existent free market under the guise of liberal democracy, the state enjoyed favorable media coverage, and criticism only within defined perimeters. Propagating terms like freedom and democracy, the neoliberal media embraced the multifaceted class war, while minimizing and distorting news about the massive wealth transfer from labor and the middle class to the wealthiest individuals.[1170]

Under neoliberalism, the media-communications-marketing networks underwent unprecedented concentration both at the national and international levels. In the transition out of the Keynesian state and into corporate welfare, the media's role was to mold public opinion. Along with depoliticizing and marginalizing those resisting the transformation model, the media's goal was to limit the public's focus to the realm of democratic consumerism, while dismissing social change as a utopian dream of the failed Communist system. Even the restoration of the Keynesian model was an anathema to the mainstream media, as Senator Bernie Sanders discovered running for president in 2016 and 2020.[1171]

Neoliberal apologists project the view that in an open society, the media is driven by cultural pluralism, linking the corporate model to democracy. The neoliberal concept of "media democratization" in essence has meant fewer government regulations and greater private sector oligopolistic control of the media whose goal has been to mold the docile consumer-citizen. Identifying a successful democracy with the "consumer society", rather than one devoted to meeting citizens' essential needs (housing, healthcare, food, recreation, etc.), the neoliberal media distracts from social problems confronting society.

The merging of news and entertainment, especially sex and violence as depicted in video games and opinion-based sensationalized news that has become mainstream reinforces the importance of distracting and indoctrinating the public. Without examining the social contract giving rise to celebrity billionaires, the media celebrates the culture of money and fame, while society's collective welfare is always in the background.[1172]

Under neoliberal transformation, the state has been subsidizing private media outlets while privatizing public entities to reflect the business model in everything from management to editorial decisions. From Chile and Argentina to the UK and US, governments removed restrictions on media foreign or domestic ownership concentration. Under concentrated international ownership, characteristics of the neoliberal globalized media include homogeneity in management, news content delivery, and consumerist and entertainment-centered programming themes. With the very obvious intent to subordinate all issues to the individual sensational-emotionally manipulative level, as though the community only exists to conform with foreign and domestic policy, the mass media celebrates individual success and drama stories, stressing the individual over collective welfare.[1173]

As oligopolistic transnational media empires consolidated, news coverage became narrower in focus, elevating the market to the realm of idealism while demonizing the Keynesian welfare state and the working class. As

Sean Phelan notes: *"The production of a "public interest" news ecology has been undermined by various cost-cutting measures, commodifying journalism "at the expense of ideal democratic objectives"; competitive pressures have resulted in a homogenization of media attention where everyone chases the same story; and journalists have been forced to adapt to a commercial environment where they are increasingly reliant on public relations source material, a regime of "news production more akin to creative cannibalization than the craft of journalism". These developments become symptomatic of a neo-liberalized news culture."*[1174]

A global phenomenon with media empires promoting the same message about neoliberal policies, ownership concentration drowned out dissent at a time of lofty claims about freedom of expression and pluralism, made possible in part by digital technology. Neoliberal transformation promoted the idea that conformity is not a deviation from the "democratic norm" but a natural evolution in harmony with the marketplace and continuation of how market-based media operated even before the Thatcher-Reagan era.

The global privatization wave of public companies that started in the 1980s and 1990s coincided with the nascent phase of the internet which formalized the media's role by reinforcing neoliberalism and hastening the twilight of the weakened Keynesian state. When Thatcher privatized British Telecom (BT), the British media as well as Reagan supporters and neoliberal academics from prestigious universities proclaimed that "peoples' capitalism" marked the beginning of Socialism's end. Immersed in the neoliberal ideology, neither the press nor neoliberal academics bothered to investigate beyond the surface to determine the degree to which privatized BT served the public interest. This was especially important not only because private companies' only goal is maximizing profit with minimal social accountability, but to secure government subsidies while clinging to the free market and efficiency myths.[1175]

Not surprisingly, the media never informed the public that privatization necessarily entailed the weakening of trade unions, a reduction of the workforce, sharply reducing the top tax rate for the rich, and government subsidizing privatization through tax cuts. Reinforcing privatization, the mass media's position reflected that of the OECD, IMF, World Bank, and stock markets cheering privatization as ostensibly "serving the public".

Privatization and outsourcing in every sector from hospital cleaning services to energy, from municipal bus services to prisons turned out to be highly costly and a burden to the taxpayer with minimal public accountability. Nevertheless, the media rarely focused on privatization disasters. Neither did academics praise the "democratization of capitalism", a euphemism for neoliberal deregulation investment policies that Thatcher and Reagan were promoting.[1176]

Claims of free speech and cultural pluralism notwithstanding, the media's rapid consolidation permitted fewer voices of expression while continuing to perpetuate the illusion of free choice. Whereas in 1983, fifty companies owned 90% of the US media market, by 2016 just six companies owned 90% - corporate giants Disney, Viacom-CBS, Time Warner-AT&T, Comcast, News-Corp, Hearst, and Gannett. Whereas in 1995 it was illegal by FCC rules for any company to own more than 40 radio stations, in 2016 Clear Channel (iHeartCommunications) owned more than 1200 stations, in a field of about 15,000.[1177]

"A 2003 study in the Columbia Journalism Review found that there were 45 of the same members on the boards of directors of Time Warner (a controlling conglomerate at the time now owned by AT&T), Viacom, and Disney. Additionally, the main conglomerates share 141 joint ventures, for example, Hulu, which is owned by both Disney

and Comcast. This means that these companies can create an echo chamber, projecting the same ideas and working together to advance mutual interests."[1178]

Tax policy is one area where the government has leverage over the media. It is no secret that the Bush administration used tax leverage with the media to secure more favorable coverage on both domestic and foreign policy, especially to prepare the public for the invasion of Iraq where the US claimed there were weapons of mass destruction and an enclave of jihadist terrorism posing a threat to the Western World and nuclear-armed Israel.

Because it had a financial and political incentive at a time when all other media had fallen in line, Viacom, the parent company of CBS, caved to administration pressure. This does not mean that the media's sole incentive has been financial, nor that it is not in the advertisers' interest for the media to promote the military-industrial complex. Making a profit while promoting neoliberal ideology and keeping the citizenry in conformity to the institutional structure has been and remains the media's central goal. Technology has helped in this regard, as it is difficult for the consumer-citizen to avoid the ubiquitous ideological net that the media represents.[1179]

Indicative of the core countries responsible for the neoliberal transformation's global reach, Chile's case provides a clear illustration of how public policy molded the media under the neoliberal model while projecting the image of pluralism. Under the US-backed Chilean military dictator Augusto Pinochet (December 1974-March 1990), the media provided a test case for other countries to pursue IMF and "Chicago School" neoliberal guidance.

"The decline of both media diversity and social mobilization during the Chilean transition are interrelated manifestations of the limitations of neoliberal democracy. Although the Chilean media no longer face the overt repression that killed or disappeared 40 journalists and communication workers, sent another 300 into exile, and left approximately 1,000 more unable to find work (Uribe, 1998: 31), the dramatic decline of media diversity since 1990 highlights the Concertación's (Concertación de Partidos por la Democracia, center-left coalition) failure to treat the media as a crucial democratic site whose openness to all sectors of civil society should be actively supported by public policy. Instead, the Concertación's embrace of the neoliberal conception of media democratization has facilitated national and transnational corporate control of the principal means of public expression and consolidated a consumerist, entertainment model incompatible with the democratic need for a diverse and vigorous public sphere." [1180]

In the dictatorship's aftermath in the 1990s, the *Concertación* regime provided neoliberalism the 'democratic' legitimacy it lacked during the Pinochet dictatorship. The media went along promoting neoliberalism's legitimacy, especially with the privatized retirement funds of the *Administradora de Fondos de Pensiones* (AFP), projecting the impression that social stability and harmony were compatible with the neoliberal model.[1181]

The media's role was the same in Argentina where structural adjustment (austerity program) became policy under the advice of IMF, World Bank, the US government, and 'the Chicago boys' neoliberal economists. Like Chile's *Concertación* regime, the conservative neoliberal regime of Argentina's Carlos Menem (1989-1999) introduced legislation to transform the media. Once severe economic dislocation resulted in a 10% drop in GDP and 17% official unemployment in 2002-03, against Latin America's 2% GDP growth and 11% unemployment, the media limited its criticism to specific individuals and policies.[1182]

Like other governments, President Menem used IMF austerity as the pretext to pursue neoliberal policies. This included the privatization of two state-owned TV stations, and authorizing telephone and media companies to corner the market on cable channels. Because the media was itself an integral part of the neoliberal model, as Pablo Castagno explains below, its only mandate was self-preservation. Continuing to promote the failed political economy, and the IMF austerity program, regardless of its impact on the middle class and workers, the media was nothing less than neoliberal transformation's PR instrument.

"In addition, Menem's legislation on foreign investments pampered the movement of capital in and out of the media market... Fifty-three new treaties on foreign investments established the state's equal treatment of foreign and national capital as well as authorized international investors to repatriate profits and capital without barriers. Menem's neoliberal policy thus facilitated media centralization and concentration, and on a transnational basis no less."[1183]

As the neoliberal transformation altered the global media landscape, the most noticeable aspect was the homogenized structure of the oligopolistic sector and news coverage focused on "analysis" and lifestyle-cult of personality perspectives, intertwined with consumerist culture that included everything from reality games to cooking programs and embedded commercial advertisements. While all 'fluff media' may seem innocuous, Despina Stratigakos (*Hitler at Home,* 2017) points out that such press coverage helped to indoctrinate German citizens who brought to power the Third Reich responsible for WWII and the Holocaust.[1184]

From propagating in favor of lower taxes for the rich to justifying US and NATO-initiated invasions and declaring militarily weak countries "national security" threats to those with nuclear warheads in their arsenal, the neoliberal media has been relentless not just in what and how it covers, but what it excludes from the coverage. News stories and events dealing with systemic injustice, legislation making it difficult for workers to unionize, and court decisions favoring corporations against government regulation affecting anti-trust issues all go through the neoliberal pro-market filter. Neoliberal constitutionalism entered the dictionary not just in the US, but all around the world where corporations use the same marketplace hegemony over the state and society.[1185]

Historically under business control, journalism has also served political parties and some trade unions in Europe and Latin America. Under neoliberalism, the homogenized mainstream media and social media fell under the control of billionaires owning corporate empires across national borders with the ability to influence public policy and the course of politics. Agents of the transformation's global reach, media empires are also the catalyst of cultural imperialism.[1186]

In 2016, the *Media Pluralism Monitor* published a study concluding that the absence of transparency prevented the public from knowing who owns what and how ownership concentration has prevented diversity of information. Some social scientists raised similar issues about billionaire media ownership and what it means for democracy. Fifteen billionaires own US mainstream media and seven own social media. As much in the US as in the rest of the world, media ownership concentration, lack of transparency, a legal system protecting the billionaires amid an incessant class war, and lack of corporate accountability coincided with the rise of the internet that companies used as a pretext for both content and labor-management decisions.[1187]

Naturally, there is a glaring contradiction between what neoliberal apologists claim about information democratization and reality, especially in social media where far rightwing ideology has played a role in the rise of populist neoliberal demagogues like Modi, Bolsonaro, and Trump, to mention only a few. Difficult to reconcile media concentration with democracy, those in the corporate media criticize the monopoly of state-dominated media in Russia, China, North Korea, and Iran where the state suppresses dissent and engages in propagandist versions of news more crudely presented than those in the West.

There is no such criticism for similar practices in Western-supported Saudi Arabia and many Afro-Arab countries practicing press censorship. The Western media criticized the Saudi government for ordering *Washington Post* reporter Jamal Khashoggi's assassination (October 2018), and the Israeli government's responsibility for Shireen Abu Akleh's assassination (*Al Jazeera,* May 2022). However, there is much greater reluctance to US policy that keeps both the Middle Eastern countries well-armed despite their human rights records.[1188]

Either from the populist right or from the liberal-pluralist perspective, corporate media empires often engage in obfuscation about structural exploitation by attacking politicians and rival news organizations for 'unbalanced coverage' or editorial decisions that cover up and/or distort news stories. The sharp rise in "fact-checking" as part of news organizations emerged out of the need not to become more balanced in reporting and stop news role in manufacturing consent, but rather as a PR exercise in support of the news organization doing the 'fact-checking'. There is also the role of the government which will provide a false or distorted story to a news organization that will never fact-check it on national security grounds. Because the media relies on advertising revenue, business promotion and government policy are intertwined in forging consensus on public policy while criticism is within the neoliberal and foreign policy perimeters.[1189]

Neoliberal media's self-serving proclamations about the "democratizing" effect on society fly in the face of authoritarianism's global rise that the media has helped to promote. The spike in far rightwing groups and political parties is one of the many contradictions of media democratizing effects. Refusing to acknowledge that the liberal elites have contributed to systemic material conditions under neoliberalism, liberal media analysts blame a revolution in values, thus, deflecting attention away from economic exploitation.[1190]

Praising social media and the internet for their "democratizing" role, many politicians, journalists, academics, and business commentators decried burdensome government regulation as an obstacle when in fact corporate control of public policy has been ubiquitous. According to a Council of Europe study: *"All democracies are undergoing unprecedented levels of media change. This change has been accompanied by a gradual decline in trust in news sources. According to the Oxford Reuters Foundation, 44% of survey respondents claim that in general, they trust the news. Levels of trust in new media are lower than those in traditional media. Only 34% of respondents say they trust news they find via search and fewer than a quarter (23%) say they trust the news they find in social media."*[1191]

A look behind the hollow rhetoric of democracy provides a clear illustration that both mainstream and social media have strengthened the far right while weakening the progressive center and the left. This is the reason that progressive politicians and activists around the world have expressed concern about the decline of liberal democracy. Like social media, mainstream media has contributed to the rise of far rightwing governments and political parties by distracting the public with identity politics and culture wars amid a relentless class war, all along benefiting from neoliberal fiscal, monetary, and labor policy.[1192]

After the election of Thatcher and Reagan, media globalization entailed cultural hybridity as a means of local market integration. Catering to specific groups, hybridity tailored to local customers focused on ideology and merchandizing neoliberal strategies with which people in a given culture have an emotional connection. Besides profits, the pluralist neoliberal media's ideological goal of globalization has been to alter the way that audiences as diverse as Latin Americans, Eastern Europeans, and East Asians develop similar tastes for media consumption under a hybrid model of content and style; in essence, cultural homogenization and institutional norm substitution to suit the neoliberal globalization framework.[1193]

Neoliberal Indoctrination and the Illusion of Popular Consent

More in the trans-Atlantic core than in the periphery, the media's self-ascribed role as society's guardian desperately tries to project the image of objectivity, neutrality-truth-based reporting, integrity, and public service. Under a thin veil of "public interest", billionaire media owners are accountable to investors and advertisers, and arch-defenders of the neoliberal model that maintains their privileged status. On everything from fiscal and monetary policy to public health and minimum wage; and from corporate welfare vs. social welfare, the media follows no mandate other than presenting all coverage to fit the mold of the social contract aiming at mass conformity.[1194]

In June 2023, the shake-up of top CNN executives was the result of corporate failure to make the company profitable, while also tilting its ideological compass to the right. Libertarian billionaire John Malone, a corporate board member in the company (WBD) that owns CNN, demanded that CNN emulate FOX. Hence, the disastrous Trump interview in April 2023, was intended to give the GOP candidate a forum on a liberal forum, but also the dismissal of anti-rightwing journalists.

Choosing Chris Licht to head the news organization was intended as a signal that the FOX model was on the way, justified presumably because it would bring in viewers and, thus, advertising revenue. Licht's mission was to make the cable news company profitable. Still, there were various modalities under which this goal could have been accomplished, rather than the chosen right under the veil of pluralism. Billionaire board member Malone had resolved that the only road to profitability was to tilt toward the right while maintaining the hollow image of pluralism.[1195]

Indispensable to capital accumulation beyond its role in mass consumption, the media is valuable for indoctrinating the masses into the market economy's ideology and tilting its focus away from the ongoing class war. It is hardly a coincidence that the rise of infomercials took place in the mid-1980s after the Reagan administration's Federal Communications Commission removed regulations regarding TV content. Projecting the illusion that class domination and ideological hegemony constitute 'public service', the media is key to forging consensual social dominance and market hegemony. Above all, the media's most important role has been to convince the public that rising inequality, poverty, and marginalization are the fault of individuals and population growth overtaking economic growth; never the political economy's structural impediments.[1196]

Amid the breakdown of the liberal consensus crisis resulting in sociopolitical polarization, neoliberal logic drives the media to tailor the news based on ideology and class warfare obfuscated by identity politics. Paradoxically, in the post-truth era, as part of the institutional structure, the media has inadvertently contributed to discrediting itself, which has helped the rise of authoritarianism. In a global public opinion survey conducted in 2022, 67% responded that journalists deliberately exaggerate and mislead the public. Beyond the ratings issue, media coverage and analysis aim at forging mass consensus amid class warfare and public confidence crisis in the social contract.[1197]

In an article intended as self-reflection, the online magazine *Politico* published several short media critics' articles touching on many causes about the young generation growing up in a social swamp. "*By 2035, most adults will have no memory of a time before polarized cable news coverage, Instagram, Snapchat, TikTok, and endless other attention-grabbing media sources yet to be invented... Most Americans will be in the swollen ranks of the informationally adrift — those lacking the means or energy to discern meaningful signals amid a cacophony that encompasses serious journalism, opinion writing, perpetual hot takes, corporate advertising, paid promotions, bloviations, disinformation, and propaganda campaigns, much of which is deliberately disguised to sound like something else. A final group will be informationally marooned — in the thrall of conspiracy theories and fakery reinforced by the archipelago-like fragmentation of social media that makes them almost impossible to reach with the truth."*[1198]

Some critics writing for *Politico* noted that hedge funds acquiring news outlets have resulted in media concentration reflecting the general trend of capital concentration and social inequality. Others criticize rising authoritarianism stifling independent journalism, amid a frenzy in entertainment news and decline in professional journalists. Naturally, not a single critic in *Politico* touched on how media reflects and promotes the social contract, regardless of social class differences within the same framework.

Mass indoctrination is as old as civilization when the first political, social, and religious elites demanded that the majority worship within a hierarchical religious and sociopolitical structure to achieve conformity in return for earthly and heavenly rewards, if not to escape punishment for non-conformity. In the age of neoliberalism, commodification of everything, including self-commodification, has been part of indoctrination, itself big business.

Coinciding with the ascendancy of digital technology applied to everything from geopolitically sensitive intelligence to the evening news, the media has a tighter grip on molding society than at any time in history. The neoliberal indoctrination formula is more or less the same as in the age of the Keynesian state. Digital technology has made everything easier, faster, more ubiquitous, and more effective on a world scale. However, it is neoliberal policies that account for media and social media monopolies as vehicles that the political and financial elites use to pave the way for authoritarianism.[1199]

Contrary to the liberal view that populist rightwing political parties are mainly responsible for mass indoctrination, the liberal-democratic camp also employed similar strategies. To achieve transformation, neoliberalism's triumph has been its ability to adapt to conditions among disparate social groups and countries. The effectiveness of indoctrination has been to convince the public that the very system responsible for the political economy impacting peoples' work, health, and education is the best possible and not the root cause of systemic flaws.

According to Rainer Mausfeld, the mass psychology of neoliberalism helps to explain indoctrination which the mass media has helped to spread throughout the world. *"Neoliberalism causes one disaster after another worldwide. In a seemingly paradoxical way, it emerges stronger out of every disaster and is immediately recommended as a "therapy." Neoliberalism not only nourishes crises but is nourished by crises and capitalizes on its inner contradictions and inconsistencies. Rather it [neoliberalism] aims at a radical redistribution from bottom to top, from public to private hand, and from South to North. To achieve this, it has to leave economically weak individuals or states without any protection to the forces of the "market" and at the same time ensure proper framing conditions are provided the economically strong for increasing their capital."*[1200]

In the age of information, digital technology and social media afford users access to all kinds of information and misinformation instantly on the web around the world. This means that propaganda today under the liberal bourgeois regime is far more effective than it was in 1945 when many countries still had censorship. A poll conducted by Ifop in May 1945, in liberated French territory, showed that people were well aware of the balance of power and the role of the Allies in the war, despite the difficulty under the occupation to access reliable news.

A clear majority of 57% replied that the USSR had contributed the most to the German defeat. The US and UK received only 20% and 12% respectively; a reality reflected in the deal between FDR and Stalin at the Tehran meeting in 1943. Public opinion polls conducted in 1994, 2004, and May 2015, the era of neoliberal pluralism, indicate that people believe that the US made the majority contribution to defeating Nazi Germany, not the USSR. This is indicative of the media's power of indoctrination.[1201]

Regardless of its systemic failures in society and regardless of government or country, neoliberal apologists are relentless in propagating from multiple platforms with the greatest public access. Not due to lack of trying, but rising inequality and autocratization have made it difficult for the mainstream media to convince the public that the world is enjoying the benefits of the neoliberal model. Max Rose and F. R. Baumgartner's empirical study of media coverage on poverty provides an excellent case of how framing the issue mirrors the political trends.

"Several studies have examined the connections between changing elite discourse, public opinion, and the national agenda on poverty policy. However, not all have suggested that shifting public opinion led to policy change. [Martin] Gilens [Why Americans Hate Welfare] (1999) argues that the media's disproportionate tendency to show welfare recipients as blacks, starting in the mid-1960s, has led directly to public misconceptions of the poor and a decrease in public support."[1202]

Even when it resorts to self-criticism, the media projects an image of a socially conscious "public servant" while turning a profit by framing news stories and analysis to promote an economic, social, and political agenda. To present the dreaded reality that tomorrow is likely to be worse than the day before under the existing social contract would only agitate the masses against the political and social elites.

Hence, the media's ceaseless quest to forge consensus around the same discredited neoliberal model has failed in its promise of sustaining liberal democracy and delivering economic benefits for workers and the middle class. Whether presenting the news entertainingly and sensationally based on hope and aspirations, or in a polemical opinion-heavy style as is the case with cable news, talk radio, and podcasts, the goal is ratings while trying not to lose credibility in the neoliberal era of pluralist vs. rightwing challenges of fake news.[1203]

Not just the world of corrupt political climate marked by extremism with the rise of the KKK, but journalism also resembles the Roaring Twenties. During the decade that culminated in the Great Depression, marketing became as popular with business and politics. Edward Bernay's *Propaganda* (1928) was as influential as Bruce Barton's *The Man Nobody Knows* (1925). Unlike Barton relying on the Bible to market corporate capitalism, Bernays used Freudian psychology when he wrote: "*If we understand the mechanism and motives of the group mind, it is now possible to control and regiment the masses according to our will without them knowing it.*"

Normalized as part of the daily routine, like drinking coffee in the morning while reading, listening, or watching news stories with slanted analysis and populist hype, even those skeptical of the media's role in society are profoundly influenced by its multi-dimensional mechanisms intended to foster loyalty to neoliberal institutions. Intertwined with social media whose journalistic standards are very low and misinformation very high, mainstream media in print and online remains important in shaping peoples' world-view.

Heavily influenced by ideology and the profit-motive, mainstream and social media feed off each other and work within the confines of the same neoliberal mode. The apparent 'unfiltered nature' of social media allows mainstream media to claim journalistic legitimacy and a bit higher level of integrity. Its short history shows that it has been an instrument of rightwing propaganda globally, despite allowing progressive voices that afford it a cloak of legitimacy.[1204]

In the quest to forge public consensus, government regulatory and fiscal policy has been the catalyst in transnational media conglomerates which in turn influence transformation policy and impact society. Pertaining both to private and publicly-funded media, the BBC is among the more significant entities in the Western world, which serves the same neoliberal model as any financial institution, government, or the IMF and World Bank. Because competitive performance criteria apply as much to publicly-funded media as to private companies, there is hardly any difference not only in what news they cover and the manner of coverage but how the entire operation is geared to promote the neoliberal logic of marketplace hegemony.[1205]

In *"Michelle Foucault, The birth of biopolitics: Lectures at the College de France, 1978-79,"* Toby Miller argues that neoliberalism has been as successful in reshaping peoples' minds as Christianity, Islam, colonialism, and Marxism. He adds: *"The grand contradiction of neoliberalism was its passion for intervention in the name of non-intervention... Neoliberalism's lust for market conduct extended to a passion for comprehending and opining on every topic imaginable, from birth rates to divorce, from suicide to abortion, and from performance-enhancing drugs to altruism. Nothing could be left outside the market, and nothing left to the chance that market relations might falter absent policing."[1206]*

The neoliberal dogma of everything within the market, nothing outside the market, and nothing against the market naturally extends to the media which plays a role in inculcating it into the public consciousness. At the urging of media companies, the considerable efforts of the state to redefine the media's role facilitate transformation across the globe, in many cases using austerity as the pretext under exigent monetary policy conditions. In South Korea, the media adopted the neoliberal model following the financial crisis of 1997-98 when IMF-style austerity resulted in a massive transfer of public capital to strengthen private banks.

Beginning with President Kim Dae-jung's (1998-2003) neoliberal reforms of health care to social policies, the media underwent a makeover to reflect the waning welfare state. Although as a presidential candidate, Kim questioned IMF fiscal austerity, he immediately embraced it as president. From 1998 to 2020, the neoliberal wave in the media led to increased restrictions on independent journalism. To muzzle news coverage about the working class opposing the neoliberal regime, the government and business supporters resorted to misinformation. Winning the Nobel Prize for Peace for his support of democracy and human rights, Kim's term overlapped with Clinton and Blair's. Like his Western counterparts who facilitated neoliberalism's institutionalization under the liberal pluralism and globalization banner, Kim fits into the same mold that led to rightwing populism.[1207]

Analyzing the marriage of technology[1] and rightwing populism, rejecting the Enlightenment[2] values and institutions of liberal democracy[3], Jeffrey Herf's *Reactionary Modernism*, (1984) examines how interwar

1. https://en.wikipedia.org/wiki/Technology

2. https://en.wikipedia.org/wiki/Age_of_Enlightenment

3. https://en.wikipedia.org/wiki/Liberal_democracy

Germany adopted the path leading to Nazism[4]. Finding expression in neoliberalism, reactionary modernism is an integral part of the rightwing media, also present in liberal media.[1208]

More social-democratic with neo-corporatist elements, Scandinavian countries followed a somewhat similar path as South Korea transitioning from the Keynesian state to neoliberalism which impacted the media's role. Not just the media's ideological orientation, but its organization and goal to serve the market while proclaiming 'objectivity' and society's collective good. Even in Sweden, the media transitioned along with the rest of the private and public sector institutions. The transformation took place even though the Nordic countries retained the most robust welfare system against the tide of neoliberalism sweeping many countries from Latin America to the US and the former Soviet republics.[1209]

In pursuit of privatization and deregulation, a collaborative relationship developed between the media and the state with the latter providing tax breaks and corporate subsidies. An integral part of the transformation, the state-media relationship reflected the mainstream political parties' agreement on neoliberal goals. As political parties, including social democrats and varieties of center-leftists, embraced neoliberalism, the media promoted transformation under the globalization label. This was throughout Western Europe, more so in Sweden and Denmark, than in Norway and Finland. Despite a long-standing tradition of maintaining a strong commitment to social democracy, the Scandinavian media became an instrument of the neoliberal elite advocating the removal of obstacles to finance capitalism's path and greater global integration.[1210]

Under the neoliberal model, the media has gone beyond the commercial culture and lifestyle emphasis as distraction and replacement for salient issues impacting the lives of the middle class and working class. Beyond the realm of conglomerates, like the Murdoch group influencing the global rightwing political landscape in Australia, the UK, and the US, programming and editorial policy in more than two dozen countries resembles the Murdoch group's rightwing networks.

The differences between the blatant propagandistic nature of the media in authoritarian societies and its pluralist counterpart in "liberal democracies" are only noticeable because the two camps within the neoliberal media vociferously criticize each other in a self-serving manner unaware of the underlying hypocrisy. Stylistics and degrees of subtleness in propaganda notwithstanding, neoliberal journalism patterns and themes are similar in Japan as in Germany, the US, Australia, Turkey, Indonesia, Brazil, and Chile.

"The decline of both media diversity and social mobilization during the Chilean transition are interrelated manifestations of the limitations of neo-liberal democracy. Although the Chilean media no longer face the overt repression that killed or disappeared 40 journalists and communication workers, sent another 300 into exile, and left approximately 1,000 more

unable to find work (Uribe, 1998: 31), the dramatic decline of media diversity since 1990 highlights the Concertación's failure to treat the media as a crucial democratic site whose openness to all sectors of civil society should be actively supported by public policy. Instead, the Concertación's embrace of the neoliberal conception of media democratization has facilitated national and transnational corporate control of the principal means of public expression and consolidated a consumerist, entertainment model incompatible with the democratic need for a diverse and vigorous public sphere."[1211]

4. https://en.wikipedia.org/wiki/Nazism

Along with the private sector, the state uses the media as the catalyst for institutional conformity. From Chile to Dubai where neoliberalism adapted to local traditions within which the elites created a world city-corporation accommodating mainstream and social media, mass indoctrination is a big profitable business as well as an instrument of the privileged class in its support of class war.[1212]

As part of its commitment to globalization, Dubai "globalized" the media sector shortly after 9/11. Sheik Maktūm bin Rāshid Āl Maktūm (House of Al Maktoum) launched Dubai Media City in 2002, offering tax breaks, government subsidies, minimal regulation, and the latest technology support. Just as he was making millions advising former Soviet bloc countries to transition into neoliberalism, Jeffrey Sachs was also active in the Gulf States with the same transformation model message. Because of 9/11, several Arab capitalists, CNN, Reuters, Sony, Showtime, and Media City, reallocated investments from the US and EU to Dubai offering multiple incentives and a modern infrastructure.[1213]

Like many countries adopting the neoliberal model, the House of Al Maktoum and its inner circle determining the course of the media in Dubai used the pretext that new technology was driving everything, including the media and social media rapidly making headway. With the advent of social media, which by 2020 was far more powerful and influential than the mainstream media, neoliberal apologists, especially corporate investors, argued that this new platform was proof of a democratized forum across the world when in fact history proved that it promoted the rise of authoritarianism.[1214]

Focused on a combination of business promotion and individualized-shared experiences, social media became a massive global forum. Besides its use for commercial purposes, raw news stories, and everything from social and cultural issues, also unfiltered, to "likes-dislikes", virtual friends, and "digital feelings", all promoted the global 'selfie culture' based on vicarious experiences. From lifestyles to the environment, often devoid of empirical or scientific framework, and often catering to the common denominator of vanity and narcissism, the hollowness of digital likes, friendships, and feelings had millions of people convinced that they are not as alone in the world. [1215]

"Social media encourages continuities of the self," Michelle Gorea observes, *"where the dedication to authenticity work and looking practices to ensure that one's visual self is interpreted as authentic by parents, friends, or imagined others is overwritten by detoxes or cleanses at life course transitions further speaks to the malleability of the visual self. However, the perceived malleability of the visual self does not mean that gendered or classed expectations have disappeared." [1216]*

A manifestation of the hedonistic culture that corporations have been promoting as the core theme in neoliberal ideology, social media exploits human vulnerabilities for profit, while giving a platform to rightwing propaganda, along with faint voices of dissidents to maintain pluralism's facade. In the postmodernist era of anti-intellectualism and cultural relativism, personal experiential instances, opinions, and feelings become a substitute for valid news coverage and analysis.

The consumer-citizen relates at the emotional level, affording political parties, especially authoritarian neoliberals, the opening to propagate more effectively. As an integral part of exclusionary rightwing populism finding expression in social media, the rise of the global "fake news-post-truth" phenomenon was as inevitable as public confidence decline in the mainstream media. Interestingly, the neoliberal pluralists and populists have been responsible for undermining public confidence in mainstream media owing to their turf culture wars that distracted from the ongoing class war.[1217]

Media Credibility under the Neoliberal Model

Despite multiple factors in its favor, the mass media has an image problem. Based on a Gallup poll in 2021, only 32% of Americans trust the mass media to report the news accurately and fairly. This percentage is the lowest since 1972, and it reflects a trend across the entire Western World. Some polling organizations rank public trust in media in the single digits. Despite acknowledging the media's lack of credibility, respondents continue to rely on it for news and analysis which shapes their views and contributes to cynicism about mainstream institutions and de-politization.[1218]

Receiving unfiltered news through social media outlets, those under thirty are more comfortable with online interactivity and apparent diversity, as well as with readily available narrowly focused groups engaged in personal opinions of news stories. Ironically, the mainstream media recirculates select content from social media which it criticizes; a transparent tactic on the part of mainstream media to remain competitive for market share, especially with younger people.[1219]

European opinion polls show a fairly high level of trust in publicly-controlled media organizations, especially in northwest Europe in comparison with southern Europe, but a very low trust level in privately-owned media. After the assassination of investigative journalist Daphne Caruana Galizia in Malta in 2017, the EU commissioned a study on media pluralism and the degree of ownership concentration. Well-known for money laundering, nepotism, and mafia business operations involving intermittent violence, Malta is an EU member. Like the rest of the EU, Malta has been pursuing neoliberal policies enmeshed with organized criminal activity involving individuals from different countries.[1220]

The extreme cases such as Malta where assassination is a last resort are made worse by the mainstream media failing to expose neoliberalism which has blurred the lines between organized crime and legal activities, the latter in many cases far worse as it facilitates organized crime globally with money laundering and sheltering operations. Empirical evidence suggests that mainstream media is undermining its credibility by representing narrow class interests and selectively recirculating social media stories that inadvertently undercut public trust. Beyond the usual liberal-conservative divide regarding the mainstream media, the neoliberal model has been responsible for the erosion of public trust. This is partly because of the lack of substantive differences between the two camps and the apparent elitism and hypocrisy in liberal media.[1221]

In *Manufacturing Consent: The Political Economy of the Mass Media* (1988), Edward S. Herman and Noam Chomsky concluded that the ideologically-driven corporate media has a long-standing history of indoctrination while all along claiming journalistic objectivity. This is especially true of the *New York Times* which Chomsky dismissed as "pure propaganda", although he concedes solid reporting in science and the environment. For its part, the *New York Times* claims that its journalistic methods and goals are carried out by 'objective' reporters, news analysts, and editors. Such claims assume that the company's operation transcends an ideological, political, and cultural setting. Somehow by magic, the newspaper is above the corporate environment which keeps the paper listed on the New York Stock Exchange.[1222]

On 8 August 2016, the *New York Times* published an article entitled *"Trump is Testing the Norms of Objectivity in Journalism"*. Implying that the newspaper upholds objective journalistic standards, this is the same newspaper that repeatedly castigated Senator Bernie Sanders, while supporting Wall Street-defense establishment neoliberal candidate Hillary Clinton in 2016 and Joe Biden in 2020. Addressing the paper's self-proclaimed objectivity, former *New York Times* reporter Christopher Hitchens noted that the paper's motto *"All the News That's Fit to Print"* makes a mockery of the concept of the idealized notion of fair and balanced journalism dedicated to the public interest beyond the narrow confines of Wall Street and the defense industry.

"I imagine most readers of the canonical sheet have long ceased to notice this bannered and flaunted symbol of its mental furniture. I check every day to make sure that the bright, smug, pompous, idiotic claim is still there. Then I check to make sure that it still irritates me. If I can still exclaim, under my breath, why do they insult me what do they take me for and what the hell is it supposed to mean unless it's as complacent and conceited and censorious as it seems to be, then at least I know I still have a pulse. You may wish to choose a more rigorous mental workout but I credit this daily infusion of annoyance with extending my lifespan."[1223]

At international conferences that corporate sponsors underwrite, including think tanks with a very clear ideological and political orientation, journalists, especially from US corporate-owned media organizations where reporting and analysis fall within the prescribed ideological and sociopolitical perimeters, Western journalists dogmatically insist on objectivity which they never practice and they know it because that is how they keep their jobs. Interestingly, many schools of journalism in US universities are usually named after corporations or wealthy donors whose donations invariably influence the school of journalism's ideology.

It especially defies credulity to have journalists and professors of journalism claim objective journalism when they know that they would not be employed if their work did not fall within the neoliberal model. This is exactly what Christopher Hitchens discovered when the *New York Times* dismissed him. Rachel Donaldo of *The Atlantic* magazine has argued that the objectivity theme is riddled with contradictions. This is largely because of the opinion-driven business model of neoliberal journalism, especially prevalent in the US. At the core of the objectivity proclamation rests the mainstream media's dictum: *"Trust us for the news but come to us for the opinions."*[1224]

In an article published in 2013, *New York Times* economics analyst Paul Krugman praised Milton Friedman, calling his version of neoliberalism "realistic" as though the European or other versions lack 'realism' in promoting the capitalist class and keeping the masses docile. The paper then paid homage to Friedman's "realistic" neoliberal ideology by convening twenty-two "experts" made up of corporate CEOs, neoliberal economists, and corporate-sponsored think tank analysts to determine the realism of Friedman's neoliberal philosophy applicable in both theory and practice. Martin Lipton, senior partner at the law firm Wachtell, Lipton, Rosen & Katz, stated that: *"the Friedman doctrine has been widely eroded, as a growing consensus of business leaders, investors, policymakers and leading members of the academic community have embraced stakeholder capitalism as the key to sustainable, broad-based, long-term American prosperity. ... Stakeholder governance is the bedrock of American capitalism now and in the future."*[1225]

From the 1970s to the Great Recession of 2008, the concept of shareholder capitalism which Freidman promoted as part of the neoliberal ideology was the underlying cause of chronic downward mobility for the working class, erosion of the middle class, race-ethnic-gender-class-based marginalization, and the richest 1% of Americans own as much as the bottom 90%. To convince the public of the pure market hegemony theory, neoliberal media apologists promoted shareholder capitalism as the new capitalist manifesto. The pillar of objective and balanced journalism, the *New York Times* also promoted this corporate doctrine by making certain that only apologists of neoliberalism were included in its panel of "experts" on Milton Friedman.[1226]

This is not to suggest that the *New York Times* and Western mainstream media, in general, are more monolithic and propagandistic in comparison to the media in China under a one-party state, or oligarchic-kleptocratic Russia where dissent does not have a place for public expression questioning government policy. Although the open society permits small operations of dissident voices usually within the social contract confines, neoliberal media is ideologically monolithic and as demanding of conformity as any other ideology. At issue, is the hypocritical claim of "objective journalism" under any social contract, not the undeniable nature of monolithic neoliberal journalism.

In February 2020, President Trump's US Attorney General William Barr dismissed liberal democracy as totalitarian, and the *"corporate—or mainstream—media press is massively consolidated...remarkably monolithic, while journalists increasingly see themselves as agents of change rather than reporters of fact, the media has the power to mobilize public opinion in a particular direction, with those mobilized becoming more powerful with the press as its ally."*[1227]

One reason that lofty claims of media objectivity, fairness, or balance are hollow is because of links between governments and the media which propagates the social contract. Although there is oligopolistic control of media conglomerates linked to political parties, neoliberals promote the thesis that corporate media is free of political control when in fact. Hence, privately-owned media allows news divisions to claim 'objectivity'. This assumption stretches credulity by asking people to believe that business-owned media is capable of delivering news in the public interest.

While the culturally pluralist neoliberal *New York Times* and the BBC insist on objectivity claims, news organizations in non-Western countries like *Living India News* and *The Times of India* refrain from making such lofty claims. From the US to Japan and Brazil, there is a global public distrust of the media that pretends to transcend class, race, ethnicity, and gender in news coverage. Besides instant accessibility, distrust in mainstream media is one reason for the popularity of social media inexorably disseminating populist propaganda. While there are disagreements between news organizations and social media about specific policies, and whether pluralism or authoritarianism best serves capital, there is agreement on the neoliberal social contract.[1228]

Despite the media's homogenized management, content, and programming structure in the age of neoliberal transformation resulting in corporate consolidation, many journalists have a sense of the profession's history, methodology, and how the profession is practiced across towns and the globe. Even during the early Cold War amid a polarized political climate, Western news organizations distanced themselves from both leftists and rightists within the same liberal bourgeois framework by giving themselves the privilege of ideological objectivity. By its very structure, the neoliberal model has relegated the media into the web of instruments of the social contract, while giving itself credibility by claiming to communicate the truth in the name of the public interest. [1229]

In the post-truth ethical crisis world of autocratization where general suspicion of reason prevails among self-baptized postmodernists, and those concealing their opportunism behind a manufactured veil, the temptation to make subjective reality into an objective science governed by natural laws is a never-ending quest of the corporate media. Because its goal is ideological, political, social, and cultural conformity, the mainstream media insists on projecting the image of objectivity which means balanced reporting. Rather than using journalism as a forum for independent critical thought to analyze the institutional structure from all perspectives to expose structural causes of social injustice, indoctrinating the worker-consumer-citizen is at the core of the media's goal.[1230]

In comparison with Medieval Western Christendom, Byzantine Empire, and the Islamic Middle East when the vast majority of the population was docile and superstitious, in the digital 21st century, there are dissenting voices, even if public avenues of expression in social media are heavily tilted toward rightwing populism. Like the Medieval institutions whose goal was to preserve the status quo by engendering spiritual conformity within the feudal/manorial order, 21st-century media has assumed an analogous role in neoliberalism's secular world on a world scale.[1231]

Because the liberal-bourgeois state thoroughly suppresses dissent in more subtle ways than the authoritarian state, the corporate media's task has not been as daunting in engendering conformity, especially because mainstream analysts present competition between mainstream and social media as a function of democracy. After all, every institution from churches to schools works toward the same goal of helping to create a consumer-citizen identity whose values emanate from the neoliberal social contract. Just as religion creates a false reality, the hegemonic capitalist ideology, especially in the metropolis, becomes the individual's only reality under neoliberalism. Hence, it is hardly surprising that a segment of the working class has internalized the neoliberal class war and turned against other workers, women, and minorities.[1232]

Without the mainstream media and social media's catalytic role, indoctrination into neoliberal transformation would not be as ubiquitous, nor as effective at the same pace. To the degree that public opinion is manipulated in support of the institutional structure, it matters to the advertising-dependent media. Within the narrow perimeters of the corporate consumerist model, given that the individual is a "consumer of news", learning about the world's daily news is no different than consuming any commodity or service. An extension of public relations departments in business and government, the media is partly responsible for the zombified citizen desperately seeking solutions within the same neoliberal political framework of liberal pluralist vs. rightwing political party structure.[1233]

More than in the conservative 1920s or 1950s, neoliberal mass journalism since the 1980s has blurred the lines between news and advertising. The difficulty differentiating between infomercials and news is indicative of the successful fusion of marketing in news and vice versa as both aim to mold and manipulate the consumer-citizen. Adding to this framework of blurring the lines between journalism and advertising, the advent of print and digital tabloid journalism has created a new norm. Although it has 19th-century roots, tabloid journalism exploded in the 1980s and swept all venues of entertainment during the ascendancy of neoliberalism by focusing on the cult of the individual devoid of a community context, often in defiance of it.[1234]

Focused on the lifestyles of the rich and famous, natural disasters, graphic petty crime, terrorism, enemies foreign and domestic, and the occasional space aliens threatening Earth's safety, all contributing to a culture of fear in tabloid journalism finding expression in all forums. Picture and video-filled sensational stories of mass neoliberal journalism aim to satisfy the senses and keep the mind distracted from life's struggle for survival. Even news presentation is often hard to distinguish from drama or melodrama, often intentionally voyeuristic and superficial, diverting attention from the essence of the news story.[1235]

Reflecting the corporate merging of media and Hollywood studios, outlets from tabloids and newspapers to TV networks and cable channels compete to entertain and provide the reader/listener/viewer with emotionally-filled stories invariably with a rightwing populist slant. Whether the story revolves around migrant workers, sensationalized working-class crime, or the occasional corporate scandal, the universality of tabloid journalism merging into the entertainment mainstream molds public opinion by manipulating values based on social justice and redirecting mass anxiety and anger toward marginalized groups. Directing the news-consumer citizen's focus away from the social contract responsible for calamities befalling the middle class and workers, this new form of journalism has been very profitable for right-wing billionaires and hedge funds.[1236]

At the core of tabloid culture, mass distraction has contributed to mold the zombified consumer-citizen helping to maintain public confidence in the social order as key to conformity, while undermining social harmony by precipitating marginalization and polarization. From news broadcasts to situation comedies, everything from radio, TV, print, and digital and social media, all present the news from the transformation model's prism. As a sector, the entertainment/communications/media corporations have played a catalytic role in redefining the public sphere as a private commodified domain, including self-commodification where the individual perceives her/his life and relationships on a market-based model. More so than the mainstream media, the digital interactive media universe converts and appropriates the user into a commodity, alienating her/him from the real world.[1237]

Faced with contradictions in the political economy and its mode of operation as a promoter of manufactured consent, the neoliberal media's objectivity conceals a dystopian machinery of a managed citizenry in socially engineered projects to maximize profit and project an image of legitimacy. Both right-wing populists and multicultural liberals agree that media social engineering is a reality. However, they accuse each other of manufacturing the news and consent, especially in the cable the social media domain.[1238]

Not only in what the West labels authoritarian non-Western countries, but in the US and Europe, media credibility has remained at very low levels under neoliberalism. A reflection of the crisis in public confidence for all authorities, this phenomenon especially affects politics and business where corruption and varieties of scandals are frequent reminders about the difference between blue-collar and white-collar criminals. In 2021, a Reuters Institute Survey of 46 countries revealed that, with Finland leading the pack, Scandinavian countries are consistently at the top of the public trust rankings. US media ranked the least trustworthy with just 29% expressing confidence, while 84% blame the media for the pre-Civil War-like political/cultural conditions in the 21st century.[1239]

An *Axios* survey of 2019 found that 80% of independent American voters did not trust the media. In 2021, just 7% expressed a great deal of trust, 29% a fair amount, while 34% had no trust at all, and 29% not much. The Rand Corporation's research confirmed that most people believe that a "subjective form of journalism" is pervasive. [1240]

As the key institutional instruments molding peoples' identities and worldviews about norms, the mainstream media and social media enjoy enormous power precisely because they allow the faint voices of the masses, with considerable algorithmic filters. All along, they commodify and monetize users' profiles, employing algorithms to promote the ideological orientation of users that concur with neoliberalism and often authoritarianism. In an article entitled *"The grotesque inequality embodied by Musk, Bezos, and Zuckerberg is a threat to democracy,"* Jeff Sparrow of *The Guardian* notes that capital concentration, especially in social media and high tech, speaks louder than beguiling rhetoric about democracy. Coincidentally, both Musk and Zuckerberg as owners of social media have had a history of promoting right-wing populism.[1241]

As opinion polls indicate, people around the world realize that the media and social media are an integral part of the status quo representing the wealthy and political class. In everything from medical data interpretation to monetary policy analyzed by charlatan ideologues and varieties of opportunists whose careers are linked to the agenda they are promoting, the post-truth culture has twisted relativism beyond the boundaries of reason, common sense, and realism. Within the capitalist class, consultants, law firms, and corporate lobbyists sweeping along unwitting followers into class war have been cashing in.[1242]

Social Media, Neoliberalism and Authoritarianism

Especially prevalent in loosely regulated social media, post-truth populist trends invariably linked with emotive language in rightwing talk radio, cable news, and social media can be traced to the convergence of technology with neoliberal transformation. Seduced by populist rhetoric, the disgruntled segment of the population embracing conspiracy theories denounces everything from globalization and global governance to scientific studies and facts in any domain from the social sciences realm to medical science. Philip Mirowski argues that neoliberalism operates based on the "double-truth doctrine", a manufactured narrative for public consumption and a realistic assessment to perpetuate the elite's privileged role in society. Indicative of the governmentality crisis, manufactured truth for the support of the social contract is an extension of forging public consent in support of the status quo.[1243]

Manifested throughout the institutional mainstream, post-truth trends and double-truth doctrine owe much of their effectiveness to social media responsible for inordinate political influence and the special role of socioeconomic elites and the media in promoting authoritarian policies globally, especially in the US. Under the ownership of billionaires molding public opinion to conform with the political and economic establishment, the oligopolistic social media and mainstream media became more concentrated and helped in the rise of neoliberal transformation helping to reproduce a hierarchical international social order.[1244]

Arguably the most controversial company in its class, Facebook sits at the top of the social media empire hierarchy, owning 91 companies, the majority hidden from public view. The poster child of data manipulation for profit, Facebook has been promoting authoritarian elements globally, and the new US Cold War, censoring only the most egregious cases of rightwing activity, such as the Bolsonaro-backed assault on Brazil's capital on 9 January 2023. With corporate hegemony over the state and society with the sole purpose of optimizing profit, Facebook stands out in Silicon Valley as an autocratization promoter projecting a democratic image.[1245]

"Facebook's rise is part of a larger autocratic movement," writes Adrienne LaFrance, *"one that's eroding democracy worldwide as authoritarian leaders set a new tone for global governance. Consider how Facebook portrays itself as a counterbalance to a superpower like China. Company executives have warned that attempts to interfere with Facebook's untrammeled growth—through regulating the currency it is developing, for example—would be a gift to China, which wants its cryptocurrency to be dominant. In other words, Facebook is competing with China the way a nation would."[1246]*

Just as transnational corporations took over mainstream media and homogenized it amid deregulated markets, enjoying corporate subsidies at all levels of government, combined with a low-tax and low-interest-rate policy favoring stock market speculation, so was the case with social media regulated far less than the mainstream media. Internet usage jumped from 16 million in 1996 to 3 billion in 2015, and up to 60 percent of the world's population by 2020. With 2.9 billion users and a net income of $29 billion on $84.1 billion in gross advertising revenue in 2020, jumping to $113 billion in 2022, the Facebook empire has easily circumvented accountability even in egregious matters of taxation, privacy issues, and promoting hate speech and rightwing propaganda for profit, as Frances Haugen, a whistleblower revealed in 2021.[1247]

In the case of Myanmar's military against the Rohingya minority in 2018, as well as the US Capitol riots of 6 January 2021, Facebook allowed right-wing elements to use the forum for their agenda. In an article entitled *"Facebook Has Always Been Right-Wing Media"*, Brain Feldman wrote that the company knows exactly what it is doing and deliberately refuses to change its policy.[1248]

Even in egregious cases involving the spread of misinformation on COVID-19, and promotion of hate speech and authoritarianism, social media managed to evade government regulation that the mainstream media has not escaped. Rationalizations about corporate bureaucracy and algorithms needing adjustment have been among distracting arguments, just as social media maximized profits. In addition to multi-million-dollar government contracts, including from the Pentagon and Homeland Security, Facebook was one of the main beneficiaries of corporate welfare. In spring 2023, Facebook censored an article by investigative journalist Seymour Hersh exposing the alleged role of the US government in the Nord Stream pipeline destruction and its cover-up. Recommending that its users refer to a NATO-funded website, Facebook followed the same line as mainstream media in suppressing freedom of speech, despite claims regarding freedom and democracy.[1249]

Just like mainstream media makes editorial decisions, so does social media by promoting rightwing voices, while censoring progressive dissent. Defaulting all blame to algorithms has helped to distract from human corporate abuse. *"For years, Facebook has known that its algorithms encourage and amplify antisocial behavior like hate speech and extreme political bias to keep users engaged, according to company documents..."*[1250]

Redefining the Enlightenment concept of individual liberty within the boundaries of the marketplace, social media has manipulated life-enhancing social interactions. Such dogmatism has subverted even Karl Popper's open society theory which in *The Poverty of Historicism* acknowledges that unlike the laws of nature, sociological laws differ in place and time, thereby rejecting dogmatism. Fostering division, chaos, and hatred among disparate rightwing groups from Myanmar to the US, social media's goal has always been the profit motive and mass distraction from structural exploitation. The quest for greater profits has played into the hands of liberal vs. authoritarian neoliberal political discourse about methods and strategies to achieve social conformity.[1251]

Within the unrestrained market of ideas, including inciting violence and promoting hatred among disparate social groups, corporate decisions about material ranging from complex scientific matters to public policy have been subject to the logic of market determinism, commodification, and subordination of the state to the market at the core of neoliberalism. Even when social media incites right-wing violence, market regulation is an anathema for neoliberals, despite its deviant sociopolitical impact. A cloak of protection for social media, neoliberal market dogmatism goes to the heart of the sector's resounding success prevailing over the state.[1252]

Neoliberal logic has led to the commercialization of intentionally misleading information, or disinformation. This is a clear illustration of corporate defiance toward the state. In May 2021, Brazilian and Indian social media influencers promoted a UK public relations script replete with disinformation about the COVID-19 vaccine. The same UK public relations firm proposed to well-paid German and French social media influencers to promote disinformation about the vaccine. Government investigations confirmed that disinformation for both the private sector and public domain using social media has become a thriving shadowy business. Nevertheless, neoliberal politicians have been reluctant to regulate, while permitting the same companies to evade taxes.[1253]

"From state-sponsored propagandists using paid troll armies, to commercially motivated data

analytics firms selling their toolkits to politicians, and platform workers producing memes for overseas clients, the global industry of disinformation production has only professionalized and diversified. This special issue for Social Media + Society aims to deepen understanding about the social identities, work arrangements, and political and commercial motivations of an emerging class of digital disinformation workers. We are interested in critical and interdisciplinary research that examines the political economy, specifically the digital and creative industries thatpropel and produce disinformation."[1254]

On 1 February 2022, congresswoman Alexandria Ocasio Cortez (D-NY) accused Facebook of exporting disinformation globally and sabotaging the effort to contain the pandemic; a view that many researchers shared as well. Refusing to address the specific accusations, the company responded that it has more than two billion users who *"express themselves freely"* on the platform. Therefore, corporate management presented the company as a "free speech" advocate, rather than offering a platform for hate speech and rightwing disinformation that only divides the working class and furthers class warfare.

According to the British-based Center for Countering Digital Hate, twelve Facebook users, among them Joseph Mercola with 1.7 million followers, were responsible for the anti-vaccine disinformation campaign. As it turns out, "free speech" was part of a well-financed disinformation campaign for which social media refused to take any responsibility. All along, Facebook was using algorithms to cancel out criticism on other matters, including the Israeli policy of more than 700,000 illegal settlements in the Palestinian West Bank, and considering that Facebook, Twitter, and other social media place right-wingers on the payroll, free speech doctrine is hollow marketing to make money.[1255]

Besides using its platform to amass hundreds of billions in profits by selling users' data and monetizing profiles, social media has helped to indoctrinate the public into neoliberal dogma and authoritarianism. Depending on the source, between 48 and 60 percent of the world's population has social media access. People in their 20s make up about one-third of users. Use drops with advanced age, although this began to change during the COVID-19 pandemic. A correlation is difficult to establish. According to some studies, heavy social media use, especially Facebook and Instagram, is linked to loneliness, anxiety, depression, smoking, and substance abuse.[1256]

"Over half of social media users have also experienced cyberbullying, with up to 20% experiencing it regularly. However, it may not be accurate to assume that social media is autonomous, and that is entirely to blame for these issues. Behind these platforms is a more deep-rooted problem; that of neoliberalism. It can easily be argued that this is the dominant ideology in our society, and whilst it is predominantly thought of as a set of economic policies, it also has social implications."[1257]

Among those arguing along similar lines, French philosopher Jacques Ranciere notes that social media affords people the opportunity to flood the web with endless topics distinguished by a blend of emotional expression, including hatred, paranoia, anger, and anxiety; more psychotherapy sessions than anything intellectually edifying. As cathartic as it may sound for the individual using the platform for psychotherapy, chronic anger and demonizing marginalized groups is not beneficial for one's mental health and it certainly has no redeeming personal or social value. It has been a source for rightwing radicalization and mobilization for populist groups and politicians. Studies by mental health professionals have shown a link between right-wing authoritarian beliefs and mental health problems.[1258]

Considering the anxiety of downward social mobility, social media's omnipresence has been the vehicle for digital entrepreneurs taking advantage of the masses who have accepted the virtual world as part of their daily routine. Surprisingly, it is not the US, Japan, or northwest Europe, but the Philippines, Colombia, Indonesia, Malaysia, and Thailand rounding out the top five countries using social media more than any developed nation. Because social media is not only shaping consumer and communications habits, but influencing mainstream culture, it has become a powerful instrument to determine the course of the neoliberal social contract, and it has done so at the expense of liberal democracy around the world.[1259]

"The most successful within this new 'marketplace of ideas' is ideological entrepreneurs disseminating (and reshaping) 'populist' political ideologies hostile to 'globalism', multiculturalism, the cultural and economic integration of minorities, feminism, and gender politics... Charismatic ideological entrepreneurs compete to reveal the follies and the 'agenda' of the 'new class', offering techniques for resisting its mystifications, 'doing your research', and coming to self-consciousness...Resistance requires a refusal to believe anything the journalists, scientists, or politicians say; the SJWs, Cultural Marxists, and universalist intellectuals will do anything, rig any election and tell any lie, to stay in power."[1260]

While Messianic populism predates the digital revolution, social media has made it possible for corrupt businessmen turned politicians in the periphery and core, especially in the US, to impose neoliberalism under measures that do not stand up to scrutiny by any definition of democracy. From Brazil's president Jair Bolsonaro, a corrupt businessman turned rightwing populist politician, to Romania's equally corrupt businessman turned politician George Becali who proclaimed hatred for everyone from cultural pluralists to humanists, mainstream and social media have given demagogues a forum to reach the masses with superficial irrational discussions about religion, nationalism, militarism, traditional values and grandiose messianic messages. Trump's election in 2016 emboldened authoritarian politicians across the globe. The danger rests with elements of the ruling class trying to conceal it or rebaptizing democracy to suit hegemony, as Jacques Ranciere points out in *Hatred of Democracy*. [1261]

Commenting about Bolsonaro's election in 2019, Zack Beauchamp, VOX senior correspondent of global affairs, captures the essence of social media's role. *"At the inauguration of Brazil's new far-right president, Jair Bolsonaro[1], in early January [2019], a crowd of his supporters began a surprising chant[2]. They weren't cheering for Bolsonaro or his running mate or their party; instead, they were reciting the names of social media platforms. "Facebook, Facebook, Facebook!" the crowd yelled. "WhatsApp, WhatsApp, WhatsApp!" They were crediting the platforms with their man's victory, and they aren't entirely wrong. During the campaign, a conservative pro-business interest group funded a massive disinformation campaign[3] on WhatsApp (the popular messaging app owned by Facebook). False and damaging information about Bolsonaro's left-wing opponent, including fake news mocked up to look like neutral fact-checks, spread like wildfire in the runup to the October 8 vote. This deluge, according to one Brazilian expert, played a role in Bolsonaro's victory[4]."[1262]*

---

1. *https://www.vox.com/2018/10/29/18037728/bolsonaro-brazil-election-guide*

2. *https://twitter.com/JotaInfo/status/1080111070516334593*

3. *https://www1.folha.uol.com.br/poder/2018/10/empresarios-bancam-campanha-contra-o-pt-pelo-whatsapp.shtml*

4. *https://theconversation.com/whatsapp-skewed-brazilian-election-proving-social-medias-danger-to-democracy-106476*

Although numerous books, articles, and case studies have concluded that profit is the motive for social media companies to promote right-wing politicians, disinformation about everything from public policy to health issues, and hate-filled postings point to an ideological cloak concealing the resolve to preserve the social order. Profit is very significant, but, even more so, molding society through the dissemination of the hegemonic culture's values while projecting the image of an open platform intertwined with the profit motive and consistent with the social contract. By advertising on social media, companies are sponsors of right-wing agendas, including some paying social media users to spread disinformation. Because advertising companies know that the entire consumer base is not made up of right-wingers, they enjoy the cover of pluralism in an otherwise populist-promoting platform.[1263]

Although it has far greater freedom under the cover of the mass user as a front to promote neoliberal transformation, social media reflects the hegemonic culture while projecting the image of a popular cultural platform. Algorithmic manipulation of users' data and professional propagandists on the payroll of companies through marketing and PR agencies with corporate and political clients makes transparency very difficult. Half to two-thirds of the population relies on social media for news and information, especially people under thirty. This is indicative that social media's impact is not confined to its defined space. It impacts the entire media landscape with the remarkable ability to be far more influential in molding public opinion about everything from what to wear to what political party people support.[1264]

To increase unique visits to the site and attract more users, social media will post almost anything, no matter how offensive, fictitious, or bordering on the absurd; no matter whether it has any redeeming social or aesthetic value, or even it is harmful to the public welfare. Yet, it is all in the name of freedom of expression, except when this too is subject to censorship and freedom is limited as the company defines it. Social media algorithms usually catch any hard-hitting material with a popular following on critical issues, including rising inequality, human rights violations, and authoritarian policies by governments claiming to be democratic.

The social media's censorship radar includes US-NATO foreign policy, the US military-industrial complex, specific defense contractors and sub-contractors, and critiques of governments violating human rights that the US and NATO support. Concerned because social media monetizes users' information, right-wing critics accuse social media of a liberal bias. Corporate cooperation with government agencies to track users' activities and disclose private information without consent has raised alarm bells with various privacy rights groups, but not as much as social media's role in promoting authoritarianism.[1265]

Social media apologists contend that the platform represents just about every ideological, political, religious, and cultural perspective in the world. Critics counter that in the absence of filters, social media often provides raw ideas and sentiments about racial purity, neo-Nazism, mass violence, and random destruction. The underlying assumption about social media vs. mainstream media is that the former tends to be more liberal than the latter because the general public associate's open access with young people prone to trendy lifestyles that high-tech executives emulate. Social media and mainstream media support political parties around the world that promote low taxes, deregulation, repatriation of profits, intellectual rights, and freedom from public scrutiny with minimal accountability to the state.[1266]

Whether in the US, India, Latin America, Eastern Europe, or sub-Saharan Africa, contemporary history has shown that social media promotes rightwing populism, along with the occasional dissident progressive voices. Permitting everything from sensationalized street crime to the war on terror and xenophobia linked to migrant non-white populations, social media has been a platform that promotes nativist polemics rooted in racism, misogyny, and xenophobia.[1267]

Like the rest of the world, African leaders have been aware that social media propelled to power both Trump and Bolsonaro. Other authoritarian leaders have demanded the freedom to use social media for self-promotion. In July 2018, Uganda introduced a social media tax impacting fifty platforms. WhatsApp, Facebook, and Twitter, among other companies vehemently objected that the government was using the "freedom of expression" card to suppress dissenting voices. Three years later, President Yoweri Museveni ended the five cent per day tax on social media, replacing it with an internet data tax.

Among other international players, the IMF, World Bank, US, and EU governments convinced Museveni to undertake neoliberal transformation at the same time that powerful social media companies were working through independent organizations toward the same goal. Under IMF Director Christine Lagarde, Uganda was a "success story". This meant that the Ugandan junta permitted transformation that afforded a pass to foreign corporations, including social media and foreign investors, to benefit from liberalization and downsizing of the public services sector.[1268]

The power struggle of the Ugandan government to manipulate social media as a means of forging consensus had pan-African dimensions. Similar situations took place in fifteen countries which on occasion restricted[5] or switched off social media access amid social protests or elections during the Afro-Arab Spring in the 2010s. Authoritarian regimes' determination to use social media as a political tool was not lost on the foreign corporations at odds with host governments. Considering that only 25% of sub-Saharan Africans used the internet by the end of the 2010s, the growth potential appeared far greater than Western Europe at 98 percent and 63 percent globally.[1269]

Corporate control ran into government demands to use social media as a tool to secure power. This entailed recurring clashes between social media companies and the government in developing countries. However, it was not so different than social media corporate clashes with the EU trying to regulate and tax a largely tax-avoidance industry. Beneath the surface of conflict between governments and social media, there has been greater cooperation than confrontation, including authoritarian regimes with a notorious record of human rights violations.[1270]

After a seven-month suspension[6], in January 2022, the Nigerian government restored Twitter. The company agreed to establish an office in Lagos, pay taxes, and *"act with a respectful acknowledgment of Nigerian laws and the national culture and history."* Echoing the Trump administration's accusations of a liberal bias, President Muhammadu Buhari's government accused social media of *"subversive purposes and criminal activities."*[1271]

"The president of Nigeria, Muhammadu Buhari, was so outraged when Twitter deleted his post... that he ordered the country's mobile networks to block access to the social network and broadcasters to delete their accounts... In the past few years, governments around the world have introduced a flurry of new laws governing online speech. In countries

5. https://www.digitalinformationworld.com/2020/12/data-reveals-social-media-restrictions.html

6. https://www.nytimes.com/2021/06/05/world/africa/nigeria-twitter-president.html

that restrict freedom of expression, social media platforms are being offered a choice between aiding repression or losing access to lucrative markets... As India was engulfed by a second surge of COVID-19, for example, the government attempted to quash online criticism of its handling of the crisis. It's a pattern of online censorship that has become increasingly common in the embattled democracy. Supporters of the farmers' protests, which brought millions out onto the streets of Delhi, were targeted in the same way earlier this year. "In the first half of 2020. Twitter tripled the number of accounts and posts removed at the request of the Indian government."[1272]

Social media companies intermittently censored African and non-Western governments, arguing that they violated democratic and human rights standards. They never applied the same standard to Israel's illegal settlements of Palestinian territory. Israel limited utility services, including water, to Palestinians, not to mention confiscating their homes, killing or injuring women, children, and journalists in clashes for which the government always blamed the victims. Social media was no different in its biased "Orientalism" coverage of the Israeli-Palestinian conflict than the mainstream media. Digital apartheid mirrors the Western mainstream media's long-standing history of directly or indirectly promoting Israeli policy, regardless of what the United Nations and human rights organizations have concluded about the apartheid policy imposed on Palestinians.[1273]

Analyzing a 50-year history of reporting and opinion columns by *The New York Times, The Washington Post, The New Republic,* and *The Nation*, Maha Nassar concluded that Edward Said's *Orientalism* (1978) theory analyzes Western media's claims of balanced reporting and measures them against empirical evidence. Mainstream and social media paid lip service to 'Palestinian rights' invariably from a paternalistic *"White Man's Burden"* perspective, rarely permitting the victims to speak for themselves. "*In the New York Times, less than 2 percent of the nearly 2,500 opinion pieces that discussed Palestinians since 1970 were written by Palestinians. In the Washington Post, the average was just 1 percent."*[1274]

In so far as it consistently censors criticism of Israel's policy toward Palestinians, while providing an open forum for discussion which mirrors the official views of the government in Tel Aviv, social media has followed a similar pattern as the Western mainstream media. Although many social media users have historically opposed Israeli policy, social media algorithms have been programmed to take down user-profiles and block material overly critical of Israeli policies. No such restrictions apply to apologists of Israeli apartheid policies, as the UN Economic and Social Commission for Western Asia has defined them since March 2017.[1275]

Long before social media's digital apartheid, Edward Said *Covering Islam* (1981) argued that Western media not only distorts Islam but rarely allows Muslims, especially Palestinians, to be heard. A theoretical principle that Western media proudly attributes to itself as a core value, nevertheless, it treats its own Orientalism coverage as balanced reporting. Faithful to Western cultural imperialist tradition, digital media has been using algorithms to perpetuate stereotypes and surreptitiously support apartheid.[1276]

"A report we recently published[7] *through the Center for Business and Human Rights*[8] *at New York University's Stern School of Business sheds light on the relationship between tech platforms and the kind of extreme polarization that can lead to the erosion of democratic values and partisan violence... Our central conclusion, based on a review of more than 50 social science studies and interviews with more than 40 academics, policy experts, activists, and current and*

7. *https://bhr.stern.nyu.edu/polarization-report-page*

8. *https://bhr.stern.nyu.edu/*

former industry people, is that platforms like Facebook, YouTube, and Twitter likely are not the root causes of political polarization, but they do exacerbate it."[1277]

Media-Defined Democracy and the Liberal-Rightwing Populist Antagonism

The mainstream media and social media have played a catalytic role in inculcating the neoliberal transformation model's ideology throughout the world. Emphasizing the new realism of neoliberal technocracy in the information age, the socioeconomic elites convinced even center-left and socialist parties to embrace neoliberalism as the only option. If one accepts Gustave Le Bon's premise regarding mass psychology of resistance to empirical reality and the social necessity of illusions, it makes sense why neoliberalism has prevailed. *"The masses have never thirsted after truth. They turn aside evidence that is not to their taste, preferring to deify error, if error seduces them. Whoever can supply them with illusions is easily their master; whoever attempts to destroy their illusions is always their victim."[1278]*

No instrument of mass communication has been as efficacious as social media in delivering illusions that the masses accept as grassroots. Presenting neoliberal ideology, values, and institutional structure as the new norm identified with progress, traditional and social media have championed the neoliberal criteria which defines what it means to be a consumer-citizen in the digital era. The media presents society's welfare as an obstacle for the community-unattached individual to achieve personal goals of entrepreneurial freedom and success equated with wealth accumulation, and the power and prestige it carries.[1279]

Daily, the media projects the image that the threat to social harmony and progress in the US, EU, and the rest of the world emanates mainly from neighborhood violence, petty crime gang-related crimes, radical groups, illegal immigrants, Islamic terrorists, and rogue enemy nations. Rarely does the media critically examine the institutional structure to determine systemic causes of social discontent that at times find expression in criminal activity. As long as the focus stays on working class and minority community crime, on liberal-pluralist identity groups accused of undermining traditional society's moral fiber, on Islamic terrorism, and belligerent Russia, Iran, North Korea, and Chinese global economic hegemony, the thin veil of the inherently self-destructive neoliberal political economy as the panacea is safe from public scrutiny.[1280]

The media's projection of 'freedom' based on disparate ideological positions through the conservative-liberal confrontation reflects the political arena, managing to camouflage the underlying consensus for neoliberal transformation on which both sides have historically agreed. Even as they disagree about managing the political economy, or how to forge popular consensus and minimize grassroots discontent, the homogenized global media empires subordinate democracy to "*emergency politics*" aimed at perpetuating class war so they can uphold the neoliberal model.

Emergency politics is invariably associated with domestic political antagonism between liberal-pluralist neoliberals vs. rightwing neoliberals combined with foreign policy crises. The trans-Atlantic US-linked governments justify everything from unilateral military interventions in the name of "freedom and democracy", to violating the Constitutional rights of citizens, including women's freedoms, and the civil rights of minorities. [1281]

As much in core countries as in semi-periphery India, Turkey, Hungary, and Brazil, the strategy of demonizing domestic and foreign enemies has been the catalyst for winning elections especially when disseminated through the popular social media platforms where post-truth doctrine is the norm.[1282] Liberal media is often subtle regarding class warfare so that class biases are not at the forefront of news coverage and analysis. Conservatives, especially rightwing journalists, and analysts, deliberately engage in hyperbolic and direct language appealing at the emotional level to propagate against domestic and foreign enemies as a means of forging a broad united front behind the establishment while the establishment is moving farther to the right. Social media uses the same messages to promote fear and hatred, thereby leading a segment of the population toward greater acceptance of authoritarianism as a paradoxical and delusional path to safety and security.[1283]

If people care more about safety and security, or at least if the media and their political, business, and community leaders have convinced the public that nothing matters more, the general public would be more likely to surrender any defense of democracy for the perceived guarantee of safety and security. In essence, the 'safety and security' bait is about the protection of the propertied classes, exactly as the father of Western liberalism, John Locke, argued almost three-and-a-half centuries ago.

If the government moves increasingly toward a more authoritarian model under the political shell of "democracy," and coincidentally cyclical economic contractions result in an increasingly smaller and weaker middle class, the media has already prepared the public for that inevitability. Unlike what the liberal media would like the public to believe, right-wing media is not solely responsible for paving the path to authoritarianism. Embedded in the doctrine of "Occidentalism", the patriarchal worldview reflecting the patron-client integration model represents the hegemonic culture. This is regardless of conservative or liberal ideological orientation. It stretches credulity to accept the thesis that rightwing populism rests solely on the shoulders of billionaire media owners, instead of focusing on the broader structural framework within which the billionaire media owners operate.[1284]

A *New York Times* essay entitled "*How Rupert Murdoch's Empire of Influence Remade the World*" (3 April 2019) maintained that the rise of global rightwing populist movements and governments, including Trump's 'Make America Great Again' elite-directed populist movement, is the result of Murdoch's media empire. The article alleges that the Murdoch family destabilized democracy in several countries and toppled governments on two continents.[1285] In the late 20th-early 21st century Murdoch is indeed something like a real-life *'Citizen Kane'.* However, it is a myth that in the US and around the world rightwing populism under the neoliberal political economy is a Murdoch-like byproduct, rather than neoliberalism making possible the Murdoch media empire. No different than the *New York Times* and other corporate media outlets, Murdoch's media empire operates as an integral part of the political economy.[1286]

As a result of his political links, which invariably involved various schemes within the political and business class, Murdoch kept spreading rightwing populist propaganda globally during the neoliberal transformation, strengthening the media empire while promoting neoliberalism from the far right by rejecting cultural pluralism. Besides company journalists hacking private mailboxes and phones of celebrities and twisting facts to the degree that it paid Dominion $787 million in damages in April 2023, the FOX NEWS media empire cleverly manipulated stories through hyperbolic populist rhetoric, scandal-style and reporting with twisted facts and figures to fit the ideological framework. The symbolic villain for liberals, the darling of conservatives, Murdoch has operated in a climate of neoliberal global media oligopoly. His model quickly became globalized, spreading the gospel of populist capitalism while making billions.[1287]

Both corporate media and state-backed media represent the same institutional neoliberal structure of which all mainstream and social media are a part. This includes the *New York Times* criticizing Murdoch for the rise of authoritarianism as a way of setting itself apart from the systemic problem that it helped to create. In 2016, the entire Western liberal media helped to elevate Donald Trump into a viable presidential candidate. By providing free coverage for Trump and promoting cult personality analysis of his candidacy, the liberal media was inadvertently promoting the candidate.

Whether emphasizing the baseless self-made billionaire "success story", or presenting him as a "Washington outsider", business maverick prepared to apply corporate models in politics, or constantly dwelling on his controversial celebrity status, good or bad, the media provided free coverage worth millions, exactly as Senator Bernie Sanders contended. With gossip-style stories surrounding Trump's personality cult, the mainstream liberal and social media did as much if not more to elect Trump as the far rightwing media.[1288]

Bluntly or subtly, the same liberal media that vilified New Deal Democrat Bernie Sanders favored the Wall Street-Cold War Democrats Hillary Clinton in 2016 and Joe Biden in 2020. All along, the media was not addressing systemic problems that would have forced a debate about corporate welfare vs. social welfare, and about diplomacy over military buildup and economically ruinous neoconservative 'forever war' doctrines. Among other liberal media outlets vilifying the Murdoch rightwing populist neoliberal propaganda machine, the *New York Times* was just as quick to embrace the militarist approach to foreign policy. Dismissing progressive principles and policies that threaten Wall Street and defense contractors, the liberal media was as responsible for strengthening the neoliberal model and illiberal democracy as the right.[1289]

According to the liberal media, the norm is a choice between Murdoch's autocratization world promising to deliver the best results for neoliberal capitalism vs. the pluralist/diverse political umbrella under a "kinder, gentler" neoliberal transformation with sprinkled elements of Keynesianism. For its part, right-wing media and its apologists want the world to believe that the monolithic liberal-democratic camp is responsible for all ills befalling society because of cultural decadence embodied in identity politics. By lumping together classical liberals, environmental center-leftists, Keynesians, Socialists, and Communists, the right created an "either-or" choice for the public. Exactly what Italian Fascists presented to the public in the 1920s and German Nazis in the 1930s, the either-or choice has been a left-over from the Cold War making a strong resurgence in the 21st century when mainstream political parties have moved to the right.[1290]

To make sense of intergroup behavior, beyond the scope of class analysis, John Turner and Henri Tajfel developed social identity theory in the nascent phase of neoliberalism during the 1970s and 1980s. Whether liberal or rightwing within the neoliberal model, Jianing Li, and Min-HsinSu maintain that peoples' disdain for the media is an integral part of political identity shaping personal identity.

"Social identity theory provides a useful framework to understand the contested nature of "fake news... This cognitive-motivational process [individuals tend to derive their self-concept based on prototypical ingroup traits] promotes category-based thinking and a sense of "us against them," which colors the perceptions of social reality against which the veracity of media content is judged. Political identification is one such important social category shaping media perceptions. Political identity has played a central role in criticisms of the media even before the rise of "fake news." Salient group identity also makes one more susceptible to elite cues that attack unfavorable content as biased or untruthful, prompting them to evaluate media based on such heuristics."[1291]

Besides mainstream and social media, watchdog groups are an outgrowth of the same neoliberal model, if not more so than the media that they analyze.[1292] The conservative *Accuracy in Media* (AIM) organization insists that mainstream media has a liberal bias. Historically, the financing for AIM has come from large oil companies. It is no surprise that the organization adamantly opposes Keynesian Democrats with an environmental and socially progressive agenda. Rather than analyzing how the media covers institutional racism in the criminal justice system, AIM castigates the favorable manner that liberal media portrays minorities, women, and environmentalists as part of liberal identity politics. Critical of the media's corporate links to biased reporting, the liberal Fairness and Accuracy in Reporting (FAIR) claims that there is a conservative predisposition in news coverage and analysis.[1293]

In *Manufacturing Consent: The Political Economy of the Mass Media,* (1988) Edward S. Herman and Noam Chomsky argue that media socially engineered consumer-citizens follow the political machines of the two parties at all levels of government. After all, the essence of neoliberally-defined democracy is the information matrix under corporate control, as Chomsky argues in *Necessary Illusions: Thought Control in Democratic Societies*[1] (1989). The key to the success of molding the neoliberal conformist citizen is for the media to project the illusion of freedom of choice within narrowly defined neoliberal perimeters and to demonstrate pluralism within those perimeters including media self-policing watchdog groups such as AIM and FAIR.

1. *https://www.goodreads.com/work/quotes/865795*

Conclusions

Contrary to how the media presents itself, it is at the heart of the political system and hegemonic culture which it propagates and perpetuates. Public interest and objectivity aside, mainstream and social media interpret stories based on neoliberal ideology and goals. Incessantly indoctrinating to maintain public consent to a system constantly generating inequality under authoritarian or pluralist neoliberal policies, the media and social media are catalysts in class warfare, with only incidental relevance to humanity's edification limited to the wealthy and derivative benefits on the descending social ladder.[1294]

In so far as it serves and benefits from the social contract, the media's role is to perpetuate the hegemonic culture, not to challenge it for the sake of creating a socially just society. Keeping the masses indoctrinated so they remain loyal to the institutional mainstream, the media contributes to the erosion of liberal democracy and inequality while claiming to serve society through the delivery of news and analysis.[1295] Important not only in influencing people receiving information, but as Jurgen Habermas contends the media molds the public sphere in its totality thereby shaping a worldview presented as the norm. Its ubiquitous role in the public sphere is far more significant in the neoliberal phase of capitalism partly because of the technological revolution than in the Keynesian phase when Habermas was analyzing it.[1296]

Because the neoliberal regime suppresses dissent and permits conflict only within the model's perimeters, including the media which presumably exists in a pluralistic society to shed light on dissent for the sake of the public interest, a corporate definition of democracy and the media contaminates with aspects of authoritarianism. Amid twentieth-century technological advancements, democracy's evolution and growth coincided with a rise in corporate public relations, and co-opting labor unions and the working class into a docile role. Employing tools of mass indoctrination through more sophisticated and covert means in a way not evident even in authoritarian societies. As Alex Carey argues in *Taking the Risk out of Democracy: Corporate Propaganda versus Freedom and Liberty,* (1996), democracy grew in the twentieth century under an authoritarian corporate model within the context of electoral politics.

Associated with non-Western dictatorships from Brazil to the Philippines, and from Central Asia to sub-Sahara Africa, authoritarianism permeated liberal-democratic parties and institutions including the media throughout the world. One manifestation of rising authoritarian tendencies has been the strengthening of the executive branch at the expense of the legislative but also the subtlety of choice within a preselected political establishment that the socioeconomic elites influence through heavy campaign donations and various other institutional avenues. Spreading like a virus infecting the entire world, political authoritarian contamination ran parallel to digital authoritarianism in the race to maintain a lock on market hegemony, especially by countries holding high the flag of democracy behind which they hide.[1297]

Influenced by Harbermas' thesis, Paul Rutherford argues that the marketplace has absorbed the public sphere, and rightly so, at least as far as the 'evangelists of neoliberalism' are concerned. "*The [public] sphere remains a site for the production of public opinion that is given concrete form by surveys and polls which, to a degree, actually fashion the opinion through the process of asking certain questions (and not asking others). Because of an excess of goods and risks competing for attention, the sphere continues to be a contested arena; however, much of the excess is manufactured by people and institutions with money, moral clout, or other forms of power. The mass media play out a double role here, both as the vehicle for competitive spectacles and as the source of news, a different kind of discourse, though again a monologue and now contaminated by the ubiquity of publicity."*[1298]

At the time that Habermas was analyzing the public sphere's role in bourgeois society, the Keynesian state was wounded because the Bretton Woods influenced policy. Nevertheless, it was still viable with deep public sector institutional roots and widespread acceptance. Four decades later when Rutherford was examining the issue, neoliberal transformation had purged much of the social welfare state in favor of corporate welfare as the new norm. All along, the media played a catalytic role in the public sphere's neoliberal colonization. Because the media's short-term objective was profit and conditioning the public into conformity with the transformation model, the slow evolution of objective macro-social realities remained beyond journalism's reach.

The crisis of neoliberal capitalism that the media analyzes from within the models' ideological perimeters in the name of the general public has eroded its credibility and obviated its effectiveness as a public instrument. Its inability to conceal corporate propaganda enmeshed in news coverage and analysis is manifested in every aspect. This is especially true in polemics of the rightwing media and identity politics populism on the part of the liberal media. An important catalyst, as Alex Carey noted analyzing corporate propaganda and the media, modern technology has had an impact on how the corporate establishment molds public opinion. The selective manner in which the state uses technology in surveillance through social media, and the commercialization of personal information further contributes to the public's erosion of institutional confidence in liberal democracy.[1299]

Because of the media's corporate control, class warfare manifests itself in news coverage and analysis. It assumes subtle forms to the degree that a segment of the working class accepts its premises and becomes a vassal in its service. This includes unrelenting propaganda that trade unions are an obstacle to economic progress, despite workers and the middle class rallying behind political parties and organizations that the hegemonic culture has co-opted.

As part of public policy and an integral part of the institutional structure and hegemonic culture, neoliberal regimes have normalized and legitimized social oppression with remarkable effectiveness, partly because of the media's role. "*One consequence of the neoliberal social-economic policies,*" Noam Chomsky notes, '*is the collapse of the social order, yielding a breeding ground for extremism, violence hatred, search for scapegoats — and fertile terrain for authoritarian figures who can posture as the savior. And we're on the road to a form of neo-fascism."*[1300]

In the incessant neoliberal class war, the army is made up of mainstream journalists and analysts, well-paid experts from academia, many of them projecting an image of open-minded liberals, think tanks, corporations, and government, all working toward the same goal of strengthening capital. Regardless of media manipulation to forge consent behind neoliberal policies precipitating inequality and authoritarianism, class warfare has been more evident in peoples' material lives. Against labor's demands for social justice, whether in France and the UK where labor struggled for wages, benefits, collective bargaining, retirement age, and terms of employment during the COVID-19 pandemic and its immediate aftermath; or in Lebanon and Sri Lanka where workers were fighting just to survive austerity throughout 2022 and 2023, the media strives to influence public opinion in favor of pro-business policy and by implication against workers. Reinforcing the neoliberal social contract rooted in market efficiency, the media has been neoliberalism's Leviathan, except that it too has been a salient factor in contributing to the capitalist crisis in so far as it has promoted financialization, derivatives, hedge funds, and corporate welfare.[1301]

Louis Althusser contended that without ideological hegemony manifesting itself in peoples' actions, class domination made possible by the state for a sustained period would not be possible. This has been evident under the neoliberal model, in which both mainstream and social media have played catalytic roles. Like Althusser, Antonio Gramsci maintained that the dominant ideology presented as normal and inevitable, instead of a social construct and a means to perpetuate the capitalist social order, blindsides the masses, a segment of which turns to the far right in hope and desperation for salvation. Interwar-era economic, social, and political conditions were like those of the neoliberal 21st century, despite some similarities. Unlike Althusser, Gramsci argued that at the core of the class struggle rests the hope of countering the normalization of systemic exploitation in which the media plays a catalytic role.[1302]

Pointing at evidence of broader national progress as reflected in GDP growth, and providing long-term hope by pointing to individual 'success stories' the media's challenge is to keep the masses loyal to the social contract. In a Calvinist-like manner, capitalism promises the possibility of riches for the chosen few who embrace the system and aspire to something better. By the manner it covers the news, the media suggests that people suspend disbelief of their realities. Although their daily lives are on the periphery of the mainstream beyond their control, people subject themselves to externally molded identities with something larger than themselves that may not necessarily be in their best interest. Celebrity-oriented media tantalizes the middle class and working class to identify with billionaires and aspire to that goal, instead of aspiring to a more just society.

As part of the ruling class ideological apparatus, the media, and social media have played substantive roles in indoctrinating, amplifying, and reenforcing globalization of norms, thereby affording legitimacy to the social contract Increasingly unable to achieve market equilibrium and stimulate economic growth, neoliberalism exacerbates social problems and undermines the model from within the institutions upholding and reproducing it. As neoliberalism's promoter in reproducing a hierarchical social order, the media has continued to suffer a credibility crisis along with the entire institutional structure amid recurring crises of capitalism.[1303]

Chapter IX:

Neoliberal Transformation and Geopolitics

Neoliberal Foreign Economic Policy

Throughout history, foreign policy reflects the social contract, although with deviations as the specific entanglement warrants. Under neoliberal globalization, one of foreign policy's goals is to minimize the state's role by permitting market hegemony across national borders. At the UN-WTO meeting in October 1996, WTO general secretary Renato Ruggiero expressed the spirit of global neoliberal transformation that the US, UK, and northwest Europe imposed on the world with the leverage of the IMF, World Bank, UN, and WTO. *"We are no longer writing the rules of interaction among separate national economies. We are writing the constitution of a single global economy."*[1304]

Given that its officially stated purpose is to help developing nations become integrated into the world economy under fair terms of trade and exchange, the UNCTAD motto is *"prosperity for all"*. The chasm between its mission statement and reality aside, UNCTAD's role affords legitimacy to neoliberalism. Regardless of its traditional role, foreign policy became increasingly an instrument of corporate power with the state catering to the market, regardless of reckless risks in regional conflicts.

Although foreign policy under neoliberalism closely resembles the Age of Imperialism (1870-1914) when smaller regional wars led to WWI, the unique element is that corporate power has had a far greater role under a thoroughly integrated neoliberal world economy than it did 150 years ago. In an essay entitled "*Three Theses on the Current Crisis of International Liberalism*", David Singh Grewal agrees that neoliberalism has undermined the liberal-democratic social contract. *"[The] shift from the inter-state orientation that characterized the first decades of international liberalism to a "dialectic of globalization," in which newly empowered transnational activity across states generates pressure for supranational governance above them."*[1305]

Operating within the confines of imperialism, as key components of US and European foreign policy, the patron-client integration model and military Keynesianism have contributed to inequality and democracy's erosion with the considerable influence of international organizations and multinationals. UNCTAD-WTO rhetoric aside about *"prosperity for all"*, the implication is not accurate that the benefits accrue to those below the richest ten percent. Owing to Pax Americana determining geopolitics as the pretext for global economic hegemony while hiding behind liberal democracy's ideology, during neoliberal globalization liberal democracy's erosion accelerated globally amid an intensified race for markets and class war. The extraction of surplus labor value while transferring capital from the Global South to the Global North took place under neoliberal foreign policy resting on the same military Keynesian foundation as the Cold War.[1306]

Military Keynesianism transitioned the US from the New Deal social welfare era to the early Cold War and into President Lyndon Johnson's "guns and butter" mixed policy which tried to keep the US both a military and economic superpower. Under neoliberalism, the US dropped the "butter" and kept the "guns". Because the chronic balance of payments deficits kept rising, the dollar was losing its real value measured in gold. Opting for military Keynesianism, in 1968 Johnson admitted that parasitic defense spending *'killed the lady I loved – the Great Society'*. Beginning with Reagan, all neoliberal presidents thereafter tried to convince the public that

Johnson's beloved lady was always sickly; society was better off with her dead. Killing the moral imperative for Keynesianism, neoliberals dismissed the government's role as an agent for social harmony and embraced class war and militarism.[1307]

The combined cost of military Keynesianism and the corporate welfare state in the US-led steadily to rising inequality and public debt of $30 trillion by the end of 2021, or 137% of GDP, along with rising household debt. With the balance of payments deficit at $821.6 billion or 3.4% of GDP in 2021, the weaponization of the dollar as an integral part of US foreign policy was a desperate resort of a chronically-ailing-declining economy whose hegemony China and BRICS challenged. The debt issue had geopolitical and geoeconomic dimensions because China was the largest foreign holder until 2022 when Japan replaced it, largely because Beijing decided to transition from the dollar as a reserve currency that the US had weaponized to the detriment of global trade growth.[1308]

With a sharp rise in defense allocations and militarism that the US formalized in February 1985 when promulgating the Regan Doctrine, essentially a continuation of previous Cold War militarist doctrines dating back to Truman in 1947, the Reagan-Thatcher neoliberal institutionalization took place concurrently with militarization. Using a more interventionist and militarist foreign policy during the neoliberal transformation entailed presenting a defensive posture against an aggressive enemy. Part of the doctrine stated that: *"We must not break faith with those who are risking their lives—on every continent from Afghanistan[1] to Nicaragua[2]—to defy Soviet-supported aggression and secure rights which have been ours from birth."* Following a long-standing US militarist interventionist policy, the Reagan Doctrine converged with neoliberalism's nascent phase.

After the US launched *"Operation El Dorado Canyon"* on April 14, 1986, US bombing of military and paramilitary installations in Tripoli, Libya, Western allies criticized Reagan for using force in such a gratuitously symbolic manner. An enthusiastic neoliberal militarist looking to military Keynesianism to stimulate capital accumulation, Margaret Thatcher had supported the war against Argentina over the Malvinas (April-June 1982), largely a distraction from radical neoliberal policies at home. From Lebanon to Nicaragua, and the sharp rise in defense allocations, Reagan's neoliberal militarism established the precedent for US convergence of geopolitics and geoeconomics that all presidents followed, especially after 9/11 under the Islamic terrorism pretext.[1309]

Heightened emphasis on militarism in the US and UK, eventually spreading to NATO was catalytic in the institutionalization of neoliberalism that defense companies fully supported and promoted as it entailed guaranteed higher profits.[1310] *"There was an insurmountable conflict between free-market capitalism and democracy,"* Darya Sinusoid points out about Thatcherism. *"Because neoliberal policies would hurt the majority of the people, they'd never vote for politicians who tried to implement them. Things changed when a seemingly insignificant military conflict altered the course of economics."*[1311]

With watered-down aspects of Keynesian macroeconomics lingering and military Keynesianism elevated, more in some countries than others beyond the 1980s, neoliberalism was ascending at the same time as militarism. Despite the end of the Soviet bloc and the Warsaw Pact, Western militarism consolidated globally in the 1990s, after George H.W. Bush declared in September 1990 that a 'New World Order' of unipolar power had emerged. No country challenged the new world order under Bush, Clinton, and George W. Bush. Inexorably tied to

---

1. *https://en.wikipedia.org/wiki/Afghanistan*

2. *https://en.wikipedia.org/wiki/Nicaragua*

neoliberal transformation, the US-globalized war on terror after 9/11, and military invasions of Afghanistan (2001) and Iraq (2003) helped to achieve popular consensus for corporate welfare, mobilizing public support behind the military-industrial complex prerogatives. As the Soviet bloc was collapsing, the US and its junior partners also abandoned the Thatcher-Bush "peace dividend" proposal (1988-1991).[1312]

Operating under a unipolar world order, the US used the war on terror pretext to strengthen Pax Americana, exactly at a time when China was placing all efforts at global economic expansion. *"The United States-led post-9/11 wars have expanded across the globe, now in over 85 countries*[3]*. The U.S. is deploying airstrikes against militant targets, engaging in combat with militants, leading military exercises, and exporting a militarized counterterrorism model to dozens of countries through "training and assistance." The narrative, tactics, funding, and institutional supports of the U.S. post-9/11 wars fuel repression and corruption, and escalate cycles of violence."*[1313]

Historically, the core of global neoliberal militarism's trans-Atlantic base, the US and northwest Europe's policies affected the periphery, including Africa and Asia subject to the war on terror offensive, where governments use national security to promote neoliberal militarism on a smaller scale to benefit domestic political, military and business circles. Besides the US, among other advanced countries, Israel has tailored neoliberal economic policies to a hawkish foreign policy, defaulting blame to Palestinian 'terrorists' as a means of rallying support among Jewish voters and Western governments. Mimicking the US, Israel's combination of militarism and neoliberalism has come at the expense of the Palestinians, but also of the Jewish middle class and working class as reflected in declining living standards from 2000 to 2020.[1314]

Israel's transformation to neoliberalism was accompanied by a sharp turn to a de facto apartheid policy which the US has supported with billions in annual military aid, interest-free guaranteed loans, and technology transfers. In *"Neoliberal Apartheid: Palestine/Israel and South Africa after 1994,"* Andy Clarno points out that both Israel's militarism and forcible expulsion of Palestinians from their property fall within the US neoliberal model which the war on terror justified. As in apartheid South Africa, Israel's perpetual colonization and police-state militarization does not preclude a Palestinian elite from collaborating with Israel and the US while presenting itself as the "realistic" force for harmony in the community.[1315]

Beginning in the first half of the 2000s', Israel under Ariel Sharon adopted neoliberal policies combined with more aggressive persecution of Palestinians to justify them. Israel's shift from Keynesian policies, to "neoliberal Zionism" permitted the state to use "exclusionary nationalism", using the Palestinians and Iran as security threats to switch from Keynesianism to corporate welfare and greater accommodations for multinational corporations.

To bolster capital, the political class defaulted Israeli working class demands state welfare capitalism and regulatory policies to the perennial Palestinian security threat and "exclusionary nationalism". This combined with the old thesis of Israel being surrounded by Arab enemies, a claim that hardly applies considering that most Arab states are not hostile toward Israel, especially after the Israeli-Arab rapprochement of the Abraham Accords in September 2020. In essence, exclusionary nationalism has resulted in a culturally and socially monolithic society, regardless of labels such as Zionism. Justified based on a religious-based definition of national identity, apartheid has been another means of denying Palestinians collective social and economic protection, while promoting a neoliberal model within the militarist state and socio-cultural milieu.[1316]

---

3. https://watson.brown.edu/costsofwar/papers/2021/USCounterterrorismOperations

With the combination of neoliberalism's financialization and corporate welfare resulting in a deeper parasitic political economy amid rising inequality and illiberal democracy, Keynesian militarism has weakened the civilian economy globally and contributed to lower working-class living standards. Between 9/11 and the end of 2018, the US spent $6.4 trillion on the wars in Iraq and Afghanistan. These costs do not include the covert and overt interventions in Libya, Syria, Yemen, Somalia, and the global 'war on terror' focused especially in the Middle East and Africa.

During that same period, the combined US corporate welfare program cost $1.5 trillion annually, while defense, intelligence, and security almost as much, accounting for about half of the US budget by 2023. Both the Republican and Democratic parties supported corporate welfare and militarism as national priorities. By contrast, healthcare and education were low priorities, and the reason that one hundred million have medical debt and 1.3 million have college debt. While the US was destabilizing the Middle East to deny Iran a balance of power role, China signed trade, investment, and reconstruction contracts, assuming a major role through economic leverage.[1317]

Rather than competing with China's civilian economy, especially in technology, the US focus is on technology with priority on defense and intelligence. Trade, technology, and commercial rather than military emphasis is a major reason China preempted the US role in the Saudi Arabia-Iran rapprochement in March 2023. Leading the world in 37 out of 44 areas of technology, China will play a major role in Saudi Arabia's proposed $1 trillion NEOM-the Line project. Datasets, including cloud and surveillance technology, will be under contract to Chinese telecoms giant Huawei which has several contracts with the Saudi government. Taking the lead in the Gulf States, Saudi Arabia resolved in 2023 that economic diversification rests with China, not the West.[1318]

Having failed in the Middle East geopolitically in the first two decades of the 21st century, geoeconomically the US did much better by preventing Israel from signing contracts with Chinese telecommunication companies during the Trump and Biden administrations. *"U.S. Deputy Secretary of Energy Dan Brouillette cautioned Israel over Chinese investment in the country, suggesting Israel's allies could limit intelligence-sharing with it as a result." [1319]* Complying with US demands, the Israeli government refused Chinese 5G telecommunications network technology, rejected Hong Kong-based Hutchison Water's bid for a desalination plant, and disqualified China Railway Construction Corp. and CRRC.[1320]

Hardly an example of the free market determining the economy's course, US foreign economic policy had a geoeconomic goal of preventing China from securing global market share at the expense of the US and companies that the US approved from allied nations. Followed by a slow recovery leading to the 2020 pandemic, and US-led anti-Russian sanctions resulted in a global economic retreat and manifested further internal contradictions in the neoliberal experiment. One of the most significant contradictions pertained to the US semiconductor policy of selective 'reshoring', as expressed in the EU and US 'Chips Act' of 2022. To justify reshoring, the EU and US used the pretext of the supply chain bottlenecks amid the COVID-19 pandemic and the fact that China, Taiwan, and South Korea control the vast majority of manufacturing. As will be seen below, the goal of reshoring foreign economic policy was to deny not just China, but East Asia dominance in the sector, and to empower EU and US companies with corporate welfare policies to achieve a larger market share.[1321]

In July 2023, China retaliated by restricting licensed exporters of gallium and germanium, the two significant metals in semiconductor, telecommunications, solar power, and electric vehicle industries. At the same time,

Beijing continued to dump US Treasury bonds, reaching a 13-year low of its holdings in 2023. These combined moves rattled the US government and private sector to the degree that the US scrambled to undo the damage through diplomacy aiming at stabilizing the relationship. Both the US and Europe became targets of Beijing's new foreign policy law aiming at countering any punitive and restrictive measures.[1322]

Oblivious to the realities of US limited power both geopolitically and geoeconomically, the neocon-dominated Biden administration stayed on the containment course against China, no matter the price to be paid. Validating the failure of the neoliberal Washington Consensus, the Biden administration came up with a revised version of that failed model. This was not necessarily to strengthen the civilian economy per se, but to maintain Pax Americana which was partly responsible for weakening the civilian economy in the first place.

"The New Washington Consensus aims to sustain the hegemony of U.S. capital and its junior allies with a new approach. [Jake] Sullivan [US National Security Advisor]: "In the face of compounding crises—economic stagnation, political polarization[4], and the climate emergency—a new reconstruction agenda is required." The U.S. must sustain its hegemony, said Sullivan, but "hegemony[5], however, is not the ability to prevail—that's dominance—but the willingness of others to follow (under constraint), and the capacity to set agendas." In other words, the U.S. will set the new agenda and its junior partners will follow—an alliance of the willing. Those who don't follow can face the consequences... The World Bank has reported just this week[6] that, economic growth in the Global South outside of China will fall from 4.1% in 2022 to 2.9% in 2023. Battered by high inflation, rising interest rates, and record debt levels many countries were growing poorer.[1323]

The contradictions, some of which the foreign economic policy of the US and EU created in the semiconductors sector, frustrated the G7 members. This is not just because they were unable to find a resolution that would restore the trans-Atlantic core to its glory from the 1950s through the 1990s, but because US foreign policy has always had a positive impact on its Western allies left paying the price for Pax Americana adventurism intended to secure greater global market share. Operating on the premise of President George H.W. Bush's "New World Order" when the US enjoyed unipolar superpower status as the trans-Atlantic core country promoting neoliberal transformation, the G7 found themselves blindsided by China's meteoric rise to economic preeminence. The Great Recession of 2007-2008 proved as much, as Russia's energy dominance during the war in Ukraine when considering that most energy producers coordinated policy with Moscow, not the US.

In January 2023, Economy, Trade, and Industry Minister Yasutoshi Nishimura called for a new world order. Japan feared that the existing world order helped 'authoritarian regimes', primarily China challenging US hegemony and its unipolar world system. More than geopolitical concerns, neoliberal contradictions led to Japan's frustration with the US-centered world order that inadvertently helped China while overshadowing Japan. Yasutoshi Nishimura made no mention of neoliberalism in both Japan and the US as the underlying structural cause of the common affliction ailing both countries.[1324]

---

4. https://www.greeneuropeanjournal.eu/the-carbon-divide-the-material-basis-of-polarisation/

5. https://osf.io/preprints/socarxiv/f8hwe/download

6. https://www.worldbank.org/en/publication/global-economic-prospects?fbclid=IwAR0g6Di2RowVYI6G3NkSYIe5IFP3SjOMoh6uuGpl6lb3Hth3oMhvGP9fk54

One unique difference between the Keynesian and neoliberal macroeconomic models is that the former has a horizontal development scheme. With an aggregate demand focus, Keynesianism stresses a strong centralized state structure stimulating economic growth and a social safety net intended for both economic and political consensus. Under the neoliberal model, military Keynesianism uses the state solely for vertical economic development with a weak social development component and heavy reliance on the defense sector.

This formula resulted in capital concentration under a weak social safety net. Especially given the pluralist/multilateralist vs. populist unilateralist foreign policy divergence on tactics, reliance on force to maintain social conformity in the name of national security becomes unavoidable. Especially for the Western Alliance member countries and those linked to the West using foreign policy as a pretext to bolster capital, the relationship between neoliberalism and geopolitics is essential.[1325]

Some critics of neoliberalism accept the thesis that every crisis resulting in severe economic contraction must necessarily lead to the end of the development model. For capitalism's survival, the transformed economic and political institutions are essential to maintain the social contract. In *The Rise and Fall of Neoliberal Capitalism,* David M. Kotz points out that only institutional change, not nuances of existing policy, can solve the perpetual stagnation that neoliberalism's structural crisis has created. Pointing to historical examples of US economic contracting cycles since the late 19th century, Kotz expects the pattern of regulated capitalism to follow neoliberalism. A prediction that others hold as well, it does not take into account geopolitics which the state uses to strengthen capital while promoting corporate welfare.[1326]

Since the Great Recession, there have been targeted policy adjustments reflecting the state's affirmation of sustaining nationally-based businesses. During COVID-19 pandemic policy adjustments, neoliberalism was strengthened not weakened. By helping domestic firms against foreign competition, the state's efforts to strengthen national capitalism represented corporate welfare continuity. Although the US-led international sanctions response to the war in Ukraine pointed to Biden's efforts presumably to strengthen globalization and multilateralism, the result was to strengthen bilateral and block trading that emboldened national capitalism but within the neoliberal policy structure in each nation. Operating under the *"New Washington Consensus"* based on the old one but with nationalist-militarist emphasis, the US-led effort to dilute neoliberalism's multilateral aspects and maintain US economic and military superpower status drove many analysts to wonder about neoliberalism's future.[1327]

To undermine globalization which favors China's global economic ascendancy, the US, EU, Japan, South Korea, Taiwan, Canada, and Australia used sanctions against Russia and its main ally China. The record shows that the US-EU policy to "punish" Russia by isolating it from the world capitalist system backfired. As a result, the Cold War-based *"New Washington Consensus"* had a much rougher start than the old Washington Consensus.

Not only did Russia have China and India as major trading partners, but its energy and grain export sector, combined with its strategic control of Black Sea ports gave it enormous global leverage. Because of the military-solution approach to the Russia-Ukraine conflict by both Russia and the West behind Ukraine, rightwing populists benefited more than the liberal pluralists identified with peace through diplomacy. Even with the global stagflation consequence of the Russia war/Western sanctions, neoliberalism adjusted into US-led G-7 regional trade blocs.[1328]

On the eve of the war in Ukraine, the inflationary spiral on the back of supply chain bottlenecks owing to COVID-19 restrictions caught up with market reality. Inflation compelled central banks to raise interest rates. Tightening monetary policy to protect financial assets, including weaponizing the dollar to preserve the US role in the core of the world economy amid global de-dollarization was in some respects similar to the British Sterling's decline in 1931 during the Great Depression. The combination of inflationary pressures and looming recession notwithstanding in 2023, the US and allied countries raised defense spending. To justify it, they pointed to Russian aggression and more defense spending as leverage against rising Chinese hegemony.[1329]

Rather than G7 vs. China inter-core competition at the root of Western geopolitics and adjustments to neoliberalism, economics professor Cedric Durand concurred with *Le Monde Diplomatique* journalist Serge Halimi that neoliberalism is on its last leg owing to stimulative (inflationary) consumer policies in the US, especially after the pandemic. Durand went so far as to agree with Biden's stimulative policies, which included a sharp rise in the defense budget, presumably a sign of supporting jobs, if not reversing neoliberalism with economic nationalism manifested in the *"New Washington Consensus"* doctrine.

"There have been many signs that the neoliberal tool-kit was proving less and less effective for the day-to-day management of capital accumulation. The Eurozone crisis, global waves of 'populist' protest, and the new assertiveness of digital monopolies were indications of growing systemic instability. On top of that the pandemic accelerated the pressure for change. At this stage, one of the few things that can be said with confidence is that the possibility of tasting once again the flavor of popular victories is a just little greater than it was five months ago."[1330]

The neoliberal model is indeed showing signs of premature aging in failing to deliver market efficiency, not to mention equilibrium, but not as a capital accumulation tool amid inter-core competition. After Russia invaded Ukraine, the US-led management of a geopolitical global crisis exposed more contradictions in the neoliberal model that the Biden administration found the need to promulgate a new version of the old Washington Consensus.

In the absence of the capitalist class opposing neoliberalism, against the backdrop of China's preponderate role in globalization, the existing development model will be stumbling along, partly owing to recurring geopolitical crises. As class warfare intensified amid trade union efforts to protect labor rights in North America, Europe, South Korea, and Japan, governments turned to geopolitics as a distraction, thereby further undermining the model from within because geopolitical conflict fuels economic nationalism.[1331]

James M. Cypher offers a realistic assessment of how weapons corporations have leveraged the state structure, using the pretext of national security while the goal is destabilization and forcing China to divert spending from the civilian economy to defense as a means of weakening its global economic role. *"Organizations such as the National Defense Industry Association, with 1,570 members, the Council of Defense and Space Industry Associations (which counts the extremely powerful 300-corporate-strong Aerospace Industry Association as a member) form, shape, and reproduce the weapon-acquisition process as administered by a deferential Pentagon... The funds appropriated by the military contracting corporations via the Titanic littoral combat ships and the Zumwalt stealth destroyer programs are but a small prelude to a massive new round of military Keynesianism designed to leapfrog U.S. high-technology industries and boost profits across the defense industrial base while forcing China to divert resources from surging technologically intensive manufacturing, thereby disrupting its bid to be the global industrial and manufacturing power."[1332]*

Especially for the US and its allies, military neoliberalism has entailed a 'forever war' doctrine and recurring humanitarian crises resulting from interventions which themselves become the focal point of prolonging multifaceted crises. Clearly, beyond the defense sector private contractors, there are corporate winners because of rising defense budgets not just in the advanced countries but also in the periphery. Considering that the profits of defense corporations far exceed non-defense company profits, there is intense lobbying in this sector to secure more lucrative contracts.[1333]

Under neoliberalism, Lebanon's defense spending rose from $0.04 billion in 1988 to $2.78 billion in 2018 when the financial crisis erupted resulting in a sharp rise in poverty. Similarly, Sri Lanka's defense went from $0.17 billion in 1986 to $1.64 billion in 2018 when it too manifested serious problems stemming from the neoliberal model. Although Lebanon's structural financial crisis and Sri Lanka's uprising of 2022 pointed to trouble for neoliberalism, as does the US-G7-led new Cold War, conditions in the first two decades of the 21st century were not as dire as the first half of the 20th century.

In contemporary neoliberal society, objective conditions are worsening for the working class, but not at the crisis juncture for capitalism to revert to some form of quasi-statism which has worked well for Chinese economic expansion. Instead, the *New Washington Consensus* of sanctions, weaponized dollar, economic nationalism, and bloc trading has been a desperate means to maintain neoliberalism, but with the US determining which country benefits and which does not.[1334]

Edward Luce of the ***Financial Times*** observed that the US wants to deny China the means to become a military superpower, but *"without provoking a US-China conflict or global economic retrenchment. A full-scale decoupling would make everyone poorer and create an Orwellian world of hostile blocs. The middle way between the old Washington consensus and the new is to preserve what was good about the old, rather than to throw out the baby with the bathwater... No power will be its sole author. But America still has an outsized say on whether the script will be dark or light."[1335]*

One reason for critics of neoliberalism predicting the end of the transformation model is China's swift move from the semi-periphery to the core of the world capitalist system. Historically, there have been such shifts reflecting the dynamic capitalist world system. Not necessarily signaling the transformation model's imminent demise, the global economy's fragmentation resulting from geopolitical struggles has worried China influencing the world's economic balance of power, as well as the US and its allies anxious to thwart China's ascendancy. This is exactly why in January 2023 the Japanese government called for a new world order and the reason for raising its defense budget from 1.2% of GDP in 2022 to 2% in 2023. This is also why Biden's National Security Advisor Jake Sullivan promulgated the New Washington Consensus in April 2023.[1336]

While the US and its allies were busy revising the old neoliberal model, China was moving forward with dreams of rapid Asian and global economic integration through the BRI project. In *"The Chinese Dream, Neoliberalism, and International Legal Ideology"* Ian Yuying Liu argues that China's global economic ascendancy coinciding with US decline was based on the country's Asian hegemony objective. Combining the *Belt Road Initiative* under statist policies, Beijing has been complying with global market forces and the Bretton Woods System as catalysts to greater global integration. What some call the neo-Confucian version of neoliberalism, Beijing has been striving toward the "Chinese Dream" as a more realistic counterpart to the elusive American Dream.[1337]

"The CCP's insistence on the Chinese Dream does not forsake neoliberalism. Rather, it perpetuates the structural inequalities between core production zones and peripheral states. OBOR's communal solidarity bends the hegemonic narrative of interstate relations to suit China's policy of materially satisfying the People. International legal ideology sustains oppression and economic inequality, endemic to capitalist relations of production. Its apparatuses present a familiar, coherent set of 'rules' by which proponents of neoliberalism can standardize political legitimacy, in a capitalist world-economy otherwise disconnected from identity and morality."[1338]

The Great Recession and its aftermath proved the validity of Yuying Liu's thesis that China under a hybrid model and the Communist Party's commitment to social development running parallel to economic growth has been a pillar of the neoliberal world economy which helps to explain the resiliency of neoliberal transformation outside China. Despite US-led efforts to intimidate China into raising its defense spending thereby weakening its civilian economy and starting a Pacific arms race to help Western defense companies, Beijing has resisted, but within certain limits. Whereas the average NATO spending has been 2.57 percent of GDP from 2014 to 2022, or comparable to China's defense allocations in 1992, the government in Beijing contained spending at about 1.7% from 2006 to 2021. This is well below the average of all developed nations, and less than half of the US at 3.48 percent of GDP in 2021.[1339]

Disagreeing about how China's economy fits into the world capitalist system, many scholars, and especially Western journalists, have excoriated everything from the one-party state to currency manipulation, and Beijing's bellicose role in Taiwan and claims in the South China Sea. After 2014 when Russia annexed Crimea, Beijing has invoked its right to draw baselines in the South China Sea and to define internal waters in four groups of islands. Despite the Taiwan Strait Crisis of the early 1950s, Beijing policy as outlined in white papers of 1993 and 2000, modified in 2022, calls for the peaceful reunification of "one country, two systems", in a way mirroring the Hong Kong model. Given the US policy of containment that President Xi has described as hostile, Beijing has stated that force is a last resort in case Taiwanese nationalists invite US-led foreign forces and overstep the boundaries of the mainland's national security.[1340]

Beyond geopolitical issues, Western neoliberal analysts have been critical of Beijing adopting the Japan-South Korea-Taiwan neo-corporatist model before neoliberalism with the state's preponderate role in the economy as a shareholder, planner, and regulator. Poised to emerge as the world's top technology superpower, China has the essential raw materials and global market share to dominate in space, robotics, energy, the environment, biotechnology, artificial intelligence (AI), advanced materials, and quantum technology. Leading in 37 out of 44 critical tech fields under a one-party state, China is thoroughly integrated into the neoliberal world economy and with domestic and international companies profiting from such achievements.[1341]

Although under a mixed capitalist model which includes aspects of neoliberalism and Japanese neo-corporatism, especially under Yasuhiro Nakasone in the 1980s, but also South Korea and Taiwan, China's contemporary economy has retained remnants of long-term state planning from the Maoist era. The *Belt and Road Initiative,* as well as fixed asset private investment vs. state asset investment in comparison with other developed countries such as Norway is based on the hybrid model, with geopolitics taken into account. Because defense allocations amount to about one-third of what the US was spending in 2021, China has been able to spend more on economic and social development.[1342]

Unlike the Chinese hybrid model, the trans-Atlantic neoliberal experiment is based on short-term chaotic market conditions from which investors realize optimal returns on the financialization/rentier parasitic system which undermines the economy's productive foundation and social development. Complicating matters for those analyzing where China fits into the capitalist system, Beijing has supported the WTO, IMF, and World Bank all of which have historically promoted austerity, deregulation, privatization, and free flow of capital across national borders. Even more significant, China's stimulative policies and purchase of US Treasury bonds helped to bail out as much of the US as the world economy during the Great Recession.

The gap between the Western fear of the aggressive China theory vs. the reality of China's global economic integration through cooperation is partly because China's ascendancy took place under the Bretton Woods System in the neoliberal era, but under a one-party state and a state-directed economy. As the engine for global integration operating within the transformation model, BRI has raised concern among the G7 nations eager not to lose global market share. Despite international corporate involvement in the BRI, and the continued steady flow of G7 corporate investment in China, the US and its allies use containment policy and sanctions as leverage to slow down China's economic progress in the hope of gaining market share for their companies, despite the negative consequences to the world economy.[1343]

Using geopolitical alliances, bloc trading, development loans, and foreign aid as a means to retain global market preeminence, the West lacks a worldwide integration scheme comparable to the *Belt and Road Initiative* on which countries can base long-term planning to provide their people with some hope for economic and social development. This does not mean that China's enterprises around the world are a panacea for the working class. In many respects, the working-class conditions of Chinese companies are worse than their Western counterparts. On the other hand, the US has remained fixated on a global military network, offering weapons sales and nothing comparable to counter China's economic focus. Despite disadvantages for workers in the host nation and heavy reliance on transported Chinese workers, BRI and association with the Shanghai Cooperation Organization and BRICS offer greater hope for development than US military bases and NATO association.[1344]

Following the US-NATO-led sanctions on Russia in the spring of 2022, the backlash on the euro and the global economy suffering stagflation forced a modicum of reality check on those banking on residual benefits. Very quickly, they discovered the self-defeating nature of extremely punitive sanctions against raw-materials-rich Russia with China and India as major markets, not to mention "fence-sitter" countries throughout the Global South.[1345]

Russia circumvented Western sanctions through various means, including the illegal trade of large ocean tankers by mysterious ownership companies. With certification and insurance from countries officially observing US sanctions, shipping companies carried on uninterrupted. *"Industry insiders estimate the size of that "shadow" fleet at roughly 600 vessels or about 10% of the global number of large tankers. And numbers continue to climb. As Europe has weaned itself off Russian energy, buyers in Asia have cut deals. China boosted imports of Russian oil to 1.9 million barrels per day on average in 2022, up 19% from 2021, according to the International Energy Agency. India ramped up purchases even more sharply, logging an 800% increase to an average of 900,000 barrels per day. Global Witness, a nonprofit, estimates that a quarter of oil tanker sales between late February 2022 and January this year involved unknown buyers, roughly double the proportion the previous year."*[1346]

Throughout the war, Europe remained Russia's second-largest buyer of oil and natural gas with China leading the list. Besides selling to Europe, Indian companies also sold to the US so adamant about punishing Russia.

Another dimension of the sanctions was the dollar's weaponization as 'soft power' diplomacy, but not without unexpected resistance in several countries, including Russia and Asia. Although the dollar gained against the weak euro, several central banks were lowering dollar holdings, some to the lowest point since the mid-1990s. For its part, Russia circumvented the Society for Worldwide Interbank Financial Telecommunication (SWIFT). Facing Western sanctions, Russia's economic resiliency was attributed to a long-standing policy of dumping the dollar as a major reserve currency before the sanctions.

At the same time, several countries were lining up behind the BRICS planning their reserve currency, thereby trying to preempt US dollar weaponization. Other than using its global military superpower status and fomenting regional instability which compelled currency investors to back the dollar at the expense of the euro and other currencies, the US had to contend with a contracting world trade and stagflation in 2022 and 2023 and nothing to show but huge costs to taxpayers for the extremely dangerous shadow war of attrition in Ukraine and the threat of nuclear holocaust under conditions where Russia realized its existence was at stake.[1347]

From the perspective of US sanctions contributing to the dollar's oversized global role, the neoliberal model suffered a setback because the war over Ukraine further strengthened China by forcing Moscow deeper into its economic embrace. At the same time, the war proved that only China had the global influence to bring about a framework for a diplomatic solution, again upstaging the US as a global destabilizing force. Undercutting the world economy, the US-NATO confrontation with Russia further weakened the Bretton Woods System. Meanwhile, the BRICS popularity rose across the Global South as the US tried to counter it with the New Washington Consensus.

By its own choice, the EU lapsed into deeper a dependency relationship on the US to the extent that President Emmanuel Macron publicly protested France's role as America's vassal from Ukraine to Taiwan policy. While US geoeconomic goals of greater market share turned into the reality of mixed blessings, it was mostly at the expense of the working class and US trading partners who diluted their multilateral trade relations to strengthen the US-led alliance. Nevertheless, they suffered economic contraction because the US used the war not just for increased weapons and energy sales, but consolidation of trade blocs with all the risks, once China and its allies began retaliating.[1348]

The EU-US geopolitical cooperation on the rivalry between the Western neoliberal model and the Chinese mixed economy contributed to modifications in Western global economic hegemony. Fomenting regional destabilization as a means of gaining an advantage in global economic competition, Western economic sanctions and military solutions exacerbated neoliberalism's inherent contradictions and provided further proof that the model is mired in contradictions, withering away from within. Several institutions and economic analysts have expressed pessimism about globalization's future which the G-7 view as benefiting China more than the rest of the world.[1349]

As evidenced in the US adopting a wide variety of protectionist measures from Obama's "returning to the Asia Pacific" policy to Biden's New Washington Consensus, the neoliberal experiment has undergone adjustments to accommodate geopolitical and geoeconomic goals of the state strategically helping certain sectors of the economy and specific companies within those sectors. Amid a power struggle between the national bourgeoisie and the comprador bourgeoisie and ongoing pressure from labor, the corporate elite is not one mind about diluting the neoliberal model. Both Trump and Biden demanded that allies follow US policy aimed to strengthen block trading benefiting mostly, but not exclusively, US-based multinational corporations. Considering that sanctions and weaponization of the dollar are a form of corporate subsidy that the state extracts from the consumer, the impact on living standards is negative and not what neoliberalism advertises.[1350]

Commercialization of foreign policy has always been an integral part of the political economy, as foreign trade, investment, and market share, are all part of geoeconomics intertwined with geopolitics. Under the neoliberal model, Bill Clinton further tilted foreign and defense policy to reflect the primacy of trade to promote US-based companies against international competitors. Considering the collapse of the Soviet bloc that permitted a strategic shift in moving foreign policy more openly to serve US economic integration, Clinton's move yielded benefits in so far as geopolitical leverage intended to raise capital accumulation and closer ties with the former Communist bloc.[1351]

The Boris Yeltsin-Bill Clinton meeting in Budapest in December 1994 illustrated that the US two-track expansion into the former Soviet sphere entailed integrating all of the former Soviet bloc economically while pushing NATO eastward to contain the Russian Federation. Formal agreements notwithstanding, history proved that NATO expansion and Western economic integration of the former Soviet republics was always the ultimate goal. Essentially a "protection racket" in international relations, post-Soviet-era Western imperialism resembled the late 19th-century militarist model. Under neoliberalism, US policy, which American advisors were offering Russia and the former Soviet republics for a hefty fee, included transactions from trade to joint ventures and massive policy transformation in the name of neoliberalism's 'market efficiency'. At the same time, the US sought the opportunity of the war in Ukraine to militarize the EU economy.

"The European Commission has been drafting a package of documents to speed up the process of militarization of the EU economy, making the arms industry one of the priorities of its economic development... In line with the package, the weapons and ammunition industry will be named a priority area of the EU economic development, along with green energy and clean production... European arms makers also have grounds to fear competition with the US military industry, the largest supplier of weapons and military equipment to the NATO countries. According to European media reports, the European Commission is discussing with the member states the possibility of assigning the priority status to European arms makers while choosing contractors for national defense procurement orders. That said, US manufacturers should be allowed to enter the market only by the residual principle. Germany, France, and Italy actively promote this approach, while Poland, Baltic countries, and several other nations are resisting it."[1352]

In the first two decades of the 21st century, the US war-geared economy has resulted in fewer jobs, less investment in infrastructure and clean energy, and higher interest rates for mass consumers because war is financed by raising the debt ceiling. Among other organizations public and private, the UN and IMF have concluded that the Ukrainian war accounted for the global rise in commodity and energy prices, which in turn exacerbated inflation and generated higher inequality. Higher inflation depleted middle-class savings, impoverished workers, and increased unemployment. As a tool of modern warfare, sanctions have had far worse consequences not only for the parties directly involved but the entire world economy which is more closely integrated than ever. According to Nicholas Mulder's *The Economic Weapon* (2022), at least one-third of the world's population lives under sanctions. Moreover, the people paying the price are completely innocent, while those in positions of power have their assets shielded. Under Trump, the US imposed on 3,900 occasions on 40 countries, and Biden continued the practice with Russia and China as main targets.

Commercialization and militarization of foreign policy further exposed the preponderate US reliance on military Keynesianism as a means of reinforcing neoliberalism. Choosing to place a lesser focus on horizontal development of the civilian economy at a time when China was competitive on a sustained basis, US military supremacy has been a means to retain the preeminent core status in the world economy. This is both a reflection and a contradiction of the trans-Atlantic neoliberal model that has led to trade fragmentation and altering of the globalization phase prevalent in the 1990s when Francis Fukuyama and Samuel Huntington were academic cheerleaders for Pax Americana's hollow triumph.[1353]

Analyzing neoliberalism's evolution in the China-centered 'Asian century' hegemony, some Western scholars concluded that the rise of neo-statism will inevitably replace neoliberalism because China became the world's top economy, in PPP terms, adhering to a hybrid formula. Oddly enough, many scholars do not take military Keynesianism into account as an integral part of neoliberalism. By reverting to historic isolationism and economic fragmentation, the US created bloc trading, thereby undermining its old neoliberal Washington Consensus. While militarizing the world as part of a strategy that diluted neoliberalism, the US and its junior partners used back channels, many in violation of WTO rules, as well as international diplomatic agreements, thereby diluting neoliberalism, contrary to the intended objective.[1354]

Some of those who see the demise of neoliberalism as necessary, also view neo-statism both as a means of expanding the capitalist economy and an effective means to compete with China. Often associating neo-statism with authoritarianism, pluralist neoliberal analysts do not see the developmental state co-existing with liberal democracy. Neither does the neoliberal pluralist or the authoritarian state that produces Third World conditions under a patron-client relationship.[1355]

In a work entitled *The Great Recoil: Politics after Populism and Pandemic,* Paolo Gerbaudo maintains that the world is grappling with neoliberalism which foments rightwing populism against statism and social democracy. In the background, the stagflation crisis of 2022-2023 (global growth dropping from 5.7% in 2021 to 2.9% in 2022) was somewhat similar to the post-1973 oil crisis. Signaling more dysfunctions in neoliberalism, the world economy which grew at a historically slow pace from 2008 to 2022, compared with the 1950-1973 and 1980-2008 cycles, will be more volatile in the years ahead. This is not necessarily because US-led geopolitical and geoeconomic blocs against China and its allies slowed world trade, but the consumer base became narrower amid greater capital concentration.[1356]

US-led Sanctions and Currency Weaponization

Instead of forging a broad social compromise to revive capitalism from deep crisis, as was the case under the Keynesian model, neoliberalism promised market efficiency only to deliver class war and rising inequality which undercut social compromise and bourgeois political consensus built around representative government. Whereas it promised growth under a minimally-regulated system to maximize economic opportunities and stability, it delivered concentrated wealth and a high degree of social instability leading to authoritarianism and militarization both in the Western metropolis and the Global South.[1357]

Combined with the glaring contradictions of what neoliberal apologists promised vs. actual results, the political economy intertwined with geopolitics undermined capitalist growth in a minimally-regulated economy where one sector undermined another exactly as was the case in the late 19th century when wars of imperialism became the "solution" to the problem of international competition for markets. Hence, neoliberalism's market efficiency and stability cause market disequilibrium, and social and political instability. Contrary to claims of some scholarly publications and newspaper articles, it took a pandemic to expose the shortcomings and contradictions of neoliberalism intertwined with geopolitics focused on expanding market share. The model always carried the same inherent contradictions, including IMF-style austerity in the 2010s, with inadvertent consequences of the geopolitical and geoeconomic clash between the US-led NATO coalition against Russia in the war in Ukraine.[1358]

Part of the US-NATO early Cold War policy, "containment militarism" (NSC 68, 1950) calling for a *"massive build-up of both conventional and nuclear arms"* added an enormous burden to the taxpayer. Along with the US decision to sustain trade deficits with Germany, Japan, South Korea, and Taiwan, containment militarism seriously undermined the civilian economy to the degree that the IMF secretly warned President Eisenhower that the chronic current account deficit was undermining the dollar's value.

In part, the IMF warning prompted Eisenhower to go public about the dangers of the military-industrial complex. Despite the self-defeating history of containment militarism, in 2023, the US planned the first $1 trillion defense budget to counter a 'hostile world' in which in 2021, the US spent more than the next ten competitors. In reality, this massive defense budgetary escalation was a corporate welfare program for the defense sector and high-tech industry, both creating greater insecurity rather than guaranteeing global security for the American people.[1359]

This is not just a conventional and nuclear arms race among major rivals, but most countries as defense sales lead to regional arms race. In some cases, weapons sales are linked to the geopolitical protection of a small country procuring weapons from a larger one. This constitutes a form of buying diplomatic support (protection) along with the weapons on the part of smaller countries. Besides selling weapons to smaller countries with weak economies, weapons manufacturers prevail upon their governments to sell weapons even to rivals as well. Such was the case of European arms transfers to Russia after the latter annexed Crimea in 2014 and the West had already imposed an embargo.[1360]

After integrating former Soviet republics into the Western economic and military orbit, the new containment policy that the US and its allies pursued against Russia was an integral part of the neoliberal transformation's global reach. At the same time, it was an ideological component carrying on the Cold War legacy and the need to demonize an enemy both as a catalyst to forge national consensus and to keep military Keynesianism vibrant. The problem for the Western alliance was that while it enjoyed overwhelming military leverage, its role in the world economy had retreated amid Asian global economic ascendancy. The inability to reconcile this asymmetry frustrated the US and its allies to the point of reverting to old Cold War solutions for a world that does not resemble the late 1940s when the US was at the zenith of its power.[1361]

As a foreign policy tool, containment was the brainchild of George F. Kennan (1946) who remolded a 19th-century strategy that the US applied to the USSR. For one country to "contain" the other effectively, tools of containment include military means, as in the 19th century and early Cold War, backed by considerable economic power and a web of alliances and alignments. Based on military means alone with ineffective economic measures, as in the case of the trans-Atlantic powers under neoliberalism, containment backfires economically.

"Russia earned twice as much cash in 2022 than in 2021, already a record year. Russia's current account rose to an unprecedented $227bn in 2022, more than doubling the previous record of $120bn. The strong expansion of exports, including oil and gas and other commodities, was the main driver of this growth. Despite a contraction of 16% in imports in 2022, this marks a recovery after a decline of 35% was seen in the early weeks of the war following the imposition of a "massive package" of sanctions. China's trade with Russia has seen significant growth since Russia's full-scale invasion of Ukraine. Sino-Russia trade has been growing explosively since the $5bn of mutual trade the two had in 1991. Trade between Russia and China reached a new all-time high in 2022, with a 29.3% increase compared to the previous year, totaling $190.27bn, according to the General Administration of Customs (GAC) of China. China's exports to Russia saw a 12.8% increase, totaling $76.12bn. Meanwhile, Russia's imports from China climbed by 43.4% to $114.15bn."[1362]

Under globalization, China benefited not just as Russia's number one energy and raw materials buyer, but with the US as well as a net exporter of finished products. In many respects, trade obviated wasteful military containment efforts very costly to the US civilian economy while China was circumventing all sorts of sanctions, especially in semiconductors. US-led containment and sanctions notwithstanding, in 2022 China experienced the highest overall trade surplus ($876.91 billion) since 1950, including a $41.3 billion surplus with the US. While the US-G7 was pursuing containment and military Keynesianism, China's economic ascendancy inadvertently resulted in a form of inadvertent economic containment at the expense of the US and its allies. Even worse for the trans-Atlantic bloc, the data on China and Russia reveal neoliberalism's structural shortcomings in terms of the model's clash with geopolitical goals intended to achieve greater global market share and determine the balance of power.[1363]

With Ukraine at the center of the US-NATO containment policy of Russia, especially after Moscow annexed Crimea in February 2014, defense, energy, and high-tech companies scored immense profits. Combined with sanctions, military Keynesianism not only impacts negatively the civilian economy to the detriment of the American middle class and working class but European and other governments anxious to keep up with what the latest technology defense companies are selling and rivals are buying. The largely parasitic sector has a depressing effect on the civilian economy and escalates regional tensions.[1364]

In addition to military Keynesianism impacting the civilian economy, sanctions have impeded global growth and kept inflation steady. Accepting foreign policy as an extension of neoliberalism, David Grewal suggests that the neoliberal post-Cold War has manifested contradictions within globalization requiring reassessment. *"Strategic consolidation, if not retreat, from the ambitions of an impossible globalization, as instantiated in the WTO, to something like the post-war GATT, which was an explicit geopolitical alliance of liberal countries that sought to deepen trade relations as part of a more general geopolitical alliance."*[1365]

Contradictions have resulted in market disequilibrium where one or more sectors assume a greater predatory position at the expense of others domestically and globally, and one nation uses exigent circumstances to secure market share for its companies at the expense of others abroad. This is precisely what took place with energy in 2022 and 2023. After Western sanctions, oil and gas exploration and production globally were estimated to generate a record $1.4 trillion in free cash flow in 2022. Energy costs hit 13% of global GDP, forcing many millions of people to cut back on essentials and some factories to reduce operations due to the high cost of energy. [1366]

As if energy profiteering, along with the defense sector, were not enough of a drain from the working class and middle-class living standards, in the summer of 2022, the US approved a $430-billion new green energy subsidy package as part of the Inflation Reduction Act (IRA), on condition that renewable energy technologies are made in North America. This is on top of fossil fuel government subsidies and windfall profits from sanctions against Russia. The EU followed a similar pattern, arguing that it cannot fall behind the US and China, the latter spending $280 billion in subsidies, or 35% less than the US.[1367]

The global economic and social consequences of trillions in windfall profits and subsidies for energy, defense, and raw materials caused market disequilibrium, economic contraction, and rising poverty and inequality. In August 2022, the *End Fuel Poverty Coalition* published a report predicting over 12 million households (42%) across the UK would face fuel poverty in the winter of 2022-2023. *Cornwall Insight* corroborated the *End Fuel Poverty Coalition's* report predicting sharp energy increases and rising inequality as a result.

The government tried to offset high energy costs not by taxing energy companies, but by providing modest consumer subsidies financed by public borrowing; a pattern repeated globally. Geopolitics precipitating market disequilibrium does not necessarily signal neoliberalism's imminent demise, though on the surface it does point in that direction. Rather, it is a manifestation of inherent contradictions that permit select sectors to engage in profiteering owing to geopolitics. This was the case in times of regional Middle East wars during the Cold War. Neoliberal authoritarian politicians use nationalism arising from wild market fluctuations to mobilize the popular base.[1368]

Not unlike "vulture capitalism" (speculating to extract value from companies in decline no matter the consequences to the company, workers, and community), which contributed to the Great Recession, the political economy of weaponized sanctions provided an advantage to the large corporations to score even greater profits. By imposing sanctions on third parties, the state paves the way for profiteering, knowing that working people pay the price. Combined with the weaponization of the dollar amid rising central bank rates, the result was economic contraction accompanied by inflation in 2022-2023.[1369]

By distracting people from structural problems impacting their material lives, history has shown that the "rally around the flag" tactics work as a mechanism of political conformity. As a tool of statecraft, weaponized sanctions as modern warfare have an impact on stirring nationalist sentiment of the sanctioned country, on third parties, and on the country imposing sanctions. As the epitome of military neoliberalism, destabilization policies leading to armed conflict, which includes weaponized sanctions as part of modern warfare, has weakened democracy, reinforced authoritarianism, and resulted in greater inequality.[1370]

"Through the use of sanctions, the US Treasury not only punishes targeted states in the name of human rights, but also promotes the interests of American corporations in global markets, enhances US state power, and advances domestic political agendas. Washington's growing enthusiasm for sanctions enjoys overwhelming bipartisan support. Sanctions originate not only in the Executive Branch but also in Congress, independently of – and at times in opposition to – the Trump administration. Also, there has been an increasing focus of lobbyists on influencing decision-making on sanctions: numerous interested parties benefit from sanctions, such as LNG producers, arms manufacturers, agro-businesses, steel and aluminum corporations, etc."[1371]

Just as there was a global struggle for markets and raw materials during the Age of Imperialism (1870-1914) leading to WWI, and an equally intense competition during the Cold War era (1945-1990), the race continued under neoliberalism which subordinates foreign policy to its mandate. The difference is that the label "empire" has been more fitting for the multinational corporations behaving like empires than for the state in the service of capital. Multinational corporations and large national companies have become key players in weaponized sanctions policy. Ideological and geopolitical considerations are a thin political veneer behind which there is a pattern and logic of the economics of imperialism. With the support of the state, multinational corporations maintain oligopolistic control of the global markets and resources with the ultimate goal of extracting the highest level of value that labor produces.[1372]

In a candid public admission, in May 2015, Obama noted that the global struggle for power included writing the rules of the global economy and denying that privilege to China; a rare honest admission about imperialist rivalry. Because Beijing's global economic integration has precluded US efforts to subordinate China in the Pax Americana orbit, the US-led anti-China Cold War campaign has had a global destabilizing effect.[1373]

The state's role as an agent of imperial hegemony on the corporation's behalf is at the heart of the neoliberal philosophy which Obama expressed by giving it a nationalist spin that no one except progressives questioned. This was two years before Trump's GOP autocratization and *"America First"* policy took hold in the US at the expense of friend and foe alike. Camouflaging the intensification of class war, the massive income transfer to the richest one percent was the common denominator for Obama and Trump alike.

Far from representing a departure from neoliberalism, the Trump-GOP administration's *"America First"* and anti-politics was the establishment's counterrevolution against liberal democracy. This was amid the neoliberal crisis under an increasingly unstable liberal order of consensus politics weakening workers and middle-class living standards, continuing to tear down the welfare state, weakening the labor movement, and chopping away wages and benefits while sabotaging trade union organizing efforts.[1374]

"Amid the sordid crimes of the American Empire, running from the Mexican-American War under Polk to the Forever Wars that have marked the 21st century...the battle between Trump and the Establishment was not actually between anti-imperialism and imperialism. Rather it was a contest between two rival forms of imperialism. Trump wanted raw imperial plunder—as practiced in its classic form by European nations during the 19th and early 20th century, and by the United States in its relationship with Central and South America. This is an imperialism of naked

territorial conquest, resource plunder, and alliances with local comprador autocrats. The Joint Chiefs of Staff—like the larger American Establishment—has little appetite for this naked policy of looting in the name of enrichment."[1375]

In the short history of neoliberalism, Western Europe and the US have been leading the world in imposing economic sanctions on rivals and occasionally on allies to strengthen home-based companies. In the name of 'national security', the West, especially the US, has imposed sanctions and import/sales bans mostly on Chinese companies and sectors to strengthen domestic sectors of the economy. Since the 1990s, the US Treasury Department's Office of Foreign Assets Control, the Bureau of Industry and Security, the Department of Commerce, and the Department of Justice used coercive sanctions, relying on the dollar as the world's most-used reserve currency, on Wall Street's influential role in global markets, and the international payments system SWIFT. The very acts of sanctions and the weaponized dollar are manifestations that the imperial state is undermining neoliberalism's global reach to strengthen home-based corporations.[1376]

Intending to effect change in foreign and defense policy, trade and tariffs, and investment and currency policy, sanctions have negatively impacted working people throughout the world. That US-led sanctions work at all is a testament to the power of the imperial matrix which includes the cooperation of international financial organizations and companies seeking to make a higher profit using the sanctions as an excuse. Although national policies still operate under the neoliberal model, sanctions lead to fragmented global trade and trading blocs which account for the rise in the politics of nationalism owing to rejection of globalization if this entails that a rival derives greater benefits from the model.[1377]

Serving a narrower market or policy interests not necessarily consistent with neoliberal dogma, there is broad scholarly consensus that sanctions rarely achieve publicly-stated goals, and always the unintended short-term and long-term negative consequences for the economy and working class. In geoeconomics competition, the government's role is essential to secure advantages in technology, energy, finance, and market share over rivals. Hiding behind national security, the US ban on Chinese tech giant Huawei Technologies, among other companies, clearly illustrates this point. The same is the case with the US liquified natural gas (LNG) industry demanding dominance in the EU market, and using Russia's invasion of Ukraine to secure market share in third countries.[1378]

Announced in April 2005, the Russian-German natural gas pipeline project (Nord Stream 2) triggered a debate about EU energy dependence on Russia, and by extension its impact on US-EU relations. Having no market-based arguments to justify its policy, the US framed the issue in national security terms. Germany insisted that national security is a means to an end for a country heavily dependent on imported energy. With the most to lose because the gas pipeline bypassed it, Ukrainian oligarchs with investments in energy and banking were as adamantly opposed to Nord Stream 2 as were American LNG suppliers. Persistent US government efforts to prevent the pipeline's completion illustrated the inordinate domestic corporate influence over the state as a vehicle to support its own companies at the expense of foreign competition where the price was much lower for LNG.[1379]

An indication that the US government was the pillar behind the energy corporations, no matter the neoliberal free trade rhetoric, the result of US pressure over the Nord Stream 2 pipeline was relentless on Germany and the EU. What the US could not accomplish with diplomacy for more than a decade under Obama and Trump, it accomplished in February 2022 with coercive sanctions after Russia invaded Ukraine under Biden who was providing subsidies to LNG and fossil fuel producers even before the outbreak of the Russian war of 2022; a practice contradicting the rhetoric regarding the administration's commitment to the green economy.[1380]

Before the US-led sanctions resulted in a sharp rise in LNG imports at an average of 40% higher cost than Russian gas, the US had convinced the EU to lessen Russian oil and gas purchases and to raise defense spending, benefit US energy and defense contractors. The first US shipment was in April 2016. By April 2021, the EU was purchasing more than 22 billion cubic meters of US gas at 12 billion euros. Right before the sanctions, the EU imported 60 billion cubic meters of American LNG out of 160 billion used annually.[1381]

Like the American LNG industry, the global oil industry also benefited when the Trump administration imposed sanctions on Iran as part of an Israeli-Saudi-backed Western containment strategy. As LNG global prices rose sharply, sanctions caused artificial shortages and sharply higher prices. Regardless of NATO members' hollow rhetoric about replacing Russian energy, while 'punishing' Putin, it was difficult to confront the reality that Russia and Iran combined are the world's largest producers with 957 billion cubic meters of global supply in 2022, benefiting from higher energy prices; a paradox of US 'punishing sanctions.'[1382]

A year before the Russian war in Ukraine, the EU Parliament commissioned a study on US sanctions, concluding that although they targeted hostile countries – Russia, China, North Korea, Iran, Venezuela, and Cuba – purporting to deter third parties under EU jurisdiction from trading with targeted countries, entities, and individuals, US-led sanctions contained multi-dimensional dangers for the EU and trading partners. Such dangers included everything from insurance to shipping companies, raw materials, and high tech. Although US and EU officials and analysts knew about inflationary risks and capital concentration at the mass consumer's expense, they proceeded with the policy resulting in economic dislocation owing to record-breaking energy and raw-materials profits.

With neoconservatives at the helm of foreign policy, Biden chose the path of containment militarism as though time stood still since the Truman presidency. The ostensible goal was to strengthen the trans-Atlantic bloc, but the real goal was to strengthen US-based corporations. The US-led coalition threw Russia deeper into China's embrace. Inadvertently, much of the Global South was looking for stability and safety within the BRICS's embrace away from G7. It also made it very profitable for India to choose Asia and Russia over the West on trade sanctions. Indian companies became the EU's largest refined fuel suppliers as a result of sanctioned Russian products. The inevitable fragmented world trade and activities making a mockery of sanctions signaled that globalization was undergoing a regional makeover with lots of war-related profiteering opportunities.[1383]

The concern on the part of many Western analysts, including EU officials, was not only that US sanctions violated World Trade Organization guidelines on free trade and neoliberal principles, but that there was nothing to stop China from retaliating in the same manner. For its part, China used the Taiwan Strait/South China Sea trouble spots as a pretext to impose punitive sanctions on Lockheed Martin Corp. and Raytheon Technologies for selling weapons to Taiwan. In July 2023, China retaliated by imposing controls on exports of gallium and germanium, key elements used to make semiconductors and electronics. At the same time, Beijing was quietly unloading US Treasury bonds as it prepared to set up a BRICS-backed reserve currency, thus undermining the dollar's artificial high level of exchange.[1384]

Using the new Cold War as an excuse for global economic advantage had winners and losers, including an impact on currency values affecting world trade and inflation. Because the entire world has been integrated under the neoliberal model where the doctrine of markets over governments implies that the power of the state is limited, EU governments, especially Germany, were uneasy about economic implications on the heels of the pandemic combined with supply-chain problems. Nevertheless, European multinationals were as eager for market share at the expense of Chinese competitors as their US counterparts.[1385]

Shaving off at least 2% of EU GDP in 2022, US-NATO sanctions demonstrated obvious contradictions between Western capitalist interests and strategic/balance of power goals that were a pretext for predatory market share acquisition in a transparent proxy war, sending a signal both to Moscow and Beijing about unrelenting Cold War-style containment. The issue of whether the US and its allies have the power to succeed with simultaneous Russia-China containment may not be at the top of Washington's list because containment, sanctions, and destabilization do the job. However, one reason that a new multipolar world order began taking shape under Beijing's sponsorship is because many countries lost trust in the trans-Atlantic model.[1386]

Considering that the state serves and promotes the national market, sanctions necessarily imply economic nationalism which strengthens the rightwing populist neoliberal camp. In the process of securing a greater market share and strengthening its currency using the war in Ukraine to impose sanctions contributed to an inevitable global trade and GDP slump.[1387] Because of its eroded status in the world economy, the US relied on regional destabilization and containment strategy, punishing enemies through sanctions, trade, and tariffs, while distracting citizens with economic nationalism and national security issues. The goal is an economic advantage over competitors, but the strategy inadvertently undermines the transformation model. A strategy that both pluralist and rightwing populist governments have adopted, this has also resulted in the rise of authoritarianism.[1388]

A form of warfare that may appear inconsistent with neoliberal dogma, extraterritorial sanctions are consistent with neoliberalism's predatory model. The dual US objective to replace Russia as Europe's LNG supplier, while reverting to the early Cold War model of Europe as America's junior partner presumably would deny Moscow geopolitical leverage emanating from energy exports. Trying to secure a strategic zone of influence through military means was a classic case of continental imperialism on the part of Moscow responding to NATO's eastward expansion.[1389]

Without the assistance of its allies, China and India, Russia would not have been able to carry on its dream of trying to at the very least neutralize Ukraine which the West wanted as part of its strategic buffer zone. In February 2023, a Bloomberg headline read: *"Oil's New Map: How India Turns Russia Crude Into the West's Fuel."* The US and the EU are keeping the Russian economy afloat by buying its energy exports through India's private energy exporting companies, NAYARA and RELIANCE accounting for 45% of Russian oil exports. From the outset of the war in Ukraine, Biden announced that he wanted to punish Russia, but then refused to punish India for buying sanctioned Russian oil and reselling it globally. US punishment policy has been so severe that the Biden administration allowed Russian oil and gas imports and refined energy products through Indian companies that claimed they had the right to resell energy because India was the third party processing it.[1390]

When it became clear that Europe did not suffer an energy shortage, except one that energy companies manufactured to spike prices when there was a steady supply, journalists revealed that all along Europe was buying sanctioned Russian oil. Amid a frenzy of confusion, profiteering thrived for anyone connected to energy and derivative industries. Once there was reporting that the reason the US refused to sanction India for buying

Russian energy was because it and the EU were the customers, the farce of sanctions was a story of energy companies profiteering with the blessing of governments on all sides. Hiding behind hollow rhetoric of freedom and democracy, opportunistic charlatan politicians and analysts were shielding Western energy companies' profiteering while the war of attrition continued. This was not an atypical situation, especially for the US which has a history of war profiteers from the Civil War to the war in Afghanistan and Iraq.[1391]

As has been the case historically since the Russo-Turkish War 1768-1774 under Catherine the Great, Putin's Russia resolved to reassert itself as a Great Power with a strategic buffer zone around its national borders. Operating under kleptocratic capitalism, the Kremlin gradually had been de-coupling its economy from the US during the Obama presidency. With sharply higher short-term inflation and reduced GDP resulting in a mild recession, Putin was willing to endure economic warfare.[1392]

Despite the risks to the global economy, savoring the windfall corporate profits was a sufficiently positive development in certain industries, even at the sacrifice of destabilizing geopolitical conditions that resulted from US foreign economic policy undermining the neoliberal model's theoretical claim of the global market as the economy's only determining factor. Even before Biden, the US did not have many alternatives, other than absorbing surplus capital from the richest one percent to strengthen the dollar amid chronically rising debt.

Throughout the Global South, the war in Ukraine brought to light several governments seeking to hold and trade hard currencies other than the dollar. With Australia, South Korea, and Japan behind the US, the Biden administration's calculation was it would emerge stronger in the short term. However, much of this strength came at the expense of Europe of Europe and many non-Western nations, like Argentina deciding to make payments to the IMF in renminbi/yuan in 2023. Despite the US military intervention disasters in Iraq and Afghanistan, the Ukrainian war of attrition still made sense to neoconservative ideologues surrounding Biden, no matter the global economic hardship and suffering of Ukrainians.[1393]

On 28 March 2022, the IMF Managing Deputy Director warned that the US-led sanctions were threatening to relegate the dollar as a reserve currency into a secondary role in the international monetary system. Despite the dollar's temporary strength against other currencies, Wall Street giants Goldman Sachs and Credit Suisse repeated the same concerns as the IMF. This was after the German government had officially accepted a US demand to terminate *Gazprom Germania (JSC Palmary and Gazprom Export Business Services LLC)* and switched to the US and other imports from the Gulf States, along with Russian energy sources indirectly through India and other illegal shipments. Paradoxically, amid the dollar's rise against the euro during the Russian war, global de-dollarization accelerated as the BRICS gained momentum after reports, including from the IMF.[1394]

An IMF study concluded that the dollar has "an outsized role", considering the chronic shrinking share of US global output, drop in global trade, rising debt, non-bank borrowing, bond issuance, and international borrowing vs. lending imbalance. Given that, during the second Obama administration, the US GDP dropped to second place in the world economy in PPP terms, dollar erosion as a reserve currency was inevitable longer-term. Even if the Russian war temporarily strengthened the dollar as the world's most-trade reserve currency, its best days were behind it. Regardless of US geopolitical maneuvering and sanctions policy, the efforts of China, Japan, and Switzerland, among a few others to maintain a strong dollar for the short term sustained it artificially at inflated levels. However, institutions and governments were hedging their bets, especially against the war in Ukraine that provided the BRICS with the opportunity for a common trading currency that much of the Global South supported because they estimated greater benefits as a result.[1395]

With China leading, in October 2022, several countries began to establish a new reserve currency for trade that would enjoy the backing of commodities, free of weaponized currency manipulation. In his meeting (April 2023) with President Xi, Brazilian President Luiz Inacio Lula da Silva proposed a BRICS trading currency, and immediately currency markets reacted because the prospect was very real. With former Brazilian president Dima Rousseff in charge of the BRICS New Development Bank (NDB), the goal was further consolidation as a means to work parallel to the Bretton Woods System. While it takes time to transition from the dollar as the dominant world currency, the neoliberal model would operate as well, if not better, assuming no manipulation under a China-BRICS-backed reserve currency that eventually competes with the dollar.[1396]

BRICS Reaction to Western Neoliberal Geopolitics

After 1995, the G-7 global GDP share began a slow decline until the dot.com bubble. By contrast, the BRICS kept rising to overtake the core countries by 2020-2021. The rise of BRICS illustrates that inter-core competition between the US and China was not going well at all for the US as the cradle of Western neoliberalism. It also helps to explain America's reliance on geopolitical destabilization as economic leverage and as a means of securing greater global market share. In a state of panic, because it was facing a retreat in global GDP share, the US-led G-7 governments scrambled for solutions. Meanwhile, Western multinational corporations made record profits.[1397]

Considering that by the time of the war in Ukraine, BRICS accounted for a larger share of the world's economic output[1] in PPP dollars than the G7, the question was how G7 governments justified policies designed to undermine China-led BRICS. In 1982, G7 accounted for half of the global GDP, dropping to 30.7 percent by 2022, or about one percent lower than the BRICS's GDP. More alarming, 23% of global assets are with China's large banks, while less than 10% of assets belong to US institutions, indicative of a massive movement of capital from West to East under neoliberalism.

According to the IMF, Asia will contribute about 70% of global growth in 2023, a much greater share than in recent years, providing a true perspective on why the G7 has become so militaristic aiming to bring down the Asian-Eurasian bloc and their allies through various destabilization means. BRICS-backed reserve currency preparedness coinciding with the dollar's weakness was another sign of structural movements in the capitalist world system.[1398]

If US and European multinational corporations are scoring record profits because the BRICS are capturing a larger share of global GDP, the task of a US or a German policymaker to justify measures designed to stop BRICS GDP growth when it would necessarily entail curtailing profits of Western multinational corporations becomes problematic. Geopolitical goals have been symptomatic of the contradictions in the neoliberal model that the state compromises with geopolitical and geoeconomic policy as the struggle for a larger market share intensifies within a highly integrated world economy which the state cannot cherry-pick without causing damage.

With all the vacuous rhetoric about G7 solidarity and playing a role in redefining the rules of the international economy, even Japan was contradicting its rhetoric as it was buying Russian oil above the G7 agreed cap price, not to mention investing heavily in China which backed Russia in the war.[1399]

When the Ukraine war erupted, the US government and private sector analysts were optimistic that sanctions imposed on Russia would strengthen the dollar in two respects. First, there would be a global rush to buy dollars as a "safe reserve currency". Second, sanctions would imply more countries would be trading in dollars, especially in energy and commodities, but also as a safety valve. In short, this scenario was sound, but that was as far as it went. The strong dollar scenario came to pass under exigent conditions. Several countries, including India, Pakistan, UAE, Saudi Arabia, Argentina, and even Israel accelerated switching from dollars to yuan/renminbi (RMB) as a reserve currency.[1400]

1. https://countercurrents.org/2023/04/brics-overtakes-g7-in-terms-of-gdp-finds-study/

Partly because energy-dependent Europe suffered worse consequences from sanctions than the US, and also because of FED rate hikes to control inflation, the flight to the dollar hurt both US manufacturing and the eurozone while further depressing the trans-Atlantic partner economies and the rest of the world. The IMF, Goldman Sachs, and private financial institutions took into account that the US would be going deeper into debt and relying more on foreign buyers of bonds.

As US GDP growth would fall below the world average at a time of continued tax-supported corporate subsidies amid higher spending on defense and foreign military aid, public debt is expected to rise by one-third between 2022 to 2032. While the FED floated bonds to back the dollar, Beijing gained even greater leverage in the world market further strengthening its economy. Mainly focused on global economic integration as the foundation of global leverage, in 2022, China, spent 1.7% of GDP on defense vs. 3.7% by the US. The US defense increase was in part intended to force China into diverting funds from the civilian sector. Forcing the rival to spend more on defense was Reagan's strategy applied against the Soviet Union. The Biden administration used the same strategy toward China without any results because China's economy was larger than the US economy with great growth prospects.[1401]

Suffering setbacks and benefiting from contradictions between US containment foreign policy and Western neoliberal economic goals mired in a destabilizing market environment as part of a Western strategy of engagement owing to inexorable economic integration, China avoided pitfalls that interfered with its global economic goals. China, Russia, and Iran's combined share of global GDP hovered around 21% and BRICS close to 32% in 2022. Russian, Iranian, and Chinese combined energy and rare earth mineral reserves dominance along with their share of world trade translated into more than sufficient leverage to circumvent US-led sanctions during the Ukrainian war.[1402]

Multinational corporations sign long-term contracts for access to raw materials and markets, but at any time the state can intervene to modify or nullify such contracts. For example, energy as key to the world economy is as much subject to market conditions as to geopolitics. Russia and Iran hold 40% of the world's gas production on which Europe was inordinately dependent, and 15% of the world's oil reserves. After the Trump administration signed an agreement with the EU in 2018 to export more natural gas, US exports rose from 16% that year to 28% in 2021.

Furthermore, the share of US arms exports rose from 33% in 2021 to 40% in 2022 with Europe the biggest buyer almost doubling its weapons imports. Leading the EU by raising defense spending to over one-third, the Macron government tried to take some of the savings from the working class by raising the retirement age. Because of the Russian war and Western sanctions, the price of natural gas temporarily rose fivefold, presenting a golden opportunity for energy companies, subcontractors, and shipping and insurance companies to make record profits and precipitate global market disequilibrium.[1403]

Technology and threats from Russia and China are the new excuses for the US proposed one-trillion-dollar defense budget by the middle of the 2020s, representing an astonishing 40% of the current spending on defense of the entire world, or an 8% jump in US share at 32% of global defense spending, and a 20% rise from the current defense budget. Other than enriching defense contractors and derivative industries, the US economy will not benefit from capital-intensive projects with immense profits leaving an added debt burden for the taxpayer.

Because of the nuclear deterrent, the extra spending was meaningless in terms of superiority, bleeding the global civilian economy. As the US continued to fall further behind China in terms of its global economic status, with lower living standards for workers and the middle class, it found the solution in more defense spending and higher debt. Heightened US militarization prompting an analogous global response has resulted in greater reliance on military in regional conflicts, often of an asymmetrical nature as the one against Afghanistan's Taliban.[1404]

US-NATO efforts to place caps on Russian energy prices and to forge bloc trading underscores one of neoliberalism's blatant contradictions, not to mention the lack of ineffectiveness in achieving the stated goal. Part of the crisis was the creation of a US-NATO foreign policy intended to punish Russia and send a message to China about its claims to safeguard historic strategic interests in Taiwan and the South China Sea. Ironically, in the first half of 2022 amid Western sanctions, Russia's current account realized the highest surplus in two decades. By contrast, the US current account deficit widened by 30% in the first quarter of 2022 and is expected to widen further owing to the strong dollar. Amid rising energy prices, defense spending had as much an impact on the US as the NATO countries operating under military Keynesianism and neoliberalism.[1405]

Militarist neoliberalism is inexorably intertwined with NATO expansion. As Pawel Vargan explains: *"the mission of NATO expansion is inseparable from the cancerous advance of the neoliberal model of globalization, which hardens within NATO member states into a condition of perpetual exploitation. States within the alliance are required to siphon a substantial portion of their social surplus away from housing, jobs, and public infrastructure toward voracious military monopolies, the largest of which are based in the United States... the logic of the neoliberal world order, constraining its field of movement and weakening its hold on the economies of the world's poorer nations."[1406]*

An integral part of militarist neoliberalism, the new Cold War targeting Russia and China has been driven by Western imperial ambitions to integrate former Soviet republics and deprive China of that zone of economic influence. China had made enormous inroads in Central Asia and the trans-Caucasus region, while the West itself becoming increasingly interdependent on China, is competing for some of those markets. The war in Ukraine did not help the EU's efforts to compete in Central Asia and trans-Caucasus. Further weakening the neoliberal model by becoming caught up in its contradictions, the US-NATO containment strategy caused economic hardships in Russia. However, it also backfired because Russia and its allies also enjoy leverage against the US and the rest of the world. According to IMF estimates, trade fragmentation resulting from the US-led efforts against the Chinese-led blocs could cost the world economy as much as 7% in GDP, or the equivalent of Japan's annual output. Not surprisingly, the Global South pays the biggest price in the global contraction. [1407]

US-China Competition and Global Consequences

US-China competition was always part of the US-led containment strategy toward Russia. Whereas the Nixon-Kissinger rapprochement with China intended to weaken Russia and help strengthen US companies interested in the Chinese market, US presidents from Obama to Biden opted for a two-front containment strategy while pursuing economic cooperation that Wall Street demanded. The competition was always part of the US-led containment strategy toward Russia sanctions, targeting China's semiconductor, AI, and high tech.[1408]

Intended to strengthen the neoliberal model under the trans-Atlantic aegis, sanctions undermined global growth, exacerbated an overdue recession artificially postponed by monetary policy, and opened the door for remolding of the Western-based neoliberal world order into more rigid trade blocs. Besides its trade zones, China's control of 37% of the world's rare earth minerals and 60% of global production of such essential minerals for both high tech and defense translates into enormous leverage in East-West relations and also affords leverage to countries lined behind it.[1409]

The US-led semiconductor war against China was intended to slow down China's race in several tech fields, especially AI. The net beneficiaries initially appeared to be European and Japanese chip makers who controlled half of the global market in the late 1980s, but whose share was reduced to 9% by 2022. One of the victims of the G7 stranglehold on China's access to proceed with the semiconductor field was Taiwan Semiconductor which controlled roughly 40% market share. Another was the South Korean chip industry which must share its latest innovations with the US, otherwise, it cannot invest in the US and benefit from government subsidies.

When Morris Chang, Taiwanese-American founder of Taiwan Semiconductor, began sounding the alarm about the end of globalization, hinting that the US was hastening the process, he knew that Warren Buffett was dumping billions worth of stock in the company shifting some investments to Japan. Buffett speculated that he would inevitably make billions from US sanctions on China, assuming he invested in the right companies.

The punitive approach of US foreign economic policy has prompted China to pour billions in new investment and to be free of the semiconductors of any country. Nevertheless, there has been a negative impact because smartphone giant OPPO closed its semiconductor subsidiary ZEKU to avoid US sanctions on its phones. The impact on Huawei's chip division has also been impacted. This then permitted greater Chinese government intervention in semiconductor development, which is exactly what the US wanted to avoid.

As much as South Korea, northwest Europe was concerned about speeding ahead to remain competitive against the background of the US Chips and Science Act of 2022. Manufactured in different countries, the chips and the equipment still find their way around the world eventually. Meanwhile, the inordinate government corporate welfare programs come at the taxpayers' expense without achieving the intended longer-term goal.

Short-term, the US scored some victories. In the long term, it was looking at bleak prospects of locking out China from the semiconductor industry. The intense but warped competition as a result of a hostile US foreign economic policy could inadvertently have positive benefits. However, these benefits would come at parallel costs of a fragmented world economy with consumers paying higher prices, not to mention the geopolitical tensions and taxpayers footing the bill for higher defense costs. Furthermore, China's dominance in the raw materials for semiconductors and its race to prevail under US efforts.[1410]

Besides challenging Western digital hegemony by engaging in a fierce technological race, China owns 3.68% of the US national debt, continuing to play a dominant role in Treasury bonds, and helping to maintain the dollar's stability as a reserve currency. At the same time, China has been the world's economic stabilizing force merely out of self-interest given its ambition to become the preeminent global economic power. A more promising destination for corporate profits in comparison with the US and EU, China attracted 21.5% year-on-year more investment in 2022, despite its pro-Russia position during the war in Ukraine.[1411]

More than any other sector, semiconductors have been at the heart of US-China competition that forces the rest of the world to choose sides as though the early 21st century is re-living themed-20th century. The US used its influence to stop China either from acquiring and/or expanding companies, services, and ports of entry around the world. Even in cases of smaller contracts involving Chinese firms that the US and EU targeted, as was the case with Malaysia and Huawei, Western governments invoked national security to prevent third parties from doing business with black-listed Chinese firms. Although Chinese shipping giant COSCO has stakes in nearly 100 ports, government measures to block it are contrary to the neoliberal model, but not inconsistent with Biden's *New Washington Consensus*.[1412]

While the US global share of chip production fell from 37% in 1990, to 12% in 2019, China began to compete aggressively by subsidizing the sector. Considering that Chinese investment was in low-tech foundries, China exported a small percentage of integrated circuits, with 75% of the global supply made either in the country or elsewhere in East Asia. Despite holding a commanding lead in the sector, US corporate subsidies rose rapidly in the first two decades of the 21st century, especially under Biden who pursued economic nationalism more vigorously than Trump, despite the Democratic multilateralism rhetoric.[1413]

To replace the benefits that corporations enjoyed by doing business in China where overall production and operational costs are 37% lower, Beijing insisted that US government subsidies will have to be at least one trillion dollars in up-front investment.[1414] Among other analysts, economist James Midway of the *New Statesman* has argued that the semiconductor wars mark the demise of neoliberalism. This is not because the sector cannot stand on its own without government subsidies, but because US action, especially against Huawei Technologies, was nothing short of aggressive economic nationalism intended to send a signal to the entire world about the US ability to determine the terms of trade and technology transfers on US terms. Beijing filed a formal complaint against the US at the WTO, but the US continued on the same course.[1415]

In a move to curb steps taken by the U.S., Beijing proposed $143 billion to assist companies by subsidizing the purchase of Chinese semiconductor equipment or plants. In a major push to cut U.S. reliance on overseas chip production, President Biden in August 2022 signed the CHIPS and Science Act $52.7 billion bill to fund U.S. semiconductor research and production through grants.[1416] As paradoxical as it may appear, the US used the CHIPS Act not necessarily to diversify semiconductor manufacturing to reduce possible disruptions from East Asia, but to lock out China by offering corporate subsidies to operate in the US and divest from China and to withhold chipmaking equipment. A counterweight to China's quasi-statist model, which in essence amounted to economic nationalism and further erosion of globalization, as Taiwan Semiconductor founder Morris Chang warned, the reshoring policy was high-risk hard-ball geoeconomics.[1417]

In March 2023, the mask of the CHIPS Act came off. The South Korean government publicly stated that the US semiconductor policy was intended to afford global preeminence to American companies and those of other countries linked to the US. Agreements to invest in the US and qualify for subsidies carried major risks for non-US CHIP makers, especially for Samsung and SK Hynix. Besides limiting their operations in China, non-US companies had to invest billions in the US to qualify for US corporate subsidies. Far more seriously, these companies must divulge chip-making secrets to the US. The conditions for investment in the US necessarily implied that the South Korean chip makers would sacrifice billions in profits by limiting operations in China while the US would be even more predatory than China when it comes to technology sharing.

"Minister [of Trade, Dukgeun] Ahn has reportedly expressed concern that those requirements mean applicants for CHIPS Act funding will need to share technology secrets, as well as so much financial information that analysis could deliver valuable competitive intelligence. The CHIPS Act also mentions profit-sharing, which matters to Korean chipmaking giants Samsung and SK Hynix. The former is considering the construction of eleven semiconductor fabs in Texas. The latter plans to invest $22 billion in the States. Neither, presumably, is keen to have US officials able to consider their innermost secrets."[1418]

Like the US and China in the early 21st century, Great Britain and Germany went through a similar cycle of inter-core competition during the Second Industrial Revolution coinciding with the Age of Imperialism. Capitalism survived the struggle for market share manifested in colonial wars from 1870 to the Great War in 1914. The ultimate winner was neither Britain nor Germany, but the US. While the US-China rivalry is not wrecking capitalism, the intense competition has precipitated diplomatic conflicts.

International competition to raise corporate subsidies for the chips sector had geoeconomic implications that emboldened China to become more self-sufficient. Inter-core competition is not only manifested in trade and investment flows but in exemptions to Western tariffs and sanctions that raise inequality and feed nationalism and rightwing populism. Such conflicts between the state and specific corporate interests reflect the tangible contradictions between national capitalism and transnational corporations that use economic nationalism to advance their interests for market share and to secure tax breaks and subsidies.[1419]

At the macroeconomic level, neoliberalism's predatory nature brings supporters of opposing trade blocs closer together. There is divergence, however, when it comes to individual corporate interests and large portfolio investors. Some embrace global transformation, as long as there is pluralism, an environmental, and social safety net, but not if it means higher production costs and sacrificing market share. Others focus strictly on capital accumulation, regardless of the type of regime, not to mention human rights violations. As the model's transformation evolves and geopolitics plays a key role, the lines between pluralist and authoritarian neoliberalism become increasingly blurred. In part, this is because technocratic neoliberalism creates a new elite absorbing the parts of the pluralist camp into the authoritarian/militarist one.[1420]

Owing to the commodification of foreign policy and militarism as leverage to offset China's global role, neoliberalism has devastated workers and marginalized groups in all domains from education to housing. In the 21st century, the US has been the world's largest exporter of weapons. In 2017, Trump signed an agreement to sell

Saudi Arabia an astonishing $110 billion in arms. Considering that in 2017, global arms sales amounted to $400 billion, the Saudi deal raised eyebrows. Moreover, Riyad was the major weapons supplier to Yemen's reactionary government involved in a civil war that resulted in the world's worst humanitarian crisis during the 2010s.

Justified based on jobs-creation in the capital-intensive defense sector, the US and other arms exporting countries never mention the link between selling arms along with a slice of foreign policy protection, depending on the buyer and its rivals. US arms transfers notwithstanding, Saudi Arabia has been forging closer ties with China as has the entire Middle East and Africa. When China brokered a rapprochement between Iran and Saudi Arabia in March 2023, followed by reinviting Syria into the Arab League, US regional military leverage proved less effective than Chinese economic power.[1421]

Long before the advent of neoliberalism, imperial states focused on military strength as a means of economic expansion for the benefit of corporate interests and the sake of power and glory. With about 750 military installations in two-thirds of the world's countries, the US consistently maintains the ostensible public relations goal to spread "freedom and democracy". From 2000 to 2017, the US sold weapons to 167 countries, 80 of which had military bases. Although neoliberalism, provided arms transfers with a market justification, the field always carries a predictable mode of operation including the occasional bribery to officials involved in arms sales and using the weapons as leverage against the seller's allies, thereby feeding the weapons procurement race.[1422]

The coincidence of the rise of neoliberalism and the end of the Soviet bloc that permitted the illusion of an eternal Pax Americana allowed China to industrialize and expand its global trade network. To slow the irreversible decline of the West, which contributes to the neoliberal model's inherent contradictions, the US and its allies accelerated destabilization policies in the Middle East and Africa, especially after 9/11. Obvious that time does not stand still for the application of anachronistic military Keynesian policies, by the Great Recession of 2008, US policymakers and analysts realized China was the emerging superpower amid the decline of the West, but refused to alter the course of military Keynesianism as an extension of neoliberalism.[1423]

China's brokered rapprochement between Iran and Saudi Arabia was the most historic geopolitical and geoeconomic development since Ibn Saud signed the Treaty of Darin with the British government in 1915. Much to the dismay of Israel expressing opposition, the EU and Western Europe voiced skepticism while welcoming the deal, and Iran and Saudi Arabia went along with China as a new patron in the new regional balance of power. Striking a deal between arch-enemies Iran and Saudi Arabia illustrated to the world that China's economic interests cannot proceed with regional destabilization policies that the US and its Western allies have historically supported. This deal opened the floodgates throughout the Middle East and Africa for closer ties with BRICS and China. A few days before the Saudi-Iran deal, Beijing had proposed a peace deal for Ukraine, but the US and EU immediately rejected it.[1424]

Eldridge A. Colby, Member of the US Council on Foreign Relations [CFR] and former Trump administration defense official, argued that the US best option against the multi-dimensional world power structure undermining Pax Americana is to forge a militarist anti-hegemonic international coalition to slow China's global ascendancy. Supported by big business, the CFR which supports neoliberalism did not raise concerns about the obvious contradiction between what Colby was preaching and globalization.[1425]

Like many enthusiasts of military solutions to diplomatic crises, Colby embraces Fukuyama's "end of history" unipolar power thesis. Like many mainstream analysts, he argues that neoliberalism was responsible for helping

China's ascendancy. Without taking into account the inherent contradictions of *Lebensraum* ('living space' Third Reich theory) assumptions applied to the political economy based on global integration without impediments of the nation-state owing to geopolitics, the Colby thesis implemented into policy found enthusiastic support in every president from George W. Bush to Biden. Devoid of any moral or intellectual validity other than the hollow and pernicious endism theory embodied in Fukuyama's "end of history", the Colby thesis put into practice was a source for the steady erosion of the US in the core status of the world economy under the aegis of both neoliberal pluralists and authoritarian populists.[1426]

A glaring contradiction in the neoliberal model, the Colby thesis finding expression in US policy illustrates that America's departure from global military and economic hegemony has not been a peaceful transition. That this thesis became a part of the New Washington Consensus speaks volumes about the policymakers' refusal to come to terms with US-China peaceful co-existence. Instead, these new Cold Warriors assume that co-existence would only strengthen China, relegating the US to a secondary supporting role in the neoliberal world economy. Questioning established rules of global trade and investment as agreed upon by the WTO, and the Bretton Woods System, the US weaponized the dollar, foreign aid, trade, loans, and investment. Using foreign policy and its allies' influence as leverage, the US has relied on early Cold War paradigms to prolong Pax Americana, both as a formal global order and an informal power structure.

Against the reality of a rapidly evolving multilateral power structure that has less to do with China's ascendancy and more with US erosion in the core of the world economy, Western analysts rarely consider that the trans-Atlantic neoliberal model and military Keynesianism have hastened economic decline. Desperately clinging to global hegemony, the US and key allies have prevented several countries from conducting business with China or permitting Chinese firms from investing in certain sectors, substituting competition under capitalism's theoretical free enterprise rules for geopolitical coercion.[1427]

In an article entitled: *"The West has so much to gain from a Cold War with China,"* Jeremy Warner, assistant editor of *The Daily Telegraph* writes: *"The fact is that we have nothing to fear from geo-economic fragmentation, provided it is done in a considered way for mutual benefit among friendly nations. Done well, it might even presage an economic rebirth, a new era of Western industrial advancement, after the dispiriting declinism of recent decades."[1428]*

A century after Oswald Spengler's *Decline of West* (1918) thesis, *declinism* became popular among some scholars in both Europe and the US, largely because the power of the ascendancy is outside of the Western World. Symptomatic of Pax Americana's decline, especially evident after the Great Recession, the US and its G7 partners were pressuring several countries to reject Chinese corporate expansion and cooperation in various domains from port leasing to high-tech applications in utilities. The irony is that the West, especially the US, which has determined the terms of trade in its favor, has used the dollar like a blank check with underfunded assets, and relied on its military muscle has maintain the hegemony of the Western-determined world order to the detriment of the Global South and workers world-wide.

Under Trump and Biden, the US pressured Israel to reject bids from Chinese companies for projects in the communications and high-tech domain. The Chinese light rail company and Israeli partner firm sued over undue political US influence. The US and EU continued to block projects linked to Chinese companies while preventing them from buying assets in several countries globally in every sector from high-tech to pharmaceuticals. Leaning heavily on the IMF and the World Bank to undermine Chinese economic expansion, the US demanded that borrowers must not use IMF money to pay back China. Competing with the IMF as the world's last resort lender, China naturally used such leverage for financial and trade integration. Both the US and IMF warned developing nations not to borrow from China and risk such dependence.[1429]

As long as it served to maintain the US at the core of the world economy, especially under the post-Soviet unipolar Western-based world order, neoliberalism was a great transformation model. Considering that neoliberalism was contributing to China's global economic ascendancy, the US political and financial elites began manipulating the model through unilateral and multilateral measures to deny the advantage to China and other competitors.

The question was how to manage the international political economy by using sanctions, tariffs, the dollar, and geopolitical, and military leverage to consolidate nationally and within regional blocs while denying market benefits to rivals like China. In some respects, the *New Washington Consensus* which articulated these goals reflects acceptance of Friedrich List's (*The National System of Political Economy*, 1841) theory of economic nationalism, although within the neoliberal model. A "neo-Listian" method to achieve capital accumulation within national borders, without necessarily realizing industrial development or even trade equilibrium, the strategy has all the implications of trade and the dollar's short-term strengths, but long-term structural weaknesses as a manifestation of an irreversible macroeconomic decline.[1430]

Capturing the malaise that goes along with decline, the Harvard Business Review article below could just as well apply to Europe. *"Strange as it may seem, a nation once celebrated for its irrepressible optimism now appears to be obsessed by decline. America's list of complaints seems endless: Real wages are falling. Productivity growth is down. Companies aren't competitive in global markets. White-collar jobs are no longer secure. The nation's infrastructure is collapsing. The federal deficit is soaring. The health system is deteriorating. The cities are unsafe. The schools are failing. The gap between rich and poor is widening."*[1431]

A desperate and utterly reckless maneuver to maintain core status by retaining what William Appleman Williams called *"Empire as a Way of Life"* (1980), the Colby thesis as applied in US policy and the *New Washington Consensus* lacks even the Schumpeterian principle of economic growth by innovation. It aims to destroy the very element of the competitor through geopolitical rather than formal bilateral and multilateral market mechanisms by which other countries abide and to which the WTO and signatories have agreed. As a method, the selective neo-Listian modality has been employed to manage neoliberal capitalism under a national system that does not obviate key aspects of the neoliberal model, especially when combined with military Keynesianism.

Therein rests the blatant contradictions, especially given that the US-led geopolitical and Western-led trading blocs, as well as the Shanghai Cooperation Organization (SCO) along with the rapidly expanding BRICS contribute to the evolving neoliberal transformation model. The more the US and its partners use geopolitics to manipulate the "pure market" model that they established, the more China inadvertently strengthens within the capitalist world system by focusing narrowly on economic growth at the national and international levels, without necessarily neglecting social development. In December 2022, Beijing announced a 12-year growth program through rising domestic consumption as a means of circumventing US-led obstacles to global trade expansion, but also as part of social development commitment, especially in the Western provinces where new railroad projects will be centered.[1432]

Frustrated with the Western inability to slow China's expansion and the decline of the West, Japan's Economy, Trade and Industry minister Yasutoshi Nishimura called for yet another new world order based on a system of bloc trading. *"We must rebuild a world order based on the fundamental values of freedom, democracy, human rights, and the rule of law. Nishimura's call to arms comes amid growing concern in the wake of Russia's invasion of Ukraine that Beijing and Moscow will use their control over energy resources and sway over manufacturing supply chains to stop the United States, Japan, Europe, and others from opposing their diplomatic and military goals. He urged that cooperation between Japan and the United States extend beyond semiconductors to biotechnology, artificial intelligence, and quantum science. "We will implement strict export controls grounded in international cooperation while engaging closely in the exchange of views with the United States and other relevant countries." On trade, Nishimura reiterated calls for the United States to join the Comprehensive and Progressive Agreement for Trans-Pacific Partnership after former President Donald Trump abandoned an earlier version of the pact in 2017." [1433]*

A version of the Colby thesis, Japan's proposal illustrates capitalism's structural crisis, the bankruptcy of the neoliberal model, and the desperation of the US and its key allies scrambling for solutions to the irreversible decline of the hegemonic West. By articulating a new version of the Washington Consensus, the neoconservative-dominated Biden administration deluded itself that a solution was on the way. As Sara Flounders points out, the declining West is using militarism as the pretext to maintain a unipolar world order with the US and its allies at the helm serving big capital.

"While the U.S.-NATO war against Russia in Ukraine continues unabated, the U.S. is preparing at breakneck speed for war with China, using Taiwan as the excuse. Taiwan, like Ukraine, is a pawn. The military and economic threats on both China and Russia are a desperate bid to quash the emergence of a multipolar world... Even more threatening to U.S. capitalists is that China is developing trade relations with the 40 countries sanctioned by Washington, and they are doing this by barter and direct currency exchanges. This works around the almighty dollar, the international reserve currency that has dominated global trade and capital flows for 100 years."[1434]

Dogmatically refusing to take into account structural determinants of neoliberalism and military Keynesianism as root causes for rising inequality and rightwing populism on a world scale, the focus of trans-Atlantic governments, institutions, and independent analysts remains on China's relative strength about the US and their bilateral and multilateral relations as salient factors in the world balance of power. Neoliberalism's structural determinants also account for the decline of the West dragging down its major partners like Japan and Germany. Predicated on the notion that diminishing China's ascending economic power would somehow magically prevent the decline of the West, instead of hastening its continued path by generating greater social inequality under autocratization regimes, the US-G7 group has been gambling with its future and it would not be the first time. Ultimately, the question is about the validity of assumptions that the Cold War economy of 1945-1990 upon which neoliberalism was built represents hope rather than the underlying causes for t twilight of the declining West.

Epilogue:

Neoliberal Twilight or the Waning of Liberal Democracy

Crisis of Neoliberal Transformation

The Freiburg School, especially Walter Eucken, father of ordoliberalism and the social market economy concept, along with the Chicago School, especially Milton Friedman, associated the pure market ideology with representative government, economic prosperity, and security. Among other things as seen in previous chapters, this entailed unleashing privatization, deregulation of business, lower corporate and direct taxes, using the state to transfer income from labor to the wealthy, and devolution of power at the local level. History has shown that neoliberalism not only entails concentrated prosperity, rising inequality, social insecurity, and social marginalization, but it also mutates liberal democracy into authoritarianism. At least some neoliberal apostles, including Hayek, Freidman, and Buchanan, had no qualms about authoritarianism, as long as it advanced capital. [1435]

A pillar of the neoliberal and neo-conservative ideological camps, Karl Popper dismissed as indefensible Hegel's historicism and holism for leading society down the path of totalitarianism, at least as Popper defines it. History has shown that the neoliberal ideology, which Popper, Hayek, Ludwig von Mises, and Milton Freidman, among many others, promoted, has led the world toward an authoritarian social contract. Operating under the thin veil of pure-market capitalism serving the "sovereign consumer", from 1980 to 2022, capitalists became richer and the state slipped down the path of authoritarianism. Because the state has been systematically redistributing income from the bottom up amid class war, inequality and authoritarianism, not market efficiency, has resulted from neoliberalism.[1436]

The irony of neoliberal apologists condemning Hegelian historicism and holism has been that neoliberal transformation has given rise to autocratization, if not its version of totalitarianism, even under Popper's definition. Because of neoliberalism's geoeconomic fragmentation and financialization crisis reflecting irreconcilable contradictions, most evident in the contracting cycles, the possibilities include a return to Keynesian social democracy as the next phase of capitalist development, a policy mix that incorporates developmentalism, one that maintains the neoliberal corporate-welfare model under rightwing populist regimes, or some new mix of libertarianism presented as democracy under the existing model's basic framework adopted to suit as much the national capitalist class as the comprador bourgeoisie.

By separating economic policy from liberal democracy, while defaulting blame to the state for anything flawed in the economy including severe dislocations as was the case with the Great Recession, neoliberal analysts and politicians, although very few identify as such, have created a protective barrier around a structurally flawed political economy that has not lived up to any of its promises. Equally detrimental for society, by attributing all blame to the state which caters to capital, neoliberal policymakers have de-legitimized the state's role and exploited public anger which they have cultivated against the public sector thereby fomenting rightwing populism.

To force Congress to keep Trump as president after he lost the election in 2020, the Capitol Hill riot of 6 January 2021 illustrates elite-guided and institutionally-directed anger finding expression in a rightwing populist movement with the president as its leader. An example of neoliberalism legitimizing authoritarianism, on 13 March 2023, Trump announced to supporters in a campaign in Iowa that the attempted rightwing coup would have succeeded had the vice president sent the votes back to the state legislators to cancel Biden's win.[1437]

The chasm between neoliberalism's image and its promise of co-existing under democracy versus what it delivers to people throughout the world has signaled the twilight of democracy inherent in the crisis of capitalism. This was evident ever since the US Savings and Loan crisis of 1986 to 1995 resulting in the collapse of 32% or 1,043 of the 3,234 S&L operations. Caused by a southwestern commercial real estate bubble in the 1980s, neoliberalism under financialization suffered a stock market bubble in the late 1990s. This was a prelude to a nationwide real estate bubble under financialization in 2007-08 and another regional banking crisis in the winter-spring 2023. The string of recurring crises of neoliberal social crimes for which capital and the state are responsible have multiplied on a world scale under the transformation model and created greater inequality and political polarization.[1438]

From the dot.com bubble to the Great Recession and its lingering effects in the 2010s, especially for the trans-Atlantic core intensifying military Keynesianism in the hope of shoring up the economy, neoliberalism's deepening crisis hastened systemic contradictions that have led to a highly polarized socioeconomic structure and authoritarianism. After the COVID-19 pandemic exposed more structural weaknesses than the contraction of 2008, the US-G7 sanctions against Russia and the weaponized dollar, and geoeconomic fragmentation during Russia's war in Ukraine found expression in the popularity of the BRICS throughout the Global South. This led some analysts to conclude that neoliberalism is in twilight mode, if not finished.[1439]

According to the UN Development Program, in the 2010s, the global twin paradoxes were progress with insecurity and polarization. This is shown in the high sense of insecurity, breakdown of trust, and low level of optimism, not just among the middle class and workers, but the elites. Finding expression in various forums, the reproduction of neoliberalism amid the chronic US-China competition altered the globalization landscape from the 1980s to 2023.[1440]

In the company of President Biden and heads of Apple, NVIDIA, AMD, and other CEOs, on 6 December 2022, Morris Chang, founder of Taiwan Semiconductor, stated: *"Globalization is almost dead, and free trade is almost dead. A lot of people still wish they would come back, but I don't think they will be back."*[1441] At the Davos World Economic Forum in 2023, political and business leaders expressed similar concerns about the inevitability of de-globalization. Hardly surprisingly, China emerged as globalization's biggest cheerleader because it had benefited the most, although the real winner was big capital. Fearing China's ascendancy, the US-led coalition remained faithful to the military as leverage, combined with sanctions, tariffs, and political influence wherever possible. The US-led anti-China coalition reiterated its 'free trade' support, but only within defined national security boundaries instead of any manipulation by China.[1442]

Joining the chorus of analysts predicting the end of neoliberalism, Luke Cooper, London School of Economics, argued that this phase of capitalism is already dead and buried, at least as an ideology, if not policy. Intertwined with the rise of rightwing populism, and nationalism, the signs of neoliberalism's early demise were evident long before the US announced the *New Washington Consensus*. Hedging his bets, Cooper noted that as an incongruous set of commitments to big business seeking corporate subsidies and opposing business regulation while favoring labor regimentation, neoliberalism could survive, but not as coherently under the "national order";

presumably based on the Westphalian system of nation-state sovereignty. The logic of such reasoning precludes nuances within the neoliberal model which thrived as much in pluralist France under Macron as in Brazil under Bolsonaro's authoritarian regime.[1443]

Among the group of scholars proclaiming the demise of neoliberalism, Gary Gerstle contends that American history can be understood in terms of the New Deal political order prevailing from the 1930s to the 1970s, followed by the neoliberal order. Focused on the Great Recession, which caused a crisis of confidence in the neoliberal order and provided an impetus to rightwing populism, New Deal progressives, and grassroots anti-neoliberal groups, Gerstle has been predicting the end of neoliberalism since 2008. Like others throughout the world, he had hoped that Obama would return to Keynesian policies, simply because America's first black president kept up the progressive rhetoric, but without ever supporting it by any policy. Once in office, he pursued neoliberalism and militarism more aggressively than his predecessor. Indicative of identity symbolism taking precedence over policy substance, neither the party faithful nor the popular base criticized him.[1444]

During the Great Recession, capital accumulation slowed, but concentration accelerated after 2009. This was due to a combination of factors, including stimulative monetary and fiscal policy adding to the richest one percent of wealth and the public debt. Corporate welfare policies and more oligopolistic conditions allow for concentrated appropriation. This was not just in the US, but globally. Pointing to its positive impact on the world economy, the World Bank's development report of 2020 pointed to empirical evidence of oligopoly resulting in capital concentration, greater inequality, and poverty.[1445]

Slowing as a result not just because of the pandemic, but the cyclical contraction built into the overheated speculative financialization system and near-zero interest-rate environment that essentially amounted to the taxpayer subsidizing capital, economic contraction coincided with the supply-chain bottlenecks and US-led sanctions-bloc-trade policies against Russia. The convergence of systemic economic causes and US-led geopolitical strategies not only slowed world GDP but manifested deep cracks in the Washington Consensus to the degree that the US had to revise it to reflect its narrow economic and geopolitical interests clashing with China and the BRICS. Nevertheless, pockets of the world economy, most notably energy and defense, but also health care-big pharma, fertilizer-agrichemicals, and portfolio management along with large law and insurance firms scored huge profits amid stagflation and geopolitical confrontation.[1446]

Even before the stagflation of 2022-2023, a new normal in cyclical recessions had developed, namely, the recovery cycle was itself recessionary for the majority of the population. This is not just in the Global South which invariably suffers much more during contracting cycles, but in core countries as well. Mainstream economists, politicians, and journalists leave the impression that the expansion cycle and rise in GDP benefit everyone, and conversely, everyone suffers proportionally during the contracting cycle. Such myths create a credibility gap between what neoliberal politicians, the media, businesses, and institutional advocates promise and the reality of peoples' declining living standards even in recovery cycles.

Analyzing the dangers of stagflation and the reaction of central banks in 2022-2023, British reformist economist Ann Pettifor (*The Production of Money*, 2017) argued that central banks deliberately chose class war over financial stability. After the collapse of Credit Suisse (March 2023) and two US regional banks, Pettifor's thesis assumed even greater validity. *"The fact is I found it hard to face up to what central bankers are doing, not just by raising rates, suppressing demand, and lowering wages. Through lack of analysis, regulation, oversight, and foresight—central bankers have shown this last week they were prepared to use high rates to risk and even precipitate bank failures and global financial instability.*"[1447]

Rather than address inflationary pressures through fiscal policy by absorbing surplus capital from windfall profits of corporations and rich investors, central banks choose to shift the burden to the working class and the lower middle class. Knowing that higher rates would kill mass consumption demand which rising unemployment worsens, regardless of pluralist liberal or rightwing populist regime, central banks chose class war to enrich the wealthiest in society and contribute to rising inequality. To some degree, rising mass anxiety amid class war has contributed to an increase in US mental health problems, including substance abuse (100,000 die annually in the US alone) and suicide (47,646 dead, 14 per 100,000) in 2021.

In 2022, neoliberal militarism contributed to the 103 million people fleeing conflict, violence, human rights violations, and persecution. According to the UN, this was a new global record. Living under the neoliberal model and military Keynesianism, these are victims of the institutional structure and the politics of counter-terrorism. Amid geopolitical chaos, institutional neoliberal reproduction has afforded an impetus to the populist political strain to maintain a popular support base.[1448]

Expressed under different political umbrellas, global grassroots opposition against the neoliberal model signals the convergence of a multi-level crisis. The model's inherent contradictions cause social unrest, and workers' demands for their rights including unionization, combined with political polarization at the same time that the US-led blocs have been undermining neoliberal transformation's global reach by pursuing geoeconomic fragmentation as an instrument of hegemony.[1449]

After several EU countries undergoing monetarist/fiscal austerity in the 2010s, the far-reaching multifaceted financial, economic, political, and social crisis in Lebanon signaled an extreme case of capitalism's systemic dysfunction. Sri Lanka's uprising in the summer of 2022 was a reaction to predatory neoliberalism similar in many respects to what took place in Lebanon which brought the country's economy to its knees. Amid the trans-Atlantic's central role in the world economy, the combination of geopolitical crises from the US-led war on terror after 9/11 to the new Cold War targeting China and Russia in the aftermath of Moscow's annexation of Crimea revealed more inherent contradictions in neoliberalism's ultimate goal of capital accumulation both under a liberal-democratic regime and authoritarianism.[1450]

Even in countries never under the suspicion radar screen because of their division and separation of powers, a strong executive branch and weak legislative have been an autocratization characteristic. By 2021, 20% of the EU and 33 countries worldwide representing more than one-third of the world's population were under some form of autocratization. According to one estimate, 72% of the world's population lives under a regime of some type with authoritarian tendencies, regardless if it claims to be democratic. Interestingly, the other 28% just happen to be primarily in the Western World, New Zealand, Australia, and Japan, all countries closely linked to the G7, while the authoritarian world is linked to BRICS and the Global South under China's aegis. Because the word democracy is in essence fairly meaningless outside of its historical context and when divorced from social justice, this gives license to all governments, including authoritarian ones, to claim that they too are under the generic democratic umbrella.[1451]

Although core countries are no exception, the strong market, and weak social welfare state phenomenon has been especially evident in the EU periphery, Africa, Latin America, and Asia. In a remarkably short period amid fierce class warfare, neoliberalism's global hegemony accounted for the world's acceptance of the new 'natural' and legitimate phase of capitalism increasingly under authoritarian policies.[1452] In January 2016, social scientist John Carey noted that a strong executive branch entails weak democracy. However, he did not link the rising phenomenon to neoliberalism, nor did he acknowledge that the US has suffered such a fate.

This was one year before Trump became president, strengthening the executive more than his predecessors against a weak legislative, and promising to strengthen the executive more if elected in 2024. What took place in the US was part of a global trend, from Israel where Prime Minister Benjamin Netanyahu placed checks on the judicial branch's role in limiting executive authority to Australia using COVID as a pretext for autocratization. In August 2022, Australia's newly-elected Prime Minister Anthony Albanese announced an investigation into his predecessor Scott Morrison secretly appointing himself to multiple ministries during the pandemic. The patterns of a strong executive-weak legislative, accompanied by a strong market-weak social welfare state have been characteristic of the neoliberal model intended to enhance corporate power and push through pro-capital policies with greater ease.[1453]

Combined with geopolitical conflicts in the race for market share and the competition to determine the balance of power, the neoliberal governance crisis cannot conceal fissures in the transformation model indicative of a deeper capitalist crisis. Despite contradictions in neoliberal governance, capitalists have taken advantage of the structural global crisis for further capital concentration, especially amid social conflict and *depoliticization* in the southern hemisphere and the largest economies.[1454]

During the COVID-19 pandemic, neoliberal governance responded opportunistically to the model's rationale. This was no different than previous neoliberal crises converting economic dislocation into an opportunity for capital accumulation. Concluding that the pandemic was the worst economic devastation for workers, the poor, and the socially marginalized since the Great Depression, the World Bank estimated a widening rich-poor gap on a world scale; an estimate which the World Economic Forum corroborated.[1455]

As a result of the pandemic, an additional 97 million fell into extreme poverty, living under $2 per day, as the World Bank defines poverty. By 2021, poverty rose to 9.1% from 7.8% in 2020, a remarkable rise considering that China had eliminated extreme poverty. Meanwhile, the world's richest one percent absorbed two-thirds of the world's newly-created wealth. Enjoying the judicial system's support, the capitalist class was relatively safe from prosecution for large-scale white-collar crime. From the 1980s S&L crisis to the collapse of Silicon Valley Bank in March 2023, not only has the state refused to punish bank criminals creating havoc in society, but it allowed them to keep billions collectively in salaries and bonuses while passing on the cost of bankruptcy to the taxpayer. The combined support of the legislative and judicial branches behind the owners of capital resulted in increased white-collar questionable or illegal activity involving billions.[1456]

"A divided federal appeals court on Tuesday threw out the insider trading convictions of four defendants, including two former hedge fund partners, over leaks from a U.S. healthcare agency about planned changes to Medicare reimbursement rates. In a 2-1 decision, the 2nd U.S. Circuit Court of Appeals in Manhattan dismissed fraud and theft charges against former Deerfield Management Co partners Theodore Huber and Robert Olan, former U.S. Centers for Medicare and Medicaid Services (CMS) employee Christopher Worrall, and David Blaszczak, the founder of political consulting firm Precipio Health Strategies."[1457]

Owing to widespread disillusionment with the status quo, a segment of the population embraced authoritarianism as the solution to liberal democracy and globalization as the root causes of institutional dysfunction and erosion of cultural integrity. From the Great Recession through the pandemic and rising global inflationary trends eroding living standards during the war in Ukraine, public confidence in government and institutions, in general, declined in most countries. No matter how desperately the media tries to convince the public that there is no alternative to the neoliberal social contract; that the solution is more privatization, deregulation, and tax cuts to benefit the wealthiest, confidence in public and private institutions continues to decline, while political polarization increases.[1458]

According to the UN Department of Economic and Social Affairs, from 2000 to 2019, globally there was a drop in public trust in governments, especially in financial institutions. *"Trust in financial institutions in these countries decreased by an average of nine percentage points, from 55 percent to 46 percent over the same period. Data from the Eurobarometer shows trust in political parties in countries of the European Union has remained low, hovering between 15 and 20 percent on average between 2000 and 2019, while trust in the press has also stayed relatively stable, around 45 percent over the same period. Nonetheless, substantial differences between countries and regions remain, as Figure 1 partly shows."[1459]*

According to a public opinion poll in 2010, 75% of Americans surveyed indicated that they were "angry" at the government and its policies. To distract from the class war, rightwing politicians amplified voter anger, and exploited fear and helplessness, directing public rage toward minorities, women, dissidents, and trade unionists. The root causes of public policy anger differ from one country to the other. The key issue of inability to keep up with the cost of living and to secure a better future for the next generation.

Historically, under the Keynesian state, people have looked to the government for solutions in everything from unemployment and living standards to public health and education. This is as true in countries with paternalistic state structures in Eurasia and Asia where collectivism has been part of the historic legacy, as individual rights in the Western World are an integral part of the value system. Redefining the public or common good in the context of a downsized democracy and outsourced labor market based on the gig economy of job insecurity, mainstream institutions incessantly try to convince the public to accept private-sector efficiency as the panacea and castigate the public sector as the root cause of all evil in society.[1460]

In 2019, Senator Marco Rubio best expressed this view when he invoked 'common good capitalism', by calling the neoliberal goals of convergence with the "transcendent goal" of our politics, rendering sacred the *"obligation to carry out God's will on Earth."*. A version of what President George W. Bush called 'ownership society', in essence, a categorical rejection of Keynesianism social welfare state as a safety net allowing for a modicum of social harmony in an otherwise predatory capitalist society.[1461]

Based on *Organization of Economic Cooperation and Development* (OECD) data, public opinion polling in 2013 indicates that only 35% of Americans had confidence in the government intervening on their behalf. In 2020 when the pandemic hit, this figure dropped to 20%. More than half of respondents noted that the government failed to address poverty, public health, and the environment. Although this may not be an indication that the public is aware of the state's role as an agent of income redistribution from the bottom up, it is aware that public policy is advancing the specific interests of the privileged few to the detriment of the many. Disillusioned that the elites have a lock on the entire institutional structure, young people who have been disengaged from the political process have even less confidence in the government to provide solutions.[1462]

Neoliberal indoctrination of collective faith in the market has convinced many to harbor disdain for the state as the root cause of all evil and that solutions and credibility can only be found in the market. In 2020, only 18% of US voters expressed confidence in Congress doing a good job, 44% approved of the Supreme Court, while 73% demanded that the government hold large corporations accountable. The level of institutional skepticism is far greater among the far right than among liberals and progressives. Lack of public trust in institutional credibility has propelled rightwing populist parties into competitive positions. This is as much in the US as in other countries with politicians misdirecting public rage toward the marginalized population.[1463]

Opposed to the institutional structure, the percentage of young Americans dropping out of the political process decreased in the 1990s. In 2008, that percentage rose, only to drop in the 2010s, and then rise again during the 2020 presidential election and 2022 mid-term congressional election. Rightwing voters participate more out of fear and anger against liberals who pollute society culturally, ideologically, and morally. American liberals and progressives fear that authoritarianism is already here overtly or concealed behind thinly disguised democratic policy.

Book banning and curriculum restrictions in local school districts, ending all discussion on institutionalized racism, abortion ban at the state level, and a criminal justice system set up to punish the working class and poor minorities inadvertently strengthen the wealthy privileged class. A common denominator for all political groups, alienation suits the markets and rightwing populists, pointing to the general decline of institutional credibility and the reason for a deeper dive into neoliberal legitimacy.[1464]

In a study on voter alienation, Daniella Wenger[1] and Roberto Foa[2] point out in that young people in Europe, the US, and Australia are more dissatisfied with liberal democracy than any previous generation. "*When Generation X hit 35, the majority were satisfied with how democracy worked. Most millennials today take the contrary view. Inevitably, our findings have proved something of a Rorschach test*[3] *for commentators who enjoy speculating about the attitudes of younger generations – including the usual mix of patronizing condescension and disbelief*[4]*. And yes, it is true, that in developed democracies such as the US, the UK, and Australia, millennials are less likely to join political parties or vote in elections, yet more likely to complain about the results. In the 2016 election, only 46% of young Americans voted, and that hasn't added legitimacy to millennial objections against the current administration's actions on the climate crisis, student loans*[5] *or housing affordability*[6]*.*"[1465]

Opinion polls reflect a widespread sentiment that the future under neoliberal political economy is not as bright as it was for this generation's grandparents under Keynesianism. This also holds for Eastern Europeans. Western

1. https://www.theguardian.com/profile/daniella-wenger

2. https://www.theguardian.com/profile/roberto-foa

3. *https://openpsychometrics.org/tests/HEMCR/*

4. *https://www.sott.net/article/443186-Democracy-isnt-working-for-young-people-because-cancel-culture-has-made-them-scared-of-freedom-of-speech*

5. *https://www.washingtonpost.com/opinions/trump-is-waging-a-war-on-millennials/2017/05/08/27d5c794-342a-11e7-b373-418f6849a004_story.html*

6. *https://www.politico.com/news/2020/08/23/trumplow-income-housing-suburbs-400155*

politicians and advisors had promised that integration into the capitalist world system would quickly propel the former Communist countries into a middle-class consumer heaven under liberal democracy. In the early 1990s, right after the collapse of the Soviet bloc, public opinion polls indicated that about two-thirds of respondents across all of the former Soviet republics were optimistic about regime change. This includes Ukraine where a minority of the population turned to neo-Nazism under the guise of freedom and democracy. Other East European countries, including Poland and Hungary, eventually evolved into illiberal democracies but enjoyed legitimacy as open societies because of their pro-NATO position.[1466]

From Bulgaria ranking 6th poorest and first in income inequality in Europe and one of the worst in corruption, to Latvia ranking third poorest and third in income inequality with a dozen millionaires owning much of the wealth, all former Communist countries wittingly and unwittingly adopting neoliberal transformation experienced a sharp rise in social inequality under corrupt regimes. Difficult to see where organized crime ends and the legitimate economy and government begin, this situation is hardly unique to the former Soviet republics. Whether Bulgaria is the EU mafia state with deep ties to Western banks and businesses, Russia and Ukraine under state-linked oligarchs, legal and illegal economic corruption has been the norm since the fall of Communism. [1467]

Especially after the crisis of 2008, farmers, schoolteachers, and workers of all walks of life have been protesting against neoliberal governance complicated by the endemic corruption of authoritarian rule serving oligarchs many of whom operate globally in illegal activities with the full knowledge of governments. *"While these oligarchs were buying up media resources,"* writes Michael Carpenter, *"the regime went about stacking the tax authorities, law-enforcement bodies, and courts with party loyalists. This ensured favorable treatment both for party leaders but also for regime-linked oligarchs whose wealth depended on government contracts. This gradual process of capturing independent state institutions and concentrating economic resources and political power in the hands of a small network of loyalists is emblematic of the corrupt "oligarchisation" of European politics—a phenomenon that extends well beyond Hungary."*[1468]

After thirty years of neoliberal capitalism adapted to national conditions in former Communist countries, the popularity of both liberal democracy and capitalism as the basis for the social contract has eroded. Once the dust settled, people realized that behind the mask of neoliberal capitalism, operating under the thin cloak of freedom and democracy, was a small clique of oligarchs on whose behalf the government conducted policy while launching a class war. In Europe's poorest countries, all former Soviet bloc members, dreams of riches quickly faded.[1469]

By the end of the 2010s, more than half of the population across Eastern Europe viewed socialism favorably. Many remained optimistic that the system would someday work for them, while others sought salvation in authoritarianism. In 2019, an opinion poll indicated that the majority of East Europeans feared Western democracy and mistrusted the media. In societies where the neoliberal domestic and international establishment was responsible for social inequality, it is difficult to speculate what concerned East Europeans; presumably the same material needs as their Western counterparts. Contrary to what many assumed and their leaders promised, social mobility never became a reality in Eastern Europe and the Balkans. Disillusionment led to a rise in nationalism with some looking to authoritarianism and others nostalgic for the security that the old Communist regime offered.[1470]

Deflecting attention from neoliberal governance precipitating structural poverty and inequality, the media blamed the individual, insisting that the system exists for all to take advantage of an otherwise well-functioning governance model. Considering that former Communist countries carried the legacy of a failed system, alienation and disillusionment with politics benefited authoritarian politicians. Nationalist-populists filled a political vacuum not only in Putin's Russia, but also in Kazakhstan under Nursultan Abishuly Nazarbayev (1990-2019), Belarus under Alexander Grigoryevich Lukashenko (1994-present), and Azerbaijan under Ilham Aliyev (2003-present).

All of them operated within the confines of capitalism's neoliberal phase intertwined with local oligarchic regimes based on clientelist politics with loyalty to the autocratic heads of state and a network filtering down to the local level. Critical of liberal rhetoric, East European and Balkan populists were as steeped in the neoliberal dogma as their Western counterparts. Even if it meant embracing regime characteristics of interwar Fascism, all were seeking solutions to save the new social order.[1471]

Regardless of political or ideological proclivity, the lack of confidence in public and private sector institutions throughout the world reflects a widespread recognition that the neoliberal social contract serves the interests of the small privileged political, social, and financial elites at war against the working class.

"Far from the calculating, entrepreneurial, moral, and disciplined being imagined by Hayek and his intellectual kin," writes Wendy Brown, *"this one is angry, amoral, and impetuous, spurred by unavowed humiliation and thirst for revenge. The intensity of this energy is tremendous on its own, and also easily exploited by plutocrats, rightwing politicians, and tabloid media moguls hipping it up and keeping it stupid. It does not need to be addressed by policy producing its concrete betterment because it seeks mainly psychic anointment of its wounds. For this same reason it cannot be easily pacified—it is fueled mainly by rancor and unavowed nihilistic despair."*[1472]

Wendy Brown's apt description of how neoliberalism has molded public consciousness illustrates the far-reaching sociopolitical polarization that has exposed a crisis in liberal democracy. For some, this may signal correctible flaws in neoliberalism. A more in-depth examination indicates the irreversible decline of the neoliberal West. Hardly surprisingly, neoliberals like James Buchanan fully endorsed the idea of politicians' role in curtailing democratic rights to enforce private property rights. Distrust of liberal democracy exposes disdain for Enlightenment-era philosophical notions of government by popular consent, casting doubt on social justice and environmental justice that capitalism undermines.[1473]

Even corporate environmentalism, which neoliberal pluralists often use as a distraction to structural exploitation, has fallen victim to predatory policies for privatization of public land, government subsidies to corporations, and concentrated market share. Amid the urgency of climate change and biodiversity degeneration, environmental justice has been an area that mainstream politicians, corporations, and the media have convinced much of the world to accept only within neoliberal governance perimeters where profit transcends all other considerations. This is not to argue that a fossil fuel economy is preferable until neoliberalism's eclipse. Green investment has a price tag and operates within the model's mandate.[1474]

Rightwing populists have provided a cloak of legitimacy to the very serious issue of environmental justice which the transformation model coopted and reformulated to fit the goal of capitalist appropriation. Besides the PR value of a company identifying with environmental protection, there was also the incentive of government subsidy programs for clean energy-related projects. Opting for market-oriented approaches, governments have been using climate change and 'green consumer' popularity to provide tax breaks and subsidies to corporations involved in these industries, including banks financing them.[1475]

Neoliberal Governance and Neo-enclosure under the Veil of Environmentalism

In the late 1980s-early 1990s, government agencies mostly in advanced capitalist countries began forming alliances with banks, corporations, consulting and law firms, international aid organizations, and NGOs promoting green energy. A necessary and practical goal with which scientists wholeheartedly agree, the neoliberal model compromised these goals to make sure that there is a profit to be made. Because the public takes it for granted that NGOs serve society's interests and presumably act independently of the state and businesses, the state and private enterprises enjoy a perfect cover for pursuing sustainable development in a green economy behind the NGO mask. Within the perimeters of the neoliberal model where the private sector determines environmental governance, the relationship between NGOs, businesses, and government serves as a cloak to subsidize projects. Given the urgency of global warming, governments ignore environmental goals, as many authoritarian neoliberal regimes have done, but still use the issue against liberal pluralists to rally popular support.[1476]

Neoliberal governance, which entails deregulation and optimal exploitation of every natural resource for profit, uses the green economy from a political and public relations vantage point to undertake a global enclosure movement displacing small family farmers to farm workers. From 1979 to 2017, 10% of UK public land shifted from public to private control in what scholars have labeled the "new enclosure" movement to contrast it with the original enclosure associated with the transition from subsistence to commercial agriculture from the 16th to the 18th century.[1477]

The original enclosure movement resulted in the forced dislocation of peasants, tenant farmers, and small farmer-owners. Thrown into urban areas, the dislocated population faced unemployment and a lack of a social safety net that the rural community provided even to a small degree. Other than church-linked charities and poor workhouses of servile labor, there was no means of survival. Cheap labor for the manufacturing sector was an inevitable consequence crucial to nascent industrial capital accumulation. Just as the first-wave enclosure of agriculture, forestry, and fisheries resulted in the consolidation of the primary field of production, so did the neoliberal second-wave enclosure.[1478]

Pursuing neoliberal policies, governments have sold or leased public land on generous terms to companies in mining, energy, forestry, commercial agriculture, and animal husbandry. The result has been to strengthen large commercial operations at the expense of small-scale businesses. Environmentalists have raised concerns over commercial farming including aquaculture which international financial institutions have been supporting under the privatization model at the expense of the community providing cheap labor. This has been the case throughout the Western Hemisphere, India, Africa, and Europe.[1479]

"The second wave of enclosure—from large pastures into barns and feedlots—has been equally destructive of rural communities, but this time the destructive potential of enclosure has expanded beyond the lives of rural residents, to include the people living in America's cities and suburbs. All are at risk from tainted meats, dairy products, and groundwater. But even if researchers can stay one step ahead of antimicrobial resistance, even if they can continuously discover new antibiotics, the second wave of enclosure has reintroduced feudal conditions in the countryside. Large

corporations distribute production contracts to men and women who were once independent operators but are now the modern equivalent of serfs."[1480]

Some environmental NGOs have played a salient role in providing a green cloak of legitimacy to large landowning investments driving small farmers out of business in the name of sustainable development. To attract large-scale domestic and foreign agricultural investment in India, Sri Lanka, and Bangladesh, the World Bank supported state-sponsored Special Economic Zones for which the state provided subsidies, including tax concessions and regulatory exemptions. Rather than helping sustainable agriculture as it claims, the World Bank has a history of promoting agrochemical and seed system dependence in the name of food security and sector efficiency. At the request of the G8, in 2013, with the financial support of America's largest farm owner Bill Gates, the World Bank was instrumental in the Enabling the Business of Agriculture (EBA) project. Consistent with neoliberal principles, EBA's goal is to strengthen corporate farming linked to Western fertilizer and seed companies.[1481]

To carry out the neoliberal experiment, the World Bank needed the cooperation of the host government. The state forcibly acquired land from small farmers leasing it to large investors. This turned into a nightmare for small farmers and agricultural workers throughout India, Sri Lanka, and Bangladesh. The enclosure project expanded to include various economic zones modeled after South Korea's Chittagong experiment, in essence, a modern form of a sweatshop. In July 2022, a massive anti-neoliberal uprising erupted in Sri Lanka, Similar to Sri Lanka, India, and Bangladesh went the same policy route with catastrophic results for the majority of the rural population.[1482]

With the full support of the World Bank and the United Nations Food and Agriculture Organization (FAO), the Gates Foundation, and agrochemical companies, neoliberal agrarian reform took place in the name of sustainable development and environmentalism. A trend ran across India and Bangladesh where the government empowered large investors and corporations in the name of the green economy, the result was further marginalization of small farmers amid land-ownership concentration. A similar situation took place throughout the world from Africa to Latin America where corporate and government-funded NGOs provided cover for neoliberal reforms using sustainable development and the green economy as a Trojan Horse.[1483]

Morocco and Madagascar are typical examples of how the IMF, World Bank, corporate-funded NGOs, and multinational corporations used the environmental mask behind which is the neoliberal enclosure movement and privatization agenda. Adopting export-oriented policies concurrently with privatization, government subsidies for capital, lower tariffs, and taxes, the Moroccan government used the environmental narrative to justify privatizing public land at the urging of Western governments and international lending agencies. After two decades of privatization, small farmers suffered as a result of the collective rangelands reduction, contributing to a sharp decline in subsistence farming synonymous with the small family farm. After the *"Green Morocco Plan"* of 2008, the government provided corporate subsidies for everything from machines to fertilizers and greenhouses, undercutting small and medium-sized farms.[1484]

Similar to Morocco, a pattern of neoliberal convergence under the guise of the green economy also took place in Madagascar. The government went along with the IMF, World Bank, corporate-funded NGOs, and domestic and foreign businesses and governments urging enclosure. Impacting forests and protected areas under the conservation agency System of Protected Areas in Madagascar, (SAMP) the result was rapid peasant dispossession. A big winner, the UK-Australian mining company Rio Tinto exploiting ilmenite that left drinking water resources in the Asony region with uranium and lead levels 40-52 times higher than the World Health Organization's safety recommendations.[1485]

The world's fourth largest island in the Indian Ocean, Madagascar is rich in natural resources – chromite, ilmenite, coffee, sugar, vanilla, cacao, pepper, and palm oil. Free of drought that plagues East Africa and with a relatively highly educated labor force, Madagascar has the potential for higher living standards, but it has been unable to rid itself of the colonialism legacy under a dependent export-oriented economy linked to the metropolis. Following a long decolonization struggle against France in the 1950s and 1960s, Madagascar remained under French administrative control until 1972. At that point, the government of Didier Ratsiraka pursued a mixed economy with a strong social safety net allowing for relatively higher living standards than most of sub-Sahara Africa.[1486]

With the advent of neoliberalism consolidating in 2008, the government of neoliberal president Marc Ravalomanana signed a secret deal with South Korean multinational corporation Daewoo Logistics. Madagascar leased 1.3 million hectares of palm oil and corn production land to Daewoo. Local farmers and peasants cultivating the same land carried out mass resistance against the corrupt Ravalomanana regime that deprived the rural population of its livelihood.

When a second deal with Australia's Varun International logistics company came to light, in 2009 Ravalomanana handed power to the armed forces. In the name of green neoliberalism, Madagascar has been cooperating with the US and EU governments, and international financial institutions to privatize public assets and deregulate the economy for the sake of attracting more foreign investment. Although the World Bank, US and Western European governments, and multinational corporations were well aware of the ruinous effect on the island nation's rural population, they continued urging privatization behind the pretext of sustainable development and the green economy.[1487]

Because 'green markets' are socially and politically influenced and in turn influential, the 'green' aspect of the primary sector of production operates as much within the neoliberal model as banking or high tech, thereby manipulating the environmental movement to market conditions. *"Across the world, 'green grabbing' – the appropriation of land and resources for environmental ends – is an emerging process of deep and growing significance. The vigorous debate on 'land grabbing' already highlights instances where 'green' credentials are called upon to justify appropriations of land for food or fuel – as where large tracts of land are acquired not just for 'more efficient farming' or 'food security', but also to 'alleviate pressure on forests. In other cases, however, environmental green agendas are the core drivers and goals of grabs – whether linked to biodiversity conservation, biocarbon sequestration, biofuels, ecosystem services, ecotourism, or 'offsets' related to any of these... Green grabbing builds on well-known histories of colonial and neo-colonial resource alienation in the name of the environment – whether for parks, forest reserves or to halt assumed destructive local practices."*[1488]

With the corporate sector and international financial institutions' support, neoliberal manipulation of the scientific environmental movement has been global. Knowing that the environment has middle-class consumer appeal, solid scientific support, and corporate support from companies in clean energy, the World Bank and IMF have been using the green economy, climate change, biodiversity preservation, and anything related to environmental protection as tools to move the neoliberal agenda forward. International lending agencies, mainstream media, businesses, governments, and NGOs have used the green economy as a pretext to usurp the scientific and grassroots environmental movement.

The environmental movement has afforded legitimacy to the neoliberal political agenda. Corporations paying lip service to the green economy include Archer Daniels Midlands (ADM) and Monsanto (now part of BAYER), as well as logging/timber companies that devastate forests in Brazil, Africa, and Canada under the pretext of sustainable forest management. In an article about Weyerhaeuser recasting itself as an environmental "do-gooder", the Wall Street Journal noted that the company remains in the logging business but merely trying to attract green investors, pointing to tree planting programs in the 11 million acres they own in the US and 14 million in Canada. The business of making lofty claims about sustainability commitments to distract from practices rests at the core of corporate greenwashing, reaching into government policy made possible by NGOs, educational institutions, think tanks, and the media.[1489]

"BlackRock has been accused of double standards after it refused to back landmark environmental resolutions at two big Australian oil companies just months after the world's largest asset manager warned global warming represented a risk to markets, unlike any previous crisis. The $6.5tn fund manager's voting record at annual meetings has been closely scrutinized following chief executive Larry Fink's letter to companies in January, where he announced BlackRock would put sustainability at the heart of its investment process and argued climate change could lead to a "fundamental reshaping of finance". But campaigners argued the asset manager was paying lip service to tackle climate change after it voted against resolutions calling for Woodside Energy and Santos to set targets in line with the Paris agreement, which aims to limit global temperature rises and to disclose their lobbying."[1490]

In principle, Blackrock had no problem supporting the green economy, as long as the company made money in the process. Refusing to invest for the sake of protecting the environment while losing money, Blackrock, like all companies, is only accountable to its shareholders expecting a return on their investment. The neoliberal model transcends any commitment to climate, biodiversity, sustainable development, or public welfare. Corporations, governments, the World Bank, NGOs, think tanks, consulting firms, and even educational institutions spend enormous resources on public relations campaigns to defend neoliberal goals concealed by genuine scientific concern for the environment.

Corporate and government hypocrisy regarding the green movement can be seen in the Paris Agreement of 2015 vs, the reality of public policy. Although almost all countries have agreed to observe the Paris Agreement, there is no agreement on tracking emissions and reduction goals, and how or whether to compensate hardest-hit countries. Even more astonishing, while governments have committed to the climate agreement, they provide $1.8 trillion a year in corporate subsidies proving the contradiction between neoliberalism and green economy politics.[1491]

In December 2022, EU governments weakened already weak laws on corporate abuse. *"It is a loss for the women and men who work in terrible conditions around the world to make the goods that end up in our shopping trolleys. The only one celebrating today is the regressive business lobby. "The original proposal was already a far cry from the game-changer law we expected. Now, after EU countries played their part, it is only weaker. On civil liability, [Marc-Olivier] Herman [OXFAM's economic policy expert] said: "There are more and more loopholes allowing companies to escape their obligations to clean up their business. The financial sector can continue to bankroll human rights violations and damage to the planet without being held accountable as it remains up to each European country to decide whether they want to make banks and other financial players clean up business."[1492]*

Beyond the hypocrisy of the G7 accusing the global south of lagging in environmental regulation and enforcement, the issue is corporate double standards considering that companies based in the advanced capitalist countries are in large measure operating in the periphery because they want to avoid strict environmental regulation. Meanwhile, they preach environmentalism at home to appease consumers and investors and they do the same with human rights and social justice issues in general.

The global focus on sustainability has inadvertently provided a cover to the fossil fuel industry which has been profiting from corporate welfare subsidies for both its fossil fuel business and renewable energy. As an integral part of the institutional private and public sector mainstream, the green movement has been as much a liberal as a rightwing tool to mobilize popular support. The most devious manipulation of the green movement has come from the state and corporate interests eager to privatize everything from water to public lands against the welfare of people, hardly for the sake of saving the environment.[1493]

The World Bank's long-term policy of water and sanitation projects was always used for privatization leverage under the pretext of "sustainable green development." IMF stabilization loan conditionality and World Bank development loans were linked to the privatization of public utilities, often using environmental issues as a pretext, when in reality the corporate sector's track record has been far worse than the public sector.[1494]

Using every public relations trick in the book, the corporate green marketing machine, with the state's support, has succeeded in co-opting much of the legitimate scientific and public environmental movement. Japan in the first two decades of the 21st century is a good case of a government co-opting science to deliver the neoliberal goal. The neoliberal use of "postmodern animism", which is rooted in Hinduism but took off in Japan, converged with the rise of neoliberalism as an expression of support for environmentalism. Used to justify consumerist culture, postmodern animism became popular in the aftermath of the Fukushima Daiichi nuclear plant disaster in March 2011, following an earthquake and a tsunami.

Coinciding with China overtaking Japan as the world's second-largest economy in nominal value, the Fukushima disaster marked a deeper skepticism, if not pessimism, among a segment of society about neoliberalism under the aegis of liberal democracy. Opportunistically, neoliberal governments have used various popular movements as a PR front to manufacture a mass false consciousness so that the transformation's goals are not compromised by popular opposition.[1495]

Judging by results not just in Brazil under Bolsonaro or the US under Trump, but even in Western pluralist-minded northwest Europe, neoliberal environmentalism has promoted capital accumulation to the detriment of both the environment and the working class. As Christopher Dent points out: *"many aspects of climate interventionism may still be compliant with neoliberal environmentalism's championing of green growthism, capitalist accumulation, and fundamentally unreconstructed capitalism generally. Climate change is a crisis of such significant magnitude that it cannot and should not be left mainly to free self-regulating markets to resolve it."*[1496]

Despite governments using various distractions to deceive the public of neoliberal policies behind the green economy, global popular resistance remained ongoing, though it assumed different forms depending on the country's unique problems. From historic conflict-ridden Lebanon to Sri Lanka (*Tigers of Tamil Eelam*), both subject to a few local, regional, and multinational players, and both financially bankrupt amid the pandemic and the Russian war in Ukraine, there were mass protests against the neoliberal status quo hiding behind various popular movements, including environmentalism.

Colombia, Kazakhstan, Armenia, Azerbaijan, Ethiopia, and other parts of the world have been in perpetual unrest against neoliberal policies impacting agriculture. Even in Holland, a cradle to neoliberalism's dogmatic adherence, farmers took to the streets against the government's stealthy use of the green economy to impose neoliberal measures and rising defense budget draining the civilian economy and undercutting the smaller and mid-sized firms.[1497]

Corporate Welfare and Neoliberal Response to the Pandemic

Along with public education, budgetary allocation for public health care is a manifestation of society's commitment to anthropocentric values and social development. The neoliberal model has subordinated peoples' health to corporate profits more so than at any time in the history of capitalism. Because of trillions of dollars in the healthcare sector, there was little doubt that neoliberal policy would impact public health more than education. Globally, governments spent $9 trillion by early May 2020 for COVID-19-related support. Because the amount spent represented about 10 percent of global GDP, many analysts concluded that the pandemic dealt a final blow to neoliberalism. Considering that a large percentage of expenditures were in the form of corporate subsidies, predictions about neoliberalism's demise were a premature assessment.[1498]

Well-known that there is a correlation between ill-health and low-income status, neoliberal policies aim at privatization and extracting even more capital from entitlement programs and the public health care system resulting in greater inequality. Privatization and passing health care costs to individuals through the public sector have been ongoing since the Reagan-Thatcher decade. This was the case in many countries, but especially so in the US which has the world's costliest healthcare system delivering quality based on income. Although the COVID-19 pandemic exposed the public healthcare system's weaknesses, it remains on the same course as before the outbreak.[1499]

Using the pretext of protecting workers and social development, governments found yet another opportunity during the pandemic to strengthen the corporate welfare state. From the pandemic outbreak in February 2020 to the Russian war in Ukraine in February 2022, the US spent $7.1 trillion in Federal Reserve actions, $5.9 trillion was in legislative outlays, and just under one trillion in administrative action for a total of $14 trillion, in an economy of $21 trillion in 2020.

Such massive injections of public capital erode the neoliberal credibility of 'market efficiency' and the myth that capitalism can stand on its legs in the absence of massive income transfer from the working class and middle class to strengthen capital and support a bloated defense establishment. The US defense budget rose to 3,200 times that of the National Labor Relations Board whose budget was cut from Obama to Biden by 25 percent when inflation is considered.[1500]

Contrary to the mainstream media's portrayal of public spending as beneficial for all, the near-zero central bank interest rates and $8 trillion of taxpayer money (approximately 10% of global GDP) amid the COVID-19 pandemic did not go to support the hard-hit working class, or even to strengthen the over-burdened public health sector personnel. Because there was a neoliberal institutional structure in place, a large share of the $8 trillion went to corporate welfare subsidies beyond the large pharmaceutical companies' research and development subsidies. The result was that by 2020, global public debt rose 28% amounting to 256% of GDP or $226 trillion. Spending a small percentage to combat the pandemic's impact on the general population, governments used the pandemic as a pretext to strengthen corporate welfare.[1501]

Indicative of how the pandemic became an excuse for more, not less neoliberalism, and more instead of less defense spending, the Trump administration took advantage of the pandemic panic to run an experiment for the privatization of Medicare. Without informing the public, the Medicare experiment was an example of an automatization measure at work. Because it impacted Wall Street interests, both liberal and rightwing media buried the story.

"Venture capital and private equity firms (some with ties to former Trump administration officials) are among the corporate concerns "who are lined up like pigs at the trough to get their hands on taxpayer dollars... Privatized plans generally cost the Medicare program more money[1] and can erect barriers to proper care, in the form of higher out-of-pocket costs, denied claims, and limited networks of health care providers. In other words, patients suffer while the private plans make billions. "The incentive is to deny as much care as possible," health advocate Diane Archer told The Intercept[2]. "It's also to delay as much care as possible." The Direct Contracting model has different rules than Medicare Advantage, but the pilot program incentivizes profit over patient care."[1502]

Despite Biden's campaign rhetoric about Trump gutting the health care system while providing $2 trillion in tax cuts to the richest Americans, and pouring more on defense and intelligence, the Biden administration kept Trump's Medicare experiment. Pouring even more money into defense than Trump, all along, Biden was symbolically committed to diversity as though this would make up for the class warfare he was pursuing. The pandemic allowed all corporations to demand more corporate welfare concealed behind public pronouncements about helping families and stimulating the COVID-19 economy. Campaign rhetoric aside about spending more on social welfare, Biden increased corporate welfare and defense, prompting similar increases in Europe, especially after Russia invaded Ukraine.[1503]

An indication that neoliberalism and militarism became stronger, not weaker, as a result of the pandemic, studies analyzing government allocation of taxpayer money reveal that businesses benefited both in direct and indirect subsidies. Intending to preserve 2-3 million jobs for $170,000-275,000 per worker, the US "Paycheck Protection Program" (PPP) extended $953 billion in loans when the pandemic erupted during the Trump presidency. Uncollateralized low-interest rate loans funded small businesses, while many PPP funds went to large companies. Of the aggregate amount, between 23 and 34 percent went to workers, while the rest went into the pockets of businesses, creditors, suppliers, and shareholders.[1504]

Shortly after 11 March 2020, the World Health Organization declared COVID-19 a pandemic. This signaled the need for an internationally coordinated public health policy. Initially, there were optimistic scenarios that there would be global health prevention solidarity and that society could become more community-conscious and anthropocentric. Whereas some feared a greater tendency toward world-government authoritarianism imposing vaccinations, the corporate sector focused on maintaining market strength and high profits, regardless of the economic and social hardship for the majority during the pandemic. Political polarization accelerated as rightwing populists rejected the science behind COVID-19 and blamed government cautionary policies for economic dislocation.[1505]

The media, corporate-funded think tanks, mainstream politicians, and analysts rarely questioned the historical context and political economy in which the pandemic erupted. Ignoring the World Health Organization's appeal for a coordinated global response to the pandemic, Western analysts embraced their governments' nationalist-militarist rhetoric demonizing China for the pandemic's lab-manufactured origin. Owing to a

1. *https://www.npr.org/sections/health-shots/2021/11/11/1054281885/medicare-advantage-overcharges-exploding*

2. *https://theintercept.com/2021/12/14/medicare-privatized-health-care-insurance-direct-contracting-ethics/*

manufactured supply-chain bottleneck problem used as a pretext for capital accumulation, made much worse after the US-led sanctions against Russia in 2022 and 2023, working-class conditions became worse.[1506]

Many institutions, including the IMF, confirmed higher inequality on a world scale amid massive profit windfalls especially for drug companies and online shopping amid the pandemic. An International Labour Office (ILO) report concluded that workers lost $3.7 trillion in income during the first two years of the pandemic. By contrast, billionaires' assets rose from $8.6 trillion in March 2020 to $13.8 trillion in November 2021. The rise represented an increase larger than the previous 14 years combined at a time when workers' income dropped sharply while public debt burdening workers and the middle class rose significantly in many countries. The pandemic was just another class war opportunity that would become worse only by the war in Ukraine.[1507]

From mainstream neoliberal institutions to progressive academics, there is agreement that the pandemic combined with the Russian-Ukrainian conflict continued to widen the rich-poor gap in the 2020s. It was especially devastating to developing nations after Western sanctions on Russia precipitated sharp inflationary pressures. Besides impacting Africa's food and fuel import needs, the war was responsible for a drop in global GDP by an additional percentage point. Among other organizations, the IMF warned that global contraction would affect mostly the working poor across the world, especially in the Southern Hemisphere. Amid monetary tightening, combined with sanctions imposed on Russia backfiring on the rest of the world, the UN Development Program reached similar conclusions as the IMF.[1508]

Pharmaceuticals, energy, raw materials, and defense, profited from the pandemic as they did from Western sanctions on Russia. Although a portion of public funds in many countries subsidized workers' lost wages, governments throughout the world, from the US, Japan, Brazil, Germany, and the UK subsidized corporations, especially big pharma but also the travel-hospitality sector. Some government corporate subsidies were in the form of business loans, fiscal relief such as tax credits, combined with direct subsidies a portion of which was intended for research and vaccine development, and worker relief, including flexible rules on interest deductions. [1509]

In an essay entitled: "*The COVID-19 pandemic: securitization, neoliberal crisis, and global vulnerabilization,*" Joao Nunes, like other scholars investigating the same topic, points out that government solutions to the pandemic exposed the inherent gross inequalities and contradictions of neoliberalism more than what was already known. *"The COVID-19 pandemic means not only a crisis of neoliberalism as an economic model; the pandemic itself is a neoliberal crisis."*[1510]

A collective responsibility by its very nature, the pandemic under neoliberalism became another policy tool for income redistribution from the bottom up. In January 2022, Oxfam research uncovered that during the pandemic the world's ten richest men doubled their wealth while 99% of the population was worse off. If it were not for a fiscal, monetary, investment, trade, and labor policy intended to benefit the very wealthy, income redistribution on a mass scale would not have taken place.[1511]

Rightwing populists around the world argued that the pandemic's lessons must include harsher policies toward immigrants and refugees. Such rhetoric kept feeding the nationalist-xenophobia frenzy which in turn governments use to keep high defense budgets and deflect attention from class war. Populist-nationalists defied epidemiologists and virologists, focusing instead on punishing China which was the pandemic's country of origin, and on liberals defending medical experts' advice under the influence of big pharma campaign contributions. Rather than undermine right-wing political parties, the unscientific often irrational reaction to the pandemic mobilized and consolidated the populist base in many countries.[1512]

Using the pandemic against globalization to reaffirm nationalism, rightwing populists advocated a weaker World Health Organization (WHO), and less dependence on multilateral institutions that seem to benefit China. Throughout the world, rightwing populists promoted a libertarian ideological argument against all measures from lockdowns to masks and vaccines. The libertarian position on the pandemic was ammunition for many businesses as well as the nationalist/militarists. For those adopting a cynical Social Darwinism perspective, the pandemic entailed that there was nothing wrong if people were sacrificed, namely, permitting nature to claim the world's poor falling through the cracks of a deficient public health care system.[1513]

Reflecting the position of many analysts, Matthias Quent of the German Institute for Democracy and Civil Society (IDZ) noted that: "*What unites people is the hatred of the political elite and public broadcasting.*" A variety of groups from traditional political and cultural conservatives to neo-Nazis used the pandemic as the catalyst against the liberal order as a pretext to affirm a commitment to authoritarianism.[1514]

Typical of the premature predictions about the end of neoliberalism before and during the pandemic, Joseph Stiglitz pointed to deepening neoliberalism's crisis. "*Today, as we face a retreat from the rules-based, liberal global order, with autocratic rulers and demagogues leading countries that contain well over half the world's population, Fukuyama's idea seems quaint and naive. But it reinforced the neoliberal economic doctrine that has prevailed for the last 40 years. The credibility of neoliberalism's faith in unfettered markets as the surest road to shared prosperity is on life support these days. And well it should be. The simultaneous waning of confidence in neoliberalism and democracy is no coincidence or mere correlation. Neoliberalism has undermined democracy for 40 years.*"[1515]

In September 2021, economist James Meadway argued that the four-decade-long 'free market' policies were finished. To prove his thesis, he pointed to the Biden administration's COVID-19 relief measures costing taxpayers \$4.3 trillion, excluding spending on health and social programs. The defense budget of \$800 billion, excluding intelligence, Homeland Security, and foreign military aid, money flowing back into the corporate bank accounts, is rarely part of the analysis to provide a more complete picture of the intersection between geopolitics and geoeconomics.

With an eye on China, the EU and UK muddled the neoliberal model in inter-core competition, especially after the war in Ukraine erupted. EU followed the US corporate subsidies model for industries competing with China. Following the same policy that the US applies to China, the UK government refused to approve the sale of the semiconductor ARM company to a US manufacturer. When the UK nationalized a steel company, many political and economic observers viewed it as a signal of neoliberalism's demise. Not a single one of those measures marked the end of neoliberalism or even a transition toward a new development model. Nevertheless, analysts kept looking for signs of anything to determine neoliberalism's limited lifespan.[1516]

Janice Alvarez points out that: "*Neoliberalism fails to appreciate that the ideal conditions to promote human prosperity do not rely solely on economic activity, but on a broader social foundation to address a wider range of interests that the neoliberal agenda willfully ignores. Neoliberalism does not enhance the human condition but only serves to contradict democratic ideals, undermine growth, and cause social upheaval. The promotion of the system worldwide must be recognized as a deliberate political project to legitimize the differential in wealth and power."*[1517]

The Myth of Progressive Neoliberalism and Speculation about Neoliberalism's Demise

By the time of the Great Recession, neoliberalism's contradictions were so glaring that there was a great deal of discussion on whether the rightwing populist, liberal pluralist, or progressive camp could come to the rescue of a model in its weakened phase amid challenges from all directions, especially from the far right. Desperate to sustain the model under the weight of chronic downward social mobility and rising inequality, the more progressive politicians within the pluralist political camp advocated progressive neoliberalism in alliance with mainstream social groups supporting the liberals against conservatives. Progressive neoliberalism implies that the pluralist political umbrella under which the model operates still has room for those hoping for some hybrid approach that would include aspects of the Keynesian social safety net and consumer demand stimulative policies.[1518]

To camouflage the predatory nature of the transformation model that they support, pluralist and progressive neoliberals employed identity politics. Australia's Labor Party Prime Minister Bob Hawke (1983-1991), President Bill Clinton (1993-2001), British Prime Minister Tony Blair (1997-2007) and Justin Trudeau (2015-present) presented themselves as progressive neoliberals who diluted Keynesianism by creating an informal alliance of feminist, environmental, and multicultural groups, on the one hand, and high tech and stock market support, on the other, while outsourcing hundreds of billions in government contracts to private firms. To widen the popular base and pursue the neoliberal agenda, corporations, and billionaires financing the campaigns of liberal pluralist politicians have been using identity politics that promotes a cosmopolitan corporate image suitable for a global market.[1519]

Concealing the essence of the political economy's impact on society, the "progressive" label has played a role in making neoliberalism palatable to liberal pluralists seeking to build popular consensus around inclusiveness within the market economy's confines. Obfuscating neoliberalism's molding of society and fomenting a political crisis by feeding off the populist movement, the trans-Atlantic experiment born out of the capital accumulation drive in the 1970s transformed the world capitalist system into a more predatory phase than the world had seen since the late 19th century. Just as quickly, the model developed contradictions that created fissures giving rise to a global tide of a global rightwing populist wave. Hollow in its attempt and create even more social contradictions, progressive neoliberalism has been a thinly veiled attempt to strengthen the neoliberal model through modest reforms reproducing itself without ever resolving the contradictions.[1520]

A manufactured concept confining itself to pluralism's perimeters without addressing the larger issue of market hegemony over the state, corporate welfare, and class war, progressive neoliberalism aims to preserve the model from irreconcilable internal contradictions often clashing with geopolitical strategies, especially among core competitors. Heads of state around the world who claimed to represent the progressive neoliberal camp, including Barak Obama, Nicolas Sarkozy, Shinzo Abe, Scott Morrison, and others with similar ideological dispositions, promoted financialization, deregulation, privatization, outsourcing government contracts, and class war as vigorously as rightwing neoliberals, even more hypocritically.[1521]

Nancy Fraser, who has conducted extensive scholarly work on progressive neoliberalism, concluded that the trend has run its course, exposing its true goals. *"They [progressive neoliberal presidents Clinton and Obama] eviscerated unions and drove down real wages, proliferated precarious service-sector jobs, and promoted predatory debt to enable the purchase of cheap stuff produced elsewhere. The result was to dramatically worsen the life conditions of the bottom two-thirds of Americans, especially (but not only) in the Rustbelt, southern, and rural communities, even as soaring stock markets fattened not just the one percent but also the upper reaches of the professional-managerial class. In due course, many harmed by these policies came to reject not only neoliberal political economy but also the more inclusive view of recognition they associated with it."*[1522]

Fraser's analysis of Clinton and Obama's anti-labor policies also applies to Biden, who along with Wall Street Democrats in Congress, opted against permitting 115,000 railroad workers who wanted to strike in November 2022. The anti-labor argument has always rested on inculcating fear in society that pro-labor policies and labor strikes hurt the economy, regardless of deplorable labor conditions. Emerging from the first industrial revolution, the argument that identifies the collective or national economic interest with capital against labor became the mantra of the neoliberal mainstream, institutionalized, and part of the hegemonic culture.[1523]

Differing on strategies, mainstream political parties serve capital. Some corporations and billionaires have supported progressive neoliberals, while others support right-wing populists. Without knowing the mechanics and behind-the-scenes maneuvering of corporate lobbying and campaign contributions, the public only feels the effects of the political economy and the top-down nature of both progressive and rightwing neoliberalism divorced from the material interests and needs of the working class.[1524]

Critical of concentrated capital and autocratization, George Soros, one of the world's progressive neoliberal billionaires, has been financing the pluralist political camp in many countries. Similar to 19th-century Western industrialists and financiers who embraced social issues intended to solidify the institutional framework that they supported, Soros, among others in the progressive neoliberal camp, used considerable resources to mold public acceptance of the status quo. Often critical of the populist political camps representing neoliberal governance the progressive camp readily acknowledges inequality that the system exacerbates. At the core of the progressive vs reactionary political power rivalry is not neoliberalism, but different strategies to mobilize voter support, manage the state apparatus, optimize popular consensus, and minimize popular dissent, all of which assume cohesion behind the class war ideology and its goals.[1525]

"Based on FEC [Federal Election Commission] records, Soros personally provided over $30 million[1] to Democratic candidates [in 2016], most of which was donated since the 2011 Citizens United ruling. His son, Alexander, has given over $5 million[2] since 2010. Soros has poured even more money than that into elections by way of Super-PACs, lavishing donations on Democrats in Congress, and in down-ticket races on the local level. Ignoring the corruption bred by massive funding from the billionaire class is what keeps authoritarian neoliberals in power... Editorials rife with elitist condescension are churned out by Vox[3] regularly... The Center for American Progress and Brock's propaganda

1. *http://docquery.fec.gov/cgi-bin/qindcont/CT/3049400.00/2/1290*

2. *http://docquery.fec.gov/cgi-bin/qind/*

3. *https://www.pastemagazine.com/articles/2016/08/the-sad-decline-of-vox-how-a-once-promising-media.html*

machines breed neoliberal robots to populate the Democratic machine's functioning parts—from staff members serving elected officials to mainstream media outlets, think tanks, and policy organizations."[1526]

Vacuous distracting rhetoric about alternatives within the system notwithstanding, progressive neoliberalism has been offering an alternative inadvertently leading to greater social exclusion. Considering that some billionaires readily acknowledge that the social contract favors them to the detriment of society, as the OXFAM 2023 report on the global income chasm indicates, the political question is whether the voices against systemic exploitation could become louder as inequality and marginalization continue to rise, or whether the far right co-opt some of those voices.[1527]

In September 2022, the UN World Food Program warned that an estimated 345 million people in 82 countries experienced acute food insecurity, with 70 million added because of Western sanctions imposed on Russia and its decision to disrupt grain shipments out of the Black Sea. Globally, more than 900,000 people are one step away from famine, representing a ten-fold increase between 2018 and 2023. Regardless of the political camps under which neoliberalism operates, there is a direct correlation between neoliberalism and rising poverty. Similarly, there is a correlation between neoliberalism and social instability owing to rising inequality and authoritarianism. [1528]

The likelihood for the proliferation of authoritarian policies reflecting the neoliberal social contract's ubiquitous stranglehold on society is just as likely to rise parallel with popular resistance finding expression in various political camps and grassroots organizations. This was the case in several countries, especially the British and French labor strikes of 2022-2023, and the Lebanon and Sri Lanka crisis of spring-summer 2022.

During the pandemic and Ukrainian war, few countries were as hard-hit by neoliberalism as Sri Lanka. On the surface, it was a power struggle between parliament and President Gotabaya Rajapaksa. Against the background of anti-government popular protests and demonstrations, the global neoliberal crisis was the root cause. Along with Lebanon's deep structural crisis, Sri Lanka was a warning to other developing nations including Laos, Pakistan, and Zambia, among other sub-Saharan African countries. Ignoring neoliberal structural causes, including IMF-style austerity, many analysts defaulted Sri Lanka's crisis to the pandemic, commodity shortages, and inflationary pressures owing to supply-chain issues and US-led sanctions against Russia; everything but the political economy in which these conditions took place.[1529]

Popular protests, which the government was unable to address serious basic goods shortages, including pharmaceuticals and power outages led to martial law in Sri Lanka. Rather than an extreme case of the periphery where neoliberal authoritarianism combined with the global economic contraction drove the economy into chaos impacting the working-class majority, Sri Lanka was the canary in the coalmine. Considering that India's neoliberal path is just as extreme as Sri Lanka's in its detrimental social impact, the ripple effect of the neoliberal crisis is as evident as the class war under autocratization.[1530]

As Thamil Venthan Ananthavinayagan argues, for decades, the IMF, World Bank, and Western governments have been promoting Sri Lanka's neoliberal transformation. Regardless of the downward economic pressures on the majority of the working class, the government stayed on course, reflecting a global trend. *"Sri Lanka is a prime example of a Third World country led by a post-colonial elite that is using people as collateral for their power considerations. The island nation has been surrendered to international financial organizations and regional superpowers as a battleground for neoliberal destruction and as a vessel for geopolitical power considerations. The idea of human rights of empowering people (in the Global South at least) is futile when the very international organizations ostensibly promoting human rights are also imposing their political agenda on the country. In this context, human rights are easily sacrificed for financial power."*[1531]

Because many developing nations have been in a similar mold as Sri Lanka, the Global South has suffered a similar fate amid a predatory race for capital concentration that presses down hardest on working people. The prospect of social revolution overturning the neoliberal order is more likely in developing nations than in advanced capitalist countries. If not a country like Sri Lanka with a history of leftist influences and civil war between the Sinhalese-dominated government and the *Liberation Tigers of Tamil Eelam* (LTTE), (1983-2009), then a larger one like India which has played a leadership role in integrating the Global South under the BRICS could experience grassroots revolution once it becomes apparent that BRICS is a G-7 competitor not the antidote to neoliberal class was.[1532]

In March 2022, Sri Lankans began protests against the high cost and shortage of essential goods. After protests at the US embassy in Colombo, in July 2022, there was a mass storming of President Gotabaya Rajapaksa's residence for what they perceived as the source of their economic problems. This sparked a protracted grassroots movement for social justice and human rights. Although the military brutally repressed popular opposition and the uprising's result was not the end of the neoliberal social contract, Sri Lanka stood out for its grassroots opposition to the corrupt government and to the political opposition also supporting neoliberal policies that the IMF had been promoting. Demanding social justice, Sri Lankans mobilized to reject authoritarian rule, populist demagogues, the disintegration of the legal/judicial system, ethno-nationalist-religious confrontations, and class war, people. This was a major development in a country where historic discrimination of the Tamil people and ethnic conflict had been the pretext to prevent working-class revolutionary solidarity.[1533]

Especially in core countries where the state and entire institutional structure are solidly in the hands of counterrevolutionary political and business elites, the prospects for revolution overturning the neoliberal social order are remote. Revolutionary prospects could be as remote in a BRICS country or one in the Global South as much under neoliberalism's grip as the UK. In addition to structural exploitation, social exclusion coupled with stagnation against the aspiration for a more inclusive society was among the long-term causes of 20th-century revolutions. Although the momentum has been with counterrevolutionaries strengthening authoritarian neoliberalism, twentieth-century revolutions could repeat in the periphery against the neoliberal metropolis and local authoritarian regimes. It is also possible that the BRICS challenged the G7 for global leadership as a means of projecting the image of anti-neoliberalism and Westernism.[1534]

In *"The Nature and Contradictions of Neoliberalism,"* Gerard Dumenil and Dominique Levy contend that neoliberalism will be unable to maintain and expand the relations of production that it inherited and managed to transition from the Keynesian era.[1535] Whether in the domain of corporate role in society, especially the multinational corporations; international finance involving IMF or other multilateral institutions; geopolitical power especially as exercised by the US-NATO alliance seeking global expansion as economic leverage; international labor, health, environmental and human rights issues, the neoliberal order at its core is based on destabilization and disorder. Because the predatory over-accumulation quest has necessarily suppressed mass consumption, neoliberalism's structural crisis embedded in the model obviates rational market expectations which neoliberals believe must remain self-regulated; a euphemism for no regulation, while it exacerbates economic, social, and political stability.[1536]

Combined with increased world trade fragmentation and economic bloc consolidation, the inevitability of perpetual market-share distributional power struggle, and social conflict management have exposed the model's inherent contradictions. Among the most obvious is the ideology that promotes freedom and emancipation when in practice it is a system aimed to mold society and the individual into conformity to its dogmatic market fundamentalism resting on chaos and disorder. It is hardly surprising that market fundamentalism sacrifices human rights, as was the case in Sri Lanka under the political dynasty of Mahinda and Gotabaya Rajapaksa, or Lebanon's predatory neoliberalism, especially under the Saudi-linked billionaire Hariri family representing the richest 10% who own three-fourths of the wealth, while a staggering 70% live in poverty unable to meet their daily expenses.[1537]

Expressing opposition in different ways depending on the country, grassroots movements have opposed the neoliberal model's perpetual structural crisis. Although trade unions labor and progressive groups became more active in their opposition to incessant class war, liberal-progressive scholars, including British academic Martin Jacques and American economist Joseph Stiglitz insisted that there was still hope for reformist change, while they fully acknowledged the model's systemic flaws.

Keynesianism, or some mix with Keynesian elements to save a system based on aggravated class war is a bourgeois cry for help one minute before midnight; anything to save the socially chaotic and destructive neoliberal social contract without damaging the capitalist order. Despite its record in Chile, Jacques applauded neoliberalism (*The Politics of Thatcherism,* 1983). As though the end justified the means, which includes tyranny of a brutal dictatorship's social consequences, such analysis has been mainstream in Western academia and media analysis.

By the time of the US presidential election in 2016, Jacques was predicting neoliberalism's imminent demise. Encouraged that liberal progressives like Paul Krugman and Joseph Stiglitz were signaling a keen interest in the debate about social inequality, Jacques' article entitled *"The Death of Neoliberalism and the Crisis in Western Politics"* sounded the alarm. *"A sure sign of the declining influence of neoliberalism is the rising chorus of intellectual voices raised against it. From the mid-70s through the 80s, the economic debate was increasingly dominated by monetarists and free marketeers."[1538]*

Besides reformist critics Krugman, Stiglitz, Thomas Piketty, and many others favoring a policy mix that includes Keynesian economics, Jacques enjoys influence in the pluralist-progressive camp. In *Frontiers of Development Economics* (2000), World Bank Vice President Nicholas Stern wrote the foreword to the edited volume by Joseph Stiglitz and G. M. Meier. Stern welcomed different development perspectives within the neoliberal framework.

In *The Strange Non-Death of Neoliberalism* (2011) Colin Crouch captures the lack of realism in analysis regarding neoliberalism's imminent demise. Despite his accurate assessment regarding inordinate corporate power, he too falls into the reformism trap, suggesting holding corporations 'accountable', as though this has realistic prospects. Like 'neoliberal ethics' completely redefining the concept no matter whether normative or applied to suit structural exploitation, corporate accountability, and green economy rhetoric are more obfuscations of their larger role in society.

It is not the case that arguments about reforming neoliberalism addressing inequality are as socially destructive as authoritarian neoliberal positions. From a policy perspective, reformists project sincere criticism from within the system for practical reasons. After all, people live in the present, not in the future world of social discontinuity with hope on the horizon to redress social injustice. Nevertheless, reformism provides the illusion that there is an alternative within the neoliberal social contract's global tyranny at all levels of life from clean and safe drinking water to health care access; from earning living wages and abolishing child labor to freedom from economic and political oppression. Reformists serve as critics within the system to keep centrists and progressives engaged and co-opted. Arguing that the institutional forum for critics is proof that the model is not as dogmatic as some portray it projects the legitimacy of alternatives within neoliberalism.

Regardless of how meritorious or distractingly manipulative reformist critics' arguments may be, the model's demise will not result from intellectuals' ominous warnings about its inherent contradictions and its destructive role in society. Contrary to predictions, the neoliberal social contract is solidifying, evolving within its contradictions as it reproduces itself, digging deeper roots, and ramping up militarism and authoritarianism, rather than heading toward dissolution. This is partly because the state remains solidly in its service with disparate resistance from the working class, a large segment of which the pluralist and authoritarian political parties have co-opted.

Split between rightwing nationalists and liberal pluralists, the latter resting on the hope of restoring some aspects of Keynesian social development and regulatory measures to prevent perpetual crises in the capitalist system, political division from within the neoliberal camp projects the image of irreconcilable disagreements on goals where there is none except in modalities. This leaves the very weak and divided progressive camp in most countries, especially in the metropolis, to address structural problems.

The French presidential election of April 2022 demonstrated that the choice that the neoliberal elites placed before the voters was between the rightwing populist neoliberal Marine Le Pen and the neoliberal pluralist incumbent President Emanuel Macron with a strong proclivity toward militarism and incessant class warfare. In an obvious bankruptcy of the liberal alternative, Hungarian prime minister Viktor Orban's fourth straight supermajority in parliamentary elections (April 2022), and the Italian prime minister's election of rightwing coalition behind Giorgia Meloni (September 2022) also proved the dynamism of the neoliberal authoritarianism.[1539]

Indicative of rising autocratization, there was a sharp rise in human rights violations during the nascent phase of neoliberalism. This coincided with mainstream institutional rhetoric about human rights abuses which the West selectively used since the Carter administration as a foreign policy tool against Communist and select Muslim enemies. Human rights hypocrisy could not hide from what was taking place in several countries under pro-US regimes, from apartheid South Africa and Israel to Chile, Brazil, Argentina, and other Latin American republics under authoritarian regimes. By the early 2000s, advanced and developing countries alike justified human rights violations in the name of combating terrorism, mostly targeting Muslims, but also leftists or other dissidents under the label of domestic terrorism.[1540]

Often owing to concentrated capital accumulation, rising inequality, and historical regimes targeting minorities has been the source of human rights violations. In addition to the paradox of a rise in human rights laws and policies in the age of neoliberalism, the emphasis on borderless global markets under free trade and low tariffs runs into the reality of the few advanced capitalist countries determining the terms of trade and using other leverage, including bloc trading, aid and loans, and weapons transfers.[1541]

Capitalism operates within national borders that potentially can collide regionally and/or at the global level, especially as competition intensifies for market share while geopolitics/balance of power pursuits figure prominently into the equation. Corporations and investors demand aggressive state intervention to protect and expand their interests while expecting the general public to pay for the costs of everything from infrastructure to corporate subsidies. With government and international financial organizations' backing, business-led class war necessarily leads to inequality and authoritarian policies.[1542]

Adding to the list of paradoxes, ostensible "value-free" market fundamentalism has remained at the theoretical level, while policy has very strong moral consequences in peoples' lives, in inter-elite power competition, alliances, and relations of production based on uneven income distribution both socially and geographically. In so far as the appropriation process comes at the expense of labor, market choices necessarily come with complex ethical assumptions about the individual and society.

The other side of market freedom's coin is the lack of freedom for trade unionism, collective bargaining, freedom from poverty and inequality, and the right to live in a society free of repression. Ethical egoism, the theory that humans have no moral duty other than self-promotion within society's moral boundaries is a manifestation of a decadent political economy with a history of ruinous consequences for the community as a whole but especially for workers within the community. Dogmatically determined to alter society's norms to the point of widening sociopolitical chasm precipitating authoritarianism, neoliberal apologists relegate all blame for anything dysfunctional in society to the Keynesian state and labor for capitalism's systemic crisis. Their dogmatism regarding overaccumulation responsible for economic stagnation finds vindication among class warfare promoters because the state and the entire institutional structure legitimize capitalist appropriation. [1543]

As it becomes more evident that the political economy riddled with contradictions serves an increasingly smaller percentage of the population, the elites on a world scale become more predacious about how to divide the economic pie. They become more contentious about how to appropriate labor value while mobilizing popular support behind mainstream political parties so that they can maintain the unequal and socially unjust social order. From the Great Recession through the pandemic and the Russian war in Ukraine, the rise of anti-labor policies in authoritarian and liberal-democratic regimes was an indication that the elites were determined to enforce the neoliberal social contract, no matter the cost to workers and social harmony.[1544]

A critical mass in society has not reached the point of making the connection between the pluralist inclusionary vs. the populist exclusionary authoritarian neoliberal versions. As systemic contradictions precipitate political polarization, economic disequilibrium in the name of market efficiency, and social resistance expressed in various forms, the political economy degenerates from within and drags down society with it. Although this does not signal social discontinuity, it indicates that structural flaws are leading to a deepening multi-level capitalist crisis. The BRICS's popularity as relief from the oppression of Western neoliberalism offered a false sense of hope, considering that the BRICS operate under the same model, serving the same capitalist interests as the G7.[1545]

Along with Bretton Woods' international financial architecture, neoliberalism is showing signs of aging amid reproduction and challenges that fragmentation is posing against the background of US-China rivalry. Japan's announcement in January 2023 that there is a need for a new world order, and the US announcing a revision of the Washington Consensus in April 2023 amid a rapidly shifting capitalist core from the trans-Atlantic to Asia have transformed the transformation model. The weakened US global hegemonic economic role and deliberately fragmented world trade as a means to retain US hegemony undercut the neoliberal model's integrity. The twilight of the existing model means continued protracted painful material costs for the working class and middle class.[1546]

Itself a manifestation of capitalism's inherent weakness, the corporate welfare system represents the private sector's absorption of public capital which contributes to inequality and opens wider the door to authoritarianism. Precipitating deeper and longer cyclical recessions, neoliberalism represents opportunities for some segments among capitalists, but misery on a world scale. For every sector from agriculture to pharmaceuticals and from high tech to defense, governments have provided trillions in corporate subsidies to sustain the private sector. From the 1980s to the present, trillions in corporate subsidies and tax reductions for highly profitable companies pose no problem for neoliberals. By contrast, public healthcare, education, subsidized housing, and social security constitute a burden on public debt. Oblivious to the level of widespread misery and destruction that neoliberalism delivers to people on a mass scale, the social and political elites remain dogmatically indifferent.[1547]

Placing as much value on labor's role in the economy as in its marginalization, neoliberalism has raised the bar of inequality and authoritarianism to levels not experienced since the 1930s. In the race for capital accumulation, natural and man-made disasters, and wars are subject to commodification, while in 2021, half of the world's population lived on less than $6.85 a day.[1548] Illness and death owing to pandemics, legal and illegal drug trade, human trafficking, child labor, lack of housing, poor health care, and authoritarianism masquerading as 'democracy' keep the lives of billions in misery. The middle and lower strata continue to experience downward mobility in most countries while the elite becomes smaller and richer. To maintain exclusive privileges that keep inequality growing, capital is driving public policy and leading society into the embrace of authoritarianism.[1549]

Pretending that the governance structure is not a reflection of the social contract, neoliberals insist that 'bourgeois pragmatism' is society's only option. The concept of bourgeois pragmatism has its roots in late 19th-century mass politics when trade unions were fighting to become a legitimate institutional presence. Under the neoliberal model, the working class throughout the world has been struggling for its rights as did workers two centuries ago. Apple, one of the world's preeminent companies, not only runs sweatshops in China, but in April 2023, it ran anti-unionizing meetings in its 270 US stores. In the absence of the state protecting labor rights, conditions approximate those of the early Industrial Revolution.[1550]

Despite the middle-class acting as a buffer between capital and labor, political, business, and media establishments reject any form of working-class solidarity as a force in society. As much in the 19th century as in the 21st, the political struggle to forge popular consensus projects the image of choice where there was none when it comes to public policy. This includes the illusion of "unlimited freedom", as long as it pertains to the consumer-citizen supporting the social contract.

Regardless of the specific political regime under which neoliberalism operates, all roads lead to populist, nationalist, militarist, and technocratic illiberal regimes as a means of protecting the transformation model from grassroots opposition. As the apparent consensus agent, the state becomes mired in contradictions owing to the gap between the reality of keeping the majority in conformity amid class war in a fragmented society and the unfulfilled promise of material progress for all.[1551]

From Australia and Britain's Labour parties to Europe's liberal parties, and from traditional populist-nationalist parties with or without a religious ideological tilt in India, Brazil, or Turkey, neoliberalism has prevailed in governance structure with nuances reflecting local traditions. With the help of modern technology, mass media, and social media, the model's remarkable success has been to conceal its authoritarian nature under the thin veil of sham electoral politics that the businesses and wealthy individuals finance in return for promoting certain policies. Although the ostensibly antithetical pluralist vs populist political camps have been the key to the neoliberal umbrella's triumphant ascendancy providing the façade of democracy, this same antagonism is a contributing factor in democracy's demise.[1552]

Testing the limits of liberal democracy amid the rise of the anti-science crisis-populist hysteria, a segment of the rightwing political, media and financial elites used COVID-19 testing, vaccination, and preventive measures as a symbol of individual freedom against the state's responsibility to protect public health as it impacts the economy rather than for its own sake. Seemingly defending the right of individual choice, as though the average individual has expertise in epidemiology and public health, crisis-peddling populists, who ordinarily favor trade protectionism, invoked a libertarian doctrine against the state's utilitarian approach when it pertained to preventative measures intended to secure intermediate economic viability under pandemic conditions.[1553]

Arguing that health preventative measures impact business freedom to operate profitably, populist-libertarian antivaxxers opposed regulation, even in emergency conditions regardless of community health risks. Intertwined with laissez-faire measures, selective industry-specific protectionism was also reflected in the corporate sector's demands for monetary, fiscal, and other corporate welfare assistance. Just below the surface of the populist-libertarian anti-vaxxer movements, which further eroded institutional confidence, there were corporate welfare demands and a drive to continue redistributing income from the bottom up.[1554]

Inordinate reliance on the state to bail out the private sector during the pandemic was an obvious contradiction that politicians, businesses, the media, and neoliberal apologists refused to acknowledge. Using the pretext that competing with China made corporate subsidies and state intervention necessary, the state adjusted neoliberal policies within a nationalist mold. "*In the past six months, the Conservative government in the UK has nationalized*[4]*, threatened major football clubs with fan ownership*[5]*, and moved to block the sale*[6] *of silicon chip designer ARM to a US manufacturer. Such moves towards more assertive state intervention are not limited to the UK. In Europe, the EU is in the process of overhauling its State Aid rules to allow greater government support to industry, citing the need to meet competition from China... None of this would fit easily into the 'neoliberal' playbook of previous decades when anti-union, tax-cutting, and market-first policies dominated government thinking.*"[1555]

Far from total eclipse amid global financial crises, pandemics, and geopolitical confrontations, neoliberalism relies on the impetus not just of the state whose laws and regulations it shapes, but on the continued distraction of the liberal-conservative competition, especially considering how populists weaponize the term "liberal". Although Karl Popper and Milton Friedman did not go as far as Hayek to argue that the 'free market' is the only mechanism

---

4. *https://www.theguardian.com/business/2021/jul/28/sheffield-forgemasters-nationalised-after-takeover-ministry-of-defence*

5. *https://talksport.com/football/869465/government-german-ownership-model-boris-johnson-european-super-league/*

6. *https://www.bloomberg.com/news/articles/2021-08-03/u-k-considers-blocking-nvidia-s-takeover-of-arm-over-security*

to guarantee individual participation in democracy, their ideology leads to the same result as Hayek's market authoritarianism.

To distract from neoliberalism's impact on inequality, downward social mobility, and a path toward authoritarianism, centrist and rightist politicians, the media, and businesses have been applying Hayek's consumer-citizen identity politics. Focused on class war by pursuing militarism and the politics of marginalization, the state, the media, and mainstream institutions have turned the working class against itself thereby shielding the capitalist class. While exclusionary populism harms the very people who embrace identity politics as a means of denying the ubiquitous class war, inclusionary neoliberalism has been catalytic in affording credibility and preserving the political economy.[1556]

Not surprisingly, the political correctness/identity politics trend started in the late 1970s and became more widespread especially among "yuppies" sharing liberal political ideas but practicing economic orthodoxy in the mid-1980s. Amid the UK and US neoliberal transformation, this trend served as a substitute for social justice and universal human rights that the government and the private sector rapidly undermined, along with the social welfare state. As long as the shield of political correctness was a satisfactory substitute for social justice to workers and the middle class, and a sizeable percentage felt that they were a part of a 'civilized' society, neoliberal policy continued on the barbaric path of social exclusion, rising inequality, class warfare, and autocratization.[1557]

Despite pro-business fiscal and monetary policy, and trillions of dollars in taxpayer money to subsidize the private sector mostly through direct and indirect payments to businesses, the results of market-efficiency policies were hardly encouraging for society, if we judge by living standards and quality of life criteria across the social spectrum. Although mainstream analysts insist on recycling the myth that government is not the solution for social inequities, the same analysts demand corporate subsidies, corporate tax reductions, and business deregulation, arguing that society's economic health is predicated on vertical corporate profits growth, not horizontal social development. Accepting that there is no arbiter in society to represent all social classes or collective welfare other than the state, liberals and conservatives alike confine the state's role to the domain of security, police, and military, all protecting the private sector from domestic and foreign threats.[1558]

Published in January 2020, a Pew Research poll indicates excessive inequality in the US where 70% think that the system favors the rich and powerful. The same poll shows that 82% believe the wealthy and large corporations have too much power and influence in the economy, while 84% believe politicians enjoy comparable power. A Pew Research poll of Western Europe in 2021 shows that the desire to change the economic system is strong, but not as strong as in the US. Europeans indicated a far greater desire for the state to regulate the private sector, whereas Americans were evenly divided.[1559]

To project a mythology somewhat effective in convincing a segment of the population that there is no alternative to neoliberalism, neoliberals only consider the ideal conditions in a market hegemony over society, disregarding the realities of both rising inequality and the path toward authoritarianism. "*This is where we see the barbarity of our current state of decadence find its expression in economic terms,*" Clara H. Whyte points out, "*and this mainly serves the interests of the new globalized oligarchy who is the only social class that is yielding real and huge benefits from this system... It has clear totalitarian tendencies, and if left unchecked might lead to some of the worst forms of totalitarianism ever witnessed thanks to the use of novel technologies such as biotechnologies, toxicology, microbiology, artificial intelligence, etc.*"[1560]

Merely another phase amid a long-term systemic crisis of the political economy and the state rapidly descending toward autocratization mode, neoliberalism is the latest stage of monopoly capitalism's brazen revival after its taming in the Keynesian phase. Hardly the last, the neoliberal stage remains fairly resilient even amid multifaceted crises, inherent contradictions, and uneven social and economic global development. Based on credit-debt cycle growth patterns stimulated by a massive income transfer from workers and the middle class into the bank accounts of the investor class, neoliberalism has lowered living standards and household savings for the majority, while sharply raising household debt and public debt.

As the banking crisis of 2023 revealed, Silicon Valley Bank, Signature Bank, Credit Suisse, and 186 US banks were at risk of insolvency, spilling over with secondary effects to the entire Western Hemisphere and Europe, creating turmoil in society and resulting in a few large banks enjoying even greater influence. Financialized capitalism has created a crisis in confidence in its legitimacy in genuinely searching for a political solution. Besides the failed US banks speculating on start-ups and cryptocurrency, the Swiss banking giant involved a complex web of legal and semi-legal investments from Israel, Russia, and Western Europe in Mozambique where Western speculators turned the former socialist country into a neoliberal enclave; this in a country with extreme poverty of 62 percent or 21 million people in 2023.[1561]

Hollow rhetoric about freedom from state intervention notwithstanding, under neoliberalism businesses never stopped demanding that the state provide corporate welfare, guarantee free market protection from risks by using taxpayer money for bailouts, an accommodative monetary policy of 'cheap money', and central banks buying corporate and mortgage bonds as a form of subsidy. After the Biden administration announced plans for massive corporate subsidies in the chips sector, in March 2021, INTEL CEO stated categorically that his company's policy was to reject such subsidies either in Arizona or Ohio.

By early 2023, INTEL was due to receive several billion from both the federal and state governments in subsidies. In addition, the company signed a deal with Germany, receiving almost one-third of a $33 billion investment in a plant. Besides massive corporate subsidies, a pro-business fiscal policy with loopholes reducing the effective rate lower than the official, the neoliberal state outsources contracts to the private sector, even for work that could be carried out in-house for a much lower cost. In essence, the state shields and enhances private capital, owing to the socialization of risks and costs, while calling such a system "free enterprise".[1562]

"As policymakers prioritized price stability over full employment, they had condemned the most unskilled or socially stigmatized workers to perpetual joblessness[7]. As globalization eroded barriers to the free movement of capital, it condemned entire regions to economic dispossession... Whatever else global capitalism had proffered in the 20th century's closing decades, it had also fostered a more fertile breeding ground[8] for emergent disease than any our species had ever known... Even as these pathogenic conditions kicked up periodic epidemics, investment in global public health had remained scarce...In a world of strong unions and left-wing parties, the engine of economic growth would likely be wage increases instead of debt-financed speculation and asset-price appreciation. In that more egalitarian political economy, financial crises might be less frequent. And when crashes did occur, it might be possible to resolve them

---

7. *https://rooseveltinstitute.org/publications/reimagining-full-employment-28-million-more-jobs-and-a-more-equal-economy/*

8. *https://magazine.washington.edu/feature/infectious-diseases-are-back-with-a-vengeance-uw-experts-warn/*

through structural reforms, rather than massive central-bank interventions aimed at stabilizing a wobbly, top-heavy economic order.[1563]

Rooted in the interwar, from its inception, one of neoliberalism's core themes was class warfare finding expressing in various domains of public policy. An aggressive attack on trade unions and the use of every possible means to divide and weaken the working class has been part of what neoliberals call labor market transformation. This is nothing short of a systematic attack on labor, in contrast to the Keynesian era when the state encouraged trade unionism for economic, political, and social stability considerations. Material conditions are dialectically related to the crisis of neoliberalism which points to the model's evolutionary course undergoing further transformation, in part because geopolitics has been influencing this phase of capitalism as it has all previously.[1564]

Neoliberal Culture of Narcissism

There is a body of scholarly literature linking the deleterious effects of neoliberal hegemonic culture to everything from mental health problems to community disintegration leaving people completely divorced from society's mainstream. Neoliberal transformation coincided with a sharp rise in a "self-help" and "be happy" industry promoting yuppie culture feel-good materialism. Although the late 1960s-early1970s "I'm OK, you're OK" concept was rooted in empathy, in the nascent stage of neoliberalism, such books and articles were a vehicle to promote transformation by propagating the new cultural norm of atomist and rejection of community welfare.

"Whenever narcissism becomes dominant, other people," Mariana Fotaki points out, *"(or the whole groups of other people) are seen not as others, like oneself, but as objects to be used. For instance, when markets are seen as anonymous 'virtual' structures, employees may be seen and treated as exploitable commodities. Such behaviors are pathologically perverse in that people disavow their knowledge of the situations they create through narcissistic processes... Separating risk from responsibility in the financial sector was not merely about creating perverse incentives enabling people to engage in greed through financial bubbles that were bound to burst, but about disengaging policymakers from the all too predictable consequences of such policies."*[1565]

Based on the dogma that the root of all problems rests with non-conformists of the Keynesian era, not the institutional structure reflecting the neoliberal social contract, culture has elevated narcissism to the highest virtue that the business elite exemplifies. Failure to achieve neoliberalism's narcissistic goals manifests itself in heightened anxiety, lack of self-confidence, low self-esteem, depression, a sense of failure, and rage internalized and/or externalized.[1566]

From Sigmund Freud's *On Narcissism* (1914) to Robert Pfaller's *Postmodern Aesthetics and Neoliberal Politics: A Relationship between Ornament and Crime,* (2020), narcissism has been a controversial scholarly topic, especially for those arguing that capitalism precipitates and reinforces it. The *"protestant ethic of modern times,"* narcissism as modern-day religious asceticism in the age of neoliberal digital society of alienation is a reflection of inner emptiness that comes from a zombified existence in a necro-capitalist institutional structure and culture. These objective conditions reinforce a never-ending thirst for materialism upon which identity, lack of self-esteem, and a happiness vacuum. Because consumer culture has such a far-reaching influence in society and on self-identity, it stands to reason that inner fulfillment is indeed as elusive in the 21st-century neoliberal dream world of financialization and cryptocurrency riches, as spiritual rapture in the era of St. Thomas Aquinas in 13th-century Italy.[1567]

Rejection of communitarian values rooted in the concept of the individual as an integral part of the collective encourages narcissism as civilization's inevitable outgrowth where identity is commodified and empathy diminished, and marginalized, if not replaced with a thirst for digital fulfillment as a substitute for creative self-development contributing to the community. Beyond bourgeois alienation which Jean-Paul Sartre addresses in *Being and Nothingness* as symptomatic of capitalist society's objectification of the self, neoliberal alienation drives the individual a step closer to techno-escapism owing to utter loss of control in a seemingly democratic society resting on a market-dominated culture where the delusion of free will affords false comfort of determining one's destiny. Given such regimented cultural conditions that the neoliberal model determines, narcissistic techno-escapism has contributed to the rapid rise of right-wing populism.[1568]

Under neoliberal transformation, civilization has degenerated to a level where the political and socioeconomic elites proclaim everything in the name of progress identified with the mythical market efficiency which thrives on chaos and disorder, demanding that the state continuously transfers income from labor to strengthen capital. Forged in anti-Communism, fascism was a desperate counterrevolutionary attempt to save capitalism and neoliberalism emerged from a similar social relations framework. A counterrevolutionary ideology, neoliberalism was born in reaction to both Communism and Keynesianism. No matter what liberals and conservatives proclaim, only to be contradicted by the detrimental impact of policies on working people, neoliberal ideology and culture is misanthropic, and destructive for humanity, undermining collective human welfare and civilization.[1569]

Distracted by everything from techno-solutions, nationalism, militarism, religion, and identity politics of both the right and the liberal center intended to maintain the neoliberal social order and the misanthropic culture, the mass consumer-citizen seeks therapy for having internalized structural problems in the social contract. Rooted in narcissism where the incessant marketing-generated thirst to own inanimate objects has substituted empathy for community and humanity; jettisoning the individual as part of the whole in limited time and space. Regardless of whether a country is under a pluralist or authoritarian regime, the neoliberal institutional structure and value system has been inculcated into the consciousness of the masses questioning community and humanity, empirical reality and scientific truth for aesthetically based personal truth of an alternative irrational universe analogous to religious dogma.

Considering that neoliberal commodification culture entails organizing one's life and social interactions on a marketing model of "personal branding" for everyone from famous politicians and corporate CEOs to the average person seeking employment to survive, it is hardly surprising that neoliberalism provides an impetus to the culture of narcissism, thus, to social alienation. From a young age to adulthood, the hegemonic culture molds the narcissistic personality and reproduces the toxic environment. Along with commodification, the neoliberal value system celebrating the parasitic wealthy class reinforces narcissism's vortex.

In *"Breaking away from narcissism: emotions and grassroots activism in the time of COVID-19,"* Tomaso Gravante and Alice Poma contend that neoliberalism has conditioned people to respect the socioeconomic elite to which many among the masses aspire. As manifested in the class war, the intolerance and disdain of capitalists toward working people and those that society has subjected to marginalization is the norm consistent with authoritarian neoliberalism.

"The message that is constantly repeated is that we live in the best possible system... Neoliberal emotional culture is so deeply rooted that many people have been more afraid and anxious about losing privileges, that until now they believed to be untouchable or at least safe, than about losing their lives or their loved ones. This is also influenced by what psychologists call the "myth of invulnerability", in other words: it will affect all the others but not me."[1570]

Confined within the narrow boundaries of winners and losers, which the market-dominated state creates through interventionist policies on behalf of capital, the neoliberal ideology presents a façade of personal salvation found in wealth as the single-issue criteria to the exclusion of all others. Not only do neoliberal institutions commodify the individual, but they also commodify secular and religious culture to the degree that they absorb the individual inside a cocoon of alienation, engendering community disconnectedness in celebration of narcissism as the hegemonic culture's virtue. Because neoliberal civilization harbors hostility toward democracy, social welfare, grassroots sovereignty, and animosity toward labor, gravitating toward autocratization has been inescapable. This is not only for the elites determined to preserve their privileges and becoming more sadistic toward labor, but also the middle class fearing losing what they have as well as for a segment of the working class frustrated with the social contract, expressing anger toward marginalized groups at the bottom of the social ladder.[1571]

The hegemonic cultural transformation has forged a narcissistic pathological personality whose foundations predate the Thatcher-Reagan era, as Christopher Lasch argues in *The Culture of Narcissism: American Life in an Age of Diminishing Expectations* (1979). Both Lasch and Foucault agreed that the general population surrendered to institutional experts representing the establishment and tailoring their scientific pursuits around social conformity. Psychologists, educators, managers, and journalists among others in the popular 'trendy circuit' reflect and promote the neoliberal value system of narcissism. Cashing in on the inspirational self-help industry that the establishment fully supports, neoliberal culture's focus is on the individual whose social obligation to conform to the social contract.

In one of the most perceptive analyses of this theme, Heidi Rimke writes: *"Addressing social needs rarely becomes part of the mainstream self-help rhetoric or jargon. The imperatives of governmental policies, public organizations and institutions, corporations, and employers to ensure essentials in all spheres of social life such as living wages, insurance, healthcare, education, and retirement or legislation to protect children, the disabled, consumers, the environment, workers and other marginalized groups thus falls to the wayside as self-help increasingly colonizes cultures, taking social pressure off authorities... Neoliberal subjectivities are therefore primarily shaped and evaluated based on shallow, competitive individualism articulated and governed through therapeutic cultures where health, illness, wellness, and disability are commodified, depoliticized, privatized, and monetized. Self-help culture thus largely deflects, distracts, and pacifies social subjects in the neoliberal era that promotes the ruthless pursuit of domination, power, and capital." [1572]*

Rooted in the celebration of human welfare and creativity, civilization has always been a collective achievement. A mirror of an epoch's cultural diffusion, civilization has never been an individual endeavor. No matter how capitalist ideology under various platforms from the 17th century to the present has assessed it to preserve the social order, civilization has always been a collective endeavor. Albert Einstein's (*The World As I See It,* 1934) belief that *"social justice and social responsibility has always contrasted oddly with my pronounced freedom from the need for direct contact with other human beings and human communities"* underscores the underlying oneness to put it into a Hinduist context of life. Under authoritarian and corporatist forms of government, neoliberal-digital era individualistic values are subordinated to the corporation and the state. Such strains have been very evident in liberal bourgeois societies headed toward authoritarianism in many parts of the world in the 21st century.[1573]

Human fascination with digital fiction aside, humans are not automatons in deep-space exploration making mechanical calculations devoid of a social context. Neoliberalism's success rests in diminishing human empathy and divorcing the individual from the social context. Unless linked to the corporation, and has had a direct impact on the rise of a necro-capitalist culture where the lifeless object and subdued worker constitute part of the lower echelons in a hierarchy of alienation and exploitation, the individual is of little consequence to the neoliberal institutional structure. An absence of social connectedness with a public policy intended to sustain the welfare of an inclusionary socially just society rests within the parasitic neoliberal model where class warfare takes center stage as an extension of the market subduing the individual into conformity.

No neoliberal cheerleader journalist, academic, think tank analyst, lobbyist, priest, or politician can manipulate the empirical effects of a parasitic, chaotic political economy against the reality of empirical data. Everything from global poverty, environmental degradation, and its co-optation and manipulation to the privatization of public property and public subsidies for corporations to fomenting class war and fractious political system permitting a hegemonic private sector and an authoritarian political system, all signal the depths of a deepening capitalist crisis.[1574]

Under neoliberalism's incessant dismemberment of the social fabric, the erosion of community cohesion, and the categorical rejection of cultural diffusion as a mirror of the universal collective endeavor, civilization will persevere. At an immense cost to billions of people, and the planet itself, civilization will survive the neoliberal assault on humanity, the deliberately created ubiquitous chaos, mass misery, inequality, and authoritarianism paving the way for neoliberalism to survive. It is inevitable that eventually, the weight of neoliberal institutions will collapse from within, precipitating mass grassroots resistance. Unlike neoliberalism's decline, fatalism is not an inevitable consequence of economic and sociopolitical chaos.

Capitalism undermining Western civilization survived long after Oswald Spengler predicted its decline at the end of WWI when the West feared the Bolshevik Revolution amid mass cynicism about the end of the Enlightenment's rationalist principles. In the century unfolding after Spengler's *The Decline of the West,* catastrophic cyclical economic crises and large-scale, as well as smaller wars, followed, eliminating an estimated two hundred million people and sinking hundreds of millions into a life of chronic misery. The victims of wars and economic misery were the result of militarism and economic policies designed to maintain concentrated wealth and power. Hiding behind perfidious hollow rhetoric of patriotism and economic 'national interest', the unjust social contract and man-made disasters became the norm that socioeconomic elites and the political class representing them imposed on humanity. This is the context from which neoliberalism emerged and blossomed globally; the path on which transformation evolved in the 21st century.

In its five-hundred history, capitalism has never produced socioeconomic equality or popular democracy, nor was this ever the goal for it would obviate the logic of social relations under a social contract that the bourgeoisie forged to perpetuate their interests. Amid class warfare, neoliberalism celebrates elites, inequality, and democracy as a thin veil behind which rests the reality of social injustice. Negatively impacting not just living standards and the rights for which workers fought in the last two hundred years, but also middle-class socioeconomic mobility, while delivering society toward authoritarianism around the world. Putting aside the merits of the historicist theory of universal laws of history and its application to the neoliberal phase of capitalism, it is impossible to see how this model does not self-destruct under the weight of its contradictions.

From the ashes of neoliberalism what follows may not be another model that works with any sort of cohesion within the capitalist system, not any sort of a higher synthesis as the next development model. Transformation of mainstream institutions evolves and adapts under monopoly capitalism carrying aspects of neoliberalism, but also grassroots resistance amid socioeconomic and political conditions more oppressive than what many countries experienced in the 20th century during social revolutions and decolonization movements. In the service of monopoly capitalism, the interplay of geopolitics and geoeconomics undermines neoliberalism and paves the way for new models resulting from the clash between a disgruntled middle class losing hope for retaining its status and workers struggling to survive against counterrevolutionary elites resolved to preserve monopoly over a decadent institutional structure.

Bibliography

Abramovitz, Mimi and Jennifer Zelnick. *"Double Jeopardy: The Impact of Neoliberalism on Care Workers in the United States and South Africa."* http://journals.sagepub.com/doi/abs/10.2190/HS.40.1.f

Albatazzi, Daniele and Duncan McDonnell. *Twenty-First Century Populism: The Specter of Western European Democracy.* (2007).

Althusser, Louis. *"Ideology and Ideological State Apparatuses."*https://www.marxists.org/reference/archive/althusser/1970/ideology.htm

Althusser, Louis. *On the Reproduction of Capitalism: Ideology and Ideological State Apparatuses.* (2014)

Amable[1], Bruno. *"The Road to Neoliberal Autocracy."* https://www.versobooks.com/blogs/4993-the-road-to-neoliberal-autocracy

Amagour[2], Otmane. *"The Political Economy of Education in the Arab World: An Interview with Hicham Alaoui."* https://www.jadaliyya.com/Details/42822.

Angelo, Tiago. *'Neoliberalismo precisa da violência, diz historiadora sobre 46 anos do golpe no Chile.'* https://www.brasildefato.com.br/2019/09/11/neoliberalismo-precisa-da-violencia-diz-historiadora-sobre-46-anos-do-golpe-no-chile

Arar[3], Khalid, Deniz Örücü[4], and Jane Wilkinson[5], eds. *Neoliberalism and Education Systems in Conflict: Exploring Challenges Across the Globe.* (2020).

Azar[6], Riad. *"Neoliberalism, Austerity and Authoritarianism."* http://newpol.org/content/neoliberalism-austerity-and-authoritarianism

Babb, Sarah and Alexander Kentikelenis. *"International Financial Institutions*

as Agents of Neoliberalism." http://www.kentikelenis.net/uploads/3/1/8/9/31894609/babbkentikelenis2018-international_financial_institutions_as_agents_of_neoliberalism.pdf

Badham, Rachel. *"The Neoliberal Side of Social Media."* https://thebadgeronline.com/2019/03/neoliberal-side-social-media

Bailes, Jon. *Consciousness and the Neoliberal Subject.* (2020).

Baturo, Alexander and Jos Elkink. *The New Kremlinology: Understanding Regime Personalization in Russia.* (2021).

1. https://d.docs.live.net/eb41a1b69e1e6e00/Desktop/Amable
2. https://www.jadaliyya.com/Author/10822
3. https://www.routledge.com/search?author=Khalid%20Arar
4. https://www.routledge.com/search?author=Deniz%20Örücü
5. https://www.routledge.com/search?author=Jane%20Wilkinson
6. https://newpol.org/authors/azar-riad/

Bedford, Sofie Bedford and Laurent Vinatier. *Resisting the Irresistible: 'Failed Opposition' in Azerbaijan and Belarus revisited*. (2018).

Bell, Daniel. *The End of Ideology*. (2000).

Ben Lazreg, Houssem. *"Post-Islamism in Tunisia and Egypt: Contradictory Trajectories."*

MDPI (June 2021).

Bensaada, Ahmed. *Arabesque: Enquête sur le rôle des États-Unis dans les révoltes arabes*, (2015).

Benzine, Rachid. *Les nouveaux penseurs de l'islam*. (2004).

Berdayes, Vicente John W. Murphy, eds. *Neoliberalism, Economic Radicalism, and the Normalization of Violence*. (2016).

Berman, Sherri. *Populism is not Fascism: But it could be a Harbinger"* https://www.foreignaffairs.com/articles/united-states/2016-10-17/populism-not-fascism

Bivens, Josh and Lawrence Mishel. *"Understanding the Historic Divergence Between Productivity and a Typical Worker's Pay Why It Matters and Why It's Real"* in Economic Policy Institute, (2015).

Bix, Herbert P. *"Japan Under Neonationalist, Neoliberal Rule: Moving Toward an Abyss?"* https://apjjf.org/2013/11/15/Herbert-P.-Bix/3927/article.html

Boddy, R. *"Corporate Psychopaths and Destructive Leadership in Organizations,"* in S. M. Camgöz[7] and O. T. Ekmecki, eds. *Destructive Leadership and Management Hypocrisy*. (2021).

Boggs, Carl. *The End of Politics: Corporate Power and the Decline of the Public Sphere*, (2000).

Boron, Atilio A. *"Democracy or Neoliberalism?"* http://bostonreview.net/archives/BR21.5/boron.html

Bouillaud, Christophe. *"Emmanuel Macron: toujours et encore le né**o-lib**éralisme?"* https://theconversation.com/emmanuel-macron-toujours-et-encore-le-neo-liberalisme-179680

Boykoff, Jules. *"Limiting Dissent: The Mechanisms of State Repression in the USA" Social Movement Studies,"* 6:3, (2007).

Bray, Francesca Lucia Bray. *"Neoliberalism and Empire: The American Military-Industrial Complex,"* Journal of International Studies, 11 (2020).

Brown, Ellen. *"Neoliberalism has met its match in China."*https://www.commondreams.org/views/2019/08/09/neoliberalism-has-met-its-match-china

Brown, John. *"Neoliberalization, De-democratization, and Populist Responses in Western Europe, the US, and Latin America"*. Critical Sociology, (May 2020).

Brown, Wendy. *"Neoliberalism's Frankenstein: Authoritarian Freedom in Twenty-First Century Democracies."* https://read.dukeupress.edu/critical-times/article/1/1/60/139328/Neoliberalism-s-Frankenstein-Authoritarian-Freedom

7. https://www.emerald.com/insight/search?q=Selin%20Metin%20Camgöz

Braudel, Fernand. *La Méditerranée et le Monde méditerranéen à l'époque de Philippe II.* (1949).

Brecher, Bob. *"Neoliberalism and its Threat to Moral Agency"* in Andrius Bielskis and Kelvin Knight, eds. *Virtue and Economy*. (2015).

Carvalko, Joseph. *The Techno-human Shell-A Jump in the Evolutionary Gap*. (2012).

Chang, Ha-Joon. *"2008 Global Financial Crisis in a Long-Term Perspective: The Failure of Neoliberalism and the Future of Capitalism."* https://cgd.leeds.ac.uk/events/2008-global-financial-crisis-in-a-long-term-perspective-the-failure-of-neo-liberalism-and-the-future-of-capitalism-2/

Chen, Weitseng, ed. *The Beijing Consensus? How China Has Changed Western Ideas of Law and Economic Development.* (2017).

Chollett, Donna L. *Neoliberalism, Social Exclusion, and Social Movements*, (2013).

Chomsky, Noam. *"Corporate Business Model are Hurting American Universities."* http://www.salon.com/2014/10/10/noam_chomsky_corporate_business_models_are_hurting_american_universities_partner/

Chomsky, Noam and R. W. McChesney. *Profit Over People: Neoliberalism and Global Order.* (2011).

Christophers, Brett. *The New Enclosure: The Appropriation of Public Land in Neoliberal Britain.* (2019).

Ciepley, David. *Liberalism in the Shadow of Totalitarianism*. (2007).

CIRL, "*Compte rendu des séances du Colloque Walter Lippmann, 26–30 août 1938*". (1939).

Clark, Gregory and Tatsuya Ishii, *"Social Mobility in Japan, 1868-2012: The Surprising Persistence of the Samurai."*

http://faculty.econ.ucdavis.edu/faculty/gclark/The%20Son%20Also%20Rises/Japan%202012.pdf

Clarno, Andy. *Neoliberal Apartheid: Palestine/Israel .and South Africa.* (2017).

Clemente, Dario Clemente. *El Estado Neodesarrollista en Brasil y su Crisis: Apuntes en Perspectiva Histórica.* https://www.academia.edu/39225926/
El_Estado_Neodesarrollista_en_Brasil_y_su_Crisis_Apuntes_en_Perspectiva_Hist%C3%B3rica

Colby, Eldridge A. *Strategy of Denial: American Defense in an Age of Great Power Conflict" (*2021).

Cole, Charles W. *"Colbert and a Century of French Mercantilism."* (1964).

Conway, Ben. *"How the Myths of Progressive Neoliberalism Hollowed out Australia's Left."* https://www.jacobinmag.com/2021/05/australian-labor-party-alp-left-neoliberalism

Cooney, Paul. "*Argentina's Quarter Century Experiment with Neoliberalism: from dictatorship to depression*". https://www.scielo.br/j/rec/a/TY6ScB7H7QshsgP8pQ9tcRg/?lang=en

Cornelissen, Lars. *"The 'new right' is not a reaction to neoliberalism, but its offspring."* https://www.opendemocracy.net/en/can-europe-make-it/the-new-right-is-not-a-reaction-to-neoliberalism-but-its-offspring/

Corson, Catherine. *"Corridors of Power: Assembling US Environmental Foreign Aid."* https://ida.mtholyoke.edu/bitstream/handle/10166/6005/Corson-2018-ForeignAid-Antipode.pdf?sequence=1&isAllowed=y

Christophers, Brett. *The New Enclosure: The Appropriation of Public Land in Neoliberal Britain.* (2019).

Crouzet, Francois. *De la supériorité de l'Angleterre sur la France: L'économique et l'imaginaire, XVIIe-XXe siècles.* (1985).

Cypher, J. M. *"From Military Keynesianism to Global-Neoliberal Militarism", Monthly Review* 59:2, (2007).

DeHaven, Tad. *"Republicans Join Democrats to Save Corporate Welfare (Again)."* https://www.cato.org/blog/republicans-join-democrats-save-corporate-welfare-again

Diego, Nieto. *"Neoliberalism, Biopolitics, and the Governance of Transnational Crime."* https://www.redalyc.org/pdf/812/81224569006.pdf

Dragos Aligica, Paul, et al. *The Neoliberal Revolution in Eastern Europe.* (2009).

Draï, Raphaël. *"Léon Blum ou le socialisme des comportements."* Cités, 43, (2010).

Elliott, Brian. *The roots of populism: Neoliberalism and working class lives.* (2021).

Elsenhans, Hartmut. *"World Systems Analysis and Political Economy"* in *Manuela Boatcă, et al. eds. Global Inequalities in World Systems Perspectives.* (2018).

Evans, B. M. and S. McBride. *Austerity: The Lived Experience,* (2017).

Farnsworth, K. *Social vs. Corporate Welfare.* (2012).

Ferenbach, Carl and Chris Pinney. "*Toward a 21st Century Social Contract*" Journal of Applied Corporate Finance. 24:2, (2012).

Fontenelle[8], Isleide A. and Marlei Pozzebon[9]. *'A dialectical reflection on the emergence of the 'citizen as consumer' as neoliberal citizenship: The 2013 Brazilian protests."* (2018).

Ferrero, Juan Pablo. *Democracy against Neoliberalism in Argentina and Brazil.* (2014).

Foroohar, Rona. *Makers and Takers: How Wall Street Destroyed Main Street.* (2016).

Foucault, Michel. *The Birth of Biopolitics*, 2010.

Frank, Andre Gunder. Andre Gunder Frank. *El desafío de la crisis: ensayos sobre crisis económica mundial, ironías políticas internacionales y desafío europeo.* (1988).

Galbraith, John Kenneth. *The Great Crash 1929.* (2009).

Gayo-Avello, Daniel. *"Social Media and Authoritarianism."* Social Science Research Network (July, 2015).

8. https://journals.sagepub.com/doi/10.1177/1469540518806939

9. https://journals.sagepub.com/doi/10.1177/1469540518806939

Gehl, Robert W. and Sean T. Lawson. *Social Engineering: How Crowdmasters, Phreaks, Hackers, and Trolls Created a New Form of Manipulative Communication.* (2022).

Gill, S. *"Pessimism of Intelligence, Optimism of Will."* in Joseph Francene, ed. *Perspectives on Gramsci.* (2009).

Gestle, Gary. *The Rise and Fall of the Neoliberal Order*. (2022).

Gibbs, David N. *"The military-industrial complex in a globalized context,"* in Ronald W. Cox, *Corporate Power and Globalization.* (2012).

Gillman, Nils. *Mandarins of the Future: Modernization Theory in Cold War America*, 2007; Edward D. Gonzalez-Acosta, *"CENTRAL AMERICA - CAFTA and the U.S. Patron-Client Relationship with Dominican Republic and Central America. 24 May 2007."* http://www.alterinfos.org/spip.php?article1385

Ginsberg, Benjamin. *The Fall of the Faculty: The Rise of the All-Administrative University and why it Matters.* (2011).

Girard, R. F. L. *Hugo Grotius: Natural Law and Social Contract Theory*. (2014).

Giroux, Henry. "*Teachers Are Rising Up to Resist Neoliberal Attacks on Education."* https://truthout.org/articles/teachers-are-rising-up-to-resist-neoliberal-attacks-on-education/

Giroux, Henry. *"Culture of Cruelty: The Age of Neoliberal Authoritarianism."* https://www.counterpunch.org/2015/10/23/culture-of-cruelty-the-age-of-neoliberal-authoritarianism/

Goonewardena, Kanishka. *"Populism, nationalism and Marxism in Sri Lanka: from anti-colonial struggle to authoritarian neoliberalism."* https://www.tandfonline.com/doi/full/10.1080/04353684.2020.1780146

Gramsci, Antonio. *Prison Notebooks*. (2011).

Grohmann, Rafael and Jonathan Corpus Ong. *"Disinformation-for-Hire and Click Farming around the World: Identities, Incentives, Infrastructures."* https://journals.sagepub.com/pb-assets/CfP-Disinformation-for-Hire-FINAL%20(002)-1628175552.pdf

Gross, Bertram. *Friendly Fascism: The New Face of Power in America.* (1999).

Groseclose[10], Tim. *Left Turn: How Liberal Media Bias Distorts the American Mind.* (2012).

Grzebalska, Weronika. *"Gendered voices from East-Central Europe. Breaking out of the deadlock of neoliberalism vs. rightwing populism."* http://balticworlds.com/breaking-out-of-the-deadlock-of-neoliberalism-vs-rightwing-populism/

Gupta, Arun. *"How the Democrats Became the Party of Neoliberalism."*

https://www.telesurtv.net/english/opinion/How-the-Democrats-Became-The-Party-of-Neoliberalism-20141031-0002.html

10. https://www.amazon.com/s/ref=dp_byline_sr_book_1?ie=UTF8&field-author=Tim+Groseclose+PhD&text=Tim+Groseclose+PhD&sort=relevancerank&search-alias=books

Gurumurthy, Anita. *"In a new world order driven by AI, we need to rewrite the rules of data capitalism."* https://www.opendemocracy.net/en/oureconomy/new-world-order-driven-ai-we-need-rewrite-rules-data-capitalism/

Gustave, Massiah. *"Authoritarianism reveals the limits of neoliberalism."* https://www.ritimo.org/Austeritarianism-reveals-the-limits-of-neoliberalism

Habermas, Jürgen. *"The Structural Transformation of the Public Sphere: An Inquiry into a Category of Bourgeois Society"* (1962).

Hadiz, Vedi R. *Empire and Neoliberalism in Asia.* (2006).

Hall[11], Richard and Mark Pulsford[12]. "*Neoliberalism and primary education: Impacts of neoliberal policy on the lived experiences of primary school communities.*" https://journals.sagepub.com/doi/full/10.1177/1757743819877344

Harrison, Mark. *"Military Keynesianism."* https://warwick.ac.uk/fac/soc/economics/staff/mharrison/war_and_economy/14_military_keynesianism.pdf

Harvey, David. *"Neoliberalism 'with Chinese characteristics."* in David Harvey, *A Brief History of Neoliberalism.* (2005).

Hauner, Thomas and Branko Milanovic, and Suresh Naidu. *"Inequality, Foreign Investment, and Imperialism."* https://www.gc.cuny.edu/CUNY_GC/media/CUNY-Graduate-Center/PDF/Centers/LIS/imperialism_Hauner-Milanovic-Naidu.pdf

Hayes, Calvin. *Popper, Hayek and the Open Society*, (2009).

Heath-Kelly, Charlotte, et al. eds., *Neoliberalism and Terror: Critical Engagements*, (2016).

Henales, Lydia and Beatrice Edwards. *"Neo-liberalism and Educational Reform in Latin America."* https://www.tc.columbia.edu/cice/pdf/25660_2_2_Heneles_Edwards.pdf

Herman, Edward S. and Noam Chomsky. *"Manufacturing Consent."* (1988).

Hickel, Jason. *A Short History of Neoliberalism*, http://www.newleftproject.org/index.php/site/article_comments/a_short_history_of_neoliberalim_and_how_we_can_fix_it

Hoffman, Anna and Almantas Salamavicius. *"Neoliberalism ad Higher Education in Central Europe."* https://www.eurozine.com/neoliberalism-and-higher-education-in-central-europe/

Huntington, Samuel. *"The Third Wave. Democratization in the late twentieth century."* (1991).

Iqbal, Yanis. *"Education under Neoliberal Capitalism."* https://socialistproject.ca/2021/08/education-under-neoliberal-capitalism/

Jinyi Li[13], Katherine. *"Failing and Jailing our Youth, from Seattle to Sao Paolo."* https://seattleglobalist.com/2015/11/23/sao-paulo-brazil-school-to-prison-pipeline-seattle-youth-jail/44637

11. https://journals.sagepub.com/doi/full/10.1177/1757743819877344

12. https://journals.sagepub.com/doi/full/10.1177/1757743819877344

Johnna, Montgomerie. *Neoliberalism and the Making of the Subprime Borrower*. (2010).

Johnson, Pauline. *"Sociology and the Critique of Neoliberalism"* European Journal of Social Theory, 2014.

Joppke, Christian. "*Neoliberal Nationalism." (*2021).

Juutinen, Marko. *"Neoliberal Civilization: Definition, Evaluation and Trends."* https://www.academia.edu/4186885/Neoliberal_Civilization_Definition_Evaluation_and_Trend. [14]

Kadri, Ali. *"Neoliberalism vs. China as model for the developing world"* https://www.athimar.org/en/articles/details/neoliberalism-vs-china-as-model-for-the-developing-world.

Kai-Fu Lee, *AI Superpowers. China, Silicon Valley and the New World Order* (2018).

Keiley, Ray. *From Authoritarian Liberalism to Economic Technocracy: Neoliberalism, Politics and 'De-democratization'* https://journals.sagepub.com/doi/abs/10.1177/0896920516668386

Kennedy, Scott. *"The Myth of the Beijing Consensus."* Journal of Contemporary China. https://www.tandfonline.com/doi/pdf/10.1080/10670561003666087.

Khiabany, Gholam. *"Arab Revolutions and the Iranian Uprising: Similarities and Differences"* Middle East Journal of Culture and Communication. (2012).

Kim, Eun Mee Kim. *The Four Asian Tigers: Economic Development & the Global Political Economy.* (1999).

Kipfert, Stefan. *"Macronism: Neoliberal Triumph or Next Stage in France's Political Crisis?"* https://www.globalresearch.ca/macronism-neoliberal-triumph-or-next-stage-in-frances-political-crisis/5596722.

Klein, Naomi. *The Shock Doctrine: The Rise of Disaster Capitalism*. (2008).

Kley, Ronald. *"Cultural Evolution."* In Ronald Kley, *Hayek's Social and Political Thought*. (1994).

Kofas, Jon V. *Independence from America: Global Integration and Inequality.* (2005).

Kofas, Jon V. *The Sword of Damocles: The IMF, the World Bank and US Foreign Policy in Colombia and Chile.* (2002).

Kofas, Jon V. *"Under the Eagle's Claw: Exceptionalism in Postwar US-Greek Relations"* (2003).

Kotz, David M. *The Rise and Fall of Neoliberal Capitalism.* (2017).

Kutlay[15], Mustafa & Hüseyin Emrah Karaoğuz[16]. "*Neo-developmentalist turn in the global political economy? The Turkish case"* Turkish Studies, 19:2, (2018).

13. https://seattleglobalist.com/author/katherine-jinyi-li

14. https://www.academia.edu/4186885/Neoliberal_Civilization_Definition_Evaluation_and_Trend.%20

15. https://www.tandfonline.com/author/Kutlay%2C+Mustafa

16. https://www.tandfonline.com/author/Karao%C4%9Fuz%2C+H%C3%BCseyin+Emrah

Kyriakopoulou, Kalliopi. *"Authoritarian states and internet social media: Instruments of democratisation or instruments of control?"* https://www.degruyter.com/document/doi/10.2478/s13374-011-0003-y/html?lang=en

Langwallner, David. *"Gradations of Evil: Neoliberalism and Neoconservatism"* https://cassandravoices.com/history/gradations-of-evil-neoliberalism-and-neoconservatism/

Lapavitsa, Costa. *Financialization in Crisis*, 2013.

Letterier, Orlando, *"The 'Chicago Boys' in Chile: Economic Freedom's Awful Toll."* https://www.thenation.com/article/archive/the-chicago-boys-in-chile-economic-freedoms-awful-toll/

Li, Ku-Wai. *Capitalist Development and Economism in East Asia*. (2002).

Liu, Ian Yuying. *"The Chinese Dream, Neoliberalism, and the International Legal Ideology."* https://brill.com/view/journals/cjgg/4/2/article-p81_1.xml?language=en

Lo, Dic. *Alternatives to Neoliberal Globalization.* (2012).

Lopez, F. A. et al eds. *Transitions from Dictatorships to Democracy.* (2016).

Loveday, Vik. *"Working-class participation, middle-class aspiration? Value, upward mobility and symbolic indebtedness in higher education."* The Sociological Review, September 2014.

Lutz, Ashley. *"These Corporations Control 90% of the Media."* http://www.businessinsider.com/these-6-corporations-control-90-of-the-media-in-america-2012-6

Macpherson, C. B. *The Political Theory of Possessive Individualism.* (1962).

Macedo, Macedo de la Rocha Santos, Rafael. *'O neoliberalismo chileno (1973-1990) e seus desafios à integração sul-americana*

dos anos 1980.' https://seer.ufs.br/index.php/tempo/article/download/10472/8076

McGuigan, Jim. "*The Neoliberal Self.*" http://www.cultureunbound.ep.liu.se/v6/a13/cu14v6a13.pdf

McKenna, Laura. *"The College President-to-Adjunct Pay Ratio."* https://www.theatlantic.com/education/archive/2015/09/income-inequality-in-higher-education-the-college-president-to-adjunct-pay-ratio/407029/

McLeran, Peter, Ramin Farahmandpur[17] and Juha Suoranta[18]. *"Richard Rorty's Self-Help Liberalism."* in M. A. Peters and Paolo Ghiraldelli, et al. eds. "*Richard Rorty: "education, philosophy and politics."* (2001).

Mansell, S. F. *Capitalism, Corporations, and the Social Contract*. (2013).

Marcuse, Herbert. *One Dimensional Man: Studies in the Ideology of Advanced Industrial Society.* (1964).

17. https://digitalcommons.chapman.edu/do/search/?q=author_lname%3A%22Farahmandpur%22%20author_fname%3A%22Ramin%22&start=0&context=5695533

18. https://digitalcommons.chapman.edu/do/search/?q=author_lname%3A%22Suoranta%22%20author_fname%3A%22Juha%22&start=0&context=5695533

Maronitis, Kostas. "*Robots and Immigrants: Employment, Precarisation and the Art of Neoliberal Governance.*" https://journals.openedition.org/angles/570.

Martínez Lucio, Miguel, Aristea Koukiadaki and Isabel Tavora. "*The legacy of Thatcherism in European labour relations: the impact of the politics of neo-liberalism and austerity on collective bargaining in a fragmenting Europe.*" Institute of Employment Rights Journal, 2:1 (2019).

Merkel, Wolfgang. *Systemtransformation: Eine Einführung in die Theorie und Empirie der Transformationsforschung.* (1999).

Massey, D. S. et. al. eds. *Chronicles of a Myth Foretold: The Washington Consensus in Latin America. (*2006).

Marian Myers. *Neoliberalism and the Media.* (2019).

Mavelli, Luca. *"Citizenship for Sale and the Neoliberal Political Economy of Belonging."* https://academic.oup.com/isq/article/62/3/482/4996972

Micocci, Andrea and Flavia Di Mario. *The Fascist Nature of Neoliberalism.* (2017). https://www.globalresearch.ca/macronism-neoliberal-triumph-or-next-stage-in-frances-political-crisis/5596722

Miller, Sam and Harrison Fluss. *"The 18th Brumaire of Donald J. Trump".* https://socialistworker.org/2016/12/05/the-18th-brumaire-of-trump[19]

Mintz, Beth. *"Neoliberalism and the Crisis of Higher Education."* https://marxistsociology.org/2021/10/neoliberalism-and-the-crisis-of-higher-education/

Moffitt, Benjamin. *The Global Rise of Populism.* (2017).

Mohammed, Shaheed Nick. *Communication and the Globalization of Culture.* (2011).

Monteiro, Basilio G. *"Commodification of Education is a necessary Evil."*

https://www.deccanchronicle.com/discourse/181118/commodification-of-education-is-a-necessary-evil.html

Moore, Barrington. *Social Origins of Dictatorship and Democracy.* (1966).

Moraes Valenca, Marcio. *"The Lost Decade of the Brazilian Government's Response in the 1990s"* Journal of Developing Areas. 33 (Fall 1998).

Moulier-Boutang, Yann. *Le Capitalisme Cognitif: La Nouvelle Grande Transformation.* (2008).

Nassar, Maha. *"US media talks a lot about Palestinians — just without Palestinians."* https://www.972mag.com/us-media-palestinians/

Naseer, Iram. *'Washington Consensus' vs 'Beijing Consensus."* https://nation.com.pk/18-Sep-2018/-washington-consensus-vs-beijing-consensus

19. https://socialistworker.org/2016/12/05/the-18th-brumaire-of-trump\

Neidleman, Jason. *"The Social Contract Theory in a Global Context."* http://www.e-ir.info/2012/10/09/the-social-contract-theory-in-a-global-context/[20]

Nunes, Joao. *"The COVID-19 pandemic: securitization, neoliberal crisis, and global vulnerabilization:"* https://www.scielo.br/j/csp/a/sng9pd8tLNdY3cQrDChhqPr/?format=pdf&lang=en

Ochoa, Enrique C. *"Introduction to Mexico in the 1990s: Economic Crisis, Social Polarization, and Class Struggle."* https://www.academia.edu/8903583/Introduction_to_Mexico_in_the_1990s_Economic_Crisis_Social_Polarization_and_Class_Struggle

Ong, Aihwa. *Neoliberalism as Exception: Mutations in Citizenship and Sovereignty.* (2006).

Osha, Sanya. *The Social Contract in Africa,* (2014); https://www.ecb.europa.eu/press/key/date/2013/html/sp130302.en.html; http://www.mei.edu/content/map/myanmar-transition-social-control-social-contract/

Ötsch, Walter and Stephan Pühringer. *"The Anti-democratic Logic of Right-wing Populism and Neoliberal Market-fundamentalism."* Journal of Language and Politics[21], 16:4[22], (2017).

Perez, Sofia and Manos Matsaganis. *"The Political Economy of Austerity in Southern Europe".* New Political Economy. (2017).

Peterson, J. *Revoking the Moral Order: The Ideology of Positivism and the Vienna Circle.* (1999).

Plehwe, Dieter et al. eds. *Neoliberal Hegemony.* (2006).

Polanyi, Karl. *The Great Transformation: The Political and Economic Origins of Our Time.* (1944).

Plihon, Dominique. El Mouhoub Mouhoud, *Le savoir et la finance. Liaisons dangereuses au coeur du capitalisme contemporain.* (2009).

Polanyi-Levitt, Kari. *From the Great Transformation to the Great Financialization.* (2013).

Portes, Alejandro Portes and Brandon P. Martinez. *"Latin American Cities: Their Evolution under Neoliberalism and Beyond."* https://cmd.princeton.edu/sites/cmd/files/media/latin_american_cities.pdf

Preston, John. *"Artificial Intelligence in the Capitalist University."* (2021).

Purdy, Jedediah. *"Neoliberal Constitutionalism: Lochnerism for a New Economy."* whttps://scholarship.law.columbia.edu/cgi/viewcontent.cgi?article=4253&context=faculty_scholarship

Orenstein, M. and Bojan Bugaric. *"How Populism Emerged from the Shadow of Neoliberalism"* https://blogs.lse.ac.uk/europpblog/2020/10/21/how-populism-emerged-from-the-shadow-of-neoliberalism-in-central-and-eastern-europe/

Ostolski, Adam and Wendy Brown. *"Neoliberalism Has Eviscerated the Fabric of Social Life."* https://www.greeneuropeanjournal.eu/neoliberalism-has-eviscerated-the-fabric-of-social-life/

---

20. http://www.e-ir.info/author/jason-neidleman/

21. https://www.jbe-platform.com/content/journals/15699862

22. https://www.jbe-platform.com/content/journals/15699862/16/4

Queiroz, Regina. *"From Exclusion of the people in neoliberalism to publicity without a public."* https://www.nature.com/articles/s41599-017-0032-1

Ramsay, Joshua. *"Neoliberalism as Political Theology of Chance: the politics of divination."* https://www.nature.com/articles/palcomms201539

Regalzi, Francesco. *"Democracy and Its Discontents: Walter Lippmann and the Crisis of Politics (1919-1938)."* https://journals.openedition.org/erea/2538

Reyes, Giovanni E. *"Four Main Theories of Development: Modernization, Dependency. World System and Globalization".* Nómadas. Revista Crítica de Ciencias Sociales y Jurídicas | 04 (2001.2)

Reynolds, Laurence and Bronislaw Szerszynski. *"Neoliberalism and technology: Perpetual innovation or perpetual crisis?"*

https://www.academia.edu/1937914/Neoliberalism_and_technology

Rimki, Heidi. *Self-help, therapeutic industries, and neoliberalism."* In Daniel Nehring, et al. eds. *The Routledge International Handbook of Global Therapeutic Cultures.* (2020).

Rollert, John Paul. *"How Sociopathic Capitalism Came to Rule the World."* https://www.theatlantic.com/business/archive/2016/11/sociopathic-capitalism/506240/

Rubara, Evans. *"Uneven Development: Understanding the Roots of Inequality."* https://www.pambazuka.org/governance/uneven-development-understanding-roots-inequality

Rutherford, Paul. *Endless Propaganda: the advertising of public goods.* (2000).

Rydgren, J. (Ed.), *Class Politics and the Radical Right.* 2012.

Sakellaropoulos, Spyros. "*Rereading The 18th Brumaire of Louis Bonaparte: The Phenomenon of Bonapartism as a Capitalist State Without Popular Representation."* Journal of Marxism and Interdisciplinary Inquiry. 11:1 (2020), 34-47.

Sample, Ruth J. *Exploitation; What is it and why it is Wrong.* (2003).

Sanchez, Rivas and Gaspar Alberto. *"La teoría económica de Lord John Maynard Keynes y su influencia práctica en los Estados Unidos de América, Alemania y Chile."* https://repositorio.uchile.cl/handle/2250/115205

Schumpeter, Joseph. *"Sociology of Imperialisms"* in P. J. Cain and Mark Harrison, eds. *Imperialism: Critical Concepts in Historical Studies.* Vol I, 310 (2001).

Seip, John and Dee Wood Harper. *The Trickle Down Delusion, How Republican Upward Redistribution of Economic and Political Power Undermines Our Economy, Democracy, Institutions and Health—and a Liberal Response.* (2016).

Selwyn, Benjamin. *"Friedrich Hayek: in defence of dictatorship."* https://www.opendemocracy.net/en/friedrich-hayek-dictatorship/

Sennett, Richard. *The Fall of Public Man.* (1979).

Serumaga, Mary. *"Uganda since 1986: Museveni, the World Bank and the Coming of Neoliberalism."* https://www.theelephant.info/op-eds/2019/01/27/uganda-since-1986-museveni-the-world-bank-and-the-coming-of-neoliberalism/

Smith, Linda H. *'Blaming-the-poor': Strengths and development discourses which obfuscate neo-liberal and individualist ideologies."* https://www.researchgate.net/publication/283192367_%27Blaming-the-poor%27_Strengths_and_development_discourses_which_obfuscate_neo-liberal_and_individualist_ideologies

Snyder-Hall, Claire and Cynthia Burack, eds. *Right-Wing Populism and the Media.* (2014).

Song, Jesook. *South Koreans in the Debt Crisis.* (2009)

Sumaria, Sheena. *"India's nightmare: the extremism of Narendra Modi."* http://www.counterfire.org/interview/18068-india-s-nightmare-the-extremism-of-narendra-modi; http://ac.upd.edu.ph/index.php/news-announcements/1201-southeast-asian-democracy-neoliberalism-populism-vedi-hadiz.

Therborn, Goran. *Ideology of Power and the Power of Ideology.* (1999).

Turgeon, Lynn. *Bastard Keynesianism: The Evolution of Economic Thinking and Policy-Making Since World War II.* (1997).

Turin, D. R. *"The Beijing Consensus: China's Alternative Development Model"* http://www.inquiriesjournal.com/articles/134/the-beijing-consensus-chinas-alternative-development-model

Turner, Fred. *From Counterculture to Cyberculture.* (2006).

Unver, Akin. *"Artificial Intelligence, Authoritarianism and the Future of Political Systems."* https://edam.org.tr/en/4025-2/

Valasco, Samuel and Leonardo Medina. *The Social Nature of Cryptocurrencies.* (2013).

Vanberg, Vikor J., *"Cultural evolution, group selection and downward causation."* In Francesca Gagliardi, ed. *Institutions and Evolution of Capitalism.* (2019).

Verhaeghe, Paul. *"The Struggle for Identity in a Market-based Society."* https://thehumanist.com/magazine/march-april-2015/arts_entertainment/what-about-me-the-struggle-for-identity-in-a-market-based-society.

Vinton, Kate. *"These 15 Billionaires Own America's News Media Companies."* https://www.forbes.com/sites/katevinton/2016/06/01/these-15-billionaires-own-americas-news-media-companies/?sh=76960331660a

Waddell, B. (2001) *"Limiting national interventionism in the United States: the warfare-welfare state as a restrictive government paradigm." Capital and class,* Vol. 74, pp. 109-140.

Walker, Peter. *"UN Chief Issues Warning on the Rise of Fascism."* http://www.independent.co.uk/news/world/politics/united-nations-chilling-warning-rise-fascism-human-rights-prince-zeid-a7464861.html

Wang, Jun. *"The developmental state in the global hegemony of neoliberalism: A new strategy for public housing in Singapore."* https://www.sciencedirect.com/science/article/abs/pii/S0264275111001338

Watkins, Robert E. *"Turning the Social Contract Inside Out: Neoliberal Governance and Human Capital in Two Days, One Night."* (2016).

Watson, H. A. *"Global Capitalism, Sovereign State Violence, and Human Insecurity"* in *A Future without Borders?* ed. by Eddy Souffrant. (2016).

Weippert-Fenner, Irene and Jonas Wolff, *"Socioeconomic Protests and Political Transformation: Dynamics of Contentious Politics in Egypt and Tunisia Against the Background of South American Experiences."* in Laura Ruiz de Elvira[23], Christoph Schwarz[24], Irene Weipert-Fenner[25], eds. *"Clientelism and Patronage in the Middle East and North Africa."* (2018).

Wertheimer, Alan. *Exploitation*, 1999.

Williamson, John. *"What Washington means by policy reform."* in J. Williamson, ed. *Latin American readjustment: How much has happened.* (1989).

Wolf, Richard D. *"How Fascism has Converged with Capitalism to redefine Government."* https://www.newsclick.in/How-Fascism-Has-Converged-With-Capitalism-Redefine-Government

Wolin, Sheldon. *Democracy Incorporated: Managed Democracy and the Specter of Inverted Totalitarianism.* (2008).

Wong, John and Sarah Chan. *"China-ASEAN Free Trade Agreement."* https://library.fes.de/libalt/journals/swetsfulltext/17768956.pdf

Xenakis, Sappho and Leonidas Cheliotis. *"Whiter Neoliberal Penalty? The Past, Present and Future of Imprisonment in the US."* http://eprints.lse.ac.uk/85702/1/Cheliotis_Whither%20neoliberal%20penality_2018.pdf

Yang, Rui. *"The Commodification of Education and Its Effects on Developing Countries: A Focus on China"*

https://www.mattersburgerkreis.at/dl/pttoJMJKonJqx4KooJK/JEP-4-2006_03_YANG_The-Commodification-of-Education-and-its-effects-on-developing-countries-A-focus-on-China.pdf

Yu, Fu-Lai Tony. *"Neo-Mercantilist Policy and China's Rise as a Global Power."* https://rpb115.nsysu.edu.tw/var/file/131/1131/img/2374/CCPS3(3)-Yu.pdf

Yuying Liu, Ian. *"The Chinese Dream, Neoliberalism, and the International Legal Ideology"*

The Chinese Journal of Global Governance. https://brill.com/view/journals/cjgg/4/2/article-p81_1.xml?language=en

Zamora, David. *"When Exclusion Replaces Exploitation: The Condition of the Surplus-Population under Neoliberalism"* http://nonsite.org/feature/when-exclusion-replaces-exploitation.

Zarkadakis, George. *In our Own Image: Savior or Destroyer? The History and Future of Artificial Intelligence,* (2017).

23. https://www.routledge.com/search?author=Laura%20Ruiz%20de%20Elvira

24. https://www.routledge.com/search?author=Christoph%20Schwarz

25. https://www.routledge.com/search?author=Irene%20Weipert-Fenner

---

[1] RONALD E. KUTSCHER, *"Historical trends, 1950-1992, and current uncertainties.* Https://www.bls.gov/mlr/1993/11/art1full.pdf

[2] The state absorbs surplus capital and devotes it to the defense sector as a fiscal stimulus that would presumably have derivative benefits for the civilian economy while maintaining military global superiority. Mark Harrison, *"Military Keynesianism."* https://warwick.ac.uk/fac/soc/economics/staff/mharrison/war_and_economy/14_military_keynesianism.pdf; Chalmers Johnson, *"The Economic Disaster of Military Keynesianism: Why the US has Really Gone Broke."* https://mondediplo.com/2008/02/05military; Sandra Kollen Ghizoni, *"Nixon Ends Convertibility of US."* https://www.federalreservehistory.org/essays/gold-convertibility-ends

[3] Werner Meng, *"Conditionality of IMF and World Bank Loans: Tutelage over Sovereign States."* https://www.nomos-elibrary.de/10.5771/0506-7286-1988-3-263/conditionality-of-imf-and-world-bank-loans-tutelage-over-sovereign-states-jahrgang-21-1988-heft-3?page=1; Eurodad Report, *"World Bank and IMF Conditionality."* https://assets.nationbuilder.com/eurodad/pages/1054/attachments/original/1601475891/World_Bank_and_IMF_conditionality-_A_development_injustice.pdf?1601475891

[4] Keri Polanyi-Levitt, *From the Great Transformation to the Great Financialization.* (2013).

[5] Graham Bentley, *"Trickle down Truss has a low tax problem."* https://www.moneymarketing.co.uk/opinion/trickle-down-economics-failure/

[6] Jarred Keller, *"The IMF confirms that 'trickle-down' economics is, indeed, a joke."* https://psmag.com/economics/trickle-down-economics-is-indeed-a-joke

[7] Giuseppe Ricotta, *"Neoliberalism and Control Strategies."* http://www.antoniocasella.eu/nume/Ricotta_2016.pdf

[8] **Flavio Azevedo, et al. *"Neoliberal Ideology and the Justification of Inequality in Capitalist Societies: Why Social and Economic Dimensions of Ideology Are Intertwined."* Journal of Social Issues, 75:1, (2019). Flavio Azevedo[26], John T. Jost[27], Tobias Rothmund[28], Joanna Sterling[29], *"Neoliberal Ideology and the Justification of Inequality in Capitalist Societies: Why Social and Economic Dimensions of Ideology Are Intertwined."*https://spssi.onlinelibrary.wiley.com/doi/10.1111/josi.12310; World Inequality Report 2022, *"Global wealth inequality: the rise of multimillionaires."* https://wir2022.wid.world/chapter-4/**

[9] George Monbiot, *"Neoliberalism – the ideology at the root of all our problems."* https://www.theguardian.com/books/2016/apr/15/neoliberalism-ideology-problem-george-monbiot

---

26. https://spssi.onlinelibrary.wiley.com/authored-by/Azevedo/Flavio

27. https://spssi.onlinelibrary.wiley.com/authored-by/Jost/John+T.

28. https://spssi.onlinelibrary.wiley.com/authored-by/Rothmund/Tobias

29. https://spssi.onlinelibrary.wiley.com/authored-by/Sterling/Joanna

[10] Minn Tent Bo, *"Why the West's state-building practices in Myanmar are part of the problem."* https://www.frontiermyanmar.net/en/why-the-wests-state-building-practices-in-myanmar-are-part-of-the-problem/

[11] Barrington Moore, *Social Origins of Dictatorship and Democracy.* (1966).

[12] Lynn Stout, *"How the Dominant Business Paradigm Turns People into Psychopaths."* https://www.nakedcapitalism.com/2018/08/dominant-business-paradigm-turns-nice-people-psychopaths.html; John Paul Rollert, *"How Sociopathic Capitalism Came to Rule the World."* https://www.theatlantic.com/business/archive/2016/11/sociopathic-capitalism/506240/; Clive R. Boddy, *"Corporate Psychopaths and Destructive Leadership in Organizations,"* in S. M. Camgöz[30] and O. T. Ekmecki, eds. *Destructive Leadership and Management Hypocrisy.* (2021)

[13] Nikkei Asia, *"TSMC founder Morris Chang says globalization 'almost dead.'"* https://asia.nikkei.com/Spotlight/Most-read-in-2022/TSMC-founder-Morris-Chang-says-globalization-almost-dead

[14] Viktor J. Vanberg, *"Cultural evolution, group selection and downward causation."* In Francesca Gagliardi, ed. *Institutions and Evolution of Capitalism.* (2019); Ronald Kley, *"Cultural Evolution."* In Ronald Kley, *Hayek's Social and Political Thought.* (1994).

[15] Lynn Parramore, *"Meet the Hidden Architect of Behind America's Racist Economics."* https://www.ineteconomics.org/perspectives/blog/meet-the-economist-behind-the-one-percents-stealth-takeover-of-america; Art Carden and James M. Buchanan, *"Public Choice, and the Political Economy of Desegregation."* https://www.researchgate.net/publication/322644472_James_M_Buchanan_Public_Choice_and_the_Political_Economy_of_Desegregation; Simon Glendinning, *"Varieties of Neoliberalism."* https://www.lse.ac.uk/european-institute/Assets/Documents/LEQS-Discussion-Papers/LEQSPaper89.pdf

[16] Gerard Hanlon, *"Total bureaucratization, neo-liberalism, and Weberian oligarchy."* https://www.researchgate.net/publication/296993256_Total_Bureaucratisation_neo-liberalism_and_Weberian_Oligarchy ; Stefan Kolev, *"The Abandoned Übervater: Max Weber and the Neoliberals."* https://papers.ssrn.com/sol3/papers.cfm?abstract_id=3309204; Timothy Shortell, *"Weber's Theory of Social Class."* http://www.brooklynsoc.org/courses/43.1/weber.html

[17] Barry Hindess, "Neo-liberal Citizenship." Citizenship Studies, 6, 2 (2002); Alan Finlayson, *"Public Choice Theory: enemy of democracy"* Soundings, 24, (2003); Luca Mavelli, *"Citizenship for Sale and the Neoliberal Political Economy of Belonging."* https://academic.oup.com/isq/article/62/3/482/4996972; Jedediah Purdy, *"Neoliberal Constitutionalism: Lochnerism for a New Economy."* https://scholarship.law.columbia.edu/cgi/viewcontent.cgi?article=4253&context=faculty_scholarship; Richard Lachman, *"Trump: authoritarian, just another neoliberal*

30. https://www.emerald.com/insight/search?q=Selin%20Metin%20Camgöz

***republican, or both?"* https://journals.openedition.org/spp/5340.**

[18] Jane Hardy, "*The myth of the 'neoliberal self'.* International Socialism, 121, (2021) http://isj.org.uk/neoliberal-self/

[19] Nela Porobić Isaković, *"COVID-19: What has Covid-19 Taught us about Neoliberalism?"* https://www.wilpf.org/covid-19-what-has-covid-19-taught-us-about-neoliberalism/

[20] William Davies, *"Neoliberalism and the Revenge of the Social."* https://www.opendemocracy.net/en/neoliberalism-and-revenge-of-social/

[21] Marianne, Schneider-Petsinger, *"Behind the US–China Trade War: The Race for Global Technological Leadership."* https://www.chathamhouse.org/2019/11/us-china-strategic-competition/behind-us-china-trade-war-race-global-technological; Lucas Myers, *"Essays on China and US Policy."* https://www.wilsoncenter.org/sites/default/files/media/uploads/documents/The%202021-22%20Wilson%20China%20Fellowship-Essays%20on%20China%20and%20U.S.%20Policy_0.pdf

[22] Craig Berry, *"The Substitutive State? Neoliberal state interventionism across industrial, housing and private pensions"* https://journals.sagepub.com/doi/full/10.1177/1024529421990845

[23] Ben Fine and Alfredo Saad-Filho, *"Thirteen things you need to know about neoliberalism.'* https://eprints.soas.ac.uk/22614/1/Fine_Saad-Filho_22614.pdf; Brett Christophers, *Who Owns the Economy and who Pays for it?* (2022)

[24] George Monbiot, *"A Death Foretold."* https://www.monbiot.com/2011/05/16/a-death-foretold/; John Williamson, *"The strange history of the Washington consensus."* https://www.researchgate.net/publication/5172951_The_Strange_History_of_the_Washington_Consensus; Joshua Cooper Ramo, *"The Beijing Consensus."* https://www.files.ethz.ch/isn/23013/Beijing_Consensus.pdf

[25] Vedi R. Hadiz, *Empire and Neoliberalism in Asia.* (2006)

[26] John Henry, *"The Historic Roots of the Neoliberal Program."* https://www.researchgate.net/publication/227454148_The_Historic_Roots_of_the_Neoliberal_Program; Dag Einar Thorsen, Amund Lie, *"What is Neoliberalism?"* https://jagiroadcollegelive.co.in/attendence/classnotes/files/1589998418.pdf

[27] CIRL, "*Compte rendu des séances du Colloque Walter Lippmann, 26–30 août 1938*", 1939; Louis Rougier, "*Le Colloque Walter Lippmann*", [Paris, 26-30 août 1938.]

[28] John Kenneth Galbraith, *The Great Crash 1929.* (2009).

[29] Ernest R. May, *American Cold War Strategy.* (1993).

[30] Stuart Mills, *"Ghosts of Mont Pelerin,"* https://medium.com/swlh/ghosts-of-mont-pelerin-b1db91c3a63c; Bruce Caldwell, *"Mont Pèlerin 1947."* https://hope.econ.duke.edu/sites/hope.econ.duke.edu/files/Caldwell%20Chapter%201%20Mont%20Pelerin.pdf; E. Eckes, *The United States and the Global Struggle for Minerals.* (2014); Jon Kofas, *Intervention and Underdevelopment.* (1989); Lynn Turgeon, Bastard Keynesianism: The Evolution of Economic Thinking and Policy-Making Since World War II (1997).

[31] ***"How Michel Foucault Got Neoliberalism So Wrong"*** **An Interview with Daniel Zamora. https://jacobinmag.com/2019/09/michel-foucault-neoliberalism-friedrich-hayek-milton-friedman-gary-becker-minoritarian-governments; David Hancock,** ***"Foucault and Neoliberalism."*** **https://link.springer.com/article/10.1057/cpt.2016.23**

[32] Harold James, *International Monetary Cooperation since Bretton Woods.* (1996); Greg Rosalsky, "*75 Years Ago the U.S. Dollar Became the World's Currency. Will That Last?"* https://www.npr.org/sections/money/2019/07/30/746337868/75-years-ago-the-u-s-dollar-became-the-worlds-currency-will-that-last?t=1652784826126

[33] Erich Weede, *"Geopolitics, Institutions and Economics: On the Rise and Decline of Civilizations."* Geopolitics, History and International Relations 8, (2016); Barry R. Weingast, *"War, Trade and Mercantilism."* https://web.stanford.edu/group/mcnollgast/cgi-bin/wordpress/wp-content/uploads/2016/01/smith.on-bh-empire-nma-cols_PRINT.18.0906.pdf

[34] Mangala Subramaniam, *"States and Social Movements in the Modern World System."* https://jwsr.pitt.edu/ojs/public/journals/1/Full_Issue_PDFs/jwsr-v21n1.pdf

[35] Sarah Babb and Alexander Kentikelenis, *"International Financial Institutions as Agents of Neoliberalism"* http://www.kentikelenis.net/uploads/3/1/8/9/31894609/babbkentikelenis2018-international_financial_institutions_as_agents_of_neoliberalism.pdf

[36] Oren M. Levin-Waldman, *"How Inequality Undermines Democracy."* https://www.e-ir.info/2016/12/10/how-inequality-undermines-democracy/; John Brown, *"Neoliberalization, De-democratization, and Populist Responses in Western Europe, the US, and Latin America."* https://www.researchgate.net/publication/340978256_Neoliberalization_De-democratization_and_Populist_Responses_in_Western_Europe_the_US_and_Latin_America

[37] Evans Rubara, *"Uneven Development: Understanding the Roots of Inequality"* https://www.pambazuka.org/governance/uneven-development-understanding-roots-inequality; Vinay Bahl, *"Concept of Development and Hegemonic World Order."* https://www.epw.in/journal/2021/44/book-reviews/concept-development-and-hegemonic-world-order.html.

[38] Josh Friedman and Michale Lind, *"The Past and Future of America's Social Contract."* https://www.theatlantic.com/business/archive/2013/12/the-past-and-future-of-americas-social-contract/282511/[31]

31. https://d.docs.live.net/eb41a1b69e1e6e00/Desktop/%20Josh%20Friedman%20and%20Michale%20Lind,

[39] Cliff Zukin, *"The American Public and the next Social Contract."* https://www.newamerica.org/economic-growth/policy-papers/the-american-public-and-the-next-social-contract/; Xue Fei, *"The Impact of Manifest Destiny on American Foreign Policy."* https://ijlass.org/the-impact-of-manifest-destiny-on-american-foreign-policy/

[40] Hartmut Elsenhans, *"World Systems Analysis and Political Economy"* in *Manuela Boatcă, et al. eds. Global Inequalities in World Systems Perspectives.* (2018); Olivera Kostoska, Sonja Mitikj, Petar Jovanovski and Ljupco Kocarev, *"Core-periphery structure in sectoral international trade networks: A new approach to an old theory."* https://journals.plos.org/plosone/article?id=10.1371/journal.pone.0229547; Claudius Grabner and Jakob Hafele, *"The Emergence of Core-Periphery Structures in the European Union."* https://www.econstor.eu/bitstream/10419/224134/1/172895116X.pdf

[41] Ben Biglaiser and R. J. McGauvran, *"The effects of IMF loan conditions on poverty in the developing world."* https://link.springer.com/article/10.1057/s41268-022-00263-1; Jon V. Kofas, *The Sword of Damocles: US Financial Hegemony in Colombia and Chile* (2002).

[42] Global Times, *"27-member bloc's GDP falls behind that of China in 2021, EU data shows."* https://www.globaltimes.cn/page/202202/1250282.shtml; https://knoema.com/atlas/China/topics/Economy/Inflation-and-Prices/Purchasing-power-parity; https://knoema.com/atlas/United-States-of-America/GDP-based-on-PPP

[43] **Sanya Osha, *The Social Contract in Africa*, (2014); Benoît Cœuré, *"Revisiting the European Social Contract."* https://www.ecb.europa.eu/press/key/date/2013/html/sp130302.en.html; Jonathan Bogais, *"Myanmar: The Transition from Social Control to Social Contract."* http://www.mei.edu/content/map/myanmar-transition-social-control-social-contract/; Marilyn Grell-Brisk, *"China and global economic stratification in an interdependent world."* https://www.nature.com/articles/palcomms201787; Li Xing and Raul Bernal-Meza, *"China-US rivalry: a new Cold War or capitalism's inter-core competition?"* https://www.scielo.br/j/rbpi/a/tPFgRF7VfFkZ9hjcd6hpsFG/?format=pdf&lang=en**

[44] REBECCA RAY, *"IMF Austerity is Alive and Increasing Poverty and Inequality."* https://www.bu.edu/gdp/2021/04/05/imf-austerity-is-alive-and-impacting-poverty-and-inequality/

[45] George Monbiot, *"Neoliberalism – the ideology at the root of our problem."* https://www.theguardian.com/books/2016/apr/15/neoliberalism-ideology-problem-george-monbiot

[46] **Ray Keiley, *"From Authoritarian Liberalism to Economic Technocracy: Neoliberalism, Politics and 'De-democratization."* https://journals.sagepub.com/doi/abs/10.1177/0896920516668386; Henry Giroux, *"Culture of Cruelty: The Age of Neoliberal Authoritarianism."* https://www.counterpunch.org/2015/10/23/culture-of-cruelty-the-age-of-neoliberal-authoritarianism/**

[47] Frederick R. Strobel and Wallace C. Peterson, *"Class Conflict American Style: Distract and Conquer."*, Journal of Economic Issues, 31:2 (1997); Enrique C. Ochoa, *"Introduction to Mexico in the 1990s: Economic Crisis, Social Polarization, and Class Struggle."* https://www.academia.edu/8903583/Introduction_to_Mexico_in_the_1990s_Economic_Crisis_Social_Polarization_and_Class_Struggle; Berch Berberoglu, *"Nationalism, Ethnic Conflict and Class Struggle."* https://library.fes.de/libalt/journals/swetsfulltext/11398911.pdf.

[48] Viktor J. Vanberg, *"The Freiberg School: Walter Eucken and Odorliberalism."* https://link.springer.com/article/10.1007/s12116-009-9040-5.

[49] Orlando Letelier, *"The 'Chicago Boys' in Chile: Economic Freedom's Awful Toll."* https://www.thenation.com/article/archive/the-chicago-boys-in-chile-economic-freedoms-awful-toll/; Juan Gabriel Valdes, *Pinochet's Economists: The Chicago School in Chile.* (1995).

[50] James Cooper *"Privatization and Deregulation."* in James Cooper, *Margaret Thatcher and Ronald Reagan.* (2012); John S. Earle and Solomiya Shpak *"Impact of Privatization on Employment and Earnings."* https://wol.iza.org/articles/impact-of-privatization-on-employment-and-earnings/long; Austin Frakt, *"Reagan, Deregulation and America's Exceptional Rise in Health Care Costs."* https://www.nytimes.com/2018/06/04/upshot/reagan-deregulation-and-americas-exceptional-rise-in-health-care-costs.html; Tad DeHaven, *"HUD Scandals."* https://www.downsizinggovernment.org/hud/scandals.

[51] Allen Thomas Hyde, "Neoliberalism, Finance, and Income Inequality: An Examination of Affluent Capitalist Democracies."

https://opencommons.uconn.edu/cgi/viewcontent.cgi?article=7452&context=dissertations; Jonathan D. Ostry, Prakash Loungani, and Davide Furceri, "Neoliberalism: Oversold?" https://www.imf.org/external/pubs/ft/fandd/2016/06/ostry.htm

[52] Pablo Precula, *"How the Welfare State became the Neoliberal Order."* https://www.publicbooks.org/how-the-welfare-state-became-the-neoliberal-order/

[53] **Robert Blanton and Dursun Peksen, *"The dark side of economic freedom: Neoliberalism has deleterious effects on labour rights."* https://blogs.lse.ac.uk/usappblog/2016/08/20/the-dark-side-of-economic-freedom-neoliberalism-has-deleterious-effects-on-labour-rights/; Eamon Akil Farhat, *"Nearly Half a Million UK Workers Set for Mass Strike Demanding Higher Pay."* https://www.bloomberg.com/news/articles/2023-01-19/nearly-half-a-million-uk-workers-set-for-mass-strike-on-feb-1; Euronews/AFP, *"Réforme des retraites : les jeunes manifestent leur opposition par milliers dans les rues de Paris."***

https://fr.euronews.com/2023/01/22/reforme-des-retraites-les-jeunes-manifestent-leur-opposition-par-milliers-dans-les-rues-de

[54] Ryan Matthew Womack, "The Emergence of Neoliberalism and Free Trade in the Developing World." https://trace.tennessee.edu/cgi/viewcontent.cgi?article=2030&context=utk_chanhonoproj

[55] Jon Kofas. *The Sword of Damocles: The IMF, the World Bank and US Foreign Policy in Colombia and Chile.* 2002. In March 2020, World Bank President David Malpass agued: *"Countries will need to implement structural reforms to help shorten the time to recovery and create confidence that the recovery can be strong."* https://fpif.org/the-world-needs-a-new-social-contract-not-more-structural-adjustment/

[56] J. M. Cypher, *"From Military Keynesianism to Global-Neoliberal Militarism", Monthly Review* 59:2, 2007; Jason Hickel, *"A Short History of Neoliberalism."* http://www.newleftproject.org/index.php/site/article_comments/a_short_history_of_neoliberalism_and_how_we_can_fix_it; Juan Gabriel Tokatlian, *"Argentina and peripheral neoliberal militarism."* https://www.opendemocracy.net/en/democraciaabierta/argentina-and-peripheral-neoliberal-militarism/

[57] Jordi Calvo Rufanges, *"War profiteering: the neoliberal militarism."* https://wri-irg.org/en/story/2015/war-profiteering-neoliberal-militarism

[58] Luigi Esposito and Fernando M. Perez, *"Neoliberalism and the Commodification of Mental Health."*https://www.researchgate.net/publication/274869713_Neoliberalism_and_the_Commodification_of_Mental_Health; Rajani Naidoo and Geoff Whitty, *"Students as Consumers: Commodifying or Democratizing Learning?"* https://journals.sagepub.com/doi/10.1163/22125868-12340022

[59] Venelin Ganev, *"The "Triumph of Neoliberalism" Reconsidered: Critical Remarks on Ideas-Centered Analyses of Political and Economic Change in Post-Communism."* https://www.researchgate.net/publication/249738143; Jolle Demmers, Alex E. Fernandez Jilberto, and Barbara Hogenboom, *"Good Governance in the Era of Global Neoliberalism."* https://www.econstor.eu/bitstream/10419/251156/1/9780203478691.pdf

[60] Paul Dragos Aligica, et al. *The Neoliberal Revolution in Eastern Europe.* (2009); David Broder, *"When Socialist Hungary Went Neoliberal"* an interview with Adam Fabry. https://jacobinmag.com/2019/09/hungary-neoliberalism-soviet-union; Matthew Goldstein et al. *"How Western Firms Quietly Enabled Russian Oligarchs."* https://www.nytimes.com/2022/03/09/business/russian-oligarchs-money-concord.html; Sharyn Alfonsi, *"Cyprus: Searching for the money of Russian oligarchs."* https://www.cbsnews.com/news/cyprus-russia-money-60-minutes-2023-01-15/

[61] Isleide A. Fontenelle[32], Marlei Pozzebon[33], *'A dialectical reflection on the emergence of the 'citizen as consumer' as neoliberal citizenship: The 2013 Brazilian protests."* https://www.academia.edu/Documents/in/Politics_of_Consumption; Hai Ren, *"Modes of Governance in Neo-Liberal Capitalism: An Introduction."* http://www.rhizomes.net/issue10/introren.htm

[62] Lydia DePillis, *"Is 'Greedflation' Rewriting Economics, or Do Old Rules Still Apply?" https://economictimes.indiatimes.com/small-biz/trade/exports/insights/is-greedflation-rewriting-economics-or-do-old-rules-still-apply/articleshow/91998360.cms*; Matthias Benz, *"Das Gerede von der «Gierflation» ist ein Ablenkungsmanöver."* https://www.nzz.ch/meinung/das-gerede-von-der-gierflation-ist-ein-ablenkungsmanoever-ld.1736999?mktcid=smsh&mktcval=LinkedIn

[63] Fredi De Ville, *"The End of Globalization As We Know It."* https://www.ugent.be/ps/politiekewetenschappen/gies/en/research/publications/gies_papers/2022-ukraine/the-end-of-globalisation-as-we-know-it

[64] https://www.weforum.org/reports/global-social-mobility-index-2020-why-economies-benefit-from-fixing-inequality/; Yaojun Li, Shun Zhang, Jianxun Kong, *"Social Mobility in China and Britain."* https://pure.manchester.ac.uk/ws/files/33808568/POST-PEER-REVIEW-PUBLISHERS.PDF

[65] Ian Yuying Liu, *"The Chinese Dream, Neoliberalism, and the International Legal Ideology"* The Chinese Journal of Global Governance. https://brill.com/view/journals/cjgg/4/2/article-p81_1.xml?language=en

32. https://journals.sagepub.com/doi/10.1177/1469540518806939

33. https://journals.sagepub.com/doi/10.1177/1469540518806939

[66] ***"Keynes v Hayek in China"*** **https://www.economist.com/news/2011/11/17/keynes-v-hayek-in-china; Penelope Newsome, *"Keynesian Common Sense in China."* https://www.theguardian.com/business/2009/jul/21/letters-keynesian-economics; http://foreignpolicy.com/2013/11/12/the-mother-of-all-experiments-in-authoritarian-capitalism-is-about-to-begin/**

[67] **Harvey Cox, *"The Market as God."* https://www.theatlantic.com/magazine/archive/1999/03/the-market-as-god/306397/; Joshua Ramey, *"Neoliberalism as a political theology of chance: the politics of divination."* https://www.nature.com/articles/palcomms201539**

[68] Alfredo Saad-Filho, *"Endgame: from crisis in neoliberalism to crises in neoliberalism."* https://journals.sagepub.com/doi/full/10.1177/1942778620962026

[69] Estelle Nilsson-Jullen, *"Five Elections that changed and shaped Europe in 2022."* https://www.euronews.com/my-europe/2022/12/27/five-elections-that-changed-and-shaped-europe-in-2022

[70] Vicente Navarro, *"The Consequences of Neoliberal in the Current Pandemic"* https://www.ncbi.nlm.nih.gov/pmc/articles/PMC7218352/

[71] BBC, *"Europe and right-wing nationalism."* https://www.bbc.com/news/world-europe-36130006

[72] Counter-Extremism Project, *"European Ethno-Nationalist and White Supremacy Groups."* https://www.counterextremism.com/content/european-ethno-nationalist-and-white-supremacy-groups

[73] Christophe Bouillaud, ***"Emmanuel Macron: toujours et encore le néo-libéralisme?"*** https://theconversation.com/emmanuel-macron-toujours-et-encore-le-neo-liberalisme-179680; Sahil Chinoy, *"What Happened to America's Political Center of Gravity?"* https://www.nytimes.com/interactive/2019/06/26/opinion/sunday/republican-platform-far-right.html; Bob Jessop, "From Thatcherism to New Labour: Neo-Liberalism, Workfarism, and Labour Market Regulation." https://www.lancaster.ac.uk/fass/resources/sociology-online-papers/papers/jessop-from-thatcherism-to-new-labour.pdf;

[74] Jens Beckert, *"The exhausted futures of neoliberalism: from promissory legitimacy to social anomy."* https://www.tandfonline.com/doi/pdf/10.1080/17530350.2019.1574867; Gabe Alpert, *"International COVID-19 Stimulus and Relief."* https://www.investopedia.com/government-stimulus-and-relief-efforts-to-fight-the-covid-19-crisis-5113980; Jonathan Montpetite, et al., *"Why millions of dollars in pandemic aid is going to corporations making healthy profits."* https://www.cbc.ca/news/canada/montreal/cews-wage-subsidy-jobs-covid-1.5834790

[75] Yorgos Rizopoulos, *"Economic Nationalism: Constrained and Fragmented."* https://hal.science/hal-03005871v1/file/Rizopoulos_Economic%20Nationalism%2C%20Constrained%20and%20fragmented%20if%20any%20final.pdf

[76] **David S. Jacks[34], Dennis Novy[35], '*Trade Blocs and Trade Wars during the Interwar Period.*"**

https://onlinelibrary.wiley.com/doi/full/10.1111/aepr.12276

[77] Christian Joppke, *Neoliberal Nationalism.* (2020); M. Orenstein and Bojan Bugaric, *"How Populism Emerged from the Shadow of Neoliberalism"* https://blogs.lse.ac.uk/europpblog/2020/10/21/how-populism-emerged-from-the-shadow-of-neoliberalism-in-central-and-eastern-europe/; Institute for Policy Studies, *"Rightwing Government Threat to Democracy in Brazil, India & USA"*, https://ips-dc.org/events/rightwing-government-threat-to-democracy-in-brazil-india-usa/; Lawrence Cox and Alf Gunvald Nielsen, *"Reading Neoliberalism as a Social Movement from Above."* https://www.redalyc.org/journal/124/12452111008/html/

[78] **World Bank, *"Remarks by World Bank Group President David Malpass on G20 Finance Ministers Conference Call on COVID-19."* https://www.worldbank.org/en/news/speech/2020/03/23/remarks-by-world-bank-group-president-david-malpass-on-g20-finance-ministers-conference-call-on-covid-19**

[79] Regina Queiroz, *"Individual liberty and the importance of the concept of the people."* https://www.nature.com/articles/s41599-018-0151-3#additional-information; Robert Kuttner and Catherine V. Stone, *"The Rise of Neo-Feudalism."* https://prospect.org/economy/rise-of-neo-feudalism/; Stephen C. Ferguson, *"Social Contract as Bourgeois Ideology,"* https://ojs.library.ubc.ca/index.php/clogic/article/download/191744/188744/218249; Jodi Dean, *'Neofeudalism: The End of Capitalism?"* https://lareviewofbooks.org/article/neofeudalism-the-end-of-capitalism/; Bagci S. Erhan, *"Decline of Meritocracy: Neo-Feudal Segregation in Turkey."* https://eric.ed.gov/?id=EJ1082107; https://www.macrobusiness.com.au/2018/10/problem-not-neo-liberalism-neo-feudalism/

[80] **R.F.L. Girard, *Hugo Grotius: Natural Law and Social Contract Theory*. 2014; Fernand Braudel, *La Méditerranée et le Monde méditerranéen à l'époque de Philippe II* (1949); Wallerstein, *The Modern World-System, Vol. I: Capitalist Agriculture and the Origins of the European World-Economy in the Sixteenth Century. (2011).***

[81] Tom O'Shea, *"Consent in History, Theory and Practice."* https://autonomy.essex.ac.uk/wp-content/uploads/2016/11/Consent-GPR-June-2012.pdf

---

34. https://onlinelibrary.wiley.com/action/doSearch?ContribAuthorRaw=Jacks%2C+David+S

35. https://onlinelibrary.wiley.com/action/doSearch?ContribAuthorRaw=Novy%2C+Dennis

[82] John Winfred O'Toole, *"The Right of Revolution: An Analysis of John Locke and Thomas Hobbes' Social Contract Theories."* https://dlib.bc.edu/islandora/object/bc-ir:102351/datastream/PDF/view; Nancy Fraser, *"Legitimation Crisis? On the Political Contradictions of Financialized Capitalism."*https://www.researchgate.net/publication/283520483_Legitimation_Crisis_On_the_Political_Contradictions_of_Financialized_Capitalism

[83] Jason Neidleman, *"The Social Contract Theory in a Global Context"* http://www.e-ir.info/2012/10/09/the-social-contract-theory-in-a-global-context/[36]; C. B. Macpherson. *The Political Theory of Possessive Individualism.* (1962).

[84] S. F. Mansell, *Capitalism, Corporations, and the Social Contract.* 2013.

[85] Andre Gunder Frank, *"The Development of Underdevelopment."* Monthly Review, 41:2 (1989)

[86] **Hartmut Kaelble, *Social Mobility in the 19th and 20th Centuries: Europe and America in Comparative Perspective.* (1986); Gregory Clark, Tatsuya Ishii, "Social Mobility in Japan, 1868-2012: The Surprising Persistence of the Samurai." http://faculty.econ.ucdavis.edu/faculty/gclark/The%20Son%20Also%20Rises/Japan%202012.pdf; Matthias Bernt, Laura Colini, *"Exclusion, Marginalization and Peripheralization."* https://leibniz-irs.de/fileadmin/user_upload/IRS_Working_Paper/wp_exclusion-marginalization-peripheralization.pdf; Eli Cook, *"The great marginalization: why twentieth century economists neglected inequality."* http://www.paecon.net/PAEReview/issue83/Cook83.pdf.**

[87] Aristotle A. Kallis, *"Studying Inter-war Fascism in Epochal and Diachronic Terms: Ideological Production, Political Experience and the Quest for 'Consensus.'"* https://library.fes.de/libalt/journals/swetsfulltext/18887466.pdf

[88] **John Kenneth Galbraith, *The Great Crash of 1929.* (2009); Jerry Mushin, *"The Sterling Area."* https://eh.net/encyclopedia/the-sterling-area/; Thomas I. Paley, *From Keynesianism to Neoliberalism: Shifting Paradigms in Economics."* https://fpif.org/from_keynesianism_to_neoliberalism_shifting_paradigms_in_economics/; Pierre Rosanvallon, *Histoire des idées keynésiennes en France.***

https://www.persee.fr/doc/rfeco_0769-0479_1987_num_2_4_1158 Raphaël Draï, *"Léon Blum ou le socialisme des comportements."* Cités, 43 (2010); Rivas Sanchez and Gaspar Alberto, *"La teoría económica de Lord John Maynard Keynes y su influencia práctica en los Estados Unidos de América, Alemania y Chile."* https://repositorio.uchile.cl/handle/2250/115205; Deepan[37]kar Basu, *"A Unified Marxist Approach to Accumulation and Crisis in Capitalist Economies."* https://scholarworks.umass.edu/cgi/viewcontent.cgi?article=1238&context=econ_workingpaper; US Bureau of Labor Statistics, *"Statistical Abstract of the United States."* https://babel.hathitrust.org/cgi/pt?id=mdp.39015021301612&view=1up&seq=407.

---

36. http://www.e-ir.info/author/jason-neidleman/

37. https://repositorio.uchile.cl/handle/2250/115205;%20Deepan

[89] Richard D. Wolff and Stephen A. Resnick, "Contending Economic Theories: Neoclassical, Keynesians, and Marxian." chapter. 3, (2012).

[90] Takeshi Inagami, *"On Japanese-Style Neo-Corporatism: Era of a Tripartite Honeymoon."*https://www.researchgate.net/publication/229929801_On_Japanese-Style_Neo-Corporatism_Era_of_a_Tripartite_Honeymoon

[91] Masahiro Takada, *"Japan's Economic Miracle: Underlying Factors and Strategies for Growth."* https://www.lehigh.edu/~rfw1/courses/1999/spring/ir163/Papers/pdf/mat5.pdf; Pierre Rosanvallon, *La Crise de l'État-providence.* (2014); OECD, *"Social Expenditure, 1960-1990."* https://www.oecd.org/social/soc/40836112.pdf

[92] Noam Zidron and Daneil Ziblatt, *"Center-Right Political Parties in Advanced Democracies."*

https://www.annualreviews.org/doi/10.1146/annurev-polisci-090717-092750; Daniel Andersson, *"How the Swedish Left moved right."* https://www.aljazeera.com/opinions/2018/11/9/how-the-swedish-left-moved-right; Kjell Ostberg, *'The Decline of Nordic Social Democracy,'* in Au Koivunen, et al, *The Nordic Economic, Social and Political Model.* (2021); Matt Seybold, *"Neoliberal Rationality in the old Gilded Age."* https://marktwainstudies.com/neoliberal-rationality-in-the-old-gilded-age-introductory-address-at-2018-quarry-farm-symposium/; Ayeisha Thomas-Smith, *"This is your brain on neoliberalism."* https://neweconomics.org/2020/10/this-is-your-brain-on-neoliberalism.

[93] Adam Dahl and Joe Soss, *"Neoliberalism for the Common Good? Public Value Governance and the Downsizing of Democracy."* http://citeseerx.ist.psu.edu/viewdoc/download?doi=10.1.1.455.3680&rep=rep1&type=pdf

[94] Regina Queiroz, *"From Exclusion of the people in neoliberalism to publicity without a public."* https://www.nature.com/articles/s41599-017-0032-1

[95] Adam Dahl and Joe Soss, *"Neoliberalism for the Common Good? Public Value Governance and the Downsizing of Democracy."* https://silo.tips/queue/neoliberalism-for-the-common-good-public-value-governance-and-the-downsizing-of?&queue_id=-1&v=1653047529&u=MTc4LjU5LjIyMC4yMDM=

[96] Luca Mavelli, *"Neoliberalism as Religion: Sacralization of the Market and Post-truth Politics."* International Political Sociology, 14:1, (2020)

[97] *"Margaret Thatcher: a life in quotes."* https://www.theguardian.com/politics/2013/apr/08/margaret-thatcher-quotes

[98] **Sotheby's, "The Man Whose Powerful Critique of Socialism Influenced Margaret Thatcher."**

https://www.sothebys.com/en/articles/this-is-what-we-believe-margaret-thatcher-and-f-a-hayek[38] ; Hugh McLachlan, "Why

38. https://d.docs.live.net/eb41a1b69e1e6e00/Documents/Sotheby's,%20

'there's no such thing as society' should not be regarded with moral revulsion."https://theconversation.com/why-theres-no-such-thing-as-society-should-not-be-regarded-with-moral-revulsion-136008

[99] Carla Ibled, *"The 'Optimistic Cruelty' of Hayek's Market Order: Neoliberalism, Pain and Social Selection."* https://research.gold.ac.uk/id/eprint/32696/1/02632764221126305.pdf; Andrew Ives, *"Neoliberalism and the concept of governance: Renewing with an older liberal tradition to legitimate the power of capital."* https://journals.openedition.org/mimmoc/2263?lang=en

[100] Emile Durkheim, *"L'Individualism et les intellectuels."* (1898); Smith, Steven. *Hegel's Critique of Liberalism: Rights in Context.* (1989); Finn Bowring, *"The individual and society in Durkheim: Unpicking the contradictions."* European Journal of Social Theory, 19:1 (2015); Corey Robin, *"Hayek von Pinochet."* https://coreyrobin.com/2012/07/08/hayek-von-pinochet/.

[101] Fiona D. Xu, "Solving Poverty by Reforming Moral Character: How the New Poor Law Failed 19th Century British Society." http://www.inquiriesjournal.com/articles/1823/solving-poverty-by-reforming-moral-character-how-the-new-poor-law-failed-19th-century-british-society; Timothy Besley, Stephen Coate and Timothy W. Guinnane, "Incentives, Information, and Welfare: England's New Poor Law and the Workhouse Test." https://www.russellsage.org/sites/all/files/u4/Besley,%20Coate,%20%26%20Guinnane_Incentives,%20Information,%20and%20Welfare.pdf

[102] Mary Papenfuss, *"GOP Senator Implies Those Who Aren't Millionaires Waste Money on Booze, Women."* https://www.huffingtonpost.com/entry/grassley-estate-taxes-booze-women_us_5a247d89e4b03c44072e5a04;

[103] Linda H. Smith, *'Blaming-the-poor': Strengths and development discourses which obfuscate neo-liberal and individualist ideologies"* https://www.researchgate.net/publication/283192367_%27Blaming-the-poor%27_Strengths_and_development_discourses_which_obfuscate_neo-liberal_and_individualist_ideologies

[104] Tim Barker, *"Spontaneous Order: Looking Back at Neoliberalism."* https://www.dissentmagazine.org/article/spontaneous-order-looking-back-at-neoliberalism

[105] John Hogan, *"The Paradox of Karl Popper."* https://blogs.scientificamerican.com/cross-check/the-paradox-of-karl-popper/; Kamen Dimitrov Lozev, *"Twenty-Five Years after Popper."* https://centerprode.com/conferences/3IeCSHSS/coas.e-conf.03.13143l.pdf

[106] Jim McGuigan: *'The Neoliberal Self'*, Culture Unbound, Volume 6, 2014; http://www.cultureunbound.ep.liu.se/v6/a13/cu14v6a13.pdf

[107] S. Gill, *"Pessimism of Intelligence, Optimism of Will"* in Perspectives on Gramsci, ed. by Joseph Francene (2009); Julia C. Becker Lea Hartwitch S. A. Haslam, *"Neoliberalism can reduce well-being by promoting a sense of social disconnection, competition, and loneliness."* https://bpspsychub.onlinelibrary.wiley.com/doi/full/10.1111/bjso.12438; Thomas Blanchet, Lucas Chancel and Amory Gethin, *'How unequal is Europe?'* https://wid.world/document/bcg2019-full-paper/; Anna Stahl, *"Public Opinion on an Ever More Differentiated EU."* https://www.iai.it/sites/default/files/euidea_pp_15.pdf

[108] Eugenio F. Biagini, *Liberty, Retrenchment and Reform: Popular Liberalism in the Age of Gladstone.* (2004)

[109] Eric Medlin, "*Populist Appeals to Europe and their Implications, 1883-1908*" https://cdr.lib.unc.edu/; *P. F. Clarke, "The Progressive Movement in England"*

https://www.cambridge.org/core/journals/transactions-of-the-royal-historical-society/article/abs/progressive-movement-in-England/A548A16CAFDA062DAD90395D1BCA50E4; Andrew Adonis, *"Gladstone, Marx and Modern Progressives."* https://liberalhistory.org.uk/wp-content/uploads/2014/10/8_adonis_gladstone_marx_and_modern_progressives.pdf

[110] Thorsten Beck and Hans-Helmut Kotz, eds. *Ordoliberalism: AGerman oddity?* https://carnegieendowment.org/files/Ordoliberalism_Nov22.pdf

[111] Lars Cornelissen, *"The 'new right' is not a reaction to neoliberalism, but its offspring."* https://www.opendemocracy.net/en/can-europe-make-it/the-new-right-is-not-a-reaction-to-neoliberalism-but-its-offspring/; Lasse Folke Henriksen, Leonard Seabrooke, and Kevin Young, *"Fathers of Neoliberalism: The Academic and Professional Performance of the Chicago School, 1960-1985."* https://www.ineteconomics.org/uploads/papers/Young-Fathers-of-Neoliberalism.pdf; [39]Werner Bonefeld, "Freedom and the Strong State: On German Ordoliberalism." https://eprints.whiterose.ac.uk/67263/1/s1_ln11019519_896202810_1939656818Hwf1595266051IdV_172829720011019519PDF_HI0001.pdf; Charles Barthold, *"Understanding financialization."* https://www.researchgate.net/publication/329694424_Understanding_financialization

[112] Marshall I. Steinbaum and Bernard A. Weisberger, *"The Intellectual Legacy of Progressive Economics."*https://marshallsteinbaum.org/assets/steinbaum-and-weisberger-2017-the-intellectual-legacy-of-progressive-economics.pdf

[113] John Williamson, *"What Washington means by policy reform."* in J. Williamson (Ed.), *Latin American readjustment.* Washington, D.C.: Institute for International Economics, (1989); Betül Sarı Aksakal, "Neoliberalism After the Washington Consensus." [40] https://www.researchgate.net/publication/329218357_NEOLIBERALISM_AFTER_THE_WASHINGTON_CONSENSUS_AN_EVALUATION_IN_THE_CONTEXT_OF_T

39. https://www.ineteconomics.org/uploads/papers/Young-Fathers-of-Neoliberalism.pdf;%20

40. https://www.researchgate.net/profile/Betuel-Sari-Aksakal

Juan Carlos Moreno-Brid, et al., *"The Washington consensus: a Latin American perspective fifteen years later."* https://www.researchgate.net/publication/

5172959_The_Washington_consensus_A_Latin_American_perspective_fifteen_years_later;

[114] D. S. Massey et. al., eds. *Chronicles of a Myth Foretold: The Washington Consensus in Latin America.* 2006; Rick Rowden, *From the Washington Consensus to the Wall Street Consensus.* https://us.boell.org/sites/default/files/2019 11/ Rowden%20From%20Washington%20To%20Wall%20Street.pdf; Stephen Metcalf, *"Neoliberalism: the idea that swallowed the world."* https://www.theguardian.com/news/2017/aug/18/neoliberalism-the-idea-that-changed-the-world

[115] Pritam Singh, *"The IMF's autocritique of neoliberalism?"* https://www.twn.my/title2/resurgence/2016/310-311/cover05.htm; Richard Inman and Philip Partington, *"IMF urges UK government to reconsider tax-cutting plans."* https://www.theguardian.com/politics/2022/sep/27/kwasi-kwartengs-tax-cuts-likely-to-increase-inequality-imf-says; ALJAZEERA, *"Sri Lanka receives first tranche of IMF bailout, says president."* https://www.aljazeera.com/economy/2023/3/22/sri-lanka-receives-first-tranche-of-imf-bailout

[116] Matthew Eagleton-Pierce, *"On Individualism in the Neoliberal Period"* https://www.psa.ac.uk/sites/default/files/conference/ papers/2016/On%20Individualism%20in%20the%20Neoliberal%20Period_Eagleton-Pierce_Eagleton

Pierce_PSA%20Conference%202016_Brighton_Paper_PDF.pdf; Marko Juutinen, *"Neoliberal Civilization."* https://core.ac.uk/download/pdf/250122137.pdf

[117] Sappho Xenakis and Leonidas Cheliotis, *"Whiter Neoliberal Penalty? The Past, Present and Future of Imprisonment in the US."* http://eprints.lse.ac.uk/85702/1/Cheliotis_Whither%20neoliberal%20penality_2018.pdf; Luke Telford and Daniel Briggs, *"Targets and overwork: Neoliberalism and the maximization of profitability from the workplace."* https://journals.sagepub.com/doi/10.1177/03098168211022208

[118] K. Farnsworth, *Social vs. Corporate Welfare,* (2012); Ha-Joon Chang, *"2008 Global Financial Crisis in a Long-Term Perspective: The Failure of Neoliberalism and the Future of Capitalism."* https://cgd.leeds.ac.uk/events/2008-global-financial-crisis-in-a-long-term-perspective-the-failure-of-neo-liberalism-and-the-future-of-capitalism-2/

[119] Riad Azar[41], *"Neoliberalism, Austerity and Authoritarianism."* http://newpol.org/content/neoliberalism-austerity-and-authoritarianism

[120] Brett Heinz, *"The Politics of Privatization: How Neoliberalism Took Over US Politics."* https://www.faireconomy.org/the_politics_of_privatization?recruiter_id=2; Derick Hamilton and Kyle Strickland, *"The Racism of Neoliberalism."* https://evonomics.com/racism-neoliberalism-darrick-hamilton/; Michael C. Behrent, *"Liberalism without Humanism: Michele Foucault and the Free-Market Creed."* https://history.appstate.edu/sites/history.appstate.edu/files/behrent_foucault_mih_article.pdf

[121] Pranhat Patnaik, *"Neoliberalism and Fascism."* https://journals.sagepub.com/doi/full/10.1177/2277976019901029; Christian Joppke, *"Populism and the double liberalism: exploring the links."* https://link.springer.com/article/10.1007/s11186-021-09435-3

41. https://newpol.org/authors/azar-riad/

[122] **Francesco Regalzi, *"Democracy and Its Discontents: Walter Lippmann and the Crisis of Politics (1919-1938)"* https://journals.openedition.org/erea/2538**

[123] Nathanael Collin-Jaeger, *"Reconstructing Liberalism: Hayek, Lippmann and the Making of Neoliberalism."* https://journals.openedition.org/oeconomia/108740; Bruce Caldwell and Leonidas Montes, *"Friedrich Hayek and His Visit to Chile."* https://eprints.lse.ac.uk/63318/ 1/__lse.ac.uk_storage_LIBRARY_Secondary_libfile_shared_repository_Content_Caldwell%2C%20B_Hayek%20and%20Chile_Cladwell_H

[124] Benjamin Selwyn, *"Friedrich Hayek: in defence of dictatorship."* https://www.opendemocracy.net/en/friedrich-hayek-dictatorship/

[125] John Meadowcroft and William Ruger, *"Hayek, Friedman, and Buchanan: On Public Life, Chile and the Relationship between Liberty and Democracy."* https://www.tandfonline.com/doi/abs/10.1080/09538259.2014.932066?journalCode=crpe20; Karin Fischer, *"The Influence of Neoliberals in Chile before, during and after Pinochet."* in Philip Mirowski and Dieter Plehwe, *The Road from Mont Pèlerin.* (2015).

[126] **Andrew Farrant, Edward McPhail and Sebastian Berger, *"Preventing the "Abuses" of Democracy: Hayek, the "Military Usurper" and Transitional Dictatorship in Chile?"* American Journal of Economics and Sociology. 71, 3 (2012). John McWorter, *"When People Were Proud to Call Themselves 'Neoliberal'* https://www.theatlantic.com/business/archive/2017/05/history-of-neoliberal-meaning/528276/; Charles Peters, *"A Neoliberal Manifesto."* https://www.washingtonpost.com/archive/opinions/1982/09/05/a-neo-liberals manifesto/21cf41ca-e60e-404e-9a66-124592c9f70d/?utm_term=.addfcc829916[42]; Tobias Rupprecht, *"Global Varieties of Neoliberalism."* https://online.ucpress.edu/gp/article-abstract/1/1/13278/111110/Global-Varieties-of-Neoliberalism-Ideas-on-Free**

[127] Arun Gupta, *"How the Democrats Became the Party of Neoliberalism."* https://www.telesurtv.net/english/opinion/How-the-Democrats-Became-The-Party-of-Neoliberalism-20141031-0002.html; Paul Embery *"Why on earth would socialists support neoliberal undemocratic EU?"* https://www.opendemocracy.net/uk/paul-emery/why-on-earth-would-socialists-support-neoliberal-undemocratic-eu; Richard Roman and Edur Velasco Arregui,

"Neoliberalism, Labor Market Transformation, and Working-Class Responses Social and Historical Roots of Accommodation and Protest." https://library.fes.de/libalt/journals/swetsfulltext/12735101.pdf; Jesus Albaracin, *"Neoliberal Employment Policies."* International Journal of Political Economy, 30:2 (2000) https://www.jstor.org/stable/40470773; Praveen Jha and Archana Prasad, *"Wages of Neoliberalism: Reflections on the world of work in*

42. https://www.washingtonpost.com/archive/opinions/1982/09/05/a-neo-liberals%20manifesto/21cf41ca-e60e-404e-9a66-124592c9f70d/?utm_term=.addfcc829916

contemporary India." https://econtents.bc.unicamp.br/inpec/index.php/rbest/article/download/14812/9808/34072

[128] Celia Eckert, *"Can Tech Workers Stop the Layoffs."* https://jacobin.com/2022/12/tech-worker-layoffs-organizing-unionization-recoding-power-rothstein; Keerthi Vedantam, *"Tech Layoffs: US Companies That Have Cut Jobs in 2022 and 2023."* https://news.crunchbase.com/startups/tech-layoffs/; Katharina Buchholz, *"Where Real Wages Rose and Where they Stagnated."* https://www.forbes.com/sites/katharinabuchholz/2023/01/26/where-real-wages-rose—where-they-stagnated-infographic/[43]; Statista, *"Distribution of net wealth in the United States."* https://www.statista.com/statistics/299460/distribution-of-wealth-in-the-united-states/

[129] Robert Caudle, "Ideology in Everyday Life." https://prezi.com/kha1ketnfjtd/ideology-in-everyday-life/

[130] Francis Fukuyama, *Liberalism and Its Discontents.* (2022).

[131] Leigh Claire Le Berge, *Scandals and Abstraction: Financial Fiction of the Long 1980s.* (2014); FDIC, *History of the Eighties.* https://www.fdic.gov/bank/historical/history/3_85.pdf

[132] Eliana Glaser, *"Bring Back Ideology: Fukuyama's 'End of History' 25 years on."* https://www.theguardian.com/books/2014/mar/21/bring-back-ideology-fukuyama-end-history-25-years-on

[133] Julian Gewitz, *"Milton Friedman's Misadventures in China."* https://theamericanscholar.org/milton-friedmans-misadventures-in-china/

[134] Yang Yao, *"China's Export-Oriented Growth Model."* https://www.eastasiaforum.org/2011/02/27/chinas-export-led-growth-model/; Kenji Hirashima, *"Regime Shift in Japan? Two decades of Neoliberal Reforms."* https://onlinelibrary.wiley.com/doi/pdf/10.1002/j.1662-6370.2004.tb00031.x

[135] Isabella Webber, *"Origins of China's Contested Relation with Neoliberalism"* https://online.ucpress.edu/gp/article/1/1/12271/107349/Origins-of-China-s-Contested-Relation-with

[136] C. R Hughes, *"Chinese Nationalism in the Global Era."* https://iccs.aichi-u.ac.jp/archives/report/005/005_11.pdf; A. L. Friedberg, *"Globalisation and Chinese Grand Startegy."* https://www.tandfonline.com/doi/full/10.1080/00396338.2018.1427362; An Interview with Professor Rainer Mausfeld, *"Neoliberal Indoctrination."* https://cognitive-liberty.online/wp-content/uploads/neoliberal-indoctrination-Copy.pdf

[137] Danilo Spinola, *"Uneven development and the balance of payments constrained model: Terms of trade, economic cycles, and productivity catching-up."*https://www.sciencedirect.com/science/article/pii/S0954349X19303145

43. https://www.forbes.com/sites/katharinabuchholz/2023/01/26/where-real-wages-rose--where-they-stagnated-infographic/

[138] A. Claire Cutler, *"Critical Reflections on the Westphalian Assumptions of International Law and Organization: A Crisis of Legitimacy."* Review of International Studies, 27:2 (2001); T. W. Watters, "The Momentous Gravity of the State of Things Now Obtaining: Annoying Westphalian Objections to the Idea of Global Governance." Indiana Journal of Global Legal Studies, 16:1, (2009)

[139] ***"The curious marriage of neoliberalism and nationalism."*** **https://left-flank.org/2011/01/16/the-curious-marriage-of-neoliberalism-and-nationalism/; Neil Davidson,** ***"Nationalism and Neoliberalism."*** **https://www.variant.org.uk/32texts/davidson32.html**

[140] Louis Althusser, *"Ideology and Ideological State Apparatuses"* https://www.marxists.org/reference/archive/althusser/1970/ideology.htm; Andrew Ryder, *"Althusser's Theory of Ideology."* https://isreview.org/issue/99/althussers-theory-ideology

[141] Ann Towns, *"Norms and Social Hierarchies: Understanding International Policy Diffusion from Below."* International Organization, 66:2, (2012); Jules Boykoff, *"Limiting Dissent: The Mechanisms of State Repression in the USA"* Social Movement Studies, 6:3, (2007)

[142] Steven Hill, *"Good Riddance Gig Economy."* https://www.salon.com/2016/03/27/good_riddance_gig_economy_uber_ayn_rand_and_the_awesome_collapse_of_silicon_valleys_dream_of_destroying_your_job/; Adam Ostolski and Wendy Brown, *"Neoliberalism Has Eviscerated the Fabric of Social Life."* https://www.greeneuropeanjournal.eu/neoliberalism-has-eviscerated-the-fabric-of-social-life/; Joseph Pozsgai-Alvarez, *"The Abuse of Entrusted Power for Private Gain: Meaning, Nature and Theoretical Evolution."* https://www.josephpozsgai.com/wp-content/uploads/2020/06/abuse_authors_accepted_manuscript-.pdf

[143] FDIC, *"The Banking Crises of the 1980s and Early 1990s."* https://www.fdic.gov/bank/historical/history/3_85.pdf

[144] Ernest Sternberg, *"Justifying Public Intervention without Market Externalities: Karl Polanyi's Theory of Planning in Capitalism."* Public Administration Review, 53, (March, 1993); Nuno Miguel Cardoso Machado, *"Karl Polanyi and the New Economic Sociology: Notes on the Concept of (Dis)embeddedness."*[44] https://journals.openedition.org/rccsar/309; Vančura, Matěj, *"Polanyi's Great Transformation and the concept of the embedded economy."* https://www.econstor.eu/handle/10419/83289

[145] Christopher Colford, *"Neoliberalism and its Excesses."* https://blogs.worldbank.org/psd/neoliberalism-and-its-excesses-after-sudden-cloudburst-controversy-clear-imf-insights-disquieting

[146] UN Department of Economic and Social Affairs, *"The Global Social Crisis."* Ch. II, https://www.un.org/esa/socdev/rwss/docs/2011/chapter2.pdf; Brookings, *"The closing of the jobs gap: A decade of recession and recovery."* https://www.brookings.edu/research/the-closing-of-the-jobs-gap-a-decade-of-recession-and-recovery/

[147] Carlos Moreira, *"El estado en América Latina desde los años trienta hasta nuestros días."* https://biblat.unam.mx/hevila/Revistaencrucijadaamericana/2010-11/vol4/no2/1.pdf; Charles Post, *"The New Deal and the Popular Front."* https://isreview.org/issue/108/new-deal-and-popular-front/index.html

[148] Kevin Farnsworth and Zoe Irving, *"The 2008 crisis failed to displace neoliberalism's core principles."*

https://blogs.lse.ac.uk/usappblog/2019/02/09/the-2008-crisis-failed-to-displace-neoliberalisms-core-principles/

[149] Felipe González y Mounu Prem, "La política de la privatización: el caso de Pinochet[45]."

https://nadaesgratis.es/admin/la-politica-de-la-privatizacion-el-caso-de-pinochet

[150] Orlando Letilier, *"The Chicago Boys in Chile Economic Freedom's Awful Toll."* https://www.thenation.com/article/the-chicago-boys-in-chile-economic-freedoms-awful-toll/; Andrew Leonard, *"Chicago Boys and the Chilean Earth Quake."*

https://www.salon.com/2010/03/02/chicago_boys_and_the_chilean_earthquake/; Robert N. Gwynne, Cristóbal Kay, *"The alternatives to neoliberalism"* in *Latin America Transformed: Globalization and Modernity*. 2004; Jon Kofas, *The Sword of Damocles*. 2002, 181-182; Tiago Angelo, *'Neoliberalismo precisa da violência, diz historiadora sobre 46 años do golpe no Chile.'* https://www.brasildefato.com.br/2019/09/11/neoliberalismo-precisa-da-violencia-diz-historiadora-sobre-46-anos-do-golpe-no-chile; Rafael Macedo de la Rocha Santos, *'O neoliberalismo chileno (1973-1990) e seus desafios à integração sul-americana*

dos anos 1980.' https://seer.ufs.br/index.php/tempo/article/download/10472/8076; CEIC, *"Chile External Debt: % of GDP."* https://www.ceicdata.com/en/indicator/chile/external-debt—of-nominal-gdp

[151] Fernando Henrique Cardoso and Enzo Faletto, *Dependencia y desarrollo en América Latina*. (1969); Marini Ruy Mauro, *América Latina. Dependencia y Globalización*. (2014)

[152] Atilio A. Boron, *"Democracy or Neoliberalism?"* http://bostonreview.net/archives/BR21.5/boron.html

[153] David Zamora, *"When Exclusion Replaces Exploitation: The Condition of the Surplus-Population under Neoliberalism"* http://nonsite.org/feature/when-exclusion-replaces-exploitation.

[154] C. J. Polychroniou, *"Toward a Post-Keynesian Political Economy of the 21st Century."* https://www.levyinstitute.org/pubs/pn_13_2.pdf

45. https://nadaesgratis.es/admin/la-politica-de-la-privatizacion-el-caso-de-pinochet

[155] Emily Czachor, *"Half of American Workers Made less than $35,000 in 2019."* https://www.newsweek.com/half-american-workers-made-less-35000-2019-report-shows-1539503; https://aspe.hhs.gov/topics/poverty-economic-mobility/poverty-guidelines/prior-hhs-poverty-guidelines-federal-register-references/2019-poverty-guidelines; https://www.cs.mcgill.ca/~rwest/wikispeedia/wpcd/wp/h/Household_income_in_the_United_States.htm

[156] Joseph Stiglitz, *"GDP is the Wrong Tool for Measuring What Matters."* https://www.scientificamerican.com/article/gdp-is-the-wrong-tool-for-measuring-what-matters/; Amit Kapoor Bibek Debroy, *"GDP is not a measure of human well-being."* https://hbr.org/2019/10/gdp-is-not-a-measure-of-human-well-being; Tim Koechlin, *"The Rich Get Richer, and Richer Still: Soaring Inequality in the US and why it Matters."* https://www.commondreams.org/views/2019/07/04/rich-get-richer-and-richer-still-soaring-inequality-us-and-why-it-matters; Marcus Lu, *"Is the American Dream Over?"* https://www.weforum.org/agenda/2020/09/social-mobility-upwards-decline-usa-us-america-economics/

[157] Fu-Lai Tony Yu, *"Neo-Mercantilist Policy and China's Rise as a Global Power."* https://rpb115.nsysu.edu.tw/var/file/131/1131/img/2374/CCPS3(3)-Yu.pdf; Yang Yao, *"China's export-led growth model."* https://www.eastasiaforum.org/2011/02/27/chinas-export-led-growth-model/; Paul Belesky and Geoffrey Alan Lawrence, *"Chinese state capitalism and neomercantilism in the contemporary food regime: contradictions, continuity and change."* https://www.researchgate.net/publication/324902169_Chinese_state_capitalism_and_neomercantilism_in_the_contemporary_food_regime_contradictions_continuity_and_change

[158] **"Communiqué of the Fifth Plenary Meeting of the 18th Central Committee of the Chinese Communist Party." https://chinacopyrightandmedia.wordpress.com/2015/10/29/communique-of-the-fifth-plenary-meeting-of-the-18th-central-committee-of-the-chinese-communist-party/; Sanjeev Kumar and Avinash Godbole, *"China's Sixth Plenum: Analyzing the Outcomes."* https://www.icwa.in/show_content.php?lang=1&level=3&ls_id=1754&lid=773**

[159] **Tatah Mentan, *Neoliberalism and Imperialism: Dissecting the Dynamics of Global Oppression.* (2016); Xi Jinping, *"Understanding the New Development Stage, Applying the New Development Philosophy, and Creating a New Development Dynamic."* http://en.qstheory.cn/2021-07/08/c_641137.htm**

[160] **Andrei Lungu, *"The US-China Clash is About Ideology After All."* https://foreignpolicy.com/2021/04/06/us-china-ideology-communism-capitalism/Lawrence Reynolds and Bronislaw Szerszynski, *"Neoliberalism and Technology: Perpetual Innovation or Perpetual Crisis?"* http://www.countdownnet.net/Allegati/31%20Neoliberalism%20and%20technology_Perpetual%20innovation%20or%20perpetual%20crisis.pdf; Milton Mueller, "Why we need to start talking about neo-mercantilism." https://www.internetgovernance.org/2021/08/04/why-we-need-to-start-talking-about-neo-mercantilism/; Jun Wang, *"The developmental state in the global hegemony of neoliberalism: A new***

***strategy for public housing in Singapore."* https://www.sciencedirect.com/science/article/abs/pii/S0264275111001338**

[161] OECD, *"Under Pressure: The Squeezed Middle Class."* https://www.oecd.org/els/soc/OECD-middle-class-2019-main-findings.pdf

[162] Brian Caterino and Philip Hansen, *"Critical Theory, Democracy and the Challenge of Neoliberalism."* https://library.oapen.org/bitstream/handle/20.500.12657/44125/external_content.pdf?sequence=1

[163] **Ali Kadri.** "*Neoliberalism vs. China as model for the developing world.*" https://www.athimar.org/en/articles/details/neoliberalism-vs-china-as-model-for-the-developing-world

[164] L.S. Stavrianos, *Global Rift: The Third World Comes of Age* (1981); W. Rodney. *How Europe Underdeveloped Africa*, (2012); André Gunder Frank, *El desafío de la crisis: ensayos sobre crisis económica mundial, ironías políticas internacionales y desafío europeo.* (1988); Jon Kofas, *Independence from America. Global Integration and Inequality.* (2017).

[165] Weitseng Chen, ed. *The Beijing Consensus? How China Has Changed Western Ideas of Law and Economic Development.* (2017).

[166] Ganesh Lal interviews Achin Vanaik, *"The Politics of Neoliberalism in India."* https://www.tni.org/es/node/12981; Ritesh Jain, *"How China's Real Economy Beats India in Wealth Creation."* https://www.outlookindia.com/business/how-china-s-real-economy-beats-india-in-wealth-creation—news-47808; Adnan Naseemullah, *"Dependent development in the twenty-first century,"* https://www.tandfonline.com/doi/pdf/10.1080/01436597.2022.2089104

[167] Dutin R. Turin, "*The Beijing Consensus: An Alternative Development Model.*"www.inquiriesjournal.com/articles/134/the-beijing-consensus-chinas-alternative-development-model

[168] **Christoph Nedopil, *"China Belt and Road Initiative."* https://greenfdc.org/wp-content/uploads/2022/07/GFDC-2022_China-Belt-and-Road-Initiative-BRI-Investment-Report-H1-2022.pdf; John Wong and Sarah Chan, *"China-ASEAN Free Trade Agreement."* https://library.fes.de/libalt/journals/swetsfulltext/17768956.pdf; Hunter Xiong, *"China's Belt and Road is Opening up to Foreign Companies."* https://www.brinknews.com/the-belt-road-is-opening-up-to-foreign-companies/; Christoph Nedopil Wang, *"Brief: China Belt and Road (BRI) Investment Report 2021."* https://greenfdc.org/brief-china-belt-and-road-initiative-bri-investment-report-2021/**

[169] Lin Yang, *"China: We're Still a Developing Nation. US Lawmakers: no Way."* https://www.voanews.com/a/china-we-re-still-a-developing-nation-us-lawmakers-no-way/7041814.html

[170] VINDOBONA, *"How the People's Republic of China Leverages Its Membership in Multilateral Organizations to Advance Its Geopolitical Interests."*

https://www.vindobona.org/article/how-china-leverages-its-membership-in-multilateral-organizations-advance-its-geopolitical-interests; Matthew D. Stephen, *"China's New Multilateral Institutions."* https://www.econstor.eu/bitstream/10419/216211/1/1696140412.pdf

[171] Jin Kai, *"The US, China, and the Containment Trap."* https://thediplomat.com/2014/05/the-us-china-and-the-containment-trap/; Zalmay Khalilzad, *"Congage China."* https://www.rand.org/pubs/issue_papers/IP187.html

[172] Niklas Swanström[46], *"Human Rights as a Policy Tool in Asia: Hypocrisy or Commitment?"* https://www.ispionline.it/en/pubblicazione/human-rights-policy-tool-asia-hypocrisy-or-commitment-31342; John Bellamy Foster, *"The New Cold War on China."* https://monthlyreview.org/2021/07/01/the-new-cold-war-on-china/; https://www.chinafile.com/reporting-opinion/features/here-are-fortune-500-companies-doing-business-xinjiang; https://www.chinafile.com/reporting-opinion/features/which-european-companies-are-working-xinjiang

[173] John Liu, *'China Model' Aims for Prosperity Without Democracy"* https://www.bloomberg.com/news/articles/2021-08-03/-china-model-aims-for-prosperity-without-democracy-quicktake-krvqxxd0

[174] Luis Carlos Bresser-Periera, *"Five Models of Capitalism".* March 2012, Revista de Economia Política[47] 32(1):21-35; http://www.china.org.cn/business/node_7233287.htm; OECD, *"China's Belt and Road Initiative in the Global Trade, Investment and Finance Landscape."* https://www.oecd.org/finance/Chinas-Belt-and-Road-Initiative-in-the-global-trade-investment-and-finance-landscape.pdf; BRI, *"China Belt And Road Projects Value Now Exceeds US$4 Trillion."* https://www.silkroadbriefing.com/news/2020/11/25/china-belt-and-road-projects-value-now-exceeds-us4-trillion/; Sebastian Strangio, *"Southeast Asian Nations Roll the Dice on Biden's Indo-Pacific Framework."* https://thediplomat.com/2022/05/southeast-asian-nations-roll-the-dice-on-bidens-indo-pacific-framework/.

[175] Jukka Gronow, *"The Capitalist Law of Appropriation: Kautsky's Interpretation of Karl Marx's Economic Thought."* in Jukka Gronow, *On the Formation of Marxism: Karl Kautsky's Theory of Capitalism, the Marxism of the Second International and Karl Marx's Critique of Political Economy.* (2016)

---

46. https://www.ispionline.it/en/bio/niklas-swanstrom

47. https://www.researchgate.net/journal/Revista-de-Economia-Politica-0101-3157

[176] Maxim Popov, *"Authoritarian liberalism between market capitalism and democracy: critical and neoliberal Pespectives."* https://www.researchgate.net/publication/351011620_Authoritarian_liberalism_between_market_capitalism_and_democracy_critical_and_neoliberal_perspecti

[177] Hermann Heller, *"Authoritarian Liberalism?"* https://edisciplinas.usp.br/pluginfile.php/5163411/mod_resource/content/0/Heller%20Authoritarian%20Liberalism.pdf

[178] John Brown, *"Neoliberalization, De-democratization, and Populist Responses in Western Europe, the US, and Latin America".* Critical Sociology, May 2020; Xinhua, *"Poverty Alleviation: China's Experience and Contribution."* http://www.xinhuanet.com/english/2021-04/06/c_139860414.htm; Alejandro Portes and Brandon P. Martinez, *"Latin American Cities: Their Evolution under Neoliberalism and Beyond."* https://cmd.princeton.edu/sites/cmd/files/media/latin_american_cities.pdf; Natalia Segura, *"How Neoliberalism Vandalized Latin America."* https://socialistworker.org/2018/11/21/how-neoliberalism-vandalized-latin-america; Bilge Erten, *"Uneven Development and the Terms of Trade."* https://scholarworks.umass.edu/cgi/viewcontent.cgi?article=1277&context=open_access_dissertations

[179] Flavio Azevedo, et al. *"Neoliberal Ideology and the Justification of Inequality in Capitalist Societies: Why Social and Economic Dimensions of Ideology Are Intertwined."* Journal of Social Issues, 75:4 (2019); Ilana Gershon, *"Neoliberal Agency."* Current Anthropology, 52:4 (2011)

[180] Fernand Braudel, *La Méditerranée et le Monde Méditerranéen à l'Epoque de Philippe II* (1949); Daniel Morales Ruvalcaba, *"The Semi-Peripheral States in the Twenty-First Century."* https://journals.sagepub.com/doi/pdf/10.1177/0020881719880769

[181] Ana Garcia Patrick Bond, *BRICS: An Anti-Capitalist Critique.* (2015); Dennis O'Hearn, *"Globalization, the new tigers and the end of the Developmental State?"* https://ces.uc.pt/publicacoes/oficina/ficheiros/123.pdf

[182] **Charles Edquist and Lief Hommen, eds. *Small Country Innovation Systems: Globalization, Change and Policy in Asia and Europe.* (2009); Bruno Marshall Shirley, *'The Asian Tigers from Independence to Industrialization."* https://www.e-ir.info/2014/10/16/the-asian-tigers-from-independence-to-industrialisation/.**

[183] Richard K. E. Rispens, *"Modern Economic Growth Theories and the "Miracle" of the East Asian Tigers"* Erasmus University Rotterdam, (2009); https//thesiseur.nl/pub

[184] **Eun Mee Kim, *The Four Asian Tigers: Economic Development & the Global Political Economy.* 1999; Ku-Wai Li, *Capitalist Development and Economism in East Asia.* (2002).**

[185] Benjamin Pham, *"How and why did South Korea transition to an economic model of export-led industrialization?"* https://fsi-live.s3.us-west-1.amazonaws.com/s3fs-public/2015_benjamin_pham_paper.pdf; Charlotte Severns, *"The Development of*

Four Asian Tigers". https://www.borgenmagazine.com/development-of-the-four-asian-tigers/; Paulina Restrepo Echavarria[48] , Brian Reinbold[49], *"Measuring Labor Share of the Asian Tigers."* https://www.stlouisfed.org/on-the-economy/2018/january/measuring-labor-share-asian-tigers

[186] Ellen Brown, *Neoliberalism has met its match in China."* https://www.commondreams.org/views/2019/08/09/neoliberalism-has-met-its-match-china

[187] Hee-Yeon Cho and Eun Mee Kim, *"State Autonomy and Its Social Conditions for Economic Development in South Korea and Taiwan."* In Eun Mee Kim (ed.), *The Four Asian Tigers: Economic Development and the Global Political Economy*. (1998); David A. Smith and Su-Hoon Lee, *"Limits on a Semiperipheral Success Story? State Dependent Development and the Prospects for South Korean Democratization."* in William G. Martin (ed.), *Semiperipheral States in the World-Economy*. (1990).

[188] Michelle Clark Neely, *"Paper Tigers? How the Asian Economies Lost Their Bite."* https://www.stlouisfed.org/publications/regional-economist/january-1999/paper-tigers-how-the-asian-economies-lost-their-bite; Nicola Bullard, Walden Bello, Kamal Malhorta, *"Taming the Tigers: The IMF and the Asian Crisis."* Third World Quarterly, 19:3, (1998)

[189] **David A. Smith, *'Lessons of Global Neoliberalism? The East Asia Economic Crisis Reconsidered."* https://escholarship.org/content/qt6pk7p5zz/qt6pk7p5zz.pdf?t=lnqidy; Walden Bello, *"The Asian Financial Crisis: causes, dynamics, prospects."* https://www.tandfonline.com/doi/pdf/10.1080/01436599908724669; *"The Asian Financial Crisis, 1997-98."* https://www.grips.ac.jp/teacher/oono/hp/lecture_F/lec11.htm**

[190] GARY JACOBS, "*The political economy of neoliberalism and illiberal democracy*" http://cadmusjournal.org/node/654.

[191] **David Harvey, *"Neoliberalism as Creative Destruction."* https://is.cuni.cz/studium/predmety/index.php?do=download&did=85806&kod=JMMZ108**

[192] **Baldev Raj Nayar, *The Geopolitics of Globalization.* (2007); Low Minmin, *"The Singapore Model: Advocacy in an Authoritarian State."* https://thediplomat.com/2020/02/the-singapore-model-advocacy-in-an-authoritarian-state/;MarkR.Thompson, *"Pacific Asia and Asian Values: authoritarianism, democracy, and good governance."* http://sites.asiasociety.org/asia21summit/wp-content/uploads/2010/11/PacificAsia.pdf**

[193] **Jorg Wiegrtz, *"How neoliberalism's moral order feeds fraud and corruption."* https://theconversation.com/how-neoliberalisms-moral-order-feeds-fraud-and-corruption-60946; B. Reisenberg, A. Kentikenelis and T. Stubbs, *"Creating crony***

48. https://www.stlouisfed.org/on-the-economy/2018/january/measuring-labor-share-asian-tigers#authorbox

49. https://www.stlouisfed.org/on-the-economy/2018/january/measuring-labor-share-asian-tigers#authorbox

capitalism: neoliberal globalization and the fueling of corruption." **http://eprints.gla.ac.uk/189119/; Pinar Bedirhanoğlu[50],** ***The neoliberal discourse on corruption as a means of consent building: reflections from post-crisis Turkey."*** **https://www.tandfonline.com/doi/abs/10.1080/01436590701591770?journalCode=ctwq20.**

[194] **Peter Leys,** ***"Peru's Neoliberalism Success Story is a Meltdown."*** **https://jacobinmag.com/2020/12/peru-neoliberalism-protest-congress-coup-corruption;**

[195] ASA CRISTINA LAURELL, *"Three Decades of Neoliberalism in Mexico: The Destruction of Society."* https://plataformapoliticasocial.com.br/wp-content/uploads/2015/12/30-years-of-neoliberalism-in-Mexico-IJHS-2015-246-64.pdf

[196] Paul Cooney, *"Argentina's Quarter Century Experiment with Neoliberalism: from dictatorship to depression".* https://www.scielo.br/j/rec/a/TY6ScB7H7QshsgP8pQ9tcRg/?lang=en

[197] Marcio Moraes Valenca, *"The Lost Decade of the Brazilian Government's Response in the 1990s"* Journal of Developing Areas. 33 (1998).

[198] Luis Esteban Gonzalez Manrique, *"La democracia 'iliberal' de Fujimori: Golpe de Estado permanente."* https://www.researchgate.net/publication/259830186_La_democracia_%27iliberal%27_de_Fujimori_Golpe_de_Estado_permanente; Oscar Dancourt, *"Neoliberal reforms and macroeconomic*

policy in Peru." https://www.cepal.org/sites/default/files/publication/files/10675/67051073I_en.pdf; Philip Mauceri, *State Under Siege: Development and Policy Making in Peru.* (1998); Jo-Marie Burt, *"Quién habla es terrorista": The Political Use of Fear in Fujimori's Peru."* https://www.academia.edu/5724656/Jo_Marie_Burt_Quien_habla_es_terrorista_The_Political_Use_of_Fear_in_Fujimoris_Peru_Latin_American_Researcl

[199] Kurt Weyland, *"Neopopulism and Neoliberalism in Latin America: how much affinity?"* https://library.fes.de/libalt/journals/swetsfulltext/18502013.pdf

[200] Darío Clemente, *El Estado Neodesarrollista en Brasil y su Crisis: Apuntes en Perspectiva Histórica.*https://www.academia.edu/39225926/El_Estado_Neodesarrollista_en_Brasil_y_su_Crisis_Apuntes_en_Perspectiva_Hist%C3%B3rica; Imelda Masni Juniaty Sianipar and Arthur Jeverson Maya, "Pink Tide: Neo-developmentalism in Brazil and Argentina.[51] http://repository.uki.ac.id/2205/1/NeodevelopementalisminBrazilandArgentina.pdf; Carlos Mallorquin, *A Southern Perspective on Development Studies.* (2020); Carlos Mallorquin, *"Celso Furtado and Development."* Development in Practice. 17:6 (2007)

---

50. https://www.tandfonline.com/author/Bedirhano%C4%9Flu%2C+Pinar

51. https://www.academia.edu/39225926/El_Estado_Neodesarrollista_en_Brasil_y_su_Crisis_Apuntes_en_Perspectiva_Hist%C3%B3rica;%20Imelda%20Masni%20Juniaty%20Sianipar%20and%20Arthur%20Jeverson%20Maya,%20

[201] Pedro Cezar Dutra Fonseca, Marcelo Arend, Glaison Augusto Guerrero, *"Growth, Distribution and Crisis: The Workers' Party Administration."* https://journals.sagepub.com/doi/full/10.1177/0094582X19886821

[202] Mariano Feliz, "A new Developmentalism?" https://www.phenomenalworld.org/analysis/a-new-developmentalism/; Jean Tible, *"¿Una nueva clase media en Brasil? El lulismo como fenómeno político-social."* https://nuso.org/articulo/una-nueva-clase-media-en-brasil-el-lulismo-como-fenomeno-politico-social/; Inaki Sagarzazu and Fernando Mouron , *"Hugo Chavez's Polarizing Legacy: Chavismo, Media and Public Opinion in Argentina's Domestic Politics."* https://www.scielo.cl/scielo.php?pid=S0718-090X2017000100007&script=sci_arttext

[203] S. Erdem Aytaç and Ziya Őniş, "Varieties of Populism in a Changing Global Context: The Divergent Paths of Erdoğan and Kirchnerismo." Comparative Politics, 47:1 (2014); Cornel Ban, *"What is neo-developmentalism?"* https://devl1980.wordpress.com/2012/04/24/what-is-neo-developmentalism/

[204] **Ruy Braga and Sean Purdy, *"A precarious hegemony: neo-liberalism, social struggles, and the end of Lulismo in Brazil."* https://www.researchgate.net/publication/325578652_A_precarious_hegemony_neo-liberalism_social_struggles_and_the_end_of_Lulismo_in_Brazil; Idelber Avelar, *"The June 2013 Uprisings and the Waning of Lulismo in Brazil: Of Antagonism, Contradiction, and Oxymoron."* https://www.researchgate.net/publication/316946767_The_June_2013_Uprisings_and_the_Waning_of_Lulismo_in_Brazil_Of_Antagonism_Contradiction_and_Oxymoron; Rodrigo Nunes, *"Centrists paved the way for the far right in Brazil."* https://www.aljazeera.com/opinions/2018/10/24/centrists-paved-the-way-for-the-far-right-in-brazil**

[205] **James M. Cypher and Yolanda Alfaro, *"The Triangle of Neo-Developmentalism in Ecuador."* www.scielo.org.mx/scielo.php?script=sci_arttext&pid=S0301-70362016000200161&lng=es&nrm=iso&tlng=en[52]"; Mustafa Kutlay[53] & Hüseyin Emrah Karaoğuz[54], "*Neo-developmentalist turn in the global political economy? The Turkish case"* Turkish Studies, 19:2 (2018); Thomas Chiasson-LeBel, *"Neoliberalism in Ecuador after Correa."* https://www.erlacs.org/articles/10.32992/erlacs.10500/galley/10899/download/.**

[206] YangYao, *"What Explains China's Economic Success?"* https://openknowledge.worldbank.org/bitstream/handle/10986/6098/deor_13_1_26.pdf;sequence=2

[207] **James M. Cypher, *"From Military Keynesianism to Global-Neoliberal Militarism"* https://monthlyreview.org/2007/06/01/from-military-keynesianism-to-global-neoliberal-militarism/; https://data.worldbank.org/indicator/**

---

52. http://www.scielo.org.mx/scielo.php?script=sci_arttext&pid=S0301-70362016000200161&lng=es&nrm=iso&tlng=en

53. https://www.tandfonline.com/author/Kutlay%2C+Mustafa

54. https://www.tandfonline.com/author/Karao%C4%9Fuz%2C+H%C3%BCseyin+Emrah

MS.MIL.XPND.GD.ZS; Richard Godfrey, Jo Brewis, Chris Grocott, *"The private military industry and neoliberal imperialism,"* https://journals.sagepub.com/doi/abs/10.1177/1350508412470731 https://www.nato.int/nato_static_fl2014/assets/pdf/2021/6/pdf/210611-pr-2021-094-en.pdf

[208] Jorgelina Do Rosario[55] and Rachel Savage[56], *"China development loans to emerging economies hi 13-year low."* https://www.reuters.com/markets/asia/china-development-loans-emerging-economies-hit-13-year-low-2021-study-2023-01-24/

[209] Chan, Lai-Ha and Lee, Pak K. and Chan, Gerald (2008) *"Rethinking global governance: A China model in the making?"* https://kar.kent.ac.uk/9350/1/Rethinking_global_governance_a_China_model_in_the_making.pdf; D. R. Turin, *"The Beijing Consensus: China's Alternative Development Model"* http://www.inquiriesjournal.com/articles/134/the-beijing-consensus-chinas-alternative-development-model

[210] Octasiano Miguel Valerio Mendoza, Mihaly Borsi, Flavio Comim, *"Human Capital Dynamics in China: Evidence from a club convergence approach."* https://www.researchgate.net/publication/357949442_Human_capital_dynamics_in_China_Evidence_from_a_club_convergence_approach; Rudolph Traub-Merz, "All-China Federation of Trade Unions: Structure, Functions and the Challenge of Collective Bargaining." https://global-labour-university.org/wp-content/uploads/fileadmin/GLU_Working_Papers/GLU_WP_No.13.pdf

[211] Scott Kennedy, *"The Myth of the Beijing Consensus"* Journal of Contemporary China. https://www.tandfonline.com/doi/pdf/10.1080/10670561003666087; Edmund Malesky and Jonathan London, *"The Political Economy of Development in China and Vietnam"* https://www.annualreviews.org/doi/pdf/10.1146/annurev-polisci-041811-150032; Iram Naseer, *'Washington Consensus' vs 'Beijing Consensus'"* https://nation.com.pk/18-Sep-2018/-washington-consensus-vs-beijing-consensus; Brad W. Setser, "Is China Manipulating its Currency?" https://www.cfr.org/in-brief/china-manipulating-its-currency

[212] Jonathan M. Katz, *"When America Invaded China: The Boxer Rebellion still shapes Beijing's attitude toward the United States."* https://foreignpolicy.com/2022/01/17/boxer-rebellion-us-invaded-china/; Ana Malindog- Uy, *"Human Rights: US Double Standards, Hypocrisy."* https://theaseanpost.com/opinion/2022/apr/17/human-rights-us-double-standards-hypocrisy; Randall P. Peerenboom, *"Assessing Human Rights in China: Why the Double-Standard?"* https://escholarship.org/uc/item/2t39b9rn

[213] Guoqiang Long, *"China's Policies on FDI: Review and Evaluation."* https://www.cgdev.org/sites/default/files/9780881323818-Ch12.pdf; Demetri Sevastopulo, *"US blacklists Chinese companies for allegedly supporting Russian military."* https://www.ft.com/content/a866bf53-ed1a-4329-aa01-2d7c1fcf305d

55. https://www.reuters.com/authors/jorgelina-do-rosario/

56. https://www.reuters.com/authors/rachel-savage/

[214] Matt Ferchen, *"Growing US-China Rivalry in Africa, Latin America and Southeast Asia."* https://merics.org/en/report/growing-us-china-rivalry-africa-latin-america-and-southeast-asia-implications-eu; Kristen Hopewell, *"Beyond US-China Rivalry: Rule Breaking, Economic Coercion and the Weaponization of Trade."* https://www.cambridge.org/core/journals/american-journal-of-international-law/article/beyond-uschina-rivalry-rule-breaking-economic-coercion-and-the-weaponization-of-trade/7817C37D098E8A9FC30A40FDCD7F8C35

[215] Alexandra Alper, *"US investors have plowed billions into China's AI sector."* https://www.xm.com/research/markets/allNews/reuters/us-investors-have-plowed-billions-into-chinas-ai-sector-report-shows-52883696; *"Distribution of rare earth imports to the United States between 2017 and 2020 by country."* https://www.statista.com/statistics/279895/us-rare-earth-import-value/

[216] **Amar Diwakar, *"Chip Wars: US-China and the battle for semiconductor supremacy."* https://www.trtworld.com/magazine/chip-wars-us-china-and-the-battle-for-semiconductor-supremacy-45052; Marc Schmid, *"Rare Earths in the Trade Dispute Between the US and China: A Deja Vu."* https://www.intereconomics.eu/contents/year/2019/number/6/article/rare-earths-in-the-trade-dispute-between-the-us-and-china-a-deja-vu.html**

[217] Jamie Christoff, *"Beijing orders banks to get ready for massive dollar dump."* https://newyorktodaymag.com/beijing-orders-state-banks-to-get-ready-for-massive-dollar-dump-reuters/; Michael Hudson, *"America's Financialization Policy vs. China's Industrial Socialism."* https://www.eurasiareview.com/17042021-americas-neoliberal-financialization-policy-vs-chinas-industrial-socialism-oped/; Isabella Weber, *"Origins of China's Contested Relationship with Neoliberalism."* https://online.ucpress.edu/gp/article/1/1/12271/107349/Origins-of-China-s-Contested-Relation-with; Gideon Rachman, *"US-China rivalry drives the retreat of market economics."* https://www.ft.com/content/1e749857-3cd6-453d-8cee-2c501cbfd53b

[218] David A. Ciepley, *"Neoliberalism and the Corporation: Mutually Contradicting and Corrupting."* https://papers.ssrn.com/sol3/papers.cfm?abstract_id=3230520

[219] **Jens Beckert, *"The exhausted futures of neoliberalism: from promissory legitimacy to social anomy."* https://www.tandfonline.com/doi/full/10.1080/17530350.2019.1574867; Zhenhua Su[57], Yanyu Ye[58], and Pu Wang[59], *"Social change and generalized anomie: Why economic development has reduced social trust in China."* https://journals.sagepub.com/doi/full/10.1177/0268580918812281**

[220] Ivan Franceschini, *"The Chinese Trade Union Goes Abroad: Evidence from Cambodia."* https://journals.openedition.org/chinaperspectives/11168; Ruixue Bai, *"The role of the All-China Federation of Trade Unions: Implications for Chinese Workers Today."* https://intercoll.net/IMG/pdf/all_china_federation_of_trade_unions.pdf

---

57. https://journals.sagepub.com/doi/full/10.1177/0268580918812281

58. https://journals.sagepub.com/doi/full/10.1177/0268580918812281

59. https://journals.sagepub.com/doi/full/10.1177/0268580918812281

[221] Aaron L. Friedberg, *"The Growing Rivalry Between America and China and the Future of Globalization."* https://tnsr.org/wp-content/uploads/2022/01/TNSR-Vol-5-Issue-1-Friedberg.pdf; Robert Grosse, Jonas Gamso, Roy C. Nelson, *"China's Rise, World Order, and the Implications International Business."* https://link.springer.com/article/10.1007/s11575-020-00433-8; https://statisticstimes.com/economy/united-states-vs-china-economy.php; Linda Gorman, *"How US-China Trade War Affected the Rest of the World."* https://www.nber.org/digest-202204/how-us-china-trade-war-affected-rest-world

[222] Y Zhu and M. Warner, *"An Emerging Model of Employment Relations in China."* https://www.jbs.cam.ac.uk/wp-content/uploads/2020/08/wp0012-1.pdf; Mimi Lau, *"Why labor rights issues may sink EU-China investment deal."* https://www.scmp.com/news/china/diplomacy/article/3121576/why-labour-rights-issues-may-sink-eu-china-investment-deal; Ekaterina Pokrovsky, *"What Work-Life Balance Looks Like Around the World."* https://fairygodboss.com/articles/what-work-life-balance-looks-like-around-the-world; https://www.globalpeoplestrategist.com/5-countries-with-the-best-employment-laws/; Tianlei Huang, *"Addressing ageism in China's workforce."* https://www.eastasiaforum.org/2023/03/06/addressing-ageism-in-chinas-workforce/

[223] Orange Wang, *"How much is China's foreign direct investment and is it still a good destination for overseas investors?"* https://www.scmp.com/economy/economic-indicators/article/3181037/how-much-chinas-foreign-direct-investment-and-it-still

[224] Minqui Li, *"China: Imperialism or Semi-Periphery?"* https://monthlyreview.org/2021/07/01/china-imperialism-or-semi-periphery/

[225] https://www.statista.com/statistics/270267/united-states-share-of-global-gross-domestic-product-gdp/ Aaron O'Neil, *"United States share of global gross domestic product (GDP)."* https://www.statista.com/statistics/270267/united-states-share-of-global-gross-domestic-product-gdp/; Felix Richter, *"China's Rise to Economic Superpower."* https://www.statista.com/chart/27688/chinas-share-of-global-gdp-vs-the-us-and-the-eu/

[226] Samanth Subramanian, *"Friendshoring is bad for politics but even worse for business."* https://qz.com/2173562/what-is-friendshoring/

[227] "Yukio Sakamato comments on the gap in China's semiconductor industry." https://www.newsdirectory3.com/yukio-sakamoto-comments-on-the-gap-in-chinas-semiconductor-industry-nikkei-chinese-website/[60]; Robyn Klinger-Vidra[61] and Yu-Ching Kuo[62], *"Asia tech godfathers to decide US chips fate."* https://asiatimes.com/2022/09/asia-tech-godfathers-to-decide-us-chips-fate/

60. https://d.docs.live.net/eb41a1b69e1e6e00/Desktop/Yukio%20Sakamato%20comments%20on%20the%20gap%20in%20China's%20semiconductor%20industry.

61. https://asiatimes.com/author/robyn-klingler-vidra/

62. https://asiatimes.com/author/yu-ching-kuo/

[228] ***Alex Mackle, and Oxford Economics, "The US-China Economic Relationship" https://www.uschina.org/sites/default/files/the_us-china_economic_relationship_-_a_crucial_partnership_at_a_critical_juncture.pdf; Alessandro Nicita and Carlos Razo, "China: The rise of a trade titan" https://unctad.org/news/china-rise-trade-titan;***

[229] SAM MILLER AND HARRISON Fluss, *"The 18th Brumaire of Donald J. Trump?"* https://socialistworker.org/2016/12/05/the-18th-brumaire-of-trump

[230] Spyros Sakellaropoulos, "*Rereading The 18th Brumaire of Louis Bonaparte: The Phenomenon of Bonapartism as a Capitalist State Without Popular Representation.*" Journal of Marxism and Interdisciplinary Inquiry. Vol. 11, No. 1 (Summer 2020) Pp. 34-47

[231] Jeff Goodwin, *"The Eighteenth Brumaire of Donald J. Trump."* https://www.pwsc.us/conflicted-the-pwsc-official-blog/blog/the-eighteenth-brumaire-of-donald-j-trump; Dorit Geva, *"Orban's Ordonationalism as Post-neoliberal Hegemony."* https://journals.sagepub.com/doi/full/10.1177/0263276421999435; Michael Wilkinson, *"Authoritarian Liberalism and the Transformation of Modern*

Europe." https://eprints.lse.ac.uk/115125/1/LSE_Law_working_paper_authoritarian_liberalism published.pdf; Peter McKenzie Atack, "*Caesarism, Fujimore and the Transformation of Peru into a Neoliberal Order.*" https://curve.carleton.ca/system/files/etd/807a8309-802c-4244-972d-2c95ac767014/etd_pdf/9f7ec734d904cda230186f76a1a93987/atack-caesarismfujimoriandthetransformationofperu.pdf

[232] Thomas Hauner, Branko Milanovic, and Suresh Naidu, *"Inequality, Foreign Investment, and Imperialism."* https://www.gc.cuny.edu/CUNY_GC/media/CUNY-Graduate-Center/PDF/Centers/LIS/imperialism_Hauner-Milanovic-Naidu.pdf; Ivan Vujačić and Mihail Arandarenko, eds. *"The Economic Causes and Consequences of the First World War."* https://cid.ekof.bg.ac.rs/wp-content/uploads/2017/01/The-Economic-Causes-and-Consequences-of-the-First-World-War.pdf; Intan Suwandi, *"Neoliberalism and Imperialism."* https://mronline.org/2021/02/21/neoliberalism-and-imperialism-interview-with-intan-suwandi/

[233] John Bellamy Foster, *"Late Imperialism."* https://monthlyreview.org/2019/07/01/late-imperialism/

[234] Joseph Schumpeter, *"Sociology of Imperialisms"* in P. J. Cain and Mark Harrison, eds. *Imperialism: Critical Concepts in Historical Studies.* Vol I, 310 (2001)

[235] **Jonathan Riley, *"J. S. Mill's Liberal Utilitarian Assessment of Capitalism Versus Socialism,"* https://www.cambridge.org/core/journals/utilitas/article/abs/j-s-mills-liberal-utilitarian-assessment-of-capitalism-versus-socialism/CB132C4872CA8254FC65EEA650C3CB03;**

[236] William A. Pelz, *"Economic Collapse and the Rise of Fascism"*, in *A People's History of Modern Europe.* (2016).

[237] Jens Hacke *"The Crisis of Liberalism in Interwar Europe."* https://www.his-online.de/en/research/project-details/projects/274/

[238] **Amir Lebdioui, *"El mito del «milagro» del libre mercado: cómo la política industrial permitió a Chile diversificar sus exportaciones."* https://www.ciperchile.cl/2021/11/03/el-mito-del-milagro-del-libremercado/; Benjamin Alemparte, *"Towards a theory of neoliberal constitutionalism: Addressing Chile' first constitutional laboratory."* https://www.sciencegate.app/document/10.1017/s2045381721000058**

[239] Gary Jacobs, *"The Political Economy of Neoliberalism and Illiberal Democracy."* http://www.cadmusjournal.org/article/volume-3/issue-3/political-economy-neoliberalism-and-illiberal-democracy

[240] Wendy Brown, *"Neoliberalism and the End of Liberal Democracy"* https://muse.jhu.edu/article/48659

[241] Lars Carnilleson, *"The new right is not a reaction to neoliberalism but its offspring."*

https://www.opendemocracy.net/en/can-europe-make-it/the-new-right-is-not-a-reaction-to-neoliberalism-but-its-offspring/ Jonathan Chait, *"How 'Neoliberalism' became the left's favorite insult."* https://nymag.com/intelligencer/2017/07/how-neoliberalism-became-the-lefts-favorite-insult.html

[242] Catherine Fieschi, *Populocracy: The Tyranny of Authenticity and the Rise of Populism.* (2019)

[243] Ben Burgis, *"We Don't Need a Culture War. We Need a Class War."* https://www.jacobinmag.com/2020/12/culture-war-class-polarization-medicare-for-all; William Shoki, *'The culture wars are a distraction.'* https://africasacountry.com/2020/09/the-culture-wars-are-a-distraction; S. Prasannarajan, *"The Wages of the Culture War."* https://openthemagazine.com/columns/the-wages-of-the-culture-war/.

[244] **Sheena Sumaria, *"India's nightmare: the extremism of Narendra Modi."* http://www.counterfire.org/interview/18068-india-s-nightmare-the-extremism-of-narendra-modi; http://ac.upd.edu.ph/index.php/news-announcements/1201-southeast-asian-democracy-neoliberalism-populism-vedi-hadiz; Weronika Grzebalska, *"Gendered voices from East-Central Europe. Breaking out of the deadlock of neoliberalism vs. rightwing populism."* http://balticworlds.com/breaking-out-of-the-deadlock-of-neoliberalism-vs-rightwing-populism/**

[245] Fareed Zakaria, *"The Rise of Illiberal Democracy."* https://www.foreignaffairs.com/articles/1997-11,-01/rise-illiberal-democracy

[246] Thiery Chopin, *"Illiberal Democracy or Majoritarian Authoritarianism?"* https://institutdelors.eu/en/publications/illiberal-democracy-or-majoritarian-authoritarianism-contribution-to-the-analysis-of-populisms-in-europe/; Richard A. Pildes, *"The Inherent Authoritarianism in Democratic Regimes."* https://www.researchgate.net/publication/228186411_The_Inherent_Authoritarianism_in_Democratic_Regimes; Andrea Pozas Loyo, *"Rousseau's Supermajoritarian Justification for Majority Rule."* https://www.scielo.org.mx/scielo.php?script=sci_arttext&pid=S2007-43872014000100012

[247] ***Manuela Cadelli, "The President of Belgian Magistrates: Neoliberalism is a form of Fascism"***

http://www.defenddemocracy.press/president-belgian-magistrates-neoliberalism-form-fascism/

[248] Antonio Gramsci, *"The Peasants and the Dictatorship of the Proletariat"* in *Selections from Political Writings, 1921–1926*, (1978); Cecilia Green, *"Advanced Capitalist Hegemony and the Significance of Gramsci's Insights."* https://www.academia.edu/45316497/
Advanced_Capitalist_Hegemony_and_the_Significance_of_Gramscis_Insights_A_Restatement

[249] **Palmiro Togliatti, *Lectures on Fascism*. (1935); Domenico Settembrini, *"Mussolini and the Legacy of Revolutionary Socialism."* Journal of Contemporary History, 11:4 (1976); Regina Quiroz, *"From the exclusion of the people in neoliberalism to publicity without a public."* https://www.nature.com/articles/s41599-0107-0032-1**

[250] Shoshana Zuboff, *"Surveillance Capitalism as Epistemic Inequality."* https://www.cambridge.org/core/books/after-the-digital-tornado/caveat-usor-surveillance-capitalism-as-epistemic-inequality/9EB949FA5BD07CF448C7D8F6A226B975; Guy Redden, *"Is Reality TV Neoliberal?"* https://www.researchgate.net/publication/319677180_Is_Reality_TV_Neoliberal

[251] Nick Couldry, *"Reality TV or the secret theater of neoliberalism."* Hermès, La Revue[63], .44:1 (2006).

[252] Bernd Schmidt, J Joško Brakus, Alessandro Biraglia, *"Consumption Ideology."* https://academic.oup.com/jcr/article/49/1/74/6358727; Aiden James Kosciesza *"It's Do or Die: Cultural Labor, Competitive Reality TV, and the Reproduction of Neoliberal Capitalism."* https://ijoc.org/index.php/ijoc/article/viewFile/16927/3404; Shoshana Zuboff[64], *"The Age of Surveillance Capitalism: The Fight for a Human Future at the New Frontier of Power."* (2019)

[253] Anism Shivani, *"This is our Neoliberal Nightmare."*https://www.salon.com/2016/06/06/this_is_our_neoliberal_nightmare_hillary_clinton_donald_trump_and_why_the_market_and_the_wealthy_win_every_time/

[254] United Nations, *"The Millennium Campaign: Successes and Challeges in Mobilizing Support for the MDGs."* https://www.un.org/en/chronicle/article/millennium-campaign-successes-and-challenges-mobilizing-support-mdgs[65]; Max Roser, *"Global Economic Inequality."* https://ourworldindata.org/global-economic-inequality; United Nations, *"Global impact of war in Ukraine: Billions of people face the greatest cost-of-living crisis in a generation."* https://news.un.org/pages/wp-content/uploads/2022/06/GCRG_2nd-Brief_Jun8_2022_FINAL.pdf

63. https://www.cairn-int.info/journal-hermes-la-revue.htm

64. https://www.amazon.com/Shoshana-Zuboff/e/B001H6O73W/ref=dp_byline_cont_book_1

65. https://d.docs.live.net/eb41a1b69e1e6e00/Desktop/United%20Nations,%20

[255] Paul Mason, *'Neoliberalism has Destroyed Social Mobility."* https://neweconomics.opendemocracy.net/neoliberalism-destroyed-social-mobility-together-must-rebuild/; *"A Promise Broken: The late 20th century manifestation of welfare capitalism spread outwards from post-war America into western democracies across the world."* https://atelier.net/social-mobility/a-promise-broken/

[256] Peter Walker, *"UN Chief Issues Warning on the Rise of Fascism."* http://www.independent.co.uk/news/world/politics/united-nations-chilling-warning-rise-fascism-human-rights-prince-zeid-a7464861.html

[257] Despina Lalaki, *"Enzo Traverso: Neoliberalism is the Totalitarianism of our Time."*https://academicworks.cuny.edu/cgi/viewcontent.cgi?article=1515&context=ny_pubs

[258] Aylin Ünver Noi and Sasha Toperich *"Challenges of Democracy in the European Union and its Neighbors."* https://archive.transatlanticrelations.org/wp-content/uploads/2016/08/Challenges-of-Democracy.pdf; Benjamin Moffitt, *The Global Rise of Populism* (2017; H. A. Watson, *"Global Capitalism, Sovereign State Violence, and Human Insecurity"* in *A Future without Borders?* ed. by Eddy Souffrant. (2016).

[259] *Melshal, "Neoliberalism, Fascism and Sovereignty"* http://readersupportednews.org/pm-section/78-78/41987-neoliberalism-fascism-and-sovereignty/

[260] Joel Rose and Jim Baker *"6 in 10 Americans say that democracy is in crisis as the big lie takes root."* https://www.npr.org/2022/01/03/1069764164/american-democracy-poll-jan-6?t=1653731082182; Ruth Igielnik, *"70% of Americans say U.S. economic system unfairly favors the powerful."* https://www.pewresearch.org/fact-tank/2020/01/09/70-of-americans-say-u-s-economic-system-unfairly-favors-the-powerful/

[261] **Doug Miller, *Can the World be Wrong? Where Global Public Opinion Says We're Headed.* (2015); David Chidester, *Authentic Fakes Religion and American Popular Culture*. (2005).**

[262] Gary Jacobs, *"The Political Economy of Neoliberalism and Illiberal Democracy." op. cit.*

[263] Catherine Chaput, *"Neoliberalism and the rhetorical invention of counterpublic attunement."* https://journals.sagepub.com/doi/10.1177/2057047318794688

[264] Ugur Aytac, *"Global political legitimacy and the structural power of capital."* https://onlinelibrary.wiley.com/doi/full/10.1111/josp.12464

[265] **Stefan Kipfert, *"Macronism: Neoliberal Triumph or Next Stage in France's Political Crisis?***

https://www.globalresearch.ca/macronism-neoliberal-triumph-or-next-stage-in-frances-political-crisis/5596722; Sam Miller and Harrison Fluss, *"The 18th Brumaire of Donald J. Trump".* https://socialistworker.org/2016/12/05/the-18th-brumaire-of-trump

[266] ***"What the world thinks about globalization,"* https://www.economist.com/blogs/graphicdetail/2016/11/daily-chart-12.**

[267] **Sebők Miklós, Jasper Simons, *"How Orbán won? Neoliberal disenchantment and the grnd strategy of financial nationalism to reconstruct capitalism and regain autonomy."***

https://academic.oup.com/ser/advance-article/doi/10.1093/ser/mwab052/6414337; NewsClick, *"Neoliberalism Returns to Uruguay With the new Right-Wing President."* https://www.newsclick.in/neoliberalism-returns-uruguay-with-new-right-wing-president; Nicola Lebourg, *"2007-2017: Ten Years of Marino-Lepenism."* https://progressivepost.eu/2007-2017-ten-years-marino-lepenism/; Ajay Gudavarthy, *"Populism and Rhetoric Amidst the Farmers' Protest in India."* https://www.e-ir.info/pdf/89949

[268] **Sheri Berman, *"Populism Is Not Fascism. But It Could Be a Harbinger"* https://www.foreignaffairs.com/articles/united-states/2016-10-17/populism-not-fascism; Joel Rose and Jill Baker, *"6 in 10 Americans say US democracy is in crisis as the big lie takes root."* https://www.npr.org/2022/01/03/1069764164/american-democracy-poll-jan-6?t=1659009198727; Isabell Hoffmann, *"Only 60 percent of EU citizens are satisfied with the state of democracy in the union."* https://www.bertelsmann-stiftung.de/en/topics/latest-news/2021/july/only-60-percent-of-eu-citizens-are-satisfied-with-the-state-of-democracy-in-the-union.**

[269] Wendy Brown, *"Neoliberalism and the End of Liberal Democracy"* http://lchc.ucsd.edu/cogn_150/Readings/brown.pdf.

[270] David M. Kotz, *"Neoliberalism and the Social Structure of Accumulation Theory of Long-Run Capital Accumulation."* https://journals.sagepub.com/doi/pdf/10.1177/0486613403255542

[271] Richard D. Wolff, *"How Fascism has Converged with Capitalism to redefine Government."* https://www.newsclick.in/How-Fascism-Has-Converged-With-Capitalism-Redefine-Government

[272] Yuen Yuen Ang, *"The Clash of Two Gilded Ages."* https://www.noemamag.com/the-clash-of-two-gilded-ages/; Martin Arnold, *"Eurozone's long-stagnating wages start to rise as cost of living soars."* https://www.ft.com/content/2c555bc7-4285-44bb-88cb-c2489e1f8304; Lawrence Mishel[66], Elise Gould[67], and Josh Bivens[68], *"Wage Stagnation in Nine Charts."* https://www.epi.org/publication/charting-wage-stagnation/

[273] Bruce N. Waller, *The Deep Roots of American Neoliberalism.* (2022)

---

66. https://www.epi.org/people/lawrence-mishel/

67. https://www.epi.org/people/elise-gould/

68. https://www.epi.org/people/josh-bivens/

[274] Waddell, B. (2001) *"Limiting national interventionism in the United States: the warfare-welfare state as a restrictive government paradigm." Capital and class,* Vol. 74, pp. 109-140; Christopher Sims, *"The Misdirection of Military Keynesianism."* https://defenceindepth.co/2018/12/03/the-misdirection-of-military-keynesianism/

[275] James Cypher, *"From Military Keynesianism to Global-Neoliberal Militarism"* Monthly Review. https://monthlyreview.org/2007/06/01/from-military-keynesianism-to-global-neoliberal-militarism/

[276] Max Losche, *"How has Neoliberalism influenced US foreign politics?"*

https://www.diva-portal.org/smash/get/diva2:317574/FULLTEXT01.pdf

[277] James Cypher, *"The Political Economy of US Systemic Militarism."* https://jussemper.org/Resources/Economic%20Data/Resources/JamesCypher-USMilitarism.pdf; David Ottaway, *"Saudi Arabia Faces the Missing 28 Pages."* https://www.wilsoncenter.org/publication/saudi-arabia-faces-the-missing-28-pages

[278] Francesca Lucia Bray, *"Neoliberalism and Empire: The American Military-Industrial Complex,"* Journal of International Studies, 11 (2020); Michael Schwartz, *"Military Neoliberalism."* https://scholarlycommons.law.case.edu/cgi/viewcontent.cgi?article=1100&context=swb

[279] David Langwallner, *"Gradations of Evil: Neoliberalism and Neoconservatism"* https://cassandravoices.com/history/gradations-of-evil-neoliberalism-and-neoconservatism/; Jon Kofas, *"American Police-State Militarism and Gun Violence."* https://www.academia.edu/31278937/AMERICAN_POLICE_STATE_MILITARISM_AND_GUN_VIOLENCE; Center for Defense Information, *"Security After 9/11: Strategy Choices and Budget Tradeoffs."* https://www.files.ethz.ch/isn/28261/security-after-911.pdf; George Baca, *"Neoliberal narratives of crisis."* https://link.springer.com/article/10.1007/s10624-017-9474-5

[280] M.B. Steger and R.V. Roy, *"Three waves of neoliberalism."* in M.B. Steger and R.V. Roy *Neoliberalism* (2021)

[281] Kaelble, Hartmut, *"Social inequality in the 19th and 20th centuries."* https://www.ssoar.info/ssoar/bitstream/handle/document/34098/ssoar-1987-kaelble-

Social_inequality_in_the_19th.pdf;jsessionid=D2240EF4038474848ECD00D124DBA490?sequence=1; Walter LeFeber, *"The Tension between Democracy and Capitalism during the American Century."* Diplomatic History 23:2 (1999); Brian D. Palmer, *"Nineteenth Century Canada and Australia: The Paradoxes of Class Formation."* Labour / Le Travail 38 (1996)

[282] Allan C. Ornstein, *"Social Justice: History, Purpose and Meaning."* https://link.springer.com/article/10.1007/s12115-017-0188-8

[283] Larry Diamond, Marc F. Plattner, Yuan-han Chu, Hung-Mao Tien, eds. *Consolidating the Third Wave Democracies.* (1997).

[284] Samuel Huntington, *"The Third Wave. Democratization in the late twentieth century."* (1991); Anna Luhrmann and S.I. Lindberg, *"A third wave of autocratization is here: what is new about it?"* https://www.tandfonline.com/doi/full/10.1080/13510347.2019.1582029.

[285] Nils Gilman, Mandarins of the Future: Modernization Theory in Cold War America, 2007; Edward D. Gonzalez-Acosta, *"CENTRAL AMERICA - CAFTA and the U.S. Patron-Client Relationship with Dominican Republic and Central America. 24 May 2007."* http://www.alterinfos.org/spip.php?article1385; Rhoda H. Halperin, *Cultural Economies Past and Present*, 1994.

[286] G. Williams Domhoff, Myth of Liberal Ascendancy: Corporate Dominance from the Great Depression to the Great Recession, 2013.

[287] Joseph Schumpeter, *"Capitalism, Socialism and Democracy"* (1942); https://blogs.ubc.ca/justanothernumber/2011/01/13/schumpeter-and-the-elite-model-of-participatory-democracy/; Edward S. Herman and Noam Chomsky, *"Manufacturing Consent."* (1988).

[288] D.C. Tipps, *"Modernization Theory and Comparative Study of Societies."* https://www.brooklyn.cuny.edu/web/aca_socialsciences_polisci/150422_IA_Comps_Modernization-Theory-Comparative-Study-Of-Societies.pdf; Giovanni E. Reyes, *"Four Main Theories of Development: Modernization, Dependency. World System and Globalization".* Nómadas. Revista Crítica de Ciencias Sociales y Jurídicas | 04 (2001.2)

[289] Ankie Hoogvelt, *Globalization and the Postcolonial World: The New Political Economy of Development.* (2001); S. C. Chew, P. Lauderdale, *"The Development of Underdevelopment."* In: S. C. Chew, S.C. and P Lauderdale, eds. *Theory and Methodology of World Development. The Evolutionary Processes.* (2010).

[290] W.W. Rostow, *The Stages of Economic Growth: A Non-Communist Manifesto.* (1960).

[291] Raymond Lotta, *"World Economy and Great Power Rivalry: The Challenge to U.S. Global Dominance."* http://www.globalresearch.ca/world-economy-and-great-power-rivalry-the-challenge-to-u-s-global-dominance/9747.

[292] Nicholas Xenos, *"Democracy as Method: Joseph A. Schumpeter."* https://democracyjournalarchive.files.wordpress.com/2015/06/xenos_democracy-as-method-democracy-1-4_-oct-1981.pdf

[293] Michael Kennedy and Miguel Centeno, *"Internationalism and Global Transformations in American Sociology"* 680-85, in *Sociology in America: A History* ed. by Craig Calhoun, 2007.

[294] **Catherine Demangeot and Kizhekepat Sankaran, *"Cultural pluralism: Uncovering consumption patterns in a multicultural environment."* https://www.researchgate.net/publication/241731761_Cultural_pluralism_Uncovering_consumption_patterns_in_a_multicultural_environment; Kostis Kornetis, et al. eds. *Consumption and Gender in Southern Europe since the Long 1960s.* (2016); Guillermo A. O'Donnell, Philippe Schmitter and Laurence Whitehead, eds. *Transitions from authoritarian rule. Southern Europe.* (1986); Emma De Angelis and Eirini Karamouzi, *"Enlargement and the Historical Origins of the European Community's Democratic Identity, 1961–1978."***

https://www.researchgate.net/publication/

301277297_Enlargement_and_the_Historical_Origins_of_the_European_Community%27s_Democratic_Identity_1961-1978.

[295] Antonio de Spinola, *Portugal e o futuro.* (1974); Raquel Varela, *"Today we celebrate the Carnation Revolution"*; https://www.jacobinmag.com/2019/04/portugal-carnation-revolution-national-liberation-april

[296] McDonald, Robert. "The Colonel's Dictatorship". In *Background to Contemporary Greece,*

edited by Marion Sarafis and Martin Eve. London: Merlin Press, 1990; Jon V. Kofas, *Under the Eagle's Claw; Exceptionalism in US-Greek Relations.* (2003), Ch. 3.

[297] Kofas, *"Under the Eagle's Claw,"* Ch. 3; Louie Dean Valencia-García[69], *"Pluralism at the Twilight of Franco's Spain: Antifascist and Intersectional Practice.*[70]" https://brill.com/view/journals/fasc/9/1-2/article-p98_98.xml?language=en

[298] **Nicos Poulantzas, *"The Crisis of the Dictatorships"* (1976); Jon Kofas, *Independence from America: Global Integration and Inequality.* (2005) Ch. 2, 3, 4; Alexandre Guedes Viana, Patricia Elena Cunha, *"The Swedish model: an alternative to macroeconomic policy."* https://www.scielo.br/j/rep/a/tPDjQgDJpZV4PwTVxR6p6xz/**

[299] **Mark Franklin, Michael Marsh and Lauren McLaren, *"Uncorking the Bottle: Popular Opposition to European Unification in the Wake of Maastricht."* Journal of Common Market Studies. 32:4, (1994).**

[300] F. A. Lopez, et al eds, *Transitions from Dictatorships to Democracy,* 2016.

[301] Andre Abner, *"Capital Inflows to Greece, Spain, Portugal and Ireland: A Sector-Level View."* International Finance, 16, 3, (2013); https://data.worldbank.org/indicator/BX.KLT.DINV.WD.GD.ZS?locations=GR; https://data.worldbank.org/indicator/BX.KLT.DINV.WD.GD.ZS?locations=ES; https://data.worldbank.org/indicator/BX.KLT.DINV.WD.GD.ZS?locations=PT

[302] Konstantinos Myrodias, *"The Eurozone crisis and the 'intermediate' economies: The*

Political Economies of Greece and Portugal."

http://etheses.lse.ac.uk/4308/1/Myrodias__Eurozone-crisis-intermediate-economies.pdf

[303] Antonio Sergio, *"Is Germany Paying for Southern Europe?"*

69. https://brill.com/search?f_0=author&q_0=Louie+Dean+Valencia-Garc%C3%ADa

70. *https://brill.com/view/journals/fasc/9/1-2/article-p98_98.xml?rskey=L8UEcm&result=1*

https://www.opendemocracy.net/en/openeconomy/is-germany-paying-for-southern-europe/; Hasan Bakir, Görkem Bahtiyar, S. Isik, *"Political Economy of the Eurozone Debt Crisis"*

https://dergipark.org.tr/tr/download/article-file/228092

[304] Martin J. Rhodes, Rachel Epstein, Tanja A. Borzel, *"Introduction: peripheries in competition? Political and economic development in the EU."* https://www.tandfonline.com/doi/abs/10.1080/01402382.2019.1609195

[305] Stephanie Bonhomme, at al., *"Inequality in Europe: What Can Be Done? What Should Be Done?"* http://archive.intereconomics.eu/year/2013/6/inequality-in-europe-what-can-be-done-what-should-be-done/; James Wickham, *Unequal Europe: Social Divisions in an Old Continent,* 2016. For in-depth analysis of the patron-client model, see Kofas, *Independence from America.*

[306] CREMed, *"Euro-Mediterranean Trade Integration and its Relationship to Trade Liberalisation Processes."* https://www.iemed.org/publication/euro-mediterranean-trade-integration-and-its-relationship-to-trade-liberalisation-processes/; Simon Neaime, *"The Effects of European Austerity Measures on the South and East Mediterranean Countries."* https://www.iemed.org/publication/the-effects-of-european-austerity-measures-on-the-south-and-east-mediterranean-countries/#_ftn2

[307] Μαίρυλιν Κορκοβήλου, *Το κόμμα-εγκληματική οργάνωση και το Σύνταγμα. Η περίπτωση της Χρυσής Αυγής στην Ελλάδα. (The political party-criminal organization and the Constitution. The case of the Golden Dawn in Greece.)* https://amitos.library.uop.gr/xmlui/handle/123456789/2228; Nikos Hasapopoulos, *"Χρυσή Αυγή, η ιστορία, τα πρόσωπα και η αλήθεια."* [*Golden Dawn, history, people and the truth.*] (2013).

[308] **Susannah Verney, *"Euroscepticism in Southern Europe: A Diachronic Perspective."* https://www.tandfonline.com/doi/full/10.1080/13608746.2010.570124; Daphne Halikiopoulou, *"Economic Crisis, Poor Governance and the Rise of Populism: The Case of Greece"* https://www.intereconomics.eu/contents/year/2020/number/1/article/economic-crisis-poor-governance-and-the-rise-of-populism-the-case-of-greece.html; Alkman Granitsas, *"Previously Unknown Group Says I Shot Greek Extremists."* https://www.wsj.com/articles/previously-unknown-group-says-it-shot-greek-extremists-1384644127?tesla=y; Rocio Gil Grande, *"El programa de vox para 'reconquistar' Espana."* https://lab.rtve.es/las-claves/el-programa-de-vox-para-reconquistar-espana-2018-12-03/; Ethan J. vander Wilden. *"Ending the Spanish Exception: Explaining the Rise of Vox"* https://digitalcommons.colby.edu/cgi/viewcontent.cgi?article=1990&context=honorstheses**

[309] Ilaria Giglioli, *"Migration, Austerity and the Crisis at the Periphery in Europe."* http://www.otheringandbelonging.org/migration-austerity-and-crisis-at-the-periphery-of-europe/; Saaransh Mishra, *"Rising far-right, declining center-left, and the future of refugees in Europe."* https://www.orfonline.org/expert-speak/rising-far-right-declining-centre-left-future-refugees-europe/

[310] **Ambrose Evans Pritchard, *"Greece is being treated like a hostile occupied state."* http://www.telegraph.co.uk/finance/**

economics/11736779/Greece-is-being-treated-like-a-hostile-occupied-state.html.

[311] Patrick Saurin, *"La 'Crise grecque', une crise provoquée par les banques."* http://www.cadtm.org/La-Crise-grecque-une-crise; Christos Laskos, Euclid Tsakalotos, *Crucible of Resistance: Greece, the Eurozone & the World Economic Crisis.* (2013); P. Tsakloglu, G. Oikonomidis, G. Pagoulatos, Ch. Triantopoulos, A. Filippopoulos, *"Πώς Έφτασε Η Ελλάδα Στα Μνημόνια;"* [*How did Greece get to the Memorandum?*] https://www.dianeosis.org/2016/04/pos_ftasame_sta_mnimonia/

[312] Mark Blyth, *Austerity: The History of a Dangerous Idea.* (2013); Gareth Gory and Sudip Roy, *"German Banks Win Big from Spain's Bailout."* https://www.reuters.com/article/spain-germany-bailout-ifr/german-banks-win-big-from-spain-bailout-idINL6E8HTFC820120629; Thomas Fazi, *"The TROIKA saved banks and creditors, not Greece."* https://www.opendemocracy.net/en/can-europe-make-it/troika-saved-banks-and-creditors-not-greece/

[313] Heather Whitesde, *"Profiting off Austerity: Private Finance for Public Infrastructure."* https://www.degruyter.com/document/doi/10.3138/9781487515171-013/htmlDuncan Cameron, *"Who Profits from Austerity?"* https://rabble.ca/columnists/who-profits-austerity/; Miguel Martínez Lucio, Aristea Koukiadaki and Isabel Tavora, *"The legacy of Thatcherism in European labour relations: the impact of the politics of neo-liberalism and austerity on collective bargaining in a fragmenting Europe."* https://www.jstor.org/stable/10.13169/instemplrighj.2.1.0028#metadata_info_tab_contents; Cornel Ban, *"Dependent Development and Its Limits: Romania Capitalism after the Great Recession."*https://www.bu.edu/gdp/files/2018/12/GEGI-GDP.WP_.Dependent-Development-and-Limits.pdf;

[314] Jeffry Frieden and Stefanie Walter, *"Understanding the Political Economy of the Eurozone Crisis."* https://www.annualreviews.org/doi/10.1146/annurev-polisci-051215-023101#_i16; Dalphine Cavalier, *"Southern European (Italy, Spain, Portugal) Banks: Mirrors of Crisis"* https://economicresearch.bnpparibas.com/Views/DisplayPublication.aspx?type=document&IdPdf=24226

[315] Elias Isquith, *"Austerity is Americanizing European labor markets."* https://www.salon.com/2013/12/04/austerity_is_americanizing_european_labor_markets/

[316] Raquel Rego, et. al., *"The crisis impact of the political discourse of Portuguese social partners."* https://www.ics.ulisboa.pt/books/book2/ch07.pdf; Ingo Schmidt, *"The Downward March of Labor Halted: The Crisis of Capitalism and the Rethinking of the Working Classes."* https://www.researchgate.net/publication/260756776_The_Downward_March_of_Labor_Halted_The_Crisis_of_Neoliberal_Capitalism_and_the_Remaking_of_Working_Classes

[317] Miguel Martínez Lucio, Aristea Koukiadaki and Isabel Tavora, *"The legacy of Thatcherism in European labour relations: the impact of the politics of neo-liberalism and austerity on collective bargaining in a fragmenting Europe."* Institute of Employment Rights Journal. Vol. 2, No. 1 (2019); Brendan Skip Mark, *"Compliance with IMF Austerity: Labor Rights, Protest and Repression."*https://orb.binghamton.edu/cgi/viewcontent.cgi?article=1102&context=dissertation_and_theses; *Juan Pablo*

Bohoslavsky, "Financial institutions complicit in impact of austerity measures on human rights, says UN expert." https://www.ohchr.org/en/NewsEvents/Pages/DisplayNews.aspx?NewsID=24967&LangID=E

[318] Konstantinos Poulis, *"The Greek Left on a Rough Path of Realpolitik."* https://aspeniaonline.it/the-greek-left-on-the-rough-path-of-realpolitik/; Cesar Rendueles and Jorge Sola, *"The Rise of Podemos: Promises, Constraints and Dilemmas."* https://www.researchgate.net/publication/321150265_The_Rise_of_Podemos_Promises_Constraints_and_Dilemmas

[319] Takis Fotopoulos, *"Left mythology and neoliberal globalization: Syriza and Podemos"* https://www.inclusivedemocracy.org/journal/vol11/vol11_no1_Left_mythology_and_neoliberal_globalization_Syriza_and_Podemos.html; Diego Lotito, "*SYRIZA and PODEMOS: A Necessary Balance Sheet."* https://www.leftvoice.org/syriza-and-podemos-a-necessary-balance-sheet/

[320] Carlos de la Torre, *"In the Name of the People: Democratization, Popular Organizations, and Populism in Venezuela, Bolivia, and Ecuador."* https://www.jstor.org/stable/23595691?seq=1#metadata_info_tab_contents

[321] Diego Lotito and Josefina L. Martinez, *"Syriza and Podemos: A Necessary Balance Sheet."* https://www.leftvoice.org/syriza-and-podemos-a-necessary-balance-sheet/; Belen Fernandez-Garcia, *"The Triumph of (Underlying) Ideology Over Populism in Western Europe"* https://www.frontiersin.org/articles/10.3389/fpos.2021.667320/full

[322] Cas Mudde, *"Nothing Left? In Search Of [a new] Social Democracy."* https://www.socialeurope.eu/a-new-social-democracy

[323] Gerasimos Livitsanos, *"ΣΥΡΙΖΑ και ΝΑΤΟ... το ίδιο συνδικάτο."[SYRIZA and NATO...the same syndicate]* https://www.imerodromos.gr/syriza-kai-nato-to-idio-syndikato/; Tad Tietze. *"The Failed Strategy"* Strategyhttps://www.jacobinmag.com/2015/08/syriza-referendum-podemos-austerity/; Cas Mudde, *"Podemos, and the beginning of the end for Europe's radical left.*[71] https://www.theguardian.com/commentisfree/2015/dec/21/podemos-europe-radical-left-party-syriza-pablo-iglesias-spanish-elections; NATO, Public Diplomacy Division, *"Defence Expenditure of NATO Countries (2013-2020."* https://www.nato.int/nato_static_fl2014/assets/pdf/2021/3/pdf/210316-pr-2020-30-en.pdf

[324] Sofia Sakorafa, "*SYRIZA let us down - but we can still end austerity.*" https://www.jacobinmag.com/2019/11/diem25-mera25-syriza-greek-elections-european-union; Andres Gil, *"Pablo Iglesias apoyará a Alexis Tsipras en el mitin central de Syriza"*, El diario (16 September 2015), www.eldiario.es/politica/pablo-iglesias-participara-tsipras-atenas_1_2485533.html[72]; Oscar Rickett, *"From latte socialist to gauche caviar – how to spot good-time leftwingers around the world."* https://www.theguardian.com/politics/shortcuts/2017/oct/23/latte-socialist-gauche-caviar-how-spot-good-time-

---

71. https://www.jacobinmag.com/2015/08/syriza-referendum-podemos-austerity/;%20Cas%20Mudde,%20

72. https://www.eldiario.es/politica/pablo-iglesias-participara-tsipras-atenas_1_2485533.html

leftwingers-around-world

[325] Nuria Font[73], Paolo Graziano[74] and Myrto Tsakatika[75] *"Varieties of Inclusionary Populism? SYRIZA, Podemos and the Five Star Movement."* https://www.cambridge.org/core/journals/government-and-opposition/article/varieties-of-inclusionary-populism-syriza-podemos-and-the-five-star-movement/2DA84524E62A5BA84656D0D10AD33E68; Joe Galbo, *"Making Sense of Italian Populism."* http://www.alternateroutes.ca/index.php/ar/article/download/22508/18300/

[326] Michael Dauderstädt, *"Cohesive Growth in Europe: A Tale of Two Peripheries."* https://www.intereconomics.eu/contents/year/2021/number/2/article/cohesive-growth-in-europe-a-tale-of-two-peripheries.html; Eshe Nelson, *"Italy's economy is barely bigger than it was back in 2000."* https://qz.com/757016/italys-economy-is-barely-bigger-than-it-was-way-back-in-2000/

[327] Eurostat, *"Government debt down to 93% of GDP in euro area."* https://ec.europa.eu/eurostat/documents/2995521/15725185/2-23012023-AP-EN.pdf/02f734a3-f3fe-df4d-db84-f1671933a5c6

[328] Mauro Serapioni and Pedro Hespanha, *"Crisis and Austerity in Southern Europe"* Centro de Estudios Sociais da Universidad de Coimbra (2019; BNP Paribas *"Southern Europe: Why such low growth potential?"* https://economic-research.bnpparibas.com/Views/DisplayPublication.aspx?type=document&IdPdf=39584; Kenneth Roberts, *"Populism and Polarization in Comparative Perspective: Constitutive, Spatial and Institutional Dimensions."* https://www.cambridge.org/core/journals/government-and-opposition/article/populism-and-polarization-in-comparative-perspective-constitutive-spatial-and-institutional-dimensions/460EFC95AE70DC5A4AAFF21D437B58D6.

[329] Bastiaan van Apeldoorn, *"The European Capitalist Class and the Crisis of its Hegemonic Project."* https://www.researchgate.net/publication/263425045_The_European_Capitalist_Class_and_the_Crisis_of_its_Hegemonic_Project; Chris Marsden *"What does the euro mean for the working class?"* https://www.wsws.org/en/articles/2002/01/euro-j08.html

[330] **Renato Miguel do Carmo[76] and Ana Rita Matias[77], *"Income inequality in Portugal and in Europe: the impact of austerity?"* https://www.observatorio-das-desigualdades.com/2014/06/12/income-inequality-in-portugal-and-in-europe-the-impact-of-austerity-by-renato-miguel-do-carmo-e-ana-rita-matias/?print=print; Tao Papaioannou[78], Suman Gupta[79], *Media***

---

73. https://www.cambridge.org/core/search?filters%5BauthorTerms%5D=Nuria%20Font&eventCode=SE-AU

74. https://www.cambridge.org/core/search?filters%5BauthorTerms%5D=Paolo%20Graziano&eventCode=SE-AU

75. https://www.cambridge.org/core/search?filters%5BauthorTerms%5D=Myrto%20Tsakatika&eventCode=SE-AU

76. http://www.cies.iscte.pt/investigadores/ficha.jsp?pkid=295

77. http://www.cies.iscte.pt/investigadores/ficha.jsp?pkid=549&a=-1591662683&subarea=todos

***Representations of Anti-Austerity Protests in the EU Grievances, Identities and Agency.* (2018); Jolle Demmers, Sameer S. Mehendale, *"Neoliberal Xenophobia: The Dutch Case."* https://www.researchgate.net/publication/48317999_Neoliberal_Xenophobia_The_Dutch_Case**

[331] Daniele Grasso and Montse Hidalgo Perez, *"The Pandora Papers: Secret files from 14 law firms reveal more than 700 offshore companies linked to Spain."* https://english.elpais.com/usa/2021-10-03/the-pandora-papers-secret-files-from-14-law-firms-reveal-more-than-700-offshore-companies-linked-to-spain.html

[332] Klára Bakk-Simon, et al., *"Shadow Banking in the Euro Area: An Overview."* https://www.ecb.europa.eu/pub/pdf/scpops/ecbocp133.pdf; Lucie Middlemiss and Ross Gillard, *"Fuel poverty from the bottom-up: Characterising household energy vulnerability through the lived experience of the fuel poor."* https://www.sciencedirect.com/science/article/pii/S2214629615000213; Susana Narotzky, *"Grassroots Economies: Living with Austerity in Southern Europe."* (2020)

[333] Derek Thompson, *"Nearly 50% of the Young People in Greece and Spain Are Unemployed."* https://www.theatlantic.com/business/archive/2011/11/nearly-50-of-the-young-people-in-greece-and-spain-are-unemployed/249286/; Werner Eichhorst and Franziska Neder, *"Youth Unemployment in the Mediterranean Countries."* https://docs.iza.org/pp80.pdf

[334] Enrico Padoan, *Anti-Liberal Populisms in Comparative Perspectives.* (2021); Sofia Perez and Manos Matsaganis, *"The Political Economy of Austerity in Southern Europe"*. https://www.researchgate.net/publication/319600397_The_Political_Economy_of_Austerity_in_Southern_Europe

[335] Tim Bale Cristobal Rovira Kaltwasser, *"What has happened to western Europe's centre right?"* https://theconversation.com/what-has-happened-to-western-europes-centre-right-169849; Nathalie Brack[80], Nicholas Startin[81], *"Introduction: Euroscepticism, from the margins to the mainstream."* https://journals.sagepub.com/doi/full/10.1177/0192512115577231?cookieSet=1; Yves Bertoncini and Nicole Koenig *"Euroscepticism or Europhobia: Voice vs. Exit."* https://institutdelors.eu/wp-content/uploads/2018/01/euroscepticismoreurophobia-bertoncini-koenig-ne-jdi-nov14.pdf

[336] Jessica Quirk, *"Has neoliberal globalization contributed to growing levels of nationalism across Europe?"* https://openjournals.library.usyd.edu.au/index.php/ANZJES/article/download/15857/13856; Colin Hay, *"Brexit and the (Multiple) Paradoxes of Neoliberalism."* http://sase.org/wp-content/uploads/2018/04/1-Hay-final.pdf;

[337] Jan Erik Grindheim, *"Why Right-Leaning Populism has Grown in the Most Advanced Liberal Democracies of Europe"* https://onlinelibrary.wiley.com/doi/full/10.1111/1467-923X.12765; https://www.brookings.edu/blog/order-from-chaos/2018/03/

---

78. https://www.routledge.com/search?author=Tao%20Papaioannou

79. https://www.routledge.com/search?author=Suman%20Gupta

80. https://journals.sagepub.com/doi/full/10.1177/0192512115577231

81. https://journals.sagepub.com/doi/full/10.1177/0192512115577231

08/the-rise-of-european-populism-and-the-collapse-of-the-center-left/; Nina Obermeir, *"Right-Wing Populism and the Rise of Internationalism in Europe."* https://www.internationalpoliticaleconomysociety.org/sites/default/files/paper-uploads/2021-10-13-00_34_00-keo44@cornell.edu.pdf; Nick Ferris, *"The UK is facing two lost decades for living standards."* https://www.newstatesman.com/chart-of-the-day/2022/03/the-uk-is-facing-two-lost-decades-for-living-standards

[338] David Dawkins, *"Europe's Billionaires are $1 Trillion Richer Than A Year Ago."* https://www.forbes.com/sites/daviddawkins/2021/04/06/europes-billionaires-are-1-trillion-richer-than-a-year-ago/; Perry Anderson, *The New Old World.* (2011); George Souvlis, *"The Antinomies of Perry Anderson"* https://www.jacobinmag.com/2020/08/perry-anderson-marxist-historian; https://www.statista.com/statistics/546486/people-at-risk-of-poverty-in-the-eu/

[339] Max Bergmann, *"Europe's Lost Decade Demands a Progressive Response."* https://www.americanprogress.org/article/europes-lost-decade-demands-progressive-response/

[340] Susan Milner[82], Andrew Mathers, Graham Taylor, *"Euroscepticism and Trade Unionism: The Crisis of 'Social Europe."* https://uwe-repository.worktribe.com/OutputFile/883391

[341] Grigoris Markou, *"The Defeat of Inclusionary Populism in Greece."* https://www.opendemocracy.net/en/can-europe-make-it/defeat-of-inclusionary-populism-in-greece-what-happens-next-0/; Saaransh Mishra, *"Rising far-right, declining centre-left, and the future of refugees in Europe"* https://www.orfonline.org/expert-speak/rising-far-right-declining-centre-left-future-refugees-europe/

[342] William S. Smith, *"Samuel Huntington was not like Steve Bannon."* https://css.cua.edu/ideas_and_commentary/samuel-huntington-was-not-like-steve-bannon/; Emad El-Din Aysha, *"Samuel Huntington and the Geopolitics of American Identity."* https://www.researchgate.net/publication/
229733291_Samuel_Huntington_and_the_Geopolitics_of_American_Identity_The_Function_of_Foreign_Policy_in_America%27s_Domest
Carlos Lozada, *"Samuel Huntington, a prophet for the Trump era."* https://www.washingtonpost.com/news/book-party/wp/2017/07/18/samuel-huntington-a-prophet-for-the-trump-era/

[343] A. Abushouk, *"The Arab Spring: A fourth wave democratization."* https://www.semanticscholar.org/paper/The-Arab-Spring%3A-A-Fourth-Wave-of-Democratization-Abushouk/5ff7a824fecda8529e30dd9cd856fa455ce1ab87.

[344] Heather Brown Emily Guskin, and Amy Mitchell, *"The Role of Social Media in the Arab Uprisings."* https://www.pewresearch.org/journalism/2012/11/28/role-social-media-arab-uprisings/; Gadi Wolfsfeld, Elad Segev, and Tamir Sheafe, *"Social Media and the Arab Spring: Social Media and the Arab Spring: Politics Comes First."* https://journals.sagepub.com/doi/pdf/10.1177/1940161212471716

[345] Shadi Hamid, *"The Struggle for Middle East Democracy."* https://www.brookings.edu/articles/the-struggle-for-middle-east-democracy/

---

82. https://researchportal.bath.ac.uk/en/persons/susan-milner

[346] Seumas Milne, *"The 'Arab Spring' and the west: seven lessons from history."* https://www.theguardian.com/commentisfree/2011/dec/19/arab-spring-seven-lessons-from-history

[347] Oz Hassan, *"Undermining the transatlantic democracy agenda? The Arab Spring and Saudi Arabia's counteracting democracy strategy."* https://www.tandfonline.com/doi/pdf/10.1080/13510347.2014.981161

[348] Nils Naumann and Julia Elvers-Guyot[83], *"Tunisia's Ousted President Zine El-Abidine Ben Ali: A Robber Baron in Disguise."* https://thewire.in/world/tunisias-ousted-president-zine-el-abidine-ben-ali-a-robber-baron-in-disguise; Stephen Zunes, *"US Backs Tunisian Dictatorship in the Face of Pro-Democracy Uprising."* https://www.huffpost.com/entry/us-backs-tunisian-dictato_b_808886

[349] Joseph N. Agbo and Jonathan O. Chimakonam, *"Democratizing in Excess: A Marxist Interpretation of the Jasmine Revolutions in North Africa"* UFAHAMU: Journal of African Studies, https://escholarship.org/uc/item/7855m1sc

[350] Hamed El-Said and Jane Harrigan, *"Economic Reform, Social Welfare, and Instability: Jordan, Egypt, Morocco, and Tunisia, 1983–2004."* https://www.researchgate.net/publication/263196522_Economic_Reform_Social_Welfare_and_Instability_Jordan_Egypt_Morocco_and_Tunisia_1983-2004; Mhamed Biygautane, Mohammed Lahuel, *"The Political Economy of Privatization in the Maghreb Region."* https://mbrsgcdn.azureedge.net/cmsstorage/mbrsg/files/26/266843a6-409c-4526-9fd1-931ac5a84f5c.pdf

[351] Koen Bogaert, *"Global dimensions of the Arab Spring and the potential for anti-hegemonic politics."* https://www.academia.edu/1402376/Global_dimensions_of_the_Arab_Spring_and_thepotential_for_anti_hegemonic_politics

[352] Jethro Norman, *"Neoliberal Globalization and Arab Spring."* https://www.e-ir.info/pdf/51946; Youssef Khalil, *"Neoliberalism and the Failure of Arab Spring."* https://newpol.org/issue_post/neoliberalism-and-failure-arab-spring/

[353] Manochehr Dorraj[84], *"Populism and Corporatism in the Middle East and North Africa: a Comparative Analysis."* https://link.springer.com/article/10.1007/s41111-017-0072-0

[354] Philip Murphy, *"Churchill and India: imperial chauvinism left a bitter legacy."* https://theconversation.com/churchill-and-india-imperial-chauvinism-left-a-bitter-legacy-36452

[355] C. Michelle Kleisath, *"The Costume of Shangri-La: Thoughts on White Privilege, Cultural Appropriation, and Anti-Asia Racism."* https://www.potsdam.edu/sites/default/files/Thoughts.pdf; Daniel Lerner, *The Passing of Traditional Society: Modernizing the Middle East.* (1958); Hermant Shah, *The Production of Modernization: Daniel Lerner, Mass Media and the Passing of Traditional Society*, 2011; Terry Maley, *Democracy and the Political in Max Weber's Thought.* (2011).

83. https://thewire.in/author/nils-naumann-julia-elvers-guyot

84. https://link.springer.com/article/10.1007/s41111-017-0072-0#auth-Manochehr-Dorraj

[356] Ahmed Abushouk, *"The Arab Spring: A Fourth Wave of Democratization?"* https://www.researchgate.net/publication/301672188_The_Arab_Spring_A_Fourth_Wave_of_Democratization_The_Arab_Spring

[357] Said Amir Arjomand, ed. *The Arab Revolution of 2011: A Comparative Perspective*, (2015), 233-35; Geoffb Brown, *"Pakistan, failing state or neoliberal crisis?"* http://isj.org.uk/pakistan-failing-state-or-neoliberalism-in-crisis/.

[358] Henner Fürtig, *"Iran and the Arab Spring: Between Expectations and Disillusion."* https://www.econstor.eu/bitstream/10419/87741/1/772038554.pdf; Kurt Weyland, *"The Arab Spring: Why the Surprising Similarities with the Revolutionary Wave of 1848?"* https://www.researchgate.net/publication/259429426_The_Arab_Spring_Why_the_Surprising_Similarities_with_the_Revolutionary_Wave_of_1848;

[359] Cæcilie Lyndgaard Andersen, *"The Arab Spring - in Egypt."* http://projekter.aau.dk/projekter/en/studentthesis/the-arab-spring—in-egypt%283c923170-55d5-4190-b469-744f5e79d4d6%29; html[85]; Nadine Naber, *"Women and the Arab Spring: Human Rights from the Ground up."* https://www.peacewomen.org/assets/file/women_in_the_arab_spring-human_rights_from_the_ground_up.pdf; Nader Hashemi, *"The Arab Spring Two Years On,"* http://www.ethicsandinternationalaffairs.org/2013/the-arab-spring-two-years-on-reflections-on-dignity-democracy-and-devotion-full-text/; Thomas Torp, *"Why Divide and Rule Survived Arab Spring."* https://institute.global/policy/why-divide-and-rule-survived-arab-spring.

[360] Kamal Dib, *"Predator Neoliberalism: Lebanon on the Brink of Disaster."* https://www.researchgate.net/publication/339878502_Predator_Neoliberalism_Lebanon_on_the_Brink_of_Disaster; Kareem Chehayeb, *"Lebanon Is the Experiment That Shows Neoliberalism's Failure."* https://tcf.org/content/commentary/lebanon-experiment-shows-neoliberalisms-failure/?agreed=1; https://www.hrw.org/world-report/2022/country-chapters/lebanon

[361] Samir Amin, *The Reawakening of the Arab World: Challenge and Change in the Aftermath of the Arab Spring.* (2016)

[362] Aaron Maté, *"Al Qaeda is on our side': how Obama/Biden team empowered terrorist networks in Syria."* https://mronline.org/2022/04/23/al-qaeda-is-on-our-side/; Peter Bartu and Maurice Ruttimann, *"North East Syria: The Good, the Bad and the Oil."* https://www.internationalaffairs.org.au/australianoutlook/north-east-syria-the-good-the-bad-the-oil/

[363] M. A. Mohamed Salih, *Economic Development and Political Action in the Arab World*, (2014); Fatima al-Samak, Islam and Democracy: An Obscure Relationship, in http://www.al-islam.org/articles/islam-and-democracy-an-obscure-relationship-fatima-al-samak; M. K. Bhadrakumar[86] *"Ten years on, Syria is almost destroyed. Who's to blame?"* https://mronline.org/2021/03/22/ten-years-

85. http://projekter.aau.dk/projekter/en/studentthesis/the-arab-spring--in-egypt%283c923170-55d5-4190-b469-744f5e79d4d6%29;%20html

86. https://mronline.org/author/mkbhadrakumar/

on-syria-is-almost-destroyed-whos-to-blame/; UNHCR, *"Eleven years on mounting challenges push many displaced Syrians to the brink."* https://www.unhcr.org/news/briefing/2022/3/623055174/eleven-years-mounting-challenges-push-displaced-syrians-brink.html

[364] Shamiran Mako M.V. Moghadam, *After the Arab Uprisings.* (2021) Ch. IV

[365] Mostafa El Sharka[87], *"Soldiers of God: The Muslim Brotherhood and Egyptian Democracy."* http://yris.yira.org/essays/5475; Amr[88] Mohammed Kandil, *"Why Muslim Brotherhood's Morsi Failed to Complete the Revolution."* https://www.egypttoday.com/Article/1/72268/Why-Muslim-Brotherhood-s-Morsi-failed-to-complete-presidential-term Lee Sustar, *"Will Morsi Hijack the Revolution?"* https://socialistworker.org/2012/11/28/will-morsi-hijack-the-revolution.

[366] Mohamed Metawe, *"How and Why the West Reacted to the Arab Spring: An Arab Perspective."* https://www.insightturkey.com/file/397/how-and-why-the-west-reacted-to-the-arab-spring-an-arab-perspective-summer-2013-vol15-no3

[367] Mariela Cuadro, *"Islam, Democracia y Neoliberalismo: Los Hermanos Musulmanes Egipcios en el Poder."* http://www.scielo.org.mx/pdf/eaa/v51n3/2448-654X-eaa-51-03-00571.pdf; David Butter, *"Egypt and the Gulf."* https://www.chathamhouse.org/2020/04/egypt-and-gulf/sisis-debt-his-gulf-arab-backers; Ismail Numan Telci, *"Understanding Al-Sisi's Western-backed Oppression Policy."* https://www.orsam.org.tr/en/understanding-al-sisi-s-western-backed-oppression-policy/

[368] **Al-Jazeera, *"Egypt upholds life sentences for 10 Muslim Brotherhood figures."* https://www.aljazeera.com/news/2021/7/12/egypt-upholds-life-sentences-for-10-muslim-brotherhood-figures; *"Egypt and the Coup: Inside the 11 days that toppled Morsi."* https://www.middleeasteye.net/news/egypt-and-coup-inside-11-days-toppled-morsi; Abdel Fattah el-Sisi, *"Egypt under Sisi: Criticism not is accepted."* http://www.aljazeera.com/news/2015/06/egypt-sisi-criticism-accepted-150609102315807.html.**

Kenneth Ross, *"Egypt's Tiananmen"*, https://www.hrw.org/news/2014/08/12/egypts-tiananmen; http://www.worldbulletin.net/news-analysis/164428/how-long-will-el-sisi-commit-murder-of-democracy-in-egypt/

[369] *"US Unlocks Military Aid to Egypt, backing President Sisi"*

https://www.bbc.com/news/world-middle-east-27961933

[370] Mamdouh Habashi, *"Egypt 2016: Who was worse? Mubarak, Morsi or Sisi?"* https://mronline.org/2017/03/01/egypt-2016-who-was-worse-mubarak-morsi-or-sisi/

87. http://yris.yira.org/essays/5475

88. http://yris.yira.org/essays/5475;%20Amr

[371] Zeinab Abul-Magd, *"The Generals' Secret: Egypt's Ambivalent Market."* https://carnegieendowment.org/sada/47137; Lydia Assouad, *"Inequality and its Discontents in the Middle East."* https://carnegie-mec.org/2020/03/12/inequality-and-its-discontents-in-middle-east-pub-81266

[372] Maged Mandoor, *"Sisi's War on the Poor."* https://carnegieendowment.org/sada/82772; Sarah Smirciak, *Cronyism and Elite Capture in Egypt.* (2021).

[373] M. Hakan Yavuz[89] and Ahmet Erdi Öztürk[90], eds. *Islam, Populism and Regime Change in Turkey.* (2020); Karem Morgul, *"Beyond the inclusion–exclusion dichotomy in populism studies: Erdoğan's Muslim nationalist discourse on Syrian refugees."* https://www.researchgate.net/publication/
365753015_Beyond_the_inclusion-exclusion_dichotomy_in_populism_studies_Erdogan%27s_Muslim_nationalist_discourse_on_Syrian_ref

[374] Malek Lakhal, *"The ghost people and populism from above: the Kais Saied case."* https://www.arab-reform.net/publication/the-ghost-people-and-populism-from-above-the-kais-saied-case/ John Hursh, *"How Kais Said Betrayed Tunisia's Democratic Revolution."* https://dawnmena.org/how-kais-saied-betrayed-tunisias-democratic-revolution/.

[375] Seifeddine Ferjani, *'What Tunisia has become under Kais Faied."* https://dawnmena.org/what-tunisia-has-become-under-kais-saied/; https://ecfr.eu/publication/back-from-the-brink-a-better-way-for-europe-to-support-tunisias-democratic-transition/; Tarek Magerisi, *'Back from the Brink: A better way for Europe to support Tunisia's democratic transition.'* Al-Jazeera, *"Tunisian President sacks dozens of judges as he consolidates rule."* 'https://www.aljazeera.com/news/2022/6/2/tunisias-president-sacks-dozens-of-judges; Fikret Adaman, Bengi Akbulut, *"Erdogan's three-pillared neoliberalism: Authoritarianism, populism and developmentalism."* https://www.sciencedirect.com/science/article/abs/pii/S0016718519303513

[376] Reuters staff, *"From War room to boardroom: Military Firms Flourish in Sisi's Egypt."* https://www.reuters.com/investigates/special-report/egypt-economy-military/; Rula Jebreal, *It's Time for the US to Support Democracy, Not Dictatorship, in Egypt.* http://www.thenation.com/article/its-time-us-support-democracy-not-dictatorship-egypt/; Zeinab Abul-Magd *"Two Paths to Dominance: Military Businesses in Turkey and Egypt."* https://carnegie-mec.org/2020/06/03/two-paths-to-dominance-military-businesses-in-turkey-and-egypt-pub-81869; Osama Gaweesh, *"The crime in Sisi's Egypt is not being corrupt, it is exposing corruption.'* https://www.middleeastmonitor.com/20211214-the-crime-in-sisis-egypt-is-not-being-corrupt-it-is-exposing-corruption/; Chris Dite, Maha Ben Gadha, *"How the Exploitation of Africa Helps Fuel Global Capitalism."* https://www.cadtm.org/How-the-Exploitation-of-Africa-Helps-Fuel-Global-Capitalism

89. https://www.routledge.com/search?author=M.%20Hakan%20Yavuz

90. https://www.routledge.com/search?author=Ahmet%20Erdi%20Öztürk

[377] Margaret Crable, *"Ten Years after the Arab Spring."* https://dornsife.usc.edu/news/stories/3489/10-years-after-the-arab-spring/; Lazae Berman, *"How Israel Kept the Arab Spring from becoming the Winter of its Discontent."* https://www.timesofisrael.com/how-israel-kept-the-arab-spring-from-becoming-the-winter-of-its-discontent/

[378] Houssem Ben Lazreg, *"Post-Islamism in Tunisia and Egypt: Contradictory Trajectories" https://www.researchgate.net/publication/352101859_Post-Islamism_in_Tunisia_and_Egypt_Contradictory_Trajectories*;

Irene Weipert Fenner and Jonas Wolff, *"Socioeconomic Protests and Political Transformation."* https://www.researchgate.net/project/Socioeconomic-Protests-and-Political-Transformation-Dynamics-of-Contentious-Politics-in-Egypt-and-Tunisia-Against-the-Background-of-South-American-Experiences.

[379] Michael Bellon, *"Rashid Benzine: On Women and the Revolution."* http://www.bruzz.be/en/stage/rachid-benzine-women-and-revolution; Rachid Benzine, *Les nouveaux penseurs de l'islam,* 2004.

[380] Roel Meijer, *"The Problem of the Political in Islamist Movements."* https://www.clingendael.org/sites/default/files/2016-02/20120000_meijer_whatever_happened_to_the_islamists.pdf; Agbo & Chimakonam, *"Democratizing in Excess" op. cit;* Gholam Khiabany, *"Arab Revolutions and the Iranian Uprising: Similarities and Differences"* Middle East Journal of Culture and Communication. (January 2012).

[381] Osama Abi-Mershed, *Apostles of Modernity: Saint Simonians and the Civilizing Mission in Algeria* (2010); Ruhul Amin, *"Domination of European Culture all Over the World."* https://digitalcommons.uncfsu.edu/cgi/viewcontent.cgi?article=1206&context=jrihttps://digitalcommons.uncfsu.edu/cgi/viewcontent.cgi?article=1206&context=jri.

[382] Neil Davidson, *"Islam and the Enlightenment."* https://socialistworker.co.uk/socialist-review-archive/islam-and-enlightenment/

[383] Ahmed Bensaada, Arabesque: Enquête sur le rôle des États-Unis dans les révoltes arabes. (2015).

[384] **Irene Weippert-Fenner and Jonas Wolff, *"Socioeconomic Protests and Political Transformation: Dynamics of Contentious Politics in Egypt and Tunisia Against the Background of South American Experiences."* in Laura Ruiz de Elvira[91], Christoph Schwarz[92], Irene Weipert-Fenner[93], eds. *Clientelism and Patronage in the Middle East and North Africa.* (2018).**

[385] RAGIP GÖKÇEL, EUGEN Lungu, *"Pan-Arabism and the Arab Spring."* https://www.researchgate.net/publication/260203557_PAN-ARABISM_AND_THE_ARAB_SPRING

[386] **Patricia Zengerle[94], *"U.S. military aid for Egypt seen continuing despite rights concerns."***

http://www.reuters.com/article/us-egypt-usa-aid-idUSKCN0T22E520151113; Charles Tiefer, *"US Resumes Military Aid to Egypt, reports show how little we know on how it's being used."* http://www.forbes.com/sites/charlestiefer/2015/04/07/us-military-aid-for-al-sisi-in-egypt-state-dept-fails-to-review/#9a093236c7f3[95]

[387] Afshin Molavi, *"China's economic impact in the Arab world has soared since the Arab Spring but jobs haven't."* Quartz Africa (2020). https://qz.com/africa/1947343/chinas-impact-since-arab/

[388] Gerard Epstein, *"The Financial Crisis of 2023: Protecting Big Finance Coming and Going."* https://www.ineteconomics.org/perspectives/blog/the-financial-crisis-of-2023-protecting-big-finance-coming-and-going; Luiz Carlos Bresser-Pereira, *"The Global Financial Crisis and a New Capitalism?"* https://www.levyinstitute.org/pubs/wp_592.pdf

[389] Per H. Hansen, *"From Finance Capitalism to Financialization: A Cultural and Narrative Perspective on 150 Years of Financial History."*

https://www.researchgate.net/publication/274623203_From_Finance_Capitalism_to_Financialization_A_Cultural_and_Narrative_Perspective_on_150_Years_

[390] **T. I. Palley, *"Financialization: What it is and Why it Matters"*. https://www.levyinstitute.org/pubs/wp_525.pdf; Ronald Dore, *"Financialization of the global economy".* Industrial and Corporate Change, 17:6 (2008), https://doi.org/10.1093/icc/dtn041; Olivier Godechot, *Financialization Is Marketization! A Study of the Respective Impacts of Various Dimensions of Financialization on the Increase in Global Inequality."* https://sociologicalscience.com/articles-v3-22-495/**

[391] Guoping Li and Hong Zhou, "*Globalization of Financial Capitalism and its Impact on Financial Sovereignty."* https://wapescholar.pure.elsevier.com/ws/portalfiles/portal/8604993/Globalization_of_Financial_Capitalism_and_Its_Impact_on_Financial.pdf; Kristine Plys, *"Financialization, Crisis, and the Development of Capitalism in the USA."* https://wapescholar.pure.elsevier.com/ws/portalfiles/

91. https://www.routledge.com/search?author=Laura%20Ruiz%20de%20Elvira

92. https://www.routledge.com/search?author=Christoph%20Schwarz

93. https://www.routledge.com/search?author=Irene%20Weipert-Fenner

94. https://www.reuters.com/journalists/patricia-zengerle

95. http://www.forbes.com/sites/charlestiefer/2015/04/07/us-military-aid-for-al-sisi-in-egypt-state-dept-fails-to-review/#a5c02393e59c943d6a75a9241140faca39a093236c7f3

portal/8604846/
Financialization_Crisis_and_the_Development_of_Capitalism_in_the_USA_Kristin_Plys.pdf; Kang-Kook Lee and MD Abu Bakkar Siddique, *"Financialization and Income Inequality."* https://www.tandfonline.com/doi/abs/10.1080/2329194X.2021.1945465

[392] Marc Quintyn and M.W. Taylor, *"Should Financial Sector Regulators be Independent?"* https://www.imf.org/external/pubs/ft/issues/issues32/

[393] Petra Dünhaupt, "The effect of financialization on labor's share of income." https://www.econstor.eu/bitstream/10419/68475/1/734374437.pdf

[394] Max Zahn, *"CEO pay with workers widened at low-paying companies in 2021."* https://abcnews.go.com/Business/ceo-pay-gap-workers-widened-low-paying-companies/story?id=85233479

[395] Jonathan Michie, *"The degeneration of capitalism from a system of production to a speculative orgy."* https://www.tandfonline.com/doi/full/10.1080/02692171.2020.1720164; Gerald F. Davis and Suntae Kim, *"Financialization of the Economy."* The Annual Review of Sociology. 41, (2015). Jonathan Michie, *"The degeneration of capitalism from a system of production to a speculative orgy."* https://www.tandfonline.com/doi/full/10.1080/02692171.2020.1720164

[396] Andrew Ross Sorkin and Loren Hirsch *"New Questions About Goldman Sachs's Work With Silicon Valley Bank."* https://www.nytimes.com/2023/03/15/business/goldman-svb-silicon-valley-bank.html

[397] Costas Lapavitsas, *The Financialization of Capitalism: 'Profiting without producing'* http://www.tandfonline.com/doi/full/10.1080/13604813.2013.853865

[398] Adil Abdela and Marshall Steibaum, *"The United States has a Market Concentration Problem."* https://www.ftc.gov/system/files/documents/public_comments/2018/09/ftc-2018-0074-d-0042-155544.pdf; Shelly Gottfried, *"Contemporary Oligarchies in Developed Democracies."* (2019).

[399] Haleyluya Hadero, *"A growing worry for charities: Tax havens for the rich."* https://apnews.com/article/business-philanthropy-b8acb10f529ac2dbaff7631021d823c9

[400] Trilochan Sastry, *"Exploring the role of business in society."* https://www.sciencedirect.com/science/article/pii/S097038961100098X; CADTM, "Concentration of wealth in the hands of the 1%" http://www.cadtm.org/Concentration-of-wealth-in-the-hands-of-the-1; Juliana Kaplan and Madison Hoff, *"The bottom half of Americans hold 2% of the country's wealth - while the top 1% of families have a third."* https://www.businessinsider.com/bottom-half-americans-hold-2-percent-wealth-richest-have-third-2022-9; Lucas Chancel, et al. *"World Inequality Report, 2022."* https://wir2022.wid.world/www-site/uploads/2022/01/Summary_WorldInequalityReport2022_English.pdf.

[401] Zarco Paic, *"Neoliberalism, Oligarchy and Politics of the Event: At the Edge of Chaos."* (2020) https://www.cambridgescholars.com/product/978-1-5275-4478-9

[402]http://eurodad.org/uploadedfiles/whats_new/news/food%20speculation%202%20pager%20final.pdf

[403] Sharon Zhang, *"CEO Pay Has Grown by 1460 Since 1978 as Workers' Wages Stagnate."* https://truthout.org/articles/ceo-pay-has-grown-by-1460-percent-since-1978-as-workers-wages-stagnate/

[404] Amanda Fischer, *"The rising financiailization of the US economy harms workers."* https://equitablegrowth.org/the-rising-financialization-of-the-u-s-economy-harms-workers-and-their-families-threatening-a-strong-recovery/; C. J. Polychroniou, *"Financialization has turned the Global Economy into a House of Cards."* http://www.truth-out.org/opinion/item/41359-financialization-has-turned-the-global-economy-into-a-house-of-cards-an-interview-with-gerald-epstein; Costas Lapavitsas, *Financialization in Crisis*, (2013); Rona Foroohar, *Makers and Takers: How Wall Street Destroyed Main Street*, (2016)

[405] D. Gabor, *Central Banking and Financialization: A Romanian Account of how Eastern Europe became Subprime.* (2011); Shigeyuki Hattori[96], *"Financialization in Japan"*; https://www.researchgate.net/publication/338815898_Financialization_in_Japan

[406] Timo Walter, Leon Wansleben, *"How central bankers learned to love financialization: The Fed, the Bank, and the enlisting of unfettered markets in the conduct of monetary policy."* https://academic.oup.com/ser/article/18/3/625/5418589

[407] Wolfgang Streeck, *"The Politics of Public Debt: Neoliberalism, capitalist development, and the restructuring of the state."* http://www.publicseminar.org/2014/02/the-politics-of-public-debt/; Jeremy Green[97], *"The politics of quantitative easing: recovery through regressive distribution."* http://speri.dept.shef.ac.uk/2013/09/24/politics-quantitative-easing-recovery-regressive-redistribution/; Chiara Perillo, Stefano Battiston, *"Financialization and unconventional monetary policy: a financial networks analysis."* https://link.springer.com/article/10.1007/s00191-020-00698-0#Fn28

[408] Julie MacLeavy, *"Neoliberalizing Subjects: The Legacy of New Labour's construction of social exclusion in local governance."* http://www.sciencedirect.com/science/article/pii/S0016718508000924; Vicente Navarro, *"The Worldwide Class Struggle."* https://monthlyreview.org/2006/09/01/the-worldwide-class-struggle/

[409] Montgomerie Johnna, *Neoliberalism and the Making of the Subprime Borrower*. (2010).

[410] David Floyd, *"26 Goldman Sachs Alumni who Run the World."* https://www.investopedia.com/news/26-goldman-sachs-alumni-who-run-world-gs/; Sandy Brian Hager, *"Investment Bank Power and Regulation:From the Volker Shock to the Volker Rule."* https://www.econstor.eu/bitstream/10419/157984/1/
bna-330_20120000_hager_investment_bank_power_and_neoliberal_regulation.pdf

[411] OECD, *"An Overview of Growing Income Inequalities in OECD Countries."* https://www.oecd.org/els/soc/49499779.pdf

---

96. https://www.researchgate.net/profile/Shigeyuki-Hattori

97. http://www.publicseminar.org/2014/02/the-politics-of-public-debt/;%20Jeremy%20Green

[412] Servaas Storm, *"Financialization and Economic Development: A Debate on the Social Efficiency of Modern Finance."* https://onlinelibrary.wiley.com/doi/full/10.1111/dech.12385; Marco Lombardi, Madhusudan Mohanty and Ilhyock Shim, *"The real effects of household debt in the short and long run."* https://www.bis.org/publ/work607.pdf;

[413] Alana Samuels *"The Economy is Great. The Middle Class in Mad."* https://us.yahoo.com/news/economy-great-middle-class-mad-100055431.html

[414] Luke Lattanzi-Silveus, "*Consumer Finance and Labor Exploitation.*" https://www.researchgate.net/publication/327841502_Consumer_Finance_and_Labor_Exploitation

[415] Marco Lombardi, Madhusudan Mohanty and Ilhyock Shim, *"The real effects of household debt in the short and long run."* https://www.bis.org/publ/work607.pdf; Jonathan Chait, *"No, the Richest One Percent Don't Pay 40 Percent of the Taxes."* https://nymag.com/intelligencer/article/fact-check-richest-1-dont-pay-40-of-the-taxes.html

[416] Hadrien Saiag, *"Financialization from the margins."* https://www.berghahnjournals.com/view/journals/focaal/2020/87/fcl870102.xml; Science Direct, *"Financialization."* https://www.sciencedirect.com/topics/social-sciences/financialization; Sebastian Kohl, "*Too much mortgage debt? The effect of housing financialization on housing supply and residential capital formation.*" https://academic.oup.com/ser/article/19/2/413/5913145

[417] Dylan Leclair, *"The Growing Financialization of Bitcoin."* https://bitcoinmagazine.com/markets/the-growing-financialization-of-bitcoin; Angelica Alonso-Rivera, "*Impact of Monetary Policy on Financial Markets Efficiency under Speculative Bubbles: a Non-Normal and Non-Linear Entropy-based Approach.*" http://www.scielo.org.mx/scielo.php?script=sci_arttext&pid=S2448-66552019000200157; MacKenzie Sigalos, Rohan Goswami, *"FTX founder Sam Bankman-Fried arrested in the Bahamas after US files criminal charges."* https://www.cnbc.com/2022/12/12/ftx-founder-sam-bankman-fried-arrested-in-the-bahamas-after-us-files-criminal-charges.html

[418] Jeremy Hill, *"Enron's Liquidator to Oversee FTX's Massive Crypto Bankruptcy."* https://news.bloombergtax.com/crypto/enrons-liquidator-to-oversee-ftxs-massive-crypto-bankruptcy; David Yaffe-Bellany[98] and Matthew Goldstein[99], *"Third Top FTZ Executive Pleads Guilty in Fraud Investigation."* https://www.nytimes.com/2023/02/28/technology/ftx-guilty-plea-fraud.html

[419] Nelson Wan, "*FTX and the crypto collapse: the bubble bursts, but the gambling goes on.*" https://www.marxist.com/ftx-and-the-crypto-collapse-the-bubble-bursts-but-the-gambling-goes-on.htm

98. http://www.nytimes.com/by/david-yaffe-bellany

99. https://www.nytimes.com/by/matthew-goldstein

[420] Will Daniel, *"JPMorgan CEO Jamie Dimon says Bitcoin is a 'hyped-up fraud' and cryptocurrencies are a 'waste of time'—but blockchain is a 'deployable' technology."* https://fortune.com/2023/01/19/jpmorgan-ceo-jamie-dimon-bitcoin-hyped-up-fraud-cryptocurrencies-waste-of-time-but-blockchain-deployable-technology/

[421] David Z. Morris, *"FTX's collapse Was a Crime, Not an Accident."* https://www.coindesk.com/layer2/2022/11/30/ftxs-collapse-was-a-crime-not-an-accident/

[422] Samuel Valasco and Leonardo Medina, *The Social Nature of Cryptocurrencies*, (2013)

[423] Denis Bouneau, *"Friedrich von Hayek, the father of Neoliberalism."* www.voltaire.org/article30058.html[100])

[424] John Collins, *"Crypto, Crime and Control."* https://globalinitiative.net/wp-content/uploads/2022/06/GITOC-Crypto-crime-and-control-Cryptocurrencies-as-an-enabler-of-organized-crime.pdf; Europol, *"Cryptocurrencies: Tracing the Evolution of Criminal Finances."* https://www.europol.europa.eu/cms/sites/default/files/documents/Europol%20Spotlight%20-%20Cryptocurrencies%20-%20Tracing%20the%20evolution%20of%20criminal%20finances.pdf

[425] Jarred Cummens, *"J.P. Morgan's Fines to Date."* https://www.dividend.com/dividend-education/a-brief-history-of-jp-morgans-massive-fines-jpm/; Eric Wallerstein, *"Crypto Banks Borrow Billions From Home-Loan Banks to Plug Shortfalls."* https://www.wsj.com/articles/crypto-banks-borrow-billions-from-home-loan-banks-to-plug-shortfalls-11674263424

[426] Pam Martens and Russ Martens, *"Four Crypto-Friendly Banks are Being Bailed out with Billions from a Federal Housing Program."* https://wallstreetonparade.com/2023/01/four-crypto-friendly-banks-are-being-bailed-out-with-billions-from-a-federal-housing-program/

[427] Protos, *"Federal Home Loan Banks are Bailing out Crypto."* https://protos.com/federal-home-loan-banks-are-bailing-out-crypto/

[428] Gertude Chavez-Dreyfus, *"Crypto money laundering rises in 2021: Chainalysis."* https://www.reuters.com/technology/crypto-money-laundering-rises-30-2021-chainalysis-2022-01-26/; D. Towne Morton, "The Future of Cryptocurrency: An Unregulated Instrument in an Increasingly Regulated Global Economy" Loyola University International Law Review, 16, 1 (2020)

[429] Chase Harrison and John Orbach, *"Explainer: Crypto in Latin America."* https://www.as-coa.org/articles/explainer-crypto-latin-america; Leo Schwartz, *"Why the Crypto crash hits different in Latin America."* https://restofworld.org/2022/why-crypto-crash-different-latin-america/

100. http://www.voltaire.org/article30058.html

[430] US Securities and Exchange Commission, *"SEC Charges Eleven Individuals in $300 Million Crypto Pyramid Scheme."* https://www.sec.gov/news/press-release/2022-134; US Department of Justice, *"Crypto Enforcement."* https://www.justice.gov/criminal-fraud/crypto-enforcement; MSG, *"The Problem with Venezuelan Cryptocurrency."* https://www.managementstudyguide.com/problem-with-venezuelan-cryptocurrency.htm

[431] *"Bitcoin: UK and EU plan crackdown amid crime and tax evasion fears."* https://www.theguardian.com/technology/2017/dec/04/bitcoin-uk-eu-plan-cryptocurrency-price-traders-anonymity; *"Venezuela cerró 2017 con una inflación de 2616% pero para Nicolás Maduro no hay crisis"* http://www.lanacion.com.ar/2099017-venezuela-inflacion-nicolas-maduro-crisis-precios; Justine Muzinich, *"America's Crypt Conundrum."* https://www.foreignaffairs.com/articles/united-states/americas-crypto-currency-conundrum; Camilo Vega Barbosa, *"Cryptocurrency Laundering? Colombian Drug Traffickers Eye Bitcoin."* https://worldcrunch.com/business-finance/cryptocurrency-laundering-colombia-drug-traffickers-eye-bitcoin; Spencer S. Hsu, *"US issues charges in first US criminal cryptocurrency sanctions case."* https://www.washingtonpost.com/dc-md-va/2022/05/16/first-us-criminal-cryptocurrency-sanctions/

[432] Tom Fairless and Hans Bentzien, *"European Central Bank Says Russians Use Crypto to bypass Sanctions."* https://www.wsj.com/livecoverage/russia-ukraine-latest-news-2022-03-21/card/european-central-bank-says-russians-use-crypto-to-bypass-sanctions-UatArIBsW9h8pfiXVuGDRFE/RL, "*Study: Iran Using Crypto Mining To Evade Sanctions.*"

https://www.rferl.org/a/iran-crypto-mining-sanctions/31267432.html; *"Have Cryptocurrencies Really Helped Venezuela Sidestep US Sanctions?"* https://insightcrime.org/news/brief/have-cryptocurrencies-helped-venezuela-sidestep-us-sanctions/

[433] Naomi Hayase, *"Bitocin's Unlimited Potential Lies in its Apolitical Core."* https://www.coindesk.com/bitcoins-unlimited-potential-lies-in-apolitical-core/; Robert Hackett, *"IMF Head: Cryptocurrency Could be the Future."* http://fortune.com/2017/10/02/bitcoin-ethereum-cryptocurrency-imf-christine-lagarde/

[434] Editor of Oilprice.com *"Fake Money is Fueling a very Real Debt Crisis."* https://finance.yahoo.com/news/fake-money-fueling-very-real-170000066.html

[435] **William Callison, *"Ordoliberalism's Trans-Atlantic (Un)Intelligibility: From Friedman and Eucken to Geithner and Schäuble."* Josef Hien and Christian Joerges, eds. *Ordoliberalism, Law and the Rule of Economics.* (2017); Howard Davies, *"Bernanke, Paulson, and Geithner: revisiting the 2008 crisis."* https://www.theguardian.com/business/2019/may/29/bernanke-paulson-and-geithner-revisiting-the-2008-financial-crisis; Tim Geithner, *"Liquidity Risk and the Global Economy."* https://www.newyorkfed.org/newsevents/speeches/2007/gei070515**

[436] **Hans Kundnani, *"Der deutsche Neoliberalismus und die Krise Europas."* https://www.blaetter.de/ausgabe/2016/september/der-deutsche-neoliberalismus-und-die-krise-europas; Christoph Butterwegge[101], *"Vererbte Privilegien."***

https://www.blaetter.de/ausgabe/2015/september/vererbte-privilegien

[437] John Bellamy Foster, *"The Financialzation of Capitalism."*https://monthlyreview.org/2007/04/01/the-financialization-of-capitalism/; Desiree Fields and Tom Gillespie, *"Dawn of the Indebted: Zombie Neoliberalism hits the Big Screen."* https://metropolitics.org/Dawn-of-the-Indebted-Zombie.html

[438] Adam Harmes, *"The Trouble with Hedge Funds."* https://www.academia.edu/11963537/The_Trouble_With_Hedge_Funds?auto=download

[439] Mehrsa Baradaran *'The Neoliberal Looting of America.'* https://www.nytimes.com/2020/07/02/opinion/private-equity-inequality.html

[440] *'SEC Charges Goldman Sachs with Fraud in Structuring and Marketing of CDO Tied to Subprime Mortgages.'* https://www.sec.gov/news/press/2010/2010-59.htm

[441] Binoy Kampmark, *"Cooking Books and Limiting Responsibility: The Goldman Sachs Playbook[102]"* https://countercurrents.org/2018/12/cooking-books-and-limiting-responsibility-the-goldman-sachs-playbook/; Louise Story[103], Landon Thomas Jr.[104] and Nelson D. Schwartz[105], *"Wall Street Helped to Mask Debt Fueling Europe's Crisis"*, https://www.nytimes.com/2010/02/14/business/global/14debt.html

[442] Matt Taibbi, *"The People vs. Goldman Sachs."* https://www.rollingstone.com/politics/politics-news/the-people-vs-goldman-sachs-245191/

[443] Frank James, *"Goldman Sachs Director Tied to Insider Trading Scandal."* https://www.npr.org/sections/thetwo-way/2010/04/goldman_sachs_director_linked.html

[444] Jodi Dean, *"The Neoliberal Trap."* https://www.opendemocracy.net/en/neoliberal-trap/

[445] Mark Chediak[106], Greg Farrell[107], and Naureen S Malik[108] *"Enron's Cast of Characters."* https://www.bloomberg.com/news/articles/2021-12-02/enron-scandal-executives-20-years-later-where-are-they-now#xj4y7vzkg; Robin Blacburn, *"The ENRON Debacle*

---

101. https://www.blaetter.de/autoren/christoph-butterwegge

102. https://countercurrents.org/2018/12/cooking-books-and-limiting-responsibility-the-goldman-sachs-playbook/

103. https://www.nytimes.com/by/louise-story

104. https://www.nytimes.com/by/landon-thomas-jr

105. https://www.nytimes.com/by/nelson-d-schwartz

106. https://www.bloomberg.com/authors/APj9IOx5Yhk/mark-chediak

107. https://www.bloomberg.com/authors/AQWsQD2WBvw/greg-farrell

108. https://www.bloomberg.com/authors/AQqaChh9K0s/naureen-s-malik

and the Pension Crisis." https://newleftreview.org/issues/ii14/articles/robin-blackburn-the-enron-debacle-and-the-pension-crisis; https://www.ocregister.com/2006/07/08/lessons-from-enron-scandal-are-lost-on-some-investors/

[446] Matt Taibbi, *"Turns Out That Trillion Dollar Bailout Was, In Fact, Real."* https://www.rollingstone.com/politics/politics-features/2008-financial-bailout-809731/

[447] Brian Orsak, *"Justice Department Seeks Largest Ever Laundering Penalties in Suits Against Lloyds TSB and Bank of Cyprus."* https://www.moneylaundering.com/news/u-s-justice-department-seeks-largest-ever-laundering-penalties-in-suits-against-lloyds-tsb-bank-of-cyprus/; Ed Caesar, *"Deutsche Bank's $10 Billion Scandal."* https://www.newyorker.com/magazine/2016/08/29/deutsche-banks-10-billion-scandal

[448] Maira Martini, *"European Banks in Money Laundering Scandals: What Lessons for the EU."* https://www.transparency.org/en/blog/european-banks-in-money-laundering-scandals-what-lessons-for-the-eu; *"Scandals involving Central Banks."* https://projects.exeter.ac.uk/RDavies/arian/scandals/centralbanks.html; Yves Smith, *"Corruption, Euro Style: ECB Chief Draghi Fudged Italy's Books to Secure Eurozone Entry, Italy Stuck with Derivative Losses."* https://www.nakedcapitalism.com/2013/06/corruption-eurostyle-mario-draghi-fudged-italys-books-to-secure-eurozone-entry-italy-stuck-with-derivative-losses.html

[449] **Reuters, *"UK fines Goldman Sachs £96.6 million in global action over 1MDB scandal."* https://www.reuters.com/article/us-goldmansachs-1mdb-settlement-britain-idUSKBN2772J6; Rozanna Latiff, *"Malaysia's ex-prime minister Najib and the multi-billion dollar scandal."* https://www.reuters.com/world/asia-pacific/malaysias-ex-pm-najib-multi-billion-dollar-1mdb-scandal-2022-08-23/; Matthew Goldstein, *"Jho Low Will Give Up as Much as $900 Million in Assets in 1MDB Scandal."* https://www.nytimes.com/2019/10/30/business/jho-low-1mdb-malaysia.html**

[450] Todd C. Frankel, *"The Search for Oligarchs."* https://www.yahoo.com/news/search-oligarchs-wealth-u-hindered-185905015.html

[451] Paul Toscano, *"What Does $1 Trillion Look Like?"* https://www.cnbc.com/2009/04/08/What-Does-$1-Trillion-Look-Like.html; Walaa' Ismael Alnassar, et al. *"Credit Derivatives: Did They Exacerbate the 2007 Global Financial Crisis? AIG: Case Study."* Procedia - Social and Behavioral Sciences 109: (2014)

[452] William K. Sjostrom, Jr., *"The AIG Bailout."* https://law2.wlu.edu/deptimages/Law%20Review/66-3Sjostrom.pdf

[453] William Greider, *"The AIG Scandal."* https://www.thenation.com/article/archive/aig-bailout-scandal/; Gerald Epstein and Robert Pollin, *"Neoliberalism's Bailout Problem."*https://bostonreview.net/articles/neoliberalisms-bailout-problem/

[454] Lynn Parramore *"Greece, Goldman Sachs, and the Dark Side of International Finance."* https://www.ineteconomics.org/perspectives/blog/revealed-greece-goldman-sachs-and-the-dark-side-of-international-finance; Von Beat Balzli, "How *Goldman Sachs Helped Greece to Mask its True Debt."* https://www.spiegel.de/international/europe/greek-debt-crisis-how-goldman-sachs-helped-greece-to-mask-its-true-debt-a-676634.html

[455] Nick Dunbar, *"Revealed: Goldman Sachs' mega-deal for Greece."* https://www.risk.net/derivatives/structured-products/1498135/revealed-goldman-sachs-mega-deal-greece

[456]https://www.latimes.com/archives/la-xpm-1998-sep-25-mn-26363-story.html; Serena NG and Carrick Mollenkamp, *"Hedge Funds Tapped Rescue Program"* https://www.wsj.com/articles/SB10001424052748703865004575649233598560948;

Robert Reich, *"How Goldman Sachs Profited from the Greek Debt Crisis"* https://www.thenation.com/article/archive/goldmans-greek-gambit/

[457] Christian Edelmann and Patrick Hunt, *"How the Great Recession Changed Banking."* https://hbr.org/2017/10/how-the-great-recession-changed-banking; Frank Partnoy, *"The Looming Bank Collapse."* https://www.theatlantic.com/magazine/archive/2020/07/coronavirus-banks-collapse/612247/; Tony Swash, *"2008 Changed the concentration of Global Finance Capital."* https://fromtone.com/2008-changed-the-the-concentration-of-global-finance-capital/; Kiril Sokoloff, *"Has Capital Concentration become too Extreme?"* https://latest.13d.com/has-capital-concentration-become-too-extreme-foreign-capital-us-financial-assets-6efe66a13bd5

[458] C. J. Polychroniou, *"Reconceiving Change in the Age of Parasitic Capitalism."* https://truthout.org/articles/reconceiving-change-in-the-age-of-parasitic-capitalism/

[459] Randall D. Guynn, Davis Polk & Wardwell, *"The Financial Panic of 2008 and Financial Regulatory Reform."* https://corpgov.law.harvard.edu/2010/11/20/the-financial-panic-of-2008-and-financial-regulatory-reform/

[460] Robert J. Antonio, *"Plundering the Commons: The Growth Imperative in Neoliberal Times."* The Sociological Review, vol. 61, 2 (2013); Eric Catchman, *"The corruption behind the crash of 2008."* https://thefulcrum.us/Elections/Campaign-Finance/economic-crisis; Matt Taibbi, *"Secrets and Lies of the Bailout."* https://www.rollingstone.com/politics/politics-news/secrets-and-lies-of-the-bailout-113270/; Adam Levitin, *"The Bailout Cronyism and Corruption have already begun."* https://www.creditslips.org/creditslips/2020/03/the-bailout-cronyism-and-corruption-have-already-begun.html.

[461] Bloomberg, *"Hedge fund charged with running Ponzi scheme."* https://www.investmentnews.com/hedge-fund-charged-with-running-ponzi-scheme-20244; Lee F. Monaghan and Michael O'Flynn, *"The Madoffization of Society: A Corrosive Process in an Age of Fictitious Capital"* Critical Sociology, 39, (2012); Lee F. Monaghan and Michael O'Flynn, *"The Madoffization of Irish Society: from Ponzi finance to sociological critique."* The British Journal of Sociology, 68:4 (2017); Charles P. Pierce, *"Wall Street Execs Allegedly Traded*

on Insider Info While the World Collapsed in 2008." https://www.esquire.com/news-politics/politics/news/a49046/wall-street-insider-trading-2008-crash/; Peter Cziraki *"Trading by Bank Insiders before and during the Financial Crisis."* http://www.eief.it/files/2012/02/02-jm-paper_cziraki.pdf.

[462] Ian Crowther, "A critique of post-crisis structural and prudential bank regulation: the UK case." https://www.research.manchester.ac.uk/portal/files/163053101/FULL_TEXT.PDF

[463] Nouriel Roubini, *'Most U.S. banks are technically near insolvency, and hundreds are already fully insolvent,'* https://www.marketwatch.com/story/most-u-s-banks-are-technically-near-insolvency-and-hundreds-are-already-fully-insolvent-roubini-says-18b89f92

[464] Madeline Coggins, *"Financial world legend sounds alarm over "biggest bank that's going down."* https://www.yahoo.com/finance/news/financial-world-legend-sounds-alarm-200129104.htmlhttps://www.yahoo.com/finance/news/financial-world-legend-sounds-alarm-200129104.html

[465] Jonathan Barrett[109], Swati Pandey[110], *"Australia vows to clean up financial sector after landmark misconduct inquiry."* https://www.reuters.com/article/us-australia-banks-inquiry-idUSKCN1PT099

[466] Kevin Farnsworth and Zoe Irving, "The 2008 crisis failed to displace neoliberalism's core principles." https://blogs.lse.ac.uk/usappblog/2019/02/09/the-2008-crisis-failed-to-displace-neoliberalisms-core-principles/

[467] John Bellamy Foster, "The Financialization of Capital and the Crisis." https://monthlyreview.org/2008/04/01/the-financialization-of-capital-and-the-crisis/; Mike Konczal, "Did Regulation Cause the Financial Crisis?" https://www.theatlantic.com/business/archive/2009/09/did-regulation-cause-the-financial-crisis/26880/

[468] Kenneth Roth, *"Barrack Obama's Shaky Legacy on Human Rights."* https://www.hrw.org/news/2017/01/09/barack-obamas-shaky-legacy-human-rights

[469] Carlos Ramirez, *"Obama's Neoliberal Foreign Policy in a Neoliberal World."* https://www.ia-forum.org/Content/ViewInternal_Document.cfm?contenttype_id=5&ContentID=8401; Jonathan Chait, *"Does the Left Have Any Better Ideas Than Obama's?"* https://nymag.com/intelligencer/2019/12/obama-legacy-liberalism-leftism-bernie-sanders-socialism-democrats.html

[470] Max B. Sawicky, *"The Sunset of Neoliberalism."* https://jacobinmag.com/2019/08/neoliberalism-democratic-party-donald-trump-hillary-clinton-barack-obama; Lester K. Spence, *The Neoliberal Turn in Black Politics.* (2013); Farhad Manjoo, *"Barrack Obama's Biggest Mistake."* https://www.nytimes.com/2019/09/18/opinion/obama-2008-financial-crisis.html; Michael Schwartz, *"Military Neoliberalism" Endless War and Humanitarian Crisis in the Twenty First Century."* https://scholarlycommons.law.case.edu/cgi/viewcontent.cgi?article=1100&context=swb; Gretchen Morgenson, and Louise Story, *"Banks Bundled Bad Debt, Bet Against it and*

---

109. https://www.reuters.com/journalists/jonathan-barrett

110. https://www.reuters.com/journalists/swati-pandey

Won." https://www.nytimes.com/2009/12/24/business/24trading.htmlhttps://www.nytimes.com/2009/12/24/business/24trading.html

[471] **Lionel D. Lyle, *"The role of wealth and neoliberalism in Barack Obama's selection, election, and presidency."*https://go.gale.com/ps/i.do?p=LitRC&u=googlescholar&id=GALE|A356354197&v=2.1&it=r&sid=LitRC&asid=6e89d156[111]; Robert Yoon, *"Goldman Sachs was top Obama donor."* http://edition.cnn.com/2010/POLITICS/04/20/obama.goldman.donations/index.html**

[472] Karl Evers-Hilstrom et al. *"More Money, Less Transparency: A Decade Under Citizens United."* https://www.opensecrets.org/news/reports/a-decade-under-citizens-united

[473] Daniel Strauss, *"How a Supreme Court case paved the way for 2020s money-soaked election."* https://www.theguardian.com/us-news/2020/jan/21/citizens-united-v-fec-supreme-court-ruling-billionares; Andrew Perez [112], Julia Rock [113]& Rebecca Burns, [114]*"The Supreme Court's Next Gift for its Billionaire Benefactors."* https://www.levernews.com/the-supreme-courts-next-gift-for-its-billionaire_benefactors/

[474] Michan Connor, *"Uniting Citizens after Citizens United: Cities, Neoliberalism, and Democracy.* "https; David Singh Grewal and Jedediah Purdy, *"Law and Neoliberalism."* https://scholarship.law.duke.edu/cgi/viewcontent.cgi?article=4705&context=lcp

[475] John Weeks, *"By the numbers: Barack Obama's contribution to the decline of US democracy."* https://www.opendemocracy.net/en/by-numbers-barack-obama-s-contribution-to-decline-of-us-democracy/

[476] Leah Wright-Rigueur, "*Neoliberal Social Justice: From Ed Brooke to Barak Obama.*" https://items.ssrc.org/reading-racial-conflict/neoliberal-social-justice-from-ed-brooke-to-barack-obama/; Peter Custers. *"Military Keynesianism under the Obama Presidency."* https://www.epw.in/journal/2009/04/commentary/military-keynesianism-under-obama-presidency.html; David Hursch, *"Explaining Obama: The Continuation of Free Market Policies in Education and the Economy."* https://files.eric.ed.gov/fulltext/EJ1134701.pdf

[477] Reed Hunt, *A Crisis Wasted: Obama's Defining Decisions.* (2019)

[478] Stephen Maher and Scoot Aquanno, *"From Neoliberalism to the New Finance Capital." https://socialistproject.ca/2021/04/from-neoliberalism-to-new-finance-capital/*

---

111. https://go.gale.com/ps/i.do?p=LitRC&u=googlescholar&id=GALE%7CA356354197&v=2.1&it=r&sid=LitRC&asid=6e89d156

112. https://www.levernews.com/author/andrew-perez/

113. https://www.levernews.com/author/julia-rock/

114. https://www.levernews.com/author/rebecca/

[479] *"Ten Years After Madoff, Updated Ponzi Database Shows Schemes Are Thriving[115]."* https://www.ponzitracker.com/home/2019/2/7/ten-years-after-madoff-ponzi-schemes-are-thriving.html

[480] Nick Buxton, *"Contagion, how the crisis spread."* https://www.redpepper.org.uk/contagion-how-the-crisis-spread/; Robert N McCauley, *"The 2008 crisis: transpacific or transatlantic?"* https://www.bis.org/publ/qtrpdf/r_qt1812f.htm; https://chicagounbound.uchicago.edu/cgi/viewcontent.cgi?article=1573&context=law_and_economics; Kenneth W. Dam, *"The Subprime Crisis and Financial Regulation: International and Comparative Perspectives."* https://chicagounbound.uchicago.edu/cgi/viewcontent.cgi?article=1573&context=law_and_economics.

[481] Mark Landler, "*The US Financial Crisis is Spreading to Europe.*" https://www.nytimes.com/2008/10/01/business/worldbusiness/01global.html

[482] Ming Zang, *"The Impact of the Global Crisis on China and its Reaction."* https://www.realinstitutoelcano.org/en/analyses/the-impact-of-the-global-crisis-on-china-and-its-reaction-ari/; John Whalley et. Al. *"China and the Financial Crisis."* https://www.cigionline.org/sites/default/files/task_force_2.pdf

[483] **Yi Wen, *"China's Rapid Rise: From Backward Agrarian Society to Industrial Powerhouse in Just 35 Years."* https://www.stlouisfed.org/publications/regional-economist/april-2016/chinas-rapid-rise-from-backward-agrarian-society-to-industrial-powerhouse-in-just-35-years; Tania Branigan, *"Beijing to pump 4tn yuan into economy to offset fall in exports."* https://www.theguardian.com/world/2008/nov/10/china-credit-crunch**

[484] Chris Buckley and Terry Wait, *"Hu signals ambitious China role in fighting crisis."* https://www.reuters.com/article/idINIndia-36639020081122; Wayne M. Morrison, *"China and the Global Financial Crisis."* https://sgp.fas.org/crs/row/RS22984.pdf; Ma Jingjing, *"China Pulled US out of 2008 crisis."* https://www.globaltimes.cn/content/1170724.shtml

[485] Heidi N. Moore, "*China: the Power Behind the $700 billion Bailout.*" https://www.wsj.com/articles/BL-DLB-3968; https://www.sfgate.com/news/article/Government-bailout-hits-8-5-trillion-3183181.php; https://www.bizjournals.com/phoenix/stories/2008/11/24/daily46.html

[486] Ben Reid, *"China's "South-South" Trade: Unequal Exchange and Uneven and Combined Development."* In Radhika Desai, *Analytical Gains of Geopolitical Economy*. (2016); Zak Cope, *"Unequal Exchange."* https://isreview.org/issue/107/unequal-exchange/index.html

[487] **Long Guoqiang,** *"Twenty Years since China's WTO Accession."* https://china-cee.eu/2022/04/28/twenty-years-since-chinas-wto-accession-looking-back-and-forward/; United States Trade Representative, *"2020 Report to Congress on China's WTO Compliance."*

---

115. https://www.ponzitracker.com/home/2019/2/7/ten-years-after-madoff-ponzi-schemes-are-thriving.html

https://ustr.gov/sites/default/files/files/reports/2020/2020USTRReportCongressChinaWTOCompliance.pdf; Minqi Li, *"China: Imperialism or Semi-Periphery."* https://monthlyreview.org/2021/07/01/china-imperialism-or-semi-periphery/

[488] Liqing Zhang, "China's Policy Responses to the Global Financial Crisis: Efficacy and Risks." https://www.die-gdi.de/fileadmin/_migrated/content_uploads/Berlin_workshop_090831.pdf

[489] Gary Jacobs, *"The political economy of neoliberalism and illiberal democracy."* http://cadmusjournal.org/node/654

[490] Anjan Thakor, *"Anniversary of Lehman's collapse reminds us – booms are followed by busts."* https://theconversation.com/anniversary-of-lehmans-collapse-reminds-us-booms-are-often-followed-by-busts-102758; A.V. Thakor, *"Anniversary of Lehman's collapse reminds us booms are often followed by busts."* https://theconversation.com/anniversary-of-lehmans-collapse-reminds-us-booms-are-often-followed-by-busts-102758; Robert Samuelson, *"Lehman Brothers Collapsed 10 years ago. Whose fault was it?"* https://www.washingtonpost.com/opinions/lehman-brothers-collapsed-10-years-ago-whose-fault-was-it/2018/08/26/79137b2e-a7dd-11e8-a656-943eefab5daf_story.html; *"Financial crisis anniversary"* https://www.ft.com/financial-crisis-anniversary?page=2; Hyun Song Shin[116], *"Reflections on the Lehman Collapse."* https://www.bis.org/speeches/sp180917.htm

[491] Ians, *"How global financial crisis of 2008 hurt liberal democracy and open borders."* https://www.business-standard.com/article/international/how-global-financial-crisis-of-2008-hurt-liberal-democracy-open-borders-118091100265_1.html; Sebastian Dullien, *"Ten Years after Lehman: Can liberal democracy survive another financial crisis?"* https://ecfr.eu/article/commentary_ten_years_after_lehman_can_liberal_democracy_survive/; Ziya Onis, *"The Crisis of Democracy in the Post-Hegemonic World Order."* https://www.networkideas.org/wp-content/uploads/2017/06/Age_of_Anxiety.pdf; Erin Coghlan[117], Lisa McCorkell[118] and Sara Hinkley[119], *"What Really Caused the Great Recession?"* https://irle.berkeley.edu/what-really-caused-the-great-recession/

[492] **Sara Boboltz, *"Obama Warns Americans Against Following In The Path Of Nazi Germany."* https://www.huffingtonpost.com/entry/obama-warns-americans-against-following-in-the-path-of-nazi germany_us_5a2c032ce4b0a290f0512487**[120]

[493] Ryan Cooper, *"Obama the Pretender."* https://theweek.com/articles/950908/obama-pretender

Paul Heideman, *"The Cost of Voting for the Lesser Evil."* https://socialistworker.org/2012/10/30/cost-of-the-lesser-evil

116. https://www.bis.org/author/hyun_song_shin.htm

117. https://irle.berkeley.edu/people/erin-coghlan/

118. https://irle.berkeley.edu/people/lisa-mccorkell/

119. https://irle.berkeley.edu/people/sara-hinkley/

120. https://www.huffingtonpost.com/entry/obama-warns-americans-against-following-in-the-path-of-nazi%20germany_us_5a2c032ce4b0a290f0512487

[494] Conor Friedersdorf, *"An Intra-Left Debate: Is Obama the More Effective of 2 Evils?"* "https://www.theatlantic.com/politics/archive/2012/09/an-intra-left-debate-is-obama-the-more-effective-of-2-evils/262134/

[495] Diego Chauvet, *"Violences: à Montreuil, les habitants ont encore la « chair de poule."* https://www.humanite.fr/monde/cisjordanie/cisjordanie-jenine-la-punition-collective-contre-la-resistance-801675; Reuter, *"France Deploys 45,000 police, armored vehicles to quell riots."* https://www.rawstory.com/france-deploys-45000-police-armoured-vehicles-to-quell-riots/

[496] Keida Kostreci, *"Are Illiberal Democracies on the March in Europe?"* https://www.voanews.com/a/are-illiberal-democracies-on-the-march-in-europe/4358311.html

[497] Rebecca Rosman, *"Is Emmanuel Macron Pandering to the Far Right?"* https://www.aljazeera.com/features/2020/11/30/is-frances-emmanuel-macron-pandering-to-the-far-right

[498] **Gaspar d'Allens, *"Geoffroy de Lagasnerie: «Macron est un chef de guerre sociale»"* https://reporterre.net/Geoffroy-de-Lasganerie-Macron-est-un-chef-de-guerre-sociale; Pierre Chailan, *"Macron avait oublié... la lutte des classes."* https://www.humanite.fr/politique/emmanuel-macron/macron-avait-oublie-la-lutte-des-classes-660574**

[499] **Romain Herreros, Albane Guichard et Marie Hayne, *"Jean-Luc Mélenchon « maudit » Emmanuel Macron pour sa réforme des retraites."*https://www.huffingtonpost.fr/politique/video/jean-luc-melenchon-maudit-emmanuel-macron-pour-sa-reforme-des-retraites_213046.html; Ernesto Gallo and Giovanni Biava, *"Democracy in the Asian Century."* https://www.opendemocracy.net/ernesto-gallo-giovanni-biava/democracy-in-asian-century.**

[500] Ganesh Sitaraman, *"The Collapse of Neolib4567eralism."* https://newrepublic.com/article/155970/collapse-neoliberalism

[501] **Sarah Sheets, *The Myths of Far Right Populism: Orban's Fence and Trump's Wall."* https://bpr.berkeley.edu/2017/02/28/the-myths-of-far-right-populism-orbans-fence-and-trumps-wall/; Stephen Moore[121] and Dean Stansel, *"How Corporate Welfare Won: Clinton and Congress Retreat from Cutting Business Subsidies."* https://www.cato.org/policy-analysis/how-corporate-welfare-won-clinton-congress-retreat-cutting-business-subsidies#[122]; https://kottke.org/21/07/new-labour-and-the-end-of-the-welfare-state-for-artists**

[502] Mike Kuhlenbeck, *"Exporting Fascism: US Imperialism in Latin America."* https://www.foreignpolicyjournal.com/2015/01/24/exporting-fascism-us-imperialism-in-latin-america/; Sarah Churchwell, *"It will be called 'Americanism': the US writers who imagined a fascist future."* https://www.theguardian.com/books/2017/feb/03/americanism-us-writers-imagine-fascist-future-fiction;

---

121. https://www.cato.org/people/stephen-moore

122. https://www.cato.org/policy-analysis/how-corporate-welfare-won-clinton-congress-retreat-cutting-business-subsidies

http://www.softpanorama.org/Skeptics/Political_skeptic/Corporatism/neofascism.shtml; Bertram Gross, *Friendly Fascism: The New Face of Power in America,* 1999; Ayse Dayi, *"Neoliberal Health Restructuring, Neoconservatism and the Limits of Law."* https://www.ncbi.nlm.nih.gov/pmc/articles/PMC6927387/.

[503] Andrea Peto, *"'The goal of the anti-abortion movement is to create a desirable counteroffer to liberal democracy'."* https://www.lemonde.fr/en/opinion/article/2022/05/17/the-goal-of-the-anti-abortion-movement-is-to-create-a-desirable-counteroffer-to-liberal-democracy_5983782_23.html

[504] Shankar Gopalakrishnan , *"Neoliberal Fascism: Free Markets and the Restructuring of Indian Capitalism,"* https://mronline.org/2008/11/14/neoliberalism-and-hindutva-fascism-free-markets-and-the-restructuring-of-indian-capitalism/

[505] D. K. Williams, *God's Own Party: The Making of the Christian Right.* (2012); The American Yawp, *"The Triumph of the Right."* https://www.americanyawp.com/text/29-the-triumph-of-the-right/

[506] David A. Ciepley, *"Neoliberalism and the Corporation: Mutually Contradictory and Corrupting."* https://papers.ssrn.com/sol3/papers.cfm?abstract_id=3230520; Jorg Wietzgratz and David Whyte, *"How neoliberalism's moral order feeds fraud and corruption."* https://theconversation.com/how-neoliberalisms-moral-order-feeds-fraud-and-corruption-60946

[507] Vinod Vyasulu,*"India's Neoliberal Path to Perdition."* https://www.catchnews.com/india-news/india-s-neoliberal-path-to-perdition-77371.html; Monica Prasad, *The Politics of Free Markets,* 2006)

[508] G. M. Tamas, *"What Is Post-Fascism?"* https://www.opendemocracy.net/people-newright/article_306.jsp

[509] Michael Hudson, *"The Counter-Enlightenment."*[123] https://www.prosper.org.au/2010/05/25/the-counter-enlightenment/

[510] Kristina Birke Daniels and Josefin Fürst *"Mapping the Far Right."* https://library.fes.de/pdf-files/bueros/stockholm/19155.pdf; Eszter Szenes *"RADICALISATION: "We're not neo-Nazis anymore": Radicalization Strategies in Online Far-right Propaganda and Disinformation Campaigns."* https://www.ceu.edu/project/radicalisation; Seyed Nader Nourbakhsh et al., "Rise of the Far Right parties in Europe: from Nationalism to Euroscepticism." http://journal.iag.ir/article_129481_6e23e152c58ba9f4e04dbf7072dbdcf0.pdf?lang=en

[511] **Jan Rettig, *"Zwischen neoliberalem Marktradikalismus und etatistischem Protektionismus Polit-ökonomische Positionen der extremen Rechten."* http://www.beigewum.at/wp-content/uploads/KuWe-4_16-Rettig_zwischen-neoliberalem-Marktradikalismus-und-etatistischem-Protekionismus.pdf; Sabine Volk, *"What the pediga movement tells us about divisions within German society."* https://blogs.lse.ac.uk/europpblog/2020/11/16/what-the-pegida-movement-tells-us-about-divisions-within-german-society/; David A. Bell, Marko Valenta and Zan Strabac, *"A comparative analysis of changes in anti-immigrant and anti-Muslim attitudes in Europe: 1990–2017."* https://comparativemigrationstudies.springeropen.com/articles/10.1186/**

123. *https://www.prosper.org.au/2010/05/25/the-counter-enlightenment/*

s40878-021-00266-w; William Peter Fitz, *"Reactionary Postmodernism? Neoliberalism, Multiculturalism, the Internet and the Ideology of the Far Right in Germany."* https://scholarworks.uvm.edu/cgi/viewcontent.cgi?article=1302&context=hcoltheses

[512] Alfred W. McCoy, *"The Bloodstained Rise of Global Populism."* https://lobelog.com/the-bloodstained-rise-of-global-populism/; Marisa von Bullow and Rebecca Neaera Abers, *'Denialism nd Populism; Two Sides of a Coin in Jair Boldonaro's Brazil.'* https://www.cambridge.org/core/services/aop-cambridge-core/content/view/94FF980F8CF1D28AEAC72F96DD3516E6/S0017257X22000148a.pdf/denialism_and_populism_two_sides_of_a_coin_in_jair_bolsonaros_brazil.pdf; Elise[124] Massicard, *"Populism in Turkey; Towards the Demise of Democracy?"* https://www.sciencespo.fr/research/cogito/home/populism-in-turkey-towards-the-demise-of-democracy/?lang=en

[513] **Hans-Georg Betz, "Exclusionary Populism in Western Europe in the 1990s and Beyond A Threat to Democracy and Civil Rights?" https://www.files.ethz.ch/isn/45939/9.pdf; Gabor Scheiring, *"The Populist Backlash Against Globalization: Economic Insecurity or Culture War?"* https://www.illiberalism.org/the-populist-backlash-against-globalization-economic-insecurity-or-culture-war/**

[514] Aihwa Ong, *Neoliberalism as Exception: Mutations in Citizenship and Sovereignty*, 2006; http://www.e-ir.info/2012/08/22/globalization-does-not-entail-the-weakening-of-the-liberal-state/

[515] Muhammad Nadeem Mirza, Haleema Azhar, *"Why Democracies Give Rise to Populist Leaders."* https://halshs.archives-ouvertes.fr/halshs-03606858/document; Federico Finchelstein, *From Fascism to Populism in History.* (2019); Mark Mardell, *"Fascism, the 1930s and the 21st Century."* https://www.bbc.com/news/uk-politics-38317787

[516] Wolfgang Streeck, *"The Crisis in Context: Democratic Capitalism and its Contradictions."* https://www.idos-research.de/fileadmin/user_upload/pdfs/messner/Streeck_The-crisis_in_context.pdf; Louis Makowski and Joseph M Ostroy, *"Appropriation in a competitive theory of value."* https://www.cairn.info/revue-cahiers-d-economie-politique-1-2012-2-page-25.htm

[517] Prabhat Patnaik, *"Why Neoliberalism Needs Neofascists."* https://www.bostonreview.net/articles/why-neoliberalism-needs-neofascists/; Nancy Fraser, *'Progressive Neoliberalism, versus Reactionary Populism.'* http://www.thegreatregression.eu/progressive-neoliberalism-versus-reactionary-populism-a-hobsons-choice/; Massimo Pendenza and Vanessa Lamattina, *"Rethinking Self-Responsibility: An Alternative Vision to the Neoliberal Concept of Freedom."* https://journals.sagepub.com/doi/full/10.1177/0002764218816827; Racheal Fest, *"Culture and Neoliberalism."* https://mediationsjournal.org/articles/culture-and-neoliberalism

[518] Andrea Micocci and Flavia Di Mario. *The Fascist Nature of Neoliberalism*, (2017).

---

124. https://lobelog.com/the-bloodstained-rise-of-global-populism/;%20Marisa%20von%20Bullow%20and%20Rebecca%20Neaera%20Abers,%20'Denialism%20nd%20Populism;%20Two%20Sides%20of%20a%20Coin%20in%20Jair%20Boldonaro's%20Brazil.'%20https://www.cambridge.org/core/services/aop-cambridge-core/content/view/94FF980F8CF1D28AEAC72F96DD3516E6/S0017257X22000148a.pdf/denialism_and_populism_two_sides_of_a_coin_in_jair_bolsonaros_brazil.pdf;%20Elise

[519] W.I. Robinson, *"Democracies Under Pressure. Authoritarianism, Repression, Struggles."* https://www.ritimo.org/ROBINSON-William-I

[520] John Bellamy Foster, *"The New Irrationalism."* https://monthlyreview.org/2023/02/01/the-new-irrationalism/

[521] Sheldon Wolin, *Democracy Incorporated: Managed Democracy and the Specter of Inverted Totalitarianism. (*2008)

[522] Charlie Savage, *"C.I.A. Is Collecting in Bulk Certain Data Affecting Americans."* https://www.nytimes.com/2022/02/10/us/politics/cia-data-privacy.html; *"Lawmakers allege 'secret' CIA spying on unwitting Americans."* https://www.bbc.com/news/world-us-canada-60351768

[523] Nancy Murray, *"Profiling in the age of total information awareness."* https://www.researchgate.net/publication/47402551_Profiling_in_the_age_of_total_information_awareness; David H. Price, *The American Surveillance State.* (2022)

[524] Malkia Amala Cyril, *"Black America's State of Surveillance."* https://progressive.org/magazine/black-america-s-state-surveillance-cyril/; David Carroll, *"China embraces its surveillance state. The US pretends it doesn't have one."* https://qz.com/1670686/the-us-has-a-lot-in-common-with-chinas-surveillance-state/;Seth G. Jones and Katrina Doxsee, *"The escalating terrorism problem in the United States."* https://www.csis.org/analysis/escalating-terrorism-problem-united-states; Elizabeth Gotein, *"How the CIA is Acting Outside the Law to Spy on Americans."* https://www.brennancenter.org/our-work/analysis-opinion/how-cia-acting-outside-law-spy-americans

[525] J.M. Cypher, *"The origins and evolution of military Keynesianism in the United States."* https://www.tandfonline.com/doi/abs/10.1080/01603477.2015.1076704?journalCode=mpke20

Robert Higgs, *"Military Keynesianism to the Rescue?"* https://www.independent.org/news/article.asp?id=2399; Scott Burchill, *"Biden's China Policy, US Business and Australia."* https://johnmenadue.com/bidens-china-policy-us-business-and-australia/

[526] Bastiaan van Apeldoorn and Nana de Graaff, *American Grand Strategy and Corporate Elite Networks.* (2016); Charlotte Heath-Kelly et al. eds., *Neoliberalism and Terror: Critical Engagements*, 2016; Chris Hedges, *"The Great Unravelling."* https://www.truthdig.com/articles/the-great-unraveling/

[527] *"Globalization has lowered wages for American workers, new EPI study finds."* https://www.epi.org/press/globalization-lowered-wages-american-workers/; Suresh Naidu, Eric Posner, Glen Weyl, *"More and more companies have monopoly power over workers' wages. That's killing the economy."* https://www.vox.com/the-big-idea/2018/4/6/17204808/wages-employers-workers-monopsony-growth-stagnation-inequality; A. J. Stewart, Nolan McCarty and Joanna J. Bryson, *"Polarization under rising inequality and economic decline"* https://www.science.org/doi/10.1126/sciadv.abd4201

[528] Cemal Burak, *States of Discipline: Authoritarian Neoliberalism and the Contested Reproduction of Capitalist Order (Transforming Capitalism)*. (2017)

[529] Glenn Greenwald and Ewen, MacAskill, *"NSA Prism program taps in to user data of Apple, Google and others."* https://www.theguardian.com/world/2013/jun/06/us-tech-giants-nsa-data; Katherine Kemp, *"Here is how tech giants profit from invading our privacy and how we can start taking it back."* https://theconversation.com/heres-how-tech-giants-profit-from-invading-our-privacy-and-how-we-can-start-taking-it-back-120078; McAfee, *"What Personal Data do Companies Track?"* https://www.mcafee.com/blogs/tips-tricks/what-personal-data-do-companies-track/

[530] Carolyn W. Veldstra, *"Stuck in the Impasse: Cynicism as Neoliberal Affect."* https://macsphere.mcmaster.ca/bitstream/11375/14115/1/fulltext.pdf

[531] Prabhat Patneik, *"Neoliberalism and Fascism."* https://journals.sagepub.com/doi/full/10.1177/2277976019901029

[532] Larry M. Bartels, *"Political Effects of the Great Recession."* https://www.vanderbilt.edu/csdi/research/CSDI_WP_06-2013.pdf; Jeff Nesbitt, *"The Secret Origins of the Tea Party."* https://time.com/secret-origins-of-the-tea-party/

[533] Nancy MacLean, *"Since We Are Greatly Outnumbered. Why and How the Koch Network Uses Disinformation to Thwart Democracy."* https://nationalhumanitiescenter.org/wp-content/uploads/2021/09/MacLean-How-the-Koch-Network-Uses-Disinformation-copy.pdf

[534] Thorsten Hellmann, Pia Schmidt, Sascha Matthias Heller, *"Social Justice in the EU and OECD."* https://www.politico.eu/wp-content/uploads/2019/12/Social-Justice-Index-2019.pdf

[535] Daniel Broudy and James P. Winter, *"Propaganda in a Neoliberal Universe: An Interview with James Winter."* https://scholar.uwindsor.ca/cgi/viewcontent.cgi?article=1028&context=communicationspub; John Bellamy Foster and R.W. McChesney, *"The 'Left Wing' Media?"* https://monthlyreview.org/2003/06/01/the-left-wingmedia/

[536] Norman Eisen, Mansi Patel and Kai Smith, *"The corruption and autocracy nexus: The case of King Bibi,"* https://www.brookings.edu/articles/the-corruption-and-autocracy-nexus-the-case-of-king-bibi/

[537] Victor M. A. Nascimento, *"The Hegemony of the Neoliberal Narrative: Right Wing Discourses of 'Common Sense', the Weaponization of the Term 'Liberal', and the Shifting of the Political*

*Spectrum.*https://dspace.library.uvic.ca/bitstream/handle/1828/12841/
Nascimento_Victor_MA_2021.pdf?sequence=1; Pankaj Mishra, "[125]*This Poisonous Cult of Personality."* https://www.nybooks.com/daily/2017/12/01/this-poisonous-cult-of-personality/ *"The Guardian's View on Erdogan's Turkey: illiberal democrat takes power."* https://www.theguardian.com/commentisfree/2018/jun/25/

125. https://dspace.library.uvic.ca/bitstream/handle/1828/12841/Nascimento_Victor_MA_2021.pdf?sequence=1;%20Pankaj%20Mishra,%20

the-guardian-view-on-erdogans-turkey-illiberal-democrat-takes-power; Ligaya Lindio-McGovern, *'Neoliberalism, Fascism, and Peoples' Resistance in the Philippines.'* Dahlia Scheindlin, *'Do Israelis vote for ideology or cult of personality?'* https://www.972mag.com/do-israelis-vote-for-ideology-or-cult-of-personality/;

[538] OXFAM, *"An Economy of the 99%."* https://www-cdn.oxfam.org/s3fs-public/file_attachments/bp-economy-for-99-percent-160117-en.pdf

[539] UN General Assembly *"World Altered by Neoliberal Outsourcing of Public Services to Private Sector."* https://www.un.org/press/en/2018/gashc4239.doc.htm

[540] Abby Innes, *"Corporate State Capture."* https://blogs.lse.ac.uk/politicsandpolicy/corporate-state-capture/; United Nation, *"World Altered by 'Neoliberal' Outsourcing of Public Services to Private Sector, Third Committee Experts Stress, amid Calls for Better Rights Protection."* https://www.un.org/press/en/2018/gashc4239.doc.htm; Andrew Moravcsik and Andrea Sangovanni, *"On Democracy and the Public Interest in the European Union."* https://citeseerx.ist.psu.edu/viewdoc/download?doi=10.1.1.525.8888&rep=rep1&type=pdf; Hadriana Lowenkron, *"Parents Sue Elite Schools for Indoctrinating their Kids With Anti-Racist Curriculum."* https://www.yahoo.com/news/parents-sue-elite-schools-indoctrinating-130000200.html; Kali Holloway, *"Jim Crow is Resurrected in Mississippi."* https://www.thedailybeast.com/jim-crow-is-resurrected-in-mississippi?via=rss&source=articles_fancylink

[541] Luca Mavelli, *"Citizenship for Sale and the Neoliberal Political Economy of Belonging."* International Studies Quarterly, 62:3 (2018).

[542] George Baca, *"Neoliberalism's prologue: Keynesianism, myths of class compromises and the restoration of class power."* https://philpapers.org/archive/BACNPK-2.pdf; T. I. Paley, *"From Keynesianism to Neoliberalism: Shifting Paradigms in Economics."* https://fpif.org/from_keynesianism_to_neoliberalism_shifting_paradigms_in_economics/

[543] **Chris Muellerleile and Susan Robertson, *"Digital Weberianism: Bureaucracy, Information, and the Techno-rationality of Neoliberal Capitalism."* https://www.researchgate.net/publication/339938853_Digital_Weberianism_Bureaucracy_Information_and_the_Techno-rationality_of_Neoliberal_Capitalism; Regina Queiroz, *"From the exclusion of the people in neoliberalism to publicity without a public."* https://www.nature.com/articles/s41599-017-0032-1**

[544] Rainer Mausfeld, "Neoliberal Indoctrination." https://cognitive-liberty.online/wp-content/uploads/neoliberal-indoctrination-Copy.pdf

[545] Juha Siltala, *"In Search of the Missing Links Between Economic Insecurity and Political Protest: Why Does Neoliberalism Evoke Identity Politics Instead of Class Interests?"* https://www.frontiersin.org/articles/10.3389/fsoc.2020.00028/full.

[546] Juan Francisco Palma, *"Advocacy NGOs and the neoliberal manufacture of the street voice."* https://www.researchgate.net/publication/348754050_Advocacy_NGOs_and_the_neoliberal_manufacture_of_the_street_voice

[547] Dieter Plehwe, *"Schumpeter Revival: How Neoliberals Revised the Image of the Entrepreneur."* https://www.econstor.eu/bitstream/10419/215869/1/Full-text-chapter-Plehwe-Schumpeter-Revival.pdf; M. Ozgur Kayalica,[1] Rafael Salvador Espinosa Ramírez, *"Political Contributions, Subsidy and Merger."* https://www.scielo.org.mx/scielo.php?script=sci_arttext&pid=S1870-66222012000200004

[548] **Beth Daley, "*Failing Union of Capitalism and Democracy Fuels Rise in Inequality.*" https://theconversation.com/failing-union-of-capitalism-and-democracy-fuels-rise-in-inequality-27217; Arash Emamzadeh, Why People Support Far-Right Political Views https://www.psychologytoday.com/us/blog/finding-new-home/201911/why-people-support-far-right-political-views**

[549] Jennifer M. Silva, *Coming Up Short: Working-Class Adulthood in the Age of Uncertainty.* (2013)

[550] Ganesh Sitaraman, *"The Collapse of Neoliberalism."* https://newrepublic.com/article/155970/collapse-neoliberalism

[551] Wendy Brown, *"In the Ruins of Neoliberalism: The Rise of anti-Democratic Politics in the West."* (2019); Henry Giroux, *"Neoliberalism Paved the Way for Right Wing Populism."* https://truthout.org/articles/neoliberalism-paved-the-way-for-authoritarian-right-wing-populism/

[552] **Nicholas Vrousalis, "*How Exploiters Dominate.*" https://www.tandfonline.com/doi/full/10.1080/00346764.2019.1618483; Hanes Kuch, "*The market, competition, and structural exploitation.*" https://onlinelibrary.wiley.com/doi/full/10.1111/1467-8675.12443; Göran Therborn, "*What does the ruling class so when it rules?*" https://library.fes.de/libalt/journals/swetsfulltext/10590661.pdf; Ronald Fischer, Katja Hanke, C.G. Sibley, "*Cultural and Institutional Determinants of Social Dominance Orientation: A Cross-Cultural Meta-Analysis of 27 Societies.*" https://www.researchgate.net/publication/259928560_Cultural_and_Institutional_Determinants_of_Social_Dominance_Orientation_A_Cross-Cultural_Meta-Analysis_of_27_Societies**

[553] Thorsten Hellmann, Pia Schmidt, Sascha Matthias Heller, *"Social Justice in the EU and OECD"* https://www.politico.eu/wp-content/uploads/2019/12/Social-Justice-Index-2019.pdf; Celi Scalon, Andre Salata, *"Inequalities, stratification and social justice."* https://www.researchgate.net/publication/314101487_Inequalities_stratification_and_social_justice

[554] Matthew Mahutga, *"The Persistence of Inequality? A Network Analysis of International Trade, 1965-2000."* https://matthewcm.ucr.edu/Mahutga%202006_final%20unpublished%20draft.pdf

[555] Roemer, John, *"Should Marxists be Interested in Exploitation?"* in John Remer, ed. *Analytical Marxism: Studies in Marxism and Social Theory*. (1986) 261-265; L. J. Warshaw, *"Precarious Employment and Child Labour."* https://www.iloencyclopaedia.org/part-iii-48230/work-and-workers/item/351-precarious-employment-and-child-labour; Hester Eisenstein, *"The Sweatshop Feminists."* https://jacobin.com/2015/06/kristof-globalization-development-third-world/; Gillian MacNaughton and Diane Frey, *"Challenging Neoliberalism: ILO, Human Rights, and Public Health Frameworks on Decent Work."* https://www.hhrjournal.org/2018/10/challenging-neoliberalism-ilo-human-rights-and-public-health-frameworks-on-decent-work/

[556] Pierre Bourdieu, *"The essence of neoliberalism."* https://mondediplo.com/1998/12/08bourdieu; David Harvey, *The Condition of Postmodernity*. 1991; David Harvey, *"Neoliberalism as creative destruction."* https://is.cuni.cz/studium/predmety/index.php?do=download&did=85806&kod=JMMZ108

[557] Jeremiah Traeger, *"Indoctrination and Free Will."* http://www.patheos.com/blogs/tippling/2017/05/15/indoctrination-and-free-will/

[558] Gerard Dumenil and Dominique Levy, *"The Nature and Contradictions of Neoliberalism."* http://www.cepremap.fr/membres/dlevy/dle2004k.pdf

[559] Boaventura de Sousa Santos, *"Governance: Between Myth and Reality."* https://journals.openedition.org/rccsar/95; Benjamin Ginsberg and Matthew A. Crenson, *"Downsizing Democracy: How America Sidelined its Citizens and Privatized its Public."* https://muse.jhu.edu/book/72712/pdf;

[560] Jacques Rupnik, *"Explaining Eastern Europe: The Crisis of Liberalism."* https://www.journalofdemocracy.org/articles/explaining-eastern-europe-the-crisis-of-liberalism/; Carlos March, *Fictiocracy: Democracy as an illusion.* https://www.opendemocracy.net/en/democraciaabierta/fictiocracy-democracy-as-illusion/; Ran Hirschl, *"The Nordic Counternarrative: Democracy, human development and judicial review."* I-CON-9 (2011).

[561] Armin Ishkanian, *"What protests in Athens, Cairo and London tell us about opposition to neoliberalism."* https://blogs.lse.ac.uk/europpblog/2018/03/19/what-protests-in-athens-cairo-and-london-tell-us-about-opposition-to-neoliberalism/; Max Zahn, *"Amazon and Starbucks workers led a union resurgence in 2022."* https://abcnews.go.com/Business/amazon-starbucks-workers-led-union-resurgence-2022/story?id=95090198; Socialist Equality Party, *"Form rank-and-file committees to lead a UK general strike!"* https://www.wsws.org/en/articles/2022/11/29/leaf-n29.html; Mario Pianta Paolo Gerbaudo, *"In Search of European Alternatives: Anti-Austerity Protests in Europe."* https://www.researchgate.net/publication/304883722_In_Search_of_European_Alternatives_Anti-Austerity_Protests_in_Europe

[562] Remy Herrera, *"The Neoliberal 'Rebirth' of Development Economics."* https://monthlyreview.org/2006/05/01/the-neoliberal-rebirth-of-development-economics/; Stephen Metcalf, *"Neoliberalism: The Idea that Swallowed the World."* https://www.theguardian.com/news/2017/aug/18/neoliberalism-the-idea-that-changed-the-world; Moises Arce, *"Parties and Social Protest in Latin America's Neoliberal Era."* https://biblioteca.cejamericas.org/bitstream/handle/2015/407/Parties-and-Social-Protest-in-Latin-Americas-Neoliberal-Era.pdf?sequence=1&isAllowed=y

[563] OECD, *"Inequality and Growth."* https://www.oecd.org/social/Focus-Inequality-and-Growth-2014.pdf; World Inequality Report, *"Global income inequality."* https://wir2022.wid.world/chapter-1/

[564] Patrick Henry, *"Economic Inequality has deepened during the pandemic."* https://www.weforum.org/agenda/2022/04/economic-inequality-wealth-gap-pandemic/

[565] Lucas Chanchel et al., *"World Inequality Report."* https://wir2022.wid.world/www-site/uploads/2022/02/WIR_2022_FullReport.pdf; David Neilson, *"Bringing in the 'neoliberal model of development."* https://journals.sagepub.com/doi/full/10.1177/0309816819852746

[566] Jonathan Malesic, *"Your work is not your god: welcome to the age of burnout epidemic."* https://www.theguardian.com/lifeandstyle/2022/jan/06/burnout-epidemic-work-lives-meaning

[567] Vasilie Sebastian Dancu, *"UBERIZATION: A struggle for power and control in the neoliberal paradise."* https://www.researchgate.net/publication/333059059_UBERIZATION_A_struggle_for_power_and_control_in_the_neoliberal_paradise; David Silva Franco and Diese Luiza de Silva Ferraz, *"Uberization of Labor and Capitalist Accumulation."* https://www.scielo.br/j/cebape/a/9NJd8xMhZD3qJVwqsG4WV3c/?format=pdf&lang=en

[568] Paul B. Ferrell, *"Myth of Perpetual Growth is Killing America."* Permaculture News (15 June 2012). https://permaculturenews.org/2012/06/15/myth-of-perpetual-growth-is-killing-america/; Lawrence Reynolds Bronislaw Szerszynski, *"Neoliberalism and technology: Perpetual innovation or perpetual crisis?"* http://www.countdownnet.net/Allegati/31%20Neoliberalism%20and%20technology_Perpetual%20innovation%20or%20perpetual%20crisis.pdf

[569] Adam Dahl and Joe Soss, *"Neoliberalism for the Common Good? Public Value -Governance and the Downsizing of Democracy."* https://www.researchgate.net/publication/262115820_Neoliberalism_for_the_Common_Good_Public_Value_-Governance_and_the_Downsizing_of_Democracy

[570] Rebecca Onion, *"Oh My God, It's Milton Friedman for Kids."* https://slate.com/human-interest/2020/02/choose-your-own-adventure-books-conservative-neoliberal-ideology-capitalism.html; *Douglas Rushkoff, "Corporate Growth for the Sake of Corporate Growth."* https://www.theatlantic.com/business/archive/2016/04/corporate-growth-for-the-sake-of-corporate-growth/479136/; Ursula Le Guin, *"On the Left/Right Paradigm Capitalism's Grow or Die Imperative and Murray Bookchin."* https://truthout.org/

articles/on-the-left-right-paradigm-capitalism-s-grow-or-die-imperative-and-murray-bookchin/; Leonard Gentle, *"Corruption and Neoliberalism."* https://www.thejournalist.org.za/spotlight/corruption-and-neoliberalism-we-are-caught-between-those-who-have-captured-the-state-and-those-who-want-to/

[571] Engelbert Stockhammer, *"Neoliberalism, Income Distribution and the Causes of the Crisis."* https://www.researchgate.net/publication/254449175_Neoliberalism_Income_Distribution_and_the_Causes_of_the_Crisis

[572] John Bellamy Foster, R. Jamil Joanna, and Brett Clark, *"The Contagion of Capital."* https://monthlyreview.org/2021/01/01/the-contagion-of-capital/

[573] Melissa Smith, *"What does the Stock Market do for Workers' Wages? Nothing."* Peoples' Policy Project.https://www.peoplespolicyproject.org/2017/08/24/what-does-the-stock-market-do-for-workers-wages-nothing/; John Seip and Dee Wood Harper, *The Trickle Down Delusion*, (2016); Paul A. Grout, et al. *"One-Half Billion Shareholders and Counting."* https://papers.ssrn.com/sol3/papers.cfm?abstract_id=1364765; Benjamin Landy, *"A Tale of two Recoveries: Wealth Inequality after the Great Recession."* https://tcf.org/content/commentary/a-tale-of-two-recoveries-wealth-inequality-after-the-great-recession/

[574] Jonathan Rothwell, *"Myths of the 1 Percent: What Puts People at the Top."* https://www.nytimes.com/2017/11/17/upshot/income-inequality-united-states.html; Max Roser, and Esteban Ortiz-Ospina, *"Income Inequality."* https://ourworldindata.org/income-inequality/

[575] An Economic Sense, *"The Highly Skewed Growth of Incomes Since 1980: Only the Top 0.5% Have Done Better Than Before."* https://aneconomicsense.org/2015/07/13/the-highly-skewed-growth-of-incomes-since-1980-only-the-top-0-5-have-done-better-than-before/;

[576] Bert Hoffman, *"China's Role in Efforts to Eradicate Poverty."* https://www.worldbank.org/en/news/opinion/2016/10/17/chinas-role-in-efforts-to-eradicate-poverty

[577] Lawrence Mishel, Elise Gould and Josh Bivens, *"Wage Stagnation in None Charts."* http://www.epi.org/publication/charting-wage-stagnation/; John Smith, *"Outsourcing, financialization and the crisis."* https://www.academia.edu/2074588/Outsourcing_financialisation_and_the_crisis; Tax Justice Network, *"How much money is in tax havens?"* https://taxjustice.net/faq/how-much-money-is-in-tax-havens/

[578] Josh Bivens and Lawrence Mishel, *"Understanding the Historic Divergence Between Productivity and a Typical Worker's Pay Why It Matters and Why It's Real".* http://www.epi.org/publication/understanding-the-historic-divergence-between-productivity-and-a-typical-workers-pay-why-it-matters-and-why-its-real/

[579] Dries Lesage and Mathias Vermeiren, *"Neo-Liberalism at a Time of Crisis: The Case of Taxation."* https://www.researchgate.net/publication/227391681_Neo-Liberalism_at_a_Time_of_Crisis_The_Case_of_Taxation; https://taxfoundation.org/publications/

corporate-tax-rates-around-the-world/; https://www.oecd.org/tax/tax-policy/corporate-tax-statistics-database-first-edition.pdf; T. L. Hungerford, *"Corporate Tax Rates and Economic Growth."* https://www.epi.org/publication/ib364-corporate-tax-rates-and-economic-growth/; Duane Swank, *"The Spread of Neoliberalism:* U.S. Economic Power and the Diffusion of Market-Oriented Tax Policy." https://ces.fas.harvard.edu/uploads/files/Working-Papers-Archives/CES_WP120.pdf; Amir Jina, *"The $200 Billion Fuel Subsidy You've Never Heard of."* https://www.forbes.com/sites/ucenergy/2017/02/01/the-200-billion-fossil-fuel-subsidy-youve-never-heard-of/?sh=2634729f652b; Médecins Sans Frontières, *"Governments must demand pharma make all COVID-19 vaccine deals public."* https://www.msf.org/governments-must-demand-all-coronavirus-covid-19-vaccine-deals-are-made-public

[580] **Duncan K. Folley, *"Rethinking Financial Capitalism and the Information Economy."* https://journals.sagepub.com/doi/10.1177/0486613413487154; Christian Élongué, *"Micro-labor, a new globalized digital proletariat."* https://cursus.edu/en/11851/micro-labor-a-new-globalized-digital-proletariat; Dave Elder-Vass, *"Digital Monopoly Capitalism"* in Dave Elder-Vass, *Profit and Gift in the Digital Economy.* (2016); Alto Jimenez Gonzalez, *"Law, Code and Exploitation: How Corporations Regulate the Working Conditions of the Digital Proletariat."* https://journals.sagepub.com/doi/10.1177/08969205211028964;**

[581] Shelton Stromquist, *Reinventing 'The People': The Progressive Movement, the Class Problem, and the Origins of Modern Liberalism.* (2005).

[582] Dieter Plehwe et al. eds., *Neoliberal Hegemony*, 2006; Carl Ferenbach and Chris Pinney, "*Toward a 21st Century Social Contract*" Journal of Applied Corporate Finance, 24:2, (2012) http://onlinelibrary.wiley.com/doi/10.1111/j.1745-6622.2012.00372.x/abstract

[583] https://bsr17.org/agenda/sessions/the-21st-century-social-contract

[584] NPR, *"1 in 10 Workers Is An Independent Contractor, Labor Department Says."* https://www.cpr.org/2018/06/07/1-in-10-workers-is-an-independent-contractor-labor-department-says/; Elaine Profeldt, *"Survey: Nearly 30% Of Americans Are Self-Employed."* https://www.forbes.com/sites/elainepofeldt/2020/05/30/survey-nearly-30-of-americans-are-self-employed/; Neil Stolovitsky, *"The Uberization of the Services Workforce in the Gig Economy."* https://uplandsoftware.com/psa/resources/blog/the-uberization-of-the-services-workforce-in-the-age-of-the-gig-economy/

[585] David Rotman, *Technology and the Inequality."*

https://www.technologyreview.com/s/531726/technology-and-inequality/; Corey Husak, "*How US Companies Harm Workers by Making them Independent Contractors.*" https://equitablegrowth.org/how-u-s-companies-harm-workers-by-making-them-independent-contractors/; Elaine Profeldt, *"Survey: Nearly 30% of Americans are Self-Employed."* https://www.forbes.com/sites/elainepofeldt/2020/05/30/survey-nearly-30-of-americans-are-self-employed/?sh=78be9c012d21

[586] Sean F. Johnston, *"The Technological Fix as a Cure for all."* https://philarchive.org/archive/JOHTTF-2v1; *"The EU Crisis and Europe's Divided Memories."* Ricerche Storich. http://www.ricerchestoriche.org/?p=749;

[587] Juliana Manasce Horowitz, Ruth Igielnik, Rakesh Kochhar, *"Trends in income and wealth inequality."* https://www.pewresearch.org/social-trends/2020/01/09/trends-in-income-and-wealth-inequality/; Peter G. Peterson Foundation, *"Income inequality has been on the rise since the 1980s and it continues its upward trajectory."* https://www.pgpf.org/blog/2021/11/Income-Inequality-Has-Been-on-the-Rise-since-the-1980s-and-Continues-Its-Upward-Trajectory

[588] Juliana Menasce Horowitz, *"Trends in Income and Wealth Inequality."* https://www.pewresearch.org/social-trends/2020/01/09/trends-in-income-and-wealth-inequality/; Marc Morgan and Theresa Neef, *"What's New About Income Inequality in Europe?"* https://wid.world/document/whats-new-about-income-inequality-in-europe-1980-2019/; https://housing4thehomeless.org/cost-of-living/

[589] Laurence Reynolds and Bronislaw Szerszynski, *"Neoliberalism and technology: Perpetual innovation or perpetual crisis?"* https://www.academia.edu/1937914/Neoliberalism_and_technology; Jessica Hall, *"Social Security's COLA could be 3.1% in 2024, and buying power has dropped 36% since 2000."* https://www.marketwatch.com/story/social-security-benefits-lose-36-of-buying-power-since-2000-study-f90f67d5?mod=home-page https://www.cbpp.org/research/poverty-and-inequality/a-guide-to-statistics-on-historical-trends-in-income-inequality; Diego Sanchez-Ancochea, *"Latin America: inequality and political instability have lessons for the rest of the world."* https://theconversation.com/latin-america-inequality-and-political-instability-have-lessons-for-the-rest-of-the-world-152929; Lwazi Siyabonga Lushaba, *"Development as modernity, modernity as development."* https://www.ascleiden.nl/Pdf/workingpaper69.pdf

[590] Colin Jenkins, *"Monopoly Capitalism in the 21st Century: Neoliberalism, Monetarism and the Perversion of Finance."* https://www.hamptonthink.org/read/monopoly-capitalism-in-the-21st-century-neoliberalism-monetarism-and-the-pervasion-of-finance

[591] EPI, *"The Productivity-Pay Gap."* https://www.epi.org/productivity-pay-gap/; Inequality.org, *"Income Inequality in the United States."* https://inequality.org/facts/income-inequality/#wage-inequality; Tanya Kaushai, *"What's driving the gap between the richest and poorest Americans."* https://finance.yahoo.com/news/whats-driving-the-gap-between-the-richest-and-poorest-americans-165307278.html

[592] Klaas V. *"Imperialism and the Concentration of Capital."* https://anti-imperialism.org/author/klaasvelija/

[593] Larry Polivka[126] and Baozhen Luo, *"The Neoliberal Economy and the Erosion of Retirement Security."* https://claudepeppercenter.fsu.edu/the-neoliberal-economy-and-erosion-of-retirement-security/

[594] David Ciepley, *"Liberalism in the Shadow of Totalitarianism."* https://americanaffairsjournal.org/2017/05/corporate-contradictions-neoliberalism/

---

126. http://claudepeppercenter.fsu.edu/about-our-staff/larry-polivka/

[595] Global Initiative, *"The Global Illicit Economy."* https://globalinitiative.net/wp-content/uploads/2021/03/The-Global-Illicit-Economy-GITOC-Low.pdf; Edward E. Williams and John Dobelman, *A Random Walk to Nowhere.* (2020); Agence France-Presse, *"Jackson, Mississippi situation is reminiscent of Flint, Michigan as residents have gone a week without drinking water."* https://www.scmp.com/news/world/united-states-canada/article/3191265/week-without-safe-drinking-water-jackson

[596] P. D. S. Martin, *"Nicos Poulntzas Theory of the State in the European Periphery Today.'* https://www.academia.edu/3339001/Nicos_Poulantzas_theory_of_the_state_and_the_neo_liberal_state_in_the_European_periphery_today; Ian Bruff, *"The Rise of Authoritarian Neoliberalism."* https://www.researchgate.net/publication/271994127_The_Rise_of_Authoritarian_Neoliberalism

[597] National Institute of Corrections, *"Private Prisons in the United States."* https://nicic.gov/private-prisons-united-states-2021; Loic Wacquant, *"The punitive regulation of poverty in the neoliberal age."* https://www.crimeandjustice.org.uk/publications/cjm/article/punitive-regulation-poverty-neoliberal-age

[598] Bill Alpert, *"How a Prominent Russian Oligarch Helped Start America's Cannabis Industry."* https://www.barrons.com/articles/russian-oligarch-roman-abramovich-curaleaf-cannabis-industry-51674507683; Beatrice Hibou, *"Economic Crime and Neoliberal Modes of Government: The Example of the Mediterranean."* https://academic.oup.com/jsh/article/45/3/642/1746036?login=true;

David Bacon, *"Stories from the Borderland."* in Teo Balve, ed. *Dispatches from Latin America.* (2006); Jacob Laderman, *"Flint's Water Crisis Is No Accident: It's the Result of Years of Neoliberalism Free Market Reforms."* https://inthesetimes.com/article/flint-water-crisis-neoliberalism-free-market-reforms-rick-snyder; Jorg Weigratz, *"How neoliberalism's moral order feeds fraud and corruption."* https://theconversation.com/how-neoliberalisms-moral-order-feeds-fraud-and-corruption-60946; D.R. Simon, *Elite Deviance.* (2018); Arjan Reurnik, *"From Elite Lawbreaking to Financial Crime."* https://d-nb.info/1116426684/34.

[599] Jamie Redman, *"5 Major Banks Exposed for Moving Trillions for Mobsters Onecoin, and Drug Cartels."* https://news.bitcoin.com/5-major-banks-exposed-for-moving-trillions-for-mobsters-onecoin-and-drug-cartels/; Ed Vulliamy, *"How a big US bank laundered billions from Mexico's murderous drug gangs."* https://www.theguardian.com/world/2011/apr/03/us-bank-mexico-drug-gangs; Jack Ewing, *"Credit Suisse is fined for helping a Bulgarian drug ring launder money."* https://www.nytimes.com/2022/06/27/business/credit-suisse-fine-bulgarian-drug-ring.html

[600] UK-FCA, *"Barclays fined £59.5 million for significant failings in relation to LIBOR and EURIBOR."* https://www.fca.org.uk/news/press-releases/barclays-fined-%C2%A3595-million-significant-failings-relation-libor-and-euribor

[601] Ryan Cooper, *"A Brief History of Crime, Corruption and Malfeasance at American Banks."* https://theweek.com/articles/729052/brief-history-crime-corruption-malfeasance-american-banks; Loic Wacuant, *Punishing the Poor: The Neoliberal Government of Social Insecurity.* (2009); Chris Hedges, *"The Mafia State."* https://www.truthdig.com/articles/the-mafia-state/

[602] Noam Chomsky and R. W. McChesney, *Profit Over People: Neoliberalism and Global Order*, (2011); Pauline Johnson, *"Sociology and the Critique of Neoliberalism"* European Journal of Social Theory, (2014).

[603] Jörg Wiegratz and David White, *"How neoliberalism's moral order feeds fraud and corruption."* https://theconversation.com/how-neoliberalisms-moral-order-feeds-fraud-and-corruption-60946

[604] John Gerring and Strom C. Thacker, *"Do Neoliberal Policies Deter Neoliberal Political Corruption?"* http://www.bu.edu/sthacker/files/2012/02/IO2005.pdf; *"Neoliberalism and Corruption."* https://staff.blog.ui.ac.id/dnh60/index.php/2008/08/19/neoliberalism-and-corruption/; Leonard Gentle, *"Corruption and Neoliberalism."* http://www.thejournalist.org.za/spotlight/corruption-and-neoliberalism-we-are-caught-between-those-who-have-captured-the-state-and-those-who-want-to/

[605] Michael Teague, *"Probation, People and Profits: The Impact of Neoliberalism."* https://mmuperu.co.uk/bjcj/articles/probation-people-and-profits-the-impact-of-neoliberalism/; R.T. Naylor, *Wages of Crime: Black Markets, Illegal Finance, and the Underworld economy.* (2002); Andrew R. Smolski, *"Introduction: Violence, Capital Accumulation, and Resistance in Contemporary Latin America."* https://journals.sagepub.com/doi/full/10.1177/0094582X20975005; Stefan Klein and Ricardo Pagliuso Regatien, *"Unfettered Capitalism: On rackets, cronies and mafiosi."* https://www.scielo.br/j/ts/a/tyrbJWzbQjwgqBYWdY84H9y/?format=pdf&lang=en; Emma Bell, *"Criminal Justice and Neoliberalism."* https://www.researchgate.net/publication/215775748_Criminal_Justice_and_Neoliberalism

[606] Beth Daley, *"How neoliberalism's moral order feeds fraud and corruption."* https://theconversation.com/how-neoliberalisms-moral-order-feeds-fraud-and-corruption-60946; UNODC, *"Illegal Betting and Sport,"* ttps://www.unodc.org/res/safeguardingsport/grcs/section-9_html/SPORTS_CORRUPTION_2021_S9.pdf

[607] Patrick Hamm, David Stuckler Hamm, Lawrence King, *"The Governance Grenade: Mass Privatization, State Capacity, and Economic Growth in Post-Communist Countries."* https://peri.umass.edu/fileadmin/pdf/working_papers/working_papers_201-250/WP222.pdf

[608] Michael A. Lebowitz. *The Contradictions of "Real Socialism": The Conductor and the Conducted*[127]. (2012). Mirjana Kasapović *"Parliamentarism and Presidentialism in Eastern Europe."* https://hrcak.srce.hr/file/155698; Lyubov Kholova, *"Social And Cultural Phenomenon "Soviet" In The Post-Soviet Space."* https://www.researchgate.net/publication/346506902_Social_And_Cultural_Phenomenon_Soviet_In_The_Post-Soviet_Space; Patrick Hamm, David Stickler and Lawrence King, *The Governance Grenade: Mass Privatization, State Capacity and Economic Growth in Post-Communist Countries.* (2010); David D. Laitin, *"Post-Soviet Politics."* https://www.annualreviews.org/doi/10.1146/annurev.polisci.3.1.117

---

127. https://monthlyreview.org/product/contradictions_of_real_socialism/

[609] Nancy Holmstrom and Richard Smith, *"The Necessity of Gangster Capitalism."* https://monthlyreview.org/2000/02/01/the-necessity-of-gangster-capitalism/

[610] Oliver Bullough, *"Russian oligarchs are more connected to the Kremlin than previously thought."* https://www.codastory.com/newsletters/russian-oligarchs-ukraine-war/; Anders Aslund, *"Russia's Crony Capitalism: The Path from Market Economy to Kleptocracy."* (2019); Dorina Rosca, *"The post-Soviet Moldovan Capitalism: Between Oligarchic Political Economy and Reciprocity."* https://www.tandfonline.com/doi/abs/10.1080/14631377.2020.1793583; Djoomart Otorbaev, *"Chaos and Opportunism in Kazakhstan."* https://www.project-syndicate.org/commentary/kazakhstan-protests-opportunities-for-russia-and-oligarchs-by-djoomart-otorbaev-2022-01; James O. Finckenauer and Yuri A. Voronin, *"The Threat of Russian Organized Crime."* https://www.ojp.gov/pdffiles1/nij/187085.pdf

[611] Ariel Ackerman, Leonardo Weller, Joao Paulo Pessoa, *"The West's Teeth: IMF conditionality during the Cold War."* The World Economy, 45:7 (2022); Marek Dabrowski, *"Western Aid Conditionality and the Post-Communist Transition."* The Moscow Times, *"Russia's 500 Super Rich Wealthier Than the Poorest 99.8%."* https://www.case-research.eu/upload/publikacja_plik/3414795_037.pdf; https://www.themoscowtimes.com/2021/06/10/russias-500-super-rich-wealthier-than-poorest-998-report-a74180

[612] Gareth Dale and Adam Fabry, *"Neoliberalism in Eastern Europe and the former Soviet Union."* https://www.academia.edu/36295873/Neoliberalism_in_Eastern_Europe_and_the_former_Soviet_Union; F. Joseph Dresen, *"The Privatization of Russia: Russian Reform Goes Awry."* https://www.wilsoncenter.org/publication/the-piratization-russia-russian-reform-goes-awry;

Andrei Shleifer and Daniel Treisman, *"A Normal Country: Russia after Communism."* https://scholar.harvard.edu/files/shleifer/files/normal_jep.pdf; Nikos Passas, *"Global Anomie and Economic Crime: Hidden Consequences of Neoliberalism and Globalization in Russia and Around the World."* http://facpub.stjohns.edu/~tillmanr/global%20crime%20readings/passas%20article.pdf

[613] Justinas Šuliokas, *"Neoliberal zeal spelled two decades of 'absolute tragedy' for Baltic development – interview."* https://www.lrt.lt/en/news-in-english/19/1406217/neoliberal-zeal-spelled-two-decades-of-absolute-tragedy-for-baltic-development-interview;

Vladimir Papava, *"Economic models of Eurasianism and the Eurasian Union: why the future is not optimistic."* https://www.cacianalyst.org/publications/analytical-articles/item/13296-economic-models-of-eurasianism-and-the-eurasian-union-why-the-future-is-not-optimistic.html; Jorum Duri, *"Corruption and Economic Crime."* https://knowledgehub.transparency.org/assets/uploads/kproducts/2021-Corruption-and-economic-crime_final.pdf

[614] Adam Harmes, *"Neoliberalism and Multilevel Governance."* https://www.researchgate.net/publication/233152950_Neoliberalism_and_Multilevel_Governance; Sheri Berman, *"The consequences of neoliberalism in Eastern Europe."* https://www.ips-journal.eu/topics/democracy-and-society/the-consequences-of-neoliberal-capitalism-in-eastern-europe-5401/

[615] Peter Rutland, *"Neoliberalism and the Russian Transition."* http://prutland.faculty.wesleyan.edu/files/2015/07/PR-Neoliberalism-in-Russia.pdf; Mark Baker, *"East: The Black Economy - How can you Measure what is Hidden?"* https://www.rferl.org/a/1053278.html; Branko Milanovic, *"Income, Inequality, and Poverty during the Transition from Planned to Market Economy."* https://documents1.worldbank.org/curated/en/229251468767984676/pdf/multi-page.pdf

[616] **Yevgeny Primakov, *"Russia's Problems; Why Neoliberal Policy is Unacceptable Today."* https://valdaiclub.com/a/highlights/russia_s_problems_why_neoliberal_policy_is_unacceptable_today/**

[617] Paul Massaro and Amelie Rausing, *'Russia's Weaponization of Corruption [and Western Complicity].'* https://www.csce.gov/international-impact/russia-s-weaponization-corruption-and-western-complicity?page=2

[618] Tahir Zaman, *"Political Islam in neoliberal times."* https://www.opendemocracy.net/en/north-africa-west-asia/political-islam-in-neoliberal-times/

[619] Jason Hackworth, *Faith Based: Religious Neoliberalism and the Politics of Welfare in the United States.* (2012); Clayton Crockett, *"Neoliberalism, Postsecuralism, and the End of Religion."* https://www.mdpi.com/2077-1444/12/8/631

[620] François Gauthier, *"Religion is not what it used to be: Consumerism, neoliberalism and the global reshaping of religion."* https://blogs.lse.ac.uk/religionglobalsociety/2017/10/religion-is-not-what-it-used-to-be-consumerism-neoliberalism-and-the-global-reshaping-of-religion/; Roger Kurt Green, *"Neoliberalism and eurochristianity."* Religions, 12, 9 (2021); Mona Atia, *"A Way to Paradise:*

Pious Neoliberalism, Islam and Faith-Based Development." https://www.tandfonline.com/doi/abs/10.1080/00045608.2011.627046; Zeynep Atalay, *Authoritarian and Islamist civil society in Turkey.* (2018)

[621] Humeira Iqidar, *"How Long is Life? Neoliberalism and Islamic Piety."* https://kclpure.kcl.ac.uk/portal/files/73722484/How_Long_Is_Life_IQTIDAR_Publishedonline1June2017_GREEN_VoR.pdf; J.A. Mohammed, *"The ethical system in Islam: implications for business practices."* https://www.researchgate.net/publication/319357849_The_ethical_system_in_islam_-_implications_for_business_practices

[622] James Carr, *"Islamophobia, Neoliberalism, and the Muslim Other."* https://www.insightturkey.com/articles/islamophobia-neoliberalism-and-the-muslim-other; Hayat, Azmat and Muhammad Shafiai, Muhammad Hakimi and Haron, Sabri, *"Neoliberalism vs Islam, An analysis of Social Cost in case of USA and Saudi Arabia."* https://mpra.ub.uni-muenchen.de/105746/1/MPRA_paper_105746.pdf; Katerina Dalacura, *"Islamism and neoliberalism in the aftermath of 2011 uprisings: the Freedom and Justice Party in Egypt and Nahda in Tunisia."* http://eprints.lse.ac.uk/64909/1/Dalacoura_Islamism_Neoliberalism.pdf; Bryan S. Turner and K.M. Nasir, *Islam, Capitalism and the Weber Thesis.* (2013); Siti Nur Hidayah, "Pesantren for Middle-Class Muslims in Indonesia (Between Religious Commodification and Pious Neoliberalism)." https://journal.iainkudus.ac.id/index.php/QIJIS/article/download/7641/pdf

[623] J N and Mariyah LM, *"Jakarta is returning: The 'neoliberal cookbook' that guides Indonesia's Omnibus Bill."* https://lausan.hk/2020/jakarta-is-returning-omnibus-bills/; John Calabrese, *"China-Iraq Relations Poised for a Quantum Leap?"* https://www.mei.edu/publications/china-iraq-relations-poised-quantum-leap

[624] Junaid Rana, *"The Racial Infrastructure of the Terror-Industrial Complex."* https://islamophobiaisracism.files.wordpress.com/2017/03/rana-racial-infrastructure-social-text-2016-rana-111-38.pdf; [128] Firyal Bawab, ed. *"US Foreign Policy in the Middle East: Changes in the Neoliberal Age."* https://luskincenter.history.ucla.edu/wp-content/uploads/sites/66/2021/06/U.S.-Foreign-Policy-in-the-Middle-East-Changes-in-the-Neoliberal-Age.pdf

[625] Naomi Klein, *The Shock Doctrine: The Rise of Disaster Capitalism.* (2008), part 6; Kevin D. Reyes, "We Must Help Them Build Free Institutions: Neoliberal Modernization and American Nation-Building in Iraq." https://escholarship.org/content/qt23w0n5sw/qt23w0n5sw.pdf?t=o7zoit&v=lg; Benjamin R. Barber, *Jihad vs. McWorld.* (1995)

[626] Naomi Klein, *No War: America's Real Business in Iraq.* (2005); Lily Hamourtziadou and Bulent Gokay, *"Iraq's security 2003-2019: death and neoliberal destruction par excellence."* https://www.opendemocracy.net/en/north-africa-west-asia/iraqs-security-2003-2019-death-and-neoliberal-destruction-par-excellence/

[627] Basav Sen, Hope Chu, *"Operation Corporate Freedom: The IMF and World Bank in Iraq."* https://archive.globalpolicy.org/social-and-economic-policy/financing-for-development-1-45/debt-relief/37224.html

---

128. https://islamophobiaisracism.files.wordpress.com/2017/03/rana-racial-infrastructure-social-text-2016-rana-111-38.pdf;%20

[628] Cited in Yousef K. Baker, *"Global Capitalism and Iraq: The Making of a Neoliberal State."* https://www.academia.edu/23159123/GLOBAL_CAPITALISM_AND_IRAQ_THE_MAKING_OF_A_NEOLIBERAL_STATE

[629] Dave Whyte, *"The Crimes of Neoliberal Rule in Occupied Iraq."* https://academic.oup.com/bjc/article/47/2/177/519163

[630] Joy Gordon, *"Accountability and Global Governance: The Case of Iraq."* https://www.cambridge.org/core/journals/ethics-and-international-affairs/article/abs/accountability-and-global-governance-the-case-of-iraq/7B57CC4FB5547E5C4A2A5040B1DAE97F; John S. Duffield, *"Oil and the Iraq War: How the US Could Have Expected to Benefit, and Might Still."* https://scholarworks.gsu.edu/cgi/viewcontent.cgi?article=1080&context=political_science_facpub

[631] James G. Stewart, *Corporate War Crimes.* (2010); Robin Wright, *"Trump's Baffling Plan to Pillage Syria's Oil."* https://www.newyorker.com/news/our-columnists/trumps-baffling-plan-to-pillage-syrias-oil

[632] Thomas Sommer Huddeville, *"Remaking Iraq: Neoliberalism and a System of Violence after the US Invasion, 2003-2011."* http://www.diva-portal.org/smash/get/diva2:1066079/FULLTEXT01.pdf; Dave Whyte, *"The Crimes of Neoliberal Rule in Occupied Iraq."* https://academic.oup.com/bjc/article/47/2/177/519163

[633] Victorios Bayan Shams, *"Introduction to the Thought of the Arab Marxist Mahdi Amel."* https://litci.org/en/introduction-to-the-thought-of-the-arab-marxist-mahdi-amel/

[634] Arhama Siddiqa, Muhammad Abbas Hassan, Assad Ullah Khan, *"Saudi-Israeli Nexus."* https://iramcenter.org/d_hbanaliz/Saudi_Y_Israeli_Nexus_Implications_for_Iran.pdf; By Aziz El Yaakoubi[129], Andrew Mills[130] and Matt Spetalnick[131], *"US, Israel push Arab allies for joint defense pact amid Iran tensions."* https://www.reuters.com/world/middle-east/us-israel-push-arab-allies-joint-defence-pact-amid-iran-tensions-2022-07-07/

[635] Rima Majed, *"Lebanon and Iraq in 2019: Revolutionary uprisings against sectarian neoliberalism."* https://longreads.tni.org/lebanon-and-iraq-in-2019; Kareem Chehayeb, *"Lebanon is the Experiment that Sows Neoliberalism's Failure."* https://tcf.org/content/commentary/lebanon-experiment-shows-neoliberalisms-failure/?agreed=1; *"Iraq's Tishreen Uprising: From Barricades to Ballot Box."* https://www.crisisgroup.org/middle-east-north-africa/gulf-and-arabian-peninsula/iraq/223-iraqs-tishreen-uprising-barricades-ballot-box; Ishac Diwan, et al. *Crony Capitalism in the Middle East: Business and Politics from Liberalization to the Arab Spring.* (2019); Michael Schwartz, *"Military Neoliberalism: Endless War and Humanitarian Crisis in the Twenty First Century."* https://scholarlycommons.law.case.edu/cgi/viewcontent.cgi?article=1100&context=swb

[636] **Husnul Amin, *"Neoliberal Globalisation and Islamic Social***

129. https://www.reuters.com/authors/aziz-el-yaakoubi/

130. https://www.reuters.com/authors/andrew-mills/

131. https://www.reuters.com/authors/matt-spetalnick/

***Movements: Critical Reflections on Approaches and Models."* https://www.academia.edu/10719393/ Neoliberal_Globalisation_and_Islamic_Social_Movements_Critical_I Tuğal, *"Fight or Acquiesce? Religion and Political Process in Turkey's and Egypt's Neoliberalizations."* https://sociology.berkeley.edu/sites/default/files/faculty/tugal/ Tugal%2C%20neoliberalization%2C%20Turkey%20and%20Egypt.pd Alexander C. Chandra, *"A Dirty Word? Neo-liberalism in Indonesia's foreign economic policies."* https://www.iisd.org/ system/files/publications/dirty_word.pdf**

[637] **Tahir Zaman, *"Political Islam in Neoliberal Times."* https://www.opendemocracy.net/en/north-africa-west-asia/political-islam-in-neoliberal-times/; https://www.transparency.org/en/cpi/2021 https://tradingeconomics.com/indonesia/corruption-index; Neil Robinson, *"The political is personal: Corruption, clientelism, patronage, informal practices and the dynamics of post-communism."* https://www.researchgate.net/publication/237086550_The_political_is_personal_Corruption_clientelism_patronage_informal_practices_and_the_dynamics_of_post-communism**

[638] Alexandra C. Chandra, *"A Dirty Word? Neoliberalism in Indonesia's foreign economic policy."* https://www.iisd.org/system/files/publications/dirty_word.pdf

[639] Toby Carroll, *"Social Development' as Neoliberal Trojan Horse: The World Bank and the Kecamatan Development Program in Indonesia."* https://www.academia.edu/3129800/Social_Development_as_Neoliberal_Trojan_Horse_The_World_Bank_and_the_Kecamatan_Development_Program_

[640] Yenny Tjoy, *"Two decades of economic growth benefited only the richest 20 percent: How severe is inequality in Indonesia?"* https://theconversation.com/two-decades-of-economic-growth-benefited-only-the-richest-20-how-severe-is-inequality-in-indonesia-101138; Hal Hill, *"What's Happened to Poverty and Inequality in Indonesia over Half a Century?"* https://direct.mit.edu/adev/article/38/1/68/98303/What-s-Happened-to-Poverty-and-Inequality-in; https://www.macrotrends.net/countries/IDN/indonesia/urban-population; Richard Grabowski jnand Sharmistha Self, *"Industrialization and Deindustrialization in Indonesia."* https://onlinelibrary.wiley.com/doi/full/10.1002/app5.295.

[641] **H. Ahmad Muzani, *"Gerindra party represents Indonesia at BRICS forum."* https://observerid.com/gerindra-party-represents-indonesia-at-brics-forum/; Vedi R. Hadiz, *"Indonesian Political Islam: Capitalist Development and the Legacies of the Cold War."* https://journals.sagepub.com/doi/10.1177/186810341103000101**

[642] Daromir Rudnyckyj, *"Spiritual Economies: Islam and Neoliberalism in Contemporary Indonesia."* Cultural Anthropology, 24, 1 (2007)

[643] **Laurens Bakker, *"Perceiving neoliberalism beyond Jakarta."* Michaela Haug, Martin Rössler, Anna-Teresa Grumblies, eds., *Rethinking Power Relations in Indonesia.* (2016); Tania Li, *"Neo-Liberal Strategies of Government through Community: The Social Development Program of the World Bank in Indonesia."* https://www.academia.edu/33771276/ Neo_Liberal_Strategies_of_Government_through_Community_The_S**

[644] Greg Acciaioli[132] and Suraya Afiff[133], *"Neoliberal Conservation in Central Kalimantan, Indonesia."* https://www.tandfonline.com/doi/abs/10.1080/13639811.2018.1531968?journalCode=cimw20

[645] **Bosman Batubara, Noer Fauzi Rachman, *"Extended Agrarian Question in Concessionary Capitalism: The Jakarta's Kaum Miskin Kota."***

https://journals.sagepub.com/doi/full/10.1177/22779760221095121; Paul K. Gellert, "." https://www.tandfonline.com/doi/abs/10.1080/14747731.2018.1560189?needAccess=true&journalCode=rglo20

[646] Andry Anshari, Mia Aulina Lubis, "Influence of the WTO's Agreement on Agriculture (AOA) Policy on Indonesian Coffee Imports 2007-2013," https://talenta.usu.ac.id/jpr/libraryFiles/downloadPublic/96

[647] Anne Booth, *"Indonesia's inconsistent income distribution data."* https://www.eastasiaforum.org/2020/05/15/indonesias-inconsistent-income-distribution-data/

[648] Agasta Amaliya Khusna, *"The Economy of Indonesia and South Korea: a comparison"* https://www.kompasiana.com/agastaamaliyakhusna0002/5aece6ebbde5757272170a34/the-economy-of-indonesia-and-south-korea-a-comparison; Dimas Muhamad, et al. *"Made in Somewhere Else: How Premature Deindustrialization Undermines the Development of Indonesia and other Emerging Economies."* https://www.aminef.or.id/

---

132. https://www.tandfonline.com/author/Acciaioli%2C+Greg

133. https://www.tandfonline.com/author/Afiff%2C+Suraya

made_in_somewhere_else_how_premature_deindustrialization_undermines_the_development_of_indonesia_and_other_emerging_economi https://knowledgehub.transparency.org/assets/uploads/helpdesk/Country-profile-Indonesia-2018_PR.pdf

[649] Suryaputra Wijaksana[134], *"Indonesia's Economic Reform Deeper than Recognized."* https://asiatimes.com/2023/05/indonesias-economic-reform-deeper-than-recognized/; The World Bank, *"Indonesia's Rising Divide."* https://www.worldbank.org/en/news/feature/2015/12/08/indonesia-rising-divide

[650] Transparency International, *"Corruption Perceptions Index."* https://www.transparency.org/en/cpi/2021?gclid=Cj0KCQjwwJuVBhCAARIsAOPwGAR7ksJnqKgyaCfhlo-W6EHFoEce-mXUJ3-JFs8hTmNYB215ckWEmzcaAm27EALw_wcB

[651] Julian E. Zelizer, *"This is Reagan's Party."* https://www.theatlantic.com/politics/archive/2016/02/this-is-reagans-party/459603/

[652] Noëlle Burgi, *"Societies Without Citizens: The Anomic Impacts of Labor Market Restructuring and the Erosion of Social Rights in Europe."* https://hal.archives-ouvertes.fr/hal-01967995/document

[653] Susan George, *"History of Neoliberalism."* https://www.tni.org/en/article/short-history-neoliberalism

[654] Agtilio A. Boron, *"Democracy or Neoliberalism."* http://bostonreview.net/archives/BR21.5/boron.html

[655] Anisha Tamana, *"Biden, Neo-Liberalism and Homelessness."* https://www.streetsheet.org/biden-neo-liberalism-and-homelessness/; https://www.sfchronicle.com/politics/article/S-F-officials-want-15-million-for-tent-sites-16269998.php#photo-20702792

[656] Matt Taibi, *"US Sues Wells Fargo."* https://www.rollingstone.com/politics/politics-news/u-s-sues-wells-fargo-yet-another-bailed-out-bank-accused-of-fraud-242163/; Luke Savage, *"We Should Have Jailed the Bankers After the Last Crisis."* https://jacobinmag.com/2021/05 https://www.sfchronicle.com/politics/article/S-F-officials-want-15-million-for-tent-sites-16269998.php#photo-20702792/wall-street-bankers-white-collar-crime-financial-crisis-wells-fargo[135]; Southern District of California "*Wells Fargo Bank Personal Banker Pleads Guilty to Money Laundering and Bank Fraud.*" https://www.justice.gov/usao-sdca/pr/wells-fargo-bank-personal-banker-pleads-guilty-money-laundering-and-bank-fraud

[657] **Max Roser, *"Global Economic Inequality."* https://ourworldindata.org/global-economic-inequality; https://www.oxfam.org/en/5-shocking-facts-about-extreme-global-inequality-and-how-even-it; David Enrich, Ben Protess and W. K. Raushbaum, *"Deutsche Bank Faces Criminal Investigation for Potential Money Laundering Lapses."* https://www.nytimes.com/2019/06/19/business/deutsche-bank-money-laundering-trump.html; Ronald Hamowy, *"Hayek's***

134. https://asiatimes.com/author/suryaputra-wijaksana/

135. https://jacobinmag.com/2021/05/wall-street-bankers-white-collar-crime-financial-crisis-wells-fargo

Concept of Freedom: A Critique." **https://oll.libertyfund.org/page/hamowy-s-critique-of-hayek-s-concept-of-freedom**

[658] *"Eight Billionaires Own as Much as Poorest Half of Global Population."* https://philanthropynewsdigest.org/news/eight-billionaires-own-as-much-as-poorest-half-of-global-population; Hanna Duggal[136] and Marium Ali[137], *"Why do more than 800 million people live in hunger?"* https://www.aljazeera.com/news/2023/5/28/why-is-global-hunger-on-the-rise-2

[659] Alan Wertheimer, *Exploitation*, 1999; Ruth J. Sample, *Exploitation; What is it and why it is Wrong*, (2003).

[660] Susan George, *Shadow Sovereigns: How Global Corporations are seizing Power.* (2015).

[661] Nooshi Dadgostar, *"Sweden's Left Has to Show Working People that the State Will Protect Them."* https://jacobinmag.com/2021/03/sweden-left-party-chair-nooshi-dadgostar; Ashlley Lavelle, *"Social Democracy of Neoliberalism? The Cases of Germany and Sweden."*

https://research-repository.griffith.edu.au/bitstream/handle/10072/18534/49600_1.pdf;sequence=1; Madison Rousseau, *"The Sweden Democrats as an Example of the Mainstreamization of the far-right."* https://www.illiberalism.org/the-sweden-democrats-as-an-example-of-the-mainstreamization-of-the-far-right/; Daniel Zamora, *"When Exclusion Replaces Exploitation."* https://nonsite.org/when-exclusion-replaces-exploitation/; Robert Blanton and Dursun Peksen, *"The side of economic freedom: Neoliberalism has deleterious effects on labour rights."* https://blogs.lse.ac.uk/usappblog/2016/08/20/the-dark-side-of-economic-freedom-neoliberalism-has-deleterious-effects-on-labour-rights/

[662] Richard Wike[138], Katie Simmons[139], Bruce Stokes[140] and Janell Fetterolf[141], *"Many unhappy with current political system."* http://www.pewglobal.org/2017/10/16/many-unhappy-with-current-political-system/

[663] Larry Diamond, *"Facing up to the Democratic Recession."*https://www.journalofdemocracy.org/wp-content/uploads/2015/01/Diamond-26-1_0.pdf; Abdurashid Solijonov, *"Voter Turnout Trends Around the World."* https://www.idea.int/sites/default/files/publications/voter-turnout-trends-around-the-world.pdf

[664] Shaheed Nick Mohammed, *Communication and the Globalization of Culture.* (2011); Pierre Dardot, *"Hegemony and Neoliberalism."* https://www.transform-network.net/publications/yearbook/overview/article/journal-112012/hegemony-and-neoliberalism/; Joseph Stiglitz, *"Three decades of neoliberal policies have decimated the middle class, our economy, and our democracy."* https://www.marketwatch.com/story/three-decades-of-neoliberal-policies-have-decimated-the-middle-class-our-economy-and-our-democracy-2019-05-13

---

136. https://www.aljazeera.com/author/duggalhaljazeera-net

137. https://www.aljazeera.com/author/alimar

138. https://www.pewresearch.org/staff/richard-wike

139. https://www.pewresearch.org/staff/katie-simmons

140. https://www.pewresearch.org/staff/bruce-stokes

141. https://www.pewresearch.org/staff/janell-fetterolf

[665] **Marcia Ghidina, *"Deconstructing Victim-Blaming, Dehumanization, and Othering: Using Empathy to Develop a Sociological Imagination."* https://www.researchgate.net/publication/332653926_Deconstructing_Victim-Blaming_Dehumanization_and_Othering_Using_Empathy_to_Devel**

[666] Necati Aydin, *"Seeking self-worth through commodity narcissism and commodity nihilism in the light of secular and Tawhidi Paradigms."* 18:2 Al-Shajarah: Journal of the International Institute of Islamic Thought and Civilization. (2013)

[667] Neil Vallelly, *"The Self-Help Myth."* https://newint.org/features/2020/04/07/feature; Alexandra Schwartz, *"Improving Ourselves to Death."* https://www.newyorker.com/magazine/2018/01/15/improving-ourselves-to-death

[668] Mitch Ciuria, *"A Tale of Two Resiliencies: The Emergence of Neoliberal Resilience and Radical Resilience."* https://biopoliticalphilosophy.com/2021/09/30/a-tale-of-two-resiliences-the-emergence-of-neoliberal-resilience-and-radical-resilience%EF%BF%BC/

[669] David Lauer, *"Facebook's ethical failures are not accidental; they are part of a business model."* https://www.ncbi.nlm.nih.gov/pmc/articles/PMC8179701/; Julia C. Wong, *"Sri Lankans fear violence over Facebook fake news ahead of election."* https://www.theguardian.com/world/2019/nov/11/facebook-sri-lanka-election-fake-news; Michel Martin, Will Jarvis, *"Far-Right Misinformation is Thriving on Facebook."* https://www.npr.org/2021/03/06/974394783/far-right-misinformation-is-thriving-on-facebook-a-new-study-shows-just-how-much; Mark Travers, *"Facebook Spreads Fake News Faster Than Any Other Social Website."* https://www.forbes.com/sites/traversmark/2020/03/21/facebook-spreads-fake-news-faster-than-any-other-social-website-according-to-new-research/

[670] Ellen Huet and Davey Alba, *"Sheryl Sandberg resigns from Facebook, leaves a tainted legacy."* https://www.news24.com/fin24/companies/sheryl-sandberg-resigns-from-facebook-leaves-a-tainted-legacy-20220602; Michele Martin, Will Jarvis, *"Far Right Misinformation in Thriving on Facebook."* https://www.npr.org/2021/03/06/974394783/far-right-misinformation-is-thriving-on-facebook-a-new-study-shows-just-how-much?t=1655190423296

[671] Jodi Melamed, *"Represent and Destroy: Rationalizing Violence in the new Racial Capitalism."* https://manifold.umn.edu/read/represent-and-destroy/section/be3128ae-62b8-4574-be7f-b07407cf1505; Carla Lou Andrea Ibled, *"Beyond limits: a psychoanalytical study of neoliberal imaginary."* https://research.gold.ac.uk/id/eprint/30356/1/POL_thesis_IbledC_2021.pdf; Jeremy K. Kessler, *"Nietzsche's Neoliberalism? A Response to Corey Robin."* https://www.dissentmagazine.org/blog/nietzsches-neoliberalism-a-response-to-corey-robin

[672] J. Rydgren (Ed.), *Class Politics and the Radical Right.* (2012).

[673] Bruce Stokes, *"Public Attitudes toward the Next Social Contract."* http://www.pewglobal.org/2013/01/15/public-attitudes-toward-the-next-social-contract/

[674] Clara Dewey, *"How Neoliberalism has Caused Income Inequality."* https://medium.com/of-course-global/how-neoliberalism-has-caused-income-inequality-9ec1fcaacb

[675] Calvin Hayes, *Popper, Hayek and the Open Society.* (2009); Charlotte Sleigh, *"The abuses of Popper."* https://aeon.co/essays/how-popperian-falsification-enabled-the-rise-of-neoliberalism.

[676] Michelle Lamont and Jonathan Mijs, *"Neoliberal Policy Implementation Goes Hand in Hand with Stronger Symbolic Boundaries."* https://epicenter.wcfia.harvard.edu/blog/neoliberal-policy-implementation-goes-hand-hand-stronger-symbolic-boundaries; Louise M. Prendergast, Dave Hill and Sharon Jones, "Social Exclusion, Education and Precarity: neoliberalism, neoconservatism and class war from above." http://www.jceps.com/wp-content/uploads/2017/10/15-2-2.pdf

[677] Louise M Prendergast, Dave Hill, Sharon Jones, "Social Exclusion, Education and Precarity: neoliberalism, neoconservatism and class war from above" http://www.jceps.com/wp-content/uploads/2017/10/15-2-2.pdf

[678] *"A 164-year Old Idea Helps Explain the Huge Changes Sweeping the World's Workforce."* https://www.bloomberg.com/news/articles/2016-07-20/a-164-year-old-idea-helps-explain-the-huge-changes-sweeping-the-world-s-workforce; Jon V. Kofas, "U.S. Foreign Policy and the World Federation of Trade Unions, 1944-1948," Diplomatic History, 26:1 (2002); Todd E. Vachon1, Michael Wallace1, and Allen Hyde, *"Union Decline in the Neoliberal Age."* https://www.asanet.org/sites/default/files/attach/journals/jul19sociusfeature.pdf

[679] Paulus Zulu, *"The Aetiology of Social Exclusion."* http://www.pass.va/content/scienzesociali/en/publications/acta/participatorysociety/zulu.html; Kathomi Gatwiri[142], Julians Amboko[143], and Darius Okolla[144], *"The Implications of Neoliberalism on African Economies, health outcomes and wellbeing."* https://www.ncbi.nlm.nih.gov/pmc/articles/PMC7223727/

[680] Grace Maich, *"Precarious Work and Communities: The Impact of Neoliberalism on Working Class Politics."* https://dr.library.brocku.ca/handle/10464/13598

[681] Elísio Estanque and Hermes Augusto Costa. *"Labour Relations and Social Movements in the 21st Century."* http://cdn.intechopen.com/pdfs/34149/InTech-Labour_relations_and_social_movements_in_the_21st_century.pdf

[682] Sotiris Rizas, *"The End of Middle Class Politics."* https://www.cambridgescholars.com/resources/pdfs/978-1-5275-0654-1-sample.pdf

---

142. https://www.ncbi.nlm.nih.gov/pubmed/?term=Gatwiri%20K%5BAuthor%5D&cauthor=true&cauthor_uid=32435159

143. https://www.ncbi.nlm.nih.gov/pubmed/?term=Amboko%20J%5BAuthor%5D&cauthor=true&cauthor_uid=32435159

144. https://www.ncbi.nlm.nih.gov/pubmed/?term=Okolla%20D%5BAuthor%5D&cauthor=true&cauthor_uid=32435159

[683] Jordan Weissmann, *"53% of Recent College Graduates are Jobless or Underemployed and Living with their Parents."* https://www.theatlantic.com/business/archive/2012/04/53-of-recent-college-grads-are-jobless-or-underemployed-how/256237/; Aimee Picchi, *"For young Americans, living with their parents is now the norm."*

https://www.cbsnews.com/news/for-young-americans-living-with-their-parents-is-now-the-norm/; Ami Sedghi and George Arnett, *"Europe's young adult living with parents."* https://www.theguardian.com/news/datablog/2014/mar/24/young-adults-still-living-with-parents-europe-country-breakdown; Iliana Magra, *"Most young people live with their parents."* https://www.ekathimerini.com/society/1162893/most-young-adults-live-with-their-parents/

[684] Iain Ramsay, *Personal Insolvency in the 21st Century: A Comparative Analysis of the US and Europe,* 2017); Paul Camack, *Making Poverty Work.* Socialist Register. (2009) https://socialistregister.com/index.php/srv/article/view/5783; Guy Standing, *The Corruption of Capitalism.* (2016); Bronson Argyle, et. al., *"Running Up the Tab: Personal Bankruptcy, Moral Hazard, and Shadow Debt."* https://www.fdic.gov/analysis/cfr/consumer/2020/argyle.pdf

[685] Philip C. C. Huang, Gao Yuan and Yusheng Peng, *"Capitalization without Proletarianization in China's Agricultural Development."* Sage, 38:2 (2012); Carter C. Price and Kathryn Edwards, *"Trends in Income from 1975 to 2018."* https://www.rand.org/pubs/working_papers/WRA516-1.html[145]; OECD, *"Inequality and Income."* https://www.oecd.org/social/inequality.htm; OECD, *"Under Pressure: The Squeezed Middle Class."* https://www.oecd.org/social/under-pressure-the-squeezed-middle-class-689afed1-en.htm

[686] Ricardo Antunes, *"The New Service Proletariat."* https://monthlyreview.org/2018/04/01/the-new-service-proletariat/; Jan Lucassen, *"The Rise, Organization, and Institutional Framework of Factor Markets."* http://www.iisg.nl/hpw/papers/lucassen.pdf; Ali Kadri, *"Proletarianisaton in the Arab World under Neoliberalism."* https://www.athimar.org/en/articles/details/proletarianisation-under-neoliberalism-in-the-arab-world; Jenna Demeter, "The Oppressive Pressures of Globalization and Neoliberalism on Mexican Maquiladora Garment Workers." https://trace.tennessee.edu/cgi/viewcontent.cgi?article=1387&context=pursuit; Marcel van der Linden, "The Social Question in Western Europe: Past and Present." www.degruyeter.com/[146]; https://indianexpress.com/article/opinion/columns/the-proletarianisation-of-teachers-7134080/Europe and India: http://www.iisg.nl/hpw/papers/lucassen.pdf; https://www.researchgate.net/publication/

288407053_Neoliberal_proletarization_along_the_urban-rural_divide_in_postsocialist_Romania.

[687] Jordan Dobrowski, *"Displacement: Neoliberal Land Welfare and Points of Intervention."* https://crownschool.uchicago.edu/student-life/advocates-forum/displacement-neoliberal-land-warfare-and-points-intervention

145. https://d.docs.live.net/eb41a1b69e1e6e00/Desktop/%20Philip%20C.%20C.%20Huang,%20Gao%20Yuan%20and%20Yusheng%20Peng,

146. http://www.degruyeter.com/

[688] Vikas Rawal, *"Indian Farmers Resist Neoliberalism."* https://arena.org.au/indian-farmers-resist-neoliberalism/; Benny Kuruvilla, *"Sri Lanka: a cautionary tale of authoritarian neoliberalism."* https://focusweb.org/sri-lanka-a-cautionary-tale-of-authoritarian-neoliberalism/; FT *"Subsidy in Agriculture"* https://thefinancialexpress.com.bd/views/opinions/subsidy-in-agriculture-1512751118

[689] Stephanie Findlay and Hudson Lockett, *"Modi's Rockefeller': Gautam Adani and the concentration of power in India."* https://www.ft.com/content/474706d6-1243-4f1e-b365-891d4c5d528b;

[690] Achin Vanaik, *"The Indian Farmers' Movement Has Shown Us How to Fight Narendra Modi."* https://jacobin.com/2021/12/indian-farmers-movement-narendra-modi-protest-farm-laws-repeal; Zeba Siddiqui[147], Rajendra Jadhav[148], Mayank Bhardwaj[149], *"Many Indian farmers voted for Modi the strongman, but now hope he tackles their woes."* https://www.reuters.com/article/uk-india-election-farmers-idUKKCN1SU1EH; India International Trade Administration, *"Food and Agriculture Value Chain."* https://www.trade.gov/country-commercial-guides/india-food-and-agriculture-value-chain

[691] Simin Fadaee, *"Politics of alliance in the farmers' march to Parliament in India."* https://journals.sagepub.com/doi/pdf/10.1177/02685809211051273; Bhuma Shrivastava, Bibhudatta Pradhan & P R Sanjai, *"Billionaires-Led 'Gilded Age' Comes Under Attack in Modi's India."* https://www.bloombergquint.com/business/two-of-india-s-richest-men-caught-in-crossfire-over-farming; - Zainab Lokhandwala, *"Neoliberalization of Indian Agriculture."* https://www.sociolegalreview.com/post/neoliberalization-of-indian-agriculture-undermining-of-the-right-to-food-of-farmers; Rakesh Kochhar, *"China's middle class surges while India's lags behind."* https://www.pewresearch.org/fact-tank/2015/07/15/china-india-middle-class/

[692] Nick Hanauer and David M. Rolf, *"The Top 1% of Americans Have Taken $50 Trillion From the Bottom 90%—And That's Made the U.S. Less Secure."* https://time.com/5888024/50-trillion-income-inequality-america/; Megan Leonhardt, *"The top 1% of Americans have about 16 times more wealth than the bottom 50%."* https://www.cnbc.com/2021/06/23/how-much-wealth-top-1percent-of-americans-have.html

[693] Megan Leonhard, *"The top 1% of American have about 16 times more wealth than the bottom 50%."* https://www.cnbc.com/2021/06/23/how-much-wealth-top-1percent-of-americans-have.html

[694] https://www.washingtonpost.com/us-policy/2019/02/27/top-tax-rate-has-been-cut-six-times-since-usually-with-democrats-help/; Sean Bray, *"Corporate Tax Rates around the World, 2021."* https://taxfoundation.org/publications/corporate-tax-rates-around-the-world/; Christian E. Weller, *"Supply-Side Follies: Wasteful Tax Cuts Will Not Boost the Economy."* https://www.americanprogress.org/article/supply-side-follies-wasteful-tax-cuts-will-not-boost-the-economy/; Josh Mound, *"The US Tax Code Should Not Allow Billionaires to Exist."* https://jacobinmag.com/2021/07/us-tax-code-reform-billionaire-wealth-inequality-propublica-expose

---

147. https://www.reuters.com/journalists/zeba-siddiqui

148. https://www.reuters.com/journalists/rajendra-jadhav

149. https://www.reuters.com/journalists/mayank-bhardwaj

[695] John Csizar. *"Here are the Most and Least Tax-Friendly Countries." https://www.gobankingrates.com/taxes/filing/lowest-highest-taxed-countries/*

[696] Kathy Le Mons Walker, *"Gangster capitalism and peasant protest in China."* https://www.tandfonline.com/doi/abs/10.1080/03066150600624413?journalCode=fjps20; Kaiser Kuo, *"Corrupt and competent: A paradox of China's economic growth."* https://supchina.com/2021/09/02/corrupt-and-competent-unpacking-the-relationship-between-corruption-and-economic-growth-in-chinas-gilded-age/

[697] Yen Yuen Ang, *China's Gilded Age* (2021); Dave Levinthal, *"67 members of Congress have violated a law designed to prevent insider trading and stop conflicts-of-interest."* https://www.businessinsider.com/congress-stock-act-violations-senate-house-trading-2021-9.

[698] Katie Wilson, *"Congress, Public Debt and the end of Neoliberalism."* https://crosscut.com/opinion/2021/10/congress-public-debt-and-end-neoliberalism

[699] Bryan Rooney, Grant Johnson, Miranda Priebe, *"How Does Defense Spending Affect Economic Growth?"* https://www.rand.org/content/dam/rand/pubs/research_reports/RRA700/RRA739-2/RAND_RRA739-2.pdf; Peter G. Peterson Foundation, *"The United States Spends More than the Next 9 countries combined."* https://www.pgpf.org/blog/2022/06/the-united-states-spends-more-on-defense-than-the-next-9-countries-combined; Bloomberg, *"China. Readies $1.1 Trillion to Support Xi's Infrastructure Push."* https://www.bloomberg.com/news/articles/2022-07-14/china-readies-1-1-trillion-to-support-xi-s-infrastructure-push

[700] Genevieve LeBaron, *"Confining Social Insecurity: Neoliberalism and the Rise of the 21st Century Debtors' Prison."* https://www.research.manchester.ac.uk/portal/files/19845834/POST-PEER-REVIEW-PUBLISHERS.PDF

[701] Tom Hall, "Child labor returns to the United States: A society moving in reverse" https://www.wsws.org/en/articles/2023/04/22/pers-a22.html; Steve Fraser, *"The Child Labor of Early Capitalism is Making a Big Comeback in the US."* https://jacobin.com/2023/07/child-labor-early-capitalism-law-right-wing-exploitation

[702] Dillon, Wamsley *"Neoliberalism, mass incarceration, and the US debt–criminal justice complex."* Critical Social Policy, 39:2 (2018); John L. Campbell, *"Neoliberalism's penal and debtor states."* https://citeseerx.ist.psu.edu/viewdoc/download?doi=10.1.1.377.8888&rep=rep1&type=pdf

[703] Anne Helen Petersen, *"America's Hollow Middle Class."* https://www.vox.com/the-goods/22166381/hollow-middle-class-american-dream; Judith Derndorfer and Stefan Kranzinger, *"The Decline of the Middle Class: New Evidence for Europe."* http://www.ecineq.org/ecineq_paris19/papers_EcineqPSE/paper_64.pdf; Marilyn Reid, *"Inequality, neoliberalism, and the unmaking of the middle class."* https://theindependent.ca/uncategorized/inequality-neoliberalism-and-the-unmaking-of-the-middle-class/;

Joseph Stiglitz, *"Three decades of neoliberal policies have decimated the middle class, our economy, and our democracy."* https://www.marketwatch.com/story/three-decades-of-neoliberal-policies-have-decimated-the-middle-class-our-economy-and-our-democracy-2019-05-13; Liliana Rojas-Suarez, *"The Gradual Rise and Rapid Decline of the Middle Class in Latin America and the Caribbean."* https://www.cgdev.org/event/gradual-rise-and-rapid-decline-middle-class-latin-america-and-caribbean; https://www.nytimes.com/2020/06/29/world/africa/Africa-middle-class-coronavirus.html; Rakesh Kocchar, *"The Pandemic Stalls Growth in the Global Middle Class, Pushes Poverty Up Sharply."* https://www.pewresearch.org/global/2021/03/18/the-pandemic-stalls-growth-in-the-global-middle-class-pushes-poverty-up-sharply/

[704] Neil L. Sobol, *"Charging the Poor: Criminal Justice, Debt and Modern-Day Poor."* https://scholarship.law.tamu.edu/cgi/viewcontent.cgi?article=1727&context=facscholar; Tayyab Mahmud, *"Debt and Discipline: Neoliberal Political Economy and the Working classes"* https://digitalcommons.law.seattleu.edu/cgi/viewcontent.cgi?article=1125&context=faculty; Neal Gabler, *"The Secret Shame of Middle Class Americans."* https://www.theatlantic.com/magazine/archive/2016/05/my-secret-shame/476415/; Francisco Velasquez, *"Over half of Americans have less than 3 months of emergency savings."* https://www.cnbc.com/2021/07/28/51percent-of-americans-have-less-than-3-months-worth-of-emergency-savings.html; Atif Mian, Ludwig Straub and Amir Sufi, *"The Saving Glut of the Rich and the Rise in Household Debt."* https://www.bankofengland.co.uk/-/media/boe/files/events/2020/june/paper-amir-sufi-the-saving-glut-of-the-rich-and-the-rise-in-household-debt.pdf?la=en&hash=AF4989A153F3D379EEBAC8FFF978F32DB808BE9F

[705] Subodh Varma[150], *"Indebted Country: People, Governments Both Buried Under Loans."* https://www.newsclick.in/indebted-country-people-governments-both-buried-under-loans

[706] Richard Weikart, *"Laissez-Faire Social Darwinism and Individualist Competition in Darwin and Huxley."* https://www.csustan.edu/sites/default/files/History/Faculty/Weikart/Laissez-Faire-Social-Darwinism.pdf; Bruno Amable, *"Morals and politics in the ideology of neo-liberalism."* https://www.mpifg.de/pu/mpifg_ja/SER_9_2011_Amable.pdf; Justine Doody, *"The Ranks Working Poor."* https://socialeurope.eu/the-ranks-of-the-working-poor; Claire Goldstein, *"Our Social Darwinist Then and Now."* https://inequality.org/research/american-social-darwinism/

[707] Wolfgang Streeck, *"The politics of public debt: Neoliberalism, capitalist development, and the restructuring of the state."* https://www.econstor.eu/bitstream/10419/78032/1/755988647.pdf; David Michael Ellis, *"Culture, Economy and the Normalization of Debt."* https://livrepository.liverpool.ac.uk/2014221/2/EllisDav_Dec2014_2014221.pdf

[708] David Micheal Ellis, *"Culture, Economy and the Normalization of Debt."* https://livrepository.liverpool.ac.uk/2014221/2/EllisDav_Dec2014_2014221.pdf; Pierre Bourdieu, *"The Essence of Neoliberalism."* https://mondediplo.com/1998/12/08bourdieu https://newleftreview.org/issues/ii57/articles/leo-panitch-martijn-konings-myths-of-neoliberal-deregulation.pdf; Dominico Johnston, *Enslaved by Consumption: How frivolous consumption fueled by debt is leading to your voluntary enslavement.* (2015); Daniel

150. https://www.newsclick.in/author/subodh-varma

Miller, *"A Theory of Virtualism: Consumption as Negation"* in Marc Edelman and Angelique Haugerud, eds. *Anthropology of Development and Globalization.* (2005).

[709] Jodi Dean, *"The Neoliberal Trap."* https://www.opendemocracy.net/en/neoliberal-trap/

[710] David Graeber, *Debt: the First 5000 Years,* 2014); Jodi Dean, *"The Neoliberal Trap."* https://www.opendemocracy.net/en/neoliberal-trap/

[711] Dhara Ranasinghe[151], *"Global Debt is fast approaching record $300 trillion."* https://www.reuters.com/business/global-debt-is-fast-approaching-record-300-trillion-iif-2021-09-14/; https://www.newyorkfed.org/microeconomics/hhdc; https://data.oecd.org/hha/household-debt.htm; Kimberly Amaded, *"Current US Consumer Debt."* https://www.thebalance.com/consumer-debt-statistics-causes-and-impact-3305704; Michael Corkery and Stacy Cowley, *"Household Debt Makes a Comeback in the US."* https://www.nytimes.com/2017/05/17/business/dealbook/household-debt-united-states.html; Jamie Ballard, *"In 2020, do people see the American Dream as attainable?"* https://today.yougov.com/topics/politics/articles-reports/2020/07/18/american-dream-attainable-poll-survey-data; European Commission, *"Special Eurobarometer: How fair do Europeans think life in the EU is."* https://ec.europa.eu/commission/presscorner/detail/en/IP_18_3427

[712] Jacob Bogage[152] and María Luisa Paúl[153], *"The conservative campaign to rewrite child labor laws."* https://www.washingtonpost.com/business/2023/04/23/child-labor-lobbying-fga/

[713] Harm Venhuizen, *"Kids could fill labor shortages, even in bars, if these lawmakers succeed."* https://apnews.com/article/child-labor-laws-alabama-ohio-c1123a80970518676be44088619c6205

[714] Ryan Edwards and Francesc Ortega, *"The Economic Contribution of Unauthorized Workers: An Industry Analysis."* https://www.nber.org/system/files/working_papers/w22834/w22834.pdf

151. https://www.reuters.com/authors/dhara-ranasinghe/

152. https://www.washingtonpost.com/people/jacob-bogage/?itid=ai_top_bogagej

153. https://www.washingtonpost.com/people/maria-luisa-paul/?itid=ai_top_Paulm

[715] ILO, *"Profits and Poverty: The Economics of Forced Labour."* https://www.ilo.org/global/publications/ilo-bookstore/order-online/books/WCMS_243391/lang—en/index.htm[154]; Dursun Peksen, Shannon Lindsey Blanton, Robert Blanton, *"Neoliberal Policies and Human Trafficking for Labor: Free Markets, Unfree Workers?"* https://www.researchgate.net/publication/317287611_Neoliberal_Policies_and_Human_Trafficking_for_Labor_Free_Markets_Unfree_Workers; Katie McQue, *"Up to 10,000 Asian migrant workers die every year."* https://www.theguardian.com/global-development/2022/mar/11/up-to-10000-asian-migrant-workers-die-in-the-gulf-every-year-claims-report

[716] Creola Johnson, *"Creditors' use of Consumer Debt Criminalization Practices and their Financial Abuse of Women."* https://academiccommons.columbia.edu/catalog/ac:4b8gtht779; *"Day 9 – Neoliberalism, Biden Style, First Hundred Days."* https://lumpenproletariat.org/tag/neoliberalism/

[717] Ignar Solty, *"German Reunification Brought a Wave of Neoliberal Triumphalism — And a Social Disaster."* https://jacobin.com/2020/10/german-reunification-gdr-east-germany-anniversary-neoliberalism;

[718] Thomas Klikauer *"Torturing the Poor, German Style."* https://www.counterpunch.org/2017/10/20/torturing-the-poor-german-style/

[719] Marcel Lewandowsky, *"Alternative fur Deutchland."* https://library.fes.de/pdf-files/id/ipa/10644.pdf; WELT, *"Alternative fur Deutchland."* https://www.welt.de/themen/alternative-fuer-deutschland/

[720] *"The Rise of Neo-Fascism in Germany: Alternative fur Deutschland Enters Parliament."* https://crimethinc.com/2017/10/01/the-rise-of-neo-fascism-in-germany-alternative-fur-deutschland-enters-the-parliament/

[721] Ralph Havetz, *"Strategy of Ambivalence: AFD Between Neoliberalism and Social Populism."* https://kirj.ee/wp-content/plugins/kirj/pub/Trames-4-2020-549-565_20201119113151.pdf

[722] Jonathan Mijs and Michelle Lamont, *"Neoliberal Policies go hand-in-hand with social exclusion."* https://news.harvard.edu/gazette/story/newsplus/neoliberal-policies-go-hand-in-hand-with-social-exclusion/

[723] Anna Luhrmann and Stefan I Lindberg, *"A third wave of autocratization is here: what is new about?"* https://www.tandfonline.com/doi/full/10.1080/13510347.2019.1582029 ; Charles Tilly, *Democracy.* (2007).

[724] Marina Ottaway, *Democracy Challenged: The Rise of Semi-authoritarianism.* (2004); CEU Democracy Institute, *"De-Re-democratization."* https://democracyinstitute.ceu.edu/research/de-re-democratization

154. https://www.ilo.org/global/publications/ilo-bookstore/order-online/books/WCMS_243391/lang--en/index.htm

[725] Livia Gershon, *"Racism and American Exceptionalism."* https://daily.jstor.org/american-exceptionalism/

[726] Jongwoo Han and L. H. M. Ling, *"Authoritarianism in the Hypermasculinized State: Hybridity, Patriarchy, and Capitalism in Korea."* International Studies Quarterly, 42, 1 (1998).

[727] IDEA, *"The Global State of Democracy Report 2021."* https://www.idea.int/gsod/

[728] Jessica Whyte, *"The invisible hand of the market': Freidrich Hayek's neoliberal faith."*Hoften ttps://www.abc.net.au/religion/jessica-whyte-invisible-hand-hayek-neoliberal-faith/12044338

[729] Lindsey A. O'Rourke, *"The US tried to change other countries' governments 72 times during the Cold War."* https://www.washingtonpost.com/news/monkey-cage/wp/2016/12/23/the-cia-says-russia-hacked-the-u-s-election-here-are-6-things-to-learn-from-cold-war-attempts-to-change-regimes/; Ben Norton, *"The US launched 251 military interventions since 1991 and 469 since 1798."* https://mronline.org/2022/09/16/u-s-launched-251-military-interventions-since-1991-and-469-since-1798/

[730] Micchael Head, *"Far from Universal: The Cold War and its impact on human rights discourse."* https://historyhub.info/far-from-universal-the-cold-war-and-its-impact-on-human-rights-discourse/

[731] https://www.gu.se/en/research/varieties-of-democracy-v-dem

[732] Rafael Khachaturian, *"Rights Without Bounds: An Interview with Wendy Brown."* https://www.dissentmagazine.org/online_articles/rights-without-bounds-wendy-brown

[733] Jamie Peck and Nik Theodore, *"Still Neoliberalism?"* https://read.dukeupress.edu/south-atlantic-quarterly/article/118/2/245/138018/Still-Neoliberalism

[734] Marine Dassé, *"The Neoliberalization of Public Spaces and the Infringement of Civil Liberties."* https://journals.openedition.org/angles/595; Eric A. Posner, *"Neoliberalism and Human Rights."* https://www.lawfareblog.com/neoliberalism-and-human-rights

[735] Prabhat Patnaik[155], "*Neoliberalism and Fascism.*" https://journals.sagepub.com/doi/full/10.1177/2277976019901029

[736] David Langwallner, *"Gradations of Evil: Neoliberalism and Neoconservatism."*https://cassandravoices.com/history/gradations-of-evil-neoliberalism-and-neoconservatism/

[737] Claudio Gallo, *"Global Totalitarianism: Change not Forbidden, Change is Impossible."* https://www.rt.com/op-edge/171240-global-totalitarianism-change-neoliberalism/

155. https://journals.sagepub.com/doi/full/10.1177/2277976019901029

[738] M. McDonald, et al., *"Social Psychology, Consumer Culture, and Neoliberal Political Economy."* https://eprints.leedsbeckett.ac.uk/id/eprint/3561/7/Social%20Psychology%2C%20Consumer%20Culture%20and%20Neoliberal%20Political%20Economy.pdf

[739] Mathew McDonald, Brendan Gough, Stephen L. Wearing, Adrian Deville, *"Consumer Culture & Neoliberal Political Economy."* https://eprints.leedsbeckett.ac.uk/id/eprint/3561/7/Social%20Psychology%2C%20Consumer%20Culture%20and%20Neoliberal%20Political%20Economy.pdf; Rosana Pinheiro-Machado[156], Lucia Mury Scalco[157], *"The right to shine: Poverty, consumption and (de) politicization in neoliberal Brazil."* https://journals.sagepub.com/doi/10.1177/14695405221086066.

[740] **Paul Verhaeghe, *"The Struggle for Identity in a Market-based Society."* https://thehumanist.com/magazine/march-april-2015/arts_entertainment/what-about-me-the-struggle-for-identity-in-a-market-based-society; Michael Welton, *"American Nightmare: the Depravity of Neoliberalism."* https://www.counterpunch.org/2015/12/04/american-nightmare-the-depravity-of-neoliberalism/; Paul Verhaeghe, *"Neoliberalism has Brought out the worst in us."* https://www.theguardian.com/commentisfree/2014/sep/29/neoliberalism-economic-system-ethics-personality-psychopathicsthic; Julia Fursova, *"Neoliberal Illusions of Freedom."* https://www.academia.edu/28509196/Neoliberal_Illusions_of_Freedom; Jürgen Habermas, *"Freedom and Determinism Is Human 'Freedom of Will' an Illusion?"* https://www.kyotoprize.org/en/workshop/jurgen-habermas/**

[741] Hans van Zon, *"The unholy alliance of neoliberalism and postmodernism."*http://www.imavo.be/vmt/13214-van%20Zon%20postmodernism.pdf

[742] Julia Lethbridge, "*Has Neoliberalism Defined Postmodernity?*" https://www.mq.edu.au/Downloads/history_initiates_vol_3_no_1_april_2015-julia_lethbridge-2.pdf; Joshua Ramsay, *"Neoliberalism as Political Theology of Chance: the politics of divination."* https://www.nature.com/articles/palcomms201539

[743] Timothy Shenk, *"The Long Shadow of Mont Pèlerin."* https://www.dissentmagazine.org/article/the-long-shadow-of-mont-pelerin

[744] Thomas I. Palley, *"From Keynesianism to Neoliberalism: Shifting Paradigms in Economics."* http://fpif.org/from_keynesianism_to_neoliberalism_shifting_paradigms_in_economics/

[745] J. Peterson, *Revoking the Moral Order: The Ideology of Positivism and the Vienna Circle*, 1999; Naomi Klein, "*It was the Rise of the Davos Class that Sealed America's Fate.*" https://www.commondreams.org/views/2016/11/09/it-was-rise-davos-class-sealed-americas-fate; Corey Robin, *The Reactionary Mind: From Edmund Burke to Sarah Palin.* (2011)

---

156. https://journals.sagepub.com/doi/10.1177/14695405221086066

157. https://journals.sagepub.com/doi/10.1177/14695405221086066

[746] Agnus Burgin, *The Great Persuasion: Reinventing Free Markets since the Depression.* (2012); Bob Brecher, *"Neoliberalism and its Threat to Moral Agency."* in Andrius Bielskis and Kelvin Knight, eds. *Virtue and Economy.* (2015); Craig McLean et al. *"Exploring the Relationship between Neoliberalism and Homicide: A Cross-National Perspective."* https://www.tandfonline.com/doi/full/10.1080/00207659.2018.1560981; Nieto Diego, *"Neoliberalism, Biopolitics, and the Governance of Transnational Crime."* https://www.redalyc.org/pdf/812/81224569006.pdf

[747] Robert Smith, *"Credit Suisse asks investors to destroy documents linked to the oligarch and tycoon yacht loans."* https://www.ft.com/content/bfea0069-4143-4e4b-accb-9712ce95a282; Brenna Hughes Neghaiwi[158] and Silke Koltrowitz[159] *"Credit Suisse faces money laundering charges in Bulgarian cocaine traffickers trial."* https://www.reuters.com/business/finance/credit-suisse-faces-money-laundering-charges-trial-bulgarian-cocaine-traffickers-2022-02-07/; Stacy Vanek Smith, *"UBS rescues Credit Suisse in a deal brokered by the Swiss government."* https://www.npr.org/2023/03/19/1164620384/ubs-rescues-credit-suisse-in-deal-brokered-by-swiss-government; Marion Halftermeyer[160], et al., *"UBS to buy Credit Suisse for more than $3 billion in government-brokered deal to restore confidence."* https://fortune.com/2023/03/19/ubs-to-buy-credit-suisse-for-more-than-2b-in-government-brokered-deal-aiming-to-restore-confidence/

[748] RiskScreen, *"The Credit Suisse scandal 2022: What went wrong this time?"* https://riskscreen.com/blog/the-credit-suisse-scandal-2022-what-went-wrong-this-time/; Mariam Mufti, *"What Do We Know About Hybrid Regimes after two Decades of Scholarship?" https://www.researchgate.net/publication/325938348_What_Do_We_Know_about_Hybrid_Regimes_after_Two_Decades_of_Scholarship*

[749] Dawn Brancati, *"Democratic Authoritarianism: Origins and Effects."* https://www.annualreviews.org/doi/10.1146/annurev-polisci-052013-115248

[750] Leonardo R. Arriola, *"Patronage and Political Stability in Africa."* https://polisci.berkeley.edu/sites/default/files/people/u3618/Arriola_2009.pdf; Network of Democracy Research Institute *"Political Clientelism, Social Policy and the Quality of Democracy."* https://fsi-live.s3.us-west-1.amazonaws.com/s3fs-public/evnts/media/Quito_Conference_Report—Final.pdf[161]; James C. Scott, *"Patron-Client Politics and Political Change in Southeast Asia."* http://www.la.utexas.edu/users/chenry/pmena/coursemats/2009/Scott-1972-clientelism.pdf; Jeanp-Louis Briquete, Frederic Sawicki, *Le clientélisme politique dans les sociétés contemporaines.* (1998).

[751] GUE/NGL group in the European Parliament, *"Panama Papers: Dirty Money and Tax Tricks."* https://left.eu/content/uploads/2017/12/dirtymoneyandtaxtricks.pdf; Will Fitzgibbon and Michael Hudson, *"Five years later, Panama Papers still having a big impact."* https://www.icij.org/investigations/panama-papers/five-years-later-panama-papers-still-having-a-big-impact/; Transparency

---

158. https://www.reuters.com/authors/brenna-hughes-neghaiwi/

159. https://www.reuters.com/authors/silke-koltrowitz/

160. https://fortune.com/author/marion-halftermeyer/

161. https://fsi-live.s3.us-west-1.amazonaws.com/s3fs-public/evnts/media/Quito_Conference_Report--Final.pdf

International, *"Licence to Bribe? Reducing corruption risks around the use of agents in defe procurement."* http://ti-defence.org/publications/licence-to-bribe-reducing-corruption-agents-defence-procurement/

[752] Beatrice Hibou, *"Economic Crime and Neoliberal Modes of Government: The Example of the Mediterranean."* Journal of Social History, 45:3 (2012). Stephen Bittle, Dean Curran and Laureen Snider. *"Crimes of the Powerful."* https://link.springer.com/article/10.1007/s10612-018-9423-x; Sarah Jassem, *"The Paradise Papers: Central to S."* https://pirsoc.com/2018/01/11/the-paradise-papers-central-to-society/

[753] Davis Richardson, *"The Koch Brothers and Robert Mercer Bankrolled Right-Wing Firm Project Veritas."* https://observer.com/2017/12/koch-brothers-and-robert-mercer-funded-project-veritas/

[754] Fabio Armao, *"Mafia-owned democracies: Italy and Mexico as patterns of criminal neoliberalism."* http://revistes.uab.cat/tdevorado/article/view/v2-n1-armao; Jose Manuel Sanchez Bermudez, *The Neoliberal Pattern of Domination: Capital's Reign in Decline,* 2012; https://www.globalresearch.ca/neoliberalisms-world-of-corruption-money-laundering-corporate-lobbying-drug-money/5519907

[755] Behrouz Alikhani, *"Post-Democracy or Processes of De-Democratization? United States Case Study."*https://www.ssoar.info/ssoar/bitstream/handle/document/55221/ssoar-hsr-2017-4-alikhani-Post-Democracy_or_Processes_of_De-Democratization.pdf?isAllowed=y&lnkname=ssoar-hsr-2017-4-alikhani-Post-Democracy_or_Processes_of_De-Democratization.pdf&sequence=1

[756] Corinna Lotz and Penny Cole, *"Deconstructing Neoliberal Hegemony."* https://www.researchgate.net/publication/335198390_Deconstructing_neoliberal_hegemony; Alikhani, Behrouz, *"Post-Democracy or Processes of De-Democratization? United States Case 'Study."* https://www.ssoar.info/ssoar/bitstream/handle/document/55221/ssoar-hsr-2017-4-alikhani-Post-Democracy_or_Processes_of_[162]Democratization.pdf?isAllowed=y&lnkname=ssoar-hsr-2017-4-alikhani-Post-Democracy_or_Processes_of_De-Democratization.pdf&sequence=1

[757] Leonie Huddy and Alexa Bankert, *"Political Partisanship as Social Identity.* https://oxfordre.com/view/10.1093/acrefore/9780190228637.001.0001/acrefore-9780190228637-e-250; Constance Duncombe and Ronald Bleiker, *"Popular Culture and Political Identity."* https://www.e-ir.info/2015/05/02/popular-culture-and-political-identity/; Ming M. Boyer, Loes Aalderin Sophie Lecheler, *"Motivated Reasoning in Identity Politics: Group Status as Moderator of Political Motivations."* https://journals.sagepub.com/doi/full/10.1177/0032321720964667

[758] Pippa Norris and Ronald Inglehart, *Cultural Backlash: Trump, Brexit and Authoritarian Populism.* (2019); Roger Eatwell and Matthew Goodwin, *National Populism: The Revolt Against Liberal Democracy.* (2018); Mike Konczal, *"The Failures of Neoliberalism are Bigger than Politics."* https://rooseveltinstitute.org/2019/03/05/the-failures-of-neoliberalism-are-bigger-than-politics/; Ray Kiley and Richard Saull, *"Neoliberalism and the Far Right: An Introduction."* Critical Sociology, 43:6, (2017)

---

162. https://www.ssoar.info/ssoar/bitstream/handle/document/55221/ssoar-hsr-2017-4-alikhani-Post-Democracy_or_Processes_of_D

[759] Boris Frankel, *"Confronting Neoliberal Regimes: The Post-Marxist Embrace of Populism and Realpolitik."* https://newleftreview.org/issues/i226/articles/boris-frankel-confronting-neoliberal-regimes-the-post-marxist-embrace-of-populism-and-realipolitik.pdf; Hans Blockalnd, *"How Postmodernism advanced Populism: An Inside Story from the Netherlands."* https://socialscienceworks.org/how-postmodernism-advanced-populism-an-inside-story-from-the-netherlands/

[760] Cecilia Jaques, Mine Islar and Gavin Lord, *"Post-Truth: Hegemony on Social Media and Implications for Sustainability Communication." https://www.researchgate.net/publication/332331237_Post-Truth_Hegemony_on_Social_Media_and_Implications_for_Sustainability_Communication;* Alfred Moore, *"Beyond populism and technocracy: The challenges and limits of democratic epistemology."* https://scholar.harvard.edu/files/zpamuk/files/moore_et_al-2020-contemporary_political_theory.pdf; William Peter Fitz, *"Reactionary Postmodernism? Neoliberalism, Multiculturalism, the Intern, and the Ideology of the New Far Right In Germany."* https://scholarworks.uvm.edu/cgi/viewcontent.cgi?article=1302&context=hcoltheses

[761] Zia Kureshi, *"Inequality in the Digital Era."* https://www.bbvaopenmind.com/en/articles/inequality-in-the-digital-era/

[762] Paul Rosenberg, *"A moment of Moral and Political Nihilism: Theologian Adam Kotsko on our current crisis."* https://www.salon.com/2021/02/06/a-moment-of-moral-and-political-nihilism-theologian-adam-kotsko-on-our-current-crisis/; Pamela Duncan[163], Jennifer Rankin[164] in Brussels and Mark Rice-Oxley[165], *"European countries gloomiest in the developed world."*https://www.theguardian.com/world/2019/may/03/european-countries-gloomiest-developed-world-poll; Kennedy School, *"Harvard Youth Poll."* https://iop.harvard.edu/youth-poll/fall-2021-harvard-youth-poll; Rebecca Ratcliff and Cattrmen Aguilar, *"Our time is now."* https://www.theguardian.com/global-development/ng-interactive/2018/sep/24/our-time-is-now-world-youth-poll-reveals-unexpected-optimism.

[763] Thomas Greven, *"Right Wing Populism and Authoritarian Nationalism in the US and Europe."* http://library.fes.de/pdf-files/id/13395.pdf

[764] Francesco Laruffa, *"Neoliberalism, Economization and the Paradox of the New Welfare State."* https://www.cambridge.org/core/journals/european-journal-of-sociology-archives-europeennes-de-sociologie/article/neoliberalism-economization-and-the-paradox-of-the-new-welfare-state/B3D839010EDEAF4F3949D9396D46017E; John Brown, *"Neoliberalization, De-democratization, and Populist Responses in Western Europe, the US, and Latin America."* https://www.researchgate.net/publication/340978256_Neoliberalization_De-democratization_and_Populist_Responses_in_Western_Europe_the_US_and_Latin_America

---

163. https://www.theguardian.com/profile/pamela-duncan

164. https://www.theguardian.com/profile/jennifer-rankin

165. https://www.theguardian.com/profile/mark-rice-oxley

[765] Elena Cristina Mitrea, Monika Muhlbock and Julia Warmuth, *"Extreme Pessimists? Expected Socioeconomic Downward Mobility and the Political Attitudes of Young Adults."* https://link.springer.com/article/10.1007/s11109-020-09593-7

[766] **Alfred Sohn-Rethel, *Economy and Class Structure of German Fascism.* (1978); Mari Lilleslåtten, *"Both Mussolini's and Hitler's rise to power followed the rules of democracy."* https://partner.sciencenorway.no/democracy-history-university-of-oslo/both-mussolinis-and-hitlers-rise-to-power-followed-the-rules-of-democracy/2000160**

[767] Rene Cuperus, *"The Populist Revolt Against Globalization"* https://www.clingendael.org/pub/2017/3/the-populist-revolt-against-globalisation/; Marek Rewizorski[166], *"Backlash Against Globalisation and the Shadow of Phobos."* https://link.springer.com/article/10.1007/s40647-020-00308-0

[768] Jan-Werner Müller[167], *"Why culture wars are an elite device: Plutocratic populists reduce economic conflicts to questions of belonging."* https://www.newstatesman.com/culture/2021/09/beyond-the-culture-wars; *"We Don't Need Culture War. We Need a Class War."* https://www.jacobinmag.com/2020/12/culture-war-class-polarization-medicare-for-all

[769] Milan Babic, *"Let's talk about the interregnum: Gramsci and the liberal world order."* https://academic.oup.com/ia/article/96/3/767/5712430

[770] Dalibor Ruhak, Liz Kennedy and Vikram Singh, *"Drivers of Authoritarian Populism in the United States."* https://cf.americanprogress.org/wp-content/uploads/2018/05/USPopulism-report-1.pdf

[771] Bilal Berady, *"The deceptive coherence of Marine Le Pen's electoral base."* https://www.rosalux.eu/en/article/2003.the-deceptive-coherence-of-marine-le-pen-s-electoral-base.html

[772] Branko Milanovic, *"Shrinking middle class encourages populism and challenges the economy."* https://temas.folha.uol.com.br/global-inequality/united-states/shrinking-middle-class-encourages-populism-and-challenges-the-economy.shtml

[773] Mindy Isser, *"The Union Members Who Voted for Trump Have to be Organized – Not Ignored."* https://inthesetimes.com/article/trump-voters-labor-unions-election-2020; Jeffrey R. Webber, *"Late Fascism in Brazil? Theoretical Reflections."* https://www.academia.edu/42903753/Late_Fascism_in_Brazil_Theoretical_Reflections; C. W. Barrow, *The Dangerous Class: The Concept of the Lumpenproletariat.* (2020); Daniel Oesch, *"Explaining Workers' Support for Right-Wing Populist Parties in Western Europe: Evidence from Austria, Belgium, France, Norway, and Switzerland."* https://journals.sagepub.com/doi/pdf/10.1177/0192512107088390

[774] Jonathan Strauss, *"Engels and the theory of Labour aristocracy."* International Journal of Socialist Renewal. http://links.org.au/node/45; Ed Kilgore, *"The Rotten Core of Republican Appeals to the Working Class"* https://nymag.com/intelligencer/article/jim-banks-

---

166. https://link.springer.com/article/10.1007/s40647-020-00308-0#auth-Marek-Rewizorski

167. https://www.newstatesman.com/author/janwernermuller

memo-republican-working-class.html; Brian Elliott, "*The roots of populism: Neoliberalism and working lives.*" (2021); Katheryn Roister, *"New Political Science Research Debunks Myth About White Working Class Support for Trump."* https://as.vanderbilt.edu/news/2020/07/29/political-science-research-debunks-myths-about-white-working-class-support-for-trump/

[775] Andrew Hartman, *"The Culture Wars are Dead."* https://thebaffler.com/outbursts/culture-wars-are-dead-hartman

[776] Bjorn Toelstede, *"Social hierarchies in democracies and authoritarianism: The balance between power asymmetries and principal-agent chains."* https://journals.sagepub.com/doi/10.1177/1043463120904051

[777] Paul Stewart[168], Brian Garvey[169], Mauricio Torres[170], and Thais Borges de Farias[171], *"Amazonian destruction, Bolsonaro and COVID-19: Neoliberalism unchained."* https://www.ncbi.nlm.nih.gov/pmc/articles/PMC7689255/; Thomas Greven, *The Rise of Right-wing Populism in Europe and the United States."* http://dc.fes.de/fileadmin/user_upload/publications/RightwingPopulism.pdf; Simina Ghit, *"The Impact of Neoliberal Policies on Cambodian Society."* https://www.e-ir.info/2012/09/13/the-impact-of-neoliberal-policies-on-cambodian-society/; Michael Hudson, *"Central Asia's Neoliberal Tragedy."* https://mronline.org/2021/10/18/central-asias-neoliberal-tragedy/; James A. Tyner, *"Violent Neoliberalism: Development, Discourse, and Dispossession in Cambodia."* https://www.tandfonline.com/doi/full/10.1080/2325548X.2019.1650552

[778] Maria de Lourdes Rollemberg Mollo [172]and Alfredo Saad-Filho, *"Neoliberal economic policies in Brazil (1994–2005)."* [173] https://www.tandfonline.com/doi/abs/10.1080/13563460500494933?journalCode=cnpe20; Felipe Antunes de Oliveira[174], *"Lost and Found: Bourgeois Dependency Theory and the Forgotten Roots of Neodevelopmentalism."* https://journals.sagepub.com/doi/full/10.1177/0094582X211037341

[779] Koenraad Bogaert, *Globalized Authoritarianism.* (2018); Anthony Robert Pahnke[175] and Marcelo Milan[176], *"The Brazilian Crisis and the New Authoritarianism."* https://monthlyreview.org/2020/06/01/the-brazilian-crisis-and-the-new-authoritarianism/; Tom Horley, Ann Meng, and Mila Versteeg, *"The World is Facing a New Form of Autocracy."* https://www.theatlantic.com/ideas/archive/2020/03/new-authoritarianism/607045/; Paula Armendariz Miranda, *"Unrest in Latin America makes authoritarianism look more appealing to some."* https://theconversation.com/unrest-in-latin-america-makes-authoritarianism-look-more-appealing-to-some-127774

---

168. https://pubmed.ncbi.nlm.nih.gov/?term=Stewart%20P%5BAuthor%5D

169. https://pubmed.ncbi.nlm.nih.gov/?term=Garvey%20B%5BAuthor%5D

170. https://pubmed.ncbi.nlm.nih.gov/?term=Torres%20M%5BAuthor%5D

171. https://pubmed.ncbi.nlm.nih.gov/?term=Borges%20de%20Farias%20T%5BAuthor%5D

172. https://www.tandfonline.com/author/Mollo%2C+Maria+de+Lourdes+Rollemberg

173. https://www.tandfonline.com/author/Saad-Filho%2C+Alfredo

174. https://journals.sagepub.com/doi/full/10.1177/0094582X211037341#con

175. https://monthlyreview.org/author/anthonyrobertpahnke/

176. https://monthlyreview.org/author/marcelomilan/

[780] Scott Timcke, *"The Imperial Republic and Pax-Americana: State Formation, Inequality, and the New American Way of War."* Triple C 12:1 (2014)

[781] AlJAZEERA, *"US blacklists ex-Paraguay President Horacio Cartes for corruption."* https://www.aljazeera.com/news/2022/7/22/us-blacklists-ex-paraguay-president-horacio-cartes-for-corruption

[782] Alborada, *"From Stroessner to Syngenta: Paraguaysssssss's Soy Conflicts."* https://alborada.net/stroessner-syngenta-paraguay-soy-neoliberalism-lugo/; GIZ, *"Paraguay."* https://www.giz.de/en/worldwide/387.html. Unlike the US ranking number one economy in the world, and Brazil 12th, Paraguay is one of the poorest. In a country with 7.8 million and rich in natural resources, ranking among the world's top five in soybean production and organic sugar, 161 people own 90 percent of the wealth, while 40% live in poverty and 18% in extreme poverty.

[783] Nancy LeTourneau *"Trump isn't an Aberration of the Conservative Movement."* https://washingtonmonthly.com/2018/05/31/trump-isnt-an-aberration-of-the-conservative-movement/

[784] Andrew Romano, *"Poll: Half of Americans now predict the US may 'cease to be a democracy' someday."* https://us.yahoo.com/news/poll-half-of-americans-now-predict-us-may-cease-to-be-a-democracy-someday-090028564.html

[785] Tim Sharp, *"Fighting the anti-strike law."* https://www.tuc.org.uk/blogs/fighting-anti-strike-law; Davide Basso, *"French unions warns of 'major social conflict' over Macron's pension reform."* https://www.euractiv.com/section/economy-jobs/news/french-unions-warn-major-social-conflict-over-macrons-pension-reform/; https://www.pewresearch.org/global/2021/03/31/many-in-us-western-europe-say-their-political-system-needs-major-reform/#democratic-satisfaction-lower-in-u-s-than-european-countries-surveyed; David Renton, *"A Brief History of Britain's Anti-Trade Union Laws."* https://tribunemag.co.uk/2022/06/trade-union-laws-rmt-strike-industrial-relations-legislation; Tom Hall, Jerry White, *"Opposition to union bureaucracy, class war monetary policies to fuel of US class struggle in 2023."* https://www.wsws.org/en/articles/2023/01/06/uscs-j06.html

[786] https://www.pewresearch.org/fact-tank/2019/05/31/the-countries-where-people-are-most-dissatisfied-with-how-democracy-is-working/

[787] **Patrick Wintour, *"US saw as a bigger threat to democracy than Russia or China."* https://www.theguardian.com/world/2021/may/05/us-threat-democracy-russia-china-global-poll; Javier Romelo-Vidal, *"War in Ukraine has widened a global divide in public attitudes toward US, China and Russia."* https://www.cam.ac.uk/stories/worlddivided; Sandra Polaski and David Dollar, *"How have Trump's trade wars affected Rust Belt Jobs?"* https://www.brookings.edu/podcast-episode/how-have-trumps-trade-wars-affected-rust-belt-jobs/**

[788] Arthur Paulson, *"Donald Trump and the Prospect for American Democracy."* (2020)

[789] Samantha Smith, *"Most think the American Dream is within reach for them."* https://www.pewresearch.org/fact-tank/2017/10/31/most-think-the-american-dream-is-within-reach-for-them/; Marcus Lu, *"Is the American Dream over? Here is what the data says."* https://www.weforum.org/agenda/2020/09/social-mobility-upwards-decline-usa-us-america-economcs/; Ghada Alshariff, *"."* https://www.thestar.com/business/2023/07/06/gap-between-canadas-rich-and-poor-increasing-at-record-speed.html

[790] Marc Pavlopoulos, *"Has the Canadian Dream replaced the American Dream."* https://syndesus.com/has-the-canadian-dream-replaced-the-american-dream/

[791] Sophia Landress, *"Rugged Individualism in American Political Thought."* https://repository.upenn.edu/cgi/viewcontent.cgi?article=1307&context=curej; Robert Reich, *"The Myth of the Rugged Individual."* https://prospect.org/economy/myth-rugged-individual/

[792] Dalibor Rohac, Liz Kennedy, and Vikram Singh, *"Drivers of Authoritarian Populism in the United States."* https://www.americanprogress.org/article/drivers-authoritarian-populism-united-states/; Lawrence K. Pettit, *"America is Transforming into an Authoritarian State."* https://missoulian.com/opinion/columnists/america-is-transforming-into-an-authoritarian-state/article_3e887f32-925d-59a4-9e54-db6d1c6d2e3a.html; Pew Research, *"Most Americans Point to Circumstances, not Work Ethic, for why People are Rich or Poor."* https://www.pewresearch.org/politics/2020/03/02/most-americans-point-to-circumstances-not-work-ethic-as-reasons-people-are-rich-or-poor/

[793] Kai Hafez, *"Lost in discourse: The mass media's role in right-wing populism."* https://www.arabmediasociety.com/lost-in-discourse-the-mass-medias-role-in-creating-trump-and-right-wing-populism/

[794] Grace Blakeley, "*The US-China war is a distraction from the true failures of liberal globalization."* https://www.newstatesman.com/world/2012/06/us-china-trade-war-distraction-true-failures-liberal-globalisation

[795] Tam Harbert, *"Here is how much the 2008 bailouts cost."* https://mitsloan.mit.edu/ideas-made-to-matter/heres-how-much-2008-bailouts-really-cost Matt Taibbi, *"Looting the Pension Funds."* https://www.rollingstone.com/politics/politics-news/looting-the-pension-funds-172774/; *"Ireland must find €17.5bn from its pension fund and reserves for bailout."* https://www.theguardian.com/business/2010/nov/28/ireland-bailout-contribution-pensions; **Susanne Soederberg,** *"Cannibalistic Capitalism: The Paradoxes of Neoliberal Pension Securitization."* https://socialistregister.com/index.php/srv/article/view/14337

[796] Lee Rainie and Andrew Perrin, *"Key findings about Americans' declining trust in government and each other."* https://www.pewresearch.org/fact-tank/2019/07/22/key-findings-about-americans-declining-trust-in-government-and-each-other/

[797] Amy Fried and D.B. Harris, *"At War with Government: How Conservatives Weaponized Distrust from Goldwater to Trump."* (2021); https://www.niskanencenter.org/how-the-left-and-right-undermined-trust-in-government/

[798] Stanley Greenberg, *"Did most Americans lose wealth, income under Barak Obama?"* https://www.politifact.com/factchecks/2019/sep/10/stanley-greenberg/did-most-americans-lose-wealth-income-under-barack/; Chad Stone et al., *"A Guide to Statistics on Historical Trends in Income Inequality."* https://www.cbpp.org/research/poverty-and-inequality/a-guide-to-statistics-on-historical-trends-in-income-inequality

[799] Michael Greenstone et al. *"Unemployment and Earnings losses."* https://www.brookings.edu/blog/jobs/2011/11/04/unemployment-and-earnings-losses-a-look-at-long-term-impacts-of-the-great-recession-on-american-workers/; Hibah Yousuf, *"Obama admits 95% income gains gone to top 1%."* https://money.cnn.com/2013/09/15/news/economy/income-inequality-obama/index.html; Jena Kasperkevic, *"The 1% are recovering from 2008 recession while 99% are still waiting."* https://www.theguardian.com/business/2016/jul/06/one-percent-2008-recession-recovery-income; Anthony DiMaggio, *Rising Fascism in America.* (2022)

[800] Paolo Demuru, *"Conspiracy theories, messianic populism and everyday social media use in contemporary Brazil: A global semiotic perspective."* https://glocalismjournal.org/wp-content/uploads/2021/03/Demuru_gjcpi_2020_3.pdf; Michael Magcamit, *"Explaining the three-way linkage between populism, securitization and foreign policy."* World Affairs, 180 (3): 30 (2017)

[801] Erin Graham, *"Conspiracy Theories and World Government."* https://drexel.edu/coas/faculty-research/fellowships/coas-undergraduate-fellowships/06-graham-19/ John Savage, *"The John Birch Society is Back."* https://www.politico.com/magazine/story/2017/07/16/the-john-birch-society-is-alive-and-well-in-the-lone-star-state-215377/

[802] Vanessa A. Boesse, *"State of the world 2021: autocratization changing its nature?"* https://www.tandfonline.com/doi/full/10.1080/13510347.2022.2069751

[803] Jordan Kyle et al. *"Populists in Power Around the World."* https://institute.global/policy/populists-power-around-world.

[804] Davis Richardson, *"The Koch Brothers and Robert Mercer Bankrolled Right-Wing Firm Project Veritas."* https://observer.com/2017/12/koch-brothers-and-robert-mercer-funded-project-veritas/; Jane Mayer, *"The Reclusive Hedge-Fund Tycoon Behind the Trump Presidency."* https://www.newyorker.com/magazine/2017/03/27/the-reclusive-hedge-fund-tycoon-behind-the-trump-presidency

[805] Edward Lempinen, *"How plutocrats, populists are driving a precarious moment in U.S. history."* https://news.berkeley.edu/2020/07/10/how-plutocrats-populists-are-driving-a-precarious-moment-in-u-s-history/; Theda Skocpol[177] and Alexander Hertel-Fernandez[178], *"The Koch Network and Republican Party Extremism."* https://www.cambridge.org/core/journals/perspectives-on-politics/article/abs/koch-network-and-republican-party-extremism/035F3D872B0CE930AF02D7706DF46EEE; Robert Busch,

---

177. https://www.cambridge.org/core/search?filters%5BauthorTerms%5D=Theda%20Skocpol&eventCode=SE-AU

178. https://www.cambridge.org/core/search?filters%5BauthorTerms%5D=Alexander%20Hertel-Fernandez&eventCode=SE-AU

"The Culture War is Actually the Battle of the Billionaires." https://medium.com/discourse/the-culture-war-is-actually-the-battle-of-the-billionaires-1a7720801b8b; https://www.washingtonpost.com/outlook/2020/07/07/republican-party-uses-populist-politics-advance-plutocratic-policy/

[806] Jamie Peck, *"Decoding Obamanomics,"* in Jamie Peck, *Constructions of Neoliberal Reason.* (2010); Naomi Klein, *"It was the Democrats' embrace of neoliberalism that won it for Trump."* https://www.theguardian.com/commentisfree/2016/nov/09/rise-of-the-davos-class-sealed-americas-fate

[807] Max B. Sawicki, *"The Sunset of Neoliberalism."* https://jacobinmag.com/2019/08/neoliberalism-democratic-party-donald-trump-hillary-clinton-barack-obama; Howard Schneider, *"Middle-cl decline looms over final years of Obama presidency."* https://www.reuters.com/article/us-usa-obama-economy/middle-class-decline-looms-over-final-years-of-obama-presidency-idUSKBN0KR0HD20150118; Rakesh Kochhar and Stella Sechopoulos, *"How the American middle class has changed in the past five decades."* https://www.pewresearch.org/fact-tank/2022/04/20/how-the-american-middle-class-has-changed-in-the-past-five-decades/

[808] Alex Samuels and Neil Lewis, *"Democrats Helped Build The Social Safety Net. Why Are Many Now Against Expanding It?"* https://fivethirtyeight.com/features/democrats-helped-build-the-social-safety-net-why-are-many-now-against-expanding-it/

[809] Jennifer McCoy and Benjamin Press, *"What Happens When Democracies Become Perniciously Polarized?"* https://carnegieendowment.org/2022/01/18/what-happens-when-democracies-become-perniciously-polarized-pub-86190

[810] Sheri Berman, *"Why identity politics benefits the right more than the left."* https://www.theguardian.com/commentisfree/2018/jul/14/identity-politics-right-left-trump-racism; Ben Norton, *"Adolph Reed: Identity Politics is Neoliberalism."* https://bennorton.com/adolph-reed-identity-politics-is-neoliberalism/; Luca Di Blasi, *"The Rightist Appropriation of Identity Politics and its Boundaries.* in Dominik Finkelde, Rebekka Klein, eds., *In Need of a Master. Politics, Theology, and Radical Democracy.* (2021).

[811] Branko Marcetic, *"There is no 'Mainstream' Conservatism."* https://jacobinmag.com/2018/11/there-is-no-mainstream-conservatism-far-right-steve-king

[812] Bruce Caldwell, Leonidas Montes, *(Friedrich Hayek and his visits to Chile.)* http://eprints.lse.ac.uk/63318/1/__lse.ac.uk_storage_LIBRARY_Secondary_libfile_shared_repository_Content_Caldwell,%20B_Hayek%20and%2C

[813] Noam Chomsky, *Who Rules the World.* (2017); Andrew Farrant, Edward Mcphail, Sebastian Berger, *"Preventing the "Abuses" of Democracy: Hayek, the "Military Usurper" and Transitional Dictatorship in Chile?"* American Journal of

Economics and Sociology. 71:3 (2012); Benjamin Selwyn, *"Friedrich Hayek: In defense of dictatorship."* https://www.opendemocracy.net/en/friedrich-hayek-dictatorship/

[814] David Sirota, *"Why is it always the Wrong Time to Criticize Democrats from the Left?"* https://jacobinmag.com/2020/08/joe-biden-rahm-emanuel-democratic-party-election

[815] David Henderson, *"Did the Tax Cut Leave the Majority of Americans Behind?"* https://www.econlib.org/did-the-2017-tax-cut-leave-the-majority-of-americans-behind/

[816] Doug Stokes, *"Trump, American Hegemony and the future of the liberal international order."* https://www.chathamhouse.org/sites/default/files/images/ia/INTA94_1_8_238_Stokes.pdf Adam S. Posen, *"The Cost of Trump's Economic Nationalism."* https://www.piie.com/blogs/trade-and-investment-policy-watch/cost-trumps-economic-nationalism-loss-foreign-investment

[817] Grace Dean, *"Wall Street spent $2.9 billion on political contributions and lobbying in 2019 and 2020, a new study shows."* https://www.businessinsider.com/wall-street-political-contributions-lobbying-election-trump-biden-president-2021-4[179]; Ashley Smith and Charlie Post, *"The Lesser Evil Trap."* https://www.tempestmag.org/2020/08/lesser-evil-trap/

[818] Shom Mazumder, *"Why the Progressive Left Fits so Uncomfortably within the Democratic Party."* https://fivethirtyeight.com/features/why-the-progressive-left-fits-so-uncomfortably-within-the-democratic-party/

[819] David Sirota, *"Democrats are Fueling Corporate Counterrevolution against Progressives."* https://www.theguardian.com/commentisfree/2020/may/26/democrats-trump-corporate-counter-revolution

[820] T. J. Coles, *"The Billionaires Behind the Far Right."* https://www.counterpunch.org/2019/05/03/the-billionaires-behind-the-far-right/; Adam IP Smith, *"A brief history of election rigging in the United States."* https://www.historyextra.com/period/modern/a-brief-history-of-election-rigging-in-the-united-states/ Jacob A. Fortinsky, *"The Rigged Electoral System."* https://www.thecrimson.com/article/2020/2/4/fortinsky-rigged-electoral-system/

[821] Jerry Sanders, *"Peddlers of Crisis: The Committee on the Present Danger and the Politics of Containment."* (1999); Defenseinfo, *"Lunch Committee on the Present Danger: China."* https://defense.info/re-thinking-strategy/2019/03/launch-of-committee-on-the-present-danger-china/; https://medcitynews.com/2021/04/survey-1-in-5-americans-cant-afford-necessary-care/; Wendy Wu, *"Cold War is Back: Bannon helps revive US committee to target 'aggressive totalitarian foe' China."* https://www.politico.com/story/2019/03/26/steve-bannon-china-1238039

[822] Sean McElwee, *"Six Ways America is Like A Third World Country."* https://www.rollingstone.com/politics/politics-news/six-ways-america-is-like-a-third-world-country-100466/; Steve Tombs and Dave Whyte, *"Researching Corporate and White-Collar Crime*

179. https://d.docs.live.net/eb41a1b69e1e6e00/Desktop/Grace%20Dean,

in an Era of Neoliberalism." https://www.researchgate.net/publication/302371738_Researching_Corporate_and_White-Collar_Crime_in_an_Era_of_Neo-Liberalism; PBS, *"Capitol riot: The 'third world' trope offends, misreads history."* https://www.pbs.org/newshour/show/capitol-riot-the-third-world-trope-offends-misreads-history; C.D. Leonnig, *"Pentagon, FBI, DHS failed on Jan. 6, former Capitol Chief says."* https://www.stripes.com/theaters/us/2023-01-01/fbi-dhs-pentagon-capitol-riot-8609065.html

[823] Stephen Shapiro, *"Caesarism Revisited: Cultural Studies and the Question of Trumpism."* in Liam Kennedy, ed. *Trump's America: Political Culture and National Identity*. (2020).

[824] Michael Goldfarb, *"Trump was no accident: And the America that made him is still with us."* https://www.theguardian.com/commentisfree/2020/nov/08/trump-was-no-accident-the-america-that-made-him-is-still-with-us; Arley Gill, *"An America where Trump is not an Anomaly."* https://www.nowgrenada.com/2021/01/an-america-where-trump-is-not-an-anomaly/; Thomas Mills, *"Trump is not an Anomaly. He's an Embodiment"* https://www.politicsnc.com/trump-is-not-an-anomaly-hes-an-embodiment/

[825] Mikael Nilsson, *"Trump is a Warning that Fascism Didn't Die with Hitler and Mussolini."* https://www.haaretz.com/us-news/.premium-trump-legacy-fascism-far-right-biden-1.9463419; Olivia B. Waxman, *"Today's Authoritarian Leaders Aren't Fascists—But They Are Part of the Same Story."* https://time.com/5908244/strongman-fascism-history/

[826] Thorsten Hellmann, Pia Schmidt, Sascha Matthias Heller, *"Social Justice in the EU and OECD."* https://www.politico.eu/wp-content/uploads/2019/12/Social-Justice-Index-2019.pdf

[827] Zach Yearwood, *"America prides itself as a beacon of democracy, but is it?"* httpssss://unfspinnaker.com/88047/opinions/election-opinion-america-prides-itself-as-a-beacon-of-democracy-but-is-it-really/[180]; Richard Wike et al. *"What People Around the World Like and Dislike about American Society and Politics."* https://www.pewresearch.org/global/2021/11/01/what-people-around-the-world-like-and-dislike-about-american-society-and-politics/

180. https://unfspinnaker.com/88047/opinions/election-opinion-america-prides-itself-as-a-beacon-of-democracy-but-is-it-really/

[828] **Tyler Cowen, *"No Fascism Can't Happen Here."* https://www.politico.com/magazine/story/2018/03/01/no-fascism-cant-happen-here-217092/; Helmut Walser Smith, *"No America is not succumbing to fascism."* https://www.washingtonpost.com/outlook/2020/09/01/no-america-is-not-succumbing-fascism/; Christianna Sliva, *"Fascism Scholar says the US is Losing it Democratic Status."* https://www.npr.org/2020/09/06/910320018/fascism-scholar-says-u-s-is-losing-its-democratic-status; News Literary Project, *"Is press freedom eroding in the US?"* https://newslit.org/tips-tools/press-freedom-eroding-in-us/; ACLU, *"Threats to Civil Liberties Post-September 11: Secrecy, Erosion of Privacy, Danger of Unchecked Government."* https://www.aclu.org/press-releases/threats-civil-liberties-post-september-11-secrecy-erosion-privacy-danger-unchecked**

[829] Henry Armand Giroux, *"The Emerging Authoritarianism in the United States. Political Culture under the Bush/Cheney Administration."* https://www.researchgate.net/publication/236804650_The_Emerging_Authoritarianism_in_the_United_States_Political_Culture_under_the_BushCheney_Adı

[830] Gianvito Brindisi, *"Brief Reflections on Authoritarian Neoliberalism."* http://www.softpowerjournal.com/web/wp-content/uploads/2021/09/16_Brindisi_BRIEF-REFLECTIONS-ON-AUTHORITARIAN-NEOLIBERALISM.pdf

[831] Ernesto Gallo, *"Three Varieties of Authoritarian Neoliberalism."* https://journals.sagepub.com/doi/full/10.1177/10245294211038425

[832] Cameron Easley, *"U.S. Conservatives Are Uniquely Inclined Toward Right-Wing Authoritarianism Compared to Western Peers."* https://morningconsult.com/2021/06/28/global-right-wing-authoritarian-test/

[833] **Brianna Richardson, *"Axios/Momentive Poll: January 6th Revisited."* https://www.surveymonkey.com/curiosity/axios-january-6-revisited/**

[834] Amanda Taub, *"The Rise of American Authoritarianism."* https://www.vox.com/2016/3/1/11127424/trump-authoritarianism; Dalibor Rohak, Liz Kennedy, and Vikram Singh, *"Drivers of Authoritarian Populism in the United States."* https://www.americanprogress.org/article/drivers-authoritarian-populism-united-states/; Timothy M. Gill, *"Why the power elite continues to dominate American politics."* https://www.washingtonpost.com/outlook/2018/12/24/why-power-elite-continues-dominate-american-politics/

[835] Zach Beauchamp, *"Call it Authoritarianism."* https://www.vox.com/policy-and-politics/2021/6/15/22522504/republicans-authoritarianism-trump-competitive.

[836] Rick Perlstein, *"The Long Authoritarian History of the Capitol Riot."* https://nymag.com/intelligencer/2021/06/long-authoritarian-history-january-6-insurrection.html

[837] Ishena Robinson, *"Anti-CTR Mania and Book Bans are the Latest Tactics to Halt Racial Justice."* https://www.naacpldf.org/critical-race-theory-banned-books/; G.B. Slater, *"Neoliberalism Paved the Way for Book Banning to Take Hold in US Schools."* https://www.academia.edu/79243412/Neoliberalism_Paved_the_Way_for_Book_Banning_to_Take_Hold_in_US_Schools

[838] Jason Stanley, *"Banning ideas and authors is not a culture war – it's fascism."* https://www.theguardian.com/us-news/2023/feb/13/african-american-studies-republican-ban-florida; Eric Kauffman, *"The Politics of Culture Wars in Contemporary America."* https://manhattan.institute/article/the-politics-of-the-culture-wars-in-contemporary-america

[839] Tom McCarthy, *"Florida banned state workers from using terms like climate change."* https://www.theguardian.com/us-news/2015/mar/08/florida-banned-terms-climate-change-global-warming; Peter[181] Greene, *"Not just Florida: How don't say gay compares in other states."* https://www.forbes.com/sites/petergreene/2022/04/14/not-just-florida-how-dont-say-gay-legislation-compares-in-other-states/; Daniel Little, *"False Consciousness."* http://www-personal.umd.umich.edu/~delittle/iess%20false%20consciousness%20V2.htm; Steve Hanson, *"False Consciousness, what's not to Dislike?"* https://www.opendemocracy.net/en/opendemocracyuk/false-consciousness-whats-not-to-dislike/ P.A. Meyers, *"Speaking Truth to Ourselves: False Consciousness and a Dilemma of Identity Politics in Democracy."* https://www.tandfonline.com/doi/abs/10.1080/03906700600931376?journalCode=cirs20; György Lukács, *History and class consciousness; studies in Marxist dialectics*. 1920.

[840] Spencer Ackerman, *"The Disappeared: Chicago police detain Americans at abuse-laden black site."* https://www.theguardian.com/us-news/2015/feb/24/chicago-police-detain-americans-black-site; Sahil Kapur and Frank Thorp *"Oklahoma county leaders caught on audio talking about killing reporters and complaining they can no longer lynch Black people."* https://www.cnbc.com/2023/04/17/oklahoma-county-leaders-caught-on-audio-talking-about-killing-reporters-complaining-they-can-no-longer-lynch-black-people.html

[841] Nizar Saghieh, *"Lebanon Unlimited: Neoliberalism Dominates the Workplace."* https://english.legal-agenda.com/lebanon-unlimited-neoliberalism-dominates-the-workplace/ Oliver Dalichau, *"Colombia votes for Social Justice."* https://www.ips-journal.eu/topics/future-of-social-democracy/colombia-votes-for-social-justice-6006/; Charlie Kimber, *"French elections: neoliberal Macron loses parliamentary majority."* https://socialistworker.co.uk/international/french-elections-neoliberal-macron-to-lose-majority/

[842] Nelson Lichtenstein, *"The Next Amazon Union Drive."* https://www.dissentmagazine.org/online_articles/the-next-amazon-union-drive; Eszter Covats, *"Solidarity in Struggle: Feminist Perspectives on Neoliberalism in Eastern Europe."* https://library.fes.de/pdf-files/bueros/budapest/12796.pdf; Scott Neuman, *"Anti-Globalization Protests Spark Violence in Hamburg for Second Day."* https://www.npr.org/sections/thetwo-way/2017/07/07/535959974/flames-subside-but-protests-continue-as-g20-leaders-gather-for-hamburg-summit?t=1650172642203; Emma Moon, *"Neoliberalism, Political Action on Climate Change and Youth in Aotearoa New Zealand."* Thesis, Victoria University of Wellington. (2013)

[843] Eduardo Silva, *"Capitalist Conditions, the State and Neoliberal Economic Restructuring: Chile, 1973-88"* World Politics 45, 4 (1993); Barbara Stallings, *"The Political Economy of Economic Adjustment: Chile, 1973-1990"*

181. https://www.theguardian.com/us-news/2015/mar/08/florida-banned-terms-climate-change-global-warming;%20Peter

in Robert H. Bates, ed. *'Political and Economic Institutions in Economic Policy Reform.'* (1993); Jane Esberg, *"Anticipating Dissent"*. The Journal of Politics, 83, 2 (2021).

[844] CNDH, *"Insurgencia del Ejército Zapatista de Liberación Nacional (EZLN)."* https://www.cndh.org.mx/noticia/insurgencia-del-ejercito-zapatista-de-liberacion-nacional-ezln Leigh Thermadater, *"In fighting globalism, the Zapatistas brought the world to Chiapas."* https://mexiconewsdaily.com/culture/zapatistas-brought-world-to-chiapas/

[845] John K. Watson and David Seddon, *"Free Markets and Food Riots: The Politics of Global Adjustment."* (1994); Jarred Olsen, *"How the Zapatistas Resisted Neoliberalism."* https://thoughtcatalog.com/jared-olson/2017/06/how-the-zapatistas-resisted-neoliberalism/

[846] W. F. Fisher and Thomas Ponniah, *Another World is Possible: Possible Alternatives to Globalization and the World Social Forum.* (2003).

[847] Roberto Savio, *"Farewell to the World Social Forum?"* https://greattransition.org/gti-forum/wsf-savio

[848] Judite Stronzake and Wendy Wolford[182], *"Brazil's Landless Workers Rise Up."* https://www.dissentmagazine.org/article/brazils-landless-workers-rise-mst-land-occupation; **Cibele Rizek and André Dal'Bó, *"The Growth of the Brazil's Homeless Workers' Movement."*** https://globaldialogue.isa-sociology.org/the-growth-of-brazils-homeless-workers-movement/; Jam Sprague, *"The Fanmi Lavalas Political Project."* https://nacla.org/article/fanmi-lavalas-political-project; Nikhil Eapen, *"Movements are not like governments that come and go: 34 years of the Narmada Project."* https://caravanmagazine.in/communities/narmada-bacaho-andolan-sardar-sarovar-dam

[849] Jyoti Sharma, *"Avoiding the Neoliberal Trap in Social Entrepreneurship."* https://ssir.org/articles/entry/a_neoliberal_takeover_of_social_entrepreneurship; http://anticsr.com/ngos-csr/; http://anticsr.com/csr-created-risk/.

[850] Jacob Middleton, *"Friends of the Poor or of Neoliberalism."* http://socialistreview.org.uk/310/friends-poor-or-neo-liberalism; Maximilien C. Forte, *"Civil Society, NGO's and Saving the Needy: Imperial Neoimperialism."* https://zeroanthropology.net/2014/08/28/civil-society-ngos-and-saving-the-needy-imperial-neoliberalism/

[851] Tiina Seppala, *"Biopolitics, Resistance and the Neoliberal Development Paradigm."* https://www.mattersburgerkreis.at/dl/qNqNJMJLLmJqx4KooJK/JEP-1-2014_05_SEPP_L__Biopolitics_-Resistance-and-the-Neoliberal-Development-Paradigm.pdf Tiina Seppala, *"Autonomy versus Conformism, Co-optation, De-politicization? Social Movements and Institutions in the Neoliberal Era."* https://ecpr.eu/Events/PaperDetails.aspx?PaperID=34958&EventID=96

[852] Adam Hanieh, *"Gulf States Neoliberalism and Liberation in the Middle East"* https://rs21.org.uk/2014/10/06/adam-hanieh-on-the-gulf-states-neoliberalism-and-liberation-in-the-middle-east/; http://links.org.au/node/4095

[853] Jim Yong Kim, *"Dying for Growth: Global Inequality and the Health of the Poor."* http://www.mit.edu/~thistle/v13/2/imf.html

182. https://www.dissentmagazine.org/author/judite-stronzake-and-wendy-wolford

[854] Lawrence Cox and Alf Gunvald Nielsen, *"Neoliberalism and Social Movements,"* https://www.e-ir.info/2014/07/30/neoliberalism-and-social-movements/; Sindhu M. Zagoren, *"Another World was Possible: 9/11 and the Struggle Against Neoliberalism in the United States."* https://cdr.lib.unc.edu/downloads/bn9997633?locale=en

[855] Anthony Giddens, *"Anthony Giddens on Globalization Excerpts from a Keynote Address at the UNRISD Conference on Globalization and Citizenship."* https://www.unrisd.org/unrisd/website/newsview.nsf/0/3F2A5BF8EF7300D480256B750053C7EC?OpenDocument&cntxt=5758C&cookielang=es#top; N. C. Georgantzas, Evangelos Katsamakas, and Dominic Solowiej, *"Giddens' globalization: Exploring dynamic implications."* https://proceedings.systemdynamics.org/2009/proceed/papers/P1072.pdf

[856] The Express Tribune, *"Worldwide demonstration: Wall-Street-inspired protests spread across Asia."* https://tribune.com.pk/story/275044/worldwide-demonstrationoccupy-wall-street-inspired-protests-spread-across-asia; Simon Rogers, *"Occupy protests around the world: full list visualized."* https://www.theguardian.com/news/datablog/2011/oct/17/occupy-protests-world-list-map; Patrick Heller, *"BRICS from below: counterpower movements in Brazil, India and South Africa."* https://www.opendemocracy.net/en/brics-from-below-counterpower-movements-in-brazil-india-and-south-africa/

[857] Nathan Schneider, *"The Real Story of Occupy Wall Street is Happened Since."* https://www.rollingstone.com/politics/political-commentary/occupy-wall-street-10-year-anniversry-1227856/; Jenny Pickerill et al. eds. *"Occupy! A Global Movement"* (2015); *"A brief history of resistance to neoliberalism"* https://ebrary.net/103466/sociology/history_resistance_neoliberalism; Armine Ishkanian and Marlies Glasius, *"Resisting Neoliberalism? Movements against Austerity and for Democracy in Cairo, Athens and London.* http://eprints.lse.ac.uk/85656/1/Ishkanian_Resisting_FINAL_.pdf; https://timesofindia.indiatimes.com/city/chandigarh/indian-amp39occupy-wall-streetamp39-movement-takes-rootshape/articleshow/11161287.cms; Arran Gare, *"Post-Modernism as the decadence of the Social Democratic state."* https://www.researchgate.net/publication/240528020_Postmodernism_as_the_Decadence_of_the_Social_Democratic_State

[858] Vijoo Krishnan, *"A Quarter Century of Neoliberal Economic Policies: Unending Distress and Peasant Resistance."* https://www.cpim.org/views/quarter-century-neo-liberal-economic-policies-unending-distress-and-peasant-resistance; Juan Pablo Ferrero, *Democracy against Neoliberalism in Argentina and Brazil,* 2014; Mimi Abramovitz and Jennifer Zelnick, "*Double Jeopardy: The Impact of Neoliberalism on Care Workers in the United States and South Africa*", http://journals.sagepub.com/doi/abs/10.2190/HS.40.1.f;

[859] Patrick Bond, *"Uneven citizen advocacy within the BRICS, within global governance."* https://www.ohchr.org/sites/default/files/Documents/Issues/IntOrder/GlobalGovernanceSpaces/PatrickBond.pdf; Annita Diloris Montoute, *"The BRICS Group and Global Economic Governance."* https://www.researchgate.net/publication/336817898_The_BRICS_Group_and_Global_Economic_Governance

[860] Fatima Moosa, *"BRICS: Continuation of Neoliberal Machine?"* https://www.thedailyvox.co.za/brics-continuation-of-neoliberal-machine-fatima-moosa/; Mihika Chatterjee[183] and Ikuno Naka[184], *"Twenty years of BRICS: Political and economic transformations through the lens of land."* https://www.tandfonline.com/doi/full/10.1080/13600818.2022.2033191

[861] Alexandria Vasileva-Dienes and Vivien A. Schmidt, *"Conceptualizing capitalism in the twenty-first century: the BRICS and the European periphery."* https://www.tandfonline.com/doi/full/10.1080/13569775.2018.1555746

Walden Bello, *The BRICS: Challenges to the Global Status Quo."* https://www.thenation.com/article/brics-challengers-global-status-quo/

[862] Joao Pedro Stedile, *"Contemporary Challenges for the Working Class & Peasantry in Brazil."* https://grassrootsonline.org/in-the-news/contemporary-challenges-for-the-working-class-peasantry-in-brazil/; https://www.mstbrazil.org/news/lula-landless-workers-movement-%E2%80%9Cwe-are-right-side-history%E2%80%9D

[863] Anthony Robert Pahnke[185] and Marcelo Milan[186], *"The Brazilian Crisis and the New Authoritarianism."* https://monthlyreview.org/2020/06/01/the-brazilian-crisis-and-the-new-authoritarianism/; Malu Gaspar, *"The Guarantor: The rise and controversies of the economist Paulo Guedes, the ultraliberal who has entered into a marriage of convenience with Jair Bolsonaro."* https://piaui.folha.uol.com.br/materia/the-guarantor/

[864] Luis Henrique Paiva, *"Poverty and Inequality Reduction in Brazil."*

https://www.iberoamericana.se/articles/10.16993/iberoamericana.4/; Gianna Amendolara, *"Inequality on the Rise: A Study of Inequality in Mexico and Brazil."* https://www.american.edu/cas/economics/ejournal/upload/global_majority_e_journal_13_1_amendolara.pdf

183. https://www.tandfonline.com/author/Chatterjee%2C+Mihika

184. https://www.tandfonline.com/author/Naka%2C+Ikuno

185. https://monthlyreview.org/author/anthonyrobertpahnke/

186. https://monthlyreview.org/author/marcelomilan/

[865] Enrico Padoan, *Anti-Neoliberal Populisms in Comparative Perspective: A Latinamericanisation of Southern Europe?* (2020); Pablo Mira, *"El Plan Convertibilidad."* https://eleconomista.com.ar/aniversario-70/el-plan-convertibilidad-n44693

[866] Fernando Rugitsky, *"Austerity reaches Brazil."* https://www.jacobinmag.com/2015/09/brazil-pt-austerity-dilma-rousseff-petrobas-real/; Laura Carvalho, *"Facing unemployment, austerity and scandal, Brazil tries to keep it together."* https://theconversation.com/facing-unemployment-austerity-and-scandal-brazil-struggles-to-keep-it-together-71663; Alfredo Saad-Filho[187], Juan Grigera[188], and Ana Paula Colombi[189], *"The Nature of the PT Governments: A Variety of Neoliberalism?"* https://journals.sagepub.com/doi/full/10.1177/0094582X19891140

[867] Patricia Justino and Bruno Martorano, *"Populism in Brazil: How Liberisation and Austerity Led to the Rise of Lula and Bolsonaro."* https://ourworld.unu.edu/en/populism-in-brazil-how-liberalisation-and-austerity-led-to-the-rise-of-lula-and-bolsonaro

[868] William Aviles, *The Drug War in Mexico: Hegemony and Global Capitalism*; https://www.researchgate.net/publication/231966134_Grassroots_Movements_and_Political_Activism_in_Latin_America_A_Critical_Comparison_of_Chile_and_Brazil; Patrick Clark, Jacobo Garcia, *"Left Populism, State Building, Class Compromise, and Social Conflict in Ecuador's Citizen's Revolution."* https://journals.sagepub.com/doi/10.1177/0094582X18807723; S.K. O'Neil, *"Mexico's Underground Economy and Illicit Money Outflows."* https://www.cfr.org/blog/mexicos-underground-economy-and-illicit-money-outflows;

The Global Economy.com, *"Mexico: Shadow Economy."* https://www.theglobaleconomy.com/Mexico/shadow_economy/

[869] Carlos Eduardo Martins, *Dependency, Neoliberalism and Globalization in Latin America.* 2020; Elizabeth Farny, *"Dependency Theory: A Useful Tool for Analyzing Global Inequalities Today?"* https://www.e-ir.info/2016/11/23/dependency-theory-a-useful-tool-for-analyzing-global-inequalities-today/; Jerome Roos, *"South Africa's untold tragedy of neoliberal apartheid."* https://roarmag.org/essays/south-africa-marikana-anc-poor/

[870] Mark Engler, *"The Legacy of Anti-Globalization."* https://www.dissentmagazine.org/blog/the-legacy-of-anti-globalization; Martin Weber and P. H. Graeme, *"Forging World Order Paradigms: 'Good Civilization' vs. 'Global Terror'."* https://www.prio.org/publications/2457.

187. https://journals.sagepub.com/doi/full/10.1177/0094582X19891140#con1

188. https://journals.sagepub.com/doi/full/10.1177/0094582X19891140#con2

189. https://journals.sagepub.com/doi/full/10.1177/0094582X19891140#con3

[871] Colin Gordon, *"Growing Apart: A Political History of American Inequality."* https://scalar.usc.edu/works/growing-apart-a-political-history-of-american-inequality/a-tattered-safety-net-social-polic; Premilla Nadasen, *"How a Democrat Killed Welfare."* https://jacobin.com/2016/02/welfare-reform-bill-hillary-clinton-tanf-poverty-dlc/

[872] Lily Geismer, *"Democrats and Neoliberalism."* https://www.vox.com/polyarchy/2019/6/11/18660240/democrats-neoliberalism

[873] Michael Meeropol, *Surrender: How the Clinton Administration Completed the Reagan Revolution.* (2000).

[874] Denis Sanders, *"Democrats and the myth of the lesser evil."* https://socialism.com/fs-article/democrats-and-the-myth-of-the-lesser-evil/

[875] *"Cornel West: "Bernie Was Crushed by Neoliberalism"* https://www.jacobinmag.com/2020/12/cornel-west-interview-bernie-black-lives-matter

[876] Robert Wright, *"Why Neoliberals Should Love Bernie."* https://nonzero.org/post/neoliberals-bernie; https://www.washingtonpost.com/outlook/2019/02/21/progressives-beware-centrists-attempts-co-opt-your-platform/

[877] Peter Dreier, *"Black Lives Matter Joins a Long Line of Protest Movements that Have Shifted Public Opinion Most Recently—Occupy Wall Street."* https://www.salon.com/2015/08/15/black_lives_matter_joins_a_long_line_of_protest_movements_that_have_shifted_public_opinion_most_recently_occupy_wall_street/

[878] Bob Jessop, *"From Thatcherism to New Labour: Neo-Liberalism, Workfarism, and Labour Market Regulation."* https://www.lancaster.ac.uk/fass/resources/sociology-online-papers/papers/jessop-from-thatcherism-to-new-labour.pdf; Alex Niven, *"Tony Blair Failed Working Class People."* https://www.jacobinmag.com/2021/04/tony-blair-working-class-new-labour-inequality

[879] Lars Cornilissen, *"The new right is not a reaction to neoliberalism, but its offsrping."* https://www.opendemocracy.net/en/can-europe-make-it/the-new-right-is-not-a-reaction-to-neoliberalism-but-its-offspring/; Daniel Zamora Niklas Olsen, *"How Decades of Neoliberalism Led to the Era of Right Wing Politics."* https://jacobinmag.com/2019/09/in-the-ruins-of-neoliberalism-wendy-brown.

[880] **Walden Bello, *"The Death of Neoliberalism."* https://greattransition.org/gti-forum/pandemic-scenario-bello; Jannick Alimi, *"Législatives : comment la Nupes est devenue la force majeure d'opposition."* https://www.leparisien.fr/elections/legislatives/legislatives-comment-la-nupes-est-devenue-la-force-majeure-dopposition-19-06-2022-W6HWOTKSUJCTXP6U6EUZA3QO4M.php; Ayelén Oliva, *"Gustavo Petro logra una victoria historica de la izquierda en Colombia."* https://www.eldiario.es/internacional/izquierdista-gustavo-petro-gana-elecciones-presidenciales-colombia_1_9099056.html**

[881] Walden Bello, *"The Race to Replace a Dying Neoliberalism is on. As of Now, the Right Wing is Ahead."* https://thewire.in/political-economy/the-race-to-replace-a-dying-neoliberalism-is-on-as-of-now-the-right-wing-is-ahead

[882] Ruth Igielnik, *"70% of Americans say US economic system unfairly favors the powerful."* https://www.pewresearch.org/fact-tank/2020/01/09/70-of-americans-say-u-s-economic-system-unfairly-favors-the-powerful/

[883] Eliane Glasser, *"Elites, Right Wing Populism, and the Left."* https://www.opendemocracy.net/uk/eliane-glaser/elites-right-wing-populism-and-left;

Robert E. Watkins, *"Turning the Social Contract Inside Out: Neoliberal Governance and Human Capital in Two Days, One Night."* (2016).

[884] **Bidisha Chakraborty, *"Education as an instrument of social change and enhancing teaching-learning process with the help of technological development."* https://www.researchgate.net/publication/325143953_Education_as_an_instrument_of_social_change_and_enhancing_teaching-learning_process_with_the_help_of_technological_development; *"A History of Assembly Line Education."* http://www.nisce.org/blog/features/a-history-of-assembly-line-education/; Carl L. Bankston, *"The Mass Production of Credentials."* https://www.independent.org/pdf/tir/tir_15_03_1_bankston.pdf; Mathew Phelan, *"$50,000 a year... to get taught by AI: Harvard announces it will teach students using an artificial intelligence instructor next semester."* https://www.dailymail.co.uk/sciencetech/article-12251763/Harvard-announces-teach-students-using-artificial-intelligence-instructor-semester.html**

[885] JAY NEWMAN, *"Education as Civilization."* The Journal of Educational Thought (JET) / Revue de la Pensée Éducative. 11:3 (1977).

[886] Hantian Wu, Kiang Zha, *"History of Chinese Higher Education."* https://www.researchgate.net/publication/331574378_History_of_Chinese_Higher_Education

[887] **Olaf Pederson, *The First Universities: Studium Generale and the Origins of University Education in Europe.* (1998);**

Asharq Al-Awsat, *"Oldest Arab Universities Founded 1000 Years Ago."* https://eng-archive.aawsat.com/theaawsat/features/oldest-arab-universities-founded-1000-years-ago[190]; Hastings Rashdall, *The Universities of Europe in the Middle Ages, Volume I: Salerno, Bologna, Paris.* (2010). Rebecca Mortimer, *"Fatima al-Fihri."* https://manchesteruniversitypress.co.uk/blog/2018/03/08/fatima-al-fihri-founder-worlds-first-university/

[888] Fred van Leeuven, *"Education, the Enlightenment and the 21st Century."* https://www.thersa.org/blog/2016/07/education-the-enlightenment-and-the-21st-century; Angelo Letizia, *"Battle for the Enlightenment: Neoliberalism, Critical Theory and the role of Circumvential Education in Fostering a new Phase of the Enlightenment."* http://www.jceps.com/wp-content/uploads/PDFs/11-3-08.pdf

[889] Joel Krieger, *"Social Policy in the Age of Reagan and Thatcher"* Socialist Register. 23, (1987).

[890] Christina L. Davis, *"The Myth of Universal Education."* http://commonplace.online/article/myth-universal-education/; Donna Ferguson, *"Working-class children get less of everything in education, including respect.*[191] https://www.theguardian.com/education/2017/nov/21/english-class-system-shaped-in-schools; Ayman K. Agbaria, *"Israeli education and the Apartheid in South Africa."* https://www.tandfonline.com/doi/abs/10.1080/14675986.2018.1429573?journalCode=ceji20; stopthewall.org *"Denial of education: An Israeli Apartheid tool to annex the Jordan Valley."* https://www.stopthewall.org/right2exist/denial-of-education-an-israeli-apartheid-tool-to-colonize-the-jordan-valley/; Georges Felouzis, Barbara Fouquete-Chauprade, *"School Segregation in France."* https://www.researchgate.net/publication/346848170_School_Segregation_in_France_The_Role_of_Public_Policies_and_Stakeholder_Strategies;

[891] Basilio G. Monteiro, *"Commodification of Education is a necessary Evil."* https://www.deccanchronicle.com/discourse/181118/commodification-of-education-is-a-necessary-evil.html; Rui Yang, *"The Commodification of Education and Its Effects on Developing Countries: A Focus on China."* https://www.mattersburgerkreis.at/dl/pttoJMJKonJqx4KooJK/JEP-4-2006_03_YANG_The-Commodification-of-Education-and-its-effects-on-developing-countries-A-focus-on-China.pdf; Chris McNutt, *"Unpacking Neoliberal Schooling."* https://medium.com/human-restoration-project/unpacking-neoliberal-schooling-aa3a2add66e8

[892] Marnie Holborow, *"Neoliberalism, human capital and the skills agenda in higher education – the Irish case."* https://dcu.academia.edu/MarnieHolborow

[893] Rodrigo Cornejo Chávez, *"El Experimento Educativo Chileno 20 Anos Despues: Una Mirada Critica a los Logros y Falencias Del Sistema Escolar."* https://revistas.uam.es/reice/article/view/10074/10181; Pallavi Sreedhar, *"Chile: An Invaluable Case Study for School Vouchers."* http://www.cpreview.org/blog/2019/10/chile-an-invaluable-case-study-for-school-vouchers; Nelly P. Stromquist, Anita Sanyal, *"Student resistance to neoliberalism in Chile."* https://www.researchgate.net/publication/274431004_Student_resistance_to_neoliberalism_in_Chile

---

190. https://d.docs.live.net/eb41a1b69e1e6e00/Desktop/Asharq%20Al-Awsat,

191. http://commonplace.online/article/myth-universal-education/;%20Donna%20Ferguson,%20

[894] Yanis Iqbal, *"Education under Neoliberal Capitalism."* https://socialistproject.ca/2021/08/education-under-neoliberal-capitalism/; Richard Hall and Mark Pulsford, *"Neoliberalism and primary education: Impacts of neoliberal policy on the lived experiences of primary school communities."* https://journals.sagepub.com/doi/full/10.1177/1757743819877344; Paul Michael Garrett, *"How to be Modern: New Labour's Neoliberal Modernity and the Change for Children Progamme."* British Journal of Social Work, 38 (October, 2006);

[895] *"Critical Race Theory with David Gillborn."* http://www.forwardpartnership.org.uk/?p=1648; Jaycee Fortin, *"Critical Race Theory: A Brief History."* https://www.nytimes.com/article/what-is-critical-race-theory.html

[896] Utsav Kumar Singh *"How India's New Education Structure is Narrowing the Idea of Dissent."* https://thewire.in/education/how-indias-new-education-structure-is-narrowing-the-idea-of-dissent; Robert Austin, Henry and Bernadete Beserra, *"Neoliberalism and Higher Education in Latin America."* Latin American Perspectives, 49:3 (2022); Sevgi Doğan Ervjola Selenica, *"Authoritarianism and academic freedom in neoliberal Turkey."* https://www.researchgate.net/publication/350070158_Authoritarianism_and_academic_freedom_in_neoliberal_Turkey; Richard Hall[192], Mark Pulsford[193], "*Neoliberalism and primary education: Impacts of neoliberal policy on the lived experiences of primary school communities.*" https://journals.sagepub.com/doi/full/10.1177/1757743819877344; Bruno Amable, "*Morals and Politics in the Ideology of Neoliberalism.*" https://www.mpifg.de/pu/mpifg_ja/SER_9_2011_Amable.pdf

[897] Vikram Singh, *"4 Years of Systematic Destruction of Education under Modi Regime."* https://www.newsclick.in/4-years-systematic-destruction-education-under-modi-regime

[898] Kemal İnal and Güliz Akkaymak, *Neoliberal Transformation of Education in Turkey*. (2012); Sunad, *"3 Years of Modi: Assault on Education Continues Unabated."* https://www.cpim.org/views/3-years-modi-assault-education-continues-unabated.

[899] David Hill, *"Class, Capital and Education in this Neoliberal Neoconservative Period."* in Sheila Macrine, Peter McLaren and Dave Hill, eds. *Revolutionizing Pedagogy Education for Social Justice Within and Beyond Global Neo-Liberalism.* (2009).

[900] Khalid Arar[194], Deniz Örücü[195], Jane Wilkinson[196], eds. *Neoliberalism and Education Systems in Conflict: Exploring Challenges Across the Globe.*(2020); Garth Stahl, *Ethnography of a Neoliberal School.* (2018); David Lundie, Andrej Zwietter Dipayan Ghosh,

---

192. https://journals.sagepub.com/doi/full/10.1177/1757743819877344

193. https://journals.sagepub.com/doi/full/10.1177/1757743819877344

194. https://www.routledge.com/search?author=Khalid%20Arar

195. https://www.routledge.com/search?author=Deniz%20Örücü

"Corporatized education and State sovereignty." https://www.brookings.edu/blog/techtank/2022/01/31/corporatized-education-and-state-sovereignty/

[901] Julie Hare, *'Private education driving the global divide between rich and poor.'* https://www.afr.com/work-and-careers/education/private-education-driving-the-global-divide-between-rich-and-poor-20211212-p59guu[197]; Nelly P. Stromquist, *Inequality as a Way of Life: education and social class in Latin America.* Pedagogy, Culture and Society. 12:1 [2004]; Inga Ting, *'Rich school, poor school; Australia's great education divide.'* https://www.abc.net.au/news/2019-08-13/rich-school-poor-school-australias-great-education-divide/11383384; Hannah Richardson, *"Top state schools 'dominated by richest families."* https://www.bbc.com/news/education-39076204; Krista Watson, *"Why Richer Areas Get More Funding than Poorer Ones."* https://www.globalcitizen.org/en/content/cost-of-education-in-us/; Alana[198] Samuel, *'Good School, Rich School; Bad School, Poor School."* https://www.theatlantic.com/business/archive/2016/08/property-taxes-and-unequal-schools/497333/

[902] Sol Gamsu, *"From assisted places to free schools: subsidizing private schools for the Northern English middle classes."* https://www.tandfonline.com/doi/full/10.1080/01425692.2020.1833180 Richard Hall, Mark Pulsford, *"Neoliberalism and primary education: Impacts of neoliberal policy on the lived experiences of primary school communities."* https://dora.dmu.ac.uk/handle/2086/17885; Lydia Henales and Beatrice Edwards, *"Neo-liberalism and Educational Reform in Latin America."* https://www.tc.columbia.edu/cice/pdf/25660_2_2_Heneles_Edwards.pdf; The Commonwealth Institute, *"Unequal Opportunities: Fewer Resources, Worse Outcomes for Schools with Concentrated Poverty."* https://thecommonwealthinstitute.org/research/unequal-opportunities-fewer-resources-worse-outcomes-for-students-in-schools-with-concentrated-poverty/

[903] Hicham Alaoui and Robert Springbord, *"Education in the Arab World: A Legacy of Coming Up Short."* https://www.wilsoncenter.org/article/education-arab-world-legacy-coming-short

[904] Otmane Amagour[199], *"The Political Economy of Education in the Arab World: An Interview with Hicham Alaoui."* https://www.jadaliyya.com/Details/42822

[905] Report Linker, *"Global Private Tutoring Industry."* https://www.reportlinker.com/p0552740/Private-Tutoring-Industry.html?utm_source=GNW

[906] Jaekyung Lee, *"Two Worlds of Private Tutoring: The Prevalence and Causes of After-School Mathematics Tutoring in Korea and the United States."*https://asset-pdf.scinapse.io/prod/163434870/163434870.pdf

[907] Henry Giroux, *"Teachers Are Rising Up to Resist Neoliberal Attacks on Education."* https://truthout.org/articles/teachers-are-rising-up-to-resist-neoliberal-attacks-on-education/; Katherine Jinyi Li[200], *"Failing and Jailing our Youth, from Seattle to Sao Paolo."*

---

196. https://www.routledge.com/search?author=Jane%20Wilkinson

197. https://d.docs.live.net/eb41a1b69e1e6e00/Desktop/Julie%20Hare,%20'Private%20education%20driving%20the%20global%20divide%20between%20rich%20and%20poor.'%20https:/www.afr.com/work-and-careers/education/private-education-driving-the-global-divide-between-rich-and-poor-20211212-p59guu

198. https://www.globalcitizen.org/en/content/cost-of-education-in-us/;%20Alana

199. https://www.jadaliyya.com/Author/10822

https://seattleglobalist.com/2015/11/23/sao-paulo-brazil-school-to-prison-pipeline-seattle-youth-jail/44637; Peter Grey, *"School is a Prison – and damaging our kids."* https://www.salon.com/2013/08/26/school_is_a_prison_and_damaging_our_kids/.

[908] Nancy MacLean, *"How Milton Friedman Exploited White Supremacy to Privatize Education."* https://www.ineteconomics.org/uploads/papers/WP_161-MacLean.pdf; Michael Apple, *"Comparing Neoliberal Projects and Inequality in Education."* https://www.researchgate.net/publication/233492110_Comparing_Neo-Liberal_Projects_and_Inequality_in_Education

[909] Adam Matthews, *"The Idea and Becoming of a University Across Time and Space: Ivory Tower, Factory and Network."* https://link.springer.com/article/10.1007/s42438-022-00341-0; Shiela Macrine, *"Pedagogies of Neoliberalism."* https://www.researchgate.net/publication/292311481_Pedagogies_of_Neoliberalism; Younis Fareed Abu Alhaija, *"Higher Education in the Shadow of Neoliberalism"* Turkish Journal of Computer and Mathematics Education. 12:7 (2021); Daniel B. Saunders, *"Students as customers: The influence of neoliberal ideology and free-market logic on entering first-year college students."* https://scholarworks.umass.edu/dissertations/AAI3465082/

[910] John Hood, *"Why College Costs Are Rising."* https://fee.org/articles/why-college-costs-are-rising/

[911] Alexander L. Q. Chen, *"The Neoliberal University and Digital Learning."* https://criticaledges.com/2021/05/05/the-neoliberal-university-and-digital-learning/; India News *"India's Worthless Degrees Undercut World's Fastest-Growing Economy."* https://www.ndtv.com/india-news/worthless-degrees-are-creating-an-unemployable-generation-in-india-3957341

[912] Ian McKay, *"A Pandemic's Punitive Pedagogy: Education and the Organic Crisis of the Global Neoliberal Order."* https://ojs.library.queensu.ca/index.php/encounters/article/download/14804/9959; Report Linker, *"Global Private Tutoring Industry."* https://www.reportlinker.com/p0552740/Private-Tutoring-Industry.html?utm_source=GNW; TBS Staff, *"Online Colleges vs. Diploma Mills."* https://thebestschools.org/magazine/online-college-vs-diploma-mills/; HLS, *"96% of Students defrauded by For-Profit Colleges Report Their Lives Are Worse Now than Before They Went to School."* https://clinics.law.harvard.edu/blog/2019/08/96-of-students-defrauded-by-for-profit-colleges-report-their-lives-are-worse-now-than-before-they-went-to-school/

[913] Bibhudatta Pradhan and Vrishti Beniwal, *"Worthless Degree are Creating an Unemployable Generation in India."* https://www.yahoo.com/finance/news/worthless-degrees-creating-unemployable-generation-230006069.html

[914] Kristin Natalier and Robert Clarke, *"Online Learning and Education Encounter in a Neo-Liberal University."* Higher Education Studies, 5:2 (2015)

---

200. https://seattleglobalist.com/author/katherine-jinyi-li

[915] Gustavo A. Yamada, Pablo Lavado, *"Labor market consequences of the college boom around the world."* https://wol.iza.org/articles/boom-in-university-graduates-and-risk-of-underemployment/long

[916] Rollin Kent, *"Two Positions in the International Debate About Higher Education: The World Bank and UNESCO."* http://lanic.utexas.edu/project/lasa95/kent.html

[917] Roberto Leher, *"A New Lord of Education? World Bank Policy for Peripheral Capitalism."* http://www.jceps.com/wp-content/uploads/PDFs/02-1-05.pdf; Kapil Dev Regmi[201], *"World Bank in Nepal's education: three decades of neoliberal reform."* Globalization, Societies and Education. 15:2, (2017); https://www.worldbank.org/en/news/press-release/2021/10/26/government-of-nepal-and-the-world-bank-launch-60-million-nurturing-excellence-in-higher-education-program; https://www.worldbank.org/en/news/feature/2019/11/12/world-bank-launches-initiative-to-tackle-education-financing-challenges

[918] Adrian Zancaro, Antoni Verger and Clara Fontdevila, *"The instrumentation of public subsidies for private schools."* https://journals.sagepub.com/doi/10.1177/14749041211023339; Maria Nikolakaki, *"The Hope of Critical Pedagogy in the New Dark Ages of Neoliberal Globalization and Imperialism."* http://www.jceps.com/wp-content/uploads/2020/04/18-1-10-marnik-.pdf; Vik Loveday, *"Working-class participation, middle-class aspiration? Value, upward mobility and symbolic indebtedness in higher education."* The Sociological Review. (September 2014)

[919] Linda Raimondi, *"Neoliberalism and the Role of the University."* https://www.iup.edu/pse/files/programs/graduate_programs_r/instructional_design_and_technology_ma/paace_journal_of_lifelong_learning/volume_21/raimondi.pdf; Philip Mirowski, *Science Mart: Privatizing American Science.* (2011) Sean Phelan, *"The Corporate University and its Threat to Academic Freedom."* https://www.opendemocracy.net/en/corporate-university-and-its-threat-to-academic-freedom/

[920] Zeena Feldman and Marisol Sandoval, *"Metric Power and the Academic Self: Neoliberalism, Knowledge, and Resistance in the British University."* https://www.researchgate.net/publication/323252595_Metric_Power_and_the_Academic_Self_Neoliberalism_Knowledge_and_Resistance_in_the_British_Uni

[921] Alpesh Maisuria and Mike Cole, *"The neoliberalization of higher education in England: An alternative is possible."* https://journals.sagepub.com/doi/pdf/10.1177/1478210317719792; Daniel Saunders, *"Neoliberal Ideology and Public Higher Education in the United States."* http://www.jceps.com/wp-content/uploads/PDFs/08-1-02.pdf; David Hursch and A. F. Hall, *"Politicizing Higher Education Assessment within Neoliberal Globalization."* https://journals.sagepub.com/doi/pdf/10.2304/pfie.2011.9.5.560; Stanley Fish, *"Neoliberalism and Higher Education."* https://opinionator.blogs.nytimes.com/2009/03/08/neoliberalism-and-education/

[922] Walter D. Valdivia, *"The States in Bayh-Dole; Public Values Beyond the Pace of Innovation."* https://link.springer.com/article/

201. https://www.tandfonline.com/author/Regmi%2C+Kapil+Dev

10.1007/s11024-011-9162-6; Daniel B. Saunders, *"Neoliberal Ideology and Public Higher Education in the United States."* http://www.jceps.com/wp-content/uploads/PDFs/08-1-02.pdf

[923] Amanda Shufang Yang, *"Meritocracy and Marketization of Education: Taiwanese Middle Class Strategies in a Private Secondary School."* https://digitalcommons.lsu.edu/cgi/viewcontent.cgi?article=6556&context=gradschool_dissertations

[924] Marin Armstrong, *"The World's Highest and Lowest Tuition Fees."* https://www.statista.com/chart/11058/bachelor-tuition-fees-international-comparison/; Preston Cooper, *"America Spends More on College than Virtually any other Country."* https://www.forbes.com/sites/prestoncooper2/2019/09/22/america-spends-more-on-college-than-virtually-any-other-country/; Guilherme and Bruno Antonio Picoli, *"Neoliberalism and Education in the Global South: A New Form of Imperialism."* https://link.springer.com/referenceworkentry/10.1007%2F978-3-319-91206-6_144-1; J. Scott MacPhail, *"The OECD, Neoliberalism, and the Learning City: Promoting Human Capital in the Guise of Lifelong Learning."* http://dc.msvu.ca:8080/xmlui/bitstream/handle/10587/99/ScottMacPhail-MAED-2008.pdf?sequence=3

[925] Anna Hoffman and Almantas Salamavicius, *"Neoliberalism ad Higher Education in Central Europe."* https://www.eurozine.com/neoliberalism-and-higher-education-in-central-europe/

[926] Adem Y. Elveren, *"Brain Drain: Causes and Consequences."* https://www.researchgate.net/publication/325288727_Brain_Drain_Causes_and_Consequences; Matt Annunziato, *"Brain Drain."* https://blogs.umb.edu/cecsprogram/2018/08/01/brain-drain-neocolonialism/

[927] Michael B. Katz, *"Public Education as Welfare."* https://www.dissentmagazine.org/article/public-education-as-welfare

[928] Zareen Zaidi, et al., *"Cultural hegemony? Educators' perspectives on facilitating cross-cultural dialogue."* https://www.ncbi.nlm.nih.gov/pmc/articles/PMC5124632/

[929] B. Ginsberg, *The Fall of the Faculty: The Rise of the All-Administrative University and Why It Matters.* (2011); Paul F. Campos, *"The Real Reason College Tuition Costs so Much."* https://www.nytimes.com/2015/04/05/opinion/sunday/the-real-reason-college-tuition-costs-so-much.html; Randall Smith, *"Bureaucratic bloat in Higher Education."* https://www.thepublicdiscourse.com/2015/01/14235/

[930] Heather MacDonald, *"Call it a Ponzi Scheme."* https://www.city-journal.org/higher-ed-diversity-bureaucracy; Beth Mintz, *"Neoliberalism and the Crisis of Higher Education."* https://marxistsociology.org/2021/10/neoliberalism-and-the-crisis-of-higher-education/

[931] Haochen Sun, *"Higher Education as a Luxury Good."* https://www.lawtech.hk/higher-education-as-a-luxury-good/; Jamil Salmi, *"Equity in access and success in HE is no longer a luxury."* https://www.universityworldnews.com/post.php?story=20230123142239831

[932] Gene A. Budig, *"Higher education crisis and how to beat them."* https://eu.usatoday.com/story/opinion/2013/01/06/college-student-loans-higher-education/1812275/; Andrew Rossi, *"How American Universities Turned into Corporations."* https://time.com/108311/how-american-universities-are-ripping-off-your-education/; OECD, *"Student Fees and student financial support."* https://www.oecd-ilibrary.org/sites/30a75d15-en/index.html?itemId=/content/component/30a75d15-en

[933] Emmie Martin, *"Here is how much more expensive it is for you to go to college than it was for your parents."* https://www.cnbc.com/2017/11/29/how-much-college-tuition-has-increased-from-1988-to-2018.html

[934] Scott Winstead, *"The Cost of Going to College Has Risen at Nearly 5x the Rate of Inflation Over the Last 50 Years."* https://myelearningworld.com/cost-of-college-vs-inflation/; Chad Stone et al., *"A Guide to Statistics on Historical Trends in Income Inequality."* https://www.cbpp.org/research/poverty-and-inequality/a-guide-to-statistics-on-historical-trends-in-income-inequality

[935] Michael Mitchell, Michael Leachman and Matt Saenz, *"State Higher Education Funding Cuts Have Pushed Costs to Students, Worsened Inequality."* https://www.cbpp.org/research/state-budget-and-tax/state-higher-education-funding-cuts-have-pushed-costs-to-students

[936] Melanie Hanson, *"Student Loan Default Rate."* https://educationdata.org/student-loan-default-rate; Daniel Kurt, *"Student Loan Debt."* https://www.investopedia.com/student-loan-debt-2019-statistics-and-outlook-4772007; Latoya Irby, *"US Student Loan Debt Statistics."* https://www.thebalance.com/student-loan-debt-statistics-4173224; https://www.bestcolleges.com/research/student-loan-default-rate-facts-statistics/

[937] The Economic Times, *"Buffett reveals 'outrageous' acts that lifted college endowment."* https://economictimes.indiatimes.com/markets/stocks/news/buffett-reveals-outrageous-acts-that-lifted-college-endowment/articleshow/69149389.cms

[938] Beth Mintz, *"Neoliberalism and the crisis of higher education."* https://mronline.org/2021/10/29/neoliberalism-and-the-crisis-of-higher-education/

[939] Abigail J Hess, *"U.S. student debt has increased by more than 100% over the past 10 years."* https://www.cnbc.com/2020/12/22/us-student-debt-has-increased-by-more-than-100percent-over-past-10-years.html; Peter G. Peterson Foundation, *"How does student debt affect the economy?*[202]*"* https://www.pgpf.org/blog/2021/10/how-does-student-debt-affect-the-economy; Bryan Soika, *"Who is Most Affected by the Student Loan Debt Crisis?"* https://rossier.usc.edu/who-is-most-affected-by-the-student-loan-debt-crisis/

[940] Tara Golshan, *"Bernie Sanders' free college proposal just got a whole lot bigger."* https://www.vox.com/policy-and-politics/2019/6/23/18714615/bernie-sanders-free-college-for-all-2020-student-loan-debt

[941] Drew Desilver, *"For most US workers, wages have barely budged for decades."* https://www.pewresearch.org/fact-tank/2018/08/07/for-most-us-workers-real-wages-have-barely-budged-for-decades/[203]; Andrew Krieghbaum, *"How Families Navigate the Growing*

202. https://www.cnbc.com/2020/12/22/us-student-debt-has-increased-by-more-than-100percent-over-past-10-years.html;%20Peter%20G.%20Peterson%20Foundation,%20

203. https://d.docs.live.net/eb41a1b69e1e6e00/Desktop/Drew%20Desilver,

Cost of College." https://www.insidehighered.com/news/2019/09/04/author-talks-about-how-paying-college-defines-middle-class; Gerardo del Cerro Santamaria, *"Challenges and Drawbacks in the Marketisation of Higher Education Within Neoliberalism."* Review of European Studies, 12, 1, (January 2020).

[942] Dave Hill, Ravi Kumar, *"Global Neoliberalism and Education and its Consequences."* http://www.untag-smd.ac.id/files/Perpustakaan_Digital_2/NEOLIBERALISM%20Global%20neoliberalism%20and%20education%20and%20its%20consequences.pdfGershom Kabaso, jr. *"How Neoliberal Policies Have Contributed to the deterioration of Education in LDC's Lack of Resources."* https://www.un.org/ldc5/sites/www.un.org.ldc5/files/zambia_social_forum_statement.pdf

[943] Frank A. Fear, *"Neoliberalism Comes to Higher Education."* https://futureu.education/welcome-to-futureu/neoliberalism-comes-to-higher-education/; Michael T. Nietzel, *"Elite University Endowments Soar as Higher Ed Divide Grows."* https://www.forbes.com/sites/michaeltnietzel/2021/10/15/elite-university-endowments-soar-to-record-highs/?sh=28fa0f842d5f; Amanda Ciafone, *"Work and Culture. Endowing the Neoliberal University."* https://wggc.yale.edu/sites/default/files/files/ciafone%20endowing%20neoliberal%20university.pdf

[944] Jenna A. Robinson, *"University Foundations Enable Waste, Fraud, and Abuse."* https://www.jamesgmartin.center/2018/03/university-foundations-host-plenty-scandals-avoid-transparency/

[945] Matthew Cunningham-Cook, *"Rutgers Is Shortchanging Faculty While Pumping Millions Into Hedge Funds."* https://jacobin.com/2023/04/rutgers-strike-endowment-faculty-pay-hedge-funds

[946] Graham Bowley, *"The Academic Industrial Complex."* https://www.nytimes.com/2010/08/01/business/01prez.html

[947] Deanna Issacs, *"Who's Buying Shimer?"* https://chicagoreader.com/columns-opinion/whos-buying-shimer/; Jake Johnson, *"Right-Wing Dark Money Group Gets $1.6 Billion Donation from Tax Dodging Business Mogul."* https://www.commondreams.org/news/2022/08/22/right-wing-dark-money-group-gets-16-billion-donation-tax-dodging-business-mogul

[948] Ali Hachem, *"Higher Education in the Era of Illusions: Neoliberal Narratives,*

Capitalistic Realities, and the Need for Critical Praxis." https://scholarworks.sfasu.edu/cgi/viewcontent.cgi?article=1002&context=secondaryed_facultypubs

[949] Clifton Mark, *"A belief in meritocracy is not only false" it's for you."* https://press.princeton.edu/ideas/a-belief-in-meritocracy-is-not-only-false-its-bad-for-you

[950] Marc Andelman, *"University Endowments as a Major Source of Corruption."* https://www.linkedin.com/pulse/university-endowments-major-source-corruption-marc-andelman/

[951] Jo Littler, *"Meritocracy as a Neoliberal Mantra."* https://archive.discoversociety.org/2018/10/02/meritocracy-as-neoliberal-mantra/; Steve Dubb, *"College Admissions Scandal Exposes Moral Rot at the Heart of US Plutocracy."* https://nonprofitquarterly.org/college-admissions-scandal-exposes-moral-rot-at-the-heart-of-us-plutocracy/

[952] Terry Cogwill, *"Corruption and the 'commodification of college admissions."* https://theberkshireedge.com/bits-corpse-flowers-at-darrow-school-bcd-head-elect-on-education-ulrike-grannis-at-camphill-ghent; Aiden Lee, *"Lee: Bribery? Not Shocking."* https://yaledailynews.com/blog/2019/03/26/lee-bribery-not-shocking/; Arran Gare, *"The neoliberal assault on Australian universities and the Future of Democracy."* https://core.ac.uk/download/pdf/131214012.pdf

[953] Richard March, *"Edtech: between neoliberalism and social justice."* https://edtechnology.co.uk/features/edtech-between-neoliberalism-and-social-justice/

[954] Chris Jones, *"Capital, Neoliberalism and Educational Technology."* https://www.researchgate.net/publication/332598335_Capital_Neoliberalism_and_Educational_Technology

[955] US Department of Education, *"A Nation at Risk: The Imperative for Educational Reform."* https://edreform.com/wp-content/uploads/2013/02/A_Nation_At_Risk_1983.pdf

[956] Trevor Norris, *"Tax 'pandemic profiteering' by tech companies to help fund public education."* https://theconversation.com/tax-pandemic-profiteering-by-tech-companies-to-help-fund-public-education-155705; Grand View Research, *"Education Technology Market Size, Share & Trends Analysis Report."* https://www.grandviewresearch.com/industry-analysis/education-technology-market; Harish Agrawal, *"How Can Technology Mitigate Inequity in Education Systems?"* https://elearningindustry.com/how-can-technology-mitigate-inequity-in-education-systems; Jaya McKeown, *"Goodbye Middle Class: 51 Percent of All American Workers Make Less Than 30,000 dollars a year."* https://washingtonindependent.com/2015/10/goodbye-middle-class-51-percent-of-all-american-workers-make-less-than-30000-dollars-a-year/

[957] Chris Jones, *"Capital, Neoliberalism and Educational Technology."* https://link.springer.com/article/10.1007/s42438-019-00042-1; Jonas Hallström, *"Embodying the past, designing the future: technological determinism reconsidered in technology education."* https://www.diva-portal.org/smash/get/diva2:1443382/FULLTEXT02; M. Oliver, *"Technological determinism in education technology research."* https://citeseerx.ist.psu.edu/viewdoc/download?doi=10.1.1.972.422&rep=rep1&type=pdf

[958] Fiona Patrick, *"Neoliberalism, the Knowledge Economy, and the Learner: Challenging the Inevitability of the Commodified Self as an Outcome of Education."* https://www.hindawi.com/journals/isrn/2013/108705/

[959] **Sarah Emerson, *"Online Learning Was Supposed to Democratize Education. Coronavirus Shows It Hasn't."* https://onezero.medium.com/online-learning-was-supposed-to-democratize-education-coronavirus-shows-it-hasnt-cf07a604a474**

[960] Valerie Strauss, *"How poverty and race affect who goes to college."* https://www.washingtonpost.com/education/2018/11/08/how-poverty-race-affect-who-goes-college-charts/

[961] Amy Walker, *"Half of Universities in England have fewer than 5% poor whites."* https://www.theguardian.com/education/2019/feb/14/half-of-universities-england-have-fewer-than-5-poor-white-students'; Paul Fain, *"Wealth's Influence on Enrollment and Completion."* https://www.insidehighered.com/news/2019/05/23/feds-release-broader-data-socioeconomic-status-and-college-enrollment-and-completion; Richard Fry, *"First Generation College Graduates Lag Behind their Peers on Key Economic."* https://www.pewresearch.org/social-trends/2021/05/18/first-generation-college-graduates-lag-behind-their-peers-on-key-economic-outcomes/; https://nces.ed.gov/pubs2020/2020460.pdf; https://seoulz.com/education-inequality-in-korea-is-a-problem-that-needs-to-be-solved/; Tachibanaki Toshiaki, *"Increasing Indifference to Japan's Education Inequality."* https://www.nippon.com/en/in-depth/d00659/; Max Planck Institute for Human Development, *"Educational Inequality in Germany."* https://www.mpib-berlin.mpg.de/press-releases/educational-inequality-in-germany; House of Commons, *"Higher education and social class."* https://researchbriefings.files.parliament.uk/documents/SN00620/SN00620.pdf; Xianglei Chen

Annaliza Nunnery, *"Profile of Very Low-and Low-Income Undergraduates in 2015-16."* https://nces.ed.gov/pubs2020/2020460.pdf; Marcus Lu, *"The Decline in Upward Mobility in One Chart."* https://www.visualcapitalist.com/the-decline-of-upward-mobility-in-one-chart/

[962] **Bradley Robinson, "*Policies and People: A Review of Neoliberalism and Education Technologies in P-12 Education Research.*" https://escholarship.org/content/qt991770tc/qt991770tc_noSplash_170447d2240619c64fd85b82e83a5104.pdf?t=q5e4y8; Alyson Fleming, "*The Perils and Promise of Personalized Learning.*" https://pdxscholar.library.pdx.edu/cgi/viewcontent.cgi?article=1047&context=nwjte; Heidi Hallman, "*Personalized learning through 1:1 technology initiatives: implications for teachers and teaching in neoliberal times.*" https://www.researchgate.net/publication/324768098_Personalized_learning_through_11_technology_initiatives_implications_for_teachers_and_teaching_in_neoliberal_times**

[963] **David Armano, "*The Digitial Disruption of Higher-Ed is Inevitable: Alternative Models Will Challenge the Status Quo.*"[204] https://www.forbes.com/sites/davidarmano/2021/04/28/the-digital-disruption-of-higher-ed-is-inevitable-alternative-models-will-challenge-status-quo/?sh=3ddd52cf156a; Alexander L. Q. Chen, "*The Neoliberal University and Digital Learning.*" https://criticaledges.com/2021/05/05/the-neoliberal-university-and-digital-learning/; https://elmlearning.com/blog/the-corporate-university-shift/; Smiljana Gartner Marjan Krasnan, "*Online learning efficiency in the humanities.*" https://www.researchgate.net/publication/285610770_Online_learning_efficiency_in_the_humanities**

[964] B. Williamson, *"New pandemic edtech power networks."* https://codeactsineducation.wordpress.com/2020/04/01/new-pandemic-edtech-power-networks/

[965] Younis Abu Al-Haija and Hatim Mahamid, *"Trends in higher education under neoliberalism: Between traditional education and the culture of globalization."* https://academicjournals.org/journal/ERR/

---

204. https://d.docs.live.net/eb41a1b69e1e6e00/Desktop/David%20Armano,

article-full-text/E2262E066060; Dalya Markovich, *"Barred from the Ivory Tower,"* https://www.haaretz.com/life/books/1.4921552

[966] Rille Raaper, *"Mark Olssen on neoliberalisation of higher education and academic lives: An interview."* https://journals.sagepub.com/doi/pdf/10.1177/1478210315610992

[967] Beth Mintz, *"Neoliberalism and the Crisis of Higher Education."* https://marxistsociology.org/2021/10/neoliberalism-and-the-crisis-of-higher-education/

[968] Caroline Simon, *"Bureaucrats and Buildings: The Case for why college is so expensive."* https://www.forbes.com/sites/carolinesimon/2017/09/05/bureaucrats-and-buildings-the-case-for-why-college-is-so-expensive/?sh=687f4dad456a

[969] https://www.higheredjobs.com/salary/salaryDisplay.cfm?SurveyID=57; Jessica Bryant, *"Who are the Highest-Paid University Presidents?"* https://www.bestcolleges.com/news/analysis/2021/05/08/highest-paid-university-presidents/;https://reports.aashe.org/institutions/university-of-california-san-diego-ca/report/2018-03-30/IN/exemplary-practice/IN-21/[205]; New Faculty Majority, *"Facts about Adjuncts."* https://www.newfacultymajority.info/facts-about-adjuncts/; Laura McKenna, *"The College President-to-Adjunct Pay Ratio."* https://www.theatlantic.com/education/archive/2015/09/income-inequality-in-higher-education-the-college-president-to-adjunct-pay-ratio/407029/

[970] Ernst Benjamin, *"The Erosion of the Tenure System and Academic Collective Bargaining."* https://thekeep.eiu.edu/cgi/viewcontent.cgi?article=1185&context=jcba

[971] **Jon D. Wisman and Quinton Duroy, *"The Proletarianization of the Professoriate and the Threat to Free Expression, Creativity, and Economic Dynamism."* https://dra.american.edu/islandora/object/auislandora%3A85210/datastream/PDF/view; Daryl Douglas, Kelly H. Summers and Lindsay N Harris, *"Shrinking Budgets, Growing Demands: Neoliberalism and Academic Identity Tension at Regional Public Universities."* https://journals.sagepub.com/doi/10.1177/2332858418757736; Scott Jaschik, *"The Shrinking PH.D. Job Market."* https://www.insidehighered.com/news/2016/04/04/new-data-show-tightening-phd-job-market-across-disciplines; Stephanie Ross, Larry Savage and James Watson, *"University Teachers and Resistance in the Neoliberal University."* Journal of Labor Studies (2019), https://www.researchgate.net/publication/336972763_University_Teachers_and_Resistance_in_the_Neoliberal_University; Dionne Elvira, *"Teacher Demoralization: Neoliberal Influence on the Complex Education System and Teacher Morale."* https://scholarworks.lib.csusb.edu/cgi/viewcontent.cgi?article=2294&context=etd**

[972] The Economist, *"Why doing a PhD is often a waste of time: the disposable academic."* https://medium.economist.com/why-doing-a-phd-is-often-a-waste-of-time-349206f9addb; Ivan F. Pacheco, *"Your PhD oversupply crisis is our opportunity."*

205. https://www.bestcolleges.com/news/analysis/2021/05/08/highest-paid-university-presidents/;https:/reports.aashe.org/institutions/university-of-california-san-diego-ca/report/2018-03-30/IN/exemplary-practice/IN-21/

https://www.universityworldnews.com/post.php?story=20150603160027984; Noah Smith, *"America is Pumping Out Too Many Ph.D.'s"* https://www.bloomberg.com/opinion/articles/2021-01-04/america-is-pumping-out-too-many-ph-d-s

[973] Alison Berg and Carter Moore, *"Charles Koch gave $25 million to our university. Has it become a rightwing mouthpiece?"* https://www.theguardian.com/us-news/2019/may/02/charles-koch-gave-25m-to-our-university-has-it-become-a-rightwing-mouthpiece; Dave Levinthal, *"Spreading the Free Market Gospel."* https://www.theatlantic.com/education/archive/2015/10/spreading-the-free-market-gospel/413239/; Roger Riddell, *"Howthe world's 10 richest billionaires are shaping education."* https://www.highereddive.com/news/how-the-worlds-10-richest-billionaires-are-shaping-education/234949/

[974] Scott Jaschik, *"Just because its legal doesn't make it right."* https://www.insidehighered.com/admissions/article/2019/03/18/admissions-scandal-focuses-attention-legal-donations-parents

[975] Julian J. Giordano[206] *https://www.thecrimson.com/article/2023/4/11/gsas-renamed-ken-griffin/*

[976] **Jeffrey Mervis, *"House spending panel does its best to hide large cut to NSF social and geosciences research."* http://www.sciencemag.org/news/2015/05/house-spending-panel-does-its-best-hide-large-cut-nsf-social-and-geosciences-research; National Humanities Alliance, *"Recent Cuts to Federal Humanities Funding are Wide-Reaching."* https://www.nhalliance.org/shrinking_federal_support_for_the_humanities; William Bianco, *"Republicans don't like the National Science Foundation, and there's a perfectly good reason for it."* https://www.vox.com/mischiefs-of-faction/2019/3/6/18252793/why-republicans-hate-nsf.**

[977] Joel Westheimer, *"Higher Education or Education for Hire? Corporatization and the Threat to Democratic Thinking."* http://www.academicmatters.ca/2010/04/higher-education-or-education-for-hire-corporatization-and-the-threat-to-democratic-thinking/

[978] Tim Schwab, *"The Corporate Hijacking of America's Land-Grant Universities."* https://civileats.com/2012/05/03/the-corporate-hijacking-of-america%E2%80%99s-land-grant-universities/

[979] Wenonah Hauter, *"How Big Business Poisons Academic Research."* https://www.commondreams.org/views/2012/12/27/how-big-business-poisons-academic-research;

[980] Devon Douglas Bowers, *"The College Bureaucracy."* http://www.occupy.com/article/college-bureaucracy-how-education-forgot-students-and-became-business#sthash.G22kz58h.dpuf;

[981] Melanie Hansen, *"Average Student Loan Debt by Year."* ttps://educationdata.org/average-student-loan-debt-by-year[207]; Andrea Koncz, *"Salary Trends Through Salary Survey: A historical perspective on starting salaries for new college graduates."*

206. https://www.thecrimson.com/writer/1217495/Julian_J._Giordano/

207. https://d.docs.live.net/eb41a1b69e1e6e00/Desktop/Melanie%20Hansen,

https://www.naceweb.org/job-market/compensation/salary-trends-through-salary-survey-a-historical-perspective-on-starting-salaries-for-new-college-graduates/.

[982] Lewis Stockwell, *"Socratic pedagogy and citizenship formation in Higher Education."* https://www.herts.ac.uk/link/volume-1,-issue-2/socratic-pedagogy-and-citizenship-formation-in-higher-education; Chris Jones, *"Capital, Neoliberalism and Educational Technology."* https://link.springer.com/article/10.1007/s42438-019-00042-1

[983] https://www.qu.edu/news-and-events/quinnipiac-university-poll/national/release-detail?ReleaseID=2275; Raven Clabough, *"Harvard Survey Shows Millennials Oppose Capitalism: But do they really?"* http://www.thenewamerican.com/economy/commentary/item/23078-harvard-survey-shows-millennials-oppose-capitalism-but-do-they-really; https://www.higheredjobs.com/salary/salaryDisplay.cfm?SurveyID=57; Marc Bousquet, *"Who's Against "College for All"?* http://www.truth-out.org/opinion/item/31994-who-s-against-college-for-all

[984] A. Kuntsman, *Selfie Citizenship* (2017); Rebecca L. Stein, Adi Kuntsman, Negar Mottahedeh, *Political Consciousness of a Selfie.* (2015).

[985] Gary Anderson, *"Media's Impact on Educational Policies and Practices: Political Spectacle and Social Control."* https://www.researchgate.net/publication/233366144_Media%27s_Impact_on_Educational_Policies_and_Practices_Political_Spectacle_and_Social_Control; Jill Anderson, *"The Effect of Media Coverage on Education."* https://www.gse;.harvard.edu/news/08/04/effect-media-coverage-education

[986] Paul Bocking, *Public Education, Neoliberalism, and Teachers.* (2020); Emma Garcia, Lawrence Mishel, *"Unions and the allocation of teacher quality in public schools."* https://www.epi.org/publication/unions-and-the-allocation-of-teacher-quality-in-public-schools/

[987] Zane C Wubbena, Derek R Ford, and Brad Porfilio, eds. *News Media and the Neoliberal Privatization of Education.* (2016).

[988] Marta P. Baltodano, *"The power brokers of neoliberalism: philanthrocapitalists and public education."* https://journals.sagepub.com/doi/full/10.1177/1478210316652008

[989] Edward Graham, *"Who is Behind the Attacks on Educators and Public Schools?"* https://www.nea.org/advocating-for-change/new-from-nea/who-behind-attacks-educators-and-public-schools; Cheryl-Ann Griffin, *"Media give anti-black perception of public schools."* https://www.royalgazette.com/letters-to-the-editor/article/20190520/media-give-anti-black-perception-of-public-schools/

[990] Eric Haas, *"The News Media and the Conservative Heritage Foundation: Promoting Education Advocacy at the Expense of Authority,"* [208]in Dave Hill, Ravi Kumar, eds. *Global Neoliberalism and Education and its Consequences* (2008); Geo Saura, "*Think Tanks*

---

208. *https://www.taylorfrancis.com/chapters/edit/10.4324/9780203891858-14/news-media-conservative-heritage-foundation-promoting-education-advocacy-expense-authority-eric-haas?context=ubx&refId=a6583fe6-4fac-4494-a553-922314e5766e*

y educación. Neoliberalismo de FAES en la LOMCE." Education Policy Analysis Archives Education Policy Analysis Archives (October, 2015)

[991] Rebecca A. Goldstein, Sheila Macrine and Nataly Z. Chesky, *"Welcome to the "New Normal": The News Media and Neoliberal Reforming Education."* https://files.eric.ed.gov/fulltext/EJ1134638.pdf

[992] Charles Lane, *"College Doesn't Need to be Free."* https://www.washingtonpost.com/opinions/college-doesnt-need-to-be-free/2015/05/21/4453fc94-ff0f-11e4-805c-c3f407e5a9e9_story.html; Evan Horowitz, *"Can America Afford Sanders Big Plans?"* https://www.bostonglobe.com/news/politics/2016/02/11/can-america-afford-sanders-big-plans/MtEoDAEbF9EhtGeCkW8QvK/story.html

[993] Catherine Hill, *"Free Tuition is not the Answer."* http://www.nytimes.com/2015/11/30/opinion/free-tuition-is-not-the-answer.html?_r=0

[994] Justin Wolfers, *"How to Think About Corporate Tax Cuts."* https://www.nytimes.com/2018/03/30/business/how-to-think-about-corporate-tax-cuts.html

[995] Michael T. Nietzel, *"Sanders Panders: Four Flaws in Bernie Sanders' Higher Education Plan."* https://www.forbes.com/sites/michaeltnietzel/2019/06/25/sanders-panders-four-flaws-in-bernie-sanders-higher-education-plan/; David H. Feldman and Robert B. Archibald, *"Bernie Sanders' Free College Plan Doesn't Make Sense"* https://www.washingtonpost.com/news/grade-point/wp/2016/04/22/why-bernie-sanderss-free-college-plan-doesnt-make-sense/

[996] Andrea Szameitat, *"Comparing Education in the US and Germany."* https://www.herbnestler.com/blog/2018/4/20/comparing-education-in-the-us-and-germany; *"Education Rankings by Country 2022."* https://worldpopulationreview.com/country-rankings/education-rankings-by-country

Andrea Szameitat, *"Comparing Education in the US and Germany."* https://www.herbnestler.com/blog/2018/4/20/comparing-education-in-the-us-and-germany; *"Education Rankings by Country 2022."* https://worldpopulationreview.com/country-rankings/education-rankings-by-country

[997] **Kevin James, *"Why Bernie Sanders' Free Public College Plan is a Bad Idea."* http://www.usnews.com/opinion/knowledge-bank/2015/05/27/why-bernie-sanders-free-public-college-plan-is-a-bad-idea; Sam Binkley, *"Emotionalisation, Neoliberalism and Academic Freedom in US."* https://www.socialsciencespace.com/2016/09/emotionalisation-neoliberalism-and-academic-freedom-in-the-us/**

[998] Ariel Gelrud Shiro and Richard V. Reeves *"The for-profit college system is broken and the Biden administration needs to fix it."* https://www.brookings.edu/blog/how-we-rise/2021/01/12/the-for-profit-college-system-is-broken-and-the-biden-administration-needs-to-fix-it/

[999] Eleanor J. Bader, *"College Faculty Against Billionaire Donors."* https://progressive.org/latest/college-faculty-against-billionaire-donors-bader-200511/; Mark J. Drozdowski, *"Donor Influence on the Academic Experience."* https://www.bestcolleges.com/news/analysis/2021/07/15/donor-influence-academic-experience/; Ellie Bothwell, *"Billionaire donors 'increasingly shaping' research agenda."* https://www.timeshighereducation.com/news/billionaire-donors-increasingly-shaping-research-agenda

[1000] **Andrew Dewson, *"Phil Knight donates $400m to Stanford: why do billionaires donate to universities?"* https://www.independent.co.uk/news/business/analysis-and-features/phil-knight-nike-stanford-universities-billionaire-donate-a6894716.html**

[1001] Harvard University, *"Index of Emerging Nonprofit Media and Donors."* https://projects.iq.harvard.edu/futureofmedia/index-emerging-nonprofit-media-and-donors. Derek R. Ford, *"The News Media, Education, and the Subversion of the Neoliberal Social Imaginary."* https://scholarship.depauw.edu/cgi/viewcontent.cgi?article=1000&context=educ_facpubs

[1002] Robin Howarth, Lisa Stifler, *"The Failings of Online for-profit Colleges."* https://www.brookings.edu/wp-content/uploads/2019/03/The-Failings-of-Online-For-profit-Colleges.pdf; Zane Wubena, *News Media and the Privatization of Education.* (2016)

[1003] **Richard Van Heertum, *Neoliberalism, Neopopulism, and Democracy in Decline: The University Under Attack on Multiple Fronts.* (2020); Michael Ian Cohen, *"Education Populism? A Corpus-Driven Analysis of Betsy DeVos's Education Policy Discourse."* https://files.eric.ed.gov/fulltext/EJ1288201.pdf; James Putzel[209], *"The 'Populist' Right Challenge to Neoliberalism: Social Policy between a Rock and a Hard Place."* https://onlinelibrary.wiley.com/doi/full/10.1111/dech.12578**

[1004] **Douglas Belkin, *"Is This the End of College as we Know it?"* https://www.wsj.com/articles/is-this-the-end-of-college-as-we-know-it-11605196909; Stephen Hopper, *"What Higher Education Needs to Stop from Becoming Obsolete."* https://thestevenpost.medium.com/what-higher-education-needs-to-stop-from-becoming-obsolete-28dcd6f8da96; Stephen Yates, *"Higher Education as we Know it is Obsolete."* https://stevenyates.medium.com/higher-education-as-we-presently-know-it-is-obsolete-596a4d05f024**

[1005] Jason Brannon and Phillip Magness, *Cracks in the Ivory Tower: The Moral Mess of Higher Education* (2019); Jason Brannon, *Against Democracy.* (2017)

[1006] Emiliano Grimaldi and Stephen Ball, *"The blended learner: digitalization and regulated freedom – neoliberalism in the classroom."* https://www.researchgate.net/publication/338253049_The_blended_learner_digitalisation_and_regulated_freedom_-_neoliberalism_in_the_classroom

209. https://onlinelibrary.wiley.com/action/doSearch?ContribAuthorRaw=Putzel%2C+James

[1007] Stephen Vassallo, *"Untangling Higher Order Thinking from Neoliberalism and Moving Toward a Democratic Vision of Schooling."* https://www.academia.edu/5738116/Untangling_Higher_Order_Thinking_from_Neoliberalism_and_Moving_Toward_a_Democratic_Vision_of_Schooli

[1008] Daniel Calderón Gómez, *"Technological Socialization and Digital Inclusion: Understanding Digital Literacy Biographies among Young People in Madrid."* https://eprints.ucm.es/id/eprint/71333/1/SI%208(2)%20-%20Technological%20Socialization%20and%20Digital%20Inclusion_%20Understanding%20Digital

[1009] Cem Dilmegani, *"100+ AI Use Cases and Applications: In-Depth Guide for 2023."* https://research.aimultiple.com/ai-usecases/; Eric Hobsbawm, *Industry and Empire.* (1999); Leslie Tomory, *"Technology in the British Industrial Revolution."* https://www.academia.edu/21565459/Technology_in_the_British_Industrial_Revolution; Raquel Dias and Ali Torkamani, *"Artificial Intelligence in clinical and genomic diagnostics."* https://genomemedicine.biomedcentral.com/articles/10.1186/s13073-019-0689-8.

[1010] Frank Asbrock et al, *"Authoritarian ambivalence towards artificial intelligence,"* https://psyarxiv.com/; Kevin Körner *"Digital Politics: AI big data and the future of democracy."* https://www.dbresearch.com/PROD/RPS_EN-PROD/PROD0000000000497768/Digital_politics%3A_AI%2C_big_data_and_the_future_of_d.pdf?undefined&realload=Wzi58x8i91w0UuxRsjGpCgO79bTrDB9Q~/z2BeI94qa6ZqLlT6r~R3dIMUK~~; H. Akın Ünver, *"Artificial Intelligence, Authoritarianism and the Future of Political Systems."* https://edam.org.tr/wp-content/uploads/2018/07/AKIN-Artificial-Intelligence_Bosch-3.pdf; *"Trouble in Paradise: The Technological Upheaval of Modern Political and Economic Systems."* https://madsciblog.tradoc.army.mil/130-trouble-in-paradise-the-technological-upheaval-of-modern-political-and-economic-systems/

[1011] Benjamin Cheatham, Kia Javanmardian, and Hamid Samandari,*"Confronting the risks of artificial intelligence."* https://www.mckinsey.com/capabilities/quantumblack/our-insights/confronting-the-risks-of-artificial-intelligence Rowena Rodriguez, *"Legal and human rights issues of AI: Gaps, challenges and vulnerabilities."* https://www.sciencedirect.com/science/article/pii/S2666659620300056

[1012] World Bank, *"Harnessing Artificial Intelligence for Development in the Post-Covid-19 Era."* https://thedocs.worldbank.org/en/doc/2e658ef2144a05f30e254221ccaf7a42-0200022021/original/DD-Analytical-Insights-Note-4.pdf; Dorota Glowacka, et al. *"Digital technologies as a means of repression and social control."* https://www.europarl.europa.eu/RegData/etudes/STUD/2021/653636/EXPO_STU(2021)653636_EN.pdf

[1013] Seth Lloyd, *"What Would the Father of Cybernetics Think of AI Today?"* https://slate.com/technology/2019/02/norbert-wiener-cybernetics-human-use-artificial-intelligence.html; Julia Bossmann, *"Top 9 ethical issues in artificial intelligence."* https://www.weforum.org/agenda/2016/10/top-10-ethical-issues-in-artificial-intelligence/

[1014] **Corine Lasnes, *"The US Unites 60 countries against digital authoritarianism."* https://www.lemonde.fr/en/international/article/2022/04/29/internet-the-u-s-unite-60-countries-against-the-rise-of-digital-authoritarianism_5981989_4.html; Amnesty International, *"Israeli authorities are using facial recognition technology to*** *entrench apartheid."* https://www.amnesty.org/en/latest/news/2023/05/israel-opt-israeli-authorities-are-using-facial-recognition-technology-to-entrench-apartheid/

[1015] **Aim Singpend, *"Digital media, political authoritarianism, and Internet controls in Southeast Asia."* https://journals.sagepub.com/doi/10.1177/0163443719884052**

[1016] Sociedade Portuguesa de Inovação (SPI) *"Overview of Cybersecurity Status in ASEAN and the EU."* https://ec.europa.eu/documents

[1017] Dirk Helbing et al, *"Will Democracy Survive Big Data and Artificial Intelligence?"* https://www.scientificamerican.com/article/will-democracy-survive-big-data-and-artificial-intelligence/; Aidan Powers-Riggs, *"COVID-19 is Proving a Boon for Digital Authoritarianism."* https://www.csis.org/blogs/new-perspectives-asia/covid-19-proving-boon-digital-authoritarianism; Stephen Feldstein, *"How Artificial Intelligence if Reshaping Repression."* https://carnegieendowment.org/2019/01/09/how-artificial-intelligence-is-reshaping-repression-pub-78093; Marc Marmino, *"Culture, Surveillance and Power: Understanding Compliance to Digital Pandemic Surveillance in Taiwan."* https://www.airuniversity.af.edu/JIPA/Display/Article/3047875/culture-surveillance-and-power-understanding-compliance-to-digital-pandemic-sur/

[1018] Читайте на русском[210] / Қазақ тілінде оқыңыз[211], ***"Digital dictatorship: authoritarian tactics and resistance in Eastern Europe and Central Asia."*** https://www.accessnow.org/digital-dictatorship-and-resistance-in-eastern-europe-and-central-asia/; Seva Gunitsky, *"The Great Online Convergence: Digital Authoritrianism Comes to Democracies."* https://warontherocks.com/2020/02/the-great-online-convergence-digital-authoritarianism-comes-to-democracies/

[1019] Sara Brown, *"A new study measures the actual impact of robots on jobs. It's significant."* https://mitsloan.mit.edu/ideas-made-to-matter/a-new-study-measures-actual-impact-robots-jobs-its-significant

[1020] Akin Unver, *"Artificial Intelligence, Authoritarianism and the Future of Political Systems."* https://edam.org.tr/en/4025-2/; Erol Yaybok, *"Promote and Build: A Strategic Approach to Digital Authoritarianism."* https://www.csis.org/analysis/promote-and-build-strategic-approach-digital-authoritarianism; Marc Marmino, *"Culture, Surveillance, and Power: Understanding Compliance to Digital Pandemic Surveillance in Taiwan."* https://www.airuniversity.af.edu/JIPA/Display/Article/3047875/culture-surveillance-and-power-understanding-compliance-to-digital-pandemic-sur/; Mona Shtaya, *"Nowhere to hide: The impact of Israel's digital surveillance regime on the Palestinians."* https://www.mei.edu/publications/nowhere-hide-impact-israels-digital-surveillance-regime-palestinians

[1021] Vincent Boulanin, *The Impact of Artificial Intelligence on Strategic Stability and Nuclear Risk.* https://www.sipri.org/sites/default/files/2019-05/sipri1905-ai-strategic-stability-nuclear-risk.pdf

---

210. https://drfl.kz/ru/digital-dictatorship/

211. https://drfl.kz/kk/digital-dictatorship/

[1022] Sam Biddle, *"Can the Pentagon use ChatGPT? OPENAI Won't Answer."* https://theintercept.com/2023/05/08/chatgpt-ai-pentagon-military/

[1023] https://historyofcomputercommunications.info/section/2.16/the-entrance-of-ibm-1952/; Gregory S. Dawson, Kevin C. Desouza, James N. Denford, *"Understanding artificial intelligence spnding by the US federal government."* https://www.brookings.edu/blog/techtank/2022/09/22/understanding-artificial-intelligence-spending-by-the-u-s-federal-government/Yanilda Maria Gonzalez, *Authoritarian Police in Democracy.* (2020); Thomas Metzinger, *"Toward a Global Artificial Intelligence Charter,"* in European Parliament, "*Should we Fear Artificial Intelligence?"* https://www.philosophie-e.fb05.uni-mainz.de/files/2018/10/Metzinger_2018_Global_Artificial_Intelligence_Charter_PE_614.547.pdf ; Howard Zinn, *"The Toll of War."* https://www.howardzinn.org/collection/the-toll-of-war/; Ben Gansky, Michael Martin and Ganesh Sitaraman, *"Artificial Intelligence is Too Important to Leave to Google and Facebook Alone."* https://www.nytimes.com/2019/11/10/opinion/artificial-intelligence-facebook-google.html; Jean Barroca and Miguel Elias Antunes, *"Surveillance and Predictive Policing Through AI."*

https://www2.deloitte.com/global/en/pages/public-sector/articles/urban-future-with-a-purpose/surveillance-and-predictive-policing-through-ai.html

[1024] Eve Tahmincioglu and Barbara Wenger, *"The Revolving Door From Government to the Boardroom."* https://www.directorsandboards.com/articles/singlerevolving-door-government-boardroom; Jeff Green, Brandon Kochkodin and Blacki Migliozzi[212], *"The Lucrative Road from Congress to Corporate Boards."* https://www.bloomberg.com/graphics/2016-congressional-board-pay/; Hannah Norman, *"These former government officials rake in the big bucks bay are atech."* https://www.bizjournals.com/sanfrancisco/news/2019/04/30/these-former-government-officials-rake-in-the-big.html

[1025] Tim Hornyak, *"Insanely human-like androids have entered the workplace and may take your job."* https://www.cnbc.com/2019/10/31/human-like-androids-have-entered-the-workplace-and-may-take-your-job.html; The University of Texas, College of Natural Sciences, *"As AI Becomes Ubiquitous, There are Risks, Says New AI100 Report."* https://cns.utexas.edu/news/as-artificial-intelligence-becomes-ubiquitous-there-are-risks-says-new-ai100-report; UK Ministry of Defense, *"Human Augmentation: The Dawn of a New Paradigm."* https://assets.publishing.service.gov.uk/government/uploads/system/uploads/attachment_data/file/986301/Human_Augmentation_SIP_access2.pdf;

[1026] Joseph *Carvalko,* ***The Techno-human Shell-A Jump in the Evolutionary Gap.*** *(2012); Cristiano Radaelli, "AI as a tool for improving life."* https://www.planetsmartcity.com/2020/05/11/ai-as-a-tool-for-improving-life/*; "The benefits and harms of algorithms: a shared perspective from the four digital regulators."* https://www.govuk/government/publications/findings-from-the-drcf-algorithmic-processing-workstream-spring-2022/the-benefits-and-harms-of-algorithms-a-shared-perspective-from-the-four-digital-regulators*; David R. Blake, "The Invisible Hand of the Unaccountable Algorithm." https://www.researchgate.net/publication/320295150_The_Invisible_Hand_of_the_Unaccountable_Algorithm_How_Google_Facebook_and_Other_Tech_Companies_Are_Changing_Jour*

[1027] Sarah Chander, *"Artificial Intelligence: Reinforcing Discrimination."* https://www.theparliamentmagazine.eu/news/article/reinforcing-discrimination

212. https://twitter.com/BlackiLi

[1028] Michael A. Peters, *"Semiconductors, geopolitics, and technological rivalry."* https://www.tandfonline.com/doi/full/10.1080/00131857.2022.2124914; Niky Brugnatelli, *"The US-China battle for the semiconductor industry."* https://www.eastasiaforum.org/2022/06/04/the-us-china-battle-for-the-semiconductor-industry/; Mathieu Duchâtel, *"Semiconductors at the heart of the China-U rivalry."* https://www.polytechnique-insights.com/en/braincamps/economy/the-technology-war-between-china-and-the-usa/semiconductors-at-the-heart-of-the-china-us-rivalry/

[1029] Erik Brattberg[213], Raluca Csernatoni[214], Venesa Rugova, *"Europe and AI: Leading, Lagging or Carving its Own Way?"* https://carnegieendowment.org/2020/07/09/europe-and-ai-leading-lagging-behind-or-carving-its-own-way-pub-82236; Jon Harper, *"Federal AI pending to Top $6 Billion." https://www.nationaldefensemagazine.org/articles/2021/2/10/federal-ai-spending-to-top-$6-billion; Sarah Zhang, "China's Artificial Intelligence Boom."* https://www.theatlantic.com/technology/archive/2017/02/china-artificial-intelligence/516615/; Dylan Love, *"The next arms race: artificial intelligence."* http://www.nbcnews.com/mach/features/next-global-arms-race-aims-perfect-artificial-intelligence-n685911; Rasmus Björklund, *"Semiconductors in the Global Race for AI."* https://isdp.eu/semiconductors-in-the-global-race-for-ai/

[1030] Akin Unver, *"Motivations for the Adoption and use of Authoritarian AI Technology."* https://carnegieendowment.org/2021/10/19/motivations-for-adoption-and-use-of-authoritarian-ai-technology-pub-85510

[1031] Ausma Bernot, *"Digital authoritarianism not just a China problem."* https://www.lowyinstitute.org/the-interpreter/digital-authoritarianism-not-just-china-problem; Seva Gu, *"The Great Online Convergence: Digital Authoritarianism Comes to Democracies."* https://warontherocks.com/2020/02/the-great-online-convergence-digital-authoritarianism-comes-to-democracies/

[1032] Peter Bool and Carl Rhodes, *"Corporate Authoritarianism and the New American Anti-Democracy."* https://www.commondreams.org/views/2016/10/23/corporate-authoritarianism-and-new-american-anti-democracy

[1033] Clarisa Diaz, *"Annual corporate investment in AI is 13 times greater than a decade ago."* https://qz.com/annual-corporate-investment-in-ai-is-13-times-greater-t-1850308964

[1034] Vyacheslav Polonski, "Why AI can't solve everything." https://theconversation.com/why-ai-cant-solve-everything-97022l; Shanhong Liu, *"Global total corporate artificial intelligence (AI) investment from 2015 to 2020."* https://www.statista.com/statistics/941137/ai-investment-and-funding-worldwide/; Venture Beat, *"Report: AI investments largest year-over-year growth in 20 years."* https://venturebeat.com/2021/12/06/report-ai-investments-see-largest-year-over-year-growth-in-20-years/; Kevin Frecking, *"House passes $280 billion package to boost chip production in the US."* https://fortune.com/2022/07/28/house-passes-280-billion-package-chip-production-semiconductor-industry/; Jenny Leonard, Ian King, Debby Wu, *"China's chipmaking power grows despite US effort*

213. https://carnegieendowment.org/experts/1342

214. https://carnegieeurope.eu/experts/1709

to counter it." https://www.bloomberg.com/news/articles/2022-06-13/china-s-growing-clout-in-global-chip-market-rings-alarm-bells-in-washington

[1035] Internet of Business, *"AI 2030/ $13 trillion boost to economy, deepening disparity: McKinsey."* https://internetofbusiness.com/a-i-2030-13-trillion-boost-to-economy-but-deep-disparity-mckinsey/; Indermit Gill, *"Whoever leads in artificial intelligence in 2030 will rule the world."* https://www.brookings.edu/blog/future-development/2020/01/17/whoever-leads-in-artificialintelligence-in-2030-will-rule-the-world-until-2100/ [215]

[1036] Nathaniel Comfort, *"Sociogenomics is opening a new door to eugenics."* https://www.technologyreview.com/2018/10/23/139420/sociogenomics-is-opening-a-new-door-to-eugenics/

[1037] https://icn.sap.com/article/neuromorphic-computing; Orit Halpern, *"The Future Will not Be Calculated: Neutral Nets, Neoliberalism and Reactionary Politics."* https://www.journals.uchicago.edu/doi/10.1086/717313

[1038] J. R. Miller, *"Eugenics, Transhumanism, and Artificial Intelligence."* https://mindmatters.ai/2022/01/eugenics-transhumanism-and-artificial-intelligence/; Heledd Straker, *"AI, ethics and eugenics."* https://www.linkedin.com/pulse/ai-ethics-eugenics-what-a-level-debacle-says-how-use-our-straker; Brian Wang, *"Data driven eugenics, Genetic Enhancement, computer cloud AI via devices and Memristor Neuromorphic Devices over the next ten years."* https://www.nextbigfuture.com/2013/03/data-driven-eugenics-genetic.html; Julia Love, "*US tech execs hone approach to counter unions amid growing worker interest."* https://www.reuters.com/markets/us/us-tech-execs-hone-approach-counter-unions-amid-growing-worker-interest-2021-11-23/; Jon Brodkin, *'Verizon, AT&T to pay $127 million for allegedly overcharging government agencies.'* https://arstechnica.com/tech-policy/2020/09/verizon-att-to-pay-127m-for-allegedly-overcharging-government-agencies/

[1039] John Preston, *Artificial Intelligence in the Capitalist University.* (2021); George Zarkadakis, *In our Own Image: Savior or Destroyer? The History and Future of Artificial Intelligence.* (2017).

[1040] Jacques Bughin, Jeongmin Seong[216], James Manyika[217], Michael Chui[218], and Raoul Joshi, *"Notes from the AI frontier: Modeling the Impact of AI on the world economy."* https://www.mckinsey.com/featured-insights/artificial-intelligence/notes-from-the-ai-frontier-modeling-the-impact-of-ai-on-the-world-economy

215. https://www.brookings.edu/blog/future-development/2020/01/17/whoever-leads-in-artificialintelligence-in-2030-will-rule-the-world-until-2100/%20%20

216. https://www.mckinsey.com/our-people/jeongmin-seong

217. https://www.mckinsey.com/our-people/james-manyika

218. https://www.mckinsey.com/our-people/michael-chui

[1041] Alexis Ong, *"This company is making digital humans to serve the metaverse."* https://www.theverge.com/2021/10/27/22746679/soul-machines-metaverse-digital-humans-labor; Jim Poole *"Interconnection is bringing the future together faster than ever."* https://www.networkworld.com/article/3250673/interconnection-is-bringing-the-future-faster-than-ever.html

[1042] Karam Adibifar, *"Technology and Alienation in Modern-Day Societies."* https://core.ac.uk/download/pdf/228083912.pdf

[1043] Erik Chia-yi Lee, *"Thinking Cyber-Subjectivity: Ideology and the Subject."* https://web.archive.org/web/20160103053908/http://www.isoc.org/inet96/proceedings/e3/e3_4.htm; Erik Chia-yi Lee, *"Thinking Cyber-Subjectivity: Ideology and the Subject."* https://web.archive.org/web/20160103053908/http://www.isoc.org/inet96/proceedings/e3/e3_4.htm; Tatiana Kuzmina, Nelli Galaktionova, *"Virtualization as Factor of Socialization."* Vol. 312, Atlantis Press, (2018).

[1044] Anita Gurumurthy, *"How to Make AI work for people and planet."* https://www.opendemocracy.net/en/oureconomy/how-make-ai-work-people-and-planet/

[1045] Tony Raval, *"Digital Transformation In The Age Of Millennials And Gen Z."* https://www.forbes.com/sites/forbestechcouncil/2019/08/20/digital-transformation-in-the-age-of-millennials-and-gen-z/?sh=2ba9cad02708

[1046] Henry Armand Giroux, *"Selfie Culture at the Intersection of the Corporate and the Surveillance States."* https://www.counterpunch.org/2015/02/06/selfie-culture-at-the-intersection-of-the-corporate-and-the-surveillance-states/

[1047] Chaise LaDousa, *"Subject to Address in a Digital Literacy Initiative: Neoliberal Agency and the Promises and Predicaments of Participation."* https://www.journals.uchicago.edu/doi/full/10.1086/677657

[1048] Jack Kelly *"Artificial Intelligence Has Caused 50- To 70 Decrease in Wages Creating Income Inequality and Threatening Millions of Jobs."* https://www.forbes.com/sites/jackkelly/2021/06/18/artificial-intelligence-has-caused—50-to-70-decrease-in-wages-creating-income-inequality-and-threatening-millions-of-jobs/?sh=4e2c0ac61009

[1049] Harry Collins, *Artifictional Intelligence: Against Humanity's Surrender to Computers"* (2018); Janna Anderson and Lee Rainie, *"Concerns about human agency, evolution and survival."* https://www.pewresearch.org/internet/2018/12/10/concerns-about-human-agency-evolution-and-survival/; Jens Hoff, Ivan Horrocks, Pieter Tops, eds., *Democratic Governance and New Technology.* (2000).

[1050] Mihaela Nedelcu, Ibrahim Soysüren, *"Precarious migrants, migration regimes and digital technologies: the empowerment-control nexus."* https://nccr-onthemove.ch/publications/precarious-migrants-migration-regimes-and-digital-technologies-the-empowerment-control-nexus/; Pracirty Lab, *"The Precarity Effect."* https://goldsmithspress.pubpub.org/pub/y5a49njp/release/1

[1051] Fabio Rerocco, "*Work Precarisation and New Inequalities: The Role of Migration.*" https://madeinchinajournal.com/2019/01/11/work-precarisation-and-new-inequalities-the-role-of-migration/

[1052] Frank Lenzen, "*The impact of digital transformation on employment law.*" https://www.businessgoing.digital/the-impact-of-digital-transformation-on-employment-law/

[1053] Fernando Galindo-Rued, Stephanie Cairns, "*A new approach to measuring government investment in AI-related RD.*" https://oecd.ai/en/wonk/government-investment-ai-related-r-and-d

[1054] Kostas Maronitis, *Robots and Immigrants: Employment, Precarisation and the Art of Neoliberal Governance.*" https://journals.openedition.org/angles/570?lang=en

[1055] Alex Kantrowitz, "*If a Press Release Says 'Artificial Intelligence', there is a Good Chance it's Meaningless.*" https://slate.com/technology/2023/05/artificial-intelligence-hype-ibm-ftc-twitter-threadbois.html

[1056] Alessandro Nicolo Tirapani, Hugh Willmott, "*Revisiting Conflict: Neoliberalism at work in the gig economy.*" https://journals.sagepub.com/doi/full/10.1177/00187267211064596

[1057] **Miron Wolnicki and Ryszard Piasecki, "*The New Luddite Scare: The Impact of Artificial Intelligence on Labor, Capital and Business Competition between US and China.*" https://www.researchgate.net/publication/335122857_The_New_Luddite_Scare_The_Impact_of_Artificial_Intelligence_on_Labor_Capital_and_Business_Competition_betwe**

Peter Fleming "*Robots and Organization Studies: Why Robots Might not Want to Steal Your Job. https://journals.sagepub.com/doi/pdf/10.1177/0170840618765568*"

[1058] Jugi Genda and Jean Hoff, "*A Nagging Sense of Job Insecurity: The New Reality Facing Japanese Youth.*" https://www.researchgate.net/publication/44371123_A_Nagging_Sense_of_Job_Insecurity_The_New_Reality_Facing_Japanese_Youth

[1059] Lonny E. Carlile, "*The Japanese Labor Movement and Institutional Reform.*" https://swopec.hhs.se/eijswp/papers/eijswp0200.pdf; Marie Okabe, "*Nakasone vows Japan's first tax reform in 37 years.*" https://www.upi.com/Archives/1987/03/03/Nakasone-vows-Japans-first-tax-reform-in-37-years/6894541746000/

[1060] CBR Staff, *"Chip Wars: US Lifts 17% of Sanctions on Japan."* https://techmonitor.ai/technology/chip_wars_us_lifts_17_of_sanctions_on_japan

[1061] Noel Gaston and Tomoko Kishi, *"Part-Time Workers Doing Full-Time Work in Japan."* https://www.researchgate.net/publication/222904967_Part-time_Workers_Doing_Full-time_Work_in_Japan

[1062] Kenji Hirashima, *"Regime Shift in Japan? Two Decades of Neoliberal Reforms."* https://onlinelibrary.wiley.com/doi/pdf/10.1002/j.1662-6370.2004.tb00031.x; Todd Schneider, Gee Hee Hong, and Anh Van Le[219], *"Land of the Rising Robots."* https://www.imf.org/external/pubs/ft/fandd/2018/06/japan-labor-force-artificial-intelligence-and-robots/schneider.htm; Kyriaki "Sandy" Galaiou, *"Neoliberalism and Labour Inequality in Japan."* https://studenttheses.universiteitleiden.nl/access/item%3A2658168/view

[1063] Anita Gurumurthy, [220]*"How to make AI work for people and planet."* http:www.opendemocracy.net/en/oureconomy/how-make-ai-work-people-and-planet/; Stephen Cullenberg, *"Exploitation, Appropriation and Exclusion: Locating Capitalist Injustice."* Rethinking Marxism, 10:2 (1998)

[1064] Upwork, *"53 Million Americans Now Freelance."* https://www.upwork.com/press/releases/53-million-americans-now-freelance-new-study-finds-2; Nancy Worth and E. Alkim Karaagac, *"Accounting for Absences and Ambiguities in the Freelancing Labour Relation."* https://onlinelibrary.wiley.com/doi/epdf/10.1111/tesg.12491; Errol Salamon, *"Digitizing freelance media labor: a class of workers negotiates entrepreneurialism and activism."* https://journals.sagepub.com/doi/pdf/10.1177/1461444819861958

[1065] Varun, *"How Will 100 million Independent Workers find and Manage Work in 2030?"* https://medium.com/@startuphackers/how-will-100-million-independent-workers-find-manage-work-in-2030-51b21ca40343; Erik Brynjolfsson and Andrew McAfee, *The Second Machine Age: Work, Progress and prosperity in a Time of Brilliant Technologies.* (2016).

[1066] Philippe Aghion, Céline Antonin and Simon Bunel. *"Artificial Intelligence, Growth and Employment: The Role of Policy."* Economie et Statistique/Economics and Statistics, No. 51-511-512, 2019

[1067] Daron Acemoglu[221] and Pascual Restrepo[222], *"Tasks, Automation, and the Rise in US Wage Inequality."* https://www.nber.org/papers/w28920

[1068] Cristian Alonso, Siddharth Kothari and Sidra Rehman, *"How Artificial Intelligence Could Widen the Gap Between Rich and Poor Nations."* https://blogs.imf.org/2020/12/02/how-artificial-intelligence-could-widen-the-gap-between-rich-and-poor-nations/;

219. https://www.imf.org/external/pubs/ft/fandd/2018/06/japan-labor-force-artificial-intelligence-and-robots/schneider.htm#author

220. https://www.opendemocracy.net/en/author/anita-gurumurthy/

221. https://www.nber.org/people/daron_acemoglu

222. https://www.nber.org/people/pascual_restrepo

Paul Cooney, *"The Mexican Crisis and the Maquiladora Boom."* https://library.fes.de/libalt/journals/swetsfulltext/12735094.pdf; Frederic Deyo, *Reforming Asian Labor Systems: Economic Tensions and Worker Dissent.* (2012)

[1069] Adrienne Williams, Milagros Miceli, and Timnit Gebru, *"The Exploited Labor Behind Artificial Intelligence,"* https://www.noemamag.com/the-exploited-labor-behind-artificial-intelligence/

[1070] Andrew Soergel, "*Robots Cut Labor Costs 16 Percent by 2025."* https://www.usnews.com/news/articles/2015/02/10/robots-could-cut-international-labor-costs-16-percent-by-2025-consulting-group-says

[1071] Juan F. Jimeno, *"Fewer babies and more robots: economic growth in a new era of demographic and technological changes."* https://link.springer.com/article/10.1007/s13209-019-0190-z

[1072] **Kostas Maronitis, "*Robots and Immigrants: Employment, Precarisation and the Art of Neoliberal Governance",* https://journals.openedition.org/angles/570; Dominic Rushie, et al, *"Twitter slashes nearly half its workforce as Musk admits 'massive drop' in revenue."* https://www.theguardian.com/technology/2022/nov/04/twitter-layoffs-elon-musk-revenue-drop**

[1073] Stacy Liberatore, *"Is YOUR job at risk? White House warns AI could soon leave 'millions' of Americans unemplyed."* http://www.dailymail.co.uk/sciencetech/article-4068986/Is-job-risk-White-House-report-warns-AI-soon-leave-millions-Americans-unemployed.html;

[1074] Gavin Kelly, *"The robots are coming. Will they bring wealth or a divided society?"* https://www.theguardian.com/technology/2014/jan/04/robots-future-society-drones; Emma Escott, *"AI Will Create 97 Million Jobs, But Workers Don't Have the Skills Required (Yet)."* https://allwork.space/2021/11/ai-will-create-97-million-jobs-but-workers-dont-have-the-skills-required-yet/; Laura Wronski, *"Momentive Poll: Fortune Brainstorm AI 2021."* https://www.surveymonkey.com/curiosity/fortune-brainstorm-ai-2021/

[1075] Revanth, *"Toward Future Farming: How Artificial Intelligence is Transforming the Agriculture Industry."* https://www.wipro.com/holmes/towards-future-farming-how-artificial-intelligence-is-transforming-the-agriculture-industry/

[1076] Johan Swinnen, Gulia Meloni, Mara Squicchiarini, '*The Economics and Politics of Food and Economic Development."* https://www.cairn.info/revue-reflets-et-perspectives-de-la-vie-economique-2016-1-page-47.htm; The World.org, *"Millions go hungry despite world food surplus."* https://theworld.org/stories/2013-07-22/millions-hungry-despite-world-food-surplus; United Nations, *"World population projected to reach 9.8 billion and 11.2 billion by 2100."* https://www.un.org/development/desa/en/news/population/world-population-prospects-2017.html

[1077] James Pethokoukis, *"A Nobel Laureate Economist Explains How AI Could Bring Back the Age of Malthus."* https://www.aei.org/economics/a-nobel-laureate-economist-explains-how-ai-could-bring-back-the-age-of-malthus/[223]; Jeff Desjardins, *"Animation: The*

223. https://d.docs.live.net/eb41a1b69e1e6e00/Desktop/James%20Pethokoukis,

World's Population in 2100 by Region." http://www.visualcapitalist.com/animation-world-population-2100-region/; https://www.statista.com/statistics/997040/world-population-by-continent-1950-2020/

[1078] UNESCO, *"What are the effects of AI on the working lives of women?"* https://www.unesco.org/en/articles/what-are-effects-ai-working-lives-women-global-experts-weigh[224]; Carl Benedikt Frey and Michael A. Osborne, *"The Future of Employment: How Susceptible are Jobs to Computerisation?"* http://www.oxfordmartin.ox.ac.uk/downloads/academic/The_Future_of_Employment.pdf; Jacques Bughin, Jeongmin Seong[225], James Manyika[226], Michael Chui[227], and Raoul Joshi, *"Notes from the AI Frontier: Modeling the Impact of AI on the World Economy."* https://www.mckinsey.com/featured-insights/artificial-intelligence/notes-from-the-ai-frontier-modeling-the-impact-of-ai-on-the-world-economy

[1079] Anton Korinnek, Martin Schindler and Joseph Stiglitz, *"Technological Progress, Artificial Intelligence, and Inclusive Growth."* https://www.elibrary.imf.org/view/journals/001/2021/166/article-A001-en.xml

[1080] Mark Harvey, *"Slavery, coerced labour and the development of industrial England."* https://www.historyworkshop.org.uk/slavery-coerced-labour-and-the-development-of-industrial-capitalism-in-britain/

[1081] Herbert Marcuse, *One-Dimensional Man: Studies in the Ideology of Advanced Industrial Society.* (1964).

[1082] Shweta Mishra, *"Is AI Deepening the Divide between the Global North and South?"* https://www.newsweek.com/ai-deepening-divide-between-global-north-south-opinion-1574141

[1083] Cristian Alonso[228], Siddharth Kothari[229], and Sidra Rehman[230], *"How Artificial Intelligence Could Widen the Gap Between Rich and Poor Nations."* https://blogs.imf.org/2020/12/02/how-artificial-intelligence-could-widen-the-gap-between-rich-and-poor-nations/

[1084] Mike Walsh, *"Algorithms are Making Economic Inequality Worse."* https://hbr.org/2020/10/algorithms-are-making-economic-inequality-worse; Toni Ruuska, *"Conditions for Alienation: Technological Development and Capital Accumulation."* https://www.academia.edu/45632157/Conditions_for_Alienation_Technological_Development_and_Capital_Accumulation; Clingendael Spectator, *"The Saudi Dream."* https://spectator.clingendael.org/en/publication/saudi-dream-dark-side-utopian-city-neom; Edwin Heathcote, *"Saudi's Neom is dystopia portrayed as Utopia."* https://www.ft.com/content/04fcb9d4-5907-45b0-9388-

---

224. https://d.docs.live.net/eb41a1b69e1e6e00/Desktop/

225. https://www.mckinsey.com/our-people/jeongmin-seong

226. https://www.mckinsey.com/our-people/james-manyika

227. https://www.mckinsey.com/our-people/michael-chui

228. https://blogs.imf.org/bloggers/cristian-alonso/

229. https://blogs.imf.org/bloggers/siddharth-kothari/

230. https://blogs.imf.org/bloggers/sidra-rehman/

f84b34bc4bea; *"Saudi Arabia: UN experts alarmed by imminent executions linked to NEOM project."* https://www.ohchr.org/en/press-releases/2023/05/saudi-arabia-un-experts-alarmed-imminent-executions-linked-neom-project

[1085] Klint Finley, *"Obama Wants the Government to Help Develop AI."* https://www.wired.com/2016/10/obama-envisions-ai-new-apollo-program/; Joseph DiStefano, *"Under Trump, science isn't dead."* https://www.inquirer.com/business/phillydeals/trump-administration-science-research-ai-quantum-computing-20191228.html Eliza Strickland, *"4 Experts Respond to Trump's Executive Order on AI."* https://spectrum.ieee.org/4-experts-respond-to-trumps-executive-order-on-ai; Jacob Pramuk, *"Biden sings $1 trillion bipartisan infrastructure bill into law."* https://www.cnbc.com/2021/11/15/biden-signing-1-trillion-bipartisan-infrastructure-bill-into-law.html

[1086] Margueritte McNeal, *"Rise of the Machines: The Future has Lots of Robots, Few Jobs for Humans."* https://www.wired.com/brandlab/2015/04/rise-machines-future-lots-robots-jobs-humans/; The White House, *"Maintaining American Leadership in Artificial Intelligence."* https://www.federalregister.gov/documents/2019/02/14/2019-02544/maintaining-american-leadership-in-artificial-intelligence; Norman Anderson, *"AI & the Biden Infrastructure Plan."* https://www.forbes.com/sites/normananderson/2021/03/09/ai-and-infrastructurethe-

[1087] Fred Schulenburg, *"New technologies are stirring up an anti-tech backlash from the very people who helped create them."* https://www.rolandberger.com/en/Insights/Publications/Tech-pioneers-and-the-neo-Luddite-revolution.html; Theodore Roszak, *The Cult of Information: A neo-Luddite Treatise on High Tech, Artificial Intelligence, and the True Art of Thinking.* (1994)

[1088] Gloria Gonzalez Fuster, *"Artificial Intelligence and Law Enforcement."* https://www.europarl.europa.eu/RegData/etudes/STUD/2020/656295/IPOL_STU(2020)656295_EN.pdf; Will[231] Douglas Heaven, *"Predictive policing algorithms are racist."* https://www.technologyreview.com/2020/07/17/1005396/predictive-policing-algorithms-racist-dismantled-machine-learning-bias-criminal-justice/

[1089] **Stan Neilson, *Robot Nation: Surviving the Greatest Socio-economic Upheaval of All Time*. (2011); Makoto Arakaki, *"Who Wants to Be a Slave? The Technocratic Convergence of Humans and Data."* https://www.frontiersin.org/articles/10.3389/fcomm.2020.00037/full**

[1090] Max More and Natasha Vita-More, ***"The Transhumanist Reader."*** (2013).

[1091] Thomas Hauer, *"Technological Determinism and new media."* https://ijels.com/upload_document/issue_files/1%20IJELS-MAR-2017-8-Technological%20determinism%20and%20new%20media.pdf; B. L. Dey, Dorothy Yen, L. Samuel, *"Digital consumer culture and digital acculturation."* https://www.sciencedirect.com/science/article/abs/pii/S026840121930876X

[1092] **Claus Thomasberger, *"The Belief in Economic Determinism, Neoliberalism, and the Significance of Polanyi's***

231. https://www.europarl.europa.eu/RegData/etudes/STUD/2020/656295/IPOL_STU(2020)656295_EN.pdf;%20Will

***Contribution in the Twenty-First Century."* https://www.researchgate.net/publication/ 260141607_The_Belief_in_Economic_Determinism_Neoliberalism_and_the_Significance_of_Polanyi%27s_Contribution_in_the_Tw First_Century; Radoslav Baltezarevic et. al. *"The Impact of Virtual Communities on Cultural Identity."* https://philarchive.org/ archive/BALTIO-3; Lourdes Arizpe Schlosser, *Culture, International Transactions and the Anthropocene.* (2019); Monmouth University, *"Artificial Intelligence use Prompts Concerns."* https://www.monmouth.edu/polling-institute/reports/ monmouthpoll_us_021523/**

[1093] Sarah Gordon, *"Using Technology to Preserve Military Loyalty: Tatmadow in Myanmar."* in Stephen Feldstein, ed. *Issues on the Frontlines of Technology and Politics.* (2021); UN Human Rights, *"Myanmar: UN experts condemn military's 'digital dictatorship."* https://www.ohchr.org/en/press-releases/2022/06/myanmar-un-experts-condemn-militarys-digital-dictatorship; Eda Keremoğlu[232], Nils B. Weidmann[233], *"How Dictators Control the Internet: A Review Essay."* https://journals.sagepub.com/doi/full/10.1177/ 0010414020912278;

[1094] Julia Carrie Wong, *"Meet the rightwing power players lurking beneath Silicon Valley's liberal Facade."* https://www.theguardian.com/technology/2017/feb/10/silicon-valley-right-wing-donald-trump-peter-thiel

[1095] Cameron Costa, *"How Palantir's tech-based patriotism and politics grew into a multi-billion dollar company."* https://www.cnbc.com/2022/10/13/how-palantirs-tech-patriotism-became-a-multi-billion-dollar-idea.html; Daphne Leprince-Ringuet[234], *"Evil AI: These are the 20 most dangerous crimes that artificial intelligence will create."* https://www.zdnet.com/ article/evil-ai-these-are-the-20-most-dangerous-crimes-that-artificial-intelligence-will-create/; Vincent Huynh-Watkins, *"Abstracting Injustice: An Analysis of the Use in Artificial Intelligence in Criminal Justice."* https://www.cs.uoregon.edu/Reports/ UG-202106-Huynh-Watkins.pdf; Internet of Business, *"Propaganda chatbots and manipulative AI: Worse to come, says MIT."* https://internetofbusiness.com/propaganda-bots-social-media-manipulation/

[1096] *John Markoff, "As Artificial Intelligence Evolves, So Does Its Criminal Potential."* https://www.nytimes.com/2016/10/24/ technology/artificial-intelligence-evolves-with-its-criminal-potential.html?_r=0*; Laurence Cerulus, "One group that's embraced AI: Criminals." https://www.politico.eu/article/artificial-intelligence-criminals/*

[1097] **Pallab Ghosh,** *"Web 're-defining' human identity says chief scientist."* http://www.bbc.com/news/technology-21084945; Brandt Dainow, *"Digital alienation as the foundation of online privacy concerns."* https://www.researchgate.net/publication/ 316939869_Digital_alienation_as_the_foundation_of_online_privacy_concerns

[1098] Clive Lawson, *Technology and Isolation.* (2017).

232. https://journals.sagepub.com/doi/full/10.1177/0010414020912278

233. https://journals.sagepub.com/doi/full/10.1177/0010414020912278

234. https://www.zdnet.com/meet-the-team/uk/daphne+leprince-ringuet/

[1099] UN *"Urgent action needed over artificial intelligence risks to human."* https://news.un.org/en/story/2021/09/1099972

[1100] Nicole Salomons et al., *"Humans Conform to Robots; Disambiguating Trust, Truth and Conformity."* https://hri.cs.uchicago.edu/publications/HRI_2018_Salomons.pdf; Elfindah Princes[235] and Adler Haymans Manurung, *"Taking Advantage of Social Conformity in Entrepreneurship."* https://www.researchgate.net/publication/339741287_Taking_Advantage_of_Social_Conformity_in_Entrepreneurship

[1101] **Yuval Noah Harari[236], *"Sapiens: A brief history of mankind."* (2018); Prahlad Srihari, *"The future is sci-fi: Metropolis' critique of capitalism endures, even if its solution to class conflict does not."* https://www.firstpost.com/entertainment/the-future-is-sci-fi-metropolis-critique-of-capitalism-endures-even-if-its-solution-to-class-conflict-does-not-7841971.html**

[1102] Steven Swier, Video Games, *"Influence, and Identification: The Perpetuation of Culture Through Digital Worlds."* https://dsc.duq.edu/cgi/viewcontent.cgi?article=2788&context=etd; Dave Malyon, *"CIA And Mossad-Linked Surveillance System Quietly Being Installed Throughout the United States."* https://knewz.com/cia-and-mossad-linked-surveillance-system-quietly-being-installed-throughout-the-united-states-report/?utm_source=rss_google; Juan Francisco Jimenez Alcazar, *"Video Games and the Middle Ages."* https://www.academia.edu/8910665/Videogames_and_the_Middle_Ages

[1103] Adriene Shaw, *"What is Video Game Culture? Cultural Studies and Game Studies."* https://citeseerx.ist.psu.edu/viewdoc/download?doi=10.1.1.863.6217&rep=rep1&type=pdf; Jon Bailes, "Ideology and the Virtual City" (2019); Patrick Jagoda, *"Playing Through a Serious Crisis of the Neoliberal Art of Video Games."* https://post45.org/2020/08/playing-through-a-serious-crisis-on-the-neoliberal-art-of-video-games/

[1104] **Daniel Doughan, *"Digital Conquerors: Minecraft and the Apologetics of Neoliberalism."* https://journals.sagepub.com/doi/full/10.1177/1555412016655678; Daniel Muriel Garry Crawford, *"Video Games and Agency in Contemporary Society."* http://www.ctcs505.com/wp-content/uploads/2016/01/Muriel_Crawford_2018_Video-Games-and-Agency-in-Contemporary-Society.pdf; Hong Jun Jeon, et al., *"Is Internet overuse associated with impaired empathic in Korean college students?"* https://www.ncbi.nlm.nih.gov/pmc/articles/PMC6181547/; S.F. Lin, *"Effect of Opponent Type on Moral Emotions and Responses to Video Game Play."* https://www.researchgate.net/publication/51112758_Effect_of_Opponent_Type_on_Moral_Emotions_and_Responses_to_Video_Game_Play**

[1105] **Tom Jacobs, *"Does Gaming Teach Kids that Gun Control is a Bad Idea?"* https://psmag.com/news/does-gaming-teach-kids-that-gun-control-is-a-bad-idea; Jason Schreier, *"Blockchain in Gaming Is all the Rage and for No Good Reason."* https://www.bloomberg.com/news/newsletters/2021-11-12/crypto-in-video-games-is-all-the-rage-but-why; Charlie Wells &**

235. https://www.researchgate.net/profile/Elfindah-Princes

236. https://www.theguardian.com/profile/yuval-noah-harari

Misyrlena Egkolfopoulou, *"Into the Metaverse: Where Crypto, Gaming and Capitalism Collide."* https://www.bloombergquint.com/wealth/what-is-the-metaverse-where-crypto-nft-capitalism-collide-in-games-like-axie; Cathy Yi Hsuan Chen, *"Are There 'Winner-Takes-It-All' Effects in Blockchain User Adoption?"* https://papers.ssrn.com/sol3/papers.cfm?abstract_id=3933704

[1106] Justin Schumaker, *"The Labor of Play: the Political Economy of Computer Game Culture."* https://dc.uwm.edu/cgi/viewcontent.cgi?article=2918&context=etd

[1107] Adam Posamai, *"The i-zation of Society, Religion, Neoliberalism, Postsecularism."* (2018); Elizabeth A. Povinelli and Kim Turcot DiFruscia, *"A Conversation with Elizabeth A. Povinelli."* https://cpb-us-e2.wpmucdn.com/sites.uci.edu/dist/f/1861/files/2014/10/2012_02_07.pdf; Pierre Dardot, *"Hegemony and Neoliberalism."* https://www.transform-network.net/publications/yearbook/overview/article/journal-112012/hegemony-and-neoliberalism/; Rosario Forlenza, *"Antonio Gramsci on Religion."* https://journals.sagepub.com/doi/10.1177/1468795X19865119

[1108] United Nations, *"193 countries adopt first-ever agreement on the Ethics of Artificial Intelligence."* https://news.un.org/en/story/2021/11/1106612

[1109] Meeta Ramnani, *"Is AI fast becoming a technology built on worker exploitation from Global South?"* https://analyticsindiamag.com/is-ai-fast-becoming-a-technology-built-on-worker-exploitation-from-global-south/; Alexa Haggerty and Igor Rubinov, *"Global AI Ethics: A Review of the Social Impacts and Ethical Implications of Artificial Intelligence."* https://www.sciencedirect.com/science/article/pii/S0016328721001269; Katalin Feher and Attila I. Katona, *"Fifteen shadows of socio-cultural AI: A systematic review and future perspectives."* https://arxiv.org/ftp/arxiv/papers/1907/1907.07892.pdf; Pratyusha Kalluri, *"Don't ask if artificial intelligence is good or fair, ask how it shifts power."* https://www.nature.com/articles/d41586-020-02003-2; Valerio De Stefano, *"Negotiating the algorithm: Automation, artificial intelligence and labour protection."* https://www.ilo.org/wcmsp5/groups/public/—-ed_emp/—-emp_policy/documents/publication/wcms_634157.pdf

[1110] Jack Flynn, *"36+ Alarming Automation & Job Loss Statistics [2023] Are Robots, Machines and AI Coming for your Job?"* https://www.zippia.com/advice/automation-and-job-loss-statistics/

[1111] NETSMIAMI, *"Transhumanism: The economic and biological impact of automation."* https://netsmiami.com/transhumanism-the-economic-and-biological-impact-of-automation/

[1112] Simone Arnadi, *"The End of History and the Search for Perfection."* in Marja Ylönen and Luigi Pellizzoni, eds. "*Neoliberalism and Technoscience.*"

https://www.taylorfrancis.com/chapters/edit/10.4324/9781315597775-9/end-history-search-perfection-conflicting-teleologies-transhumanism-neo-liberal-democracy; Ana Teixeira Pinto, *"Capitalism with a Transhuman Face: The Afterlife of Fascism and the Digital Frontier."* https://www.academia.edu/40093604/Capitalism_with_a_Transhuman_Face_The_Afterlife_of_Fascism_and_the_Digital_Frontier; Celia Sampol,

"AI, Transhumanism, Post-Humanity: Fear and Imagination." https://emag.medicalexpo.com/artificial-intelligence-transhumanism-post-humanity-between-fear-and-imagination/;

[1113] Special Committee on Artificial Intelligence. *"AI and the Future of Democracy."* https://www.europarl.europa.eu/cmsdata/237000/Working%20Paper%20on%20AI%20and%20the%20Future%20of%20Democracy.pdf

[1114] Luca Paltinieri, *"Neoliberal Selves: Human Capital between Bourdieu and Foucault."* in Stephen W. Sawyer and Daniel Steinmetz-Jenkins, eds., *Foucault, Neoliberalism and Beyond* (2019)

[1115] **Francesc Torralba Roselló, *"The alliance between transhumanism and global neoliberalism. The need for a new technoethics."* http://www.pass.va/content/scienzesociali/en/publications/studiaselecta/dignity_of_work/torralba.html**

[1116] **Jun-E Tan, *"Alternative ethical frameworks for AI: A critical view of AI ethics."* https://www.apc.org/en/blog/engagemedia-alternative-ethical-frameworks-ai-critical-view-ai-ethics; Scott H. Hawley, "'*Challenges for an Ontology of Artificial Intelligence."* https://arxiv.org/ftp/arxiv/papers/1903/1903.03171.pdf**

[1117] **David M. Kleinberg-Levin, *"The Invisible Hands of Capital and Labour: Using Merleau-Ponty's Phenomenology to Understand the Meaning of Alienation in Marx's Theory of Manual Labour."* Philosophy and Social Criticism, 31:1 (2005); Avi S. *"A.I. and Humanity's Self-Alienation."* https://towardsdatascience.com/a-i-and-humanitys-self-alienation-69a2fddf9b9c**

[1118] JOHN ARMITAGE, *"Resisting the Neoliberal Discourse of Technology."* https://journals.uvic.ca/index.php/ctheory/article/view/14620/5486

[1119] Karl Marx, *"Economic and Philosophical Manuscripts of 1844,"* in *Karl Marx, Friedrich Engels: Collected Works.* Volume 3, (1975).

[1120] Sebastian Kaempf, *"The Digital Divide: Scarcity, Inequality and Conflict."* In Glen Creeber and Royston Martin, eds. *Digital Cultures. Understanding New Media.* (2009).

[1121] Institute for Employment Rights, *"AI: Alienating Intelligence."* https://morningstaronline.co.uk/article/f/ai-alienating-intelligence

[1122] Mikko Vesa[237] and Janne Tienari[238], *"Artificial intelligence and rationalized unaccountability: Ideology of the elites?"* https://journals.sagepub.com/doi/full/10.1177/1350508420963872; Sascha Engel, *"Minding Machines: A Note on Alienation."*

237. https://journals.sagepub.com/doi/full/10.1177/1350508420963872

238. https://journals.sagepub.com/doi/full/10.1177/1350508420963872

https://fastcapitalism.journal.library.uta.edu/index.php/fastcapitalism/article/view/108/439

[1123] Daisy Jones, *"Gen Z Love Cocaine as Much as Their Parents."* https://www.uc https://www.vice.com/en/article/qj8d7q/gen-z-cocaine-usage; l.ac.uk/news/2021/apr/substance-use-and-depression-more-closely-linked-generation-z-teens; Seyyed Salman Alavi, et al., *"Behavioral Addiction versus Substance Addiction: Correspondence of Psychiatric and Psychological Views."* https://www.ncbi.nlm.nih.gov/pmc/articles/PMC3354400/; Yasha Sazmand Asfaranjan, et al., *"Alleviating the sense of isolation and alienation in the virtual world."* https://www.researchgate.net/publication/335259325_Alleviating_the_senses_of_isolation_and_alienation_in_the_virtual_world_Socialization_in_distance_education

[1124] Anna Zeira, *"Mental Health Challenges Related to Neoliberal Capitalism in the United States."* https://www.ncbi.nlm.nih.gov/pmc/articles/PMC8145185/; Maria Epele, *"Survival, Drugs and Social Suffering during the Argentine Neoliberal Collapse."* Human Organization, 67, 3 (2008); Fred Turner, *From Counterculture to Cyberculture.* (2006); Noël Ingram, *"Suicide and Neoliberalism: An Imminent Critique of Cognitive-Behavioral Therapy."* https://digitalcommons.pepperdine.edu/cgi/viewcontent.cgi?article=1507&context=scursas; Anna Zeira[239], *"Mental Health Challenges Related to Neoliberal Capitalism in the United States."* https://www.ncbi.nlm.nih.gov/pmc/articles/PMC8145185/; https://www.macrotrends.net/countries/NAC/north-america/suicide-rate.

[1125] Francesco Rodella, *"Making Robots More Human and More Social."* https://www.sacyr.com/en/-/robots-mas-humanos-y-sociales-el-gran-reto-de-la-inteligencia-artificial; Cliff Saran, *"Pioneering companies use AI to drive profit."* https://www.computerweekly.com/news/252492422/Pioneering-companies-use-AI-to-drive-profit; Alen Toplišek, *"Liberal Democracy in Crisis: Redefining Politics and Resistance through Power."* https://qmro.qmul.ac.uk/xmlui/bitstream/handle/123456789/23844/Toplisek_A_PhD_final_171116.pdf?sequence=1&isAllowed=y

[1126] Ken Klippenstein, *"FBI Hired Social Media Surveillance Firm that Labeled Black Lives Matter Organizers "Threat Actors"."* https://theintercept.com/2023/07/06/fbi-social-media-surveillance-zerofox/

[1127] France24, *"Private Israeli malware "Pegasus" used to spy on journalists, activists and politicians."* https://www.france24.com/en/technology/20210718-private-israeli-malware-used-to-spy-on-journalists-activists-and-politicians

[1128] Priya Anand and Mark Bergen, *"Big Teacher is Watching: How AI Spyware Took Over Schools."* https://www.bloomberg.com/news/features/2021-10-28/how-goguardian-ai-spyware-took-over-schools-student-devices-during-covid

[1129] H. James Wilson and Paul R. Daugherty, *"Collaborative Intelligence: Humans and AI are Joining Forces."* https://hbr.org/2018/07/collaborative-intelligence-humans-and-ai-are-joining-forces

---

239. https://www.ncbi.nlm.nih.gov/pubmed/?term=Zeira%20A%5BAuthor%5D&cauthor=true&cauthor_uid=34032963

[1130] Francisco Dao, *"The Commoditizing of Humans."* https://venturebeat.com/2014/12/07/internet-marketplaces-have-turned-human-beings-into-commodities/; Aviva Rutkin, *"Why granny's only robot will be a sex robot."* https://www.newscientist.com/article/2096530-why-grannys-only-robot-will-be-a-sex-robot/ Jeremy Gilbert, *"Against the Commodification of Everything."* Cultural Studies, 22, 5 (2008)

[1131] Paul F. Christiano, *"Machine intelligence and capital accumulation."* https://rationalaltruist.com/2014/05/14/machine-intelligence-and-capital-accumulation/; Garvey, *"Artificial Intelligence and Japan's Fifth Generation."* Pacific Historical Review. 88, 4 (2019); Robert C. Allen. *"Capital Accumulation, Technological Change, and the Distribution of Income*

during the British Industrial Revolution." http://www.piketty.pse.ens.fr/files/Allen05.pdf

[1132] J. M. Hude, *"Ethics in artificial Intelligence."* http://www.viirj.org/vol12issue1/43.pdf; Ben Vermeulen, Andreas Pyka, and Mirheta Omeroviv, *"The Economic Impact of Robotics and Artificial Intelligence."* https://reeler.eu/fileadmin/ingen_mappe_valgt/wp6.pdf; Philip Jensen and Philip Brey, *"Ethical Analysis of AI and Robotics Technologies"* http://en.philosophylab.philosophy.uoa.gr/fileadmin/philosophylab.ppp.uoa.gr/uploads/D4.4_Ethical_analysis__AI_R_.pdf

[1133] Steven Goldstein, *"The Global Expansion of AI Surveillance."* https://carnegieendowment.org/2019/09/17/global-expansion-of-ai-surveillance-pub-79847; C. D. Bourne, *"AI Cheerleaders: Public Relations, Neoliberalism and Artificial Intelligence."* https://research.gold.ac.uk/id/eprint/25962/1/AI-Neoliberalism-PR-Jan2019%20(1).pdf; Colin

[1134] Dinah, PoKempner, *"A Shrinking Realm: Freedom of Expression since 9/11."* https://www.hrw.org/legacy/wr2k7/essays/shrinking/ashrinkingrealm.pdf; ACLU, *"More About FBI Spying."* https://www.aclu.org/other/more-about-fbi-spying

[1135] John Laider, *"High tech is watching you."* https://news.harvard.edu/gazette/story/2019/03/harvard-professor-says-surveillance-capitalism-is-undermining-democracy/

[1136] ***"60 Minutes/Vanity Fair poll: Artificial Intelligence."*** **http://www.cbsnews.com/news/60-minutes-vanity-fair-poll-artificial-intelligence/; James Vincent,** ***"More Americans in favor of AI than fear it."*** **https://www.theverge.com/2019/1/10/18176645/ai-robot-survey-america-public-opinion-future-of-humanity-institute; Mike Thomas,** ***"7 Dangerous Risks of Artificial Intelligence."*** **https://builtin.com/artificial-intelligence/risks-of-artificial-intelligence**

+[1137] Daphne Leprince-Ringuette, *"AI's big problem; Lazy humans just trust the algorithms too much."* https://www.zdnet.com/article/ai-needs-to-be-controlled-but-lazy-humans-may-not-be-up-to-the-job/; Monty Munford, *"Artificial Intelligence: Enemy of the People or Friend of the Lazy and Inept?"* https://www.forbes.com/sites/montymunford/2018/10/28/artificial-intelligence-enemy-of-the-people-or-friend-of-the-lazy-and-inept/

[1138] Stephen Hsu, *"Don't Worry, Smart Machines Will Take Us With Them."* http://nautil.us/issue/28/2050/dont-worry-smart-machines-will-take-us-with-them; Anna Zeira, *"Mental Health Challenges Related to Neoliberal Capitalism in the United States."* https://www.ncbi.nlm.nih.gov/pmc/articles/PMC8145185/

[1139] Diana Gasparyan and Svetlana Klimova, *"Why Badly-Trained AI is a Bigger Threat than a Robot Uprising."* https://www.hse.ru/en/news/research/508226580.html

[1140] **James Barrat, *Our Final Invention: Artificial Intelligence and the of the Human Era*. (2013); Abigail Higgins, *"Stephen Hawking's final warning for humanity: AI is coming for us."* https://www.vox.com/future-perfect/2018/10/16/17978596/stephen-hawking-ai-climate-change-robots-future-universe-earth; Vernon Vinge, *"Technological Singularity."* https://frc.ri.cmu.edu/~hpm/book98/com.ch1/vinge.singularity.html; Nick Bostrom, *Superintelligence: Paths, Dangers, Strategies*. (2015)**

[1141] JONATHAN SHAW, *"Artificial Intelligence and Ethics."* https://www.harvardmagazine.com/2019/01/artificial-intelligence-limitations

[1142] Anita Gurumurthy, *"In a new world order driven by AI, we need to rewrite the rules of data capitalism."* https://www.opendemocracy.net/en/oureconomy/new-world-order-driven-ai-we-need-rewrite-rules-data-capitalism/

[1143] Wim Naude, *"Artificial intelligence; neither Utopian nor apocalyptic impacts soon."* https://www.tandfonline.com/doi/full/10.1080/10438599.2020.1839173; Vincent Bulanin, *"AI & Global Governance: AI and Nuclear Weapons – Promise and Perils of AI for Nuclear Stability."* https://cpr.unu.edu/publications/articles/ai-global-governance-ai-and-nuclear-weapons-promise-and-perils-of-ai-for-nuclear-stability.html

[1144] Jeff Haden, *"Mark Cuban: The World's First Trillionaire is Learning 1 Skill and Discovering how to use it in Now Unimaginable Ways."* https://www.inc.com/jeff-haden/mark-cuban-worlds-first-trillionaire-is-learning-1-skill-discovering-how-to-use-it-in-now-unimaginable-ways.html

[1145] Chris Weller, *"Mark Cuban thinks the world's first trillionaire will work in artificial intelligence."* https://www.businessinsider.com/worlds-first-trillionaire-mark-cuban-2017-3.

[1146] Gregory A. Daneke, *"Machina-economicus or homo-complexicus: Artificial intelligence and the future of economics?"* http://www.paecon.net/PAEReview/issue93/Daneke93.pdf

[1147] Kieran Markov, *"The dangers of artificial intelligence under capitalism."* https://www.marxist.ca/article/the-dangers-of-artificial-intelligence-under-capitalism; **Kai-Fu Lee, *AI Superpowers. China, Silicon Valley and the New World Order* (2018); Raphael Koster, et al. *"Human-centered mechanism design with Democratic AI."* https://arxiv.org/ftp/arxiv/papers/2201/2201.11441.pdf**

[1148] Emile Durkheim, *Sociologie et Philosophie.* (1898); Bruno Karsenti, *La société en personnes - études durkheimiennes.* (2005).

[1149] Michał Krzyżanowski, *"Normalization and the discursive construction of "new" norms and "new" normality: discourse in the paradoxes of populism and neoliberalism."* https://www.diva-portal.org/smash/get/diva2:1459676/FULLTEXT01.pdf

[1150] Vu Anh Ngoc Nguyen, *"Reality Television as a Neoliberal Technology of Citizenship?"*https://www.lse.ac.uk/media-and-communications/assets/documents/research/msc-dissertations/2016/Dissertation-Vu-Anh-Ngoc-Nguyen.pdf; Saif Shahin[240], *"News, Nations, and Power Relations: How Neoliberal Media Reproduce a Hierarchical World Order."* https://journals.sagepub.com/doi/full/10.1177/08969205211072455; Aihwa Ong, *Neoliberalism as Exception: Mutations in Citizenship and Sovereignty*. (2006).

[1151] Burton Lee Artz, *"Global Media Practices and Cultural Hegemony: Growing, Harvesting, and Marketing the Consuming Audience,"* in Savaş Çoban[241], ed. *Media, Ideology and Hegemony* (2018).

[1152] Andrew Pettegree, *The Invention of News.* (2014); Sabrina Alcorn Baron[242] and Brendan Dooley[243], eds., *The Politics of Information in Early Modern Europe.* (2011).

[1153] Todd Gitlin, *The Whole World is Watching.* (2003).

[1154] John Nerone, *"The Historical roots of the normative model of journalism."* https://journals.sagepub.com/doi/10.1177/1464884912464177; Amelia Bonea, *The News of Empire.* (2016).

[1155] Charlotte Ann Legg, *The New White Race: Settler Colonialism and the Press in French Algeria, 1860-1914.* (2021); Amanda Frisken, *Graphic News: How Sensational Images Transformed Nineteenth-Century Journalism.* (2020); Frankie Hutton and Barbara Straus Reed, eds. *Outsiders in 19th Century Press History: Multicultural Perspectives.* (1995).

[1156] Johan Lindell, *"Battle of the classes: news consumption inequalities and symbo lic boundaries work."* https://www.tandfonline.com/doi/full/10.1080/15295036.2020.1829670

---

240. https://journals.sagepub.com/doi/full/10.1177/08969205211072455

241. https://brill.com/search?f_0=author&q_0=Sava%C5%9F+%C3%87oban

242. https://www.amazon.com/s/ref=dp_byline_sr_book_1?ie=UTF8&field-author=Sabrina+Alcorn+Baron&text=Sabrina+Alcorn+Baron&sort=relevancerank&search-alias=books

243. https://www.amazon.com/s/ref=dp_byline_sr_book_2?ie=UTF8&field-author=Brendan+Dooley&text=Brendan+Dooley&sort=relevancerank&search-alias=books

[1157] Gerald J. Baldasty, *The Commercialization of News in the Nineteenth Century.* (1992); Gerald J. Baldasty and Jeffrey B. Rutenbeck. *"Money, Politics, and Newspapers: The Business Environment of Press Partisanship in the Late 19th Century."* Journalism History 15:2/3 (1988); Karmen Erjavec and Jožica Zajc, *A Historical Overview of Approaches to Journalism Studies*

https://hrcak.srce.hr/file/119671; Randall Sumpter, *"Being a journalist could have been worse than it is now."* https://www.salon.com/2018/10/08/being-a-journalist-could-have-been-worse-than-it-is-now_partner/.

[1158] John Simkin, *"Muckraking Journalism."* https://spartacus-educational.com/Jmuckraking.htm; C. C. Regier, *The Era of the Muckrakers,* (1933).

[1159] Delia Dumitrescu, Anthony Mughan, *Mass Media and Democratic Politics.* in K. T. Leicht and J. C. Jenkins, eds. *Handbook of Politics. Handbooks of Sociology and Social Research.* (2010); D. M. Chalmers, *"The Muckrakers and the Growth of Corporate Power: A Study in Constructive Journalism."* American Journal of Economics and Sociology. 18 (1959).

[1160] Jürgen Habermas, *The Structural Transformation of the Public Sphere: An Inquiry into a Category of Bourgeois Society.* (1991); Ann Bausum, *Muckrakers: How Ida Tarbell, Upton Sinclair, and Lincoln Steffens Helped Expose Scandal, Inspire Reform, and Invent Investigative Journalism.* (2007).

[1161] Sarah Hinchliff Pearson[244], *"Objective Failure: Why the debate about media objectivity threatens the viability of general-interest news outlets."* http://cyberlaw.stanford.edu/blog/2010/05/objective-failure-why-debate-about-media-objectivity-threatens-viability-general

[1162] Francesco Regalzi, *"Democracy and Its Discontents: Walter Lippmann and the Crisis of Politics (1919-1938)."* https://journals.openedition.org/erea/2538

[1163] Nancy E. Bernhard, *U.S. Television News and Cold War Propaganda, 1947-1960.* (2003); Matthew P. Valdespino, *"American Communism and Cold War Censorship: The Creation of a New American Citizen."* https://repository.upenn.edu/cgi/viewcontent.cgi?article=1192&context=curej

[1164] R. A. Schwartz, *Cold War Culture: Media and the Arts, 1945-1990.* (1990); David S. Allen, *"The Pen and the Secret Sword: The CIA-News Media Relationship."* PhD dissertation, Penn State University. (1986)

[1165] Beverly Cage, *"McCarthyism was never defeated. Trumpism won't be either."* https://www.washingtonpost.com/outlook/joseph-mccarthy-movement-trumpism/2020/12/04/d6e807ee-3460-11eb-b59c-adb7153d10c2_story.html

244. http://cyberlaw.stanford.edu/about/people/sarah-hinchliff-pearson

[1166] Alexander Satfford, *"The Rose of the Media during the Cold War."* https://www.e-ir.info/2013/10/26/the-role-of-the-media-during-the-cold-war/[245]; Charlotte Lepri, *De l'usage des médias à des fins de propagande pendant la guerre froide."* Revue internationale et stratégique[246]. 78, (2010). https://www.cairn.info/revue-internationale-et-strategique-2010-2-page-111.htm#xd_co_f=N2ZiNDhiNmUtNjlhYS00YzVhLThkODgtZDk5ODIxNWM1NWUy~

[1167] Henrik G. Bastiansen & Rolf Werenskjold, *"The Nordic Media and the Cold War."* http://www.diva-portal.org/smash/get/diva2:1534764/FULLTEXT01.pdf; John Jenks, *"British Propaganda and the News Media in the Cold War."* https://edinburgh.universitypressscholarship.com/view/10.3366/edinburgh/9780748623143.001.0001/upso-9780748623143; Oana Godeanu-Kenworthy[247], *"How 'socialism' became a bad word in hyper-capitalist America."* https://scroll.in/article/954941/how-socialism-became-a-bad-word-in-hyper-capitalist-america

[1168] Alexander Safford, *"The Role of the Media during the Cold War."* https://www.e-ir.info/2013/10/26/the-role-of-the-media-during-the-cold-war/

[1169] Kevin Grieves, *Cold War journalism: Between Cold Reception and Common Ground.* (2021).

[1170] H. A. Giroux, *"The Terror of Neoliberalism: Rethinking the Significance of Cultural Politics."* https://www.researchgate.net/publication/236696050_The_Terror_of_Neoliberalism_Rethinking_the_Significance_of_Cultural_Politics; George Monbiot, *"Free Market does not exist."* https://www.theguardian.com/guardianweekly/story/0,,1672097,00.html; A. T. Rowland, *"From authoritarian dirty war to neoliberal, 'democratic' class war neoliberalism as class struggle in Argentina."* https://trace.tennessee.edu/cgi/viewcontent.cgi?article=7375&context=utk_gradthes;

245. https://d.docs.live.net/eb41a1b69e1e6e00/Desktop/Alexander%20Satfford,

246. https://www.cairn.info/revue-internationale-et-strategique.htm

247. https://scroll.in/author/18520

[1171] **Nicholas Garnham, *Emancipation, the Media, and Modernity: Arguments about the Media and Social Theory*. (2000).**

[1172] **Gilles Lipovetsky, *Le bonheur paradoxal: Essai sur la société d'hyperconsommation*. (2009); Aeron Davis et al, *Media, Democracy and Social Change: Re-imagining Political Communication*. (2020); Deregulation or democracy? Natalie Fenton, *"New media, news, neoliberalism and the public interest."* https://research.gold.ac.uk/id/eprint/5976/2/Dereg.pdf; *"Propaganda of consumerism in mass-media."* https://what-is-good.com/consumerism/**

[1173] Victor Pickard, *America's Battle for Media Democracy: The Triumph of Corporate Libertarianism and the Future of Media Reform*. (2015; Yuxi Wen, *"The Political and Economic of Media Ownership Structures and Concentration of Global Communication."* https://digitalcommons.butler.edu/cgi/viewcontent.cgi?article=1306&context=bjur;

[1174] Sean Phelan, *"Articulating Neoliberalism in Critical Media and Communication Studies."* in Sean Phelan, *Neoliberalism, Media and the Political* (2014).

[1175] Letza Steve, Clive Smallman, William Xiuping Sun, *"Reframing privatization: Deconstructing the myth of efficiency."* https://www.researchgate.net/publication/5153616_Reframing_privatisation_Deconstructing_the_myth_of_efficiency

[1176] Mike Berry, *"Media and Neoliberalism."* https://www.researchgate.net/profile/Mike-Berry-5/publication/336717428_Media_and_Neoliberalism/links/60cc777fa6fdcc01d47f15b7/Media-and-Neoliberalism.pdf; John Moore, *"British Privatization: Taking Capitalism to the People."* https://hbr.org/1992/01/british-privatization-taking-capitalism-to-the-people; Dexter Whitfield, *"Privatization Failures in the UK."* https://www.tni.org/es/node/14588

[1177] Ashley Lutz, *"These 6 Corporations Control 90% of the Media in America."* http://www.businessinsider.com/these-6-corporations-control-90-of-the-media-in-america-2012-6

[1178] Kira Rao Poolla, *"The Dangers of the Concentration of Media Ownership."* https://berkeleyhighjacket.com/2021/entertainment/the-dangers-of-the-concentration-of-media-ownership/

[1179] Charlie Cray et al. *"Dissecting Bush Administration Policies under the Microscope."* http://www.multinationalmonitor.org/mm2004/05012004/may-june04corp1.html

[1180] Rosalind Bresnahan, *"The Media and the Neoliberal Transition in Chile: Democratic Promise Unfulfilled."* https://library.fes.de/libalt/journals/swetsfulltext/18006615.pdf

[1181] Adolfo Rodríguez Herrera, Fabio Durán Valverde, *"Costos e incentivos en la organización de un sistema de pensiones."* https://www.cepal.org/sites/default/files/publication/files/5306/S00060522_es.pdf; Raul Madrid, *"The Politics and Economics of Pension Privatization in Latin America."* https://www.researchgate.net/publication/292543034_The_politics_and_economics_of_pension_privatization_in_Latin_America

[1182] Alan McLeod, *"Chile: A revolt against neoliberalism the media refuses to acknowledge."* https://www.twn.my/title2/resurgence/2019/341-342/world1.htm; Tomas Undurraga, *"Neoliberalism in Argentina and Chine: common antecedents, divergent paths."* https://www.scielo.br/j/rsocp/a/Hjyw9CtYFgkMRMYR87bGHfn/?format=p"df&lang=en

[1183] Pablo Castagno, *"Marxist Theory in Critical Transitions: The Democratization of the Media in Post-Neoliberal Argentina."* Triple C-communication, capitalism and critique. 10:2, (2012)

[1184] George Monbiot, *"Our cult of personality is leaving real life in the shade."* https://www.theguardian.com/commentisfree/2018/oct/03/cult-personality-politics-boris-trump-corbyn-george-monbiot

[1185] Jedediah Purdy, *"Neoliberal Constitutionalism: Lochnerism for a new economy."* https://scholarship.law.duke.edu/cgi/viewcontent.cgi?article=4713&context=lcp; Benjamin Alemparte, *"Towards a theory of neoliberal constitutionalism: Addressing Chile's first constitutionalism."* https://www.cambridge.org/core/journals/global-constitutionalism/article/towards-a-theory-of-neoliberal-constitutionalism-addressing-chiles-first-constitutionmaking-laboratory/AFEC4BE02411DA7466F1F4CE4F578913

[1186] **Colin Sparks, *"Media and cultural imperialism reconsidered." Media and cultural imperialism reconsidered."* https://www.researchgate.net/publication/254250992_Media_and_cultural_imperialism_reconsidered; Michael Griffin, *"From Cultural Imperialism to Transnational Commercialization: Shifting Paradigms in International Media Studies."* https://www.academia.edu/182484/From_Cultural_Imperialism_to_Transnational_Commercialization_Shifting_Paradigms_in_International_Media_Studies**

[1187] Kate Vinton, *"These 15 Billionaires Own America's News Media Companies."* https://www.forbes.com/sites/katevinton/2016/06/01/these-15-billionaires-own-americas-news-media-companies/?sh=353a929a660a; https://www.europarl.europa.eu/doceo/document/P-8-2018-004860_EN.html; Reporters Without Borders, *"Latin American media: under control of families, economic and political elites."* https://rsf.org/en/news/latin-american-media-under-control-families-economic-and-political-elites

[1188] Al Jazeera, *"UN: Israelis fired shots that killed journalist Shireen Abu Akleh."* https://www.aljazeera.com/news/2022/6/24/un-israelis-fired-shots-that-killed-journalist-abu-akleh; Shane Harris, Greg Miller and Josh Dawsey, *"CIA concludes Saudi crown prince ordered Jamal Khashoggi assassination."* https://www.washingtonpost.com/world/national-security/cia-concludes-saudi-crown-prince-ordered-jamal-khashoggis-assassination/2018/11/16/98c89fe6-e9b2-11e8-a939-9469f1166f9d_story.html

[1189] Robert W. McChesney[248], *"Global Media, Neoliberalism, and Imperialism."* https://monthlyreview.org/2001/03/01/global-media-neoliberalism-and-imperialism/; Jose Ruas Araujo, John P. Wihbey, and Daniel Barredo-Ibanez, *"Beyond Fake News and Fact-Checking."* https://www.mdpi.com/2673-5172/3/2/19; George Monbiot, *"Champions of the Overdog."* https://www.monbiot.com/2009/11/09/champions-of-the-overdog/; Steven Barnett, *"What's wrong with media monopolies? A lesson from history and a new approach to media ownership policy."* https://www.lse.ac.uk/media-and-communications/assets/documents/research/working-paper-series/EWP18.pdf

[1190] Larry Diamond, et al. eds. *Authoritarianism Goes Global; The Challenge to Democracy.* (2016).

[1191] Damian Tambini, *"Media Freedom, Regulation and Trust."* https://rm.coe.int/cyprus-2020-new-media/16809a524f

[1192] Hüseyin Pusat Kildiş, *"Post-truth and Far-Right Politics on Social Media."* https://www.e-ir.info/2020/11/17/post-truth-and-far-right-politics-on-social-media/; *Eli M. Noam, "Who Owns the World's Media? Media Concentration and Ownership around the World."* https://oxford.universitypressscholarship.com/view/10.1093/acprof:oso/9780199987238.001.0001/acprof-9780199987238; Paweł Surowiec[249] and Václav Štětka[250] *"Introduction* E. S. Habermas, *"Media in the US political economy."* in Brett Mills and David M. Barlow, eds., *Reading Media Theory.* (2012); Henry Jenkins, *Convergence Culture.* (2008).

[1193] Oliver Lloyd Barret and Tanner Mirrlees, eds. *Media Imperialism; Continuity and Change.* (2019) Ruby Z. *"Transnational Media in Globalized and Hybridized Environment."* https://medium.com/@ruiqianz/transnational-media-in-globalized-and-hybridized-environment-212d9fca5b68; Marwan M. Kraidy, *"Globalization of Culture Through the Media."* https://repository.upenn.edu/cgi/viewcontent.cgi?article=1333&context=asc_papers; Alexander Kentikelenis, Sarah Babb, *"The Making of Neoliberal Globalization: Norm Substitution and the Politics of Clandestine Institutional Change."* https://www.researchgate.net/publication/333638170_The_Making_of_Neoliberal_Globalization_Norm_Substitution_and_the_Politics_of_Clandestine_Institutional_Change

[1194] E. S. Habermas, *"Media in the US political economy."* in Brett Mills and David M. Barlow, eds. *Reading Media Theory.* (2012); Henry Jenkins, *Convergence Culture: Where old and new media collide.* (2008).

[1195] Julie Hollar, *"CNN needs more than a new CEO - it needs a new model of journalism."* https://mronline.org/2023/06/10/cnn-needs-more-than-a-new-ceo-it-needs-a-new-model-of-journalism/?utm_source=rss&utm_medium=rss&utm_campaign=cnn-needs-more-than-a-new-ceo-it-needs-a-new-model-of-journalism; Clare Malone, *"What the Shakeup of CNN Says about the Future of Cable News."* https://www.newyorker.com/news/annals-of-communications/what-the-shakeup-at-cnn-says-about-the-future-of-cable-news

---

248. https://monthlyreview.org/author/robertwmcchesney/

249. https://www.tandfonline.com/author/Surowiec%2C+Pawe%C5%82

250. https://www.tandfonline.com/author/%C5%A0t%C4%9Btka%2C+V%C3%A1clav

[1196] C. J. Kollmeyer, *"Explaining Consensual Domination: Moving Beyond the Concept of Hegemony."* https://escholarship.org/content/qt0rj9f4dm/qt0rj9f4dm_noSplash_e55b2b34e105f09ad5e32b224eae5c13.pdf; Hallvard Sandven, *"Systemic domination social institutions and the coalition problem."* https://journals.sagepub.com/doi/full/10.1177/1470594X20927927

[1197] Thomas Klikauer, *Media Capitalism: Hegemony in the Age of Mass Deception.* (2021); **IPSOS, "Trust in the Media." https://www.ipsos.com/sites/default/files/ct/news/documents/2019-06/global-advisor-trust-in-media-2019.pdf;** Aisha Majid, *"Almost seven-in-ten people worry they are being lied to by journalists according to latest Edelman survey."* https://pressgazette.co.uk/almost-seven-in-ten-people-worry-they-are-being-lied-to-by-journalists-according-to-latest-edelman-trust-survey/

[1198] POLITICO, *"Is the Media Doomed?"* https://www.politico.com/news/magazine/2022/01/21/media-journalism-future-527294

[1199] Luís Francisco Carvalho João Rodrigues, *"Drawing the Line? Critical Notes on Commodification."* https://www.hetecon.net/wp-content/uploads/2019/12/CarvalhoRodrigues2006.pdf; Daniel Broudy, *"Propaganda in a Neoliberal Universe: An Interview with Hames Winter."* https://scholar.uwindsor.ca/cgi/viewcontent.cgi?article=1028&context=communicationspub

[1200] Jens Wernicke, *"Neoliberal Indoctrination: Interview with Professor Rainer Mausfeld."* https://cognitive-liberty.online/wp-content/uploads/neoliberal-indoctrination-Copy.pdf

[1201] Olivier Berruyer, *"L'enseignement de l'ignorance : Quelle est la nation qui a le plus contribué à la défaite de l'Allemagne en 1945?"* https://www.les-crises.fr/la-fabrique-du-cretin-defaite-nazis/

[1202] Max Rose and F. R, Baumgartner, *"Framing the Poor: Media Coverage and US Poverty Policy."* https://fbaum.unc.edu/articles/PSJ-Framing-the-poor.pdf

[1203] Des Friedman, *"Media and the Neoliberal Swindle: From Fake News to Public Service."* in S. Dawes, M. Lenormand, eds., *Neoliberalism in Context.* (2019).

[1204] **Ed Heil, "*What Impact does Social Media have on Mainstream Media?*" https://www.storytellermn.com/blog/impact-social-media-has-on-mainstream-media; Annika Bergström[251] & Maria Jervelycke Belfrage[252], "*News in Social Media: Incidental consumption and the role of opinion leaders.*" https://www.tandfonline.com/doi/full/10.1080/21670811.2018.1423625**

[1205] SIMON DAWES, *British Broadcasting and Public-Private Dichotomy: Citizenship and the Public Sphere.* (2016); Simon Dawes and Terry Flew, *"Neoliberalism, Voice and National Media Systems."* https://ojs.meccsa.org.uk/index.php/netknow/article/download/467/288

---

251. https://www.tandfonline.com/author/Bergstr%C3%B6m%2C+Annika

252. https://www.tandfonline.com/author/Jervelycke+Belfrage%2C+Maria

[1206] Toby Miller, *"Foucault: The birth of biopolitics: Lectures at the College de France, 1978-79"* in Oliver Bennett, ed., *Cultural Policy Review of Books.* (2012).

[1207] You-Il Lee, *"South Korea's globalization in the late twentieth century: An end to economic nationalism."* https://www.researchgate.net/profile/You-Il-Lee; Jesook Song, *South Koreans in the Debt Crisis.* (2009); Julian Ryall, *"South Korean journalists fear new laws will muzzle media."* https://www.dw.com/en/south-korean-journalists-fear-new-laws-will-muzzle-media/a-58999070

[1208] William Peter Fitz, *"Reactionary Postmodernism? Neoliberalism, Multiculturalism, the Internet and the Ideology of the New Far Right in Germany."* https://scholarworks.uvm.edu/cgi/viewcontent.cgi?article=1302&context=hcoltheses; C. Son, *"Transformation of the media system under a neoliberal government, 1998-2008."* Political Science, (2012).

[1209] Uwe Becker, ed. *The Small Political Economies of Small West European Countries.* (2011).

[1210] Lars Nord, *"Comparing Nordic Media Systems. Between the West and East?"* https://www.researchgate.net/publication/239587745_Comparing_Nordic_media_systems_North_between_West_and_East; Peter Jakobsson[253], Johan Lindell[254], Fredrik Stiernstedt[255], *"A Neoliberal Media Welfare State? The Swedish Media System in Transformation."* https://www.tandfonline.com/doi/full/10.1080/13183222.2021.1969506; Eli Skogerbø, et al. eds., *Power, Communication and Nordic Politics.* (2020).

[1211] Rosalind Bresnahan, *"The Media and the Neoliberal Transition in Chile."* https://library.fes.de/libalt/journals/swetsfulltext/18006615.pdf

[1212] Noam Chomsky, *"What Makes Mainstream Media Mainstream."* https://chomsky.info/199710__/; Ahmed Kanna, *Dubai, the City as Corporation.* (2011).

[1213] **Mara Hvistendahl, *"The Price of Happiness."* https://theintercept.com/2021/12/29/jeffrey-sachs-uae-happiness/**

Michael Curtin, *"Between State and Capital: Asia's Media Revolution in the Age of Neoliberal Globalization."* https://ijoc.org/index.php/ijoc/article/download/5156/1980

[1214] **https://uaecabinet.ae/en/details/news/mohammed-bin-rashid-emphasises-role-of-media-amid-current-challenges;** Ahmed Kanna, "Making Cadres of the City-Corporation: Cultural and Identity Politics in Neoliberal Dubai." https://www.researchgate.net/publication/290586524_Making_Cadres_of_the_City-Corporation_Cultural_and_Identity_Politics_in_Neoliberal_Dubai

253. https://www.tandfonline.com/author/Jakobsson%2C+Peter

254. https://www.tandfonline.com/author/Lindell%2C+Johan

255. https://www.tandfonline.com/author/Stiernstedt%2C+Fredrik

[1215] Theresa M. Senft and Nancy Baym, *"What Does the Selfie Say? Investigating a Global Phenomenon."* International Journal of Communications. 9, (2015); Jeremiah Morelock and Felipe Ziotti Narita, *The Society of the Selfie*. (2021).

[1216] **Michelle Gorea, "Becoming Your 'Authentic' Self: How Social Media Influences Youth's Visual Transitions." https://journals.sagepub.com/doi/10.1177/20563051211047875**

[1217] Jim Aitken, *"Philosophy, cultural relativism, anti-intellectualism and the far right."* https://www.culturematters.org.uk/index.php/culture/theory/item/3871-philosophy-cultural-relativism-anti-intellectualism-and-the-far-right; Robert Caruana, *"Alternative Hedonism: Exploring the Role of Pleasure in Moral Markets."* https://link.springer.com/article/10.1007/s10551-019-04123-w; **John M. Roberts, New media and public activism: Neoliberalism, the state and radical protest in the public sphere. (2014).**

[1218] Megan Brennan, *"Americans' Trust in Media Dips to Second Lowest on Record."* https://news.gallup.com/poll/355526/americans-trust-media-dips-second-lowest-record.aspx

[1219] Pitabas Bradhan, Niky Kumari, Aligarh Muslim, *"A study on Journalistic use of social media."* https://amity.edu/UserFiles/asco/journal/ISSUE68_6.%20Pitabas%20%20-%20AJMCS%20Vol%208%20No%201.pdf; Devin J. Christensen, John Lovett and John A. Curiel, *"Mainstream Media Recirculation of Trust-Reducing Social Media Messages."* https://journals.sagepub.com/doi/full/10.1177/1532673X211023931; Nic Neman, *"Mainstream media and the distribution of news in the age of social discovery."* https://ora.ox.ac.uk/catalog/uuid:94164da6-9150-4938-8996-badfdef6b507/
download_file?file_format=application%2Fpdf&safe_filename=Mainstream%2BMedia%2Band%2Bthe%2BDistribution%2Bof%2BNews%2

[1220] Elda Brogi, et al., *"Monitoring Media Pluralism in Europe."* https://cmpf.eui.eu/wp-content/uploads/2018/11/CMPF_MPM2017_FINAL_REPORT.pdf; Beatrice Hibou, *"Economic Crime and Neoliberal Modes of Government: The Example of the Mediterranean."* https://www.researchgate.net/publication/254953831_Economic_Crime_and_Neoliberal_Modes_of_Government_The_Example_of_the_Mediterranean; Teodor Reljic, *"How neoliberal capitalism shaped Tigne Point to sell the Valleta view."* https://www.maltatoday.com.mt/arts/valletta_2018/82339/how_neoliberal_capitalism_shaped_tign_point_to_sell_the_valletta_view#.ZAK1dR9BxD8

[1221] Katerina Eva Matsa, *"Across Western Europe, public news media widely used and trusted."* https://www.pewresearch.org/fact-tank/2018/06/08/western-europe-public-news-media-widely-used-and-trusted/; Art Swift, *"Americans' Trust in Mass Media Sinks to New low."* http://www.gallup.com/poll/195542/americans-trust-mass-media-sinks-new-low.aspx; J. M. Ladd, *"Why is Everyone Mad at the Media?"* http://assets.press.princeton.edu/chapters/s9607.pdf

[1222] Edward S. Herman and Noam Chomsky, *"Manufacturing Consent: Political Economy of the Mass Media."* (1988). http://www.nytimes.com/2016/08/08/business/balance-fairness-and-a-proudly-provocative-presidential-candidate.html?_r=0; Noam Chomsky, *"The New York Times is Pure Propaganda."* https://www.salon.com/2015/05/25/noam_chomsky_the_new_york_times_is_pure_proganda_partner/

[1223] *"Christopher Hitchens Quotes"*, https://www.goodreads.com/author/quotes/3956.

[1224] Lisa Kraege, *"Objectivity and the News: Reexamining Facts, Truth and Fairness."* https://journalism.princeton.edu/2021/02/19/journalists-and-professors-discuss-objectivity-and-the-news/

[1225] Peter Isackson, *"The NY Times: Liberal or Neoliberal?"* https://www.fairobserver.com/region/north_america/peter-isackson-new-york-times-liberal-neo-liberalism-milton-friedman-economics-american-world-news-76916/

[1226] *Jomo Kwame Sundaram, "Milton Freidman's Shareholder Capitalism and its Discontents."* https://www.miamisocialsciences.org/home/a7glsn38uobrz8cog85t2ftzvtlrcg

[1227] John Eggerton, *"Barr Slams 'Totalitarian Democracy' and 'Monolithic Media'."* https://www.nexttv.com/news/barr-slams-totalitarian-democracy-and-monolithic-media

[1228] Asia Society, *"Interview: How India's Media is 'Often Fearless, But Seldom Objective."* https://asiasociety.org/blog/asia/interview-how-indias-media-often-fearless-seldom-objective; Hayashi Kaori, *"Japan's Media: Facing Public Indifference More than Distrust."* https://www.nippon.com/en/currents/d00398/; Mads Damgaard, "*Cascading corruption news: explaining the bias of media attention to Brazil's political scandals.*" https://www.scielo.br/j/op/a/FRgsxyphwkpfFLkmjVVSv6t/?lang=en

[1229] Matt Guardino, *"No One Wants to Change the System as Much as Those who are Trapped by the System."* in *Framing Inequality: News Media, Public Opinion, and the Neoliberal Turn in U.S. Public Policy.* (2019).

[1230] W. Lance Bennett, *"Global Media and Politics."* https://www.annualreviews.org/doi/10.1146/annurev.polisci.7.012003.104804; Rosalind Bresnahan, *"The Media and the Neoliberal Transition in Chile."* https://library.fes.de/libalt/journals/swetsfulltext/18006615.pdf

[1231] Terézia Ronˇcáková, *"Media as Religion"* https://mdpi-res.com/d_attachment/religions/religions-11-00568/article_deploy/religions-11-00568-v3.pdf?version=1604477204; Burton Lee Artz, *"Global Media Practices and Cultural Hegemony."* in *Media, Ideology and Hegemony.* (2018).

[1232] Corina Lotz, Penny Cole, *"Deconstructing Neoliberal Hegemony."* https://www.tandfonline.com/doi/abs/10.1080/10286630500411168?journalCode=gcul20

[1233] **Jacques Ellul, Propaganda: The Formation of Men's Attitudes. (1962); Herbert Marcuse, One Dimensional Man: Studies in the Ideology of Advanced Industrial Society (1964);** Jon Bailes, *Consciousness and the Neoliberal Subject.* (2020); E. Bernays, *"Manipulating Public Opinion."* https://www.semanticscholar.org/paper/Manipulating-Public-Opinion%3A-The-Why-and-The-How-Bernays/726c724946dfa67ef1ad8ed549452993c6c6f484

[1234] Kevin Glynn, *Tabloid Culture.* (2000); Andrew Hoskins, John Tulloch, *"From Tabloids to Broadsheets: A Case Study of "Everyday" and "Premediated" Journalism during the Global Financial Crisis."* in *Risk and Hyperconnectivity: Media and Memories of Neoliberalism.* (2016).

[1235] Lene Bech Sillesen, Chris Ip, and David Uberti, *"Journalism and the Power of Emotions."* https://www.cjr.org/analysis/journalism_and_the_power_of_emotions.php; M.A. Milburn and Ann B. McGrail, *"The Dramatic Presentation of News and Its Effects on Cognitive Complexity."* Political Psychology, 13:4 (1992).

[1236] **Helena Chmielewska-Szlajfer, "What do journalists writing for right-wing tabloids think about their work?"** https://blogs.lse.ac.uk/polis/2017/10/25/what-do-journalists-writing-for-right-wing-tabloids-think-about-their-work-a-new-research-project/; Andy Becket, *"Revenge of the Tabloids."* https://www.theguardian.com/media/2016/oct/27/revenge-of-the-tabloids-brexit-dacre-murdoch; Bethany Usher, *"Tabloidism, television and the neoliberal soap opera."* in Bethany Usher, ed. *Journalism and Celebrity*. (2020).

[1237] P. David Marshall, *"When the private becomes public: commodity activism, endorsement, and making meaning in a privatised world"* in P. David Marshall, et al., eds., *Contemporary publics: shifting boundaries in new media, technology and culture.* (2016); Shrija Agrawal, *"How self-commodification is becoming the future of ecommerce."* https://www.livemint.com/industry/retail/how-self-commodification-is-becoming-the-future-of-ecommerce-11611585413486.html; Goran Bolin, *"Media Use and the Extended Commodification of the Lifeworld."* In Paško Bilić, Jaka Primorac and Bjarki Valtýsson, eds., *Technologies and Labour and the Politics of Contradictions.* (2018).

[1238] **Justin Lewis, *Beyond Consumer Capitalism: Media and the Limits to Imagination.* (2013); Rutger Claassen, *"Communication as Commodity: Should the Media be on the Market?"* https://www.academia.edu/510240/Communication_as_Commodity_Should_the_Media_be_on_the_Market; Robert W. Gehl and Sean T. Lawson, *Social Engineering: How Crowdmasters, Phreaks, Hackers, and Trolls Created a New Form of Manipulative Communication.* (2022).**

[1239] Joe Concha, *"US just finished dead last in media trust among 46 countries in media trust."* https://thehill.com/opinion/international/560480-us-finishes-dead-last-in-media-trust-among-46-countries-heres-why; Allen Able, *"America is deeply divided - and some say another civil war is a possibility."* https://www.macleans.ca/society/america-is-deeply-divided-and-some-say-its-only-going-to-get-worse/; Barbara F. Walter, *"Trump Could Still Lead the US to Civil War."* https://time.com/6141468/trump-us-civil-war/

[1240] https://www.foxnews.com/media/gallup-poll-media-distrust-us-political-divide; Megan Brenan, *"Americans' Trust in Media Dips Second Lowest on Record."* https://news.gallup.com/poll/355526/americans-trust-media-dips-second-lowest-record.aspx

[1241] Jeff Sparrow, *"The grotesque inequality embodied by Musk, Bezos and Zuckerberg is a threat to democracy,"* https://www.theguardian.com/commentisfree/2022/nov/18/the-grotesque-inequality-embodied-by-musk-bezos-and-zuckerberg-is-a-threat-to-democracy

[1242] Karl Thompson, *"The postmodernist tmodel of audience effects."* https://revisesociology.com/2019/10/30/postmodern-theory-media-audience/[256]; Pratap Antony, *"The Truth About our Acceptance of Manufactured Truth."* https://countercurrents.org/2017/02/

the-truth-about-our-acceptance-of-manufactured-truth/; Toby Miller and Pal Ahlu, *"Neoliberalism and the Manufacture of Truth."* https://www.tandfonline.com/doi/full/10.1080/13504630.2021.1896447

[1243] Philip Mirowski, *"Neoliberalism: The Movement That Dare Not Speak Its Name."* https://americanaffairsjournal.org/2018/02/neoliberalism-movement-dare-not-speak-name/

[1244] Saif Shahin, *"News, Nations, and Power Relations: How Neoliberal Media Reproduce a Hierarchical World Order."* https://journals.sagepub.com/doi/10.1177/08969205211072455

[1245] Amar Diwakar, *"Our 'post-truth' era goes back further than you think."* https://www.trtworld.com/magazine/our-post-truth-era-goes-back-further-than-you-think-53660; Ryan Cooper, *"Facebook's Monstrous Empire."* https://theweek.com/tech/1004986/facebooks-monstrous-empire; https://www.theguardian.com/technology/2018/sep/30/facebook-zuckerberg-empire-instagram-whatsapp-antitrust

[1246] Adrienne LaFrance, *"The Largest Autocracy on Earth."* https://www.theatlantic.com/magazine/archive/2021/11/facebook-authoritarian-hostile-foreign-power/620168/

[1247] Serena Bhandari, *"Facebook and media accountability: a tale of power, politics and ignorant entrepreneurs."* https://medium.com/@saibhandari/facebook-and-media-accountability-a-tale-of-power-politics-and-ignorant-entrepreneurs-f5c252a42eab; https://www.statista.com/statistics/271258/facebooks-advertising-revenue-worldwide/; Alex Cranz and Russell Brandom, *"Facebook encourages hate speech for profit."* https://www.theverge.com/2021/10/3/22707860/facebook-whistleblower-leaked-documents-files-regulation

[1248] Angshuman Choudhury *"How Facebook is Complicit in Myanmar's Attacks on Minorities."* https://thediplomat.com/2020/08/how-facebook-is-complicit-in-myanmars-attacks-on-minorities/Alexandra Stevenson, *"Facebook Admits it was used to Incite Violence in Myanmar."* https://www.nytimes.com/2018/11/06/technology/myanmar-facebook.html; Craig Tiberg, Elizabeth Dwoskin and Reed Albergotti, *"Inside Facebook: Jan. 6 violence fueled anger over missed warning signs."* https://www.washingtonpost.com/technology/2021/10/22/jan-6-capitol-riot-facebook/; Brian Feldman, *'Facebook has Always Been Right Wing Media.'* https://www.vice.com/en/article/n7vvwq/facebook-has-always-been-right-wing-media

[1249] Ben Norton, *"Facebook censors journalist Seymour Hersh report on Nord Stream pipeline attack."* https://mronline.org/2023/04/26/facebook-censors-journalist-seymour-hershs-report-on-nord-stream-pipeline-attack/?utm_source=rss&utm_medium=rss&utm_campaign=facebook-censors-journalist-seymour-hershs-report-on-nord-stream-pipeline-attack

---

256. https://d.docs.live.net/eb41a1b69e1e6e00/Desktop/Karl%20Thompson,

[1250] Linette Lopez, *"Facebook's algorithm is a sociopath and Facebook is too greedy to stop it."* https://www.businessinsider.com/facebook-algorithm-socopath-management-too-greedy-to-stop-it-2020-5

[1251] Pat Garofalo, *"Facebook's tax breakage thoroughly undeserved. But local governments think they are worth it."* https://www.nbcnews.com/think/opinion/facebook-s-tax-breaks-are-thoroughly-undeserved-local-governments-think-ncna1004561; Marian Myers, *Neoliberalism and the Media.* (2019); Sean Phelan, *Neoliberalism, Media and the Political.* (2014); https://www.investopedia.com/articles/personal-finance/051815/top-11-companies-owned-facebook.asp; https://researchoutreach.org/articles/hate-speech-regulation-social-media-intractable-contemporary-challenge/; Zachary Laub, *"Hate Speech on Social Media."* https://www.cfr.org/backgrounder/hate-speech-social-media-global-comparisons; Branko Marcetic *"Facebook Harms its Users Because That's Where the Profits Are."* https://jacobinmag.com/2021/10/facebook-whistleblower-haugen-profits-addiction-public-utility-regulation-censorship-moderation-zuckerberg

[1252] October Karreman, *"Out of bounds: how media monopolies keep radical ideas off the agenda."* https://www.peoplesworld.org/article/out-of-bounds-how-media-monopolies-keep-radical-ideas-off-the-agenda/

[1253] Max Fisher, *"Disinformation for Hire, a Shadow Industry, Is Quietly Booming."* https://www.nytimes.com/2021/07/25/world/europe/disinformation-social-media.html

[1254] Rafael Grohmann and Jonathan Corpus Ong, *"Disinformation-for-Hire and Click Farming around the World: Identities, Incentives, Infrastructures."* https://journals.sagepub.com/pb-assets/CfP-Disinformation-for-Hire-FINAL%20(002)-1628175552.pdf

[1255] Max Zahn and Andy Sewer, *"AOC: Facebook sabotaged the global response with disinformation."* https://news.yahoo.com/aoc-facebook-sabotaged-the-global-covid-response-with-misinformation-180254381.html; Human Rights Watch, *"Israel/Palestine: Facebook Censors Discussion of Rights Issues."* https://www.hrw.org/news/2021/10/08/israel/palestine-facebook-censors-discussion-rights-issues; Angelo Carusone, *"Facebook and Twitter don't censor conservatives. They hire and promote them."* https://www.nbcnews.com/think/opinion/facebook-twitter-don-t-censor-conservatives-they-hire-promote-them-ncna1245308

[1256] **Brian Dean, "Social Network Usage and Growth Statistics." https://backlinko.com/social-media-users; Osman Ulvi "Social Media Use and Mental Health: A Global Analysis." https://mdpi-res.com/d_attachment/epidemiologia/epidemiologia-03-00002/article_deploy/epidemiologia-03-00002.pdf?version=1641905768**

[1257] Rachel Badham, *"The Neoliberal Side of Social Media."* https://thebadgeronline.com/2019/03/neoliberal-side-social-media/

[1258] L. Allan Furr, Wayne Usui, Vicky Hines-Martin, *"Authoritarianism and Attitudes Toward Mental Health Services."* https://www.researchgate.net/publication/9016817_Authoritarianism_and_Attitudes_Toward_Mental_Health_Services; Jessica Stern, Megan K.

McBride, *"Three Factors Drive Rightwing Violence."* https://time.com/6178689/violence-extremism-how-to-stop/

[1259] **Interview with Jacques Rancière[257] by Mathieu Dejean and Jean-Marc Lalanne, "*The Issue is to manage to maintain dissensus.*" https://www.versobooks.com/blogs/5132-jacques-ranciere-the-issue-is-to-manage-to-maintain-dissensus; John Bone, "*Neoliberal precarity and primalization: A biosocial perspective on the age of insecurity, injustice, and unreason.*" British Journal of Sociology. 72, 4 (2021); Gil Appel[258], Lauren Grewal[259], Rhonda Hadi[260] & Andrew T. Stephen[261], "*The future of social media in marketing.*" https://link.springer.com/article/10.1007/s11747-019-00695-1; DMI, "*SocialMedia.*" https://digitalmarketinginstitute.com/blog/social-media-what-countries-use-it-most-and-what-are-they-using**

[1260] Alan Finlayson, *"Neoliberalism the Alt-Right and the Intellectual Dark Web."* https://journals.sagepub.com/doi/full/10.1177/02632764211036731

[1261] Carolina Caiero, *"Bolsonaro's social media plan shows his election worry."* https://www.chathamhouse.org/2021/09/bolsonaros-social-media-plan-shows-his-election-worry; Marina Alina Asavei, *"Radical right populist entrepreneurs and the use of religious representations through popular culture: George Becali as the 'Saviour of Romania"* https://journals.sagepub.com/doi/10.1177/1367549420973205

[1262] Zach Bauchamp, *"Social media is rotting democracy from within."* https://www.vox.com/policy-and-politics/2019/1/22/18177076/social-media-facebook-far-right-authoritarian-populism

[1263] Jenni Frazer, *"The reason social media companies tolerate hate? Profit."* https://www.jewishnews.co.uk/meet-the-man-trying-to-drive-antisemitism-offline/

[1264] Jeffrey Gottfried and Elisa Shearer, *"New use across social media platforms."* http://www.journalism.org/2016/05/26/news-use-across-social-media-platforms-2016/

[1265] Lois Beckett, *"Yes, Companies Are Harvesting and Selling your Social Media Porfiles."* https://www.propublica.org/article/yes-companies-are-harvesting-and-selling-your-social-media-profiles; Christopher Boyd, *"How social media platforms mine personal data."* https://blog.malwarebytes.com/privacy-2/2020/04/how-social-media-mine-data-sell-personal-information-for-profit/; Zak Doffman *"Your social media is (probably) being watched right now."* https://www.forbes.com/sites/zakdoffman/2019/11/06/new-government-spy-report-your-social-media-is-probably-being-watched-right-now/?sh=1d2e54f99a43

---

257. https://www.versobooks.com/authors/194-jacques-ranciere

258. https://link.springer.com/article/10.1007/s11747-019-00695-1#auth-Gil-Appel

259. https://link.springer.com/article/10.1007/s11747-019-00695-1#auth-Lauren-Grewal

260. https://link.springer.com/article/10.1007/s11747-019-00695-1#auth-Rhonda-Hadi

261. https://link.springer.com/article/10.1007/s11747-019-00695-1#auth-Andrew_T_-Stephen

[1266] Kalliopi Kyriakopoulou, *"Authoritarian states and internet social media: Instruments of democratisation or instruments of control?"* https://www.degruyter.com/document/doi/10.2478/s13374-011-0003-y/html?lang=en

[1267] Daniel Gayo-Avello, *"Social Media and Authoritarianism."* Social Science Research Network (2015).

[1268] Mary Serumaga, *"Uganda since 1986: Museveni, the World Bank and the Coming of Neoliberalism."* https://www.theelephant.info/op-eds/2019/01/27/uganda-since-1986-museveni-the-world-bank-and-the-coming-of-neoliberalism/; Oryem Nyeko, *"Uganda's Troubling Social Media Tax."* https://www.hrw.org/news/2018/07/02/ugandas-troubling-social-media-tax; World Bank Group, *"Digital Solutions in a Time of Crisis."* https://thedocs.worldbank.org/en/doc/61714f214ed04bcd6e9623ad0e215897-0400012021/related/Uganda-Economic-Update-Fifteenth-Edition.pdf; Juliet Nanfuka, *"How Social Media Taxes Can Buren News Outlets: The Case of Uganda."* https://www.cima.ned.org/publication/how-social-media-taxes-can-burden-news-outlets-the-case-of-uganda/; Daniel Mwesigwa, *"Uganda."* https://cipesa.org/2021/07/uganda-abandons-social-media-tax-but-slaps-new-levy-on-internet-data/

[1269] Nita Bhalla, *"Digital authoritarianism threatening basic rights in Africa."* https://www.reuters.com/article/us-rights-privacy-africa-trfn/digital-authoritarianism-threatening-basic-rights-in-africa-study-says-idUSKBN2AW0YS; https://www.statista.com/statistics/269329/penetration-rate-of-the-internet-by-region/

[1270] Qi Jiang, Yanli Chen, Tianjun Sun, *"Government social media and corporate tax avoidance."* https://www.sciencedirect.com/science/article/pii/S175530912300014X

[1271] Nimi Pricewill and Stephanie Busari, *"Nigeria bans Twitter after company deletes President Buhari's tweet."* https://edition.cnn.com/2021/06/04/africa/nigeria-suspends-twitter-operations-intl/index.html Ruth Maclean, *"Nigeria Lifts 7-Month Ban on Twitter."* https://www.nytimes.com/2022/01/13/world/africa/nigeria-lifts-twitter-ban.html.

[1272] Laurie Clarke and Katharine Swindles, *"How social media companies help authoritarian governments censor the internet."* https://www.newstatesman.com/science-tech/2021/06/how-social-media-companies-help-authoritarian-governments-censor-internet

[1273] Nooran Alhmadan and Eliza Campbell, *"How Social Media is Failing Palestinians."* https://www.mei.edu/publications/how-social-media-failing-palestinians;https://www.amnesty.org/en/latest/campaigns/2022/02/israels-system-of-apartheid/; Omar Zahzah, *"Palestinians being silenced on social media."* https://www.aljazeera.com/opinions/2021/5/13/social-media-companies-are-trying-to-silence-palestinian-voices

[1274] Maha Nassar, *"US media talks a lot about Palestinians — just without Palestinians."* **https://www.972mag.com/us-media-palestinians/**

[1275] Yara Hawari, *"UN report confirms that Israel is guilty of apartheid and endorses BDS."* https://www.opendemocracy.net/en/north-africa-west-asia/un-report-confirms-that-israel-is-guilty-of-apartheid-and-endorses-bds/

[1276] Vivian Yee and Mona El-Naggar, *"Social Media is the Mass Protest: Solidarity with Palestinian grows online."* https://www.nytimes.com/2021/05/18/world/middleeast/palestinians-social-media.html; **Nooran Alhamdan and Eliza Campbell "How social media is failing Palestinians." https://www.mei.edu/publications/how-social-media-failing-palestinians**

[1277] Paul Barrett, Justin Hendrix and Grant Sims, *"How tech platforms fuel US political polarization and what government can do about it."* https://www.brookings.edu/blog/techtank/2021/09/27/how-tech-platforms-fuel-u-s-political-polarization-and-what-government-can-do-about-it/

[1278]**Gustave Le Bon, *The Crowd: A Study of the Popular Mind and Mass Formation*. (2022).**

[1279] Eli Cook, *"How Money Became the Measure of Everything."* https://www.theatlantic.com/business/archive/2017/10/money-measure-everything-pricing-progress/543345/; Briana Thomas, *"Unfortunate definition of success in society."* https://coppellstudentmedia.com/68779/opinions/the-unfortunate-definition-of-success-in-society/; R. J. Rienhart, *"Americans' Perceptions of Success in the US."* https://news.gallup.com/opinion/gallup/266927/americans-perceptions-success.aspx

[1280] Nick Couldry and Clemencia Rodriguez, *"Why the media is a key dimension in global inequality."* https://theconversation.com/why-the-media-is-a-key-dimension-of-global-inequality-69084

[1281] Des Freedman Daya Kishan Thussu, *Media and Terrorism: Global Perspective*; Bonnie Honnig, *Emergency Politics: Paradox, Law, Democracy*; Pippa Norris, Montague Kern, Marion Just, eds., *Framing Terrorism: The News Media, the Government and the Public.* (2003); Douglas Kellner, *Media Spectacle and the Crisis of Democracy: Terrorism, War, and Election Battles.* (2005).

[1282] Francesco Petricone, *"Social Media and the Post-Truth World Order: The Global Dynamics of Disinformation."* https://www.tandfonline.com/doi/full/10.1080/23753234.2021.1945936

[1283] Mark Scott and Lawrence Cerulus, *"Europe's populists are flooding social media, research shows."* https://www.politico.eu/article/europe-far-right-groups-noisier-than-others-on-twitter-research-shows-afd-germany-facebook-google-alto-analytics/; Laura Alonson-Munoz and Andreu Casero-Ripolles, *"Populism Against Europe in Social Media: The Eurosceptic Discourse on Twitter in Spain, Italy, France, and United Kingdom During the Campaign of the 2019 European Parliament Election."* https://www.frontiersin.org/articles/10.3389/fcomm.2020.00054/full; Claire Snyder-Hall and Cynthia Burack, eds., *Right-Wing Populism and the Media.* (2014); Daniele Albatazzi and Duncan McDonnell, *Twenty-First Century Populism: The Specter of Western European Democracy.* (2008).

[1284] Lilith Mahmud, *"We Have Never Been Liberal: Occidentalist Myths and the Impending Fascist Apocalypse."* https://culanth.org/fieldsights/we-have-never-been-liberal-occidentalist-myths-and-the-impending-fascist-apocalypse; Ben Witham, *"It's no surprise liberal democracy is giving way to authoritarianism."* https://theconversation.com/its-no-surprise-liberal-democracy-is-giving-way-to-authoritarianism-174509

[1285] Jonathan Mahler and Jim Rutenberg, *"How Rupert Murdoch's Empire of Influence Remade the World."* https://www.nytimes.com/interactive/2019/04/03/magazine/rupert-murdoch-fox-news-trump.html

[1286] Joe Allen, *"The Fall of Citizen Murdoch."* https://socialistworker.org/2011/07/20/fall-of-citizen-murdoch.

[1287] Bernd Debusmann Jr., *"After $787.5m Dominion settlement, what's next for Fox?"* https://www.bbc.com/news/world-us-canada-65328457; Alvaro de Miranda, *"The Death and Rebirth of 'Class War' (1979-2012) + Class War in Post-World War II Historical Perspective."* https://www.researchgate.net/publication/319354406_The_Death_and_Re-birth_of_%27Class_War%27_1979-2012_Class_War_in_PostWorld_War_II_Historical_Perspective; Barney Warf, *"Oligopolization of Global Media and Telecommunications and its Implications for Democracy."* https://www.researchgate.net/publication/228630234_Oligopolization_of_Global_Media_and_Telecommunications_and_its_Implications_for_Democracy; Bulent Kenes, *"Rupert Murdoch: A Populist Emperor of the Fourth Estate."* https://www.populismstudies.org/rupert-murdoch-a-populist-emperor-of-the-fourth-estate/

[1288] David Silito, *"Donald Trump: How the media created the president."* https://www.bbc.com/news/entertainment-arts-37952249; Charlie Becket, *"What does the Trump triumph mean for journalism, politics and social media?"* https://blogs.lse.ac.uk/polis/2016/11/13/what-does-the-trump-triumph-mean-for-journalism-politics-and-social-media/

[1289] Michael Sainato, *"Liberal Mainstream Media Continues Blacking out Progressives, Hires Conservatives."* https://observer.com/2017/05/mainstream-media-hires-conservatives-lacks-progressives/

[1290] Tim Groseclose[262], *"Left Turn: How Liberal Media Bias Distorts the American Mind."* (2012).

[1291] Jianing Li and Min-HsinSu, *"Real Talk About Fake News: Identity Language and Disconnected Networks of the US Public's "Fake News" Discourse on Twitter."* https://journals.sagepub.com/doi/full/10.1177/2056305120916841

[1292] Savaş Çoban[263], *"Hegemony, Ideology, Media"* in Savaş Çoban[264], ed. *Media, Ideology and Hegemony.* (2018).

262. https://www.amazon.com/s/ref=dp_byline_sr_book_1?ie=UTF8&field-author=Tim+Groseclose+PhD&text=Tim+Groseclose+PhD&sort=relevancerank&search-alias=books

263. https://brill.com/search?f_0=author&q_0=Sava%C5%9F+%C3%87oban

264. https://brill.com/search?f_0=author&q_0=Sava%C5%9F+%C3%87oban

[1293]; Walker Bragman, *"The Sad Decline of VOX: How a once Promising Media Outlet Became a Bastion of Neoliberal Corporatism."* https://www.pastemagazine.com/politics/vox/the-sad-decline-of-vox-how-a-once-promising-media/; https://www.patreon.com/fairnessandaccuracyinreporting; https://mediabiasfactcheck.com/accuracy-in-media-aim/

[1294] **Nouf Alhouzami, *"Social Media and Interculturality: Promise, Threat, or Mirror."* https://www.researchgate.net/publication/347588326_Social_Media_and_Interculturality_Promise_Threat_or_Mirror; Mita Bandyopadhyay, *"Literature in the changing socio-cultural milieu: From digital humanities to digital media."* https://www.researchgate.net/publication/318777507_Literature_in_the_changing_socio-cultural_milieu_From_digital_humanities_to_digital_media; Jan Servaes and Toks Oyedemi, eds. *Social Inequalities, Media and Communication.* (2016).**

[1295] Burton Lee Artz, *"Global Media Practices and Cultural Hegemony: Growing, Harvesting, and Marketing the Consuming Audience"* in Burton Lee Artz, *Media, Ideology and Hegemony.* (2018).

[1296] **Jürgen Habermas, *"The Structural Transformation of the Public Sphere: An Inquiry into a Category of Bourgeois Society"* (1962).**

[1297] Julio C. Teehankee, *"Authoritarian contamination after EDSA."* https://www.rappler.com/voices/thought-leaders/analysis-authoritarian-contamination-post-edsa-people-power-political-parties/; Angelos Giannakopoulos, *"Introduction: Media, Freedom and Democracy. Fundamental Aspects Retold."* Angelos Giannakopoulos, ed., *Media, Freedom of Speech, and Democracy in the EU and Beyond.* https://europeanjournalists.org/wp-content/uploads/2019/07/Media-Freedom-of-Speech-and-Democracy-min.pdf

[1298] Paul Rutherford, *Endless Propaganda: the advertising of public goods.* (2000).

[1299] Valentine Roux and Marie-Agnes Courty, *"Introduction to Discontinuities and Continuities."* https://www.researchgate.net/publication/257577985_Introduction_to_Discontinuities_and_Continuities_Theories_Methods_and_Proxies_for_a_Historical_and_Sociological_Appro Alex Carey, *"The Ideological Management Industry."* https://www.scribd.com/document/303377018/Alex-Carey-The-Ideological-Management-Industry#

[1300] C. J. Polychroniou, *"Noam Chomsky. We're on the Road to a Form of Neofascism."* https://www.globalpolicyjournal.com/blog/09/12/2022/noam-chomsky-were-road-form-neofascism

[1301] Euronews, *"Trade union workers march across France in protest against rising cost of living."* https://www.euronews.com/my-europe/2022/11/10/trade-union-workers-march-across-france-in-protest-over-rising-cost-of-living; Thomas Scripps, *"How the trade unions suppressed the class struggle during UK's "Summer of Discontent."* https://www.wsws.org/en/articles/2022/09/16/plga-s16.html;

"Lebanon and Sri Lanka share economic collapse." https://en.qantara.de/content/which-country-will-be-next-lebanon-and-sri-lanka-share-economic-collapse

[1302] Louis Althusser, *On the Reproduction of Capitalism: Ideology and Ideological State Apparatuses.* (2014); Antonio Gramsci, *Prison Notebooks.* (2011).

[1303] Saif Shahin, *"News, Nations, and Power Relations: How Neoliberal Media Reproduce a Hierarchical World Order."* https://journals.sagepub.com/doi/full/10.1177/08969205211072455

[1304] UNCTAD, *"UNCTAD and WTO: A Common Goal in a Global Economy."* https://unctad.org/press-material/unctad-and-wto-common-goal-global-economy

[1305] David Singh Grewal, *"Three Theses on the Current Crisis of International Liberalism."* https://www.researchgate.net/publication/325182873_Three_Theses_on_the_Current_Crisis_of_International_Liberalism

[1306] A. J. Hurrell, *"Pax Americana or the Empire of Insecurity?"* https://www.researchgate.net/publication/249284721_Pax_Americana_or_the_empire_of_insecurity; Dominique Plihon, El Mouhoub Mouhoud, *Le savoir et la finance. Liaisons dangereuses au coeur du capitalisme contemporain.* (2009); Yann Moulier-Boutang, *Le Capitalisme Cognitif: La Nouvelle Grande Transformation.* (2008); William I. Robinson, *"Giovanni Arrighi: Systemic Cycles of Accumulation, Hegemonic Transitions, and the Rise of China."* https://escholarship.org/content/qt34b5s46w/qt34b5s46w.pdf?t=lfbx87&v=lg

[1307] Julian E. Zelizer, *"The Nation: Guns and Butter; Government Can Run More than a War."* https://www.nytimes.com/2001/12/30/weekinreview/the-nation-guns-and-butter-government-can-run-more-than-a-war.html; Mary Hawksworth, *"Neoliberalism and the Micropolitics of Domination in the United States."* In L. Macdonald and A. Ruckert, *Post-neoliberalism in the Americas.* (2009).

[1308] James M. Cypher, *"From Military Keynesianism to Global Neoliberal Militarism."* https://monthlyreview.org/2007/06/01/from-military-keynesianism-to-global-neoliberal-militarism/; https://tradingeconomics.com/united-states/government-debt-to-gdp; https://www.bea.gov/news/blog/2022-03-24/us-current-account-deficit-widens-2021

[1309] Kiron K. Skinner, *"Margaret Thatcher led in fighting terrorism."* https://edition.cnn.com/2013/04/11/opinion/skinner-thatcher-terrorism/index.html; https://www.jstor.org/stable/24361630

[1310] Walden Bello, *"Short-lived legacy: Margaret Thatcher, neoliberalism and the Global South."* https://www.theguardian.com/global-development/poverty-matters/2013/apr/16/legacy-margaret-thatcher-neoliberalism

[1311] Darya Sinusoid, *"How the Falklands War Brought Neoliberalism to the UK."* https://www.shortform.com/blog/neoliberalism-uk/

[1312] Gordon Lafer, *"Neoliberalism by Other Means: The War on Terror at Home and Abroad."* https://www.researchgate.net/publication/248966674_Neoliberalism_by_Other_Means_The_War_on_Terror_at_Home_and_Abroad; Charlotte Heath-Kelly, Christopher Baker-Beall, Lee Jarvis, eds. *Neoliberalism and Terror.* (2018)

[1313] Catherine Besteman and Stephanie Savell, *"Global Expansion of Post-9/11 Wars."* https://watson.brown.edu/costsofwar/costs/social/global-expansion

[1314] Jeff Halper, *War Against the People: Israel, the Palestinians and Global Pacification*. (2015).

[1315] Andy Clarno, *Neoliberal Apartheid: Palestine/Israel .and South Africa.* (2017).

[1316] Arie Krampf, *"Israel's Neoliberal Turn and its National Security Paradigm."* Polish Political Science Yearbook, 47:2, (2018); J. F. Getzoff, *"Start-up Nationalism: The Rationalities of neoliberal Zionism."* https://www.semanticscholar.org/paper/Start-up-nationalism%3A-The-rationalities-of-Zionism Getzoff/670fde24a8e6be8d592fb91e13ab4d17ba915265[265]; Ryan Waters and Cory Blad, *"In the Land of Whose People? Inequality, Neoliberalism, and Shifting Nationalisms in Israel."* https://www.sociostudies.org/almanac/articles/in_the_land_of_whose/

[1317] Tad DeHaven, *"Republicans Join Democrats to Save Corporate Welfare (Again)."* https://www.cato.org/blog/republicans-join-democrats-save-corporate-welfare-again; George Leef, *"Corporate Welfare Is Terrible Policy, But Democrats and Republicans Do it Anyway."* https://www.forbes.com/sites/georgeleef/2015/05/15/corporate-welfare-is-terrible-policy-but-democrats-and-republicans-do-it-anyway/

[1318] **Helsinki Times, *"China world leader in 37 out of 44 critical technologies, Finland out of chart[266]"* https://www.helsinkitimes.fi/themes/themes/science-and-technology/23435-china-world-leader-in-37-out-of-44-critical-technologies-finland-out-of-chart.html; Tom Porter, *"The Saudi crown prince wants to build a trillion-dollar utopia in the desert. His deals with China reveal a darker vision."* https://www.yahoo.com/news/saudi-crown-prince-wants-build-081700837.html; REUTERS, *"Saudi Arabia Seeks Cooperation with China, 'Ignores' Western Worries."* https://www.voanews.com/a/saudi-arabia-seeks-cooperation-with-china-ignores-western-worries/7132507.html.**

[1319] Reuters, *"Israeli minister reassures US over Chinese telecom investment."* https://www.reuters.com/article/us-israel-china-usa-idUSKCN1PC0ZX

[1320] Casey Babb, *"Proceed with Caution: Israeli Research Collaboration with China."* https://www.inss.org.il/publication/academic-relations-china/

---

265. https://www.semanticscholar.org/paper/Start-up-nationalism%3A-The-rationalities-of-Zionism%20Getzoff/670fde24a8e6be8d592fb91e13ab4d17ba915265

266. https://www.helsinkitimes.fi/themes/themes/science-and-technology/23435-china-world-leader-in-37-out-of-44-critical-technologies-finland-out-of-chart.html

[1321] European Parliament, *"The EU chips act: Securing Europe's supply of semiconductors."* https://www.europarl.europa.eu/RegData/etudes/BRIE/2022/733596/EPRS-Briefing-733596-EU-chips-act-V2-FINAL.pdf; https://commission.europa.eu/strategy-and-policy/priorities-2019-2024/europe-fit-digital-age/european-chips-act_en; PWC, *"The CHIPS Act."* https://www.pwc.com/us/en/library/chips-act.html

[1322] Anton Shilov, *"China Retaliates: Restricts Vital Chipmaking Materials Gallium and Germanium."* https://www.yahoo.com/lifestyle/china-retaliates-restricts-vital-chipmaking-155120380.html

[1323] Michael Roberts, *"Modern supply-side economics and the New Washington Consensus."* https://mronline.org/2023/06/13/modern-supply-side-economics-and-the-new-washington-consensus/?utm_source=rss&utm_medium=rss&utm_campaign=modern-supply-side-economics-and-the-new-washington-consensus

[1324] Kevin Farnsworth and Zoe Irving, *"The 2008 crisis failed to displace neoliberalism's core principles."* https://blogs.lse.ac.uk/usappblog/2019/02/09/the-2008-crisis-failed-to-displace-neoliberalisms-core-principles/; Barney Warf, *"The Coronavirus Pandemic and American Neoliberalism."* https://www.tandfonline.com/doi/pdf/10.1080/00167428.2021.1884981; Joseph Stiglitz, *"Shock Therapy for Neoliberals."* https://www.project-syndicate.org/commentary/russia-war-covid-global-shocks-reveal-bankruptcy-of-neoliberalism-by-joseph-e-stiglitz-2022-04?barrier=accesspaylog; The Straits Times, *"Japan minister calls for new world order to counter rise of authoritarian regimes."* https://www.straitstimes.com/world/united-states/japan-minister-calls-for-new-world-order-to-counter-rise-of-authoritarian-regimes

[1325] Amitava Krishna Dutt and Peter Skott, *"Keynesian Theory and the Aggregate-Supply/Aggregate-Demand Framework: A Defense."* Eastern Economic Journal, 22:3, (1993); Amir Hussain, "*From MDGs to SDGs.*" https://www.thenews.com.pk/print/851530-from-mdgs-to-sdgs; Michael Schwartz, *"Military Neoliberalism: Endless War and Humanitarian Crisis."* https://scholarlycommons.law.case.edu/cgi/viewcontent.cgi?article=1100&context=swb

[1326] David M. Kotz, *The Rise and Fall of Neoliberal Capitalism.* (2017).

[1327] Guy Standing, *"The Neoliberal Origins of Russia's War."* https://progressiveeconomyforum.com/blog/the-neoliberal-origins-of-russias-war/; Franklin Foer, *"The New Washington Consensus."* https://www.theatlantic.com/ideas/archive/2023/05/biden-economics-industrial-policy-trump-nationalism/673988/

[1328] Kai Ryssdal and Andi Corban, *"How Russian sanctions could speed up the corrosion of globalization."* https://www.marketplace.org/2022/03/23/how-russian-sanctions-could-speed-up-the-corrosion-of-globalization/; Esfandyar Batmanghelidj and Francisco Rodriguez *"The Danger of Sanctions."* https://www.noemamag.com/the-danger-of-sanctions/; Ira Kalish, *"How sanctions impact Russia and the global economy."* https://www2.deloitte.com/us/en/insights/economy/global-economic-impact-of-sanctions-on-russia.html

[1329] Paul Gifford, *"The Hybrid Model at the Heart of a Vibrant New China"* in Paul Gifford, *The China Paradox.* (2017); Jukka Aukia, *"China as a hybrid influencer: Non-state actors as state proxies."* https://www.hybridcoe.fi/wp-content/uploads/2021/06/20210616_Hybrid_CoE_Research_Report_1_China_as_a_hybrid_influencer_Non_state_actors_as_state_proxies_WEB.pdf; Miloš Šumonja[267], *"Neoliberalism is not dead – On political implications of Covid-19"* https://journals.sagepub.com/doi/full/10.1177/0309816820982381; Craig Stirling, *"Weaponizing Dollar Risks Echo of Sterling's Decline, Study Says."* https://www.bnnbloomberg.ca/weaponizing-dollar-risks-echo-of-sterling-s-decline-study-says-1.1596920

[1330] Cedric Durand, *"1979 in Reverse."* https://newleftreview.org/sidecar/posts/1979-in-reverse

[1331] Kate Hudson, *"The Problem with the G-7."* https://cnduk.org/the-problem-with-the-g7/

[1332] James M. Cypher, *"The Political Economy of Systemic US Militarism."* https://monthlyreview.org/2022/04/01/the-political-economy-of-systemic-u-s-militarism-2/

[1333] Michael Schwartz, *"Military Neoliberalism: Endless War and Humanitarian Crisis in the Twenty-First Century."* https://scholarlycommons.law.case.edu/cgi/viewcontent.cgi?article=1100&context=swb; Francesca Lucia Bray, *"The American Military Industrial Complex."* https://core.ac.uk/download/322535234.pdf; Robert Higgs, *"Profits of US Defense Contractors."*

https://www.independent.org/publications/article.asp?id=129

[1334] Joseph Daher, *"Lebanon: How the Post War's Political Economy Led to the Current Economic and Social Crisis."* https://cadmus.eui.eu/bitstream/handle/1814/73856/QM-01-22-031-EN-N.pdf; https://www.macrotrends.net/countries/LBN/lebanon/military-spending-defense-budget; https://www.macrotrends.net/countries/LKA/sri-lanka/military-spending-defense-budget

[1335] Edward Luce, *"The New Washington Consensus."* https://www.ft.com/content/42922712-cd33-4de0-8763-1cc271331a32

267. https://journals.sagepub.com/doi/full/10.1177/0309816820982381

[1336] **Dennyza Gabiella, *"How Does Neo-Liberalism Explain the Likelihood of China's Threat towards United States' Global Hegemony in the 21st Century?"* https://media.neliti.com/media/publications/70556-EN-how-does-neo-liberalism-explain-the-like.pdf; *"Japan approves 2023 draft budget at $862 billion with record defense allocation."* https://www.business-standard.com/article/international/japan-approves-2023-draft-budget-at-862-bn-with-record-defence-allocation-122122300762_1.html; *"Remarks by National Security Advisor Jake Sullivan on Renewing American Economic Leadership at the Brookings Institution."* https://www.whitehouse.gov/briefing-room/speeches-remarks/2023/04/27/remarks-by-national-security-advisor-jake-sullivan-on-renewing-american-economic-leadership-at-the-brookings-institution/**

[1337] Abdul Wasay Ajmal, *"Neo-Confucian and Neo-Liberal school of thought: A study of US-China Economic systems."* https://moderndiplomacy.eu/2022/01/03/neo-confucian-and-neo-liberal-school-of-thought-a-study-of-u-s-china-economic-systems/

[1338] Ian Yuying Liu, "*The Chinese Dream, Neoliberalism, and International Legal Ideology*." https://brill.com/view/journals/cjgg/4/2/article-p81_1.xml?language=en

[1339] Gearoid Reidy, *"Japan's Standing is Rising: Not so its Leader's."* https://www.washingtonpost.com/business/japans-standing-is-rising-not-so-its-leaders/2023/01/12/2f1f21a0-92c3-11ed-90f8-53661ac5d9b9_story.html; Xinhua, *"China Focus: China to lower defense budget growth to 7.5 percent."*http://www.xinhuanet.com/english/2019-03/05/c_137871426.htm

[1340] Michael Cunningham, *"China's Taiwan Policy in 2023."* https://globaltaiwan.org/2023/01/chinas-taiwan-policy-in-2023/

[1341] **Al Jazeera, *"China beating West in race for critical technologies, report says."* https://www.aljazeera.com/economy/2023/3/3/china-beating-west-in-race-for-critical-technologies-report-says**

[1342] Takeshi Inagami, *"On Japanese-Style Neo-Corporatism: Era of a Tripartite Honeymoon?"* https://www.researchgate.net/publication/229929801_On_Japanese-Style_Neo-Corporatism_Era_of_a_Tripartite_Honeymoon; Yasuhiro Kamimura, *"Big Deal and Small Deal. The New Corporatism in South Korea and Taiwan."* https://www.researchgate.net/publication/228955156_Big_Deal_and_Small_Deal_The_New_Corporatism_in_South_Korea_and_Taiwan; Celal Bayari, "*The Neoliberal Globalization Link to the Belt and Road Initiative: The State and State-Owned-Enterprises in China.*" https://mpra.ub.uni-muenchen.de/104471/; Subhayu Bandyopadhyay[268], Praew Grittayaphong[269], *"Military Expenditures: How do the top spending nations compare?"* https://www.stlouisfed.org/on-the-economy/2023/jan/military-expenditures-how-top-spending-nations-compare

268. https://www.stlouisfed.org/on-the-economy/2023/jan/military-expenditures-how-top-spending-nations-compare#authorbox

269. https://www.stlouisfed.org/on-the-economy/2023/jan/military-expenditures-how-top-spending-nations-compare#authorbox

[1343] Servaas Storm, *"Financialization and Economic Development: A Debate on the Social Efficiency."* https://onlinelibrary.wiley.com/doi/full/10.1111/dech.12385; David Harvey, *"Neoliberalism 'with Chinese characteristics."* in David Harvey, *A Brief History of Neoliberalism*. (2005).

[1344] Jennifer Hillman, Alex Tippett, *"Who Built That? Labor and the Belt and Road Initiative."* https://www.cfr.org/blog/who-built-labor-and-belt-and-road-initiative; D. R. Russell and Blake Berger, *"Navigating the Belt and Road Initiative."* https://asiasociety.org/sites/default/files/2019-06/Navigating%20the%20Belt%20and%20Road%20Initiative_0.pdf.

[1345] Josh Lipsky and Sophia Busch, *"Where do the 'fence-sitters' sit on trade with Russia?"* https://www.atlanticcouncil.org/blogs/econographics/where-do-the-fence-sitters-sit-on-trade-with-russia/

[1346] Julia Horowitz, *"A mysterious fleet is helping Russia ship oil around the world."* https://edition.cnn.com/2023/03/01/business/russia-oil-shadow-fleet/index.html

[1347] Hung Tran, *"The Euro at parity with the USD: Implications for the global economy."* https://www.atlanticcouncil.org/blogs/econographics/the-euro-at-parity-with-the-usd-implications-for-the-global-economy/; Serkan Arslanalp[270], Barry J. Eichengreen[271], and Chima Simpson-Bell[272], *"The Stealth Erosion of Dollar Dominance: Active Diversifiers and the Rise of Nontraditional Reserve Currencies."* https://www.imf.org/en/Publications/WP/Issues/2022/03/24/The-Stealth-Erosion-of-Dollar-Dominance-Active-Diversifiers-and-the-Rise-of-Nontraditional-515150; Tracy Alloway and Joe Weisenthal, ***"Zoltan Pozsar on Russia, Gold, and a Turning Point for the U.S. Dollar."*** https://www.bloomberg.com/news/articles/2022-03-02/zoltan-pozsar-on-russia-gold-and-a-turning-point-for-the-u-s-dollar; John Letzing, *"This is why the US dollar isa potent sanctions weapon for now."* https://www.weforum.org/agenda/2022/06/this-is-why-the-us-dollar-is-a-potent-sanctions-weapon-for-now/; Will Daniel, *"Mohamed El-Erian says the relentless appreciation of the dollar is terrible news for the global economy."* https://fortune.com/2022/09/26/mohamed-el-erian-economic-outlook-strong-dollar-bad-news-global-economy/

[1348] Gérard Duménil[273] and Dominique Lévy[274] *The Crisis of Neoliberalism*. (2013); Yoichi Funabashi, *"Forget Bretton Woods II: the Role for U.S.–China–Japan Trilateralism."* https://www.tandfonline.com/doi/pdf/10.1080/01636600902772620

---

270. https://www.imf.org/en/Publications/Publications-By-Author?author=Serkan+Arslanalp&name=Serkan%20Arslanalp

271. https://www.imf.org/en/Publications/Publications-By-Author?author=Barry+J.+Eichengreen&name=Barry%20J.%20Eichengreen

272. https://www.imf.org/en/Publications/Publications-By-Author?author=Chima+Simpson-Bell&name=Chima%20Simpson-Bell

273. https://www.hup.harvard.edu/results-list.php?author=6568

274. https://www.hup.harvard.edu/results-list.php?author=6569

[1349] Kaye Wiggins[275], Antoine Gara[276], and Jamie Smyth[277], *"Business leaders warn that three-decade era of globalization is ending."* https://www.ft.com/content/0599878e-a820-4657-8e52-f069bb10d512; Ian Bremmer, *"Globalization Isn't Dead. The World Is More Fragmented, but Interdependence Still Rules."* https://www.foreignaffairs.com/world/globalization-isnt-dead

[1350] William Krist, *"US Trade Policy in Crisis."* https://www.wilsoncenter.org/chapter-1-us-trade-policy-crisis; A.W. Wolff, *"Paradigm: Lost US Trade Policy as an Instrument of Foreign Policy."* https://www.wcl.american.edu/impact/lawwire/paradigm-lost-us-trade-policy-as-an-instrument-of-foreign-policy/; Jin Canrong, *"How America's relationship with China changed under Obama."* https://www.weforum.org/agenda/2016/12/america-china-relationship/

[1351] Chalmers Johnson, *"Bill Clinton: A Bigger Imperialist than George W. Bush?"* https://www.theglobalist.com/bill-clinton-a-bigger-imperialist-than-george-w-bush/; FP Editors, *"Think Again: Clinton's Foreign Policy."* https://foreignpolicy.com/2009/11/19/think-again-clintons-foreign-policy/; Jonathan Hua, *"Clintonian Policy in a Changing World."* http://www.cornellpolicyreview.com/clintons-war/?pdf=2125

[1352] Tass *"EU set to include weapons industry into its economic priorities."* https://tass.com/world/1612575

[1353] Svetlana Savranskaya and Tom Blanton, *"What Yeltsin Heard: From Cold War to "Cold Peace": Clinton's Two Tracks Collide – NATO Enlargement and Russia Engagement."* https://nsarchive.gwu.edu/briefing-book/russia-programs/2021-11-24/nato-expansion-budapest-blow-1994; Pietro S. Nivola, Commercializing Foreign Policy? American trade policy then, and now." https://www.brookings.edu/articles/commercializing-foreign-policy-american-trade-policy-then-and-now/; Michael Hirsh, *"Is Biden Fighting the Last War on Trade?"* https://foreignpolicy.com/2022/05/05/biden-trade-policy-war-economy/

[1354] **Julian Gruin, *"The epistemic evolution of market authority: Big data, blockchain and China's neostatist challenge to neoliberalism."* https://journals.sagepub.com/doi/full/10.1177/1024529420965524; Paolo Gerbaudo, *"The demise of neoliberalism and the dawn of a new era of neo-statism."* https://theloop.ecpr.eu/the-demise-of-neoliberalism-and-the-dawn-of-a-new-era-of-neo-statism/; C. A. McNally, *"Chaotic mélange: neo-liberalism and neo-statism in the age of Sino-capitalism."* https://www.researchgate.net/publication/337043439_Chaotic_melange_neo-liberalism_and_neo-statism_in_the_age_of_Sino-capitalism**

[1355] Samuel Hall, *"Neoliberalism vs. Neostatism."* https://nuipe2015.wordpress.com/2015/02/20/neoliberalism-vs-neostatism/; Rajeev Patel and Philip McMichael, *"Third Worldism and the lineages of global fascism: the regrouping of the global South in the neoliberal era."* https://www.tandfonline.com/doi/abs/10.1080/0143659042000185426

---

275. https://www.ft.com/kaye-wiggins

276. https://www.ft.com/antoine-gara

277. https://www.ft.com/jamie-smyth

[1356] **World Bank, *"Stagflation Risk Rises Amid Sharp Slowdown in Growth."* https://www.worldbank.org/en/news/press-release/2022/06/07/stagflation-risk-rises-amid-sharp-slowdown-in-growth-energy-markets; Paolo Gerbaudo, *"The demise of neoliberalism and the dawn of a new era of 'neo-statism'.* https://theloop.e/cpr.eu/the-demise-of-neoliberalism-and-the-dawn-of-a-new-era-of-neo-statism/**

[1357] **Mehmet Erman Erol, Çağatay Edgücan Şahin, *"Labour unions under neoliberal authoritarianism in the Global South: the cases of Turkey and Egypt."* https://www.tandfonline.com/doi/full/10.1080/02255189.2022.2119945**

[1358] Isabel Ortiz, et. al., *"The Decade of Adjustment: A Review of Austerity Trends 2010-2020 in 187 Countries."* https://www.social-protection.org/gimi/gess/RessourcePDF.action?ressource.ressourceId=53192

[1359] **Office of the Historian, *"NSC 68, 1950."* https://history.state.gov/milestones/1945-1952/NSC68; Walter R. Gardner, "An Exchange-Market Analysis of the U.S. Balance of Payments." https://www.elibrary.imf.org/configurable/content/journals$002f024$002f1961$002f001$002farticle-A003-en.xml?t:ac=journals%24002f024%24002f1961%24002f001%24002farticle-A003-en.xml; *"President Dwight D. Eisenhower's Farewell Address (1961)."* https://www.archives.gov/milestone-documents/president-dwight-d-eisenhowers-farewell-address**

[1360] Laure Brillaud, et. al., *"EU member states exported weapons to Russia after the 2014 embargo."* https://www.investigate-europe.eu/en/2022/eu-states-exported-weapons-to-russia/

[1361] Wendy Brown, *"American Nightmare: Neoliberalism, Neoconservatism and De-Democratization,"* https://sxpolitics.org/wp-content/uploads/2018/05/Wendy-Brown-American-Nightmare.pdf

[1362] BNE IntelliNews, *"China steps into sanctions trade hole to supply Russia."* https://intellinews.com/china-steps-into-the-sanctions-trade-hole-to-supply-russia-269679/

[1363] Joe MacDonald, *"China's trade surplus swells to $877 billion as exports grow."* https://apnews.com/article/inflation-shanghai-business-0c0f7946bc3c08db1df13eb78911f4aa; https://tradingeconomics.com/china/balance-of-trade

[1364] AKM Khairul Islam, *"Cooperation under Anarchy: Neoliberal Institutional Explanations."* The Indian Journal of Political Science, LXX, 3, (2009); Charlie Richards, *"On Neoliberal Foreign Policy"* https://exponentsmag.org/2019/07/31/on-neoliberal-foreign-policy/; Carlos Ramirez, *"Obama's Neoliberal Foreign Policy in a Neoliberal World."* https://www.ia-forum.org/Content/ViewInternal_Document.cfm?contenttype_id=5&ContentID=8401

[1365] New Common Sense Newsletter, *"The breakdown of neoliberalism as foreign policy agenda."* https://hewlett.org/the-breakdown-of-neoliberalism-as-foreign-policy-agenda-5-questions-for-david-grewal/

[1366] *"Deloitte: Oil & Gas Industry Could Have Highest-Ever Cash Flows and Become Debt-Free, Primed to Accelerate the Energy Transition."* https://www.prnewswire.com/news-releases/deloitte-oil—gas-industry-could-have-highest-ever-cash-flows-and-become-debt-free-primed-to-accelerate-the-energy-transition-301611955.html[278]; Tsvetana Paraskova, *"Energy spending to Hit Record 13% of Global GDP."* https://oilprice.com/Latest-Energy-News/World-News/Energy-Spending-To-Hit-Record-13-Of-Global-GDP-In-2022.html; Kyra Buckley, *"Oil and gas producers on track to generate $1.4 trillion in free cash flow this year."* https://www.houstonchronicle.com/business/energy/article/Oil-and-gas-producers-on-track-to-generate-1-4-17397559.php; Joe Deaux[279] and Naureen S Malik[280], *"The US Industrial Complex is Starting to Buckle from High Power Costs."* https://www.bloomberg.com/news/articles/2022-07-07/high-power-costs-force-us-industrials-factories-to-shut#xj4y7vzkg

[1367] Enel SpA, *"US subsidies better than EU ones on manufacturing, Enel says."* https://www.reuters.com/business/energy/us-subsidies-better-than-eu-ones-energy-re-shoring-enel-ceo-says-2022-12-01/; Philip Blenkinsop, *"EU sets out green industry deal to take US and China."* https://www.reuters.com/business/sustainable-business/eu-lay-out-green-industry-plan-counter-us-china-subsidies-2023-02-01/; https://www.enerdata.net/about-us/company-news/energy-subsidies.html

[1368] EFPC, *"Fuel poverty levels set to rocket as petition passes 100,000."* https://www.endfuelpoverty.org.uk/fuel-poverty-levels-set-to-rocket-as-petition-passes-100000-mark/; Anna Cooban, *"A third of Brits face poverty with energy bills set to hit $5000."* https://edition.cnn.com/2022/08/09/economy/uk-energy-bills-poverty/index.html

[1369] Kazuto Suzuki, *"Can Economic Sanctions Replace Armed Forces in Modern Warfare?"* https://www.orfonline.org/research/can-economic-sanctions-replace-armed-forces-in-modern-warfare/; Brian O'Toole and Daniel Fried, *"What's Left to Sanction in Russia? Wallets, Stocks and Foreign Investments."* https://www.atlanticcouncil.org/blogs/new-atlanticist/whats-left-to-sanction-in-russia-wallets-stocks-and-foreign-investments/

[1370] Lauren Smith, *"United States Imposed Economic Sanctions: The Big Heist."* https://mronline.org/2020/03/10/united-states-imposed-economic-sanctions-the-big-heist/; Sahil Jai Dutta et. al., *"The Military Roots of Neoliberal Governance."* https://www.ppesydney.net/forums/the-military-roots-of-neoliberal-governance/

[1371] Ksenia Kirkham, *"The Political Economy of Sanctions in the Era of Global Neo-Protectionism."* https://valdaiclub.com/a/highlights/the-political-economy-of-sanctions/.

[1372] **James Petras, Henry Veltmeyer[281], Luciano Vasapollo[282], Mauro Casadio[283], *Empire with Imperialism: The***

278. https://www.prnewswire.com/news-releases/deloitte-oil--gas-industry-could-have-highest-ever-cash-flows-and-become-debt-free-primed-to-accelerate-the-energy-transition-301611955.html

279. https://www.bloomberg.com/authors/AR-UdU62fNE/joe-deaux

280. https://www.bloomberg.com/authors/AQqaChh9K0s/naureen-s-malik

281. https://www.google.gr/search?hl=el&tbo=p&tbm=bks&q=inauthor:%22Henry+Veltmeyer%22

Globalizing Dynamics of Neoliberal Capitalism. (2005); Intan Suwandi and John Bellamy Foster, _"Multinational Corporations and the Globalization of Monopoly Capital."_ https://monthlyreview.org/2016/07/01/multinational-corporations-and-the-globalization-of-monopoly-capital-from-the-1960s-to-the-present/; Gregory Albo, _"The Old and New Economics of Imperialism."_ Socialist Register 40, (2004)

[1373] Barak Obama, *"Writing the Rules for 21st Century Trade."* https://obamawhitehouse.archives.gov/blog/2015/02/18/president-obama-writing-rules-21st-century-trade; Adrian Budd, *"China and Imperialism in the 21st century."* http://isj.org.uk/china-imperialism-21/; Xi Ling and Raul Bernal-Meza, *"China-US rivalry: a new Cold War or capitalism's intra-core competition?"* https://doaj.org/article/f4d46074bb6b40c69b049698a5b25fb3

[1374] Pia Figuerola, *"Economic Sanctions' Effectiveness in a World with Interdependent Networks and Powerful MNC's: The Role of Governance in the Target State."* https://repository.upenn.edu/cgi/viewcontent.cgi?article=1226&context=curej; Jonathan Hopkin, *Anti-System Politics: The Crisis of Market Liberalism in Rich Democracies.* (2020).

[1375] Jeet Heer, *"The Surprisingly Durable Myth of Donald Trump, Anti-Imperialist."* https://www.thenation.com/article/politics/trump-anti-imperialist/ [284]

[1376] Jonathan, Hackenbroich, *"Tough Trade: Th hidden costs of economic coercion."* https://ecfr.eu/publication/tough-trade-the-hidden-costs-of-economic-coercion/; NPR, *"U.S. bans the sale and import of some tech from Chinese companies Huawei and ZTE."* https://www.npr.org/2022/11/26/1139258274/us-ban-tech-china-huawei-zte

[1377] Prabhat Patnaik, *"Sanctions within a regime of neoliberalism."* https://mronline.org/2022/03/12/sanctions-within-a-regime-of-neo-liberalism/; Jonathan Cini, "*Geoeconomic competition: global disruptions from the new frontline.*" https://www.files.ethz.ch/isn/192598/GCSP%20Strategic%20Security%20Analysis%20-%20Geo-economic%20competition.pdf

[1378] Lee Jones, *Societies Under Siege: Exploring How International Economic Sanctions (Do Not) Work. (*2015); Todd Prince, *"More Nord Stream 2 Sanctions On Horizon? U.S. Senator And Ukraine's Naftogaz Discuss Ways To Halt Controversial Gas Pipeline[285]."* https://www.rferl.org/a/more-nord-stream-2-sanctions-on-horizon-u-s-senator-and-ukraine-naftogaz-kobolyev/30475104.html; Ivan Timofeev, *"Rethinking Sanctions Efficiency[286]."* https://eng.globalaffairs.ru/articles/rethinking-sanctions-efficiency/

---

282. https://www.google.gr/search?hl=el&tbo=p&tbm=bks&q=inauthor:%22Luciano+Vasapollo%22

283. https://www.google.gr/search?hl=el&tbo=p&tbm=bks&q=inauthor:%22Mauro+Casadio%22

284. https://www.thenation.com/article/politics/trump-anti-imperialist/%20

285. https://www.rferl.org/a/more-nord-stream-2-sanctions-on-horizon-u-s-senator-and-ukraine-naftogaz-kobolyev/30475104.html

286. https://eng.globalaffairs.ru/articles/rethinking-sanctions-efficiency/

[1379] Illya Levelev, *"Neo-Realism Meets Neo-Liberalism: Nord Stream and its Implications for EU-Russia Energy Relations."* https://www.grin.com/document/175801; Daniel Fried, R. L. Morningstar and D. D. Stein, *"Reconciling transatlantic differences over Nord Stream 2."* https://www.atlanticcouncil.org/blogs/energysource/reconciling-transatlantic-differences-over-nord-stream-2/; Andy Powell, *"American Gas Lobby Spins Ukraine Crisis to Push for Expansion of Dirty LNG."* http://priceofoil.org/2022/02/16/american-gas-lobby-spins-ukraine-crisis-to-push-for-expansion-of-dirty-us-lng/

[1380] Jeff Brady, *"Fossi 'l fuel subsidies are proving harder to end than first thought."* https://www.npr.org/2021/12/14/1064011237/fossil-fuel-subsidies-are-proving-harder-to-end-than-first-thought

[1381] **Maria Shagina, *"A Tale of Two Pipelines."* https://ridl.io/en/a-tale-of-two-pipelines/; European Commission, *"EU-US LNG Trade."* https://ec.europa.eu/energy/sites/ener/files/eu-us_lng_trade_folder.pdf; Luke Harding, *"Deutsche Bank faces action over $20bn Russian money-laundering scheme."* https://www.theguardian.com/business/2019/apr/17/deutsche-bank-faces-action-over-20bn-russian-money-laundering-scheme**

[1382] Jesse Richman and Nurullah Ayyilmaz, *"Can the US and Europe contain Russian power in the European energy market? A game theoretic approach."* https://www.sciencedirect.com/science/article/pii/S2211467X19300860; EIA, *"Despite sanctions, Iran's dry natural gas grew steadily over the past 20 years."* https://www.eia.gov/todayinenergy/detail.php?id=50276; Melissa Pistilli, "*10 Top Natural Gas Producers by Country."* https://investingnews.com/top-natural-gas-producers/

[1383] European Parliament, Policy Department, *"Extraterritorial sanctions on trade and investments and European Responses."* https://www.europarl.europa.eu/RegData/etudes/STUD/2020/653618/EXPO_STU(2020)653618_EN.pdf

[1384] Joe McDonald, *"China imposes sanctions on Lockheed Martin and Raytheon over sales to Taiwan."* https://www.pbs.org/newshour/world/china-imposes-sanctions-on-lockheed-martin-and-raytheon-over-sales-to-taiwan; ING, *"China strikes back in the tech war, restricting exports of gallium and germanium."* https://www.ing.com/Newsroom/News/China-strikes-back-in-the-tech-war-restricting-exports-of-gallium-and-germanium.htm; GT, *"China cuts US Treasury holdings in Feb.to 13-year low, raises economic security."* https://www.globaltimes.cn/page/202304/1289349.shtml

[1385] Greg Ip, *"How the West Can Win a Global Power Struggle."* https://www.wsj.com/articles/how-the-west-can-win-a-global-power-struggle-11647615557; W. I. Robinson, *"What are the real reasons behind the New Cold War?"* https://mronline.org/2021/05/10/what-are-the-real-reasons-behind-the-new-cold-war/; OC, *"The impact of financial sanctions on supply chains."* https://www.osborneclarke.com/insights/impact-financial-sanctions-supply-chains

[1386] Dale Aluf, *"China ramps up its efforts to shape a multipolar world."* https://thechinaproject.com/2023/03/31/china-ramps-up-its-efforts-to-shape-a-multipolar-world/

[1387] Monica Duffy Toft. *"The US isn't at war with Russia, technically, but its support for Ukraine offers a classic case of a proxy war."* https://theconversation.com/the-us-isnt-at-war-with-russia-technically-but-its-support-for-ukraine-offers-a-classic-case-of-a-proxy-war-192064

[1388] Jaime Dettmer, *"Ban on Russian gas risks reviving populism in Europe."* https://www.politico.eu/article/ban-on-russian-gas-risks-reviving-populism-in-europe/; Penny M. Von Eschen, *"Neoliberalism, the Decline of Diplomacy and the Rise of the Global Right."* https://networks.h-net.org/node/28443/discussions/174976/issf-policy-series-neoliberalism-decline-diplomacy-and-rise-global

[1389] Joseph Choonara, *"The devastation of Ukraine: NATO, Russia and imperialism.* "https://isj.org.uk/devastation-of-ukraine/

[1390] Yongchang Chin, Rakesh Sharma. *"Oil's New Map: How India Turns Russia Crude into the West's Fuel."* https://www.bloomberg.com/news/articles/2023-02-05/oil-s-new-map-how-india-turns-russia-crude-into-the-west-s-fuel

[1391] The Wire, *"Analysts See Link Between Rising Indian Oil Product Exports to US and Surge in Russian Crude Imports."* https://thewire.in/political-economy/experts-link-rise-of-indian-refineries-product-sales-to-us-and-surge-in-russian-crude-imports

[1392] **Ken Silverstein, "*Is The U.S. Using Sanctions To Elbow Russia Out Of The European Natural Gas Market?*[287]" https://www.forbes.com/sites/kensilverstein/2020/05/04/is-the-us-using-sanctions-to-elbow-russia-out-of-the-european-natural-gas-market/; Mathias Neunkirch and Florian Neumeier, "*The impact of US sanctions on poverty.*" https://www.researchgate.net/publication/301234868_The_impact_of_US_sanctions_on_poverty**

[1393] Colin M. Barry and Katja Kleinberg, *Profiting from Sanctions: Economic Coercion and US Myths and Realities of US Energy Independence."* https://www.cfr.org/blog/iranian-oil-sanctions-myths-and-realities-us-energy-independence; Branko Marcetic, *"End the Sanctions."* https://jacobinmag.com/2017/09/united-states-sanctions-venezuela-maduro; Peter Keoning, *"Sanctions, sanctions, sanctions, the final demise of the dollar hegemony."* https://mronline.org/2018/08/24/sanctions-sanctions-sanctions-the-final-demise-of-the-dollar-hegemony/

[1394] Reuters, *"IMF warns Russia sanctions threaten to chip away at dollar dominance."* https://www.reuters.com/business/imf-warns-russia-sanctions-threaten-chip-away-dollar-dominance-ft-2022-03-31/; Harry Robertson, *"Goldman Sachs warns the dollar is at risk of losing its dominance, and could end up a lesser player like the UK pound."* https://www.businessinsider.in/stock-market/news/goldman-sachs-warns-the-dollar-is-at-risk-of-losing-its-dominance-and-could-end-up-a-lesser-player-like-the-uk-pound/articleshow/90598081.cms; FT, *"Financial warfare: will there be a backlash against the dollar?"* https://www.ft.com/content/220db8f2-2980-410f-aab8-f471369ac3cf

---

287. https://www.forbes.com/sites/kensilverstein/2020/05/04/is-the-us-using-sanctions-to-elbow-russia-out-of-the-european-natural-gas-market/#a5c02393e59c943d6a75a9241140faca332fa09562109

[1395] Xu Wenong, *"Russia's de-dollarization drive more than symbolic."*

https://global.chinadaily.com.cn/a/202202/24/WS6216be34a310cdd39bc88834.html; Aisling Ní Chúláin[288], *"The US dollar is the mightiest of all world currencies, but its position is under threat."* https://www.euronews.com/next/2022/05/04/watch-the-us-dollar-is-the-mightiest-of-all-world-currencies-but-is-its-position-under-thr; Gary Springfield, *"Are we Witnessing a Global de-dollarization Spree?"* https://internationalbanker.com/finance/we-are-witnessing-a-global-de-dollarisation-spree/

[1396] Reuters, *"Brazil's Lula supports trading currency for BRICS countries."* https://www.reuters.com/article/spain-brazil-lula-idUSL1N36T1WW

[1397] Jim O'Neill, Alessio Terzi, *"The G-7 is dead, long live the G-7."* https://www.bruegel.org/blog-post/g7-dead-long-live-g7

[1398] Ramesh Thakur, *"The Fraying of the Liberal International Order."* Thomas Helbling[289], Shanaka J. Peiris[290], Krishna Srinivasan[291], *"Asia Poised to Drive Global Economic Growth, Boosted by China's Reopening."*

https://brownstone.org/articles/fraying-liberal-international-order/; https://www.imf.org/en/Blogs/Articles/2023/05/01/asia-poised-to-drive-global-economic-growth-boosted-by-chinas-reopening; Zhou Xin, *"US will come to regret holding back China at the IMF ."* https://asia.nikkei.com/Opinion/U.S.-will-come-to-regret-holding-back-China-at-the-IMF

[1399] East Asia Forum, *"Japan's G-7 high-wire balancing act."* https://asiatimes.com/2023/04/japans-g7-high-wire-balancing-act/

[1400] Dipanjan Roy Choudry, *"BRICS working on new global reserve currency and alternative mechanism for international payments: Vladimir Putin"* https://economictimes.indiatimes.com/news/international/world-news/brics-working-on-new-global-reserve-currency-and-alternative-mechanism-for-intl-payments-vladimir-putin/articleshow/92407851.cms; Jonathan Wheatley and Colby Smith, *"Russia sanctions threaten to erode dominance of US dollar, says IMF."* https://www.ft.com/content/3e0760d4-8127-41db-9546-e62b6f8f5773; Sumner Said, and Stephen Kalin, *"Saudi Arabia Considers Accepting Yuan Instead of Dollars for Chinese Oil Sales."* https://www.wsj.com/articles/saudi-arabia-considers-accepting-yuan-instead-of-dollars-for-chinese-oil-sales-11647351541; *US Dollar at Risk of Losing Dominance."* https://www.tasnimnews.com/en/news/2022/04/04/2690625/us-dollar-at-risk-of-losing-dominance-wall-street-bank-warns; Daniel Avis *"Israel Adds Yuan to $206 Billion Reserves in Philosophy Change."* https://www.bloomberg.com/news/articles/2022-04-20/israel-adds-yuan-to-206-billion-reserves-in-philosophy-change

---

288. https://twitter.com/euronews

289. https://www.imf.org/en/Blogs/authors?author=Thomas%20Helbling

290. https://www.imf.org/en/Blogs/authors?author=Shanaka%20J%20Peiris

291. https://www.imf.org/en/Blogs/authors?author=Krishna%20Srinivasan

[1401] **William J. Norris, *"China's Post-Cold War Economic Statecraft: A Periodization."* https://journals.sagepub.com/doi/full/10.1177/18681026211058186; Oren Liebermann, Ellie Kaufman and Jeremy Herb, *"Biden administration proposes larger defense budget to counter China, Russia."* https://edition.cnn.com/2022/03/28/politics/defense-budget-biden-administration/index.html Medea Benjamin and N. J. S. Davis, *"The US Leaves Ukraine to Fight New Cold War with Russia."* https://www.fairobserver.com/region/north_america/medea-benjamin-nicolas-davies-russia-ukraine-war-usa-america-cold-war-joe-biden-vladimir-putin-39184/**

[1402] Maria Shagina *"Business as Usual: Sanctions Circumvention by Western Firms in Crimea."* https://www.researchgate.net/publication/335543264_Business_as_Usual_Sanctions_Circumvention_by_Western_Firms_in_Crimea

[1403] Jasper Jolly and Jessica Elgot, *"Profits at world's seven biggest oil firms soar to almost £150bn this year."* https://www.theguardian.com/business/2022/oct/27/profits-at-worlds-seven-biggest-oil-firms-soar-to-almost-150bn-this-year-windfall-tax; BBC, *"Russia sanctions: How can the world cope without oil and gas?"* https://www.bbc.com/news/58888451; Reuters, *"European arms imports climb, US dominance in exports grows."* https://finance.yahoo.com/news/european-arms-imports-climb-u-230001867.html; AL JAZEERA, *'Multiple threats': Macron raises France's military budget 40%." https://www.aljazeera.com/news/2023/1/20/macron-boosts-french-military-spending-by-over-a-third*

[1404] John M. Donnelly, *"Watershed $1 trillion defense budget on the horizon."* https://rollcall.com/2023/03/14/watershed-1-trillion-defense-budget-on-the-horizon/

[1405] C. J. Atkins, *"Pipeline ploy: How US natural gas interests are fueling the Ukraine crisis."* https://www.peoplesworld.org/article/pipeline-ploy-how-u-s-natural-gas-interests-are-fueling-the-ukraine-crisis/; Trading Economics, *"Russia's Current Account."* https://tradingeconomics.com/russia/current-account; Trading Economics, *"United States Current Account."* https://tradingeconomics.com/united-states/current-account

[1406] **Pawel Wargan, *"NATO and the Long War on the Third World."* https://monthlyreview.org/2023/01/01/nato-and-the-long-war-on-the-third-world/**

[1407] Daniel Larison, *"We should've known sanctions on Russia wouldn't work as intended."* https://responsiblestatecraft.org/2022/06/17/we-shouldve-known-sanctions-on-russia-wouldnt-work-as-intended/; David Uren, *"History Shows that the West's Sanctions Could Backfire."* https://www.realcleardefense.com/articles/2022/04/06/history_shows_the_wests_sanctions_on_russia_could_backfire_825674.html; Hannah Ward-Glenton, *"IMF says fragmentation could cost global economy up to 7 percent of GDP."* https://www.cnbc.com/2023/01/16/imf-says-fragmentation-could-cost-global-economy-up-to-7percent-of-gdp.html

[1408] Matthew Gooding, *"The US wants to muzzle China's semiconductor industry: It could end up shooting itself in the foot."* https://techmonitor.ai/technology/silicon/china-semiconductor-us-sanctions-nvidia-amd; Courtney McBride, *"Kissinger Warns Biden Against Endless Confrontation with China."* https://www.bloomberg.com/news/articles/2022-07-19/kissinger-warns-biden-against-endless-confrontation-with-china

[1409] Ekaterina Arapova, *"How the US Forces Third Countries to Support Sanctions."* https://valdaiclub.com/a/highlights/how-the-us-forces-third-countries-to-support-sanct/; Esfandyar Batmanghelidj, Francisco Rodriguez, *"The Danger of Santions."* https://www.noemamag.com/the-danger-of-sanctions/; Anastasia Lyrchikova, Gleb Stolyarov, *"Russia has $15 billion plan to dent China's Rare Earth dominance."* https://www.reuters.com/article/russia-rareearths-idUSL8N2F73F4

[1410] Jeff Pao, *"China's chip sector needs change after OPPO setback."* https://asiatimes.com/2023/05/chinas-chip-sector-needs-change-after-oppo-setback/; Che Pan, *"Smartphone giant Oppo's closure of chip design unit Zeku triggers speculation on cause of action, as 3,000 engineers are laid off."* https://www.scmp.com/tech/big-tech/article/3220642/smartphone-giant-oppos-move-disband-chip-design-unit-zeku-triggers-speculation-cause-action-3000

[1411] Li Xing and Raul Bernal-Meza *"China-US rivalry: a new Cold War or capitalism's intra-core competition?"* https://www.scielo.br/j/rbpi/a/tPFgRF7VfFkZ9hjcd6hpsFG/?format=pdf&lang=en; Shobhit Seth *"Why China Buys US Debt with Treasury Bonds."* https://www.investopedia.com/articles/investing/040115/reasons-why-china-buys-us-treasury-bonds.asp; Sam Olsen, *"China is winning the war for global tech dominance."* https://thehill.com/opinion/technology/518773-china-is-winning-the-war-for-global-tech-dominance; GT, *"China vows new measures to expand market access, attract foreign investment."* https://www.globaltimes.cn/page/202208/1274233.shtml

[1412] Demetri Sevastopulo, *"US to add Chinese chipmaker to trade blacklist."* https://www.ft.com/content/7aabf066-1cc7-4eee-a963-f863bdbbb08c; Mercedes Ruehl, *"EU and US warn Malaysia of 'national security' risk in Huawei's bid for 5G role."* https://www.ft.com/content/3da9a1bd-a49c-46f4-acc2-60333e55eaaa; Didi Kristen Tatlow, *"China's Stake in World Ports Sharpens Attention on Political Influence."* https://www.globaltimes.cn/page/202208/1274233.shtml; Jenny Leonard, *"US to Add Than 30 Chinese Companies to Trade Blacklist."* https://www.bloomberg.com/news/articles/2022-12-14/us-to-add-more-than-30-chinese-companies-to-trade-blacklist;

[1413] David Shepardson, *"China opposes semiconductor bill because it gives US advantage."* https://www.reuters.com/technology/china-opposes-semiconductor-bill-because-it-will-give-us-advantage-us-commerce-2022-05-11/; Scott Lincicome and Llana Blumsack, *"The Top Seven Reasons to Oppose New Semiconductor Subsidies."* https://www.cato.org/blog/top-seven-reasons-oppose-new-semiconductor-subsidies; Yaling Jiang, *"Semiconductor imports to China shrink for first time in two years, but value jumps."* https://www.scmp.com/tech/policy/article/3169723/semiconductor-imports-china-shrink-first-time-two-years-value-jumps

[1414] SZ Tan and Peter W. Singer, *"How China is Trying to Turn the US CHPIS Act to its Favor."* https://www.defenseone.com/ideas/2022/11/how-china-trying-turn-us-chips-act-its-favor/379828/

[1415] Edward White, Demetri Sevastpulo, and Eleanor Elcott, *"China hits back at US chips sanctions with WTO dispute."* https://www.ft.com/content/4eaedee4-5267-4e3a-b9da-5d2bb6f356ee

[1416] James Midway, *"How the semiconductor industry crisis signals the end of neoliberalism."* https://www.newstatesman.com/business/economics/2021/11/how-the-semiconductor-crisis-signals-the-end-of-neoliberalism

[1417] Vishnu Kannan, Jacob Feldgoise, *"After the CHIPS Act: The Limits of Reshoring and Next Steps for US Semiconductor Policy."* https://carnegieendowment.org/2022/11/22/after-chips-act-limits-of-reshoring-and-next-steps-for-u.s.-semiconductor-policy-pub-88439

[1418] Simon Sharwood, *"South Korea Warns US: The Chips Act leaves a sour taste." https://www.theregister.com/2023/03/09/south_korea_warns_usa_chips_act/*

[1419] Aaron Thomas Rowland, *"From authoritarian dirty war to neoliberal 'democratic' class war: neoliberalism as class struggle in Argentina."* https://trace.tennessee.edu/cgi/viewcontent.cgi?article=7375&context=utk_gradthes

[1420] **Gavin Bade, *"Corporate America fights uphill battle against anti-China push."* https://www.politico.com/news/2021/09/01/business-us-china-trade-508239; Ryan Hass, "*The new normal in US-China relations: Hardening competition and deep interdependence.*" https://www.brookings.edu/blog/order-from-chaos/2021/08/12/the-new-normal-in-us-china-relations-hardening-competition-and-deep-interdependence/; William K. Carroll and Jean Philippe Sapinski, "*Neoliberalism and the transnational capitalist class.*" in *The Handbook of Neoliberalism*, ed by Kean Birch, Julie MacLeavy and Simon Springer (2016). Haley C. Cuccinello, *"Michael Dell, Laurene Powell Jobs And Other Billionaires Hit By Trump's Orders For U.S. Companies To Find 'Alternative To China.'"* https://www.forbes.com/sites/hayleycuccinello/2019/08/23/trump-tariffs-china-alternative-billionaires/?sh=70912e721ac6**

[1421] Trevor Thrall[292] and Caroline Dorminey[293], *'Risky Business: The role of Arms Sales in us Foreign Policy.'* https://www.cato.org/policy-analysis/risky-business-role-arms-sales-us-foreign-policy; A. Trevor Thrall, Jordan Cohen and Caroline Dorminey, *"Power, Profit, or Prudence? US Arms Sales since 9/11."* https://www.airuniversity.af.edu/Portals/10/SSQ/documents/Volume-14_Issue-2/Thrall.pdf; Ethan B. Kapstein[294] and Jonathan D. Caverley[295], *"Biden Must Base Arms Sales on US Interests not US Jobs."* https://foreignpolicy.com/2021/02/25/biden-must-base-arms-sales-on-u-s-interests-not-u-s-jobs/; Christina Lu, *"China and Saudi Arabia Reinforce Economic Ties."* https://foreignpolicy.com/2022/12/07/china-saudi-arabia-xi-jinping-trip-trade-oil/; Francesca[296]

292. https://www.cato.org/people/trevor-thrall

293. https://www.cato.org/people/caroline-dorminey

294. https://foreignpolicy.com/author/ethan-b-kapstein/

295. https://foreignpolicy.com/author/jonathan-d-caverley/

296. https://foreignpolicy.com/2021/02/25/biden-must-base-arms-sales-on-u-s-interests-not-u-s-jobs/;%20Christina%20Lu,%20

Lucia Bray, *"Neoliberalism and Empire: The American Military-Industrial Complex."* https://gjis.journals.yorku.ca/index.php/gjis/article/download/40265/36443/50340

[1422] Trevor Thrall and Caroline Dorminey, *"Risky Business: The Role of Arms Sales in US Foreign Policy."* https://www.cato.org/policy-analysis/risky-business-role-arms-sales-us-foreign-policy

[1423] Abdol-Madjid Bayat Mossadegh, *Mossadegh pages d'histoire de l'Iran.* (2012).

[1424] Frédéric Lemaître, *"La Chine, nouvel acteur politique au Moyen-Orient."* https://www.lemonde.fr/international/article/2023/03/11/pekin-nouvel-acteur-politique-au-moyen-orient_6165064_3210.html; Peter Baker, *"Chinese-Brokered Deal Upends Mideast Diplomacy and Challenges US."* https://www.nytimes.com/2023/03/11/us/politics/saudi-arabia-iran-china-biden.html

[1425] Eldridge A. Colby*, Strategy of Denial: American Defense in an Age of Great Power Conflict."* (2021).

[1426] Sean Speer, *"Canada should be worried: Eldridge Colby offers a realist perspective on the rise of China."* https://thehub.ca/2021-12-01/elbridge-colby-offers-a-realist-perspective-on-the-rise-of-china/; Laurence H. Shoup, *"Giving War a Chance."* https://monthlyreview.org/2022/05/01/giving-war-a-chance/.

[1427] Christopher Layne, *"This Time It's Real: The End of Unipolarity and the Pax Americana."* https://www.carlanorrlof.com/wp-content/uploads/2013/03/This-Time-Its-Real-The-End-of-Unipolarity-and-the-Pax-Americana.pdf; Cristopher Layne, *"The US-Chinese Power Shift and the end of Pax Americana."* https://www.chathamhouse.org/sites/default/files/images/ia/INTA94_1_6_249_Layne.pdf

[1428] Jeremy Warner, *"The West has so much to gain from a Cold War with China,"* https://www.telegraph.co.uk/business/2023/04/19/west-has-much-gain-from-new-economic-cold-war-china/

[1429] Yonah Jeremy Bob, *"China sues Israeli government for denying light rail tender under US pressure."* https://www.jpost.com/business-and-innovation/energy-and-infrastructure/article-704417; George Calhoun, *"War With China? The Economic Factor that Could Trigger it."* https://www.forbes.com/sites/georgecalhoun/2021/09/12/war-with-china-the-economic-factor-that-could-trigger-it/?sh=795c23125d26;Tom Hussain, *"Why is the US trying to bully Pakistan with empty China Threats?"* https://www.scmp.com/week-asia/politics/article/2158234/why-us-trying-bully-pakistan-empty-china-threats; Astha Rajvanshi, *"How China Became a Global Lender of Last Resort."* https://time.com/6266658/china-emerges-major-global-lender/

[1430] David Levi-Faur, *"Friedrich List and the political economy of the nation-state."* https://www.researchgate.net/publication/233153408_Friedrich_List_and_the_political_economy_of_the_nation-state; Andrea Andromidas, *"Free Trade Monetarism is the Road to Serfdom."* https://archive.schillerinstitute.com/economy/2013/list-vs-von_hayek.html

[1431] Michael Prowse, *"Is America in Decline?"* https://hbr.org/1992/07/is-america-in-decline

[1432] Zhao Mingwen, *"Shanghai Cooperation Organization."* https://www.ciis.org.cn/english/ESEARCHPROJECTS/Articles/202007/t20200715_3591.html; Janko Šćepanović, *"Russia and the Shanghai Cooperation Organization: a question of the commitment capacity."* https://saias.ecnu.edu.cn/t/9279

[1433] **David Brunnstrom and Michael Martina, *"Japan minister calls for new world order to counter rise of authoritarian regimes."* https://www.reuters.com/world/japan-minister-calls-new-world-order-counter-rise-authoritarian-regimes-2023-01-05/**

[1434] Sara Flounders, *"Taiwan – A Pawn for US War on China."* https://covertactionmagazine.com/2023/04/27/taiwan-a-pawn-for-u-s-war-on-china/

[1435] Stefan Kolev, Ekkehart A. Koelher *"Old Chicago and Freiburg: Why Ordoliberalism Was No German Oddity."* https://www.promarket.org/2021/07/25/chicago-freiburg-ordoliberalism-neoliberalism-germany/; Helen V. Milner, *"Is Global Capitalism Compatible with Democracy? Inequality, Insecurity, and Interdependence."* https://academic.oup.com/isq/article/65/4/1097/6318891; Mike Douglas, *"Globopolis or Cosmopolis?—Alternative Futures of City Life in East Asia."* https://www.academia.edu/34405495/Globopolis_or_Cosmopolis_Alternative_Futures_of_City_Life_in_East_Asia

[1436] **Stefan Schwarzkopf, *"The Political Theology of Consumer Sovereignty Towards an Ontology of Consumer Society."*https://www.researchgate.net/publication/258192297_The_Political_Theology_of_Consumer_Sovereignty_Tow**

[1437] William Davies and Nicholas Gane, *"Post-Neoliberalism? An Introduction."* https://journals.sagepub.com/doi/10.1177/02632764211036722; S.V. Date *"Trump Blames Mike Pence for Jan 6 Violence for not Going Along with his Coup Attempt."* https://www.yahoo.com/news/trump-blames-mike-pence-jan-221444807.html

[1438] Kitty Calavita,[297] Henry N. Pontell[298], Robert Tillman, [299]*Big Money Crime: Fraud and Politics in Savings and Loan Crisis.* (1997); Leigh Clair La Berge, *Scandals and Abstraction: Financial Fiction of the Long 1980s.* (2014), ch. 4.

297. https://www.ucpress.edu/search.php?q=Kitty+Calavita

298. https://www.ucpress.edu/search.php?q=Henry+N.+Pontell

299. https://www.ucpress.edu/search.php?q=Robert+Tillman

[1439] C. J. Polychroniou, *"Ukraine War Is Exposing Still More Flaws in Neoliberalism's Economic Structures - An Interview with C. P. Chandrasekhar."* https://www.globalpolicyjournal.com/blog/07/04/2022/ukraine-war-exposing-still-more-flaws-neoliberalisms-economic-structures-interview

[1440] Pedro Conceição, *"Uncertain Times, Unsettled Lives."*

https://hdr.undp.org/system/files/documents/global-report-document/hdr2021-22pdf_1.pdf; Bonn Juego, *"The Reproduction of Neoliberalism and the Global Capitalist Crisis."* https://journals.aau.dk/index.php/ijis/article/view/510

[1441] Philippe Escande, *"At Davos, the end of globalization is on everyone's mind."* https://www.lemonde.fr/en/economy/article/2023/01/17/at-davos-the-end-of-globalization-is-on-everyone-s-mind_6011910_19.html

[1442] Simon Kennedy, *"What's worrying the global elite in Davos?"* https://www.bloomberg.com/news/newsletters/2023-01-16/what-s-happening-in-the-world-economy-the-fractured-world-is-worrying-davos

[1443] Luke Cooper, *"From I won't protect you to I will: Why the new authoritarian protectionism marks the end of neoliberalism."* https://www.transformingsociety.co.uk/2021/06/25/from-i-wont-protect-you-to-i-will-why-the-new-authoritarian-protectionism-marks-the-end-of-neoliberalism/

[1444] Gary Gertsle, *"The Age of Neoliberalism is Ending in America. What will Replace it?"* https://www.theguardian.com/commentisfree/2021/jun/28/age-of-neoliberalism-biden-trump; Gary Gestle, *The Rise and Fall of the Neoliberal Order.* (2022). Gary Gestle, "*The Resilient Power of the States across the long Nineteenth Century.*" in Lawrence Jacobs and Desmond King, eds., *The Unsustainable American State.* (2009).

[1445] Benjamin Selwyn and Dara Leyden, *"Oligopoly-driven development: The World Bank's Trading for Development in the Age of Global Value Chains* in perspective." https://journals.sagepub.com/doi/full/10.1177/1024529421995351; https://www.worldbank.org/en/publication/wdr2020/brief/world-development-report-2020-data

Benjamin Selwyn and Dara Leyden, *"Oligopoly-driven development: The World Bank's Trading for Development in the Age of Global Value Chains* in perspective." https://journals.sagepub.com/doi/full/10.1177/1024529421995351; https://www.worldbank.org/en/publication/wdr2020/brief/world-development-report-2020-data;

[1446] Axel Leijonhufvud, *"Shell Game: Zero-interest policies as hidden subsidies to banks."* https://cepr.org/voxeu/columns/shell-game-zero-interest-policies-hidden-subsidies-bank; Philip Inman, *"We face a global economic crisis and no one knows what to do about it."* https://www.theguardian.com/business/2022/jun/18/we-face-a-global-economic-crisis-and-no-one-knows-what-to-do-about-it; Patricia Cohen, *"Global Growth Will Be Chocked."* https://www.nytimes.com/2022/06/07/

business/world-bank-forecast.html; Rajesh Mehta and Sunny Sabharwal, *"Financial Crisis: How Catastrophic is it?"* https://www.businessworld.in/article/Financial-Crisis-How-Catastrophic-Is-2022-/20-06-2022-433246/

[1447] Tristan Bove, *"An economist who correctly predicted the Great Financial Crisis says the world's central banks have chosen 'class war over financial stability.'"* https://www.yahoo.com/finance/news/economist-correctly-predicted-great-financial-215332088.html

[1448] Tom Clark and Anthony Heath, *Hard Times: Inequality, Recession and Aftermath*, (2014); UN, *"100 million displaced, 'a record that should have never been set."* https://news.un.org/en/story/2022/12/1131957; UNHCR, *"Mid-Year Trends 2022."* https://reliefweb.int/report/world/unhcr-mid-year-trends-2022

[1449] Thomas Da Costa Vieira, *"'In time, every worker a capitalist': Accumulation by legitimation and authoritarian neoliberalism in Thatcher's Britain."* https://journals.sagepub.com/doi/10.1177/10245294231153028

[1450] Taylor C. Boas and Jordan Gans-Morse, *"Neoliberalism: From New Liberal Philosophy to Anti-Liberal Slogan."* https://link.springer.com/article/10.1007/s12116-009-9040-5; Joseph Daher, *"Continuous Crisis in Lebanon."* https://internationalviewpoint.org/spip.php?article7350

[1451] Grace Blakely, *"True Democracy is Incompatible with Capitalism."* https://jacobin.com/2023/06/democracy-retreat-capitalism-authoritarianism-crisis

[1452] Vanessa Boese, *"State of the world 2021: autocratization changing its nature."* https://www.tandfonline.com/doi/full/10.1080/13510347.2022.2069751; H Sabelo J Ndlovu-Gatsheni, *"Weak states and the growth of the private security sector in Africa: Whither the African state?"*

https://issafrica.org/chapter-2-weak-states-and-the-growth-of-the-private-security-sector-in-africa-whither-the-african-state-sabelo-j-ndlovu-gatsheni; Luiz Carlos Bresser-Peirera, *"Assault on the State and on the Market: Neoliberalism and Economic Theory."* https://www.scielo.br/j/ea/a/F8tmPL4Z7PBjDtnhzHV7hVm/?lang=en&format=pdf

[1453] Rahmane Idrissa, *"Weakened States and Market Giants: Neoliberalism and Democracy in Niger and West Bengal."* African Development. 43:3, (2018); Xiaoming Huang, ed. *The Political and Economic Transition in East Asia: strong market, weakening state.* (2001); John Carey, *"Strong presidencies may threaten democracies. Luckily, we don't have one."* https://www.washingtonpost.com/news/in-theory/wp/2016/01/14/strong-presidencies-may-threaten-democracy-luckily-we-dont-have-one/; Al Jazeera, "Australi[300]a *announces inquiry into Morrison's secret ministries."* https://www.aljazeera.com/news/2022/8/23/australia-announces-inquiry-into-morrisons-secret-ministries; Terry Hathaway, *"Neoliberalism as Corporate Power."* [301] https://journals.sagepub.com/doi/pdf/10.1177/1024529420910382

[1454] Jolle Demmers, Alex E.Fernández Jilberto and Barbara Hogenboom, eds. *Good Governance in the Era of Global Neoliberalism.* (2004); Keith Jacobs and Tony Manzi, *"Neoliberalism as entrepreneurial governmentality: contradictions and dissonance within contemporary English housing associations."* https://www.tandfonline.com/doi/abs/10.1080/02673037.2019.1617411?journalCode=chos20

[1455] Magnet Editorial Team, *"European Wealth Report: The pandemic has increased wealth centration."* https://www.lgt.com/en/magnet/financial-markets/european-wealth-report-the-pandemic-has-increased-wealth-concentration/#button2; Matthew Sparke[302], Owain David Williams[303], *"Neoliberal disease: COVID-19, co-pathogenesis and global health insecurities."* https://journals.sagepub.com/doi/full/10.1177/0308518X211048905; World Bank Group, *"COVID-19 and Human Capital: Europe and Central Asia Economic Update."* https://openknowledge.worldbank.org/bitstream/handle/10986/34518/9781464816437.pdf; WEF *"Economic inequality has deepened during the pandemic."* https://www.weforum.org/agenda/2022/04/economic-inequality-wealth-gap-pandemic/

[1456] W.D. Cohan, *"How Wall Street's Bankers Stayed out of Jail."* https://www.theatlantic.com/magazine/archive/2015/09/how-wall-streets-bankers-stayed-out-of-jail/399368/; Julia Conley, *"Warren Calls for Clawing Back Pay, Bonuses for Silicon Valley Bank Eecutives."* https://www.commondreams.org/news/warren-silicon-valley-bonuses

[1457] Larry Neumeister, *"Divided court rejects 4 insider trader convictions."* https://apnews.com/article/politics-legal-proceedings-new-jersey-state-government-district-of-columbia-b9d68cb82117443be765f2ca560368cc

[1458] **Michael Husson, *"Neoliberalism: The Highest Stage?"* https://www.cairn-int.info/article-E_AMX_051_0086—neoliberalism-the-highest-stage.htm[304]; Susi Dennison, *"Crisis of Confidence: How Europeans see their place in the world."* https://ecfr.eu/publication/crisis-of-confidence-how-europeans-see-their-place-in-the-world/; Richard Wike et al. *"Many in U.S., Western Europe Say Their Political System Needs Major Reform."* https://www.pewresearch.org/global/2021/03/31/many-in-us-western-europe-say-their-political-system-needs-major-reform/**

[1459] UN, *"Trust in public institutions: Trends and implications in economic security."* https://www.un.org/development/desa/dspd/2021/07/trust-public-institutions/

300. https://www.washingtonpost.com/news/in-theory/wp/2016/01/14/strong-presidencies-may-threaten-democracy-luckily-we-dont-have-one/;%20Al%20Jazeera,%20

301. https://www.aljazeera.com/news/2022/8/23/australia-announces-inquiry-into-morrisons-secret-ministries;%20Terry%20Hathaway,%20

302. https://journals.sagepub.com/doi/full/10.1177/0308518X211048905

303. https://journals.sagepub.com/doi/full/10.1177/0308518X211048905

304. https://www.cairn-int.info/article-E_AMX_051_0086--neoliberalism-the-highest-stage.htm

[1460] Hassan Kilani, *"The impact of outsourcing on labour market."* https://www.researchgate.net/publication/290195202_The_Impact_of_outsourcing_on_labour_market; Adam Dahl Joe Soss, *"Neoliberalism for the Common Good? Public-Value Governance and the Downsizing of Democracy."* https://www.researchgate.net/publication/262115820_Neoliberalism_for_the_Common_Good_Public_Value_-Governance_and_the_Downsizing_of_Democr

[1461] Marco Rubio, *"Common Good Capitalism and the Dignity of Work."* https://www.thepublicdiscourse.com/20+19/11/58194/

[1462] **Drew Desilver, *"Confidence in government falls in much of the developed world."* https://www.pewresearch.org/fact-tank/2013/11/21/confidence-in-government-falls-in-much-of-the-developed-world/; Andy Barr, *"Poll: 75% angry at government."* https://www.politico.com/story/2010/02/poll-75-angry-at-government-032680**

[1463] **Gallup, *"Congress and the Public,"* https://news.gallup.com/poll/1600/congress-public.aspx; Pew Research Center, *"Americans' Views of Government: Low Trust, but Some Positive Performance Ratings."* https://www.pewresearch.org/politics/2020/09/14/americans-views-of-government-low-trust-but-some-positive-performance-ratings/; https://www.statista.com/statistics/1086979/public-opinion-accountability-wall-street-us/**

[1464] Julia Manchester *"Majority of young adults in US hold negative view of capitalism."* https://thehill.com/homenews/campaign/560493-majority-of-young-adults-in-us-hold-negative-view-of-capitalism-poll; Owen Jones, *"Eat the rich: why millennials and Generation Z have turned their backs on capitalism."* https://www.theguardian.com/politics/2021/sep/20/eat-the-rich-why-millennials-and-generation-z-have-turned-their-backs-on-capitalism; https://www.statista.com/statistics/1096299/voter-turnout-presidential-elections-by-age-historical/

[1465] Daniella Wenger[305] and Roberto Foa[306], "*Young voters are disconnecting from democracy – but who can blame them?"* https://www.theguardian.com/commentisfree/2020/oct/23/young-voters-disconnecting-democracy-centre-politics

[1466] Arlind Qori, *"How Neoliberal Shock Therapy Brought Albania to the Brink of Civil War."* https://jacobinmag.com/2022/05/albania-pyramid-schemes-capitalist-transition-conflict-socialists; Maritn Orr, *"The Failure of Neoliberal Globalization and the end of Empire,"* in Berch Berbeloglu, *Globalization in the 21st Century*. (2010); Veronika Sušová-Salminen, *"After Neoliberal Transformation: Authoritarian Tendencies in Central and Eastern Europe."* https://www.transform-network.net/en/publications/issue/after-neoliberal-transformation-authoritarian-tendencies-in-central-and-eastern-europe/; Ben Slay, *"Poverty, Inequality, and Social Policy Reform in the Former Soviet Union."* https://www1.undp.org/content/dam/rbec/docs/Poverty-inequality-and-social-policy-reform-in-the-former-Soviet-Union.pdf

---

305. https://www.theguardian.com/profile/daniella-wenger

306. https://www.theguardian.com/profile/roberto-foa

[1467] Timofey Agarin and Ryo Nakai, *"Political Dejection in a divided society: a challenge for Latvia's democracy."* https://www.tandfonline.com/doi/full/10.1080/01629778.2021.1968917; Ernesto Gallo, *"Three varieties of Authoritarian Neoliberalism: Rule by the experts, the people, the leader."* https://journals.sagepub.com/doi/full/10.1177/10245294211038425; Beatrice Hibou[307], *"Economic Crime and Neoliberal Modes of Government: The Example of the Mediterranean."* Journal of Social History 45:3 (2012); Adriaan Alsema, *"The ties between Colombia's government and organized crime."* https://colombiareports.com/ivan-duques-ties-to-colombias-organized-crime/; Christian Oliver, *"How Bulgaria became the EU's mafia state."* https://www.politico.eu/article/bulgaria-how-it-became-mafia-state-of-eu/

[1468] Michal Carpenter, *"The Europe Whole and Free: Europe's Struggle Against Illiberal Oligarchy."* https://pism.pl/publications/The_Europe_Whole_And_Free_Europes_Struggle_Against_Illiberal_Oligarchy

[1469] Archana Kabra, *"14 Poorest Countries in Europe, 2022."* https://www.thetealmango.com/featured/poorest-countries-in-europe/#google_vignette; Iveta Ķešāne, *"Neoliberalization and Politics of Shaming: Ruling Elites' Response to Protests by Schoolteachers and Farmers in Post-Soviet Latvia (1994–2000)."* https://www.academia.edu/55440876/Neoliberalization_and_Politics_of_Shaming_Ruling_Elites_Response_to_Protests_by_Schoolteachers_and_Farmers_in_Post_Soviet_Latvia_

[1470] Julia Rone, *"Divided by a Common Purpose."* https://blogs.lse.ac.uk/europpblog/2021/02/24/divided-by-a-common-purpose-why-do-activists-in-central-and-eastern-europe-rarely-collaborate-with-those-in-the-west/; Kurt Biray, *"Communist Nostalgia in Eastern Europe: longing for the past."* https://www.opendemocracy.net/en/can-europe-make-it/communist-nostalgia-in-eastern-europe-longing-for-past/; *"Neoliberalism and the Cultural Politics of Shame."* https://thenewpolis.com/2019/09/03/neoliberalism-and-the-cultural-politics-of-shame-samantha-pinson-wrisley/; Jon Henley, *"Poll reveals majority of eastern Europeans fearful of democracy."* https://www.theguardian.com/world/2019/nov/04/poll-reveals-majority-of-eastern-europeans-fearful-for-democracy; Mihaly Simai, *"Poverty and Inequality in Eastern Europe and the CIS Transition Economies."* https://www.un.org/esa/desa/papers/2006/wp17_2006.pdf; Sanja Potkonjak and Tea Skokic, *"Working Class Gone to Heaven: From Working Class to Middle Class and Back."* https://www.academia.edu/30235229/_Working_Class_Gone_to_Heaven_From_Working_Class_to_Middle_Class_and_Back

[1471] **Sherri Berman, *"The Consequence of Neoliberalism in Eastern Europe."* https://www.ips-journal.eu/topics/democracy-and-society/the-consequences-of-neoliberal-capitalism-in-eastern- atwaragainst europe-5401/[308]; Alexander Baturo and Jos Elkink, *The New Kremlinology: Understanding Regime Personalization in Russia.* (2021); Sofie Bedford and Laurent Vinatier, *Resisting the Irresistible: 'Failed Opposition' in Azerbaijan and Belarus revisited.* (2018)**

[1472] Wendy Brown, *"Neoliberalism's Frankenstein: Authoritarian Freedom in Twenty-First Century "Democracies"* https://read.dukeupress.edu/critical-times/article/1/1/60/139328/Neoliberalism-s-Frankenstein-Authoritarian-Freedom

---

307. https://journals.sagepub.com/doi/full/10.1177/10245294211038425;%20Beatrice%20Hibou

308. https://www.ips-journal.eu/topics/democracy-and-society/the-consequences-of-neoliberal-capitalism-in-eastern-%20atwaragainst%20europe-5401/

[1473] James Buchanan, *"Public Choice: Politics Without Romance."* https://www.cis.org.au/wp-content/uploads/2015/04/images/stories/policy-magazine/2003-spring/2003-19-3-james-m-buchanan.pdf; Nancy MacLean, *Democracy in Chains: The Deep History of the Radical Right's Stealth Plan for America.* (2017).

[1474] Richard Fairchild, *"What motivates corporations to make green decisions?"* https://blogs.bath.ac.uk/business-and-society/2021/11/03/what-motivates-corporations-to-make-green-decisions/; Robert Rapier, *"The big money of environmentalism."* https://www.csmonitor.com/Business/Consumer-Energy-Report/2012/0728/The-big-money-of-environmentalism

[1475] Ellie-Anne Jones and Rick Stafford, *Neoliberalism and the Environment: Are We Aware of Appropriate Action to Save the Planet and Do We Think We Are Doing Enough?"* MDPI Earth (June, 2021).

[1476] Catherine Corson, *"Shifting Environmental Governance in a Neoliberal World: US AID for Conservation."* https://www.researchgate.net/publication/229576135_Shifting_Environmental_Governance_in_a_Neoliberal_World_US_AID_for_Conservation

[1477] Brett Christophers, *The New Enclosure: The Appropriation of Public Land in Neoliberal Britain.* (2019).

[1478] Bas van Bavel[309], Auke Rijpma[310], *"How important were formalized charity and social spending before the rise of the welfare state? A long-run analysis of selected western European cases, 1400–1850."* https://onlinelibrary.wiley.com/doi/full/10.1111/ehr.12111

[1479] Nathan Young and Ralph Matthews, *The Aquaculture Controversy in Canada: Activism Policy and Contested Science.* (2010); Evelyn Pinkerton and Reade Davis, *Neoliberalism and the politics of enclosure in North American small-scale fisheries.* https://www.sciencedirect.com/science/article/pii/S0308597X15000743

[1480] Paul Theobald and Ronald S. Rochon, *"Enclosure Then and Now: Rural Schools and Communities in the Wake of Market-Driven Agriculture."* https://jrre.psu.edu/sites/default/files/2019-08/21-12.pdf[311]

[1481] Oakland Institute, *"Calling on the USAID, DFID, DANIDA, The Netherlands, and the Bill and Melinda Gates Foundation to Stop Financing the World Bank-Managed Enabling the Business of Agriculture (EBA) Project."* https://www.oaklandinstitute.org/stop-financing-world-bank-enabling-business-agriculture; The Oakland Institute, *"Down on the Seed"* https://www.oaklandinstitute.org/sites/oaklandinstitute.org/files/down-on-the-seed.pdf

[1482] **Shapan** Adnan, *"Alienation in Neoliberal India and Bangladesh: Diversity of Mechanisms and Theoretical Implications."* https://journals.openedition.org/samaj/4130; John Vidal, *"Are export processing zones sweatshops or drivers of development?"* https://www.theguardian.com/global-development/poverty-matters/2012/apr/30/export-processing-zones-sweatshops-development

---

309. https://onlinelibrary.wiley.com/action/doSearch?ContribAuthorRaw=Bavel%2C+Bas

310. https://onlinelibrary.wiley.com/action/doSearch?ContribAuthorRaw=Rijpma%2C+Auke

311. https://jrre.psu.edu/sites/default/files/2019-08/21-12.pdf%20%20

[1483] Amar Diwakar, *"Neoliberal reforms sowed the seeds of Despair for India's farmers."* https://www.trtworld.com/magazine/neoliberal-reforms-sowed-the-seeds-of-despair-for-india-s-farmers-42038; Mark Everingham, *"Agrarian Reform, Neoliberal Adjustment and Democracy in Central America and East Africa."*

http://biblioteca.clacso.edu.ar/ar/libros/lasa97/everingham.pdf

[1484] **Diana K Davis and Edmund Burke, *Environmental Imaginaries of the Middle East and North Africa.* (2013); Attac Moroc, *"The state-led decline of subsistence farming in Morocco."* https://waronwant.org/news-analysis/state-led-decline-subsistance-farming-morocco; Razai Sara, *"L'universel au détriment du particulier: la tension entre « sécurité alimentaire » et « souveraineté alimentaire."* https://www.ritimo.org/L-universel-au-detriment-du-particulier-la-tension-entre-securite-alimentaire**

[1485] **Amber Huff and Yvonne Orengo, *"Resource warfare, pacification and the spectacle of 'green' development: Logics of violence in engineering extraction in southern Madagascar."***

https://www.sciencedirect.com/science/article/pii/S0962629819301532; Mongabay, *"Rio Tinto Mine is Polluting Malagasy Water with Uranium."* https://news.mongabay.com/2021/09/rio-tinto-owned-mine-is-polluting-malagasy-water-with-uranium-and-lead-ngos-say/; Ross Hemmingway, *"the new Colonialism: Rio Tinto in Madagascar."* https://www.redpepper.org.uk/the-new-colonialism-rio-tinto-in-madagascar/

[1486] **Catherine Corson, *"Territorialization, enclosure and neoliberalism: non-state influence in struggles over Madagascar's forests."* Journal of Peasant Studies, 38, (2011)**

[1487] Catherine Corson, *"Corridors of Power: Assembling US Environmental Foreign Aid."* https://ida.mtholyoke.edu/bitstream/handle/10166/6005/Corson-2018-ForeignAid-Antipode.pdf?sequence=1&isAllowed=y; Benjamin D. Neimark, *"The Land of Our Ancestors: Property rights, social resistance, and alternatives to land grabbing in Madagascar."* https://www.iss.nl/sites/corporate/files/LDPI_WP_26.pdf

[1488] James Fairhead, Melissa Leach and Ian Scoones, *"Green Grabbing: A new appropriation of nature?"* https://www.tandfonline.com/doi/full/10.1080/03066150.2012.671770

[1489] **Sylvaine Poret, *"Corporate–NGO Partnerships through Sustainability Labeling Schemes: Motives and Risks."* https://hal.archives-ouvertes.fr/hal-02154666/document; Caroline Dale Ditlev-Simonsen, *"Beyond sponsorship - exploring the***

***impact of cooperation between corporations and NGOs."* https://jcsr.springeropen.com/articles/10.1186/s40991-017-0017-9; Ryan Dezember, *"America's Most Prolific Logger Recasts Itself as Environmental Do-Gooder."* https://www.wsj.com/articles/weyerhaeuser-logging-carbon-emissions-offset-market-environment-76850c01**

[1490] Attracta Mooney, *"Blackrock accused of climate change hypocrisy."* https://www.ft.com/content/0e489444-2783-4f6e-a006-aa8126d2ff46

[1491] Patrick Greenfield, *"World spends $1.8 trillion a year on subsidies that harm the environment."* https://www.theguardian.com/environment/2022/feb/17/world-spends-18tn-a-year-on-subsidies-that-harm-environment-study-finds-aoe

[1492] Oxfam International, *"European countries water down landmark EU law to clean up business."* https://www.oxfam.org/en/press-releases/european-countries-water-down-landmark-eu-law-clean-business

[1493] **Douglas A. McIntyre, *"The "Green" Hypocrisy: America's Corporate Environment Champions Pollute The World."* https://247wallst.com/energy-business/2009/04/02/the-green-hypocrisy-americas-corporate-environment-champions-pollute-the-world/; Xiaobei Liang, Xiaojuan Hu and Hu Meng, *Truly Sustainability or Hypocrisy: The Effects of Corporate Sustainable Orientation on Consumers' Quality Perception and Trust Based on Evidence from China."* Sustainability, MDPI (2020);**

[1494] **United Nations, *"World Altered by 'Neoliberal' Outsourcing of Public Services to Private Sector, Third Committee Experts Stress, amid Calls for Better Rights Protection."* https://press.un.org/en/2018/gashc4239.doc.htm.**

[1495] P. Raja Siregar, *"World Bank and ABD's Role in Privatizing Water in Asia."* https://www.circleofblue.org/wpcontent/uploads/2012/06/WorldBank_ADB_Privatization_Asia.pdf; Sara Grusky, *"Bearing the Burden of IMF and World Bank Policies."* https://www.iatp.org/sites/default/files/Bearing_the_Burden_of_IMF_and_World_Bank_Polic.htm; Clayton Crockett, *"Neoliberalism, Post-secularism and the end of Religion."* https://www.mdpi.com/2077-1444/12/8/631/htm; Rane Willerslev, *"Taking Aminism Seriously, but Perhaps Not too Seriously?"* https://anthropolojamz.wordpress.com/2015/12/29/willerslev-taking-animism-seriously-but-perhaps-not-too-seriously/

[1496] Christopher Dent, *"Neoliberal Environmentalism, Climate Interventionism and the Trade-Climate Nexus.* Sustainability 2022, 14, 15804. https://doi.org/10.3390/su142315804

[1497] Joseph Daher, *"What's left of Lebanon's 2019 uprising?"* https://www.ips-journal.eu/topics/democracy-and-society/whats-left-of-lebanons-2019-uprising-5936/; Devaka Gunawardena and Ahilan Kadirgamar, *"Sri Lankan Peoples' Protests."* https://www.theindiaforum.in/article/sri-lanka-people-protests; Jon Kofas, *"Overview of the Iran-Azerbaijan Confrontation and the Regional Balance of Power."* https://www.transcontinentaltimes.com/overview-of-the-iran-azerbaijan-confrontation-and-the-regional-balance-of-power/; Noé Hochet-Bodin, *"Ethiopia and the Tigray Peoples' Liberation Front sign a fragile peace accord."* https://www.lemonde.fr/en/international/article/2022/11/04/ethiopia-and-the-tigrayan-people-s-liberation-front-sign-a-fragile-peace-accord_6002952_4.html; Jennifer Pedraza, *"Colombia's Uprising Isn't About Duque. It's About Overturning Neoliberalism."* https://jacobin.com/2021/06/colombia-ivan-duque-government-neoliberalism-protest-general-strike; Brunel University, *"When revolutionary moments arise again – and they will – what will we do?"* https://www.brunel.ac.uk/news-and-events/news/articles/When-revolutionary-moments-arise-again-and-they-will-what-will-we-do; Thomas Brooke, *"Dutch farmers ramp up protests against government's crippling environmental demands."* https://rmx.news/article/dutch-farmers-ramp-up-protests-against-governments-crippling-environmental-demands/

[1498] Bryn Battersby[312], Elif Ture[313], Raphael Lam[314], *"Tracking the $9 Trillion Global Fiscal Support to Fight Covid-19."* https://www.imf.org/en/Blogs/Articles/2020/05/20/tracking-the-9-trillion-global-fiscal-support-to-fight-covid-19

[1499] **Rama V. Baru[315] and Malu Mohan[316], *"Globalisation and neoliberalism as structural drivers of health inequities."* https://health-policy-systems.biomedcentral.com/articles/10.1186/s12961-018-0365-2**

[1500] Michelle Jamrisko & Gregor Stuart Hunter, *"When $8 Trillion in Global Stimulus Still isn't Enough."* https://www.bloombergquint.com/china/when-8-trillion-in-global-fiscal-stimulus-still-isn-t-enough; Committee for a Responsible Federal Budget, *"COVID Money Tracker,"* https://www.covidmoneytracker.org/; Amy Livingston Sarah Lazar, *"Military Budget Hike is 3,200 Times the NLRB Increase."* https://inthesetimes.com/article/military-budget-hike-for-2023-is-3-200-times-the-nlrb-increase

[1501] Vitor Gaspar[317], Paulo Medas[318], Roberto Perrelli[319], "*Global Debt Reaches a Record $226 trillion.*" https://www.imf.org/en/Blogs/Articles/2021/12/15/blog-global-debt-reaches-a-record-226-trillion

[1502] NCPSSM[320] *"Trump Plan to Plan to Privatize is Alive and Well."* https://www.ncpssm.org/entitledtoknow/trump-plan-to-privatize-medicare-still-alive-and-well/

---

312. https://www.imf.org/en/Blogs/authors?author=Bryn%20Battersby

313. https://www.imf.org/en/Blogs/authors?author=Elif%20Ture

314. https://www.imf.org/en/Blogs/authors?author=Raphael%20Lam

315. https://health-policy-systems.biomedcentral.com/articles/10.1186/s12961-018-0365-2#auth-Rama_V_-Baru

316. https://health-policy-systems.biomedcentral.com/articles/10.1186/s12961-018-0365-2#auth-Malu-Mohan

317. https://www.imf.org/en/Blogs/authors?author=Vitor%20Gaspar

318. https://www.imf.org/en/Blogs/authors?author=Paulo%20Medas

319. https://www.imf.org/en/Blogs/authors?author=Roberto%20Perrelli

320. https://www.ncpssm.org/entitledtoknow/author/ncpssm/

[1503] Zolan Kanno-Youngs, Allan Rappaport and Emily Cochrane, *"Biden's $5.8 Trillion Budget Pivots Toward Economic and Security Concerns."* https://www.nytimes.com/2022/03/28/us/politics/biden-proposes-increases-in-defense-and-social-spending.html

[1504] David Autor, et al., *"The $800 Billion Paycheck Protection Program: Where Did the Money Go and Why Did it Go There?"* https://www.nber.org/papers/w29669https://www.nber.org/papers/w29669

[1505] Brian Levy, *"How Inequality and polarization Interact: America's Challenges Through South Africa's Lens."* https://carnegieendowment.org/2022/04/27/how-inequality-and-polarization-interact-america-s-challenges-through-south-african-lens-pub-86935

[1506] Benjamin L. McKean Emma M. MacKinnon, J.R. Winters, E.R Pineda and Paul Apostolidis. *"The political theory of global supply chains."* https://link.springer.com/article/10.1057/s41296-022-00587-0; Steve Banker, *"The Biggest Supply Chain Fallacies."* https://www.forbes.com/sites/stevebanker/2018/04/09/the-biggest-supply-chain-fallacies/?sh=e4d6a0f263d0

[1507] Juliana Kaplan, *"Workers lost 3.7 trillion in earnings during the pandemic."* https://www.businessinsider.com/workers-lost-37-trillion-in-earnings-during-the-pandemic-2021-1; Anna Cooban, *"Billionaires added $5 trillion to their fortune during the pandemic."* https://edition.cnn.com/2022/01/16/business/oxfam-pandemic-davos-billionaires/index.html

[1508] Reshma Kapadia, *"IMF Cuts Global Growth Outlook."* https://www.barrons.com/articles/imf-global-growth-outlook-warning-signs-51650326199;

UNCTAD, *'UN Sees Worsening Prospects for Global Growth in 2022 due to Ukraine War and Monetary Tightening.'* https://unctad.org/press-material/un-sees-worsening-prospects-global-growth-2022-due-ukraine-war-and-monetary

[1509] Colin M. Barry and Bailey Kleinberg, *"Profiting from Sanctions: Coercion and US Foreign Direct Investment in Third Party States."* https://www.researchgate.net/publication/278729748_Profiting_from_Sanctions_Economic_Coercion_and_US_Foreign_Direct_Investment_in_Third-Party_States; Maxime Combes, *"Corporate Welfare in a Time of the Pandemic."* https://www.rosalux.eu/en/article/1848.corporate-welfare-in-a-time-of-pandemic.html

[1510] Joao Nunes, *"The COVID-19 pandemic: securitization, neoliberal crisis, and global vulnerabilization:"* https://www.scielo.br/j/csp/a/sng9pd8tLNdY3cQrDChhqPr/?format=pdf&lang=en

[1511] David Myer, *"Elon Musk and the rest of the world's 10 richest doubled their wealth during the pandemic, but 99% of humanity if worse off."* https://fortune.com/2022/01/17/elon-musk-inequality-oxfam-davos-99-percent/

[1512] Bret Meyer, *"Pandemic Populism: An Analysis of Populist Leaders' Responses to COVID-19."* https://institute.global/policy/pandemic-populism-analysis-populist-leaders-responses-covid-19;Aline Burni, *"The Populists and the Pandemic."* https://internationalepolitik.de/en/populists-and-pandemic

[1513] Miroslav Mareš, *"Tirer avantage des crises Comment les différentes forms d'extrémisme violent de droite exploitent la pandémie de COVID–19, et enseignements à tirer pour la prévention et la lute contre l'extrémisme violent."* https://ec.europa.eu/home-affairs/system/files/2022-02/ran_capitalising_crises_how_vrwe_exploit_covid-19_pandemic_082021_fr.pdf

[1514] Christina Gossner, *"Anti-lockdown protests in Germany infiltrated by far-right extremists."* https://www.euractiv.com/section/coronavirus/news/anti-lockdown-protests-in-germany-infiltrated-by-far-right-extremists/

[1515] Joseph Stiglitz, *"The End of Neoliberalism and Rebirth of History."* https://www8.gsb.columbia.edu/articles/chazen-global-insights/end-neoliberalism-and-rebirth-history

[1516] **James Meadway, *"Neoliberalism is Dying – now we must replace it."* https://www.opendemocracy.net/en/oureconomy/neoliberalism-is-dying-now-we-must-replace-it/**

[1517] Janice Alvarez, *"Neoliberalism: A History of Broken Promises."* https://natoassociation.ca/neoliberalism-a-history-of-broken-promises/

[1518] Joanna Brenner and Nancy Fraser, *"What is Progressive Neoliberalism? A Debate."* https://www.researchgate.net/publication/315883314_What_Is_Progressive_Neoliberalism_A_Debate

[1519] Ben Conway, *"How the Myths of Progressive Neoliberalism Hollowed Out Australia's Left."* https://www.jacobinmag.com/2021/05/australian-labor-party-alp-left-neoliberalism; Nancy Fraser, *"The End of Progressive Neoliberalism."* https://www.dissentmagazine.org/online_articles/progressive-neoliberalism-reactionary-populism-nancy-fraser

[1520] Olga Baysha, *"On "progressive neoliberalism" from a discursive perspective: "Progress" as an empty signifier."* https://www.researchgate.net/publication/350606760_On_progressive_neoliberalism_from_a_discursive_perspective_Progress_as_an_empty_signifier; Kevin Young, *"How Neoliberalism Reproduces itself."* https://www.researchgate.net/publication/271313539_How_Neoliberalism_Reproduces_Itself

[1521] Herbert P. Bix, *"Japan Under Neonationalist, Neoliberal Rule: Moving Toward an Abyss?"* https://apjjf.org/2013/11/15/Herbert-P.-Bix/3927/article.html; Katharine Murphy, *"Scott Morrison unleashes foreign policy fetish while staying passive on economy."* https://www.theguardian.com/australia-news/2019/oct/05/scott-morrison-unleashes-foreign-policy-fetish-while-staying-passive-on-economy; John Passant, *"Prime Minister Scott Morrison: The new face of neoliberalism."* https://independentaustralia.net/politics/politics-display/prime-minister-scott-morrison-the-new-face-of-neoliberalism,11829

[1522] Nancy Fraser, *"The Crisis of Progressive Neoliberalism."* https://lpeproject.org/blog/the-crisis-of-progressive-neoliberalism/

[1523] Hamilton Nolan, *"Biden Just Knifed Labor Unions in the Back."* https://www.theguardian.com/commentisfree/2022/dec/01/joe-biden-rail-strike-labor-unions; Emily Peck, Erin Doherty, *"Congressional leaders vow to consider bill to avoid rail strike."* https://www.axios.com/2022/11/28/biden-calls-on-congress-to-act-fast-to-avoid-rail-strike

[1524] Chris Hedges, *"On strike for a better world: Labor conflict is coming and the ruling class will fight back hard."* https://www.salon.com/2022/09/21/on-strike-for-a-better-world-labor-conflict-is-coming—and-the-ruling-class-will-fight-back-hard/[321]

[1525] George Soros, *Open Society: Reforming Global Capitalism.* (2000); Rebecca Fisher, *Managing Democracy, Managing Dissent.* (1996); https://corporatewatch.org/wp-content/uploads/2017/09/MDMD-Master-PDF1.pdf; Nicolas Guilhot, Reforming the World: George Soros, "*Global Capitalism and the Philanthropic Management of the Social Sciences.*" Critical Sociology, 33, 3 (2007)

[1526] Michael Sainato, *"George Soros and Neoliberalism Still Own the Democrats."* https://observer.com/2017/01/george-soros-democratic-party-involvement/

[1527] https://www.oxfam.org/en/press-releases/richest-1-bag-nearly-twice-much-wealth-rest-world-put-together-over-past-two-years

[1528] Al Jazeera, *"UN warns 345 million face starvation worldwide."* https://www.aljazeera.com/news/2022/9/16/un-warns-up-to-345-million-people-marching-towards-starvation; Guy Feldman, *"Neoliberalism and Poverty."* https://www.researchgate.net/publication/336700342_Neoliberalism_and_poverty_An_unbreakable_relationship; WFP, *"A Global Food Crisis."* https://www.wfp.org/global-hunger-crisis

[1529] Abhishek G. Bhaya, *"Sri Lanka crisis offers lessons for middle income developing countries."* https://news.cgtn.com/news/2022-07-11/Sri-Lanka-crisis-offers-lessons-for-middle-income-developing-countries-1bAfJCDG17G/index.html

[1530] Shashi Tharoor, *"Neoliberalism and Sri Lanka."* https://english.mathrubhumi.com/columns/i-mean-what-i-say/neo-liberalism-and-sri-lanka-shashi-tharoor-1.7581890; Nagesh Rao, and Nimanthi Rajasingham, *"Sri Lankan Uprising: Struggle against neoliberal austerity."* https://www.cadtm.org/Sri-Lankan-Uprising-Struggles-against-neoliberal-austerity; Agense France-Presse, *"Sri Lanka crisis timeline: from galloping inflation to a president's resignation."* https://www.theguardian.com/world/2022/jul/10/sri-lanka-crisis-timeline-from-galloping-inflation-to-a-presidents-resignation

321. https://www.salon.com/2022/09/21/on-strike-for-a-better-world-labor-conflict-is-coming--and-the-ruling-class-will-fight-back-hard/

[1531] Thamil Venthan Ananthavinayagan, *"Sri Lanka and the Neocolonialism of the IMF."* https://thediplomat.com/2022/03/sri-lanka-and-the-neocolonialism-of-the-imf/

[1532] Nithyani Anandakugan, *"The Sri Lankan Civil War and Its History, Revisited in 2020."* https://hir.harvard.edu/sri-lankan-civil-war/

[1533] Kanishka Goonewardena, *"Populism, nationalism and Marxism in Sri Lanka: from anti-colonial struggle to authoritarian neoliberalism."* https://www.tandfonline.com/doi/full/10.1080/04353684.2020.1780146; Nalika Gajaweera, *"Sri Lanka's Dual Crisis: Ethnic Conflict & the Debt Economy."* https://www.jamhoor.org/read/sri-lankas-dual-crisis-ethnic-conflict-the-debt-economy; Nithyani Anandakugan, *"The Sri Lankan Civil War and its History."* https://hir.harvard.edu/sri-lankan-civil-war/; [322]**Thamil Venthan Ananthavinayagan, *"Sri Lanka and the Neocolonialism of the IMF."*** https://thediplomat.com/2022/03/sri-lanka-and-the-neocolonialism-of-the-imf/

[1534] Leonid Grinin, Andre Grinin and Andrey Korotayev, *"20th century revolutions: characteristics, types and waves."* https://www.nature.com/articles/s41599-022-01120-9; Donna L. Chollett, *Neoliberalism, Social Exclusion, and Social Movements*, (2013).

[1535] Gerard Dumenil and Dominique Levy, *"The Nature and Contradictions of Neoliberalism,"* https://socialistregister.com/index.php/srv/article/download/5776/2672/7703

[1536] Sahil Jai Dutta, Samuel Knafo, Ian A. Lovering, *"Neoliberal failures and the managerial takeover of governance."* https://www.cambridge.org/core/journals/review-of-international-studies/article/neoliberal-failures-and-the-managerial-takeover-of-governance/FA0C2CB2F90C9EADF9693CFF3E53C28F/share/6a2604da8c9e5f3a569824d5d0cd212c6f5c4d39; Gary Teeple and Stephen McBride, *Relations of Global Power: Neoliberal Order and Disorder.* (2010); Anis Chowdhury[323] and Piotr [324]Zuk, *"From Crisis to Crisis: Capitalism, Chaos and Constant Unpredictability."* https://www.cambridge.org/core/journals/the-economic-and-labour-relations-review/article/abs/from-crisis-to-crisis-capitalism-chaos-and-constant-unpredictability/9E21382598FF32CE033932C2CA37E354

[1537] **Harshana Rambukwella, *"Sri Lankan Uprising is a Cry for Regaining Democracy Brutalized by the Rajapaksas."* https://thewire.in/south-asia/sri-lankan-uprising-is-a-cry-for-regaining-democracy-brutalised-by-the-rajapaksas; DW, *"Rajapaksa: The rise and fall of Sri Lanka's powerful political dynasty."***

https://www.dw.com/en/rajapaksa-the-rise-and-fall-of-sri-lankas-powerful-political-dynasty/a-62458780; HRW, *"Lebanon: Rising Poverty, Hunger Amid Economic Crisis."* https://www.hrw.org/news/2022/12/12/lebanon-rising-poverty-hunger-amid-economic-crisis; Lydia Assouad, *"Lebanon's Political Economy: From*

322. https://hir.harvard.edu/sri-lankan-civil-war/;%20

323. https://www.cambridge.org/core/search?filters%5BauthorTerms%5D=Anis%20Chowdhury&eventCode=SE-AU

324. https://www.cambridge.org/core/search?filters%5BauthorTerms%5D=Piotr%20%C5%BBuk&eventCode=SE-AU

Predatory to Self-Devouring." https://carnegie-mec.org/2021/01/14/lebanon-s-political-economy-from-predatory-to-self-devouring-pub-83631

[1538] **Martin Jacques, *"The death of neoliberalism and the crisis in western politics."*https://www.theguardian.com/commentisfree/2016/aug/21/death-of-neoliberalism-crisis-in-western-politics**

[1539] Allan, Patience, *"If we are reaching neoliberal capitalism's end days, what comes next?"* https://theconversation.com/if-we-are-reaching-neoliberal-capitalisms-end-days-what-comes-next-72366; Kim Lane Scheppele, *"How Viktor Orban Wins."* https://www.journalofdemocracy.org/articles/how-viktor-orban-wins/; Mattia Zullianello, *"Italian General Election 2022: The Populist Right Goes Mainstream."* https://journals.sagepub.com/doi/10.1177/20419058221147590

[1540] Jeanne Morefield, *"When Neoliberalism Hijacked Human Rights."* https://jacobin.com/2020/01/morals-markets-human-rights-rise-neoliberalism-jessica-whyte

[1541] Mauro Cristeche, *"Capital Accumulation, the Role of the State and Human Rights in Argentina: Contributions for Debates on Economic and Social Right.* https://papers.ssrn.com/sol3/papers.cfm?abstract_id=3710850

[1542] Paolo Gerbaudo, *"After Globalization."* https://www.dissentmagazine.org/article/after-globalization

[1543] **Jörg Wiegratz and David Whyte, *"How neoliberalism's moral order feeds corruption."* https://theconversation.com/how-neoliberalisms-moral-order-feeds-fraud-and-corruption-60946; Daniel Moura Borges, *"Neoliberalism's Moral Bankruptcy."* https://www.thecommoner.org.uk/neoliberalisms-moral-bankruptcy/**

[1544] Maria Pentaraki, *"COVID-19 response-lessons learned: challenging the neoliberal TINA discourse through social work education."* https://www.tandfonline.com/doi/full/10.1080/02615479.2021.2018416; Miloš Šumonja[325], "Neoliberalism is not dead: On political implications of COVID-19" https://journals.sagepub.com/doi/10.1177/0309816820982381

[1545] Robert Skidelsky, *"Keynes, Globalization and the Bretton Woods Institutions in the light of Changing Ideas about Markets."* http://oxonia.org/WE%20articles/WE_skidelsky.pdf; Massiah Gustave, *"Authoritarianism reveals the limits of neoliberalism."* https://www.ritimo.org/Austeritarianism-reveals-the-limits-of-neoliberalism

[1546] Valentina Pop, Sam Fleming, James Politi, *"Weaponization of finance: how the west unleashed shock and awe on Russia."* https://www.ft.com/content/5b397d6b-bde4-4a8c-b9a4-080485d6c64a; Marina Gržinić, *"Biopolitics, Necropolitics and De-coloniality."* https://monoskop.org/images/3/32/Pavilion_14_Biopolitics_Necropolitics_and_De-Coloniality_Jan_2010.pdf; Aaron Major, *"Neoliberalism and the new International financial architecture."* https://www.jstor.org/stable/41697933; IMF, *"Co-economic puzzle: Policymaking in a more fragmented world."* Finance and Development. (June 2022).

[1547] **Suhaib, *"Governments throughout the world offer $536B in annual subsidies to this 1 business — and billionaire***

325. https://journals.sagepub.com/action/doSearch?target=default&ContribAuthorStored=%C5%A0umonja%2C+Milo%C5%A1

investor Mario Gabelli is acquiring in on the motion." **https://trendswide.com/governments-throughout-the-world-offer-536b-in-annual-subsidies-to-this-1-business-and-billionaire-investor-mario-gabelli-is-acquiring-in-on-the-motion-heres-how-you-can-way-too/; IRENA, *"Energy Subsidies."* https://irena.org/-/media/Files/IRENA/Agency/Technical-Papers/IRENA_Energy_subsidies_2020.pdf**

[1548] Elena Suckling, Zach Christensen, Dan Walton, *"Poverty Trends: Global, Regional, National."* https://devinit.org/resources/poverty-trends-global-regional-and-national/; Marta Schoch, et al., *"Half of the global population lives on less than US$6.85 per person per day."* https://blogs.worldbank.org/developmenttalk/half-global-population-lives-less-us685-person-day

[1549] Mark LeVine, *"From neoliberalism to necrocapitalism in 20 years."* https://www.aljazeera.com/opinions/2020/7/15/from-neoliberalism-to-necrocapitalism-in-20-years; Gundula Ludwig, *"Promises of Freedom in Violent Times: On the neoliberal entanglement of biopolitics and necropolitics."* https://ecpr.eu/Events/Event/PaperDetails/29733; Subhabrata Bobby Banerjee, *"Necrocapitalism."* https://openaccess.city.ac.uk/id/eprint/6088/1/Necrocapitalism_OS2008FINAL2.pdf; Eve Darian-Smith, *"Dying for the Economy: Disposable People and the Economies of Death in the Global North."* Pluto Journals, 10, 1 (2021) https://www.jstor.org/stable/pdf/10.13169/statecrime.10.1.0061.pdf

[1550] The Paradise, *"Apple reportedly held anti-union meetings in all of its US stores."* https://theparadise.ng/apple-reportedly-held-anti-union-meetings-at-all-of-its-us-stores/

[1551] **Andrew Ives, *"Neoliberalism and the Concept of governance: Renewing with an older liberal tradition to legitimate the power of capital."* https://journals.openedition.org/mimmoc/2263; Athena D. Mutua, *"Framing Elite Consensus, Ideology and Theory and ClassCrits Response."* https://www.swlaw.edu/sites/default/files/2017-04/2%20Framing%20Elite%20Consensus%2C%20Ideology%20and%20Theory%20%26%20A%20Classcrits%20Response.pd**

[1552] **Ernesto Gallo, *"Three varieties of Authoritarian Neoliberalism: Rule by the experts, the people, the leader"* https://journals.sagepub.com/doi/full/10.1177/10245294211038425; Olivier Dartigolles, *Macron, entreprise de démolition: Forces, failles, farces.* (2018); https://www.counterfire.org/articles/opinion/19592-macron-is-a-snake; Katerina Hatzikidi, *"The tamed and the untamable: How the establishment is serving Bolsonaro's authoritarianism."* https://www.opendemocracy.net/en/democraciaabierta/how-brazil-establishment-serves-bolsonaro-authoritarian-project/; Ben Conway, *"How the Myths of Progressive Neoliberalism Hollowed out Australia's Left."* https://www.jacobinmag.com/2021/05/australian-labor-party-alp-left-neoliberalism**

[1553] Nils Ringe and Lucio Renno, *"Populists and the Pandemic. How populists around the world responded to COVID-19."* https://library.oapen.org/bitstream/handle/20.500.12657/57268/1/9781000634877.pdf

[1554] Rogers Brubaker, *"Paradoxes of Populism during the Pandemic."*

https://journals.sagepub.com/doi/10.1177/0725513620970804; AFR, *"Mad anti-vax populism no mainstream outbreak."* https://www.afr.com/policy/health-and-education/mad-anti-vax-populism-no-mainstream-outbreak-20211123-p59bga; Leyland Cecco, *"Canada's Covid protests highlight rise of rightwing populist movements."* https://www.theguardian.com/world/2022/feb/01/canada-protests-covid-vaccines-mandates-rightwing-movement.

[1555] James Meadway, *"Neoliberalism is dying - now we must replace it."* https://www.opendemocracy.net/en/oureconomy/neoliberalism-is-dying-now-we-must-replace-it/

[1556] Victor M. A. Nascimento, *"The Hegemony of the Neoliberal Narrative: Right Wing Discourses of 'Common Sense', the Weaponization of the Term 'Liberal', and the Shifting of the Political Spectrum."*https://dspace.library.uvic.ca/bitstream/handle/1828/12841/Nascimento_Victor_MA_2021.pdf?sequence=1&isAllowed=y; Walter O. Ötsch and Stephan Pühringer, *"The Anti-democratic Logic of Right-wing Populism and Neoliberal Market-fundamentalism."* Journal of Language and Politics[326], 16: 4[327], (2017); Ganesh Sitaraman, *"The Collapse of Neoliberalism."* https://newrepublic.com/article/155970/collapse-neoliberalism.

[1557] Bill Fletcher Jr. *"To Fight the Right, We Need to Understand It Better."* https://www.dissentmagazine.org/online_articles/fighting-trump-right-wing-populism-vs-neoliberalism/; Jessica Gantt Shafer, *"Donald Trump's "Political Correctness": Neoliberalism as Frontstage Racism on Social Media."* http://www.thecyberhood.net/documents/papers/Shafer.pdf;

[1558] Anna Zeira, *"Mental Health Challenges Related to Neoliberal Capitalism in the United States."* https://www.ncbi.nlm.nih.gov/pmc/articles/PMC8145185/; Vishal Bhavsar and Dinesh Bhugra, *"Globalization: Mental Health and Socioeconomic Factors."* https://www.researchgate.net/publication/249723717_Globalization_Mental_Health_and_Social_Economic_Factors; https://www.macrotrends.net/countries/WLD/world/gdp-growth-rate; Noel Ingram and Jason Blakley, *"Suicide and Neoliberalism."* https://digitalcommons.pepperdine.edu/cgi/viewcontent.cgi?article=1507&context=scursas; Telesur, *"Drugs Don't Kill People, Neoliberalism Kills People."* https://www.telesurenglish.net/analysis/Drugs-Dont-Kill-People-Neoliberalism-Kills-People—20171122-0007.html[328]

[1559] Ruth Igielnik[329], *'70% of Americans say U.S. economic system unfairly favors the powerful.'* https://www.pewresearch.org/fact-tank/2020/01/09/70-of-americans-say-u-s-economic-system-unfairly-favors-the-

---

326. https://www.jbe-platform.com/content/journals/15699862

327. https://www.jbe-platform.com/content/journals/15699862/16/4

328. https://www.telesurenglish.net/analysis/Drugs-Dont-Kill-People-Neoliberalism-Kills-People--20171122-0007.html

329. https://www.pewresearch.org/staff/ruth-igielnik

powerful/; Kat Devlin[330], Shannon Schumacher[331] and J.J. Moncus[332], *"Many in Western Europe and U.S. Want Economic Changes as Pandemic Continues."* https://www.pewresearch.org/global/2021/04/22/many-in-western-europe-and-u-s-want-economic-changes-as-pandemic-continues/

[1560] Clara H. Whyte, *"Getting Back to the Roots of Nihilism and Cynicism in Modern Democracies: How to Rebuild Trust?"* https://www.paideiamundi.org/fr-fr/getting-back-to-the-roots-of-nihilism-and-cynicism-in-modern-democracies-how-to-rebuild-trust/

[1561] Richard Peet, *"Contradictions of Finance Capitalism."* https://monthlyreview.org/2011/12/01/contradictions-of-finance-capitalism/; Pranav Dixit, *"186 US banks at risk of failure similar to Silicon Valley, says research."* https://www.businesstoday.in/industry/banks/story/186-us-banks-at-risk-of-failure-similar-to-silicon-valley-bank-says-research-heres-why-373895-2023-03-18; Mark Thompson and Julia Horowitz, *"Europe's banks are still at risk."* https://edition.cnn.com/2023/03/27/business/bank-risks-europe/index.html; Nancy Fraser, *"Legitimation Crisis? On the Political Contradictions of Financialized Capitalism."* https://www.researchgate.net/publication/283520483_Legitimation_Crisis_On_the_Political_Contradictions_of_Financialized_Capitalism; John Nichols, *"Bankers Lobbied for Deregulation, Congress Capitulated, and Now Banks are Collapsing."* https://www.federalreserve.gov/monetarypolicy/bst_recenttrends.htm; Joseph Hanlon, *"Mozambique: Credit Suisse is liable for the $2 billion in secret debt."* https://www.cadtm.org/Mozambique-Credit-Suisse-is-liable-for-the-2-bn-secret-debt; https://www.statista.com/statistics/1243825/extreme-poverty-rate-in-mozambique/

[1562] Gerard Dumenil and Dominique Levy, *"The Nature and Contradictions of Neoliberalism."* http://www.cepremap.fr/membres/dlevy/dle2004k.pdf; Christian Stark, *The Neoliberal Ideology, Its Contradictions, the Consequence and Challenges for Social Work."* https://hrcak.srce.hr/file/300257; Tobias Mann, *"Chipmakers, you can have these billions – but Uncle Sam wants a cut of your profits."* https://www.theregister.com/2023/02/28/us_chips_conditions/; Friederike Heine[333], Supantha Mukherjee[334] and Andreas Rinke[335], *"Intel spends $33 billion in Germany in landmark expansion."* https://www.reuters.com/technology/berlin-sign-agreement-with-intel-after-chip-plant-talks-2023-06-19/

[1563] Eric Levitz, *"Neoliberalism Died of Covid. Long Live Neoliberalism! How the predominant ideology of our time survived the pandemic."* https://nymag.com/intelligencer/2021/10/neoliberalism-died-of-covid-long-live-neoliberalism.html

---

330. https://www.pewresearch.org/staff/kat-devlin

331. https://www.pewresearch.org/staff/shannon-schumacher

332. https://www.pewresearch.org/staff/jerry-joseph-moncus

333. https://www.reuters.com/authors/friederike-heine/

334. https://www.reuters.com/authors/supantha-mukherjee/

335. https://www.reuters.com/authors/andreas-rinke/

[1564] Jon V. Kofas, *"US Foreign Policy and the World Federation of Trade Unions, 1944-1948."* Diplomatic History, 26:1 (2002); Renato Perim Colistete, *"Trade Unions and the ICFTU in the Age of Developmentalism in Brazil, 1953—1962."* https://www.researchgate.net/publication/260103756_Trade_Unions_and_the_ICFTU_in_the_Age_of_Developmentalism_in_Brazil_1953-1962; Jon V. Kofas, *The Struggle for Legitimacy: Latin American Labor and the United States, 1930-1960.* (1992); Luiz Carlos Bresser-Pereira, *"The global financial crisis, neoclassical economics, and the neoliberal years of capitalism."* https://journals.openedition.org/regulation/7729

[1565] Mariana Fotaki, *"Narcissistic elites are undermining the institutions created to promote public interest."* https://blogs.lse.ac.uk/politicsandpolicy/narcissism-and-perversion-in-public-policy/

[1566] Joanna Moncrieff, *"The Political Economy of the Mental Health System."* https://www.frontiersin.org/articles/10.3389/fsoc.2021.771875/full; Megan Linton, *"Mental health under neoliberalism: From self-help to CBT."* https://canadiandimension.com/articles/view/mental-health-under-neoliberalism-from-self-help-to-cbt; Earl Gammnon, *"Narcissistic Rage and Neoliberal Reproduction."* http://sro.sussex.ac.uk/id/eprint/66742/1/Narcissistic_Rage_170206_final.pdf

[1567] Richard Sennett, *The Fall of Public Man, (*1992*);* Marina Grzinic, *"Biopolitics and Necropolitics in relation to the Lacanian four discourses."* https://www.ub.edu/doctorat_eapa/wp-content/uploads/2012/09/Marina.Grzinic_Biopolitics-Necropolitics_Simposio_2012.pdf; Matthew McDonald, Stephen Wearing, and Jess Pointing, *"Narcissism and Neo-Liberalism: Work, Leisure and Alienation in an era of Consumption."* https://www.researchgate.net/publication/261680045_Narcissism_and_Neo-Liberalism_Work_Leisure_and_Alienation_in_an_Era_of_Consumption

[1568] GREG SHARZER, *"Escapism and Contemporary Neoliberalism: Alienation, Work and Utopia."* https://www.academia.edu/46871181/Late_Escapism_and_Contemporary_Neoliberalism_Alienation_Work_and_Utopia; James Arvanitakis, *"The Commodification and Reclaiming of Trust."* https://www.westernsydney.edu.au/__data/assets/pdf_file/0008/365399/Arvanitakis_CommodificationReclaimingTrust_ICS_Pre-Print_Final.pdf ; Melissa May Racho, *"Assessing the Cultural Effects of Neoliberalism on Empathy."* https://digscholarship.unco.edu/cgi/viewcontent.cgi?article=1426&context=dissertations

[1569] **Dan Sinykin, *American Literature and the Long Downturn: Neoliberal Apocalypse.* (2020), Introduction, Ch. 4, and Conclusion; Carolyn Veldstra, *"Bad feeling at work: emotional labour, precarity, and the effective economy."* https://www.tandfonline.com/doi/abs/10.1080/09502386.2018.1555269 Jeremiah Howe, *"The Neoliberal Periah."* https://via.library.depaul.edu/cgi/**

viewcontent.cgi?article=1148&context=soe_etd

[1570] TOMASO GRAVANTE AND Alice Poma, *"Breaking away from narcissism: emotions and grassroots activism in the time of COVID-19."* https://www.opendemocracy.net/en/openmovements/breaking-away-narcissism-emotions-and-grassroots-activism-time-covid-19/

[1571] Marko Juutinen, *"Neoliberal Civilization: Definition, Evaluation and Trends."* https://www.academia.edu/4186885/Neoliberal_Civilization_Definition_Evaluation_and_Trend; Matthew McDonald, Stephen Wearing and Jess Ponting, *"Narcissism and Neoliberalism: Work Leisure and Alienation in an era of consumption."* https://opus.lib.uts.edu.au/bitstream/10453/10289/1/2008002436.pdf

[1572] Heidi Rimke. *Self-help, therapeutic industries, and neoliberalism."* In Daniel Nehring, et al. eds. *The Routledge International Handbook of Global Therapeutic Cultures.* (2020)

[1573] Bryan S. Turner, *"Individualism, Capitalism and the Dominant Culture."* https://journals.sagepub.com/doi/abs/10.1177/144078338802400103?journalCode=josa

[1574] Richard Heinberg[336], Melody Travers[337], Rob Dietz[338], *"Four Reasons Civilization Won't Decline: It Will Collapse."* https://www.resilience.org/stories/2020-08-10/four-reasons-civilization-wont-decline-it-will-collapse/

336. https://www.resilience.org/resilience-author/richard-heinberg/

337. https://www.resilience.org/resilience-author/melody-travers/

338. https://www.resilience.org/resilience-author/rob-dietz/

About the Author

Jon Kofas is a retired professor of history. His field of specialization was international political economy. He was in higher education from 1979 until 2005. He was with the Department of Sociology, History, and Political Science, Indiana University Kokomo from 1992 until 2005. His most recent publication is PHANTOM of APOCALYPSE: A Dystopian novel

THE LITTLE FRENCH

The Little Frenche Media.

About the Publisher

]Welcome to The Little French eBooks a press dedicated to publishing erotica, romance and mystery eBooks in multiple formats for compatibility with the variety of eBook reader devices. Our commitment is to provide quality and exciting works to the public. For submission guidelines visit our website.

www.thelittlefrenchebooks.com

www.thelittlefrenchebookstore.com

www.ingramcontent.com/pod-product-compliance
Lightning Source LLC
LaVergne TN
LVHW082011200926
848481LV00010B/2834